**UTSA DT LIBRARY RENEWALS 458-2440**
## DATE DUE

| | | | |
|---|---|---|---|
| | | | |
| | | | |
| | | | |
| | | | |
| | | | |
| | | | |
| | | | |
| | | | |
| | | | |
| | | | |
| | | | |
| | | | |
| | | | |
| | | | |
| | | | |
| | | | |
| | | | |
| | | | |
| | | | |
| | | | |
| GAYLORD | | | PRINTED IN U.S.A. |

# Conservation of Furniture

# Butterworth-Heinemann Series in Conservation and Museology

# Conservation of Furniture

**Shayne Rivers**
**Nick Umney**

ELSEVIER
BUTTERWORTH
HEINEMANN

AMSTERDAM • BOSTON • HEIDELBERG • LONDON • NEW YORK • OXFORD
PARIS • SAN DIEGO • SAN FRANCISCO • SINGAPORE • SYDNEY • TOKYO

Elsevier Butterworth-Heinemann
Linacre House, Jordan Hill, Oxford OX2 8DP
30 Corporate Drive, Burlington, MA 01803

First published 2003
Reprinted 2005

**British Library Cataloguing in Publication Data**
A catalogue record for this book is available from the British Library

ISBN 0 7506 09583

For information on all Butterworth-Heinemann
publications visit our website at www.bh.com

Composition by Scribe Design, Gillingham, Kent
Printed and bound in Great Britain

# Contents

Series editors' preface     xix

Contributors     xxi

Acknowledgements     xxv

Illustration acknowledgements     xxvii

**PART 1 HISTORY**

**1   Furniture history**     3

1.1   Introduction     3
1.2   Earliest times to the Middle Ages     3
    1.2.1 Egypt     3
    1.2.2 Greece     4
    1.2.3 Rome     5
    1.2.4 Byzantium and the Romanesque period     5
1.3   Medieval     6
    *Background*     6
    *Functional types*     6
    *Design and construction*     7
    *Materials used*     8
    *Tools and techniques*     8
    *Surface decoration and finish*     8
    *Organization of the trade*     9
1.4   Renaissance to Industrial Revolution     9
    1.4.1 1500–1600     9
       *Background*     9
       *Functional types*     9
       *Design and construction*     10
       *Materials used*     11
       *Tools and techniques*     11
       *Surface decoration and finish*     11
       *Organization of the trade*     12
    1.4.2 1600–1700     12
       *Background*     12

       *Functional types*     13
       *Design and construction*     14
       *Materials used*     16
       *Trade practice, tools and techniques*     16
       *Surface decoration and finish*     18
    1.4.3 1700–1800     20
       *Background*     20
       *Functional types*     20
       *Design and construction*     21
       *Materials used*     23
       *Tools and techniques of conversion and construction*     24
       *Surface decoration and finish*     25
       *Organization of trades*     26
1.5   The nineteenth century     26
    *Background*     26
    *Functional types*     28
    *Style and type of construction*     29
    *Materials used*     30
    *Tools and techniques*     31
    *Surface decoration and finish*     33
    *Organization of trades and manufacturing*     34
1.6   The twentieth century     35
    *Context*     35
    *Materials used*     37
    *Tools and techniques of conversion and construction*     40
    *Surface decoration and finish*     40
    *Organization of trades and manufacturing*     41

1.7   Conclusion                          41
Bibliography                             41

**PART 2  MATERIALS**

**2   Wood and wooden structures        49**
2.1   Introduction to wood as material  49
2.2   The nature of wood:
      appearance, cellular structure
      and identification                 51
      2.2.1 Gross features               51
            *Grain*                      52
            *Texture*                    53
            *Figure*                     53
            *Colour*                     54
            *Taxonomy – the
            classification of plants*    54
      2.2.2 Wood anatomy: softwoods      55
      2.2.3 Cell structure: hardwoods    57
      2.2.4 Wood identification          60
      2.2.5 Hand–lens examination        61
      2.2.6 Microscopic examination      70
      2.2.7 Other methods                74
2.3   Chemical nature of wood            74
      2.3.1 Chemical constituents of
            wood                         74
      2.3.2 The cellulose structure
            within cell walls            75
2.4   Wood–water relations and
      movement                           76
      2.4.1 Hygroscopicity               77
      2.4.2 Measuring moisture
            content of wood              77
      2.4.3 Dimensional change           79
      2.4.4 Estimating dimensional
            change                       80
2.5   Mechanical properties              83
      2.5.1 Defining mechanical
            properties                   83
      2.5.2 Relative strength properties 85
      2.5.3 Factors affecting the
            strength of wood             85
      2.5.4 Role of wood strength in
            furniture                    86
2.6   Manufactured timber products       87
      2.6.1 Veneers                      87
      2.6.2 Plywood and related
            materials                    88
      2.6.3 Reconstituted wood
            products                     89
2.7   Wooden structures                  89
      2.7.1 Types of joints              89

      2.7.2 Critical success factors for
            joints                       90
      2.7.3 Dovetail joints             91
      2.7.4 Mortise and tenon joints    92
      2.7.5 Other joint types           93
Bibliography                            95

**3   Upholstery materials and
    structures                         97**
3.1   Introduction to upholstery        97
      3.1.1 Classification and
            terminology                  97
      3.1.2 Historical development       98
      3.1.3 Technical examination       100
3.2   Top surface/simple structures    100
      3.2.1 Leather/skin/parchment     100
            *Skin*                      100
            *Leather*                   101
            *Structure processing and
            properties*                 102
            *Methods of working and
            uses of leather*            102
            *Parchment*                 104
            *Skins 'in the hair'*       104
            *Shark and ray skin*        104
            *Identification of leather
            and skin products*          105
      3.2.2 Simple structures –
            interworked materials
            (including rush and cane)   105
            *Cordage*                   105
            *Rush*                       106
            *Wicker*                     106
            *Rattan or cane*            106
            *Reed*                       107
            *Splints*                    107
      3.2.3 Textiles                    107
            *Fibres*                     108
            *Dyes and dyeing*           109
            *Textile structures*        109
            *Surface decoration and
            finishing*                  110
            *Identification of textiles
            and fibres*                 111
      3.2.4 Synthetic polymers and
            plastics                    112
            *Polystyrene*               112
            *Polyester urethane and
            polyether urethane*         112
            *Rubber*                     112
            *Identification of polymer
            systems*                    113

3.2.5 Coated fabrics and 'leather
cloths' 113
*Oil cloths* 113
*Rubber cloths* 113
*Cellulose nitrate* 113
*Polyvinyl chloride (PVC)* 113
3.2.6 Trimmings 113
3.3 Hardware 114
3.4 Under structures 115
3.4.1 Fillings 116
*Animal materials* 116
*Vegetable materials* 118
*Elastomers, synthetic*
*materials and latex* 118
3.5 Support systems 119
3.5.1 Webbing 119
3.5.2 Springs 120
3.5.3 Fabrics and twines used
as part of the structure 120
3.6 Adhesives 120
Bibliography 121

4 **Plastics and polymers, coatings and**
**binding media, adhesives and**
**consolidants** 124
4.1 Plastics and polymers 124
4.1.1 Chemical structure 124
4.1.2 Physical properties 126
4.1.3 Polymer materials history
and technology 128
4.1.4 Identification of plastics
and polymers 134
4.2 Introduction to coatings,
binding media, adhesives and
consolidants 134
4.3 Coatings – functions and
properties 135
4.3.1 Protection against handling
and soiling 136
4.3.2 Strength and elasticity 136
4.3.3 Barrier properties 137
4.3.4 Optical properties 138
4.3.5 Solubility and working
properties 140
4.4 Coatings – structures and
preparations 141
4.4.1 Supports 142
*Stoppings* 142
*Grain fillers* 142
4.4.2 Grounds 142
*Gesso grounds* 142
*Bole* 143
*Composition* 144

4.4.3 Paints and paint media 144
4.4.4 Transparent coatings 146
*Historical use of varnishes* 147
4.4.5 Gilding 148
4.4.6 Oriental lacquer (urushi) 149
*Preparing the lacquer* 149
*Refining raw lacquer* 150
*Making a cured film* 150
*Applying lacquer to*
*substrate* 151
*Decoration* 152
*Identification* 152
4.4.7 Japanning 153
4.5 Adhesives 156
*Glue line thickness,*
*adhesive failure* 158
*Starved joints* 159
*Roughening surfaces* 159
4.5.1 Factors governing the
choice of an adhesive 159
*Health and safety* 160
*Characteristics of cured*
*adhesive* 160
*Relativity of choice factors* 160
4.5.2 Adhesives used in
woodworking 160
4.5.3 Hot melt adhesives 161
4.5.4 Contact cements 161
4.6 Consolidants 161
4.7 Review of materials: coatings,
media, adhesives and
consolidants 162
4.7.1 Oils and fats 162
4.7.2 Waxes 165
*Animal waxes* 166
*Plant waxes* 166
*Mineral waxes* 166
*Commercial products* 167
4.7.3 Carbohydrates: sugars and
polysaccharides 167
*Alginates* 167
4.7.4 Proteins 169
*Collagen* 169
*Albumins* 173
*Casein and milk* 173
4.7.5 Natural resins and lacquers 174
*Shellac* 174
4.7.6 Synthetic materials 179
*Thermoplastics* 179
*Poly(vinyl acetate) PVAC* 179
*Poly(vinyl alcohol)* 180
*Poly(vinyl acetals)* 180
*Acrylics* 180

Cyclohexanone resins                181
Cellulose nitrates                  182
Other thermoplastic
materials                           183
Thermosetting resins                184
Alkyds                              185
Epoxies                             185

4.8   Examination and identification of
adhesives, coatings and media   187
Bibliography                            189

**5   Other materials and structures    194**
5.1   Ivory, ivory-like teeth, bone and
antler                            194
Ivory 194
Bone and antler                 197
Ivory substitutes               197
Identification of ivory,
bone and antler                 199
5.2   Keratinaceous materials – horn
and turtleshell                   201
General information             201
Turtleshell                     201
Horn                            202
Properties                      202
Identification                  203
5.3   Mollusc shell                     204
5.4   Paper and paper products          205
Identification of paper
and paper products              206
5.5   Metals                            206
Iron and steel                  208
Copper alloys                   209
Common white metals             210
Gold leaf                       210
Shell and powdered gold         211
Finishes and coatings on
metals                          211
Identification of metals        212
Identification of structure
and fabrication of metal
objects                         212
Dating metals                   213
5.6   Ceramics and glass                213
Flat glass                      214
Identification of glass
and ceramics                    217
5.7   Stone and related materials       217
Marble                          217
Identification of stone and
related materials               218
5.8   Colorants: pigments, dyes and
stains                            219

5.8.1 Colour                            219
Why objects appear
coloured                        219
5.8.2 Pigments                          221
Chemical properties             221
Physical properties             222
5.8.3 Dyes                              230
5.8.4 Stains                            230
5.8.5 Identification of pigments,
dyes and stains                 232
Bibliography                            233

**PART 3   DETERIORATION**

**6   General review of environment
and deterioration                241**
6.1   Introduction                      241
6.1.1 Organizational and political
context                         241
6.1.2 Use versus preservation      242
Change and damage               242
6.1.3 Managing the object life
cycle                           243
6.2   The environment                   244
6.2.1 Background chemistry         244
6.2.2 Light                             246
Light energy, colour
temperature and damage          247
Reciprocity                     248
Control of light                248
Lighting and heating            251
6.2.3 Heat                              252
Measurement and control
of temperature                  252
6.2.4 Absolute humidity and
relative humidity               253
Measuring RH                    254
RH and damage                   256
Control of RH                   257
6.2.5 Pollution                         260
Particulate pollution           260
Gaseous pollution               263
6.2.6 Biological agents            266
Fungi                           266
Insects                         267
6.2.7 Mechanical handling,
packing and moving              273
Touch                           273
Clothing                        274
Forces applied to objects
(lifting, moving and
placing)                        274

*The actual move* 275
*Protection of objects* 276
*Damage* 276
6.2.8 Environmental management
for preventive conservation 277
*Stores and storage* 277
6.3 Disaster preparation 279
6.3.1 Disaster planning 279
*Prevention* 279
*Preparation* 280
6.3.2 When a disaster occurs 281
6.3.3 After a disaster 282
Bibliography 282

7 **Deterioration of wood and
wooden structures** 285
7.1 Deterioration of wood as
material 285
7.1.1 Natural defects in wood in
living trees 285
7.1.2 Artificial defects –
conversion and seasoning 288
*Conversion* 289
*Seasoning defects* 289
7.1.3 Deterioration of 'normal'
seasoned wood 290
*Light* 290
*Heat* 291
*Moisture* 292
*Pollution* 294
*Fungi* 294
*Insects* 296
*Mechanical deterioration
of wood* 301
7.2 Deterioration of wooden
structures – causes 302
7.2.1 General – dimensional
response of wooden
structures 302
7.2.2 Faulty construction and
conservation 303
*Design faults* 303
*Faults in execution of the
design* 305
*Poor quality materials
used* 306
*Inappropriate use of
material* 306
*Role of fashion and
technical innovation* 306
*Conservation treatment
errors* 306

7.3 Deterioration of wooden
structures – consequences 307
7.3.1 Broken and damaged parts
and losses 307
7.3.2 Loose and lifting veneer 307
7.3.3 Loose and broken joints 308
7.3.4 Shrinkage, splitting and
warping 308
7.3.5 Accretions and other
surface disfigurement 310
7.3.6 Review of damage by
structure 310
*Carcase furniture* 311
*Tables* 312
Bibliography 313

8 **Deterioration of other materials
and structures** 315
8.1 Ivory, ivory-like teeth, bone and
antler, horn and turtleshell 315
8.2 Mollusc shell – mother-of-pearl
and related materials 316
8.3 Paper and paper products 317
8.4 Metals 317
*Role of moisture* 321
*Chlorides* 322
*Light* 322
*Heat* 322
*Pollutants* 322
*Mechanical damage* 323
8.5 Ceramics and glass 323
8.6 Stone and related materials 324
8.7 Colorants – pigments, dyes and
stains 324
8.8 Plastics and polymers 326
*Environmental stress
cracking and crazing* 327
*Oxidation* 327
*The effect of light on
polymers* 328
*The effect of heat on
polymers* 329
*The effect of RH on
polymers* 329
*The effect of pollution on
polymers* 329
*Biological damage to
polymers* 330
*Prevention and care* 330
8.9 Coatings – deterioration of some
common systems of surface
decoration 331
8.9.1 The support 332

8.9.2   The ground                   333
8.9.3   The paint                    335
8.9.4   Transparent top coatings
        – varnishes                  337
        *Development of insoluble
        matter*                      339
8.9.5   Gilding                      340
8.9.6   Oriental lacquer             342
8.9.7   Japanning                    343
8.10  Adhesives                      345
8.11  Deterioration of specific
      materials                      345
      8.11.1 Oils and fats           345
      8.11.2 Waxes                   346
      8.11.3 Carbohydrates: sugars
             and polysaccharides     346
      8.11.4 Proteins                346
      8.11.5 Natural resins and
             lacquers                346
      8.11.6 Synthetic materials     348
8.12  Deterioration of upholstery
      materials and structures       348
             *Prevention conservation*  348
      8.12.1 Top surface/simple
             structures              348
             *Leather, skin and
             parchment*              348
             *Rush, reed and cane*   349
             *Textiles*              350
             *Chemical degradation*  351
             *Biodeterioration*      352
             *Structure of textiles* 353
             *Dyes and finishes*     353
             *Preventive conservation
             of textiles*            354
             *Plastics*              354
             *Rubber*                355
             *Polyurethanes*         356
             *Polyvinyl chloride (PVC)*  357
             *Cellulose nitrate*     358
             *Trimmings*             358
             *Understructures*       359
             *Hardware*              359
      Bibliography                   360


**PART 4   CONSERVATION**

**9   Conservation preliminaries**   367
9.1   Context                        367
      9.1.1 Historical background     367
      9.1.2 Definition of the
            profession               368
9.1.3 Professional organizations     369
9.1.4 The business of
      conservation                   370
9.2   Ethics                         370
      9.2.1 Codes of ethics and
            practice                 370
      9.2.2 Historical conflict between
            restoration and
            preservation             371
      9.2.3 Conservation as a cultural
            discipline               372
      9.2.4 Tools for balanced ethical
            judgement                374
            *The V&A ethics checklist*  375
9.3   Examination                    380
      9.3.1 Purpose of examination   380
      9.3.2 What to look for         381
            *Structural damage*      383
            *Surface effects*        383
      9.3.3 Methods of examination   384
            *General aspects of
            characterization*        385
            *Estimating*             386
            *Gross examination*      386
            *Simple mechanical tests*  388
            *Microscopic examination*  390
            *Sampling*               391
            *General aspects of
            analytical methods*      393
            *Dating methods*         394
9.4   Documentation                  396
      9.4.1 What is documentation and
            why is it important?     396
      9.4.2 Information needs        396
      9.4.3 Documentation methods    398
      9.4.4 Setting up a documentation
            system                   400
      9.4.5 Photography              401
            *The film*               402
            *The light source*       402
            *Alternative light sources*  405
            *The camera*             406
9.5   Studio organization and layout  407
      9.5.1 Workshop processes and
            procedures               408
            *Examination and
            recording of condition*  408
            *Dismantling the object*  408
            *Repair of existing
            components and making
            of new ones*             408
            *Re-assembly*            408
            *Finishing and colouring*  408

Recording and reporting
treatment                                        409
9.5.2 The location                               409
9.5.3 The building/space                         409
      Entrance/loading bay                       410
      Client reception and
      administration area                        410
      Object storage                             410
      Examination and
      photography                                411
      The main work area                         411
      Machine room                               411
      Retouching area/clean
      room                                       412
      The wood store                             412
      Upholstery workshop                        412
      Metalworking area                          413
      Recreational areas                         414
9.5.4 Detailed requirements                      414
      Storage                                    414
      Wet areas                                  415
      Electrical power supply                    415
        Lighting and heating                     415
        Extraction                               416
9.6   Tools and equipment                        417
      9.6.1  Woodworking tools and
             equipment                           417
      9.6.2  Other tools and
             equipment                           418
9.7   Health and safety                          420
      9.7.1  Health and safety
             requirements                        421
             Principal legal
             requirements                        421
             What you should know
             about health and safety
             law                                 421
      9.7.2  The process of managing
             health and safety                   422
      9.7.3  Documentation for health
             and safety management               422
      9.7.4  Risk assessment                     423
             Generic assessments                 424
             Five steps to risk
             assessment                          424
             Step 1: Look for the
             hazards                             424
             Step 2:Decide who or
             what might be harmed
             and how                             426
             Step 3:Evaluate the risks           426
             Step 4: Record your
             findings                            427

             Step 5: Review your
             assessment                          427
      9.7.5  Control risk                        427
             The hierarchy of control            428
             The life cycle of control           428
      9.7.6  Maintain controls                   428
      9.7.7  Monitor exposure                    429
      9.7.8  Survey health                       429
      9.7.9  Inspect the workplace               429
             Checklist for health and
             safety review                       430
      9.7.10 Inform, instruct and train          430
             Shared workplace and
             visiting workers                    430
             Duties of employees                 430
             Labelling and signage               430
      9.7.11 Audit                               430
      9.7.12 Accidents and
             emergencies                         430
             Fire prevention                     431
             Fire precautions                    431
      9.7.13 Further information on
             health and safety                   431
      Bibliography                               432

10  Principles of conserving and
    repairing wooden furniture                  436
10.1 General principles                         437
     10.1.1 Diagnosing the cause of
            failure                             437
     10.1.2 Selection of repair method
            and repair material                 438
     10.1.3 Selection of wood for a
            repair                              438
     10.1.4 Transferring shapes, profiles
            and measurements                    439
     10.1.5 Making the repair piece            439
     10.1.6 Fitting the repair to the
            object                              439
     10.1.7 Adhesion and surface
            preparation                         440
     10.1.8 Selecting an adhesive              442
     10.1.9 Assembly                            444
     10.1.10 Cramping/clamping                  444
     10.1.11 Levelling repairs                  448
     10.1.12 Preparation of repair for
             finishing                          449
10.2 General techniques                         454
     10.2.1 Dismantling furniture               454
     10.2.2 Cleaning joints after
            dismantling                         458
     10.2.3 Repairs after insect
            infestation                         458

10.2.4 Reinforcing joints 459
10.2.5 Frames 459
        *Handling mirror frames* 459
10.3 Repair by damage type 460
10.3.1 Loose and broken joints 460
10.3.2 Shrinkage checks and
        splits 461
10.3.3 Hinges 465
10.3.4 Warping 465
10.3.5 Breaks and losses 468
10.3.6 Faulty construction 470
10.4 Veneer, marquetry and boulle 470
10.4.1 Laying veneer 471
10.4.2 Cleaning 473
10.4.3 Consolidation 474
10.4.4 Transferring the outline
        of a loss 476
10.4.5 Replacing losses 476
10.4.6 Lifting original veneer 480
10.4.7 Coatings for boulle
        work 481
10.4.8 Stringing and metal
        inlay 481
10.5 Moulding and casting 482
10.5.1 General procedure 482
10.5.2 Selection of materials 483
10.5.3 Release agents 488
10.5.4 Making a mould 489
10.5.5 Colorants and fillers 489
10.5.6 Finishing 489
10.5.7 Gilders composition 490
        *Ingredients* 490
        *Mixing* 490
Bibliography 491

**11 Principles of cleaning** 494
11.1 Preliminaries 495
11.1.1 Cleaning objectives 495
11.1.2 Examination 496
11.1.3 Pre-cleaning checklist 496
11.1.4 General approach 496
11.1.5 Cleaning tests 497
11.1.6 Dirt 499
11.1.7 Removal of varnish or
        overpaint 500
11.2 Mechanical cleaning 501
11.2.1 Dusting 501
11.2.2 Cleaving 501
11.2.3 Abrasives 503
11.2.4 Dry cleaning methods 503
11.3 Solvent cleaning 504
11.3.1 Classes of solvents that
        may be encountered in

furniture conservation 505
        *Hydrocarbon solvents* 505
        *Chlorinated hydrocarbons* 509
        *Alcohols* 510
        *Aldehydes and ketones* 510
        *Ethers* 511
        *Esters* 511
        *Organic nitrogenous
        compounds* 511
11.3.2 Physical properties of
        solvents 512
        *Evaporation rates, vapour
        pressure and density* 513
        *Viscosity* 513
        *Surface tension and
        capillary action* 514
        *Toxicity* 514
        *Flammability* 515
11.3.3 Solubility 515
        *Process of dissolution* 515
        *Solubility parameters* 518
        *Predicting solubility* 518
        *Solvent removal of varnish* 524
        *Mixing solvents* 525
11.3.4 Proprietary paint strippers 526
11.4 Chemical cleaning 527
11.4.1 Introduction to acids and
        bases 527
11.4.2 Ka and pKa 528
11.4.3 Acids 529
11.4.4 Bases 529
11.5 Aqueous cleaning 529
11.5.1 pH and aqueous cleaning 531
11.5.2 pH buffers 532
        *Choosing a buffer* 532
11.5.3 Ionic concentration/
        conductivity 533
11.5.4 Soaps, detergents and
        surfactants 534
        *Detergents* 535
        *Emulsions and hydrophilic
        lipophilic balance (HLB)
        numbers* 535
        *Critical micelle
        concentration (CMC)* 536
        *Choosing a detergent* 539
        *Residues and rinse
        procedures* 540
11.5.5 Chelating agents 540
        *Formation constants* 542
        *Effects of pH and
        conditional stability
        constants* 543

11.5.6 Enzymes 548
11.5.7 Blanching and blooming 551
11.6 Thickened solvent delivery
systems – pastes, poultices
and gels 552
11.6.1 Controlled vapour
delivery 553
11.6.2 Gelling materials 553
*Clays* 553
*Cellulose ethers* 554
*Polyacrylic acid
(Carbopol)* 556
Bibliography 557

**12 Principles of consolidation, aesthetic
reintegration and coatings** 560
12.1 Basic principles 560
12.1.1 Making solutions 561
*Concentration* 561
*Molar solutions* 561
*Dilution* 561
*Measuring small quantities
without a balance* 562
12.2 Consolidation 562
12.2.1 Introduction to
consolidation treatment 562
12.2.2 Penetration of consolidant
and reverse migration 563
12.2.3 Consolidation of wood 563
*Materials used to
consolidate wood* 564
12.2.4 Consolidation of painted
and decorated surfaces 566
*Traditional vs. modern
materials* 567
*Materials used for the
consolidation of
decorative surfaces* 567
*Application techniques* 571
*Flakes, cups, tents and
blisters* 572
*Facing* 573
12.3 Aesthetic reintegration 574
12.3.1 Fills 574
*Introduction to filling* 574
*Fill materials* 576
12.3.2 Retouching 578
*Introduction to
retouching* 578
*Light, colour and
metamerism* 579
*Materials for retouching* 582

*Making paint tablets* 585
*Commercial preparations* 586
12.4 Coatings 586
12.4.1 Introduction to coating 586
12.4.2 Saturation and gloss 587
*Refractive index* 588
*Gloss* 589
*Molecular weight* 589
12.4.3 Varnish formulation 589
12.4.4 Matting down varnishes 590
12.4.5 Stabilizers 592
12.4.6 Selecting a coating 593
12.4.7 Coating materials 593
*Natural resins* 593
*Acrylics* 594
*Synthetic low molecular
weight varnishes* 595
12.4.8 Application methods for
coatings 598
*Brush application* 598
*Spray application* 598
Bibliography 602

**13 Conserving transparent coatings
on wood** 606
13.1 Introduction to transparent
finishes 606
13.1.1 Photochemical oxidation
and patina 607
13.1.2 Revivers 607
13.2 Cleaning 608
13.3 Selective layer removal 610
13.4 Surface blemishes 611
13.4.1 Dents and scratches 611
13.4.2 Watermarks 611
13.4.3 In-filling varnish losses 612
13.5 Colour matching repairs to
varnished wood 612
13.5.1 Introduction to colour
matching processes 612
13.5.2 Surface preparation 613
13.5.3 Materials for colour
matching wood repairs 614
*Precautionary measures* 614
*Bleaches* 614
*Addition of colour to
wood repairs: pigments,
lakes and stains* 616
13.5.4 Grain fillers 620
13.5.5 Stoppings and filling
materials 622
13.5.6 Colour matching methods 624

*Binding media for*
*colour matching*
*varnished wood*                                      624
*Applying pigments*                                   625
*Applying stains*                                     625
*Sealing coats*                                       626
13.6  Treatment of degraded varnish    627
13.7  Application of coatings to
        varnished wood                                628
        13.7.1  Non-traditional materials    628
        13.7.2  Traditional materials        629
                *Wax*                                 629
                *Oils*                                630
                *Natural resins*                      631
                *French polishing*                    633
                *Glazing*                             637
13.8  Craquelure, crazing and
        crocodiling                                   637
13.9  Polishing or dulling a varnished
        surface                                       638
13.10 Distressing                                     639
Bibliography                                          639

14  **Introduction to traditional gilding**  642
14.1  Background                                      642
        14.1.1  Water and oil gilding        642
        14.1.2  Tools for gilding            643
        14.1.3  Gold and metal leaf          646
        14.1.4  Surface preparation          647
        14.1.5  Gesso putty                  647
14.2  Water gilding                                   647
        14.2.1  Conditions for gilding       647
        14.2.2  Size                         648
        14.2.3  Preparation of glue size     648
        14.2.4  Assessing gel strength       648
        14.2.5  Sizing the wood              649
        14.2.6  Gesso                        649
        14.2.7  Application of gesso         650
        14.2.8  Faults in the gesso          652
        14.2.9  Smoothing the gesso          652
        14.2.10 Decorative details           653
        14.2.11 Recutting                    653
        14.2.12 Yellow ochre                 655
        14.2.13 Bole                         655
        14.2.14 Laying the leaf              658
        14.2.15 Faulting                     660
        14.2.16 Matte water gilding          660
        14.2.17 Double gilding               661
        14.2.18 Burnishing                   661
        14.2.19 Punched decoration           662
        14.2.20 Coatings                     662
14.3  Oil gilding                                     663
        14.3.1  Mordants for oil gilding     663

        14.3.2  Surface preparation          664
        14.3.3  Applying the oil size        664
        14.3.4  Applying gold leaf           664
        14.3.5  Coatings                     665
14.4  Composition                                     665
Bibliography                                          666

15  **Conserving other materials I**       667
15.1  Ivory, bone and antler, turtleshell
        and horn, mother-of-pearl                     667
        15.1.1  Ivory, bone and antler       667
                *Cleaning*                            667
                *Staining*                            668
                *Consolidation*                       669
                *Humidification*                      669
                *Adhesives*                           669
                *Replacements*                        670
                *Staining ivory*                      670
                *Polychrome ivory*                    670
                *Coatings*                            671
                *Antler*                              671
                *Repair and replacement*              671
        15.1.2  Turtleshell and horn         671
                *Cleaning*                            671
                *Consolidation*                       671
                *Replacing losses*                    672
                *Coatings*                            673
        15.1.3  Mother-of-pearl              673
                *Cleaning*                            673
                *Consolidation*                       674
                *Replacing losses*                    674
                *Coatings*                            674
15.2  Paper labels and linings on
        furniture                                     674
        15.2.1  Labels                       675
                *Options for dealing with*
                *a label on furniture*                675
        15.2.2  Paper liners                 676
15.3  Metals                                          677
        15.3.1  Introduction                 677
                *Patina*                              678
                *Removal of metal fittings*           678
        15.3.2  Cleaning                     678
        15.3.3  Removal of corrosion
                products                              679
                *Mechanical removal of*
                *corrosion products*                 680
                *Electrochemical and*
                *electrolytic reduction*             681
                *Chemical removal of*
                *corrosion products*                 682
        15.3.4  Rinsing and drying           682

15.3.5   Repairs                         683
15.3.6   Replacement elements            683
15.3.7   Application of coatings
         after conservation              684
         Method of application           685
         Preferential corrosion          685
         Coating materials for
         metals                          686
15.3.8   Ferrous metals                  688
         *Patination of iron*            688
         *Mechanical removal of
         corrosion products*             689
         *Rust converters*               690
         *Chemical removal of
         corrosion products*             691
         *Coatings*                      692
15.3.9   Brass and bronze                692
         *Stabilization*                 692
         *Mechanical removal of
         corrosion products*             693
         *Chemical removal of
         corrosion products*             693
         *Stress corrosion cracking*     693
         *Dezincification and the
         deposition of insoluble
         metal complexes*                694
         *Reagents for the chemical
         removal of corrosion
         products*                       694
15.3.10  Ormolu                          696
         *Cleaning*                      697
         *Removal of corrosion
         products*                       697
15.3.11  Silver                          698
         *Removal of corrosion
         products*                       699
         *Reshaping*                     700
         *Prevention of tarnish*         700
         *Coatings*                      700
15.3.12  Lead                            700
         *Removal of corrosion
         products*                       701
         *Coatings*                      701
15.4  Ceramics and enamels               701
15.4.1   Cleaning                        702
15.4.2   Bonding                         702
15.4.3   Filling losses                  703
15.4.4   Retouching                      703
15.4.5   Enamels                         704
15.5  Flat glass, mirrors, reverse
      painted and gilded glass           705
15.5.1   Flat glass                      705
15.5.2   Mirrored glass                  705

15.5.3   Painted and decorated
         glass                           706
15.5.4   Repairs to adjacent
         wood                            707
15.5.5   Removing glass                  707
15.5.6   Refitting decorated and
         mirrored glass                  708
15.5.7   Cleaning undecorated
         glass                           708
15.5.8   Cleaning mirrored and
         decorated glass                 709
15.5.9   Repair of glass                 709
15.5.10  Consolidation                   709
15.5.11  Restoration and
         retouching                      710
15.5.12  Coatings                        710
Bibliography                             710

16  **Conserving other materials II**    714
16.1  Stone and related materials        714
16.1.1   Marble                          714
         *Cleaning*                      714
         *Consolidation*                 716
         *Repair and reintegration*      716
         *Coatings*                       717
16.1.2   Scagliola                       717
         *Cleaning*                      717
         *Consolidation*                 717
         *Fills*                         718
         *Coatings*                      718
16.1.3   Piètre dure                     718
         *Cleaning*                      718
         *Fills/losses*                  718
         *Coatings*                      718
16.2  Plastics                           719
16.2.1   Introduction to plastics        719
16.2.2   Cleaning                        719
16.2.3   Adhesives and
         consolidation                   720
16.2.4   Filling                         721
16.2.5   Retouching                      721
16.2.6   Coatings                        721
16.3  Upholstery                         721
16.3.1   Introduction to upholstery
         conservation                    721
16.3.2   Ethics                          722
16.3.3   Examination and
         documentation of
         upholstery                      723
16.3.4   Previous interventions          723
16.3.5   Condition of the frame          724
16.3.6   Materials                       724
16.3.7   Non-invasive treatments         725

*Surface cleaning* 725
*Semi-transparent
coverings* 725
*Case covers* 726
*Stabilizing with repairs* 726
*Supports* 726
16.3.8 Invasive treatments 726
*Removal and
documentation* 726
*Metal fixings* 727
*Cleaning* 727
*Supports* 728
*Reapplication of lined
textiles* 729
*Storage for study as an
alternative to
reapplication* 729
*Independent sub-frames* 729
16.3.9 Rush, reed and cane 729
*Rehumidification* 729
*Deacidification* 730
*Repair* 730
16.3.10 Imitation leather 730
16.4 Leather, parchment and
shagreen 731
16.4.1 Leather 731
*Evaluating the surface
of the leather* 731
*Cleaning* 732
*Chemical stabilization* 732
*Consolidation* 733
*Infills* 734
*Backing materials* 736
*Coatings* 736
16.4.2 Parchment and vellum 736
*Cleaning* 737
*Repair and support* 738
*Coatings* 739
16.4.3 Shagreen 739
*Cleaning* 740
*Lifting edges and tears* 740
16.5 Textiles 740
16.5.1 Cleaning 742
16.5.2 Loose and lifting linings 742
16.6 Painted furniture 743
16.6.1 Introduction to
conservation of painted
furniture 743
16.6.2 Cleaning 744
16.6.3 Removal of varnish 745
*Mechanical removal* 747
*Solvents* 747
*Alkaline reagents* 749

*Aqueous methods* 749
*Removal of synthetic
varnishes* 751
16.6.4 Removal of overpaint 751
16.6.5 Consolidation 752
16.6.6 Reintegration 752
16.6.7 Coatings 752
16.6.8 Matte paint 753
16.7 Japanned furniture 753
16.7.1 Introduction to japanning 753
16.7.2 Examination of objects 754
16.7.3 Cleaning 755
16.7.4 Removal of overpaint and
later varnishes 757
16.7.5 Consolidation 757
16.7.6 Infilling 758
*Fills for grounds* 758
*Fills for papier mâché* 759
*Fills for japanned layers* 759
16.7.7 Varnishes 759
16.8 Lacquered (urushi) furniture 760
16.8.1 Introduction and
definition 760
16.8.2 Handling lacquer 760
16.8.3 Distinguishing Oriental
lacquer from japanning 761
16.8.4 Eastern and Western
approaches to restoration
and conservation 762
16.8.5 Cleaning 763
*Potential problems* 763
*Removal of surface dirt
and accretions* 763
*Cleaning decorative
elements* 764
*Removing unwanted
coatings* 764
16.8.6 Consolidation 766
*Softening brittle lacquer
before consolidation* 766
*Flattening distorted
lacquer* 767
*Materials* 767
*Shell inlay* 768
16.8.7 Infilling 768
16.8.8 Retouching 768
16.8.9 Restoring a degraded
matte surface 769
16.8.10 Coatings 769
16.9 Gilded furniture 770
16.9.1 Introduction to
conservation of gilded
surfaces 770

16.9.2  General care          771
16.9.3  Cleaning              771
16.9.4  Removal of overgilding  773
16.9.5  Removal of bronze
        paint                 773
16.9.6  Consolidation         773
16.9.7  Reintegration         774

16.9.8  Composition           776
16.9.9  Coatings              776
16.9.10 Distressing           776
16.9.11 Toning                777
Bibliography                  777

*Index*                       785

# Series editors' preface

The conservation of artefacts and buildings has a long history, but the positive emergence of conservation as a profession can be said to date from the foundation of the International Institute for the Conservation of Museum Objects (IIC) in 1950 (the last two words of the title being later changed to Historic and Artistic Works) and the appearance soon after in 1952 of its journal *Studies in Conservation*. The role of the conservator as distinct from those of the restorer and the scientist had been emerging during the 1930s with a focal point in the Fogg Art Museum, Harvard University, which published the precursor to *Studies in Conservation, Technical Studies in the Field of the Fine Arts* (1932–42).

UNESCO, through its Cultural Heritage Division and its publications, had always taken a positive role in conservation and the foundation, under its auspices, of the International Centre for the Study of the Preservation and the Restoration of Cultural Property (ICCROM), in Rome, was a further advance. The Centre was established in 1959 with the aims of advising internationally on conservation problems, co-ordinating conservation activators and establishing standards of training courses.

A significant confirmation of professional progress was the transformation at New York in 1966 of the two committees of the International Council of Museums (ICOM), one curatorial on the Care of Paintings (founded in 1949) and the other mainly scientific (founded in the mid-1950s), into the ICOM Committee for Conservation.

Following the Second International Congress of Architects in Venice in 1964 when the Venice Charter was promulgated, the International Council of Monuments and Sites (ICOMOS) was set up in 1965 to deal with archaeological, architectural and town planning questions, to schedule monuments and sites and to monitor relevant legislation. From the early 1960s onwards, international congresses (and the literature emerging from them) held by IIC, ICOM, ICOMOS and ICCROM not only advanced the subject in its various technical specializations but also emphasized the cohesion of conservators and their subject as an interdisciplinary profession.

The use of the term *Conservation* in the title of this series refers to the whole subject of the care and treatment of valuable artefacts, both movable and immovable, but within the discipline conservation has a meaning which is distinct from that of restoration. *Conservation* used in this specialized sense has two aspects: first, the control of the environment to minimize the decay of artefacts and materials; and, second, their treatment to arrest decay and to stabilize them where possible against further deterioration. Restoration is the continuation of the latter process, when conservation treatment is thought to be insufficient, to the extent of reinstating an object, without falsification, to a condition in which it can be exhibited.

In the field of conservation conflicts of values on aesthetic, historical, or technical grounds are often inevitable. Rival attitudes and methods inevitably arise in a subject which is still developing and at the core of these differences there is often a deficiency of technical knowledge. That is one of the principal *raisons d'être* of this series. In most of these matters ethical principles are the subject of much discussion, and generalizations cannot easily cover (say) buildings, furniture, easel paintings and waterlogged wooden objects.

A rigid, universally agreed principle is that all treatment should be adequately documented.

There is also general agreement that structural and decorative falsification should be avoided. In addition there are three other principles which, unless there are overriding objections, it is generally agreed should be followed.

The first is the principle of the reversibility of processes, which states that a treatment should normally be such that the artefact can, if desired, be returned to its pre-treatment condition even after a long lapse of time. This principle is impossible to apply in some cases, for example where the survival of an artefact may depend upon an irreversible process. The second, intrinsic to the whole subject, is that as far as possible decayed parts of an artefact should be conserved and not replaced. The third is that the consequences of the ageing of the original materials (for example 'patina') should not normally be disguised or removed. This includes a secondary proviso that later accretions should not be retained under the false guise of natural patina.

The authors of the volumes in this series give their views on these matters, where relevant, with reference to the types of material within their scope. They take into account the differences in approach to artefacts of essentially artistic significance and to those in which the interest is primarily historical, archaeological or scientific.

The volumes are unified by a systematic and balanced presentation of theoretical and practical material with, where necessary, an objective comparison of different methods and approaches. A balance has also been maintained between the fine (and decorative) arts, archaeology and architecture in those cases where the respective branches of the subject have common ground, for example in the treatment of stone and glass and in the control of the museum environment. Since the publication of the first volume it has been decided to include within the series related monographs and technical studies. To reflect this enlargement of its scope the series has been renamed the Butterworth-Heinemann Series in Conservation and Museology.

Though necessarily different in details of organization and treatment (to fit the particular requirements of the subject) each volume has the same general standard, which is that of such training courses as those of the University of London Institute of Archaeology, the Victoria and Albert Museum, the Conservation Center, New York University, the Institute of Advanced Architectural Studies, York, and ICCROM.

The authors have been chosen from among the acknowledged experts in each field, but as a result of the wide areas of knowledge and technique covered even by the specialized volumes in this series, in many instances multi-authorship has been necessary.

With the existence of IIC, ICOM, ICOMOS and ICCROM, the principles and practice of conservation have become as internationalized as the problems. The collaboration of Consultant Editors will help to ensure that the practices discussed in this series will be applicable throughout the world.

# Contributors

**Part 1 History**

1    Furniture history
*Clive Edwards*

**Part 2 Materials**

2    Wood and wooden structures
*Bruce Hoadley, Nick Umney and
Antoine Wilmering*

3    Upholstery materials and structures
*Sherry Doyal, Kathryn Gill, Nick Umney
and Roger Griffith*

4    Plastics and polymers, coatings and
binding media, adhesives and consoli-
dants
*Jonathan Thornton, Nick Umney,
Shayne Rivers, Gregory Landrey,
Christopher McGlinchey, Susan May,
Brian Considine, Merete Winness and
Albert Neber*

5    Other materials and structures
*Jonathan Thornton, Nick Umney,
Gregory Landrey, Mechthild Baumester
and Susan May*

**Part 3 Deterioration**

6    General review of environment and
deterioration
*Nick Umney*

7    Deterioration of wood and wooden
structures
*Nick Umney, Bruce Hoadley, Antoine
Wilmering and Gregory Landrey*

8    Deterioration of other materials and
structures
*Jonathan Thornton, Nick Umney,
Gregory Landrey, Sherry Doyal, Kathryn
Gill, Roger Griffith and Shayne Rivers*

**Part 4 Conservation**

9    Conservation preliminaries
*Nick Umney and Shayne Rivers*

10    Principles of conserving and repairing
wooden furniture
*Shayne Rivers, Jonathan Thornton, Neil
Trinder, Nick Umney, Antoine
Wilmering and Albert Neber*

11    Principles of cleaning
*Shayne Rivers, Gregory Landrey,
Richard Wolbers and Julie Arslanoğlu*

12    Principles of consolidation, aesthetic
reintegration and coatings
*Shayne Rivers, Gregory Landrey and
Stephen Gritt*

13    Conserving transparent coatings on
wood
*Shayne Rivers, Gregory Landrey and
Nick Umney*

14    Introduction to traditional gilding
*Susan May, Brian Considine and
Shayne Rivers*

15    Conserving other materials I

15.1 Ivory, bone and antler, turtleshell and
horn, mother-of-pearl
*Frank Minney, Shayne Rivers and
Jonathan Thornton*

15.2 Paper labels and linings on furniture
*Jodie Lee Utter and Shayne Rivers*

15.3 Metals
*Francis Brodie, Shayne Rivers and
Jonathan Thornton*

15.4 Ceramics and enamels
*Fi Jordan and Shayne Rivers*

15.5 Flat glass, mirrors, reverse painted and
gilded glass
*Patricia R. Jackson and Shayne Rivers*

16    Other materials II
16.1 Stone and related materials
        *Charlotte Hubbard and Shayne Rivers*
16.2 Plastics
        *Brenda Keneghan and Shayne Rivers*
16.3 Upholstery
        *Sherry Doyal and Kathryn Gill*
16.4 Leather
        *Timothy Hayes and Shayne Rivers*
16.4 Parchment and shagreen
        *Roy Thomson and Shayne Rivers*
16.5 Textiles
        *Marion Kite and Shayne Rivers*
16.6 Painted furniture
        *Shayne Rivers and Richard Wolbers*
16.7 Japanned furniture
        *Marianne Webb and Shayne Rivers*
16.8 Oriental lacquer
        *Shayne Rivers and Nick Umney*
16.9 Gilded furniture
        *Shayne Rivers*

## Alphabetical list of contributors

**Julie Arslanoğlu**
Paintings Conservator, Organic Chemist
USA

**Mechthild Baumeister**
Conservator
The Metropolitan Museum of Art
New York, NY
USA

**Francis Brodie**
Horologist
London
UK

**Brian Considine**
Conservator of Decorative Arts and Sculpture
J Paul Getty Museum
Santa Monica, CA
USA

**Sherry Doyal**
Upholstery Conservator, specialising in the
conservation of plant materials
Devon Conservator
The National Trust
UK

**Dr Clive Edwards**
Senior Lecturer
Loughborough University
Leicester
UK

**Kathryn Gill**
Textile Conservator, specialising in the
conservation of upholstered furniture
and furnishing textiles
Textile Conservation Centre
University of Southampton
UK

**Roger Griffith**
Associate Conservator
Museum of Modern Art
New York, NY
USA

**Stephen Gritt**
Lecturer in Conservation
Courtauld Institute of Art
London
UK

**Timothy Hayes**
Senior Objects Conservator
Heritage Conservation Centre
Singapore

**Dr R. Bruce Hoadley**
Professor of Wood Science and Technology
University of Massachusetts at Amherst
USA

**Charlotte Hubbard**
Senior Conservator, Sculpture
Victoria and Albert Museum
London
UK

**Patricia Jackson**
Conservator specialising in glass, mirrors and
flat decorated glass
UK

**Fi Jordan**
Senior Conservator, Ceramics and Glass
Victoria and Albert Museum
London
UK

**Brenda Keneghan**
Senior Conservation Scientist, Polymers
Victoria and Albert Museum
London
UK

**Marion Kite**
Senior Conservator, Textiles
Victoria and Albert Museum
London
UK

**Gregory Landrey**
Director of Conservation
Winterthur Museum, Garden and Library
Delaware
USA

**Susan May**
Gilding Conservator
Arnold Wiggins and Son
London
UK

**Christopher W. McGlinchey**
Conservation Scientist
The Museum of Modern Art
New York, NY.
USA

**Frank Minney**
Senior Conservator, Organic Artefacts
British Museum
London
UK

**Albert Neher**
Head, Furniture Conservation
Victoria and Albert Museum
London
UK

**Shayne Rivers**
Senior Conservator, Furniture
Victoria and Albert Museum
London
UK

**Roy Thomson**
Chief Executive
Leather Conservation Centre
Northampton
UK

**Jonathan Thornton**
Professor
Art Conservation Department
Buffalo State College
Buffalo, NY.
USA

**Neil Trinder**
Furniture Conservator, specializing in the
conservation of boullework
Sheffield
UK

**Nick Umney**
Director of Collections Services
Victoria and Albert Museum
London
UK

**Jodie Lee Utter**
Paper Conservator
Memphis, TN.
USA

**Marianne Webb**
Decorative Arts Conservator
Royal Ontario Museum
Canada

**Antoine M. Wilmering**
Professor
Graduate Institute Conservation of Cultural
Relics
Tainan National College of the Arts
Taiwan, R.O.C.

**Merete Winness**
Conservator
Norwegian Institute for Cultural Heritage
Research (NIKU)

**Richard Wolbers**
Associate Professor
Winterthur/University of Delaware Art
Conservation Program
Delaware
USA

**Liz Wray**
Illustrator
UK

# Acknowledgements

It would take a very large space indeed to acknowledge everyone who has helped this book to come to fruition and it is inevitable that I will leave out the names of many who deserve to be mentioned individually. First, I wish to thank profoundly all those authors and contributors whose names are given in the contributors' list, especially those who promptly delivered finished text and then had to wait many years before seeing their work in print. I would like to thank the staff of the Conservation Department at the V&A Museum, particularly Charles Wright, John Kitchin, and John Bornhoft, who got me started in conservation and Jonathan Ashley Smith for his support, encouragement and opportunity for professional development in his department. Many professional colleagues have also assisted with advice, references, illustrations and in other ways and I would like to thank particularly Stephen Copestake for allowing me to use material from his third year undergraduate thesis, Merete Winness and Roger Griffith for use of material from their Masters theses, David Pinniger and Jonathan Stein for help with insect pest material, and Junka Mori for picture research. The staff at Butterworth-Heinemann have been very supportive over the years and I would like to thank Anne Berne, Caroline Lacy, Marie Milmore, Clare Sims and Alison Yates, and particularly Neil Warnock Smith. My wife, Lydia and children, Michael and Georgina had to put up with me stuck in front of a keyboard for untold weekends but have been endlessly tolerant and supportive throughout this endeavour. Finally, I have to say a very special thank you to Shayne, without whom this book would never have been finished.

*N.U.*

I am grateful to the many friends and colleagues who assisted, supported or offered constructive criticism during the preparation of this book, in particular Albert Neher, Jonathan Ashley-Smith, Liz Wray, Tim Hayes, Colin Piper, Jonathan Thornton, Gregory Landrey, Julie Arslanoğlu, Alan Cummings, Simon Hogg, Dr A.G. Holton, Brenda Keneghan, Alan Phenix, Christine Powell, Carolyn Sargentson, Terry Vincent (John Mylands Ltd), Marianne Webb, Judith Wetherall, David Widdowson, Richard Wolbers and Yoshihiko Yamashita. My heartfelt thanks goes to my partner, Izzy and son, Dan who have offered me unstinting love and support throughout this project.

*S.R.*

# Illustration acknowledgements

The authors wish to thank the many individuals and institutions, as well as authors, illustrators and publishers, who have generously supplied or given permission to reprint illustrations in this book.

**Plate 1** Courtesy of The Art Conservation Department, Buffalo State College, Buffalo, NY

**Plate 2** Courtesy of the Victoria and Albert Museum, London: (*a,b,c*) photographs by Nanke Schellmann; (*d,e,f*) photographs by Clara von Engelhardt

**Plate 3** Courtesy of the Victoria and Albert Museum, London: photograph by Shayne Rivers

**Plate 4** Photograph by Herb Crossan, Winterthur Museum Garden and Library, with kind permission to reprint.

**Plate 5** Courtesy of Winterthur Museum, Garden and Library

**Plate 6** Photograph by Herb Crossan, the Winterthur, University of Delaware Art Conservation Programme (WUDPAC), with kind permission to reprint

**Plate 8** (*a,c*) Photographs by Shayne Rivers; (*b*) Photograph by Dr Lucia Burgio

**Figure 1.1** Courtesy of the Griffith Institute, Oxford

**Figure 1.2** Courtesy of the V&A Picture Library

**Figure 1.3** Courtesy of the V&A Picture Library

**Figure 1.4** Drawings by Liz Wray

**Figure 1.5** Drawing by Liz Wray

**Figure 1.6** Drawing by Liz Wray

**Figure 1.7** Drawings by Liz Wray

**Figure 1.8** Courtesy of the V&A Picture Library

**Figure 1.9** Courtesy of the V&A Picture Library

**Figure 1.10** Drawing by Liz Wray

**Figure 1.11** Drawing by Liz Wray

**Figure 1.12** Drawings by Liz Wray

**Figure 1.13** Courtesy of the V&A Picture Library

**Figure 1.14** Courtesy of the V&A Picture Library

**Figure 1.15** Courtesy of the V&A Picture Library

**Figure 1.16** Courtesy of Christies Images Ltd, 2002

**Figure 1.17** Courtesy of the V&A Picture Library

**Figure 1.18** Courtesy of the V&A Picture Library

**Figure 1.19** Courtesy of the V&A Picture Library

**Figure 1.20** Courtesy of the V&A Picture Library

**Figure 1.21** Courtesy of the V&A Picture Library

**Figure 1.22** Courtesy of the V&A Picture Library

**Figure 1.23** Courtesy of the V&A Picture Library

**Figure 1.24** Courtesy of the V&A Picture Library

**Figure 1.25** Courtesy of the V&A Picture Library

**Figure 1.26** Courtesy of the V&A Picture Library

**Figure 1.27** Courtesy of the V&A Picture Library

**Figure 1.28** Courtesy of the V&A Picture Library

**Figure 2.1** Reproduced from Hoadley, R.B. (1990) *Understanding Wood: A Craftsman's Guide to Wood Technology*, The Taunton Press, with permission

**Figure 2.2** Reproduced from Hoadley, R.B. (1990) *Understanding Wood: A Craftsman's Guide to Wood Technology*, The Taunton Press, with permission

**Figure 2.3** provided by Bruce Hoadley

**Figure 2.4** Reproduced from Hoadley, R.B. (1990) *Understanding Wood: A Craftsman's Guide to Wood Technology*, The Taunton Press, with permission

**Figure 2.5** Reproduced from Hoadley, R.B. (1990) *Identifying Wood: Accurate Results with Simple Tools*, The Taunton Press, p. 38, with permission

**Figure 2.6** Drawings by Liz Wray

**Figure 2.7** Reproduced from Hoadley, R.B. (1990) *Identifying Wood: Accurate Results with Simple Tools*, The Taunton Press, pp. 38, 39, with permission

**Figure 2.8** Reproduced from Hoadley, R.B. (1990) *Identifying Wood: Accurate Results with Simple Tools*, The Taunton Press, with permission

**Figure 2.9** Reproduced from Hoadley, R.B. (1990) *Identifying Wood: Accurate Results with Simple Tools*, The Taunton Press, Bruce Hoadley, p. 18, with permission

**Figure 2.10** Reproduced from Hoadley, R.B. (1990) *Identifying Wood: Accurate Results with Simple Tools*, The Taunton Press, p. 36, with permission

**Figure 2.11** Reproduced from Hoadley, R.B. (1990) *Identifying Wood: Accurate Results with Simple Tools*, The Taunton Press, pp. 37, 40, with permission

**Figure 2.13** Drawing provided by Bruce Hoadley

**Figure 2.14** Reproduced from Hoadley, R.B. (1990) *Understanding Wood: A Craftsman's Guide to Wood Technology*, The Taunton Press, with permission

**Figure 2.15** Reproduced from Hoadley, R.B. (1990) *Understanding Wood: A Craftsman's Guide to Wood Technology*, The Taunton Press, with permission

**Figure 2.16** Drawings by Liz Wray

**Figure 2.17** Reproduced from Hoadley, R.B. (1990) *Understanding Wood: A Craftsman's Guide to Wood Technology*, The Taunton Press, with permission

**Figure 2.18** Drawing by Bruce Hoadley/Liz Wray

**Figure 2.19** Reproduced from Hoadley, R.B. (1990) *Understanding Wood: A Craftsman's Guide to Wood Technology*, The Taunton Press, with permission

**Figure 2.20** Reproduced from Hoadley, R.B. (1990) *Understanding Wood: A Craftsman's Guide to Wood Technology*, The Taunton Press, with permission

**Figure 2.21** Drawing by Bruce Hoadley/LizWray

**Figure 2.22** Drawing by Liz Wray

**Figure 2.23** Drawing by Liz Wray

**Figure 2.24** Drawing by Liz Wray

**Figure 2.25** Drawing by Liz Wray

**Figure 2.26** Drawing by Liz Wray

**Figure 2.27** Drawing by Liz Wray

**Figure 2.28** Drawing by Liz Wray

**Figure 2.29** Drawing by Liz Wray

**Figure 2.30** Drawing by Liz Wray

**Figure 3.1** Drawing by Liz Wray

**Figure 3.2** Drawing by Liz Wray

**Figure 3.3** Courtesy of the V&A Picture Library

**Figure 3.4** Courtesy of the V&A Picture Library

**Figure 3.5** Drawing by Sherry Doyal/Liz Wray

**Figure 3.6** Courtesy of the Victoria and Albert Museum, London

**Figure 3.7** Drawing by Kathryn Gill

**Figure 3.8** Drawing by Kathryn Gill/Liz Wray

**Figure 3.9** Courtesy of Kathryn Gill

**Figure 4.1** Drawing by Liz Wray

**Figure 4.2** Drawing by Liz Wray

**Figure 4.3** Drawing by Liz Wray

**Figure 4.4** Drawing by Liz Wray

**Figure 4.6** Drawing by Liz Wray after Kumanotani, J, (1988) The Chemistry of Oriental Lacquer (Rhus Verniciflua) in Brommelle, N.S., and Smith, P., (eds) *Urushi: Proceedings of the 1985 Urushi Study Group* Getty Conservation Institute, Figure 7, p. 248

**Figure 4.7** Drawing by Liz Wray

**Figure 4.8** Drawing by Liz Wray

**Figure 4.9** Drawing by Liz Wray

**Figure 4.14** (*a,c,d*) Drawing by Liz Wray

**Figure 5.1** Courtesy of the V&A Picture Library

**Figure 5.2** Courtesy of The Art Conservation Department, Buffalo State College, Buffalo, NY

**Figure 5.3** Drawing by Liz Wray

**Figure 5.4** Courtesy of The Art Conservation Department, Buffalo State College, Buffalo, NY

**Figure 5.5** Courtesy of The Art Conservation Department, Buffalo State College, Buffalo, NY

**Figure 5.6** Courtesy of The Art Conservation Department, Buffalo State College, Buffalo, NY

**Figure 5.7** From E.O. Espinoza and M. Mann (1992) *Identification Guide for Ivory and Ivory Substitutes*, 2nd edn, World Wildlife Fund, Baltimore, with permission

**Figure 5.8** Courtesy of The Art Conservation Department, Buffalo State College, Buffalo, NY

**Figure 5.9** Courtesy of The Art Conservation Department, Buffalo State College, Buffalo, NY

**Figure 5.10** Courtesy of the V&A Picture Library

**Figure 5.11** Courtesy of The Art Conservation Department, Buffalo State College, Buffalo, NY

**Figure 5.12** Courtesy of The Art Conservation Department, Buffalo State College, Buffalo, NY

**Figure 5.13** Courtesy of the V&A Picture Library

**Figure 5.14** Courtesy of the V&A Picture Library

**Figure 5.15** Courtesy of the V&A Picture Library

**Figure 5.16** Courtesy of the V&A Picture Library

**Figure 5.17** Courtesy of the V&A Picture Library

**Figure 5.18** Courtesy of The Art Conservation Department, Buffalo State College, Buffalo, NY

**Figure 5.20** Drawing by Liz Wray

**Figure 6.1** Drawing by Liz Wray

**Figure 6.2** Drawing by Liz Wray

**Figure 6.3** Drawing by Liz Wray

**Figure 6.4** Drawing by Liz Wray

**Figure 7.1** Drawing by Liz Wray

**Figure 7.2** Drawing by Liz Wray

**Figure 7.3** Photograph by Shayne Rivers

**Figure 7.4** Reproduced from Hoadley, R.B. (1990) *Identifying Wood: Accurate Results with Simple Tools*, The Taunton Press, p. 73, with permission

**Figure 7.5** Photograph by Nick Umney

**Figure 7.6** Reproduced by generous permission of the Central Science Laboratory (CSL) of the Department for Environment, Food and Rural Affairs (DEFRA) © Crown Copyright

**Figure 7.7** Reproduced by generous permission of the Central Science Laboratory (CSL) of the Department for Environment, Food and Rural Affairs (DEFRA) © Crown Copyright

**Figure 7.8** Courtesy of David Pinniger

**Figure 7.9** Courtesy of the Victoria and Albert Museum, London

**Figure 7.10** Reproduced by generous permission of the Central Science Laboratory (CSL) of the Department for Environment, Food and Rural Affairs (DEFRA) © Crown Copyright

**Figure 7.11** Courtesy of the Victoria and Albert Museum, London

**Figure 7.12** Courtesy of the Victoria and Albert Museum, London

**Figure 7.13** Courtesy of Mr and Mrs M.J. Luxton

**Figure 7.14** Courtesy of the Victoria and Albert Museum, London

**Figure 7.15** Drawing by Liz Wray, derived from Thomson (1986)

**Figure 7.16** Data compiled by Nick Umney; tabulated by Liz Wray

**Figure 7.17** Courtesy of the Victoria and Albert Museum, London

**Figure 8.1** Courtesy of The Art Conservation Department, Buffalo State College, Buffalo, NY and the Victoria and Albert Museum, London

**Figure 8.2** Drawing by Liz Wray

**Figure 8.4** Courtesy of Winterthur Museum, Garden and Library

**Figure 8.5** Drawing by Liz Wray

**Figure 8.6** Courtesy of the Victoria and Albert Museum, London; photograph by Shayne Rivers

**Figure 8.7** Courtesy of the Victoria and Albert Museum, London; photograph by Nigel Bamforth

**Figure 8.8** Courtesy of Winterthur Museum, Garden and Library

**Figure 8.9** Courtesy of Winterthur Museum, Garden and Library

**Figure 8.11** Courtesy of the Victoria and Albert Museum; photograph by Roger Griffith

**Figure 8.14** Courtesy of the Victoria and Albert Museum; photographs by Roger Griffith

**Figure 8.15** (*b*) Courtesy of the Victoria and Albert Museum, London; photograph by Roger Griffith

**Figure 9.1** Courtesy of the V&A Picture Library

**Figure 9.2** Photograph by Shayne Rivers

**Figure 9.3** Courtesy of Winterthur Museum, Garden and Library

**Figure 9.4** Photograph by Shayne Rivers

**Figure 9.5** Photographs by Shayne Rivers

**Figure 9.6** Photographs by Shayne Rivers

**Figure 9.7** Photograph by Shayne Rivers

**Figure 9.8** Photograph by Shayne Rivers

**Figure 9.9** Photograph by Shayne Rivers

**Figure 9.10** Photograph by Shayne Rivers

**Figure 9.11** Photograph by Shayne Rivers

**Figure 10.1** Drawing by Liz Wray

**Figure 10.2** Drawing by Liz Wray

**Figure 10.3** Drawing by Liz Wray

**Figure 10.4** Drawings by Liz Wray: (*a*) after Hayward, C.H. (1967) *Furniture Repairs*, Evans, ch.8, Fig. 5, with permission

**Figure 10.5** Drawings by Liz Wray

**Figure 10.6** (*a,b*) Courtesy of Leeds Museums and Galleries (Lotherton Hall); (*c,d,e*) Courtesy of the Victoria and Albert Museum, London

**Figure 10.7** Drawing by Liz Wray

**Figure 10.8** Drawing by Liz Wray

**Figure 10.9** Courtesy of The Art Conservation Department, Buffalo State College, Buffalo, NY

**Figure 10.10** Drawing by Liz Wray

**Figure 10.11** Drawings by Liz Wray

**Figure 10.12** Drawing by Liz Wray

**Figure 10.13** Courtesy of the Victoria and Albert Museum, London

**Figure 10.14** Courtesy of the Victoria and Albert Museum, London

**Figure 10.15** Drawing by Liz Wray

**Figure 10.16** Drawings by Liz Wray: (*a*) after Rodd, J. (1976) *Repairing and Restoring Antique Furniture*, David & Charles, Fig. 38, with permission

**Figure 10.17** Drawings by Liz Wray

**Figure 10.18** Photograph by Shayne Rivers

**Figure 10.19** Drawings by Liz Wray

**Figure 10.20** Courtesy of the Victoria and Albert Museum, London, photograph by Shayne Rivers

**Figure 10.21** Drawings by Liz Wray

**Figure 10.22** Drawings by Liz Wray

**Figure 10.23** (*a,b,c*) Courtesy of the Victoria and Albert Museum, London

**Figure 10.24** Drawing by Neil Trinder/Liz Wray

**Figure 10.25** Drawings by Liz Wray

**Figure 11.1** Drawing by Liz Wray after Moncrieff, A. and Weaver, G. (1992) *Science for Conservators*, Vol. 2: *Cleaning*, Routledge, Fig. 1.1, with permission

**Figure 11.2** (*a,b*) Drawings by Alan Cummings/ Liz Wray; (*c*) courtesy of the Victoria and Albert Museum, London

**Figure 11.3** Courtesy of the Victoria and Albert Museum, London; photograph by Timothy Hayes

**Figure 11.4** Photograph by Herb Crossan, the Winterthur, University of Delaware Art Conservation Programme (WUDPAC), with kind permission to reprint

**Figure 11.5** Courtesy of the Victoria and Albert Museum, London

**Figure 11.6** Drawings by Alan Cummings/Liz Wray

**Figure 11.7** Courtesy of the Victoria and Albert Museum, London; photograph by Timothy Hayes

**Figure 11.8** Courtesy of the Victoria and Albert Museum, London

**Figure 11.9** Julie Arslanoğlu based on a graph by Michalski, S, (1990) A Physical Model of the Cleaning of Oil Paint in *Cleaning Retouching and Coatings* Conference Preprints, IIC, Figure 4, p. 87

**Figure 11.10** Based on data from Horie, V. (1992) *Materials for Conservation*, Butterworth-Heinemann, with permission

**Figure 11.11** Based on data from Banik, G. and Krist, G. (eds) (1986) *Lösungsmittel in der Restaurierung*, Verlag der Apfel, p. 101 as reproduced in Tímár-Balázsy, A. and Eastop, D. (1998) *Chemical Principles of Textile Conservation*, Butterworth-Heinemann, with permission

**Figure 11.12-11.14** Based on data from Horie, V. (1992) *Materials for Conservation*, Butterworth-Heinemann, App. 3, p. 219

**Figure 11.15** Drawing by Liz Wray

**Figure 11.16** Drawing by Liz Wray

**Figure 11.17** Drawing by Liz Wray

**Figure 11.18** Drawing by Liz Wray

**Figure 11.19** Drawing by Liz Wray

**Figure 11.20** Based on Moncrieff, A. and Weaver, G. (1992) *Science for Conservators*, Vol. 2: *Cleaning*, Routledge, Fig. 5.7, p. 84, after De Jong (1966), with permission

**Figure 11.22** Derived from tabulated data in *Keys to Chelation: Versene Chelating Agents*, Dow Chemical Company, 1985, with permission

**Figure 11.23** Courtesy of the Victoria and Albert Museum, London, photograph by Nigel Bamforth

**Figure 11.24** Courtesy of Richard Wolbers

**Figure 11.25** Courtesy of Hercules

**Figure 11.26** Manufacturer's information, Carbopol Resins Handbook, BFGoodrich 1991, Figs 4 and 5, with permission

**Figure 12.1** Drawings by Liz Wray

**Figure 12.2** Photographs by Shayne Rivers

**Figure 12.3** Courtesy of Richard Wolbers

**Figure 12.4** Courtesy of Victoria and Albert Museum, London, photographs by Shayne Rivers

**Figure 12.5** Drawing by Liz Wray after Thomson, G. (1988) *The Museum Environment*, Butterworth-Heinemann, Fig. 59, with permission

**Figure 12.6** Julie Arslanoğlu based on (1) Thomson, G. (1988) *The Museum Environment*, Butterworth-Heinemann, Fig. 59; (2) Mayer, R. (1991) *The Artist's Handbook of Materials and Techniques*, 5th edn, Faber and Faber, p. 70; (3) Staniforth, S. (1985) Retouching and colour matching: the restorer and metamerism, *Studies in Conservation*, 30, 101-11, Fig. 4a

**Figure 12.7** Drawing by Liz Wray

**Figure 12.8** Courtesy of Kate Duffy, Associate Scientist, Analytic Laboratory, Winterthur Museum

**Figure 12.9** Courtesy of Degussa-Hüls

**Figure 12.10** Drawing by Liz Wray after Brill, T.B. (1980) *Light: Its Interaction with Art and Antiquities*, Plenum Press, p. 103, with permission

**Figure 12.11** Courtesy of Degussa-Hüls

**Figure 12.12** Courtesy of Degussa-Hüls

**Figure 12.13** Drawing by Liz Wray

**Figure 12.14** Drawing by Liz Wray

**Figure 12.15** Drawing by Liz Wray

**Figure 12.16** Drawing by Liz Wray

**Figure 13.1** Courtesy of the Victoria and Albert Museum, London

**Figure 13.2** Courtesy of Kate Duffy, Associate Scientist, Analytical Laboratory, Winterthur Museum

**Figure 13.3** Photograph by Shayne Rivers

**Figure 13.4** Photograph by Shayne Rivers

**Figure 13.5** Tímár-Balázsy, A. and Eastop, D. (1998) *Chemical Principles of Textile Conservation*, Butterworth- Heinemann, pp. 226, 232, with permission

**Figure 13.6** Courtesy of Kate Duffy, Associate Scientist, Analytical Laboratory, Winterthur Museum

**Figure 13.7** Photograph by Shayne Rivers

**Figure 13.8** Photographs by Shayne Rivers

**Figure 13.10** Courtesy of the Victoria and Albert Museum, London; photograph by Nanke Schellmann

**Figure 13.11** Courtesy of Winterthur Museum, Garden and Library

**Figures 13.12** Drawing by Liz Wray after Hayward, C. (1988) *Staining and Polishing*, Evans Bros, London/Unwin Hyman, Fig. 14, with permission

**Figure 13.13** Drawing by Liz Wray after Hayward, C. (1988) *Staining and Polishing*, Evans Bros, London/Unwin Hyman, Fig. 16, with permission

**Figure 13.14** Drawing by Liz Wray after Hayward, C. (1988) *Staining and Polishing*, Evans Bros, London/Unwin Hyman, Fig. 15, with permission

**Figure 13.15** Courtesy of the Victoria and Albert Museum, London

**Figure 13.16** Courtesy of Degussa Hüls

**Figure 13.17** Courtesy of Degussa Hüls

**Figure 14.1** Courtesy of Arnold Wiggins and Sons Ltd

**Figure 14.2** Courtesy of Arnold Wiggins and Sons Ltd

**Figure 14.3** Courtesy of The Art Conservation Department, Buffalo State College, Buffalo, NY

**Figure 14.4** Courtesy of Arnold Wiggins and Sons Ltd

**Figure 14.5** Courtesy of Arnold Wiggins and Sons Ltd

**Figure 14.6** Courtesy of Arnold Wiggins and Sons Ltd

**Figure 14.7** Courtesy of Arnold Wiggins and Sons Ltd

**Figure 14.8** Courtesy of Arnold Wiggins and Sons Ltd

**Figures 14.9** Courtesy of Arnold Wiggins and Sons Ltd

**Figure 14.10** Courtesy of Arnold Wiggins and Sons Ltd

**Figure 14.11** Courtesy of The Art Conservation Department, Buffalo State College, Buffalo, NY

**Figure 14.12** Courtesy of Arnold Wiggins and Sons Ltd

**Figure 14.13** Courtesy of Arnold Wiggins and Sons Ltd

**Figure 14.14** Courtesy of Arnold Wiggins and Sons Ltd

**Figure 14.15** Courtesy of Arnold Wiggins and Sons Ltd

**Figure 14.16** Courtesy of Arnold Wiggins and Sons Ltd

**Figure 14.17** Courtesy of Arnold Wiggins and Sons Ltd

**Figure 14.18** Courtesy of Arnold Wiggins and Sons Ltd

**Figure 14.19** Courtesy of The Art Conservation Department, Buffalo State College, Buffalo, NY

**Figure 14.20** Courtesy of The Art Conservation Department, Buffalo State College, Buffalo, NY

**Figure 15.1** Courtesy of The Art Conservation Department, Buffalo State College, Buffalo, NY

**Figure 15.2** Courtesy of Jodie Lee Utter

**Figure 15.3** Courtesy of The Art Conservation Department, Buffalo State College, Buffalo, NY

**Figure 15.4** Courtesy of the Victoria and Albert Museum, photograph by Shayne Rivers

**Figure 15.5** Courtesy of The Art Conservation Department, Buffalo State College, Buffalo, NY

**Figure 15.6** Courtesy of the Victoria and Albert Museum, London, photograph by Simon Metcalf

**Figure 15.7** Courtesy of the Victoria and Albert Museum, London

**Figure 15.8** Courtesy of the Victoria and Albert Museum, London, photographs by Shayne Rivers

**Figure 15.9** Courtesy of the Victoria and Albert Museum, London, photographs by Sophia Wills

**Figure 15.10** Courtesy of The Art Conservation Department, Buffalo State College, Buffalo, NY

**Figure 15.11** Courtesy of the Victoria and Albert Museum, London

**Figure 15.12** Courtesy of the Victoria and Albert Museum, London

**Figure 15.13** Courtesy of the Victoria and Albert Museum, London, photograph by Shayne Rivers

**Figure 15.14** Courtesy of the Victoria and Albert Museum, London

**Figure 15.15** Courtesy of P.R. Jackson

**Figure 15.16** Courtesy of the Victoria and Albert Museum, London, photographs by Shayne Rivers

**Figure 15.17** Courtesy of P.R. Jackson

**Figure 15.18** Courtesy of the Victoria and Albert Museum, London

**Figure 16.1** Courtesy of the Victoria and Albert Museum, London

**Figure 16.2** Courtesy of the Victoria and Albert Museum, London

**Figure 16.3** Courtesy of the Victoria and Albert Museum, London, photograph by Roger Griffith

**Figure 16.4** Courtesy of the Victoria and Albert Museum, London, photograph by Paul Robins

**Figure 16.5** Drawings by Kathryn Gill/Liz Wray

**Figure 16.6** Drawings by Kathryn Gill/Liz Wray

**Figure 16.7** Courtesy of the Leather Conservation Centre, Northampton, UK

**Figure 16.8** Drawing by Timothy Hayes/Liz Wray

**Figure 16.9** Courtesy of the Leather Conservation Centre, Northampton, UK

**Figure 16.10** Courtesy of the Victoria and Albert Museum, London, photographs by Shayne Rivers

**Figure 16.11** Courtesy of the Victoria and Albert Museum, London

**Figure 16.12** Courtesy of the Victoria and Albert Museum, London, photograph by Shayne Rivers

**Figure 16.13** Courtesy of the Victoria and Albert Museum, London, photograph by Marion Kite

**Figure 16.14** Courtesy of the Victoria and Albert Museum, London

**Figure 16.15** Photograph by Herb Crossan, Winterthur Museum Library and Gardens, with kind permission to reprint

**Figure 16.16** Drawing by Liz Wray after Feller, R.L., Stolow, N. and Jones, E.H. (1985) *On Picture Varnishes and their Solvents*, National Gallery of Art, Washington, DC, Fig. 4-2, with permission

**Figure 16.17** Layout by Brenda Keneghan

**Figure 16.18** Courtesy of Shayne Rivers

**Figure 16.19** Courtesy of the Victoria and Albert Museum, London, photograph by Shayne Rivers

**Figure 16.20** Courtesy of Günther Heckmann

**Figure 16.21** Drawing by Liz Wray

**Figure 16.22** Courtesy of Günther Heckmann

**Figure 16.23** Courtesy of the Victoria and Albert Museum, London, photographs by Shayne Rivers

**Figure 16.24** Courtesy of the Victoria and Albert Museum, London, photograph by Rowan Carter

**Figure 16.25** (*a*) photograph by Hiroshi Kato (*b*) photograph by Shayne Rivers

**Figure 16.26** Courtesy of The Art Conservation Department, Buffalo State College, Buffalo, NY

**Figure 16.27** Courtesy of The Art Conservation Department, Buffalo State College, Buffalo, NY

**Figure 16.28** Courtesy of The Art Conservation Department, Buffalo State College, Buffalo, NY

**Figure 16.29** Courtesy of The Art Conservation Department, Buffalo State College, Buffalo, NY

# Part 1

# History

# 1

# Furniture history

## 1.1 Introduction

The importance of furniture as an indicator of the way people live has been recognized by many social historians as well as those interested solely in furniture. This recognition has led to a distinction between historians of antiques and decorative arts, and those who take a 'material culture' approach. The latter examine furniture as part of an effort to understand the society that made and used it. The analysis of furniture is often the same for both groups: it is the emphasis put on the results that varies along with the types of furniture examined.

Locating furniture types and their usage within the society that produced them will help to reveal the social structure, wealth and intellectual values that society had. In addition to this, the historical events and circumstances which influenced art and design, the economic, political, religious and intellectual climate had an effect on the way furniture was designed, made and used. All these strands help in explaining how ideas about function, comfort, style and use of materials are manifested in furniture. The production and use of furniture were also dependent on the materials and technology available to the makers. Therefore, to gain a fuller understanding, one also needs to investigate the construction, quality of workmanship and available tools.

Each subsequent section is therefore planned so that a brief historical context is followed by an analysis of functional types and the development of particular forms of furniture. This is supplemented by a discussion of stylistic features and constructional elements. Materials used in the process of making are then discussed, followed by an evaluation of the tools and techniques used in construction, from the conversion of timber to the final finish. The sections conclude with a brief discussion of the organization of the trade and the role of the craftsman.

This account is necessarily focused predominantly on England, America and France, but a similar approach can be applied to other traditions. We apologize to all colleagues for whom this is not the most relevant axis. We hope, however, that the approach taken together with the reference points provided in the text and bibliography will still be helpful in illuminating the range of materials, structures and techniques encountered by the furniture conservator. Some further discourse of the history of technology will be found in Part 2 with reference to upholstery and other non-wood materials.

## 1.2 Earliest times to the Middle Ages

### 1.2.1 Egypt

The earliest evidence of true furniture is found in the Egyptian society that existed some five thousand years ago. The exceptional circumstances of survival in royal tombs have given us famous examples of furniture. It is apparent that beds, chairs, stools, tables and storage boxes had all been created by 3000 BC, and there is no doubt that a skilled workforce existed in Egypt.

Beds were developed from crude frames lashed together, to sophisticated jointed frames and proper suspensions of leather thongs. They were supported on short legs, usually in the form of a bull's foot. Beds were often supplied with a separate head-rest, as headboards were unknown.

**Figure 1.1**  Golden throne, tomb of Tutankhamun (1336–1327 BC). The chair is almost completely covered with thick gold sheet. The seat, a flat board of wood covered in gold, is decorated with over 2000 squares of gold, calcite and faience. The chair back depicts the seated young pharaoh who is being anointed by his wife, Ankhesnamun. Their skins are depicted in chiselled red glass, wigs in light blue faience, whilst their robes are made from sheet silver embellished with calcite, faience and coloured glass

Seats were derived from backless stools, initially having framed seats with carved bull's legs to the front, and then developing to armchairs by the fourth dynasty (c.2600–2500 BC). The most well-known example of an Egyptian seat is Tutankhamun's gold throne, both as a model of furniture-making and also as the embodiment of the symbolic authority of the chair (*Figure 1.1*). On a more mundane level, stools remained popular, often designed with braced struts and a white paint finish. Folding stools were also used: they often had hide seats, and cross-frames decorated as carved duck's heads inlaid with ivory.

Tables were usually small, hardly more than stands for food or offerings. Gaming boards were mounted onto legged frames to create the earliest example of games tables. Most boxes, whether of wood, papyrus or reed, were rectangular with short feet. Some were fitted with divisions for toiletries, jewellery and the like.

The selection of materials began in the locality and was extended to other sources. The only local timbers – acacia, sycamore, fig and tamarisk – were supplemented by imported woods, such as cedar, cypress ebony, juniper and thuya. The shortage of timbers resulted either in the use of veneer or a build up of smaller pieces of wood. In other cases, furniture was occasionally overlaid with gold or silver or made from solid ivory.

The construction of cabinets was based on the mortise and tenon, dovetail and mitred joints. Hinges were used from the eighteenth dynasty (1575–1300 BC) as a replacement for wooden pivots in chests, but locks were rare.

Woodworking tools included mallets, saws with copper or bronze blades, axes and drills. For levelling timber, adzes were used since the woodworking plane was not invented until later. This is perhaps one reason why the Egyptians ground the timber surface with sand and overlaid it with gesso, ready for gilding or painting. In some cases a transparent varnish was used.

The origins of the techniques of wood-turning and bending have been the subject of some dispute amongst experts. It is probable that whilst bending was known in Egypt, the lathe originated in Syria (c.1000 BC) and was not known to the Egyptians. However, the establishment of many type-forms, tools and techniques originated from this time.

### 1.2.2   Greece

Very few pieces of Greek furniture survive, so the main sources are the illustrations on pottery and a few remaining stone-carved items. Nevertheless, there is enough evidence to identify the main furniture types. It is not surprising that the main categories resembled Egyptian prototypes but there were other developments that had a long-lasting influence.

The most important of these was the introduction of the couch as a development of the Egyptian bed. It was used not only as a bed but also as a sofa for reclining upon. This developed stylistically into the Greek sofa with its well-known curved head and footboards.

Seating arrangements were based on a range of stools and chair types. Stools were basic four-legged versions or box-like constructions. In addition there was the diphros, a four-legged stool with stretchers. The famous

**Figure 1.2** Klismos chair, English, *c.*1805. The design for this chair is based on the classical Greek Klismos form

klismos chair form (*Figure 1.2*), originally with well-proportioned outward-curving legs and a back panel at shoulder height, gradually developed a top-heavy back board, thus making it rather clumsy in appearance.

The use of chests is evident but no such item as a cupboard was made, as most items were hung on the wall. Low tables were used for dining purposes, then subsequently removed.

Due to the plentiful supply of timber, the Greeks avoided the need for veneers and it was only in Roman times that the art returned. However, materials such as marble, bronze, inlaid ivory and precious stones were used to decorate important pieces of furniture, often in conjunction with wood.

Etruscan furniture often relied on Greek models. The main Etruscan contribution to furniture-making was the use of bronze for tripods, candelabra and a particular circular casket called a cista. They also produced a chair type which was based on a barrel shape, having a back made in either wood or sheet bronze, curving round to form arms.

### 1.2.3 Rome

The continuation of Greek ideals, through the spread of Roman civilization around the Mediterranean, ensured that furniture of Graeco-Roman style was used all over the Empire. For example, straight-legged folding stools have been found in Belgium and England, cross-legged stools in Holland, and a remarkable silver tripod-table in Germany. Greek forms naturally continued, with couches and klismos chairs being the most popular. Some Roman chairs were based on an upright panelled chair and there are instances of tub-shaped chairs being made from wicker.

Tables were small and round, often made in bronze or silver, with three or four legs in the shape of animal legs. Storage furniture was still mainly in the form of chests, but later came the idea of a cupboard with doors and shelves.

The Romans used a great variety of materials which included imported veneers and highly prized woods, bronze, marble, silver and materials peculiar to a specific region.

The invention of the plane, arguably the most important advance in woodworking, seems to have occurred in Roman times, as no evidence has been found of its use previously. The manufacture of furniture was aided by the development of the plane which removed a continuous shaving rather than a chip, and so allowed not only shaping, but also close fitting of parts and a smooth finish.

### 1.2.4 Byzantium and the Romanesque period

The collapse of the Roman Empire in the fifth century AD moved the centre of culture to Byzantium. The Byzantine aesthetic was based on an amalgam of a new Christian tradition, mixed with Hellenistic taste and an oriental interest in rigid abstract ornamentation. In addition to this stylistic mix was the continuity of the cabinet-making tradition which resulted in the survival of the skilled craft.

Chairs and thrones remained important and were now based on a box shape with a back. X-framed chairs, often made of metal, were typically fitted with a slung leather seat. Combinations of desk and lectern were significant, indicating the importance of manuscripts and reading. Tables followed classical models, sometimes with drawers and lecterns, in a variety of shapes including circular. Chests were important and the open cupboard was fairly common. Some beds were magnificent structures with high canopies and curtains.

The skill of Byzantine woodworkers was demonstrated by their use of the lathe. They also used the panelled construction process to avoid the cracking of ivory panels due to shrinkage. As in other parts of the Mediterranean, limited amounts of wood meant that stone, metal and other materials were also used to make furniture.

The cataclysmic changes in the Western economy and political map resulted in an amalgam of classical styles, Byzantine skills and northern traditions. This period, called Romanesque (AD 1000–1300) was notable for its unsettled and unstable way of life, which resulted in generally sparsely furnished homes which had furniture that could be easily moved at will. This mobility is remembered in a variety of European languages in words such as *mobili*, *möbel* and *meubles*.

Chests and boxes of all sizes were the commonest articles of furniture. They ranged from the simple dugout tree trunk, through dome-topped and detachable lidded versions, to six-plank or boarded chests. Cupboards and presses were sturdily constructed and brightly decorated, and tables were trestle types or semicircular in shape.

Chairs were still a sign of rank, and the style of a chair reflected one's position in society. Both simple turned chairs with pegged members and box-seated chairs were decorated with carving, applied mouldings and arcading. Stools with turned legs were common, but the X-shaped or faldsthul (folding stool) was more convenient.

## 1.3   Medieval

### Background

For much of the Medieval or Gothic period, a large part of Europe was at war or in an unsettled state. The feudal system limited the ability of most of the population to own any furniture other than the basic necessities, and most craftsmen were only employed by powerful churches or nobles. In 1215 the Magna Carta was signed and became a basis for an English Parliament and system of law which gradually developed to support a growing merchant class. During the 1350s the Black Death led to

serious depopulation, which indirectly brought about the end of the feudal system. It was not until 1485, when the Wars of the Roses were brought to an end by a victorious Henry Tudor, that a firm monarchy could be established and bring peace and prosperity to England.

Owing to these difficult conditions, few items of furniture were needed and those that were available were made to be portable or collapsible. Scanty furniture contrasted with the prestige of textiles, hangings, gold and silver plate and carpets, which were portable as well as useful and luxurious.

In the history of furniture, the architectural shell has always had a great influence on design. Gothic architectural forms are overriding in any discussion of medieval furnishings or designs. The Gothic style was all pervasive over much of Europe, and is evident in all furniture forms in most countries. However, the beginning of a Renaissance in Italy in the early fifteenth century changed forever the way furniture was made, decorated and used.

### Functional types

It is important to remember that domestic requirements were generally very limited, although there are records of very finely furnished interiors for elite residences. Seating remained a prime use of furniture. Benches were made in the same way as three-legged stools, i.e. legs were pushed into holes and pegged with wedges. Thrones remained symbols of authority: examples could include the Coronation chair, Dagobert's bronze throne and the silver throne of King Martin of Aragon. Chairs developed in England, France and the Netherlands, based on a box-like panelled structure, possibly derived from chest construction.

The chest was arguably the most important piece of medieval furniture. Chests, which, as previously mentioned began as dugouts or trunks, had developed by the fourteenth century into a type that was made up from solid planks, nailed or pegged together. From the fifteenth century, some chests were made using a framed construction thus reducing the undesirable consequences of both shrinkage in inadequately seasoned timber and the normal movement of wood in service.

Apart from chests, cupboards began to be made for storage (*Figure 1.3*). German exam-

**Figure 1.3** Late medieval oak English livery cupboard. Planked and nailed construction with carved gothic open tracery forming the ventilation panels in the doors

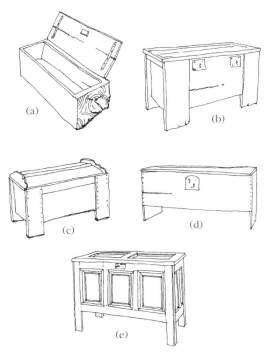

**Figure 1.4** Chest types
(*a*) Solid hewn or dugout chest (up to the fifteenth century). These were made from a solid baulk of timber from which the interior had been bored out or dug out with an adze, axe or chisel. The unhewn end walls varied in thickness but were prone to shakes and splits that radiated from the pith of the log. The timber was often reinforced with multiple iron straps. (*b*) Clamped front chest (thirteenth to seventeenth century). These were constructed from planks rather than hewn from solid baulks of timber. 'Clamp' refers to the boards that form part of the front and rear of the chest and extend past the base of the chest to act as feet. (*c*) Ark type chest (thirteenth to eighteenth century). These were a variation of the clamped front form that were usually, though not exclusively, used for storage of grain or bread. The lid was not originally hinged or fixed to the base. This allowed the lid to be removed and used as a kneading trough or hand barrow. (*d*) Six plank or boarded chest (through the Middle Ages and up to the nineteenth century). These were made from thick planks of wood, usually oak, that were pegged or nailed together and often reinforced with iron strapwork. The grain of the front and back planks ran horizontally. The sides were often extended in length to form feet and as a result the grain ran vertically. This method of construction restrains the movement of the timber in service and as a result splits in the front and back panels are common. (*e*) Framed and panelled chest (from the sixteenth century onwards). The panels are fitted (not glued) into grooves in the (mortise and tenoned) frame components. Movement in service of the panels is unrestricted and therefore the panels do not split. Frame and panel construction produced chests that were strong and comparatively lightweight

ples of Gothic armoires were most impressive, originally having been painted in vivid colours. The buffet, another display and storage item, was made with a stepped-tier construction for displaying silver items. It depended on rank how many tiers were made and used. A second type, not stepped but canopied, evolved into a cupboard as it became enclosed. The armoire or aumbry, originally a safe, became a livery cupboard, used to store food. Tables were based on the trestle principle.

The four-poster image of beds is not always an accurate description, as many had testers suspended from the ceiling or were fitted with a headboard instead. Italian beds were different, having head and footboards rather than a tester. Box beds remained popular as they were built into the fabric of the house.

### Design and construction
The relationship between architectural decoration and furniture was important, so it is evident that there would be some use of the same

motifs. For example the shallow geometric carving that is found on much medieval furniture is clearly taken from the stonemason's tradition.

In the early part of this period, furniture-making was a branch of carpentry. This was because there was no demand, in England, for a separate trade of cabinetmaker, because the nature of house building and furnishing allowed for the carpenter, and later the joiner, to manage all the work required. Indeed, the relation between the building and its furnishing was often close. Some furniture was dependent upon the wall and bedsteads were often part of the wall. Other receptacles were formed by building doors over recesses in the wall thickness. The construction of chests, stools and trestles all came within the remit of the carpenter. Boards were pegged to each other, and chests and boxes were bound with iron bands to try to minimize the effects of warping. Chests were sometimes made with internal vertical stiles that formed feet as well as a frame. Although uncommon, a crude dovetail joint was known in chest construction. Examples of chest construction are shown in *Figure 1.4.*

### Materials used

Timber dominated, the most common in use being ash, elm and oak, with oak the most popular. However, it was often the case that the local material was the inevitable choice.

The forging of metal was a highly skilled trade and the use of metal fittings occurred from the first furniture in this period. Straps were made for chests, to ensure that there was as little movement as possible: these as well as hinges, hasps and protective scrollwork, were all worked in wrought iron. By the fourteenth century, chests were often fitted with a lock, the movement of which was sunk into the woodwork. Strap hinges were used so that the strap round a chest combined to make a hinge in one piece. On cupboard doors, butterfly hinges were common until the fifteenth century when they were elongated to form a decorative strap. Metals were occasionally used for more than just fittings and examples of iron furniture are known. Very rarely, silver, gold, pewter and ivory were used to decorate important pieces.

### Tools and techniques

Perhaps one of the most important changes in furniture-making in this period was that from nailed and pegged board construction, to framed-up construction. The reasons for these constructional changes and the pace at which they occurred are difficult to fathom, but three separate theories have been proposed. First, the desire for lighter, more easily moved furniture, which introduced sawn timber and panels rather than baulks and boards. Secondly, the invention of the water-powered saw mill in Germany in the early fourteenth century could have made it easier to convert logs into thinner panels and more manageable boards, especially in comparison to the older methods of two-handed pit sawing. Thirdly, there is an obvious benefit in not having timbers that split. Whatever the reason, the class of workmen called joiners, from the end of the fifteenth century, were encouraged to develop skills of artistry only previously known to masons and smiths. Panelling of 'wainscot' (quarter-sawn oak) became popular for interiors once timber conversion had become easier. This new-found delight encouraged changes such as allowing the wood members of bed-testers, posts and headboards to be exposed rather than hidden beneath cloth, and, more important, for ornament to be produced from the wood itself, rather than the painting or applied metal work. The construction method still necessitated mouldings to be worked in the solid and for masons' mitres (where joint and mitre do not coincide) to be used. This was discontinued in the sixteenth century when true mitres began to be constructed. Frame and panel construction is illustrated in *Figure 2.29.*

### Surface decoration and finish

Carving was one of the most popular methods of furniture decoration in the Gothic period. Chip carving and piercing made it possible to reproduce many of the designs (tracery and roundels for example) that were based on stonemasons' work. The carving motif most recognized is the linenfold design that was used on wall panelling and furniture towards the end of the fifteenth century.

Apart from these carving techniques, inlay or intarsia, painting and gilding were also used to decorate furniture. Painting was particularly important during the period 1200–1500 and the conjunction of polychromy and carving generally falls into two groups, those items in which painting makes the design and those in which painting is a colouring medium for ironwork or carving. In the later Gothic period there was a trend towards less decoration in England, whilst in France and the Netherlands more decoration and elaborations were demanded.

### Organization of the trade

As with many medieval trades, the superior craftsmen organized themselves into guilds. Furniture-making guilds were established for carpenters, carvers, gilders, joiners, turners, smiths and leather workers. One of the earliest was a turner's guild, established in Cologne by 1180, and in the late fourteenth century a *menuisier's* guild was founded in Paris, but the differentiation between 'furniture-makers' and carpenters existed, in France, well before the fourteenth century. Carpenters were responsible for large-scale structural work, whilst joiners developed techniques for exacting and accurate construction of interior furnishings. The trade of coffer-maker apart from making trunks and coffers was also responsible for the embryonic craft of upholstery.

## 1.4  Renaissance to Industrial Revolution

### 1.4.1  1500–1600

#### Background

The revival of classical thinking in Italian city-states combined with a new way of thinking about man's role in the world order, had begun to change the whole way of life by the sixteenth century. There was a search for a replacement to the all-pervading Gothic style and the Renaissance was the result. The Italian achievement soon permeated most of Europe and inspired men to master the sciences, engineering and literature as well as the arts. The invention of printing, around 1440, encouraged the dissemination of pattern books which ensured that the new ideas, patterns and designs would be available to a wide marketplace.

In England, the Wars of the Roses destroyed the old feudal system and encouraged the growth of a middle class. The economy improved, and the role of the monarch was secured by Henry VII and his Tudor dynasty. The new wealth encouraged house building using braced-timber methods of post and beam construction. There was subsequently a demand for furniture to equip them.

Voyages of discovery, linked to trade with the East and the eventual opening of markets in the colonies led to an increase in profits, but also became the route by which new ideas of decoration and construction, as well as a variety of exotic materials, could be introduced. For example, there is an interesting connection between Florentine pietre dure and the same sort of work being undertaken in India at the same time.

The Renaissance spirit was developed into Mannerism in Italy and France during the sixteenth century. This had the effect of introducing the Grotesque, the Moresque, strapwork and perspective into designs. It was during Elizabeth I's reign (1558–1603) that the Mannerist style manifested itself in England with a vigour appropriate to the times.

### Functional types

The range of furniture types was influenced by the decline of the hall as the most important room, and the rise of a variety of other rooms for private use. The distinction between furniture and fittings was also more marked as a greater variety of moveable furniture was made to accommodate the demands of the new and more stable society.

In England the trestle table was now longer, and made with a fixed top using a panelled construction and a fixed underframe. The most important innovation, however, was the extending table mechanism, which allowed the leaves to be drawn out upon tapered bearers (lopers) so virtually doubling the size of the table top (*Figure 1.5*).

Chairs, developed from a box-panelled shape possibly based on the chest with a back added, gradually began to be less heavy, more open and usually fitted with arms. They were given a slight rake to the back, but the legs remained straight. Chairs continued to be made by joiners, often with prestigious ornament inlaid into the backs of joined chairs.

The bed was usually the most expensive piece of furniture and was considered an heirloom. Four-poster beds were enlarged and fitted with highly carved canopies and testers,

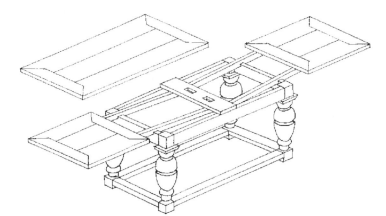

**Figure 1.5** Diagram of a draw-leaf table, shown fully extended and with the centre panel removed. This design was introduced into England around 1600 by European craftsmen and is often associated with the drawings of Hans Vredeman de Vries (1527–*c*.1604)

often with the frame separate from the end posts.

Storage became more important and the idea of a cupboard made the transition from 'a cupboard with things on, to one with things in'. The raising of a chest on tall legs gave the first sideboard or table, and the planked hutch gradually developed into the court cupboard and buffet. Nevertheless, chests remained the most important storage devices and were available in a wide variety of forms, shapes and sizes.

France developed two items that deserve mention: the '*lit de repos*' or daybed, lavishly decorated with drapes and materials, and the '*caquetoire*' chair with its trapezoidal seat and narrow carved back, which was invariably decorated with carved or pierced back panels.

### Design and construction
During the early part of the sixteenth century, tenon-jointed frames, pegs and dowels were used to make the panelled construction that was in general use. This had been introduced from Flanders in the fifteenth century. The frame and panelling technique could be either left open for chairs, stools or tables, or enclosed with the panels for wall covering, boxes, chests and settles. During the sixteenth century the development of the true constructional mitre allowed the mouldings to be pre-cut on the stiles and posts before assembly rather than being cut like masons' mouldings over the true joint. Thus the basic techniques of making were established and would serve the joiner well, until the advent of the cabinet-maker in the later seventeenth century.

Turning created some of the more elaborate chair forms during the sixteenth and early seventeenth century (*Figure 1.6*). The description 'turned all over' gives an indication of the design. These chairs, the work of turners, were different from traditional chair construction in that their joints were usually dowelled and pegged rather than mortised and tenoned.

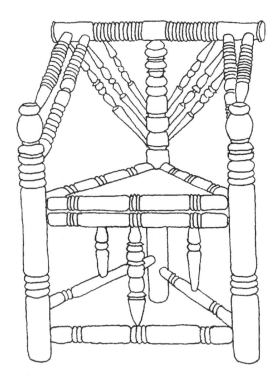

**Figure 1.6** Turned or 'thrown' chair with triangular seat, early seventeenth century

### Materials used

The choice of materials during this period remained limited to native woods, especially oak, linked with other materials such as leather, iron and textiles for the particular requirements of an item.

### Tools and techniques

The conversion of timbers to useful sizes for joinery has always been of prime concern to woodworkers. In the early period, oak logs were converted by splitting with a beetle and wedge, or riving iron, or by being sawn in a saw pit. The first method was quite successful as it did not waste anything in sawdust and the split timber followed its natural grain. It was also less labour-intensive than the two-man saw pit. It did not, however, give such a level surface and this unevenness may have suggested the linenfold motif. For levelling processes the adze was used. During the 1560s the first wooden bow fretsaw was introduced to enable joiners to cut small pieces for inlaying. For working mouldings, a simple scratch tool was used.

### Surface decoration and finish

The trades of turner, carver, inlayer, painter-stainer and blacksmith all assisted the joiner in decorating furniture.

It was only in the 1560s that the merits of turning were fully appreciated. Although it had been used for making rudimentary chairs, it was in the middle of the century that turning became an essential part of furniture decoration. Large bulbous melon-like turnings, sometimes called cup and cover, were popular on table legs and bedposts. Constructionally unnecessary, they illustrate the fashionable nature of furniture decoration by this time. Some authorities also relate the shapes to the male clothing fashions of the time. These bulbous shapes were often carved with gadroon motifs, scrolled acanthus leaf work and capitals.

During the sixteenth century, carving was a highly prized method of decoration which comprised mixed Gothic and Renaissance motifs followed by Mannerist hyperbole (*Figure 1.7*). In the early part of the century,

(a)

(b)

(c)

**Figure 1.7** Examples of carving styles: (*a*) gothic; (*b*) strapwork; (*c*) Renaissance

these included the so-called 'Romayne panels', which were carved profile heads set in medallions; Gothic curved rib panels; tracery designs and Grotesque ornament. These were mostly achieved by shallow chip-carving using a chisel and gouge. Later in the century the Mannerist strapwork, an intricate arabesque or geometric ornament, carved in low relief, was used on flat panels, along with developments of the grotesque which encouraged virtuoso work in the form of carving 'in the round' for table and buffet supports.

Inlays of woods such as holly, box and Irish bog oak were chosen to produce polychrome effects which were particularly used on chair backs and the so-called 'Nonesuch' chests with their pictures in perspective (*Figure 1.8*). *Trompe l'oeil* perspective techniques of intarsia, particularly in Italy, are good examples of the Mannerist decoration of interiors which influenced furniture decoration.

**Figure 1.8**   Nonesuch chest (English, 1570–1600). The front and sides of the chest are decorated with marquetry depicting architectural scenes, geometric and checkerboard designs. The top of the chest is undecorated

Although there were examples of painted and gilded finishes, the fashion for wood inlays and carvings resulted in the use of other methods to protect the surfaces. Oil polishing with linseed and nut oils was the first method to be used, with the use of beeswax and turpentine following towards the end of the sixteenth century.

### Organization of the trade
From the fifteenth century, guilds or companies represented the interests of woodworkers. The Carpenters' Company was incorporated in 1477 and the Joiners' Company in 1570. The Turners' Company was incorporated in 1604 whilst the Upholders' (who dealt with beds, hangings and cushions) were recognized as a separate 'mystery' in 1360 though waited until 1626 for a charter.

### 1.4.2   1600–1700
### Background
The period between 1600–1700 is marked by a number of significant changes; economic, political and religious. Economically the period was one of relative prosperity and growth, with the 'mercantile system' being established in which a favourable trading balance was to be maintained. Politically it was a time of upheaval, culminating in the Civil War of 1642–49, the Commonwealth and the reduction of the powers of the monarchy. With the Restoration of the monarchy in 1660, Charles II introduced manners and ideas from European courts. Newly fashionable furniture and craftsmen were imported into Britain, and trading links further encouraged an interchange of ideas and designs with Holland, Portugal and the Far East. This flow of continental talent was enhanced after 1685, when Louis XIV revoked the Edict of Nantes which resulted in Protestant Huguenot craftsmen coming to Britain, particularly with textile weaving skills.

This period was also the beginning of architect-builders. Under the patronage of Charles I and his court, for example, Inigo Jones developed the ideas of Palladio and the Baroque. The extensive building programme with luxurious interiors was not limited to London: many fine country houses were built at this time which incorporated classical planning and detail.

Although having emphasized the fashionable bases for changes in furniture design and making, it must be pointed out that there was also a development of regional styles based on local centres of production which contrasted with the internationalism of the capital cities of Europe.

In addition, the colonization of North America brought existing European traditions to that area, which could exploit the vast tracts of timber including oaks, maple and pine. Although some American furniture of the period reflects the dour and simple Pilgrim style, many surviving examples demonstrate a healthy delight in the use of paint, carving, mouldings and turnings to decorate surfaces. Apart from the English traditions, the influence of Dutch work was also important at this time. The Dutch immigrants of the seventeenth century who settled in isolated areas in New Jersey, Long Island and the Hudson river valley brought the kas, for storage, which remained a staple (either plain oak, painted, or inlaid) piece of furniture. Other design features such as elaborate turnings, complex curves on cupboards as well as sensible multi-purpose furniture resulted from Dutch originals.

### Functional types

Between 1600 and 1640 the demand for fashionable furnishings and the desire to keep up with the court encouraged the growth of the trade, as furniture became more common and began to be regarded as a necessity rather than a luxury. Although comfort became a major consideration, furniture was now as important for show, as for practical use. There was a move to develop furniture types for special purposes, especially to increase comfort. The farthingale chair is one of the best-known, made to accommodate the fashionably wide skirts of the period, but at other end of the century also the tea table is a response to the social habit of tea drinking. In addition to this, houses were divided into more special purpose rooms, each demanding a particular set of furniture.

The chief characteristics of furniture in the first half of the seventeenth century include a smaller and lighter feel than the Elizabethan, with more restrained ornament.

Chairs continued to be made in massive and solid forms, but there was a demand for comfort and luxury, such as was found abroad. The result of this was the beginning of upholstery. The earliest examples were simply based on stretched coverings over a frame. This developed into the X-frame chair which was supplied with loose cushions. The farthingale chair mentioned above was often covered in Turkey work, a canvas with a knotted pile, introduced to imitate Turkish carpets. The settle was sometimes further developed into a combination piece, with the back turning into a table (called a monk's bench). In America, the chairs characterized by turned spindles have been known as Brewster or Carver chairs, based on the possible original owners, but many chairs still relied on English models as the basis of their design.

The Elizabethan models for tables continued into the new century but with a tendency to reduce the amount of carving and the thickness of legs. Initially made from built-up sections, they were later made just from the thickness of the leg timber. Gate-leg tables, with circular, rectangular or oval tops, were developed to suit smaller family living quarters. This form of table demanded some improvement to the hinge so that the leaves could be dropped more carefully.

The development of the court cupboard and the buffet was a major feature of the Jacobean period. Both forms originated in the previous century but the later versions were noticeably less decorated and were not made with a canted upper stage (*Figure 1.9*). By the 1650s they were a shadow of their former glory and gradually disappeared from fashion. The development of the chest into its final form with drawers, began with the introduction of the 'mule' chest which had a single drawer in the base. It was not then a big step to introduce the drawers into the whole carcase.

During the period the range of chests, cupboards and boxes expanded and examples relate to regional styles as much as any other furniture type. In America they range from the simple six-boarded variety to more decorated panelled and carved versions. The famous Hadley and Hartford types attest to this local tradition. These sometimes have a drawer underneath the proper chest, a harbinger of a new form – the chest of drawers. The forms of court cupboards and presses in America again followed English traditions.

The Commonwealth period (1649–1660) is often seen as a severe style with little emphasis on comfort or convenience and with few new initiatives in design or production. Fashion was in abeyance during this Puritan period, which was clearly one of little ornament. However, turned work became more elaborate, as exemplified by bobbin and ball turning. During the 1640s the 'Yorkshire and Derbyshire' chairs were produced with their distinctive knob-turned front legs, and back consisting of two wide carved crescent-shaped rails. In this period, leather was no longer slung as a seat but instead used as a close covering, fitted by brass studs.

The exuberant epoch that occurred during the reign of Charles II (1660–1688) was followed by a restrained period under William and Mary (1689–1702). Nevertheless, the whole period was one of change in form, construction and decoration. There was a rise in the taste for Oriental objects, and a further increase in the desire for comfort. Pieces were scaled to fit the smaller rooms in the newer townhouses and there was generally a lighter touch to furniture designs. The period was one of success in economic and political terms and this was reflected in a demand for more and better furniture.

To satisfy this demand a number of new or improved items of furniture came into the repertoire of the furnisher. These included: clocks with long cases; easy chairs with high backs and wings (at the end of the period); chests of drawers; chests on stands; cabinets on stands; bureaux; scrutoires; card tables; daybeds; chandeliers and sconces; girandoles; looking glasses; hanging corner-cupboards; dressers.

### Design and construction

The first half of the century saw the culmination of the 'age of oak'. Conservative attitudes to design and change resulted from the unsettled political situation. By the mid-century there was a diminution in the influence of architecture which gave cabinetmakers the opportunity to develop decorative techniques of their own, without being tied by the strict constraints of classical detailing and architectural features. The influence of styles and techniques based on the original homes of immigrants to North America meant that particular traditions were taken across the Atlantic and established in localities that continued these ways of designing and working.

Without a doubt the most momentous change in this latter part of the seventeenth century was the need to introduce new methods of construction. These were required so that the new fashions from the Continent could be supplied by English makers. The introduction of veneering, using walnut, hastened the transition from oak panelled and joined construction to bring the true cabinetmaker to the forefront of the trade.

**Figure 1.9** Hall cupboard, English, oak, *c.*1610. The panels in the upper section are decorated with geometric inlay, whilst the pilasters form secret compartments. The cornice moulding is not original. The hall cupboard developed from the court cupboard, which had an open, three-tiered structure

Joined chairs remained important and backstools or armless chairs were an innovation. By the Restoration, twist turning had become a typical feature of the period, and the tallbacked walnut chairs with caned seats and back panels are easily recognizable (*Figure 1.10*). Constructionally they were not always sound, since in many cases, seat-rails were simply placed on top of the legs and dowelled instead of being tenoned in between. However, the introduction of the splayed back leg does show some consideration for the possibility of overbalancing. The double-scroll Flemish leg changed to a Dutch bandy-leg which gradually led to the cabriole shape. By the 1690s an inverted cup and trumpet were used for legs on tables, tallboys and cabinets. These leg shapes are illustrated in *Figure 1.11*. Castors, using leather or wood rollers, were

**Figure 1.10** High-backed cane chair, English, *c.*1680–1700. Usually executed in walnut, or painted or stained beech

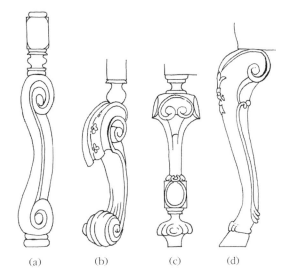

| (a) | (b) | (c) | (d) |

**Figure 1.11** Leg shape comparison: (*a*) double scroll leg, *c.*1675; (*b*) S-scroll or 'bandy' leg, *c.*1690; (*c*) cup and trumpet leg, *c.* 1690; (*d*) cabriole leg, early eighteenth century

introduced around 1690. Daybeds or couches, with six legs, had cane and carved or turned wood decoration to match the chairs. Settee-backs were divided to resemble chairs joined together, and in dining chairs drop-in seats and the stuff-over method were both used.

Tudor storage forms continued with some modification until the Restoration when the court cupboard was abandoned in favour of the cabinet-on-stand, with either a twist-turned or scroll-legged base. Chests became the dominant furniture item in many rooms but dressers, cupboards, china cabinets, writing desks and bureaux, and bookcases were all made to meet the particular requirements of the time. Bookcases, some with hooded pediments and most with nailed shelf-bearers,

became popular: the first one recorded was made for Samuel Pepys. By 1670, small hand-made brass screws, which were tapered and slotted, had begun to be used for hinge fixing in place of nails. In America one particular form of storage developed which clearly shows the influence of a European homeland. The 'kas' was based on original models from the Low Countries, particularly Holland, where a painted finish tradition was also borrowed.

With the increase in business, letter writing and the spread of literature, the need for specialist furniture again became evident. Bureaux were first made in two halves and later the sides were of one piece. They are distinguished by the panelled doors which were sometimes fitted with mirrors. Writing tables were often designed with recesses for knees and were usually made with cabriole legs and apron pieces. The secretaire is made so that the whole of the front drops down to form a writing top, with the interior invariably fitted out with various pigeonholes and cupboards. The decoration was often in the form of marquetry but in some of the bigger items the veneers were not large enough to cover in one piece, so the quartering technique was devised which turned a necessity into a decorative practice.

The large panel size also caused difficulties with the fall front groundwork. The drop-flaps were often made with the grain of the main panel(s) running horizontally and the sides fixed with frames in a vertical manner. This led to differential movement and resulted in cracked veneers.

China cabinets were another example of objects designed to meet specific needs. The collecting of Oriental chinaware and 'curiosities' was very popular in the later seventeenth century and it was a matter of course that a display case was required which included glazed doors. The subdivision of doors by small glazing bars appears to have been necessary, due to the size of the glass panes, but it was so successful, decoratively, that it remained popular even when the glass was big enough to fill the space in one piece.

Beds became very tall and exuberant, surmounted by testers with all the woodwork covered with fabric. Beds are good examples of changing taste, for whilst at the beginning of the century they would have been proudly carved, they were now hung with expensive fabrics, being demonstrations of the upholsterer's art rather than the carver's.

Mirrors and picture frames were considered essential to a stylish interior, but mirror glass was still expensive and only made in small panes. Nevertheless, freestanding and wall-mounted mirrors were extremely popular by the end of the century. Lime-wood carving in naturalistic forms is associated with the last part of the century and particularly with Grinling Gibbons. It is his style rather than his artefacts that are memorable though.

Tables with space-saving attributes were made including those with gate-leg mechanisms, butterfly tables and even chair-tables.

### Materials used

The early part of the century was still dominated by the use of oak, and all the time that wood was seen as a constructional material, rather than a decorative one in its own right, this would remain the case. However, by the reign of Charles II, oak was becoming displaced by walnut, beech, cherry, cedar, olive, yew and laburnum, as well as burrs of various woods. These woods worked well in veneer form, thus encouraging the replacement of oak for carcases with the more stable yellow pine.

The use of veneers opened up the decorative possibilities of parquetry, marquetry and oyster veneering (see below). The use of ebony in some cabinets in the first half of the seventeenth century, combined with bright, contrasting inlays of ivory, tortoiseshell, pietre dure etc., showed how the architecturally influenced form was becoming subservient to the cabinet-made surface effect. In America the use of local woods continued. In addition to oak, ash, maple and pine were widely employed in both joined furniture and chair work.

Canework, originally of Chinese origin, found instant success in the 1660s, and by the end of the century cane-workers had established themselves as part of the furniture-making fraternity. Cane never usurped the position of textiles, but its use as a flexible and decorative material for chair seats and backs ensured its popularity. It was most commonly used in this period in conjunction with carved and perforated splats for chair backs and seats.

Metal working began to be subdivided from the work of smiths into the more specialized trades of locksmiths and mount-makers. A certain interest in a more sophisticated approach to metalwork is evidenced by the growth of the process of chamfering the edges of metal mounts. Stop-chamfering was a further development which made an even more decorative outline by leaving some parts of the edge straight.

During the second half of the century, brass began to displace iron, and began its monopoly in the manufacture of cabinet mounts. This was due to the fact that brass was a good colour, easy to work and, by casting, could be reproduced accurately. The results were ideal for use on the lighter forms of furniture that were characteristic of the later seventeenth century.

In the seventeenth century, 'tortoiseshell' (actually turtleshell) was widely used both in Italy and the Low Countries. As it was malleable when heated, it could be used as a veneer. Laid in conjunction with metals such as brass and pewter on coloured grounds, it represented a high point in marquetry work. This process is usually associated with André-Charles Boulle (see below).

### Trade practice, tools and techniques

The qualities of furniture-making still depended on the skill of the joiner, who began to use the continental dovetailing methods of joining boards which foreign craftsmen had introduced into England.

The ardent desire of tradesmen to maintain differentials resulted in the London Court of Aldermen (in 1632) deciding that carpenters should be restricted to making nailed and boarded work and that only joiners could use glue, mortise and tenon and dovetail joints. It was this process that divided the joiner's craft into those who fitted up rooms, for example with panelling, and those who would be called cabinetmakers.

By the second half of the century the cabinetmaker was supreme, one of the earliest references to a 'cabinetmaker' being in Samuel Pepys's diary in 1664. The increasing division of crafts and trades continued with chair makers, cane chair makers, japanners, turners and other crafts, developing their specialities.

Drawer construction is a reference point for the skill of cabinetmakers, and drawer development is related to the rise of the cabinetmaker (*Figure 1.12*). The frames were invariably of oak, possibly due to the wearability on sliding surfaces, whereas oak and

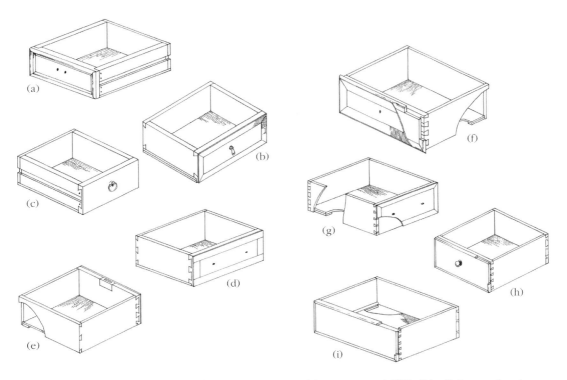

**Figure 1.12** Development of dovetailed drawer construction. (*a*) Up to around 1650: Sides fit into a rebated drawer front and are butt jointed at the back. Note that sides are thick (up to one inch) to accommodate the groove. Grain of drawer bottom runs front to back. (*b*) Up to about 1700: Drawer sides have a single coarse through dovetail at the front and are butt jointed at the back. The drawer front was veneered. Runners sometimes added to lift the drawer bottom clear of cross rails in the carcass. (*c*) From around 1670: Coarse lap dovetailing may be found. (*d*) Around 1700: Drawer sides have two or more coarse lapped dovetails at the front and through dovetail/s at the back. Drawer sides can be thinner now they are not grooved. (*e*) Around 1700: Drawers now slide on runners and both drawer bottom and runners may be rebated into the drawer side. (*f*) Early eighteenth century: Lipped drawers concealed through dovetails with an applied cross grain moulding. (*g*) From the early eighteenth century: Dovetails further refined as multiple pins and tails introduced. (*h*) From around 1715: cockbeading added to drawer fronts to protect veneer and as a decorative feature. Drawer bottoms with the grain running from side to side begin to be used from the first quarter of the eighteenth century. (*i*) From the last quarter of the eighteenth century: Dovetails become finer. Whilst the side and bottom cockbead remain in rebates, the top cockbead is the width of the drawer front and requires a half mitre. Drawer bottom fitted into rebated slips that are glued to the drawer sides

pine were used for drawer fronts. The fixing of drawers by hanging them on runners and grooves was improved by drawers sliding on the dust board. The grain of drawer bottoms at first ran from front to back but was later changed to run from side to side. Drawers with dovetailed fronts replaced nailed and rebated ones. After 1670, the crude through dovetailing of the fronts of drawers used in the early part of the century was replaced with lapped or stopped dovetailing which gave a better ground for veneering.

Early panelled work used mouldings that were run on oak and used as a framing surround. By the seventeenth century, mouldings for cornices, plinths, friezes, edges of tables, drawers and so on were important for decorative effect and were usually finished with cross-grained veneer. The cavetto (hollow) shape was used on tall chests and the half-round on carcase fronts; the double half-round was used between 1700 and 1715. On drawers after 1710, an ovolo moulding was set so that the join between the opening and the drawer was hidden when closed.

*Turning* Until the early seventeenth century turnings were produced on dead-centre lathes, driven by treadle or wheel or on the pole lathe. For much of the century, knop and ring turning and bobbin turning were repeated but towards the end of the century there were some contrivances introduced that allowed a twist or spiral to be put in on the lathe rather than by using hand-rasping to achieve the effect.

### Surface decoration and finish

In the first half of the seventeenth century, cabinet work was often decorated with split turnings and raised faceted mouldings that were applied to surfaces and sometimes painted black and inlaid with bone or mother-of-pearl. Carving was generally flatter than previously, with acanthus scrolls, guilloche, lunettes and gadrooning. The Commonwealth period encouraged simpler decoration. From the Restoration, decorative processes became very important again due to the practice of veneering cabinets.

The techniques associated with the use of veneer (*Figure 1.13*) include cross banding, marquetry, parquetry and oyster veneering. All these practices involved applying veneers of

**Figure 1.13** Detail of a marquetry table top, English, *c.*1674. Oyster work (walnut), cross banding and pictorial decoration executed using contrasting wood veneers

decorative wood to a suitable substrate, sometimes separately, other times in conjunction with each other. In most cases banding was part of the scheme as it provided a finished edge treatment. Parquetry and oyster work used woods to create a geometric effect, whilst 'seaweed' marquetry used arabesque designs to great advantage. Although seaweed marquetry appears to be the height of the marquetry cutter's skill, it was relatively straightforward in that only two woods were used – box or holly for the pattern and walnut for the ground. The skill in seaweed marquetry was in using a very fine saw to keep to the design lines and at the same time cut at an angle, to ensure as close a fit as possible between the pieces. These methods were often the only way certain woods could be used satisfactorily.

There was a great demand for floral marquetry in the last part of the century, perhaps because it depicted the popular Dutch flower painters' scenes; at any rate it certainly showed the skills of the cabinetmaker. By the end of the century, marquetry was toned down to two shades of brown. Veneers were also carefully matched to form geometric patterns by book-matching or quartering.

Interest in oriental products, particularly imported lacquer wares, encouraged European makers to attempt to copy them. Oriental lacquer imported into Europe had two distinct type characteristics. One type had the orna-

**Figure 1.14** Japanned cabinet on stand, English, 1680–1730

ment in relief; the other, sometimes known as Bantam work, had the ornament incised or cut into the surface. The process was imitated by 'japanners' who cut out a pattern in a gesso ground then coloured and gilded the result. In 1688 John Stalker and George Parker published their *Treatise of Japanning and Varnishing*. This publication identified three elements essential to the art of japanning. These were gums, metals and colours. The gums were used to prepare varnishes; metals were used in powder or dust form and were worked into the varnish, and colours were put down to make backgrounds (*Figure 1.14*).

Around 1660, varnishing was introduced as an alternative wood finish. Stalker and Parker (1688) also gave recipes for shellac spirit-varnish which was used for coating all sorts of wood products. After the application of each coat, the spirits evaporated leaving a thin film of shellac on the surface. After this had been built up to ten or twelve coats, it was given a high polish with a mineral called Tripoli. This high quality finish was favoured for walnut and later for mahogany and satinwood. In other cases oil was used hot, to rub into walnut to give it a 'black and sleek' appearance.

Japanned cabinets were often made to fit onto gilded or silvered stands. These stands were roughly bosted and then gesso was applied in thin coats. Once it had hardened, it was re-carved, sanded and gilded. After the Restoration, the fashion for gilding required both water gilding and oil gilding processes to be used. Water gilding required a wet clay base, which was sometimes double gilded and usually burnished. Although this was the finer finish, oil gilding was the more durable method and hence more popular.

Other decorative processes included verre eglomisé (the process of decorating glass by drawing and painting on the underside and backing this with metal foil). Mirror surrounds at the end of the century were most likely to incorporate this process, using red or black ground, and silver or gold foil. In the 1670s straw work was introduced as a decorative finish using marquetry designs and continued in popularity through the eighteenth century with an impetus from the French prisoners of the Napoleonic wars.

Around 1680 the earliest Tunbridge ware was recorded. Originally produced in Tunbridge Wells, the process flourished for the next one hundred and fifty years. The process was initially one of tiny cuts of veneers built into a mosaic pattern, often with a cubic or elongated rectangular theme. It should not be confused with the end-grain mosaic work produced there in the nineteenth century.

The use of metal in furniture decoration in the period was not common but did occur. Furniture covered in sheet silver or made from solid cast silver was produced in the Restoration period, though little now survives. During the last quarter of the seventeenth century, boulle work was introduced which used brass or pewter inlays in a tortoiseshell base, sometimes framed by an ebony veneer. André-Charles Boulle worked in Paris as *ébéniste du Roi* from 1672 and his distinctive process was adapted by Gerritt Jensen for his work in London. The boulle process is considered similar to marquetry in that both sheet materials, metal and shell, were cut simultaneously. Recent research seems to show that early boulle work was not necessarily cut in this way, but individually from the same pattern. It was only in the eighteenth century that multiple cutting (of several pattern repeats at one time) was adopted.

### 1.4.3   1700–1800

*Background*

Despite the wars that were a feature of parts of the period (War of the Spanish Succession, 1702–14; Seven Years War, 1756–63; War of American Independence, 1775–83; French Revolutionary and Napoleonic Wars, 1789–1815), this century was a period of sustained growth in wealth. In England the monopoly on colonial trade, the growth of a National Debt and the economy of war all led to this new affluence. Landowners controlled the country, finances and industries and encouraged a market for luxury furnishings, but the general population growth also encouraged development of cities, agriculture and internal trade.

In America, developing cultural and trading conditions combined to make Boston and Philadelphia important furniture-making centres, with Newport, New York and Charleston not far behind. Distinctive regional characteristics continued to develop, often based on the original location of immigrants. However, American colonists also gradually took on the Classical revival principles of order, balance and reason which were manifested in their architecture and furnishings.

Another tradition which was away from the mainstream was the 'folk art' furniture made in centres such as coastal New England which acted as a transmitter of design ideas to the interior. The furniture produced in rural New Hampshire, the Delaware valley, Chesapeake Bay, Carolina, Piedmont, Tennessee, Mississippi and Ohio, and by particular groups such as the Pennsylvania Germans, or Norwegian Americans in Wisconsin and Iowa, demonstrates the very particular design and technical vocabulary that each represents. In addition, the Spanish territories in New Mexico continued a different tradition. Simple models of Spanish origin and in traditional form included *alacenas* (wall cupboards), *repisos* (shelves), *tarmita* (stools) and *trasteros* (cupboards). They were often made in pine and simply decorated with painted motifs or chip carvings.

By the mid-eighteenth century, the need to import furniture into America had declined as increasingly sophisticated designers and makers competed for trade, so that furniture-making was a well established urban craft. The development of an infrastructure of craftsmen and raw material suppliers and wholesalers combined with freedom from guild restrictions and other regulations helped to develop a healthy trade within North America. Examples of well-known craftsmen include Thomas Afleck, William Savery and Benjamin Randolph, all exponents of the Rococo style. In Newport the Townsend-Goddard family dominated furniture-making for well over one hundred years. By the later eighteenth century Samuel McIntyre and John Seymour were among the famous craftsmen.

The eighteenth century saw vast changes in the development of the applied arts and furniture and furnishings to meet the various demands put upon the trade. Often called the 'Golden Age of Furniture', this century included some of the greatest names in English furniture history and witnessed the change from the Baroque (*c*.1670–1720) to the Rococo (*c*.1720–1760) and then a Classical revival (*c*.1760–1800). These three divisions coincide with the major designers and craftsmen of the century. William Kent was the major design influence along with the Gumley family, Benjamin Goodison and Mathias Lock; all representing a high quality interpretation of Baroque/Palladian designs. The second or Rococo period centres on Thomas Chippendale, Ince and Mayhew, Johnson and Manwaring. It was also the age of the pattern book. By the third period, the Classical revival, spurred on by excavations in Italy and the eastern Mediterranean, was the fashionable and popular style. Robert Adam is synonymous with the period but he alone was not responsible for the style. Both Hepplewhite in the 1777–90 period and Sheraton from the 1790s to 1806 were important exponents of the neo-classical style.

*Functional types*

At the beginning of the eighteenth century, Queen Anne's reign saw an English taste assert itself, characterized by using walnut with plain, simple elements. For its effect it relied both upon the Baroque outline, and the natural beauty of the timbers used. Early Georgian furniture by contrast was generally heavier and with larger proportions, due to the influence of William Kent, who developed coherent furnishing schemes under his architectural direction.

Queen Anne chairs were noticeably restrained in their added decoration, although the most important feature to come out of this period was, without doubt, the cabriole leg. Introduced in the late seventeenth century, and perfected in the beginning of the eighteenth, the cabriole leg with its uniting of two opposing curves was seen as the epitome of the curvilinear design. Compound curves were introduced into the hoop backs of chairs, and stretcher braces disappeared as construction techniques improved. Chair types began to proliferate and included hall chairs with hard seats, often decorated with coats of arms; upholstered easy chairs with embroidered coverings; two-seater sofas or love seats and the vernacular Windsor chair type. From around 1745 the Rococo influence and the use of mahogany allowed chairs to be made in a lighter and more delicate fashion.

Settees by Kent included solid hall seats with carved scroll arms, and an upholstered type in velvet or damask with parcel gilt and mahogany, or gilded-gesso frames. The second half of the century saw the introduction of confidantes, settees with seats at each end with upholstered divisions between them.

Numerous table types were introduced during the century. These included: console tables with marble tops and painted frames; dumb waiters; writing desks; kidney tables; tea tables; sofa tables; library tables, and toilet tables. For dining, the gate-leg table, still in use in the early part of the century, was superseded by the swing-leg table. Other tables included a tripod tea table, essential for the ritual of tea-drinking. In addition to tables, sideboards with cutlery boxes and wine cisterns were prerequisites for the fully furnished dining room by the second half of the century.

A vast range of storage furniture was designed and made in the eighteenth century for the requirements of the new age: China cases for displaying or storing; bookcases to furnish libraries; collectors' cabinets for curios; corner cabinets for the display of ornaments, and a wide variety of double chests, clothes presses and commodes.

Other items that were introduced in the period were chamber or exercising horses, pole screens, pedestals for supporting decorative items and elaborate girandoles for lighting schemes.

### Design and construction

The eighteenth century has been divided into a variety of eras for different purposes. The most suitable for furniture studies is either the stylistic distinction between Baroque, Rococo and the Neo-Classic, or the dynastic division between early Georgian, mid-Georgian and late Georgian or Regency. Throughout these divisions other stylistic influences occur either disparately or in conjunction. The Chinese taste from the middle of the century to the end is evidence of an Oriental passion; a Gothic mode was popular from the middle of the century onwards and both the Classical revival (under the influence of Adam), and the Greek revival, in the last decade of the century were part of the Neo-Classical revival (*Figure 1.15*). The period was also important for the influence of particular cabinetmakers and their publications which have also been used as period names.

The conjunction between material and method is best seen in the Rococo designs that were suited to mahogany. Due to this material's strength, ribbon back chairs, cabriole legs, Chinese style frets and lattice-pierced galleries

**Figure 1.15** Neo-Classical commode, 1773, designed by Robert Adam, from the Drawing Room, Osterley Park House. The commode is veneered with satinwood, harewood, rosewood and other woods, some stained green, and has ormolu mounts

could be made in profusion. The Rococo style was promoted by the Saint Martin's Lane Academy, set up by William Hogarth. The close geographical connection with furniture-makers ensured a speedy application of the style in furniture designs.

Around 1700 Daniel Marot introduced a style of chair with a narrow back which enclosed a vertical solid vase or splat. Cabriole legs changed chair construction by doing away with the stretcher bars, which resulted in a wider knee. Shoe-pieces for backs were now pinned and glued to back rails, and seat rails were rebated to accept drop-in seats. Chair seats were now broader. Legs were decorated with carved acanthus foliage on knees, and were finished in a ball and claw foot. Upholstered backs became common. During George II's reign, legs became even more elaborate, with high relief carving and decorated seat rails, with solid splats replacing pierced ones. These features remained essentially the ingredients of armchairs through the mid-century. There were, though, innovations, changes of scale and detail, for example: the introduction of the square section leg with stretcher bars; the ladder-back dining chair; fretted and latticed work in the Chinese style, and various Gothic motifs. Adam's French influence is apparent in his chair designs based on the oval back and taper-turned leg, whereas the neo-classical influence was found in the round, or rectilinear style of backs. Hepplewhite introduced the shield-back, oval and heart shapes for chair backs. It is noticeable that most of his chair backs are supported by the upward elongation of the back legs. Sheraton's chairs were generally designed with square backs and frequently had square section legs which were slightly tapered. For economy they were often made from beech and finished with paint.

In America regional preferences were manifested in the design and construction of chairs. For example, New England side chairs were tall and had legs formed by turned and joined stretchers. New York side chairs were broader and lower than the New England ones. Whilst in Philadelphia the chairs were larger in proportion, did not usually have stretchers and were sculptural in form. The importance of Windsor chairs should also be stressed. Probably first developed for outdoor use, painted green, they soon became an important furnishing item and were made in a wide range of shapes and styles that reflected local taste and craft. A particular Windsor form with a writing arm was developed in America.

Early Georgian cabinets were relatively plain if made from solid wood. This return to plain, solid wood, as opposed to the veneering practices of the previous period, encouraged architectural detail to be applied, to relieve the surface. Heavy cornices or broken pediments, fluted pilasters and mouldings were added as decoration, and some cabinets were supported on cabriole legs. The heavier chest bases used the angle-bracket foot for supporting carcases on the floor. Cabinets with serpentine fronts and convex sides and front were popular in Europe and sometimes received interest in England. Details include the use of bail or loop handles and astragal mouldings on glazed bookcase doors.

From 1750 onwards the influence of France is seen in the Rococo mounts used. Sometimes they were supplied by the French or they were indifferently copied and chased by English workmen. In 1762, Boulton's factory in Birmingham began to make high quality mounts, which were sometimes gilded by the mercury process – the result being known as ormolu. From the 1750s solid back-plates on handles were replaced by two roses, one at each end. By 1800, ball or loop handles were replaced by brass knobs or lion masks, holding rings.

In American cabinet work the flat topped high boy was a particular development and so was the use of a decoration called blocking, which refers to the concave and convex profiles of panels on the fronts of cabinets or chests. This was almost exclusively used in New England. Much other American cabinet work relied on English models.

Mahogany flap dining tables often had four or six legs with oval or circular tops and used the gate-leg principle to support the flaps. By the mid-century it was common to extend a dining table by adding two semicircular pier tables at each end of the gate-leg table. From 1715 folding-hinged frames were introduced on card tables, in contrast to the swing-legs used previously. By 1710 kneehole writing tables had been introduced as one example of a number of special-use objects. Around 1730 card tables with square corners were introduced. By 1750 the tea table or tripod table

**Figure 1.16**   A mahogany English Regency Carlton House table

**Figure 1.17**   Upholstered wing chair, English, mahogany, second half of the eighteenth century. The textile cover, embroidered with silks and wool, is somewhat earlier

was used and it soon developed a tilting mechanism by being hinged to a small cage. From 1770 the 'Carlton House' style table was introduced (*Figure 1.16*).

The early part of the eighteenth century is marked by the use of needlework for upholstery, and the rise of the wing chair, which remained popular throughout the century (*Figure 1.17*). From around 1725, bergère chairs, characterized by a long seat and a raked back, were introduced from France. By the middle of the century, upholstery had become less visually important, but was used in conjunction with carved wooden frames for chairs and a wide variety of special types of seating furniture and hangings.

Beds remained important pieces of furniture, but gradually became lighter in construction with draperies reduced to a minimum and the woodwork again becoming important, the posts being reeded and slender and the canopy often pierced and carved. The so-called Angel bed, which had its tester hung from the ceiling, was introduced. Other new bed designs included the French 'Lit à la Polonaise' and the 'Lit à la Turque'. Field and tent beds also became popular towards the end of the century. When draperies were used they often included crewel work or other embroidery.

### Materials used

The range of woods available to eighteenth century cabinetmakers had gradually increased as trade with America, West Indies and the coasts of south America developed. In America itself, walnut, tulipwood, gumwood, cedar, cherry and mahogany as well as maple and walnut veneer were added to the cabinetmaker's repertoire. In England the fashionable taste for walnut encouraged the importation of Virginia black walnut to augment European supplies. Although the era is well known for the use of mahogany, walnut was still acceptable as a fashionable timber up to the 1750s. However, in 1721 the abolition of duty on mahogany encouraged the first major imports, which were mainly from Jamaica. Spanish mahogany (sometimes known as Baywood) from Cuba or Honduras was also shipped to England, and towards 1750 it came into general use. San Domingo shipped another variety, which was very hard and straight grained, and was ideal for carved designs that would require a crispness to them. All mahoganies were used extensively in the solid and in large boards (avoiding joined up panels for table

**Figure 1.18**   Chair, mahogany, English, *c.*1760. The backsplat resembles designs for 'Ribband-Back' chairs in Chippendale's 1754 *Gentleman and Cabinet Maker's Director*

tops), as well as in veneer form. Apart from its rich colour and handsome figure, several other virtues established mahogany as an ideal cabinet wood that allowed the extraordinary designs in chair backs to be executed by Chippendale and his followers (*Figure 1.18*). It is strong, hard, tough, uniform in structure, dimensionally stable, durable and resistant to splitting. Mahogany remained important for the rest of the century. Satinwood was used in the second half of the century for its fine figuring and rich golden yellow colour. Supplied from both the West and East Indies, it was mainly used in veneer form. Robert Adam and Sheraton both incorporated it into their designs, as it suited the lighter touch furniture of the latter part of the century.

The trade in timber was international. In 1747 Campbell in his *London Trades* mentions '... deal from Norway, wainscot from Sweden, mahogany from Jamaica and wall-nut from Spain'. Yellow deal from the Baltic, and red cedar from North America (after 1750), were extensively used for carcasses. Many other foreign woods were used especially in veneer

form for marquetry and banding. Calamander or Coromandel came from India and Ceylon. Woods from South America, especially from Brazil, included kingwood, partridge, zebra, and tulip woods. Amboyna came from the East Indies and red cedar from North America, whilst thuja was imported from Africa. Domestic woods were used to imitate the imported ones. Birch and horse chestnut were substituted for satinwood and acacia for tulipwood. Harewood was produced by staining maple or sycamore, using salts of iron, which resulted in a green–grey tint. The Windsor chair used only indigenous timbers, usually elm for the seats, beech for the spindles and yew for the frames. In America these timbers were often hickory, ash, maple or tulip.

The principle woods used during this period in America were walnut, and a little later, mahogany. Maple was also used in New England and Pennsylvania, and cherry was used in New York.

*Scagliola*   This was an imitation marble or rare stone material made from fine-ground plaster of Paris mixed with glue and colourings and marble or stone chips. It was originally made in Italy and was very popular for table tops. Although table and commode tops were often imported from Italy, by the second half of the century there were some makers in England supplying the needs of the furniture and carving trades.

### Tools and techniques of conversion and construction

During the eighteenth century there were few developments in methods of construction or of the use of new tools. There were, however, some efforts made that were to assist developments in the long term. These early attempts included the 1761 Society of Art's Prize to Stansfield, for his sawmill design, and in 1793, Bentham's comprehensive patent for woodworking machinery. Developments such as lathe-turned screws which were being produced with slotted heads to fix handles, and Maudsley's construction of a sliding tool holder in 1797 which enabled screws to be made more easily, were aimed at woodworkers other than furniture-makers. Their influence was not to become important until the nineteenth century.

One process of construction that continued without question was the use of plies and laminates of wood for the construction of chair splats and fretted galleries. The use of plies in mid-eighteenth century work was merely a solution to a problem; it was not seen as a momentous technical advance. It was evidently common practice for larger plies to be used as well. Sheraton describes the construction of his Universal table by saying '... the pannels are sometimes glued up in three thicknesses, the middle piece being laid with the grain across, and the other two lengthways of the pannel to prevent it warping.' More deliberate developments occurred in the work of Chapius in Belgium, and Samuel Gragg in the United States. Both men made chairs with bentwood components but the process was subordinate to the ruling taste in design terms. Tambour doors were introduced from France in the latter part of the century and were used as decorative falls or covers for night tables, pot cupboards and desks.

Furniture historians are indebted to the design books of the eighteenth century not only for their designs, but also for general practical details of construction. The works of Plumier, Diderot, Roubo and Bimont are invaluable for their extremely detailed accounts and illustrations of furniture and woodworking practices in eighteenth century France.

### Surface decoration and finish

The eighteenth century was a period of ever-increasing choice in matters of decoration and finish. Marquetry, turned work and lacquer work gradually went out of fashion. Carving and free-flowing curves became popular as Rococo forms were introduced in the 1730s. These were based on imaginative compositions of scrolls, shells, foliage, figures, masks and animal forms, and were undertaken by a specialized group of chair-carvers. These hardwood carvers were distinct from the frame-carvers who worked picture and mirror frames in softwood.

Gilding became popular in the first half of the century due to the influence of William Kent. He designed parcel-gilt decoration for furniture objects as well as wholly gilded pieces, especially console tables with matching gilded looking-glasses. The gilding process became part of the repertoire of the softwood carver as it became associated with mirror and picture frames. Many businesses advertised themselves as carvers, gilders and picture frame makers.

In 1770 there was a revival of painted furniture, due mainly to the influence of Robert Adam. Painting direct onto primed wood was the usual method, with the designs forming garlands, medallions and borders. Sometimes the base veneer was visible; otherwise, the whole cabinet might be painted in light colours as a background for the designs. Adam motifs included festoons of husks, vase figures, honeysuckle, paterae, ram heads and medallions. The painting was linked with various finishing methods such as carving, inlay and ormolu. There was a close association between painting and japanning, often with the japanner painting the ground and applying the varnish whilst the more artistic furniture painter applied the detail. By 1800 painted furniture was far more popular than marquetry.

The combination of other materials with timber was most fashionable in the case of ceramic plaques and medallions. France's use of porcelain plaques during the reign of Louis XVI was also copied in England by the use of Wedgwood plaques in the latter part of the eighteenth century.

Finishing processes included lacquering or japanning, varnishing and polishing. Japanning remained popular through much of the century although the process gradually was simplified and cheapened by omitting priming, and substituting materials such as bronze powder for gold. Fine examples of japanning can be found on Chippendale's work for the bedroom at Nostell Priory, but the decoration on Garrick's famous suite is executed in tinted varnish on an oil paint ground, a more common technique by the last quarter of the century. In North America carving began to supersede turning, except on Windsors, as a major decorative technique and japanning was also important. The japanning technique was highly developed in Boston. In this work, the use of smooth maple wood fronts with pine frames obviated the need for gesso to be used so the ground was prepared using white size covered with numerous coats of varnish.

Transparent finishes for woodwork, such as clear lacquer, improved during the eighteenth century, the most famous being 'Vernis Martin', patented by the Martin Brothers in France. In 1730 they were granted a monopoly for imitations of Oriental lacquer, but their best-known products are the smooth lacquered panels used in many applications and often based on grey, green or blue base colours with painted decorative scenes. The painting was then given an antique effect by craquelure which was then lacquered over with a clear glaze.

Sheraton's *Dictionary* gives four methods of polishing wood surfaces. These are (a) unsoftened wax rubbed with a cork for interior surfaces; (b) turpentine and beeswax with a little red oil applied and polished off; (c) linseed oil (which may be coloured with alkanet) and brick dust which produces a polishing 'putty' which will secure a fine polish; (d) a hardish composition of wax, turpentine, copal varnish, red-lead and colour worked into a ball, used for polishing chairs.

### Organization of trades

Eighteenth century furniture-making was characterized by the variety of crafts that were the constituent parts of the trade: carvers; turners; joiners; chairmakers and fancy chairmakers; cabinetmakers; clock-case makers; japanners; turners; gilders; looking-glass and picture frame-makers; and upholsterers. The success of many businesses is exemplified by the description from 1747, when it was said in a *General Description of all Trades* that: '... many of their shops are so richly set out they look more like palaces, and their stocks are of exceeding great value'. An example of the entrepreneur–maker was the business of Thomas Chippendale, first recorded working in Long Acre. By 1753 Chippendale had opened a workshop in Saint Martin's Lane, London and in 1754 he had published *A Gentleman And Cabinet-Maker's Director*. This was to be one of the most influential pattern books published in the period. Among other designer-makers were Vile and Cobb from Saint Martin's Lane. Between 1759 and 1763 the business of Ince and Mayhew was responsible for publishing a Universal System of Household Furniture, which had over 300 designs in it.

In 1788 George Hepplewhite's *Cabinet-Makers' and Upholsterers' Guide* was published. This was in fact two years after his death, when the business was being run by his widow, Alice. The publication was a successful

venture and ran into three editions before 1794.

Between 1791 and 1794 Thomas Sheraton's *The Cabinet-Maker's and Upholsterer's Drawing Book* was published. It encouraged an economic approach to design with a light delicate touch. This economy in materials, space use and cost resulted in simple, elegant or compact furniture items. In 1803 his *The Cabinet Dictionary* was published. It is doubtful that Sheraton ever made furniture or had a workshop as his business was teaching and drawing, nevertheless his designs demonstrated the delicacy, strength and desire for utility that are hallmarks of the last part of the eighteenth century.

The situation in America developed slightly differently. Although the apprentice, journeyman, master system based on the old guild practice continued, there was a degree of freedom of movement and flexibility of employment that allowed craftsmen to move around whilst learning the whole business of furniture-making. This had the effect of maintaining local styles of construction, design and decoration but also allowed for some influence from other shops and traditions.

For much of the eighteenth century the French trade was controlled very strictly by the guild system, which did not allow the several distinct trades to cross over. The divisions were *menuisier* (solid wood and joiner), *ébéniste* (veneered cabinetmaker), *fondeur* (metal mounts), *ciseleur* (bronze chaser), *vernisseur* (lacquer-worker), *marqueteur* (marquetry–panel maker) and *doreur* (gilder). From 1743 the guilds demanded that all pieces made were stamped with the maker's initials and the JME (*juré des menuisiers et ébénistes*) mark. The control of the guilds was limited to an extent, as royal makers were exempt from the controls, as were makers outside the city boundaries. In addition to the makers, the businesses of the *marchands-merciers* must be stressed in their role of taste-makers and decorators.

## 1.5   The nineteenth century

### Background

The growth of nationalism and liberalism, in part stemming from the French Revolution, provided the background for the changes that were to make this the century of transition. The reforms in education (1870 Elementary Education Act), representation (1832 First Reform Act), transportation and communication were all part of a tendency towards improvement, growth and material gain.

The so-called 'Industrial Revolution' has been blamed or praised as a prime mover in changing the way furniture was designed, made and used during the nineteenth century. There is no doubt that there was a redistribution of wealth that encouraged more spending on furniture and furnishings but overall there was only a gradual change in the furniture industry and this was piecemeal.

Other changes such as accessible steam (and later electric) power, personal communications and the mechanization of many parts of industry all helped to improve the infrastructure that was necessary for a burgeoning economy. Living conditions improved immeasurably assisted by medical improvements and this in turn laid stress on the notions of comfort and well being.

Following the Revolutionary War of 1776 in America, the taste for a neo-classical style was further developed in the Federal period (1780–1810), which was followed by a Graeco-Roman revival up to 1835, both of which continued to echo European fashions. As in Europe, fashionable historical revivals followed.

Architecturally the search for a style for the new century was confounded by the demands of the new age. Railway stations, hospitals, courts, museums, factories and warehouses all made demands on architecture that it was ill equipped to handle. The search for and the subsequent battle of styles, led to an eclectic approach to architecture, and consequently furniture design, which resulted in a series of revivals and other configurations. This was combined with what was perhaps the most important social change, the usurpation of the aristocracy as arbiters of taste in favour of a prosperous middle class.

The romantic literature of the period, exemplified by Sir Walter Scott, led to a troubadour or medieval style. This vied with a more scholastic Gothic revival urged by A.W.N. Pugin. Associated with these was the Tudor or Jacobean style. In contrast there was a demand for a continuation of the classical taste, which included a Greek and an Egyptian revival. The French Rococo was seen as an especially suit-

able style for the newly wealthy. All these styles led to an interest in old furniture and the reproduction of original pieces. In France there were similar movements: a Gothic revival; a Louis XVI revival between 1815 and 1840; a Louis XV revival between 1830 and 1930; and a further Louis XVI revival between 1850 and 1900.

In the United States a Rococo revival was manifested in the work of Henry Belter, Charles Baudouine and Alexander Roux. A Gothic revival was advocated by A.J. Downing and Clarence Cook, whilst the so-called Eastlake style was popular, perhaps due to the relatively inexpensive production processes associated with it.

This muddled state of affairs was recognized at the time and one of the aims of the Great Exhibition of 1851 was to identify the weaknesses of English design and compare it to foreign efforts. The confusion led to some attempts at combining reforms of a social nature with design and making in the form of the Arts and Crafts movements. In 1860 William Morris's business was founded, and in 1875 Arthur Liberty's first shop was opened. In 1882 the Art Workers Guild was founded and in 1888 the Art and Crafts Exhibition Society was established. In 1902 the Guild of Handicraft was founded by C.R. Ashbee.

The linking of progressive architects with the ideals of the Arts and Crafts movement has been seen as one of the foundations for the modern movement that was to come in the twentieth century.

In the United States of America two different evolutionary paths were evident, the major one being the trades connected with enterprises in the major cities and populous areas. They followed the trends set and maintained standards appropriate to the growing moneyed classes. Both cabinet-work and upholstery was made to reflect the growing status of the new establishment. In contrast were the settlers moving west, who were often only part-time craftsmen. Whatever furniture was not brought with them had to be built. Furniture was based on a make-do philosophy when there were more important issues to consider. Once there was some settlement, some furniture was made with care and thoughtful use or reuse of materials. Once frontier establishments had grown to a sufficient size the exchange of labour was possible and specialist chair or furniture-makers could set up shop. The obvious conjunction between raw materials and a market place with water or steam power meant expansion as the towns became regional centres of supply. When the physical frontier had been reached, another trend was noticed. The wealthy eastern consumers were looking to the wild and the rustic as a source of design inspiration and purchased furniture made from cattle horns, or established summer camps in the wilder parts of the east. The Adirondacks were home to a complete style of rustic furniture which to some extent reflected the romantic vision of the frontier and the 'good life'.

One important American group who produced a very particular 'style' of furniture were the Shakers. A religious group, the Shakers reached their peak in the 1840s. They lived in communal groups in centres across the United States. Shaker design follows simple traditions that would have reflected the vernacular origins of the group members. Although they made for themselves and their own use, the Mount Lebanon community also made furniture for public sale. The practicality and simple lifestyle encouraged furniture that was easily stored and cleaned, that was functional and not overtly decorative. Early furniture was painted, but later the simple varnishing of plain wood resulted in a functional and decorative surface. The range of woods reflects their attitudes. Hickory or oak for chair slats being easily shaped; maple for door knobs as it is durable; cherry for table tops as it dense and solid. Many other slight differences such as the number of slats, the seating method etc., can often identify the workshops. The qualities of the Shaker furniture are once again appreciated both in the original models and in numerous reproductions.

### Functional types

*1800–1830*  The fashion for classical purity was introduced from France by Henry Holland, developed by Thomas Hope in his *Household Furniture and Interior Decoration* of 1807, and popularized in the trade by George Smith's *Collection of Designs for Household Furniture* of 1808. Graeco-Roman ornament was precisely reproduced and Grecian chairs, with wide shoulder boards and sabre legs, became fashionable. Two new types of table are asso-

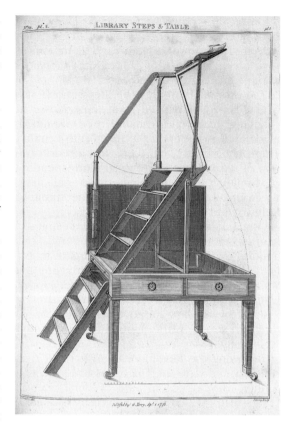

**Figure 1.19**  Design for metamorphic library steps and table from Sheraton's *Cabinet Maker's and Upholsterer's Drawing Book* (3rd edition), published in London in 1802

ciated with the early nineteenth century: the centre pedestal table and the sofa table. Smaller tables included quartetto table nests and work tables with pouches. Small writing tables abounded. There was also a return to fashion of longer dining tables. Sideboards gave way to large serving tables, and small bookcases with wire trellis doors became a feature. There were developments in the manufacture of metal bedsteads and campaign furniture and a craze for so-called patent furniture, which was often able to be converted from one use to another (*Figure 1.19*).

*1840–1900*  During this period two new chair designs were introduced: the balloon-backed dining or bedroom chair and the prie-dieu or kneeling chair. Various other furniture types were introduced including canterburies, chesterfields, chiffoniers, davenports and cosy corners.

From the mid-century onwards there was a growing variety of new and exciting furniture designs that were not slavishly copying traditional designs. This furniture, designed by architects, craftsmen or artists was gradually associated with the beginnings of the modern style. North America and most European countries were affected. In Britain the rise of 'Art Furniture' was initially encouraged by designers such as Bruce Talbert and E.W. Godwin, whilst the craftsman–designer was represented by Ernest Gimson, Lethaby and Barnsley. By the end of the century, Voysey and Mackintosh represented the new designers. In the United States, Herter Brothers, Associated Artists and Tiffany, Stickley and the Roycrofters, the Greene Brothers, and a little later, Frank Lloyd Wright all exemplified the new thinking.

In France the two schools of Paris (represented by Guimard, Gaillard) and Nancy (Galle, Majorelle) were style leaders by the end of the century. In Belgium Van de Velde and Horta were developing the Art Nouveau, whilst in Austria, the Vienna Secession (Hoffman, Moser, Olbrich, Loos, Wagner) were using modern geometric shapes. In Germany the Jugendstil was represented by Behrens, Endell, Riemerschmid and Pankok. Other more exotic designs were produced by Gaudi in Barcelona and Carlo Bugatti in Italy.

### Style and type of construction

The early nineteenth century is called the Regency period in England or the Empire style in France. The style of the period in both countries aimed to adapt newly discovered archaeological remains and the furniture therein to represent their new society. In 1804 Baron Denon published the results of his exploration in Egypt following Napoleon's campaign, and this provided authentic sources for copying models for the Egyptian craze that followed. In addition to this style there was a taste for the Oriental and Chinese in particular. To achieve these effects the use of beech, turned and painted to imitate bamboo, was common. The use of lacquered or japanned panels in carcase furniture was also part of the taste.

Regency furniture can be identified by dark, glossy wood offset by brass inlay, trellis work galleries, lion's paw feet, masks, star-shaped bolt heads and studs. Angularity of shapes was often accentuated by reeding on chair legs and cabinets as it was considered that ancient furniture was nearly always angular.

Early Victorian furniture was characterized by the revivals mentioned above but from the 1850s onwards upholstered lounge suites were popular, comprising: sofa, a pair of spoon-back chairs and a number of smaller balloon-back side or dining chairs. These remained available well into the next century in one form or another.

High-quality cabinet work was produced during the period and is evidenced in the international exhibitions where countries and manufacturers tried to outdo each other with the spectacle of their products. However, it is as well to remember that the exhibition pieces were just that, and are not representative of the productions made for the retail market.

In Germany and Austria, the rectangular, plain, neo-classical style named Biedermeier was popular. It had similarities with the more academic classicism of Schinkel. The success of the bentwood industry run by Thonet and others is discussed below. It was not until the unification of Germany in 1870 that the individual states and their local traditions began to be subsumed into a German style.

In France, the high-quality eighteenth century traditions continued, with Paris remaining the centre of the trade. Oak continued to be used as a base timber for cabinets, whilst beech was used for chair frames. There are examples of drawer linings and chair frames being made in walnut, but these are exceptions. The French construction process continued to use the goujon or peg that was used in the eighteenth century though its use gradually died out during the nineteenth century.

From the 1870s, attempts to influence furniture design by the Aesthetic movement were successful. The ideas taken from Japanese art and design produced a lighter and more delicate range of furniture. This was made by art furniture-makers. E.W. Godwin was the most important designer in this field, his productions using carefully balanced components, combined with Japanese materials such as stamped leather and netsuke. They were often ebonized and fitted with silver components. The Japanese taste extended to poor copies of art furniture, often comprising standard designs embellished with fretwork. Far more successful on a less elite level was the use of bamboo and other Japanese products such as grass cloth, lacquer panels and leather papers.

The last quarter of the century saw a taste for Moorish and Middle Eastern styles characterized by pierced and carved fretwork (sometimes imported from Cairo and named Cairene), inlay, carpets and cushions and potted palms.

In the United States this style was also promoted by designers and makers such as the Herter Brothers and Louis Comfort Tiffany who worked for clients who wanted furniture to reflect the contemporary aesthetic sensibilities. On the other hand the Colonial revival of the 1870s onward, revealed a nostalgia for America's past, whether it be from 1620 or 1820. As well as an interest in the antiques of the past, the revival was also a response to the fully blown Victorian furniture that was rejected by other groups such as the Arts and Crafts movement and often for similar reasons.

During the century the attempts by the furniture industry to meet the demands of the growing population for stylish and even ostentatious furniture were decried by design reformers. The problem was that reformers could not break out of the system. Reviving traditional methods and materials would inevitably have been very expensive and the introduction of plain, simple furniture would not have been appreciated by most people. This is not to say that efforts were not made to attempt to improve taste. The reformers mentioned above all tried to introduce new ways of thinking about furniture design but most missed the point about the public's demand for quantity of 'work' and costly looking materials.

### Materials used

The search for novelty and control of material and cost resulted in an eclectic range of materials being used during the nineteenth century.

The Regency period favoured striped figured timber, especially rosewood, calamander and zebrawood, all of which would contrast with the use of brass. From 1840 African mahogany was imported as a substitute for the expensive Central American type. Walnut remained popular in Scandinavian countries where exotic woods were too expensive. The Biedermeier style in Germany favoured mahogany in the north, and yew, cherry, or maple in the south.

The developments in using plies of wood continued with experiments in Europe and the United States. One of the most successful was the Gardner company of New Jersey, who patented a chair seat using perforated three ply.

The search for substitutes encouraged many inventions associated with the imitation of wood. The simplest was the method of mixing fine glue and sawdust or wood raspings to a paste to be put into a mould and allowed to dry under weight. Composition ornament (a mixture of whiting, animal glue, rosin, and linseed oil) was pressed into a mould and allowed to dry. It was then applied to a surface.

J.C. Loudon recommended the use of metal for furniture in his *Encyclopaedia* and illustrated some very advanced, as well as revivalist styles. The use of cast iron reached a high point during the mid-century. Established manufacturers turned to the expanding furniture market to supply garden seats, tables, jardinières, hallstands and other static items. Metal was also used in upholstery. From 1830 coiled springs were used and iron-framed chair backs were produced in quantity to give a flexible but strong support to easy chairs. Twisted wire for all kinds of furniture was especially popular around 1870 in the United States.

In the early part of the century a taste for tabletops of marble or stone became fashionable. British marbles and spars became popular and it was inevitable that attempts would be made to imitate them. The use of enamelled slate by E.G. Magnus was so successful that the marble industry gradually declined.

The period from 1835 to 1870 can be considered the heyday of English papier mâché (*Figure 1.20*). There were several varieties of papier mâché, the two main ones being pulped paper and layered paper. The first was mainly used for small-scale applied decoration, e.g. cornices, mouldings canopies and other applied ornament that could be used on furniture. The second type was used to make parts of furniture using a mould. This process produced blanks which could then be decorated. In 1825, Jennens and Bettridge took out a patent for pearl shell 'inlaying' for papier mâché. This well-known process, which was not actually inlaying, used slivers of pearl shell applied to the surface and varnished over. The important decorating process was based on a black background and an applied painted design.

**Figure 1.20** Papier mâché chair, English *c.*1840. Japanned with gilded decoration and painted mother-of-pearl inlay

During the 1850s gutta percha was introduced as a furniture material. It was a rubber-like material that could be moulded into a variety of shapes and designs. However, due to cost increases and problems with damage, it was discontinued before it could become fully established. Other organic materials such as deer antlers and other animal horn were used to produce eccentric chairs particularly. Rustic furniture was also made from logs and roots. Bamboo and its painted imitation has been mentioned above in association with the Regency style, but it was revived again in the latter part of the century for whatnots, hall-stands, flimsy tables, and so on. Basketwork, wicker and rattan were all pressed into service to make furniture, but especially chairs. The distinctions between the various materials cause confusion. Wicker refers to the plaited twigs or osiers of willow; cane is the outer bark of the rattan palm used for weaving seats, whilst reed is the inner core of the rattan. Cane is also a generic name for bamboo and malacca reeds which are made into a large variety of utensils and equipment, as well as

furniture. The role of Cyrus Wakefield and Walter Heywood in the development of cane and reed in furniture is important. By the mid-century Wakefield had developed the rattan used for packaging into a furniture-making material by processing the reed and the cane. Heywood introduced power looms to weave cane into a continuous web to avoid hand-work; he also substituted the rattan with its pith, the reed, which was susceptible to staining (and could therefore be coloured).

The period experimented with a variety of other materials that were essentially unsuitable for furniture-making or decoration. Coal, glass, lava, liquefied quartz, ferns and even seaweed were experimented with and in some cases patented. More important developments included machine-made screws in the 1850s and the first machine-made tacks in 1860.

Innovations in upholstery related to springing, and metal frames have been mentioned. Much effort was expended in trying to find substitutes or improvements in fillings. The use of curled horsehair was standard but other ideas included plant fibres, seaweed, and natural sea-sponge. The more likely stuffings were wood-wool, shredded fibres, animal hair and flock. An interesting substitute for leather was developed in the period. Although known since the fourteenth century, oil or leather cloth or Rexine, was originally made with a linseed oil coating. In the second half of the nineteenth century it was coated with a mixture of oil and liquid celluloid (cellulose nitrate).

### Tools and techniques

The use of machines in the conversion of raw material and the construction of furniture during the nineteenth century is a story of both important changes and minor developments. The development of machines such as circular saw planers, mortisers, borers, dovetail-cutters and veneer cutters for preparing and shaping timber was the most important change, which affected all woodworking industries, including particularly shipbuilding and house building. Machines for processing and shaping parts (bandsaws, fretsaws and lathes) were also being used in larger quantities, as was the third category of machines (embossers, moulders and carving machines), that produced decoration. Similar developments in the textile industry made soft furnishings more widely available.

In 1805, Brunel took out a patent for large circular saws particularly associated with veneer-cutting and in 1807 developed the saw further in association with block-making machinery. The importance of large powered saws for converting timber has been recognized in the development of the timber, joinery and furniture trades. However, one of the most important developments was not on this scale at all. The small circular saw of up to seven inches diameter, often operated by a treadle, was one of the keys to the success of small-scale furniture-makers. This saw enabled makers of cheap furniture to square up, mitre and rabbet cleanly, accurately and quickly, allowing the frames of cheap carcase work to be simply rebated and nailed. This method of rebating, using a circular saw, was particularly useful for drawer-making, which was traditionally a place for using dovetail joints. The advantage of this cheap method was that a dozen drawers could be made in the time it took to dovetail joint just one. This obviously had great advantages when such objects as Davenports and chests were being made.

In the same way as saws, planing machines had been developed by simply trying to replicate the reciprocating human action and in 1776 the first machine was invented by Leonard Hatton. Bentham improved upon this patent, first with a reciprocating plane and then with one based on the rotary principle. Joseph Bramah developed a trying-up machine for use in the Woolwich Arsenal that used a disc cutter mounted on a vertical spindle. These machines were called Daniels planers in the United States and in later models all had horizontal cutter blocks in place of the vertical spindle. All subsequent planing machines were then based on the rotary knife principle.

Attempts to apply machinery to joint cutting again originated with Bentham and his comprehensive patents of 1791 and 1793, but were not commercially viable until the 1850s. In this case it was the United States that led the way. For example, the Burley dovetailing machine, patented in 1855 was alleged to have been able to produce seventy-five to one hundred dovetail joints per hour. Improvements continued to occur in these machines but one that is worthy of special mention is the Knapp dovetailing machine, patented in 1870. It has been pointed out that this machine was significant because it was the first machine that did not attempt to reproduce the hand cut dovetail but rather produced its own peculiar 'modern machined joint'. Ironically, interest in traditional furniture towards the end of the century contributed to the decline of this obviously modern joint.

The development of bandsaws originated with an invention by William Newberry in 1808. However, it was not until the success of a Msr Perin of Paris, who produced a bandsaw blade that lasted reasonably well, that the machine was really viable and operated satisfactorily. It was again the Woolwich Arsenal that ordered some of the first to be used in England in 1855. The fretsaw or jig or scroll saw, developed from the simple marquetry cutter's saw, was one of the simplest and most useful tools for the cabinetmaker. Often treadle-operated with a single blade, it could cut out intricate shapes, and satisfy the demand for the most elaborate decoration.

The third group of machines includes two different divisions. First, the patent processes run by companies producing such items as carvings, mouldings and embossed ornament for sale to cabinetmakers (see below) and secondly, the machines that allowed a cabinetmaker to produce the decoration for his own work. The most important of this second group would seem to be the spindle or toupie moulder. It was said that it was particularly useful for Gothic or medieval work 'as more chamfering can be done by it in one hour than could be done by handwork in a day'.

From a technical point of view the developments in bent and laminated wood were amongst the most innovative in the century. Thonet, with his initial experiments in laminations and subsequent bending of solid timber, began the first large-scale production system based on interchangeable parts in furniture-making. He introduced simple functional designs which enabled him to have a commercial, as well as technical success (*Figure 1.21*). John Henry Belter came from the same tradition as Thonet but developed his ideas in the United States. His patents related to the bending of laminates of wood in two directions around formers to shape such items as chair backs and bed frames. Belter's technique was usually hidden behind a large amount of decorative carving.

**Figure 1.21** Thonet bentwood chair, Viennese *c.*1865, stamped Thonet Austria 6811

## Surface decoration and finish

The demand for novelty, and the reproduction of expensive processes by imitation, were the two main driving forces behind developments in surface decoration and finish. Many old techniques were revived, along with a range of new patented processes, some of which became established while others were unsuccessful.

The most well-known revival and its mechanized equivalent is carving. During the early years of the century the carving trade was in a poor state. With the revival of historical styles and a demand for 'old' pieces, carving was stimulated. However, much of the work for the general taste and fashion was destined to be cut on carving and routing machines. This taste was fuelled by a few schools of carving, developed by the Rogers family in London, Tweedy and Robinson in Tyneside and Kendal and Cooke in Warwick. Most of their work was based on anecdotal scenes, often of great complexity, which remained examples for other makers to copy.

To satisfy the demand for carving, particularly in the Gothic style, machine carving, which had been known to sculptors previously, was applied to architectural woodwork. It was soon used to make carvings suitable for furniture. The most successful of three major companies was the Jordan process, which allowed the model to be copied by moving the material towards a fixed cutting tool.

Pyrography, in which wood is charred by heated iron moulds being applied to the surface, was developed with the result that the surface had an 'old' finish built in. Pressure carving or moulding was another technique for imitating the work of the chisel. It was effected by applying moulds, with a design stamped into them, to wood under great pressure. It was especially useful for end-grain medallions. Finally, there was a range of mouldings and applied decoration made from wood waste and other material including colourings and adhesives.

*Painting* The decoration of furniture by painting is divided between that with painted ornament on a timber ground and that with an all-over painted ground which is then decorated. The latter process was usually confined to cheaper woods and is often called japanning by contemporary writers: a particular type was called pen-work. This was an imitation of etching which was made by first japanning the furniture black and then painting the design in white japan. Following this was the final process of adding line work with Indian ink and a pen.

Sheraton in his *Cabinet Dictionary* gives full details on the subject of painting, including the process of painting rush seats. In this instance he warns against the practice of using water colour which was designed to deceive the purchaser. This warning was repeated much later in the century by another commentator talking about painted bedroom furniture which was deceitfully decorated with water colours rather than proper varnishes.

*Marquetry and equivalents* During the 1850s and 1860s a number of methods of imitation decoration were invented and patented in response to the demand and the rising cost of the original processes. The boulle revival of the nineteenth century was supported by stamping brass (especially borders) directly into timber or by substituting other materials in place of metal and shell.

Marquetry was reproduced by embossing or printing decorative designs onto paper that were then transferred to woods and varnished over. This process was patented as xylography. Another method called diachromatizing used stains to produce a pattern which penetrated the wood. Ready-made marquetry, mouldings and carvings were available from wholesale suppliers in increasing numbers throughout the period.

The revival of interest in pietre dure, where coloured stones were let into an ebony or stone face, continued a tradition that started in Italy in the seventeenth century.

*Tunbridge Ware*   Already known in the eighteenth century, the technique of the process was changed in the early part of the nineteenth century. The method used was to glue a selection of thin strips or rods together in a predetermined way. Once these bunches were dry, they would be sawn transversely to reveal a pattern that could be laid down as a veneer. The mini mosaic effect was best suited to small items, such as trays, boxes, tea caddies and small table tops (*Figure 1.22*). It is thought that only woods in natural colours were used.

*Finishing*   Graining, staining and marbling were all processes that were well known to furniture-makers and were practised widely in the first half of the nineteenth century. These processes enjoyed a revival not only for cost saving reasons, but also because regular supplies of timber were interrupted by the Anglo-

French wars. Graining was acceptable and strongly recommended by commentators on interior decoration. However, by the mid-century these practices were criticized as deceits, and towards the end of the century were only associated with low-grade furniture.

The finishing processes were explicitly described in contemporary trade manuals, the most important being Nathaniel Whittock's *The Decorative Painters' and Glaziers' Guide*. Staining was important as a finishing process and it was acknowledged that the method was especially suited to bulk treatments. Whittock mentions how chairs are dipped in large copper vats and allowed to hang and dry. The dye for this process was made from Brazilwood chips and pearlash (potassium carbonate). Other methods included the use of alkanet dye mixed with linseed oil, as a colour enhancer and reviver for mahogany. During the 1820s French polish was introduced. This was originally designed to give a thick transparent coating which would impart a highly glazed effect without changing the colour of the timber. By the mid-century the process had acquired a bad name because staining caused by the polish obliterated the natural colours of the wood and stopped it 'ageing' naturally.

### Organization of trades and manufacturing

In 1803, Sheraton could say that the furniture trade was 'one of the leading mechanical professions in every polite nation in Europe'. It is still often considered that the so-called 'Industrial Revolution' brought furniture-making into a factory situation during the nineteenth century, which, combined with the use of machines, dramatically changed the way furniture was made over the period. This is not the case, although there were undoubtedly some changes. The enduring nature of the trade and its attitudes to change were such that new methods were only espoused if they contributed to profitability. Technological change was not necessary while the older ways met the demand. This is not to say that factories did not exist, simply that there was no dramatic change from one system to another; it was rather a gradual process that is still not really complete.

In England the rise of wholesalers and retail outlets which gradually took over from the comprehensive manufacturing firms was a

**Figure 1.22**   Tunbridge Ware writing box, English, 1830–70

major feature, and confirmed the separation of maker and seller. In France, the trade was centred on Paris, often with businesses run by German cabinetmakers alongside French ones. The businesses of Joseph-Emanuel Zwiener and François Linke were two of the most well known. By the 1880s there were around 17,000 workers in the Paris industry alone. By 1790 the marking of goods was no longer a requirement, following the disbandment of the guilds, but was revived in the early nineteenth century by makers stamping furniture or engraving the brass-work with the firm's name. Rather than a guild control, the stamp was a promotional device encouraged by retailers.

The main input by Austria during the nineteenth century was the development of the bentwood furniture industry. By 1900, the Thonet company employed 6000 workers producing 4000 pieces per day and there were another 25,000 workers employed in Austria alone in other bentwood businesses.

Publications remained an important part of the trade's network and are indicative of the conservative approach to design. In 1788 the *Cabinet-Makers' Book of Prices* was published and was reissued throughout the nineteenth century. In 1802 came the *London Chair-makers' and Carvers' Book of Prices*. In 1803 Thomas Sheraton's *Cabinet Dictionary* was published and in 1829 Thomas King brought out *The Modern Style of Cabinet Work Exemplified*. This was reissued unaltered in 1862, testimony to conservative style. In 1833, Loudon's *Encyclopaedia of Cottage Farm and Villa Architecture* was produced. Later in the century the decorators and pundits of various styles wrote 'how to decorate' books. These included works by Charles Eastlake, Clarence Cooke, Ogden Codman and Edith Wharton, Christopher Dresser as well as a growing number of magazines and journals.

One of the most important developments in the United States was the expansion of the furniture industry into the mid-west and southern states. Improved transportation and an abundance of water and timber in states such as Indiana, Illinois and Ohio meant that firms like Mitchell and Rammelsburg of Cincinnati or whole cities like Chicago or Grand Rapids and (later) South Carolina and High Point could trade with the East and West Coast centres successfully.

## 1.6 The twentieth century

### Context

The twentieth century, sometimes called the machine age, has seen such a great variety of designs of furniture that generalizations are meaningless. Advances in materials use and production techniques led to major changes in the production of furniture. Designers with a knowledge of materials and techniques that were developed to meet the new demands were employed to design furniture for large-scale production. The division between production furniture and designers' limited editions grew as the market for furniture increased rapidly.

The twentieth century has produced such a wide ranging variety of forms of furniture that any general statements are not very useful. The variety of factors that have always affected furniture design, i.e. the nature of consuming, the training of craftsmen, the intellectual background, the technical aspects, the critical acceptance of work, and the prevailing style and fashion have been even more varied in the twentieth century so that we can see sculptural fine art furniture through to full blown reproductions of historical styles in modern plastic materials.

These factors led to two separate developments: one, the rise of modernism and machine production and the other, the continued development of the craftsman–designer's influence. Two important examples of the first are the Bauhaus metal products of the 1920s (*Figure 1.23*) and the post-war use of synthetics, such as plastics.

The complicated story of the rise of modern furniture can only be hinted at here. Artistic movements including Cubism, De Stijl, Constructivism, Expressionism and Futurism have had degrees of influence on furniture design. However, architects who designed furniture for specific interiors, including Lutyens, Le Corbusier, Mies van der Rohe, Frank Lloyd Wright and Rietveld (to name a few), produced icons of modern design that often have little relation to the productions of the major furniture factories but are symbolic of the twentieth century. After the First World War the fashionable Art Deco style was adopted for commercial as well as high-style furniture. The work of the French designers Jean Dunand, Pierre

**Figure 1.23** Armchair, 'Wassily', designed by Marcel Breuer (1902–81), Bauhaus, Dessau, 1925

**Figure 1.24** Desk and chair, oak, designed by Sir Ambrose Heal (1872–1959), 1929

Chareau, Paul Poiret, Ruhlmann and Sue et Mare stand as examples of the high quality of craftsmanship and ingenious use of materials. Based on a wide variety of inspirations, it remained popular into the 1930s, when it began to draw inspiration from the Modern movement and streamlining.

The British tradition of Arts and Crafts was continued during the first half of the century, with subtle alterations by Ambrose Heal, Sidney Barnsley and Gordon Russell (*Figure 1.24*).

In the United States the continuing importance of immigrants is highlighted by early twentieth century designers such as Kem Weber, Paul Frankl and Gilbert Rohde who were to stamp an individuality on American design in the 1920s and 1930s. By the 1930s the oppression in Europe resulted in Bauhaus luminaries being employed in American schools of design, Josef Albers, Walter Gropius and Mies van der Rohe being amongst the most well-known emigres who brought European modernism to America. A version of Art Moderne was developed in furniture and interiors by a number of designers, including Donald Deskey and Bel Geddes. These styles were characterized by streamlined shapes and modern materials, including stainless steel, glass and aluminium.

During the Second World War the inevitable shortages meant that there was a curtailing of decoration, and the Utility scheme was introduced into Britain in 1942. The need to conserve materials resulted in a stark simplicity that was a precursor of contemporary modernism.

After the Second World War, Scandinavian and Italian influences became important through much of Europe and North America. The Scandinavian designers such as Alvar Aalto, Hans Wegner, Arne Jacobsen and manufacturers including Fritz Hansen, were responsible for the successful combination of machine and handwork which had been established by Danish designer Kaare Klint.

In the United States organic design became important after the war. Charles and Ray Eames, Noguchi, and Bertoia were all designing more fluidly shaped furniture which was facilitated by the new materials available. Eero Saarinen's 'tulip chair' is an icon of the period (see *Figure 1.27*). The importance of manufacturing companies such as Hermann Miller and Knoll Associates encouraged modern design as a commercial enterprise.

In the latter part of the century there has been a craft revival or a continuation of the woodworking tradition. In the United States this has been spearheaded by the work of Wharton Esherick, George Nakashima, Sam Maloof and Wendell Castle and in Britain by John Makepeace, Rupert Williamson and others.

Since the early 1980s, there has been a revolt against the orthodoxy of modernism. The

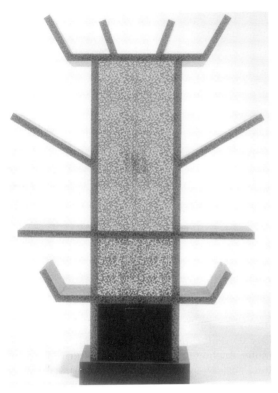

**Figure 1.25** Sideboard, 'Casablanca', designed by Ettore Sottsass (1917– ), manufactured by Memphis, Italy, 1981

Italian design group Memphis, and individual designers such as Danny Lane, Ron Arad and Phillipe Starck, have introduced a new sense of fun and excitement into furniture design (*Figure 1.25*).

The major advances in furniture types relate to usage in the twentieth century. Built-in furniture and unit furniture reflect the changing use of space in rooms, and the introduction of do-it-yourself (DIY) and knock-down (KD) forms of construction reflect a new marketing approach to furniture. In addition, the enormous expansion of the contract furniture market has resulted in a whole range of office furniture and equipment that represents a completely new typology.

### Materials used

The choice and range of materials available to furniture-makers in the twentieth century have been extremely wide. The continued develop-ment of metal, plastics, and wood-based products has been essential to complement the traditional materials still in use.

*Metals* The use of metal was revived in the twentieth century by Frank Lloyd Wright who developed office furniture made from metal which started a trend that has remained as a type form. The nineteenth century experiments with metal tubing were ignored until Mart Stam and Marcel Breuer in the 1920s developed a cantilever chair. The potential of tubular steel as a truly modern material, ideal for series production, has been vindicated as a number of models from the 1920s were still in production in the 1990s. In other cases, steel bar was bent and polished to produce a highly sophisticated design such as Mies van der Rohe's (1929) 'Barcelona chair'. In many instances the use of chromium plate gave the metal a bright finish and there are also examples of a gold colour being applied. Many of the modernist icons were made in chromed steel, including the chaise longue (1928) by Le Corbusier, the Wassily chair (1925) and the Cesca chair (1928) also by Breuer.

Aluminium, prized for its lightweight and non-corroding properties, was used for decorating and making frames for furniture in the 1930s. Marcel Breuer exploited it for his chaise longue (1932) and it was used in 1938 for outdoor chairs in Switzerland to the design of Hans Coray. After the Second World War, Ernest Race produced the BA chair, made from aluminium sections complete with a padded seat. Aluminium went on to be used in cast or spun form in many furniture designs, especially for chair and stool bases and special applications like the frame of the Plia chair (1968). In the 1980s aluminium was again a designer material with outdoor chairs designed by Jorge Pensi (1986) and the sculptural Lockheed Lounge (1986) by Marc Newsom.

The use of wire for furniture had its roots in the nineteenth century but in the 1950s the sculptural chair designs of the Eames (DKR 1951) and Harry Bertoia (Diamond chair 1952) introduced the 'see-through' chair which was ideal for the open plan interiors of the period.

Metal has continued to be at the avant-garde of furniture design with the work of Ron Arad, Tom Dixon and Kuramata using sheet steel, scrap iron and wire respectively.

*Wood-based*  For much of the century traditional furniture woods have been used with little change. Oak, mahogany and walnut have been used to make reproduction furniture of varying quality. Other traditional woods have been used in the making of modern furniture. The design phases of sapele mahogany, makore, rio rosewood, American walnut and pine are all testimony to the longevity of taste for particular species. The major twentieth-century timbers that were apparently new to furniture were teak and afromosia. Although previously used in boat-building and furniture-making, these woods were reintroduced to European furniture via Scandinavia.

The century is best known for its technical advances in the treatment of wood. Whether it be improvements in seasoning, veneer-cutting, laminations and plywood, or reconstituted wood materials such as block-board or particle board, the advances were highly important. The developments in manmade boards began with plywood, prepared in sheet form for use as a constructional material in the early part of the century. Its value as a panel board was soon acknowledged. The use of plywood as a 'designer material' was developed especially by Alvar Aalto in 1930–1. He then worked on laminated plies in 1936, producing some of the twentieth century's most famous chairs. Other examples of plywood work include Gerald Summers, Marcel Breuer and the Isokon company (*Figure 1.26*). Although successfully used in much inexpensive production furniture, the three-dimensional chair forms made from plywood by Charles Eames in the 1940s are amongst the most famous results obtained using this material. Plywood was further developed by other designers such as Arne Jacobsen in his Ant chair (1952) and it continues to be a valuable material. Hardboard or Masonite was a later invention which involved pressing a mixture of wood fibres and adhesives into sheets. It has been used for back panels of cabinets and for packing. Block board and laminboard are two further developments of nineteenth century cabinetmaking techniques that were taken over by timber merchants and made and marketed as constructional panels. However, the most important product in the second half of the century was particle board or chipboard. This board, developed during the Second World War, comprises wood chips of varying shapes

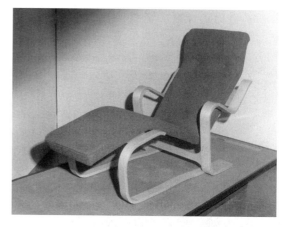

**Figure 1.26**  Isokon Long Chair, beech, bent laminated frame, padded plywood seat. Designed by Marcel Breuer (1902–81), made in England, 1936

with adhesives and fillers which are bonded under great pressure. The board thus produced is extremely strong and flat with no natural faults, making it ideal for the box-like designs of the later twentieth century. This process was developed to use other materials such as flax residues (flax-board) and sugar cane residues (bagasse board). One of the latest innovations is medium density fibreboard (MDF), which is made from wood fibres bonded together with a resin to make a variety of thicknesses of an easily machined and finished board.

*Synthetic materials*  The astounding advances in synthetic chemistry and the development of plastics have brought unprecedented changes to the way furniture is made. In many cases the skills of the cabinetmaker have been overtaken by engineers skilled in machine development or by semi-skilled assemblers putting together prefabricated parts.

Plastics have been known since the nineteenth century with the work of Alexander Parkes, but their commercial application to furniture-making is a twentieth century phenomenon. In furniture use, plastics have been used for construction, decoration and finishing. The replacement of animal glues with synthetic resins in most assembly and laminating processes is a result of the development in adhesives science. The development of urea-formaldehyde adhesives for veneering and laminating, polyvinyl acetate adhesives for gen-

**Figure 1.27**  Tulip chair, designed by Eero Saarinen (1910–61), 1956. White moulded fibre glass shell on an aluminium pedestal with blue woven textile seat cushion

**Figure 1.28**  Polyprop chair Mark II designed by Robin Day (1915– ). Injection moulded polypropylene made by S. Hille and Co. from 1963

eral wood jointing, and other specialist adhesives for special applications, releases some of the original constraints on furniture designers. Plastics were used for construction before the Second World War but it was immediately afterwards that they came into their own. The use of sheet acrylics such as Lucite and Perspex was developed in the 1940s along with further experiments with glass-fibre and an increasingly wide range of special plastics. In 1940 Charles Eames and Eero Saarinen developed moulded polyester seats that could be fixed to a variety of underframes and in 1956 Saarinen designed his 'Tulip chair' using glass-reinforced plastic for the seat and aluminium for the base (*Figure 1.27*).

The development of glass fibre reinforced plastic led to a new range of multi-shaped objects, including the Womb chair designed by Saarinen in 1948 and the DAX chair designed by Charles and Ray Eames in the same year. The injection moulding of plastics was a great advance as one-piece furniture items could be made. The most ubiquitous was Robin Day's chair design for Hille, made from polypropylene (*Figure 1.28*). Italian designers developed

plastics and their processing to a high degree. Two examples from the 1960s demonstrate this. The Blow chair, an inflatable PVC chair (1967), and the Sacco (1968), a bag of polystyrene chips which could be used in a multitude of ways, show how plastics could reflect lifestyles and develop new furniture types. By the 1980s plastics were revived as one of the materials of postmodernism. The use of the ubiquitous plastic laminates was one example.

*Upholstery*  The technical changes in upholstery have been related to both the internal structure and the external coverings. At the beginning of the century the spiral compression spring was supreme but in the 1930s spiral tension springs were introduced into Germany and England. This released the designer from having to create a deep section to a chair to accommodate the spiral springs: he could produce a more elegant easy chair whilst retaining the benefits of metal springing. In 1929 the development of latex-rubber cushioning was patented by Dunlop. When made up into cushions, this became an ideal partner to the tension-sprung chair. Post-war developments included the four-point suspension (a one-piece rubber platform) and the introduction of rubber webbing by Pirelli. Both these processes hastened the demise of the traditional spring until the introduction of serpentine metal springs, which enabled manufacturers to produce a traditional-looking upholstery range without the cost of a fully sprung interior.

Plastics also earned a place in post-war upholstery with the introduction of polyether and polyester foams for cushions and padding. Developments continued with substitutes for most traditional materials, e.g. man-made fibre-fill in place of cotton-fibre wrap. The constructional use of plastics in chairs has been mentioned, but the development of polystyrene shells to create an extremely light-weight frame should be noted. External coverings have been revolutionized by the use of PVC-coated fabrics as substitutes for the earlier leather cloths.

*Other* There seem to be few materials that have not at one time or another been pressed into service in the name of furniture-making. However, two significant materials that have not been discussed deserve a brief mention. The use of paper, discussed in connection with papier mâché, was reintroduced in a product called Lloyd Loom (1917). This was a material made from metal wire with paper wrapped around which was then woven into sheets so that it could be fixed to bentwood chair shapes. In recent years, cardboard and corrugated board have both been used in the making of furniture, in the case of Frank Gehry (1972), as very limited editions, in another case as throwaway children's chairs. Glass is the other important material that has been used throughout the century for constructional, decorative and finishing purposes. As a table top, it became synonymous with the 1960s style known as 'chrome and glass', although it has been exploited by Art Deco designers such as Lalique as well as contemporary artists such as Danny Lane.

### Tools and techniques of conversion and construction

There have been great advances in the application of woodworking machines to furniture-making, but no really major advances in machine type. Accuracy and speed increased through the mechanical adaptation of hand operations powered by various independent sources, and by the electrification of hand tools. However, many furniture-making operations remain a mix between machine processes and hand work. Various techniques have been adopted in particular fields to match materials development with technical competence. The Thonet company adapted their experience in bending wood to producing bent metal furniture. Other developments outside the industry also contributed to change. Developments in both World Wars had an effect on furniture production, these included changes in factory management, the increase in the range of new materials, the de-skilling of labour and the application of technology once unrelated to furniture-making. For example, the Chrysler Corporation's experience of cycle welding to join wood, rubber, glass, or metal was invaluable in the experiments of Charles Eames. He was able to use this technology to fix metal legs, via rubber grommets, to plywood seats.

Undoubtedly, one of the most important changes in furniture-making has been the development of prepared parts and specialist fittings that have enabled semi-skilled operators to make furniture. Precut and finished panels, KD fittings and pre-sewn upholstery covers complete with fillings attached are examples of this simplified approach to production.

The twentieth century furniture factory, making cabinet furniture on a large scale, is organized so that there is a logical sequence of event that takes full advantage of flow line productions systems, semi-skilled labour and intensive machinery. The rough end receives lumber and deals with the processes of sawing, planing and moulding as well as veneer preparation. The shaping department follows with mortising, lathe work, boring, bandsawing and jointing. This is followed by sanding. Once these preliminaries are complete the assembly can begin. Work such as sub-assemblying, clamping, drawer work and door hanging occur at this point. Finally the finishing stain, filling, sealing and glazing occur before items are ready for packing and shipping.

### Surface decoration and finish

Again, innovative techniques and application of novel materials have played a large part in the story of decoration and finish in the twentieth century.

The range of finishes has increased enormously over the century. French polish and wax finishes remained popular during the early part of the century but after the First World War they were gradually replaced by nitro-cellulose lacquers. These lacquers, developed from the dopes used on aircraft frames, produced a quick-drying finish that was more resistant than French polish to heat and water. They could also be applied by spray gun. Post-war synthetic lacquers including acid catalysed urea-formaldehyde and melamine-formaldehyde, polyurethane and polyester (all with varying properties) have been developed for special applications. Oiled finishes were popular on teak and rosewood furniture.

The Art Deco period (1910–30) was instrumental in incorporating unusual and exotic materials in furniture decoration and finish. In addition to exotic woods, such as Macassar ebony, burr walnut and amboyna, cabinetmakers incorporated mother-of-pearl, ivory, snakeskin, sharkskin (shagreen or Galuchat), leather, vellum, brass and lacquer into their repertoire of novel materials. There was a revival of Oriental lacquer decoration in the period, particularly with the work of Eileen Grey and Jean Dunand.

In the latter half of the century the use of plastics, apart from lacquers, is most noticeable in laminates and paper foils. Other finishes, popular at various times during the century, include fumed oak (subjecting objects to ammonia fumes), limed oak (slaked lime rubbed into grain leaving white flecks), and for metals, oxidizing, anodizing, and stove enamelling.

The twentieth century is unique in the wide range of opportunities that furniture-makers have had in the making, decoration and finishing of their furniture.

### Organization of trades and manufacturing

With the vast increase in the choice of materials and methods of making, the role of traditional furniture-makers and retailers has been whittled away. There are still many small businesses in the trade but the turn of the century saw the beginning of a tendency to move towards factory production on a larger scale. This occurred especially in the United States, in centres such as Grand Rapids.

In England a move away from London's East End towards the Lea Valley Trading Estate was exemplified by the Lebus company who at one time had the largest furniture factory in the world. In the second half of the century the trade has become international in its markets. This has been helped greatly by the development of the knock-down (KD) method of construction.

## 1.7  Conclusion

Like all material objects, the history and background of furniture is a mirror of change in societies. The continuing development of societies in economic, political, cultural and philosophical terms, as well as changes of physical and geographic nature are all reflected in furniture. The understanding of the context of furniture therefore has value far beyond questions of attribution, rarity, value, association or other equally interesting aspects. It is very much part of the material culture of a society. From the meanest stool to the grandest cabinet, all furniture and furnishings are part of the jig-saw that represents particular moments in history.

The careful study of artefacts and their cultural context will enable us to understand a little more of how materials, techniques, tools, trade and consumer usage were understood in their own time. In conjunction with the practical physical analysis and inspection by conservators and historians, other sources of history are needed to develop what can be learnt from the objects themselves. These other sources include, inventories, account books, diaries, journals, design and price books, paintings and drawings as well as aspects of interior design and architecture. The important contributions to be made from other disciplines need to be acknowledged but there is some way to go before they are fully part of the furniture historian's armoury. However, anyone interested in learning more about furniture, those who made and used it, as well as its wider role in various societies will enjoy following the multifarious paths that make up the history of furniture.

## Bibliography

This bibliography is a limited selection of works that will be useful to furniture scholars. It omits any monographs on individual designers or any commentaries on particular design groups. The vast resource of journal articles is also omitted. For further bibliographies see in the works listed below as well as in the following:

*American Furniture* (annual) Chipstone Foundation

Ames, K. and Ward, G. (1989) *Decorative Arts and Household Furnishings in America 1650–1920, An Annotated Bibliography*, Winterthur, The Henry Francis duPont Museum

Bunston, J. (1971) *English Furniture Designs 1800–1914, A Bibliography of 120 Pattern Books and Trade Catalogues in the Library of the Victoria and Albert Museum*, V&A Publications

Edwards, C. (2000) *Encyclopaedia of Furniture Making Materials, Techniques and Trades*, Ashgate

*Furniture History, The Journal of the Furniture History Society*, London (annual bibliographies published from 1970 to 1985)

Russell, T. (1989) *The Built Environment: A Subject Index 1800–1960*, 4 vols, Gregg Publishing

Shoreditch Public Library (1950) *Bibliography of Books Relating to Furniture*, Shoreditch, London

## General texts

Beard, G. and Gilbert, C. (eds) (1986) *Dictionary of English Furniture Makers, 1660–1840*, Furniture History Society, London

Cescinsky, H. (1931) *The Gentle Art of Faking Furniture*. Chapman and Hall

Cooke, E.S. (ed.) (1987) *Upholstery in America & Europe from the Seventeenth Century to World War 1*, W.W. Norton

Cotton, B. (1990) *English Regional Chairs*, Antique Collectors Club

Edwards, R. (1983) *Dictionary of Furniture from the late Middle Ages to late Georgian Period*, 3 vols, Antique Collectors Club

Fairbanks, J.C. and Bates, E.B. (1981) *American Furniture 1620 to the Present*, Marek

Giedion, S. (1948) *Mechanisation takes Command*, Oxford University Press

Gilbert, C. (1991) *English Vernacular Furniture 1750–1900*, Yale University Press

Gloag, J. (1990) *Dictionary of Furniture*, revised edition, Unwin Hyman

Hayward, H. (ed.) (1965) *World Furniture*, Hamlyn

Heckscher, M. (1985) *American Furniture in the Metropolitan Museum of Art*, MMA

Kreisel, H. (ed.) (1968–74) *Die Kunst des Deutsches Mobels*, 3 vols, Munich

Nutting, W. (1948) *Furniture Treasury*, 3 vols, Macmillan

Thornton, P. (2000) *Authentic Decor: the Domestic Interior, 1620–1920,* Cassell

Verlet, P. (ed.) (1972) *Styles, meubles décors du Moyen âge à nos jours*, 2 vols, Larousse

## General texts on period and countries

### Earliest times to the Middle Ages

Aldred, C. (1954–1955) Fine woodwork, in Singer, Holmyard and Hall, *A History of Technology*, vol. I, Oxford University Press

Baker, H. (1966) *Furniture in the Ancient World: Origins and Evolution 3100–475 BC*, The Connoisseur

Eames, P. (1977) Furniture in England, France and the Netherlands 12th–15th centuries, *Furniture History*, 12

Killen, G. (1980) *Ancient Egyptian Furniture*, Aris and Phillips

Lucas, A. (1948) *Ancient Egyptian Materials and Industries*, 4th edn, Arnold; revised by J.R. Harris, Hutchinson, 1962; repr. *Histories and Mysteries of Man*, 1989

Mercer, E. (1969) *Furniture 700–1700*, Weidenfeld and Nicolson

Richter, G. (1960) *The Furniture of the Ancient Greeks, Etruscans and Romans*, Phaidon

### Renaissance to Industrial Revolution

Beard, G. (1986) *Craftsmen and Interior Decoration in England 1660–1820*, Bloomsbury Books

Burr, G. (1964) *Hispanic Furniture from the Fifteenth through the Eighteenth Century*, Archive Press

Chinnery, V. (1979) *Oak Furniture: The British Tradition*, Antique Collectors Club

Chippendale, T. (1966) *A Gentleman and Cabinet Maker's Director*, Facsimile of the 1762 edition, Dover Press

Comstock, H. (1968) *The Looking Glass in America, 1700–1825*, Viking Press

Cooke, E.S. (1996) *Making Furniture in Pre-industrial America: The Social Economy of Newtown and Woodbury, Connecticut*, Johns Hopkins University Press

Edwards, C.D. (1996) *Eighteenth Century Furniture*, Manchester University Press

Fitzgerald, O.P. (1982) *Three Centuries of American Furniture*, Prentice-Hall

Forman, B. (1988) *American Seating Furniture, 1630–1730*, W.W. Norton

Gilbert, C. (1978) *The Life and Works of Thomas Chippendale*, Tabard Press

Gusler, W.B. (1993) *Furniture of Williamsburg and Eastern Virginia, 1710–1790*, Colonial Williamsburg Foundation

Hepplewhite, G. (1969) *The Cabinet Maker and Upholsterer's Guide,* Facsimile of the 1794 edition, Dover Press

Hurst, R.L. and Prown, J. (1997) *Southern Furniture, 1680–1830*, Colonial Williamsburg Foundation/Abrahms

Jervis, S. (1974) *Printed Furniture Designs Before 1650*, W.S. Maney and Son Ltd for the Furniture History Society

Jourdain, M. (1924) *English Decoration and Furniture of the Early Renaissance 1500–1650*, Batsford

Kane, P. (1976) *300 Years of American Seating Furniture: Chairs and Beds from the Mabel Brady Garvan and other collections at Yale University*, New York Graphic Society

Montgomery, C. (1967) *American Furniture, The Federal Period*, Thames and Hudson

Morrazzoni, G. (1940) *Il Mobilio Italiano*, Florence

Sheraton, Thomas (1972) *The Cabinet Maker and Upholsterer's Drawing Book*, Facsimile reprint of material from various early editions published by the author between 1793 and 1802, Dover

Thornton, P. (1978) *Seventeenth Century Interior Decoration in England, France and Holland*, Yale University Press

Trent, R. (1976) *Pilgrim Century Furniture, An Historical Survey*, Universe Books

Vandal, N. (1990) *Queen Anne Furniture*, The Taunton Press

Viaux, J. (1962) *Le Meuble en France*, Presses Universitaires de France

Wills, G. (1971) *English Furniture, 1550–1760*, Doubleday

Wills, G. (1971) *English Furniture, 1760–1900*, Doubleday

Wolsey, S.W. and Luff, R.W. (1968) *Furniture in England: the Age of the Joiner*, Barker

### The nineteenth century

Agius, P. (1978) *British Furniture, 1880–1915*, Antique Collectors Club

Aslin, E. (1962) *Nineteenth Century English Furniture*, The Collectors Book Club

Briggs, A. (1988) *Victorian Things*, Batsford

Cathers, D. (1996) *Furniture of the American Arts and Crafts Movement*, Turn of the Century Editions

Collard, F. (1985) *Regency Furniture*, Antique Collectors Club

Cooper, J. (1987) *Victorian and Edwardian Furniture and Interiors*, Thames and Hudson

Darling, S. (1984) *Chicago Furniture. Art and Industry, 1833–1933*, Chicago Historical Society in association with Norton

Edwards, C.D. (1993) *Victorian Furniture*, Manchester University Press

Gloag, J. (1973) *Victorian Comfort: A Social History of Design from 1830–1900*, David and Charles

Grier, K.C. (1988) *Culture and Comfort, People Parlours and Upholstery, 1850–1930*, University of Massachusetts Press

Himmelheber, G. (1974) *Biedermeier Furniture*, Faber

Joy, E. (1974) *English Furniture, 1800–1851*, Sotheby Parke Bernet Publications/Ward Lock Ltd

Loudon, J.C. (2000) *An Encyclopaedia of Cottage Farm and Villa Architecture and Furniture*, Facsimile of the 1846 edition, Donhead

Madigan, M. (1982) *Nineteenth Century Furniture Innovation, Revival and Reform*, Billboard Publications

Mayes, L.J. (1960) *The History of Chair Making in High Wycombe*, Routledge and Kegan Paul

Metropolitan Museum of Art (1970) *19th Century America: Furniture and Other Decorative Arts*, New York, Graphic Society

Montgomery, C. (1967) *American Furniture, The Federal Period*, Thames and Hudson

Naylor, G. (1990) *The Arts and Crafts Movement*, Trefoil, London

Payne, C. (1988) *19th Century European Furniture* [NB: excl. British], Antique Collectors Club

Symonds, R.W. and Whineray, B. (1987) *Victorian Furniture*, Studio Editions

### The twentieth century

The Cantilever Chair, Exhibition Catalogue, Stuhl Museum Burg Beverungen, Alexander Verlag, Berlin, 1986

Dormer, P. (1987) *The New Furniture*, Thames and Hudson

Edwards, C.D. (1994) *Twentieth Century Furniture*, Manchester University Press

Fiell, P. and Fiell, C. (1991) *Modern Furniture Classics since 1945*, Thames and Hudson

Greenberg, C. (1995) *Mid-century Modern; Furniture of the 1950s*, Thames and Hudson

Hiesinger, K. (ed.) (1983) *Design since 1945*, Thames and Hudson in association with the Philadelphia Museum of Art

Logie, G. (1947) *Furniture from Machines*, G. Allen and Unwin

McFadden, D. (1982) *Scandinavian Modern Design, 1880–1980*, Abrahms

Sembach, K. (1982) *Contemporary Furniture: an International Review of Modern Furniture 1950 to the present*, Design Council, London

Sparke, P. (1988) *Italian Design, 1870 to the Present*, Thames and Hudson

Wilk, C. (1980) *Thonet: 150 years of Furniture*, Barron's

## Texts relating to design and construction

NB: Many of the other texts have sections on the subject of design and construction.

Alexander, J. (1978) *Make a Chair from a Tree: An Introduction to Working Green Wood*, Greenwoodworking

Bairstow, J. (1984) *Practical and Decorative Woodworking Joints*, Batsford

Blackie and Son (1970) *Victorian Cabinet Makers Assistant 1853*, Facsimile edition, Dover

Bonnett, D. (1956) *Contemporary Cabinet Design and Construction*, Batsford

Evans, N.G. (1996) *American Windsor Chairs*, Hudson Hills Press

Hayward, Charles (1979) *Antique or Fake?* Evans Brothers

Rider, L.Z. (1960) *The Ornamented Chair*, Rutland

Stephenson, S. (1979) *Rustic Furniture*, Van Nostrand

Symonds, R.W. (1955) *Furniture Making in 17th and 18th Century England*, The Connoisseur

Wells, P. and Hooper, C. (1924) *Modern Cabinet Work, Furniture and Fitments*, 4th edn, Batsford

## Texts relating to materials

NB: Many of the other texts have sections on the subject of materials.

Adamson, J. (1993) *American Wicker: Woven Furniture from 1850 to 1930*, Rizzoli

Boulton, B. (1921) *The Manufacture and Use of Plywood and Glue*, Pitman

Bourne, J. (1984) *Lacquer: An International History and Collectors Guide*, Bracken Books in association with Phoebe Phillips Editions

Buttrey, D.N. (1964) *Plastics in the Furniture Industry*, MacDonald and Co.

Campbell-Cole, B. (ed.) (1979) *Tubular Steel Furniture*, Art Book Co.

Child, G. (1990) *World Mirrors, 1650–1900*, Sothebys

Curtis, L. (1997) *Lloyd Loom Woven Fibre Furniture*, Salamander

DeVoe, S. (1971) *English Papier Mâché of the Georgian and Victorian Periods*, Barrie and Jenkins

Evelyn, J. (1670) *Sylva, A Discourse of Forest Trees*, London

Fennimore, D. (1996) *Metalwork in Early America: Copper and its Alloys from the Winterthur Collecton*, Winterthur, The Henry Francis duPont Museum

Gilbert, C. and Murdoch, T. (1993) *John Channon and Brass-inlaid Furniture, 1730–1760*, Yale University Press

Giusti, A.M. (1992) *Pietre Dure Hardstone in Furniture and Decoration*, Philip Wilson

Gonzalez-Palacios, A. (1981) *Mosaici e Pietre Dure*, Milan

Hanks, D. (1981) *Innovative Furniture in America from 1800 to the Present*, Horizon Press

Himmelheber, G. (1996) *Cast Iron Furniture*, Philip Wilson

Hinckley, F.L. (1960) *Directory of the Historic Cabinet Woods*, Crown

Huth, H. (1971) *Lacquer of the West: The History of a Craft and an Industry, 1550–1950*, University of Chicago Press

Jervis, S. (1972) *Antler and Horn Furniture*, V&A Museum Yearbook 111, Victoria and Albert Museum

Knight, E.V. and Wulpi, M. (eds) (1927) *Veneers and Plywood*, The Ronald Press Co.

Latham, B. (1957) *Timber: Its Development and Distribution: a Historical Survey*, Harrap

Thompson, F. (1979) *The Complete Wicker Book, the History of Wicker Furniture and Accessories from Antique to Modern*, Wallace Homestead Books

Viaux-Loquin, J. (1997) *Les Bois d'ébénisterie dans les mobilier français*, Leonce Laget

Walkling, G. (1979) *Antique Bamboo Furniture*, Bell and Hyman

Waterer, J.W. (1968) *Leather Craftsmanship*, Praeger

Wills, G. (1965) *English Looking Glasses*, Country Life

Wood, A.D. and Linn, T.G. (1963) *Plywoods of the World, Their Development and Manufacture*, Edinburgh

## Specific texts relating to tools and techniques

NB: Many of the other texts have sections on the subject of tools and techniques.

Adair, W. (1983) *The Frame in America, 1700–1900: a Survey of Fabrication Techniques and Style*, The American Institute of Architects Foundation, Washington, DC

Austen, B. (1992) *Tunbridge Ware and Related European Decorative Woodware*, Foulsham

Beecroft, E. (1976) *Carving Techniques*, Batsford

Bigelow, D. *et al.* (eds) (1992) *Gilded Wood, Conservation and History*, Sound View Press

Bruggemann, E. (1988) *Kunst und Technik des Intarsien, Werkzeug und Material*, Munich

Ettema, M. (1981) Technological innovation and design economics in furniture manufacture, in *Winterthur Portfolio*, 16

Fales, D. (1979) *American Painted Furniture, 1660–1880*, E.P. Dutton

Gaynor, J. and Hagedorn, N. (1993) *Tools: Working Wood in Eighteenth Century America*, Colonial Williamsburg Foundation

Goodman, W. (1976) *The History of Woodworking Tools*, David McKay

Holtzappfel, C. (1994) *Turning and Mechanical Manipulation*, Facsimile of the 1843 edition, Astragal Press

Jones, P. and Simons, E.N. (1961) *Story of the Saw*, Newman Neame for Spear and Jackson

Massie, F. (1990) *La Marqueterie Boulle*, Biro

Moxon, J. (1970) *Mechaniks Exercises or the Doctrine of Handy Works etc.*, reprint of 1703 edition, Astragal Press

Ostergard, D. (ed.) (1987) *Bentwood and Metal Furniture: 1850–1946*, American Federation of Arts

Oughton, F. (1976) *History and Practice of Woodcarving*, Stobart

Pattou and Vaughn (1944) *Furniture Finishing, Decoration and Patching*, F. Drake and Co.

Ramond, P. (1989) *Marquetry*, Taunton Press

Roubo, Jacques-Andre (1984) *L'Art du Menuisier*, Slatkine reprints of Paris 1761–89 editions

Salaman, R. (1989) *A Dictionary of Woodworking Tools*, Unwin Hyman

Sims, W. (1985) *200 Years of History and Evolution of Woodworking Machinery*, Walders Press

Stalker, J. and Parker, G. (1960) *A Treatise of Japanning and Varnishing*, Alec Tiranti reprint of 1668 edition

Welsh, P.C. (1966) *Woodworking Tools: 1600–1900*, Smithsonian Institution/US Government Printing Office

Zimmerman, P. (1981) Workmanship as evidence, a model for object study, in *Winterthur Portfolio*, 16, 4, Winter, pp. 301–5

## Specific texts relating to upholstery

Beard, G. (1997) *Upholsterers and Interior Furnishing in England, 1530–1840*, Yale University Press

Bimont, Jean François (1766) *Manuel des Tapissiers*, Paris

Bimont, Jean François (1770) *Principes de l'art du Tapissier; ouvrage utile aux gens de la profession, et à ceux qui les emploient*, Paris

Bitmead, R. (1876) *Practical Upholsterer and Cutter-Out*, London

Bland, S. (1995) *Take a Seat. The Story of Parker-Knoll, 1834–1994*, Baron Birch

Cooke, E.S. (1988) *Upholstery in America and Europe from the Seventeenth Century to World War 1*, W.W. Norton

Houston, J.F. (1993) *Featherbedds and Flock bedds, Notes on the history of the Worshipful company of Upholders*, Three Tents Press also www.upholders.co.uk/ffbindex.htm

Michie, A.H. (1985) Upholstery in all its branches: Charleston, 1725–1820, *Journal of Early Southern Decorative Arts*, XI:2

Montgomery, F. (1970) *Printed Textiles. English and American Printed Cottons and Linens, 1700–1850*, Thames and Hudson

Montgomery, F. (1984) *Textiles in America, 1650–1870*, W.W. Norton

Ossut, C. (1994) *Le Siège et sa garniture*, Vial

Passeri, A., Trent, R. and Jobe, B. (1987) The Wheelwright and Maerklin inventories and the history of the upholsterer's trade in America, 1750–1900, *Old Time New England* 72, 312–54

Walton, K.M. (1973) *The Golden Age of English Furniture Upholstery, 1660–1840*, Temple Newsam House

Williams, M. (ed.) (1990) *Upholstery Conservation*, American Conservation Consortium Symposium Preprints

## Specific texts relating to trade organization

NB: Many of the other texts have sections on the subject of trade organization.

Alford, B. and Barker, T. (1968) *A History of the Carpenters Company*, Allen and Unwin

Auslander, L. (1996) *Taste and Power, Furnishing Modern France*, University of California Press

Campbell, R. (1973) *The London Tradesman*, 1747, reprinted David and Charles

Earl, P. (1973) Craftsmen and machines. Nineteenth century furniture industry, *19th annual Winterthur Conference Report*, Winterthur, The Henry Francis duPont Museum

Kirkham, P. (1988) *The London Furniture Trade, 1700–1870*, Furniture History Society, London

Oliver, J. (1966) *The Development and Structure of the Furniture Industry*, Pergamon

# Part 2

# Materials

# 2

# Wood and wooden structures

It is essential for furniture conservators to understand the properties and behaviour of wood. Only when the underlying basis of the working properties, identification and appearance of wood is understood can conservators make responsible decisions in their work. Proper knowledge of wood as a material will help in building an understanding of issues such as deterioration, preventive conservation and restoration. This chapter covers the structure and properties of wood and how they relate to each other. It also includes information on the behaviour of wooden structures and basic data on manufactured timber products.

## 2.1 Introduction to wood as material

Wood has always been indispensable to human needs, and it is therefore not surprising that we find wood at the heart of our cultural heritage. Because of its unique physical properties, wood holds honoured status as an engineering material and functional commodity. But the beauty of the material itself, when considered with tactile properties and working characteristics, assures that wood has prevailed as a medium in the decorative arts. Although the manner in which wood has been used often takes advantage of its aesthetic values, historical use is most closely related to its material properties. Only by studying wood as an engineering material, while remembering its biological origin, can we fully appreciate the craft and arts which developed around it.

The virtues and properties of wood are so well known to everyone that it is sometimes difficult to step back and consider them objectively – and scientifically. Given that there are tens of thousands of species that yield usable timber, an obviously wide array of characteristics can be expected. However, certain basic features are common to all woody plants and it is appropriate to begin by considering those generalities which are most important yet generally understated.

One idea is paramount: *wood comes from trees*. While such a statement seems foolishly elementary, it is fundamental to understanding the complex nature of wood. Remembering this basic reality will help to prevent or solve many problems associated with wood. The structure of wood is the outcome of a complex series of chemical reactions. It begins with photosynthesis, which takes place in the living tree. Photosynthesis is the process whereby carbon dioxide and water are converted, using sunlight energy captured by chlorophyll in the leaves, into simple sugars. These simple sugars ultimately form both the food and structural materials of the tree. The stem provides mechanical support for the crown, serves as an avenue of conduction between the crown and the roots, and, on occasion, stores appreciable amounts of reserve food material. Wood is therefore strong yet, once seasoned, is relatively light in weight, since its cells are then largely full of air. Being of plant origin, it is soft, in comparison with iron or stone (other materials of equivalent strength), and is therefore relatively easily worked, yet it is surprisingly durable. These properties, together with the rich variation in decorative characteristics arising from grain patterns and colour markings on the longitudinal surfaces, make wood unique among building materials.

Although its fabrication and many of its applications are comparatively simple, wood itself is a substance of great complexity. To make the best use of this material a degree of scientific and technical understanding is necessary. Technically defined, wood is the xylem from the stem (trunk or bole) of plants which are vascular, perennial and persistent and capable, by virtue of the activity of the cambium or growing layer, of secondary thickening. Wood may also usefully be described as *a cellular polymeric composite*. This short phrase encapsulates many important ideas about wood. First, wood is cellular tissue. The appearance, identification and working properties of wood can best be understood and interpreted through the nature, arrangement and distribution of the different types of its cells. In the second place, it is the polymeric composite nature of wood that best explains the mechanical properties and wood–water relationships.

The study of wood routinely begins at the cellular level. It is both appropriate and important to think of wood as a mass of cells. Woody cells evolved in satisfying the needs of the tree, on the one hand to be good structural beams and columns, on the other hand to provide systems for conduction of sap and for storage of food materials. The cells specialized for these mechanical and physiological functions are primarily elongated and fibre-like, and parallel to the tree stem axis. The alignment of these longitudinal cells in wood determines its 'grain direction'. The stem of a tree 'grows' in diameter by adding cylindrical layers of cells, which we recognize as growth rings. The combination of the axial direction of longitudinal cells, and their arrangement in growth rings, gives wood tissue a three-dimensional orientation, and the properties of wood are significantly different along its three structural directions.

The principal chemical components of cell wall substance – namely, cellulose, hemicelluloses, and lignin – are strikingly similar across the array of different woods. However, as living sapwood (an outer, functionally active portion of the stem) transforms to non-living heartwood, the formation of chemical substances known as extractives even in rather trace amounts, may impart significant changes to certain properties.

While many generalities can be applied to all woods, it is important to appreciate the wide range of differences that exist. For example, overall, *density* is probably the one physical characteristic of a wood that best predicts many other properties and determines its potential uses. Density is the mass of a unit volume of a substance, that is, mass divided by volume. In SI units, density may be expressed in kilograms per cubic metre ($kg/m^3$), in grams per cubic centimetre (g/cc) or in pounds per cubic foot ($lb/ft^3$). The term *specific gravity* was the former term for the ratio of the density of a substance to that of water. The term *relative density* is now used instead. The realization that the range of relative density of less than 0.1 for the lightest woods to greater than 1.3 for the heaviest illustrates an obvious diversity among woods.

In the traditional approach to classifying wood, botanical taxonomy serves as the logical framework, in which timber trees are categorized in one of two broad groups, called softwoods and hardwoods. The words softwoods and hardwoods, however, are unfortunate terminology as they do not accurately apply to the relative hardness or density of woods they represent. Rather, woods of the two groups differ in the types and arrangement of cells comprising them. The softwoods belong to a group of trees called the Gymnosperms, primitive, conifers or cone-bearing trees with naked seeds and mostly needle-like leaves. Correspondingly, hardwoods belong to a group of trees more accurately called Angiosperms. In fact, on the basis of cellular differences, woods of the two groups can be readily distinguished visually at relatively low magnification. Further separation of woods within each group for identification involves examination of additional cellular detail, commonly with microscopic magnification. The systematic study of anatomy goes hand in hand with wood identification, although familiarity with anatomy is fundamental to the understanding of many other aspects of wood properties as well.

Wood–moisture relationships are probably at the source of more problems in using wood and in the conservation of objects than any other aspect of wood properties. Although such problems can be complex, the underlying principles can be easily summarized. First, trees are wet, containing large amounts of moisture in the form of sap. Second, as the timber taken from trees is dried to a condition appropriate for use, it loses most of its moisture. Third, the loss of this moisture affects many properties, such as increasing strength, but decreasing dimensions (shrinkage). Fourth, after initial drying, wood remains hygroscopic, and will continue to adsorb or desorb moisture, and consequently change dimensions and other properties, in response to changes in relative humidity of its environment.

The following account will highlight in more detail the various aspects of relationships between the appearance, structure and function of wood that are needed properly to understand many of the problems encountered by furniture conservators.

## 2.2 The nature of wood: appearance, cellular structure and identification

Virtually all wood found in furniture is the product of the stem portions of mature trees. The stem, also referred to as the trunk or bole, is harvested as a 'log' and further processed into lumber, turning squares and the like. Therefore each component of furniture, whether it is the flat-lumber leaf of a table top or the turned leg of a chair, can be interpreted in terms of its original position in a tree. Many characteristics are common to all trees and can be discussed without regard to a specific type of wood. In considering the eventual details of cell structure, however, it will be fitting to discuss softwoods and hardwoods separately.

### 2.2.1 Gross features

The crosscut or 'end-grain' surface of a log immediately reveals important features, as shown in *Figure 2.1a*. At the periphery of the log the layer of bark (also called the phloem) is easily recognized. Within the bark, the main portion of the stem is wood (xylem). A microscopically thin layer of cells, the cambium, separates the bark from the wood. In viewing an end-grain surface, individual wood cells usually cannot be seen without magnification but in certain hardwood species, the largest cells, vessel elements, may be visible on cleanly cut surfaces (*Figure 2.1b*). However, we recognize the familiar pattern of circular growth rings, concentrically arranged around the central pith. Within each ring, and depending on the species, a first-formed early-wood layer may be distinct from an outer late-wood layer. The pat-

terns of longitudinal surface appearance or 'figure' by which we recognize wood are most commonly the result of this early-wood–late-wood variation. Distinct early-wood–late-wood contrast usually indicates variation in cell characteristics resulting in late-wood having greater density than early-wood, but in some woods, there may be no significant difference in properties within growth rings.

Individual wood cells usually have an elongated shape, although they vary in proportions from short and barrel-shaped to long and needle-like (see *Figure 2.4*). Most cells are longi-

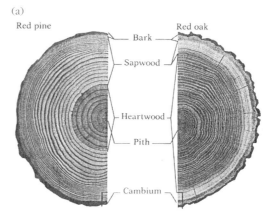

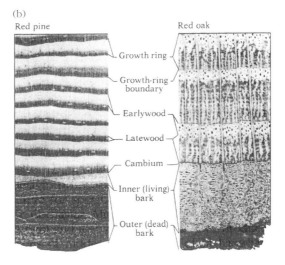

**Figure 2.1** Cross-section or end-grain surface of a typical softwood (red pine, *Pinus resinosa*) and a typical hardwood (northern red oak, *Quercus rubra*): (*a*) shows gross features (bark, sapwood, heartwood, pith), (*b*) shows fine structures (inner and outer bark, cambium and growth rings)

tudinal, that is, they are elongated parallel to the stem axis. On an end-grain surface we therefore see them in cross-section. Scattered through the longitudinal wood cells are groups of cells whose long axes are horizontal in the tree. These groups extend radially outwards from the pith and are called rays. Rays are flattened ribbons of cells oriented horizontally with the plane of the ribbon vertical. Individual ray cells are always too small to be seen without magnification and therefore narrow rays are not apparent. However, some hardwood species have rays of up to several cells wide that are distinctly visible on cross-sections. Collectively, the ray cells in most species account for less than 10% of the volume of the wood. It is important to remember that rays are present in every species and, whether visible or not, have an important influence on many properties of wood.

The arrangement of the growth rings in the tree stem, along with the vertical and horizontal arrangement of cells, establishes a three-dimensional orientation to the cell structure (*Figure 2.2*). A plane perpendicular to the stem axis is termed the transverse plane or cross-sectional plane, typically represented by the end of a log or board. Because the tree cross-section is analogous to a circle, a plane pass-ing through the pith of the stem (as would a radius of the circle) is a radial plane or surface. A plane parallel to the pith, but not passing through it forms a tangent to the circular growth ring structure, and is termed a tangential plane or surface. The curvature of the growth ring is not geometrically regular, and the surface in question is most ideally tangential where the plane is perpendicular to the radial plane. However, any slabbed log surface is usually accepted as a tangential surface. In a small cube of wood, the curvature of the rings is insignificant, so the cube can be oriented to contain quite accurate transverse, radial and tangential faces. Thin slices or sections of wood tissue, as commonly removed from the surfaces for study, are termed transverse, radial and tangential sections. These planes are often designated simply by the letters X, R and T, respectively.

### Grain

The surface qualities by which wood is so highly prized as a decorative material arise from variations in the number and arrangement of different cells and can be classified under the headings of grain, texture and figure. Properly speaking, the term grain refers to the longitudinal alignment of wood cells. That is, the direction of the fibres relative to the axis of the tree or the longitudinal edges of individual pieces of timber. This term is extensively misused to describe a number of other characteristics, including texture and figure. Texture refers to the relative size, and the amount of variation in size, of the cells. Figure refers to the pattern produced on longitudinal surfaces of wood as a result of the arrangement of the different tissues and the nature of the grain.

Six types of grain may be distinguished. These are straight, irregular, diagonal, spiral, interlocked and wavy. In straight-grained timber the fibres and other elements are more or less parallel to the vertical axis of the tree. This is a contributory factor in strength and ease of working but does not give rise to ornamental figure. Where strength is the primary consideration it is usual to specify that timber shall be straight grained. A slope of 1 in 25 reduces bending strength by 4% while a slope of 1 in 5 reduces it by up to 45%. Stiffness is also reduced by sloping of the grain and it will be readily apparent that this is therefore an import-

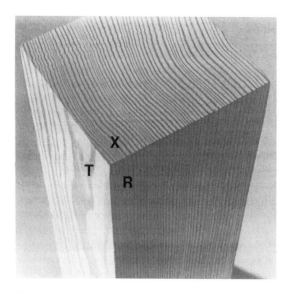

**Figure 2.2** A block of Douglas fir cut to demonstrate the three planes used to describe the structural orientation of wood: transverse (cross-sectional or end-grain), tangential and radial (quarter-sawn) surfaces

ant consideration in the selection of material.

Timber in which the fibres are inclined at varying and irregular angles to the vertical axis in the log is said to have irregular grain. Although this is frequently restricted to knots and other similarly limited areas it is a very common defect and, when excessive, seriously reduces strength as well as making working difficult. It may produce attractive figure, however. Pronounced irregularities in the direction of the fibres, resulting from knot-like elevations or conical depressions in the annual rings, produce blister figure and bird's eye figure respectively.

Diagonal grain is a defect arising during conversion and results from otherwise straight grained timber being cut so that the fibres do not run parallel to the long edges of the board or plank.

Spiral grain results when the fibres follow a left- or right-handed spiral course in the living tree. It is not always readily apparent but may often be detected from the direction of surface seasoning checks. Spiral grain is a serious defect in timber intended for important structural work.

Interlocked grain, or interlocked fibre, results from the fibres of successive growth layers being inclined in opposite directions. This produces a ribbon or stripe figure on quarter-sawn surfaces. Interlocked grain is relatively uncommon in temperate woods but is a characteristic of many tropical hardwoods. It may not appreciably affect the strength of timber but can cause serious twisting during seasoning and severe difficulties in working, especially in planing when the timber picks up leaving a very rough finish. In timber with heavily interlocked grain sawing difficulties may be very great and special machinery and modified techniques are needed to overcome these difficulties. It may be an advantage in some cases that such wood is virtually impossible to split.

When the direction of the fibres is constantly changing, so that a line drawn parallel with them appears as a wavy line on a longitudinal surface, the grain is said to be wavy. This type of grain gives rise to a series of diagonal, more or less horizontal, darker or lighter stripes on longitudinal surfaces. This is due to variations in the angle at which light is reflected from the surfaces of the fibres and is called fiddle-back figure. This type of grain is exploited entirely

for its decorative possibilities, any reductions in strength being regarded as of secondary importance. Wavy grain and interlocked grain may occur together in the same piece of timber giving rise to a broken ripple called roe figure on quarter-sawn surfaces.

### Texture

Wood may be of coarse or fine, even or uneven texture, or any intermediate grade. The classification as to the degree of coarseness or fineness is made on the basis of the dimensions of the vessels and the width and abundance of the rays. Timbers, such as oak, in which the vessels are large or the rays broad are said to be of coarse texture. Where, as in sycamore or box, the vessels are small and the rays narrow the timber is said to be of fine or very fine texture. The texture of a timber is an important factor in determining its suitability for a particular application. For example, boxwood is more appropriate for a finely detailed carving or turning than is oak. Texture is also related to surface smoothness and to the performance of stains and finishes applied to wood. All softwoods are fine or at most relatively coarse textured as their cells are all of relatively small diameter. The texture of softwoods is influenced by alternation of zones of early-wood and late-wood. When the contrast between zones is marked, as in Douglas fir and larch, the wood may be said to be of uneven texture. Timbers such as spruce, in which there is little or no contrast in the early-wood and late-wood, are even textured. These terms may also be applied to hardwoods where ring-porous woods can be considered as uneven and diffuse-porous woods, unless they have broad rays or wide layers of wood parenchyma, as even textured.

### Figure

Many kinds of figure are recognized. Those mentioned above are the principal types arising from the variety of grain present (from which many of the other types arise). In addition, figure may be derived from the distribution of certain types of tissue in wood. The broad high rays of the true oaks and Australian Silky oak are an example of figure, called silver figure derived from the particular distribution of ray tissue in these woods. The alternating layers of dark, dense late-wood and lighter, less dense early-wood give rise to the flame figure of certain softwoods, for example Douglas fir, when flat sawn or rotary peeled. The distribution of wood parenchyma in broad conspicuous bands may, in hardwoods, also give rise to flame figure known as watered silk. A similar figure may also be produced in timbers with alternating layers of different colours, such as the striped ebonies. The prominence and decorative effect of figure depend not only on correct conversion of the timber but also on the natural lustre of the wood, which is the ability of the cells to reflect light. Also important, though not necessarily related to lustre, is the ability of the wood to take a good polish.

### Colour

The colour of a timber, which is important from a practical point of view, because it may enhance or detract from the decorative value of timber, is caused largely by infiltrates in the cell wall. These may be affected by light, air, or heat causing the colour of the timber to change over a period of time. They may also interact with other materials, as for instance when oak reacts with iron a marked colour change may be induced. The infiltrates and cell contents of some timbers may, during planing, sawing, sanding and so forth, cause irritation of mucous membranes or dermatitis which may in some cases be severe. Mansonia, makore and teak are particular examples of timbers that may elicit a more severe adverse reaction. In other cases a distinctive odour or taste may render a timber particularly suitable or particularly unsuitable for a given application.

### Taxonomy – the classification of plants

To delve further into the anatomical nature of wood, generalities must now give way to specifics, and individual types and species must be considered at the cellular level. Taxonomy, the science of classifying living things, provides a logical approach to studying the cellular nature of wood, because, as expected, closely related trees will have similar wood tissue. It follows that wood identification is based on the systematic knowledge and recognition of cell structure.

The plant kingdom is classified into divisions (phyla), subdivisions (classes), orders, families, genera and species (*Figure 2.3*). It is customary to refer to a tree, or its wood, by its species name. In the system of scientific nomenclature, a species is designated by a binomial term consisting of its genus (generic name) followed by the species (specific name). The complete scientific name also includes an abbreviation of the name of the botanist who first discovered and classified the plant, although this is frequently omitted in general texts. For example, the scientific name for European ash is *Fraxinus excelsior L.* The L in this case is an abbreviation for Linnaeus. Scientific names in Latin are uniformly accepted in the scientific world. A species within a genus may be referred to in general terms by the roman abbreviation sp. (plural spp.). Each wood of course has one or more common names in the local language, and this can lead to confusion through inconsistency. Use of scientific names is therefore advantageous, and reference to authoritative checklists for both scientific and common names is recommended. The scientific and common names of woods found in furniture are given by British Standards Institution (1974) and Little (1980).

The woods of most temperate zone trees can be identified to the genus, but among many genera the individual species cannot be distinguished on the basis of wood tissue alone. In such cases the wood is designated by the genus name followed by the abbreviation sp. For example, *Picea sp.* would indicate a species of spruce.

Within the plant kingdom, timber producing trees are found in the division Spermatophytes, the seed plants. Within this division are two classes, the Gymnosperms and Angiosperms. Trees belonging to the Gymnosperms (principally in the order Coniferales) are called softwoods. In the Angiosperms, a subclass known as 'dicots' (dicotyledonous plants) includes hardwoods.

Within the Angiosperms, a second subclass, the monocotyledons or 'monocots', includes such woody plants as palms, rattan and bamboo. Materials of these plant groups are not generally thought of under the term timber and are not included in this discussion. However, they are used extensively in some parts of the world, and those that are commonly encountered in furniture are discussed in Chapter 3.

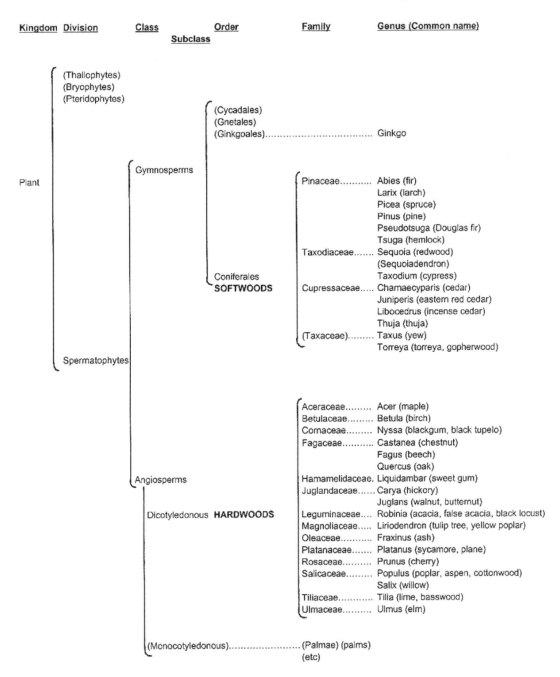

**Figure 2.3** Plant classification chart showing the relationship of genera of many common woods found in furniture

## 2.2.2  Wood anatomy: softwoods

The cell structure of softwoods is relatively simple compared to that of the hardwoods (see *Figure 2.4*). Most of the cells found in conifer-ous woods are tracheids, which comprise 90–95% of the volume of the wood. Tracheids are fibre-like cells with lengths of approxi-mately 100 times their diameter. Average tra-cheid length ranges from 2 to 6 millimetres

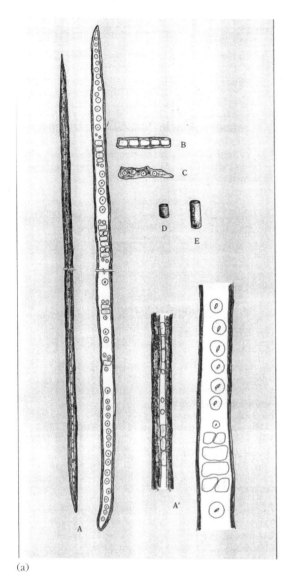

(a)

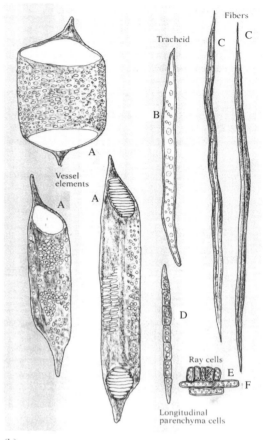

(b)

**Figure 2.4** Diagrams of representative cell types (*a*) Softwood cell types: Tracheids (A, enlarged view, A') make up 90–95% of the volume of the wood. The rest is mainly ray tissue in the form of ray parenchyma cells (B) or ray tracheids (C). Some species (e.g. larch) also have a small percentage of epithelial cells (D) that line the resin canals or longitudinal parenchyma cells (E). (*b*) Hardwood cell types: Vessel elements (A) may vary in shape and size. In hardwoods, tracheids (B) serve an intermediate function between vessel elements and fibres. Fibres (C) are long, slender straight cells that, in comparison to vessel elements, are smaller in size and have thick cell walls. They impart strength to the wood. Parenchyma cells, used for transport and storage, may be longitudinal (D) or radial. They are similar in cross-section to tracheids, though parenchyma are shorter. Ray cells may be upright (E) or procumbent (F)

among coniferous species, with a corresponding diameter range of approximately 20–60 μm (1 μm = 0.001 mm). The relative diameter of tracheids is a basis for classifying texture among conifers. Texture can be estimated by how clearly individual tracheids can be seen on a cross-sectional surface with a hand lens, and is therefore a valuable aid in wood identification. For example yew (*Taxus* spp.) is fine textured, redwood (*Sequoia sempervirens*) is coarse textured.

For a given species, average tangential diameter of tracheids is fairly consistent. Across a growth ring, late-wood is distinguished from early-wood by decreased radial diameter and increased cell wall thickness. The transition may be gradual in some woods, abrupt in others. The early-wood–late-wood contrast may be slight in some woods (even-grained woods) or may be pronounced (uneven-grained woods). In uneven-grained woods such as hard pines or larches, there may be as much as a threefold difference in density (relative density 0.3–0.9) from early-wood to late-wood.

Some coniferous species have resin canals, tubular passageways lined with epithelial cells, which exude resin or pitch into the canals. Resin canals are a constant feature of genera in the family Pinaceae (the pine family), including *Pinus* (pine), *Picea* (spruce), *Larix* (larch) and *Pseudotsuga* (Douglas fir), and are therefore an important feature for initial identification screening of unknown wood samples. Resin canals are largest and most numerous in the pines, usually distinct to the naked eye. In other species, magnification may be required to locate them. The resin from canals may bleed through paint films and result in yellowish speckling of finished surfaces.

Some softwoods also have a longitudinal cell type called longitudinal parenchyma (parenchyma is the collective name for cells specialized for the storage of food materials). If present, these cells represent a very small percentage of the wood's volume and are of importance mainly as an identification feature.

The rays in softwoods are narrow, usually one cell wide (except for occasional rays with horizontal resin canals in some species) and therefore cannot be seen without magnification. With a hand lens they are barely visible as light streaks across radial surfaces. Microscopic examination of softwood rays provides valuable information on how many cells high or wide a ray is, the type(s) of cell(s) present and the type of pitting and other features present on the cell walls. This information is very important for identification of softwoods.

Most narrow softwood rays contain two types of cells, ray tracheids and ray parenchyma. A softwood ray with both types of cells is termed heterocellular or heterogeneous. A ray composed of either ray tracheids or ray parenchyma alone is termed homocellular or homogeneous (it should be noted that these terms have different meanings in hardwoods).

The pitting that occurs between ray parenchyma cells and early-wood longitudinal tracheids is called cross-field pitting. Cross-field

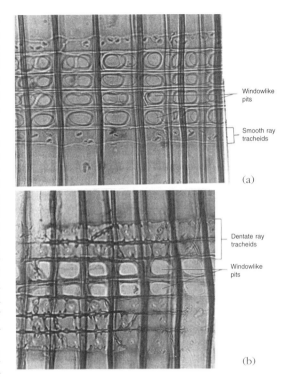

Windowlike pits

Smooth ray tracheids

(a)

Dentate ray tracheids

Windowlike pits

(b)

**Figure 2.5** Radial microscopic views of eastern white pine, *Pinus strobus* (*a*) and Scots pine *Pinus sylvestris* (*b*) showing cross-field pitting. The term 'cross field' refers to the area where a ray parenchyma cell (seen here where the cells run horizontally) crosses an earlywood longitudinal tracheid (seen here where the cells run vertically). The two cell types share a cell wall and the shape inside the cell wall (here the pitting is described as 'windowlike') can be used as a diagnostic feature in softwoods. An additional diagnostic feature can be seen in the ray tracheids above and below the cross fields. In the case of eastern white pine (*a*) the ray tracheids are smooth, whilst in Scots pine (*b*) the ray tracheids are jagged in appearance and are described as 'dentate'

pitting may be window-like (*Figure 2.5*), pinoid, piceoid, cupressoid, or taxodoid. For further information see Grosser (1977), Hoadley (1990), Phillips (1960), Schweingruber (1990) and the anatomical features list produced by the International Association of Wood Anatomists (IAWA).

### 2.2.3   Cell structure: hardwoods

In comparing the anatomy of the hardwoods with that of the softwoods several general differences are apparent. There are many more cell types present in hardwoods, and there is more variation in their arrangement. Rays in hardwoods vary widely in size, from invisibly small to conspicuous to the eye. Hardwoods do not have resin canals as such but may have gum canals in rays.

Hardwood trees have evolved specialized conductive cells called vessel elements, which are distinct in having relatively large diameters and thin cell walls (see *Figure 2.4*). They form in the tree in end-to-end series in which the end walls become perforated, thus forming continuous vessels ideal for sap conduction. Vessel elements stand out as the largest diameter cells in a given hardwood species. When vessels are cut transversely, the exposed open ends are referred to as pores. Pores vary in size among and within species. In certain woods such as chestnut and oak the largest pores up to 300 µm in diameter can be easily seen without magnification, whereas in some species such as holly the pores are no larger than 40 µm in diameter and are barely perceptible with a hand lens. Among hardwoods, pore size serves as a measure of texture. Oaks having large pores are coarse textured; maple has small-diameter pores and is fine textured.

In some (temperate) species such as oak, ash, elm and sweet chestnut the largest pores are concentrated in the early wood. Such woods are said to be ring-porous; they are inherently uneven-grained and therefore have a distinct growth-ring related figure. Ring porous structure results in uneven density and expectedly affects woodworking behaviour such as uneven resistance to abrasive paper and uneven retention of pigmented stains. Woods (maple, birch, lime, poplar etc.) whose pores are more uniform in size and evenly distributed across the growth ring are said to be diffuse-porous. Such woods may show inconspicuous figure, or figure may be associated with uneven pigmentation or density of fibre mass in the outer late wood. Most diffuse-porous woods of the temperate regions have relatively small diameter pores, but among tropical woods, some diffuse porous species (e.g. mahogany) have rather large pores. A third classification, semi-ring porous (also called semi-diffuse porous), refers to woods in which the first-formed pores in a growth ring are large, but decrease in size gradually to small pores in the late wood, without apparent

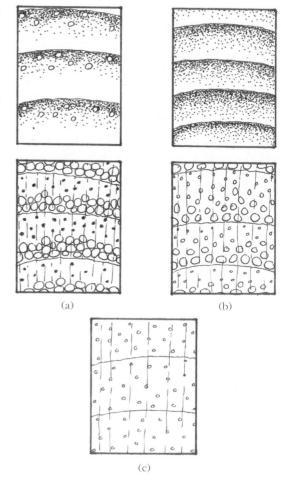

(a)   (b)   (c)

**Figure 2.6**  Hardwoods are classified as (*a*) ring-porous (e.g. ash, chestnut, oak), (*b*) semi-ring-porous (e.g. walnut), or (*c*) diffuse-porous (e.g. lime, birch) on the basis of the pore size and distribution within a growth ring when the end-grain (transverse section) is viewed with a hand lens (10×)

distinction of early-wood and late-wood layering. Walnut is an important example of this type. Ring porosity is illustrated in *Figure 2.6*.

Not all vessels have contents, but where present, contents can be a valuable aid in identification. Tyloses are bubble-like structures that form in the cell cavities of some species (see, for example, *Figure 2.8* B). Other significant vessel contents include whitish or chalky deposits, and reddish or brown gummy deposits.

Hardwoods have three other types of longitudinal cells: fibres, tracheids and parenchyma cells. All are uniformly small in diameter

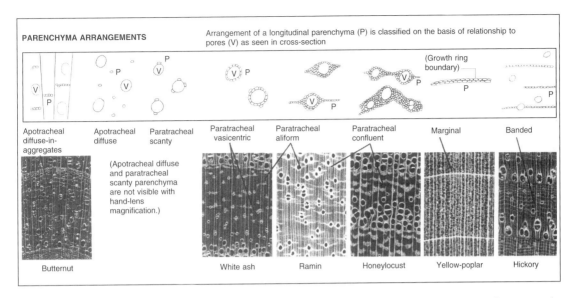

PARENCHYMA ARRANGEMENTS — Arrangement of a longitudinal parenchyma (P) is classified on the basis of relationship to pores (V) as seen in cross-section

| Apotracheal diffuse-in-aggregates | Apotracheal diffuse | Paratracheal scanty | Paratracheal vasicentric | Paratracheal aliform | Paratracheal confluent | Marginal | Banded |

(Apotracheal diffuse and paratracheal scanty parenchyma are not visible with hand-lens magnification.)

Butternut — White ash — Ramin — Honeylocust — Yellow-poplar — Hickory

**Figure 2.7** The arrangement of longitudinal parenchyma (P) is classified on the basis of the relationship to vessels (V) when viewed in cross-section

(mostly in the range of 15–30 µm), and therefore can be seen individually only under a microscope. Fibres are present in all woods and are characteristically long and needle-like with tapering, pointed ends and relatively thick walls. On transverse surfaces, masses of fibres appear as the darkest areas of the tissue. Among hardwood species, tracheids and parenchyma cells range from absent or sparse to fairly abundant. They are thinner walled cells than fibres and when present in sufficient numbers, the resulting areas of tissue usually appear lighter in colour than adjacent fibre masses. Parenchyma and tracheids can be distinguished with certainty only with microscopic examination. Tracheids are elongated cells roughly similar to tracheids in softwoods. Parenchyma cells occur as vertical series of rather short cells arranged end to end. On transverse surfaces viewed with a hand lens, characteristic patterns of lighter tissue (mostly parenchyma, but sometimes including tracheids) are valuable in identifying hardwoods.

The various arrangements of parenchyma are referred to in *Table 2.1* and illustrated in *Figure 2.7*. Longitudinal parenchyma is termed paratracheal if associated with the pores and apotracheal if independent of the pores. A complete halo or sheath of parenchyma more or less concentric with a pore is termed vasi-

centric. Cells of parenchyma along the growth ring boundary, referred to as marginal parenchyma, are termed initial if they occur at the inner edge of the growth ring or terminal if they occur at the outer edge. Single isolated cells of apotracheal parenchyma are called diffuse parenchyma. Diffuse parenchyma in short tangential lines is described as diffuse-in-aggregates parenchyma. More or less continuous tangential or wavy lines or bands of parenchyma within the growth ring are called banded parenchyma. Paratracheal parenchyma with wing-like lateral extensions is termed aliform. When parenchyma forms a continuous tangential or diagonal zone connecting two or more pores, it is termed confluent.

Rays are quite variable among hardwood species. The size of rays is expressed by cell count as viewed microscopically on tangential sections, in particular, ray width or seriation of the largest rays present. In woods such as chestnut and willow, the rays are uniseriate, that is, only one cell wide, and therefore visible only with a microscope. At the other extreme, such as the white oaks, the largest rays are up to 40-seriate and up to several inches in height. Rays in oak are conspicuous to the unaided eye.

Although hardwood rays consist entirely of ray parenchyma cells, there are two types of these distinguished on the basis of overall shape. As seen in radial view, procumbent ray cells are elongated horizontally; upright ray cells are either square or they are vertically oriented. If only one type of cell is present in the ray, it is termed homocellular or homogeneous. If both types are present, it is called heterocellular or heterogeneous.

In some species, the rays are of fairly even height and are spaced at even horizontal levels throughout the tree. These storied rays appear as even horizontal rows when the wood is sectioned tangentially. Ripple marks, horizontal striations of lighter and darker wood 0.4 mm to 0.8 mm apart, frequently seen in tropical woods are due to storied rays.

The distinct appearance of rays on radial surfaces is termed ray fleck, and in many woods, such as oak, plane, beech and lace wood, their prominent rays are a characteristic feature of the figure. Rays also profoundly influence physical and mechanical behaviour. Rays, especially larger ones, represent planes of weakness in the wood. Shrinkage stresses associated with the seasoning of wood may develop checks through the ray tissue. Also, the restraining effect of the rays contributes to differential radial and tangential shrinkage, a common cause of cupping of flat sawn boards and radial cracking of timbers.

Detailed illustrations of microscopic wood anatomy beyond the scope of the present work are provided by Brazier and Franklin (1961), Détienne and Jacquet (1983), Fahn *et al.* (1986), Grosser (1977), Hart and Jay (1971), Hoadley (1990), Panshin and deZeeuw (1980), Phillips (1960) and Schweingruber (1990).

## 2.2.4   Wood identification

Identification of furniture woods plays a vital part in historical studies and in the authentication of furniture. In addition, identification enables the furniture conservator to select the most appropriate materials for a good match to the original. Traditionally, wood identification in furniture focused on the principal primary wood or woods as a fashionable reference to the objects. We routinely refer to a card table as 'a mahogany card table'. But increasingly it is considered important to evaluate all wooden components, primary and secondary, as critical information in the analysis and attribution of

an object. In identifying wood, the usual objective is to determine the species of the tree from which a particular piece of wood was obtained. Whether or not this goal can be achieved is dependent largely on the wood in question, namely, whether or not the particular wood has physical and anatomical characters that distinguish it from all others. Many woods cannot be separated on their wood anatomy to a single species (e.g. *Tilia* sp.). In applying wood identification to interpretative analysis, it is important to know the level of identification possible as well as the geographic ranges of the woods under consideration.

Unfortunately, there is no single technique or method of wood identification which fits every situation or which is best for every species. An identification procedure often begins by taking advantage of any obvious or unique features, such as unusual colour, recognizable odour, distinguishing figure, or extremes of density, which immediately suggest the identity of the wood. Occasionally, the answer is immediate, as from the unusual weight and dotted pigmentation of snake wood or the distinctive bee-wing figure and golden colour of satin wood. Usually, however, visual or tactile hints must be checked by more precise and reliable means. Ultimately, wood identification requires the presence of a defined set of known features that will verify each species encountered. These may be macroscopic features, microscopic features, or a combination of the two. Anatomical features of an unknown are assessed and compiled for comparison with known features of familiar woods, with information in anatomy texts or computer databases, or with direct observations of actual reference specimens.

Many publications on wood anatomy include dichotomous keys. These keys are based on a system that offers (usually) two options at each stage in the selection process. Only one feature can be selected, which leads to the next two options. At the final stage, one or more taxa are suggested as possible candidates for the unknown wood. The final result always has to be checked against reliable reference material. Keys exist for specific regions, for example, Grosser (1977) and Schweingruber (1990) have keys for Europe, and Panshin and deZeeuw (1980) have a key for the United States. In the UK, the Timber Research and Development Association (TRADA) has published simple keys of this type for both hardwood and softwood identification. Dichotomous identification keys, accompanied with 10× to 15× photographs of transverse cross-sections of wood provide useful supportive data with the hand-lens identification method (Normand, 1972). The main disadvantage of this approach is that no match will be found when that particular genus or species is not included in the key, means that it is often useful to adopt a more flexible approach (Brazier and Franklin, 1961; Hoadley, 1990).

Multiple entry key systems exist that are based on either perforated cards or computer systems. Examples of multiple entry perforated card systems are published by the Forest Products Research Laboratory (FPRL) and described by Brazier and Franklin (1961), Phillips (1960) and Henderson (1960). Multi-entry computer sorting systems have been developed based on the traditional FPRL perforated card system. Especially within the International Association of Wood Anatomists (IAWA), there is an ongoing discussion about some of these programs, combined with reviews of suitable wood anatomical features. The General Unknown Entry Search System (GUESS) by Wheeler (Wheeler *et al.*, 1986) is a useful and inexpensive PC program containing more than five thousand taxa in eight different databases, and is accompanied by an excellent textbook. Miller (1980), and Miller *et al.* (1981, 1987) has described more elaborate systems that operate with a larger number of features. Other programs were developed for specific regions or countries. Jiaju and Fang (1990) describe the Wood Identification Program (WIP) for woods mostly from China. A review of current computer search programs is given by Wheeler and Baas (1998).

Reference material should consist of microscope slides made of vouchered wood samples, wood descriptions and photo-micrographs of wood sections (Détienne and Jacquet, 1983; Fahn *et al.*, 1986; Grosser, 1977; Miles, 1978; Panshin and deZeeuw, 1980; Schweingruber, 1990). Vouchered wood samples are specimens of woody plants of which the leaves, fruits or flowers also were collected of the same exact plant, and identified to the

species level for taxonomic purposes. Gregory (1980) provides an annotated bibliography on wood identification including a listing by botanical family, growth regions and microscopic features with cross references to more than 450 bibliographic entries.

Wood identification is typically an invasive and destructive process, at least to the extent that some wood tissue must be disturbed. The process usually consists of removing small samples or sections, or at least in cleanly cutting into a surface to expose cell structure for examination. In identifying woods of historic objects, a primary responsibility is to utilize approaches that accomplish identification with the least possible disturbance to the object.

### 2.2.5  Hand–lens examination

A routine starting point in identifying a given piece of wood is to locate a tiny area of end-grain surface where the wood can be cut cleanly with a razor blade or equally sharp tool to expose longitudinal cells in cross-section. When the exposed surface is examined with a good quality 10× magnifier or hand lens, it can immediately be identified as a hardwood (pores visible) or softwood (pores absent). In addition, placement of growth rings and rays indicates the orientation of radial and tangential planes in the wood.

In cases where pores (and in some cases conspicuous rays) give immediate indication that the unknown is a hardwood, the pore distribution and size range suggests whether the wood is ring-porous, semi-ring-porous or diffuse-porous. This process of examination and deduction continues until all features have been evaluated. In summary, among hardwoods, hand lens observation of transverse surfaces reveals the relative width and distinctiveness of rays, the size and distribution of pores, and characteristic patterns of parenchyma cells.

An acetate measuring gauge, which can be ordered from most forest products laboratories, is helpful in measuring features such as pore quantity and size. Careful evaluation of typical characteristics will usually suggest an identification, at least to the genus, for most temperate region hardwoods. However, it is routinely recommended to follow through with microscopic examination of thin sections to confirm

**Table 2.1** Representative woods found in furniture

| Common and systematic names related/similar species | Key identification features — Macroscopic | Key identification features — Microscopic | Average relative density[a] | Typical strength properties[b] $C\|$ | $C\bot$ | MoR | MoE | SH | Shrinkage (%)[c] $S_t$ | $S_r$ |
|---|---|---|---|---|---|---|---|---|---|---|
| Oak – *Quercus* spp. – Red oaks<br>(1) *Q. rubra* – Northern red oak<br>(2) *Q. falcata* – Southern red oak<br>(3) *Q. coccinea* – Scarlet oak<br>(4) *Q. kelloggii* – Calif. Black oak<br>(5) *Q. palustris* – Pin oak<br>(6) *Q. velutina* – Black oak | Heartwood light brown, usually with flesh coloured cast. Ring porous. Up to four rows of large solitary pores in early-wood. Late-wood pores solitary in radial lines, few and distinct ('countable'). Tyloses absent or sparse in early-wood. Largest rays conspicuous; tallest less than 1 in. Late-wood pores are the most reliable method for separating red and white oaks | Narrow rays, uniseriate or in part biseriate. Late-wood vessels thick-walled | (1) 0.63<br>(2) 0.59<br>(3) 0.67<br>(4) 0.57<br>(5) 0.63<br>(6) 0.61 | 46.6<br>42.0<br><br>44.9 | 8.61<br>7.44<br><br>7.92 | 98.5<br>75.1<br><br>95.8 | 12 500<br>10 300<br><br>11 300 |  | 8.6<br>11.3<br><br>11.1 | 4.0<br>4.7<br><br>4.4 |
| Oak – *Quercus* spp. – White oaks<br>(1) *Q. alba* – White oak<br>(2) *Q. prinus* – Chestnut oak<br>(3) *Q. lyrata* – Overcup oak<br>(4) *Q. robur* – European oak<br>(5) *Q. petraea* – Sessile oak<br>(6) *Q. stellata* – Post oak | Heartwood light to dark brown to greyish brown. Ring porous. Up to four rows of large solitary pores in early-wood. Late-wood pores small, solitary or in multiples, in spreading radial arrangement, numerous and indistinct ('uncountable'), grading to invisibly small with lens. Tyloses abundant. Largest rays conspicuous; tallest greater than 1.25 in | Narrow rays, uniseriate or in part biseriate. Late-wood vessels thin-walled | (1) 0.68<br>(2) 0.66<br>(3) 0.63<br>(4) 0.62<br>(5) 0.62<br>(6) 0.67 | 51.3<br><br><br>45.5 | 7.37<br><br><br>12.1 | 105<br><br><br>90.9 | 12 300<br><br><br>10 400 |  | 10.5<br><br><br>12.7 | 5.6<br><br><br>5.3 |
| Chestnut – *Castanea* spp.<br>(1) *C. dentata* – American chestnut<br>(2) *C. sativa* – European sweet chestnut | Heartwood greyish brown or medium to dark brown. Ring porous. Early-wood pores several pores wide; pores oval, surrounded by lighter tissue. Late-wood pores very numerous in radial dendritic or wandering patches. Tyloses present. Rays barely visible with lens | Rays almost exclusively uniseriate | (1) 0.43<br>(2) 0.54 | 36.7 | 5.24 | 59.3 | 8480 |  | 6.7 | 3.4 |
| Elm – *Ulmus* spp.<br>(1) *U. rubra* – Slippery elm<br>(2) *U. americana* – American elm<br>(3) *U. procera* – English elm<br>(4) *U. glabra* – Wych elm<br>(5) *U. alata* – Winged elm | Heartwood light brown to brown or reddish brown, except (1) red to dark brown or reddish brown. Ring porous. Early-wood varies with species: (1) 2–6 pores, (2) fairly continuous row of large, uniformly sized evenly spaced early-wood pores, (3) and (4) similar, (5) early-wood pores small and indistinct in intermittent row. Late-wood pores in wavy bands. | (1) Rays homocellular, 1–7 (mostly 4–5), seriate. (2,3,4) Rays homogeneous, 1–7 (mostly 4–6), seriate. (5) Rays homogeneous, 1–7, seriate | (1) 0.53<br>(2) 0.50<br>(3) 0.49<br>(4) 0.60<br>(5) 0.66 | 38.0 | 5.86 | 81.3 | 9230 |  | 9.5 | 4.2 |

Tyloses generally sparse in early-wood. Rays not distinct without lens. Heartwood of (1) fluoresces dim yellow-green

| | Description | Rays | Density | | | | | | |
|---|---|---|---|---|---|---|---|---|---|
| Ash – *Fraxinus* spp.<br>(1) *F. americana* – White ash<br>(2) *F. pennsylvanica* – Green ash<br>(3) *F. latifolia* – Oregon ash<br>(4) *F. excelsior* – European ash<br>(5) *F. nigra* – Black ash | Heartwood colour light brown or greyish brown (1–4) greyish brown to medium or dark brown (5). Ring porous. Early-wood 2–4 pores wide, moderately large to large (5) surrounded by lighter tissue. Late-wood pores solitary and in radial multiples of 2–3 (not numerous in (5)). In (1–4), late-wood pores are surrounded by vasicentric parenchyma or connected by aliform parenchyma. In (5), aliform or confluent parenchyma in outer late-wood is rare. Tyloses fairly abundant. Rays not distinct to eye but clearly visible with hand lens. | Rays 1–3 seriate. Late-wood pores thick-walled | (1) 0.60<br>(2) 0.56<br>(3) 0.55<br>(4) 0.61<br>(5) 0.49 | 51.1 | 9.71 | 106 | 12 200 | 7.8 | 4.9 |
| | | | | | | | | 7.8 | 5.0 |
| Walnut – *Juglans* spp.<br>(1) *J. nigra* – Black walnut<br>(2) *J. regia* – English walnut/Circassian French walnut/Circassian walnut | (1): Heartwood medium brown to deep chocolate brown. Semi-ring porous. Early-wood pores fairly large, decreasing gradually to quite small in outer late-wood; pores solitary or in radial multiples of 2 to several. Tyloses moderately abundant. Short tangential lines of banded or diffuse in aggregates parenchyma visible with lens. Rays fine, visible but not conspicuous with lens. (2): very similar but appears lighter and less uniform in colour and more diffuse porous | Rays 1–5 seriate; ray cells appear round in tangential view. Crystals in longitudinal parenchyma and 'gash-like pits' in late-wood vessels occasionally found in (1) but not in (2) | (1) 0.55<br>(2) 0.56 | 52.2 | 8.61 | 101 | 11 600 | 7.8<br>6.4 | 5.5<br>4.3 |
| Plane – *Platanus* spp.<br>(1) *P. occidentalis* – American sycamore<br>(2) *P. acerifolia* – London plane | Heartwood light to dark brown usually with a reddish cast. Diffuse porous; growth rings distinct due to unusual lighter colour of late-wood. Pores small, solitary, and in irregular multiples and clusters, numerous and evenly distributed throughout most of the growth ring. Late-wood zone evident by fewer, smaller pores and lighter colour. Rays easily visible without lens on all surfaces, appear uniform in size and spacing on transverse and tangential surfaces. Conspicuous dark ray fleck on radial surfaces | Largest rays up to 14 seriate. Uniseriate rays not common | (1) 0.49<br>(2) 0.55 | 37.1 | 5.93 | 68.9 | 9780 | | |

*continued*

**Table 2.1** Continued

| Common and systematic names related/similar species | Key identification features | | Average relative density[a] | Typical strength properties[b] | | | | | Shrinkage (%)[c] | |
| --- | --- | --- | --- | --- | --- | --- | --- | --- | --- | --- |
| | Macroscopic | Microscopic | | C\|\| | C\|- | MoR | MoE | SH | $S_t$ | $S_r$ |
| Beech – *Fagus* spp.<br>(1) *F sylvatica* – European beech<br>(2) *F grandifolia* – American beech | Heartwood creamy white with reddish tinge to medium reddish brown. Diffuse porous; growth rings distinct. Pores small, solitary and in irregular multiples and clusters, numerous and evenly distributed throughout most of the ring; narrow but distinct late-wood in each ring due to fewer, smaller pores. Largest rays conspicuous on all surfaces; darker ray fleck against lighter background on radial surfaces | Largest rays 15–25 seriate; uniseriate rays common. Occasional crystals in longitudinal parenchyma in (2) but not in (1) | (1) 0.64<br>(2) 0.64 | 50.3 | 8.61 | 103 | 11 900 | | 11.9 | 5.5 |
| Maple – *Acer* spp.<br>Hard maple group:<br>(1) *A. saccharum* – Sugar maple<br>(2) *A. nigrum* – Black maple<br>(3) *A. pseudoplatanus* – English sycamore<br>Soft maple group<br>(4) *A. rubrum* – red maple<br>(5) *A. saccharinum* – silver maple<br>(7) *A. campestre* – Field maple<br>(8) *A. platanoides* – Norway maple | Heartwood creamy white to light reddish brown. Soft maples, red maple in particular may have an overall greyish cast or streaks. Diffuse porous. Growth rings are distinct due to narrow zone of darker brown cells at outer margin of growth ring. Pores small and solitary or in radial multiples of 2 to several – fairly uniform in size and quite uniform in distribution. Rays very distinct, the largest about as wide as the diameter of the largest pores. On radial surfaces, rays produce a conspicuous ray fleck – dark against lighter background | Fine, evenly spaced spiral thickenings. Simple perforation plates. Alternate, large intervessel pitting. In hard maples the largest rays are 7–8 seriate, and uniseriate rays are numerous. In soft maples, rays are 1–5 seriate | Hard 0.56 – 0.63<br>(1) 0.63<br>(2) 0.57<br>(3) 0.56<br>Soft 0.46 – 0.54<br>(4) 0.54<br>(5) 0.47 | 54.0<br><br><br><br>45.1 | 12.5<br><br><br><br>8.54 | 109<br><br><br><br>92.3 | 12 600<br><br><br><br>11 300 | | 9.9<br><br><br><br>8.2 | 4.8<br><br><br><br>4.0 |
| Cherry – *Prunus* spp.<br>(1) *P. serotina* – black cherry<br>(2) *P. avium* – European cherry<br><br>Plums, peaches and apricots similar. Also in Rosaceae family, *Malus* (apple) spp. and *Pyrus* (pear) spp. – 'fruitwood' | Light to dark cinnamon or reddish brown. Diffuse porous; growth rings sometimes distinct because of narrow zone or row of numerous slightly larger pores along initial early-wood. Pores through growth ring solitary and in radial or irregular multiples and small clusters. Gum defects common. Rays: not visible on tangential surface; conspicuous light ray fleck on radial surfaces; distinct bright lines across transverse surface, conspicuous with lens. Plums, peaches and apricots similar, apple and pear have narrower rays 1–3 (mostly 2) seriate | Rays 1–6 (mostly 3–4) seriate. Spiral thickenings variable from thick to very thin, irregularly spaced (sparse in apple and pear). Simple perforation plates. Alternate intervessel pitting. Vessels with orange to ruby red contents | (1) 0.50 | | | | | | 7.1 | 3.7 |

## Birch – *Betula* spp.

(1) *B. alleghaniensis* – Yellow birch
(2) *B. lenta* – Sweet birch
(3) *B. papyrifera* – Paper birch
(4) *B. pubescens* – European birch
(5) *B. pendula* – European birch

Heartwood light to dark brown or reddish brown. Diffuse porous. Growth rings may not be distinct – terminated by narrow zone of slightly denser, darker fibre mass. Pores small to medium, solitary or in radial multiples of 2 to several. With lens, pores clearly larger than width of rays. Some pores filled with whitish substance. Rays barely visible to unaided eye but distinct with lens on X section

Rays 1–5 seriate. No spiral thickenings. Scalariform perforation plates with many fine bars. Intervessel pitting alternate, very small with confluent apertures

| | | | | | | |
|---|---|---|---|---|---|---|
| (1) 0.62 | 56.3 | 8.20 | 114 | 13 800 | 9.2 | 7.2 |
| (2) 0.65 | 39.2 | 5.10 | 84.7 | 11 000 | 8.6 | 6.3 |
| (3) 0.55 | | | | | | |
| (4) 0.59 | | | | | | |
| (5) 0.59 | | | | | | |

## Lime – *Tilia* spp.

(1) *T. americana* – Amer. basswood
(2) *T. heterophylla* – White basswood
(3) *T. vulgaris* – European lime

Heartwood creamy white to pale brown. Faint but characteristic musty odour. Diffuse porous. Growth rings indistinct or faintly delineated by marginal parenchyma, sometimes with blurry whitish spots along the growth-ring boundary. Pores small, mostly in irregular multiples and clusters. Rays distinct but not conspicuous on transverse surface with lens

Rays 1–6 seriate. Ray cells appear laterally compressed in tangential view. Rays have bright yellow cast. Thick, evenly spaced spiral thickenings. Simple perforation plates. Intervessel pitting alternate

| | | | | | | |
|---|---|---|---|---|---|---|
| (1) 0.37 | 32.6 | 3.10 | 59.9 | 10 100 | 9.3 | 6.6 |
| (3) 0.48 | | | | | | |

## Poplar – *Populus* spp.

N. American cottonwood/poplar:
(1) *P. balsamifera* – Balsam poplar
(2) *P. deltoides* – Eastern cottonwood
(3) *P. heterophylla* – Swamp cottonwood
(4) *P. trichocarpa* – Black cottonwood

European poplars:
(5) *P. alba* – White poplar
(6) *P. canescens* – Grey poplar
(7) *P. nigra* – Black poplar

Aspens:
(8) *P. grandidentata* – Bigtooth aspen
(9) *P. tremuloides* – Quaking aspen
(10) *P. tremula* – European aspen

Heartwood in aspen typically light greyish brown. Cotton wood heartwood is greyish to light greyish brown, sometimes with an olive cast. In aspen, wood may be lustrous, cotton wood usually dull. Moist cottonwood has foul odour which disappears on drying. Growth rings distinct due to narrow margins of slightly darker denser fibres. Diffuse porous but larger, more numerous and crowded pores in early-wood grading to small in outer late-wood suggest a semi diffuse porous arrangement. Pores solitary and in radial multiples of 2 to several. In aspen, all pores are invisibly small. In cottonwood, the largest pores are usually barely visible to the unaided eye. Rays very fine, not easily seen with hand lens

Rays uniseriate, homocellular. Spiral thickenings absent. Perforation plates simple. Intervessel pitting, large alternate

| | | | | | | |
|---|---|---|---|---|---|---|
| (1) 0.33 | 33.8 | 3.24 | 58.6 | 9 440 | 9.2 | 3.9 |
| (2) 0.40 | | | | | 6.7 | 3.5 |
| (4) 0.35 | | | | | | |
| (6) 0.40 | | | | | | |
| (8) 0.39 | | | | | | |
| (9) 0.38 | | | | | | |

*continued*

**Table 2.1** Continued

| Common and systematic names related/similar species | Key identification features | | Average relative density[a] | Typical strength properties[b] | | | | | Shrinkage (%)[c] | |
|---|---|---|---|---|---|---|---|---|---|---|
| | Macroscopic | Microscopic | | C‖ | C⊥ | MoR | MoE | SH | S_t | S_r |
| African mahogany – *Khaya* spp. | Heartwood pale rosy red to dark reddish brown, often with purplish cast. Grain typically interlocked producing even stripe figure. Growth rings usually indistinct but sometimes distinct due to increased fibre density in outer late-wood or weakly defined terminal parenchyma. Diffuse porous. Pores medium to medium-large, visible without lens, relatively few to numerous, evenly distributed, solitary and in radial groups of 2–8. Some pores with red gum contents (but usually not white). Parenchyma usually not distinct without lens; terminal parenchyma occasionally present, poorly defined; vasicentric parenchyma narrow. Rays distinct on cross section without lens. On radial surfaces, ray fleck darker than background. Ripple marks usually not present, but if present are indistinct and irregular | Rays of two sizes: smaller mostly 2–3 seriate, larger 4–7 seriate, with larger cells on flanks of rays (tangential view). Marginal cells and longitudinal parenchyma may contain crystals. Intervessel pitting alternate, very small | 0.63 | | | | | | | |
| Central American mahogany – *Swietenia* spp. | Heartwood pale brown or pink to dark reddish brown. Grain straight or roey. Growth rings distinct due to concentric lines of terminal parenchyma easily visible without a lens. Diffuse porous. Pores medium-large, visible without lens, rather numerous, evenly distributed, solitary and in radial groups of 2–10. Some pores with red gum contents or whitish deposits. Parenchyma terminal and vasicentric. Rays barely visible without lens on cross section. On radial surfaces, ray fleck darker than background. Ripple marks usually distinct and regular; occasionally irregular, all elements storied | Rays 1–6 (mostly 3–4) seriate. Crystals in some marginal ray cells; longitudinal parenchyma occasionally contains crystals. Intervessel pitting alternate, very small | 0.58 | | | | | | 5.1 | 3.7 |
| Teak – *Tectona grandis* | Heartwood dark golden yellow turning dark brown or nearly black with age. Waxy feel. | Rays 1–5 (mostly 3–4) seriate. Ray and | 0.57 | | | | | | 4.0 | 2.2 |

| Species | Gross features | Microscopic features | Density | | | | | | | |
|---|---|---|---|---|---|---|---|---|---|---|
| | Straight grain. Characteristic spicy odour. Growth rings distinct, wood usually ring porous. Early-wood pores very large, solitary and in radial groups of 2–3; late-wood pores smaller, not numerous, evenly distributed; vessels with tyloses or with yellowish or whitish deposits. Parenchyma terminal and vasicentric. Rays distinct without lens on cross section | longitudinal parenchyma with brown gum contents. Intervessel pitting alternate, medium | | | | | | | | |
| Rosewood – *Dalbergia* spp. *D latifolia* – Indian rosewood | Heartwood light to dark violet brown to purple with near-black pigment layering that resembles growth rings. Grain irregular to roey. Growth rings indistinct. Diffuse porous. Pores variable in size, large to small, irregularly distributed, solitary and in radial multiples. Parenchyma aliform with short to very long wings; confluent forming wavy tangential bands; also apotracheal forming broken tangential lines or in smaller patches. Rays not visible without a lens. Ripple marks distinct and regular; all elements storied | Rays 1–3 (mostly 2–3) seriate; up to 15 cells high. Intervessel pitting alternate, medium-large | 0.76 | | | | | | | |
| Pine – *Pinus* spp. Hard pine group (1) *P. sylvestris* – Scots pine (2) *P. resinosa* – red pine (3) *P. palustris* – longleaf pine | Coniferous wood. Heartwood distinct, pale reddish-brown. Resinous odour. Wood medium texture, uneven grained (v. dense late-wood). Early-wood/late-wood transition abrupt, resin canals numerous, large, mostly solitary, evenly distributed | Epithelial cells thin-walled. Rays heterocellular. Ray tracheids dentate. Crossfield pitting window-like (1–2) or pinoid (3) | 0.46 – 0.60 (1) 0.46 (2) 0.44 (3) 0.58 | 41.8 56.6 | 4.48 6.55 | 75.8 98.5 | 11 200 13 300 | 254 | 7.2 7.5 | 3.8 5.1 |
| Larch – *Larix* spp. (1) *L. laricina* – Eastern larch (2) *L. occidentalis* – Western larch (3) *L. decidua* – European larch | Coniferous wood. Heartwood distinct yellowish to orange brown or russet (1) through to reddish brown (2) or brick red (3) in colour. Odourless. Uneven (1) to moderately uneven (2) grain. Early wood/late-wood transition abrupt. Rings in (2) generally narrow. Resin canals small, relatively few and variable in distribution, solitary or up to several in tangential groups. Texture medium-fine (1) to medium-coarse (2) | Epithelial cells thick-walled. Ray tracheids with *Larix*-type pits. Cross-field pitting piceoid. Longitudinal parenchyma absent | (1) 0.53 (2) 0.51 (3) 0.53 | 49.3 55.9 | 6.82 6.75 | 79.9 96.8 | 11 300 13 500 | 9.1 | 4.5 | |
| Spruce – *Picea* spp. (1) *P. rubens* – red spruce | Heartwood light in colour; indistinct from sapwood. Odourless. Grain fairly even to | Epithelial cells thick-walled. Ray tracheids | (1) 0.41 (2) 0.40 | 37.7 | 3.72 | 67.5 | 9 200 | | 7.8 | 3.8 |

*continued*

**Table 2.1** Continued

| Common and systematic names related/similar species | Key identification features | | Average relative density[a] | Typical strength properties[b] | | | | | Shrinkage (%)[c] | |
|---|---|---|---|---|---|---|---|---|---|---|
| | Macroscopic | Microscopic | | $C\|\|$ | $C\perp$ | MoR | MoE | SH | $S_t$ | $S_r$ |
| (2) *P. glauca* – white spruce<br>(3) *P. mariana* – black spruce | moderately even. Early-wood/late-wood transition gradual. Resin canals small, relatively few and variable in distribution, solitary or up to several in tangential groups | with *Picea* Type I and II pits. Large bordered pits on radial walls of tracheids seldom paired. Longitudinal parenchyma absent | (3) 0.40 | | | | | | | |
| Fir – *Abies* spp.<br>(1) *A. balsamea* – balsam fir<br>(2) *A. concolor* – white fir<br>(3) *A. grandis* – grand fir<br>(4) *A. alba* – Norway fir or silver fir | Heartwood indistinct and light in colour. Odourless but may have bitter taste (2,3). Grain moderately uneven to moderately even. Early-wood/late-wood transition gradual (2–3) to very gradual (1). Resin canals absent. Texture medium (1) to medium-coarse or coarse (2,3). Norway fir is a low-density species similar to (1) | Cross-field pitting taxodioid. Ray tracheids absent. Ray parenchyma end walls nodular. Crystals sometimes present in ray parenchyma (2,3) absent in (1). Longitudinal parenchyma usually absent. Rays in (4) consistently exceed 30 cells in height | (1) 0.36<br>(2) 0.37<br>(3) 0.40<br>(4) 0.43 | 31.2<br>36.9 | 2.62<br>4.13 | 52.4<br>64.1 | 8470<br>9500 | | 6.9<br>7.1 | 2.9<br>3.2 |

[a] Numbers in parentheses refer to named species in first column on left of table. The number sequence in this column is preserved in columns to the right so that, for example, in the shrinkage column values are given for Q. rubra, Q. falcata and Q. velutina but not for the other red oaks listed.

[b] Typical strength properties: C|| = compression parallel to grain MN/m² maximum crushing strength. C⊥ = compression at right-angles to grain MN/m² at proportional limit – when measuring compression perpendicular to grain, there is no meaningful maximum load – after reaching the proportional limit the piece is compacted more and more and resistance increases. MoR = modulus of rupture MN/m². MoE = modulus of elasticity MN/m². SH = side hardness kg.

[c] Approximate shrinkage as % of green dimension from green to oven-dry moisture content. $S_t$ = tangential shrinkage; $S_r$ = radial shrinkage.

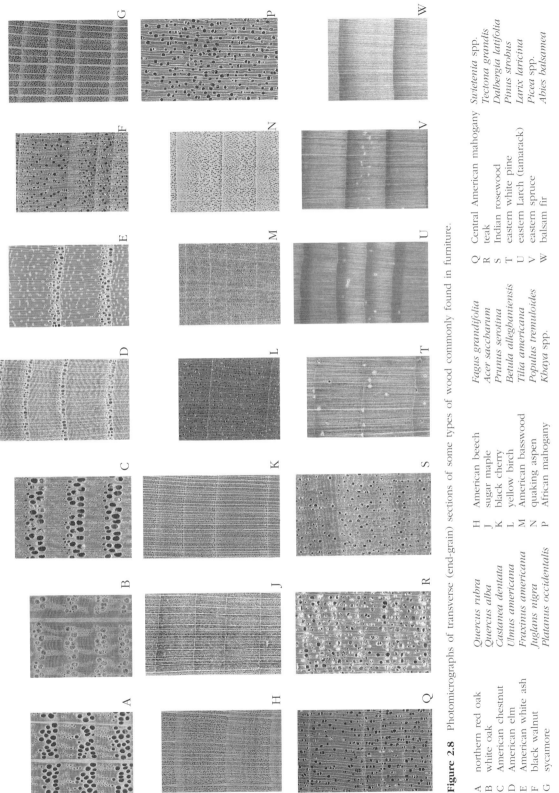

**Figure 2.8** Photomicrographs of transverse (end-grain) sections of some types of wood commonly found in furniture.

| | | | |
|---|---|---|---|
| A | northern red oak | *Quercus rubra* | |
| B | white oak | *Quercus alba* | |
| C | American chestnut | *Castanea dentata* | |
| D | American elm | *Ulmus americana* | |
| E | American white ash | *Fraxinus americana* | |
| F | black walnut | *Juglans nigra* | |
| G | sycamore | *Platanus occidentalis* | |
| H | American beech | *Fagus grandifolia* | Q | Central American mahogany | *Swietenia* spp. |
| J | sugar maple | *Acer saccharum* | R | teak | *Tectona grandis* |
| K | black cherry | *Prunus serotina* | S | Indian rosewood | *Dalbergia latifolia* |
| L | yellow birch | *Betula allegbaniensis* | T | eastern white pine | *Pinus strobus* |
| M | American basswood | *Tilia americana* | U | eastern Larch (tamarack) | *Larix laricina* |
| N | quaking aspen | *Populus tremuloides* | V | eastern spruce | *Picea* spp. |
| P | African mahogany | *Khaya* spp. | W | balsam fir | *Abies balsamea* |

the analysis, or to make further separation to species, if indeed this is possible.

*Table 2.1* gives data for selected woods representative of those commonly found in furniture. For each wood a general description is given, with principal identification features and summary data for physical and mechanical properties. *Figure 2.8* shows cross-sectional views of the main genera represented in *Table 2.1*. These photographs enable a general comparison of representative types of hardwoods and softwoods. Macroscopic features that are useful for identification purposes can be observed. Further detailed information is given by Henderson (1960) and by Hoadley (1990).

With softwoods, hand lens identification is tentative at best, since for all conifers the bulk of the wood tissue consists mainly of tracheids. Some initial screening can be accomplished by determining the presence or absence of resin canals, the coarseness of texture, the unevenness of grain (texture) caused by early-wood/late-wood contrast, and whether the transition from early-wood to late-wood is gradual or abrupt. This information will lead to educated guesses, but conscientious identification of softwoods requires the microscopic evaluation of radial and tangential sections. *Figure 2.8* T–W shows transverse surfaces of selected softwoods commonly found in furniture. For further information see Hoadley (1990).

### 2.2.6  Microscopic examination

Using a cross-section to provide orientation, surfaces can subsequently be split or shaved along the radial or tangential planes. For microscopic examination, tissue sections must be accurately cut along radial, tangential or transverse surfaces using a razor blade or comparably sharp instrument. When working on objects, it is sometimes possible to cut sections from furniture parts directly. In other cases it is more expedient to dissect first a tiny piece from the object, which can then be further prepared as required. Typically, a fragment $3 \times 3 \times 10$ mm will be sufficient. To obtain the best results it is normally advisable to soften this initial sample by boiling to enable very thin slices of wood tissue from each of the three principal planes to be taken for microscopic examination. These should normally be approximately $3 \times 3$ mm and as thin as possible. Ideally, the section should be thinner than the diameter of the smallest cells, that is less than 0.020 mm (i.e. 20 µm). It is possible to achieve such thin cuts using a razor blade but more consistently even results can be obtained with a microtome. In reality, sections cut by hand will be variable in thickness, and some portions of the sample will be too thick to show detail. Useful cellular detail will usually be found along thin edges of hand-cut sections. The section is placed on a glass microscope slide, moistened with a drop of water, and then covered with a thin cover glass. When placed on the stage of a standard compound light microscope, the translucent section is illuminated with transmitted light and the cellular detail can be examined at magnification in the range of $100 \times$–$500 \times$. Ideally, the microscope should have facilities for using polarized light as this is useful for identifying crystals (for choice of a suitable instrument see Hoadley, 1990; also Normand, 1972; Core *et al.*, 1979). Samples can be stained or bleached to enhance the microscopic image of the wood section (Blanchette, 1992a; Florian *et al.*, 1990; Grosser, 1977; Walter, 1980). The stain Safranin 'O' is commonly used to increase contrast of wood section. Sections can be permanently mounted for safe storage and long term use (Florian *et al.*, 1990).

Among the conifers, microscopic details offer the most distinctive differences from one species to another and thus provide the most reliable basis for separation. Among the routinely useful features are the height and width of the rays, the types of ray cells present, the shape and number of cell-wall pits (voids in the cell walls connecting adjacent cells), the smoothness of the cell walls, the presence and colour of contents of the cells, or spiral thickenings in the tracheids. Such detail is often quick and easy to see and evaluate. For example, among the pines, the cell walls of ray tracheids are smooth in the soft pines (such as eastern white pine, *Pinus strobus*), providing a certain separation from the hard pines (such as Scots pine, *Pinus sylvestris*), which have dentate ray tracheids with jagged walls (see *Figure 2.5b*). As another example, the characteristic spiral thickenings observed in yew, *Taxus* spp. (*Figure 2.9*) quickly separate this wood from other conifers found in furniture.

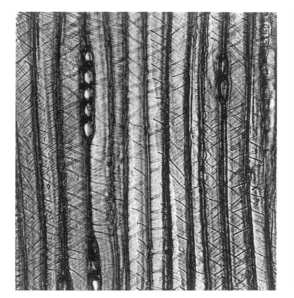

**Figure 2.9** Tangential microscopic view showing spiral thickening in tracheids in yew. This distinctive feature, along with the absence of both resin canals and longitudinal parenchyma, distinguishes yew from other conifers

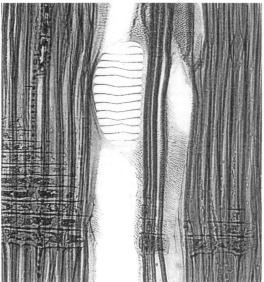

**Figure 2.10** The scalariform perforation plate (the ladder-like feature also seen in *Figure 2.4b*) in combination with the numerous tiny pits (minute alternate inter-vessel pitting) are distinguishing features of birch (*Betula* spp.)

Among the hardwoods – the diffuse-porous hardwoods especially – microscopic analysis also provides the best means of confirming many genera, and in most cases, the only way of separating species within a genus. For example, in *Betula* (birch), the multiple grate-like end walls (scalariform perforation plate) separating consecutive vessel elements together with the numerous tiny pits (minute alternate inter-vessel pitting) laterally connecting vessels, are distinguishable features of this genus (*Figure 2.10*).

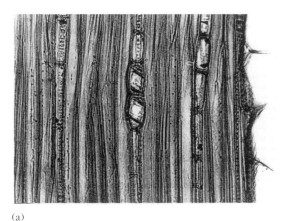

(a)

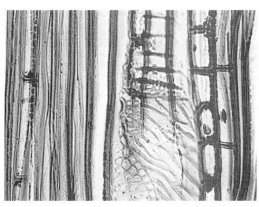

(b)

**Figure 2.11** Radial microscopic views of black walnut: (*a*) shows crystals in longitudinal parenchyma cells; (*b*) shows reticulate thickenings, called 'gash-like pits', in late-wood vessel elements. These two features can be used to separate North American black walnut (*Juglans nigra*) from European walnut (*Juglans regia*) as they are present only in the North American species

**Table 2.2**   List of microscopic features for the identification of hardwoods

**Anatomical features**

1   Growth ring boundaries distinct *or* absent
2   Vessels
       Porosity – ring porous *or* semi-ring porous *or* diffuse porous
       Arrangement – tangential bands *or* diagonal/radial pattern *or* dendritic pattern
       Groupings – solitary *or* radial multiples *or* clusters
       Solitary vessel outline angular
       Perforation plates – simple *or* scalariform including number of bars *or* other types
       Intervessel pits arrangement and size
           intervessel pits scalariform *or* opposite *or* alternate *or* polygonal
           intervessel pits minute *or* small *or* medium *or* large
           range of intervessel pit size
       Vestured pits present
       Vessel ray pitting
           with distinct borders *or*
           with much reduced borders, pits rounded or angular *or*
           with much reduced borders, pits horizontal to vertical *or*
           of two distinct sizes or types in the same ray cell *or*
           pits unilaterally compound and coarse (over 10 μm) *or*
           pits restricted to marginal rows
       Spiral thickenings
           present throughout body of vessel element *or* only in vessel element tails *or*
           only in narrower vessel elements
       Mean tangential diameter of vessel lumina ≤ 50 μm *or* 50–100 μm *or* 100–200 μm *or* ≥ 200 μm
           vessels of two distinct diameter classes, wood not ring-porous
       Vessels per mm$^2$ – ≤ 5 *or* 5–20 *or* 20–40 *or* 40–100 *or* ≥ 100
       Mean vessel element length – ≤ 350 μm *or* 350–800 μm *or* ≥ 800 μm
       Tyloses and deposits in vessels
           tyloses common *or* sclerotic *or* gums and other deposits in heartwood vessels
       Wood vessel-less
3   Tracheids and fibres
       Vascular/vasicentric tracheids present
       Ground tissue fibres
           with simple to minutely bordered pits
           with distinctly bordered pits
           fibre pits common in both radial and tangential walls
           spiral thickenings in ground tissue fibres
       Septate fibres and parenchyma-like fibre bands
           septate fibres present *or*
           non-septate fibres present
           parenchyma-like fibre bands present
       Fibre wall thickness – very thin-walled *or* thin- to thick-walled *or* very thick-walled
       Mean fibre lengths – ≤ 900 μm *or* 900–1600 μm *or* ≥ 1600 μm
4   Axial parenchyma
       Axial parenchyma absent or extremely rare
       Apotracheal axial parenchyma – diffuse *or* diffuse-in-aggregates
       Paratracheal parenchyma – scanty *or* vasicentric *or* aliform *or* confluent *or* unilateral
       Banded parenchyma – more than three cells wide *or* narrow bands up to three cells wide *or* reticulate *or* scalariform *or* marginal
       Axial parenchyma cell type/strand length – fusiform *or* three to four cells per strand *or* five to eight cells per strand *or* more than eight cells per strand *or* unlignified
5   Rays
       Ray width – rays exclusively uniseriate *or* one to three cells wide *or* larger rays commonly four to ten seriate *or* larger rays commonly more than 10 seriate *or* rays with mulitseriate portion as wide as uniseriate portion
       Aggregate rays present
       Ray height greater than 1 mm
       Rays of two distinct sizes
       Cellular composition of rays
           all cells procumbent
           all cells upright and/or square
           body ray cells procumbent with one row of upright and/or square marginal cells
           body ray cells procumbent with mostly two to four rows of upright and/or square marginal cells

*continued*

> body ray cells procumbent with over four rows of upright and/or square marginal cells
>
> rays with procumbent, square and upright cells mixed throughout the ray
>
> Sheath cells present
>
> Tile cells present
>
> Perforated ray cells present
>
> Disjunctive ray parenchyma cell walls present
>
> Ray per mm – ≤ 4/mm *or* 4–12/mm *or* ≥ 12/mm
>
> Wood ray-less

6  Storied structure

> All rays storied
>
> Low rays storied, high rays non-storied
>
> Axial parenchyma and/or vessel elements storied
>
> Fibres storied
>
> Rays and/or axial elements irregularly storied
>
> Number of ray tiers per axial mm

7  Secretory elements and cambial variants

> Oil and/or mucilage cells associated with ray parenchyma *or* associated with axial parenchyma *or* present among fibres
>
> Intercellular canals
>
> > axial canals in long tangential lines *or* short tangential lines *or* diffuse
> >
> > radial canals
> >
> > intercellular canals of traumatic origin
>
> Tubes or tubules present
>
> Cambial variants – included concentric phloem *or* included diffuse phloem *or* other

8  Mineral inclusions

> Prismatic crystals present – in upright and/or square ray cells *or* in procumbent ray cells *or* in radial alignment in procumbent ray cells *or* in chambered upright and/or square ray cells *or* in non-chambered axial parenchyma cells *or* in fibres
>
> Druses present in ray parenchyma cells *or* in axial parenchyma cells *or* in fibres *or* in chambered cells
>
> Other crystal types – raphides *or* acicular crystals *or* styloids and/or elongate crystals *or* crystals of other shapes *or* crystal sand
>
> Other diagnostic crystal features – more than one crystal of about the same size per cell or chamber *or* two distinct sizes of crystal per cell or chamber *or* crystals in enlarged cells *or* crystals in tyloses *or* cystoliths
>
> Silica
>
> > Silica bodies present – in ray cells *or* in axial parenchyma cells *or* in fibres
> >
> > Vitreous silica present

**Non-anatomical information**

> Geographical distribution
>
> Specific gravity – low *or* medium *or* high
>
> Heartwood colour
>
> Odour
>
> Heartwood fluorescence
>
> Water and ethanol extracts – fluorescence and colour
>
> Froth test
>
> Chrome Azurol-s test
>
> Burning splinter test

*Source:* Derived from Wheeler, Baas and Gasson (eds) (1989) IAWA list of microscopic features for hardwood identification, *IAWA Bulletin*, 10 (3), 219–332

In the walnut genus, *Juglans*, two important microscopic features – crystals in longitudinal parenchyma cells and reticulate thickenings, (called gash-like pits) on some vessel walls – provide a positive separation of North American black walnut (*Juglans nigra*) from European walnut (*Juglans regia*) (*Figure 2.11*).

*Table 2.2* lists the features used for accurate microscopic identification of hardwoods. These features are extensively described by Brazier and Franklin (1961), Core *et al.* (1979), Grosser (1977), Hoadley (1990), Panshin and deZeeuw (1980), Phillips (1960), and Schweingruber (1982, 1990). The quarterly bulletin of the International Association of Wood Anatomists (IAWA) provides excellent up-to-date information on microscopic features, reviews of botanical families, book reviews and articles on wood anatomy.

### 2.2.7 Other methods

Both transmission electron microscopy and scanning electron microscopy (SEM) are useful in examining features (such as vestured pits) that may otherwise be difficult to observe.

SEMs equipped with an Energy Dispersive X-ray Spectrometry (EDS) system can be helpful in analysing wood inclusions such as naturally occurring calcium deposits (Core *et al.*, 1979). Blanchette *et al.* (1992b) used TEM and SEM-EDS to determine the source of the green coloration of decorative furniture woods. This showed that colour was due to the presence of the hyphae of *Chlorociboria* and associated coloured deposits rather than copper stains.

When only a tiny fragment of wood is available, too small to be sectioned, it may be practical to make a maceration. A mixture of glacial acetic acid and hydrogen peroxide (Franklin's method) can be used to break down the wood into individual cell-elements. These elements are then mounted and examined (Jane, 1970; Panshin and deZeeuw, 1980).

Dyer (1988), Avella *et al.* (1988) and Hoadley (1990) have shown that some wood species display autofluorescence examined by long wave UV light. The ideal opportunity for observing autofluorescence of wood is to examine the fresh surface where a sample for wood identification has been taken.

Chemical spot tests sometimes can provide additional information in differentiating wood species. Chrome azurol, for example, will turn bluish when brought in contact with species containing elevated levels of aluminium (Kukachka and Miller, 1980). Chemical methods for discriminating between the heartwood of red and white oak and between red maple and sugar maple are described by Panshin and deZeeuw (1980).

## 2.3 Chemical nature of wood

Considering that wood is a biological product and is derived from thousands of different species of plants, it is not surprising that its chemical nature is extremely complex. It is likely that more remains to be discovered about the chemistry of wood than has yet been established. Any attempt to address the subject of wood chemistry within a few brief pages must understandably be a sweeping summary at best. However, there are specific fundamentals of the chemical nature of wood which are critical to the basic understanding of wood properties. Certainly, chemical reactions with wood are inherently involved with such practical conservation procedures as finishing, gluing, stabilization and preservative treatment. Even more important, attention to the major chemical constituents provides the key to our understanding of the very structure of the individual wood cell, and, in turn, the anisotropic physical and mechanical properties of wood, its hygroscopicity and dimensional behaviour.

### 2.3.1 Chemical constituents of wood

The cell substance of wood is described chemically as a composite material consisting of three types of organic polymers: cellulose (40–50%), hemicelluloses (20–30%) and lignin (25–30%). These constituents serve as skeletal, matrix and encrusting substances, respectively. In addition, a minor amount of inorganic (ash) content (0.1–0.5%) is present in wood. Depending upon species, extractives (extraneous substances, 1–5%) may also be present, mainly in heartwood.

Cellulose, the major chemical constituent of wood, is in many respects the most important. It is also the most easily defined and described. Wood cellulose is chemically defined as $(C_6H_{10}O_5)_n$. The basic monomer units of glucose anhydride are alternately linked in forming long linear-chain polymeric cellulose with an average degree of polymerization (DP) of about 10,000. *Figure 2.12* illustrates a representative portion of the cellulose molecule.

The hemicelluloses found in wood are linear polysaccharides of moderate size (DP averaging 150–200 or greater) of the types that are invariably associated with cellulose and lignin in plant cell walls. Predominant types include xylan (the principal hemicellulose in hardwoods), glucomannan, and galactoglucomannans (the major hemicellulose of softwoods). A small percentage of hemicellulose in all woods is acetylated and capable of releasing acetic acid on hydrolysis, especially under conditions of elevated temperature and relative humidity.

Lignin has complex three-dimensional polymeric structure comprising various phenyl propane units. Lignin apparently infiltrates and

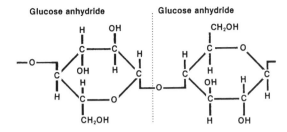

**Glucose anhydride**          **Glucose anhydride**

**Figure 2.12** A representative portion of a molecule of cellulose, the major chemical constituent of wood. The cellulose polymer is composed of glucose anhydride monomers

encrusts the cell wall structure after the polysaccharides are in place. Although lignin contributes to the compressive strength of wood, tensile strength is provided principally by its cellulose.

Extractives are typically low-molecular weight compounds which are principally associated with heartwood formation and are located as much outside the cell wall as within. Extractives represented among the various species of wood fall within classifications such as tannins, terpenes, polyphenols, lignans, resin acids, fats, waxes and carbohydrates. In addition to changing appearance of the wood – mainly as colour – extractives may contribute to other properties of the wood, such as the

significant decay resistance of cedars that results from the presence of tropolones.

### 2.3.2 The cellulose structure within cell walls

As the most important constituent of wood, the nature and orientation of cellulose determine the architecture of the cells. Insight into the configuration of the cellulose within cell walls provides an important key to understanding and anticipating many of the properties and the behaviour of wood. As a basis for discussion, *Figure 2.13* depicts a conceptual model representing a typical longitudinal wood cell, such as a hardwood fibre or a softwood tracheid. The cell wall is layered. The outer layer, the primary wall, was the functional cell wall during cell division in the cambium and during subsequent enlargement/elongation of the developing daughter cell. Next, the secondary wall formed within, giving permanence to the cell dimensions and shape. The primary wall is very thin and lacks any apparent structural orientation; by contrast, the secondary wall occupies the dominant portion of the cell wall and has three layers, designated as $S_1$, $S_2$ and $S_3$. When examined with an electron microscope, the substance comprising the secondary wall appears to have oriented striations. These striations indicate the general direction of cellulose mole-

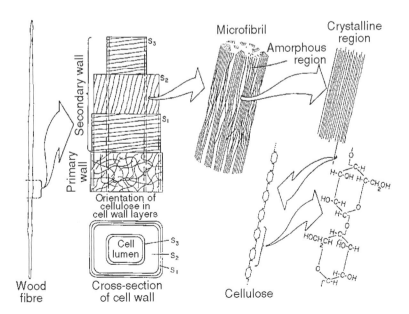

**Figure 2.13** Diagrammatic representation of the structure of a wood fibre. Fibres give wood its strength, have closed ends and thicker walls than vessels, which are used to conduct fluid and nutrients. The lumen is the void or hole in the centre of the cell. The cell wall has four layers and is composed of microfibrils. The microfibrils are arranged randomly in the primary wall. The direction of the microfibrils in the three secondary walls alternates. There are both amorphous and crystalline regions within the microfibrils, which are themselves composed largely of cellulose

cules, the apparent groupings referred to as fibrils (sub-groupings sometimes termed micro fibrils). It is the orientation of fibrils which defines the layering of the secondary wall. Within the thinner $S_1$ and $S_3$ layers, the fibril orientation is nearly perpendicular to the cell axis, whereas fibrils within the dominant $S_2$ layer are oriented more nearly parallel with the cell axis.

Experimental evidence provides a theoretical explanation of the arrangement of cellulose within fibrils. In random areas, called crystallites, cellulose molecules (or more likely, portions of cellulose molecules) are aligned into compact crystalline arrangement. Adjacent areas where cellulose is non-parallel are called amorphous regions. The hemicelluloses and lignin are also dispersed between crystallites and through the amorphous regions.

Within the fibrils, water molecules cannot penetrate or disarrange the crystallites. Water molecules can, however, be adsorbed by hydrogen bonding in one or more layers to the exposed surfaces of crystallites and components of amorphous regions, namely at the sites of available hydroxyl groups. Such polar groups of the polysaccharide fractions on exposed wall surfaces provide the principal active sites for bonding of adhesives and finishes and for other chemical reactions with wood.

Because the average length of cellulose molecules is far greater than the apparent length of the crystallites, it is concluded that an individual cellulose molecule may extend through more than one crystalline region, being incorporated in crystal arrangement at various points along its total length. Therefore, within the fibrillar network, the random end-wise connection of crystallites would appear to offer linear strength to the fibril. Since crystallites would be more readily displaced laterally from one another due to the intrusion or loss of water molecules (or other chemicals capable of entering the fibrils), dimensional response would be expected perpendicular to the fibril direction. In summary, the linear organization of cellulose within the fibrils, the dominance of the $S_2$ layer, and the near-axial orientation of fibrils within the $S_2$ layer, together provides a foundation of understanding of the greater strength and dimensional stability of the cell in its longitudinal direction. It follows that wood itself – as the composite of its countless cells – has oriented properties.

## 2.4  Wood–water relations and movement

No other area of wood science and technology is more important to object conservation than wood–moisture relationships. The moisture condition of wood is related to properties ranging from thermal conductivity and strength to adhesive bonding and fungal development. However, the most telling influence of moisture in wood is upon dimensional behaviour. Solving and preventing the array of problems related to dimensional movement in wooden objects begins by recognizing the fundamental relationships involving wood, moisture and the atmosphere. It is customary to express the amount of water in wood as moisture content. The moisture content (MC) of wood is defined as the ratio of the weight of water in a given piece of wood to the weight of the wood when it is completely dry. The water-free weight of wood is also referred to as its oven-dry weight, determined by drying a wood specimen at 100–105 °C until it ceases to lose weight. Moisture content is expressed as a percent and is calculated as follows:

$$MC = W_i - W_{od} \times 100/W_{od}$$

where

$MC$ = moisture content, expressed as a percentage
$W_i$ = initial weight
$W_{od}$ = oven-dry weight.

Water exists in wood in two forms, as bound water and as free water. Water adsorbed and held within the cell wall by hydrogen bonding is called bound water. Water in wood in excess of the fibre saturation point exists as liquid water in the cell cavities and is called free water. The fibre saturation point (FSP) is the moisture condition of wood wherein the cell walls are completely saturated with bound water but the cell cavities are devoid of free water. It is usually expressed as a numerical value of moisture content and is generally in the range 25–30%.

The sap contained in living trees is primarily water, with small amounts of dissolved minerals and nutrients. Wood in living trees is always above the fibre saturation point, although the moisture content may vary from slightly above the fibre saturation point to 200–300%, depending upon species, whether sapwood or heartwood, and so forth. When trees are harvested and the timber is seasoned for use, all of the free water and some of the bound water is dried from the wood. In any portion of the wood tissue, bound water is not lost until all free water has evacuated.

### 2.4.1 Hygroscopicity

Wood is hygroscopic, that is, it has the capability of exchanging moisture by adsorption or desorption directly with the atmosphere. When wood is seasoned, how much bound water is lost – and how much remains in the wood – is determined by the relative humidity of the atmosphere in which the drying takes place. After initial drying, wood remains hygroscopic. It responds to changes in atmospheric humidity and loses bound water as the relative humidity decreases or regains bound water as the humidity increases. The moisture condition established when the amount of bound water is in balance with the ambient relative humidity is called the equilibrium moisture content (EMC). For example, for interior woodwork in most parts of the United States a moisture content of 5–10% is recommended, but in the damp southern coastal regions a range of 8–13% is suggested and in the dry southern regions, 4–9% (Desch, 1973). In the United Kingdom and most regions of the United States, thoroughly air-dry timber seasoned under the most favourable conditions contains 15–18% moisture.

The relationship between the equilibrium moisture content and relative humidity is shown in *Figure 2.14*. The figure represents average data for white spruce, a typical species, shown as having a fibre saturation point of about 30% moisture content. The FSP varies somewhat among different species. In woods having a high extractive content such as rosewood or mahogany, the FSP can be as low as 22–24%; for those low in extractives, such as beech or birch, the FSP might be as high as 32–35%. Temperature also has an effect on equilibrium moisture content. The curves shown are for 70 °F (21.1 °C), but at intermediate humidity levels the EMC would be about 1% lower for every 25–30 °F elevation in temperature. The EMC curves always converge at 0% RH and 0% EMC, so variation due to extrac-

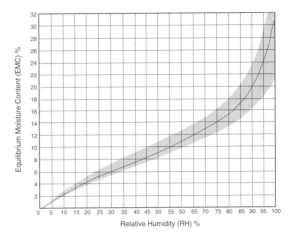

**Figure 2.14** The relationship between relative humidity (RH) and equilibrium moisture content (EMC) in white spruce is shown by the solid line. Most other species fall within the shaded band. The curve shows EMC as a function of RH at constant temperature and is called a moisture sorption isotherm. The moisture content of wood is directly related to the humidity and temperature of the surrounding air (RH). As RH rises or falls, the wood absorbs or desorbs moisture until it is in equilibrium with its environment (hence *equilibrium moisture content*)

tives and temperature will be most pronounced towards the FSP end of the relationship.

Under conditions where the relative humidity is closely controlled, as in laboratory treatments or experiments, the curve for wood that is losing moisture (desorption curve) is slightly higher than that for wood which is gaining moisture (adsorption curve). This effect is called hysteresis. Under normal room or outdoor conditions of fluctuating relative humidity, an averaging effect results, as indicated by the oscillating curve.

### 2.4.2 Measuring moisture content of wood

Any property of wood that varies in some known and predictable way with moisture content could in theory be used to measure moisture content. According to Skaar, there are as many as fifteen methods that have been used (Skaar, 1984). Methods of moisture measurement commonly used or potentially useful in conservation are based on one or other of the following: changes in mass; changes in electrical resistance: change in the dielectric constant.

In the gravimetric method, wood is weighed then dried to constant weight in a convection oven at $103 \pm 2$ °C. The MC is then calculated from the formula given earlier. This method assumes that the oven is completely dry and that only water is lost from the sample. It provides an absolute measure of moisture content at one point in time.

The mass of an applied load can be measured as an electrical signal by a device called a load cell. Typically these devices measure $20\,mm \times 10\,mm$ in size. A wide range of load cells is available that can be used to provide a continuous record of changes in mass of large or small furniture objects as water is absorbed or desorbed from the atmosphere. Although they can be extremely sensitive, load cells cannot readily provide information about the location of moisture in an object or the absolute amount present.

The Karl Fischer reagent, consisting of pyridine, sulphur dioxide, iodine and methanol, can be used to measure the moisture content of wood, and a wide variety of other materials, by titration. It gives the best results of any of the standard methods but is not practical for large samples (Kollman and Hockele, 1962).

Two types of moisture meter are routinely used to determine moisture in wood. They are the electrical resistance type and the dielectric type.

Dry wood is an effective electrical insulator but water is a conductor of electricity. As the moisture content of wood increases its electrical resistance decreases (approximately halving for each 1% increase in MC between 6% and the FSP). The electrical resistance meter, measuring the flow of direct current parallel to the grain between two electrodes inserted into the wood, is commonly used to measure moisture content over this range. Below about 6% MC, resistance metres are not reliable because resistance is too high ($> 10^{11}$ Ohms). Above about 24%, MC readings become less reliable, partly due to loss of sensitivity as resistance falls and partly due to polarization and heating effects. AC metres and those using short repetitive pulses rather than continuous current are able to overcome these shortcomings to some extent.

As electricity takes the path of least resistance, the electrical resistance meter tends to measure the highest MC in the area between the electrodes. However, by insulating the probes along their length except for the penetrating tips that are to serve as the electrodes, resistance metres can be used to measure the magnitude of moisture gradients in wood by measuring the MC at different depths from the surface. Resistance metres require pin electrodes to be inserted into the wood so their use on presentation surfaces of furniture is not acceptable. However, a possible way round this is to take measurements on wood of identical size, species and finish that is kept with the object and allowed to reach the same equilibrium conditions of RH and temperature. Given a suitable meter, electrodes can be left in situ and readings taken as required. The English firm of Hutton and Rostron have developed a small, cheap resistance electrode that can be inserted in multiples into structural timbers and used to monitor moisture content remotely by PC. This system is employed in the Royal Pavilion, Brighton, where it is used to monitor moisture levels in the fabric of the building as part of the decay prevention strategy.

The resistance of wood increases with decrease in temperature, and correction for temperature is therefore required. Some meters can achieve this automatically through a temperature probe connected to the meter. The change in resistance of wood is also to some extent dependent on species. However, variation between species is not as marked with the electrical resistance meter as with the dielectric type of moisture meter.

Dielectric moisture metres use alternating current (AC), usually at radio frequencies and are of two types, the capacitance type and the power loss type. The capacitance type measures the dielectric constant of wood. The more common power loss meter measures the rate of energy absorption as the product of dielectric constant and loss factor. At a given frequency, the dielectric constant increases with increasing moisture content, increasing density and increasing temperature. Power loss generally increases with wood moisture content and with temperature. Usually a concentric arrangement of electrodes placed on one surface is used by both types of dielectric meter. This is normally fixed for a particular meter and the field generated penetrates to a standard depth so that the reading obtained is more or less an average value. Dielectric metres are normally calibrated to read between

0 and 25% moisture content. They have the distinct advantage of being able to take readings without damaging wood surfaces but the disadvantage of operating at a fixed depth of field.

To get the best out of either type, familiarity with the nature of wood–moisture relations and with the meter is necessary and it is a good idea to experiment with different methods and compare the results. Other instrumental methods that have been used to measure moisture content include the neutron moisture meter and nuclear magnetic resonance (Skaar, 1984).

The curve in *Figure 2.14* showing equilibrium moisture content as a function of relative humidity (or relative vapour pressure) at constant temperature is called a moisture sorption isotherm. After initial seasoning, a sample of wood taken through repetitive cycles of RH exposure between 0 and 100% tends to follow the same adsorption and desorption curve repetitively. Therefore, an indirect method of estimating moisture content is to place the wooden object inside a well-sealed container with a hygrometer and to measure the RH produced.

### 2.4.3 Dimensional change

Of all the properties affected by moisture content, dimensional stability commands the greatest attention. Not only is wood hygroscopic, it is also *anisotropic*. That is, it exhibits different properties when tested along axes in different directions. Because of this, dimensional change in wood is usually considered separately in the three principal linear directions: longitudinal, radial and tangential. In previous sections the general effects of bound water sorption were reviewed relative to the cellulose structure within the cell wall. Discussion here will concentrate on the quantitative effects of moisture content on the anisotropic dimensional behaviour of wood tissue. In the initial drying of wood, there is no dimensional response to the loss of free water. Only when a portion of wood tissue has reached the fibre saturation point and begins to lose bound water does shrinkage begin.

The common basis for indicating the relative dimensional instability of a given wood is to measure the total amount of linear shrinkage

that takes place in a given direction from the green to the oven-dry condition, expressed as a percentage of the green dimension. Thus, the total shrinkage percentage is calculated as follows:

$$S = (D_g - D_{od})/D_g \times 100$$

where $S$ = total shrinkage, expressed as a percentage ($S_t$ = tangential shrinkage, $S_r$ = radial shrinkage, $S_l$ = longitudinal shrinkage) and $D$ = change in dimension ($D_g$ = green dimension, $D_{od}$ = oven-dry dimension). *Figure 2.15* illustrates the application of the formula in the determination of tangential shrinkage based on green and oven-dry measurements of a tangentially sawn strip of wood.

Total of shrinkage of wood along the grain (i.e. longitudinal shrinkage) is normally in the range of 0.1–0.2%. In practical situations involving typical moisture content changes over a moderate range, only a portion of this small quantity would be effected and the resulting dimensional change becomes insignificant. It is reasonable to assume that wood is stable along its grain direction, and for most purposes longitudinal shrinkage and swelling are ignored. In fact, longitudinal shrinkage data

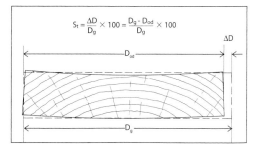

**Figure 2.15** The calculation for percentage of tangential shrinkage ($S_t$) based on green and oven-dry measurements of a tangentially sawn strip of wood. $\Delta D$ = the change in dimension, $D_g$ = the dimension of the wood when green, $D_{od}$ = the dimension of the wood when oven-dried. Note that this formula is only applicable to shrinkage starting from the green condition. For dimensional change of partly seasoned wood this formula will introduce an average error of about 5% of the calculated change in dimension. Calculation of the dimensional change of partly seasoned wood is described in section 2.4.4

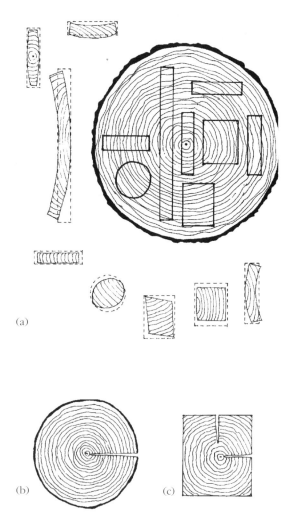

(a)

(b)    (c)

**Figure 2.16** Roughly speaking, tangential shrinkage is double radial shrinkage. This difference in dimensional change when wood is seasoned causes the distortion seen in representative shapes cut from logs (*a*) and commonly results in radial cracks in logs (*b*), or squared timbers (*c*) containing the pith of the tree

Shrinkage across the grain (transverse shrinkage), however, is significant, and tangential shrinkage is always greater than radial shrinkage. Average tangential shrinkage varies between species over the range of about 4 to 12%, with an overall average of about 8%. Average radial shrinkage values range from about 2 to 8%, averaging slightly over 4%. The result of differences in radial and tangential shrinkage is illustrated in *Figure 2.16*.

### 2.4.4 Estimating dimensional change

There is a difference between shrinkage, which occurs as the change in dimensions of wood on initial drying from the green condition, and movement, the dimensional change which takes place when wood that has been dried is subjected to changes in atmospheric conditions below the fibre saturation point (Farmer, 1972). It is possible that a wood may shrink quite appreciably in drying from the green condition yet it may undergo comparatively small dimensional changes when subjected to a given range of atmospheric conditions in service. The reason is that the fibre saturation point, the moisture content value at which appreciable shrinkage begins to take place, varies between different species. In addition, the moisture con-

are not commonly available, as are data for perpendicular shrinkage (i.e. shrinkage across the grain). It should be cautioned, however, that abnormal wood tissue, such as juvenile wood, reaction wood, or pieces with cross-grain, may exhibit longitudinal shrinkage of up to 10–20 times normal. In addition, it should be expected that abnormal wood will occur unevenly in severity and in distribution, and that the resulting uneven longitudinal shrinkage may produce warping.

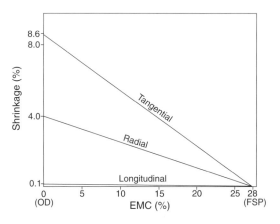

**Figure 2.17** Typical relationships of tangential, radial and longitudinal shrinkage to equilibrium moisture content, shown from oven dry (OD) to fibre saturation point (FSP). Note that shrinkage along the grain (longitudinal) is negligible. Tangential shrinkage is roughly double radial shrinkage, thus the historical preference for quartersawn boards when maximum dimensional stability was required

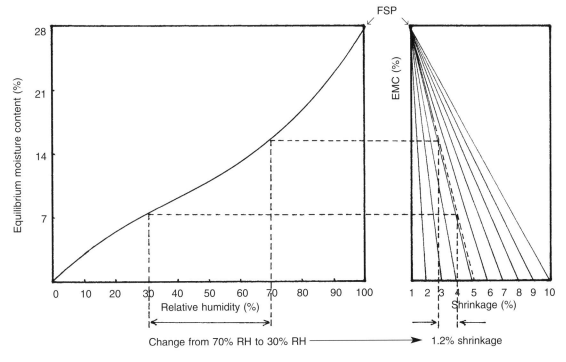

**Figure 2.18**  The relationship between relative humidity, equilibrium moisture content and shrinkage. Choose shrinkage according to species and growth ring orientation, for example, 5.1% for a tangentially sawn mahogany board (shown as a dotted line on the graph on the right). In this case a change from 70% RH to 30% RH will cause 1.2% shrinkage. In a board one metre wide, this produces 12 mm of shrinkage

tent change of one timber corresponding to any given range of atmospheric conditions often varies considerably from that of another. However, in a given direction, dimensional change is roughly proportional to moisture content over the range of bound water loss, as shown in *Figure 2.17.*

Because the shrinkage percentages are based upon shrinkage from the green condition, the formula given in section 2.4.3 is accurate only for shrinkage starting from the green condition. For dimensional change of wood starting at a partially dry condition this formula will introduce an average error of about 5% of the calculated change in dimension. For most purposes, such error is insignificant in view of other inherent sources of error. However, where a more refined estimate is desirable the following formula should be used:

$$D = \frac{D_i\,(MC_i - MC_f)}{\dfrac{FSP}{S} - FSP + MC_i}$$

where

$D$ = dimensional change, in linear units
$D_i$ = initial dimension
$MC_i$ = initial moisture content, per cent
$MC_f$ = final moisture content, per cent
$FSP$ = fibre saturation point, per cent
$S$ = published value for shrinkage, as percentage ($S_t$ for tangential, $S_r$ for radial etc.) of green dimension from green to oven-dry moisture content.

In using this formula, the shrinkage percentages are taken as average published values for the species, which are listed as either radial or tangential. In specific cases involving a piece of wood with intermediate growth ring placement, an approximate value would have to be deduced by rough interpolation between the radial and tangential values. It should be noted that since shrinkage takes place only below fibre saturation, neither $MC_i$ nor $MC_f$ can be greater than the FSP. Positive values of dimensional change indicate shrinkage; negative values indicate swelling.

To illustrate, suppose a flat-sawn mahogany board had been conditioned to an outdoor

environment of 70% RH (from *Figure 2.14*
assume an EMC = 13%). The board is then
moved to an indoor environment of 30% RH
(EMC = 6%). From *Figure 2.14* assume an FSP
of 30%. Published data for mahogany indicate
a 5.1% tangential shrinkage (Hoadley, 1980).
Therefore, the estimated change in the width
of the board is calculated as:

$$D = \frac{14.5 \text{ in } (0.13 - 0.06)}{\dfrac{0.30}{0.051} - 0.30 + 0.13}$$

$$= \frac{1.015}{5.712} = 0.178 \text{ in}$$

Thus the board would shrink by 0.178 inches.

Where direct measurement of moisture content is impossible and where precise numerical
values are unrealistic, the above formula may
be of more academic than practical use. An
equally useful and reasonable approach is a
graphic method of estimating dimensional
change. Combining the oscillating curve of
*Figure 2.14* with the idea of *Figure 2.17*, a
composite working graph can be devised, as
shown in *Figure 2.18*.

Based on the species and growth-ring orientation of a piece of wood in question, the
appropriate shrinkage percentage ($S_t$, $S_r$, or
interpolated estimate) is taken from published
data. On the right-hand side of *Figure 2.18*,
choose the EMC/$S$ line that most closely
matches the shrinkage percentage of the subject. Estimates of changes in RH can now be
translated into percentage dimensional change
by following RH values up and over to corresponding EMC values, then over and down to
corresponding $S$ values.

The graphic relationship between relative
humidity, moisture content and shrinkage
draws attention to the important point that relative humidity is the important controlling parameter and dimensional change is the eventual
consequence. Too often, relative humidity is
not given the serious attention it deserves.
Although moisture content is usually not of
direct concern, it can be important indirectly, if
we remember that the weight of wood reflects
the moisture content. A furniture object probably loses or gains weight primarily as a
response to changes of moisture content of its
wooden components. This change takes place
before any significant dimensional change

(where wood is restrained, it may not actually
be possible to observe dimensional change).
Placing of furniture on a weighing device such
as a load cell could be used as a quite accurate
and relatively inexpensive means of monitoring
the weight of an object. It could therefore be
an excellent way to detect and prevent changing conditions which might eventually result in
dimensional change problems, especially when
wooden objects are being transported or relocated in a new environment. Such a device
could actually be connected to humidification
equipment thereby allowing the object to control its own environment.

Although dimensional change alone may be
a serious consequence of moisture variation,
shrinkage and swelling that is uneven, even
though in minor amounts, can cause distortion
of a piece from its desired or intended shape.
Various forms of distortion include cup (deviation from flatness across the width of a board),
bow (deviation from lengthwise flatness of a
board), crook or spring (departure in end-to-
end straightness along the edge of a board),
and twist (where four corners of a flat face do
not lie in the same plane).

A common source of uneven dimensional
change is simply the greater tangential than
radial shrinkage percentage, a routine cause of
cup in boards, as shown in *Figure 2.16*. Note
that flat sawn boards located closest to the pith
have most severe cup, concentrated near the
centre. Unequal radial and tangential shrinkage
causes round turnings to dry to ovals, squares
with diagonal ring placement to become dia-
mond-shaped (as a rule of thumb, growth ring
lines tend to straighten). In log sections, or timbers containing the pith of the tree, the greater
tangential shrinkage develops circumferential
stresses which may exceed the strength of the
wood, resulting in radial cracks.

The fact that dimensional change is greater
at right-angles to the grain than parallel to it
also produces problems. The opening of mitre
joints and the loosening of mortise and tenon
joints are classic examples. Other causes of
uneven shrinkage are uneven drying, or material with abnormal wood (such as reaction
wood, juvenile wood etc.) This topic is discussed in more detail in Chapter 7.

With time, the dimensional response of
wood may lessen, in part because hygroscopicity of the wood may decrease, or because of

mechanical effects of repeated shrinkage/ swelling cycles, or stress-setting of the wood. However, experiments with wood taken from artefacts thousands of years old have shown the wood to have retained its hygroscopicity and its capacity to dimensionally respond to changes in moisture content. The assumption should therefore prevail that wooden objects, regardless of age, can demonstrate dimensional movement when subjected to variable relative humidity conditions.

## 2.5 Mechanical properties

In the evolution of trees, wood tissue has developed which has highly effective axial compression (i.e. compression along the grain) and bending strength characteristics. For its weight, this wood demonstrates amazing stiffness as well as fracture resistance and it is therefore utilized in structural products such as furniture. However, although axial strength of wood is impressive, the comparative weakness of wood perpendicular to the grain, in both compression and tension, can often be the limiting factor of mechanical performance. This is indicated by examples ranging from surface indentation and splitting to the failure of joints. Given the anisotropic nature of wood, the many possible modes of loading wood tissue, the many environmental conditions and defects which influence strength, and the array of different structural applications of wood in furniture, a thorough discussion of mechanical properties is hardly feasible here. Therefore this section will merely highlight selected aspects of the strength of clear (defect-free) wood and the major factors that influence it in relation to furniture.

### 2.5.1 Defining mechanical properties

In recognition of the anisotropic nature of wood, it is traditional to consider the strength of wood along its three principal axes: longitudinal, radial and tangential. Parallel to grain (longitudinal) strength is significantly greater than strength across the grain; however, since there may be only minor difference between radial and tangential directions, it is appropriate to simply consider average strength perpendicular to the grain.

Strength measures the ability of a material to resist applied force or load. The strength of material is commonly expressed in terms of a stress value. Stress is defined as load per unit area, and is calculated by dividing the magnitude of the applied load or force by the cross-sectional area over which it is distributed. A general formula:

stress = load/area

In English-speaking countries, loads have traditionally been measured in pounds (lb) and areas in square inches (sq. in). In continental Europe, kilograms and centimetres were used. In SI units, Mega Newtons per square metre ($MN/m^2$) are used.

The basic modes of load application are compression, tension and shear. The components in *Figure 2.19* are subjected to a single type of stress. In practice, a combination of stresses may occur, as in the bending of a beam. A beam is an elongated member supported at various points along its length with one or more loads acting perpendicular to its axis. For example, the beam of *Figure 2.20* is supported at each end with a concentrated load at its mid span. As a result of the consequent bending deformation, the upper surface is shortened and stressed in longitudinal compression; the lower surface is stretched and thereby stressed in tension. These axial stresses in tension or compression are referred to simply as bending stresses; they are maximal at the upper and lower surfaces of the beam and diminish to zero at the mid plane of the beam

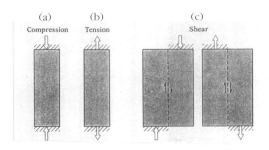

**Figure 2.19** Modes of load application. Compression (*a*) occurs where applied forces are aligned and tend to crush a material. Tension (*b*) occurs where applied forces are aligned and tend to pull a material apart. Shear (*c*) occurs where applied forces are not aligned and tend to slide one part of a material in one direction and the other part of the material in the opposite direction

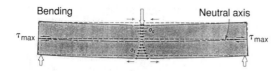

**Figure 2.20** Diagrammatic representation of a beam supported at each end with a load concentrated at its mid span. The large arrows indicate the direction of the applied load on the beam, whilst the small arrows indicate the resulting stresses within the beam as it bends. Compression and tension are concentrated on the surface of the beam at mid span, whilst shear stress is concentrated along the neutral axis at the ends of the beam

(the neutral axis). Given the span, cross-sectional dimensions and the magnitude and position of loads on a beam (regardless of the material used), the magnitude of the bending stresses can be computed using an engineering concept known as the Flexure Formula

(Hoadley, 1980). In wood, the level of bending stress which results in failure of a wooden beam, i.e. the breaking strength, is called the modulus of rupture.

It is tempting to consider strength to mean simply the maximum resistance of wood. However, another important aspect of strength is the reality that mechanical loading of a material is always accompanied by deformation. Deformation in an object under load is expressed as strain. Strain is defined as the change in dimension per unit of original dimension:

$$\text{strain} = \frac{\text{change in dimension (in)}}{\text{original dimension (in)}}$$

Though strain is expressed in units per unit (e.g. inches per inch), it is nevertheless simply a fraction or ratio.

Consider the simultaneous stress and strain behaviour during the progressive loading of a

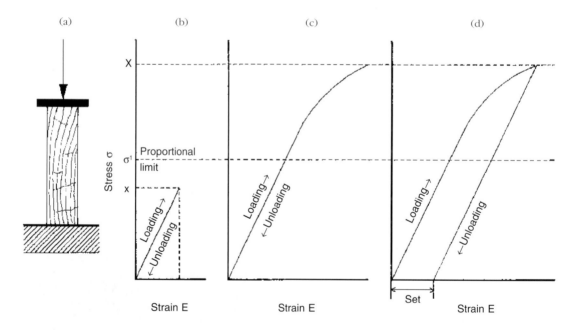

**Figure 2.21** Stress strain diagram. A block of wood under a load in compression perpendicular to the grain is shown in (*a*). The relationship between stress and strain (defined in section 2.5.1) is shown in (*b*), where moderate loading is applied and stress (e.g. x) does not exceed the proportional limit ($\sigma'$). Behaviour in this range is elastic, i.e. when the load (stress) is removed, the wood returns to its original dimension (strain is recovered). In (*c*), as additional load (stress) is applied (X) and the proportional limit ($\sigma'$) is exceeded, dimensional change (strain) is no longer proportional to the applied load (stress). In the graph, this is the point at which the line that shows the effect of loading begins to curve. With most wood properties, the proportional limit is also the elastic limit, and dimensional change (strain) beyond the elastic limit is not reversible when the load (stress) is removed. Once the proportional limit has been exceeded in (*d*), even though the applied load (stress) is removed, the wood does not return to its original dimension (residual strain). Residual strain in wood is called set

wood member, for example, a block of wood under a load in compression perpendicular to grain, as shown in *Figure 2.21a*.

Under moderate loading, the relationship between stress and strain is indicated by *Figure 2.21b*. Note that strain is proportional to stress, and behaviour in this range is elastic, that is, when stress is removed, strain is recovered. However, as shown in *Figure 2.21c*, as additional stress is applied, a proportional limit, σ, is reached, beyond which strain is no longer proportional. With most wood properties, the proportional limit is also the elastic limit, and strain beyond the elastic limit is not reversible; when stress is removed, strain is not reversible. As shown in *Figure 2.21d*, removal of stress beyond the proportional limit results in residual strain, called set. Dents in the surfaces of furniture or the loosening of mortise and tenon joints are examples commonly associated with compressing wood perpendicular to grain beyond its proportional limit. In most cases, there is no meaningful maximum load, since continued compression would result in increasing resistance, even after the wood had been crushed beyond usefulness.

With many strength properties, such as compression parallel to grain (i.e. along the grain) or bending, a maximum load is reached at levels of 1.5–2 times the proportional limit load. Maximum load may be accompanied by fracture or other consequential failure.

Within the proportional limit, the ratio of stress to strain is called the modulus of elasticity, or Young's Modulus ($E$):

$E$ = stress/strain

Since the units of strain cancel out to give a ratio or number without dimensions, the result of this calculation is still a stress. It is that stress which would in theory double the length of a specimen if it did not break first. It can also be regarded as the stress to produce 100% strain (Gordon, 1976). Whereas strength is a measure of the force or stress needed to break an object, Young's modulus or $E$ is concerned with how stiff, flexible, springy or floppy a material is. To quote from J.E. Gordon's excellent *The New Science of Strong Materials*: 'A biscuit is stiff but weak, steel is stiff and strong, nylon is flexible (low $E$) and strong, raspberry jelly is flexible (low $E$) and weak. The two properties (*modulus and strength*) together

describe a solid about as well as you can reasonably expect two figures to do' (Gordon, 1976).

The modulus of elasticity is especially important in bending as it serves as a convenient rating of relative stiffness among different woods. In many applications, the rigidity of the wood may be as critical as its breaking strength.

Certain strength characteristics of wood cannot be described in terms of pure stress values, as they involve complex loading or resistance which cannot be readily analysed. An example is the hardness value of wood, which measures the indentation resistance of wood. This property is determined by an empirical test which simply measures the amount of force required to embed a standard tool (a hemisphere of 0.44 in diameter) into a wood surface.

### 2.5.2 Relative strength properties

For a given species of wood, relative density is perhaps the best single predictor of relative strength. It seems logical that the higher the relative density, the harder and stronger the wood. This is illustrated by the following comparison of figures for a typical white oak with those for a typical species of poplar.

| Timber | Relative density | Modulus of elasticity | Modulus of rupture |
|---|---|---|---|
| *Quercus* spp. | 0.68 | 11 700 MN/m$^2$ 1.7 × 10$^6$ psi | 105 MN/m$^2$ 15 200 psi |
| *Populus* spp. | 0.34 | 7600 MN/m$^2$ 1.1 × 10$^6$ psi | 47 MN/m$^2$ 6800 psi |

Within a given species of wood, there is striking superiority of strength parallel to grain compared with that perpendicular to the grain. For example, among softwoods with average relative densities in the range of approximately 0.3–0.55, the tensile strength parallel to grain of air-dry woods is in the range of approximately 70–140 MN/m$^2$ (10 000–20 000 psi), perpendicular-to-grain tensile strength averages only about 3–8% as great. Compression strength parallel to grain of dry softwoods is in the range of 30–60 MN/m$^2$ (4000–9000 psi), perpendicular to grain only 8–25% of this value.

Strength properties for common species of cabinet wood are presented in *Table 2.1*.

### 2.5.3   Factors affecting the strength of wood

Besides the normal variability of strength among and within species, many other factors may affect the strength of wood. These factors may be broadly grouped into natural defects and irregularities, factors related to the environment and the effects of biological agents.

When the grain direction is not parallel to the long axis of a wooden component, it is said to be cross-grained (sometimes referred to as short-grained). Cross grain may occur from spiral grain in the tree or by the manner in which the timber is sawn. In linear furniture parts such as legs and spindles, whose performance depends on longitudinal properties such as bending resistance, cross grain may result in serious strength loss. A slope-of-grain of one in five, for example, may result in 50–60% reduction in the modulus of rupture. Knots in wood are another major weakening defect. Loss in strength results not only from the abnormal tissue and grain direction of the knot itself, but from the cross grain of wood distorted around the knot. Compression wood, the reaction wood formed in conifers as a result of crooked or leaning stems, is usually higher in density and compression strength than normal wood, but the wood is weaker in tensile strength and in both modulus of rupture and modulus of elasticity in bending. In hardwoods, tension wood is exceptionally weak in compression parallel to the grain though it may be stronger in tension and tougher than normal wood of the same density. It exhibits abnormally high longitudinal shrinkage and slightly increased tangential, but normal radial, shrinkage. The lignin content of the cell wall is deficient compared with normal wood and gelatinous fibres may be present.

As wood dries below the fibre saturation point, strength increases with the loss of bound water. The greatest increases are in compression along the grain: strength is approximately doubled when wood is dried to 12% moisture content, tripled when oven-dried. Modulus of rupture is increased much less, and modulus of elasticity is increased least upon drying. Strength of wood is also affected by temperature, increased as temperature is lowered, decreased as temperature is increased. Over the range and duration of naturally occurring temperature changes, strength changes are tempo-

rary. However, if exposed to higher than natural temperatures, or for prolonged periods, permanent loss of strength may result. Effects of heat in reducing strength are least in dry air, greatest in moist air or steam. The use of steaming to temporarily plasticize wood for permanent bending of furniture parts is well known. Strength of wood is also related to duration of loading. Time-related creep in wood reduces strength over long-term load periods. For example, a beam might carry a short-term (5 minutes) load three times as great as it could carry for a long term (a hundred years or longer).

The destructive effects of wood-inhabiting insects such as termites, carpenter ants and beetles need little elaboration, as the physical loss of wood will result in proportional loss of strength. Fungi are a major cause of deterioration in wood. In order for the threadlike hyphae of fungi to develop in wood, four major requirements are necessary: favourable temperature (70–85 °F is ideal), oxygen (20% or more air volume in the wood), moisture (fibre saturation point or above is ideal), and food. Wood-staining fungi utilize the residues of stored materials in parenchyma cells of sapwood but they do not attack cell walls. Therefore, although the staining fungi discolour the wood, they do not reduce its strength. However, the wood-destroying fungi utilize enzymes to break down and assimilate the cell wall substance, producing various forms of decay or rot. Initial stages of fungal invasion, termed incipient decay, may at first have insignificant effect on strength. Impact strength is the first strength property to be affected. If allowed to continue, total loss of strength may result. It should be noted that *Chlorociboria* both deposits a green stain in the wood and causes losses of strength. Controlling moisture is the principal approach to preventing decay. If wood is maintained below 20% moisture content, decay fungi cannot develop.

### 2.5.4   Role of wood strength in furniture

In furniture, strength of wood plays a critical role in various ways. Bending strength may determine the integrity of legs and stretchers in chairs and tables, the rails or posts of beds, or the planks of benches and leaves of tables. Hardness usually predicts how well surfaces resist indentation under practical use or abuse.

The strength of wood in compression perpendicular to the grain – in particular, the elastic strain limit – is important to the performance of joints such as mortise and tenon and dowel joints. Racking loads may concentrate excessive compression loads on mating parts of joints, but in addition, self-induced compression set resulting from restrained swelling under variable moisture conditions is a major cause of joint failure. In evaluating the failure of furniture, it is rare that components break in two; it is more common that objects seem to simply fall apart, indicating that the limiting strength was related to joints. In turn, the root of the failure might well be attributed to the manner in which the object or its joints were designed or fabricated, rather than to the strength properties of the wood *per se*. The nature and properties of various forms of furniture construction are discussed below and their deterioration and failure are discussed in Chapter 7.

## 2.6 Manufactured timber products

In addition to traditional forms of solid wood, mention must also be made of the many forms of manufactured wood products. These are based on veneers, on veneers combined with solid wood and on reconstituted wood particles, fibres, flakes and chips. A concise guide to these materials is given by Schniewind (1989). Their production and properties are discussed by Hoadley (1980) and more comprehensively reviewed in the United States Department of Agriculture *Handbook of Wood and Wood-based Materials* (Forest Products Laboratory, 1989). The use of these materials in the production of furniture is reviewed by Hanks (1981) and the chemistry of wood polymer composites is discussed by Meyer (1984). Deterioration of these materials in relation to their production and use in furniture is discussed by Klim (1990), who also reviews conservation treatment.

### 2.6.1 Veneers

Veneers, thin sheets of wood cut with the grain parallel to the surface, can vary in thickness, before use, from 0.25 mm up to about 6.4 mm. All decorative veneers produced in Europe are cut into 0.6–0.9 mm for face quality, average thickness 0.7 mm (1/40 in). In the United States

and Australia most veneers produced are cut 0.9 mm (1/28 in). They are produced by three basic methods, sawing, rotary peeling and slicing. Those of high value or striking appearance are used for surface decoration but veneers are also used structurally to make plywood boards and to make bent laminated and moulded shapes that could not otherwise be achieved in a single thick piece of wood without chemical modification. The original method of production by sawing has been replaced in all but a very few cases by knife cutting for commercial production. Logs intended for slicing are cut open and examined for figure, grain, texture and defects before cutting into suitable sections for veneer production. The halved, quartered, or flitched log sections are then usually steamed or soaked in hot water for one to several days before cutting. Logs intended for rotary peeling are treated in the round.

In rotary cutting, the log is held at either end in a large lathe and rotated against the knife, which is moved forward at each rotation to preserve the thickness of the cut. This method of cutting is specially suited for high volume production of large sheets of veneer used to make plywood. However, it is also used in one or other of its five basic variations to produce many freak figured decorative veneers, such as bird's eye maple, figured betula and masur birch, that cannot be extracted by any of the other cutting methods.

In slicing, a flitch of wood held in a frame is moved against a knife. Four different methods of cutting and mounting the flitch are used to extract the best figure. Veneer slices are kept in sequence during subsequent drying operations so that the sequence of a figure from one leaf to another is preserved. They are usually sold in this form as a flitch that may subsequently be broken up and sold in books or individual leaves or sheets.

Whether rotary peeling or slicing is used, the cutting action is essentially similar in both. As the knife separates the veneer from the flitch, the separated layer of wood is severely bent and stresses build up in the region near the knife edge. When these stresses exceed the strength of the wood, failure occurs resulting in a series of knife checks across the side of the veneer that was against the knife. This side of the veneer is called the loose side and the side away from the knife is called the tight side. By using a pressure bar to restrain the veneer as it is cut, it is possible to substantially reduce this problem and in some cases to eliminate it. The extent to which this is possible is determined by the species, by the thickness of cut, by the setting up of the machine and by the temperature of the wood. Diffuse porous hardwoods with well-distributed rays, such as birch, are more likely to yield tight veneers than ring porous hardwoods such as oak.

Holding a piece of veneer with one edge in each hand and flexing it will usually reveal tight and loose sides; veneers feel stiffer when flexed to close the checks and more limp when they are flexed open. If the veneer feels the same in both directions it is probably tight. Knife checks often show up months or years after the veneer has been laid, as parallel-to-grain cracks through the finish. Whenever possible therefore the tight side (also called the face side) should be laid face up and great care should be taken not to sand through it during finishing. A comprehensive review of all aspects of the preparation, selection and use of veneers is given by Lincoln (1984).

### 2.6.2 Plywood and related materials

Plywood consists of layers of thin veneers or plies glued together under huge pressure with the grain directions at right-angles in each successive layer. This allows the production of large sheets of dimensionally stable material in which most properties are approximately equalized across the surface with the strength of wood parallel to the grain predominating. Shrinkage and swelling are very small, being about 0.18% along the grain and 0.27% across it over the range of 7–20% moisture content (Joyce, 1970). Normally an uneven number of plies is used to give a balanced construction but even-numbered plywoods, in which the grain of the central pair of veneers is parallel, are made. Plywood is highly resistant to splitting parallel to the face grain but splits relatively easily in its thickness. Although cross-ply laminations of wood are known from antiquity, plywood made from thin veneers and used as a substitute for solid wood is essentially a modern material that owes much to the development of economical, moisture-resistant adhesives.

Where one outermost ply is of better quality than the other, the better-quality veneer is referred to as the face and the other as the back. Where they are of equal quality, both are referred to as faces. The central ply is referred to as the core and in plywoods with more than three plies those lying immediately beneath the face and back are referred to as cross bands or cross banding. Manufactured boards in which the central plies are replaced by particle board or wood core strips glued together side by side typically retain only the face veneer and cross banding, or less commonly the face veneer only. Examples illustrated in *Figure 2.22* include blockboard, in which the core strips may not exceed 25 mm, and laminboard, in which the strips must not exceed 7 mm wide.

Plywood is graded according to the strength and stiffness of the face veneers, the quality of the face veneers including the size and num-

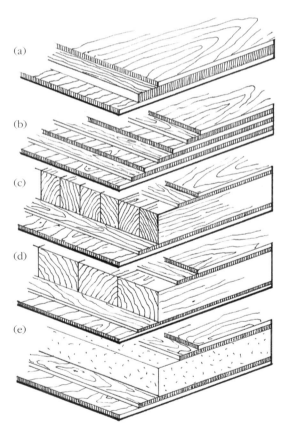

**Figure 2.22** Examples of manufactured board construction: (*a*) three ply (thicker veneer core); (*b*) multiply (seven-ply); (*c*) laminboard (veneered outer layers, laminated core); (*d*) blockboard (veneered outer layers, blocked core); (*e*) five ply particle board core

ber of defects and repairs, and the suitability of the material for interior or exterior use, or immersion in water etc. The precise form in which this is expressed differs between countries.

### 2.6.3  Reconstituted wood products

The desire to extend and modify natural wood sizes and properties and the need to use manufacturing waste and residues and smaller and lower grade trees to produce more versatile and more consistent products has lead to a vast array of materials known as wood composites or reconstituted wood products. Wood composites can be broadly grouped into fibre products on one hand and solid wood composites on the other.

Fibre products include cardboard or pasteboard, low density fibreboard and medium density fibreboard (MDF) and hardboards (e.g. Masonite). In this class of product, wood is broken down to its individual constituent wood cells or fibres and is then reformed to the desired shape with or without pressure by re-establishing chemical bonding of lignin between the fibres with little or no added resin binder.

In solid wood composites, often referred to as particle boards, particles, chips, flakes, shavings and other reduced dimensions of whole wood arc rc-bondcd using a resin adhesive. These materials are classified by particle type, by adhesive type, by density, and by strength. Uniform properties and reduced dimensional response are typical of these materials but increasingly they are being engineered for specific purposes. See Schniewind (1989) for further information.

### 2.7  Wooden structures

Furniture is generally expected to be functionally sound, fit for its intended purpose, good to look at, strong enough to withstand applied loads during a useful lifetime, able to accommodate fluctuations in environmental conditions, affordable and reasonably transportable. Except for a few turned or carved items, very few pieces of furniture are able to meet these criteria when formed from a single piece of wood. For example, the most beautiful cuts of wood are frequently the least stable, the least

strong and also the rarest and most expensive. They are often more effectively used as veneers. Wood is comparatively weak perpendicular to the grain in both tension and compression. Dimensional change is greater at right-angles to the grain than parallel to it. Hence, over the centuries a seemingly bewildering variety of methods of joining pieces of wood together has evolved in an attempt to optimize the production and performance of wooden structures. New and more complex forms of wood products are constantly being developed and with them new ways of joining pieces together.

It is necessary to understand something of the nature of joined wooden constructions if the conservator is to recognize and reduce potential dangers to wooden structures from use, display, transport etc. An overview of the main types of joints used in cabinetmaking is followed by a review of the critical factors that determine the success of any given joint with a more detailed analysis of some representative joints. This review is illustrative rather than exhaustive, dealing with basic considerations and leaving the reader to apply them to specific situations.

### 2.7.1  Types of joints

Any junction between two components or materials that are intended to stay together could be considered a joint. Joints may rely on adhesion (e.g. butt joints) or they may be mechanically interlocked (e.g. dovetail joints) or they may involve some form of mechanical fastening such as screws, nails or other more specialized hardware. Many specialized types of worked or interlocking joints have been developed for use in joining wood in cabinetmaking and these can be classified into three main groups: widening joints; angle or box joints; and framing joints.

Widening joints are used to produce wide boards from a number of narrow boards by joining them edge to edge. Examples of widening joints are shown in *Figure 2.23*.

Angle joints are generally used for fixing together pieces which have their faces at right-angles and edges flush. This includes corner angle joints used in box-like constructions such as solid cabinets, boxes and drawers and joints where one piece meets another, with the faces

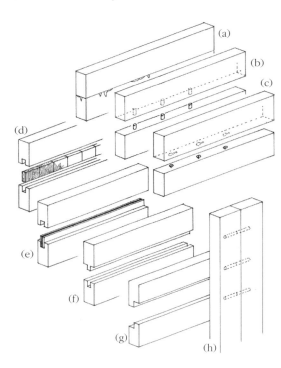

**Figure 2.23** Examples of widening joints: (*a*) rubbed joint; (*b*) short dowels; (*c*) slot screws; (*d*) tongue and groove (traditional cross-grained tongue); (*e*) loose tongue and groove (plywood tongue); (*f*) tongue and groove; (*g*) rebate; (*h*) long dowels

of the pieces at right-angles, but not at an end, as occurs for example with shelves and partitions in cupboards. Examples of angle joints, of which the dovetail is perhaps the most well known, are shown in *Figure 2.24.*

Framing joints are used in frame-like constructions such as chairs, tables, panelled doors and some picture frames. The members are usually jointed end to edge with their edges at right-angles and where the face sides of the members are usually flush. Examples, including the familiar mortise and tenon, are shown in *Figure 2.25.*

### 2.7.2  Critical success factors for joints

Whatever the type of joint under consideration, there are four crucial factors that determine success. These are, the nature of the stresses imposed on it and that it is designed to withstand, the grain direction of the joined parts, wood movement in response to moisture and the surface quality of the mating parts.

Although it is not usually important to be able to calculate loads precisely, it is essential to understand the types and relative sizes of loads that joints are able to support for furniture in use, in transit or in conservation treatments such as dismantling and cramping up. Most furniture is well designed for compression but trouble often arises from tension and racking (a racking load on a frame causes it to deform diagonally from a rectangle to a diamond shape).

The most difficult combination of grain to join is end to end. Although such a joint could easily support loads purely in compression, there is normally some bending as well. Many of the elaborate scarf joints designed by those who work with timber frames are designed to convert end-to-end grain combinations in joints to side-to-side combinations. End-grain to side-grain is a commonly encountered situation that works well for most loads except those of pure tension, when it tends to pull apart. In compression, this joint is usually limited by the strength across the grain of the side-grain member. In bending, either part may be the limiting factor. This type of joint is usually either made to be interlocking, as in the mortise and tenon, or reinforced by external members across the join. When adhesive-bonded, side-grain to side-grain joints can be as strong as the wood itself but when the grain of the two pieces is not parallel, complications arise in service as a result of moisture-induced dimensional change.

Dimensional change in response to changes in relative humidity can cause problems in joints when the response of the two members is different. This situation could arise because different timbers were used, or because of the difference in radial and tangential movement in two pieces that were cut differently but is most likely to cause serious problems when grain directions are at right-angles, such as a mortise and tenon jointing a chair leg to a seat rail (see *Figure 2.28*). This is particularly true if tangential and longitudinal cuts are opposed. Such joints are always apt to self-destruct no matter how firm they may be at first, and this is further discussed in Chapter 7.

Ideally, joints should have uniform dimensions, and regular, smooth, even surfaces that mate perfectly across 100% of their surface area so that applied loads are evenly distributed and unwanted movement in the joint is restricted. Deviation from this ideal may result in loads being unevenly distributed, stress concentrations arising, or movement that will lead to the destruction of glue lines, bearing surfaces and failure of the joint and the structure of which it is a part.

There are so many possible combinations of the above factors that may arise in different joints that only a few can be selected for further discussion.

### 2.7.3 Dovetail joints

The dovetail (*Figure 2.24*) is the strongest joint for joining pieces of wood together at right-angles in their thickness (side-grain to end-grain) and is widely used at corners for box, drawer and carcase construction. It consists of interlocking tails and pins that resist tension along the tail member but not along the pin member. In drawers, the joint is therefore oriented with the pins in the front and back of the drawer and the tails in the sides while in carcases the tails should be in the top to prevent the sides from moving outwards. The joint relies on the wedging action of pins and tails to hold it together in tension and on glue between side-grain to side-grain mating faces of tails and pins to hold it together. Therefore, the factors that affect both the strength and appearance of the joint are the number and size of the tails and pins and their slope. Provided that an adequate amount of wood remains across the narrow part of the tail, increasing the number of tails will increase the strength of the joint by providing an increased side-grain to side-grain gluing area. It is common to make the tails at their widest part about twice that of the pins but for the strongest work they can be equal. The slope or rake of the tails is a compromise, if it is too small the wedging-locking action will be lost but if too

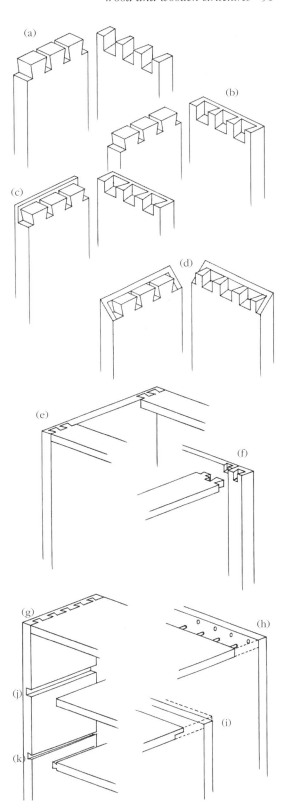

**Figure 2.24** Examples of angle joints: dovetail joints: (*a*) through dovetail; (*b*) lapped dovetail; (*c*) double lapped dovetail; (*d*) secret mitred dovetail. Joints used in carcases: (*e*) cross rails dovetailed into solid side; (*f*) cross rails dovetailed into framed side; (*g*) top dovetailed to side; (*h*) top dowelled to side; (*i*) top rebated; (*j*) housing; (*k*) tapered dovetail housing

great then a fragile component of end-grain will be introduced at the splayed tips of the tails that will also impair the side-grain integrity of the gluing surfaces. A slope of 1:5 or 1:6 for dovetails in carcase work, where appearance is of little consequence, is recommended whilst for show work such as drawer sides a slope of 1:7, and for very fine decorative dovetailing a slope of 1:8, has been suggested (Joyce, 1970).

### 2.7.4 Mortise and tenon joints

The classic, and a most successful, way of join-ing end-grain to side-grain, the mortise and tenon joint (*Figure 2.25*) can have hundreds of different variations. The mating parts can be rectangular (traditional mortise and tenon) or round (dowels). A well-made joint offers mechanical restraint in all directions except direct withdrawal of the tenon from the mor-tise and is therefore able to offer good resist-ance to compression, shear and racking. The basic joint can be improved in several ways. Providing a shoulder to the tenon gives addi-tional bearing surfaces on the outside of the mortise to share resistance to compression. Pegging the shoulder increases resistance to racking and greatly improves performance in tension (*Figure 2.25a*). Gluing will also improve performance in some respects partic-ularly by adding side-grain to side-grain shear resistance that will oppose rotation. A mortise and tenon joint functions like a cantilever beam, so increasing the height of the beam (normally the tenoned member) will reduce the axial stress on the joint for the same load on the beam (*Figure 2.25b*). For further ex-planation of this phenomenon see Hoadley (1980). Increasing the depth of insertion of the tenon will similarly provide an increased area for gluing. However, it will also increase the dimensional conflict caused by the opposing grain directions of the components. Arranging the grain direction so that the longitudinal grain of the tenon is matched to the radial grain of the mortise and the longitudinal grain of the mortise is matched to the radial grain of the tenon will give the best dimensional stabil-ity. Dividing the joint into multiple tenons will provide greater bonding surface and minimize dimensional restraint (*Figure 2.25c–e*). In some cases, such as carcase pinning, multiple tenons are preferable to a single wide joint (*Figure*

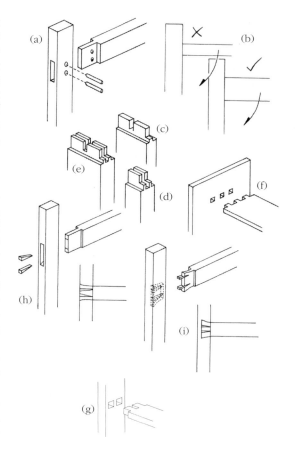

**Figure 2.25**   Examples of framing joints: mortise and tenons: (a) mortise and tenon pegged close to the shoulder of the joint; (b) increasing the height of the tenoned member will reduce the axial stress on the joint; (c) double tenon; (d) twin tenons; (e) twin double tenons; (f) carcase pinning using multiple tenons; (g) carcase pinning used on a drawer rail; (h) through-wedged mortise and tenon; (i) fox-wedged mortise and tenon

*2.25f,g*). Tenon depth more than compensates for the loss of width and the increase in tenon height and the number of side-grain to side-grain surfaces greatly increases the strength of the joint.

Wedged mortise and tenon joints are pri-marily intended to provide lateral pressure on glued surfaces and dovetail-style mechanical interlock (*Figure 2.25h,i*). They may also pro-vide an effective stress relief slot that helps to preserve the glue line during shrinkage of the tenon caused by compression set arising from moisture cycling.

### 2.7.5 Other joint types

Among other commonly encountered joint types the mitre and the dowel joint will be briefly mentioned here. Parallel side-grain to side-grain mitres make a very efficient corner joint. Mitre joints where the grain meets at right-angles, for example in picture frames, are attractive but present serious technical problems because of the difference in dimensional change along and across the grain. They are apt to open up if the moisture content change is large or the joint is wide (*Figure 2.26a,b*). Gluing is relatively ineffective because of the large end-grain component in the joint. Joint strength can be improved by introducing dowels or splines that increase side-grain to side-grain gluing surfaces (*Figure 2.26c,d*).

Dowels are widely used in joints for a variety of different purposes, as tenons, as pins and as gluing accessories to hold parts in alignment. Where dowels are used to modify end-grain to side-grain joints, a mortise and tenon joint is effectively created (*Figure 2.27*). In a joint with two dowels that is subjected to racking, one of the dowels carries a critical share of the load in tension and the remaining load is transferred as surface compression. Increasing the height of the end-grain member (e.g. a seat rail) allows the dowels to be spaced more widely, reducing the stress on the joint for a given load (Hoadley, 1980). Dowels need to be large enough to carry the tensile stress and deep enough to resist pulling out. They should also be able to carry and transfer the shear load parallel to the side-grain member of the joint.

Great care is needed when using dowels or splines as gluing accessories to help locate the components of a joint to avoid both loss of gluing area and restraint of normal movement. Dowels can be used to help align boards that are to be edged-joined (*Figure 2.23b*) provided that the dowels themselves are kept reasonably short and are not glued into their sockets. If they are glued in then the restraint to normal movement of the boards may cause the wood to fail at or near the glue joint. Loss of surface gluing area when using dowels for alignment is likely to be small. In contrast, when using traditional short crossgrained tongues (*Figure 2.24d*) the loss of gluing area may be substantial if the splines are used dry, whilst if they are glued in position and restrain movement of the timber, splits may result.

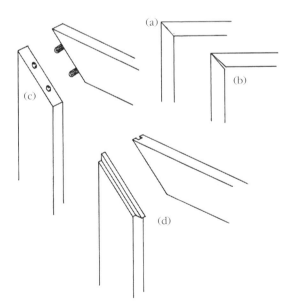

**Figure 2.26** Corner framing joints: (*a*) picture frame mitre; (*b*) picture frame mitre after shrinkage; (*c*) mitre reinforced with dowels; (*d*) mitre reinforced with a loose tongue or spline

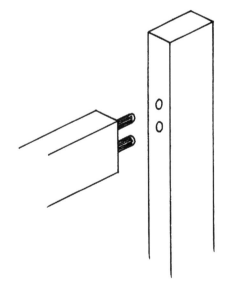

**Figure 2.27** Dowel joint. Although dowel joints date from the nineteenth century, pegs may be found in earlier furniture, for example in the eighteenth century spiral fluted urn illustrated in *Figure 10.6a*

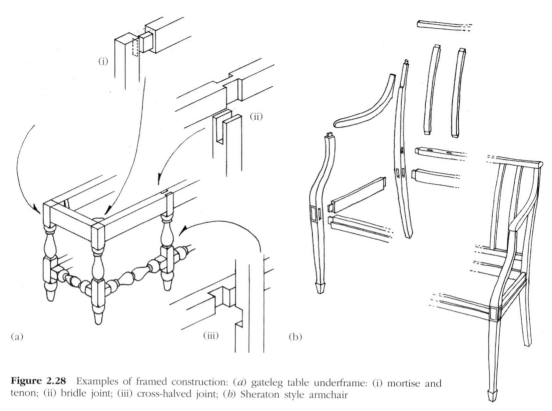

**Figure 2.28**  Examples of framed construction: (*a*) gateleg table underframe: (i) mortise and tenon; (ii) bridle joint; (iii) cross-halved joint; (*b*) Sheraton style armchair

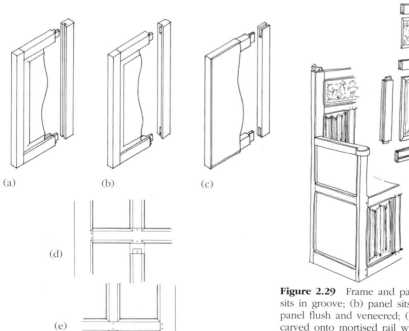

**Figure 2.29**  Frame and panel construction: (*a*) panel sits in groove; (*b*) panel sits in rebate; (*c*) frame and panel flush and veneered; (*d*) mason's mitre (mitre carved onto mortised rail whilst the shoulder of the tenoned stile is square), pegged; (*e*) true mitre (both stile and rail are mitred), pegged; (*f*) framing and panelling used to construct a mid-sixteenth century English box chair

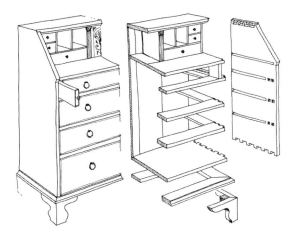

**Figure 2.30** Dovetails and associated joints used in an early nineteenth century mahogany bureau

The topic of joining wood is more exhaustively discussed by Hoadley (1980). Use of the joints described above in the construction of furniture is illustrated in *Figures 2.28–2.30*.

## Bibliography

Avella, T., Dechamps, R. and Bastil, M. (1988) Fluorescence study of 10,610 woody species from the Tervuren Collection, Belgium, *IAWA Bulletin*, 9 (4), 346–52

Barefoot, A.C. and Hawkins, F.W. (1982) *Identification of Modern and Tertiary Woods*, Oxford University Press

Baumeister, M. and Müller-Arnecke, S. (1989) Die Veränderung eines barocken Chorgestühldorsals aus der ehemaligen Kartause zu Mainz, *Zeitschrift für Kunsttechnologie und Konservierung*, 3 (2), 378–93

Blanchette, R.A. and Simpson, E. (1992a) Soft rot and wood pseudomorphs in an ancient coffin (700 BC) from Tumulus MM at Gordion, Turkey, *IAWA Bulletin*, 13 (2), 201–13

Blanchette, R.A., Wilmering, A. and Baumeister, M. (1992b) The use of green-stained wood caused by the fungus Chlorociboria in intarsia masterpieces from the 15th century, *Holzforschung*, 46, 225–32

Brachert, T. (ed.) (1986) *Beiträge zur Konstruktion und Restaurierung alter Möbel*, Callwey

Brazier, J.D and Franklin, G.L. (eds) (1961) *Identification of Hardwoods (A Microscope Key)*, Forest Products Research Bulletin No. 46, Forest Products Research Laboratory, Her Majesty's Stationery Office

British Standards Institution (1974) *Nomenclature of Commercial Timbers, including Sources of Supply,* BS 881 and BS 589, BSI

Butterfield, B.G. and Maylan, B.A. (1980) *Three Dimensional Structure of Wood*, Chapman and Hall

Core, H.A., Côté, W.A. and Day, A.C. (1979) *Wood Structure and Identification*, 2nd edn, Syracuse University Press

Chudnoff, M. (1984) *Tropical Timbers of the World*. Agricultural Handbook 607, US Department of Agriculture, Forest Service, Washington, DC

Corkhill, T. (1979) *A Glossary of Wood*, Stobart Davies

Cutler, D.F., Rudall, P.J., Gasson, P.E. and Gale, R.M.O. (1987) *Root Identification Manual of Trees and Shrubs*, Chapman and Hall

Desch, H.E. (1973) *Timber: Its Structure and Properties*, 5th edn. Macmillan, London

Détienne, P. and Jacquet, P. (1983*) Atlas d'Identification des Bois de L'Amazonie et des Regions Voisines*, Centre Technique Forestier Tropical, Nogent-Sur-Marne

Dyer, S.T. (1988) Wood fluorescence of indigenous South African trees, *IAWA Bulletin* 9 (1), 75–87

Espinoza De Pernia, N. and Miller, R.B. (1991) Adapting the IAWA list of microscopic features for hardwood identification to Delta, *IAWA Bulletin*, 12 (1), 34–50

Fahn, A., Werker, E. and Baas, P. (1986) *Wood Anatomy and Identification of Trees and Shrubs from Israel and Adjacent Regions*, The Israel Academy of Sciences and Humanities

Farmer, R.H. (1972) *Handbook of Hardwoods*, HMSO

Florian, M., Kronkright, D.P. and Norton, R.E. (1990) *The Conservation of Artefacts Made from Plant Materials*, The Getty Conservation Institute

Forest Products Laboratory, Forest Service, USDA (1989) *Handbook of Wood and Wood based Materials for Engineers, Architects, and Builders*, Hemisphere Publishing Corporation, NY (Contains complete text of Forest Products Laboratory (1987) *Wood Handbook; Wood as an Engineering Material*, Agriculture Handbook 72, US Department of Agriculture, Forest Service, Washington, DC)

Forman, B.M. (1988) *American Seating Furniture, 1630–1730*, The Winterthur Museum, W.W. Norton

Gill, K. (1990) Approaches in the treatment of twentieth century upholstered furniture, *Upholstery Conservation*, Preprints of a Symposium held at Colonial Williamsburg, East Kingston, pp. 305–17

Gill, K., Soultanian, J. and Wilmering, A. (1990) The conservation of the Seehof Furniture, *Metropolitan Museum Journal*, 25, 205

Gordon, J.E. (1976) *The New Science of Strong Materials: or Why You Don't Fall Through the Floor*, 2nd edn, Pelican, p. 41

Gordon, J.E. (1978) *Structures – Or Why Things Don't Fall Down*, Pelican

Gregory, M. (1980) Wood identification: an annotated bibliograpy, *IAWA Bulletin* (new series), 1 (1/2), 3-41

Grosser, D. (1977) *Die Hölzer Mitteleuropas*, Springer- Verlag

Hanks, D.A. (1981) *Innovative Furniture in America from 1800 to the Present*, Horizon Press

Hart, G. and Jay, B.A. (1971) *Microscopic Structure of Hardwoods with Terms Definitions and Drawings*, Teaching Aid No. 6, Timber Research and Development Association, High Wycombe, Bucks

Haygreen, J.G. and Bowyer, J.L. (1989) *Forest Products and Wood Science*, 2nd edn, Iowa State University Press

Hayward, C.H. (1970) *Antique or Fake?*, Evans

Henderson, F.Y. (ed.) (1960) *Identification of Hardwoods (A Lens Key)*, Forest Products Research Bulletin No. 25, Forest Products Research Laboratory, Her Majesty's Stationery Office

Henderson, F.Y. (1977) *Handbook of Softwoods*, Her Majesty's Stationery Office

Hinckley, F.L. (1960) *Directory of the Historic Cabinet Woods* [A complete guide to all hardwoods used in furniture making 1460–1900], Crown

Hoadley, R. Bruce (1980) *Understanding Wood: A Craftsman's Guide to Wood Technology*, The Taunton Press

Hoadley, R.B. (1990) *Identifying Wood: Accurate Results with Simple Tools*, The Taunton Press

Hoadley, R.B. (1991) Appendix A: Identification of Woods in the [Milwaukee/Layton] Furniture Collection, in *American Furniture with Related Decorative Arts, 1660–1839: The Milwaukee Art Museum and the Layton Art Collection*, Hudson Mills Press, pp. 273–81

International Association of Wood Anatomists (IAWA) (1964) *Multilingual Glossary of Terms used in Wood Anatomy*, International Association of Wood Anatomists

Jane, F.W. (1970) *The Structure of Wood*, 2nd edn, completely revised by K. Wilson and D.J.B. White, A. and C. Black

Jiaju, Y. and Fang, C. (1990) A computerized system for features image display and identification of woods from China, *IAWA Bulletin*, 11 (1), 105

Joyce, E. (1970) *The Technique of Furniture Making*, Batsford

Klim, S. (1990) Composite wood material in twentieth century furniture, *AIC Wooden Artifacts Group Conference Postprints*, Richmond, Virginia

Kollman, F. and Hockele, G. (1962) *Holz Roh-Werkst*, 20 (12), 461–73

Kribs, D.A. (1968) *Commercial Foreign Woods on the American Market*, Dover Publications

Kukachka, B.F. and Miller, R.B. (1980) A chemical spot-test for aluminium and its value in wood identification, *IAWA Bulletin*, 1 (3), 104–9

Kuroda, K. (1987) Hardwood identification using a micro computer and IAWA codes, *IAWA Bulletin*, 8 (1), 69–77

LaPasha, C.A. and Wheeler, E.A. (1987) A microcomputer based system for computer-aided wood identification, *IAWA Bulletin*, 8 (4), 347–54

Levitan, A. (1987) Conservation of furniture from Russia and Alaska, *CRM Bulletin*, 10, National Park Service, pp. 7–15

Lincoln, W.A. (1984) *The Complete Manual of Wood Veneering*, Stobart & Son

Lincoln, W.A. (1986) *World Woods in Colour*, Macmillan

Little, E.L. Jr (1980) *Checklist of United States Trees (Native and Naturalised)*, United States Department of Agriculture, Agriculture Handbook No. 541, US Government Printing Office, Washington, DC

Meyer, J.A. (1984) Wood–polymer materials, in R. Rowell (ed.), *The Chemistry of Solid Wood*, Advances in Chemistry Series, No. 207, American Chemical Society, Washington, DC, pp. 257–90

Miles, A. (1978) *Photomicrographs of World Woods*, Building Research Establishment, HMSO

Miller, R.B. (1980) Wood identification via computer, *IAWA Bulletin*, 1 (4), 154–60

Miller, R.B. and Baas, P. (Coordinators) (1981) Standard list of characters suitable for computerized hardwood identification, *IAWA Bulletin*, 2 (2–3), 99–145

Miller, R.B., Pearson, R.G. and Wheeler, E.A. (1987).

Creation of a large database with IAWA standard list characters, *IAWA Bulletin*, 8 (3), 219–35

Normand, D. (1972) *Manuel d'Identification des Bois Commerciaux*, vol. I, Centre Technique Forestier Tropical, Nogent-Sur-Marne

Odell, S. (1972) The identification of wood used in the construction of 17th and 18th century keyboard instruments, *Bulletin of American Group – IIC*, 12 (2), 58–61

Panshin, A.J. and deZeeuw, C. (1980) *Textbook of Wood Technology*, 4th edn, McGraw-Hill

Pendleton, M. and Warlock, P. (1990) Scanning electron microscope aided wood identification of a Bronze Age wooden diptych, *IAWA Bulletin*, 11 (3), 255–60

Phillips, E.W.J. (ed.) (1960) *Identification of Softwoods by their Microscopic Structure* (Forest Products Research Bulletin No. 22), Forest Products Research Laboratory, Her Majesty's Stationery Office

Rendle, B.J. (1969, 1970) *World Timbers:* Vol. I *Europe and Africa*; Vol. II *North and South America*; Vol. III *Asia and Australia & New Zealand*, University of Toronto Press

Rowell, R. (ed.) (1984) *The Chemistry of Solid Wood*, Advances in Chemistry Series, No. 207, American Chemical Society, Washington, DC

Rowell, R.M. and Barbour, R.J. (eds) (1990) *Archaeological Wood: Properties, Chemistry & Preservation*, Advances in Chemistry Series, No. 225, American Chemical Society, Washington, DC

Schniewind, A. (ed.) (1989) *Concise Encyclopaedia of Wood and Wood-based Materials*, Pergamon Press and The MIT Press

Schweingruber, F.H. (1978) *Microscopic Anatomy of Wood: Structural Variability of Stems and Twigs in Recent and Sub-fossil Woods from Central Europe*, Swiss Federal Institute of Forestry Research; Zurcher, Zug, Switzerland

Schweingruber, F.H. (1982) *Microskopicshe Holzanatomie* (Microscopic Wood Anatomy), F. Flück-Wirth

Schweingruber, F.H. (1990) *Anatomie Europaischer Holzer* (Anatomy of European Woods), Eidgenossische Forschungsanstalt fur Wald, Schnee und Landschaft, Birmensdorf (Hrsg.) Haupt

Skaar, C. (1984) Wood–water relationships, in R. Rowell (ed.), *The Chemistry of Solid Wood*, Advances in Chemistry Series, No. 207, American Chemical Society, Washington, DC, pp 127–74

Walter, F. (1980) *The Microtome*, 2nd edn, revised by W. Schmitt, Wetzlar

Walton, J.A. (1979) *Woodwork in Theory and Practice*, 6th edn, Australasian Publishing Co.

Wheeler, E.A. and Baas, P. (1998) Wood identification – a review, *IAWA Journal*, 19 (3), 241–64

Wheeler, E.A. and Pearson, R.G. (1985) A critical review of the IAWA standard list of characters formatted for the Ident. programs, *IAWA Bulletin*, 6 (2), 151–60

Wheeler, E.A., Baas, P. and Gasson, P.E. (1989) IAWA list of microscopic features for hardwood identification, *IAWA Bulletin*, 10 (3), 219–332

Wheeler, E.A., Pearson, R.G., LaPasha, C.A., Zack, T. and Hatley, W. (1986) *Computer-Aided Wood Identification*, Bulletin 474, The North Carolina Agricultural Research Service, NC State University

# 3

# Upholstery materials and structures

Although upholstery conservation is generally separate from furniture conservation, many objects that the furniture conservator has to deal with are upholstered. Frequently, liaison between furniture conservators and upholstery conservators is required. Understanding the nature and behaviour of upholstery materials and structures and their significance in a piece of furniture is a prerequisite to understanding the deterioration, care and conservation of upholstery presented in later chapters. It is the purpose of this chapter to provide basic information that will lead to better appreciation and care of upholstery and better liaison with other conservators.

It is outside the scope of this book to give details of upholstery technique. Indeed it would be counterproductive, as there are national and regional differences in style. The reader is advised to consult upholstery technique manuals appropriate to the type of furniture, e.g. French manuals for French or French Colonial furniture and period manuals where possible (see Bibliography).

The chapter begins with an introduction to the classification, terminology, historical development and technical examination of upholstery. This serves as a foundation for the systematic exploration of upholstery materials and structures that forms the bulk of the chapter.

## 3.1   Introduction to upholstery

In simple terms, the history of upholstery could be said to be the quest for comfort by an enlarging consumer market at decreasing cost. Innovations in upholstery techniques and materials have developed in response to the market. In modern times these advances have been communicated rapidly and widely, though this was not always so.

### 3.1.1   Classification and terminology

Upholstered furnishings can generally be placed in one of three groups:

(1)  Soft or loose furnishings such as bed curtains and cushions.
(2)  Adhered furnishings such as desktops and textile-covered carving.
(3)  Tight or fixed furnishings such as woven plant material and tacked down upholstery.

Some furniture, such as state beds, may include furnishings from all three groups. Those items in group 1 may be independently considered by a textile conservator but those in groups 2 and 3 will almost certainly require liaison between conservators of textiles, upholstery and furniture.

Group 3, fixed furnishings, includes the widest range of structures and may be further grouped into simple structures and complex structures. Simple structures include cane, rush, woven, web or splint, cordage techniques and shallow fixed upholstered slings or platforms (see *Figure 3.6*). Simple structures may be supplemented with cushions. Complex structures include multiple layered upholstery using mixed materials such as hardware, loose filling (stuffing) material and the materials which encapsulate the fills (stuffing) within the structure, a top covering and trimmings. Four main types of upholstery seat structures are simple dome, stitched edge, sprung and pre-formed (see *Figure 3.8*).

For purposes of clarity, upholstered structures are normally described sequentially from the frame to the top surface. The first layer on a frame may be a web, a base fabric or a combination of the two to form a continuous surface upon which the rest of the upholstery is built. The last layer on a frame is usually called the top cover or the show cover (including trim if used). The layers between the base and the top are called fills and filling covers.

There may be a single fill, or multiple fills. Where there are several fillings these are usually encapsulated by a fabric which separates one from another. For simplicity, the fills are numbered from the frame. The first layer above the base is called the first fill and the fabric which covers this is called the first fill cover. It is rare to find more than three types of filling layers on a single unit. The layers may be shaped by ties or stitching (*Figure 3.2*). The layers closest to the frame are the firmest (for shape) while those closest to the user are the softest (for comfort). The final filling layer, called a skimmer layer, may be very thin.

Each layer within an upholstered structure has a function. The material chosen to fulfil that function may be selected because it best meets the needs of the function, e.g. ability to take up or resist shape deformation, because the material is traditionally used in that position or for economic reasons. Any of these considerations may apply to a given structure. It is entirely possible that a seat may be made out of best quality materials throughout but in reality qualities within an upholstered structure usually vary. Quality may be related to the material type (for example linen would be a more stable and more expensive choice for a filling cover than a jute product) or to the weight of the material (for example, closely woven jute would be more expensive than loosely woven jute).

An awareness of the qualities of upholstery materials should be developed so that informed judgements can be made about what lies between a top covering and base layer in an upholstered structure. However, one should avoid making assumptions. For example, although in conventional upholstery from a particular period it is common to find cotton fabrics as a layer directly below top coverings, this has not always been so. It is therefore only after examination that the names of specific materials should be ascribed to each layer within the structure.

For the purpose of explanation, it is convenient to describe seat construction but the same techniques are employed for arms and backs. The differences are marginal, usually being of horizontal or vertical plane and of strength of materials. For example, a sprung back is constructed in a similar way to a sprung seat but the tacks, web, springs and twine may all be of a lighter quality because they do not bear the same loads as a seat.

### 3.1.2 Historical development

The sling seat is one of the simpler types and has been known since the beginning of upholstery in ancient times. It consists of a single layer of sturdy material such as leather stretched across and attached to a (usually wooden) framework by means of tacks or dome headed nails. This type of seat was used on folding chairs and stools and was usually provided with cushions for added comfort. Some sling style seats were quilted, an early form of layered upholstery. The seat and back of a late sixteenth century example in the collection of the Metropolitan Museum of Art, New York (41.100.321) (*Figure 3.1*) consists of a layer of leather and a layer of linen stitched together in a scale pattern in which the individual scales are padded out with hair stuffed through holes in the linen layer.

The first fixed upholstery types, that is upholstery which is attached to a rigid rather than a folding structure, are the simple dome and boxed edge types of the late sixteenth and early seventeenth centuries. These consist basically of pin, or boxed edge, cushions stuffed with one type of loose filling such as animal hair or down, attached to a wooden framework by means of tacks and dome-headed nails. Due to lack of structure across the base and sides of the upholstered seat, both of these simple types easily became misshapen during use. The introduction of narrow bands of coarsely woven linen or hemp stretched across, and tacked to, the seat base provided a sturdier foundation to take the weight of the sitter and the overlying layers of upholstery. Early attempts to maintain an even distribution of upholstery were achieved with a form of quilting (*Figure 3.1*), though deep structures were not possible using this technique.

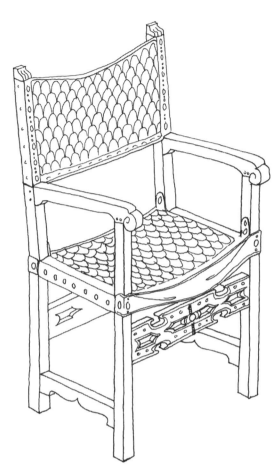

**Figure 3.1** A late sixteenth century folding armchair, Spanish, walnut, with quilted sling style seat (Metropolitan Museum of Art, New York, gift of George Blumenthal, 1942)

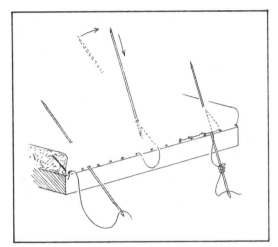

(a)

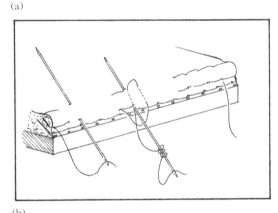

(b)

**Figure 3.2** (*a*) blind stitch, used to build the depth of an upholstered seat; (*b*) top stitch, shown here above a row of blind stitches, is used to bring the edge outwards and form the roll edge of an upholstered seat

Shallow tufting, an eighteenth century practice, served to hold fills in place as stitches went through all upholstery layers. These were sometimes purely functional and sometimes more decorative.

By the middle of the eighteenth century, upholstery structures were quite technically advanced and more complex than ever before. They consisted of multiple layers of fillings of different densities separated from each other and contained by various types of woven cloths. Full advantage could be taken of the different qualities of different fills. Denser, less resilient, fills were used near the base of the structure with less dense and more resilient fills closer to the top cover providing more comfort

for the sitter. An example can be seen in the wing chairs of the mid-eighteenth century (e.g. *Figure 1.17*). The rounded edges of the seat rail and inner wings were formed with densely packed straw or dried grass encased in narrow strips of linen and hemp cloth tacked under tension to form a firm roll-edge that did not distort during use or from the tension of the overlying layers (particularly leather). The well created in the middle of the seat and wings was fitted with a less dense filling for purposes of comfort. The loose filling was evenly distributed and held with very large stitching thread passed through a foundation of stretched linen and webbing, and then covered (including the roll edge) with a filling cover, held under tension to the frame with tacks. *Figure 3.9* shows some examples of loose filling materials.

The next development was the stitched edge, in which two basic types of stitches were used, blind stitch to build the depth of the seat and top stitch to bring the edge outwards and form the roll edge (see *Figure 3.2*). These stitches enabled the shape of the edge to be controlled during manufacture and maintained during use. By the late eighteenth or early nineteenth century all of these developments, and variations, were being used both alone and in combination with each other.

The major innovation in the nineteenth century was the use of coiled springs. Individual coil springs were used in groups on the seat frame. These were held together under compression on the webbed base with cords and stitching to form a unit. The sprung unit was used in combination with various stitched layered fills forming deep stuffed upholstery. In comparison to previous upholstery structures, the sprung seat was extremely comfortable (see *Figure 3.8c*).

Buttoning is a nineteenth century development, not to be confused with eighteenth century tufting. It consists of a textile covered deep filling laid onto a tensioned cloth base on the frame. The filling is compressed at regular intervals by stitching through all the upholstery layers and knotting off the thread under tension to buttons forming a pattern of deep stuffed padded pockets. An exaggerated version of this technique is known as deep buttoning.

By the twentieth century, technology made it possible to manufacture the upholstery for a chair in the form of a single preformed foam unit with variations in density created by cavities moulded into the foam (see *Figure 3.8d*). Spring units, rubberized webs and tension springs are all twentieth century developments of earlier upholstery structural components rather than true innovations but each has had an effect on furniture design. Essential reading on the historical development of upholstery is provided by Beard (1997), Clabburn (1990), Cooke (1987) and Montgomery (1984). For further information see also Desbrow (1951), Fowler and Cornforth (1986), Grier (1988), Holley (1981), Kirkham *et al.* (1987), Milnes (1983), Murphy (1966), Nylander (1990), Passeri (1988), Schoeser and Dejardin (1991), Schoeser and Rufey (1989), Thornton (1978) and Walton (1979).

### 3.1.3　Technical examination

Upholstered objects are multi-media pieces in which several trade techniques may be represented. The skills of examination are rarely embodied in one individual; successful collaboration between curators, upholsterers, conservation scientists and conservators of upholstery, textiles, furniture, leather and plastics is needed. A basic level of knowledge in each area of expertise would provide a sound vocabulary allowing for informed discussions with these specialists and an understanding of published material and research.

Simple analytical techniques include:

• Examination of fabrics and thread structures
• Microscopic examination to identify fibres, fillings and pigments
• Burning tests for fibre and plastic identification
• Wet chemical spot tests for identification of metals and leather tannins
• Solubility tests for identification of fibres and dyes
• Staining tests for the identification of fibres, dyes, dressings and adhesives.

More complex analytical techniques include:

• Thin layer chromatography to identify dyestuffs
• Gas chromatography to identify natural finishes and adhesives
• Infra red spectroscopy (including Fourier Transform Infra Red) to identify synthetic and semi-synthetic finishes, adhesives and fillings
• Energy dispersive X-radiography for the identification of metals in threads, finishes and hardware.

The application of these techniques to specific materials is further discussed below. Details of the techniques are provided by Sibilia (1996).

## 3.2　Top surface/simple structures

Top coverings may be loosely classified as fabrics, skins or plastics.

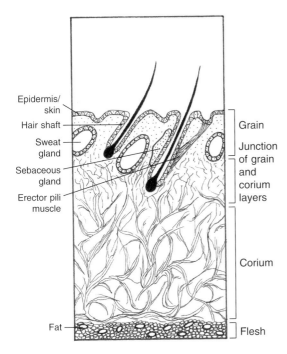

Epidermis/
skin

Hair shaft

Sweat
gland

Sebaceous
gland

Erector pili
muscle

Fat

Grain

Junction
of grain
and
corium
layers

Corium

Flesh

**Figure 3.3**  A cross-section of animal skin (cattle hide). Mammal skin has three layers: the epidermis or grain, the corium and the flesh. The epidermis contains the hair follicles, sebaceous and sweat glands. The corium is made up of a complex three dimensional network of fibre bundles. Once tanned, it is the corium layer that is responsible for the characteristic strength and tear resistance of leather. The flesh layer consists of subcutaneous membrane and fat cells and is usually removed before the leather is tanned

### 3.2.1  Leather/skin/parchment

Tanned, semi-tanned and raw hides and skins, with or without hair or wool from mammals (mostly from cattle sheep, goats and pigs), birds, fish and reptiles have been used as furnishings from ancient times. Consideration is given here to the nature of the raw material, the processes used to convert skin to leather, and the relation between structure, processing and properties. Methods of working leather and the uses to which it has been put are also briefly discussed and short sections on parchment, skins in the hair and sharkskin are included.

#### Skin

A cross-section through animal skin is shown in *Figure 3.3*. The central fibrous dermis or corium layer is composed of long fine fibrils of

the protein collagen, grouped together in units of between twenty and fifty to form fibres. The fibres are then further associated in bundles held together by reticular tissue. Fibre bundles interweave in a three-dimensional network that in all skins is larger and coarser towards the central thickness and finer and more compact in the layer close to the surface. Each animal type also shows characteristic variations in the pattern of the weave that markedly determine the properties of the leather made from it. The fibre structure also varies in different regions of the skin and in all skins there is a predominating direction in which the fibres run – aligned with the hair and the underlying muscle – that confers oriented properties of strength and elasticity on the skin and on leather prepared from it.

Rawhide is dried, untanned skin, usually a split cattle hide (see below) that, unlike tanned leather, will putrefy in warm moist environments. Its tendency to shrink on drying has been exploited to make drum seats.

#### Leather

The aim when producing leather from skin is to preserve the fibrous structure from which the principal characteristics of strength and flexibility arise and to modify the proteins in the skin to avoid decay in damp conditions.

Early methods of preparation involved cleaning and scraping the skin to remove flesh and hair followed by sun drying, smoking or salting. By the eleventh century AD, three principal methods – oil chamoising, alum tawing and vegetable tanning – had evolved and remained in use little altered until the nineteenth century. The term tanning is now used generally to describe conversion of skin to leather rather than in the more limited original sense of treatment with vegetable materials rich in tannin.

There is no exact definition for tanning but modern criteria relate to shrinkage temperature, microbiological stability, chemical stability and retention in the dry state of the fibrous structure to produce an opaque flexible material.

If raw collagen is heated in water a point is reached at which it transforms from a regular coiled structure to a disordered random coil. This is accompanied by sudden shrinkage and the point at which this occurs is called the shrinkage temperature. For raw collagen this occurs at about 65 °C. Introducing materials into the skin that form chemical cross links in the protein structure alters the temperature at which this change takes place. Oil tans and alum tawed skins have shrinkage temperatures in the range 50–63 °C, vegetable tans 75–85 °C and modern chrome tans 95–105 °C (pre-treatment of skin with alkalis reduces shrinkage temperature).

Removal of excess bound water and of water soluble plasma proteins (such as albumins and globulins that surround collagen fibres) from the skin already gives leather increased resistance to micro-organisms when compared to untanned skin. Ultimately, however, the increased resistance of leather to biological deterioration in comparison to skin is a reflection of the tanned product to resist enzymatic attack. Digestibility of collagen diminishes as tanning proceeds, with chrome tans being more effective than vegetable tans and vegetable tans more effective than alum tawing. Alum tawing, however, does increase resistance to enzyme attack.

Once tanned, it is important that the leather should remain tanned to prevent deterioration in normal use. It is important for example that the tanning agent is not readily washed out on contact with water. Chrome and vegetable tanned leathers are very resistant to removal of the tan but alum tawed leather readily reverts to the untanned condition on washing.

Removal of excess water from the spaces between the fibres during tanning can lead to the collapse of the fibre network and the production of a glassy, hard, inflexible, translucent material rather than the opaque, soft, and flexible result that is leather. To prevent this, materials introduced during tanning, either the tanning agent itself (as with vegetable tans) or other material such emulsified oil (as with chrome tans) must be introduced before the leather is allowed to dry out. This renders the fibres hydrophobic and permanently non-adhesive thereby preserving the fibre structure.

Early methods of chamoising with oils and fats would have lead to separation and dehydration of the fibres, providing them with a water-resistant film and producing flexible and tough leathers though these would count as only partially tanned. Use of alum alone led to a stiff and imperfect leather which was improved by addition of salt to the tan but still lacked some important qualities such as water resistance and which would therefore qualify

as a partial or pseudo tan. Alum tawing was often combined with treatments including egg, flour and oil to improve the result. Vegetable tanning, in which skins were immersed in successively stronger baths of vegetable matter (e.g. oak bark, oak galls, pomegranate rind or sumac) for periods of fifteen months or longer, produced a true tan.

### Structure processing and properties

While the chemical properties of a leather are indicative of the mechanism of tanning, the mechanical and physical properties of a leather are the result not only of the method of tanning but also of changes induced in the collagen during its preparation for tanning and of the subsequent lubricating and mechanical working of the tanned fibres. It is possible to produce leathers of quite markedly different structure and properties from skin of the same animal type by varying the degree of opening up of the fibre network and the angle at which the fibres interweave.

Pre-tanning processes, used to remove the epidermal layer and non-collagen proteins, lead to opening up of spaces between and within fibre bundles in the network. Mechanical manipulations such as pummelling (or chewing) can break down large fibre bundles into smaller units with more freedom of movement that will be reflected in greater flexibility of the final product. The angle of the fibres changes with the extent of swelling of the collagen and according to whether skin is under tension or not. By choosing the angle during tanning and the tension during drying the tanner can to some extent control the properties of the leather produced. In sole leathers for shoes, for example, large fibre bundles and a high angle of weave give a high degree of resistance to abrasion. In a flexible belting leather the large amount of splitting up of the fibre bundles gives greater flexibility. The lower angle allows the direction of pull to be more closely aligned with the long axis of the fibres giving increased tensile strength and reduced extensibility.

Post-tanning processing may be carried out to improve durability, mechanical properties or appearance. Sole leathers may be hammered or harness leathers stuffed with grease (curried) to improve durability. Leather may be oiled and/or worked, for example by rubbing it over a blunt metal blade or by pounding with wooden mallets, to soften it. Goat skins are folded, hair side in, and rubbed back and forth over a curved board causing them to develop the typical pebbly or grainy appearance of morocco leather. The original shagreen was made by trampling seeds into the surface of moist leather and shaking them out when dry. Thick hides may be split into two or more thickness and surfaces may be dyed or painted, sized waxed, or buffed to finish. In the United States, under rulings of the Federal Trade Commission, a split must be so marked and cannot be called 'genuine leather' or 'genuine cowhide' (Tanners Council of America, 1983).

### Methods of working and uses of leather

Numerous methods of working leather have been used, of which a few will be mentioned here. Apart from sewing and riveting used to assemble three-dimensional leather structures, leather has been fastened to rigid foundations using animal glue to cover boxes, coffers, caskets, sword hilts and scabbards or stretched across frames to produce litters, sedan chairs, coaches, wall panels, screens and chairs. Skins were prepared and applied to forms both in a wet and dry state by stitching, riveting or gluing. The marked ability of vegetable tanned leather to conform to a mould when wet and to remain permanently set on drying with moderate heat has been known as cuir bouilli since at least the fourteenth century and exploited for the production of a large variety of domestic and industrial objects. Leather for moulded objects has also been laminated, either alone or with canvas or paper. Decoration of leather has been achieved using lines impressed into the surface with hot metal tools and by modelling, cutting, punching, incising or bruising over a relief in wood, blind stamping and gold tooling. The practice of gilding all over was used for panelling and hangings but although gold leaf was sometimes used it is more common to find silver or tin foil adhered to the surface with shellac or white of egg and covered with yellow varnish (see *Figure 3.4* and *Figure 11.5*). Specialized tools were developed for stretching, cutting, skiving, finishing edges and joining and for creating decorative surfaces on leather (see Scholten, 1989).

Stretched leather was used for seats of chairs and stools in Egypt but its use for fixed uphol-

**Figure 3.4** Wallpaper and leather panels; crimson flock and embossed gilt leather, Dutch and/or English, *c.*1680

stery is not definitely known to be older than the mid-seventeenth century (Waterer in Taylor and Singer, 1956). Quilted leather is one of the earliest forms of layered upholstery (see *Figure 3.1*). Eighteenth century, down-filled cushion cases have been made from alum tawed leather and drum seats from rawhide.

'Spanish' leather was popular all over Europe in the sixteenth and seventeenth centuries for chair seats and backs, hangings, screens and many other purposes. French, Flemish, Spanish and Dutch leather were embossed using large wooden blocks cut in relief. Embossing was done after gilding but before painting or varnishing. Many seventeenth century examples of rooms panelled with this type of leather survive. Towards the end of the eighteenth century embossed leather was replaced, particularly for screens, by painted leather.

Leather and skins continue to be used in simple upholstery systems such as sling/platform or woven seats, backs or bed bases or as top covers in more complex systems. The materials are used on furniture for functional reasons. For example, a desk top where the pressure of writing is absorbed by the resilience of the skin, or as the cushioning material on castors, which can be renewed when worn. George Hepplewhite's *Cabinet Maker's and Upholsterer's Guide* of 1788 recommends leather as a covering for dining room furniture because of its resistance to food smells.

### Parchment

Parchment, made from the skins of calves, goats, lambs and sheep, differs from leather in that it is not tanned but prepared by a special drying process on a frame. All, or nearly all, grease is removed in the process giving a surface suitable for writing but in sheep the natural high grease content may lead to a partial oil tan. The finest parchment is made from the skins of very young animals, usually calves, and hence is called vellum (though definitions of parchment and vellum may vary from country to country). In a typical sequence of preparation, little changed in two thousand years, a well-washed skin is left in a bath of 30% slaked lime for 8–16 days depending on temperature, de-haired, limed again then washed and stretched. The quality depends on careful control of the drying process on the frame. The skin is dried at about 20 °C, washed with cold water, partly dried and washed again to give a smooth glue-like surface. At the same time it is scraped and shaved thin. This process gives an arrangement of collagen in lamellae more or less parallel to the surface in contrast to the interwoven structure of leather. After scraping the skin is rubbed smooth with pumice or other abrasive material and allowed to dry in its stretched state.

If subsequently wetted, the dermal network may revert to a random arrangement with the skin becoming hard, horny, transparent, cockled and shrunken. Components of the skin will hydrolyse and dissolve in hot water and advantage is taken of this in the preparation of parchment size for gilding. In furniture parchment has been used as a constituent material of elaborate trimmings or passementerie (see *Figure 16.14*) and occasionally for seat coverings and panelling, as seen in the Bugatti armchair in *Figure 3.5*.

### Skins 'in the hair'

This group includes furs and sheepskin. The subcutaneous side is very thoroughly scraped

**Figure 3.5** Armchair with painted parchment panels, 1895–1900, designed by Carlo Bugatti (1856–1940)

and dried to remove unwanted flesh that would putrefy and spoil the skin. After drying the skin is manipulated to soften the handling. Sometimes the skins are oil or alum dressed on the flesh side, for example Eames's 1946 Slink Skin seat illustrated in Miller (1990).

### Shark and ray skin

The skins of sharks and rays of the class Chondrichthyes have had various uses in furniture making and are often confused. Both types of skin are covered with raised horny 'pellicles' (dermal denticles). These contain osteodentin, a material resembling the dentin of teeth but having the mineralized tissue organized into a structure of tightly packed tubes. In shark skins these are quite small and sharp, and have made sharkskin useful as an abrasive for finishing woodwork. Ray skins, particularly the various stingray species of the family Dasyatidae, are covered with light coloured rounded polygons packed tightly together. These have been used to cover Japanese sword hilts with the pellicles left intact. In Europe, sting ray skins were ground down flat, and often dyed from the flesh side to produce a beautiful pearl-patterned material which was used to cover boxes and cases for high quality instruments. This 'shagreen' (also known as Galuchat after a French craftsman who excelled in its use) was used to cover furniture, particularly in French Art Deco style pieces such as those by Jacques Emile Ruhlman.

### Identification of leather and skin products

It may be possible to identify the type and maturity of the skin by examining various gross features including grain surface patterns and grouping and sizes of hair or feather follicles, or scale patterns (Haines 1981, 1985; Munn, 1989; Waterer, 1968). Also, different tanning and finishing techniques give leather its variety in appearance (Kühn, 1986). Under magnification, further identification can be made by examining cross-sections of the internal structure since skins vary in total thickness, in dimensions of fibre bundles, in weave patterns and in the ratios of grain to corium. Imitation leather such as polyvinyl-chloride can be identified macroscopically or in cross-section (Haines, 1981; Thorp, 1990). Methods of analysis are available to determine tanning method used, fat and

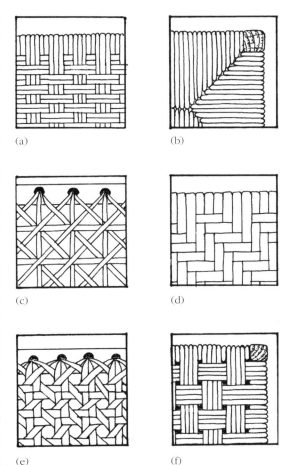

**Figure 3.6** Simple woven structures of rush/reed/cane: (*a*) binder cane; (*b*) rush; (*c*) 4-way cane; (*d*) spline; (*e*) 6-way cane; (*f*) cordage

moisture contents and acidity (Haines, 1985; Hallebeek, 1984; O'Flaherty *et al.*, 1965).

For further information on skins parchment and leathers see Calnan and Haines (1991), Fogle (1985), Reed (1972), Sharphouse (1983), Stambolov (1969), Thomas *et al.* (1983), Thomson (1981a, 1981b, 1985), Waterer (1968, 1972), and occasional papers published by the Leather Conservation Centre in the UK and by Leather Conservation News in the USA.

### 3.2.2   Simple structures – interworked materials (including rush and cane)

These materials are used in the production of simple upholstery systems which include flat woven or sling/platform seats which may be augmented by cushions. Woven plant materials include cordage, rush, wicker, rattan and splint (*Figure 3.6*). The weaves may be plain or decorative. The surface may be painted, gilt or the material may be stained before use.

Similar working techniques may be employed using animal material (leather, parchment/vellum and rawhide) or manufactured materials (textile and paper webs, rubber webs, PVC spaghetti or tube). Choice of materials may be due to vagaries of fashion or to local availability, for example skin may be employed in cordage techniques in desert areas with limited vegetation.

### Cordage

This term refers to materials which are spun and plied with a finished diameter of less than one inch. It may also be applied to materials that are plaited or knotted in construction. These materials have been used to produce seating and bedding since ancient times, as seen in surviving Egyptian furniture. Types of cordage include Sea Grass (Chinese sedge, family Cyperaceae, genus *Carex*) and Danish cord, a three-ply paper string popularized by the twentieth century Danish Modern high style. Danish cord is used on Wegner's 1950 Chair 24, and cellophane cordage is used on Ponti's 1957 side chair Superlegga 699. The cordage technique requires frames with a dowel rail type construction and the cord tends to be of the whip cord type, that is a closely twisted hard cord, resistant to stretching.

### Rush

The stem of the rush, an example of the monocotyledons referred to in Chapter 2, consists of cellulose micro-fibrils embedded in an amorphous matrix of hemicellulose, pectin and small amounts of protein. Rush has been used since ancient times in the middle east (4000 BC Egypt). Rush furnishings include products of the common bulrush (*Scirpus lacustrus*), marsh flag (*Juncus effusus*) and cattail (or reed *Typha latifolia*). Both fresh water and salt water ('Dutch') varieties are used. A paper product – fibre rush – is made in imitation of these materials and has been available since the First World War. In 1917, Marshall Lloyd developed a loom to weave fibre mesh in large sheets. This mechanization brought Lloyd Loom furniture into the marketplace. In this type of furniture, the fibre mesh is often sized and strengthened by a central wire.

Rush, as a commercial product, is harvested biannually in late summer/autumn. The harvested rush is normally dried and bunched into 'bolts' for transport, though some workers prefer to use the green product. A bolt is about 3 m tall, 100 cm in diameter and weighs about 2.5 kg. This amount is sufficient to seat about three side chairs. Before use, the dried rush is moistened, laid end (butt) to tip and twisted together to make an even coil for weaving. The technique, described in detail by Brown (1984) and Danssy (1979), requires frames of the dowel railed type, often with raised corner posts. There are regional differences in technique between the Anglo and Scandinavian traditions. A type peculiar to Normandy employs sedge with a corn overwrapping. Rush will keep but care must be taken to ensure good air circulation to prevent mould growth.

### Wicker

Wicker furnishings are made from the whole or split rods (osiers) of immature willow trees (genus *Salix*) grown in Northern Hemisphere wetlands. The basketry techniques used are described by Crampton (1972), Heseltine (1982) and Hodges (1976). The material is adaptable and can be made into a range of goods, from small containers to whole pieces of furniture including tables, chests, chairs and even settees, suitable for both indoor and outdoor use. Immature stems of willow contain the pith and only one or two layers of secondary xylem. The properties of the material and of the woven structure together mean that wicker furniture is light and flexes in use. The 'give' in wicker chairs provides great comfort to the sitter. This furniture has been produced since Classical times as documented by a Roman relief of AD 200 in the Treves Museum which illustrates a basket chair (Crampton, 1972). The osiers are cut during the winter at the end of a season's growth when they are about 2 m high. The bark is sometimes left on but is more often removed. The natural colour of the wicker under the bark is white but if the osiers are boiled before bark removal, the familiar buff coloured wicker results. The osiers are soaked before weaving. For further information on durability see Chapter 8.

### Rattan or cane

The cane that is used for chair seating is called rattan and comes from a form of climbing palm that is native to South East Asia. The material was introduced to Europe in the seventeenth century by trade and became popular for dining and bedroom weight furniture and for use in the damp atmospheres of conservatories and gardens. The material was perceived to be dust and pest free. Cane is the pared outer surface (inner bark) from the stem of several species of the genera *Calamus* and *Doemonorops*. It contains the epidermis and some of the cortex. The long, dense longitudinal fibres of this monocot stem are closely packed towards the epidermis giving a dense exterior with strength in the length and suppleness. Cane splits easily across its width. It is supplied in various sizes (1–6), which relate to the size of the holes through which the material is threaded in the frame. Suppliers' catalogues may grade the material in a variety of ways. For example, some British suppliers grade the product as 'red tie' (top quality), 'blue tie' (second quality) or 'white tie' (bleached), the 'tie' being literally the colour of the thread or tape used to tie up the hank. Different widths of cane have common names, for example common, medium, fine. However, suppliers are inconsistent about the widths to which these names are applied so some queries to the supplier are usually required or the catalogue should be used as an information source for an individual supplier. The terms used are not internationally transferable so local enquiries should be made. Cane may be washed, bleached or oil dressed during processing. It is resistant to colouring because of the silicaceous nature of its surface. The surface may need to be rubbed down with abrasive paper to provide a key for varnishing, painting or gilding to be successful. Spray painting with compressed air is advised. The materials may be dyed using reactive dyes in a bath or by sponge application (Florian *et al.*, 1990).

*Identification of cane, rush and wicker*  Cane, rush and wicker can be examined macroscopically, or in cross-sections as for wood identification (Florian *et al.*, 1990; Hoadley, 1990) and macerations can be made for examination of individual cell elements.

### Reed

Reed is a by-product of the cane industry, being the core (cortex and stele) which remains after cane is split. Its use in furniture making was developed by Wakefield, an American, in the 1850s and exploited in China and Northern Europe.

### Splints

Splints are strips of wood split from the tangential surfaces of green saplings, including white oak, hickory and ash. The strips are used to produce woven seats and backs in North American country furniture. The frames used are of the dowel railed type.

Further information on the interworked materials discussed above is given by Edwards (1954), Holdstock (1989), Johnson *et al.* (1990), Kirkham (1985), Miller and Widess (1986), Roubo (1988) and Walkling (1979). Another important furniture type, which utilized coiled straw, is discussed by Gilbert (1991).

### 3.2.3   Textiles

The term 'textile' refers specifically to a woven fabric, though in modern usage the term has wider application. Fabric is a general term used for any manufactured, woven or non-woven, cloth-like material made for use in clothing, hangings and coverings. The term textile is used here to refer to woven, non-woven and knitted structures made of any combination of spun or plied, cellulosic, proteinaceous, or synthetic fibres, or metal threads. The processes involved in textile production are many and varied depending on the desired end product. They include extraction of the fibre, dyeing and spinning into yarn followed by weaving, felting, or knitting to produce a textile structure. These structures may be dyed or further embellished with surface decoration such as embroidery, printing, stamping, or calendaring. The processes are briefly reviewed below. For definitions of textile terms see Burnham (1982) and Emery (1980). For a complete account of the making of a textile see Hodges (1976).

Textiles may be used as loose or fixed top coverings over upholstery structures and frames. Choice of material may depend on the status of the user, function of the object and availability of materials. The fibre, colouring, structure, finish and the width and pattern scale (that is, the height and width of the pattern relative to the fabric width) are all relevant to the appropriateness of a fabric to a period frame and should, where possible, be examined and recorded. For example, fibre type and weave structure may indicate the status and function of the seat furniture of which it is a part. In the past, luxurious textiles such as silk brocades, velvets and damasks, often embellished with gold and silver threads, embroidery and trimmings, were reserved for thrones, canopies and beds of state apartments. In comparison, woollen textiles (stamped being of a higher status than plain), linens and cottons were more commonplace and used, for example, to cover the outer backs of chairs or made into case covers. Leather or a cloth with the weft of horsehair was used for dining room furniture since it absorbed food smells less readily.

Factors such as dye type may indicate the date of manufacture. For example, the first man-made aniline dye was not introduced until 1856. The style of the textile design, scale of pattern and width of a textile may distinguish a dress fabric from a furnishing fabric and indicate provenance and date, since there were differences in style and loom widths between different countries and over time. Also, the height, width and scale of the textile relative to the width of the fabric may distinguish sixteenth-century, seventeenth-century and eighteenth-century textiles from nineteenth- or twentieth-century reproductions. This is possible since earlier patterns were rewoven on different looms without allowance being made for the different dimensions of the looms used. Consequently, most of the designs of later reproductions have become elongated in width and shortened in length. All of these factors are relevant in dating, assigning provenance and assessing the appropriateness of a textile in relation to the frame to which it is attached.

Knowledge of the chemical, physical and mechanical properties of fibres, textiles, structures and finishes is essential to assess their suitability for use, environmental response and interaction with other materials in the composite upholstered structure. These aspects of textiles are more fully discussed by Clabburn (1990), Landi (1992), Montgomery (1984), Nylander (1990), Schoeser and Rufey (1989) and Tímár-Balázsy and Eastop (1998).

### Fibres

Fibres for textiles are obtained from a wide variety of sources but are simply categorized as cellulosic (from plants), proteinaceous (from animals) and synthetic. There is considerable diversity in their chemistry, structure and properties but this can be addressed through a common vocabulary, of which it is useful for the conservator to be aware. Some general observations on the nature of textile fibres are followed by data for specific types, and this section concludes with some discussion of identification of textiles and fibres.

Fibre structures are made up of a mass of fibrils covered by a cuticle. For example, in wool the fibrils are contained in the central cortex and covered with a cuticle of scales (Landi, 1992). In silk they are parallel to the axis of the fibre. In cotton they are laid in spiralling layers round the lumen and similarly in flax in a different spiral form. Textile fibres are illustrated in Cook (1984). Regenerated and synthetic fibres vary depending on the processes used. Important mechanical properties of fibres include their strength, ability to stretch and recover (elasticity) and flexibility. These properties are affected by external factors such as relative humidity and temperature. For an explanation of fibre properties in relation to their structure see Gohl and Vilensky (1987) and Tímár-Balázsy and Eastop (1998).

*Cellulosic* or *ester cellulosic* fibres include cotton, linen, jute and hemp. Cotton is obtained from the seed hair of *Gossypium herbaceum* and *G. hursutuin* by ginning, a mechanical process used to remove plant waste from fibres. The average length of the fibres or 'staples' is 12–55 mm. Flax, the raw material of linen is obtained from bast stem fibres of *Linium usitatissimum*. The unidirectional fibres which have an average length of 150–1000 mm are loosened from the stems by retting, a process of rotting in water, and further processed by scutching to remove the outer bark. Other bast (flexible, fibrous bark) fibres are processed in similar fashion. Jute is obtained from bast stem fibres of *Corchorus capsularis* and hemp from bast stem fibres of *Cannabis sativa*. All these plant fibres are formed from long chain molecules of cellulose that are flexible and very strong.

Also included in this category are man-made regenerated celluloses, including viscose from wood pulp and cellulose acetate from cotton waste. Regenerated cellulose is formed through various chemical processes in which the cellulose is dissolved, reformed and extruded through fine spinarettes to form homogeneous filaments. The properties of regenerated celluloses and synthetics vary according to the manufacturing process used.

*Proteinaceous fibres* include wool, silk and horsehair. Wool includes the body hair of sheep and some other animals. Wool fibres range in length from 12.5 to 250 mm. After shearing or plucking from the animal, wool is washed and carded to clean, separate and align the fibres. Silk is a continuous filament that is extruded from the head of the silk worm (e.g. *Bombyx mori*) to form the protective cocoon at the stage of pupation. The cocoons are degummed to remove unwanted materials and loosen the filament so that it can be unwound. Horsehair is the body hair from the tails and manes of horses. All proteins consist of polypeptides which in turn are made up of amino acids. The type and formation of these in wool are partially responsible for its ability to stretch, and those in silk for its strength.

Many *synthetic* and *semi-synthetic* polymers have been used from the early part of the twentieth century to produce textile fibres. They include casein, rayon, nylon, polyester and polypropylene. Fibres may be used alone or may be combined, or blended, in a spun thread or in a textile structure.

*Spinning* Bundles of aligned fibres are drawn out to a uniform thickness and spun into a yarn by a process which involves twisting the fibres to bind them together. They may be twisted clockwise (S) or anticlockwise (Z). The higher the number of twists per unit length, the stronger the thread. Two or more threads may be plied together to increase strength. Generally speaking, threads that are 'S' spun will be 'Z' plied and vice versa.

### Dyes and dyeing

Dyes are organic materials used to impart colour to textile fibres. Textiles may be dyed in the yarn or in the piece. Dyes have four important properties:

(1) Intense colour.
(2) Solubility in aqueous solution (with a few exceptions), either permanently or during dyeing.
(3) The ability to be absorbed and retained by the fibre (substantivity) or to be chemically combined with it (reactivity).
(4) Fastness, that is the ability to withstand the treatments the fibre undergoes in manufacture and in use.

Until 1856 all dyes were of natural origin, mostly extracted from plants and a few from insects and shell fish. These dyes all belonged to a small number of groups of chemicals and the dyeing process was similar for all but a very few. All museum textiles made before about 1860 have been dyed with natural dyes but very few natural dyes remain in use in any quantity today. Synthetic dyes replaced them remarkably quickly because they were easier to apply, cheap, provided colours unobtainable with natural dyes and shades could be accurately matched from batch to batch. The early synthetic dyes were often of strident colours (mauves and purples) and had very poor light fastness. Subsequently synthetic dyes have been developed to provide an enormous range of colour and intensity for many different purposes – the Colour Index of the Society of Dyers and Colourists contains references to more than 6000 synthetic dyes marketed under 35 000 trade names (Society of Dyers and Colourists, 1971). The first synthetic dyes were applied to natural fibres but whole new classes of dyes have had to be made for use on regenerated and synthetic fibres. The dye chemist is able to modify the dye molecule to give the most satisfactory properties for any particular use.

Dyes are usually classified according to two different classification schemes. One scheme is based on their chemical constitution, the other on the basis of their dyeing properties. However, there is little relation between the two classifications. Azo dyes, for example, may be found among various classifications according to their dyeing properties. The various chemical groups are illustrated by Trotman (1984). Classification according to application, which is most important to the dyer, is as follows:

- Acid (usually on proteins and synthetics)
- Azoic (usually on celluloses)
- Basic/cationic (usually on acrylics)

- Direct (usually on celluloses and ester celluloses)
- Disperse (usually on synthetics especially polyester)
- Mordant/pre-metallized (usually on proteins)
- Reactive (used on most fibre types)
- Sulphur (usually on celluloses or ester celluloses)
- Vat (usually on cellulose)
- Optical brighteners (for most fibres; they include 'bluing' and fluorescent brighteners).

Some textile printing techniques employ dyes rather than inks on fabrics. The science of dyeing and the chemical technology of textile fibres is comprehensively discussed by Trotman (1984). The art and craft of natural dyeing are covered by Bemiss (1973) and by Liles (1990). The history of dyes is reviewed by Taylor and Singer (1956) and in a series of papers on the history of dyes published by the Paper Conservation Institute. Dyes may be identified by wet chemical means using solubility or liquid chromatography techniques (Schweppe, 1979).

### Textile structures

*Woven*  All woven structures are made of two sets of interlaced threads worked at right-angles to each other. Those parallel to the length of a cloth are known collectively as the warp and individually as ends. Those parallel to the width are known collectively as the weft and individually as picks. The warp threads are set up under tension on a loom and sometimes the warps are sized (e.g. with cornstarch or vegetable gum) to hold down loose fibres to aid in the weaving process (size is usually washed out after weaving). The weft thread is passed back and forth under and over one or more ends across part or all of the set of warps. The main types of woven structures are plain, twill, pattern, and pile.

*Plain* or *tabby* weave is the simplest structure. Each pick passes under alternate ends. *Tapestry weave* is a plain weft faced weave having weft threads of different colours worked over portions of the warp to form the design.

The weft of the *twill* weave is passed over two or more ends, the binding point being shifted sideways on each successive warp to form a diagonal effect. Variations on this theme include a herringbone pattern. *Satin* weave is similar to twill except that the weft is passed over five or more picks creating a smooth surface of floats. The binding point is spaced randomly to avoid a distinctive pattern forming, as is the case with twill. The floats on the face side reflect light while the reverse side does not. *Damask* combines the effects of twill and satin weaving to form a pattern in which the background is a form of twill and the pattern a form of satin weave. Another form of pattern weaving is when supplementary threads are introduced to create a pattern. When a supplementary weft is introduced into a ground weave for decorative effect, this is known as a *brocade* weave. When supplementary warp and weft threads are introduced into a ground weave for decorative effect, this is known as a *lampas* weave.

*Pile* woven fabrics are formed by a supplementary weft or warp whose ends or picks form a pile above the ground weave. The pile may be cut or uncut. The ground weave may be of any one of the three basic weaves. Examples of warp pile include velvets. Examples of weft piles include velveteen and velour.

Different effects are possible with the above weaves when yarns of different weights, colours and fibres, including metals, are used in combination.

*Non-woven*  The term non-woven is reserved for textile cloths, such as *felt*, which are formed by the matting together of loose fibres under pressure or heat or with the aid of adhesives.

*Knit*  Knitted structures consist of successive rows of continuous open loops worked by hand on two or more needles or on machines with one or more continuous threads. The two main structures, knit and purl, may be used in different combinations for different effects. Knitted structures have great elasticity.

### Surface decoration and finishing

Textiles may be embroidered (e.g. canvas work, or crewel work), decorated by painting or printing with coloured pigments or inks (e.g. chintz), stamped or embossed (e.g. watered and pressed pile fabrics), or calendared (e.g. polished cottons).

The surfaces of both woven and non-woven cloths may be embellished with embroidery and applied cloths. Embroidery, executed with needle and thread, may partially or totally cover the ground cloth. An example of partial covering is *crewel work*, in which a woven ground, often of satin weave linen, is embroidered with designs worked in lines and solid areas of coloured wools. *Canvas work* is worked on a plain, open and even weave canvas. Generally speaking, canvas work, usually executed in wool with silk highlights, completely covers the canvas ground. Sometimes a second woven cloth is cut to shape and attached to the surface of the ground weave by stitching or gluing, as in two types of work known as hands and faces and stumpwork.

Another form of surface decoration or finishing is created by applying pressure and/or heat to the textile cloth surface by means of heavy smooth-finished metal or wooden rollers. If the rollers are etched with a design, the raised area of the design flattens the threads in those areas. As a result, the light is reflected differently off the pressed and unpressed areas. Textile cloth, with a pile or non-pile surface, may be embellished this way. The effect is not unlike a damask weave in appearance. If the rollers are not etched, a different finish is achieved. Calendaring is formed in this way. The process renders a smooth, sometimes polished, surface – particularly if gum water is added to the surface. If the fabric, particularly warp-faced wool, is folded in half and then pressed together the imprint of one textile surface against the other produces a wavy effect often known as moire, moreen or watered (Montgomery, 1984).

*Finishes* Natural or synthetic materials may be applied to textiles for practical or aesthetic reasons. For example, starch may be added to give body to either a thread or a fabric and bleaches are used to remove undesirable colour. Textile finishes include bleaching, weighting (with metal salts), stiffening (with starch or other adhesive), dressing/filling, flame retardants, water repellents, antistatic treatments, anti-bio-predation, anti-shrink. Other examples of materials used for finishing and details of the processes involved are given in Grier (1988), Montgomery (1984) and Tímár-Balázsy and Eastop (1998).

### Identification of textiles and fibres

Textile fibres from upholstery or embroidered panels, and fibres from leather-covered furniture, paper decorations, papier mâché and cardboard furniture can be examined under low power magnification for their structure and pattern, or microscopically for composition and origin. A 10× lens with a scale, for example, is useful in examining and counting the warp and weft threads, and for examining their condition (Adrosko, 1990; Emery, 1980). Upholstery conservators use a hand-lens, or binocular microscope in examining the nail pattern, and textile fragments of upholstery on the furniture, in order to discriminate original from later interventions (Francis, 1990; Howlett, 1990).

Fibres can be examined longitudinally and in cross-section to determine their composition and possibly their origin. For example, longitudinal sections of wool in good condition show characteristic scales covering the central cortex. On degraded wool fibres the scales may be worn away. Cotton fibres are twisted with frequent changes in direction. In transverse section, a cotton fibre is a collapsed hollow tube. Flax shows bundles of polygonal cells. Procedures are described by the American Association of Textile Chemists and Colourists (Weaver, 1984; Farnfield *et al.* (1985) and by Tímár-Balázsy and Eastop (1998). Excellent descriptions are also given by Appleyard (1978), Howlett (1990), King (1985) and Catling and Grayson (1982). Fibres can also be examined for additives and finishes. Techniques for sample preparation are mentioned by Annis *et al.* (1992a, 1992b), Farnfield *et al.* (1985), Florian *et al.* (1990), King (1985), Weaver (1984) and Tímár-Balázsy and Eastop (1998). The type of microscope required for fibre identification is similar to that needed for wood identification (McCrone, 1987; Weaver, 1984). A polarized light microscope with bright field and dark field illumination is recommended. A hot-stage for observing melting points of synthetic fibres is useful (Farnfield *et al.*, 1985). Cross-sections can be cut by hand or on a microtome; good results have been obtained by Annis *et al.* (1992b) with a plate style microtome. Excellent results have also been achieved by embedding the fibre sample in a resin block before cutting the cross section (Rogerson, 1997).

Fibres can be identified using simple methods such as burning tests and wet chemical tests (Burnham, 1982; Emery, 1980; Roff and Scott, 1971; Tímár-Balázsy and Eastop, 1998). For example, when held over a naked flame, protein fibres will curl away from the flame and will produce a smell of burning hair, rendering a black brittle ash. Cellulosic fibres smell of burnt paper and render a soft grey ash when burned.

Textiles can be examined by eye or under low magnifications to determine their spun structure (twist/ply), weight (thread count) and technique (weave, knit) This serves as an aid to identification of a particular textile and as a guide to what may need to be considered in treatment. Sophisticated methods like X-ray diffraction, or pyrolysis gas chromatography, can be useful in further identification of textiles or textile blends (Farnfield *et al.*, 1985; Hardin and Wang, 1989). DNA mapping may prove to be invaluable in analyses of organic material (Pääbo, 1993}.

Some finishes, such as calendaring, are physical and may be detected by visual examination alone under low magnification. Chemical finishes may be detected by various wet chemical tests. The Beilstein test may be used as a simple means of screening organic and polymeric materials for the presence of chlorine (CCI, 1988a). The diphenylamine spot test can be used for cellulose nitrate (CCI, 1988b) and the amido black test for protein dressings (Martin, 1977). Further tests are described by Champion (1987), Martin (1977) and Tímár-Balázsy (1998).

### 3.2.4   Synthetic polymers and plastics

Plastics occur in upholstered furniture in many different guises. These include structural usage in frames or 'shells', support systems and filling materials, fittings and fastenings such as hook and loop fasteners and zips, and as seat covering materials. They are also widely used in the form of paints and coatings on frames, and as adhesives, fabric coatings, printing inks and dressings.

Synthetics are materials made artificially by chemical reaction. These usually consist of a polymer plus additives. Polymers of styrene, vinyl chloride and methyl methacrylate have been known since the nineteenth century,

polyester since 1936, polyurethane since 1937. Additives are used for a wide range of different purposes. Reinforcing agents, for example in fibre or rubber crumb, are used to increase strength. Fillers are used to extend the polymer to decrease cost, plasticizers to increase flexibility, and pigments or dyes to identify a density or disguise a tendency to discolour. Blowing agents are used to create foams. Stabilizers (antioxidants), flame retardants and many other additives may also be used.

Chlorinated fluorocarbons (CFCs) were previously extensively used as blowing agents but since 1989, 'environmentally friendly' flame retardant upholstery foams have been available. These carry a blue/grey four-dove logo and omit ozone-depleting CFCs.

A good introduction to plastics and rubbers is provided by Blank (1990). The uses of plastics in furniture and the developments in upholstery that have occurred as a result of the introduction of these materials are discussed by Buttery (1976), Gill and Eastop (2001), James (1990), Kovaly (1970), McDonald (1981), Tímár-Balázsy and Eastop (1998) and Wilson and Balfour (1990). Further information is given in Chapter 4.

### *Polystyrene*
Polystyrene is a thermoplastic, rigid, inexpensive hydrocarbon polymer, formed by the polymerization of styrene. It was used for upholstery shells from 1935. It was also used for 'Sacco', the 1960s bean bag chair by Gatti, Paolini and Teodora for the furniture manufacturer Zanotta, each Sacco chair contains twelve million polystyrene beads expanded under pressure (Sparke, 1986).

### *Polyester urethane and polyether urethane*
Polyester urethane and polyether urethane are synthetics produced by the reaction between a hydroxyl rich material (polyether or polyester) with polyisocyanates (usually diisocyanate). The material produced may be thermoplastic or thermosetting. Various grades of material are produced, ranging from the rigid to the flexible. Although in commercial production for furnishings since 1943, polyether urethane had a poor reputation due to inconsistency in early production, though it was favoured by modern furniture designers during the 1960s and 1970s

(Gill and Eastop, 2001). 'Throwaway', designed by Landel for the manufacturer Zanotta in 1967, was the first piece of upholstered furniture that had no separate supporting frame (Sparke, 1986). Polyester urethane has largely replaced polyether urethane since the 1960s in the production of upholstered furniture, especially for the production of foam backed fabrics.

### Rubber

The rubber hydrocarbon is synthesized by a wide range of plants, most of which are found in wet tropical areas. Three important botanical families cultivated for the product are the Apocynaceae, Artocarpaceae and Euphorbiaceae. The material was first introduced to Europe in 1735 but was not much exploited until the nineteenth century. The natural thermoplasticity of rubber is overcome by a process called vulcanization. Vulcanization, the modification of rubber latex by sulphur and heat, is used to improve the resilience and strength of rubber and to produce a hard rubber product by producing sulphide links between rubber molecules (see Blank, 1989). The process was discovered in 1839 by Goodyear and patented in 1843 by Hancock and in 1844 by Goodyear. In 1929 the Dunlop Rubber Co. patented latex foam – 'sponge rubber'. Shortages caused by supply difficulties during the Second World War increased research, leading to synthetic latex developed by Pirelli and others. The properties of rubber are reviewed by Roff and Scott (1971).

### Identification of polymer systems

Accurate identification of materials may help to differentiate an early production of a furniture model from a recent production. Plastics are not easy to identify with certainty by visual inspection alone and simple tests (e.g. Mossman, 1988; Nuttgens, 1999) although useful are not always completely reliable or may require burning or heating of objects. Techniques such as Fourier Transform Infra Red spectroscopy (see Shearer, 1989) require expensive equipment and trained staff. However, more reliable and simplified tests are being developed in response to the needs of the plastics industries (Mucci, 1997). Further information on the identification of these materials is given in Chapter 4.

### 3.2.5 Coated fabrics and 'leather cloths'

#### Oil cloths

In Europe, from the fourteenth century, oil cloths were made in imitation of leather and came to be used for upholstery. The cloth was made by applying coatings of a filling, typically a paste of china clay or lithopone in thickened linseed oil, to one side of a suitable cloth base, typically unbleached, plain woven cotton or linen. Several applications of these materials would be required to produce the finished cloth, which was allowed to dry at moderate temperature between applications. The better qualities of cloth were rubbed down between coatings, dusted with chalk and calendared. The results were variously known as American cloth, wax cloth, toile cire and Lancaster cloth.

#### Rubber cloths

Textiles, commonly unbleached plain weave cottons coated with rubber, were used to produce inflatable cushions from 1813 and waterbeds from 1832. The material was exploited for its waterproof properties in clothing (e.g. the Macintosh) and carriage work. However, it was hard and inflexible during cold weather, soft and sticky in hot weather – two disadvantages which led to its being superseded, first by superior forms of rubber and later by synthetic materials such as those based on cellulose nitrate.

#### Cellulose nitrate

Introduced in the 1850s, most cellulose nitrate imitation leathers are essentially combinations of castor oil and cellulose nitrate with colouring added (Thorp, 1990). Much in use until the 1950s for carriage work, prams and motor cars, where waterproof or leather-like qualities were

**Figure 3.7** An early example of textile trimmings from a bed valance, English, *c.*1675

desired, it was superseded by polyvinyl chloride fabrics.

### Polyvinyl chloride (PVC)

PVC has been in commercial production since 1928. It is thermoplastic, low cost, flame resistant (due to chloride content) and, in the presence of a plasticizer, rigid but flexible. It replaced earlier coated fabrics as it had less tendency to crack. The coating can be laid on woven fabrics or knits, which have more stretch and are better for buttoned or curved work. The coated surface can be printed, textured by embossing or flocked to resemble suede.

### 3.2.6   Trimmings

Trimmings are known by names which vary by country, shape, function, scale and materials type. However, they are best described simply as: flat tapes and braids; cords, including piping and welts; fringes; tassels (parts known as mold and skirt); tufts, including buttons and rosettes; metal trims (includes decorative nails, mouldings, bosses).

Materials and techniques found in trimmings are diverse and may be used singly or in combination (*Figure 3.7*). Lustrous threads may be worked over metal wire, wood moulds or skin bases. Metal threads, glass beads and gelatine sequins may be included. Top covering materials may be worked around lead mouldings with integral nails bent to shape and tapped into position (Todd, 1993). Top covering materials may also be used over cord to form piping or welting. Button moulds may be covered in the same way.

Techniques employed include weaving, braiding, needle lace, bobbin lace, crochet, knotting, knitting and embroidery, including appliqué and cut work. Since ancient times textile trimmings and metal fasteners have been used for decorative effect on furniture. Trimmings were at the height of opulent development in the seventeenth century, particularly in France where they are called passementerie. These very elaborate and costly trimmings often completely concealed the furniture framework. The perfected hand-executed techniques of the seventeenth century have been copied in the following centuries but the huge costs of intensive labour required in hand finishing these items has led to subsequent designs being simplified. In the eighteenth century, tastes were simpler and flat braids and dome headed nails predominated to compliment elaborately carved furniture or the clean lines of neo-classical furnishing. In the nineteenth century, industrial developments made elaborate textile trimmings widely available as some processes were mechanized. The resulting loss of status of elaborate trims led to a decline in their popularity.

Trimmings have evolved partly for practical reasons, for example a fringe formed of knotted off warps which prevents a textile from unravelling. Trimmings have been used to conceal details of construction such as seams, raw edges, and tack lines; to hold back curtains or hangings; to secure loose fillings in buttoned or tufted seats, cushions or mattresses; and as fastenings joining one piece to another such as corners of valances or table covers. Trimmings may be attached to furniture by adhesives, stitching, or with metal fasteners.

Trimmings are also used to accentuate the lines of furniture or room hangings. Cord or decorative nails may be used to draw the eye or simply to embellish and enrich appearance. In the seventeenth century, nails were often of several sizes and might be clustered to decorative effect. In the eighteenth century close nailing was used in multiple or shaped lines within the depth of a rail.

For further information on trimmings see Clabburn (1990), Cooke (1987), Fowler and Cornforth (1986), Huette (1972), Musée des Arts Décoratifs (1973).

### 3.3   Hardware

Hand-forged, stamped and machine-cut iron tacks, pins, wire nails, staples and other hardware such as clips, hooks, clamps, braces, snaps and zips are used to attach layers of upholstery, and support systems to frames (see James, 1990; Jobe, 1987).

Eighteenth-century tacks have hand-forged iron shanks and hammered heads sometimes referred to as 'rose head'. However, this term is also used to describe some machine-made types and should therefore be avoided as confusing. By the late eighteenth century the process had developed further – shanks were machine-cut but the heads were still hammered by hand. It was not until the early nineteenth century that the heads were machine-stamped. Today upholstery tacks are generally blued cut steel and of two types, fine and improved, the latter being slightly heavier with a larger head. They have a small spur of metal used for temporary tacking and can be used with a magnetic tack hammer. Professional upholsterers commonly kept sterilized tacks in the mouth, from where they could be quickly and easily spat onto the magnetic head, temporarily placed and then driven home with the hammer head, thus keeping one hand free to hold material. Clout tacks have burred shanks to increase the anchor into the wood.

Gimp pins are small thin nails, enamelled or lacquered in a range of colours, that are used to attach gimp braid, fringes and exposed backs of outer covers. They were known in the late eighteenth century as copper pin nails (Diderot, 1771). Today they are generally of fine cut steel. Small wire nails have been used for the same purpose.

Since mechanization in the closing years of the eighteenth century, tacks have become plentiful and comparatively cheap. More are therefore used in so-called traditional upholstery as currently practised than were used in pre-industrial age furniture and this may cause more damage to the frame. It is a common misconception that traditional upholstery (using hand-built industrial age upholstery techniques) is more authentic and less damaging to the frame than modern application techniques.

Staples properly delivered from electric or pneumatic guns probably cause less stress to the frame than tacks hammered in by hand, though the staple is used by most manufacturers of commercial furniture for reasons of economy. Also, modern techniques usually involve the application of a complete pre-formed unit which only requires the application of a single row of metal fasteners to secure it to the frame. This contrasts with hand-built techniques where each separate layer of the multi-layered structure is attached to the frame with a separate row of metal fasteners.

Metal fasteners are available in a variety of sizes, gauges and metals. Standard sizes of wire from which commercially available fasteners are derived conform to certain recognized gauges (e.g. Birmingham Wire Gauge), but this differs internationally (e.g. metric, Imperial, USA). Some are plated either for decorative

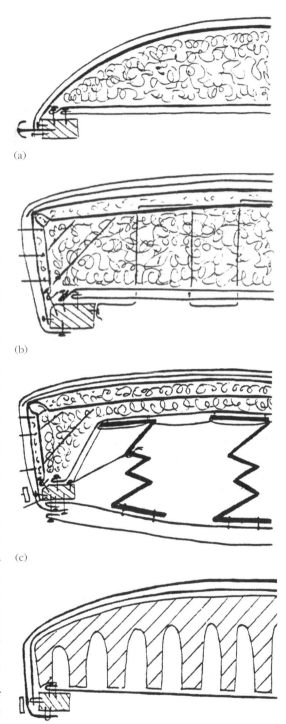

(a)

(b)

(c)

(d)

**Figure 3.8** Examples of different types of upholstery structures: (*a*) simple dome; (*b*) stitched edge; (*c*) sprung; (*d*) pre-formed foam

purposes or to increase their resistance to corrosion. Generally speaking, the larger tacks and staples are used to hold webbing, the smallest and finest to hold the top cover. Metals include iron, steel and copper alloys. Close examination of tacks and nails may indicate the type of manufacturing process (see Bradley Smith, 1966; Neilson, 1968). Features to look for include tapered and non-tapered shanks, uniform sizes and shapes, surface burrs and striations, gripper die marks and metal type. These features may indicate techniques of manufacture and may suggest a date. For example, uniform sizes with flashes may suggest casting whilst identical features may indicate machine manufacture. For additional information on nails see Bodley (1983). Identification of metals is discussed in Chapter 5.

## 3.4   Understructures

Understructures include the support system of webs, springs and fills. The understructure has several functions. It provides comfort for the sitter, it takes the weight of the sitter, it enhances the design through the lines of the frame, it prevents loose covers from slipping off and it holds the shape of the object while in use. Examples of different structures are illustrated in *Figure 3.8*. Fills are shown in *Figure 3.9*. These features, and springs, are also beautifully illustrated in James (1990).

Individual materials and upholstery structures have to withstand heavy wear over long periods of time. The higher the grade the more durable the product. In top-grade work, materials of the highest quality would be used. These include, for example, curled hair, linen cloth and webbing of flax, cotton, jute and hemp. Attention would also be paid to detail (historical correctness in profile and fabric, trim, seam construction etc.). Such work will last well but can involve much hand work. In low-grade work, materials would be of lower quality and might include coir fibre, Algerian fibre and, in particular, foamed plastics, jute cloth, textile waste, adhesives and poor quality staples. Such work will not stand up to heavy use. Lower-grade work may involve use of preformed units requiring less skill to fit. Many commercial mass-produced pieces are of poor quality – but not all. The main concern for such pieces is to look good from the outside; long-term durability is not a major concern.

There follows a survey of the most commonly extant materials and structures, however, if a material was locally available, economically viable and practical, it may have been used in upholstery. Pine needles, thistledown, leaves, bracken and chaff have all been used but are less resilient and therefore less likely to survive than more resilient materials such as curled hair.

### 3.4.1   Fillings

Fillings may be loose, prepared, sprung, or elastomeric (see *Figure 3.9*). Loose fillings are supplied as an amorphous mass which requires encasing between layers of other materials, for example cloth stretched over the fill and tacked to the frame. They may require to be teased into position and stitched to take and retain the desired shape. Prepared fillings have already been given a form, either by machine or by hand. They may consist of one or more layers ready for use, requiring only to be cut and attached to the frame. The selection of fillings is guided by price, comfort and durability. These in turn are influenced by factors such as density, resilience, ease of use and the amount of training required to use them properly.

The quality of filling is often judged and graded by its resilience, that is, its ability to recover its size and shape after deformation, especially after compression. Loose fillings require skill and judgement in handling and are therefore expensive to use. Prepared fillings have an economic advantage over loose fillings in that they may be cut to size and less skill is required to use the materials, both in judging quantities and in applications.

A common characteristic of loose fillings is that they are highly compressed for shipping and transportation. Therefore, they require opening out before use. This may be a manual or mechanical process. Different terminology is used for different grades of filling in different countries and there is no agreed international standard.

***Animal materials***
*Curled hair* is the highest quality filling as it maintains good resilience over long periods.

**Figure 3.9** Examples of upholstery fill materials: (*a*) curled hair; (*b*) coir fibre; (*c*) retted Spanish moss; (*d*) ulva marina; (*e*) tow; (*f*) pre-moulded cavity foam

Horse hair, obtained from the mane and the tail, is the highest grade, since it is the longest, strongest, and most resilient. Lower grades are shorter and more brittle. The curl is permanently set by boiling or steaming tightly twisted hair ropes. Curled hair is used for first and second fillings and skimmer layers.

*Feathers* are light, horny epidermal outgrowths and down is the soft under feather. Before using as a filling, feathers are sometimes chopped into smaller pieces or curled to give them more resilience. Feathers from live birds are preferred but most now come from dead birds reared for meat production. Eider duck down is especially valued because of its high resilience and high warmth to weight ratio.

The Drapers Dictionary of 1882 mentions that 'shoddy' (recycled shredded wool cloth) was used as a stuffing for saddles or furniture. An example of *wool* used as a secondary filling is cited in *Housecraft* of 1926: 'The filling is preferably of hair, covered "topped out" with raw wool thick enough to cover the wooden edges well.'

### Vegetable materials

These can be categorized as: seed fibres (cotton, vegetable downs); stem or stalk fibres (e.g. straw), Bast Fibres (e.g. flax, hemp, jute); leaf fibres (pine wool, tampico, esparto grass, raffia, corn shucks); fruit fibres (coir); other vegetable materials (wood, sea wrack, latex). They can also be categorized according to their suitability for first fillings, second fillings, skimmer layers and roll edges.

*Coir*, the fibre, obtained from the outer husk of the coconut (*Cocus nucifera*), was introduced to Britain around 1845. It forms a solid, densely packed filling and is a less expensive but less resilient substitute for curled hair. To obtain coir, the husk is split, retted and then beaten to loosen the fibres which are dried for use. Retting involves leaving stems to rot in water to separate the fibrous from the non fibrous parts of the plant.

*Spanish moss* (*Tilandia usneoides*) is an epiphyte, a member of the Bromiliaceae family, from the southern United States of America and from Central America. It is available in several grades though not much used today, perhaps because of environmental threats to its survival. The black variety, which is retted longer and ginned more thoroughly, is of better quality than the grey (Bast, 1946). Spanish moss is inferior to top grade hair, but superior to short hair.

*Tow* is a byproduct of the manufacture of bast fibres, during scutching or hackling, a process of beating to separate fibres from plant waste (Bast, 1946). It is a dense filling but has poor resilience.

*Algerian fibre* is obtained from the leaves of palm grass (*Chamareops humilis*) which

grows in Northern Africa and Southern Spain. The leaves are shredded and curled in a manner similar to hair. It is imported as rope and unwound at a fibre processing plant. The green fibre may be dyed black to achieve sterilization (probably because of the increase in temperature during dyeing). It is coarser than hair and best suited as a first filling. It has good resilience over a long period.

*Ulva marina* is a type of seaweed processed by washing and drying. It is a coarse filling with very poor resistance and durability. Webster's *Encyclopaedia of Domestic Economy* of 1845 says of seaweed: 'Well spoken of as a stuffing for mattresses; does not harbour vermin ... is tolerably light and soft ... If not sufficiently washed is said to attract moisture, owing to a little salt remaining in it.'

The following loose fillings are softer and less resilient than the filling materials described hitherto. Therefore, in better quality work they are only used for second fillings or cushion stuffing, though they may occur elsewhere in poor quality upholstery.

*Kapok*, a seed fibre of the Ceiba tree (Bombacaceae – *Ceiba pentandra*) is the most important but not the only source of this material. It is processed by ginning. The Drapers Dictionary of 1882 comments that 'kapok is employed to a limited degree in upholstery ... used for stuffing chairs and pillows'.

*Cotton* fillings are a byproduct of the manufacturing process of separating cotton seeds from cotton fibre. The short cotton linters, still attached to the seeds, are removed and formed into cotton felt. The earliest date for cotton wadding observed in upholstered furniture is around 1850.

*Straw* and *dried grasses* pack down hard and are most suited as a linear filling for roll edges, see Howlett (1990).

The identification of vegetable fillings is discussed by Catling and Grayson (1982).

### Elastomers, synthetic materials and latex

Elastomers include materials such as natural or synthetic rubber that are able to resume their original length after stretching. Rubber was the first such material used in furniture production but has been much replaced by synthetic materials. Synthetic loose fillings include spaghetti and chip cut foams, foam crumb, cut and curled nylon monofilament and polystyrene beads.

The ability of elastomers to be moulded was a real asset in the development of mass seating. In conventional upholstery the ability to match profiles of one seat to many others required very skilled, and therefore expensive, work. Preformed seating requires far less, and less skilled, labour but costs may still run high since the production of large runs of one type of seat are required to off-set the cost of mould production.

***Sheet ('slab stock') and moulded materials***
The selection of fillings is guided by factors such as price, comfort and durability that are in turn are influenced by density, resilience and ease of use. The production of upholstered furniture using synthetic or latex sheet or loose material still requires substantial manual labour. Various densities of the materials are cut, shaped and assembled (commonly with adhesives and staples) to form comfortable yet durable surfaces. For example, a shaped front edge of reconstituted crumb foam might be combined with a seat deck of firm sheet foam and a cushion of soft spaghetti cut foam. This is well illustrated in James (1990).

***Foams*** Foams are available in sheets, of varying densities and qualities for hand-building, made by one or other of the following methods.

*Bonded chip foam* or *reconstituted* foam is formed from off-cuts of foam crumbed and mixed into a new batch of foam to form a very high density mix for heavy use. The foam chip/crumb acts like gravel in a concrete mix or grog in a ceramic mix. Pre-shaped moulded forms are manufactured. Walls of high density chip foam may be used to enclose softer foams. The purpose of walling is to retain shape in the same way that a stitched or rolled edge would in conventional upholstery. Chip foam is difficult to cut thinly as it tends to break up.

*Cavity foams* are sheet materials containing moulded cavities. They come in a variety of depths but must be walled in with sheet material. They are often glued 'back to back' to create cushions.

*Pincore foam* is sheet material perforated with holes. Various thicknesses and densities are available. This material does not need to be walled in. In practice the sheet materials may be glued together, with adhesive applied by brush or spray, or textiles may be stuck to them for tacking to frames. Textiles may be used to encase the materials to protect them from exposure to light or handling.

*Rubberized fillings* are sheets of pre-carded loose filling which have been sprayed with latex milk and vulcanized. They may also be packed in moulds.

*Needled fillings* are sheets of pre-carded loose fillings which have been pushed into a textile ground by a machine containing barbed needles.

Sheet fibre such as *cotton flock* and *polyester*, are used as skimmer layers, second fillings and cushion filling. The material may be loose, bound, or come with a skin of adhesive, for example, polyester wadding with a skin of PVA adhesive.

Machine-made roll edges are tubes of textile containing loose jute fibre or paper fillings. Rolls are also available in moulded rubberized fill and chip foam.

Understructures and support systems are discussed by Davies (1982), Farnfield *et al.* (1985), Himmelfarb (1957), James (1990), Ossut (1996), Stenberg and Akervall (1989).

## 3.5 Support systems

Support systems include the materials and structures situated on the frame to take the direct load of the overlaying upholstery unit and the sitter. The main support systems are webbing and springs – for example, compression springs and tension springs working directly with the frame.

### 3.5.1 Webbing

Webbing comes in various widths, usually between 50 mm and 150 mm. It may be made from natural materials such as linen, jute or cotton or from synthetic materials such as reinforced rubber (from *c.*1950) or polypropylene. Metal webs in 15 mm and 18 mm widths with perforations for nails are also found. Webbing material comes in a variety of weaves, including plain and twill variations. Webbing is used in various arrangements as the foundation of the upholstery structure or edges. Webbing arrangement may be termed close woven, French webbed, open woven, or English webbed. Such nationalist terms are misleading and should be avoided in documentation since both arrangements are used world-wide.

### 3.5.2  Springs

Various types, shapes, gauges and sizes of wire springs are available, providing differing degrees of resilience and suitability for use in different locations in furniture. The three major types of springs are compression, tension and arc. Compression springs were patented in Vienna in 1822, and in England in 1828. They are available in double cone, single cone, barrel and drum shapes. Tension springs were introduced into the UK by W. Knoll around 1930. Arc springs are variously known as sinuous, serpentine and zigzag (*c*.1930). Webster and Parkes (1845) describe coil springs as 'elastic iron wire', being used extensively for easy chairs and seats of various kinds. Loose springs are manually built by the upholsterer into units or supplied preformed in strips or units.

### 3.5.3  Fabrics and twines used as part of the structure

Various textile cloths are used in upholstery structures. The different weaves, weights, fibres and dressings are relevant to the durability and stability of the structure. Choice may be governed by function, local availability or economics.

Bast fibre cloths including linen, jute and hemp are used to sandwich and contain loose fillings. Linen and hemp have been used since ancient times. Jute, commonly known as burlap in the USA and as hessian in the UK, was first introduced into Britain from India in 1830–32 (Bally, 1956). In 1833 successful attempts to spin and harvest that year increased the demand for jute cloth. The Crimean War (1854) gave a further boost to the industry because Russia cut flax export. In 1857 steam power driven looms and spinning machinery were introduced into Calcutta, expanding the availability of the textile world-wide and rapidly replacing coarse linen cloths. Jute was treated with an emulsion of whale oil and water but the Scottish whaling fleet collapsed during the 1914–1918 war. By 1957 the

Scottish industry could no longer compete. Jute is cheaper and superior to linen for its purpose since it does not stretch as much and therefore does not sag as quickly. Hemp is more durable than jute and coarser and stronger than linen.

Cotton cloths are used as covers under the top cover (muslin/calico layers). Since the nineteenth century, deep dyed cottons were commonly used under the seat rail, a practice referred to as bottoming. Over time, the use of dressed cotton largely replaced leather and dressed or closely woven linen cases for feather and down. Cotton may be expected from the late nineteenth century and polyester cotton from the mid-twentieth century as cheaper and more easily maintained alternatives to leather. The process of dressing (using starch paste and other materials) was used to add body, to give a decorative finish, to give a water-resistant finish, or to cover small imperfections in the weave thus reducing the ingress of dust and light and the escape of feathers.

Threads, twines and cords of various weights are used to make up the stitched edges of the upholstery structures (*Figure 3.2*). Spring twine, as the name implies, is used to stitch springs to the webbing foundation. Laid cord, used to tie down springs, is resistant to stretch to maintain compression of the springs. Stitching twine is used to anchor the loose fill to the webbing foundation. A finer waxed thread is sometimes used for stitching corners.

## 3.6  Adhesives

Adhesives may occur in upholstered objects as a means of fixing one layer of the upholstery structure to another (in use of slab stock elastomeric materials for example); as a means fixing a material to a substrate (silk fabric to carved wood on a bed cornice or leather to a desk top for example) or to attach trimmings. They may also be found as dressings (to dust-proof a ticking material or to stiffen a buckram for example); as a finish to a cut raw edge of a fabric, to stop the weave unravelling; or used to set an embroidery, where they are applied to the back to prevent distortion caused by stitch tensions.

Glues derived from animal proteins include gelatine, skin glue (rabbit, scotch), fish glues, isinglass and casein. Vegetable-based glues include polysaccharide gums such as gum arabic or acacia gum, and vegetable mucilages such as starch. Synthetic glues include cellulose derivatives, hot melt polyamides and rubber cements. These materials may be applied by brush, gun or spray. For further details see Masschelein-Kleiner (1985) and Chapter 4.

# Bibliography

Adrosko, R.J. (1990) Identifying late 19th century upholstery fabrics, in *Upholstery Conservation* (Preprints of a Symposium held at Colonial Williamsburg, 2–4 February 1990), American Conservation Consortium Ltd, Kingston, New Hampshire, pp. 103–35

Annis, P.A., Quigley, T.W and Kyllo, K.E. (1992a) Useful techniques in textile microscopy, *Textile Chemist and Colorist*, 24, 19–22

Annis, P.A., Quigley, T.W and Kyllo, K.E. (1992b) Hand techniques for cross-sectioning fibers and yarns, *Textile Chemist and Colorist*, 24, 78–82

Appleyard, H.M. (1978) *Guide to the Identification of Animal Fibers*, 2nd edn, WIRA, Leeds

Bally, W. (1956) *Ciba Review* No. 116, Book X, August/September 1956

Bast, H. (1946) *The New Essentials of Upholstery*, The Bruce Publishing Co., Milwaukee

Beard, G. (1997) *Upholsterers and Interior Furnishing in England, 1530–1840*, Yale University Press, London and New York

Bemiss, E. (1973) *The Dyer's Companion*, 3rd edn, Dover

Blank, S. (1989) Rubber in museums: a conservation problem, in *AICCM Bulletin*, 14 (3/4), 53–93

Blank, S. (1990) An introduction to plastics and rubbers in collections, *Studies in Conservation*, 35, 2

Bodley, H. (1983) *Nailmaking*, Shire Album No. 87

Bradley Smith, H.R. (1966) Chronological development of nails: blacksmiths and farriers tools at Shelburne Museum, *Museum*, Pamphlet Series 7, Shelburne Museum, USA

Brown, M. (1984) *Cane and Rush Seating*, Batsford

Burnham, D.K. (1982) *Warp and Weft: A Dictionary of Textile Terms*, Scribners

Buttery, D.N. (1976) *Plastics in Furniture*, Applied Science Publishers

Calnan, C.N. and Haines, E.B. (eds) (1991) *Leather: Its Composition and Changes With Time*, UKIC

Catling, D. and Grayson, J. (1982) *Identification of Vegetable Fibres*, Chapman and Hall

CCI (1988a) The Beilstein test, *CCI Notes* 17/1, Canadian Conservation Institute, Ottawa

CCI (1988b) The diphenylamine spot test for cellulose nitrate in museum objects, *CCI Notes* 17/2, Canadian Conservation Institute, Ottawa

Champion, D. (1987) Tests for adhesives and dressings in laboratory practicals, unpublished notes compiled by The Textile Conservation Centre, Hampton Court Palace

Clabburn, P. (1990) *The National Trust Book of Furnishing Textiles*, Viking/National Trust, London

Cook, J.G. (1984) *Handbook of Textile Fibres*, Merrow

Cooke, E.S. Jr (ed.) (1987*) Upholstery in America and Europe from the Seventeenth Century to World War 1*, W.W. Norton

Crampton, C. (1972) *Canework*, Dryad

Danssy, M. (1979) *Antiques – Professional Secrets for the Amateur*, Book Club Associates

Davies, M. (1982) *Tailored Loose Covers*, Stanley Paul

Desbrow, R. (1951) Latex foam in furniture design and manufacture, *Rubber Developments*, 3

Diderot, D. and D'Alembert, J. (1959) *A Diderot Pictorial Encyclopedia of Trades and Industry*, edited and introduced by C.C. Gillespie, Dover (originally published as *Recueil de planches*, 11 Volumes, Paris, Briasson et al. 1762–72)

Edwards, R. (1954) Caning, *The Dictionary of English Furniture*, Country Life Ltd.

Emery, I. (1980) *The Primary Structure of Fabrics*, The Textile Museum, Washington, DC

Farnfield, C.A. *et al.* (1985) *The Identification of Textile Materials*, 7th edn, The Textile Institute, Manchester

Florian, M-L.E., Kronkright, D.P. and Norton, R.E. (1990) *The Conservation of Artefacts Made From Plant Materials*, The Getty Conservation Institute

Fogle, S. (ed.) (1985) Recent advances in leather conservation: proceedings of a refresher course sponsored by FAIC, June 1984; editor Sonja Foyle; assistant editors Toby Raphael and Katherine Singles; hosted by National Park Service, Division of Conservation, Harpers Ferry, West Virginia. Foundation of the American Institute for Conservation of Historic and Artistic Works.

Fowler, J. and Cornforth, J. (1986) *English Decoration in the Eighteenth Century*, Barrie and Jenkins

Francis, K. (1990) Fiber and fabric remains on upholstery tacks and frames: identification, interpretation and preservation of textile evidence, *Upholstery Conservation*, Preprints of a Symposium held at Colonial Williamsburg, 2–4 February 1990, American Conservation Consortium Ltd, Kingston, New Hampshire, pp. 63–5

Gilbert, C. (1991) *English Vernacular Furniture, 1750–1900*, Yale

Gill, K. and Eastop, D. (2001) *Upholstery Conservation: Principles and Practice*, Butterworth-Heinemann

Gohl, E.P.G. and Vilensky, L.D. (1987) *Textile Science: An Explanation of Fibre Properties*, Longman

Grier, K.C. (1988) *Culture and Comfort: People, Parlors, and Upholstery, 1850–1930*, The Strong Museum, Rochester, NY in association with the University of Massachusetts Press

Haines, B.M. (1981) *The Fibre Structure of Leather*, Leather Conservation Centre, Northampton

Haines, B.M. (undated) *Leather Under the Microscope*, Leather Conservation Centre, Northampton

Haines, B.M. (1985) Identification of leather, in S. Fogle (ed.), *Recent Advances in Leather Conservation*, AIC, Washington, DC

Hallebeek, P. (1984) Examination techniques for leather: documentation and analysis, in S. Fogle (ed.), *Recent Advances in Leather Conservation*, AIC, Washington, DC

Hardin, I.R., and Wang, X.Q. (1989) The use of pyrolysis-gas chromatography in textiles as an identification method, *Textile Chemist and Colorist*, 21, 29–32

Heseltine, A. (1982) *Baskets and Basket Making*, Shire Album No. 92

Himmelfarb, D. (1957) *The Technology of Cordage Fibers and Rope*, Textile Publishers Inc. and Leonard Hill

Hoadley, R.B. (1990) *Identifying Wood – Accurate Results with Simple Tools*, Taunton Press

Hodges, H. (1976) *Artifacts*, Baker

Holdstock, R. (1989) *Seat Weaving in Rush, Cane and Cord*, The Guild of Master Craftsmen

Holley, D. (1981) Upholstery springs, *Furniture History*, XIIV, London

Howlett, C. (1990) The identification of grasses and other plant materials used in historic upholstery, in *Upholstery Conservation*, Preprints of a Symposium held at Colonial Williamsburg, 2–4 February 1990, American Conservation Consortium Ltd, Kingston, New Hampshire, pp. 66–91

Huette, R. (1972) *Le Livre de la passementerie*, H. Vidal

Indictor, N., Koestler, R.J., Wypyski, M. and Wardwell, A.E. (1989) Metal threads made of proteinaceous substrates examined by scanning electron microscopy-energy dispersive X-ray spectrometry, *Studies in Conservation*, 34, 171–82

James, D. (1990) *Upholstery: A Complete Course*, The Guild of Master Craftsman Publications

Jàro, M. (1983) The technological and analytical examination of metal threads on old textiles: conservation–restoration of church textiles and painted flags, Investigation of Museum Objects and Materials Used in Conservation–Restoration, Veszprem, Hungary 2–10 July, National Centre of Museums, Budapest, pp. 253–64

Jobe, B. (1987) The Boston upholstery trade, in E.S. Cooke Jr (ed.), *Upholstery in America and Europe from the Seventeenth Century to World War 1*, W.W. Norton

Johnson, K., Elton Barratt, O. and Butcher, M. (1990) *Chair Seating in Rush, Cane, Willow and Cords*, Dryad Press

King, R.R. (1985) *Textile Identification, Conservation, and Preservation*, Noyes Publications

Kirkham, P. (1985) Willow and cane furniture in Austria, Germany and England *c*.1900–14, in *Furniture History* XXI, The Furniture History Society, London

Kirkham, P., Mace, R. and Porter, J. (1987) *Furnishing the World – The East London Furniture Trade, 1830–1980*, Journeyman, London

Kovaly, K.A. (1970) *Handbook of Plastic Furniture Manufacturing*, Technomic

Kuhn, H. (1986) *Conservation and Restoration of Works of Art and Antiquities*, translated by Alexander Trone, Butterworth Series in Conservation and Museology, Butterworth-Heinemann

Landi, S. (1992/1985) *The Textile Conservator's Manual*, Butterworth-Heinemann

Liles, J.N. (1990) *The Art and Craft of Natural Dyeing: Traditional Recipes for Modern Use*, University of Tennessee Press

Martin, E. (1977) Some improvements in techniques of analysis of paint media, *Studies in Conservation*, 22, 63–7

Masschelein-Kleiner, L. (1985) *Ancient Binding Media, Varnishes and Adhesives*, ICCROM

McDonald, R.J. (1981) *Modern Upholstering Techniques*, Charles Scribners Sons

Miller, B.W. and Widess, J. (1986) *The Caner's Handbook*, Prentice-Hall Press

Miller, R.C. (1990) *Modern Design 1890–1990 in the Metropolitan Museum of Art*, MMA, pp. 212–13

Milnes, E.C. (1983) *History of the Development of Furniture Webbing*, private publication (Mr Milnes, 22 Elmete Hill, Leeds, LS8 2NT, UK)

Montgomery, F.M. (1984) *Textiles in America, 1650–1870*, Norton

Mossman, S. (1988) *Simple Methods of Identifying Plastics in Modern Organic Materials*, Scottish Society for Conservation and Restoration

Mucci, P.E.R. (1997) Rapid identification of plastics using external beam mid-infrared spectroscopy, *Proceedings of the Royal Society of Chemistry Symposium: Chemical Aspects of Plastics Recycling*, University of Manchester Institute of Science and Technology, Manchester 1996, Cambridge: Royal Society of Chemistry Information Services, pp. 53–70

Munn, J. (1989) Treatment Techniques for the Vellum Covered Furniture of Carlo Bughalti in Wood Artifacts Speciality Group Reprints AIC, Cincinnati

Murphy, E.A. (1966) Some early adventures with latex, *Rubber Technology*, 39, 3, June

Musée des Art Décoratifs (1973) *Des dorelotiers aux passementiers*, exhibition calalogue Musée des Art Décoratifs, Paris, Jan–March

Neilson, L.H. (1968) *Nail Chronology as an Aid to Dating Old Buildings*, The American Association for State and Local History, Technical Leaflet No. 48, vol. 24, No. 11

Nuttgens, F. (1999) Deteriorating rubber and PVC: the characterization and conservation of a World Airways Flight Bag *c*.1970, TCC Report No. 2182, Unpublished Diploma Report, Textile Conservation Centre/Courtauld Institute of Art

Nylander, J.C. (1990) *Fabrics for Historic Buildings*, 4th edn, The Preservation Press

O'Flaherty, F., Roddy, W.T. and Loller, R.M. (1965) *The Chemistry and Technology of Leather*, 4 vols, Reinhold

Oldemors Pomponger possementhandverket i Trondheim Norenfojeldske Kunstindustrimuseum, Trondheim, 1982

Ossut, C. (1996) *Tapisserie d'ameublement*, Editions H. Vial, Dourdan

Pääbo, S. (1993) Ancient DNA, *Scientific American*, 269(5), 86–92

Passeri, A. (1988) My life as an upholsterer, 1927–1986, in G.W.R. Ward (ed.), *Perspectives on American Furniture*, Norton

Reed, R. (1972) *Ancient Skins, Parchments and Leather*, Seminar Press

Roff, W.J. and Scott, J.R. (1971) *Fibres, Films, Plastics and Rubbers*, Butterworths

Rogerson, C. (1997) Evaluating the application of a cross-sectional analysis to the documentation and examination of textiles, Unpublished Diploma Report, Textile Conservation Centre/Courtauld Institute of Art

Roubo, A.J. (1988) The art of caning, in translation in B.M. Forman, *American Seating Furniture, 1630–1730*, Winterthur/W.W. Norton and Co.

Schoeser, M. and Dejardin, K. (1991) *French Textiles from 1760 to the Present*, Laurence King

Schoeser, M. and Rufey, C. (1989) *English and American Textiles from 1790 to the Present*, Thames and Hudson

Scholten, F. (ed.) (1989) *Goud Leer Kinkarakawa De geschiedenis van het Netherlands goudleer en zijn invloed in Japan*, Vitgeverij Waanders-Zwolde, p. 104

Schweppe, H. (1979) Identification of dyes on old textiles, in AIC Conference Preprints, Toronto

Sharphouse, J.H. (1983) *The Leather Technician's Handbook*, revised edn, Leather Producers Association, Northampton

Shearer, G.L. (1989) An Evaluation of Fourier Transform Infrared Spectroscopy for the Characterisation of Organic Compounds in Art and Archaeology, Thesis, Institute of Archaeology, London

Sibilia, J.P. (1996) *A Guide to Materials Characterization and Chemical Analysis*, 2nd edn. VCH, New York.

Society of Dyers and Colourists (1971) *Colour Index, prepared by the Society of Dyers and Colourists and the American Association of Textile Chemists and Colorists*, The Society of Dyers and Colourists, Bradford, England

Sparke, P. (1986) *Furniture: Twentieth Century Design*, Bell and Hyman

Stambolov, T. (1969) Manufacture, Deterioration and Preservation of Leather – a literature survey, *ICOM Plenary Meeting*, 16–19 September, Amsterdam Central Research Laboratory for Objects of Art and Science

Stenberg, B. and Akervall, T. (1989) Mobelstoppning Som Hantwerk Sveiges Tapetseraremastares Centralforening

Stephenson, J. (1941) *Practical Upholstering*, Clifford Lawton

Tanners Council of America (1983) *Dictionary of Leather Terminology*, Tanners Council of America, Washington, DC, 7th edn, p. 23

Taylor, E.S. and Singer, C. (1956) Pre-scientific industrial chemistry, in C. Singer *et al.* (ed.), *A History of Technology*, Volume II, pp. 364–9

Thomas, S., Clarkson, L.A. and Thomson, R. (1983) *Leather Manufacture Through the Ages*, Proceedings of the 22nd East Midlands Industrial Archaeology Conference

Thomsom, R.S. (1981a) Tanning: Man's first manufacturing process, *Transactions of the Newcomen Society*, 53, 139–54

Thomson, R.S. (1981b) Leather manufacture in the post medieval period, in *Post Medieval Archaeology*, 15, 161

Thomson, R.S. (1985) Chrome tanning in the nineteenth century, in *Journal of the Society of Leather Technologists and Chemists*, 69, 93

Thornton, P. (1978) *Seventeenth-Century Interior Decoration in England, France and Holland*, Yale University Press

Thorp, V. (1990) Imitation leather: structure, composition and conservation, *Leather Conservation News*, 6, 7–15

Timár-Balázsy, A. and Eastop, D. (1998) *Chemical Principles of Textile Conservation*, Butterworth-Heinemann

Todd, V. (ed.) (1993) Pin beading, *Conservation News*, 50, March, UKIC, p. 31

Trotman, E.R. (1984) *Dyeing and Chemical Technology of Textile Fibres*, Edward Arnold

Walkling, G. (1979) *Antique Bamboo Furniture*, Bell and Hyman

Walsall Leather Centre (1992) *Leather Bibliography*, Walsall Leather Centre, Walsall

Walton, K. (1979) The Worshipful Company of Upholders of the City of London, in *Furniture History* IX, The Furniture History Society, London

Waterer, J.W. (1968) *Leather Craftsmanship*, Praeger

Waterer, J.W. (1972) *A Guide to the Conservation and Restoration Objects Made Wholly or in Part of Leather*, Bell, London

Weaver, W. (1984) *Analytical Methods for a Textile Laboratory*, 3rd edn, American Association of Textile Chemists and Colorists, Research Triangle Park, NC

Webster and Parkes (1845) *The Encyclopedia of Domestic Economy*, Harper and Bros

Wilson, L. and Balfour, D. (1990) Developments in upholstery construction in Britian during the first half of the twentieth century, in *Upholstery Conservation*, Preprints of a Symposium held at Colonial Williamsburg, 2–4 February 1990, American Conservation Consortium Ltd, Kingston, New Hampshire

# 4

# Plastics and polymers, coatings and binding media, adhesives and consolidants

## 4.1 Plastics and polymers

The word 'plastic', from the Greek word for mouldable, originally described pliable materials that could be shaped by hand or tool pressure as distinguished from 'glyptik' shaping processes relying on stock removal by carving, engraving or grinding. The term aptly describes all of the modern materials, commonly called plastics, which are all soft and mouldable at some point in their manufacture. It also describes the natural materials that are their technological and functional forbears, such as horn, rawhide, turtle shell, natural rubber and gutta percha. The general historical progression of the use of these materials furniture is from the natural materials through the semi-synthetic to the entirely synthetic modern plastics.

The many uses of plastics in furniture include structural members, veneers, inlays, knobs, fittings and decorative components, upholstery foams and textiles, adhesives and coatings. They were used from the very beginning to copy, often slavishly, more costly and rare natural materials just as the cheaper and reproducible processes of moulding were used to duplicate the qualities of more laborious carving and polishing. However, plastics, and the technologies of moulding, extrusion, lamination and hot bending, have certainly exerted an influence on design and public taste. Twentieth-century furniture composed entirely of wood often owes a stylistic debt to the forms of manufactured plastics.

Plastic materials cover a wide range of chemical types, exhibit huge variation in physical, optical and dielectric properties and are fabricated in a wide range of forms for different uses. Only a brief review from the perspective of furniture applications can be attempted here. For a more extensive introduction see Young (1991).

### 4.1.1 Chemical structure

In all cases, plastic materials consist of a mass of very large molecules. Although some polymeric materials have a structure which is heterogeneous and complex, most plastics consist of long chains of repeating small molecular units, or monomers, covalently bonded together. In the bulk material, polymer chains are mechanically intertwined and may also be chemically bonded together or *crosslinked* at various points along their lengths to form a network structure. These materials are of high molecular weight and hence are referred to as high polymers or macromolecules.

Polymer chains may be linear or branched depending on the nature of the monomer and the polymerization reaction. In *homo-polymers,* the monomer units are all of one chemical type. Hydrocarbon polymers such as polyethylene are based on carbon and hydrogen alone. Other carbon chain polymers may have atoms of other elements such as chlorine incorporated into the polymer structure. The replacement of carbon atoms in the backbone itself by atoms of other elements produces *heterochain* polymers. In *co-polymers,* the monomer units are of two or more types. There are three principal types of arrangement of the units in co-polymers, *alternating, ran-*

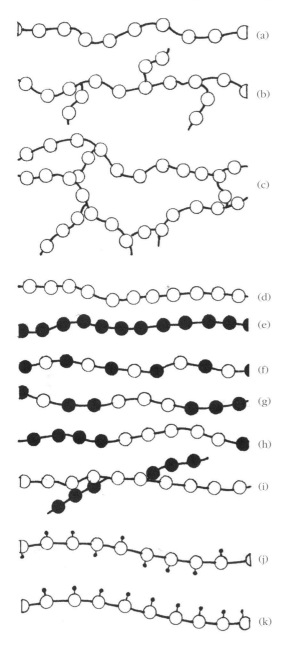

**Figure 4.1** The arrangement of atoms that make up a polymer fundamentally affects the way in which adjacent molecules can fit together, which in turn radically affects the mechanical and other properties of the molecule. Some examples of polymer terminology: (*a*) linear; (*b*) branched; (*c*) crosslinked; (*d*) homopolymer; (*e*) homopolymer; (*f*) alternating co-polymer; (*g*) random co-polymer; (*h*) block co-polymer; (*i*) graft co-polymer; (*j*) atactic form of polypropylene – has a random arrangement of units; (*k*) isotactic form of polypropylene – all units have a spatially identical arrangement of atoms

*dom* and *block*. Polymer terminology is illustrated in *Figure 4.1*.

Poly(vinyl acetate) (PVAC), one of the simplest polymers, consists of up to 20 000 repeating units of vinyl acetate joined together. This can be expressed by writing the chemical formula as $[CH_2CHOCOCH_3]_n$ where n specifies the number of monomer units in the chain and is called the degree of polymerization (DP). Synthetic polymers are formed by two major classes of chemical reactions, addition reactions and condensation reactions (Hall, 1981). Because of the nature of the reactions by which polymers are formed, not all molecules of a given compound are identical in size. Even under controlled conditions of manufacture there will be a range of molecular weights and the DP quoted for any product will be an average. The plastic may also contain some unreacted monomer and small quantities of other impurities. All these factors are important because the mechanical, chemical and ageing properties depend to a considerable extent on them (Brydson, 1991).

The simplest macromolecules are composed of fundamental units linked end to end in chains with relatively few branches or side chains. The links or primary (covalent) bonds along each chain are strong compared to the secondary forces (e.g. Van der Waals forces and hydrogen bonding) holding adjoining chains together and it is therefore possible to separate the molecules from each other. Such materials are usually both soluble and fusible, that is they are thermoplastic, becoming soft and fluid when heated and returning to the solid state on cooling. If secondary forces are sufficiently strong, a linear polymer may be insoluble or restricted in solubility and it may be infusible or fusible only at temperatures at which the polymer begins to decompose. If the composition is such that the chain molecules are flexible, but the inter-chain forces are very weak, random coiling occurs and the material shows long range elasticity. Such materials are known as elastomers (e.g. rubber). If more than two primary linkages can be formed by each fundamental unit, the structure of the polymer becomes one of chains with cross chains and may approach a fully crosslinked network which is effectively a single molecule. Polymers of this type are much less tractable than linear polymers being both insoluble and infusible. The name thermoset was originally given to them because they were only formed under the influence of heat as the result of chemical reaction. They are usually used as resin pre-polymers, the crosslinking being deferred until it can be completed in situ.

## 4.1.2   Physical properties

The properties of macromolecules result from the subtle interplay of processes operating at several different structural levels. These include the nature of the atoms in the molecules and the way in which molecules come to together in chains or other units to form the bulk material; whether in regular, ordered *crystalline* arrangements or irregular, *amorphous* arrangements and on the presence of complex microstructures, vacancies and defects within the bulk material.

Of particular importance is the *stereo regularity* or *tacticity* of the polymer. Polymers in which all units have a spatially identical arrangement of atoms are called *isotactic*, those in which a random arrangement prevails are called *atactic*, and those which show a regular alteration in configuration along the chain are called *syndiotactic*. The tacticity of polymer molecules affects the way in which adjacent molecules can fit together in the bulk material and hence controls the strength of forces between molecules from which the mechanical properties arise. Stereoregular homopolymers with strong inter-chain forces, and certain block co-polymers, tend to show significant crystallinity whereas atactic homopolymers and random co-polymers are amorphous.

As with most materials, the physical state of polymers is temperature-dependent. Unlike changes of state in simple molecules, which generally occur at definite temperatures, changes of state in polymers are less well defined and often occur over a finite temperature range. Most thermoplastics are either amorphous or only slightly crystalline and exist in different states according to average molecular weight and temperature. Generally, increasing molecular weight or degree of polymerization increases toughness, viscosity in solution and softening point, and decreases rate of solution. At low molecular weights these polymers are solid below a certain temperature and liquid above it. At higher molecular weights a clearly defined melting point no

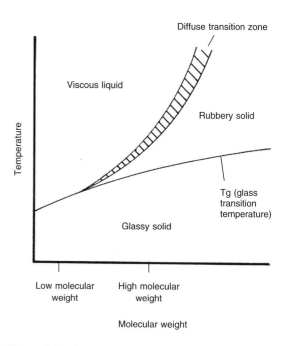

**Figure 4.2**  Glass transition temperature – the relationship of physical state to temperature for amorphous polymeric materials of different molecular weights

longer occurs and a rubbery intermediate zone is observed. In the solid state, amorphous and moderately crystalline polymers have a glassy transparent appearance, sometimes called the glassy state. The transition from a glassy or brittle state to a rubbery state occurs at the *glass transition temperature*, Tg (*Figure 4.2*). The glass transition temperature is also sometimes referred to as the *second order transition temperature*. Increase in temperature above Tg causes progressive softening until the material becomes a viscous fluid. In the glassy state, molecular movements other than bond vibrations are very limited. Above Tg the molecules have more energy and movement of molecular segments becomes possible. However, above a certain crosslink density movement of the complete molecule as a unit does not take place. Softening under heat is the basis of moulding, extrusion and heat sealing of these materials and is important in their use as coatings and adhesives in conservation. When heated, thermosets do not soften to a truly fluid condition but some become sufficiently flexible to allow them to be bent into simple shapes.

Many properties apart from hardness are affected by the change from the glassy to the rubbery state. These include specific volume, specific heat, thermal conductivity, dynamic modulus and simple stress/strain characteristics. It is important to be aware of this since a polymer in use near its Tg may show quite marked changes in properties with small changes in temperature. For example, many grades of PVAC and some methacrylates have a Tg close to room temperature.

Transition temperatures additional to Tg may occur (e.g. in some methacrylates) because at temperatures below Tg the side chains and sometimes small segments of the main chains require less energy for mobility than the main segments associated with Tg. These are designated alpha, beta, gamma etc., with alpha being Tg and the others following in order of decreasing temperature. Secondary transitions confer useful properties on particular polymers, for example, materials that have secondary transitions below room temperature tend to be tough.

For successful use a polymer must have appropriate rigidity, toughness, resistance to long term deformation, and recovery from deformation on release of stress over the range of operating conditions. The same factors will apply to selecting a polymer for use in conservation as to the care and conservation of objects made of these materials.

The rigidity of a polymer is determined by the ease with which its molecules are deformed under load. In the absence of secondary transitions, at temperatures below Tg, the load is taken by bond bending and stretching. Secondary transitions below Tg allow more response to stress resulting in a decrease in elastic modulus (i.e. a more elastic material). Changes due to such secondary transitions are usually small but the change in behaviour that occurs at Tg is highly significant. *Young's modulus*, the most widely quoted measure of elasticity, indicates the resistance of a material to reversible longitudinal extension (see also section 2.5). At the Tg in an amorphous polymer the modulus may drop from typical values of $3500 \, MN/m^2$ to less than $1 \, MN/m^2$. The effect of further temperature increases depends on molecular weight. In lower molecular weight polymers the modulus drops rapidly towards zero. In higher molecular weight material a significant rubbery modulus may be maintained

up to the decomposition temperature. It should be noted that fracture frequently occurs at defect sites which may be due to additives or processing and not just to the properties of the bulk polymer.

Similar effects occur in crosslinked polymers; the greater the degree of crosslinking, the higher the modulus. Molecular movement above the glass transition temperature is restricted by crystallinity; the greater the degree of crystallinity the more rigid the polymer. Additives may also affect the modulus (Roff and Scott, 1971). Generally, plasticizers reduce it and fillers increase it. The elastic modulus of unplasticized poly(vinyl butyral) is about $1500 \, MN/m^2$. With plasticizer this may fall below $10 \, MN/m^2$. The elastic modulus of phenol formaldehyde systems may rise from around $3000–6000 \, MN/m^2$ unfilled to over $20000 \, MN/m^2$ filled. Similar effects are noted on tensile strength (the maximum tensile stress to which a material may be subjected before breaking). The properties of some polymers (for example, poly(vinyl alcohol)) are markedly affected by humidity changes.

The toughness of a material is indicated by its resistance to the sudden application of a mechanical load. Tough materials will show greater elongation before breaking. Polymers that fracture with very little deformation are said to be brittle. Toughness is influenced by polymer structure and temperature and by the method and rate of stressing. A polymer may be tough when subjected to a tensile load but brittle when assessed by an Izod type test in which a notched sample is subjected to a bending load. In real life situations, toughness is also affected by stress concentrations due to design and manufacture. It is possible to obtain materials that are both rigid and tough by blending polymers with different properties, co-polymerization, the use of additives and by choosing the right processing conditions.

The deformation and recovery from deformation of linear polymers is a complex process having components that can be described as (1) normal elastic behaviour (Hooke's law obeyed). (2) highly elastic and (3) viscous (Brydson, 1991; Horie, 1987) One aspect of this behaviour is the phenomenon described as 'creep' or cold-flow in which a fixed stress can bring about permanent deformation. Plastic deformation of this kind is much enhanced at elevated temperatures and its presence in certain polymers (e.g. PVAC and PVAL) even at room temperature is undesirable and renders them unsuitable for applications involving prolonged periods of stress. The closer a thermoplastic material is to its Tg at room temperature, the greater the likelihood of creep.

As with all categories, the clear distinction between thermoplastic and thermosetting tends to break down if examined closely enough. Linear polymers can oxidize and crosslink as they age, becoming in essence thermosetting, while even a highly crosslinked polymer such as oriental lacquer (urushi) is somewhat thermoplastic. Although linear polymers are generally more soluble in various solvents than crosslinked polymers some, such as high density polyethylene, are insoluble due to very high molecular weight (long chain length) and/or crystallinity due to the arrangement of the chains. Properties of polymer materials relevant to their use as adhesives, coatings and consolidants are further discussed below. Chain branches and cyclic polymer structures also strongly influence solubility.

### 4.1.3 Polymer materials history and technology

Many purely natural polymers were traditionally used to manufacture small objects by moulding and pressing. Horn and turtleshell are quite thermoplastic and were die-pressed into complex shapes such as decorative snuff boxes. When used as thin veneers they could be made to conform to mouldings or turned pilasters by gluing under heated cauls.

Most natural resins are also thermoplastic. Shellac was used to polish turned wood articles in India and Europe by simply rubbing solid sticks of the material on the spinning stock until it melted by the heat of friction. This use apparently pre-dates its use as a solvent varnish. Some of the most extensively employed early thermoplastic materials were various compositions used to imitate carved detail on picture frames in architectural interiors. This craft saw its heyday during the late eighteenth and early nineteenth centuries when 'composition' ornament makers used mixtures typically consisting of rosin, linseed oil, animal glue and whiting to mould-press elaborate sculptural detail.

Ornament made from 'composition' was popularized in Britain by the Adam brothers in the last quarter of the eighteenth century. Their fine and repetitive style of decoration was difficult and expensive to reproduce by the traditional method of carving in wood so they introduced a way of manufacturing their designs more cheaply from composition pressed into reverse-carved moulds. This method of ornamentation was used extensively throughout the nineteenth-century for picture frames, furniture and interior decoration.

Gutta-percha, a natural latex tapped from trees native to Malaysia, was first brought to European notice in 1843. It was used to manufacture picture frames, book covers and various other decorative and useful objects during the Victorian era. Although chemically identical to natural 'India' rubber, it was rigid at room temperature and mouldable at around 90 °C. In fact, natural rubber and gutta percha are the cis and trans isomers respectively of polyisoprene. Imitation woods made from ground coconut shell or other wood dusts mixed with gutta percha could be mould formed or worked by standard woodworking techniques.

In 1839, Charles Goodyear patented a process by which the much more ubiquitous natural rubber could be made hard by crosslinking the polymer with sulphur. This ebony-like material was variously called ebonite, vulcanite and hard rubber. Linoleum, patented in 1860, combined the toughness of a crosslinked polymer (partially oxidized linseed oil) with the thermoplasticity of a natural resin (pine rosin). The mixture of these polymers and various fillers produced a tough, attractive and wear-resistant floor covering.

Bois-durci, an imitation ebony, was patented in 1855 and used to produce small decorative plaques for the furniture trade until the 1880s. Made from sawdust and albumen derived from blood or eggs, the protein binder was denatured and crosslinked during the hot moulding operation and so could be described as an early thermosetting resin. Likewise casein, the protein present in milk and cheese, was used as the basis for a mouldable composition patented in Germany in the late 1890s. Casein continues to be used world-wide by button manufacturers.

Because many natural polymers were highly modified to achieve different properties, the designation of the first synthetic plastic is rather arbitrary. However, this distinction is often given to the cellulose nitrates. In 1846 an explosive known as gun-cotton was made by reacting a mixture of nitric and sulfuric acids with cotton-wool. Experiments on this material showed it to be thermoplastic, but highly unstable and flammable. The extensive efforts of Alexander Parkes in England led eventually to a thermoplastic resin composed of less highly nitrated cellulose combined with various oils, fillers and pigments, and called Parkesine. Moulded objects were made from this material between 1855 and 1868 but suffered from fragility. In 1869, the Hyatt brothers of Albany, New York patented a synthetic ivory named Celluloid made from cellulose nitrate plasticized with camphor which was an immediate and lasting success. The manufacturing technologies developed to convert Celluloid and its English equivalent Xylonite into a wide range of useful and decorative objects formed the basis of a plastics industry which grew and flourished as further discoveries were made.

A thermosetting, crosslinked resin synthesized from phenol and formaldehyde was patented by Leo Baekeland in 1907 as Bakelite. Bakelite could be produced in any colour (that allowed for its natural yellow tint), was very hard and rigid and found extensive use in early radio cabinets, automobile components and other high-tech applications.

In 1922, a great impetus was given to the synthesis of further plastic compounds by the work of Hermann Staudinger. In the process of synthesizing rubber, Staudinger identified and described the essential linear structure of polymers. A more sophisticated understanding of polymer structure gave rise after 1930 to a rapidly growing list of 'plastics' arrived at by deliberate chemical engineering rather than trial-and-error or chance discovery. After the Second World War, furniture made entirely of plastics became increasingly popular (e.g. see Katz, 1984). Clear acrylic sheet (Perspex®, Plexiglas®) made from poly (methyl methacrylate) was extensively employed but was soon found to be brittle and easily scratched. A summary of the main synthetic polymer materials is given in *Table 4.1*.

Perhaps the category of plastics most important to furniture history and manufacture are the composites or laminates. Composites are combinations of dissimilar materials that show properties different from and often superior to the individual ingredients (Gordon, 1976). This is a very old concept and in many ways describes all of the materials discussed so far in that they are almost never pure substances. An early example of structural composites showing high strength combined with low weight were the papier mâché panels used to form furniture (see section 5.4). Gypsum plaster and coarse weave jute or hemp layered into moulds or built up on wooden armatures were extensively employed for the realization of complex architectural interiors and even entire exhibition buildings. Such 'fibrous plaster' or 'staff' filled the functions of what is today commonly called 'fibre-glass'.

Fibre-glass is a rather misleading term for resin and glass-fibre composites more properly called glass reinforced plastics or GRPs. Such composites use glass fibre in the form of cord, cloth or randomly oriented felt-like matt which is impregnated with thermosetting resins such as phenolics, epoxies and polyesters. They are very strong, relatively light in weight and have been used to manufacture furniture since the 1940s.

Paper-based composite laminates have also found extensive use in furniture as surface coverings. Laminates such as Formica®, based on paper and melamine resin, have been used to copy every variety of wood and stone.

Synthetic polymers had a revolutionary effect on the textile industries and synthetic fibres were quickly brought into use in upholstery. Uses of polymers in upholstery are described in Chapter 3. Polymer foams can be thought of as composites of resins and gas bubbles. They can be made either soft and flexible or hard and rigid depending on resin composition and bubble size. An extremely readable review of the technology of fibres, plastics and rubbers is given by Kaufman (1968). Kovaly (1970), Buttrey (1976) and Seymour and Mark (1990) provide further information on the utilization of plastics in furniture and as industrial finishes.

Polymers that become soft or fluid when heated have had various applications in moulding and casting. Historically they have been used to produce rigid moulds. Decorative plasterers have used mixtures of waxes, resins and fillers to produce moulds for repeat pat-

**Table 4.1**  Review of some important synthetic polymers

| Polymer group, names and trademarks | Date introduced and country | Description and use | Simple identification |
|---|---|---|---|
| **Acrylic** Poly(methyl methacrylate) (PMMA) Oroglas (Röhm & Haas – USA), Perspex (ICI – GB), Plexiglas (Röhm GmbH-D) | PMMA: 1934 UK | Amorphous, thermoplastic, carbon chain addition polymer. PMMA is usually produced by 'casting' from monomer to form clear or opaque coloured sheets or rods with good outdoor durability. Brittle unless toughened but cuts cleanly. Used as 'unbreakable' substitute for glass, for mouldings and light fittings. Various acrylics used as adhesives and as solution/dispersion type coatings. Widely used in conservation as consolidants and coatings | Burns noisily with blue-based yellow flame, little smoke, acrid fruity smell. Continues to burn after removal from flame. Not affected by cyclohexanone or by aromatic solvents |
| **Acrylonitrile-butadiene rubber (NBR)** Nitrile rubber | | Rubber formed by emulsion polymerization of acrylonitrile and butadiene. Used for oil resistant properties | |
| **Acrylonitrile-butadiene-styrene (ABS)** | 1952 USA | Amorphous thermoplastic mixture of styrene with acrylonitrile and nitrile rubber. Chemical resistant and tough with generally good impact resistance though toughness somewhat variable. Normally in opaque colours. Can be formed, moulded, extruded and calendared. Cuts cleanly | Burns with blue-based yellow flame and black smoke with faint odour of marigolds. Continues to burn after removal from flame. Softened by cyclohexane but not by aromatic hydrocarbon solvents |
| **Butyl rubber (BUTYL)** | | Formed by ionic polymerization of isobutylene with a small proportion of isoprene. Mainly used in inner tubes for tyres. Also used as adhesive | |
| **Cellulose acetate butyrate (CAB)** Uvex (Eastman Chemical Products Co., USA) | CN: 1870 USA CA: 1905 Germany | Thermoplastics formed by chemical modification of the natural polymer, cellulose, present in cotton and wood. Used with a plasticizer. CA: Moderately tough (notch brittle) with good impact resistance but poor outdoor durability. Films used in photography and for packaging are highly transparent and protective but tear easily. Found in textile fibres as cellulose acetate and triacetate. Some use as adhesive. CN used in solution type coatings | CA: Burns rapidly with blue-based orange flame and smell of burning paper. Sputters and drips while burning. Continues to burn after removal from flame. Softened by cyclohexane but not aromatic hydrocarbons |
| **Cellulosic esters** cellulose nitrate (CN) cellulose acetate (CA) | | Thermoplastic. Similar to cellulose acetate but with improved outdoor durability. May develop smell of rancid butter on ageing. Cuts cleanly. Also used in simple solution coatings | Burns with yellow flame and smell of rancid butter. Continues to burn after removal from flame. Softened by cyclohexane but not aromatic hydrocarbons |
| **Epoxy (EP)** | 1947 USA | Amorphous, thermosetting network polymer. Basic functional unit formed by reaction of epichlorhydrin with diphenylol propane can be polymerized in situ with a variety of crosslinking agents, the main ones being amines. Used for surface coatings and adhesives and some mouldings | |

| | | | |
|---|---|---|---|
| **Melamine formaldehyde (MF)** | 1938 Germany | Hard and tough, amorphous, thermosetting network polymer formed by polycondensation of melamine and formaldehyde. The resin is always mixed with one or more fillers to make it suitable for particular applications. Used to make decorative laminates and mouldings, mainly in opaque colours, that are resistant to scratching and chemicals. Chips and powders when cut. Also used as adhesive and, with or without alkyd, in reactive type coatings | Hard to ignite. Burns with pale yellow flame with bluish edge and fishy smell. Not softened by cyclohexane or aromatic hydrocarbons |
| **Phenol formaldehyde (PF)** e.g. Bakelite, phenolic resins | 1909 USA | Amorphous, network, thermoset formed by polycondensation of phenol or cresol and formaldehyde. The resin is almost always mixed with fillers to suit particular applications. Good heating and insulating properties. Used in mouldings, paints, adhesives and laminates. Chips and powders when cut | Burns with yellow flame and 'phenolic' smell with evidence of formaldehyde. Self-extinguishing on removal from flame. Not softened by cyclohexane or aromatic hydrocarbons |
| **Poly acetal (POM)** Delrin (Du Pont – USA) Hostaform (Hoechst AG-D) | | Crystalline thermoplastic. Moderately tough (notch brittle) and rigid with good solvent and heat resistance. Good electrical properties. Cuts cleanly | Difficult to ignite but burns with very pale blue lame and acrid smoke with odour of formaldehyde. Continues to burn after removal from flame. Bubbles and becomes clear when molten. Not affected by cyclohexane or aromatic solvents |
| **Polyamides (PA)** All types of Nylon. Commercially available varieties include 6, 66, 610, 7, 11, 12 and 66/610. | 1939 USA | Crystalline, heterochain thermoplastic formed by polycondensation of dibasic acids and diamino compounds or condensation of amino acids with themselves. Light, tough when wet, moderately tough (notch brittle) when dry chemically resistant and durable. Cuts easily. Used in textiles and in mouldings | Burns with blue flame with yellow tip producing drips and strings of molten polymer and smell of burning vegetation. Continues to burn after removal from flame. Not affected by cyclohexane or aromatic solvents |
| **Polybutadiene (BR)** | | Hydrocarbon rubber, formed by ionic polymerization of butadiene. Used in tyre treads | |
| **Polycarbonate (PC)** Lexan (General Electric Co USA) Makrolon (Bayer AG-D) Tuflak (Röhm & Haas – USA | 1959 W Germany/ USA | Hard, rigid thermoplastic with good impact resistance and high softening point formed by action of phosgene on diphenyol propane. Available in transparent and opaque forms. Cuts cleanly | Difficult to ignite. Burns with spluttery orange flame, black smoke and phenolic smell. Bubbles and chars when burning and continues to burn after removal from flame. Not affected by cyclohexane or aromatic solvents |
| **Polychloroprene (CR)** | | Rubber formed by addition polymerization of chloroprene. Used where non-flammability and good weathering properties required. Also used as adhesive | |
| **Polyester** linear polyesters include Hostaphan (Hoechst AG-D), Melinex (ICI – GB), Mylar (Du Pont – USA) | UP: 1946 USA | Polyesters, heterochain condensation polymers formed from polyfunctional acids and polyfunctional alcohols, including linear polyesters, unsaturated polyesters (UP) and alkyds. Linear | Linear polyesters burn rapidly with blue-based yellow flame and very faint odour, continuing to burn after removal from flame. Not |

*continued*

**Table 4.1**   Continued

| Polymer group, names and trademarks | Date introduced and country | Description and use | Simple identification |
|---|---|---|---|
| | | polyesters are thermoplastic, alkyds and UPs are thermosetting. Linear polyesters have excellent clarity, dimensional stability and chemical resistance. They are used to make textile fibres such as Terylene, Dacron and Tergal and high quality films such as Melinex and Mylar. Films make metallic sound when shaken and are difficult to tear. Unsaturated polyesters (UP) are used in glass-reinforced plastics mouldings. They are usually crosslinked with styrene but other unsaturated compounds may be used. Alkyd resins are used in (reactive type) paints | affected by cyclohexane or aromatic solvents |
| **Polyolefins** Low density polyethylene (LDPE) High density polyethylene (HDPE) Polypropylene (PP) | LDPE: 1939 UK HDPE: 1955 W. Germany PP: 1957 Italy | Thermoplastic, crystalline, stereoregular hydrocarbon chain homopolymers formed by addition. LDPE is formed by high pressure free radical polymerization whilst low pressure ionic polymerization of monomer is used for the others. Highly chemical resistant, light and strong with waxy feel. Float on water. Cut cleanly. HDPE and most PPs are moderately tough (notch brittle) but some PPs are very tough with high impact resistance. Polypropylene has greater rigidity and surface hardness than PE. Used for all kinds of mouldings and films, also as adhesives and fibres. Film stretches before tearing | Burns with blue-based yellow flame and smell of candle wax. Becomes clear when molten and continues to burn on removal from flame. Not affected by cyclohexane or aromatic solvents |
| **Polystyrene (PS)** | 1930 Germany | Thermoplastic hydrocarbon addition polymer formed mainly by bulk polymerization of styrene. Most commercial PS is hard, brittle amorphous atactic homopolymer used for mouldings, films and foams. PS alone cuts cleanly is readily moulded or formed but shatters easily (makes metallic sound when shaken) has poor resistance to solvents and poor outdoor durability. It is copolymerized with a variety of other materials to make high impact plastics, dispersion type coatings and rubbers (see ABS, SBR, SAN) | Burns with spluttery orange flame and dense black sooty smoke with faint odour of marigolds. Continues to burn after removal of flame. Softened by cyclohexane and aromatic solvents |
| **Polytetrafluoroethylene (PTFE)** Teflon, Fluon | 1943 USA | Thermoplastic, crystalline, carbon chain, addition polymer formed by emulsion polymerization of tetrafluoroethylene. Used where heat resistance, chemical resistance or low friction are required. Copolymers of TFE with other fluoro compounds are used as heat resistant rubbers | |

| | | | |
|---|---|---|---|
| **Polyurethanes (PUR)** | 1943 Germany | Polyurethanes, amorphous heterochain polymers, are formed from reaction of low molecular weight **polyesters** or **polyethers** with isocyanates and are classified accordingly into two main groups of polyethers and polyesters. Polyurethanes may be thermoplastics, rubbers or thermosets. They have been used as flexible foams in upholstery, rigid foams for insulation, solid elastomers and surface coatings | Burns with blue-based yellow flame and acrid smell. Continues to burn on removal from flame. Not affected by cyclohexane or aromatic solvents |
| **Poly(vinyl acetate) (PVAC)** | | Thermoplastic carbon chain addition polymers formed principally by emulsion polymerization of vinyl acetate. Principally used as emulsion paints and adhesives. Poly(vinyl alcohol), poly(vinyl formal), and poly(vinyl butyral) are chemical derivatives of PVAC and also find applications in conservation treatments as adhesives and consolidants and coating media | |
| **Poly(vinyl chloride) (PVC)** e.g. 'Cobex' (Storey Bros. & Co – GB), 'Darvic' (ICI – GB), 'Genotherm' (Hoechst AG-D) | 1933 Germany/ USA | Thermoplastic carbon chain addition polymer formed mainly by suspension and emulsion polymerization of vinyl chloride. PVC is used in plasticized form and as copolymer with vinyl acetate and with vinylidene chloride. It is available in clear and opaque colours in limp, flexible, rigid and self adhesive forms used for mouldings of all sorts, textiles (e.g. leather cloth) and sheetings, and in dispersion coatings. Films are difficult to tear. Cuts cleanly | Difficult to ignite, burns with green tinged orange flame, black sooty smoke and acrid acidic smell. Self-extinguishing on removal from flame. Softened by cyclohexane but not by aromatic hydrocarbons |
| **Polyvinyl fluoride (PVF)** e.g. 'Tedlar' (Du Pont – USA) | | Thermoplastic. Carbon chain addition polymer. Unaffected by wide variety of chemicals, solvents and staining agents and highly resistant to weathering. Normally used in thin sheets in both clear and pigmented forms. Cuts easily. Films difficult to tear | Burns noisily with yellow flame and black smoke with acrid, acidic smell. Shrinks on burning. Continues to burn after removal of flame. Not affected by cyclohexane or aromatic solvents |
| **Silicone (SI)** | 1943 USA | Heterochain polymers formed by polycondensation of polyfunctional silanols can exist as thermoplastics, rubbers and thermosets depending on starting materials and polymerizing conditions. They are used for laminates, rubbers, mould making materials, adhesives and other applications where good performance is required over a wide range of conditions | |
| **Styrene acrylonitrile (SAN)** | | Thermoplastic similar to polystyrene but harder with better chemical resistance. Suitable for outdoor use. Cuts cleanly | Burns with orange flame, black, sooty smoke, and odour of marigolds. Continues to burn after removal from flame. Softened by cyclohexane but not by aromatic hydrocarbon solvents |
| **Styrene butadiene (SBR)** | | Rubber | |

*continued*

**Table 4.1** Continued

| Polymer group, names and trademarks | Date introduced and country | Description and use | Simple identification |
|---|---|---|---|
| **Urea formaldehyde (UF)** | 1926 UK | Very hard, amorphous, chemically resistant thermoset formed by polycondensation of urea and formaldehyde. The resin is always mixed with one or more fillers to make it suitable for particular applications. Used for adhesives and mouldings, and, with or without alkyds in reaction type coatings., Normally available in dark, opaque colours. Chips and powders when cut | Difficult to ignite, burns with pale yellow flame with bluish edges and fishy smell. Self-extinguishing on removal from flame. Not affected by cyclohexane or aromatic hydrocarbon solvents |

*Source:* Compiled from information in Hall, 1981, Kaufmann, 1968 and others cited in Chapter 4

terns. Many nineteenth-century moulds for composition ornaments were made of pitch mixtures enclosed in a strong frame and squeezed, while hot and pliable, over an oiled carving. Gutta percha was also used as a mould material. Modern synthetic resins can also be used in this way (see section 4.7.6). Dental impression compounds have been used in picture frame restoration to make small squeeze moulds for the replacement of lost composition ornament. Commercial mould-makers and sculptors have used poly(vinyl chloride) 'hot melts' extensively for large flexible moulds.

### 4.1.4   Identification of plastics and polymers

Knowledge of the history of plastics provides useful background to their identification. Mossman (1988) and Braun (1986) provide simple tests for identifying plastics primarily based on solubility, heating and flame tests although additives for plastics are likely to modify test results (Gächter and Müller, 1985). The identification of additives in many instances can be carried out using methods described elsewhere in this chapter, however some additives are extremely difficult to identify directly and can only be inferred by the modification of properties from pure polymer or by sophisticated instrumental analytical techniques.

The increased complexity of polymeric materials has made their positive identification

correspondingly more difficult. Lebeaux (1989) has published a book known as the *Resinkit* that contains fifty samples of common plastics along with simple tests for identifying unknown plastics and comparing them to standards. This kit is helpful for observing the range of physico-mechanical properties of commercial polymers. Urbanski *et al.* (1977) provides more advanced methods for identifying plastics. Though some methods require sample amounts that may prohibit their use in conservation, the use of silicon carbide sampling of materials for examination by Fourier Transform Infra Red (FTIR) spectroscopy, as described by Martin (1988), is virtually non-destructive. FTIR microscopy is now becoming more generally available. Spectroscopic methods are further discussed by King (1992). Blank (1988) provides some simple tests relevant to conservation issues to help identify classes of polymers in order to determine proper consolidants and storage methods. Further information on the characterization of polymers is given by Campbell and White (1989) and by Hunt and James (1992). The identification of polymers used as coatings and media, adhesives and consolidants is discussed in section 4.8 below.

### 4.2   Introduction to coatings, binding media, adhesives, and consolidants

Coatings, media and adhesives are found as normal constituents of most furniture items.

Consolidants when present have usually been added by a restorer or conservator. A wide range of materials has been used to fulfil these functions, with synthetic materials having been added more recently to the range of naturally occurring materials used historically. Both groups are chemically complex, mostly organic, polymers but natural materials tend to be much more variable in composition and properties than their synthetic counterparts. These substances possess qualities of cohesiveness and adhesiveness and share a range of other properties, discussed below. In practice, the same substance was often used for different functions. An adhesive substance found to be useful in joining wood is also likely to adhere when applied in a thin layer as a coating, to bind pigment particles together or incorporate dyes and stick them to a surface as a binding or paint medium. Therefore, while it is convenient to discuss these categories separately, it is important to realize that there is considerable overlap between them.

To be useful, materials used as coatings, binding media, adhesives and consolidants need to be liquid at some point in their application and then to solidify. There are four basic mechanisms by which this occurs. Setting can occur through change in temperature alone (e.g. waxes), or through change of temperature and loss of solvent together (e.g. animal glues). It can also occur through loss of solvent or liquid phase without change in temperature (e.g. modern synthetic thermoplastics). Lastly, setting can occur by chemical reaction (e.g. thermosetting polymers, urushi, linseed oil). Chemical reaction may involve loss of a small molecule, such as water (e.g. urea formaldehyde) or may proceed without loss of volatile matter (epoxies, polyesters). Sometimes more than one setting mechanism may exist for a given chemical type. The way in which a material sets plays a large part in the way it can be used. Elimination products cause contraction. Epoxies, because they do not produce elimination products do not contract appreciably on setting.

A basic (ideal) requirement for all coatings, media, adhesives and consolidants is that they should be stable, fully compatible with the object material with which they are in contact (that is there should be no adverse chemical or physical interaction) and that they should

remain so. They should be durable under their intended service conditions and should not discolour, degrade, or crosslink. For conservation materials added to objects these are important considerations that govern our ability to undo treatments and to retreat at a later date, for example in the case of applying a coating to a paint layer. Materials must be safe to use and have the desired working properties to facilitate handling and application. Sensitivity of these materials to solvents remains important after their application.

## 4.3   Coatings – functions and properties

The general term *coating* is used here for any fluid organic material used to provide a continuous coat or cover on furniture and woodwork. It includes both clear or lightly coloured coatings commonly called varnishes and pigmented coatings called paints. Coatings may be applied to protect the surface of an object but are often of the utmost importance in themselves since it is the outer film or finish that visually represents an object to the viewer. Coatings are often encountered as *systems* of surface decoration (e.g. gilding, lacquer) rather than single materials. Therefore, a discussion of the general nature, function and properties of coatings is followed by an account of the structure of some common types of surface decoration and the preparations making up the layers found in them. This discussion covers primarily those coatings intended for interior use.

In summary, there are several properties of materials that are generically important to their function as coatings. Surface coatings are required to provide protection against handling and soiling and against damage caused by dust and atmospheric pollution. They should also impede the passage of water vapour, oxygen and prevent certain wavelengths of electromagnetic radiation. The coating must adhere well to the surface it is to protect. The cohesion and elasticity of surface coatings should allow for all ordinary changes in humidity and temperature of the air and preserve the elasticity of paint films under them. The coating should add to, rather than detract from, the appearance of the object and its colour, clarity, gloss and freedom from defects, such as bloom and wrinkling, are thus of paramount importance.

### 4.3.1   Protection against handling and soiling

Surface coatings prevent dirt from coming into contact with the object surface and protect it from abrasion during handling and dusting. The coating should therefore have appropriate resistance to abrasion and this is indicated by its hardness. Hardness expresses resistance to deformation and is a complex property. When assessed by indentation or penetration methods, it involves factors such as elastic modulus, yield strength, plasticity and rate of stressing. It is standard practice to define hardness only in terms of the methods of measurement or apparatus used, all of which measure slightly different things. A commonly used scale is Mohs hardness. This is a qualitative scale of unequal intervals based on increasing scratch resistance of minerals with talc equal to one and diamond equal to ten. It is too broad for coatings because all organic polymers rate below three on Mohs scale (they can be scratched with calcite). Pencil hardness covers a much smaller range than Mohs and is more useful to describe the hardness of coatings. It is obtained by using graphite pencils of increasing hardness (6B–9H) until a definite scratch is produced. Sward hardness can also be used. This measures the damping effect of a film on the movement of a rocker placed on the surface. Soft films damp the motion of the rocker more than hard ones.

The hardness of a coating is related to the viscosity grade of that material and hence to the average degree of polymerization. The viscosity grade of a material is usually taken as the viscosity of its solution at 20% solids concentration in toluene (Feller and Curran, 1985). Some idea of the range of hardness of different materials and of hardness within a polymer series can be obtained from the data in *Table 4.2*.

Hardness of a coating is related to the Tg of its polymer material. PVAC of viscosity grade 9 will have a Tg of about 17 °C whereas PVAC of viscosity grade 80 will have a Tg of about 24 °C. The practical lower limit to the hardness of a surface coating is that if it is too soft it will tend to pick up and imbibe dirt falling on the surface, thus defeating its purpose. This can be tested by coating some of the material on to a white surface and leaving it for a time in a dirty area at the expected service temperature. If the polymer has a Tg much below the service temperature it will resist attempts to clean it with water, detergent and a soft cloth and will remain dark grey with the collected dirt. This tends to be a problem with low viscosity grades of PVAC and with poly (n-butyl methacrylate). Shellac wears well and can be an excellent coating where hardness is desired. A balance of hardness for protection yet flexibility to accommodate movement in the substrate is desirable.

### 4.3.2   Strength and elasticity

A coating must be able to stretch and change its dimensions so that a minimum of stress is placed on the painted surface underneath. Ideally, the elastic modulus should be lower for the coating than for the paint. In practice, most polymer films have an elastic modulus considerably lower than dried linseed oil paint. A coating must be capable of reasonable elongation so that it remains continuous because if cracks develop, dirt and water vapour can penetrate and cause damage. The material therefore should not be unduly brittle. A safe limit

**Table 4.2**   Hardness of some thermoplastic resins

| Material | Viscosity grade (centipoise) | Pencil hardness | Sward hardness |
|---|---|---|---|
| PVAC | 9 | F | 63 |
| PVAC | 80 | H | |
| Poly n-butyl methacrylate | 50 | 2B | 30 |
| Poly iso-butyl methacrylate | 55 | H | 65 |
| Mastic and dammar | 1.5 | > 3H | 81 |

Films 0.0381 mm thick baked on window glass approximately 2 mm thick and measured at 21 °C and 50% RH.
*Source:* Information taken from Feller and Curran, 1971

on brittleness is not precisely defined but a figure of 1–3% elongation at break has been suggested for picture varnish coatings (Feller and Curran, 1985). Knowledge of viscosity grade is useful in comparing polymers in a series based on the same monomer. However, it does not necessarily follow that polymers of different types having the same viscosity grade will have precisely the same strength and brittleness. This applies equally to the hardness of different materials. In general, however, low viscosity grade polymers are more brittle than those of higher viscosity grade. For example, dammar and mastic (viscosity grade 1.5 cp) are much more brittle than Elvacite 2044 (poly (n-butyl methacrylate)) of viscosity grade 48 or AYAF (PVAC) of 80 cp. Brittleness can be reduced by using plasticizers. However, a better result may be achieved by suitable co-polymerization. The inclusion of material which is not part of the polymer structure can result in problems caused by its migration into paint layers. Plasticizers are generally avoided in conservation materials but have been widely used in the manufacture of plastic objects. Plasticizers reduce the modulus of elasticity, effectively reduce Tg, decrease hardness, increase creep and permeability and may result in more rapid deterioration. It is therefore better to use polymers with intrinsically desirable properties.

### 4.3.3 Barrier properties

Permeability is a general term used to describe the property of a material to allow the passage of some substance through it. Permeation takes place by diffusion. Measurements of permeability refer to the rate of transmission through a film.

Diffusion can be defined as the movement of atoms, molecules or ions through a gas, liquid or solid. In diffusion, gases, vapours (i.e. water vapour) and liquids pass through permanent or transient voids between polymer molecules. The diffusion rate therefore depends considerably on the size of the small molecules and the size of the gaps. It also depends on the partial pressure gradient across the film and intermolecular forces (hydrogen bonding, Van der Waals forces). For polymers, the size of the gaps depend on the physical state of the polymer, that is, whether it is glassy, rubbery or

crystalline. In the case of amorphous polymers above Tg, molecular segments have considerable mobility and there is an appreciable 'free volume' in the polymer mass. Also, because of segment mobility, there is a good chance that a molecular segment will at some stage move out of the way of a diffusing small molecule. Below Tg, the segments have little mobility and there is a reduction in free volume. There will be fewer voids and a diffusing molecule will have to take a much more tortuous path to get through the polymer. Around the Tg there are often complicating effects as the diffusing molecule may plasticize the polymer thus effectively reducing the Tg (e.g. PVAL and water). Crystalline structures have a much greater degree of packing and the individual lamellae can be considered to be almost impermeable. Diffusion can therefore only take place through amorphous zones or through zones of imperfection. Hence, crystalline polymers tend to resist diffusion more than either rubbery or glassy polymers. Unfortunately penetration of solvent into the polymer mass will be similarly restricted and these materials are difficult to formulate and use as coatings. Crosslinked polymers tend to resist diffusion but are generally unsuitable for conservation coatings.

Permeation can be defined as a three-part process. It involves dissolution of small molecules in the polymer, migration or diffusion through the polymer according to the concentration gradient and emergence of the small particle at the other side. Hence, permeability is a product of chemical compatibility and diffusion. Henry's law states that the solubility of a gas in a liquid is directly proportional to the partial pressure of the gas at a given temperature. Most atmospheric gases have relatively low solubilities and obey Henry's law but diffuse freely through amorphous regions of solid polymer. Vapours of organic substances with similar solubility parameters to the polymer have relatively high solubilities, with deviations from Henry's law, but diffuse more slowly as a result of comparatively larger molecular size and often strong interactions with polymer chains.

Polymers with low permeability to both gases and vapours include poly(vinylidene chloride) and co-polymers, acrylonitrile-styrene co-polymers, epoxides, poly(vinylidene fluoride), poly(ethylene terephthalate) (polyester), poly(vinyl chloride). These may be encountered in museum objects but are not suitable for use as conservation materials as they either have restricted solubility or are thermosetting.

In general, coatings are not complete vapour barriers. They do not prevent the transmission of vapours but reduce the amount transmitted in a given time. This property is valuable in the absence of stable environmental conditions. The effect of coatings in reducing the rate of dimensional change in hygroscopic materials, especially wooden panels, has been well demonstrated (Buck, 1961). Unfortunately, many sensitive objects are coated only on one side. When environmental conditions are stable, water vapour will pass through most coatings until equilibrium is established and in most cases this will happen surprisingly quickly. Some waxes, for example paraffin wax, possess good barrier properties to water vapour and are better in this respect than the synthetic thermoplastic polymers used as conservation coatings. The moisture exclusiveness of finishes on wood is reviewed by Feist *et al.* (1985).

### 4.3.4   Optical properties

The most important optical properties of coating materials are clarity (transparency), gloss, refractive index and colour. High clarity requires that the refractive index is constant throughout the sample in the viewing line. The presence of interfaces between regions of different refractive index causes scattering of light and reduction in transparency. This can be seen in otherwise transparent coatings containing very fine air bubbles, or matting agents such as wax or silica. Amorphous polymers free from impurities are transparent unless chemical groups are present that absorb visible light. Crystalline polymers may or may not be transparent. Where crystalline structures are smaller than the wavelength of light then they do not interfere with the passage of light and the polymer is transparent. Where these structures are greater in diameter than the wavelength of light then light will be scattered, providing the crystal structures have a different refractive index (i.e. a different density) from that of amorphous regions.

Transparency may be defined as the state permitting perception of objects through or beyond the material (coating). It can be assessed as the fraction of normally incident light that is transmitted with less than 0.1° deviation from the direction of the primary beam. Some coatings, although transparent, may have a cloudy or milky appearance known as haze. This can be measured as the amount of light deviating by more than 2.5 from the transmitted beam direction and is often the result of surface imperfections.

When light falls on a material some is transmitted through it, some is reflected and some is absorbed. *Transmittance* is the ratio of light passing through to the light incident and *reflectance* is the ratio of reflected to incident light. The gloss of a film is a function of the reflectance and the surface characteristics of a material. A perfect mirror-like surface, known as a specular reflector, shows one extreme of behaviour. At the other extreme, a perfect diffuse reflector reflects light equally in all directions at all angles of incidence. Several different measures of gloss exist, each defining a distinct aspect of appearance. These include specular gloss, distinctness of image gloss, contrast gloss and sheen. Specular gloss refers to the reflection that occurs at the angle of reflection equal to the angle of incidence of a beam of light. Contrast gloss is the ratio of intensity of light that is reflected at two different angles relative to the surface. Distinctness of image gloss refers to the distinctness of patterns of light reflected from a surface. Sheen is a type of reflection, possessed by velvet, where a matt surface gives rise to pronounced specular reflection at a small angle to the surface.

There is a relationship between viscosity and gloss whereby, generally, it is easier to get a high gloss with a polymer of low degree of polymerization (and low molecular weight). This is because the viscosity (resistance to relative motion within the material) is lower at a given solids concentration. Viscosity is also affected by choice of solvent and by temperature. Viscosity grade provides a convenient index. High viscosity grade material becomes resistant to flow at an earlier stage in drying. Solvent coatings that form an immobile gel at a point when they still contain appreciable solvent tend to form a surface that follows the irregularities of the underlying substrate. If a coating dries with a rough surface its contrast gloss and distinctness of image gloss will be markedly affected. The higher molecular weight PVAC and acrylic polymers tend to give semi-matt finishes whereas dammar, mastic and AW2 tend to produce high gloss surfaces. The nature of the surface therefore depends partly on the ability of the film to level itself. This in turn depends on the nature of the solvents used to formulate the coating. Using solvents that evaporate slowly will reduce the rate at which viscosity rises and allow more time for levelling of the coating before drying. However, it will also allow more time for the coating to pick up dust. Considerable experience is needed for the proper selection of solvents for coatings, particularly when using materials of high viscosity grade. Selection of solvents for coatings may, however, be restricted by the potential effect of the solvent on the underlying paint (Tsang and Erhardt, 1990). A slow evaporating solvent will remain in contact with the paint for longer and there is therefore greater risk of solvent action on the paint. Provided that a polymer material used as a coating is capable of high gloss then it is possible to obtain a full range of effects using different solvents, application techniques and matting agents.

The ability of a coating to wet the surface is important in saturating the surface and allowing colours to be seen, particularly so with porous surfaces. Penetration into porous surfaces is more easily achieved with polymers of low viscosity grade. An appropriate degree of adhesion to the surface is also important. Failure in this respect leads to light being reflected by cracks and fissures. This is often noted with polyvinyl alcohols which generally have low adhesion on most kinds of paint. The interaction of a coating with the wood on a cellular level is difficult to ascertain. Microscopy may show coatings that sit on the top of the wood exhibiting no evidence of saturation. Other coatings may be found to penetrate many cells into the wood tissue. The adhesive properties of surface coatings are similar to those of the same polymers used as adhesives. Some components of a coating such as oils can be drawn into the wood structure selectively due to the heterogenous nature of wood and this can cause uneven ageing characteristics in the coating. Coatings that are water or alcohol based are capable of swelling the wood tissue and thereby penetrating through cell walls.

This is one reason why alcohol-based coatings, or 'spirit varnishes' are known for excellent mechanical bonding with wood.

The refractive index of a coating can affect the appearance of the underlying surface. Refractive index measures the extent that light is bent in travelling from one medium to another (strictly speaking, from a vacuum but air gives a close approximation). As the refractive index of a coating increases, more light is reflected from the top surface, less light escapes from the coating into the air again and less light is reflected at the coating/paint interface. The refractive index therefore affects the success with which the surface is revealed. However, in practice the effect of variations in refractive index is often less apparent than differences in gloss due to the relative smoothness of the upper surface of the coating and the ability of the coating to penetrate and wet out the surface. This point is demonstrated by polyvinyl alcohols, cellulose ethers, and soluble nylon which are, or have been, used as consolidants of loose dry pigment. They have a minimal darkening effect because of their poor adhesive and wetting properties.

Very few polymers absorb radiation in the visible spectrum that is roughly between 380 and 760 nm. Thus, most polymers are colourless. However, some thermosets (including phenol formaldehyde, epoxies, and polyurethanes) absorb slightly more strongly at the blue end of the spectrum and thus appear yellowish or brownish in transmitted or reflected light. These substances contain alternating double and single bonds or aromatic rings which act as chromophores, absorbing light at frequencies corresponding to the excitation energies of bonding electrons. Since the eye is not sensitive to wavelengths of less than about 400 nm it is not necessary for coatings to transmit light of shorter wavelength. Indeed, it is a definite advantage if they do not since this will protect the underlying surface against damage from UV. Fresh dammar resin films absorb nearly all radiation below 280 nm and some of that between 280 and 380 nm. When aged, films of dammar and mastic absorb more of the UV component and some of the shorter wavelength visible radiation. They therefore appear yellow and later even brown thus distorting the true colours of the surface under the coating.

The extent to which a coating is known to yellow is an important consideration in its selection. The methacrylate and vinyl acetate polymers possess good stability to light and do not yellow with age. However they are transparent to short wavelength radiation and have a sharp cut off of transmission in the region of 200 nm. Coatings that are opaque to short wavelengths offer useful protection to painted surfaces in situations where UV levels are not otherwise controlled. Ideally, such coatings should remove all light below 400 nm and none above. Several compounds exist which are designed to filter UV radiation and which are suitable for incorporation in coatings. One problem with their use, however, is that of incorporating sufficient absorber for efficacy in a very thin film without the absorber migrating out of the film. The presence of traces of solvent may provide protection against UV during the drying period.

### 4.3.5   Solubility and working properties

Knowledge of the solubility of coatings is very important for several reasons. These include protection of existing coatings, deliberate removal or cleaning of existing coatings, application of new coatings, and health and safety considerations. A polymer that is to be used as a surface coating must be soluble in a solvent that does not adversely affect the underlying surface. It is also important that the coating should remain soluble in such a solvent.

A true solution is one from which the solute (the dissolved material) can be recovered unchanged by simple physical process. Two substances will only pass spontaneously into true solution if the free energy change for the solution process is negative. Whether or not this will occur depends on the various forces of attraction between molecules, the degree of randomness of the system and on the temperature. Solubility is favoured where the forces of attraction between polymer molecules and solvent molecules are greater than those between adjacent polymer molecules and where polymer and solvent molecules have similar polarity (Johnstone and Webb, 1977).

The inner cohesion of the polymer solid increases with its degree of crystallinity as the efficiency of molecular packing assists intermolecular interaction. Crystalline polymers are therefore less easily dissolved than amorphous polymers. They typically require conversion to a more amorphous form by warming (e.g. waxes). Crosslinked polymers cannot dissolve in the true sense. They may, however, show extensive swelling and softening when they come into contact with compatible solvents. A good introduction to solubility and solvents for conservation problems is provided by Torraca (1988) and by Book 2 in the Science for Conservators series (Moncrieff and Weaver, 1992).

Attempts have been made to relate the most important aspects of the compatibility of polymers and solvents through their solubility parameter. Its significance is that polymers and solvents having similar solubility parameters are likely to form solutions (Horie, 1987). A graphical representation of solubility (see *Figure 11.10*), developed by J.P. Teas of the Ashland Chemical Company and known as a Teas Diagram, is explained by Torraca (1988). For polymers used in conservation coatings, a more empirical alternative which has been used by some conservators is the concept of solubility grade. This gives a convenient measure of the relative tendencies of polymers to dissolve in hydrocarbon solvents (Feller *et al.*, 1985). The issue of solvents and solubility is discussed in Chapter 11.

Many organic solvents present serious health and safety problems through action on human physiology, through risk of fire and through damage to the environment. The best way to control the risk from organic solvents is to eliminate their use entirely. While this may not yet be practicable the hazard posed by the need to use organic solvents is playing an increasingly important part in materials selection. An alternative approach to that of solvent delivery is to apply surface coatings as emulsions. This has advantage over simple solutions that a much higher solids content can be achieved without making the preparation too viscous and is usually safer. Various acrylic and vinyl polymers can be manufactured in emulsion form. Thermoplastic resin *emulsions* contain resin particles of colloidal size ($0.001–1$ μm in diameter) dispersed in water. The process by which emulsions form films involves loss of water followed by coalescing of individual droplets of polymer to form a continuous film. For a given polymer there is a minimum film formation temperature (MFFT) below which the droplets do not flow together and therefore do not form a satisfactory film. The MFFT is important in relation to working properties, hardness and susceptibility to creep (especially important where emulsions are employed as adhesives). Emulsions can be prepared with varying sizes of dispersed particles. Small particles give good penetration and binding of pigment particles whereas large particles tend to remain more on the surface. This can be an advantage where consolidation which minimizes darkening of a chalky friable surface is required. The observations made about coatings in general apply equally to films formed from emulsions.

Before using emulsions as conservation coatings it is wise to investigate their composition since they are prepared by commercial emulsion polymerization processes and may contain undesirable additives. For an emulsion to form a satisfactory film it is necessary that the Tg of the polymer should lie some degrees below the ambient temperature. One way to achieve this is by use of a fugitive plasticizer in the formulation. Such plasticizer is slowly lost by evaporation in the final stages of drying causing Tg to rise and improving hardness. The nature of such plasticizers and other materials such as dispersing and coalescing agents should be known before use. Once dry, these films cannot normally be re-dispersed in water but require a polar organic solvent for removal. The nature of solvents needed for removal should be known before the material is applied. Emulsions are more thoroughly treated in the section on consolidation in Chapter 12.

Each time a varnish is removed there is a risk of solvent action on the underlying paint, including leaching, swelling and partial dissolution of the paint film. All coatings change chemically as they age, to an extent that is largely predictable based on the known chemistry of the coating. It is therefore important to consider carefully at the time of application of a coating, the likely requirements for its removal and the effect this will have on the paint. A resin that is prone to chain scission, or the breaking apart of the molecule into smaller units, will cause the resin to loose some of its cohesive strength. A polymer that crosslinks as the coating cures and ages becomes insoluble making it difficult to remove. Polymers that are chemically stable, undergoing minimal chain scission or crosslinking over time, are the most likely to be long-lived coatings. It is easier to predict the behaviour of a pure substance than of a formulation or mixture containing several materials.

## 4.4 Coatings – structures and preparations

The basic elements of decoration considered from a structural viewpoint are the support, the ground, the 'paint' or other decorative layer, and the varnish. The relationship of these layers is shown diagrammatically in *Figure 4.3*. Each component in a decorative scheme has a particular function to fulfil. The desirability of properties varies with different components but adhesion to adjacent layers, internal cohesion, hardness, brittleness, strength, sensitivity to light, temperature and relative humidity,

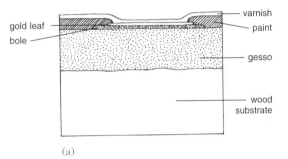

(a)

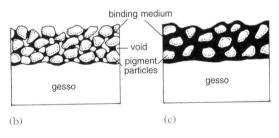

(b)                                    (c)

**Figure 4.3** (*a*) Diagrammatic representation of the layer structure of a painted and gilded surface, consisting of wood substrate and gesso ground, with paint layer/s and gilding (bole and gold leaf) covered by a varnish layer. (*b*) Underbound or 'lean' paint often appears matte. It has minimal binding medium that is often only barely sufficient to hold pigment in place. (*c*) Well-bound, medium rich or 'fat' paint usually appears glossy. The pigment particles are fully wetted by the medium

ageing properties and overall stability are all important. The following description includes the terminology used for different parts of decorative structures, some examples of the preparations used and an explanations of the layer structure of some common types of surface decoration. For definitions of a wide range of materials used in coatings see Massey (1967).

### 4.4.1   Supports

The support is the structural foundation, backing or carrier for the ground. Supports of decorative finishes on furniture are mostly wood but can be leather, metal, glass, stone, ceramics, papier mâché, or other materials. Supports may be flexible or rigid and may be more or less dimensionally stable under the influence of humidity and temperature. The stability of the support is of fundamental importance to the continued survival of the decoration placed on it.

#### *Stoppings*

Stoppings are used to repair small defects in presentation surfaces of (wooden) supports of furniture after manufacture, before further finishing. Historically, stoppings were based on oil and whiting, wood dust and glue, resin, wax or a combination of these. A representative stopping recipe for 'beaumontage' for traditional cabinet work included equal parts of beeswax and crushed rosin, a few flakes of shellac and dry pigments heated until the mixture had melted together and was used hot (Hayward, 1974). Commercially available shellac and 'lacquer' sticks are available for this purpose which are melted and dripped into the hole. Various types of plastic wood, supplied in tubes and cans, often contain cellulose and a quick drying synthetic resin binder. Two part wood stoppings that set with a catalyst are also available. Stoppings based on natural resins may have a tendency to crack and become brittle. Wax-based stoppings may be too soft for normal wear and could inhibit the adhesion of later finish work. Two part stoppings set by chemical reaction and may therefore be difficult to remove.

#### *Grain fillers*

Grain filler does not form a continuous layer over the surface and is not technically a

ground. Many different materials have been used to fill the grain of wood before polishing or painting, to prevent the finish sinking, to economize on materials and time, and to prevent grain showing. The use of brick dust is referred to by Sheraton in the *Cabinet Dictionary* (Sheraton, 1970) as a means of filling the grain partly with the dust itself and partly with wood fibres detached from the surface of the wood. Pumice can be used to the same end. Other materials include plaster, various resins and commercial grain fillers. There are many brands of filler available commercially. These divide into oil based fillers, composed of natural or synthetic resin and tung or linseed oil binders, and those containing a water-based finish (e.g. acrylic) as a binder. In either case, the bound solid is normally silica. An appropriate pigment is normally added to match the colour of the wood being filled.

### 4.4.2   Grounds

Grounds are layers or coats applied to the support to provide a suitable surface on which to paint or gild. Three important grounds in European and American painting are oil grounds, gesso grounds and emulsion grounds, though there are others (Massey, 1967). The ground fulfils some important functions. First, it buffers the surface decoration from the hygroscopic movements of the support, particularly important with wood. Secondly, it provides a smooth surface for painting or gilding and may itself be decorated with recutting or punch work. Thirdly, it gives a unified light colour against which the decoration is reflected and finally, the elasticity of the ground may permit burnishing of gold leaf applied to the surface. Different types of surface decoration require different grounds and these choices are determined by the intended use and cost. A traditional gesso ground, for example, is required for high quality water gilding, but oil gilding destined for an exterior location can be applied on a primer paint.

#### *Gesso grounds*

Gesso consists of an adhesive with an inert filler. Traditionally, animal glue is used as the adhesive but gesso can be based on casein, acrylic or other materials. The term gesso originally referred to a gypsum- (calcium sulphate) based gilding ground such as those commonly used in southern Europe. In the general context of painted, japanned or gilded furniture, the term is extended to include grounds based on calcium carbonate. This may not be the case in other conservation disciplines, where the use of the term 'gesso' may be specific to calcium sulphate grounds and where other grounds, such as those based on calcium carbonate, may be simply described as 'white ground'. Cennini's fifteenth century commentary on artists' materials recommends that the best size for gessoing panels is made from parchment prepared from the necks of goats and sheep by trimming, washing, soaking and then boiling it (Thompson, 1960). Other historic treatises such as those by Theophilus and Watin also advise on the preferred animal glue for making gesso, although interestingly, none mentions rabbit-skin glue (Souza and Derrick, 1995).

The filler is typically calcium carbonate or calcium sulphate but other materials can be used. Historically, calcium sulphate has been used in the Mediterranean basin and calcium carbonate in Northern Europe, where chalk was plentiful, but this is not invariable. Kaolin ($A_{12}O_3.2SiO_2.2H_2O$) and sometimes dolomite ($CaMg(CO_3)2$) were also used (Cession, 1990).

Large deposits of gypsum are found near Bologna and Volterra and also occur in varying grades throughout the world. Chemically, gypsum is calcium sulphate dihydrate formed by the deposition of salts in inland lakes. The raw, unburned gypsum has no function in the making of gesso and is only used once it is calcined and ground to make plaster of Paris ($CaSO_4.\frac{1}{2}H_2O$). The powder, known as *gesso* in Italian, is used in two ways. It is soaked in excess water (so that it does not set) for four or five weeks with frequent stirring and changes of water. The residue, after the water is poured off, is made into small loaves and dried. This very fine powder, known as *gesso di Bologna*, can then be crushed, sieved and mixed with size to make *gesso sottile*. To make *gesso grosso*, unadulterated plaster of Paris is sifted and mixed into a paste with either parchment or rabbit-skin size. *Gesso di Bologna* is slightly greyer than chalk whiting (see below), it feels cooler and softer, and compacts more easily. It is lumpy and therefore it is always necessary to sieve it before mixing it into the size.

In Northern European regions, particularly England and France, where the chalk deposits are plentiful and of a high quality, a very fine variety of calcium carbonate (chalk whiting – $CaCO_3$) known as gilders' whiting is used to make gesso. Natural chalk is a soft, white rock which is largely composed of the remains of minute sea organisms. It is extracted by open-surface mining of deposits with minimal impurities and a high degree of whiteness. Once the material is extracted it is dried to lower its water content from 20% to 0.2%. For gilders' whiting the rocks are ground to a particle size of 3.3 or 4 µm. The fine, soft, white powder is added to glue size, made from parchment cuttings or rabbit skins, to make gesso.

Southern European grounds prepared with gypsum (natural gypsum is calcium sulphate – $CaSO_4.2H_2O$), usually consist of a coarse preliminary preparation followed by a smoother one. Cennini describes the two stages, *gesso grosso* (coarse) and *gesso sottile* (fine). Typically, *gesso grosso* refers to anhydrite ($CaSO_4$) or plaster of Paris ($CaSO_4.\frac{1}{2}H_2O$), which is then coated with a *gesso sottile* made of calcium sulphate ($CaSO_4.2H_2O$), the difference being the degree of hydration and the consequent chemical link. Anhydrite and plaster of Paris set by hydration, regaining the water lost during heating, but when mixed with glue, they become much harder.

Von Endt and Baker (1991) explain that in a filled animal glue system, the hydrogen bonds of the glue are pulled apart to allow the filler into the matrix, which reduces the flexibility of the chains. This makes the matrix stiffer, but also weaker as less force is required to pull it apart. Fillers such as calcium carbonate and sulphate do not interact chemically with the matrix and consequently form a system that is weaker than those in which there is chemical linking between the filler and the polymer. Although filled glue system are less permeable to water than unfilled ones, gesso can be permanently deformed by the introduction of humidity because the molecules do not always go back to their original positions and less stress is required to provoke subsequent deformation.

### Bole

A type of clay also called bole is used to facilitate the burnishing of water gilding. The name *bole* or *bolus* is derived from the Greek, meaning 'clod of earth', as the clay that was first used for this purpose came from deposits in the ground. Armenian bole was considered to be the best. It is composed of pipe clay (hydrated silicate of aluminium and organic sediments) and iron oxides, which give it its distinctive blood-red or orange colour. It may now be difficult to obtain.

The colours used depended upon the clay deposits that were locally available so that, for instance, the red clay on seventeenth century Spanish work is a different colour to French red clay of the same period. In later centuries, when individual clay deposits were no longer exclusively relied upon, fashion played a role in determining the clay colour. In nineteenth-century English gilding, for example, a dark blue/black clay was often used under burnished water gilding whilst in the last quarter of the eighteenth century a pinkish brown clay was common. The clays were made using a number of different ingredients, ranging from bullock's blood to soap. These additives gave varying characteristics but the base constituents remained pipe clay and pigments.

Today, bole comes in many colours and is most often sold in the wet state, but it can also be purchased in a more limited range of colours in the dry cone form. Modern commercially produced boles are manufactured from pipe clay combined with a colouring agent and water. A few contain an oil or lead to further facilitate the burnish but in most cases it is left up to the gilder to add a little oil if required.

Bole is made by mixing clay with warmed parchment size, rabbit-skin size, fish glue or glair and applying with a soft brush onto the prepared gesso surface on which the leaf is to be laid. Glair is derived from egg white (see section 14.2.13). Two distinct layers of bole may often be found on the same piece. A yellow ochre bole was applied directly on the gesso, to hide any breaks or 'faults' in the gilding by virtue of its colour. Over the yellow bole, there may then be a second bole made of clay of a deeper colour to which beeswax, tallow, oil, suet or graphite may have been added to enhance its burnishing capabilities. Souza and Derrick (1995) has shown cross-sections of Brazilian polychrome sculptures in which graphite particles can be seen lying parallel to the surface of the bole. This second layer of bole is applied to tone the colour of the gilding, and to serve as a soft 'seat' (*assiette* in French) which deforms under an agate burnisher to take a high polish. Bole is discussed further in Chapter 14.

### Composition

There are numerous recipes for composition and the term is used to cover many forms of raised decoration including papier mâché and 'pastiglia'. However, the traditionally accepted form of 'gilders' compo' is a mixture of resin, linseed oil, animal glue and whiting. Ornament is created by pressing the warm, dough-like composition into reverse-carved moulds of boxwood or fruitwood (Thornton, 1985). When released from the mould the composition will have taken on the detail, however fine, of the mould. At this stage it is pliable and easy to cut enabling the ornament to be placed onto curved surfaces or into corners. Once dry, composition is hard and brittle and cannot be cut into or carved without the material splintering or shattering. Though composition itself is very durable, shrinkage can be a problem and regular breaks and gaps are a common feature in this type of ornament. As it shrinks and breaks it sometimes also curls away from the support.

### 4.4.3  Paints and paint media

When present, paint usually carries a vital part of the information the artist, designer or craftsman wished to convey. Paints consist essentially of a *pigment*, a film-forming *medium* or *binder,* and a liquid component composed of solvents and diluents that makes the mixture more or less fluid during application. Together, the film-forming and liquid components are often called the *vehicle*. Various additives may be used to give coatings additional structural or aesthetic properties. Many of the materials used to make transparent coatings are also used to make paints. Due to the presence of pigment particles, opaque coatings are generally more stable than transparent coatings (Roff and Scott, 1971) and generally provide better protection of the substrate due to the more complete exclusion of light, moisture and environmental fluctuations. A harmonious relationship between the ground, the pigment and the binding medium is essential (Wehlte, 1975). The ground is not only the foundation, but the underlayer for all subsequent colour. The visual character is determined by the binding medium, whether the pigment particles are simply attached or whether they are embedded in it. The absorption of the medium by the ground, and the distribution of the pigment in the medium (opacity) are critical factors. Finally the surface coating is important, not only as a protective layer, but also in giving the paint its optical properties.

Pigments are fine, solid, particles that do not dissolve in the vehicle. They are used to provide colour and body. Materials that provide body without providing colour are called *extenders*. Extenders are normally used because they are cheaper than prime pigments but they also contribute useful qualities to the paint, for example by improving adhesion, strength and ease of sanding.

A medium or binder is the substance that holds the pigment particles together in a paint. This must be capable when dry of forming a solid coating in a continuous film over the surface. This can be achieved by evaporation of solvents, by reaction of pre-polymers, or by change of temperature. The term medium may also be used for materials suitable for adding to or combining with paint to change its properties to the requirements of the artists particular techniques; for example to make it thicker or thinner, quicker or slower drying. Additives that may be used for this purpose include thickeners, flow promoters and reducers, matting agents, catalysts, accelerators, inhibitors, wetting agents and dyestuffs. Binders for pigments must satisfy most of the same criteria as for a clear finish except that they need not be transparent. Mixtures of pigments and binders, or paints, can be categorized by the ratio of pigment to binder. Paints with a high ratio of binder to pigment are called *fat* and *vehicular* and those with a low ratio are *lean* or *granular*. This terminology may be extended to lightly coloured mediums which are described as *pellicular*.

The liquid part of the vehicle can consist simply of a true solvent for the medium but frequently it contains diluents which are not true solvents for the binder but which contribute other desirable properties to the vehicle.

The formulation of paints is critical to their success and many different factors play a part. Paint must have the required appearance when dry but must permit ease of handling to allow application in the fluid state. All paints require an appropriate degree of adhesion to the substrate or preceding paint layer and good flow characteristics to wet the surface and level out to the required degree. They must then stop flowing and dry to produce hard tough durable films that will retain their decorative properties in service. Generally, it is desirable that they should be relatively easy to repair but they must be resistant to common solvents in use. Normally if a paint is being formulated for a particular application one starts with the required properties of the dry film. This determines whether the film will be thermoplastic or thermosetting and consequently the choice of drying mechanism and application techniques required. Formulation of paints in relation to application characteristics is discussed by Bentley (1998).

Pigmented varnishes are sometimes called enamels, lacquers, finish coats or topcoats. Enamels are normally based on thermosetting materials that give a hard finish superficially resembling vitreous enamel. The term lacquer is normally used for thermoplastic solution paints or varnishes but is sometimes confused with oriental lacquer (e.g. Japanese urushi), a quite different material. Although top coats can be applied directly to the support, it is often difficult to achieve the desired result with a single formulation. Stoppers, fillers, primers and undercoats which have a composition suited to fulfil their function in the system of surface decoration, are usually applied to form a ground to give optimal results from the finish layers. The function of stoppers and fillers has been discussed above. Primers promote adhesion, reduce absorption by porous surfaces and usually impart some corrosion resistance over metals. Undercoats, which frequently contain significant quantities of extender, form a highly pigmented layer that provides body to the paint and help to level out minor imperfections to permit easy smoothing and give a good base for the topcoat. Undercoats must adhere well to both the primer layer and top coat. Sealers may be applied to the substrate over another coating layer to prevent movement of material out of the substrate into the paint or from one layer of paint to another. Sealers may also be used to improve adhesion between layers where this would otherwise be weak. Suitable paint media may be used in thin layers with little (transparent) pigment to make glaze layers which permit subtle colour variations to be achieved.

A wide range of substances and mixtures of substances is found in historic paint media used in the 'polychromy' or coloured decoration of furniture. Among these are animal glue (distemper), egg tempera, casein tempera, wax emulsions, wax resin mixtures (encaustic) and various drying oils and oil–resin mixtures. Water colours are also frequently encountered in retouches. Watin's *L'Art du Peintre, Doreur, Vernisseur*, first published in 1755, gives an excellent account of artist's materials and their application. The pigments he recommended include lead and chalk whites, red and yellow ochres derived from clays, lapis and Prussian blues and lamp and ivory blacks to name only a few. He cites binders made of animal glues, egg white, oils, such as linseed, walnut and olive, resins such as mastic, copal and sandarac, and gums. These materials are discussed in more detail at the end of this chapter. A French paint system that Watin called *Chipolin* (from the Italian for garlic), consisted of parchment glue to which garlic has been added and whiting (ground) followed by two coats of a glue-based paint, and then by two coats of weak glue size. Finally, three coats of spirit varnish were applied (Watin, 1728). The garlic may have served to promote adhesion and acted as a fungicide.

Fascinating and valuable historical reference is also provided by the period treatises of Pacheco (1649) and Stalker and Parker (1688). Massey (1967) gives over 200 formulas for making paints, glazes, mediums and varnishes for a variety of painting techniques including tempera, oil, acrylic, gouache and encaustic with instruction on their purpose, manufacture and use. Knowledge and awareness of traditional paints has led to the formation of organizations such as the Traditional Paint Forum in the United Kingdom which focuses on the materials and techniques utilized for architectural paint schemes and associated furniture. The materials and techniques of medieval painting are discussed by Thompson (1956) and by Hulbert (1987). Mayer (1981) provides

the artist with a comprehensive review of all aspects of the materials and techniques of painting. A good introduction to paint chemistry and the principles of paint technology is provided by Bentley (1998).

### 4.4.4    Transparent coatings

Transparent coatings used over painted wood include varnishes and waxes. Oils may be added to the list of transparent coating materials used to finish unpainted wood. Varnishes are transparent or translucent top coatings that give a gloss (Perry, 1804). They are similar to glazes but generally unpigmented and are used to protect the finished work against moisture, pollutant gases, dust and handling. Transparent finishes increase the sheen and deepen the colour of the surface by filling pits and surface irregularities thus reflecting more light back to the eye rather than scattering it, that is they provide optical saturation. Historically varnishes were based on natural resins but waxes and oils have also been used in combination with them in various varnish formulations, as well as on their own, to enhance both bare wood and finished surfaces. The twentieth century has seen a large range of synthetic thermoplastic and thermosetting polymer materials added to the list of transparent surface coatings available for wood. For a review of traditional and modern coatings commonly found on furniture see Mills and White (1987). For coatings commonly used for conservation purposes, see Horie (1987). The chemistry of these materials is further discussed by Ash and Ash (1982), Kolesky (1995) and Bentley (1998).

To form a continuous thin film, coatings, like adhesives, need to be in liquid form at some stage in their application. This requirement can be met in various ways. Thermoplastic finishes found on furniture are relatively hard at room temperature but during their application heat can be used to make them soft or fluid. Materials such as waxes, wax-resin mixtures and shellac can be made sufficiently fluid by the vigorous motion of a hand-held rubbing tool (friction polishing) or by the motion of a lathe.

A category of thermoplastic materials, important to coating and adhesive technology but of minor use in plastics manufacturing, is materials that dissolve in solvent and harden again without undergoing any change as the solvent evaporates. This category, known as solvent release coatings, includes traditional spirit varnishes made from clear hard solvent-soluble polymers called resins and solvents such as ethanol. Two commonly used solvent release varnishes are shellac in ethanol and methyl methacrylate in petroleum benzine. Other thermoplastic resin types commonly used in the preparation of solvent release varnishes in the fabrication or conservation of furniture include the polycyclohexanones (e.g. ketone N and MS2A), poly(vinyl acetate), poly(vinyl butyral), and a range of acrylics.

Thermoplastic resin varnishes are usually easy to prepare and are sufficiently durable for interior use, having good abrasion resistance but only moderate resistance to water and other solvents. The fact that such coatings are susceptible to solvent action makes it comparatively easy to repair surface damage such as scratches and abrasions. Ageing of the coating may restrict solubility to some extent as crosslinking may occur in natural resin coatings, but they are generally resistant to this process due to lack of reactive sites on the polymer chains. Consequently they generally remain relatively soluble even after ageing. Virtually all of the solvent leaves the coating once the film has reached full hardness, though this may take weeks or months (Martens, 1968). The process of film formation and the life of the film are extensively discussed by Feller *et al.* (1985). Some solvent release coatings, for example oil/resin varnishes which contain a drying, oil have an additional film forming process involving oxygen where network polymerization takes place.

Thermosetting varnishes harden by irreversible chemical reaction which usually results in greater polymerization and crosslinking than occurs with thermoplastics. A general name for this class of coating is *reactive*, because setting takes place as the result of chemical reaction. In cases where oxygen is directly involved in the setting reaction, as with drying oils, the term *oxidative* may be used. True inter-molecular networking, or crosslinking requires a minimum of two double bonds or reactive sites on one chain and three on another (Kolesky, 1995). Important thermosetting finishes include fixed oil varnishes, oriental lacquer (urushi) and modern two-component catalysed polymers such as epoxies, polyesters, polyurethanes and some acrylics.

Traditional finishes in this class, known as fixed oil varnishes or oil/resin varnishes, include resin(s), an oil and a solvent. Such mixtures often require heat or pressure to coax the components into a solution. Typical reactive varnishes include copal and linseed oil in turpentine or alkyd resin and tung oil in a petroleum distillate. Modern polyurethane and alkyd varnishes are chemically modified drying oils which also harden by oxidation. The drying oils such as poppy, linseed and nut oils and mixtures of these oils with natural resins have been in common use at least since the fourteenth century (Gettens and Stout, 1966). The curing of oil varnishes is a function of solvent release and the oxidative polymerization of the oil component.

Thermosetting polymer coatings are harder and tougher than thermoplastics, have improved resistance to moisture, solvents and staining and thus yield greater protection for objects in use. Their lower molecular weight in solution allows for high solid content applications. However, they have generally greater potential long-term reactivity tending toward yellowing and their resistance to solvents makes them more difficult to repair and very difficult to remove independently of other coatings.

### *Historical use of varnishes*

Some of the earliest examples of glazes and stains can be found on medieval European polychrome sculpture (Serck–Dewaide, 1991). There are, however, countless examples on later European painted or gilded furniture. Theophilus, a twelfth century monk, recommended coating metal leaf with 'boiled oils added to a quart of gum called glass by the Romans'. The De Meyerne Manuscript of 1620 describes the use of shellac, saffron, aloe and gum arabic. Some common transparent coatings were lacquers or glazes of coloured resins or gums (e.g. gamboge) applied in a solvent such as spirits of turpentine over silver gilding to give it the appearance of gold. Watin (1728) describes making a good 'vernis or' from gutte, sandarac and wine spirits, while Stalker and Parker (1688) advise the use of 'size, seed-lac-varnish or lacker', which, for a deeper colour, should be mixed with dragon's blood and saffron. Pacheco (1649), Cennini (Thompson, 1960) and other well-known period sources all give such recipes, many of which were highly coloured with madder, indigo or other dyes to be applied over metal leaf or paint.

The process of distillation necessary for the production of solvents was known to the ancient Greeks but not extensively or efficiently employed. Purified alcohol was widely available in Europe after the twelfth century. Various volatile essential oils such as 'oil of spike' (spike lavender) and 'spirits of turpentine' (distilled from conifer resins) were also being prepared in Europe by the late fifteenth or early sixteenth centuries. Several clear resins could be dissolved in 'spirits of wine' (ethanol) including shellac, sandarac, mastic, gum benzoin, accroides and the brightly coloured red and yellow resins dragon's blood and gamboge. A smaller number, such as mastic and dammar, could be dissolved in turpentine. Turpentine was the primary solvent used to thin out both drying oils and oil–resin varnishes.

Until the end of the eighteenth century, the relatively high cost of alcohol soluble resins as well as the expense of the solvent confined these 'spirit varnishes' to such rarefied and time-consuming crafts as japanning and the finishing of small decorative objects. The technique of 'French polishing', by which shellac-based varnishes are applied with a cloth pad in a complex series of operations, was probably not developed until the early years of the nineteenth century when both shellac and rectified alcohol became more commonplace. It is worth noting however that shellac must have been available from at least the late seventeenth century since it is referred to by Stalker and Parker as being unsuitable for varnishing. The application of shellac with a pad creates a surface coating known as French polish. This finish technique has its origins in an eighteenth century process called French polishing which used bundles of abrasive *equisetum* stalks called a 'polissoire' and wax to create a high gloss finish (Halee, 1986; Mussey, 1982a). By the early nineteenth century, obtaining a high gloss finish with a pad and shellac became the preferred technique. In an 1827 American finisher's manual, it was noted that friction, or French polishing, was 'of com-

paratively modern date' (Mussey, 1987). The *Mechanic's Register* (1837) claimed that 'We were the first to publish any accurate information on the "French Polish" for wood, now become so universally employed'. It has been a part of the finisher's and restorer's trade ever since. For further discussion on the introduction of 'French polish', see Penn (1984).

Synthetic polymers became available as coating products toward the close of the nineteenth century with the introduction of cellulose nitrate. This and the products that have followed in the twentieth century are synthetic materials intended as improvements on traditional natural materials. These products vary greatly in chemical make-up. They can be found in transparent coatings, paints, and other finishing materials. In general, synthetic resins are high molecular weight long chain or network polymers. Synthetic resins that have been used as coatings on wood include alkyds, urethanes, phenolics, polyesters, epoxies, methacrylates (acrylics), ketone resins and cellulose nitrates.

### 4.4.5   Gilding

The term gilding usually refers to the process of covering a surface with gold or other metal leaf in imitation of solid metal. The range and characteristics of metal leaves are described in section 5.5. There are several methods by which they can be attached and these are described more fully in Chapter 14. Historically, there are two processes described as 'oil gilding' and 'water gilding' by which the extremely thin metal leaf may be attached to the surface to be gilded. Oil gilding uses a very thin layer of oil-gold size as the adhesive to attach the leaf and can be carried out on virtually any surface though the full effect of the gold is only achieved on well-prepared smooth surfaces. Oil-gold size contains principally linseed oil with the addition of copal varnish to promote thorough drying of the film and to prevent the size from forming runs, and turpentine to achieve the desired viscosity. A very thin coat is applied with a brush onto the surface to be gilded. Porous surfaces are best isolated by, for example, a shellac coating to prevent excessive or uneven absorption of the size and loss of adhesion. Water gilding uses water to activate the glue size in the surface layers of the ground. Normally the ground is a highly prepared surface of gesso and bole. Water gilding can be left matte or it can be burnished to a very high lustre. Oil gilding cannot be burnished in this way but can be lightly polished with cotton wool to achieve a sheen. Examples of the different types of gilding, with their corresponding layer structures, are discussed in Chapter 14.

### 4.4.6 Oriental lacquer (urushi)

The term 'lacquer' is sometimes rather indiscriminately used to represent various different materials including natural resin varnishes and synthetic coatings based on polyesters, acrylics and cellulose derivatives. Oriental lacquer, which the Japanese call *urushi*, is, however, a unique material. The main raw material used in the lacquer process, that is the lacquer itself, is made from the sap of several species of trees of the family Anacardiaceae, the most important of which is *Rhus vernicifera* (also called *Rhus verniciflua* and sometimes considered to belong to the genus *Toxicodendron*). Other species of importance include *Rhus succedana* from Taiwan and Vietnam and *Melanorrhoea usitata* found in Thailand and Burma. Other members of the same family growing in South East Asia and other tropical zones produce similar materials. These include mango, and cashew which is used by some commercial restorers and craftsmen working in Japan.

In China where use of the sap originated, archaeological evidence has continued to push back the earliest known date for lacquer items at least to about 700 BC (Kuwayama, 1988). In 1978 there were estimated to be 410 000 000 lacquer trees in China with an annual production of some 2 000 tons of lacquer. About 250 g of sap are obtained from each tree. This huge output reflects the use of lacquer in China as an industrial plastic used in the manufacture of insulators and oil pipelines as well as domestic wares and art objects. In Japan, where the use of lacquer is confined to art objects and domestic wares, production in the same year was estimated at five tons.

Lacquer has been used in the production of a wide range of decorative art objects, sculptures and buildings. Variations in method are found all over Asia but the technique was brought to perfection by the Japanese. *Rhus*

species are relatives of the sumac and poison ivy and are toxic, producing in most people an allergic reaction with skin rashes and blistering which can be severe. Once cured, however, the risk of unfavourable reaction is very slight. Cashew lacquer, a less toxic substitute for urushi lacquer, has been marketed as Polycite by the Mitsubishi Petrochemical Company.

### *Preparing the lacquer*

The first stage in the production of lacquer is obtaining the raw materials. *Sap* is collected from mature trees through incisions made in the bark (Quin, 1882). When first collected, the sap is a double emulsion of water in oil in water containing 27–50% water (*Figure 4.4*). During maturation the sap converts to *raw lacquer*, a water in oil emulsion. Raw lacquer contains urushiol (60–65%) and glycoprotein (2–5%) in the oil phase of the emulsion and polysaccharide (5–7%), laccase enzyme (1–2%) and water (20–25%) in the water phase.

Chemically, urushiol is a catechol – a benzene ring with two adjacent hydroxyl groups – which can have a variety of C15 or C17 carbon chains attached to it (Du, 1988) (*Figure 4.5*).

Raw lacquer is used as an adhesive for the priming layers in the manufacture of lacquer objects. However, if sap is used for the upper layers as well, the coating will be found to have very changeable properties and is not at all durable. The mechanical properties of a coating made with refined urushi remain unchanged over long periods of time

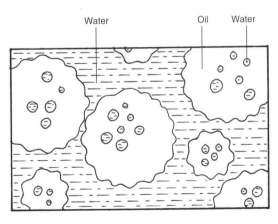

**Figure 4.4** Diagrammatic representation of the double water-in-oil-in-water emulsion nature of lacquer sap when first collected

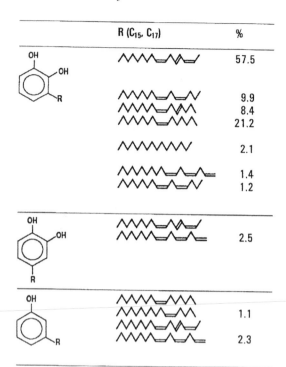

| | R (C₁₅, C₁₇) | % |
|---|---|---|

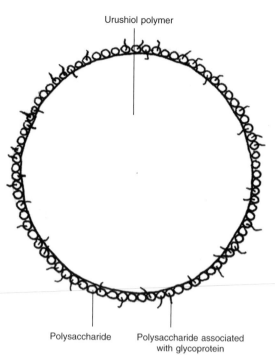

Urushiol polymer

Polysaccharide          Polysaccharide associated
                        with glycoprotein

**Figure 4.5** The chemical structure of the main urushiol constituents of Chinese and Japanese lacquer (Du, 1988). The zigzag line represents the C15 or C17 chain attached to the primary urushiol molecule, and the double lines indicate the position of double bonds on these chains

**Figure 4.6** Diagrammatic representation of a proposed structure for an urushi grain. The high molecular weight urushiol polymer has outer polar hydroxyl groups. Polysaccharides and glycoproteins are absorbed onto the urushiol molecule to form an outer layer on each urushiol grain (Kumanotani, 1988)

(Kumanotani, 1983). The process of converting sap to true lacquer is therefore very important.

### Refining raw lacquer

The matured sap is filtered and then stirred, first at room temperature then at 20–45 °C in a specially designed open vessel. The conclusion of the stirring is determined by the changing colour and viscosity of the sap under treatment. The refined urushi produced by this process has a much reduced water content and an appropriate viscosity for coating. During the processing, several important things happen:

- Excess water is evaporated off, giving 2–4% water content.
- The polysaccharides in the water droplets are at first precipitated and then broken up into fine particles which become dispersed into the urushiol.
- There is partial polymerization of some of the urushiol.

- The urushiol becomes grafted on to glycoproteins and some of these urushiol glycoprotein complexes join up with the finely dispersed polysaccharides (*Figure 4.6*).

In practice different grades and qualities of lacquer are prepared for use at different stages in the application process.

### Making a cured film

There is a great deal of variation in the technique used. This partly reflects the requirements of the final product and partly the techniques used by individual artists. It is not unusual for there to be 30–70 or more steps in the production of a plain black lacquer article, so only the main steps are reviewed here.

At each of the stages in the production of a surface it is necessary to cause the lacquer to harden. This is achieved in one of two ways. In the first method, in which lacquer is baked at 110–180 °C, oxygen reacts with unsaturated side chains of the urushiol to produce perox-ides. These peroxides can then attack the ring to produce free radicals which enter further reactions or form crosslinks with other side chains, both routes leading to a highly crosslinked polymer. This method is used for the first coats on metal articles but the method normally used on organic substrates, including wood, involves enzymatic polymerization. In this method, lacquer is cured in a humidity chamber via an enzyme catalysed reaction. At 20–30 °C, urushiol is oxidized in the presence of laccase enzyme present in the sap to form free radicals. These then react in a number of ways to give a crosslinked polymer. High humidity is required in this process for oxygen transport. The relative humidity at which poly-merization occurs significantly influences the qualities of the final product. During the 'cure', which can take anything from a few hours to several days, the net water content of the film reduces to 1–3%. Part of this water is incorp-orated in the molecular structure of the urushi and cannot be lost without damage to the lac-quer coating.

The polymerization mechanism is complex and not completely understood but involves three important stages: first, chemical enzy-matic polymerization of the urushiol; secondly some additional reaction of the polymeric urushiol with the polysaccharides to form a three-dimensional network and thirdly, physi-cal drying. The net result of the various reac-tions is to produce a film which is densely packed with grains of giant polymerized urush-iol. Each grain is surrounded with polysaccha-ride and glycoprotein and 'glued' together by polymerized urushiol and glycoprotein (*Figure 4.7*). The urushiol inside the grains is well pro-tected against degradation but material that 'glues the grains together' is more vulnerable. At a macroscopic level, the final result of applying a number of layers of lacquer is a hard, transparent, brownish-black, lustrous, durable coating of great beauty, the best of which is highly resistant to water and organic solvents and does not tend to dry up or crum-ble with time. Many of the properties of the cured film are comparable to modern plastics such as melamine. However, the quality does vary considerably depending on the quality of the raw materials and the techniques used. Lacquer articles incorporate other materials for

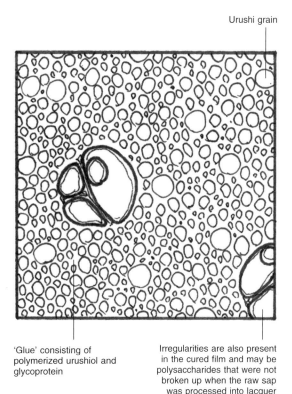

Urushi grain

'Glue' consisting of polymerized urushiol and glycoprotein

Irregularities are also present in the cured film and may be polysaccharides that were not broken up when the raw sap was processed into lacquer

**Figure 4.7** Diagrammatic representation of the morphology of a cured urushi film, characterized by densely packed grains. The grains have a diameter of around 0.1 µm and are bound together with a 'glue' composed of polymerized urushiol and glycoproteins (Kumanotani, 1988)

strength and stability in the primary layers and for the production of decorative effects in lay-ers close to the surface.

### Applying lacquer to substrate

Metal, leather, ceramic, turtleshell, ivory, horn and cloth have all been used as supports for lacquer objects but the most common sub-strate is wood. For flat objects, hinoki (Japanese cypress) or Japanese cedar are typi-cally used. For turned objects a variety of tim-bers (typically a ring-porous hardwood) is used. Timber is meticulously selected to be free of knots and other defects, with straight grain and even texture, and is then carefully prepared. Wood may be boiled to remove resins, or smoke seasoned and is often left for 10 years or more after seasoning before use. The final lacquer coating will add something like 0.75 mm all round (i.e. if piece of wood is 2 mm thick it will end up 3.5 mm thick) and this has to be allowed for in construction. A mixture of glue and lacquer is used as an adhesive for jointed pieces.

The first step in the process of creating a lacquer finish on the substrate is priming. This involves sealing the substrate against the ingress and egress of moisture and providing a foundation which effectively isolates the topmost coats from the substrate. It builds the foundation for the topcoats in the same way that gesso does for gold leaf. The first coat of the priming is raw lacquer and this penetrates and to some extent seals the wood surface and provides a good key for adhesion of subsequent coats. After this any defective parts of the wood are cut away and these and other irregularities are filled with a mixture of urushi, rice paste and wood dust (*kokuso*). This stopping is cut back when dry and cloth or paper is then applied over the entire surface with glue and lacquer. A number of layers of a mixture of lacquer, clay, and water (*sabi*) are then applied. Each one is left to dry and is rubbed down before the next is applied.

Wajima and Yamashina are the two main areas in Japan where clays suitable for urushi foundation are found. It is formed into small cakes with water then baked and ground up into a powder. The powder is sieved to give different grades. Coarser grades are used nearest the substrate and progressively finer material is used as the foundation is built up. The process of application drying and polishing continues using different grades of lacquer and abrasive until the final surface is achieved. The complete process and some of its many variations are described in detail by Quin (1882). Useful information is also given by Herberts (1963), Brommelle and Smith (1988) and in the various publications of the Tokyo National Research Institute of Cultural Properties.

### Decoration

In the Japanese repertoire of lacquer techniques, which is by far the most comprehensive of lacquer-producing cultures, there are nine major divisions of technique with many further variations. According to Jahss and Jahss (1972), the nine main divisions are: background techniques; makie; coloured lacquer;

lacquer painting; carving; imbedded lacquer; encrusted lacquer; lacquer imitating or covering other material; transparent lacquer. Nashiji, of which there are twelve or more different types, is the name given to the well-known background technique in which small flakes of gold or silver alloys are dusted over wet lacquer to give a stippled gold Venetian-glass effect. This is similar to the European techniques known as aventurine, named in turn after a type of quartz which contains scales of mica or other sparkling material which the decoration resembles. In makie techniques a design is gradually built up in layers by repeated dustings, sprinklings and rubbing down of powdered gold and silver alloys. In *togidashi*, the design is built up in gold, covered with black lacquer and is then literally 'brought out by polishing'. In *hiramakie*, subtle graduated dustings and clear lacquer are used with shading lacquer to give a flat picture. In *takamakie*, a raised design is built up. There are variations on each of these basic techniques and a further ten or so miscellaneous makie types. Carving techniques include guri in which lacquer is carved back through coloured layers, *kamakura-bori* in which wood is carved in low relief, covered with black and then with red lacquer and *chinkin-bori* (literally sunk gold) in which a design is incised and filled with gold or other material. Imbedded lacquer techniques use gold or mother-of-pearl shell stuck on with lacquer and the surrounding area is then built up flush with lacquer around it. The full range of techniques is well described from both a technical and historical perspective by Jahss and Jahss (1972) and von Ragué (1967). For further information on Chinese lacquer see Garner (1979).

### Identification

The work in good-quality Japanese lacquer is normally so highly regulated that with only a little familiarity it is fairly easily recognized. However, export lacquers, and those from other sources may be more readily confused with European imitations. Jaeschke (1994) provides useful guidelines on both simple identification and on suitable instrumental methods. Microanalytical FTIR techniques based on reference sets of samples of known origin have been used by Derrick *et al.* (1988) to distinguish between urushi and pigmented natural resins though this technique required the removal of a small sample. Classification of far eastern lacquers by pyrolysis mass spectrometry, described by Burmester (1983), requires the use of larger quantities of unrecoverable sample and complex data handling methods but provides a powerful method for the identification of restored areas and forgeries and for the relative dating of East Asian lacquer-ware. Determination by atomic absorption spectroscopy of the content of copper, iron and manganese of oriental lacquers has been used to investigate the provenance of urushi. When access to analytical facilities is limited, solvents may be used to help distinguish between Oriental and European lacquer (Westmoreland, 1988). Solvents tests are based on the fact that oriental lacquer is not soluble in polar solvents, whilst resin-based Western japanning is readily soluble in such solvents. Swabs used for solvent testing oriental lacquer may be discoloured by lacquer degradation products even when the bulk lacquer is not soluble. Oriental lacquer may have been coated or repaired with natural resins.

### 4.4.7 Japanning

Highly decorative articles of lacquer were carried to Europe first by overland trade routes and later by the ships of maritime nations such as Holland, Portugal and Britain. By 1609 the demand for wares from the Orient was sufficient to prompt the establishment of a shop by the East India Company which retailed 'East India Commodities' (Edwards, 1987). Imports of Asian lacquer lead to the production of copies executed in spirit varnish on a wooden ground in imitation of Japanese makie techniques, referred to as *japanning*. Historically this term has also included the imitation of other lacquer techniques such as *bantam* and *nambang* work as well as faux marble and tortoiseshell.

Although the decorative art of japanning has a continuous history from the sixteenth century to the early twentieth century, significant differences in technique were employed at different times. The early japanners created complex multi-layered spirit varnish surfaces in an attempt to achieve the deep translucence of the Oriental lacquer which they were imitating. This is significantly different to the techniques

employed from the mid-eighteenth century onwards when the use of thin layers of oil-based paints and varnishes superseded the earlier spirit varnish techniques. There is a distinct lack of both comprehensive secondary sources and of systematic studies of existing primary documentary sources on japanning that may have led to some confusion about the materials and techniques which have been used. John Evelyn (1664) and Stalker and Parker (1688) offered instructions for contemporary amateur japanners. Professional japanners were trained by apprenticeship. Although the professional may have employed more sophisticated techniques, there were only limited ranges of pigments and resins appropriate to the task. Those mentioned in these documentary sources are also found within a broader artistic tradition where they are employed for the same working properties that recommended them for japanning.

Evelyn's instructions begin with the preparation of the varnish. The recipe is set out as follows:

> *The Gum-lacq remaining in the Bag [four ounces], with one ounce of Sandrac (some add as much Mastick and White-amber) dissolve in a large Matras (well stopped) with the [one pint of exquisitely dephlegmed] Spirit of Wine, by a two Days Digestion, frequently agitating it, that it adhere not to the glass: Then strain and press it forth into a lesser Vessel: Some after the first Infusion upon the Ashes, after twenty-four Hours, augment the heat, and transfer the Matras to the Sand-bath, till the Liquor begins to simper; and when the upper Part of the Matras grows a little hot, and that the Gum-lacq is melted, which by that Time (if the Operation be heeded) commonly it is, strain it through a Linnen-cloth, and press it betwixt two Sticks into the Glass, to be kept for Use, which it will eternally be, if well stopped.*

Gum-lac is soluble in alcohol and was used to impart a hard, tough, flexible film. However, it has a tendency to yellow, darken and become insoluble with age (see section 4.7.5). Sandarac was added for hardness and lustre and mastic as a plasticizer. Amber, though soluble in oils when heated, is described as practically insoluble in ordinary resin solvents, including alcohol. It was often confused or adulterated with copal resins (Gettens and Stout, 1966) and thus it is unclear whether amber, copal or another unknown resin were actually used in this recipe.

Evelyn goes on to describe the method of application. Wood is to be prepared clean and smooth. Any defects are to be filled with a paste made from gum tragacanth mixed with an appropriate coloured pigment. Once flaws had been filled the wood was then to be given a coat of the varnish. Instructions are given for the preparation of coloured varnish; red from cinnabar, black from a mixture of calcined ivory and green copperas (verdigris) and blue from ultramarine. Red or black coloured varnish was prepared by mixing one part colour with seven parts varnish. Four coats of coloured varnish were applied with drying time between coats and then rubbed down with Dutch rushes (Dutch rushes or Dutch reed was obtained from members of the Equisitaceae, the Horsetail family of jointed ferns, whose stems contain large amounts of silica). This application of four coats could be repeated up to four or five times to give a total of up to twenty-four coats of coloured varnish. The final layer of coloured varnish was smoothed with Tripoli powder and either olive oil or water on a felt pad. Over the coloured varnish, two coats of a modified clear varnish without sandarac (possibly to decrease the brittleness) were given and into this gold decoration was applied. The gold was obtained by filing or cutting fine gold wire of the type used by embroiderers. Coloured details could be added to this before the whole was coated with an unspecified number of layers of clear varnish sufficient to render the surface 'like polished glass'. Final polishing was done with Tripoli powder, oil and felt.

Stalker and Parker (1688) provides detailed technical instruction for the manufacture and decoration of varnished surfaces and over a hundred patterns in the 'Indian' style with which to decorate them. So comprehensive were the instructions that the treatise became the definitive description of the japanning process for amateurs, being either plagiarized or reproduced with minor alterations in subsequent texts for the following fifty years. The success of the book would have been dependent on the success or failure of the efforts of its readers and thus it is likely that the authors

simplified the range of equipment, materials, recipes and techniques to ensure that the application of the Japan varnish was as straightforward as possible.

Pear wood, close grained, free from knots, smooth and clean, was recommended as a substrate for japanning. However, as supplies of this fruitwood were limited it was often applied as a veneer. Lime and walnut presented good alternatives, whilst oak and deal were more problematic as they required priming with 'plaisterers Size' to fill the grain and smooth the surface before japanning could begin. Stalker and Parker were aware of the problems caused by a thick priming layer and recommended that such layers be well rubbed down 'thin and smooth and even'. An alternative preparation suitable only for 'the tops of tables and boxes' was a mixture of animal glue and sawdust which needed to be scraped flat when dry.

Although Stalker and Parker lay out general rules for varnishing, they describe three distinct processes depending on the colour desired. First, for blacks and reds, seed lac varnish mixed with pigments was recommended for both ground and top varnish. Secondly, for white and blue, a ground of pigment in isinglass secured with best 'white' (i.e. transparent) varnish was recommended as a means to avoid the discoloration that would occur with gumlac. Thirdly, for chestnut and olive grounds, pigment in common glue size secured with seed-lac varnish was used. In every case a highly reflective surface, which imitated Oriental lacquer, was the desired outcome.

Lampblack was recommended for black grounds. For red grounds, vermilion was used in one of three variations; on its own for 'Common' red japan ground; glazed with dragon's blood in seed lac for dark red grounds and mixed with white lead for pale red grounds. Blue grounds were achieved with smalt and white with flake white applied over a white (gesso) ground based on calcium carbonate and isinglass. For chestnut grounds, a mixture of Indian red or brown ochre with lead white and lamp black was used. For olive grounds English pink (a yellow lake derived from a dye extracted from buckthorn berries) was mixed with lamp black, lead white and raw umber as required.

Seed-lac varnish is recommended by Stalker and Parker in seven out of nine of their recipes for coloured japan grounds and by Salmon (1701), the *Dictionarium Polygraphicum* (Barrow, 1735) and Dossie (1764). Seed-lac is a semi-refined material which has grain-like appearance and varies in colour from yellow to reddish-brown. It seems to have been preferred to the more highly refined shellac at this time probably because either the refining process itself or the adulteration which sometimes accompanied it resulted in a product that gave inferior results. The various stages and products of the refining process for shellac are discussed in Section 4.7.5. Stalker and Parker recommended one and a half pounds of seed-lac per gallon of spirit, a solution only half as strong as both Evelyn's varnish or a typical modern shellac varnish. The presence of Venice turpentine, added along with alcohol to spirit varnishes at this time (Gettens and Stout, 1966), may help to explain the increased brittleness of long-dried films and may contribute to the yellow green fluorescence seen on japanned objects. The use of lac-based varnishes has made japanned finishes highly vulnerable to damage from water and alcohol. The combined use of shellac as the vehicle for carrying pigments and securing varnishes limits the options available for the conservator wishing to clean or remove discoloured surfaces as all layers are likely to exhibit similar solubility.

Stalker and Parker's recipe for Best White Varnish includes whitest gum sandrick (64%), whitest gum mastic (4%), clearest Venice turpentine (12%), gum capal (6%), gum elemni (2%), gum benzoin (2%), gum animae (6%) and white rosine (2%) dissolved in alcohol in a concentration range equivalent to 2¼–4½ pounds per gallon. This mix of resins seems to have been a deliberate attempt to balance the properties of each ingredient to achieve as transparent and long-lasting a varnish as possible.

The general procedure was to apply three to six coats of pigment in the chosen medium to give the base colour and over this to apply tinged varnish or glaze (optionally, depending on the colour) and then up to twenty-four clear top coats of varnish polished to give a high gloss. Polishing was a multi-stage process that denibbed, flattened and then polished the surface. Tripoli powder was used with water up to the final stage of polishing which was achieved using oil and a pigment in harmony with the ground colour to remove all traces of Tripoli powder. Lamp black was used for black grounds and fine flour for white. The polished ground could be left as a flat unadorned surface or decorated with speckles, painted, or decorated with raised chinoiserie designs.

Pictorial designs could be created by simply painting the ground in imitation of the togi-dashi technique used on Japanese lacquer. A range of commercially available artists pigments could be applied in weak gum water after the ground had been degreased with Tripoli powder. Stalker and Parker recommended a weak mix, first to avoid 'spoiling the complexion of the colours' and secondly to allow the varnished surface to be polished without damaging or lifting the underlying paint. It is likely that the use of such a weak binding agent has been a factor in the deterioration of painted and similarly bound metal powder decoration.

Raised work was applied in imitation of finely executed takamakie decoration. Two methods were described by Stalker and Parker. In the first, equal parts of whiting and bole were finely ground into a paste of 'dropping consistency' with a weak solution of gum arabic (2 oz in ¾ pint of water). The paste was raised to an appropriate level, the detail painted on top in gum water and vermilion and the raised work was then cut, scraped and carved to reveal pictorial detail, hopefully without breaking the dried paste from the ground. A second, easier, method was to use a thinner paste and to raise the design in stages, each pictorial element being isolated from the next by coating the edges with seed lac varnish to preserve a crisp design. When dry, the paste was smoothed with Dutch rushes and was then ready for the application of painted or metal decoration.

A range of different metal powders was used to embellish both flat and raised japanning. Classified according to colour and based on alloys of copper, zinc, silver and tin they were applied either with oil gold size or weak gum water. When dry, this decoration was sometimes coloured with transparent pigments very finely ground in oil and thinned to an appropriate consistency with turpentine. Fine detail could then be added by incising or adding finely painted lines. Two different kinds of modified seed lac securing varnish were used to protect the surface decoration. One was applied in three to four coats over the painted or metal decoration to prevent tarnish, enhance colour and provide gloss and the second was applied in five to six coats over the whole surface.

The japanned papier mâché that was popular from about 1770–1870 was decorated using different materials and techniques to those described above, though the inspiration was largely the same – the imitation of work from Japan. Because early japanning lacked both the strength and density of its Eastern counterpart, attempts were made to develop an improved alternative. In 1757 the Society of Arts offered a premium of £20 to anyone who could produce a varnish equal to that of the famous French 'verrnisseur' Guillaume Martin and his brothers. A stronger, more satisfactory English varnish evolved based on *asphaltum*, which is a slow-drying element from the residue of petroleum or coal tar. It is also known as pitch and has been used for coatings since prehistoric times. Tar varnish was made of a mixture of linseed oil, resin, wax and asphaltum thinned with turpentine. This mixture had to be dried artificially, and as a result, its use on wooden objects was fairly hazardous. It was in fact originally developed around 1730 at an iron foundry near Pontypool in Wales for use on iron plates. The iron plates were found not to be a good surface for japanning because the lacquer easily chipped off the metal. However, on paper mâché the mixture was much more successful. The papier mâché would not warp or crack like wood, but could otherwise be treated in just the same way.

In the blacking shop the articles were treated as Henry Clay set out in his patent:

> ... it is first coated with fine lampblack mixed with tar varnish, then with tar varnish only, and when dry scraped with a plane, to remove all the loose fibrous particles from the surface of the paper, it is then varnished and well rubbed between each coat of varnish, to make the surface quite even. When sufficiently varnished to form a good even surface, it is placed in the polisher's hands, to be polished in the black state previous to painting. The polishing is performed by rubbing first with pumice stone to take off the small dust knots in the varnish, and make it

> harden better, then the surface is rubbed with sand made from pumice stone afterwards with rotten stone , and if a bright surface is required, it is produced with the hand, and a little finely powdered rotten stone ...

The 'blackers' worked quickly over the surface of the object with a large round 'stovers brush'. Speed was so crucial to the work that they could not put down their job until they had finished the process and could pass the article to the stove. Each coat of varnish had to be stove dried. In larger firms, the stoves were small rooms about 10 ft × 10 ft × 10 ft with large iron doors, into which the stove enamellers could push their trucks to stack the shelves. The earliest ovens were heated by underground fires which, because they had to be stoked from the outside, tended to be warmer near the outer wall where they were easier to stoke. Many hours of rubbing and varnishing were necessary to achieve the brilliant, glossy finish that was the hallmark of all English papier mâché. This finish is found not only on the outside, but on the inside and the back of an article as well.

Japanning became a popular art among the ladies of the eighteenth century; various magazines published articles describing the newest methods. *The Ladies Amusement or the whole art of Japanning Made Easy* (see Pillement, 1959), became a standard source book for those engaged in decorating japanned wares at an amateur level, much as Stalker and Parkers' *Treatise* was in the late seventeenth century. Walch and Koller (1997) provide analyses of German baroque and rococo japanning and an extensive exploration of their science, technology and conservation.

## 4.5   Adhesives

Adhesives are substances capable of holding other, similar or dissimilar, materials together by their own agency or, as is often the case in woodworking, by acting in concert with mechanical methods such as joints. Hence they must have good adhesion and good cohesion. *Adhesion* is the bond formed between the adhesive and the substrate (the *adherend*), whilst *cohesion* is the internal attraction of the adhesive to itself. The effectiveness of an adhesive is a result of the type of stresses experienced, the bonding area, the overall load and whether this is intermittent or continuous. If the adhesive is visible, for example as a glue line, then colour and other optical considerations may be important. The choice of an adhesive is affected by many additional practical considerations discussed below.

Adhesives may hold materials together simply by invading tiny pores and undercuts in the adherends thereby locking them together mechanically (called mechanical adhesion), or by molecular attraction of the adhesive and adherend – the same inter-molecular forces that generate cohesion. This attraction that molecules of one surface have to those of another is termed 'specific adhesion' and is greatest between materials that are chemically similar. As everyone knows, oil and water do not mix, and a polar water-based adhesive is unlikely to adhere well to an oily non-polar substrate. However, specific adhesion may also be high when hydrogen bonds are capable of being formed between dissimilar materials where one is a proton donor and the other a proton acceptor.

The forces of attraction depend on very close proximity of molecules. A non-porous solid such as steel will attract itself if the mating surfaces are so perfectly polished that air is excluded and very close contact is made, but such close contact is not possible between most solid surfaces due to roughness, or because they are porous and consist mostly of voids (e.g. wood). This dictates the use of a liquid adhesive which can flow out onto a rough and void filled surface 'wetting' it intimately and serving as an intermediate between the solid surfaces. When the adhesive itself becomes solid by cooling (heat set), chemical reaction (polymerization or thermosetting) or solvent loss, the adherends are firmly stuck together. Pressure sensitive adhesives are exceptions to this type of adhesion, being soft enough in solid form to conform very closely to surfaces.

The better a substrate is 'wet' by an adhesive, the better the bond will be because the degree of wetting is itself dictated by the attraction generated between the substrate and adhesive (specific adhesion). Wetting is dependent on the surface tension, or energy, of the liquid and the solid and on the viscosity of the liquid. Surface tension is a direct measure of intermolecular forces. The tension at the surface of a liquid or solid material is the result of the attraction for the bulk of the material to the surface layer. A molecule in the bulk of the material is attracted equally to the molecules that surround it whereas a molecule at the surface is attracted from below but not from above (*Figure 4.8*). This attraction tends to reduce the number of molecules in the surface region and causes an increase in the distance between molecules at the surface. In order to keep these molecules at the surface, energy is transferred from the body of the material to its surface (i.e. work is done). Surface energy is a measure of the energy necessary for the body of the material to hold the surface to itself (i.e. of the work being done). Thus materials whose bulk and surface are strongly bound together, such as metals, ceramics or diamond, will exhibit high melting points and hardness and will have a high surface energy (500–5000 mJ/m²). Materials which are held together only by secondary molecular bonding (e.g. hydrogen bonding or Van der Waals forces) will have a low surface energy (less than 100 mJ/m²). Water, for example, has a surface energy of 72 mJ/m² whilst paraffin wax has a

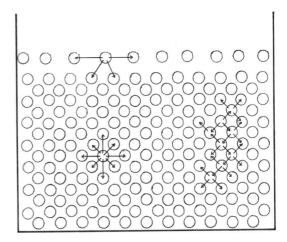

**Figure 4.8** Surface tension/energy. Diagrammatic representation of the intermolecular forces in a liquid, with arrows indicating the attraction between molecules. The molecules at the surface of the liquid are more widely separated than adjacent molecules in the bulk liquid. Surface tension (or surface energy) is a measure of the intermolecular forces between the body of the material and its surface

surface energy of 22 mJ/m². In order for a liquid adhesive to spread and wet the adherend surface, there must be a greater attraction of its constituent molecules for the substrate than for each other. Low energy liquids will therefore be attracted to high energy surfaces. A good example of the effect of relative surface energy is to use two materials that can be either liquid or solid (and thus can be either adhesive or adherend) that are relatively close in surface energy. Liquid epoxy resin (surface energy 43 mJ/m²) applied to solid polyethylene (surface energy 31 mJ/m²) will wet the surface poorly and produce a comparatively weak adhesive bond. Liquid polyethylene applied to solid epoxy will wet the surface well and produce a much stronger adhesive bond (Blomquist *et al.*, 1983). Similarly, whilst low surface energy Teflon (18 mJ/m²) will adhere to high surface energy metal, few materials will adhere to Teflon (hence the success of non-stick cookware).

A high energy surface contaminated with low energy material (e.g. a metal surface contaminated with oil) will behave as though it were a low energy surface until the contaminants are removed. Similarly some low energy surfaces present on polymeric materials will either require selection of an adhesive with an even lower surface energy or some form of pre-treatment to raise the surface energy of the adherend.

Another way to visualize surface wetting is by the *contact angle* formed between the surface of a drop of liquid on a solid and the surface of the solid. A drop of water on a piece of wax, for example, beads up into a spherical shape having a large contact angle. A drop of water that can spread and flatten on a wettable surface has a small contact angle (*Figure 4.9*). Observation of this phenomenon can be a useful guide in judging the appropriateness of an adhesive, or of the condition of the adherend surface which may be too oily to be wet with a water based adhesive.

There are various other practical aspects of adhesive bonding which can be explained by physical phenomena.

### Glue line thickness, adhesive failure

The thickness of the glue layer between the adherend surfaces can affect the strength of a joint in several ways. First, an excessively thick glue line composed of a thermoplastic adhesive will tend to 'creep' or gradually change shape and fail under a prolonged loading stress. In some situations the rigid adhered surfaces will restrain movement of the plastic adhesive (plastic constraint) but only where the adhesive line is thin enough that its internal flow characteristics (rheological properties) will not be the dominating factor.

Secondly, adhesives may be hard and brittle due to their inherent characteristics (such as low molecular weight or highly crosslinked structures), low temperatures (below the glass transition temperature at which they show fragile glass-like characteristics) or due to excessive desiccation (as with hide glues). With such brittle adhesives, a thick glue line may make it possible for flaws and fissures at the edges to serve as 'stress raisers' and propagate the cracks throughout the adhesive causing failure.

Closely mating surfaces and thin glue lines are generally desirable but even this rule has limits. If excessive clamping pressure is exerted on adherends in order to create a thin glue line, high spots on the surfaces are forced into compression and can then exert a continuous stress on the glue line after the clamps are removed. This stress can cause 'strain' resulting in a change of shape and failure due to either plastic flow or fracture. There is a theoretically ideal glue line thickness which achieves a balance between failure due to excessively thick glue lines on the one hand and failure due to starved joints on the other. Whether this can be achieved in practice is another matter. Ideal

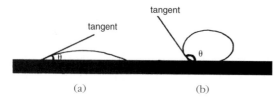

(a)                              (b)

**Figure 4.9** One way to quantify the surface wetting characteristics of a liquid is to measure the contact angle of a drop of liquid placed on a surface. The contact angle ($\theta$) is the angle formed by the solid/liquid interface and the liquid/vapour interface measured from the side of the liquid. If the contact angle is less than 90° the liquid will wet the solid well (*a*). A zero contact angle represents complete wetting. If the contact angle is greater than 90° the liquid will wet the surface poorly (*b*)

glue line thicknesses for wood are discussed in Chapter 10.

### Starved joints

Obviously sufficient adhesive must be present in a glue line to fulfil its intended function. A starved joint will result where insufficient adhesive has been applied to fill the gap between adherend surfaces, or where the porosity of the adherends has drawn adhesive away from the join by capillary action. Adhesive viscosity plays a large role in this mode of failure. Adhesives with low viscosities are generally unsuitable for use on porous substrates and have no gap filling capability where mating surfaces are less than perfect.

### Roughening surfaces

An early, and apparently naive, theoretical model for the interaction of adhesive and adherend stressed the mechanical interlocking of a dried adhesive with voids and undercuts on the substrate surface. Intuition suggested that a roughened surface would produce a stronger join and toothing planes were traditionally used by cabinetmakers to key up mating surfaces. Modern studies have demonstrated that this actually decreases adhesion in wood by damaging the fibres and creating loose detritus. The increase in surface area due to roughness should create a stronger join, but air trapped in voids tends to offset this effect. Modern adhesive science has found very few practical instances where increased roughness aids in adhesion. Although toothed surfaces may result in weaker joints, it is conceivable that a toothed surface could promote a more even glue line thickness by allowing excess glue to flow away (Hawkins, 1986). Also, it is perhaps worth mentioning that roughening surfaces removes contaminants and will increase surface area. Therefore while intentional roughening may be a poor strategy for wood, it may be more effective for other materials, such as gesso-type grounds or metals.

### 4.5.1 Factors governing the choice of an adhesive

Most adhesives have a characteristic *open time*, which is the time that may be allowed to elapse after application before assembly. The *closed time* is the length of time that may be allowed

to elapse after assembly before final positioning and clamping, after which assembly is either impossible or the strength of the final bond is adversely affected. Adhesives with very short open times can be chosen where the assembly job is simple or where clamping is not possible owing to shape, fragility or other factors. Conversely, adhesives with long open times are necessary where the assembly job is difficult or where elaborate clamping systems must be used. Open and closed times may be affected by factors such as the ambient temperature, and humidity or the age of the adhesive. Most adhesives have useful shelf lives of a few months to a few years. The problem of short shelf life can be addressed by only purchasing in small quantities and only as much as is required for a particular job. The shelf life of most materials can be extended by refrigeration or hermetically sealed storage. Liquid hide glues degrade continuously in the bottle and become less effective with age. Hot hide glues begin to degrade as soon as they are hydrated and heated, and should be made fresh at regular intervals, and not overheated while in use. Information on the preparation and use of hot hide glues is given in Chapter 10.

A great number of factors can affect the choice of an adhesive. These include shelf-life, surface preparation required, viscosity, bond strength, size of loads and types of stresses it can withstand, durability in service (effect of relative humidity and temperature), whether reversibility and/or re-treatment are possible, open time, closed time, health hazards, characteristics of cured material, colour, optical saturation, machinability, chemical stability, water resistance, gap-filling ability, reversibility, formulation, substrates, price and the pressure under which components need to be held together while the adhesive sets.

An adhesive must do its job under the operating conditions or it is unsuitable regardless of ideal characteristics of chemical stability and reversibility. Reversibility is a conservation principle that must not be seen in absolute terms, but as a concept that is influenced by service conditions. As already mentioned, a museum conservator can often make more conservative decisions because re-treatment in the event of failure is feasible, whereas a more intrusive treatment and inherently less reversible adhesive may be necessary if conservation is likely to be a unique event in the life of the object. There are various reasons why the principle of reversibility must be borne in mind by the conservator and they can be very practical (e.g. providing short-term reversibility in case things go wrong) as well as ethical or philosophical. Some adhesives and coatings will severely limit the possibility of future treatment or even subsequent operations in the same treatment. For example, consolidation with waxes or stabilization with polyethylene glycols will introduce very effective release agents that make adhesive bonding or coating virtually impossible, and such treatments are practically as well as theoretically irreversible. There may also be a conflict between durability and reversibility.

### Health and safety
Virtually all cured adhesives are of very low toxicity, but this is not true of the uncured liquid components. The chemicals used to prepare thermosetting adhesives such as epoxies, polyesters and formaldehyde resins, are associated with a variety of health hazards, as are the solvents used to apply various natural and synthetic resins. Health hazards have become an increasingly important concern as the risks have become more fully understood. Decisions regarding use of toxic materials have been left to the craftsperson or conservator in the past, but are increasingly being made by governmental regulatory agencies. Wherever good alternatives can be found to toxic materials they should be used, even if minor disadvantages are evident.

### Characteristics of cured adhesive
The physical characteristics of the cured or solid adhesive are of obvious importance. Many of these characteristics, such as hardness and fragility, softness and potential for cold flow or creep, sensitivity to moisture and heat have already been discussed. Visual characteristics can also be very important. These considerations include the initial colour of the cured adhesive as well as colour change as a result of ageing. The adhesive can affect the colour of the substrate by staining it, or by filling pores and visually darkening it as a result of optical saturation. Cured adhesives are also vulnerable to processes of chemical degradation which can result in change of colour or adhesive and cohesive failure. Adhesives

which spontaneously reverse themselves over time have obvious limitations but from the point of view of a manufacturer in our throw-away society, these times can be relatively short and still be acceptable. Claims of permanence by industry must therefore be carefully evaluated.

### Relativity of choice factors
It is important to note that there are no absolute advantages or disadvantages affecting a choice that will not be governed by service conditions and ethical and aesthetic factors. The characteristic cold-flow or creep of a soft adhesive for instance, while disadvantageous in most situations can accommodate movement in an inherently unstable material such as wood. There are no good or bad materials, only poorly considered applications. A conservator is simply eliminating tools from the kit if a prejudice concerning a material is allowed to develop as a result of poor performance under specific conditions. Care must be taken to evaluate each new situation with a clear and open mind.

## 4.5.2   Adhesives used in woodworking

Given the ingenuity and imagination of human beings it is likely that almost any substance ancient or modern that could be construed as an adhesive has been tried as such. A tremendous variety of substances have been used as adhesives, both singly and in combination. These include natural waxes, bituminous materials (asphaltum and bitumen, tars and pitches), carbohydrates (starch and plant gums), animal and vegetable proteins, natural resins and lacquers, and virtually all of the synthetic polymers or plastics. Among the synthetic thermoplastic polymers used as adhesives, simple solvent release formulations include cellulose nitrate, cellulose acetate, polystyrene, poly vinyl acetates and acrylics. Resin emulsions, familiar to most people as white glue and yellow glue, are among the most commonly used non-industrial woodworking adhesives. Thermosetting resins include urea formaldehyde, phenol formaldehyde, resorcinol formaldehyde, epoxies and cyanoacrylates. These materials are discussed in detail in section 4.7.6. Many of these materials were obviously unsuitable, many have had brief vogues and fallen out of favour, and many have continued to be used under various service conditions. Because so many of these materials have also been used as consolidants, media, coatings and as moulding and casting materials, more detail about them is given in the review of materials in section 4.7. However, the discussion of two categories of adhesive material, hot melt adhesives and contact cements will be completed here.

### 4.5.3 Hot melt adhesives

These adhesives are thermoplastics which are capable of wetting and adhering to a surface when melted and achieve their bond strengths as they cool. A wide variety of hot melts are used in industry but home and small shop use is generally confined to the commercially available sticks that are melted and applied with a hot glue 'gun'. These sticks are available in a variety of melting ranges which govern open time, and are generally composed of polyamide type resins similar to Nylon. Polyamides melt at reasonably low temperatures, are quite polar (compared to polyethylene for example) and wet substrates well. They are very useful in quick construction of jigs, fixtures and shipping crates. Polyamide glue-gun sticks have poor to fair bond strength and are generally soft and prone to creep with poor machinability. The open time varies according to grade but is generally very short (measured in seconds). Irritant fumes are given off when materials become too hot and there is a danger of serious burns by skin contact with molten adhesive. Eye protection must be worn when using these materials. They vary in colour from white to amber and have good chemical stability and water resistance.

Hot melt adhesives have also been used in sheet or film form for laminating. The adhesive known as BEVA, specially formulated for low temperature application, is based on ethylene vinyl acetate and contains various other additives. It has been used extensively in conservation for various applications, both in solvent solutions and as a dried film.

### 4.5.4 Contact cements

These adhesives can be characterized as permanently sticky or tacky coatings applied to adherends which stick firmly to themselves as soon as they are brought into close contact. A variety of polymers have been used in this way, but the commercial contact cements sold for veneering and laminating usually consist of neoprene, a synthetic rubber, in solvent solution. Most rubbers including neoprene have very poor long-term chemical stability. As a result, whilst rubber-based contact cements are widely used in new veneering and laminating, they should not be used on historic artefacts. Contact cements may also be made from resin emulsions. These are available commercially as water based contact cements, but may also be made by the conservator from appropriate grades of acrylic emulsion such as those available in the Lascaux or Rhoplex lines. These adhesives have much greater chemical stability, are non-toxic and have various applications from gilding to mount-making. Contact cements of any type have fairly low bond strengths and are soft and prone to creep.

Adhesion and adhesives are discussed by Allen (1984), Blomquist *et al.* (1983), Cagle (1973), Kinloch (1987), Lee (1991), Packham (1992), Shields (1974 and 1976), and Skeist (1977). The conservation aspects of adhesives and consolidants are discussed in Brommelle *et al.* (1984).

## 4.6 Consolidants

The object of consolidation is to impart strength to the surface, and to the structure if necessary, sufficient for the surfaces to endure handling for storage or display and to bear the loads imposed by their structures. This may range from the conservation of a friable paint layer, to the restoration of structural strength to a load-bearing member (e.g. a table supporting a heavy stone slab or a beam in a building). This can be achieved by the introduction of a liquid adhesive which is a potential solid and which can be converted into the actual solid state, ideally at a controlled rate at room temperature and without shrinkage. The requirements of consolidants are to a large extent similar to those of both adhesives and coatings. It is therefore not surprising to find that most of the materials used for these purposes in conservation have also been used as consolidants. Examples include waxes, wax resin mixtures, animal proteins, epoxies, poly vinyl acetates, poly vinyl butyrals, acrylics and other synthetic thermoplastic resins.

Grattan (1980) has listed the properties of an ideal consolidant, which are as follows:

- Good adhesive properties
- Imparts strength to the surface
- Imparts strength to the structure if required
- Flexible but hard
- Should not creep
- Solutions should combine high concentration with low viscosity
- Application should be simple, e.g. by brush
- Solvent should be non-toxic and non-damaging to the object and the conservator
- Should have short-term reversibility, at least and should not inhibit retreatment
- Should not yellow
- Should keep mechanical properties.

The three factors that contribute most to the effectiveness of a consolidant are viscosity, penetration and evaporation (see Moncrieff and Weaver, *Science for Conservators*, Book 3). Viscosity, the fluidity or 'runniness' of the consolidant, is determined by the bonding between the molecules, the molecular weight (chain length) of the polymer, the concentration in the solvent system chosen and the temperature. Porosity is the amount of open space in a material and, with the viscosity of a consolidant, it contributes to the penetration of that consolidant into a material. Evaporation of the solvent vehicle is important, chiefly for thermoplastic materials in solution, because the higher the surface tension of the consolidant, the more it will be pulled out of a material as its solvent evaporates. To be effective, the consolidant must adhere to all parts of the system being consolidated (support ground, paint etc.) and to do this it must wet the surfaces to be adhered. Other factors that must be considered in the selection of a consolidant are strength, which must be adequate but not so great as to cause original material to break, toughness, hardness, colour, long-term stability, the working properties of the material in solid form, the conditions required for its application, and the setting time. Most importantly, it must not preclude future interventions.

Among the thermoplastic materials used as consolidants, wax is unusual in solidifying through change in temperature alone. Most other thermoplastic polymers used as consolidants undergo a phase change from a liquid to solid by the evaporation of the solvent. As temperature increases, their viscosity decreases and their rates of solvent release increase. This can create two problems: first, the consolidant can follow the solvent back to the surface as it dries, reducing the penetration of the consolidant; and secondly, evaporation of the solvent can result in structural damage to the material by causing its collapse. To avoid these situations, it may help to keep the surface tension of the consolidant as low as possible and this can be achieved by the addition of a wetting agent (Allen, 1984).

## 4.7 Review of materials: coatings, media, adhesives and consolidants

This section presents basic information about materials to allow simple correlation with the lists of desirable properties of coatings and media, adhesives and consolidants presented earlier and alluded to in later chapters. The information given is also relevant to moulding and casting, another use to which some of the materials in this review are suited. The desirable properties of moulding and casting materials are reviewed in Chapter 10. The aim of this review is to avoid unnecessary duplication and simplify cross referencing. For further information see Mills and White (1987), Horie (1987), Gettens and Stout (1966), Mayer (1981), Bentley (1998) and other sources listed in the bibliography.

### 4.7.1 Oils and fats

In contrast to mineral oils which consist of mixtures of hydrocarbons, oils and fats from plants and animals are members of a rather heterogeneous chemical class of fatty acid esters called lipids. The hydrophobic, hydrocarbon nature of lipids is reflected in their very low solubility in water and considerable solubility in organic solvents. Lipids are traditionally classified as (i) neutral lipids, (ii) phosphatides and sphingolipids, (iii) glycolipids and (iv) terpenoid lipids (including carotenoids and steroids). All classes are widely distributed in nature. Neutral lipids consist of mixed triglycerides of various fatty acids. A triglyceride has the general structure shown in *Figure 4.10*. Each molecule consists of a backbone of *glycerol* in which each of the three hydroxyl groups present in the original alcohol molecule is joined via ester linkages to a fatty acid chain. There is no fundamental difference between oils and fats, the distinction being solely one of melting point. Oils are liquid at 20 °C while fats are solid at this temperature. As with the other physical properties of this class of material, this reflects the types and proportions of the fatty acids which make up the triglyceride. Fatty acids containing double bonds are termed unsaturated, those which do not are termed saturated. Most plant oils contain a large proportion of low melting point unsaturated fatty acids such as oleic, linoleic and linolenic acids and are liquid. In many animal fats a higher proportion of higher melting point saturated fatty acids, such as palmitic and stearic acid, is present leading to a solid or semi-solid state at room temperature. Certain oils, which have the property of forming tough elastic films when exposed to the air in thin layers, are classed as drying oils. They include linseed, walnut, poppy and tung oils, among others. The drying ability of these oils increases as the proportion of unsaturated fatty acids present increases and is often expressed as the *iodine number* of the oil. Iodine values of drying oils range from about 120–200. Drying oils contain a substantial proportion of fatty acids with (at least) three double bonds. *Non-drying* oils, including olive oil, castor oil and almond oil, will thicken at elevated temperature but do not

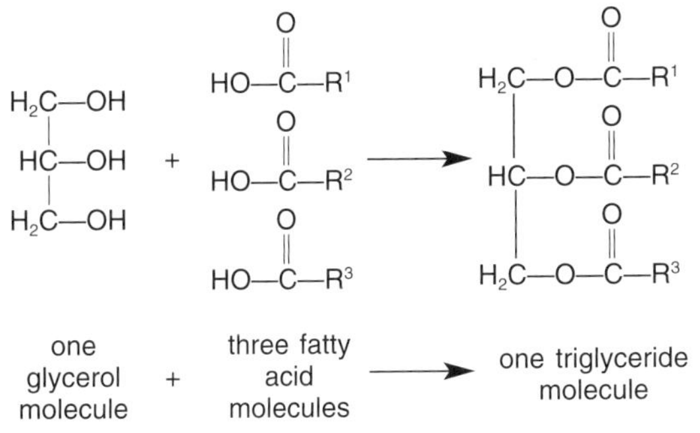

dry to a skin even with long exposure to the air. They have iodine numbers in the range 80–100 and their triglycerides contain predominantly fatty acids having only a single double bond in each molecule.

Linseed oil, the most important of the drying oils, comes from seeds of flax (*Linum usitatissimum*). The best is cold pressed. The oil may be refined with acid, alkali, brine or by mechanical means. Alkaline refined oils have are considered by Mayer (1981) to be the best choice because of their colour stability. The oil may subsequently be bleached by sunlight or by chemical methods. Linseed oil consists of mixed triglycerides of linolenic, linoleic, oleic and stearic acids with small amounts of other acids and up to about 1.5% of unsaponifiable matter (i.e. material which cannot be reacted with alkali to form a soap) (*Figure 4.11*). It has an iodine value of 170–195. Linseed oil is used for grinding oil colours and as an ingredient of paint media, when it is used alone or in a wide variety of emulsions and mixtures with egg, resins and varnishes (Massey, 1967). It is also found as an important or principal ingredient in oil-gold size, gilders' composition, grain fillers, furniture reviver, glaziers' putty, plasticine, linoleum and oil cloth.

When exposed to the air, linseed oil reacts with oxygen and at a normal temperature becomes tacky (to a stage suitable for oil gilding) in three to five days. The mechanism by which drying oils form complex, crosslinked structures involves the formation of peroxides and free-radical polymerization. It is clearly summarized by Bentley (1998) and by Mills and White (1987), though aspects of the process remain incompletely understood. The oxidation period is greatly shortened by heat and the presence of salts of certain metals such as lead, manganese or cobalt. The addition of 1% cobalt, for instance, reduces the drying time by a factor of seven. Such compounds are functionally described as siccatives or driers. Lead compounds such as lead acetate and carbonate had the greatest historic importance. Driers such as the resinates or lineolates of cobalt, zinc and manganese are more recent. Boiled oils – drying oils that have been heated at around 150 °C with various driers – are used mainly for industrial paints and varnishes including enamels and for oil size used for adhering metal leaves in oil gilding. By varying

**Figure 4.10** One glycerol molecule combined with three fatty acid molecules produces one triglyceride molecule, where $R^1$, $R^2$ and $R^3$ may be different fatty acids

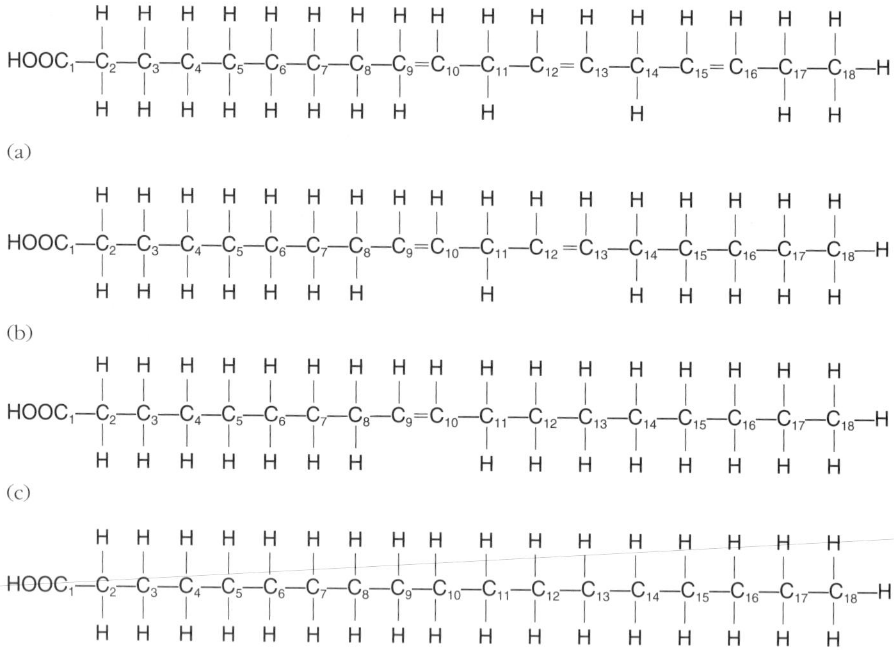

(a)

$$HOOC_1-C_2-C_3-C_4-C_5-C_6-C_7-C_8-C_9=C_{10}-C_{11}-C_{12}=C_{13}-C_{14}-C_{15}=C_{16}-C_{17}-C_{18}-H$$

(b)

$$HOOC_1-C_2-C_3-C_4-C_5-C_6-C_7-C_8-C_9=C_{10}-C_{11}-C_{12}=C_{13}-C_{14}-C_{15}-C_{16}-C_{17}-C_{18}-H$$

(c)

$$HOOC_1-C_2-C_3-C_4-C_5-C_6-C_7-C_8-C_9=C_{10}-C_{11}-C_{12}-C_{13}-C_{14}-C_{15}-C_{16}-C_{17}-C_{18}-H$$

(d)

$$HOOC_1-C_2-C_3-C_4-C_5-C_6-C_7-C_8-C_9-C_{10}-C_{11}-C_{12}-C_{13}-C_{14}-C_{15}-C_{16}-C_{17}-C_{18}-H$$

**Figure 4.11** Major fatty acids components of linseed oil
(*a*) 48–60% linolenic acid (9,12,15 octadecatrienoic acid), a polyunsaturated fatty acid
(*b*) 14–19% linoleic (9,12 octadecadiennoic acid), a polyunsaturated fatty acid
(*c*) 14–30% oleic acid (9-octadecenoic acid), a monounsaturated fatty acid
(*d*) 3–6% stearic acid (octadecanoic acid), a saturated fatty acid

the amount of drier and the length of the heating period, the oxidation period and thus the drying time of the oil can be varied. Oil gold size is available with drying times between 3 and 24 hours. Various driers speed up different stages of polymerization. Therefore, combinations of driers often have a dramatic effect. Certain classes of chemical compounds, notably the phenols, have an inhibitory effect on the drying of oil films. Phenols present in tars and bituminous earths may therefore explain the poor drying of oil paint films containing carbon black or Vandyke brown.

Films formed from oil alone are slow drying, soft, have poor gloss and relatively poor water resistance. Highly pigmented oil films overcome some of these disadvantages but oils are frequently mixed with natural or synthetic resins to improve hardness and gloss. Resins decrease drying time, harden the film and improve gloss but reduce flexibility. The weight ratio of oil to resin is called the oil length: 3–5 parts of oil to 1 of resin is described as long oil, 1.5–3:1 as medium oil and 0.5–1.5:1 as short oil. Long oil varnishes have the slowest drying but the best outdoor durability because the oil contributes the necessary flexibility.

Polymerized linseed oil films become progressively more resistant to solvent action with time and also tend to darken. Their low solubility can be an advantage during surface cleaning or removal of varnish or over paint but should be remembered when using revivers or similar preparations that may leave an oil residue on a surface where none was originally intended. Dried oil-based films remain prone to leaching and swelling by solvents.

Egg yolk contains approximately one-third lipids, as opposed to egg white in which lipids are absent. The lipids in egg are made up of triglycerides (65%), phospholipids (29%) and cholesterol (5.2%). Phospholipids consist of triglycerides in which one of the fatty acid ester groups is substituted by a phosphatide group

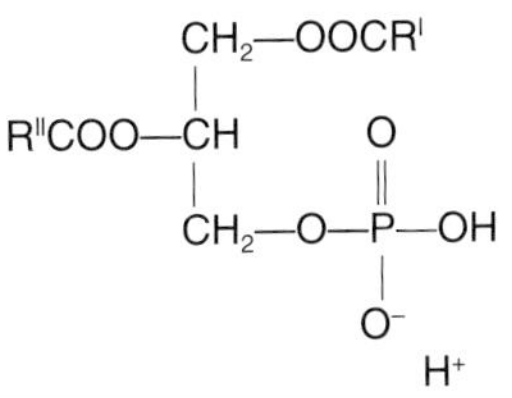

(a)

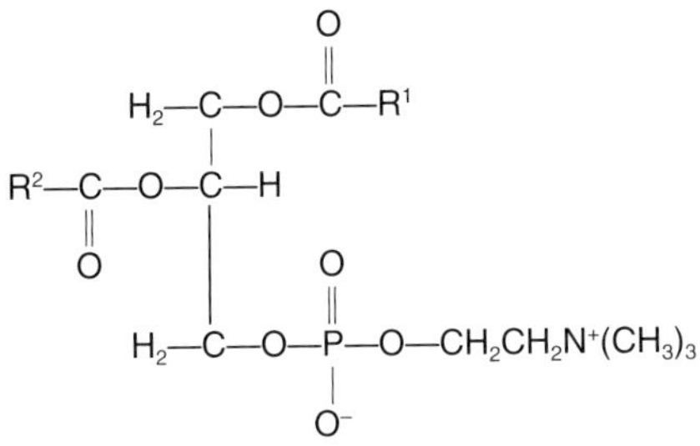

(b)

**Figure 4.12** (*a*) Phosphatidic acid; (*b*) phosphatidyl choline (lecithin)

so named because they contain a phosphorous atom. Phosphatides are tribasic (i.e. there are three atoms of acidic hydrogen in the molecule thus giving rise to three possible series of salts), phosphatidic acid and may combine further with various compounds (*Figure 4.12a*). In combination with the strong nitrogenous base choline, for example, phosphatidyl choline or *lecithin* is formed (*Figure 4.12b*). Lecithin is an *emulsifier*, that is it confers on egg yolk the property of forming and stabilizing emulsions.

An emulsion is a *colloidal system*. A colloidal solution is one in which the *solute* (*disperse phase*) is present as a system of particles of $10^{-4}$–$10^{-6}$ mm in the *dispersion medium*. Such a system has properties distinct from a true solution because of the larger size of the particles (approximately $10^{-4}$–$10^{-6}$ mm across). In an emulsion, one liquid is dispersed in the form of fine droplets throughout another liquid with which it cannot evenly mix. The most common examples are made up of oil and water. For example, mayonnaise and cream are emulsions of fat dispersed in water, and butter is a water in oil emulsion. Many paints rely on the formation of emulsions to achieve the combination of properties desired. In creating emulsions, energy is required to overcome the surface tension between two immiscible

liquids. Once this has been achieved a method of stabilizing the result is required so that the components do not simply re-coalesce into two separate phases. Certain proteins, plant resins and gums and other large carbohydrate molecules (e.g. starch) can do this by surrounding the droplets of the dispersed phase and interfering with their coalescence. An important class of emulsifier relies on the properties of fatty acids which have a fat soluble tail attached to a water soluble head. With one end immersed in the droplet phase and the other in the continuous phase, such molecules, known as surfactants, are extremely effective at preventing one droplet from recognizing another. Soaps belong to this class as do lecithin, and other related substances, present in egg yolk.

### 4.7.2 Waxes

True waxes are esters of long chain fatty acids ranging from $C_{24}$ to $C_{36}$ and monohydroxy alcohols ranging from $C_{16}$ to $C_{36}$. When obtained from natural sources, waxes also contain varying amounts of hydrocarbons, free fatty acids and alcohols and may also contain plant sterols and triterpenoids and their esters (Mills and White, 1987). Waxes are non-greasy solids at room temperature, soften or melt at fairly low temperatures, are highly insoluble in water and have very low chemical reactivity. The term wax is also applied to fully saturated high molecular weight hydrocarbons having similar properties (e.g. paraffin wax).

Waxes and wax resin mixtures have been used as adhesives, consolidants and fill materials. Waxes, especially beeswax, were finishes in early and continuous use. Beeswax is known to have been in use on wooden artefacts as early as the time of the ancient Egyptian craftsmen and its use in the fine arts can be traced back over 2000 years (Kirk-Othmer, 1985). Wax finishes have very low permeability to moisture (Gettens and Bogelow, 1933) though a buffed wax layer on top of a continuous film is exceptionally thin, much thinner than a typical resin coating, perhaps only a few molecules thick. Waxes show low optical saturation when applied cold but a high degree of optical saturation when applied hot. Their natural colour varies from white to brown depending on type but they are easily coloured using pigments or fat-soluble dyes.

Waxes show generally low bond strength and are more commonly encountered as coatings than as adhesives in woodwork. However, wax and wax–resin mixtures have been used extensively in painting conservation as adhesives for lining canvases and have also been used to consolidate biodeteriorated wood and to secure flaking polychromy to wood substrates. Waxes have also been used extensively as fill materials in conservation where they have been exploited for the range of hardness available and the ease with which they may be applied and levelled. Waxes are grouped according to their origins as animal waxes, plant waxes and mineral waxes.

### Animal waxes

Animal waxes have been obtained from a great variety of sources, of which the most important are beeswax, shellac or lac wax, Chinese insect wax, spermaceti wax from sperm whales and lanolin or wool wax from sheep. Wax synthesized by the honey bee (*Apis mellifera*) and extracted from honey comb using hot water, pressure or organic solvents, has the empirical formula $C_{15}H_{51}COOC_{30}H_{61}$. It contains about 64% esters, 14% hydrocarbons and 12% free fatty acids, a composition that is genetically determined for each species and varies to only a small extent. However, the use of paraffin wax and stearin to make artificial combs may lead to a 'contaminated' product. Beeswax varies in colour from pale yellow to dark greenish brown. Darker varieties may be bleached using a variety of methods among which the oxidizing acids tend to cause deterioration. It also varies in texture being fairly brittle when cold but plastic when warm. It becomes markedly soft and susceptible to finger printing at about 37 °C with a melting point generally in the range 63–65 °C. Bleached wax tends to be denser, more brittle and to have a smoother fracture. Beeswax is the primary traditional component of furniture wax polishes. However, because its relatively low melting point makes it prone to finger printing, it is often used in conjunction with other waxes such as carnauba and paraffin wax. Despite a reputation for being freely soluble in a wide range of solvents, there are in fact very few true solvents for this material of which Horie (1987) cites only chloroform and carbon tetrachloride. Pure gum turpentine has been widely

used as a solvent for waxes in furniture conservation. Toluene and xylene are probably the best among a wide range of partial solvents. A mixture of xylene and methanol (in unspecified proportions) is available commercially as a wax remover (Libnet® by Liberon). Less toxic substitutes may be found in a range of precision cleaning fluids available from Merck of which Dow Corning OS-120 fluid is an effective solvent for wax. Beeswax has an acid value (the number of milligrams of potassium hydroxide required to neutralize the free fatty acid in one gram) of 16–22. Another insect wax, lac wax, a byproduct of the shellac refining process, is occasionally used in furniture finishes. Lanolin, which comes from the processing of wool, is occasionally used on furniture but more commonly on leather.

### Plant waxes

A large variety of plant waxes exists, including carnauba wax, ouricuri wax, candelilla wax, esparto wax, Japan wax and jojoba oil. The most commonly used plant wax is carnauba wax which comes from the leaves of the Brazilian palm tree *Copernicia cerifera* where its function is to prevent moisture loss from the plant. A major component is melissyl cerotate ($C_{25}H_{51}COOC_{30}H_{61}$) but carnauba wax also contains triterpenes and esters of long chain acids and alcohols up to fifty-six carbon chains in length. These long chains constitute a diagnostic feature that can be used to distinguish carnauba from beeswax. Carnauba is a dark greenish brown hard and brittle wax with a melting range of 83–86 °C. In the bleached condition it is pale yellow. It will take a very high gloss when rubbed but its high melting point means that manual buffing is very laborious and it is therefore often used as an additive to increase the hardness of wax mixtures, as are some hard natural resins. Carnauba wax dissolves in pure gum turpentine and is also affected, but to a lesser extent, by the solvents listed for beeswax.

### Mineral waxes

This category includes waxes obtained from plant remains in various stages of decomposition towards coal. Montan wax is extracted from peat, and ozokerite and ceresine are obtained by mining and processing lignite. As these waxes have been altered over geological time periods, the proportion of esters and free fatty acids has decreased and the proportion of hydrocarbons has increased. Ceresin, a dazzling white, odourless plastic and non-crystalline wax with a melting range of 65–80 °C is sometimes used as a substitute for beeswax. Paraffin waxes, the most important group of mineral waxes, are obtained by distillation of shale oil, lignite and petroleum. These bluish-white, translucent, highly inert waxes consist of mixtures of saturated hydrocarbons having the general formula $C_nH_{2n+2}$. They are available in a wide range of well defined melting points from 48 °C up to 62 °C. Those with higher melting points are harder, heavier and less crystalline. Higher molecular weight hydrocarbon fractions that tend to produce very small crystals during the preparation of paraffin waxes are designated as microcrystalline wax. These waxes are tough, have a high melting point (e.g. 90 °C) and are produced with a variety of hardness properties from hard to very hard. Advantage is taken of these properties and of their clear (white) colour and inertness in the production of coatings having a high resistance to moisture and gases (e.g. Renaissance Wax®) for decorated surfaces and for metals and in their use as matting agents in wax resin varnish compositions (Plenderleith and Werner, 1971; Larson, 1979; de Witte, 1975).

### Commercial products

Most proprietary furniture paste waxes are based on beeswax (animal) with the addition of another higher melting temperature wax (vegetable) to achieve adequate hardness for furniture surfaces. They tend to be preferred in the furniture trade as they have among the best properties of application, buffing, appearance and wearability. Pigments or dyes may be used to colour the wax so that traces of wax left behind do not become noticeable as they dry. These colorants rarely impart colour to an existing finish but they may affect bare wood. Some products include UV inhibitors designed to protect finishes from the effects of ultra violet radiation. Solvents in commercial animal/vegetable waxes are commonly turpentine, white spirits or toluene. The more toxic hydrocarbon solvents such as toluene present greater health risks in their use (McCann, 1979). Wax polish recipes are given in Chapter

13. The use of waxes in moulding and modelling is discussed in Chapter 10.

### 4.7.3 Carbohydrates: sugars and polysaccharides

Carbohydrates, so called because they contain only carbon, hydrogen and oxygen, include simple sugars and polymers of simple sugars termed polysaccharides. Few simple sugars are used in object fabrication and conservation but polysaccharides are encountered in the form of starches, dextrins, water soluble gums or mucilages and alginates. Starches are present in plants in the form of complex granules with no adhesive characteristics. If starch granules are cooked they will swell and burst yielding a water-dispersed colloidal paste with good adhesive qualities. Starch adhesives are very polar and wet cellulosics such as paper and wood well. Japanese woodworkers have used rice starch extensively but in the West the use of starch-type adhesives has been mostly confined to the paper industries. Dextrins are derived from starches but have shorter chain lengths. Though extensively used in bonding paper, they have seen little use in woodworking. Water-soluble gums include acacia (gum arabic), cherry gum and gum tragacanth. They have been extensively employed as label adhesives and water colour paint binders.

All these materials are relatively weak and unlikely to cause substrate failure. They have long to moderate open times, depending on ambient humidity, with excellent machinability and no significant health hazards. They vary in colour from white (starches) to light amber (plant gums) and show only slight optical saturation depending on concentration. The chemical stability of starches is excellent and that of plant gums is fair to good. Their resistance to moisture is poor and bonds made with them are easily reversible using water.

### Alginates

Alginates are polysaccharides extracted from various species of marine algae which form hydro-colloidal gels in water quite similar to those formed by animal glues. Agar–agar is one such alginate also sometimes called Japanese isinglass. Their use in moulding is discussed in Chapter 10.

(a)

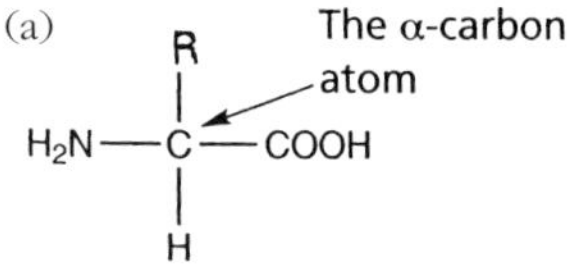

The α-carbon atom

$H_2N$—C—COOH

**Figure 4.13** (*a*) General formula of an amino acid. Each amino acid consists of an alpha (α) carbon atom that is attached to a hydrogen atom (H), an amino group ($NH_2$), a carboxylic acid group (—COOH) and one of twenty different side chains (R)

(*b*) The chemical structure of α-amino acids in their ionic form (i.e. $NH^{3+}$ instead of $NH_2$, $COO^-$ instead of COOH) at pH 7

(b) **R Group – simple alkane**

glycine　alanine　valine　leucine　isoleucine

**R Group – aromatic (arene)**　　　　　**R Group – simple hydroxy (alcoholic)**

phenylalanine　tyrosine　tryptophan　　serine

threonine

**R Group – acidic**　　　　　**R Group – amide**

aspartic acid　glutamic acid　　asparagine　glutamine

**R Group – basic**

lysine　　arginine　　histidine

**R Group – sulphur containing**　　**Proline, an imino acid**

cysteine　methionine　　proline

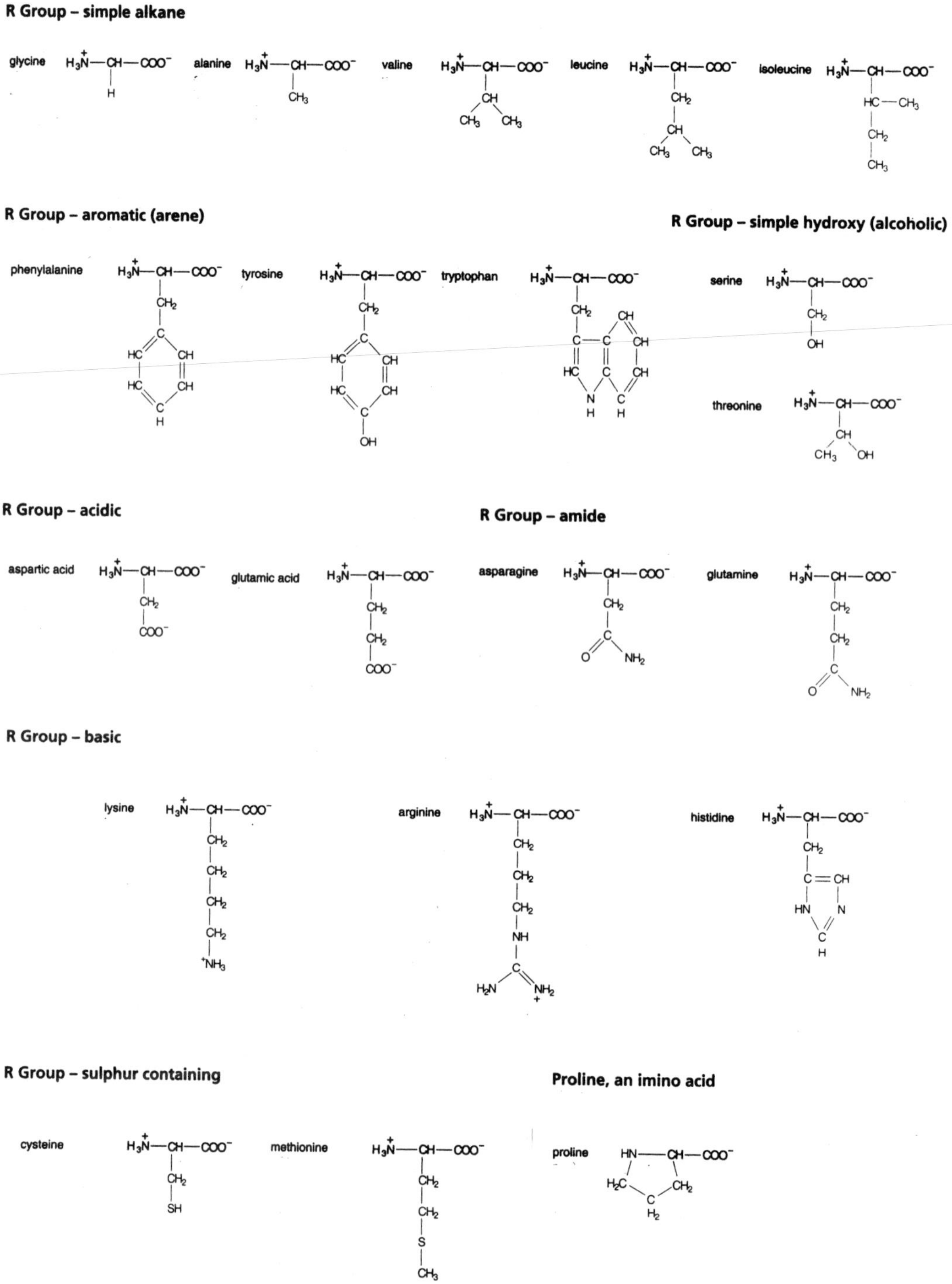

(c)

R₁ H O R₃ H O R₅

(structural diagram of polypeptide chain)

(*c*) A section of a polypeptide chain showing the peptide backbone and side chain groups or residues (R)

∕ peptide backbone
R side chain groups or residues

## 4.7.4 Proteins

Proteins are naturally occurring polymers consisting of large numbers of repeating α-amino acid units. The general formula of an amino acid is shown in *Figure 4.13a*. Each amino acid has its own side chain groups or residues (R) (*Figure 4.13b*). The term peptide bond refers to the amide group (—CO—NH—) that joins two α-amino acid units together (*Figure 4.13c*). The type and sequence of α-amino acid side chain groups gives each polypeptide unique properties.

All α-amino acids contain both acidic (—COOH) and basic (—NH₂—) groups and are therefore amphoteric (i.e. capable of reacting with both acids and bases). More complex amino acids may contain two carboxyl groups (acidic) two amino groups (basic), aromatic or heterocyclic ring structures or may also contain sulphur.

Proteins, which may have molecular weights from a few thousand to several million, are divided into two general groups, the *fibrous* (structural) proteins and the *globular* (regulatory) proteins. Fibrous proteins such as keratin and collagen consist of long thread-like chains joined laterally by various types of crosslinkages to form fairly stable and insoluble structures. Biologically active proteins such as enzymes are of the globular type in which a considerable amount of folding of the long polypeptide chains occurs to give a globular or somewhat elliptical shape overall. Four structural levels are assigned to describe the complex structure of proteins. The *primary* structure simply describes the linear sequence of amino acids in a polypeptide chain (*Figure 4.14a*). Interaction of regularly occurring groups on the polypeptide chain yields a *secondary* structure (*Figure 4.14b*). There are several types of secondary structure, of which two common examples are the α-helix and the β-

sheet. The α-helix structure has a chain of repeating amino acid units wound into a spiral which is stabilized by hydrogen bonds between carbonyl (CO) and imido (NH) groups which occur at regular intervals along the chain. In the β-sheet configuration, which occurs for example in silk, two or more peptide chains are held together laterally by hydrogen bonds into an orderly crystalline structure. The *tertiary* structure (*Figure 4.14c*) describes the overall three-dimensional structure (i.e. the coiling and folding) of a globular protein molecule. The *quaternary* structure describes the spatial arrangement of a protein characterized by a number of sub-units of identical tertiary structure (*Figure 4.14d*). This commonly occurs with enzymes.

The term 'denatured' describes the partial or complete disruption of the arrangement of polypeptide chains within a protein. Once denatured, the protein may become insoluble (e.g. a boiled egg) or lose its function (e.g. an enzyme). Changes in pH, temperature, salt concentration and the presence of reducing agents can denature proteins. Some solvents can also denature proteins.

### Collagen

By far the most common adhesive for use in furniture was animal protein glue. Before the twentieth century, the unqualified term 'glue' meant this and only this owing to the widespread use of animal glue for most purposes. Animal glues have great importance in the history of both woodworking and conservation and are discussed in detail by Grant (1980) and Ward (1977). The primary component of animal glues and sizes is gelatin derived from collagen (Greek: *colla*, 'glue'; *gen*, 'creator'), the long fibrous structural protein of connective tissue present in animal skins, muscle, bone and hide. Although collagen itself is insoluble in water, glue can be made from it by

(a)

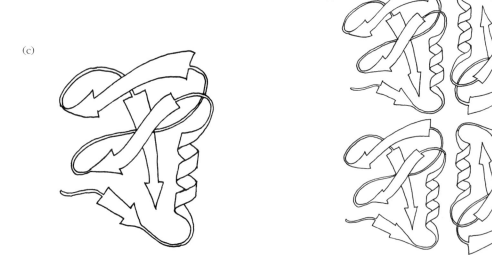

Serine    Tyrosine    Alanine    Glycine    Leucine

(b)

(i)

(ii)

(iii)

(c)

(d)

**Figure 4.14**  Structure of a protein
(*a*) Primary structure of a polypeptide chain containing serine, tyrosine, alanine, glycine and leucine
(*b*) Secondary structure of a protein – an α-helix and a β-sheet. In the α-helix configuration, the primary backbone has a helical structure (i). In the β-sheet configuration, the polypeptide backbones have a sheet structure (ii), often represented by a flattened arrow (iii)
(*c*) Tertiary structure of a protein. Diagrammatic representation of the complex folding of a single unit (one polypeptide chain or monomer) that contains both an α-helix and β-sheets. This native conformation is stabilized by secondary bonding (e.g. Van der Waals forces and hydrogen bonding). If the native structure of the protein is disrupted, the protein is said to be denatured
(*d*) Quaternary structure of a small globular protein polymer (oligomer) made up of four protein units (monomers) and stabilized by secondary bonding

hydrolysing the initial collagen in a strong acid or alkali, breaking the polymer chains into smaller extractable units by the action of water at an elevated temperature to produce gelatin. Whilst the collagen must be treated in order to break it down to produce the adhesive, the longer it is treated, and the more extreme the pH, the more protein is broken down. Bones require extended treatment whilst adhesive can be extracted from skin with much less aggressive preparation. Acid processed animal glue will be slightly acidic whilst that prepared using alkaline processing will be slightly alkaline.

Collagen molecules are characterized by a triple stranded helix with frequently repeating glycine-proline-hydroxyproline amino acid units. The overall structure is maintained by strong hydrogen bonding between the hydroxyl group of the hydroxyproline and the amino hydrogens of adjacent glycine units. Gelatin results from the separation of the three strands as a consequence of the scission of the hydrogen bonds between them and their replacement with hydrogen bonds to solvent water. As the solution cools the coils cannot re-form exactly but become misaligned resulting in a gel formation.

The bulk of animal glue is made from cattle hides (scraps from tanneries being a readily available supply) and is called hide glue. Other starting stock such as bones (bone glue) fish skins and rabbit skins are also used to produce distinctive adhesives. The glue stock (starting material) is first prepared by washing. Fats and oils are removed by saponification in a lime solution, and acid solutions are used to neutralize the lime and to remove unwanted mucus-type proteins and polysaccharides. The glue stock is then steeped in water at controlled temperatures and a series of broths removed by pressing and draining the stock as the desired protein concentration is reached. Because the collagen will continue to break down by hydrolysis as the temperature rises and the steeping time increases, a series of broths of progressively lower molecular weight (shorter chain) proteins can be extracted at progressively higher temperatures until the glue stock is exhausted. Below a molecular weight of about 20 000, adhesive properties of the extract are lost. The highest quality glue comes from the first draining of the glue-broth.

The broth is dehydrated by low temperature boiling in a vacuum (to prevent further damage by high temperatures) until it gels and is then air-dried to the final product (Cummins, 1986).

Hide glues possess unique properties that have made them useful in a wide range of applications. A small amount of glue can tie up large quantities of water into a hydro-colloidal gel structure. The flexible and rubbery gels consist of expanded open networks of protein polymer chains which hold water in the structure by hydrogen bonding and other forces. This gel state is temperature dependent being fluid when moderately hot but gelled and rubbery at room temperature. When animal glue is heated in water, the coiled strands dissolve into single strands. Animal glue is applied hot and fully fluid in a water solution that can readily wet a polar substrate such as wood. On cooling, hydrogen bonding allows animal glue molecules to bond to each other and to appropriate substrates. Gelling occurs when the glue gels upon cooling into a rubbery elastomeric state. The gel then dehydrates and contracts until it is a set, hard and tough solid (Von Endt and Baker, 1991).

Animal glues were among the earliest adhesives and continued to be virtually the only adhesives employed in furniture construction until relatively recently. In addition to their use as woodworking adhesives they are also used as binding media for gesso and bole in gilding, as components of fillers and moulding materials and as a simple but surprisingly durable paint medium. Animal glues have proven extremely durable under ideal circumstances and intact glue joints can be found that are centuries old. Optimum animal glue joints are stronger than the wood itself but even under less ideal circumstances offer adequate strength. They do not stain wood or impede the application of stains and coatings, are non-toxic and easily cleaned from areas where they are unwanted. Disadvantages of animal glue include limited working time at room temperatures, poor gap filling abilities, and biodeterioration under some circumstances. As water-soluble adhesives, animal glues are moisture-sensitive. This makes them unsuitable for some applications but this ease of reversibility continues to recommend them for furniture conservation. Because they are most likely to be the original adhesive in a glue joint, regluing an old joint with animal glue is usually the best choice in terms of compatibility and strength.

An understanding of molecular weight and its relation to glue properties can help the user make decisions regarding use. The molecular weight of a glue largely accounts for its properties. Generally, high molecular weight glues have greater cohesive strength in the gelled state, and greater toughness and flexibility in the fully dried state. They will take up more water at a given concentration, swell slowly in water, gel at a higher temperature, form more viscous solutions at fluid temperatures and have high gel strengths at given concentrations. The reverse applies to low molecular weight animal glues. Commonly used animal glues may be roughly ranked in order of increasing molecular weight as follows: bone glue, lower quality hide glue, higher quality hide glue, rabbit-skin glue and 'parchment size'. The form in which the glue is sold is not an indication of strength or purity. Although wood-workers' animal glue is still supplied in pearly form, modern manufacturers supply glue across a range of strengths and purity in granular form.

A hide glue of high molecular weight and gel strength is prepared from fresh rabbit skins that have not been subjected to any of the damaging processes of tanning. Rabbit-skin glue is strong and flexible and has been used extensively in gilding as the binder for calcium carbonate or calcium sulphate to make gesso and in canvas painting preparation. Although occasionally still found in sheets, the most common form is granules. The sheets are generally a uniform brown but the granules range in colour from brown to almost grey. France is the main source of the glue, where it is still extracted in much the same way as it was in the sixteenth century when it was first used for gesso making. Donkey skins were once used in the manufacture of skin glues but rabbit skins are now more readily available. Rabbit-skin glue is an excellent binder for gesso and bole in gilding, because its high strength even at low concentrations forms a tougher gesso than would a low molecular weight glue. It also resists redissolving which is advantageous when laying the gold with aqueous 'gilder's liquor' particularly when the solution is cool. Rabbit-skin glue is a poor choice for most

wood joinery however because rapid gelling decreases the time available to assemble and clamp, it is a poor gap filler and has low cohesive strength.

The industrial standard for the strength of gelatin adhesives is Bloom strength. This is measured on glue in the gel phase using a Bloom gelometer. A gel is made up from 7.5 g of dry glue placed in a Bloom bottle and well mixed with 105 ml distilled water. The mixture is allowed to stand until it is completely swollen. It is then heated in a 65 °C waterbath until the gelatin has dissolved. The bottle is then placed in a 10 °C chill bath where it matures for 16–18 hours. Finally, a flat bottomed plunger 12.7 mm (half an inch) in diameter is used to depress the surface of the gelatin by 4 mm. The weight required to do this to the nearest gram is expressed as gram strength, Bloom strength or grams Bloom (gB). Commercially available glues range from around 75 to 400 gB. The Bloom scale allows comparison of gelatin products. Modern animal/pearl glues have a bloom strength of 150–210 whilst a typical rabbit-skin glue may range from 380–400. A higher bloom number indicates more weight is required to depress the gel and this in turn indicates more sites which are involved in adhesive bonding along the polymer. The higher the Bloom strength, the higher the viscosity for a given solids content, the faster the glue will gel, the higher its adhesive properties but the poorer its cohesive/gap-filling properties.

Other factors, aside from molecular weight, which affect the adhesive strength of a given glue are the purity of the product and the degree of degradation. Inclusions of naturally occurring non-collagen products, such as polysaccharides, which contribute to the adhesion of the glue as a whole. Polysaccharides contribute to the gapfilling properties and cohesive strength. Degradation can occur during manufacture but will also occur in the workshop. The further above 55 °C and the longer the glue is above the temperature the more degraded, dark and weak the glue will become.

Bone glues are used for gummed labels and stamps because they re-hydrate very rapidly.

Fish glues do not gel at room temperature because of chemical factors other than molecular weight. Although weaker than most hide weight glues they are strong enough to perform well in most situations and offer very long open time for complicated assembly before hardening by water loss alone.

Isinglass is an animal glue with a rich lore. It consists of the swim bladders of sturgeons, though other fish are sometimes substituted. The name is derived from the Dutch word *huisenblas*, meaning bladder of the huso, or large sturgeon. The glue is extracted by washing the swim bladders in hot water to remove extraneous material, after which they are cut open to expose the inner membranes to the air. When almost dry the outer membranes are removed by beating and rubbing. Isinglass is supplied in a dry state as thin, transparent strips, or in sheet form. The best isinglass is milky white and free from any yellowness. Other varieties of fish yield a glue which is darker in colour and less soluble. Even though it is not generally classed as a fish glue, it behaves as one. Compared to gelatin and rabbit-skin glue it has greater tack, lower viscosity and a lower gelation temperature. Very high molecular weights are reported, but solutions of isinglass do not gel at room temperature. Gelation is a highly complex chemical phenomenon in which a number of factors aside from molecular weight operate. Compared to gelatins and rabbit-skin glues, isinglass forms brittle dried films and is highly moisture-sensitive. It has been used for gilding on glass and in conservation for consolidation of flaking gesso and paint. Light colour and lack of gelling may well be advantageous in such conservation procedures as consolidating flaking paint but these properties are achievable with other adhesives and one suspects that the continuing mystique of isinglass is based as much on scarcity and exoticism as on intrinsic properties. Haupt (Haupt *et al.*, 1989; Haupt *et al.*, 1990) has characterized animal glues in terms relevant to conservators and has studied the ways in which the properties of glue may vary with type of glue and with the means of preparation used.

Some gilders make fresh 'size' or dilute glue from parchment clippings to provide a colourless high strength binder for gesso and bole. The glue stock is very clean and the size obtained corresponds to a high molecular weight first batch in glue manufacture being almost pure gelatin. It is ideal for mixing with the clay bole for water gilding and for the protective size coat on the gold. It was used extensively in the gilding process until the more convenient rabbit-skin size replaced it in most uses. Parchment is now almost always made from sheep skins but can also be made from calf and goat skins. The inside layer of skin, called the flesh or lining, is carefully scraped, stretched and dried to produce a fine writing surface. The shredded parchment cuttings that gilders use are the trimmings from the finished skins.

### Albumins

Another binder described in historic literature is glair, prepared from egg white, the principal ingredient of which is the globular protein albumin. Albumins quickly become insoluble under the effects of heat and light. Besides carbon, hydrogen, nitrogen, and oxygen, egg albumin contains about 1.6% of sulphur. Egg white and egg yolk contain the same amino acids but differ in the amounts of each that they contain. Also, egg white shows a much higher water content than the yolk, a lower protein content and an absence of lipids. Egg white is sometimes used to mix with the clay in water gilding, for gilding on glass, and has been used as a protective coat on oil and water gilding.

### Casein and milk

Casein glues are one of the oldest thermosetting adhesives. 'Cheese glues', based on the milk protein casein and calcium hydroxide (lime), are described in many early treatises such as those by Theophilus and Cennini. By the beginning of the twentieth century prepared casein glues that could be mixed with water to form an adhesive or paint binder were available. Casein is made by heating skimmed milk to 35 °C, and adding hydrochloric acid until the mixture reaches a pH of 4.6. It is allowed to settle and is then washed with hydrochloric acid (Gettens and Stout, 1966). Casein forms a sludge with water, but in alkaline solutions forms a colloidal suspension. Prepared casein glues consist of the dry sodium salts of dry milk protein (sodium caseinate) from skim milk, and calcium hydroxide. When water is added the soluble sodium caseinate gradually converts to an insoluble calcium caseinate which hardens as the water evaporates. Casein glues were the most water-resistant glues available until the introduction of other thermosetting adhesives in the 1930s and 40s but they are not water-proof. Casein adhesives were popular before emulsions were available and may be found in small shop construction and do-it-yourself repairs. Due to their high alkalinity they bond very well to oily and resinous woods such as teak, yew and resinous pine. They are hard and creep resistant with good machinability. Their open time is intermediate between hide glues and other thermosets. Toxicity is low but their strong alkalinity can cause staining on some woods, such as oak and maple). Their light tan colour may be an advantage or dis-advantage depending on the application. They are insoluble in organic solvents and only resoluble in strongly alkaline solutions. Similarly, casein based paints tend to form very durable coatings that are not easily redissolved.

### 4.7.5   Natural resins and lacquers

Natural resins form a chemically diverse group of water-insoluble materials secreted or excreted by plants. Most resins belong to the class of chemicals known as terpenoids which are formed from units of the compound iso-prene. Isoprene has the empirical formula $C_5H_8$ and the terpenoids are classified according to the number of carbon atoms in the structure of their compounds as follows: monoterpenoids ($C_{10}$), sesquiterpenoids ($C_{15}$), diterpenoids ($C_{20}$), sesterterpenoids ($C_{25}$), triterpenoids ($C_{30}$), carotenoids ($C_{40}$). Higher molecular weight compounds of isoprene form polymers (poly isoprenoids) with the general formula $(C_5)n$. Resins from living plants are collected by inten-tional tapping or slashing. Copal resins, the semi-fossilized products of long dead trees, and amber, a fossil resin aged over geological time scales, are collected by surface prospect-ing or mining. Shellac, an insect resin, is secreted by tropical scale insects that feed on various trees found in India, Burma and Thailand.

Mono and sesquiterpenoids form the main components of the essential oils of plants and are responsible for the initial fluidity of the oth-erwise solid and involatile di- and triterpenoids as they occur in nature. Such mixtures, classi-fied as oleo-resins and balsams are sometimes

used as they occur (e.g. Venice turpentine, Canada balsam) but are more frequently treated by distillation or other processes to sep-arate the oil component from the harder resin component. Oleo-resins from pines are dis-tilled, yielding a hard resin known as rosin or colophony and a volatile essential oil known as spirits-of-turpentine or gum turpentine.

Natural resins have been relatively little used as adhesives in recent times and, like waxes, are now more commonly encountered as coat-ings than as adhesives. However, mixtures of waxes and resins such as beeswax and dammar have been widely used as adhesives (e.g. for lining paintings) and solid shellac resin has been used as a thermoplastic gap-filling adhe-sive in situations such as the joining of a ceramic knob to a metal screw post for exam-ple. Examples of primary natural resins used as transparent coatings on wood include sandarac, mastic and shellac. Oil soluble rosin could be combined with a drying oil in a heated kettle to make common varnish. Oleo resins have also been added to harder resin compositions to soften or plasticize them and increase tough-ness. More expensive varnishes with greater final hardness were often made with hard fos-sil resins by first subjecting these insoluble resins to a destructive distillation process called 'cracking' after which they could be combined with oil. Oil-resin varnishes were normally thinned for use with either turpentine or petro-leum solvents. While they are soluble in a vari-ety of polar and non-polar solvents, resins are by definition insoluble in water. Gums, how-ever, are water soluble. Many resins, such as 'gum mastic', are misnamed since they are not gums. The natural resins become less soluble over time and some may be capable of crosslinking. Solid shellac sticks called burn in sticks have also been extensively employed by furniture restorers to fill small areas of damage. A summary of the main resins is given in *Table 4.3* on page 176. For further information the reader is referred to Gettens and Stout (1966), Mills and White (1987), Horie (1987) and Thorpe and Whiteley (1937). Natural lacquers, film forming emulsions obtained from plants, are discussed in section 4.4.6.

### Shellac

Best known as the principal ingredient of French polish, shellac is obtained from the secretions of a scale insect *Laccifer lacca* which infests a variety of host trees in certain regions of Southern Asia. In India the principal host is *Butea monosperma*. The raw lac product consists of resin encrusted sticks and twigs (hence *stick lac*) intermixed with insect remains, dyestuff and other unwanted contaminants. The first stage of refining traditionally involved crushing this raw material, sieving off the larger sticks and twigs and washing in water to remove the dye. The dye was valued for colouring leather and imparting a beautiful red to silk and was precipitated from solution by the addition of lime. When dry, the resin was winnowed to remove small fragments of stick. This produced the semi-refined *seed-lac* which had a grain like appearance and varied in colour from yellow to reddish brown depending on the district in which it was cultivated and the type of tree from which it was derived. Further purification involved heating long sausage shaped bags about two inches in diameter filled with seed lac and gently squeezing the molten shellac through the cloth. It was then stretched into a thin sheet. The thinner central portion of the sheet was broken up into *shellac flakes* while the thicker edges were mixed with the subsequent batch. The indigenous use of shellac buttons for applying a decorative glaze by friction heating was assisted by the addition of other natural resins particularly cheap and brittle rosin. A small quantity of orpiment could also be added to lighten the appearance of both flakes and varnish and this made it slightly opaque. These adulterations were likely to have been undertaken before the shellac was exported but it is also entirely conceivable that unscrupulous importers or retailers could have further adulterated their supplies. At any rate shellac as such was shunned in favour of seed lac by Stalker and Parker and their contemporaries.

The chemistry of shellac is extremely complex and only recently understood. Raw lac contains 70–80% resin, 6–7% wax, 4–8% coloured matter and some moisture. The resin fraction divides into a hard (ether-insoluble) fraction and a soft (ether-soluble) fraction. Shellac resin consists largely of low molecular weight polymers (oligomers) formed by esterification of polyhydroxy carboxylic acids with one another. It is possible by rigorous purification under laboratory conditions to obtain a

material that has been designated 'pure lac resin'. This is a fairly low molecular weight (2100) polyester formed by reaction of aleuritic acid and a sesquiterpene acid. In this esterification reaction, aleuritic acid, an aliphatic polycarboxylic acid related to the common fatty acids, functions as the acid and sesquiterpene acid functions as the alcohol. It appears that the hard and soft resin fractions are essentially similar but differ in the number of polymer units (oligomers) present in the molecule. Shellac also contains aldehyde groups which may be gradually converted by oxidation to carboxylic acid groups. As there are plenty of hydroxyl groups available in the molecular structure of shellac, it is possible that the esterification process could continue in a shellac film and that this could explain the gradual reduction in alcohol solubility of shellac that occurs over time.

Historically, shellac has been used both alone and in combination with other resins. An early reference documenting the use of shellac by itself is in the hand written notes of tradesman Isaac Byington from Bristol, Connecticut (Byington, 1795). It is produced in various forms and grades as buttons, pellets, and flakes, seedlac, garnet lac, orange, blonde and white. These are all essentially soluble in ethanol or blends of alcohols being usually made in about a 25% solution (roughly a 2 pound cut). The less refined shellacs have a fairly dark hue while the most thoroughly processed, blonde, is quite clear. Commercially available white shellac is bleached through a chlorination process resulting in a less stable material both before and after its use (Flexner, 1994). Copestake (1992) has shown that decoloration using activated charcoal results in a much more stable product.

Shellac is important in furniture conservation where it is often used for finishing new wood that is being matched to an old surface. It has several qualities which make it particularly useful in conservation. It has desirable colour and refractive qualities for wood substrates, is consistent with the visual qualities of traditional coatings, and can saturate and adhere well to them. It is relatively easy to formulate and use, has a short drying time, is resistant to abrasion and chipping and can easily be redissolved in alcohols. Although shellac does change chemically over time, practical experience suggests

**Table 4.3** Summary of principal natural resins

| Class | Family/ (subfamily) | Genus and species (spp. = various species) | Common name | Notes |
|---|---|---|---|---|
| Monoterpenoid | (Pinaceae) | *Pinus* spp. | Oil of turpentine | A mixture of monoterpenes of variable composition obtained by distillation of crude pine resin (gum turpentine) or pine stumps (wood turpentine). Oxygenated/polymerized materials may remain and may cause yellowing when turpentine is used as a solvent. Known since the sixteenth century |
| | Labiatae | *Lavandula spica* | Oil of spike (spike lavender) | Complex mixture of monoterpenes and some sesquiterpenes. Includes oxygenated components. Less volatile than oil of turpentine. In use from the sixteenth century |
| | | *Rosmarinus officinalis* | Oil of rosemary | |
| | Lauraceae | *Cinnamomum camphorae* | Camphor | Used as a plasticizer |
| Diterpenoid | Coniferae (Pinaceae) | *Pinus* spp. | Common or Bordeaux turpentine, rosin or colophony | Pine resins are the most important of the Pinaceae resins. Mainly soft, soluble, unpolymerized resins or balsams. Abundant and cheap. Composition variable and inconstant with principally acid components. Colophony or rosin, the harder involatile component remaining after distillation of crude pine resin has melting point of 100–130 °C and good solubility in turpentine and aromatic hydrocarbons |
| | | *Picea* spp. | Burgundy pitch | |
| | | *Abies* spp. | Strasbourg turpentine; Canada balsam | Canada balsam used as a mounting medium in microscopy |
| | | *Larix* spp. especially *L. decidua* | Venice turpentine | Used as a varnish as such, as a modifier for other resin varnish compositions, and as raw material for preparation of copper resinate 'pigment'. Dries slowly to yellow, brittle film. Due to high cost not regularly used for preparation of oil of turpentine |
| | | *Pseudotsuga menziessii* (Douglas fir) | Oregon balsam | |
| | Coniferae (Cupressaceae) | *Tetraclinis articulata* | Sandarac | Cupressaceae resins contain polycommunic acid, an important component of fossil resins, that gives rise to polar materials such as |

|  |  |  |  | sandarac soluble in alcohol but insoluble in turpentine and white spirit. Also insoluble in drying oils unless heat treated. Melting point 135–145 °C |
|---|---|---|---|---|
|  |  | *Juniperus* spp. |  | May have been confused with sandarac in past |
|  |  | *Cupressus* spp. |  |  |
|  | Coniferae (Araucariaceae) | *Agathis australis* | Kauri copal | Copal is a general name given to a large variety of hard resins obtained both as fossils and taken fresh from living trees. Accumulations in soil of Araucariaceae resins from Agathis (the main resin producing genus of the Southern hemisphere) gave rise to hard and durable 'semi-fossil' resins extensively exported and used in the nineteenth century for making high quality varnish. Manila copal is described by various different names according to hardness. Fresh resin is softer and semi-fossil resin is hard |
|  |  | *Agathis dammara* (also known as *A. alba*) | Manila copal |  |
|  | Leguminosae | *Hymeneae* spp. | East African or Zanzibar copal; Brazil copal | Resin producing trees of the Leguminosae are tropical. Exact source of resin is often not known due to complexity of supply chain. Though difficult to distinguish one from another, leguminous copals as a group have characteristic composition which allows them to be readily distinguished from coniferous resins. Zanzibar copal is the hardest of the copals and has very high melting point 240–360 °C |
|  |  | *Copaifera* spp. | Copaiba balsams | Very liquid resin containing sesquiterpenes |
|  |  | *Guibortia* spp.; *Tessmannia* spp.; *Daniela* spp. | Copal | Other African copals from e.g. Congo, Accra, Benguela, Sierra Leone |
| Triterpenoids | Dipterocarpaceae (Dipterocarpoideae) | Triterpenoid resins come from numerous genera of broad-leaved trees, mainly but not exclusively tropical. Approximately 500 species in 15 genera principally *Hopea* spp. and *Shorea* spp. | Dammars | Much more varied taxonomy and chemistry than diterpenoid resins. Triterpenoid resins are generally non-polymerizing but easily oxidized and occur in mixtures with sesquiterpenoids rather than monoterpenoids. Dammars are less yellowing than most conifer resins and more readily soluble than leguminous copals. They dissolve completely in aromatic hydrocarbons and turpentine but only partially in alcohol. Pale in colour with very good optical properties, though some yellowing does occur over time and film has a tendency to remain slightly tacky. Melting point 100–105 °C. Dammars come mainly |

*continued*

**Table 4.3** Continued

| Class | Family/ (subfamily) | Genus and species (spp. = various species) | Common name | Notes |
|---|---|---|---|---|
| | | | | from Malaya and Indonesia and were first used as varnish resins in the second quarter of the nineteenth century |
| | Anacardiaceae | *Pistacia* spp. principally *P. lentiscus* | Mastic | Mastic has similar properties to dammar producing a light coloured glossy and elastic varnish that becomes somewhat yellow, brittle and fissured with age and blooms readily in moist atmospheres. Known from antiquity and may have been used as a varnish from the ninth century. Dissolves readily in oil of turpentine, aromatic hydrocarbons and alcohol but is mostly insoluble in petroleum spirit. Melting point 95 °C |
| | Burseraceae | Various genera including: *Carium, Bursera, Ayris, Protium* have been called elemi. Now restricted to *Canarium luzonicum* | Elemis | Elemis contain high proportion of liquid sesquiterpenes. Soft and malleable with strong citrus odour. Used as plasticizing components of varnishes though this effect may disappear as more volatile components evaporate |
| Fossil resin | | | Amber | Resin of plant origin (originally from tree with chemistry similar to Araucariaceae) modified over geological time scales. Found chiefly on shores of Baltic. Used in jewellery, for decorating and constructing small objects and as component of oil varnish. Very hard high molecular weight polymer material only slightly soluble in organic solvents (e.g. 20% of mass soluble in ether) |
| Polyisoprenoids | Euphorbiaceae | Many different plants. *Hevea brasilensis* is very important | Natural rubber | See Chapter 3 |
| Insect resin | | *Laccifer lacca* | Shellac | See below |
| Miscellaneous resins | | *Styrax* spp.; *Benzoin* spp. | Benzoin | Dark resinous material containing mainly esters of benzenoid acids and alcohols (cf. terpenoids). Characteristic odour of vanilla. Used as plasticizer for varnishes |
| | | *Calamus draco* | Dragon's blood | Comes from species of rattan palm. Used to colour spirit varnishes and for lacquering metals |

that this does not normally occur to the extent that removal of an old shellac coating becomes unacceptably difficult. Shellac readily wets onto existing shellac and many other spirit-soluble coatings. Shellacs are tinted and may therefore cause some colour change to substrates to which they are applied. This drawback makes them inappropriate as a coating for an existing painted surface. Shellac can be applied by brush, spray, or pad. French polishing and other application techniques are described in Chapter 13. Further information on shellac is given by Gardner (1938), Hicks (1962), Parry (1935), Williams (1988) and in the Bulletin of the London Shellac Research Bureau.

### 4.7.6  Synthetic materials

Synthetic resins are polymers which generally mimic or improve upon the properties of natural resins. Synthetic resins or 'plastics' have been and continue to be used as coatings and media, adhesives and consolidants and for moulding and casting applications. Virtually all of the tremendous variety now available have had some use, however brief, in the wood working industries. Synthetic resins vary greatly in chemical make-up in structure, properties and uses.

### *Thermoplastics*

Resins dissolved in various solvents have seen extensive use as coatings, but have also been used by conservators as consolidants for degraded wood and poorly bound or adhered coatings. Solvent type adhesives based on cellulose-nitrate resin (H.M.G., Duco etc.) and emulsions based on acrylics and PVACs have also seen extensive use in conservation.

### *Poly(vinyl acetate) PVAC*

Poly(vinyl acetate) (*Figure 4.15a*) was one of the earliest synthetic materials available to conservators and has been used as a consolidant, adhesive and coating. Although never popular as a transparent coating on wood it is liked by some people for retouching and to make an occasionally used varnish that is soluble in toluene or in ethanol/water mixtures. Commercially available poly(vinyl acetate) resins include the Rhodopas series by Rhône Poulenc, the Mowilith series by Hoechst, and

the Vinylite series by Union Carbide. PVA emulsions used in conservation include the Vinamul series by Vinyl Products, the Mowilith series by Hoechst and Jade 834-403N by Aabbitt.

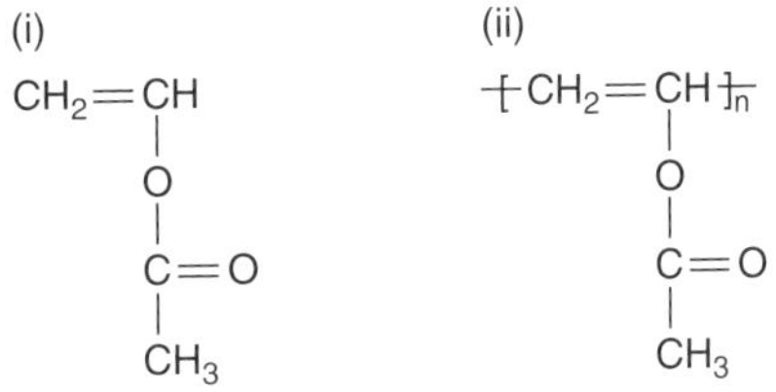

**Figure 4.15(a)**  Structure of some common polymeric materials. (i) Vinyl acetate monomer; (ii) poly(vinyl acetate) (PVAC)

PVAC resins are water clear and relatively stable have little tendency for crosslinking and are relatively unaffected by light. They are soluble in a wide range of solvents including toluene, acetone, and methanol but insoluble in petroleum type solvents, hexane, water and butanol. They are only partially soluble in ethanol and xylene. PVACs whiten in contact with water, have generally low glass transition temperatures and have different optical properties to natural resins including a generally lower refractive index.

Poly(vinyl acetate) emulsions were the first resin emulsions to be used as wood adhesives and are familiar to most people as white glue. They bond well to wood and a variety of other substrates, are easy to use and clean up, and are readily available. This combination of factors has made them the most commonly used non-industrial woodworking adhesives and the choice of DIY enthusiasts everywhere. While emulsions are initially dispersible in water, they dry to tough films that are only swellable in water but have greater solubility in organic solvents such as ketones. Owing to their high molecular weights they are also not completely resoluble in organic solvents as are the parent resins.

'Yellow glues' are emulsion-type adhesives consisting principally of poly(vinyl acetate) and ethylene vinyl acetate co-polymers. They are generally more viscous than white glues and as a result do not squeeze out as much under clamping pressure. They set very quickly, are easier to sand and more creep resistant than white glues. Yellow glues have a shelf life of six months to a year, give excellent bond strength and moderately good gap filling ability although thicker glue lines will creep more than thin ones. Hardness is variable depending on resin and formulation but they have good machinability. They have very low toxicity, are non-flammable and have good chemical stability. Water resistance is good in regard to high relative humidity but poor in liquid water.

### Poly(vinyl alcohol)

Poly(vinyl alcohol) PVAL (*Figure 4.15b*) is prepared from PVAC by a process of alcoholysis (hydrolysis with alcohol). The proportion of alcohol groups in the end product can be varied between 70 and 100% to give products with varied properties. PVAL is insoluble in most organic solvents at room temperature but dissolves in water. PVAL that is less than 80% hydrolysed will dissolve only in cold water. Above about 93% hydrolysis, PVAL will dissolve only in hot water and will form a gel or precipitate on cooling. Grades between about 85 and 90% are stable and soluble in both hot and cold water. PVAL adheres poorly to most organic materials and therefore does not saturate and darken them. Fully hydrolysed materials have the greatest tensile strength but films formed from them tend to shrink on drying. PVAL is hygroscopic and the properties of dried films are therefore affected by the relative humidity of their environment. The hydroxyl groups in PVAL are highly reactive and it participates in a range of reactions that result in crosslinking and the formation of insoluble complexes. It has been widely used for fixing of pigment, particularly where absence of darkening is required, and as an adhesive for temporary facing of friable surfaces. It is also widely used as a release agent in moulding and casting. Commercially available poly (vinyl alcohols) include the Gelvatol range by Monsanto, the Mowiol range by

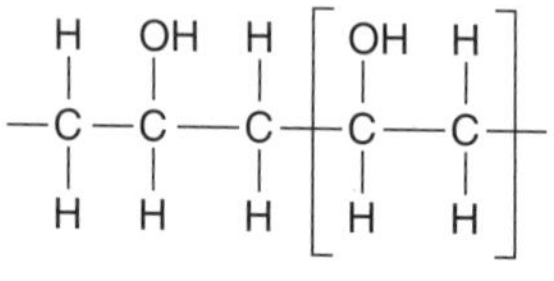

**Figure 4.15(b)**   Poly(vinyl alcohol) (PVAL)

Hoechst, the Rhodoviol range by Rhône Poulenc, the Elvanol range by Du Pont and the Polyviol range by Wacker.

### Poly(vinyl acetals)

Poly(vinyl acetals), another PVAC-derived polymer, are formed by the reaction of PVAL with an aldehyde. Poly(vinyl butyral) (PVB), the most widely used material of this type, is available in various molecular weights with different proportions of residual hydroxyl groups present (*Figure 4.15c*). PVBs in which a high proportion of OH groups remain have high Tg, require more highly polar (hydrogen bonded) solvents or solvent mixtures for solution, and tend to be more difficult to use as adhesives. Conversely, lower hydroxyl PVBs have a lower Tg and are soluble in a wider range of solvents. Examples of PVBs include the Butvar series from Monsanto, the Mowital series from Hoechst and the Rhovinal series from Rhône Poulenc. PVBs have been widely used as consolidants and adhesives for wood and as consolidants for paint films.

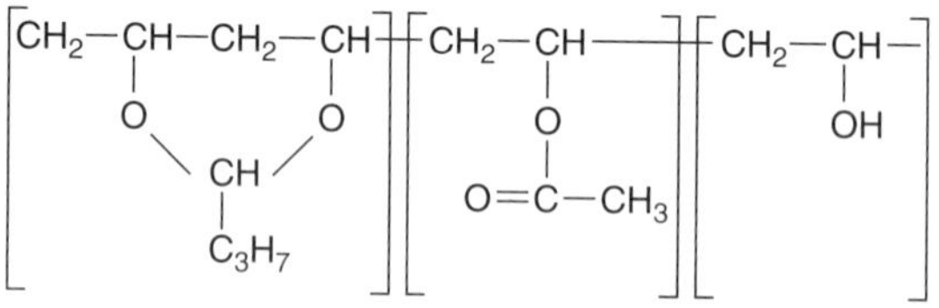

**Figure 4.15(c)**   Poly(vinyl butyral) (PVB): structure of PVB, with typical proportions of monomer components

### Acrylics

These water clear synthetic resins are polymers produced from two families of monomers, the acrylates derived from acrylic acid and the methacrylates derived from methacrylic acid. The acrylics were developed by Otto Röhm and Otto Haas in the 1920s. These are usually used as singular resins in a solvent, usually aromatic hydrocarbons, ketones or esters. Some of the common acrylics found in conservation include the Paraloid and Rhoplex (Primal) series from Röhm and Haas, the Elvacites from Du Pont, the Plexigums and Plexisols from Röhm and the Lascaux range. The Paraloid series includes Paraloid B67 (isobutyl methacrylate), Paraloid B72 (ethyl methacrylate/methyl acrylate 70/30 co-polymer), and Paraloid B44 a material similar to, but slightly harder than, B72 (*Figure 4.15d*). The Paraloid series was previously known in the United States under the name Acryloid. The names Acryloid and Paraloid are both trade marks of Röhm and Haas. Acrylics are mostly easily prepared for use, are clear, and have solubility parameters that are often different from an extant coating making it possible to remove them without causing harm. Shellac will mostly adhere adequately to the acrylics making it possible to use them as an interface between a shellac and an original surface. The more apparent draw backs of the acrylics are possibly inadequate adherent properties due to high molecular weight/long-chain structure and different optical qualities to natural resin coatings being matched. Acrylics are usually soluble in aromatic hydrocarbon solvents. For further information on the acrylics see Kolesky (1995).

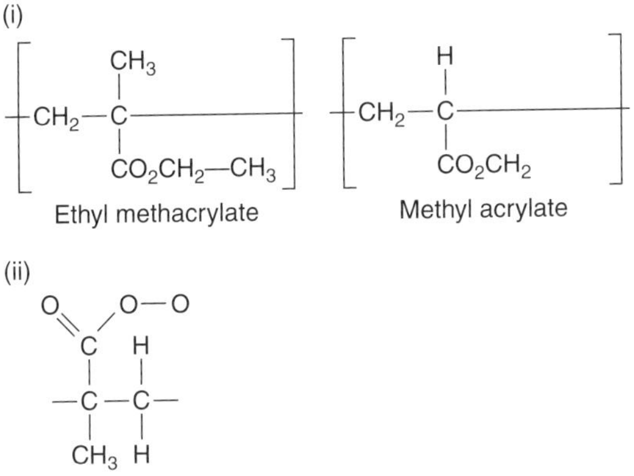

resins of this type to be used in conservation as a picture varnish. It was later replaced by Ketone Resin N, also called Laropal K80 (BASF), a product based on cyclohexanone alone. MS2, another product resembling AW2, was based on methyl cyclohexane. MS2 formed the starting point for a reduced derivative, MS2A, in which all the carbonyl groups were converted to hydroxyl groups by catalytic hydrogenation (*Figure 4.15e*). MS2A is much more stable to light-induced oxygenation and less sensitive to water vapour with less tendency to bloom. It has therefore remained soluble in non-polar solvents for much longer and has enjoyed considerable popularity in the UK as a final varnish on cleaned painted surfaces. However, at some point in the history of manufacture of this material (*c*.1963) the starting material was changed from methyl cyclohexanones to cyclohexanone itself. MS2A prepared from this starting material was found to be too brittle for satisfactory use as a coating. Another reduced cyclohexanone material MS2B prepared from AW2 had similar good properties to

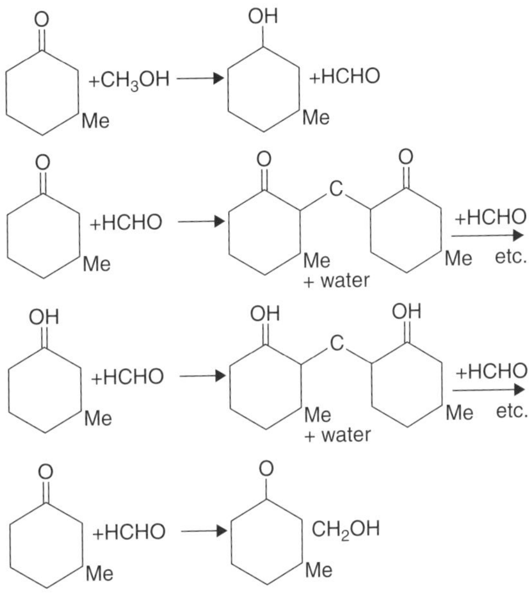

Figure 4.15(d)

**Figure 4.15(d)** (i) Paraloid B72: the monomer units are arranged randomly in the polymer chain; (ii) Paraloid B67 monomer

### Cyclohexanone resins

This class of low molecular weight resins has somewhat variable properties depending on starting materials and processing. Generally, they are hard but somewhat brittle, optically similar to natural resins and with similar solubility characteristics to them, initially more stable than natural resins but tending to require more polar solvents for removal as they age. AW2 (BASF) a co-polymer of cyclohexanone and methyl cyclohexanone, was one of the first

**Figure 4.15(e)** MS2A (Routledge, 2000): MS2A is the product of a complex mixture formed by reactions involving methyl cyclohexanone, methanol and their derivatives. Routledge (2000) states that 'typical' MS2A has a weight average molecular weight of 1800, a number average molecular weight of 800, and will contain around eight ring units per molecule

the earlier type of MS2A. However the MS2B prepared from Ketone N (when Ketone N replaced AW2) was again found to have unsatisfactory properties. For further information on the structure of these resins see Mills and White (1987) and Routledge (2000).

### Cellulose nitrates

Two important classes of polymers derived from cellulose are the cellulose esters and the cellulose ethers. Of the various esters of cellulose that have been manufactured, cellulose nitrate and cellulose acetate are the most important to the conservator (*Figure 4.15f*). Cellulose nitrate is produced through the conversion of cellulose to nitrate esters by reacting it with sulfuric and nitric acids. As a coating, cellulose nitrate has been used extensively in the furniture industry but is not commonly employed in conservation. It has a high Tg which is reduced by the addition of plasticizers. The composition of cellulose nitrate products varies significantly depending on the blend with an assortment of plasticizers, solvents, catalysts and other additives. They cure initially by the rapid loss of solvent followed by crosslinking and eventual decomposition releasing acid forming nitrogen dioxide. Cellulose nitrates are quick drying, and provide initially durable surface resistant to moisture and many solvents, though they remain largely removable even after significant ageing. In the long term they show poor ageing properties, with problems occurring due to migration of plasticizers out of the coating and lack of saturation of substrate. Cellulose nitrate coatings show both crosslinking and reduction of molecular weight through ageing. Typically cellulose nitrate coatings require fairly aggressive, toxic and flammable solvents both for application and removal. They tend to dry too fast for brush application therefore requiring spray application to achieve a good result. HMG® (H. Marcel Guest) is a quick drying, clear, cellulose nitrate based adhesive of moderate strength suitable for a wide variety of substrates that has been widely used in conservation.

Cellulose ethers (*Figure 4.15g*) form a large class of materials used in conservation principally for the consolidation of pigment and as

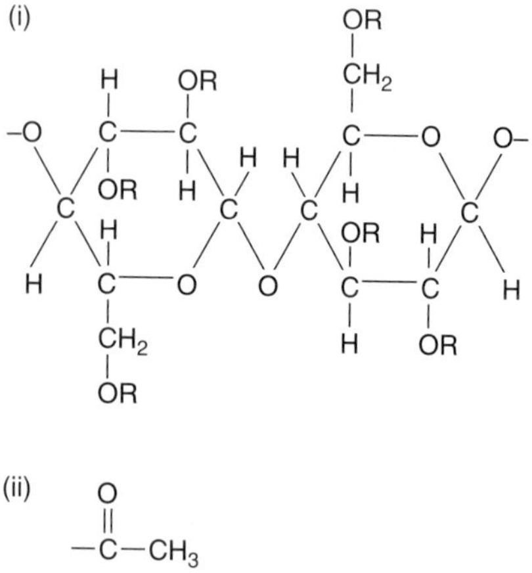

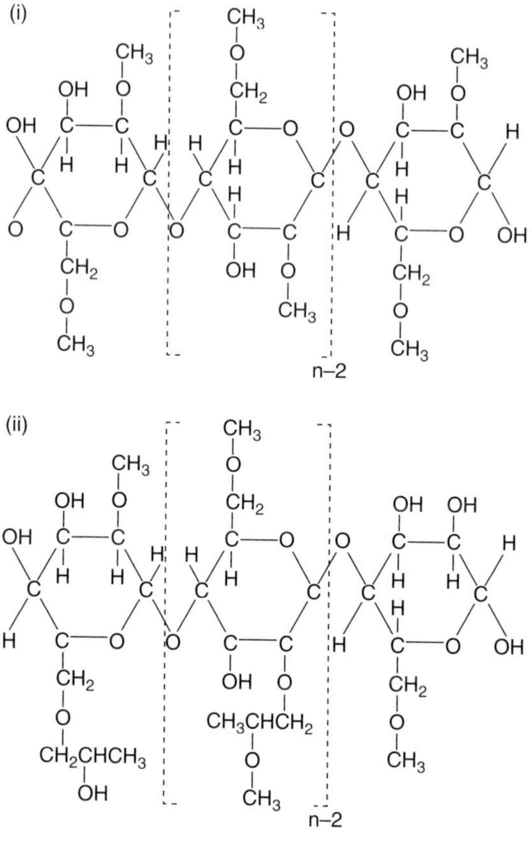

**Figure 4.15(g)**  Cellulose ethers: (i) methyl cellulose; (ii) hydroxypropylmethyl cellulose (*from* Dow Methocel Cellulose Ethers product literature)

**Figure 4.15(f)**  (i) Two monomer units of a cellulose ester (Horie, 1992). In cellulose nitrate, about 2.1 of the R groups (12% by weight) are —$NO_2$. In cellulose acetate, about 2.4 of the R groups are acetate groups (ii)

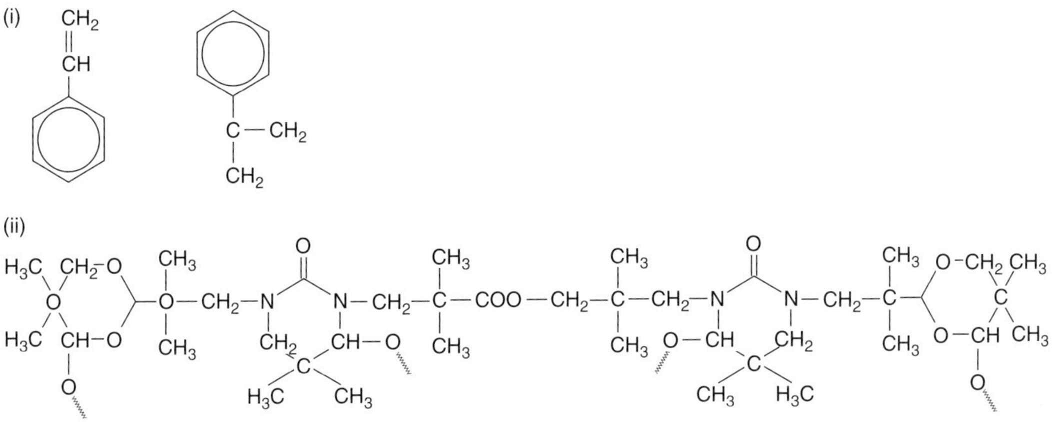

(i)

(ii)

**Figure 4.15(h)** (i) Regalrez: the Regalrez series are hydrogenated oligomers of styrene (vinyl benzene, ethenyl benzene) and α-methyl styrene (isopropyl benzene or 1-methyl-1-phenyl ethylene). An oligomer is a polymer that has relatively few monomer units (usually an upper limit of about ten units). Hydrogenation is a chemical reaction involving the addition of hydrogen across a double or triple bond, to produce a singe or double bond respectively. In the context of resins such as Regalrez, the removal of double bonds produces a more chemically stable varnish. (ii) Proposed structure of Laropal A81 (Arslanoğlu and Learner, 2001)

an adhesive in paper conservation. These materials generally have very low strength and relatively poor adhesion. However, methyl cellulose (e.g. Methocel A by Dow Corning) has been used as a consolidant for waterlogged wood (Rosenquist, 1959) and for basketry (Thomsen, 1981). Hydroxy propyl cellulose (e.g. Klucel G and Klucel J by Hercules) has been used as a 2% solution in ethanol for the consolidation of pigment where non-aqueous treatment and absence of darkening are required (Berger, 1976; Hofenk de Graaf, 1981). For further information see Horie (1987).

### Other thermoplastic materials

Several other industrially manufactured low molecular weight (LMW) resins have been investigated for their potential use in picture varnishes (de la Rie and McGlinchey, 1990). Three synthetic LMW resins that are claimed to be considerably more stable than natural resins and the ketone resins are reviewed by de la Rie (1993). These include the hydrogenated hydrocarbon resin Regalrez 1094 (Hercules) and an aldehyde resin produced by BASF. Two synthetic low molecular weight resins that have found application in furniture conservation are Regalrez 1094 and 1126 and Laropal A81 (*Figure 4.15b*).

### Thermosetting resins

These generally consist of two chemical components which react to form highly crosslinked polymers. The reaction frequently proceeds without the formation of elimination (condensation reaction) products and usually therefore causes relatively little shrinkage, so they generally have fair to excellent gap-filling capabilities when used as adhesives. The final polymer is mostly quite chemically inert making these materials water and solvent resistant. Their rigid crosslinked nature gives them high hardness and internal strength, high resistance to creep and excellent machinability.

Blood and milk protein adhesives must be regarded as thermosets because they harden by irreversible chemical reaction. Blood glues were extensively used in plywood manufacture during the middle of this century but are little used today. A variety of thermosetting resins became available as a result of advances in polymer chemistry. Phenol-formaldehyde (phenolic) adhesives were produced in film form for hot pressing soon after 1910, and in liquid form in 1935. Urea-formaldehyde adhesives were introduced around 1937, epoxies during the 1940s and resorcinol-formaldehyde in 1943. These are the primary adhesives used in industrial wood bonding applications such as plywood and particle-board manufacture, but they have also been available for small shop use where a water proof adhesive is required. All of these adhesives form chemically resistant crosslinked polymers and should be considered irreversible in wood bonding applications.

*Urea-formaldehyde* (UF) adhesives are formed from the reaction of urea and formaldehyde (*Figure 4.15i*). These adhesives are cheaper than phenolics and epoxies but are less water-resistant. They liberate formaldehyde during and after curing, and cure poorly under about 21 °C though bond strength is excellent, especially on woods with high moisture content. They are hard and creep resistant, with good machinability but gap filling ability is relatively poor. Also, they tend to be brittle which is more of a problem in thicker glue lines. Open time is highly temperature dependent, and they may be cured rapidly with heat. Urea-formaldehyde resins are highly toxic when uncured and long term release of formaldehyde from cured resin is a significant conservation problem. The water resistance of UF resins is intermediate between casein and phenolics. The colour may be light brown or white.

*Phenol-formaldehyde* (PF) resins developed in the early 20th century by Leo H. Baekeland are the basis of phenolic varnishes and adhesives (*Figure 4.15j*). An early form of phenolic resin was produced as a possible shellac replacement in the early 1900s. Early phenolic varnishes were heated to high temperatures and reacted with oils. Later phenolics were developed that were combined with oils at more moderate temperature (Fry, 1995). As with other modern coatings, high solid content phenolic formulations are available to conform to various government regulations designed to limit solvent pollution. Phenol-formaldehyde adhesives remain fluid until set by heat (170–300 °F) when they develop excellent bond strength. They are hard and creep resistant yet moderately flexible, with good machinability and good gap filling ability but become increasingly brittle on ageing. They are toxic before curing and can release small amounts of formaldehyde after curing. They are highly resistant to solvents, water and stains, brown in colour and are used to make exterior and marine grade plywood.

*Resorcinol-formaldehyde* (RF) resins develop excellent bond strength but require curing

**Figure 4.15(i)**   Urea formaldehyde (e.g. Cascamite adhesive)

above 21 °C. They are hard and creep resistant with good machinability and good gap filling ability. After mixing, open time is about an hour but this is highly temperature dependent. Formaldehyde is released while curing but relatively low rates of release occur after curing. RF resins are dark reddish brown and are highly waterproof.

*Polyurethanes* contain urethane linkages, —NHCO—, based on reaction products of isocyanates with hydroxyl group bearing materials (*Figure 4.15k*). As coatings they are valued for their resistance to solvents and abrasion and are among the most durable of thermoset polymers. However, they may lack transparency and may not adhere well to some substrates. The development of urethane coatings as a viable commercial and industrial product is attributed to Otto Bayer in the late 1930s (Wells, 1974). There are different properties within this class of materials and the American Society for Testing and Materials (ASTM) has classified them into six groups. Polyurethanes are often combined with other products, particularly alkyds.

**Figure 4.15(j)**   Phenol formaldehyde (Bakelite)

## Alkyds

Alkyds are a type of oil-modified polyester resin. They are produced from polyhydric alcohol, polybasic acid and a fatty monobasic acid or triglyceride. The term alkyd comes from 'al' for alcohol and 'kyd' for acid structure (Martens, 1968). The polymeric networking is commonly a function of oxygen and carbon-carbon double bond reactions. Alkyds are often formulated in conjunction with a drying oil and classified according to the use of short, medium or long oils. High solid content alkyds with low viscosity are available to limit the amount of solvent released in the drying process. Metallic driers may be used to accelerate the crosslinking process but are not usually required for alkyds because they are pre-polymerized to relatively high molecular weights and require relatively little further polymerization to gel. Alkyd coatings are highly resistant to moisture and solvents, durable, and have greater initial transparency than some other common thermosetting polymers. However, they tend to discolour, particularly in the presence of vegetable oil modifiers.

*Thermosetting acrylics* are very similar to thermoplastic acrylics except that the polymer includes reactive sites such as carboxyl and hydroxyl functional groups. Acrylics can be reacted with epoxies, amino acids and isocyanates. They are good performers on an industrial level lacking any glaring disadvantages and are used extensively in enamels and emulsion paints (Friel, 1995). Thermosetting acrylics are found in high gloss 'lacquer' finishes on some furniture. They are highly durable but difficult to remove.

## Epoxies

Epoxies are a chemically and physically diverse family of thermosetting compounds which have in common the presence of the epoxide functional group, a three-membered ring composed of two carbon atoms and one oxygen (*Figure 4.15l*). Adhesives and casting resins normally consist of two components; a resin and a hardener which when mixed together react to form a rigid crosslinked polymer. Epoxy resins are more expensive than the previously discussed thermosetting resins, but they have important advantages. A large number of epoxy resins and adhesives are on the market permitting a wide choice of properties and potential applications. Epoxies are solvent-free systems which shrink very little on curing and do not off-gas toxic or reactive compounds once cured. This makes them good gap fillers which can be used with very low clamping pressure. Their chemical reactivity is low after curing and while they are prone to darken with age they do not lose adhesive or cohesive strength to any significant degree as a result of ageing. Epoxies are highly polar adhesives, with excellent adhesive and cohesive strength, which bond very well to a variety of substrates including wood, metal, glass and stone. Conversely, they do not bond well to non-polar oily and resinous materials. A wide range of resins and hardeners is used in epoxy formulations but a few generalizations can be made. Quick-setting epoxies are more viscous, initially darker in colour and more prone to darken with age. They build higher temperatures in curing because there is less time for heat-of-reaction to dissipate. The reverse is true of slower setting epoxies which are available in clear ('water white'), highly fluid grades. Hardness varies from hard and brittle to rubbery depending on formulation, creep is very low even for soft varieties. Open time is highly variable depending on formulation. Epoxies are waterproof and their optical saturation of substrates is high. Uncured resins and hardeners are toxic, cured films are not. Reversibility is very limited on porous substrates but good on hard and non-porous substrates such as porcelain and glass although it requires use of chlorinated solvents to swell the polymer matrix. Examples of epoxy resins

(i)

(ii)

Urethane units

**Figure 4.15(k)**   (i) A urethane monomer; (ii) a polyurethane

which have been used in conservation include the Araldite range from Ciba Geigy, the Ablebond range from Ablestick, the Rutapox range from Bakelite, and Hxtal-Nyl-1 from Conservation Materials.

*Cyanoacrylates* adhesives are popularly called 'SuperGlue' after an early trade name (*Figure 4.15m*). The first of these adhesives (Eastman 910) was introduced in 1958 and the number of available brands and range of physical properties have increased markedly since then. Unlike the previously described thermosetting resins, no separate hardener is required for curing. The clear fluid adhesive polymerizes very rapidly in contact with a weak base, such as the water that is present in or on virtually all substrates. The chief advantage of cyanoacrylates is their very rapid cure which eliminates the need for any clamping other than hand pressure. They will stick to a wide variety of substrates (including skin!) and so are useful in bonding dissimilar materials. Open time is measured in seconds but is shorter on alkaline substrates and longer on acidic substrates such as wood. Cyanoacrylates initially had virtually no gap-filling abilities and would not cure in any but very thin glue lines. New varieties are available which have good gap-filling characteristics. They are hard and machinable with low creep. Cyanoacrylates have short shelf lives and show poor long term chemical stability when cured. Adhesive joins become weaker and prone to failure as they age. They can be extremely useful in quick assembly and can function as clamps in difficult circumstances but should be considered temporary in conservation terms unless backed up by another adhesive or fastener system. The cured material is swollen, but not dissolved, by acetone which can be used to effect its removal from non-porous substrates.

Thermosets used in moulding and casting are discussed in Chapter 10.

## 4.8    Examination and identification of adhesives, coatings and media

The difficulties inherent in the identification of surface finishes are reviewed by Mussey

**Figure 4.15(l)**   (i) A small molecule with epoxy groups at each end (resin); (ii) a diamine (hardener); (iii) a crosslinked epoxy network

**Figure 4.15(m)**   Methyl cyanoacrylate monomer + water → polycyanoacrylate (Super glue)

(1980). A single layer of finish often contains several different materials including resins, oils and waxes making precise identification of individual components difficult or impossible without (or even with) sophisticated technology. A mid-eighteenth century document which illustrates this problem recommends a furniture varnish that contains no fewer than six natural resins: sandarac, copal, mastic, amber, shellac and colophony (Brachert, 1978). While exact identification may not always be possible, an understanding of the nature of the materials present can be instructive as to the characteristics, history and conservation needs of a coating. The overall identification of any waxes, varnishes and paints present on a furniture piece is thus the first consideration during examination of the surface. Examination of the gross optical and mechanical properties of materials, their solubility, melting point, appearance under light of different wavelengths, and simple microscopy can be used to obtain contextual information about them before subjecting them to more advanced analytical methods. Scrutinizing coatings in the proximity of joints, damages, blemishes and unexposed areas will help evaluate the relationship of the coating to the original construction date of the furniture. Simple methods of analysis that can be applied to investigating surface coatings on furniture are described by Krupa (1991). For a thorough and systematic description of the application of more advanced techniques to the analysis of organic materials see Mills and White (1987).

Waxed surfaces may be confused with burnished surfaces when superficially examined. With the aid of a magnifying loupe, waxes in the pores of wood and wood-grain compression become more apparent. Thickly waxed surfaces take on a cloudy appearance because there are sufficient randomly oriented crystalline domains to scatter visible light. In general, wax surfaces can be distinguished from resinous finishes by their difference in compliance. Resin coatings such as shellac and dammar are hard surfaces that are usually somewhat brittle.

The general solubility testing of surface coatings can be performed on areas as small as 2 mm across with a tightly wrapped and pointed cotton swab along with the aid of a magnifying loupe. Surfaces that appear to have

aged yet have solubility properties akin to fresh materials should elicit further technical examination. Tests of the solvent polarity necessary to solubilize aged varnish using blends of cyclohexane, toluene and acetone were devised by Feller and Curran (1975) to examine the change in solubility during the ageing process of both historic and modern varnishes. Traditional urushi, obtained from the tree *Rhus verniciflua*, is an extremely hard, insoluble material. Westmoreland (1988) has used its relative insolubility to distinguish it from eighteenth century European lacquers that may contain such resins as dammar, mastic, sandarac, copal and shellac and drying oils.

The melting point of a wax is one simple method for identification (White, 1978). Heat-programmable microscope stages help to determine the melting point of small samples (*c*. 0.1 mm thick, sample placed on edge) while viewing under low power magnification. The wax will change into an amorphous (hence transparent) liquid at the melting point, for accurate measurements a second melting point must be taken. Miscible wax blends have a melting point that is a weighted average of the separate waxes.

The illumination of painted surfaces by monochrome sodium vapour light has been investigated by Hours (1976). It has been observed that chromatic aberrations disappear under monochrome light, rendering a sharper detail albeit shifted to a yellow monochromatic range. The authors suggest that pentimenti are more easily detected with this particular monochrome light than when illuminated by more conventional polychromatic lighting methods. Information on under drawings may also be obtained using infra red imaging devices.

Auto-fluorescence excited by ultra-violet illumination is useful for providing information about the character and condition of furniture finishes (see section 13.3). For more accurate interpretation of the emission colour of the fluorescence, a spectrophotometer can be used to supplement visual perception. Amber and related fossil resins fluoresce in a wide range of colours and with varying intensity (Rice, 1980; Werwein, 1982). Some Dominican and Sicilian ambers also fluoresce under normal light. Newly fractured surfaces are more fluorescent than those that have had exposure to air (Rice, 1980). Many stable, synthetic materials and proteins maintain a pale blue/lavender fluorescence, even after extensive exposure. De la Rie (1982) showed that sandarac, dammar, mastic, Venetian turpentine and drying oils shift from this bluish fluorescence to yellowish after natural ageing. Larsen *et al.* (1991) has observed that fresh, unbleached shellac immediately fluoresces orange. The UV fluorescence of shellac shows a variety of colours as is reported by Baumeister (1988), Hering and Buchholz (1990) and Wolbers and Landrey (1987). Larsen *et al.* (1991) has reported changes in emission spectra from orange to yellow for two separate lots of orange shellac film. One film was 38 years old and the other was recently cast. Orange shellac can contain up to 10% dyestuffs (Mills and White, 1987). If this dye was originally present in both samples in approximately equal amounts and after 38 years it had begun to fade, it is possible that the observed shift in fluorescence is associated with fading of the dyestuff and not solely indicative of lot variance.

Optical microscopy is frequently the first method used when further investigation of paint samples is necessary. Transmitted and incident microscopy can be used to view the stratigraphy of the organic materials that make up these complex coatings. The layer stratification can be studied in areas of losses or, if sampling is possible, on an embedded cross-section. Sample removal techniques, mounting and examination of cross-sections taken from a broad range of paintings representing different artistic techniques are described by Plesters (1956). Waentig (1993) has a range of casting materials. The mounting of samples from a polychrome sculpture using a polyester casting resin and a glass knife microtome to expose the cross-section is described by Stodulski and Dorge (1991).

Stains that are reactive towards specific functional groups have been employed to characterize organic adhesives, mediums and resins. Johnson and Packard (1971) note that it is important to first test for proteins since egg yolk also contains a significant amount of oil that would in addition test positive for oil. Martin (1977) makes visual observations while heating a thin section to 225 °C to detect oils; since resins may degrade in appearance similar to oils she used bromo creosol purple to first test for resins. It is necessary to test the sample with this stain prior to embedding since this is a non-specific stain for acids and will react with acids commonly found in embedding materials. Wolbers and Landrey (1987) has used fluorochromes to test for triterpenoid resins. The reactivity of fluorochrome stains can be difficult to determine when pigments interfere with the auto fluorescence of the medium or on occasions where absorbent passages have localized intensities of dyes present. To reduce this false-positive assessment, thin sections taken from embedded cross sections or high magnifications (e.g. 800×) may need to be used. Even then, interpretation remains subjective and though results may suggest the presence of a particular substance, more advanced methods should be used for positive identification.

Gas chromatography (GC) will characterize many organic materials by resolving the heterogenous components according to molecular composition. Glastrup (1989) and Mills and White (1977) used GC to identify resins. White (1978) showed that original components of waxes and their mixtures are easily separated and identified with GC since they are chiefly composed of non-glyceryl esters which are more stable than components of resins and oils. Drying oils differ dramatically after they have thoroughly set; Mills (1966) reports that it is possible to distinguish linseed, poppy and walnut oil according to the ratio of methyl palmitate to stearate obtained from the chromatogram and in 1982 reported some success in distinguishing stand from raw linseed oil by noting the ratio of dicarboxylic acid esters present.

Pyrolysis gas chromatography (PGC) has been used to identify synthetic resins and binders by de Witte and Terfve (1982) and Sonoda and Rioux (1990) whilst a range of alkyds were analysed by Bates *et al.* (1989). De Witte and Bates reported data that were obtained from a gas chromatography apparatus coupled to a mass spectrometer to enable the identification of peaks according to their molecular fragmentation pattern. Mills and White (1982) has discussed the benefits of mass spectrometry in identifying artists' materials. Hyphenated techniques such as GC-MS, LCMS and PY-GC-MS have greatly enhanced detection capabilities and separation methods.

Proteinaceous materials are too high in molecular weight to identify easily with gas chromatography and their constituent amino acids are too polar to identify with the set up required for routine analysis of resins, waxes and oils. Liquid chromatography has been used by Halpine (1992) to identify proteins using derivatized amino acids of fifteenth century painting samples. An additional method of directly analysing proteins using an immunoassay technique originally suggested by Johnson and Packard (1971), has been used by Tomek and Pechova (1992) to identify ovalbumin in egg (see also Kockaert *et al.*, 1989).

Derrick *et al.* (1992) has used Fourier Transform Infra Red (FTIR) microscopy for analysing resin finishes on furniture from both laboratory prepared samples and historic furniture. The spectra were obtained from samples that were microtomed in 20 µm increments, though the authors subsequently commented on obtaining thinner samples using a glass blade microtome. Godla (1991) has also used FTIR to evaluate historic surface finishes on pre-industrial American furniture. Derrick *et al.* (1988) has reported the FTIR spectra of urushi and compared it to library spectra of known resins and lacquers, though no characteristic infra red band assignments were made in the investigation. In addition to infra red microscopy, infra red spectral depth profiling has identified layered components of coatings, though on a limited scale due to the complexity of the technique. The application of photo thermal beam deflection spectroscopy to identify a nitrocellulose print on polyethylene is described by Low and Varlashkin (1986). This is a non-destructive technique provided the sample holding cell can be properly manufactured to accommodate the object. Unfortunately, the technique is not widely commercially available. Differences in the fluorescence of layers help clarify the stratigraphy of cross-sections taken from surface coatings. Baumeister (1988), Hering and Buchholz (1990) and Landrey (1987) have used UV microscopy for examining cross-sections of transparent furniture finishes. UV microscopy is generally suited to broad characterizations rather than specific identification of materials. The laser microspectral analysis of paint is discussed by Roy (1979).

The ageing of organic materials depends on their history and on the presence of other materials that may accelerate or delay degra-dation mechanisms. It is therefore difficult to determine the age of organic material based on degradation products. Identification of pigments can help establish the provenance of an object. Gettens and Stout (1966) and Harley (1982) may be consulted for chronologies of historic pigments. Gottsegen (1987) provides dates for the manufacture of many contemporary artists' pigments. The identification of Oriental lacquer is discussed in section 4.4.6.

# Bibliography

Allen, K.W. (1984) Adhesion and adhesives: some fundamentals, in *Adhesives and Consolidants*, Conference Preprints, IIC, pp. 5–12

Arslanoğlu, J. and Learner, T. (2001) The evaluation of Laropal A81: Paraloid B72 polymer blend varnishes for painted and decorative surfaces – appearances and practical considerations, *The Conservator*, 25, 62–71

Ash, M. and Ash, I. (1982) *Encyclopaedia of Plastics, Polymers and Resins*, Vols I–III, Chemical Publishing Co.

Barrow, J (1735) *Dictonarium Polygraphicum or The Whole Body of the Arts*, C. Hitch and C. Davis

Bates, J.W., Allinson, T. and Bal, T.S. (1989) Capillary pyrolysis gas chromatography: a system employing a Curie Point Pyrolyser and a stationary phase of intermediate polarity for the analysis of paint resins and polymers, *Forensic Science International*, 40, 25–43

Baumeister, M. (1988) Die Fluoreszenzmikroskopie als Untersuchungsmethode für historische Möbeloberflächen, *Restauro*, 94, 100–4

Bentley, J. (1998) *Introduction to Paint Chemistry and the Principles of Paint Technology*, 4th edn, Chapman and Hall

Berger, G.A. (1976) Formulating adhesives for the conservation of paintings, in N.S. Brommelle and P. Smith (eds), *Conservation and Restoration of Pictorial Art*, Butterworths, pp. 169–81

Bikales, N.M. (1971) *Adhesion and Bonding*, Wiley Interscience

Blank, S. (1988) Practical answers to plastic problems, in *Modern Organic Materials*, The Scottish Society for Conservation and Restoration, Edinburgh, pp. 115–22

Blomquist, R., Christiansen, A.W., Gillespie, R.H. and Myers, G.E. (eds) (1983) *Adhesive Bonding of Wood and Other Structural Materials*, Pennsylvania State University

Brachert, T. (1978) Historical transparent varnishes and furniture polishes: Part I, in *Maltechnik Restauro*, pp. 56–65

Brannt, W.T. (1900) *India Rubber, Gutta–Percha and Balata*, Henry Carey Baird

Braun, D. (1986) *Simple Methods for Identification of Plastics*, 2nd edn, Hanser Publishers

Brommelle, N.S and Smith, P. (eds) (1988) *Urushi*, Proceedings of the Urushi Study Group, 10–27 June 1985, Tokyo, The Getty Conservation Institute

Brommelle, N.S., Pye, E., Smith, P. and Thomsen, G. (eds) (1984) *Adhesives and Consolidants*, Conference Preprints, IIC

Brydson, J. (1991) *Plastics*, HMSO

Buck, R.D. (1961) Use of moisture barriers in panel paintings, *Studies in Conservation*, 6, 9–20

Burmester, A. (1983) Far Eastern lacquer: classification by pyrolysis mass spectrometry, *Archaeometry*, 25, 1, 45–58

Buttrey, D.N. (ed) (1976) *Plastics in Furniture*, Applied Science Publisher, London

Byington, I. (1795) *Issac Byington Manuscript, Diaries and Recipes*, Joseph Downs Collection of Manuscripts and Printed Ephemera, Library, Winterthur Museum

Cagle, C.V. (1973) *Handbook of Adhesive Bonding*, McGraw-Hill

Campbell, D. and White, J.R. (1989) *Polymer Characterization Physical Techniques*, Chapman and Hall

Cennini, C. (1960) *The Craftsman's Handbook* (trans. D.V. Thompson, 14th century *Il Libro dell'Arte*), Dover

Cession, C. (1990) The surface layers of Baroque gildings: examination, conservation, restoration, in J.S. Mills and P. Smith (eds), *Cleaning, Retouching and Coatings*, Conference Preprints, IIC, pp. 33–5

Copestake, S. (1992) The ageing and stabilisation of shellac varnish resin, Third Year Undergraduate Research Project Report, Department of Chemistry, Imperial College of Science, Technology and Medicine, London

Cummins, J. (1986) Visit to a glue factory, *Fine Woodworking*, March/April, 57, 66–9

de la Rie, R. (1982) Fluorescence of paint and varnish layers, *Studies in Conservation*, Part I: 27, 1–7; Part II: 27, 65–9; Part III: 27, 102–8

de la Rie, R. (1993) Polymer additives for synthetic low molecular weight varnishes, in ICOM Committee for Conservation, Preprints 10th Triennial Meeting, Washington, DC, II, pp. 566–75

de la Rie, R. and McGlinchey, C.W. (1990) New synthetic resins for picture varnishes, in J.S. Mills and P. Smith (eds), *Cleaning, Retouching and Coatings*, Conference Preprints, IIC

Derrick, M. (1989) Fourier Transform Infra Red spectral analysis of natural resins used in furniture finishes, *Journal of the American Institute for Conservation*, 28(1), 43–56

Derrick, M., Druzik, C. and Preusser, F. (1988) FTIR analysis of authentic and simulated black laquer finishes on eighteenth century furniture, in N.S. Brommelle and P. Smith (eds), *Urushi*, Proceedings of the Urushi Study Group, 10–27 June 1985, Tokyo, The Getty Conservation Institute

Derrick, M., Stulik, D.C., Landry, J.M. and Bouffard, S.P. (1992) Furniture finish layer identification by infrared linear mapping microspectrometry, *Journal of the American Institute for Conservation*, 31, 225–36

de Witte, E. (1975) The influence of light on the gloss of matt varnishes, in ICOM Committee for Conservation, Preprints 4th Triennial Meeting, Venice, 13–18 October 1975

de Witte, E. and Terfve, A. (1982) The use of a PY–GC–MS technique for the analysis of synthetic resins, in *Science and Technology in the Service of Conservation*, IIC Congress, Washington, DC, pp. 16–18

Dossie, R. (1764) *The Handmaid to the Arts*, J. Nourse

Du, Y. (1988) The production and use of Chinese raw urushi and the current state of research, in N.S. Brommelle and P. Smith (eds), *Urushi*, Proceedings of the Urushi Study Group, 10–27 June 1985, Tokyo, The Getty Conservation Institute, pp. 189–97

Edwards, R. (1987) *The Shorter Dictionary of English Furniture*, Spring Books

Evelyn, J., *Silva*, 2nd edn, London 1670, 5th edn 1729, facsimile 5th edn 1979, Stobart & Son, London

Feist, W.C., Little, J.K. and Wennesheimer, J.M. (1985) *Moisture-excluding Effectiveness of Finishes on Wood Surfaces*, US Forest Products Laboratory, Part 1 Research Tape FPL 462; Part 2 support data publication available through the National Technical Information Service, PB86–147717

Feller, R.L. and Curran, M. (1975) Changes in solubility and removability of varnish with age, *AIC Bulletin*, 15, 17–26

Feller, R.L., Stolow, N. and Jones, E. (1985) *On Picture Varnishes and Their Solvents*, National Gallery of Art, Washington, DC

Flexner, R. (1994) *Understanding Wood*, Rodale Press

Friel, J.M. (1995) Acrylic polymers as coatings binders, in J.V. Kolesky (ed.), *Paint and Coating Testing Manual*, ASTM

Fry, J.S. (1995) Phenolics, in J.V. Kolesky (ed.), *Paint and Coating Testing Manual*, ASTM

Gächter, R. and Müller, H. (1985) *Plastics Additives*, Hanser Publishers

Gardner, W.H. (1938) *Shellac and Some of Its Uses in Protective Coatings*, Polytechnic Institute of Brooklyn, Shellac Research Bureau Technical Paper No. 24, Reprinted from Official Digest No. 180, pp. 473–8 November 1938; Drugs, Oils and Paints, No. 12, pp. 438–41, December 1938

Garner, H. (1979) *Chinese Lacquer*, Faber

Gettens, R.J. and Bogelow, E. (1933) The moisture permeability of protective coatings, *Technical Studies II*, pp. 15–25

Gettens, R.J. and Stout, G.L. (1966) *Painting Materials: A Short Encyclopedia*, Dover

Glastrup, J. (1989) An easy identification method of waxes and resins, *Archaeometry: Proceedings of the 25th International Symposium* (ed. Y. Maniatis), Elsevier, pp. 245–52

Godla, J. (1991) The use of wax finishes on pre–industrial American furniture, in AIC Wooden Artifacts Group, Conference Papers, Albuquerque

Gordon, J.E. (1976) *The New Science of Strong Materials*, 2nd edn, Pelican

Gottsegen, M.D. (1987) *A Manual of Painting Materials and Techniques*, Harper and Row

Grant, R.A. (ed.) (1980) *Applied Protein Chemistry: Properties and Uses of Gelatin*, Applied Science Publishers

Grattan, D. (1980) Consolidants for degraded and damaged wood, in *Proceedings of the Furniture and Wooden Objects Symposium*, July 2–3 1980, Canadian Conservation Institute, pp. 27–42

Halee, P.J. (1986) *French Polishing*, The Amsterdam Academy for Restoration, SAAR, pp. 3–4

Hall, C. (1981) *Polymer Materials – an Introduction for Technologists and Scientists*, Macmillan

Halpine, S. (1992) Amino acid analysis of proteinaceous media from Cosimo Tura's 'The annunciation with St. Francis and St. Louis of Tuolouse', *Studies in Conservation*, 37, 22–38

Harley, R.D. (1982) *Artists' Pigments c. 1600–1835*, 2nd edn, Butterworths

Haupt, M., Dyer, D. and Hanlan, J. (1989) An examination

of animal glues, in *Papers presented by trainees at the Fifteenth Annual Art Conservation Training Programs Conference*, Conservation Analytical Laboratory of the Smithsonian Institution

Haupt, M., Dyer, D. and Hanlan, J. (1990) An investigation into three animal glues, *The Conservator*, 14, 10–16

Hawkins, D. (1986) *The Techniques of Wood Surface Decoration: Intarsia to Boullework*, Batsford

Hayward, C.H. (1974) *Staining and Polishing*, Drake

Heaton, N. (1928) *Outlines of Paint Technology*, Charles Griffin & Co

Herberts, K. (1963) *Oriental Lacquer: Art and Technique*, Abrams

Hering, B. and Buchholz, R. (1990) Zur Identifiizierung von Holzüberzügen aus organischen Naturstoffen in *Arbeitsblätter für Restauratoren*, 25, 86–91

Hicks, E. (1962) *Shellac, Its Origins and Applications*, MacDonald and Co. (originally published Chemical Publishing Co.)

Hofenk de Graaf, J. (1981) Hydroxypropyl cellulose, a multipurpose conservation material, in ICOM Committee for Conservation, Preprints 6th Triennial Meeting, Ottawa

Hollander, H.B. (1972) *Plastics for Artists and Craftsmen*, Watson Guptill

Horie, C.V. (1987) *Materials for Conservation*, Butterworth Heinemann

Hours, M. (1976) *Conservation and Scientific Analysis of Painting*, Van Nostrand Reinhold

Hulbert, A. (1987) Notes on techniques of English medieval polychromy on church furnishings, in *Recent Advances in the Conservation and Analysis of Artifacts*, Summer Schools Press

Hunt, B.J. and James, M.I. (eds) (1992) *Polymer Characterization*, Blackie Academic

Jaeschke, H. (1994) Examination of lacquer for conservation, in *Lacquerwork and Japanning*, postprints of the Conference held by UKIC at the Courtauld Institute of Art in London, May 1994, pp. 6–10

Jahss, M. and Jahss, B. (1972) *Inro and Other Miniature Forms of Japanese Lacquer Art*, Kegan Paul

Johnson, M. and Packard, E. (1971) Methods used for the identification of binding media in Italian paintings of the fifteenth and sixteenth centuries, *Studies in Conservation*, 16, 145–64

Johnstone, A.H. and Webb, G. (1977) *Energy, Chaos and Chemical Change*, Heinemann

Katz, S. (1984) *Classic Plastics*, Thames and Hudson

Kaufman, M. (1968) *Giant Molecules*, Aldus

King, J. (1992) *Spectroscopy of Polymers*, American Chemical Society

Kinloch, A.J. (1987) *Adhesion and Adhesives*, Chapman Hall

Kirk-Othmer (1985) *Encyclopedia of Chemical Technology*, Wiley

Kockaert, L., Gausset, P. and Dubi–Rucquoy, M. (1989) Detection of ovalbumin in paint media by immunofluorescence, *Studies in Conservation*, 34, 183–8

Kolesky, J.V. (ed.) (1995) *Paint and Testing Manual*, 14th edn of the Gardner–Sward Handbook, American Society for Testing and Materials, Ann Arbor, MI

Kovaly, K.A. (1970) *Handbook of Plastic Furniture Manufacturing*, Technomic Publishing

Krupa, A. (1991) Möglichkeiten und Grenzen der Erkennung klarer Überzüge auf Möbeln und anderen Holzobjekten mit Hilfe einfacher Methoden, *Restauro*

Kumanotani, J. (1983) Japanese lacquer – a super durable coating, in C.E. Carraher and L.H. Sperling (eds), *Polymer Application of Renewable–Resource Materials*, Plenum

Kumanotani, J. (1988) The chemistry of Oriental lacquer (*Rhus verniciflua*), in N.S. Brommelle and P. Smith. (eds), *Urushi*, Proceedings of the Urushi Study Group, 10–27 June 1985, Tokyo, The Getty Conservation Institute, pp. 243–51

Kuwayama, G. (1988) Chinese *Guri* lacquers, in N.S. Brommelle and P. Smith (eds), *Urushi*, Proceedings of the Urushi Study Group, 10–27 June 1985, Tokyo, The Getty Conservation Institute, pp. 13–22

Landrey, G. (1987) Transparent finishes on furniture and fluorescent microscopy, in AIC Wooden Artifacts Group, Conference Papers, Vancouver

Larsen, E.B. (1993) *Moulding and Casting of Museum Objects*, The School of Conservation, The Royal Danish Art Academy

Larsen, L.J., Kim Shin, K.S. and Zink J.I. (1991) Laser spectroscopy of materials used in paintings, *Materials Research Society*, 185, 133–8

Larson, J. (1979) The conservation of alabaster monuments in churches, *The Conservator*, 3, 28–33

Lebeaux, R.A. (1989) *The Resinkit: A Complete Guide for Identifying and Testing Plastic Resins*, The Resinkit Company

Lee, L.-H. (1991) *Fundamentals of Adhesion*, Plenum

LeSota, Stanley (ed.) (1978) *Paint and Coatings Dictionary*, Federation of Societies for Coatings Technology

Low, M.J.D. and Varlashkin, P.G. (1986) Application of Infrared Fourier Transform spectroscopy to problems in conservation II: photothermal beam deflection spectroscopy, *Studies in Conservation*, 31, 77–82

Martens, C.E. (1968) *Technology of Paints, Varnishes and Lacquers*, Robert E. Krieger Publishing

Martin, E. (1977) Some improvements in the techniques of analysis of paint media, *Studies in Conservation*, 22, 63–7

Martin, G. (1988) The identification of modern polymer systems using FTIR, in Preprints of Modern Organic Materials Meeting, Edinburgh 14–15 April 1988, pp. 47–50

Massey, R. (1967) *Formulas for Painters*, Watson Guptill

Mayer, R. (1981) *The Artist's Handbook of Materials and Techniques*, 4th edn (ed. E. Smith), Faber

McCann, M. (1979) *Artist Beware*, Watson–Guptill Publications

Mills, J. (1966) The gas chromatographic examination of paint media Part 1. Fatty acid composition and identification of dried oil films, *Studies in Conservation*, 11, 92–108

Mills, J. and White, R. (1977) Natural resins of art and archaeology: their sources, chemistry and identification, *Studies in Conservation*, 22, 12–31

Mills, J. and White, R. (1982) Organic mass spectrometry of art materials: work in progress, *National Gallery Technical Bulletin* 6, 3–18

Mills J.S. and White, R. (1987) *The Organic Chemistry of Museum Objects*, Butterworths

Moncrieff, A. and Weaver, G. (1992) *Science for Conservators*, Crafts Council Conservation Teaching Series, Routledge

Morgan, J. (1991) *The Conservation of Plastics, an Introduction to their History, Manufacture, Deterioration,*

*Identification and Care*, Plastics Historical Society and The Conservation Unit of the Museums and Galleries Commission

Mossman, S. (1988) Simple methods of identifying plastics, in *Modern Organic Materials*, The Scottish Society for Conservation and Restoration, Edinburgh, pp. 41–6

Mussey, R. (1980) Transparent furniture finishes in New England – 1700–1820: a documentary study, in *Proceedings of the Furniture and Wooden Objects Symposium*, Canadian Conservation Institute, Ottawa, Ontario, Canada, 2–3 July, pp. 77–101

Mussey, R. (1982a) Old finishes – what put the shine on furniture's Golden Age, *Fine Woodworking*, 33, March/April, 71–75

Mussey, R. (1982b) Early varnishes: the 18th century's search for the perfect film finish, *Fine Woodworking*, 35, July/August, 54–8

Mussey, R.D. Jr (1982c) Old finishes, French polishing with wax, *Fine Woodworking*, July–August, 35

Mussey, R.D. Jr (ed.) (1987) *The First American Finisher's Manual*, Dover Publications (originally published as *The Cabinet-Maker's Guide* in 1825)

Mustoe, George (1983) Which glue do you use?, *Fine Woodworking*, 43, 62–5

Mustoe, G. (1984) Glues for woodworking, *Fine Woodworking*, 44, 48–50

Newell, A.C. (1940) *Colouring, Finishing and Painting Wood*, Chas. A. Bennett Co.

Nicholson, C. (1991) Some notes on shellac, *BAFRA Newsletter*, 44 (March), 15–17

Pacheco (1649) *Arte de la Pintura*, first published in 1649 by S. Faxardo, Seville (republished in Spanish 1990 by Catedra, Madrid and in a translation by Zahira Veliz in *Artists Techniques in Golden Age Spain: six treatises* edited and translated by Z. Veliz, Cambridge University Press, 1987)

Packham, D.E. (ed). (1992) *Adhesion and Adhesives*, Longman

Parry, E.J. (1935) *Shellac: Its Production, Manufacture, Chemistry, Analysis, Commerce and Uses*, Pitman

Penn, T.Z. (1984) Decorative and Protective Finishes, 1750–1850: Materials, Processes, Craft in *APT Bulletin* [Association for Preservation Technology] Vol. XVI, No. 1, 1984, pp. 3–45; also (1966) Decorative and Protective Finishes, 1750–1850: Materials, Process and Craft, Masters Thesis, University of Delaware

Perry, W. (1804) *The Royal English Standard Dictionary*, Brookfield, Massachusetts

Pillement, J.N. (1959) *The Ladies Amusement or the Whole of Japanning Made Easy*, A facsimile of the edition of 1762, Ceramic Book Co.

Plenderleith, H.J. and Werner, A.E.A. (1971) *The Conservation of Antiquities and Works of Art*, 2nd edn, Oxford University Press

Plesters, J. (1956) Cross-sections and chemical analysis of paint samples, *Studies in Conservation*, 3, 110–55

Quin, J.J. (1882) *Report of Her Majesty's Acting Consul at Hakodate on the Lacquer Industry of Japan*, Harrison and Sons

Rice, P.C. (1980) *Amber, The Golden Gem of the Ages*, Van Nostrand Reinhold

Roff, W.J. and Scott, J.R. (1971) *Fibres, Films, Plastics and Rubbers*, Butterworths

Rosenquist, A.M. (1959) The stabilisation of wood found in the Viking ship of Oseberg – part II, *Studies in Conservation*, 4, 62–72

Routledge, V. (2000) The development of MS2A reduced ketone resin in painting conservation, *WAAC Newsletter*, 22, 2

Roy, A. (1979) The laser microspectral analysis of paint, *National Gallery Technical Bulletin*, 3, 43–50

Salmon, W. (1701) *Polygraphice*, London

Serck-Dewaide, M. (1991) The history and conservation of the surface coating on European gilded wood objects, in D. Bigelow (ed.), *Gilded Wood: Conservation and History*, Sound View Press, pp. 65–78

Seymour, R.B. and Mark, H.F. (eds) (1990) *Organic Coatings: Their Origin and Development*, Elsevier

Sheraton, T. (1970) *Thomas Sheraton's Cabinet Dictionary*, Facsimile edition, Praeger

Shields, J. (1974) *Adhesive Bonding*, Oxford University Press

Shields, J. (1976) *Adhesives Handbook*, Newnes-Butterworths

Skeist, I. (ed.) (1977) *Handbook of Adhesives*, Van Nostrand Reinhold

Sonoda, N. and Rioux, J.P. (1990) Identification des matériaux synthétiques dans les peintures modernes. I: Vernis et liants polymères, *Studies in Conservation*, 35, 189–204

Souza, L.A.C. and Derrick, M.R. (1995) The use of FTIR spectrometry for the identification and characterization of gesso–glue grounds in wooden polychromed sculptures and panel paintings, in *Materials Issues in Art and Archaeology IV*, symposium held May 16–21 1994, Cancum, Mexico, pp. 573–8

Stalker and Parker (1688) *A Treatise of Japanning and Varnishing*, London (republished A. Tiranti, London, 1971)

Stodulski, L.P. and Dorge, V.J. (1991) Analysis of materials from a late 15th–early 16th century polychromed wood sculpture, *Materials Research Society*, 185, pp. 151–75

Stout, G.L. (1975) *The Care of Pictures*, Dover

Thompson, D.V. (1956) *The Materials and Techniques of Medieval Painting*, Dover

Thompson, D.V. (1960) *The Craftsman's Handbook* (translation of *Il Libro dell'Arte* by Cenino Cennini), Dover

Thomsen, F.G. (1981) Repair of a Tlingit basket using moulded cotton fibres, ICOM Committee for Conservation, Preprints 6th Triennial Meeting, Ottawa

Thornton, J. (1985) Compo: the history and technology of plastic compositions, Preprints of papers presented at the AIC 13th annual meeting, Washington, DC

Thorpe, J.F. and Whiteley, M.A. (1937) *Thorpe's Dictionary of Applied Chemistry*, 4th edn, 12 vols, Longmans

Tomek, J. and Pechova, D. (1992) A note on the thin layer chromatography of media in paintings, *Studies in Conservation*, 37, 39–41

Torraca, G. (1988) *Solubility and Solvents for Conservation Problems*, ICCROM, 3rd edn

Tsang, Jia-Sun and Erhardt, D. (1990) The extractable components of oil paint films, in AIC Paintings Speciality Group, Vol. 3: Postprints of the 18th annual meeting of the AIC in Richmond, Virginia

Urbanski, J., Czerwinski, W., Janicka, K., Majewska, F. and Zowall, H. (1977) *Handbook of Analysis of Synthetic Polymers and Plastics*, Ellis Horwood

Von Endt, D.W. and Baker, M.T. (1991) The chemistry of filled animal glue systems, in D. Bigelow (ed.), *Gilded Wood Conservation and History*, Sound View Press

von Ragué, B. (1967) *Gesichte der Japanischen Lackkunst,* Berlin

Waentig, F. (1993) Gießharzsysteme zum Einbetten von Proben, *Restauro*, 99 (3), 195–9

Walch, K. and Koller, J. (1997) *Baroque and Rococo Lacquer*, Bayerische Landesamt für Denkmalpflege

Wall, W.E. (1946) *Graining Ancient and Modern*, Drake & Co.

Ward, A.G. (1977) *The Science and Technology of Gelatin*, Academic Press

Watin, J.F. (1728) *L'Art du Peintre, Doreur, Vernisseur*, revised and augmented edition published by L. Laget, Paris, 1977

Wehlte, K. (1975) *Materials and Techniques of Painting*, Van Nostrand

Wells, E.R. (1974) Urethane coatings, in *Technology of Paints, Varnishes and Lacquers* (ed. C.R. Martens), Robert E. Krieger Publishing Company, pp. 205–6

Werwein, E. (1982) Die Restaurierung eines Bernsteinkabinetts aus dem späten 17. Jahrhundert, *Arbeitsblätter für Restauratoren*, 15, 8–17

Westmoreland, R. (1988) Solvent testing method for identification of Oriental lacquer used in European furniture, in N.S. Brommelle and P. Smith. (eds), *Urushi*, Proceedings of the Urushi Study Group, 10–27 June 1985, Tokyo, The Getty Conservation Institute

White, R. (1978) The application of gas-chromatography to the identification of waxes, in *Studies in Conservation*, 23, 57–68

White, R. (1981) A review, with illustrations, of methods applicable to the analysis of resin/oil varnish mixtures, in ICOM Committee for Conservation, Preprints 6th Triennial Meeting, Ottawa, pp. 1–9

White, R. (1984) The characterization of proteinaceous binders in art objects, *National Gallery Technical Bulletin*, 8, 5–14

Williams, D. (1988) Shellac finishing: a traditional finish still yields outstanding results, *Fine Woodworking*, 71 (July/August), 56–9

Wolbers, R. and Landrey, G. (1987) The use of reactive fluorescent dyes for the characterization of binding media in cross-sectional examinations, AIC Wooden Artifacts Group, Conference Papers, Vancouver

Young, R.J. (1991) *Introduction to Polymers*, 2nd edn, Chapman and Hall

# 5

# Other materials and structures

## 5.1 Ivory, ivory-like teeth, bone and antler

Ivory, bone, antler and related materials have been used in furniture in a variety of ways, as structural elements comprising the bulk of the object, as decorative elements such as knobs and inlays, and as veneers. Ivory veneers for furniture were generally sawn longitudinally, but documentary sources indicate that some veneers were continuously cut from the circumference of a prepared ivory cylinder much as modern plywood veneers are cut from a log. The Parisian piano-maker Papé

had a method patented early in the nineteenth century to produce ivory veneer by a spiral paring of the tooth that was capable of producing leaves up to 43 cm by 95 cm in size (Holzapffel and Holzapffel, 1843). Pieces of furniture made entirely of elephant ivory have been occasionally produced throughout history. Furniture made from assemblages of unworked antlers were popular in European and American hunting lodges and Scottish country houses (*Figure 5.1*). An excellent introduction to the structure and properties of these materials is provided by Starling and Watkinson (1987).

### Ivory

Strictly speaking, true ivory is material from the tusks (incisor teeth) of elephants and mammoths of the Proboscidean order. Walruses, hippopotamuses, various pig species and narwhals (rare arctic whales) also produce tusks large enough to have been exploited economically and have been used as sources for ivory in furniture (*Figure 5.2*). The large teeth of sperm whales (*Physter catodon*) and killer whales (*Orcinus orca*) have been carved and decorated in their original form as teeth but are not used as a source for ivory and are unlikely to be found in furniture. Elephant ivory has always been the most sought after and commonly used of these materials in artefacts and furniture but walrus and mammoth ivory have also been historically important.

Mammoth and elephant tusks are much larger than those from other sources and are relatively soft and even in coloration and texture, with an attractive 'figure' or grain. The surviving species are the African elephant

**Figure 5.1**  Chair made from unworked antler

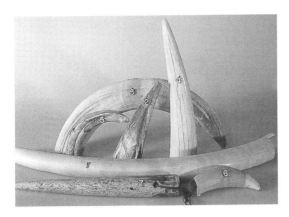

**Figure 5.2** Sources of ivory that have been exploited commercially: elephant (1), mammoth (2), hippopotamus (3), walrus (4), wart hog (5), sperm whale tooth (6). Item 7 is a sailors fid (a tapering pin used to open the strands of a rope before splicing) made from the jaw bone of a sperm whale

(*Loxodonta africana*) and the Asian or Indian elephant (*Elephas maximus*). The tusks of the African elephant grow to a larger size than those of the Indian elephant, are carried by both sexes and are generally of a whiter colour. The female Indian elephant may carry very small tusks but these do not often protrude from behind the lips. The tusks of a mature African bull elephant may reach a weight of 70–90 kg and a length of 2–2.5 m. For Indian male elephants a tusk may reach only 1.5 m in length and weigh 25–40 kg (Kühn, 1986). Mammoth tusks can be up to 5 m long and weigh up to 150 kg each. Elephants are currently restricted to small portions of their original ranges, which included virtually all of Africa, the Middle East and Asia. Trade in elephant ivory is ancient and was surprisingly widespread with elephant ivory showing up as far north as Britain and Germany during the Roman period. During the past few centuries the trade in ivory has focused on the African elephant, with huge quantities being exported during the nineteenth and twentieth centuries (Tomlinson, 1862). In recent years the trade in ivory has been restricted and the transfer of objects containing ivory across international boundaries is currently monitored and controlled.

Walruses range around the world in the Arctic latitudes and produce large tusks of even colour and texture. Walrus ivory has been traded almost as far southward as elephant ivory was traded northward and was always a source for ivory workers in the northern latitudes. Ivory from the mammoth species *Mammuthus primigenus* was a northern ivory source found in well-preserved permafrost deposits in Siberia and used extensively in the nineteenth century when the trade in ivory reached large proportions. During a visit to the London dock warehouses in 1899 Tomes noted 130 tons of elephant ivory and about ten tons of mammoth tusks. The price of mammoth ivory then was only a quarter of the price of elephant ivory (Tomes, 1923). It is thought that the tusks of at least 45 000 mammoths have been sold in the last 300 years (Krzyskowska, 1990). It has further been estimated that in recent years only one-quarter of commercial ivory has been obtained from freshly killed elephants and that the remainder derives from extinct proboscidea (Edwards *et al.*, 1998).

Tusks (elephant and mammoth) are modified elongated incisor teeth, found only in the upper jaw, the premaxilla. In other animals tusks may possibly be found elsewhere but they are still teeth. They all share a common composition and structure of inorganic salts deposited within a protein matrix composed predominantly of collagen. All vertebrate mineralized tissues have a form of calcium phosphate as the main inorganic constituent. The inorganic component of human dentine is mainly hydroxyapatite $Ca_{10}(PO_4)_6OH_2$. Ivory has long been thought to be built up from hydroxyapatite as well. However, it has been shown that a more correct composition of the inorganic component of proboscidean ivory is given by dahllite. Dahllite is also a calcium phosphate mineral but with the formula $Ca_{10}(PO_4)_6 (CO_3)H_2O$ (Matienzo and Snow, 1986). Different sources suggest varying organic/inorganic ratios in dentine. The organic part is normally said to be around 35–40% (Webster, 1958). However, a recent examination has shown the protein content of African ivory to be on average 30% greater than that of Indian ivory (Edwards *et al.*, 1998).

Teeth are composed of three structurally distinct materials – enamel, dentin and cementum (*Figure 5.3*). When present, enamel forms a thin but very hard outer covering. Dentin is

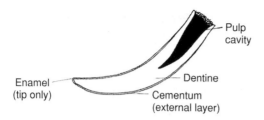

Enamel
(tip only)

Pulp
cavity

Dentine

Cementum
(external layer)

**Figure 5.3** Diagrammatic representation of elephant tusk morphology

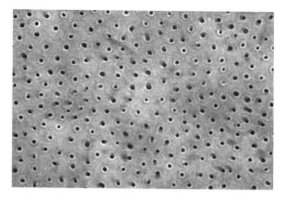

**Figure 5.4** Cross-section of a human molar (×250), visible light, showing dentinal tubules. The shape and distribution of tubules provides key information for identification

the main structural material. Cementum is present at the base or 'insertion' and serves to anchor the tooth or tusk into the jaw-bone. While dentin and enamel are formed by living cells, these cells migrate to the interior or exterior of the tooth as the dentin or enamel is laid down without becoming embedded in the material. Dentin or 'ivory' contains no cell nuclei and is therefore an acellular material in contrast to cementum, which incorporates cell nuclei. Elephant and mammoth tusks are not covered in enamel, except for a little enamel that may be present on the tip of the tusks of young animals. The other teeth of these species are covered in enamel but not the tusks. The tusks are mainly used in feeding, for purposes like prising off the bark from trees and digging for roots, and the enamel is soon worn off. Ivory is composed almost entirely of dentine, which provides the bulk and general form of all teeth. However, the complete length is covered by a thin layer of cementum. The cementum is 3–4 mm thick on elephant tusks and up to 8 mm on mammoth tusks. This soft calcified tissue is normally removed before ivory is worked.

Dentine is formed by complex processes in the so-called odontoblast and subodontoblast cells. These are specialized columnar cells the bodies of which are arranged in a layer on the pulpal surface of the dentine. As teeth and tusks grow, new material is added in the interior pulp cavity much as the length of a stack of conical paper drinking cups is increased by inserting others into the bottom of the stack. As these new layers are formed, the living cells responsible for formation migrate inwards leaving an unmineralized protein fibre behind them. These fibres dry out and collapse after the tooth or tusk is removed from the animal leaving a tiny tube called a

dentinal tubule (*Figure 5.4*). In elephant ivory these have a diameter of one micron (Soggnaes, 1960). The shape and distribution of tubules constitutes the primary and indeed only sure way of determining the species source of worked ivory. Although tubules are very small, when compared to the size of water and other solvent molecules they are vast caverns through which liquids and gases can readily and speedily move. They also retain a desiccated protein filament which is a potential food source for bacteria and fungi. Further information on the formation of dentine is given by Halstead (1974) and MacGregor (1985).

The appearance and properties of ivory are influenced by the age, species and living conditions of the animal from which it is obtained. Ivory is both hygroscopic and anisotropic with some differences in behaviour between the different parts of the tusk. The largest movement in ivory is along the tubular structure, that is radially to the axis of the tusk. The relative magnitude of maximum shrinkage and swelling in ivory is found to be radial (4.2%) > tangential (1.5%) > longitudinal (0.5%) (Jehle, 1995; Lafontaine and Wood, 1982). Ivory is denser and harder than bone but can be made flexible by treatment with phosphoric acid and rehardened by washing and drying, but not without injury to its quality. Ivory can be carved, sawn, turned, engraved, polished and painted. It takes dyes well and can be bleached by the action of sunlight and moisture or by hydrogen peroxide.

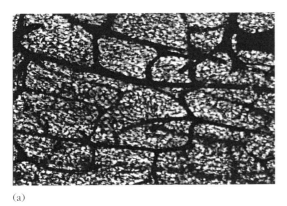

(a)

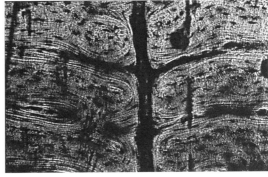

(b)

**Figure 5.5**
(*a*) Cross-section of an antler (unknown species, ×50, visible light). The cell nuclei and vascular canals are present but have a random structure
(*b*) Cross-section of a cow bone tibia (×62.5, normal light) which has regular Haversian systems of vascular canals

### Bone and antler

Bone has been used to fill the same functions as ivory in furniture and the two material types are often confused. Bone suitable for working comes mostly from the long bones of mammals. The outer portions of these bones are dense, white, relatively non-porous and readily available around the world from both wild and domesticated animals. Antlers are the paired structures found on the heads of male members of the deer family (Cervidae), such as deer, elk and moose, that are formed and shed annually. They evolved from bone and are therefore very similar to it in composition and structure.

Bone, unlike ivory, is a living cellular tissue. It is composed of essentially the same proteins and minerals as are teeth but, unlike teeth, the cell nuclei are embedded in bone as it grows and continue to live throughout the life of the animal, communicating with each other by means of tiny canals called canaliculi. Larger ducts and channels which conduct blood and fluids are also present in bone and can be seen as tiny pits and lines with the naked eye.

Like bone, antler shows embedded cell nuclei and extensive canal networks which carried blood vessels during antler formation. Antlers are formed rapidly from randomly oriented tissue called woven bone as distinct from the more regular lamellar or layered bone found in mammalian long bones (*Figure 5.5*). Antler is most compact in the outer portions and at the base where it attaches to the skull. The interior tends to be spongy or cancellous and is therefore not generally used as a decorative material.

Both bone and antler are hygroscopic and anisotropic, especially in mechanical properties. Antler is tougher and more elastic than bone and because of its high collagen content it is possible to alter the shape of compact antler by bending it after treating with steam or hot water.

### Ivory substitutes

Vegetable ivory from the hard nuts of the South American palm *Phytelephas macrocarpa* has been used for small carvings and turnings since the nineteenth century, and has found renewed favour as a replacement for elephant ivory among modern craftspeople (*Figure 5.6*). Ivory nuts (or corozo nuts) are composed of virtually pure cellulose, have a slightly warmer

**Figure 5.6** Sources of alternative ivory: ivory nut *Phytelephas macrocarpa* (1), white tail deer antler and an unknown species antler tine (2) and cattle horn cup and tips (3). Item 4 is a piece of hawksbill turtle shell *Eretmochelys imbricata*

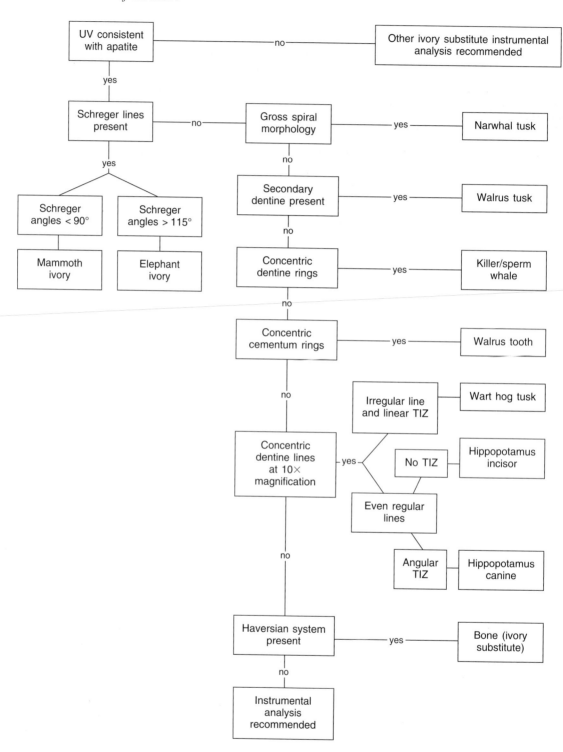

**Figure 5.7**   Scheme for the preliminary characterization of ivory and ivory substitutes in cross-section (TIZ = tusk interstitial zone)

**Table 5.1** Class characteristics of selected commercial ivories

| Source | Modified tooth | Macroscopic characteristic | Microscopic characteristic (10×) | Enamel | UV characteristic |
|---|---|---|---|---|---|
| Elephant (Asian and African) | Upper incisors | Schreger angles > 115° in cross-section | | Tip worn away | |
| Mammoth | Upper incisors | Schreger angles > 90° in cross-section | | | Vivianite may be present |
| Walrus tusk | Upper canines | Secondary dentine in cross-section | | Tip worn away | |
| Walrus teeth | All teeth | Cementum rings in cross-section; hypercementosis | | Tip may be worn | |
| Killer/sperm whale | All teeth | Dentine rings in cross-section | | Tip | |
| Narwhal | Upper incisor | Spiral; hollow centre in cross-section | | Tip worn away | |
| Hippopotamus | Upper canines | Oval cross-section angular TIZ | Fine concentric lines in cross-section | Longituinal band | |
| Hippopotamus | Lower canines | Triangular cross-section; angular TIZ | Fine concentric lines in cross-section | Longituinal band | |
| Hippopotamus | Lower incisors | Peg-shaped; no TIZ (dot) | Fine concentric lines in cross-section | Tip | |
| Wart hog | Upper and lower canines | Squared cross-section; linear TIZ | Fine concentric lines in cross-section | Longituinal band | |

TIZ = tusk interstitial zone
*Source:* Edgard O. Espinoza and Mary-Jacque Mann (1992) *Identification Guide for Ivory and Ivory Substitutes*, 2nd edn, World Wildlife Fund, Washington, DC, with permission

pinkish coloration than ivory, and on close examination show tiny striations if cut and polished. Other palm species such as the African doom palm (*Hyphaene thebaica*) and the South Pacific species *Metroxylon amicarum* also produce ivory-like nuts but are less commonly encountered or marketed than *Phytelephas macrocarpa*.

Synthetic polymers or plastics have been used to imitate ivory since they were first produced. Indeed the impetus behind the development of cellulose nitrate or celluloid, one of the earliest plastics, was the desire to find a replacement for ivory billiard balls. Pigmented and layered celluloid was made to at least superficially copy the grain of elephant ivory. Recent restrictions on the ivory trade have given fresh impetus to the manufacture of imitation ivory.

### Identification of ivory, bone and antler
Pieces of furniture composed of bulk material or unmodified structures present few problems

of identification (Burek, 1989). While microscopy is often necessary to accurately assign a species origin to small, heavily worked or degraded material, much useful identification relies on an understanding of the structures involved and examination with the naked eye. A scheme developed by Espinoza and Mann (1992) for the preliminary characterization of ivory and ivory substitutes in cross-section is shown in *Figure 5.7*. *Table 5.1* shows class characteristics of selected commercial ivories. Krzyskowska (1990) has proposed a diagnostic flow chart, based on the physical characteristics of the material, to distinguish between elephant, mammoth and hippopotamus ivory, boar tusk, bone and antler. Penniman's (1952) classic identification guide for osseous materials and vegetable ivory, with photographs of transverse and longitudinal sections at low magnification, remains valuable. A comparative study by S. O'Connor (1987) of new and archaeological samples of osseous and keratinaceous materials includes

**Figure 5.8** (*right*) Transverse view of an elephant tusk with Schreger lines (angles marked). The outer cementum is also present. (*left*) Transverse view of a walrus tusk with outer primary dentin and inner secondary dentin, sometimes called 'tapioca'

photographs of macroscopic and microscopic structures. Distinctive patterns of decay, such as the cone in cone splitting of elephant ivory, may also assist in the identification of these materials (S. O'Connor, 1987, T.P. O'Connor, 1987).

Ivory from any source is free of visible pits or channels, while antler and bone are pitted overall with the small lacunae (voids) left by the collapse of the cell nuclei. Blood vessel channels are also apparent in antler and bone. Both the lacunae and the channels often pick up dirt and become more accentuated (as seen in the sperm whale jaw bone in *Figure 5.2*).

Bone and antler are more heavily mineralized than ivory and are therefore usually more opaque and whiter in colour.

Uniquely in Proboscidean (elephant or mammoth) ivory the arrangement and form of the tiny tubules radiating outward through the dentine from the central pulp cavity gives rise to a characteristic pattern, believed to be an optical phenomenon. On cross-sectional surfaces this pattern has been described as 'engine turnings'. Small lozenge or diamond shapes are formed by the intersection of arcs which radiate out from the centre (*Figure 5.8*). These arcs, called Schreger lines, form angles at their intersections which can be used to differentiate ivory from extant and extinct species (Espinoza and Mann, 1992). The angles are obtuse in elephant ivory (> 115°) and acute in mammoth ivory (< 90°). This feature can be seen by eye, under low magnification or with crossed polarized light (Thornton, 1981).

Schreger lines are caused by the regular sine-wave form of the tubules in the radial direction (*Figure 5.9*). They are seen only on the cross-section or 'end grain' of proboscidean ivory. Longitudinal surfaces show either a layered or wood-like grain depending on the orientation of the viewing surface. Plastic substitutes can be non-destructively differentiated from the real thing by the absence of any evidence of complex structure of biological origin. Espinoza and Mann (1992) suggests a spot test with sulfuric acid to differentiate ivory from vegetable ivory.

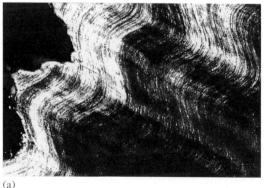

(a)

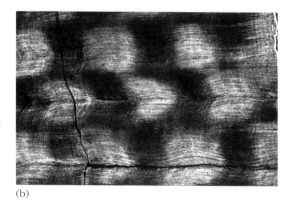

(b)

**Figure 5.9** Schreger lines are caused by the regular sine-wave form of the tubules in the radial direction (*a*) Radial section of mammoth ivory under cross-polarized light (×15.6) showing a regular tubule wave in the radial direction. (*b*) Cross-section of a mammoth tusk (20° off cross-polar light source, ×16) showing the curl of the tubules that give rise to Schreger lines and the typical grain pattern

In walrus ivory an outer primary dentin making up the bulk of the tusk is virtually featureless showing only faint concentric banding. Secondary dentin with a whorled chaotic structure resembling tapioca pudding fills the interior of mature walrus tusks and may be taken as proof of walrus origin (*Figure 5.8*).

In the absence of significant morphological features, bone and antler are difficult to differentiate without microscopy. Microscopic thin sections in transmitted light show the non-directional woven structure of antler, contrasted with the orderly layered structure of mammalian long bone (see *Figure 5.5*). Under crossed polars, antler thin sections are more strongly pleochroic than bone.

The characteristic bluish-white fluorescence of ivories, bone and antler is attributed to their collagen content (Gayathri, 1983). Vegetable ivory, in comparison, has a slight orange fluorescence (Espinoza and Mann, 1992). Mammoth ivory is sometimes stained by vivianite, an iron phosphate, which is generally brown or bluish-green but is not always visible under normal light. It shows a characteristic purplish fluorescence under ultra violet light (Espinoza and Mann, 1992). Vivianite does not occur on elephant ivory.

Ivory and related substances have rarely been examined analytically although there are several studies of these materials from archaeological sources. For further information see Matienzo and Snow (1986), Rao and Subbaiah (1983), Willisch (1990). The use of C14 for dating purposes is discussed in Chapter 9.

## 5.2  Keratinaceous materials – horn and turtleshell

### General information
Although both horns and antlers evolved for the purpose of defence and display, they are structurally and chemically distinct. Horns, carried by cattle, sheep, goats and antelopes, are permanent structures with a living core of bone and vascular tissue. Horns evolved from skin, and like the outer, dead cells of skin, are composed primarily of the protein keratin. Other skin-evolved keratinous materials include hair, hoofs, feathers, nails and claws, the mouth plates of filter feeding whales (mystacoceti), properly called baleen but historically known as whalebone, the solid fibrous horn of the rhinoceros and the shells of turtles and tortoises. Aside from turtleshell, only hair and feathers have any importance as furniture materials, where they are encountered in upholstery. Although furniture made from the horns of long horn cattle enjoyed a limited vogue in the American west, horn and tortoiseshell have been used in furniture mostly as veneers and for decorative elements such as knobs and inlays.

Keratin is a complex mixture of fibrous and globular proteins secreted by skin and held together by hydrogen bonds, polar forces and disulphide linkages in the amino acid cystine. The balance of different components and their alignment in the overall structure gives rise to variations in strength, elasticity and hardness on the basis of which the different keratinaceous materials are classified as hard or soft. Soft keratin structures such as hair and skin are continuously shed and replaced. Hard keratin structures such as horn and tortoiseshell, although dead, continue to grow by addition of layers of new material from the inside surface. The molecular structure and mechanical properties of keratins are reviewed by Fraser and Macrae (1980).

### Tortoiseshell
Although shells of land tortoises have been used in the production of objects, tortoiseshell in furniture is much more likely to have come from various species of marine turtle, notably the hawksbill turtle (*Eretmochelys imbricata*) but also the green turtle (*Chelonia mydas*) and loggerhead turtle (*Thalassochelys caretta*).

The turtle's complete shell consists of the carapace, which covers the back, the plastron which covers the belly, and a number of rigid connecting plates joining the two together. The whole structure is formed of spongy bone plates covered by keratinous scales which may be detached from the underlying bone by heating or boiling. The hawksbill's carapace may grow up to 35 inches in length while that of the loggerhead may grow to 47 inches. Typically, the carapace is made of fifty four plates or scales and the plastron of sixteen. A detailed account of the anatomy, morphology and development of turtleshell is given by Zangerl (1969).

The shells vary greatly between species in colour and pattern of markings and to a lesser extent also within species (Richie, 1970). From the Age of Discovery (the end of the fifteenth century) onwards, marine turtles supplied a beautiful and expensive alternative to horn which was used for many of the same purposes. The hawksbill turtle, with its striking gold and brown mottled back plates up to 3.5 mm thick, was particularly sought after for combs, jewellery and as a furniture veneer. Turtleshell veneer was used extensively as an overall covering for case furniture, boxes and picture frames during the seventeenth century. Marquetry panels of interspersed turtle shell and brass are most closely associated with André Charles Boulle, and the generic term boullework came to describe the later reproductions of this popular technique. Turtleshell veneers were made from the back plates of the turtle by softening them in hot water, pressing them flat, and shaving them to final thickness. Turtle shell veneers were commonly adhered to carcass work with a mixture of glue and a pigment such as vermilion that would show through the translucent shell. Hunting of the Hawksbill turtle for its shell has brought it to the brink of extinction. Farmed turtle shell is available from the Cayman Islands (Cayman Islands Turtle Farm, PO Box 645, Grand Caiman, British West Indies, www.turtle.ky/).

### Horn

Horn, like ivory, is non-living, non-nucleated tissue but unlike antler, ivory or bone, horn is almost entirely composed of protein and has only a small mineral content. Horn varies widely in colour from black through reddish brown to green and white and mixtures of these colours. The natural surface usually appears fibrous parallel to the long axis of the horn. Horn has been readily available from domestic animals and was adaptable to many of the roles now filled by modern plastics.

Horn veneers required more steps in preparation than tortoiseshell (*Figure 5.10*). The conical horn sheath was removed from the bony core, and the solid tips were cut off to be carved or turned. The remaining tapered cylinder was boiled, heated over charcoal to soften it, then split up one side and opened out into a plate. These plates could be worked as they were or further modified by heating and pressing, often with the addition of oil or fat impregnants. This further processing yielded a translucent material (green horn) that could be readily split into thin sheets and scraped and polished to a high shine (Poller, 1980). Horn could be tinted in a manner similar to tortoiseshell, using a pigment mixed into the glue used to lay it, for example the smalt used to tint horn blue when interspersed with pewter in boullework.

### Properties

Horn and turtle shell are softer and more translucent than bone or ivory, though cattle horn can also sometimes be white and opaque. Hydrogen bonding in the protein structure makes both horn and tortoiseshell hygroscopic. As horn grows from the inside, a characteristic cone-within-cone structure develops. The alignment of cells, and the keratin fibres of which these are composed, in the long axis of the cone gives horn anisotropic mechanical properties (Fraser and Macrae, 1980). Small parallel fissures are frequently seen on the surface of horn, particularly as it ages, and horn will also form small splits in plane with the surface as human finger nails are also apt to do. Tortoiseshell is much more homogeneous than horn, much less anisotropic in its properties and therefore much easier to work. It is not fibrous and not so obviously laminated though sinuous lines similar to the appearance of burr-wood grain may be perceptible on the surface of turtle shell.

Both horn and tortoiseshell are thermoplastic. In the softened state they can be shaped by bending or pressing into moulds, or embossed using hot metal dies. On cooling the new shape is retained. Tortoiseshell can be softened in boiling water (which may be salted to achieve a slightly higher temperature) and can be welded to itself by clamping two pieces together under pressure and boiling or steaming. Horn requires higher temperatures from superheated steam or hot metal cauls to achieve the same result. Both materials in powdered form can be fused in heated metal moulds. Both materials can be sawn, carved, and turned or decorated by piercing and engraving and can be given a high shine by polishing with a succession of finer and softer abrasives. Horn veneers were often dyed to

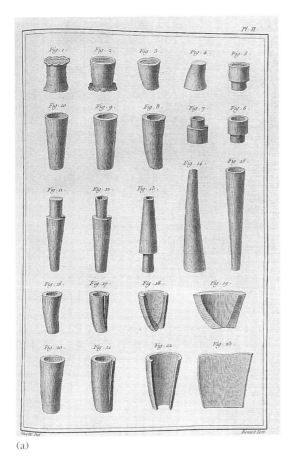

(a)

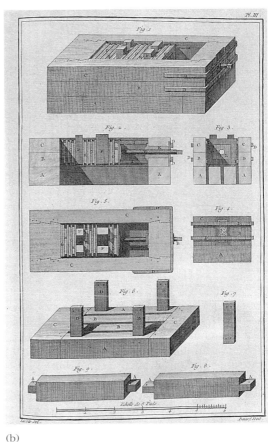

(b)

**Figure 5.10**   Plates from Diderot's *Encyclopédie ou Dictionnaire des Sciences*, 1771 showing (*a*) the process of flattening horn sections to form plates and (*b*) presses used for flattening horn plates

imitate the more costly turtle shell. Green horn was boiled in nitric acid to give the yellow colour of blonde tortoiseshell and after neutralizing and washing was coloured using a variety of materials as described by Wenham (1964), Vuilleumier (1979) and Hardwick (1981). The result is seldom subtle enough to be very convincing, especially when compared to the genuine article.

Further information on the history, tools and techniques of working tortoiseshell and horn can be found in Hardwick (1981), Jaeckel (1978), Richie (1970, 1974), Vuilleumier (1979, 1980) and Wenham (1964).

### Identification

Burek (1989) and O'Connor (1987a) suggest investigation by transmitted light to differenti-

ate between horn and tortoiseshell. Bovine horn exhibits a pattern of pigmentation that follows the longitudinal axis of the fibre, while tortoiseshell shows a mottled pattern (*Figure 5.11*). Marks in tortoiseshell go right through the thickness but change slightly in size, shape and position from one side to the other. They are formed of aggregations of pigment particles that under low power magnification in transmitted light give a granular appearance similar to photographic grain. Blonde tortoiseshell from the plastron can be distinguished from clear horn by lack of the striations or corrugations present in horn.

Marks in horn stained to imitate tortoiseshell are always on the surface, are not granular or grainy, and often show evidence of brush marks. Resin imitations of tortoiseshell may

 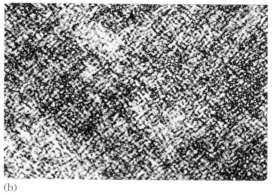

(a)  (b)

**Figure 5.11**  Differentiation of horn and turtleshell. (*a*) Cow horn in tangential section (under cross-polars, ×15.6) showing the layered structure of cattle horn with embedded melanin granules. (*b*) Shell from the marine hawksbill turtle (*Eretmochelys imbricata*) in longitudinal ('scute') section (×15.6, transmitted light) showing the scattered groupings of pigment granules that give the shell a mottled appearance

show variations in depth but pigmentation is not granular and the material tends to show the pattern of mixing of the components rather than the mottled pattern of true shell. In cross-section, resin imitations lack the organizational structure of tortoiseshell shown in *Figure 5.11b*.

A comparative study by O'Connor (1987a) of new and archaeological samples of osseous and keratinaceous materials includes photographs of macro- and microstructures.

## 5.3  Mollusc shell

Shells are produced by most members of the phylum Mollusca. These animals live on land and in the water around the world except the Arctic. Molluscs have always been an important food source, and their geometrically perfect and often beautiful shells have been appreciated by humans since the remotest prehistory. Shell is commonly used in furniture in the form of thin veneer but also as small knobs or decorative elements. Geometric shell inlay has been a part of Islamic tradition, and shell veneers have been used in European marquetry since the seventeenth century. Shell has been extensively used in the lacquerwork of China, Korea and Japan. The Japanese lacquer technique called raden employs extremely thin mother-of-pearl shell (usugai) made from abalone, nautilus and other shells.

Pearls and mother-of-pearl, as the nacreous inner layers are called, are produced by many families of molluscs (Lindner, 1977; Poppe, 1991). The most important, due to size and widespread distribution, are the Avisulidae (including the marine pearl oysters), the Haliotidae (including abalone), the Unionidae (fresh water mussels), the Mytelidae (marine mussels) and the Prochidae (top shells). A selection of these shells is shown in *Figure 5.12*. Since the most beautiful and valuable pearls have been recovered from the warm water pearl oysters (genus Pinctada), mother-of-pearl from these species, notably *P. margaritifera* (the black lipped pearl oyster) and *P. maxima* (gold lipped), was an early and valuable by-product. Abalone shells provide a beautiful material with variegated colouring that has been worked and traded by all of the cultures proximate to their Pacific ocean habitat. *Haliotis fulgens*, the splendid abalone and the large red abalone (*H. rufescens*) are the most important commercial species. Fresh water mussels have also furnished a tremendous quantity of mother-of-pearl. Various members of the Unionidae family formed the basis of a pearl and pearl shell industry in the Mississippi and Ohio river systems before it was ended by pollution. A current source of high quality mother-of-pearl is the trochus shells of the Philippines, where destruction of the marine habitat by shell collecting appears to continue unabated.

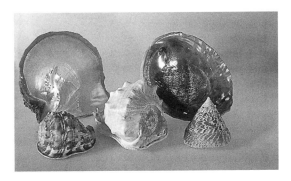

**Figure 5.12** Mollusc shells used in furniture. Pearl oyster (mother-of-pearl, *Pinctada maxima*, *rear left*), red abalone (*Haliotis rufescens*, *rear right*), red helmet (*Cassis rufa*, *front left*), pink queen conch (*Strombus gigas*, *front centre*) and great top shell (*Trochus niloticus*, *front right*)

There are various types of molluscan shell material all made of roughly the same chemical constituents but with characteristically different microstructures and different mechanical properties. Shells are composed of calcium carbonate bound together by the protein conchiolin. Both crystalline forms of calcium carbonate may be present with the hexagonal form, known as calcite, predominating in the outer layers of most shells. Many species produce a pearly iridescent material known as nacre on the interior surfaces close to their bodies and enclose irritating particles and parasites with nacre to form pearls. This nacre is composed of 10% conchiolin with the rest consisting of the orthorhombic crystalline form of calcium carbonate called aragonite. In thin layers this latter causes iridescence due to light wave interference (see Williamson and Cummins, 1983 for an explanation of this phenomenon). A detailed explanation of the properties of different shells in relation to their microstructure, including measured values of the strength and elasticity of thirty species, is provided by Currey (1980).

Shell has a Mohs hardness of 2.5–3.5 and can be cut with steel tools, particularly if lubricated with dilute acid, but grinding techniques using much harder abrasives have been preferred. Diamond saws are the best modern method of preparing thin material. Thin shell can be easily fret-sawn with fine jeweller's saw blades. Decorative patterns can also be produced on shell material by acid etching. Shell can be coloured using, for example, aniline dyes but the limited penetration obtained requires this to be done almost as the last step in finishing. Treatment with silver nitrate solution followed by exposure to sunlight produces a rich black. Methods of working shell are described by Richie (1970, 1974).

Apart from identification of whole shell (Lindner, 1977), polished samples of known origin will provide broad identification by colour, sheen etc. (Poppe, 1991). However, the authors are not aware of any text on the microscopic identification of shells.

## 5.4   Paper and paper products

Paper (thin flexible sheets made from various plant fibres) can be found in furniture as discreet sheets in labels, backings, drawer linings etc., or used as a raw material in the production of paste-board and papier mâché. Occasionally a painted paper ground over wood support is encountered. The technique of scrollwork uses rolled up paper to create images and models. Wherever paper is found in furniture it should be regarded as potentially important and worthy of attention. Labels have an obvious importance, but small shreds of printed paper may also provide clues to dating. Unique examples of historic wallpaper have been found as backings on case furniture or preparatory layers under upholstery.

Before about 1840, when ground-wood or wood-pulp paper began to be produced, Western papers were made from old rags, cut up into pieces and beaten to a pulp under large water-mill-powered hammers. In the Orient, paper was made primarily from virgin plant fibre sources, and beating was commonly carried out by hand. Such traditional papers, made from pure cellulose fibres, tend to be very durable as opposed to wood-pulp papers which degrade more rapidly due to the presence of lignin and other impurities. Paper may also contain loading materials such as kaolin or calcium carbonate, added to give weight, and sizes (animal, vegetable, or synthetic) to hold the loadings, give the material body and facilitate finishing processes. Paper is hygroscopic. Many papers are also anisotropic as a consequence of the regular orientation of fibres resulting from the process of manufacture. The materials, history and technology of paper-making have been reviewed by Collings and Milner (1990), Hunter (1978) and Krill (1987).

Three-dimensional objects have been made from sheet paper or paper pulp at various places since the invention of paper itself. The second quarter of the eighteenth century saw the establishment of a thriving trade in England producing papier mâché architectural decoration in imitation of plasterwork and carved and gilded wood. In 1772, Henry Clay took out a patent on panels made from laminated paper waterproofed with linseed oil (Aitken, 1866; De Voe, 1971). Such laminated panels laid the groundwork for large objects made of paper as distinct from the small snuff-boxes and toys which were produced in the eighteenth century. Jennens and Bettridge, the successor firm to Henry Clay, produced large objects including suites of furniture during the mid-nineteenth century, as did various other less well known manufacturers (Hughes and Hughes, 1958; Jones, 1982) (*Figure 1.20* and *Figure 5.13*). In 1847, Theodore Jennens patented a method for steaming and pressing already prepared laminated panels into shape which made the production of large trays, chair backs and other structural panels more efficient. The history and technology of papier mâché and related paper based materials are reviewed by Van der Reyden and Williams (1986) and Thornton (1993).

Most nineteenth-century papier mâché furniture is not entirely made of paper but contains key structural elements or interior armatures made of wood or metal. Papier mâché articles from both the eighteenth and the nineteenth centuries were finished with polished varnish layers. By far the most popular decoration was the black 'japanned' ground decorated with polychrome painting and gilding (Jones, 1982; Pillement, 1959). From the early nineteenth century pearl shell was extensively employed (De Voe, 1971; Dickinson, 1925).

### Identification of paper and paper products

Fibres from paper decorations, papier mâché and cardboard furniture can be examined under low power magnification for their structure and pattern, or microscopically for composition and origin, in the same way as

**Figure 5.13** Carton-pierre candelabra made by George Jackson and Son, London. (Illustration from William Miller (1897) *Plastering, Plain and Decorative,* B.T. Batsford, London)

textile or wood fibres. The fibrous components of papier mâché, and manufactured particle boards, can be microscopically examined for plant cell features after maceration (see Chapter 2; Côté, 1980; Panshin and De Zeeuw, 1980; Strelis and Kennedy, 1967).

## 5.5 Metals

Metals have exerted an enormous influence on the history of mankind, and by extension, the history of furniture. A great deal of furniture includes metal components and some items of furniture are made entirely of metal. The mechanical properties of metals allow them to be shaped and used in a wide range of structural applications, as whole pieces of furniture, as fixtures, fittings and fastenings. The colours and characteristic lustre of metals has recommended their use in a wide variety of decorative applications. Metal tools have made the most intricate woodworking operations possible. Depending on the application, metals can be manufactured and decorated in many different ways, as described in the general literature of metal manufacturing and techniques. A wide variety of metals and their alloys have been used in furniture (Koller, 1989), but those with the greatest importance in furniture production have been the ferrous metals and copper alloys. The science and technology of metals, in particular the extraction of metals from their ores, their heat treatment and compounding of alloys is called metallurgy (Shrager, 1949; Tylecote, 1976). The science relating to the internal crystalline structure of metals and alloys is called metallography (Shrager, 1949).

Metals are not simply defined but are characterized by several physical and chemical properties. They are lustrous when polished and most are denser, stronger and more malleable and ductile than non-metallic elements. Metals have great strength and toughness (i.e. the ability to withstand limited overload without catastrophic failure) and a high electrical conductivity which decreases slightly with increase in temperature. Metallic elements are generally electropositive and combine with oxygen to give bases from which alkaline hydroxides are formed. Elements having only some of these properties (e.g. antimony and arsenic) have been referred to as metalloids, semi-metals or semi-metallic elements.

Metals such as gold and platinum that do not corrode or tarnish in air or water are referred to as noble. These are found as free metals but most other metals (base metals) are found in nature almost exclusively in oxidized states as compounds of the metal. These compounds include oxides, sulphides and carbonates. After mining or quarrying and concentration of the ores, they are treated by heat, chemical or electrical processes to chemically reduce the ores and convert them to metals. This conversion is called smelting. Availability and price are affected by the amount present in the earth's crust, by the concentration of metal in the ore, by the ease of extraction, concentration and smelting. Iron ores typically contain 20–30% of metal while gold ores typically contain 1 part in 100 000

or less. The availability of metal ores and methods of obtaining metals from them are discussed by Street and Alexander (1979) and Hill and Holman (1978).

Examination of a polished and etched metal surface by reflected light, under suitable magnification, reveals that it is made up of innumerable small, three-dimensional grains varying in size from 0.25 mm or less to 2 mm or more. The grains are usually ductile and are highly cohesive requiring great force to separate them from one another. Grain size is an indicator of hardness and strength; in general, a metal with fine grains will be somewhat harder and stronger than one with coarse grains. Grain size depends on casting temperature, presence of impurities, and the mechanical working and heat treatment that a metal has received. Metallic grains are in fact crystals in which the metal atoms (each of which has a size characteristic of the metal element concerned) are arranged in characteristic regular and orderly fashion. The most frequently encountered patterns of arrangement in the crystal lattice are referred to as face centred cubic, body centred cubic and hexagonal.

The two most important ways in which the properties of metals can be modified are by alloying (blending) with other metals or with non-metals, or by heat treatment. The addition of one metal to another affects the strength, melting point, toughness, resistance to wear and corrosion, and other properties of the resulting alloy in ways which cannot be simply predicted from the behaviour of the parent materials. By blending suitable metals it is possible to produce alloys whose strength is much greater than the constituent materials. Some of these respond to heat treatment processes to enable even better mechanical properties to be obtained (Street and Alexander, 1979).

Changes in the pattern of the atomic lattice when metals are alloyed can be used to explain the changes in properties that occur. For example, the introduction of zinc into the copper lattice causes it to become distorted leading to a greater resistance to deformation, and hence greater hardness, than occurs in the pure metal. Heat treatment in particular will bring about recrystallization thereby changing the grain pattern and with it the evidence of previous historical working of the metal artefact concerned. Metal grains also display a range of imperfections in their crystalline arrangements that help to explain why they are tough and not brittle, why they will stand heavy loads, extend a little and then stop extending and why they can endure shock loads and stress reversal better than most non-metallic materials (Street and Alexander, 1979).

Metals can be shaped by a multitude of methods (Maryon, 1971; Untracht, 1968). However, these can be summarized as (i) shaping from molten metal (e.g. casting), (ii) shaping from hot solid, (iii) shaping from solid metal, (iv) joining by mechanical methods or by soldering, brazing or welding, (v) powder metallurgy.

For further information on metallurgy, that is the science and technology of metals, in particular their extraction, heat treatment and alloying, see Shrager (1949) and Tylecote (1976).

### Iron and steel

The fundamental process in the production of iron is the reduction of iron ore by carbon which may be represented as

$$FeO + C \rightarrow Fe + CO$$

| Iron oxide | Carbon | Metal | Oxides of carbon |
|---|---|---|---|

The principal oxides of iron include haematite ($Fe_2O_3$) and magnetite ($Fe_3O_4$). Though iron ores are relatively rich in metal, they contain silica which is almost impossible to melt and which tends to combine with metallic compounds when heated with them. In early times, the ore was heated in a charcoal fire to give a spongy mass or forgeable 'bloom' of iron containing relatively little carbon. This was further processed to produce the wrought iron of which most historic ferrous furniture hardware is composed.

In the fifteenth century, furnaces were developed that used a forced blast of air to obtain temperatures high enough to melt the iron which could then be poured in liquid form and cast. Much of the silica and other impurities are removed during the process of smelting by mixing limestone with the iron ore. In the great heat of the blast furnace, lime combines with silica to form a molten slag that floats on top of the molten metal and can be separated from it. The resulting iron is called pig iron. Cast iron containing between 5 and 10% of other elements including carbon, silicon, and manganese is produced by remelting pig iron from the blast furnace. Cast iron is the cheapest of all metals. It contains a higher percentage (3–5%) of carbon than wrought iron and is very brittle.

In 1709, Abraham Darby succeeded in smelting iron with coke, leading to technical improvements, cost savings and increased availability that opened the door to the use of iron on a much larger scale. In 1828, a Scot, James Neilson, developed the use of a heated blast of air leading to further increases in efficiency and cost savings. A typical output of a blast furnace in the 1780s was about 900 tons per year. By the 1980s it was common to find amounts greater than this being produced daily.

Wrought iron, which had a high reputation for strength and reliability, is usually a very pure iron mixed with an iron-rich glass (slag) made from spongy iron blooms either smelted directly in 'bloomeries' or refined from cast iron in 'fineries'. It was made on an industrial scale by puddling. Pig iron could be melted and refined by addition of iron oxide and other substances to oxidize and remove carbon, silicon and sulphur. As impurities were removed, the melting point of the iron rose to approach that of pure iron (1500 °C). At this temperature the furnace was unable to keep the metal molten and it was removed as lumps. Iron, which in this form is highly malleable, was hammered to squeeze out slag and then hot rolled and forged to the required shape. The 'wrought' of wrought iron actually refers to the process of hammer-consolidating the semi-molten blooms. This hammering resulted in elongated 'stringers' of slag running longitudinally in the stock as the iron was compacted and excess slag squeezed out. Slag stringers give wrought iron a fibrous structure that looks very much like wood grain in corroded specimens. Wrought iron is a particular and distinctive material and not an interchangeable term for ornamental ironwork. Because wrought iron is somewhat softer under the hammer and forge-welds more easily than mild steel, it continued to be preferred by hand smiths until its industrial extinction in the mid-twentieth century. After the middle of the nineteenth century, new methods of iron making gradually replaced wrought iron with a slag-free product, of generally higher carbon content, called mild steel.

Steel is iron that contains from 0.1% to 1.5% carbon in the form of cementite (iron carbide, $Fe_3C$). The properties of different steels vary according to the percentage of carbon, the presence of metals other than iron (e.g. manganese, nickel, chromium, tungsten, vanadium) and the method of preparation. Before the industrial revolution, steel was expensive and produced only in very small quantities, for swords and springs etc., while structural components were made of cast or wrought iron. In 1856, Henry Bessemer made public a description of a process for blowing air through molten pig iron to produce steel. Oxygen in the air combined with some of the iron to produce iron oxide which then dissolved in the molten metal and reacted with silicon and manganese to form a slag, with carbon being burned off as its oxides. Removal of impurities in this way took about fifteen minutes. The manganese and carbon contents of the steel were adjusted just before pouring. This was the first process to make steel at low cost and in large quantities. With some modifications it remained in use until the 1960s when it was replaced by the oxygen process. Other methods of making steel, the open hearth process, the L-D process and the electric furnace, all share the same aim of reducing silicon, phosphorous and sulphur impurities and adjusting the quantity of carbon and alloying metals to the desired level for the particular application.

The addition of carbon to iron gradually hardens it by forming iron-carbides even in the fully soft annealed state which is achieved by slow cooling. Carbon also makes it possible to carry out heat-treating operations which will yield hardness much greater than those produced by the addition of carbon alone. Tool steels containing from 0.6 to 1.7% carbon will become glass hard and brittle if heated to a red heat then quickly cooled (quenched) in a liquid. This hardening step was normally followed by a second heating called tempering which partially softened the steel and yielded a range of hardness that could be selected by the smith according to how the object was meant to function. The characteristic colours that appear on ferrous metals at different temperatures enable the point to be judged at which the required properties will be obtained (Untracht, 1968). Tool steel was always the most expensive of the ferrous materials. Most historic tools are made from a small 'bit' of steel forge welded onto a larger body of wrought iron.

Ferrous alloys above 1.7% carbon are usually hard and brittle at normal temperatures and were only shaped by casting or cold stock-removal processes such as grinding. Called cast irons, they are likely to be encountered in furniture only as fairly large cast-to-shape elements such as decorative feet and casters.

### Copper alloys

While pure copper is sometimes found as a decorative covering or inlay metal in furniture, alloys with tin (bronze) and zinc (brass) are more likely to be encountered. This sharp distinction in nomenclature and composition between brass and bronze is relatively recent. Many historic objects are mixtures of metals with variable compositions. Alloys of copper with more than 1% of tin, lead and zinc have been called lattens and gun metals.

Copper–tin bronzes are variable in colour from the pink hue of low tin bronze to the silver colour of speculum used in antiquity for mirrors (30–35% tin). Compared to brasses, they are stronger but less ductile and more expensive. Bronze alloys are normally cast and machined to shape.

Zinc was not economically available as a free metal in Europe until after 1738 (although it had been smelted in China perhaps as early as the ninth century AD), so brass was made by stacking sheets of copper with zinc carbonate (calamine) and heating so that the zinc would diffuse into the copper. Such cementation brass ranged up to 28% zinc, which was the upper limit for this process.

Most historic brasses are alpha brasses, which contain up to 38% zinc. Alpha-beta brasses (39–45.5% Zn) are stronger than alpha brasses but less ductile. Alpha brasses of around 30% zinc are the most ductile and were used for die-stamped sheet brass hardware. Unlike steel, brass cannot be hardened (tempered) by heating but it can be made hard and springy by cold rolling and softened by heating.

### Common white metals

Silver (Ag) has been used in furniture as an inlay metal, in sheet and leaf form, or cast to shape for mounts and decorative hardware. Silver is frequently alloyed with copper to increase its hardness and reduce its cost. Sterling silver, an English legal standard, is 7.5% copper and 92.5% silver. Nickel silver, a cheap imitation of silver, is an alloy of copper, nickel and tin.

Like gold, pure silver can be beaten into leaf. Though not as widely used as gold leaf, silver leaf was frequently used on frames and furniture in northern Europe in the second half of the seventeenth century and has been in continuous use in Mediterranean countries. It was sometimes used to imitate gold by the application of a yellow/brown lacquer, for which several recipes are given in gilding manuals (e.g. Scott-Mitchell, 1905), but often silver was used as a decorative material in its own right. In France after the Middle Ages it was illegal to use silver to imitate gold and therefore it was not used to the same extent as in other countries. Examples of French silvering do exist, however, and the metal was much admired. Currently, 100% pure silver leaf may be purchased in books of 25 leaves each 95×95 mm, and four to five times the thickness of gold leaf. Silver leaf is applied by the same methods as gold leaf. Because it is heavier and less ductile it is more difficult to apply with water, though if so applied a high burnish can be achieved.

Tin is the major constituent of pewter which also contained copper, antimony and lead. Pewter was used for cast hardware. In sheet form it was often used in juxtaposition with blue coloured horn in boulle style marquetry. The lead content of pewter to be used with food was regulated by law, but for other uses lead could be present in large percentages.

Zinc was a major component of oriental alloys imported into Europe as curiosities before the mid-eighteenth century: the silvery paktong (a zinc/copper/nickel alloy) from China was occasionally recast into European designs for furniture mounts.

Aluminium was only isolated from its ore in 1845 and was a rare metal until it was commercially produced by electrolytic methods after 1886. Aluminium is lightweight, strong and corrosion-resistant in normal use and has therefore become important as a structural metal in furniture. In fact, aluminium is highly reactive but the thin oxide layer that quickly forms generally prevents further reaction and the metal can therefore be considered stable under normal conditions.

### Gold leaf

Pure gold is completely resistant to atmospheric attack and will retain its lustre indefinitely. This quality, and its rarity, have given gold social and cultural value above all other metals. The most malleable of all metals, gold may be beaten into leaves of extreme thinness (0.1 m is possible) that conform to the most intricate shapes and cover large surfaces economically.

The traditional process of gold leaf production is described by Scott-Mitchell (1905) and by Wheeler and Hayward (1973). Modern leaf is made by casting, rolling and hammering, which leaves a poorly ordered pattern of plates with extensive distortion of the basic atomic arrangement with holes and tears and very little mechanical strength (Lins, 1991). The starting point for the production of leaf is gold of up to 99.95% purity alloyed with other metals in varying proportions to produce leaf of different colours. Traditionally copper and silver were used but platinum and palladium have also been used more recently. Copper gives gold a warm tone, copper and silver together give mid-range tones, and silver produces cool tones (see *Table 5.2*). Leaf alloys of less than 50% gold by weight are rare. The carat system of measuring gold content refers to a 24th part. Thus 18 carat (ct) gold contains 18 parts of gold and 6 parts of alloying metals. The gold leaf most commonly used now is 22 or 23 carat. Depending on the country and period of origin, several colours of gold may be found on a single object. Furniture and picture frames have also been gilded with leaves of Dutch metal (an alloy of copper and zinc), silver leaf, or even leaves of two different metals beaten together, known as schlagmetal.

Gold leaf is sold loose in books of 25 leaves laid between rouged tissue. A 'pack' consists

**Table 5.2** Relationship between composition and colour of different metal leaves

| Colour/carat | % Gold (Au) | % Copper (Cu) | % Silver (Ag) |
|---|---|---|---|
| Red 23.5ct | 98 | 2 | |
| Medium deep 22.75ct | 95 | 2.5 | 2.5 |
| Pale yellow 22ct | 92 | 1 | 7 |
| Yellow 24ct | 100 | | |
| Lemon 18ct | 75 | | 25 |
| Green 14.5ct | 60 | | 40 |
| White 12ct | 50 | | 50 |
| Silver | | | 100 |

of 20 books. The size of the leaf is usually 85 mm (3⅜ in.) square, but may vary between 60 and 110 mm depending on the individual goldbeater. Thickness varies between 0.36 and 0.8 μm. One troy ounce (31.1 g) of gold will produce about 80 standard books of gold leaf, that is 2000 3⅜ in. square leaves.

The thinnest gold was produced at the end of the nineteenth century and beginning of the twentieth. At this time, workshops were numerous and prosperous, allowing more specialization of tasks. This increased the skill of the beaters so that they could produce very thin leaves. There was a correspondingly high level of skill in gilders, who perfected the art of handling such fine leaves. Transfer or patent leaf is similar to loose leaf but is lightly adhered to non-rouged tissue by pressure or wax. Leaves of gold cold-welded together are sold in rolls, in widths from 3 mm to 135 mm and up to 21 m in length, for use in bookbinding and architectural gilding.

'Regular' gold is a colloquial term for the gold beater's 'own brand' and will vary between establishments in colour, carat and thickness. Double-weight gold is a thicker leaf of 22 carat or more used for exterior gilding and for areas of high burnish. Though called double-weight, the leaf in fact contains no more than 10–15% more metal than standard leaf. Again, the leaf varies according to the beater, for instance one goldbeater's regular gold maybe just as thick as another's double weight. A high carat gold is recommended for exterior use to reduce tarnishing.

### Shell and powdered gold

Shell gold and powdered gold are made from either gold leaf or the skewings thereof. Shell gold is powdered gold mixed with gum arabic and water. This paste was traditionally allowed to dry naturally in mussel shells (the source of its name), which acted as both a container and a palette. It is now sold as small blocks (0.33 g) on white plastic palettes. It dries to a dull lustre and has a slight tendency to look like bronze powder. Its advantage, however, is that it does not tarnish and it can be lightly burnished. Powdered gold is pure gold with no binder. It adheres either by the gilder breathing onto the area to be gilded, or by application onto a wetted surface. Its advantages over shell gold are that it is much brighter and can be more highly burnished. It is bought in 1 and 2 g packages in a limited range of colours, but other colours can be made by the gilder.

### Finishes and coatings on metals

Ferrous metal objects could be left with the lustrous black fire scale formed by oxidation in the forge, adhering to the surface. As such they were the work of the blacksmith. They could also be ground, filed, and polished to a high shine by the whitesmith.

Coatings of tin have always been popular on iron and copper alloy objects and could be achieved by hot-dipping or by rubbing the molten tin onto a clean, hot and fluxed metal surface. Thin tinned-iron sheet was made in large quantities in the area of south Wales from the early eighteenth century. Tinned-iron sheet (tin plate), often commonly called simply tin, was used to make pierced screens for food storage furniture. Tin-plate tends to rust through in spots, so a coating of zinc (galvanizing) was commercially used on iron after about 1838. A zinc coating will continue to protect the iron from corrosion as long as any metallic zinc remains, unlike tin which will actually accelerate corrosion of the iron once it has been exposed.

Electroplating of one metal onto another by use of a direct current became common after 1840 although electrochemical plating using metallic salts can be dated from at least a thousand years earlier. Nickel plate on both iron and copper alloys has been popular for decorative hardware since the late nineteenth century.

Before the invention of electroplating, gilding on metals was most commonly achieved by the application of gold–mercury alloys (amalgam). The silver coloured buttery amalgam was applied with a stiff wire brush to presentation surfaces. The object was then heated to vaporize the mercury leaving a dull coating of gold that was burnished to a high shine. Ormolu furniture mounts are predominantly brass alloys fire gilded using this highly toxic and dangerous mercury process.

Organic coatings have also been extensively employed on metals. Waxes and oils work well on unpolished or rough work, while spirit varnishes based on shellac or sandarac were commonly used on polished work during the eighteenth century and later. Lacquers for white metals were often coloured with dyes or with the alcohol-soluble coloured resins gamboge and dragon's blood to imitate the colour of gold. Since the age of modern plastics, a host of synthetic resins have been used as clear coatings and paint binders on metalwork. Intentional chemical patination of metals has been widely used for decorative effect (Hughes and Rowe, 1982).

For further information on the history and technology of metals see Singer *et al.* (1954–1958) and Street and Alexander (1979).

### Identification of metals

Some metals and alloys have a characteristic colour, specific gravity or corrosion product that can be used to make a preliminary identification of the material. However, when making a visual identification it should be considered that the presence of coatings, patinas, corrosion and dirt can affect the appearance of metal.

Qualitative microchemical tests, based on the formation of characteristic colours or precipitates on reaction with a specific test reagent, can be used for the identification of metals and alloys (Laver, 1978). The lower limit of detectability of an alloying element is generally between 0.2 and 1.0% (Newell, 1982). The tests are carried out either as spot tests on the metal surface or involve sampling (Laver, 1978). A disadvantage of this destructive method is that the presence of each element has to be detected individually. Thomson (1991) suggests a battery continuity tester to detect the presence of non-conductive organic coating or corrosion layers on a metal surface. The ferromagnetism of iron and

nickel makes it possible to identify them with a magnet.

Various instrumental analytical methods, including X-ray fluorescence (XRF), energy dispersive X-ray spectrometry (EDS), atomic absorption spectroscopy (AA), neutron activation (NA), emission spectroscopy (ES), proton induced X-ray/gamma-ray emission (PIXE/PIGE) and photon activation may be used to identify metals and alloys (Parkes, 1987). These analytical methods, as well as X-ray diffraction and infrared absorption spectroscopy, may also be useful in the characterization of corrosion products.

### Identification of structure and fabrication of metal objects

General methods of manufacture, e.g. casting, pressing, turning or assembling, can be recognized from the overall appearance or shape of the metal component. Visual examination, especially in raking light, may reveal features of the manufacture and decoration techniques such as mould marks from casting, incised grooves from engraving or compressed channels from chasing (Larsen, 1993; Watts, 1982). Silicon rubber casts, which provide a reversed relief of the surface, can be an aid in the study of tool marks. The regularity of the tool marks may indicate whether or not the metal was worked by hand or machine, e.g. hammering versus rolling or, as in the case of screws, hand filing versus machine threading. The identity of the maker, workshop or origin may be recognized through stamped marks (Brandner, 1976; Kisluk-Grosheide, 1991; Stratmann, 1975) or inscribed signatures (Van Duin, 1989). Visual examination may also reveal whether or not the applied hardware is original to the furniture, as the presence of outlines, marks, holes and plugs can indicate previous attachments. A hand lens and stereomicroscope may reveal further surface details such as concentric scratches from turning or the cut edge characteristic of a fretsaw blade.

Metallographic examinations reveal the internal grain structure of metals, thus providing information on the techniques employed in their fabrication. A polished and etched cross-section is prepared from a sample removed from the object and examined in reflected light using a metallographic microscope (Scott, 1991). Elemental analysis of observed features can be carried out on the cross-section with various instrumentation, such as energy dispersive X-ray spectrometry or electron microprobe, if connected to a scanning electron microscope.

X-ray images of metal objects can provide information concerning methods of manufacture. For example, cast metal may contain voids or other casting flaws, which appear in radiographs as dark spots, while hammered objects sometimes exhibit a characteristic mottled hammer blow pattern. Repairs and replacements are often detectable with X-ray radiography, for example solder is often recognizable due to its porous structure, characteristic flowed appearance and radio-opacity. However, where the solder and bulk metal have similar densities the solder join may not be detectable in radiographs. Computer aided tomography (CAT) might prove helpful in such instances because it detects very small density variations.

In contrast to the wide range of analyses which have been carried out on works of art in metal, the identification of materials and manufacture of metal components on furniture have thus far received little attention. The results of most studies are unpublished, only briefly mentioned (Koller, 1989; Pelz, 1992) or included in footnotes (Brachert, 1986; Schneider, 1990). Studies to determine the origin of several south German boulle works based on the elemental compositions of their pewter and brass inlays have been carried out by Walch (1993) and Segebade (1993, 1994) using photon activation analysis. X-ray fluorescence was used to establish that what was thought to be a gilded surface on brass casters from a nineteenth century American couch did not in fact contain gold (Thomson, 1991).

### Dating metals

Marks stamped on to metals may relate to the particular maker(s), may be characteristic of certain regions, such as the Augsburg pine cone (Kisluk-Grosheide, 1991; Stratmann, 1975), or may relate to taxation, such as the crowned C mark on French bronze mounts (de Bellaigue, 1974). Such marks may aid in dating because they often reflect documented changes in guild and state regulations.

With the exception of experimental methods for carbon-14 dating of iron (Creswell, 1992;

Riederer, 1981) there are no instrumental methods for determining the age of metal. At least until the Industrial Revolution, when geological coal or coke were introduced as fuel, the carbon incorporated into iron is generally contemporaneous with the manufacture of the object itself. The fact that previously produced iron goods were recycled is a potential source of error and must be taken into consideration. Dating of historic metal can be based on comparison to documented inventions and discoveries affecting metallurgical practices. Metallographic examinations have, for example, been carried out on the metal components of a historic wooden gate in order to determine its age (Storch, 1987).

## 5.6 Ceramics and glass

Ceramics, clay products made permanent by heat, are among the most ancient of human technologies. Vitreous glazes on ceramics predate the use of glass as a separate material. Glass vessels made their first appearance in the Middle East and Egypt around 1500 BC. Beautiful and functional ceramics and glass have been the object of increasingly complex technologies since their earliest use and occupy a central place in human technological history (see Kingery, 1986; Singer, 1958). The carbide cutting teeth on the best modern woodworking tools are a form of metallic ceramic made from carbon and various metals.

Ceramics are commonly found in furniture as tiles or decorative knobs and escutcheon plates. Knobs and pulls have also been made of glass, particularly after the development of pressed glass in the 1840s made cheaper imitations of cut glass widely available. Glass may also occur in furniture in the form of clear or coloured flat-glass glazing in case pieces, or as mirrored glass. Glass mosaics produced in Rome during the eighteenth and nineteenth centuries were used as decorative inserts or entire table tops. The Roman Mosaic technique employed a wide colour palette of thin glass rods (smalti) set closely together on end to create extremely detailed images. Glass has also been important as an abrasive (glass powder glued to paper) in woodworking.

Glass can be described as a meta-stable super-cooled liquid because as it cools from the molten state it simply gets progressively stiffer rather than crystallizing, as metals do. Ceramics, by contrast, are predominantly crystalline structures, consisting of various high temperature transformation products of clays (alumino-silicates) and various additives and impurities which constitute the final mixtures or 'body'.

Most historic glass is an essentially amorphous polymer formed from silicon dioxide ($SiO_2$), usually in the form of sand, quartz or flint, melted together with an alkaline flux such as potash or soda to bring down the melting temperature of the silica and decrease viscosity at historically achievable temperatures. Other materials, such as lime or lead, are usually added to make the glass harder and more durable. A wide variety of metallic oxides may be present, either intentionally added or present as impurities. Iron is a very common impurity and imparts a greenish tinge to the glass. Other elements serve to create a more stable corrosion resistant glass or impart colour.

Ceramics will include increasing quantities of glass as firing temperature rises, but they are given structural integrity by aluminosilicate crystals which can be thought of as internal skeletons. Thus the same fluxes present in glass (sodium, potassium, iron, lead and calcium) serve to promote fusing, or glass production, in a ceramic body, while more aluminium gives rise to refractory or non-fusing mixtures. Glazes are practical and decorative coatings composed of more highly fluxed silicates than those of the ceramics. They can be partially crystalline or entirely vitreous in nature.

Ceramics are hard and brittle, hold their shape and, unlike the parent material, cannot be reconstituted to a pliable state by the addition of water. Across the range of ceramics their precise properties vary depending on the clay used, the way it is shaped and the firing conditions used (Buys and Oakley, 1994; Kingery, 1960; Shepard, 1968).

Glass has been described as a fourth state of matter with distinctive properties too technical to allow description here. While it retains the physical characteristics of a liquid in some respects, flow does not take place at ambient temperatures except over geological time scales. Glass is hard and brittle and may

be transparent or translucent to light or almost opaque. For a description of the chemical and physical properties of glass see Newton and Davison (1989).

### Flat glass

Glass formed into flat sheets is frequently encountered as an element in furniture as clear glazing, mirrors, or as decorative panels painted or gilded on the back surface such as reverse-glass paintings, hinterglassmalerei and verre eglomisé (Brown and O'Connor, 1991). Understanding the relevant technologies is important for dating and connoisseurship as well as in making sound conservation decisions.

Glass was made into sheets by three major methods; casting, and two techniques that start with a blown bubble of glass, the crown and broad methods. Glass was undoubtedly cast into flat slabs while molten before the invention of glass blowing in the first century AD. Excavated examples of Roman glass produced in this way are thick and show a rough surface, probably from an open-face sand mould. Such ancient pieces of flat glass were essentially translucent tiles, although it is possible that high quality cast glass was ground and polished to transparency as in later centuries.

During the last quarter of the seventeenth century, the French developed a method of casting large pieces of glass on an iron table, rolling to uniform thickness with a large metal roller, then laboriously grinding and polishing the surfaces to planar perfection (*Figure 5.14*). The process could produce much larger pieces of flat glass than any other method. This plate glass was generally used to make large mirrors for the wealthy. Plate glass manufacture was established in England in 1773. Plate glass continued to be made by casting and grinding until the 1950s though with substantial improvements to the methods employed.

Broad glass, also called muff, cylinder or common glass, may well date from soon after the invention of blowing, though some authorities give the fourth century as the starting point. To make broad glass the glass is gathered on a blow pipe and blown into a sphere which is elongated by swinging (*Figure 5.15*). The ends are removed and the resulting cylinder is divided lengthways and put

**Figure 5.14** The use of a crane to move a crucible of molten glass from the furnace to the casting table where the molten glass was poured out. When cooled, the surfaces of the cast plate glass were laboriously ground and polished. (Illustration from Dionysius Lardner (1832) *The Cabinet Cyclopedia, Useful Arts Series*, Longman, Rees, Orme, Brown & Green, London)

back into a furnace until it resoftens enough to be eased out into a reasonably flat rectangular sheet (*Figure 5.16*).

Broad glass was the cheapest and most common window glass. It is characterized by irregular ripples and thickenings, by elongated straight bubbles, and a slightly dimpled surface on one side where imperfections in the flattening oven have made impressions in the soft glass. At the end of the nineteenth century the cylinder process was mechanized by J.H. Lubbers to produce very much larger cylinders up to 40 feet long but the finished product was otherwise similar in appearance and defects to earlier production. The hand cylinder method is still used to produce the most expensive full antique sheets for stained glass

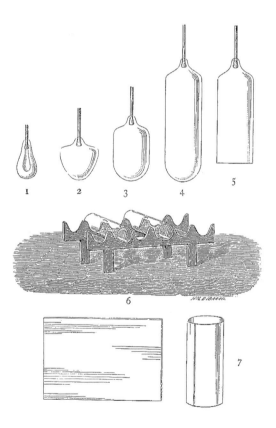

**Figure 5.15** Blowing a cylinder for sheet glass. (Illustration from George Dodd (1844–51) *British Manufactures*, C. Knight and Co., London)

**Figure 5.16** Stages in the production of blown sheet glass. (Illustration from Alexandre Sauzay (1870) *The Marvels of Glass Making in All Ages*, Sampson, Low, Son and Marston, London)

(a)                              (b)                              (c)

**Figure 5.17**   Stages in the production of crown glass. (Illustrations from Dionysius Lardner (1832) 'A treatise on The Progressive Improvement & Present State of the Manufacture of Porcelain and Glass': part of *The Cabinet Cyclopedia, Useful Arts Series*, Longman, Rees, Orme, Brown & Green, London)

work. Some broad glass was ground and polished to produce distortion-free glass for common mirrors.

Crown glass was probably produced as early as broad glass and the two methods were both used off and on during subsequent centuries. As with broad glass, the first stage is the blowing of a globe but in the crown method a solid 'pontil' rod is then attached opposite the blow pipe which is then cracked off leaving a round hole. The globe is spun on the pontil in front of a hot furnace opening until the hole enlarges. As the heat increased the globe eventually 'flashes' or opens out suddenly into a slightly convex flat crown. The disk is cooled in the air sufficiently that it will not be imprinted with anything when it is laid down and the pontil iron is removed (*Figure 5.17*). The resulting glass was the best quality that could be produced by hand methods because of its thinness and regularity and because it had a fire polished surface on both

sides. Semicircular thickenings and lines of bubbles can often be seen in crown glass (*Figure 5.18*). The centres of the sheets bearing the pontil scars (bullseyes) were used in glazing the cheapest windows.

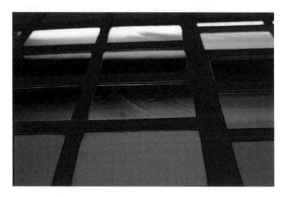

**Figure 5.18**   A window pane made from crown glass showing characteristic curved striations, in the window of a late seventeenth-century period room, Yale

Early in the fourteenth century small mirrors were produced in Nuremberg by introducing tin, bismuth and a resin into hot globes of glass. This method was superseded around 1500 by a cold process employing liquid mercury to affix a sheet of tin leaf to the polished back of a flat glass sheet. This tin/mercury amalgam method continued to be used for common broad-glass mirrors as well as the luxurious plate glass expanses of the aristocracy until a cold chemical method involving the in-situ reduction of a silver containing solution to form a thin metallic silver layer was developed in the mid-nineteenth century.

At the beginning of the twentieth century the Lubbers process had made it possible to draw a cylinder up to 40 feet long from a molten reservoir of glass. The advantages of drawing out a flat sheet of glass rather than producing a cylinder which was then flattened were appreciated during the nineteenth century but introduced with only limited success by Fourcault in France and Colburn in the United States. By 1913 the Fourcault process had been perfected in France and in the US the Libby-Owens Company, working from Colburn's patents, was producing flat drawn-glass. Innovations in the casting of plate glass were made in England and the US but it wasn't until the development of the float glass method by Pilkington Bros in England in 1952 that truly flat glass was produced without grinding and polishing. In this process a drawn sheet is floated on a molten tin bath in an inert atmosphere and kept soft until both surfaces are planar and defect free. Virtually all clear window glass is made by this process today. For further information on glass, see Newman (1977).

### Identification of glass and ceramics

For a description of the characteristics of different ceramic materials see Buys and Oakley (1994). Frank (1982) provides information about the analysis of archaeological glass. Advanced analytical methods such as XRF can be applied to the analysis of materials used in reverse glass paintings and mirror foilings (Ryser, 1991; Schott, 1988).

## 5.7  Stone and related materials

The all-encompassing term stone includes rocks and minerals which are the natural products of geological processes. Minerals are named elements and compounds of specific composition and crystalline type, and rocks are mixtures of minerals. Common usage of the term stone may also include organic materials, such as amber and jet, altered by geological conditions. Stone is commonly used in furniture as polished slabs forming surfaces such as table tops and occasionally as precious and semi-precious stones used in decoration. Rocks and minerals are also the origin of materials such as bole, clay and pigments that are components of materials such as gesso, paint and fillers found on objects. Minerals have also been used as abrasives.

Rocks can be classified into three general types: (i) igneous, solidified from the molten state; (ii) sedimentary, formed by the erosion of existing rocks followed by redeposition; and (iii) metamorphic, formed by the action of heat and pressure on existing rocks (Cox, 1972). The composition, structure, formation and properties of the rocks that make up these classes and their important degradation products, formed by mechanical and chemical degradation of the parent rock, are described by Dietrich (1989), Press and Siever (1986) and Webster (1987). This short section can only attempt to review some of the stony materials encountered in furniture conservation.

### Marble

Stone used in slabs to form surfaces such as table tops is often described as marble. This term has acquired a loose trade definition meaning any decorative facing stone cut into slabs to cover furniture or architectural surfaces.

Marble also has a more specific meaning, which excludes much of this material. True marble is completely metamorphosed limestone in which all of the original structures such as fossils have been changed into crystalline calcite. Marble may be characterized by its colour, by its texture (e.g. serpentine), or by its origin (e.g. *breccia di tivoli* – rock from Tivoli). Marble may be pure white, as is much of the material from Italy, Greece, Vermont and Georgia (USA) or a variety of colours. Colours, imparted by impurities in the form of metal salts, include green 'Connemara' from Ireland, black ('noir Belge') from Belgium and red (antico rosso). Marble is relatively soft and easy to work but is hard enough to sustain a polish. It is also a stone of even unlayered consistency which can be worked freely in any direction.

Alabaster is a massive form of hydrated calcium sulphate ($CaSO_4.2H_2O$) or gypsum which can occur in a wide variety of solid or veined colours and is often quite translucent. It takes a good polish but is very soft and easily marred. Alabaster is weakly water soluble and the polish can be removed with water.

The term limestone describes rocks composed of calcium carbonate ($CaCO_3$) which have formed directly by sedimentation. Most sedimentary limestones are composed of calcite (hexagonal $CaCO_3$) but if they contain magnesium carbonate are called dolomitic limestones (over 10% $MgCO_3$) or dolomite (over 45% $MgCO_3$). Many hard limestones containing visually interesting shell fossils, such as purbeck and frosterley marble have been used as decorative stones. Occasionally a fossiliferous limestone can be completely replaced by silicon dioxide while retaining its visual characteristics (pseudomorphic replacement). Such is the case with the beautiful snail-shell agate called 'turitella'.

Travertine is a variety of marble formed by precipitation from hot spring water and is composed of aragonite (orthorhombic $CaCO_3$). Travertine is usually characterized by a layered arrangement of small pits and voids giving a rustic character but some, such as Mexican onyx is dense, translucent and colourful.

Conglomerate and breccia are stones composed of rock detritus recemented into a stone matrix material. The stone is a conglomerate if the larger rock inclusions are rounded and a breccia if they are angular and broken.

Igneous rocks have cooled directly from melted material and are finely or coarsely crystalline depending on the cooling rate. Granite is a term commonly used to describe stone composed of roughly equal sized crystals of mixed minerals. Technically it means only light coloured stone where quartz predominates (roughly 15% dark coloured minerals) while quartz diorite (20%), diorite (30%) and gabbro (50%) are terms used to describe progressively darker stone. Porphyry describes an igneous stone where much larger crystals (phenocrysts) are embedded in a finely crystalline matrix.

Coloured stone, used in much the same way as veneers are used in marquetry and parquetry, and known as pietra dure, has been used to create decorative surfaces and table tops in furniture. This technique was developed in sixteenth century Italy and employed either hard silicate stones called pietra dure or soft calcareous stones called pietra tenere. Complex stone-marquetry designs composed of flat surfaced agate, jasper, lapis lazuli and chalcedony are sometimes called commeso di pietra dure or Florentine mosaic (Giusti, 1992; Monna *et al.*, 1983).

Sulphur, also known as brimstone, has been used as a decorative inlay material in furniture. This element melts at only 113 °C and retains a bright yellow colour if not overheated. In the molten form it can be poured into an undercut cavity in wood then flattened and polished after cooling and hardening. In solid form it has only a slight smell and is reasonably tough and hard.

Plaster has been used to imitate decorative stone for many centuries. This work, called scagliola, employs finely powdered selenite, a crystalline form of gypsum plaster, mixed with animal glue and pigments to imitate natural facing stone or stone-mosaic work. An ornate style of scagliola, imitating pietra dure, was developed in northern Italy at the end of the seventeenth century and was extensively employed in making table tops. In this work, a background colour of plaster was cast onto a stone supporting slab, then successive incised designs were filled with brightly coloured plasters and scraped flat. Lastly the entire surface was ground flat, impregnated with resins and polished to a high shine. The term marezzo describes scagliola that was cast face-down on a glass plate and required little subsequent polishing. Plaster has also been used as a moulding and casting material and in the production of gesso.

### Identification of stone and related materials

The first steps in analysing marble, semi-precious stones and other such materials are to identify colour, texture and grain. An authoritative, practical identification guide to minerals and rocks is provided by Hamilton *et al.* (1992). Samples can be examined microscopically, or with sophisticated methods such as atomic absorption spectroscopy (AA), optical emission spectroscopy (ES), X-ray diffraction, energy dispersive X-ray fluorescence spectrometry (ED–XRF), in further determining the stone's composition (Johnson and Maxwell, 1981; Lazzarini *et al.*, 1980; McMillan and Hofmeister, 1988).

Fraquet (1987) and Rice (1980) describe the physical and chemical characteristics of different ambers and give a general gemological test for their identification. Methods for determining the provenance of amber are discussed by Beck (1982).

## 5.8 Colorants: pigments, dyes and stains

A wide range of materials of very diverse origins and chemical types has been used to colour wood and other materials found in furniture. Pigments and dyes may be classified in a variety of ways according to their colour, origins, historical availability, chemistry, physical properties and permanence. Stains constitute such a diverse group that it may be more productive to consider them from the point of view of the medium in which they are used. This subsection discusses in a general way the terminology associated with this functional group of materials and is intended to be illustrative rather than exhaustive. There is an extensive and excellent literature on the history, variety, chemistry and use of pigments and dyes and the reader is referred to sources listed in the bibliography. For further information on pigments see Feller (1986), Gettens and Stout (1966), Harley (1982) and Mayer (1982). For further information on dyes see Abrahart (1977), Liles (1990) and sources listed in Chapter 3. For further information on other colorants used on furniture and woodwork see Hayward (1974), Sheraton (1803), Siddons (1830) and Stalker and Parker (1688).

### 5.8.1 Colour

The sensation of colour arises through the influence of electromagnetic radiation of wavelength 400–700 nm on the human eye. The chromatic quality or *hue* of a colour is indicated by name as red, orange, yellow etc. *Value* describes the relationship of a colour to white and black. Higher values of a colour are lighter and lower values are darker (this is equivalent to a physicist's brightness of light). To change the value of a colour we can mix it with something lighter or darker. Adding black or white changes the value but does not change the hue. The *intensity* of a colour is the strength of hue as compared to a colourless neutral grey. This is well illustrated by the comparative terms brilliant and dull. Other terms used to describe intensity of pigment colours are saturation, chroma, purity, vividness and brightness. Intensity is reduced by mixing with another colour. It is possible to change the intensity of a colour without changing its value or hue by adding neutral grey of the same value.

Because there are three independent variables of perceived colour, it is impossible to achieve a logical arrangement in two dimensions (on a paint card for example). Consequently, various systems have been developed to describe or map colour space in three dimensions. Perhaps the most well known of these is the Munsell system. The Munsell system suffers from the disadvantages that colour chips on adjacent plates show large hue differences at high chroma but very small hue differences at low chroma. Also, there are too few chips for the high chroma colours which (at least industrially) are more important. To cope with these difficulties, the Munsell system, with 1488 glossy colour chips and 1277 matte chips, has been expanded by the Japanese Chroma Cosmos system which has 5000 colour chips. Other colour atlases have also been developed including the Optical Society of America OSA-UCS system, the Natural Colour System and the ICI Colour Atlas which illustrates 27 000 different colours (McLaren, 1983). For everyday purposes, the *Methuen Handbook of Colour* (Kornerup and Wanscher, 1978) provides a useful way to compare and describe colours.

### Why objects appear coloured
Light of different wavelengths falling on the retina of the eye gives rise to the sensation of colour through the response of the cones in the retina (Gregory, 1966). Light of wavelength 400 nm gives rise to the sensation of blue and that at 700 nm to red. A mixture of all wavelengths appears white. When white light hits a surface it may be reflected, transmitted through the object, or absorbed. If all light is

absorbed the object will appear black. If all light is reflected it will appear white. If all light is transmitted it will appear transparent or translucent. If some wavelengths are absorbed more strongly than others then the object will appear to have the colour *complementary* to the wavelength absorbed. For example, strong absorption of blue will make the object appear yellow, strong absorption of red will result in a bluish green appearance, and so on. If some light is absorbed at all wavelengths, the object will appear grey.

Different wavelengths of light have different amounts of energy. Short wavelength blue light has more energy than longer wavelength red light (see Chapter 6). Particular substances preferentially absorb light of different energies (i.e. wavelengths) because these amounts of energy correspond to different excited states in which molecules can exist (Suppan, 1972). Each transition from one energy state to another higher energy state is associated with a definite amount of energy. If the amount of energy involved in the transition corresponds to energy in the visible part of the spectrum then the substance will appear coloured. Colour in inorganic molecules is frequently associated with electron movements in transition metals. These are the d block elements in Group 3a of the Periodic Table (Hill and Holman, 1978), including titanium, vanadium, manganese, iron, cobalt, nickel, copper and zinc. Charge transfer, the transfer of a valency electron from one atom or ion to another, occurs particularly with oxides, sulphides, iodides and bromides and is a another example of how colour arises in inorganic materials. Colour in organic materials is usually associated with the presence of *chromophores* usually found attached to aromatic rings such as benzene or other complex ring structures (*Figure 5.19a*). These have their colour intensified by certain other groups called *auxochromes* which include amino groups, halo groups, hydroxyl groups, and methoxy groups (*Figure 5.19b*). The colour of alizarin is a result of the presence within its chemical structure of chromophores and auxochromes (*Figure 5.19c*). In the absence of chromophores, organic molecules may still appear coloured due to *conjugation*, the pattern of alternating single and double bonds (e.g. lycopene in *Figure 5.19d*) or *resonance*, when

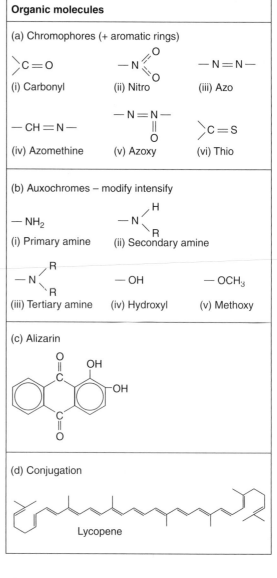

**Figure 5.19**
(*a*) Chromophoric groups, such as aromatic structures and double bonds, contain delocalized electrons. Some examples are: (i) carbonyl group; (ii) nitro group; (iii) azo group; (iv) azomethine group; (v) azoxy group; (vi) thio group. (*b*) Auxochromic groups modify or intensify the colour produced by chromophores. Some examples are: (i) primary amine; (ii) secondary amine; (iii) tertiary amine; (iv) hydroxyl group; (v) methoxy group. (*c*) The colour of alizarin is a result of the presence of chromophores (two benzene rings, two carbonyl groups) and auxochromes (two hydroxyls). (*d*) The colour of lycopene (responsible for the deep red colour seen in tomatoes, pink grapefruit, guava and watermelon) is due to conjugation, i.e. alternating single and double bonds between the carbon atoms

a substance exists as a hybrid of two different structures (e.g. malachite green).

Besides the simple absorption of light of a particular wavelength, the colour of a dye or pigment depends on several other factors including the width and profile (steepness) of the absorption band, the probability that light of the correct wavelength will actually be absorbed (the molar extinction coefficient), the change in refractive index with wavelength and the wavelength(s) at which maximum absorption occurs. The importance of these factors is further discussed by McLaren (1983).

### 5.8.2 Pigments

In contrast to dyes, true pigments are insoluble, have comparatively large particle sizes and are generally bound in a medium to create paints. Surface coating pigments may be required to fulfil a variety of functions among which providing colour is the most obvious but not the only requirement. The ability of a paint to obscure previous colours may also be important as may the effect pigments can have on the strength, durability and adhesion of paint films. Pigments may also provide increased protection against corrosion of metals, reduce gloss and modify the flow and application properties of paints.

The use of pigments began in remote prehistory with the exploitation of various brightly coloured natural materials from animal, vegetable and mineral sources. Coloured material obtained from flowers, seeds, nuts, berries, bark, roots and wood were mostly impermanent but madder and woad are more durable examples (Goodwin, 1965). Yellow, red and brown coloured earths and clays and carbon blacks from various sources are also known from the early archaeological sites. Coloured minerals of heavy metals such as malachite, azurite, cinnabar, lapis lazuli, orpiment and realgar were known and used, at least in the areas where they naturally occurred, from very early times. The history of pigments continues through the introduction of various semi-synthetic and synthetic colorants. The beginning of the development of modern synthetic pigments dates to the early years of the eighteenth century but many synthetic pigments were in fact known before this time, including Egyptian blue, artificial red and yellow oxides of lead, lead white (basic lead carbonate) and verdigris (basic copper acetate).

Pigments embrace a wide variety of different chemical types with consequent wide variation in properties. They include inorganic, organic and metallo-organic compounds, and organic/inorganic composites. In some cases they are pure homogeneous materials in other cases, mixtures of different materials and composite materials. Among the inorganic pigments are found oxides, carbonates, chromates, phosphates, silicates and sulphides, of heavy metals and transition metals. The properties of pigments that affect their performance and ability to function in the ways discussed above depend on chemical reactivity and a variety of physical properties including refractive index, particle size, particle morphology, surface energy, density and thermal stability.

### *Chemical properties*

There are several ways in which the chemical properties of pigments govern their performance, including solubility, reactions with each other and with paint media, colour fastness, stability and toxicity. Pigments are generally insoluble but not all pigments are equally insoluble in all media. In some cases, a later application of paint may pick up the colour of an earlier one. Organic reds are particularly prone to this fault of bleeding and white applied over a cured red paint film may turn pink on, or shortly after, application. Pigments may be acidic or basic and may therefore react with other basic or acidic materials including media or other pigments in mixtures. They may affect the formulation by modifying pH in emulsions or by the ease with which they can be wetted out. Zinc oxide, for example, is amphoteric, that is it can act as an acid or a base. As a base it reacts with resins containing a high proportion of acidic groups to form soaps. Because zinc is divalent this leads to cross linking of the resin and an increase in the viscosity of the paint in storage. Oxides of heavy metals in general form sufficiently strong bases to cause saponification of free fatty acids in oil media to form soaps. This is believed to be one of the reasons why oxides of lead in oil form such compact, elastic and durable paint films. Release of chromates on contact with water confers anti-corrosive properties on certain pigments, particularly the chromates of zinc, lead and strontium. Phosphate pigments and silica pigments which release calcium on an ion exchange basis can also be effective as anti corrosives.

Some pigments such as red lead exhibit poor durability in glue media. Under certain conditions, sulphides can interact with copper and lead pigments to produce black or brown copper or lead sulphides that then cause discoloration of paint films. This will not normally happen in oil because the pigment particles are well enclosed in medium and effectively separated from one another. Colour changes due to the influence of one pigment on another can also arise because some oxygen containing pigments (e.g. chromates) can oxidize some organic pigments, being themselves reduced in the process. The ability of certain pigments to speed up or retard the drying of oils has been discussed in section 4.7.1.

The nature of the chemical groups at the surface of a pigment particle will determine the degree of attraction between it and the vehicle in which it is to be dispersed and consequently the ease of wetting out and the handling properties of the paint. In some cases, pigment may be preferentially attracted to a minor component such as the drier or another additive and could interfere with the effectiveness of that component in the mixture.

Pigment toxicity varies from the innocuous (e.g. chalk) through harmful (e.g. cobalt pigments) to toxic (e.g. lead and cadmium containing materials) and very toxic (e.g. vermilion, Prussian blue). The maximum permissible limits of exposure to such materials is constantly being revised, invariably downward, as new evidence becomes available. In the absence of a positive identification it is wise to treat all pigmented materials with care and respect, taking positive steps to avoid ingestion, inhalation, or contact with skin or eyes.

### Physical properties

When a ray of light passes obliquely from one medium to another, it is bent or refracted at the surface separating the two media. This occurs because light travels at slightly differ-

ent velocities in different media and therefore there is a slight change of wavelength at the interface between media. The extent to which this is occurs is described by the refractive index ($n$) of the material. Refractive index describes the ratio of the velocity of light ($c$) in a vacuum to its velocity in a substance such as a mineral or pigment:

$$n = \frac{c \text{ vacuum (for practical purposes air)}}{c \text{ substance (in this case a pigment)}}$$

For most practical purposes, values for air can be used in place of those for a vacuum. Refractive index can also be defined as the ratio of the sine of the angle of incidence to the sine of the angle of refraction when light is refracted from a vacuum (or air) into the medium (*Figure 5.20*):

$$n \text{ (refractive index)} = \frac{\text{sine } i \text{ (angle of incidence)}}{\text{sine } r \text{ (angle of refraction)}}$$

In a paint film there are hundreds of interfaces or boundaries between pigment and medium. By successive refractions light can be returned to the surface. The bigger the difference between the refractive index of the pigment and the refractive index of the medium the more light is reflected at each interface and the more opaque the pigment

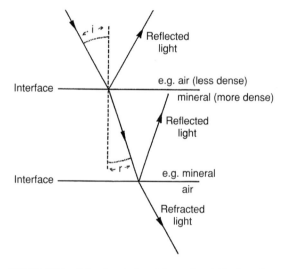

**Figure 5.20**  Refractive index ($n$) can be defined as the ratio of the sine of the angle of incidence ($i$) of light to the sine of the angle of refraction ($r$): $n = $ sine $i$/sine $r$

**Table 5.3** Pigments

| Colour/group Pigment name | Chemical composition and description | Origin/date | Properties | Refractive Index |
|---|---|---|---|---|
| **Whites** | | | | |
| Chalk (whiting) | One of many natural forms of calcium carbonate ($CaCO_3$). Fine, soft, microscopically homogeneous, white or whitish powder | Natural deposits | Low refractive index gives poor hiding power in oil but covers well in water paints. Dissolves in acids with evolution of $CO_2$. See also section 4.4.2 on grounds | 1.51–1.64 |
| Gypsum | Hydrated calcium sulphate $CaSO_4.2H_2O$. Fine, granular, crystalline | Natural deposits | | 1.52–1.53 |
| Lead white (flake white, Cremnitz white) | Basic lead carbonate ($2PbCO_3.Pb(OH)_2$), very fine white crystalline powder. The most important of the lead pigments | Artificially prepared from early times by the action of acetic acid on lead and subsequent reaction with carbon dioxide | Pure lead white in oil tends to chalk on weathering but does not crack or check and therefore leaves a good surface for repainting. Indoors, it tends to yellow. Blackened by sulphides in pigment mixtures or in air (but negligible in oil). Less good in watercolour or tempera. Toxic | 2.09 |
| Zinc white (Chinese white) | ZnO very finely divided, pure cold white, rounded particles or acicular crystals | Artificially prepared (1782). In use as water colour pigment from about 1834 and in oil from about 1850 | Oil films dry poorly. Requires more oil than lead white to form a paste. Unaffected by strong sunlight. Soluble in dilute alkalis. Can react with sulphides to form (white) zinc sulphide. Acicular form has greater tinting strength and hiding power. Non-poisonous. Oil films brittle | 2.00 |
| Titanium oxide | $TiO_2$. Extremely dense powerful opaque white. Mostly sold as a composite in which it is precipitated on a base of barium sulphate or calcium sulphate (typically 30% $TiO_2$: 70% $BaSO_4$). Both pure form and barium base form are fine and microcrystalline | Occurs in nature as Rutile but commercial pigment is prepared from titanated iron ore or Ilmenite ($FeTiO_3$). In use in paints from about 1920 | The whitest of the whites. Greatest hiding power of any white pigment. Very stable and non-reactive. Failure to react with drying oils leads to soft paint films that require additional ZnO or driers to compensate | 2.76 Rutile 1.75–2.5 Barium base |
| **Red and orange** | | | | |
| Vermilion (cinnabar) | Mercuric sulphide (HgS). Crystalline form is red, amorphous form is black. Red varies in colour due to differences in particle size. Artificial variety very finely divided and homogeneous. Translucent deep orange red particles, very deep red by transmitted light | Found as natural mineral cinnabar. Synthetic vermilion also available from very early times. Widely used in painting of nearly all periods and countries in the West since classical times | Excellent body and hiding power. Generally very stable and durable but may darken in direct sunlight especially in water colour or tempera and therefore largely replaced by cadmium red. Natural form indistinguishable from synthetic | 2.81–3.14 |
| Iron oxide reds – haematite, Indian red, light red, Mars red, Tuscan red, Venetian red | Iron oxide, anhydrous ($Fe_2O_3$) or hydrated ($Fe_2O_3.nH_2O$). Anhydrous oxide dark purple red or maroon, hydrated form warm red to dull yellow. Some varieties (e.g. haematite) transparent by transmitted light others opaque. Darker varieties show elongated splintery dark brown lustrous particles of haematite | Used since prehistoric times with continuous use in all periods. Difficult to distinguish natural from artificial varieties | Very stable. Unaffected by light or alkali | 2.78–3.01 Haematite |
| Red lead (minium) | Red tetroxide of lead ($Pb_3O_4$). Very opaque orange red, finely divided, crystalline or amorphous pigment with good hiding power | Artificially made but known from antiquity and used as a pigment into the Middle Ages | Reacts with nitric and acetic acids to form brown lead dioxide, with HCl to form white lead chloride and with sulphur to form black lead sulphide. Darkens on exposure to light and air. Artists' | 2.42 |

*continued*

**Table 5.3**  Pigments – continued

| Colour/group Pigment name | Chemical composition and description | Origin/date | Properties | Refractive Index |
|---|---|---|---|---|
| | | | use discontinued but still important in anti corrosive paints for iron. Toxic | |
| Dragon's blood | Not strictly a pigment. Dark red by reflected light but clear orange red by transmitted light | Dark red resinous exudate from fruit of the rattan palm (*Calamus draco*) | Soluble in alcohol and other organic solvents. Has been used for colouring varnishes but not much as an artists' colour. Fugitive unless locked in a resin film | |
| Madder lake | A mixture of alizarin and purpurin, both anthraquinone dyestuffs. Usually very fine crimson red powder | | Natural madder lake fluoresces under UV light but synthetic variety does not | |
| Alizarin crimson | 1,2-dihydroxyanthraquinone obtained from madder root (*Rubia tinctorum*). Lake pigment made by precipitating dye on aluminium hydrate (Al(OH)$_3$) | First isolated in 1826 and first synthesized in 1868. The first natural dyestuff to be made synthetically | Base is finely divided, semi-transparent, inert. Synthetic alizarin is among most light fast of organic red pigments but may not be permanent when mixed with earth colours | c 1.7 (base) |
| Cadmium red | Cadmium sulpho-selenide (CdS(Se)). Shades varying from deep maroon to vermilion can be prepared by varying the ratio of selenium to sulphur and the conditions of the reaction. Very small non-crystalline particles of very high refractive index | Prepared by precipitation from cadmium sulphate using sodium sulphide and selenium. Commercial production began *c.*1910 | Very good hiding power. Stable, light resistant popular modern pigment. Very toxic | 2.64–2.77 |
| **Yellow** | | | | |
| Yellow ochre | Ochres are natural earths consisting of silica and clay with colour (yellow, golden, red or brown) due to oxides of iron. Colour in yellow ochre is caused by hydrated forms of Fe$_2$O$_3$.H$_2$O chiefly goethite. Usually very small regular grains. Varies in shade, usually rather dull golden yellow by reflected light | Natural product in early and continuous use. Artificial product Mars yellow is also made | Ochres vary in hiding power, that of yellow ochre is good. Unaffected by acids and alkalis and permanent in all techniques | 2.0–2.3 |
| Massicot and litharge | Both forms of yellow lead monoxide PbO. Massicot is dull yellow, litharge usually contains a little red lead and is therefore a little more orange. Fine almost amorphous texture like lead white | Manufactured pigment known from antiquity | Good hiding power and properties similar to lead white. Unaffected by strong light but may revert to lead white on long exposure to damp air | 2.51–2.71 |
| Orpiment (King's yellow) | Arsenic trisulphide (As$_2$S$_3$). Brilliant rich lemon yellow in pure form. Crystalline, occurring in small flakes and fibrous masses. Coarsely ground to preserve rich colour. Surface appears glossy or waxy | Natural mineral known from ancient times. Once widely used but now largely abandoned because of toxicity and supply shortages | Highly refracting with fair hiding power. Stable to light, air and most chemicals but incompatible with some lead and copper pigments because of its sulphide content | 2.4–3.02 |
| Realgar | Natural orange red sulphide of arsenic (As$_2$S$_2$) closely related to orpiment and associated with it in nature | | The chemical and physical properties are similar to those of orpiment. Considered too poisonous for modern use | Slightly < orpiment |
| Mars yellow | Mars colours are artificial ochres precipitated from a solution containing alum and a soluble iron salt using alkali. This produces a yellow precipitate of variable colour depending on the proportions of alum used. When heated, the yellow gives rise to various shades of orange, red, | | | |

*continued*

**Table 5.3**   Pigments – continued

| Colour/group Pigment name | Chemical composition and description | Origin/date | Properties | Refractive Index |
|---|---|---|---|---|
| Hansa yellow | brown and violet. Very homogeneous and fine but with no significant advantages over natural yellow and red counterparts Permanent greenish yellow lake pigment made by precipitating one of a range of Hansa yellow dyes on an inert base. The dye is prepared from diazotized aromatic amines containing nitro or halogen groups coupled with aceto-acetanilide or its derivatives | | Good hiding power. Lightfast. Suitable for artists use. | |
| Naples yellow | Lead antimonate ($Pb_3(SbO_4)_2$). Varies from yellow to orange depending on the proportions of the oxides of lead and antimony chemically combined in the compound. Homogeneous, finely divided like massicot in appearance | Recipes for this pigment appear from the mid eighteenth century but a similar material was in use much earlier. Name now used to indicate shade of yellow rather than a specific compound | Good hiding power. Chemically stable but is darkened by hydrogen sulphide and is therefore more used in oil than in water based media | 2.01–2.88 |
| Chrome yellow | Lead chromate ($PbCrO_4$). Usually very fine rather opaque crystals varying in colour from lemon yellow to orange depending on particle size and conditions of preparation | Preparation described in 1809. Commercially available from c.1818. Commercially important pigment. Expensive | Pure lead chromate is fairly stable to light but may darken and become brown on ageing. May become green (by reduction to chromic oxide) in mixtures with organic pigments. Best used in oil | 2.31–2.49 |
| Barium yellow (Lemon yellow) | Barium chromate ($BaCrO_4$). Dull, pale, greenish yellow by reflected light but nearly colourless in transmitted light. Very fine crystalline or plate form | | Poor hiding power. Most stable of the chromate pigments. Soluble in dilute alkalis and mineral acids. Little affected by light but may become more greenish in strong light due to chromic oxide formation | 1.94–1.98 |
| Strontium yellow | Strontium chromate ($SrCrO_4$). Mass of finely divided needle-like crystals. Deeper and brighter than barium chromate, also sold as lemon yellow | | Greater hiding power than barium chromate | 1.92–2.01 |
| Cobalt yellow (Aureolin) | Complex compound – potassium cobaltinitrite ($CoK_3(NO_2)_6.H_2O$). Tiny crystals and crystal clusters, yellow by transmitted light | Discovered in 1848 and first used as a pigment in 1861. Expensive | Fair hiding power. Light fast but impure samples unstable. May accelerate fading of organic pigments itself turning brown in the process. Decomposed by strong alkalis and acids, slightly soluble in cold water | 1.72–1.76 |
| Cadmium yellow | Cadmium sulphide (CdS). Depending on the conditions of preparation, precipitated cadmium sulphide varies from lemon yellow to deep orange. Colour differences depend on the size and state of crystallinity of the pigment particles but all types are comparatively finely divided | Found as a mineral in nature but that used for pigments is precipitated from an acid solution of a soluble cadmium salt by the action of an alkaline sulphide or hydrogen sulphide gas. First used in 1829 commercially available from 1846 | High refractive index and therefore good hiding power. Permanent and fast to light. A very important yellow pigment. Toxic | 2.35–2.48 |
| Gamboge | Yellow resin produced by trees of the genus *Garcinia*. Used with indigo or Prussian blue as component of Hooker's green | | Used mainly in watercolour or in varnish. Permanent in oil but less so in watercolour when it fades in strong light | 1.58–1.59 |

*continued*

**Table 5.3**    Pigments – continued

| Colour/group Pigment name | Chemical composition and description | Origin/date | Properties | Refractive Index |
|---|---|---|---|---|
| **Green** | | | | |
| Green earth (terre verte) | Complex mixture of variable composition including glauconite and celadonite (hydro silicates of iron, magnesium, aluminium and potassium) ranging from neutral yellow to pale greenish grey. Coarse crystalline particles | From ancient times | Very stable and unaffected by light or chemical reagents such as acids and alkalis | 1.62 |
| Malachite | Basic copper carbonate ($CuCO_3.Cu(OH)_2$). Similar in chemical composition to azurite and often occurring in conjunction with it but containing more combined water. Crystalline fragments of a rather pale blue-green colour. | Natural mineral. Perhaps the oldest known bright green pigment. Widely used up to about 1800 | Decomposed by acids. Unaffected by light | 1.66–1.91 |
| Verdigris | Verdigris of commerce is dibasic copper acetate ($Cu(C_2H_3O_2)_2$. $2Cu(OH)_2$) but the term sometimes used for copper carbonate or other blue green corrosion products on copper. Clear blue-green crystals sometimes with pointed needles. Colour often very strong. Acetic odour | Prepared from ancient times by action of vinegar on copper. Numerous medieval recipes exist | Reactive and unstable pigment. Readily soluble in acids. Blackens readily with sulphur. Decomposes when heated. Fugitive unless locked up in protective coating | 1.53–1.56 |
| Copper resinate | Not strictly a pigment. Green compound (e.g. copper abietate) formed by dissolving verdigris in Venice turpentine or similar oleoresin | May have been used as early as the eighth century | Clear grass green when in good condition decaying to brown | |
| Cobalt green (Rinman's green, Zinc green) | Similar to cobalt blue but with aluminium oxide wholly or partly replaced by zinc oxide. Fine regular rounded transparent particles blue green in reflected light but pure green by transmitted light | Synthetic pigment discovered in 1780 but not in general use until the nineteenth century. Expensive | Semi-transparent pigment of low hiding power. Stable and inert and can be used safely in mixtures in all techniques | 1.94–2.0 |
| Chromium oxide (opaque) | $Cr_2O_3$. Dull opaque olive green of irregular and fairly coarse particle size | First used as artists' pigment c.1862. | Light-fast, stable and permanent in all painting techniques | 2.5 |
| Viridian (Guignet's green) | Transparent chromium oxide ($Cr_2O_3.2H_2O$). Deep cool green of great purity and transparency. Particles fairly large, irregular in size and slightly rounded | Synthetic. First prepared in 1838. Introduced as artists' pigment c.1860 | Exceptionally transparent pigment. High tinting strength. Stable in all media. Light-fast and unaffected by acids and alkalis | 1.82–2.12 |
| Chrome green | Homogeneous mixture of Prussian blue with chrome yellow. Colour varies from grass green to blue green. Blue and yellow particles cannot be separately distinguished as the blue coats the yellow | Described in 1809. In use from first quarter of the nineteenth century. Inexpensive | Very good hiding power. Commercially important but not sufficiently light-fast for use as artists' pigment. Sensitive to acids (turns blue) and to alkalis (turns dark orange) | 2.4 |
| Scheele's green | Copper hydro-arsenite ($CuHAsO_3$). Composition varies according to method of preparation. Rather opaque bright lime green. Irregularly shaped flakes of varying size | Synthetic. First prepared in 1778 | Blackened by lead. Decomposed by acids. Fades rapidly. Replaced by emerald green | |
| Emerald green (Paris green, Schweinfurt green), Veronese green | Copper aceto-arsenite ($Cu(C_2H_3O_2)_2.3Cu(AsO_2)_2$). Bright blue green. One of the most brilliant inorganic colours. Small rounded grains some appearing as trefoil or quatrefoil shapes | First prepared in 1814 | Fair hiding power. Very toxic and dangerous to handle. Blackened by sulphur gases and pigments containing sulphur. Fairly permanent in oil or varnish media | 1.71–1.78 |

*continued*

**Table 5.3**   Pigments – continued

| Colour/group Pigment name | Chemical composition and description | Origin/date | Properties | Refractive Index |
|---|---|---|---|---|
| Phthalocyanine green | Chlorinated copper phthalocyanine. Similar to phthalocyanine blue | Available commercially from 1938 | | 1.40 |
| **Blue** | | | | |
| Azurite (mountain blue) | A basic copper carbonate $(CuCO_3.Cu(OH)_2)$. Crystalline. Appears deep violet blue when ground coarsely but becomes paler and weaker in tinting strength if more finely ground | Natural pigment derived from the mineral azurite. Important from the fifteenth to the seventeenth centuries, now rarely used | Mostly used in tempera as it appears dark and 'muddy' in oil. Generally very stable but may discolour in contact with alkalis and can turn to green Malachite by hydration | 1.73–1.84 |
| Blue bice | Artificial basic copper carbonate similar to azurite. Usually more rounded and finer particles than azurite | Used extensively in medieval painting until the end of the eighteenth century | Once used in large quantities as cheaper, but less stable substitute for Azurite and Ultramarine. Tendency to turn green over time | 1.72–1.74 |
| Ultramarine – natural | A mixture of lazurite with calcspar and iron pyrites. Clear, often slightly purplish, blue crystalline particles of irregular size and shape. A few orange-red particles of iron pyrites are often seen with white crystalline calcite | Obtained from the semi-precious stone lapis lazuli. First occurs as pigment in sixth and seventh century wall paintings. In wide use until the early nineteenth century. Still available | | 1.50 |
| Ultramarine – synthetic (French ultramarine) | Chemically identical to natural ultramarine. A compound of sodium, silica, aluminium and sulphur. Two distinct kinds of ultramarine are made: soda ultramarine and sulphate ultramarine. It is possible to arrive at many subtly different shades according to the method of manufacture and the exact formula which can vary from $Na_8Al_6Si_6O_{22}S_4$ to $Na_{10}Al_6Si_6O_{24}S_2$. Finely divided homogeneous particles usually smaller and more rounded than those of natural product and lacking calcite and pyrites | In commercial production from about 1830 | Light-fast and stable under all conditions except in the presence of acids when it loses colour and evolves hydrogen sulphide gas. Ultramarine in oil may decolour and become grey with age due to presence of acids in the oil film. Ultramarine containing free sulphur may cause darkening when mixed with lead or copper pigments. Soda ultramarine contains a high percentage of silica and is sometimes called acid resisting. Sulphate ultramarine has a greenish tinge and lower covering power | 1.50 |
| Smalt | Formed from cobalt blue glass coloured by the addition of cobalt oxide formed by roasting cobalt containing minerals. Coarser particles give deep rich purple-blue. Finer particles only a pale blue. Very characteristic coarse glassy fragments | Used in Europe from the late sixteenth century (earlier in Asia) until the beginning of the nineteenth century when it was replaced by cobalt blue and artificial ultramarine | Stable but with very poor hiding power | 1.49–1.52 |
| Indigo | Blue vegetable colour used as both a dye and a pigment. Appears as intensely blue discrete particles at high magnification (1500×) | Obtained from plants of the genus Indigofera. Very early use in Far East. First synthesized in 1880 | Fair tinting strength. Can be used in oil but better in tempera or water colour. Very stable in tempera and resistant to fading by light but not when used in thin films | |
| Cobalt blue (Thénard's blue) | Cobalt aluminate $(CoO.Al_2O_3)$. Pure blue rounded particles, moderately fine and of irregular size. Bright blue by transmitted light | Discovered in 1802. Expensive and therefore liable to adulteration and substitution | Light-fast, very stable and permanent in all painting techniques | 1.74 |
| Cerulean blue | Cobaltous stannate $(CoO.nSnO_2)$. Finely divided rounded particles, high refractive index, green blue in transmitted light. Harmful | Known early in the nineteenth century but not commercially available until 1860 | Stable and inert, unaffected by light or strong chemicals | 1.84 |
| Prussian blue | A complex compound, technically ferric ferrocyanide $Fe_4(Fe(CN)6)_3$. | Earliest of 'modern' pigment colours first | Transparent but with high tinting strength. Fairly permanent but | 1.56 |

*continued*

**Table 5.3**   Pigments – continued

| Colour/group Pigment name | Chemical composition and description | Origin/date | Properties | Refractive Index |
|---|---|---|---|---|
| (Antwerp blue, Berlin blue, Paris blue, Chinese blue) | Very dark blue, finely divided, amorphous, green blue in transmitted light | made *c.*1704 and well known by 1750 | sensitive to alkalis. Very toxic by ingestion, inhalation and skin contact; in contact with acids liberates toxic gas | |
| Phthalo-cyanine Blue (Monastral blue) | An organic blue dyestuff having the empirical formula $C_{32}H_{16}N_8Cu$. Can be precipitated on aluminium hydroxide as a lake or used directly in non-aqueous media | Introduced in 1935 | Absorbs light almost completely in the red and yellow regions of the spectrum. Very high tinting strength. Very good light-fastness. Highly resistant to oxidation and reduction and to alkalis and most acids | 1.38 |
| **Violet** | | | | |
| Cobalt violet | Anhydrous cobalt phosphate ($Co_3(PO_4)_2$) – dark – or cobalt arsenate ($Co_3(AsO_4)_2$) – light – or a mixture of the two. Transparent reddish violet. Highly refracting irregular particles and particle clusters | Preparation of cobalt phosphate pigment first described in 1859. Expensive. | Transparent. Weak in tinting strength. Stable and unaffected by most chemical reagents. Can be used in all techniques | 1.65–1.81 |
| Manganese violet | Manganese ammonium phosphate ($(NH_4)_2Mn_2(P_2O_7)_2$). More nearly true violet than cobalt violet but dull. Rounded granules of rather irregular size bright red violet by reflected light but pale transparent mauve by transmitted light | First prepared in 1868 and introduced in 1890 | Permanent to light but with poor hiding power. Decomposed by strong acids and alkalis | 1.65–1.75 |
| Thio violet | Thio indigo red-violet B. An intense and brilliant synthetic organic pigment chemically related to indigo | | Very good resistance to light | |
| **Brown** | | | | |
| Raw sienna | A special kind of yellow ochre that comes from Sienna. Golden brown by transmitted light, it is a mixture of transparent yellow, red, brown and colourless particles with some opaque brown ones | | | 1.87–2.17 |
| Burnt sienna | Prepared by calcining raw sienna when the ferric hydroxide is converted to ferric oxide, becoming a warmer reddish brown. Amorphous, transparent | | | 1.85 |
| Raw umber | A brown earth pigment similar to ochres and siennas but containing 8–16% manganese dioxide in addition to hydrated ferric oxide. Heterogeneous in composition and particle size. Mainly fine darkish yellow brown grains but some orange, yellow and colourless particles | A natural mineral | Durable, compatible with other pigments and adaptable to all media | 1.87–2.17 |
| Burnt umber | Made by roasting the raw earth (see Burnt sienna). Slightly more transparent than raw umber | Not in general use in Europe until the end of the fifteenth century | Stable, unaffected by alkalis and dilute mineral acids. Dries well in oil because of manganese content but has a high oil absorption. Harmful by inhalation or if swallowed | 2.2–2.3 |
| Mars brown | see Mars yellow | | | |
| Brown ochre | Nearly pure limonite. See also Yellow ochre | | | |
| Bitumen | Brownish black naturally occurring mixture of hydrocarbons with oxygen, sulphur and nitrogen. | Known from ancient times. | Partially dissolves in oil to give reddish brown transparent film. Popular with English eighteenth | 1.64–1.66 |

*continued*

**Table 5.3** Pigments – continued

| Colour/group Pigment name | Chemical composition and description | Origin/date | Properties | Refractive Index |
|---|---|---|---|---|
| | Found as amorphous solid or semi-solid near oil deposits. | | century School but now little used as it never dries properly and tends to cause shrinkage leading to alligatoring and cracking of paint films applied over it. Soluble in turpentine etc. | |
| **Black** | | | | |
| Bone black (animal black, drop black) Ivory black | Blue black pigment made by charring animal bones in closed vessels. It is a mixture of carbon (10%) calcium phosphate (84%) and calcium carbonate (6%) and has a smooth dense texture. Irregular translucent blackish brown grains | | Popular pigment also sold as ivory black. Works well in oil and in water colour | 1.65–1.70 |
| | The most intense of all black pigments is made by charring waste cuttings of ivory in closed vessels. Term now also used for Bone black | | | Opaque |
| Lamp black | Nearly pure amorphous carbon prepared from burning mineral oil, tar, pitch or resin. Slightly bluish in colour. Very finely divided, uniform, homogeneous | | Makes good neutral greys. Residual oil content may make wetting by water based media difficult. Presence of phenols may retard drying of oils. | Opaque |
| Mars black Earth pigments | See Mars yellow Complex mixtures of minerals including clays, ochres, siennas, and umbers derived from mineral ores and sedimentary deposits | Used from ancient times | Mainly highly stable | Opaque |

*Sources*: Gettens and Stout (1966); Harley (1982); Mayer (1982)

will appear. The refractive index of some common pigments is shown in *Table 5.3*. The refractive index of chalk is very similar to the refractive index of fresh linseed oil medium (1.48) so that chalk in oil will be highly transparent. Rutile titanium oxide on the other hand has a much higher refractive index and is highly opaque in oil. Refractive index therefore makes a very important contribution to the covering power or hiding power of a paint. Particle size and shape are also important in this respect.

Particle size plays a large part in determining the extent to which a pigment will scatter light and to a considerable extent the amount of medium required to wet the pigment surface. For a given weight of pigment, as the size of particles is reduced, the number of interfaces available for scattering light increases but below a certain size the scatter-ing power decreases. Maximum scattering of light is achieved when the diameter of the pigment particle is approximately equal to the wavelength of light in the particle (this is about half the wavelength of light in air, or about 0.2–0.4 $\mu$m). Pigments have particle diameters ranging from about 0.01 $\mu$m to about 50 $\mu$m, although all samples of pigment contain a range of sizes of which the figure quoted will be an average. As particle size decreases, the total surface area increases and hence the amount of medium required to wet it will increase.

The shape of pigment particles is also important since it can affect hiding power, gloss and other properties such as water resistance. Some of the terms that may be used to describe pigment particles include spherical, cubic, nodular (rounded and irregular), acicular (needle-like or rod-like) and lamellar (plate like). Shape affects the way particles pack together and therefore affects hiding power. Rod shaped particles can act like reinforcing bars in concrete but can also project through the surface thereby reducing gloss but also providing a mechanical key for subsequent paint layers. Lamella particles, as found in aluminium and mica pigments, can overlap one another in paint films and confer increased water resistance on the paint film.

The tinting strength of pigments is a measure of the amount of a coloured pigment required to achieve a particular strength of colour. It is typically measured as the strength of colour achieved by one part of coloured pigment in twenty parts of pure zinc oxide. The tinting strength of a pigment is independent of its hiding power and even quite transparent pigments can have high tinting strengths.

### 5.8.3 Dyes

Dyes are organic molecules containing functional groups that absorb particular wavelengths of light giving rise to perceived colour (see section 5.8.1). The particle sizes of dyes are often on a molecular level allowing them to interpenetrate and stick to, or in some cases chemically react with, a variety of substrates. Their aggregates on fibres are too small to scatter light and therefore there are no white dyes. Unlike most pigments, most dyes can be prepared in solution. There is, however, some ambiguity of terminology in that some pigments, for example indigo and Prussian blue, are used as dyes. Some dyestuffs can also be made into pigments of larger particle size by precipitating them out of solution so that they are incorporated into an inorganic crystalline material such as aluminium hydroxide. These dye pigments are generically called lakes. Lakes are bright colours with low covering power and were especially useful in lightly pigmented paint layers or glazes. Lakes have a reputation for being highly fugitive and in may cases have only survived unchanged where protected from light. However, very high quality alizarin crimsons have been produced since the 1920s that remain permanent under conditions that cause older or inferior varieties to fail.

Dyes may be animal, vegetable or mineral in origin. Vegetable dyes are cheap and ubiquitous and may be extracted from leaves, roots, seeds, flowers and from woods that are particularly rich in coloured extractives such as Brazilwood (*Caesalpinia braziliensis* and related spp.), logwood (*Haematoxylon campechianum*) and Sanders wood (*Pterocarpus santalinus*). Dyes of animal origin include lac, kermes and cochineal (carmine) from insects and Tyrian purple extracted from shellfish of the genus Murex. Mineral dyes and stains include iron browns and blacks, and blue–green copper acetate (verdigris).

The age of synthetic dyes began with the synthesis of Perkin's Mauve by William Perkin in 1856. Many more colours were synthesized from a chemical derived from coal-tar (aniline) before the end of the century. Today there are many thousands of synthetic dyes available, some of which, such as CIBA Orasol dyes and BASF Basantol dyes, show excellent stability.

The use of dyes is as ancient as the use of pigments and many dyes have been sold as stains for wood. Dyes are far less stable than pigments, however, and tend to fade in colour or even disappear in extreme cases. Dyes have been used to colour all porous substrates, and penetrate well due to their small size. They bond to the substrates by various mechanisms including hydrogen bonding (e.g. direct dyes), non polar forces, due to matching shapes of dye and substrate molecules, ionic forces, and covalent bonding (e.g. reactive dyes).

Most natural dyes are dependent on a mordant (from the Latin word 'to bite') to help fix them to the substrate. Traditional mordants were compounds of iron, copper, tin, chrome and aluminium such as alum (potassium aluminium sulphate) and copperas (ferrous sulphate). Tin and chromium salts yield particularly bright colours but are relatively modern, their use dating from about 1630 and 1850 respectively. Many single dye sources will yield a variety of colours depending on the mordant. Madder root for example will yield orange with tin, maroon with chrome, yellow with copper and brown with iron. Further information on dyes is given in Chapter 3 and in the bibliography to that chapter.

### 5.8.4 Stains

The terms stain and staining are used to describe any sort of material and process used

**Table 5.4**  Some traditional colorants for wood

| Yellow | Brown | Red | Green and blue | Black |
|---|---|---|---|---|
| Turmeric (*Curcuma longa*) | Catechu | Alkanet root (Anchusa) | Emerald rot (*Cholorosplenium aeruginascens* (see Blanchette, 1992) (green) | Logwood + vinegar and rusty iron mixture used to stain sycamore and maple grey (harewood) |
| Saffron | Blueberry + alum + nut galls | Brazil wood (+ solution of tin in aqua regia) | Boil in alum then immerse in mixture of verdigris, ammonia and acetic acid. Used on wood and ivory for green | Lamp black + turpentine + drying oil |
| Apple + alum | Currant bush + alum | Dragon's blood | Blueberry berries + alum + iron sulphate (blue) | Sulphuric acid (on oak) |
| Ash + alum | Tannic acid from gall nuts and oak bark followed by alkali | Madder with gum or starch + iron acetate | Aniline dyes | Hot sand |
| Dilute nitric acid | Strong nitric acid | Red Sanders wood | | Anilines (e.g. nigrosine) |
| Gamboge | Dilute sulphuric acid | Quicklime slaked in urine | | |
| Aniline dyes | Potassium permanganate Potassium/sodium hydroxide Ammonia Sodium carbonate Hot sand Green husks of walnut Vandyke brown Potassium bichromate Aniline dyes | Potassium bichromate Aniline dyes (e.g. Bismarck brown) | | |

on wood to add colour while still maintaining a high degree of transparency. Stains have been used for decoration, for imitation and for faking. Up to about 1650 furniture was generally made from wood grown close to home and stains were used to increase the range of colours available. From about 1660, when timber prices were rising, stain was used to make cheaper woods simulate more expensive ones. For example, beech could be made to resemble walnut and pear to look like ebony. Stains have also been used to offset the variation in wood from tree to tree and from sapwood to heart wood, no doubt helping to reduce costs. From about the 1830s the increase in volume of furniture production and reduction in prices lead to the production of 'Old English' furniture in which stain was used to simulate age. Many different kinds of materials have been used for staining (see *Table 5.4*). Once in place, however it is often

difficult to find out what they are or even whether they have been used. Recipes for staining wood are found in the earliest technological treatises and were copied and re-copied over the centuries. Traditional colorants for wood came from a variety of sources. The textile industry was a primary source for dyes such as cochineal, Brazilwood and logwood and greatly increased the availability of useful colorants for wood finishers. Publications on textile history and conservation serve as a useful resource on traditional colorants (Landi, 1992). Aniline dyes were discovered in the mid-nineteenth century and subsequently applied in the furniture industry. More recently aniline dyes have been replaced by organic complexes of chromium, cobalt and copper that are highly stable, light fast materials. Further information on the history of furniture colorants is given by Mussey (1982, 1987).

A vast array of stains is now available for wood and it is sometimes difficult to choose the most appropriate one. Stains may be classified according to their reactivity, transparency and the vehicle in which they are applied. Different stains have various advantages and disadvantages with respect to the quality of their effect, their permanence, the extent to which they raise the grain of the wood, penetration, speed of drying and so forth. These materials may be referred to as transparent stains which are non-reactive colorants without pigment, translucent stains which are non-reactive colorants with pigments, and chemical stains which are reactive colorants without pigment. These groups of stains are further considered, in relation to their application, in Chapter 13.

### 5.8.5 Identification of pigments, dyes and stains

The colour of pigments under daylight and under ultra violet light are two macroscopic methods that may be of use. For routine identification of pigments on a day-to-day basis excellent microscopic and chemical methods are available. However, for non-destructive analysis of pigments in situ, for quantitative assessment of very small samples and for some more specialized applications, advanced instrumental methods of analysis may be required.

Some pigments fluoresce under UV light and some will also affect the natural UV fluorescence of binding media. Natural madder lake fluoresces pink, zinc white fluoresces greenish-yellow and cadmium yellow, orange and red pigments also fluoresce under UV (De la Rie, 1982). The false colour of some pigments under infra red light may serve as a guide to their identification and has been comprehensively investigated by Moon *et al.* (1992).

Microscopic techniques frequently provide positive identification of pigments on the basis of their size, shape and optical behaviour in polarized and crossed polarized light. Micro-scale sampling and identification of most artists' pigment particles has been organized in flow chart fashion arranged by each colour (McCrone, 1982). McCrone now recommends the use of Meltmount, a mounting medium free from polychlorinated bi-phenyls (PCBs).

The application of microchemical tests to pigment identification has been described by Plesters (1956). De Keijzer (1988) has analysed modern synthetic blue pigments using micro-crystallization and colour change on acidification. Complex mixtures of pigments or impurities found in paints may result in competing reactions from the chemistry outlined in the laboratory manuals cited above. It may therefore be necessary to identify unknown materials by alternative methods.

Organic pigments have been analysed by Pey (1989) and Schweppe (1989) using thin layer chromatography (TLC) and by Wouters and Verhecken (1989) and Pey (1989) with high pressure liquid chromatography (HPLC). Hofenk-de-Graaf (1969) also describes methods by which organic dyes can be analysed. TLC, HPLC and mass spectrometry have been used to identify xylindein, a green coloration produced by the fungus Chlorociboria (Michaelsen *et al.*, 1992, see also Blanchette *et al.*, 1992). The use of indigo as a wood stain has been identified by several spectroscopic methods (Buchholz, 1991).

Solution and high order derivative spectrophotometry has been used to identify the large number of organic pigments that have come into common usage in the twentieth century (Billmeyer *et al.*, 1982; Risti-Solaji, 1990). Wakeford and Wardman (1989) has used derivative reflectance spectroscopy to identify organic blue pigments from tints prepared in titanium white. Guineau (1989) reports that samples as small as 5 µg could be positively identified with Raman spectroscopy. Varlashkin and Low (1986) has demonstrated the use of the non-destructive technique, infra red photo thermal beam deflection spectroscopy (PBDS) to identify black inks on paper, and the components of a dagger. McMillan and Hofmeister (1988) provides an overview of infra red and Raman methods used to identify minerals.

The elemental composition of pigments from painted passages can be suggested by study of the X-ray image though one should be extremely cautious in arriving at such conclusions based on X-ray observations alone (see Rees-Jones in Van Schoute (1986) for information on the X-ray absorptivity of specific pigmented paints of varying thickness). Gold leaf, being so thin, is usually transparent to X-rays. X-ray diffraction (XRD) identifies crystalline materials according to their crystalline d-spacings. Amorphous material present in the sample or the mounting material will contribute to the background of the signal. Fitz (1978) has discussed the optimal working conditions for the Debye-Scherrer powder diffraction camera used to identify samples about 0.1 mm in size. The technique is most commonly employed to identify inorganic materials, though the morphology and effect of processing on polymers can also be studied by XRD. Energy dispersive X-ray fluorescence will provide a quantitative and qualitative profile of the elements present in situ in a paint layer or pigment sample. For pigment identification this technique generally needs to be used in conjunction with microscopic examination of cross sections. Autoradiography following neutron beam activation has been used by Meyers *et al.* (1982) to identify the elements Mn, Cu, Na, As, P, Hg and Co in pigments. These elements become radioactive products with unique half-life decay emissions that modify the exposure of the film. SEM-EDS is useful for elemental analysis of pigment compositions. Although no published data exist, EDS can be utilized in detecting penetration profile of chemical stains such as bichromate, or ferrous stains. The laser microprobe may be a useful technique in elemental analysis of cross-sections.

# Bibliography

Abrahart, E.N. (1977) *Dyes and Their Intermediates*, Chemical Publishing

Aitken, W.C. (1866) Papier mâché manufacture, in *The Birmingham & Midland Hardware District Journal*, reprinted in *The Quarterly*, British Association of Paper Historians Journal, 1999, No. 29

Amoroso, G.G. and Fassina, V. (1983) *Stone Decay and Conservation*, Elsevier

Anon (1798) *The Cabinet Maker's Guide*, Knight and Lacy, London (Ansel Phelps, Greenfield, Massachusetts, 1925, etc.)

Beck, C.W. (1982) Authentication and conservation of amber: conflict of interests, in *Science and Technology in the Service of Conservation*, Preprints to the Washington Congress, 3–9 September, IIC, pp. 104–7

Billmeyer, F.W Jr, Pamer, T. and Saltzman, M. (1982) Pigment analysis for conservation, in *Science and Technology in the Service of Conservation*, Preprints to the Washington Congress, 3–9 September, IIC, pp. 177–9

Blanchette, R.A., Wilmering, A. and Baumeister, M. (1992) The use of green-stained wood caused by the fungus Chlorociboria in intarsia masterpieces from the 15th century, *Holzforschung*, 46, 225–32

Brachert, T. (ed.) (1986) *Beiträge zur Konstruktion und Restaurierung alter Möbel*, Callwey

Brady, G.S. and Clauser, H.R. (1977) *Materials Handbook*, 11th edn, McGraw Hill

Brandner, W. (1976) Die Restaurierung einer Garnitur Augsburger Prunkmöbel, *Jahrbuch der Staatlichen Kunstsammlungen in Baden Württemberg* 13, 55–64

Brown, S. and O'Connor, D. (1991) *Glass Painters*, British Museum Press

Buchholz, R. (1991) Eingedrückte Streifen an Holzobjekten, *Restauro*, 97 (6), 375–83

Burek, M. (1989) *Der Fiesole-Altar Im Domschatz Zu Hildesheim*, Institut für Museumskunde an der Staatlichen Akademie der Bildenden Kunste, Stuttgart, p. 108

Buys, S. and Oakley, V. (1994) *Conservation and Restoration of Ceramics*, Butterworth-Heinemann

Clarke, C.D. (1971) *Moulding and Casting*, The Standard Arts Press

Collings, T. and Milner, D. (1990) A new chronology of papermaking technology, *The Paper Conservator*, 14, 58–62

Côté, W.A. (ed.) (1980) *Papermaking Fibers*, Syracuse University Press

Cox, K. (1972) Minerals and rocks, in I.G. Gass, P.J. Smith and R.C.L. Wilson (eds), *Understanding the Earth*, 2nd edn, Artemis, pp. 13–40

Creswell, R.G. (1992) The radiocarbon dating of iron artifacts using accelerator mass-spectrometry, *Historical Metallurgy*, 25, 78–85

Cummins, J. (1986) Visit to a glue factory, *Fine Woodworking*, 57, 66–9

Currey, J.D. (1980) Mechanical properties of mollusc shell, in J.F.V. Vincent and J.D. Curry (eds), *The Mechanical Properties of Biological Materials*, Society for Experimental Biology Symposium No. XXXIV, Cambridge University Press, pp. 75–97

de Bellaigue, G. (1974) *The James A. De Rothschild Collection at Waddesdon Manor. Furniture, Clocks and Gilt Bronzes*, National Trust, London

De Keijzer, M. (1988) The blue, violet and green modern synthetic organic pigments of the 20th century used as artist's pigments, in *Modern Organic Coatings*, Scottish Society for Conservation and Restoration, Edinburgh, pp. 97–103

De la Rie, E.R. (1982) Fluorescence of paint and varnish layers, in *Studies in Conservation*, Part I: 27, 1–7; Part II: 27, 65–9; Part III: 27, 102–8

De Voe, S.S. (1971) *English Papier Mâché of the Georgian and Victorian Periods*, Wesleyan University Press

Dickinson, G. (1925) *English Papier Mâché, Its Origin, Development and Decline*, The Courier Press

Dietrich, R.V. (1989) *Stones: Their Collection, Identification and Uses*, 2nd edn, Geoscience Press

Dresdner, M. (1989) Aniline dyes, *Fine Woodworking*, May, 50

Driggers, J.M., Mussey, R.D. and Garvin, S.M. (1991) Treatment of an ivory inlaid Anglo-Indian desk bookcase, in AIC Wooden Artifacts Group, Conference Papers, Albuquerque

Edwards, H.G.M., Farwell, D.W., Holder, J.M. and Laeson, E.E. (1998) Fourier Transform Raman spectroscopy of ivory: a non-destructive diagnostic technique, *Studies in Conservation*, 43, 9–16

Espinoza, E.O. and Mann, M. (1992) *Identification Guide for Ivory and Ivory Substitutes*, 2nd edn, World Wildlife Fund

Feller, R.L. (1972) Scientific examination of artistic and decorative colorants, *Journal of Paint Technology*, 44, 51–8

Feller, R. (ed.) (1986) *Artists Pigments*, Vol. 1, National Gallery of Art, Washington, DC

Fennimore, D.L. (1996) *Metalwork in Early America: Copper and Its Alloys from the Winterthur Collection*, Henry Francis Du Pont Winterthur Museum

Fitz, S. (1978) Identification of pigments in paintings with X-ray powder diffraction method – possibilities and limits, in ICOM Committee for Conservation, Preprints 5th Triennial Meeting, Zagreb

Fleming, J. and Honour, H. (1977) *Dictionary of the Decorative Arts*, Harper and Row

Flexner, R. (1994) *Understanding Wood*, Rodale Press

Frank, S. (1982) *Glass and Archaeology*, Academic Press

Fraquet, H. (1987) *Amber*, Butterworths

Fraser, R.D.B. and Macrae, T.P. (1980) Molecular structures and mechanical properties of keratins, in J.F.V. Vincent and J.D. Curry (eds) *The Mechanical Properties of Biological Materials*, Society for Experimental Biology Symposium, No. XXXIV, Cambridge University Press, pp. 211–47

Gayathri, P. (1983) A note on the fluorescence of ivory, *Journal of Archaeological Chemistry*, 1, 43–5

Gettens, R.J. and Stout, G.L. (1966) *Painting Materials*, Dover

Giusti, A.M. (1992) *Pietre Dure, Hardstone in Furniture and Decorations*, Philip Wilson Publishers, p. 311

Gonzelez-Polacios, A. (1982) *The Art of Mosaics: Selections from the Gilbert Collection*, Los Angeles County Museum of Art

Goodwin, T.W. (1965) *Chemistry and Biochemistry of Plant Pigments*, Academic Press

Gordon, J.E. (1976) *The New Science of Strong Materials or Why You Don't Fall Through the Floor*, 2nd edn, Pelican

Gregory, R.L. (1966) *Eye and Brain*, World University Library

Guineau, B. (1989) Non-destructive analysis of organic pigments and dyes using raman microprobe, microfluorimeter or absorption microspectrophotometer, *Studies in Conservation*, 34, 38–44

Hackney, S., Townsend, J. and Eastaugh, N. (eds) (1990) *Dirt and Pictures Separated*, Papers from the joint UKIC and Tate Gallery Conference, London

Hall, C. (1981) *Polymer Materials – an Introduction for Technologists and Scientists*, Macmillan

Halstead, L.B. (1974) *Vertebrate Hard Tissues*, Wykeham Publishers

Hamer, F. and Hamer, J. (1977) *Clays*, Pitman and Watson-Guptill

Hamilton, W.R., Woolley, A.R. and Bishop, A.C. (1992) *Minerals Rocks and Fossils*, Hamlyn

Hardwick, P. (1981) *Discovering Horn*, Lutterworth Press

Harley, R.D. (1982) *Artists' Pigments c.1600–1835*, Butterworths

Hayward, C.H. (1974) *Staining and Polishing*, Drake Publishers

Hill, G.C. and Holman, J.S. (1978) *Chemistry in Context*, Nelson

Hodges, H. (1964) *Artifacts*, John Baker

Hofenk-de-Graaf, J.H. (1969) Natural dyestuffs, chemical constitution, identification, *ICOM Committee for Conservation*, Amsterdam, 69/16, 112

Hoffman, M. (1939) *Sculpture Inside and Out*, W.W. Norton

Holzapffel, C. and Holzapffel, J.J. (1843) *Turning and Mechanical Manipulation*, Vol. 1, Holzapffel and Co. (Five volume set published 1843–1883; vols. II, IV and V available in reprint editions from The Astragal Press)

Horie, C.V. (1987) *Materials for Conservation*, Butterworths

Hughes, B. and Hughes, T. (1958) *Small Antique Furniture*, Lutterworth Press

Hughes, R. and Rowe, M. (1982) *The Colouring Bronzing and Patination of Metals*, Crafts Council

Hunter, D. (1978) *Papermaking, The History and Technique of an Ancient Craft*, Dover (1st edn, 1943)

Inman, T.B. (1990) Evaluating wood finishes, *Fine Woodworking*, May, 62–4

Jaeckel, K. (1978) Die restaurierung des Bamberger Psalters, *Maltechnik-Restauro*, 84 (2), 96–9

Jehle, H. (1995) Elfenbein – Überlegungen zum Material und zu seiner Verarbeitung, *Zeitschrift für Kunsttechnologie und Konservierung*, 9, 337–47

Jervis, S. (1972) *Antler and Horn Furniture*, Victoria and Albert Museum Yearbook, 3, 87–99

Johnson, W.M. and Maxwell, J.A. (1981) *Rock and Mineral Analysis*, 2nd edn, John Wiley & Sons

Jones, Y. (1982) *Georgian and Victorian Japanned Wares in the West Midlands*, Wolverhampton Art Gallery and Museums

Kingery, W.D. (1960) *Introduction to Ceramics*, Wiley

Kingery, W.D. (ed.) (1986) *Ceramics and Civilization*, 3 vols, American Ceramic Society, Waterville, Ohio

Kisluk-Grosheide, D. (1991) A group of early eighteenth-century 'Ausburg' mirrors, *Furniture History* (Journal of the Furniture History Society), 27, 1–18

Koestler, R.J., Indictor, N. and Harneman, R. (1990) 'Ancient Near Eastern ivories imaged and analyzed with environmental scanning electron microscope and conventional scanning electron microscopy', *Scanning*, 90, 73–4

Koller, M. (1989) Zur Technik und Restaurierung dreier Kunstschränke aus der Zeit Um 1600, *Restauratorenblätter*, 10, 88–97

Kornerup, A. and Wanscher, J.H. (1978) *Methuen Handbook of Colour*, 3rd edn, Eyre Methuen

Krill, J. (1987) *English Artists Papers*, Trefoil Publications, London

Krzyszkowska, O. (1990) Ivory and related materials, an illustrated guide, *Bulletin of the Institute of Classical Studies*, Supplement 59

Kühn, H. (1986) *Conservation and Restoration of Works of Art and Antiquities*, Butterworths

Lafontaine, R.H. and Wood, P.A. (1982) The stabilization of ivory against relative humidity fluctuations, *Studies in Conservation*, 27, 109–17

Landi, S. (1992) *The Textile Conservators Manual*, 2nd edn, Butterworth-Heinemann

Larney, J. (1975) *Restoring Ceramics*, Watson-Guptill

Larsen, E.B. (1984) *Electrotyping*, The School of Conservation, The Royal Danish Art Academy, Copenhagen

Larsen, E.B. (1993) *Moulding and Casting of Museum Objects*, The School of Conservation, The Royal Danish Art Academy, Copenhagen

Larson, J. (1978) The conservation of marble monuments in churches, *The Conservator*, 2, 20–5

Larson, J. (1979) The conservation of alabaster monuments in churches, *The Conservator*, 3, 28–33

Laver, M. (1978) Spot-tests in conservation: metals and alloys, ICOM Committee for Conservation, Preprints 5th Triennial Meeting, Zagreb

Lazzarini, L., Moschini, G. and Stievano, B.M. (1980) A contribution to the identification of Italian, Greek and Anatolian marbles through a petrological study and the evaluation of Ca/Sr ratio, *Archaeometry*, 22 (2), 173–82

Liefkes, F. (1980) De ivoren meubelen van Maurits de Braziliaan, *Antiek*, 14, 381–400

Liles, J.N. (1990) *The Art and Craft of Natural Dyeing*, University of Tennessee Press

Lindner, G. (1977) *Seashells of the World* (translated and edited by Gwynne Vevers), Blandford Press

Lins, A. (1991) Basic physical properties of gold leaf, in D. Bigelow (ed.), *Gilded Wood: Conservation and History*, Sound View Press, pp. 17–26

MacGregor, A. (1985) *Bone Antler Ivory and Horn*, Croom Helm/Barnes & Noble

Maryon, H. (1971) *Metalwork and Enamelling*, Dover

Matienzo, L.J. and Snow, C.E. (1986) The chemical effects of hydrochloric acid and organic solvents on the surface of ivory, *Studies in Conservation*, 31, 133–9

Mayer, R. (1982) *The Artist's Handbook of Materials and Techniques*, 4th edn (ed. E. Smith), Faber

McCann, M. (1979) *Artist Beware*, Watson Guptill

McCrone, W.C. (1982) The microscopical identification of artists' pigments, in *J IIC-CG*, 7, 1/2, 11–34

McLaren, K. (1983) *The Colour Science of Dyes and Pigments*, Adam Hilger

McMillan, P.F. and Hofmeister, A.M. (1988) Infrared and Raman spectroscopy: spectroscopic methods in minerals and geology, *Reviews in Mineralogy*, 18, 99–159

Mechanics Register (1837) *The Mechanics' Register, Journal of the Useful Arts*, Philadelphia, Vol. 1, No. 2, 28–9

Meilbach, D.A. (1977) *Decorative and Sculptural Ironwork*, Crown Publishers

Meyers, P., Ainsworth, M.W., Brealey, J. *et al.* (1982) The application of neutron activation autoradiography in the study of paintings by Rembrandt and related artists, in *Science and Technology in the Service of Conservation*, Preprints of the Contributions to the Washington Congress, 3–9 September, IIC, London, pp. 165–8

Michaelsen, H., Unger, A. and Fischer, C.H. (1992) Blaugrüne Färbung an Intarsienhölzern des 16. bis 18. Jahrhunderts, *Restauro*, 98, 17–25

Millar, W. (1899) *Plastering Plain and Decorative*, B.T. Batsford

Moncrieff, A. and Weaver, G. (1992) *Science for Conservators*, Crafts Council Conservation Teaching Series, Routledge

Monna, D., Pensabene, P. and Sodini, J.P. (1983) L'identificazione dei marmi: necessita, metodi, limiti, in E. Dolci (ed.), *Marmo Restauro*, Museo del Marmo, Carrara, pp. 34–60

Moon, T., Schilling, M. and Thirkettle, S. (1992) A note on the false-color IR photography in conservation, *Studies in Conservation*, 37, 42–52

Mussey, R.D. (1982) Old finishes, *Fine Woodworking*, 33 (March–Apr), 71–5

Mussey, R.D. (ed.) (1987) *The First American Finisher's Manual*, Dover (originally published as *The Cabinet-Maker's Guide* in 1825)

Newell, R. (1982) A review of methods for identifying scrap metals, *Information Circular 8902*, US Department of Interior, Washington, DC, p. 19

Newman, H. (1977) *An Illustrated Dictionary of Glass*, Thames and Hudson

Newman, L.S. and Hartley, J. (1979) *Electroplating and Electroforming for Artists and Craftsmen*, Crown Publishers

Newton, R.G. (1982) *The Deterioration and Conservation of Painted Glass: A Critical Bibliography*, Oxford University Press

Newton, R. and Davison, S. (1989) *Conservation of Glass*, Butterworth-Heinemann (2nd edn, S. Davison, 2003)

O'Connor, S. (1987a) The identification of osseous and keratinaceous materials at York, in *Archaeological Bone, Antler and Ivory*, Proceedings of a Conference held by UKIC Archaeology Section, December, Occasional Papers, 5, pp. 9–21

O'Connor, T.P. (1987b) On the structure, chemistry and decay of bone, antler and ivory, in *Archaeological Bone, Antler and Ivory*, Proceedings of a Conference held by UKIC Archaeology Section, December, Occasional Papers, 5, pp. 6–8

Osborne, H. (ed.) (1984) *The Oxford Companion to Art*, Clarendon Press

Osborne, H. (ed.) (1985) *The Oxford Companion to the Decorative Arts*, Oxford University Press

Panshin, A.J. and De Zeeuw, C. (1980) *Textbook of Wood Technology*, 4th edn, McGraw-Hill

Parkes, P.A. (1987) *Current Scientific Techniques in Archaeology*, St Martin's Press

Pelz, K. (1992) Die Restaurierung eines Schreibtisches von Johann Melchior Kambli, *Arbeitsblätter für Restauratoren*, 25, 117–25

Penniman, T.K. (1952) *Pictures of Ivory and other Animal Teeth, Bone and Antler*, Occasional Papers on Technology 5, Pitt Rivers Museum, University of Oxford

Pey, E.B.F. (1989) The organic pigments of the Hafkensheid collection, *Restauro*, 95, 146–50

Pillement, J.N. (1959) *The Ladies Amusement or the Whole Art of Japanning Made Easy*, 2nd edn. A facsimilie of the edition of 1762, Ceramic Book Co.

Plenderleith, H.J. and Werner, A.E.A. (1971) *The Conservation of Antiquities and Works of Art*, 2nd edn, Oxford University Press

Plesters, J. (1956) Cross-sections and chemical analysis of paint samples, *Studies in Conservation*, 3, 110–55

Poller, T. (1980) Die Herstellung von duennen klaren Hornblettern, *Maltechnik-Restauro*, 86 (2), 124–5

Poppe, Goto (1991) *European Sea Shells*, Verlag Christa Hemmen

Press, F. and Siever, R. (1986) *Earth*, 4th edn, Freeman

Rado, P. (1969) *An Introduction to the Technology of Pottery*, Pergamon Press

Rao, S. and Subbaiah, K.V. (1983) Indian ivory, *Journal of Archeological Chemistry*, 1, 1–10

Rhodes, D. (1973) *Clay and Glazes for the Potter*, Chilton

Rhodes, D. (1978) *Stoneware and Porcelain: The Art of High Fired Pottery*, Pitman

Rice, P.C. (1980) *Amber, the Golden Gem of the Ages*, VNR

Rich, J.C. (1947) *The Materials and Methods of Sculpture*, Oxford University Press

Richie, C. (1970) *Carving Shells and Cameos*, Barnes

Richie, C. (1974) *Shell Carving: History and Techniques*, Barnes

Riederer, J. (1981) *Kunstwerke chemisch betrachtet*, Springer-Verlag

Risti-Solaji, M. (1990) *Higher Order Derivative Spectrophotometry for Identification and Quantitative Estimation of Synthetic Organic Artists' Pigments*, Institut für Technische Chemie, Munich

Rogers, J.E. (1908) *The Shell Book*, Doubleday, Page & Co.:

Rolt, L.T.C. (1965) *A Short History of Machine Tools*, MIT Press

Ryser, F. (1991) *Verzauberte Bilder, Die Kunst der Malerei hinter Glas von der Anike bis zum 18. Jahrhundert*, Klinkhardt & Biermann

Schneider, G. (1990) Die Verwendung von Stecknadeln an spätmittelalterlichen Bildwerken, *Zeitschrift für Kunsttechnologie und Konservierung*, 4, 251–60

Schniewind, A.P. and Arganbright, D.G. (1984) Coatings and their effect on dimensional stability of wood, *Western Association for Art Conservation Newsletter*, May

Schott, F.L. (1988) Eglomise, Technik und Konservierung, *Restauro*, 94, 9–16

Schweppe, H. (1989) Identification of red madder and insect dyes by thin layer chromatography, in S.H. Zeronian and H. Needles (eds), *Historic Textile and Paper Materials II, Conservation and Characterization*, ACS Symposium Series 410, American Chemical Society: Washington, DC, pp. 188–219

Scott, D.A. (1991) *Metallography and Microstructure of Ancient and Historic Metals*, The Getty Conservation Institute

Scott-Mitchell, F. (1905) *Practical Gilding, Bronzing and Lacquering*, Trade Papers Publishing Co.

Segebade, C. (1993) Naturwissenschaftliche Untersuchungen an Boulle Marketerien Valentin Zindters In Jahrbuch (1988), *Der Bayerischen Denkmalpflege*, 42, 138–43

Segebade, C. (1994) Prinzipien und einige Anwendungen der Neutronen-und Photonegativierungsanalyse, in *Fourth International Conference: Non-Destructive Testing of Works of Art*, Berlin, 3–8 October, Berichtsband, 45, Teil 1, pp. 326–46

Shepard, A.O. (1968) *Ceramics for the Archaeologist*, Publication 609, Carnegie Institute: Washington

Sheraton, Thomas (1803) *The Cabinet Dictionary*, Praeger facsimile edition 1970

Shrager, A.M. (1949) *Elementary Metallurgy and Metallography*, Dover

Siddons, G.A. (1830) *The Cabinet Makers Guide*, 5th edn, printed for Sherwood, Gilbert and Piper, Paternoster Row, London

Singer, Charles *et al.* (eds.) (1954–1958), *A History of Technology*, 5 vols, Oxford University Press

Sinkankas, J. (1955) *Gem Cutting: a Lapidary's Manual*, Van Nostrand Reinhold

Slater, E.A. and Tennant, N.H. (eds) (1979) *The Conservation and Restoration of Metals*, Conference Proceedings, Scottish Society for Conservation and Restoration: Edinburgh

Smith, G.F.H. (1972) *Gemstones*, 14th edn, Pitman Publishing (1st edn 1912)

Snow, C.E. and Weisser, T.D. (1994) The examination and treatment of ivory and related materials, in *Adhesives and Consolidants*, IIC Preprints, pp. 141–5

Soggnaes, R.F. (1960) The ivory core of tusks and teeth, *Clinical Orthopaedics and Related Research*, 17, 43–62

Sperisen, F. (1961) *The Art of the Lapidary*, Bruce Publishing

Stalker, J. and Parker, G. (1688) *A Treatise of Japanning and Varnishing*, London (republished A. Tiranti, London, 1950)

Starling, K. and Watkinson, D. (eds) (1987) *Archaeological Bone, Antler and Ivory*, UKIC Occasional Paper No. 5, United Kingdom Institute for Conservation

Storch, P.S. (1987) The analysis and conservation of an historic wooden gate, *Recent Advances in Conservation and Analysis of Artifacts*, Summer School Press, University of London

Stratmann, R. (1975) Eine Garnitur Ausburger Prunkmöbel des frühen 18. Jahrhunderts, in *Jahrbuch der Staatlichen Kunstsammlungen*, Baden Württemberg, 12, pp. 157–70

Street, A. and Alexander, W. (1979) *Metals in the Service of Man*, Pelican

Streeter, D. (1980) *Professional Smithing*, Charles Scribner's Sons

Strelis, I. and Kennedy, R.W. (1967) *Identification of North American Commercial Pulpwoods and Pulp Fibers*, University of Toronto Press

Suppan, P. (1972) *Photochemistry*, Royal Society of Chemistry

Thomson, C. (1991) Last But Not Least – Examination and Interpretation of Coatings on Brass Hardware, AIC Wooden Artifacts Group, Conference Papers, Albuquerque

Thornton, J. (1981) The structure of ivory and ivory substitutes, in *Preprints of papers at the Ninth Annual Meeting, Philadelphia*, American Institute of Conservation, pp. 173–81

Thornton, J. (1990) A light box apparatus for the repair of glass, *Studies in Conservation*, 35, 107–9

Thornton, J. (1991) Replicating stamped brasses, *Fine Woodworking*, 86, 86–7

Thornton, J. (1993) The history, technology and conservation of architectural papier mâché, *JAIC*, 32, 165–76

Tomes, C.S. (1923) *A Manual of Dental Anatomy – Human and Comparative*, 8th edn, London (1st edition, 1876)

Tomlinson, C. (ed.) (1862) *Cyclopedia of the Useful Arts*, James Virtue

Torraca, G. (1981) *Porous Building Materials*, ICCROM

Tylecote, R.F. (1976) *A History of Metallurgy*, The Metals Society

Untracht, O. (1968) *Metal Techniques for Craftsmen*, Doubleday

Untracht, O. (1982) *Jewellery Concepts and Techniques*, Doubleday

Ure, A. (1866) *A Dictionary of Arts Manufactures and Mines*, Appleton and Co

Van der Reyden, D. and Williams, D.C. (1986) The technology and conservation treatment of a nineteenth century papier mâché chair, *AIC Preprints*, pp. 125–42

Van Duin, P. (1989) Two pairs of Boulle caskets on stands by Thomas Parker, *Furniture History*, 25, 214–17

Van Schoute, R. (1986) Art history and laboratory. Scientific examination of easel paintings, *Journal of the European Study Group on Physical, Chemical and Mathematical Techniques Applied to Archaeology*, 13, The Council of Europe

Varlashkin, P.G. and Low, M.J.D. (1986) FT–IR photothermal beam deflection spectroscopy of black inks on paper, *Applied Spectroscopy*, 40, pp. 507–13

Vuilleumier, R. (1979) Scildpatt-verarbeitungstechniken und imitationen, *Maltechnik Restauro*, 85 (1), 40–7

Vuilleumier, R. (1980) Werkstoffeder kunstschreinerei, elfenbein, knocken, horn, permutter, fischbein und fischhaut, *Maltechnik-Restauro*, 86 (2), 106–23

Waentig, F. (1993) Gießharzsysteme zum Einbetten von Proben, *Restauro*, 99 (3), 195–9

Wakeford, C.M. and Wardman, R.H. (1989) The identification of blue pigments in paint by derivative spectroscopy, *JOCCA*, 1, 22–8

Walch, K. (1993) Boulle-Marketerien an süddeutschen Klosterausstattungen des 18. Jahrunderts: Technik und Restaurierung von Arbeiten aus der Dominikanerwerkstatt Valentin Zindters, *Zeitschrift für Kunsttechnologie und Konservierung*, 7 (1), 103–25

Watts, S. (1982) Period furniture hardware, *Fine Woodworking*, 34, 86–91

Webster, D. (1987) *Understanding Geology*, Oliver and Boyd

Webster, R. (1958) Ivory, bone and horn, *The Gemmologist*, 27, 91–8

Webster, R. (1962) *Gems, Their Sources, Descriptions and Identification*, 1 and 2, Butterworths

Wenham, L.P. (1964) Hornpot Lane and the Horners of York, *Annual Report of the York Philosophical Society for 1964*, pp. 25–56

Wheeler, W. and Hayward, C.H. (1973) *Practical Woodcarving and Gilding*, Evans Bros

Williams, N. (1983) *Porcelain Repair and Restoration*, British Museum Publications

Williams, T. (1982) *A Short History of Twentieth Century Technology, 1900–1950*, The Clarendon Press

Williamson, S.J. and Cummins, H.Z. (1983) *Light and Colour in Nature and Art*, John Wiley and Sons

Willisch, S. (1990) Applications and results of xeroradiographs for the study of works of art and historical objects, Translation Bureau no. 3623315, Dept of the Secretary of State of Canada, 1990. Translation of article first published in German as Willisch, S. (1989) Anwendung und Ergebrisse der Xeroradiographie bei der Untersuchung von Kunstwerten und historischen objekts, *Zeitschrift für Kunsttechnologie*, 3(1), 197–213

Wouters, J. and Verhecken, A. (1989) The coccid insect dyes: HPLC and computerized diode-array analysis of dyed yarns, *Studies in Conservation*, 34, 189–200

Zangerl, R. (1969) The Turtle Shell, *Biology of Reptilia*, Vol. 1 (ed. C. Gans *et al.*), Academic Press, pp. 311–40

# Part 3

# Deterioration

# 6

# General review of environment and deterioration

## 6.1 Introduction

Deterioration of objects produces undesirable change leading to loss of value or utility (Ashley Smith, 1997). This can mean various different things to different people. For example, it could mean that an object loses its ability to be used as a fully functional piece of furniture, or that its market value drops, or that the information it contains is in some way lost so that it is no longer able to function as an historical record. Deterioration is a complex process but it is evident that the kind of deterioration found will reflect the way objects are used. It is therefore very important to understand the organizational and political context within which collections are maintained and used. Changes may occur through natural alteration of material or through interference and may be chemical, physical, or biological in nature. Prevention is better than cure. Our aim should be to minimize deterioration; to reduce both the rate at which change occurs and the extent to which it proceeds. To do this it is important to understand energy and especially the thermodynamics and equilibria of chemical reactions. Ultimately, the factors we can control are light, heat, relative humidity, biological activity, pollution, handling and movement. To effectively control the separate and joint actions of these factors requires carefully considered and integrated strategies for environmental management. While the possibility of disaster is small, the consequences are devastating. Proper planning for the possibility of emergencies is therefore essential.

### 6.1.1 Organizational and political context

Conservation is a time-consuming and expensive business so we should be aware of why we do it and how to obtain and give the best value for money. In most cases, museums and other heritage organizations are governed by a legal requirement to care for, preserve and add to their collections. They are required to ensure that these objects are made available to the public both by display and by provision of reference facilities to allow access for study. Also, they must add to the body of knowledge relevant to the collections through research and disseminate that knowledge. Most private owners of important objects demonstrate moral responsibility for the care of the national heritage as well as for the value of their investment. For both groups, a basic conflict is that between access and preservation. We want to be able to see and use objects but this involves exposing them to light, changes in climate and mechanical action that may cause damage. Control of these hazards is usefully viewed in simple terms such as control of light, heat and humidity but in real life, caring for collections is a complex business that involves harmonizing the aims, objectives, abilities and skills of owners, curators, conservators, engineers, scientists, administrators and others.

Although conservators do not all work for museums, such institutions do provide an important part of the work of many private conservators. Because of their need for accountability, such organizations frequently lead developments in activities such as collections management and conservation. The frequent reference to institutional needs in this chapter is not intended to exclude those working privately but to provide a benchmark for all those involved in caring for our heritage.

### 6.1.2  Use versus preservation

Many collections, both institutional and private, constitute finite groups of objects that have been built up over long periods of time which are, for practical purposes, irreplaceable. These collections are required to be used but equally must be preserved for future generations. We often seem to expect each individual object to last forever and yet to be continually used and re-used. Clearly, objects cannot last forever. It is therefore important for all those involved in the use and the maintenance of these non-renewable resources to understand how to get the best out of their objects and how to look after them so that they will last as long as possible. It is therefore necessary to understand how objects are used, what it is about them which is important, how they may be changed or damaged during use and how this change can be minimized. Conservators are expected to have detailed knowledge in this area but they can add to their effectiveness by being able to communicate their knowledge in realistic and meaningful fashion to others who require understanding but less detailed knowledge.

Collections may be used in many ways, but there are two general approaches to the use of public collections. In one the objects remain stationary and people come to them and in the other the objects themselves are moved. It is important to understand that the lives of objects are dynamic. For objects to be useful they must be used. This is especially true for objects in public collections. Despite the often mausoleum like atmosphere in museums they are in fact, at least as far as their objects are concerned, extremely busy places. To meet the requirement to give access to the public, objects are displayed in galleries, study rooms and stores, loaned to exhibitions, photographed for publication subjected to scientific examination and actively used for lecturing and teaching. These activities require a continual cycle of handling and moving. Ways in which the potentially harmful effects of this activity can be minimized are presented below in the section on handling.

We do not keep objects just because they are 'beautiful' but because of the information they contain, because they are documents in their own right. Some information is available in the form of photographs, catalogues and labels, and these are very important. However, objects themselves contain a great deal of information that may not be available elsewhere. If an object is lost this is lost with it. Much of this information – texture, colour, shape, decoration, patterns and so forth may be immediately obvious on the surface. There may also be traces of pigment or there may be tool marks – small traces that may only be visible upon very careful inspection. In some cases information is only revealed by scientific examination. A lot of this information is on or in the surface of the object and it is the surface that is, unfortunately, the part most likely to get damaged.

### Change and damage

Where the majority of the information is on the surface of the object, a small amount of damage or loss could result in the loss of a great deal of information. Also, a small amount of damage may result in the remaining information being distorted. We have therefore to be very careful about how we care for our collections because we might inadvertently lose the whole purpose of an individual part of our collection or a whole collection.

The risks associated with moving objects are in general familiar; objects may interact with each other, with the people doing the moving, or with the building, transport or equipment used. Inherent risks to the objects range from knocks and abrasions to total loss. The risks of just leaving objects at rest may not be so obvious but changes will take place very slowly, which may alter the way the objects can be used. The way in which objects will react to either being left alone or being moved will depend very much on the materials they are made of and the way they were originally constructed.

One way to preserve our objects would be to bury them deep underground hermetically sealed in thick, dark, inert containers from which water, oxygen and other reactive gases had been excluded. This would not meet our needs for access and so is not a practical solution to our problems. We must therefore find other ways to display, store and use objects in which the harmful effects of light, heat, oxygen, pollution, water vapour and other environmental hazards can be minimized. Methods of display, storage and handling have been developed and continue to be developed which allow us to preserve collections and extend the lives of objects while improving the quality of displays. As these develop, it is important that they become part of our established policy and procedure.

### 6.1.3 Managing the object life cycle

The cycle of activity in which objects are placed needs to be managed. Those responsible for collections must be able to control and monitor their activities, to set priorities and to measure performance and cost. The starting point for effective management of a collection is to have a policy which sets out rules and guidelines and provides a framework in which decisions may be made. Most large publicly funded bodies are required to have such a policy. Typically this sets out a statement of the purpose, aims and objectives of the institution, the composition and terms of reference of the governing body and management structure, the scope of the collections and the activities involved in managing them. The *scope* of the collection will include the kind of objects collected, their origins and periods and how they relate to other museums' collections. Information which is to be recorded about objects and the standards to which documentation must adhere should be defined (see Roberts, 1988). This is further discussed in Chapter 9. *Cataloguing* must include a unique identification number and normally also a photograph for identification purposes. Location records (*Inventory*) are required for stocktaking, retrieval of objects and response to losses. The policy should also set out rules governing acquisition, disposal, access, lending and borrowing of objects, standards for care and maintenance, risk management and security.

If they are not to become merely reactive, conservators need to understand, encourage and actively participate in the process of collections management, though this is not to say that conservators should become collections managers. A fairly traditional picture of the relationship of the furniture conservator to others involved in caring for collections is that the conservator was only called in once deterioration of an object had progressed to the stage where active intervention was required. Furniture conservators must be able to repair furniture but they are also very well placed to advise on many aspects of policy and collections management that can help to reduce loss and damage. An unrepaired object in good condition is to be preferred on historical and aesthetic grounds to one which has been repaired. In the long run, care is also a better economic proposition than repair.

The term 'object life cycle' refers to activities from acquisition to disposal. Conservators can help to both maintain the condition of our heritage and enhance the reputation of the profession by offering sensible, rational advice and relevant services at the appropriate time in relation to these activities. Advice at the time of acquisition may relate to technical issues having a bearing on authenticity, object condition, appropriate methods of display and environmental conditions required for display as well as treatment required. Conservators should also be able to advise on the suitability of objects for loan and on the packing, handling and transportation required. Furniture conservators should be able to survey mixed media furniture collections and advise on priorities for conservation including environmental issues related to the preservation of objects. In particular it is important that conservators should understand the effect of the condition of the building in which a collection is housed on issues such as climate, pest control and security.

Many of these activities may involve liaison with other specialists. This is especially true in an institutional setting or when working for a large organization. The final course of action chosen may depend on consideration of many different factors of which conservation is one, but not the only one. Curators, conservation scientists, collections managers, technicians, architects, engineers, educators, trustees, accountants, exhibition designers, security staff and others may be involved in decisions affecting the use of objects. It may therefore be helpful for the conservator to spend some time to understand the points of view of others involved in the cycle of management of collections and be prepared to offer solutions to conservation problems that meet the needs of a wider group of stakeholders. Such consideration for the points of view of others is usually repaid.

Discussions of aspects of the function, organization and planning of museums which may be generally helpful are offered by the Department of National Heritage (1996), Ambrose and Paine (1993), Ambrose and Runyard (1991), George and Sherrell-Leo (1987), Knell (1994) and Thompson (1984). A useful summary framework for the preservation of institutional collections is provided by the Canadian Conservation Institute (1994). Bachmann (1992) deals with conservation concerns and Keene (1996) with the management of conservation in museums.

## 6.2 The environment

The condition of furniture and wooden objects depends on the materials from which they are made, on their structures and on the conditions to which they have been exposed during their lifetime. The materials may be organic (wood, textiles) or inorganic (metals, ceramics, glass), with the former generally considered to be more susceptible to deterioration. No material, however, is stable under all conditions. This raises problems for mixed collections, especially where materials requiring different conditions for their preservation are found in the same object or need otherwise be shown together. Deterioration of furniture items can proceed through physical, chemical, or biological agents but generally more than one force is in operation at the same time. In discussing what can be done to minimize damage, it is useful to find some underlying basis for the description of the processes of decay. This is possible to a certain extent through an understanding of the thermodynamic and kinetic molecular theories of chemical change. The second law of thermodynamics, which tells us that nature is gradually moving towards a state of disorder, gives little comfort. We can, though, do something

to slow down the rate at which this affects our objects. Some points concerning chemical reactions in general will therefore be discussed first as a basis for understanding the influence of light, heat and humidity, discussion of which follows.

### 6.2.1 Background chemistry

Systems tend to move towards their most stable state. We might therefore expect that the more stable the products of a reaction are compared with the starting materials, the further towards the products any equilibrium between them might lie. In seeking their most stable condition, systems tend towards minimum energy (*enthalpy* – *H*) and maximum disorder or randomness (*entropy* – *S*). A measure of their relative stability thus embraces *H* and *S* and is provided by the Gibb's free energy (*G*). The free energy change during a reaction at a particular temperature is given by the following equation:

$$\Delta G = \Delta H - T\Delta S$$

where

$\Delta$ is used as a symbol to represent the amount of change
$G$ is Gibb's free energy
$H$ is minimum energy (or enthalpy)
$T$ is the absolute temperature (0° absolute equals −273 °Kelvin)
$S$ is maximum disorder (or entropy).

Whether or not a reaction will proceed spontaneously depends on the free energy change ($\Delta G$) for the reaction. For a spontaneous reaction to occur $\Delta G$ must be negative, that is the free energy of the products of the reaction must be lower than the free energy of the reactants. The more negative the value of $\Delta G$ the further will the equilibrium for a reaction lie in favour of the products. $\Delta G$ is related to the equilibrium constant for the change by the relation

$$-\Delta G = 2.303RT \log_{10} K$$

where $R$ is the Gas Constant and $T$ is the absolute temperature. Knowledge of the standard free energies of starting materials and products enables us to predict the extent of the conversion of the former into the latter.

Most of the materials of concern to conservators are not in their most stable state and what is therefore of greater interest is how fast any reaction will occur. For example, $\Delta G$ for the oxidation of cellulose [$(C_6H_{12}O_5)n + 6nO_2 \rightarrow 6nCO_2 + 5nH_2O$] is large and negative so that the equilibrium for the reaction lies essentially completely over in favour of carbon dioxide and water. While this would appear to favour spontaneous self-destruction, we know that a drawing or book can be viewed in the air for a long time without noticeably fading away into gaseous products. The rate of a chemical reaction, which may be defined as the speed at which the products are formed, depends on the physical state, concentration and temperature of the reactants and on the presence of catalyst. A chemical reaction cannot begin unless the reactants are in contact *at activation levels of energy* and the reaction cannot proceed if the reactants clog or prevent fresh molecular collisions from taking place (e.g. the oxide layers on aluminium and chromium). Advantage can sometimes be taken of this in the display space to make conditions as unfavourable as possible for reaction.

Molecular freedom of at least one reactant to move about and mingle with the other(s) is a prerequisite for chemical reaction. The greater the effective surface area the faster a reaction will tend to take place. Solutions are most often chosen as the medium for carrying out chemical reactions for just these reasons. Moisture on the surface of objects and pitted or porous surfaces both increase the likelihood of reactions occurring. Chemical reactions take place when the appropriate atoms, ions or molecules collide with each other. The number of collisions will be greater for light molecules as these travel faster than heavy ones and should collide more frequently. Larger molecules should also collide more frequently than smaller ones. If the number of molecules in a fixed volume (i.e. the concentration) is doubled this will result in four times the number of collisions. An increase in temperature will also increase the number of collisions but this is not the main effect of temperature. Collision between two molecules is a necessary but not sufficient condition for reaction. Each collision requires a certain amount of energy before reaction can occur and this *activation energy* represents a barrier to reaction which can be represented diagrammatically, as shown in *Figure 6.1*. At a particular temperature, not all particles have the same kinetic energy. Only collisions involving particles of sufficient (higher than average) kinetic energy will result in reaction. The well-known increase in the rate of reaction that occurs as temperature is raised is due to the growing proportion of molecules, as temperature rises, with an energy above the minimum necessary for reaction (*Figure 6.2*). As a very rough guide, a 10 °C rise in temperature will lead to a doubling of rate of reaction, though the rate of oxidation of cellulose is doubled if the temperature rises from 20 °C to 25 °C (Thomson, 1986). It may sometimes be possible to artificially raise the activation energy barrier, for example by applying lacquers to metals. The rise in temperature required to cause a doubling of rate can be found from the equation:

$$\log_{10} k_1/k_2 = -E_a/2.303R[1/T_1 - 1/T_2]$$

where $k_1$ and $k_2$ are rate constants at temperatures $T_1$ and $T_2$, $E_a$ is activation energy and $R$ is the Gas Constant.

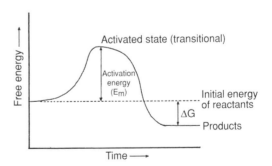

Figure showing Free energy on the vertical axis and Time on the horizontal axis, labelled: Activated state (transitional), Activation energy ($E_m$), Initial energy of reactants, $\Delta G$, Products.

**Figure 6.1** If they are to react, colliding molecules must have sufficient kinetic energy to cause chemical bonds to break or form. The minimum energy required to initiate a chemical reaction is called the activation energy. Diagrammatic representation of the path of an exothermic reaction showing the initial energy of the reactants, the activation energy ($E_a$) required to achieve an activated state, the change in free energy ($\Delta G$) caused by the reaction and the energy of the reaction products (now lower than the initial energy because this example is an exothermic reaction – a reaction that gives out energy in the form of heat)

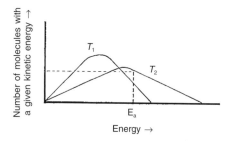

**Figure 6.2** Not all molecules at the same temperature have the same kinetic energy. This is diagrammatically represented in a Maxwell Distribution graph which plots the fraction of molecules with a given kinetic energy against kinetic energy. The kinetic energy of a molecule is directly proportional to the temperature. In order to undergo a reaction, molecules must possess an energy that is equal to or higher that the activation energy $E_a$. At a low temperature ($T_2$), only a few molecules have sufficient energy, thus the reaction will proceed, but at a slower rate. At a higher temperature ($T_1$), more molecules are able to exceed the activation energy ($E_a$), thus the reaction proceeds at a faster rate. Thus there is an increase in the rate of reaction as temperature increases

Even if molecules with sufficient energy to overcome the activation energy barrier do collide, reaction may still not occur. Reaction takes place at particular sites on molecules and the correct areas may not be in contact on collision. This becomes important with large molecules which have only a few reaction sites. A catalyst is a substance which alters the rate of a chemical reaction but remains chemically unchanged at the end of the reaction. It is generally believed that this results from an effective lowering of the activation energy barrier. This may occur through an orientation of reactant molecules on the catalyst itself. A catalyst does not alter $\Delta G$ for reaction. Examples of catalysts include iron and some other heavy metals, which, when present on the surfaces of objects and the insides of buildings, may catalyse the conversion of sulphur dioxide to sulphuric acid.

The concepts introduced here are more fully explained in the publication *Chemistry for Conservators* (Moncrieff and Weaver, 1992), especially in Book 2 of that series. Further discussion can be found at the desired level in many books of physical chemistry (see for example Brown, 1964) and in an excellent introduction to the concepts and applications

of chemical thermodynamics by Johnstone and Webb (1977).

Chemical reactions involving objects almost invariably mean deterioration. Such reactions may be endothermic (heat absorbing) or exothermic (heat releasing) but in either case a definite amount of activation energy must be supplied to start the reaction. This can occur either by heating or by illumination.

### 6.2.2   Light

Wherever objects are on display, light is a source of great potential damage. Though its action is confined mainly to the surface of most objects this is often of the greatest importance, especially on painted and decorated surfaces. All organic material is at risk under light and even some glasses, such as those with a high manganese content, may change colour after prolonged illumination. Frequently, the effects of light are aggravated by, or are only achieved in, high relative humidity and in the presence of oxygen. Paper, cotton, linen, wood, parchment, leather, silk, wool, feathers, hair, dyes, oils, glues, gums and resins can all be affected and in fact about the only classes of objects which are not generally susceptible to light are stone, metal and ceramics.

White light falling on a surface will be partly absorbed and partly reflected and in some cases a further part may pass directly through it. The characteristics of a surface, especially its colour, are perceived by the amount of light at each wavelength which is reflected (section 5.8.1). The light absorbed may, through a huge variety of chemical reactions, lead to photo oxidation of the material. Molecules of different types and complexity are usually involved and after the primary photochemical reaction a whole series of reactions may be initiated which are not necessarily dependent on light. Further information on the mechanisms of deterioration relevant to specific materials is given in the following chapters.

Objects may appear for a considerable period to be unaffected by light and may then, sometimes only after many years, show significant signs of degradation. The early changes brought about by light during the 'induction' period may mainly affect impurities or irregularities in polymer structure which effectively protect the material. When these become exhausted, changes affecting the properties of the polymer may manifest themselves and will continue until most of the damage that can be done has been done. It is not therefore wise to assume that any object can be safely exposed to light unless extended tests, or long experience, have shown this to be the case. The induction period of some methacrylates for example has been found to be in excess of ten years under well illuminated conditions.

### Light energy, colour temperature and damage

All objects are made up of millions of molecules each of which changes its state in discrete all or nothing steps. Each molecule will stay in its ground state unless energy at least sufficient to overcome the activation energy barrier is received in one go. According to quantum theory, energy exists in discrete packets or quanta. The energy of a body can only change by some definite whole number multiple of a unit of energy known as a quantum. In contrast to heat quanta which at any given temperature are spread over a range of energies, the energy of a quantum of light (known as a photon) is fixed at any given wavelength ($\lambda$) according to the expression:

$$E = hc\lambda$$

where $E$ is the value of a quantum in ergs and $h$ is Planck's constant and $c$ is the velocity of light. At room temperature, the energy of heat quanta will be sufficient to overcome activation energy barriers up to about 30 Kcal/mol. Light quanta in the near infra red region will have energies close to this. As the wavelength becomes shorter so the energy of quanta will increase through yellow, green and blue light to radiation in the ultra violet waveband (approximately 300–400 nm) which can overcome activation energy barriers of 90 Kcal/ mol. Light in the blue, violet and especially the ultra-violet wavebands is thus potentially the most damaging.

All light sources can be more or less matched, in terms of the predominant colour sensation, with the light emitted by a mythical 'black body' at a particular temperature. This is a non-combustible, completely non-reflecting body the colour of which when heated could, if it existed, be used accurately as a measure of temperature. This temperature is known as the *colour temperature* of a light source. In practice, the light from an overcast sky corresponds to a colour temperature of about 6000 °K and that of a blue sky to 10 000–20 000 °K (degrees Kelvin – see section 6.2.3). At the other end of the scale, ordinary tungsten light corresponds to about 3000 °K. Fluorescent lighting in the colour temperature range 3000–6500 °K corresponds to the range from tungsten to overcast daylight. As the colour temperature increases, the proportion of shorter wavelengths, that is of the blue, violet and ultra violet parts of the spectrum, increases. As the colour temperature decreases, the proportion of longer wavelengths, in the red and infra red parts of the spectrum increases. Rather confusingly, light of low colour temperature is warmer in appearance due to the greater proportion of longer (red and infra red) wavelengths. Lights of high colour temperature actually appear 'cool' due to the greater proportion of shorter (blue and violet) wavelengths. The UV component of tungsten light is quite small but that of a blue sky is an appreciable percentage of the total radiation. There is, however, much less UV than visible light in all light sources, even daylight.

When lighting objects for display purposes it is important to consider which colour temperature in the range 3000–6500 °K will produce the least damage to vulnerable objects. Since the energy associated with radiation is greater the shorter the wavelength, there is an a priori argument in favour of lighting of low colour temperature. However, because of the complexity of photo degradation processes and the vast range of materials, especially dyes, it is impossible to apply this argument quantitatively. Fading, especially of fugitive dyes, can be produced by wavelengths over the whole of the visible spectrum. A very fugitive material will be damaged by either visible or UV radiation and since visible radiation is more plentiful most of the damage will be done by visible light. A material which is fairly fast to light but nevertheless susceptible in the long run may be secure against most of the visible spectrum and will therefore be changed mainly or wholly by UV. It is therefore clear that ultraviolet radiation, which in any case makes no contribution towards the goal of seeing the object, should be eliminated. Visible radiation, on the other hand, should be reasonably balanced, with no major gaps or very large peaks in the spectrum, for proper colour rendering and this therefore has to be controlled.

### Reciprocity

The amount of damage will in general be related to the amount of light received. This in turn depends on the illuminance and on the time of exposure. If the illuminance is doubled and the time of exposure is halved the degree of deterioration will be the same. Similarly, if the illuminance is doubled only half the time will be required to produce the same degree of deterioration. This is a loose statement of the *Reciprocity Law* which suggests that light acts cumulatively and that it is the total dose or exposure which matters. The exposure is the simple product of illuminance and time. Illuminance is measured in *lux* (1 lux = 1 lumen/m$^2$ or approximately 10 foot candles) and time in hours. Thus an object illuminated at 100 hours lux for 10 hours will receive an exposure of 1000 lux-hours. Fifty lux for 20 hours would give it the same exposure.

There are some conditions of very high and very low illuminance where reciprocity may not apply. In the discussion of activation energy, it was implied that a photochemical reaction involves the absorption of one photon only since the reaction, if it occurs at all, takes place so fast that there is insufficient time for a second photon to arrive at the same site. At high light intensities this can break down because the density of photons is such that an excited molecule may have its energy increased even further by the absorption of a second photon. In addition to this, some excited species do not have short lives. It is therefore possible for two photon absorption to occur conferring energy by addition in excess of anything in the 'daylight through glass' UV range and therefore be very potent indeed. Rates of damage on a pure two photon basis are proportional not to the light intensity itself but to its square. For practical purposes, illuminance levels should never be allowed to exceed 2000 lux, even for short periods. Some idea of the light fastness of different dyed fabrics and paints can be obtained using the Blue Wool standard (British Standard BS1006 – 1961).

### Control of light

Since the effectiveness of displays is largely dependent on the contributions made by lighting, damage by light can never be entirely eliminated. However, the rate of damage can be greatly reduced, first by eliminating UV radiation, secondly by reducing the level of illumination to the minimum necessary for comfortable viewing and thirdly by reducing the amount of time for which objects are illuminated. Each of these approaches is briefly reviewed below. For further discussion of this complex topic see Brill (1980), Cassar (1995) and Thomson (1986).

*Measurement of light*  Measurement of light levels is an important aspect of control. The light or lux meter measures the energy of white light sources, not directly, but as the eye sees it. Thus the meter does not respond to infra red or ultra violet radiation and is more sensitive to green than to either red or blue. It consists of a photocell which converts light energy into electrical energy and a meter relating the voltage obtained to the light level. This is read as the incident light and the meter is normally calibrated directly in lux. The proportion of UV in a light source is measured as micro watts per lumen by a UV monitor which contains two photosensitive devices, one for UV and one for visible radiation. A method for using the exposure meter in a camera as a tool to measure lux levels is described in the Canadian Conservation Institute's Note number 2/5. Devices for continuous monitoring of light levels, as opposed to spot readings, are also available. See for example SSCR (1989) and Child (1993).

*Control of UV radiation*  All white light sources emit some UV radiation, as shown in *Table 6.1*. Seventy-five micro watts per lumen is usually taken as a threshold above which it is necessary to provide a filter to remove the excess UV radiation. However this should not be taken to indicate that this amount of UV is somehow harmless. If the means exist to reduce UV to levels lower than this then they should be employed. Most of the UV radiation in sunlight of wavelength below 300 nm is filtered out by the ozone layer in the upper

**Table 6.1** UV Component of various light sources

| Light source | UV (micro watts per lumen) |
|---|---|
| Blue sky @ 15 000 °K | 1600 |
| Cloudy overcast sky (north light) | 800 |
| Direct sun | 400 |
| Fluorescent lamps | 40–250 |
| Tungsten halogen (iodine) | up to 130 |
| Normal tungsten | 60–80 |

atmosphere. This still leaves potentially damaging radiation in the waveband 300–400 nm and this must be removed by a filter. Ordinary window glass absorbs only the shorter wavelengths of UV and is transparent to UV in the region 300–400 nm. However, certain chemicals, such as the substituted benzophenones, have the property of being able to absorb almost all of the UV without absorbing visible light. Such materials can be added to a varnish or a transparent plastic sheet or film to make an effective UV filter. With currently available technology, it is possible to reduce UV levels to the threshold of measurement and this should be the goal. UV filters must be placed between the light source and the object illuminated. Complete protection can be provided by placing filters over windows, skylights and light fittings as necessary. Filters can also be used in display cases and in the glazing of pictures. However as increasing amounts of blue light are removed by the UV absorber, films appear increasingly yellow. This can be overcome by slightly reducing the strength of the UV absorber to the point where a colourless material is obtained or by adding a complementary dye or pigment to the film to produce a neutral grey. A yellow cast will usually only be noticeable if the plastic material is close to an exhibit and not if a whole room is so treated. Where possible, it is in any case better in principle to remove UV at source rather than on an item by item basis.

The choice of UV filter varnish or sheet is influenced by cost and fitting considerations. Sheet can be invisible if it is behind diffusing glass but may be too apparent behind plain glass. Varnish may show if applied by brush or spray but can be applied by special flow techniques to make it practically invisible. It is

also cheaper though less durable than sheet. These materials are more liable to scratching than glass and are also liable to attract an electrostatic charge which will result in the accumulation of dust. An antistatic coating is required to reduce this effect.

Most UV filters may be expected to last about ten years but their effectiveness should be checked from time to time using a UV meter. They can conveniently be replaced during redecoration of rooms. Under conditions of very strong sunlight the filter may degrade in an uneconomically short time. Under these conditions, it may be possible to arrange that all light reaching a sensitive object has been reflected at least once from a wall which has been coated with a white pigment having a high absorption in the UV range. Titanium dioxide and zinc oxide are both suitable for this purpose.

Most fluorescent tubes are coated on the inside with a material which absorbs some of the UV and re-emits radiation of a longer wavelength. However, most fluorescent lamps still emit levels of UV that require filtration. Quartz halogen lamps (e.g. tungsten iodide) have a quartz envelope which is transparent to UV and take advantage of higher operating temperatures than ordinary tungsten lamps to obtain more light per watt of electricity consumed. The small but powerful amount of short wave radiation emitted by these lamps makes filtration a necessity.

*Control of visible radiation*　All objects, unless known to be insensitive to UV radiation, should be protected in the ways outlined above. In considering control of visible radiation, it is necessary to find levels of illumination which will be satisfactory for both conservation and display purposes. A certain amount of damage will be caused by the very act of display and yet it will not be worthwhile to exhibit an object at all unless an adequate level of detail can be perceived by the viewer. Just where this level of detail should be fixed is a matter of judgement taking into account the form and surface qualities and susceptibility to light of different objects. Therefore, when an object is not being viewed there is no need to illuminate it. Objects should be illuminated only when it is necessary for display or study and the illumination should be no more than that needed for the task. When the light level is lower than 50 lux the object cannot be seen properly. Increasing the light level above 250 lux does not greatly increase the viewer's appreciation of the object. Deliberately lighting an object at less than 50 lux or more than 250 lux causes damage without any compensating benefit. Rooms should remain unlit or at reduced light level when not in use. The current goal in the reduction of illumination for conservation purposes is to keep the level below 150 lux for oil and tempera painting, undyed leather, lacquer, wood, horn, bone and ivory and to reduce the level to 50 lux for costumes, water colour painting, tapestries, furnishing textiles, prints and drawings, stamps, manuscripts, miniatures, wall papers, dyed leather and most natural history exhibits. Within these limits it is also desirable that the lighting should meet with several other conditions. It should be fairly evenly distributed over walls and should facilitate comfortable appreciation of small detail. The illumination level provided for exhibits should be higher than that provided for general room lighting. The incident light should give an acceptable colour rendering, without undue distortion and the colour and brightness of the walls and ceilings should not distract from appreciation of the objects or provoke visual discomfort. The lighting should be as inconspicuous as possible.

Two major faults which should be avoided are glare and gross inequalities in lighting of adjacent areas. Glare is well known as a dazzling brilliance or strong fierce light which can arise, for example, from the surface of glazed paintings or showcases, when light sources are not placed at the correct angle to the objects being illuminated. It interferes with the ability to see things properly, especially at low light levels and leads to visual discomfort. Deep shadows can produce a similar effect. Large inequalities in lighting adjacent areas should, as far as possible, be avoided since a room may be adequately lit and still look gloomy if there is a much brighter room beside it. The converse is also true. The human eye has very little ability to measure illumination values as such but readily detects differences in brightness. This fault can lead to the sometime unpleasant necessity of continually adapting the eye in passing from one room to another. Control of lighting to 150 lux should not present too much difficulty in this respect but the lower limit of 50 lux requires considerable thought to be exercised to avoid creating an excessively gloomy environment.

*Control of daylight* Access for daylight is often considered desirable both for its spectral quality and as a corollary of providing exterior views from a room to aid visitor orientation. Daylight has the advantage of being free but because it varies in intensity, direction and spectral quality throughout the year, an object in a daylit gallery may receive a hundred times more light on a bright sunny day than on a dull one. If it is to be ensured that there is always sufficient light for comfortable viewing and yet the illumination never exceeds 150 lux, the illumination must be continuously controlled and must be fairly evenly distributed throughout the exhibition area. Daylight cannot be very easily directed as can, for example, spot lights and the simplest and most commonly used solution to this problem is diffusion. Very low levels of daylight create an impression of gloom, especially when highly diffused. Furthermore, diffuse light, coming equally from all directions throws none of the shadows necessary for appreciation of surface texture and will make colours appear paler. For these reasons, control of daylight to 50 lux is not generally attempted. At this level, tungsten is a more appropriate choice that enables surface texture and colour to be appreciated more easily and, for the same degree of illumination, creates a warmer and more cheerful appearance.

Several approaches have been adopted to the problem of controlling daylight to 150 lux. Using blinds or other means of blocking out light (such as titanium sputtered films), the level of daylight entering a gallery or room can be reduced to the point where it only rises to 150 lux at the brightest time of day or year. This can then be supplemented at other times with artificial light. In this way, the quality of daylight is essentially lost since at most times the lighting will be mainly artificial. A way in which this can be overcome is to paint skylights in spring with a paint that wears away by the end of the summer so that natural lighting makes a more significant contribution throughout the year. Another scheme is to use a translucent ceiling through which daylight is highly diffused so that all exhibits are illuminated at the agreed level. Light can be admitted through blinds which are automatically controlled by a photocell. As daylight fails, artificial light is introduced under dimmer control also operated by photocells. Although this sounds an attractive proposition, the constancy of illumination and its degree of diffusion again results in light which is very like that from an overcast sky in both colour temperature and directional quality. There is also an increased probability of failure in such complex systems. As an alternative to the above, which aim at a steady illumination of 150 lux, the equivalent annual exposure can be worked out and an average exposure value calculated based on meteorological data. A level of control can be set which allows light levels to go over the 150 lux limit during the summer months but averages out to around 150 lux over the whole year (i.e. the same equivalent dose measured in lux-hours). If automatic blinds are used they can be adjusted hourly on a monthly schedule. Lighting can thus retain some connection with the weather outside and some of the essential features of daylight are retained.

*Reducing time of exposure* Another important aspect of the control of lighting is reduction of the time of exposure. For very sensitive objects, including some upholstered furniture, an excellent way to reduce exposure is for objects to be put on display for a limited period only before being replaced by another, possibly similar, object. This is commonly known as rotation. The period of rotation can be varied to suit the circumstances. It might be, for example, one year in ten or it could be one month per year. Obviously it can more easily be achieved with a large collection, or where there is only a small space available for display. In general, illumination, apart from that required for security purposes, can be restricted to institutional opening hours. Exposure can be further restricted by means of curtains or covers around or over a display and by the use of time switches so that very sensitive objects are only illuminated when they are actually being viewed. Objects in conservation workshops and in stores should be similarly protected when they are not being worked on. Black plastic sheeting in the workshop or Tyvek covers in stores may be used for this purpose. Some

items can be quite conveniently arranged on racking systems so that they can be pulled out for observation and then pushed back into dark conditions when this has finished. The use of replicas is another possibility.

*Artificial lighting* Artificial lighting has to be used both for supplementing daylight and as a substitute for it, during the winter months, where a source of natural light is not available and at the lower level of 50 lux where use of daylight is not really feasible. Artificial light offers many advantages in flexibility and ease of control. A range of lights of different colour temperatures is available with tungsten and tungsten halogen lamps in the 'warm' category – around 3000–4000 °K – and fluorescent tubes in the 'cool' category – up to 6500 °K. A warm light may give good effect to reds and golds, especially under low levels of illumination while a cooler light may look more effective with blues. Once the decision is made, a lamp of good colour rendering must be chosen. Although a tungsten lamp can look yellow in direct comparison to daylight when the two are in close proximity (say on a white wall), if the whole area is illuminated by tungsten it will appear white. Within each category of colour temperature, lamps are available which the eye will still read as white provided that there are no very large deficiencies of any wavelength in their spectra. Fluorescent lamps, however, can present more problems in this respect. Fluorescent tubes have a greater luminous efficiency than tungsten and are well suited for general illumination as they come in a wide range of colour temperatures and sizes and can be very conveniently used with various types of diffusing panels in ceilings and so on. They require a greater bulk of control gear than tungsten lights and some of this tends to get quite hot in operation so that siting of it has to be carefully considered. Tungsten is more suitable for spot lights that provide accent lighting.

### Lighting and heating

One aspect of lighting which should be remembered is that most lamps, and of course the sun, produce not only UV and visible radiation but also infra red radiation and heat. These long wavelength radiations in fact comprise by far the greatest part of the output of tungsten and fluorescent lamps. Heat conducted and convected away from light fittings will affect the general environment and may require thermostatic control to maintain suitable, stable conditions. A more serious worry, however, is the extent to which different kinds of light sources radiate heat and thus warm the surfaces of objects above general room temperature.

### 6.2.3   Heat

Heat is the energy possessed by a substance in the form of kinetic energy of atomic or molecular motion. The heat contained by an object, normally measured in joules, calories or British Thermal Units, is the product of its mass, temperature and specific heat capacity. Heat may be transmitted from places of higher temperature to those of lower temperature by *conduction,* the direct transfer of energy from one molecule or free electron to another, *convection,* the transfer of heat through movement of a liquid or gas, and *radiation,* the transfer of energy independently of matter.

The chief observable physical effects of an increase in heat content include a rise in temperature; an increase in the rates of physical processes, such as the movement of water and gases through solids; change of state, for example from solid to liquid or from liquid to gas; expansion; and various electrical effects. An increase in the rate of physical processes will in turn increase rates of chemical reactions as previously discussed. Typically, a 5 °C rise in temperature will result in a one-and-one-third times increase in reaction rates and this will also apply to the evaporation of traces of volatile material, perhaps formed by deterioration, since such evaporation is primarily limited by diffusion. Age embrittlement is related to these processes. Materials will mostly expand by a very small amount but for moisture-containing materials like wood, paper, bone, ivory, leather, textiles and paint this effect will be of secondary importance to changes caused by moisture induced dimensional change. For brittle, non-moisture absorbent, composite objects, such as enamel on metal, whose parts expand at different rates, an unusual change in temperature might be dangerous. The activity of fungi and bacteria generally increases in warm weather. Most importantly, changes in temperature

cause changes in relative humidity unless this is kept independently constant. An increase in temperature will lower relative humidity. Where this is caused by radiant heat the effect will take place directly on the surface of the object and will not be adequately controlled by room RH adjustments. This might be advantageous for some textiles, where the rate of fading could be reduced, but on the other hand it could also lead to a decrease in flexibility. For other materials this effect can be extremely dangerous, leading to splitting of veneers and even complete fragmentation of materials such as ivory. One possible effect of the surface heating caused by lighting is to set up a fatigue cycle of heating by day and cooling by night thus leading to alternate expansion and contraction of objects either directly, or indirectly, through changes in moisture content, that has enormous potential for long-term damage.

***Measurement and control of temperature***

For ordinary purposes, temperature is measured on the Celsius (Centigrade) or Fahrenheit scales, each of which has set points defined by the freezing point and boiling point of water under standard atmospheric pressure. The units of Kelvin (K) and Celsius temperature interval are identical. A temperature expressed in degrees Celsius is equal to the temperature in Kelvins less 273.15 °C (i.e. freezing point of water = 273.15 °K). Temperatures in display areas should be kept reasonably low, compatible with human comfort and constant. A figure of 20 °C ± 1 °C is a common target. For storage of archival material, particularly cellulose, a lower temperature could be employed subject to the consideration that moving an object straight from a cold to a warm environment may cause water vapour to condense from the air on to its surface. The temperature at which this happens is called the *dew point*. For a room at 55% RH (relative humidity) and 20 °C the dew point is 11 °C.

Sources of heat in buildings housing furniture collections include the sun, people, radiators and other components of heating systems such as pipes and internal lighting. The effect of the sun depends among other things on the aspect of the building, materials from which it is made, on the number of windows and on climate. An important aspect of the control of temperature is to ensure that the internal space of the building is properly insulated from external conditions. Excessive radiant heat must be avoided and to this end both spotlights and control gear carefully sited. The temperature rise which can occur through lighting depends on the illuminance, on the spectral quality of the light (notably the proportion of infra red) and on the colour of the object (more for a black object than for a white one). Halving the distance between the light source and the object will result in four times the amount of light falling on the surface of the object (an example of the *inverse square law*). Tungsten spotlights can be obtained with a special 'dichroic' reflector which allows infra red radiation to pass through the back of the lamp so that only visible radiation is directed at the object. A standing person emits about the same amount of heat as a 100 W light bulb. The effect of different heat sources on the internal temperature of buildings and the control of temperature are further discussed by Thomson (1986) and Cassar (1995). The effect of temperature changes on relative humidity is of very great importance.

### 6.2.4 Absolute humidity and relative humidity

Absolute humidity is a measure of the actual amount of moisture in the air and is expressed as grams of water per cubic metre of air (g water/m³ air). The higher the amount of water vapour in the air, the higher the absolute humidity. The amount of moisture (water vapour) the air can hold before becoming saturated varies with temperature (*Figure 6.3a*). In other words, warm air can hold more moisture than cold air. Relative humidity (RH) measures the amount of moisture in the air, relative to the amount of moisture the air could hold at a given temperature and is expressed as a percentage.

Relative humidity may be defined as:

$$\frac{\text{Amount of water in a given amount of air at a given temperature}}{\substack{\text{Maximum amount of water that} \\ \text{amount of air can hold at that} \\ \text{temperature}}} \times 100\%$$

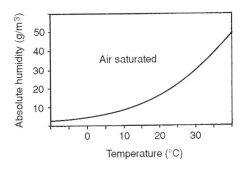

(a)

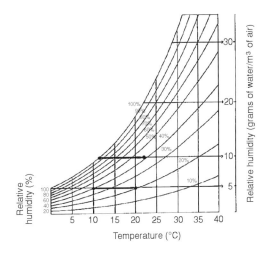

(b)

**Figure 6.3** Relationship between humidity and temperature
(*a*) Graphical representation of the relationship between absolute humidity and temperature.
The amount of moisture the air can hold before becoming saturated is dependent on temperature. This graph illustrates that the warmer the air, the more moisture it can hold. The line plotted on this graph represents the maximum amount of moisture air can hold at a range of temperatures. Above the line, the air is saturated, whilst below the line it is not
(*b*) Representation of the relationship between relative humidity and temperature. Whilst the amount of moisture in the air may remain constant, changes in temperature will affect the relative humidity. Thus, in this example, air with an absolute humidity of 5 g/m³ will have a relative humidity of about 40% at 10 °C. If temperature increases to 20 °C, the same absolute humidity will produce an RH of about 20%. Similarly, air containing 10 g/m³ of water at 22 °C will have an RH of about 45%, but if the temperature falls below 12 °C the RH will rise to 100% and moisture will begin condensing out of the air. Note that the figures in this graph are approximate and should not be used for RH calculations

The relationship between absolute humidity, relative humidity and temperature is illustrated in *Figure 6.3b*.

All organic materials contain water in life which is gradually given up when the object is no longer part of a living organism. A level is reached at which the moisture content of the material is in equilibrium with the relative humidity on the air. The moisture content of wood at 50% RH is about 11%. If the relative humidity of the air falls, the object will give up some water to the air and if the RH rises the object will absorb water. Material displaying these properties is called hygroscopic and this applies to most organic materials encountered in objects and to some inorganic materials.

The origin of changes in RH may lie with the weather, penetration of rain water (e.g. from the roof or drains), condensation due to temperature differences, or other effects of changes in temperature. An important aspect of changes in RH is that they are often accompanied by dimensional changes. Materials such as wood expand on absorption of water from the air when the RH rises and contract on loss of water when the RH falls. Relative humidity changes are much more potent than temperature changes in this respect; the same amount of expansion will result from a rise of 4% RH as from a rise of 10 °C at constant relative humidity. It is important to maintain the dimensional stability of materials and hence the scale of relative humidity is used. If the RH of the air is kept constant then, within reasonable temperature limits, the moisture content of materials will remain constant.

## Measuring RH

Perhaps not surprisingly, dimensional change can be used to measure relative humidity. Any organic material, even wood, could be used for this purpose. Hair is a more rapidly responding material and hair hygrometers are still in use, especially where continuous recording of RH is required. In practice, these machines need to be calibrated fairly often against another more accurate device such as the wet and dry bulb hygrometer. This instrument consists essentially of two thermometers arranged in a framework so that air can be moved past the bulbs. One thermometer has a small sleeve of fabric fitted over it the other end of which rests in a reservoir of distilled water. Air moving past this 'wet bulb' cools it by evaporation of the water so that a lower temperature is read at the wet bulb than at the dry bulb. The depression of the wet bulb temperature compared to the dry bulb reading depends on the amount of water in the air and so can be used to calculate relative

**Figure 6.4** Originally developed by Willis Carter (USA) in the early twentieth century, the hygrometric chart graphically represents the interrelationship of air temperature and moisture content. More sophisticated psychrometric charts also contain specific volume (the weight per unit volume of air), enthalpy (the relative energy content per unit weight of air) and a correction for variations in atmospheric pressure (see, for example, Thomson, 1986).

(*a*) A hygrometric chart. The chart appears very complicated because it contains four scales: the dry bulb temperature, the wet bulb temperature, the dew point temperature and relative humidity. The humidity ratio (grams of water/kg of air) is sometimes indicated on the right side of the chart. Thomson (1986) uses absolute humidity (grams of water/m³ of dry air) to aid visualization of the concept, although this results in a small loss of accuracy because air expands as it is heated, so the grams of water per cubic metre falls slightly as temperature rises

(*b*) Dry bulb temperature, which is the air temperature as measured by a thermometer. The dry bulb temperature is indicated by vertical lines running from the base of the chart

(*c*) Wet bulb temperature, which shows the cooling effect of evaporating water. It is measured by a thermometer with its sensing bulb covered by a wet wick that also has air being drawn across it. The wet bulb temperature is indicated by sloping lines running from the curved edge at the left of the chart

(*d*) Dew point temperature, which is the temperature below which moisture will condense out of the air and form droplets of water. The dew point temperature is indicated by horizontal lines running from the curved edge at the left of the chart

(*e*) Relative humidity, which measures the moisture content of the air in comparison to how much moisture the air could hold at a given temperature. Relative humidity is indicated by the curved lines that originate from the vertical line at the left edge of the chart

(*f*) In conjunction with a hygrometer or psychrometer, which measure dry and wet bulb temperatures, the hygrometric chart can also be used to calculate relative humidity. Plotting hygrometer readings of 20 °C (dry bulb) and 15 °C (wet bulb), indicates a relative humidity of 50%. Note that an 8 °C drop in temperature (indicated by the broken line) will cause relative humidity to rise to 95%, and conversely, a rise in temperature to 28 °C will lower RH to about 30%. The effects of such fluctuations in RH on the equilibrium moisture content of wood and the movement that results is described in Chapter 2

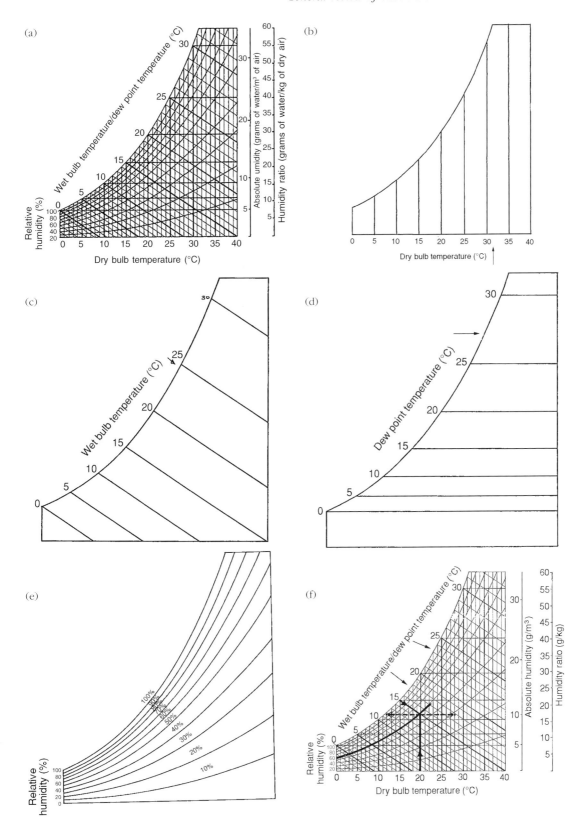

humidity. Standard tables (see Thomson, 1986) and other aids are available to make this a relatively simple routine calculation (*Figure 6.4f*). The traditional version of this instrument, known as the whirling hygrometer or sling psychrometer, has a handle arranged at right angles to the frame containing the thermometers and can be swung round rather like a football rattle through 360° so that air moves past the bulbs. When carefully used, the accuracy of such devices is adequate to meet the needs of most furniture conservators but they should be carefully calibrated at regular intervals against a more accurate and reliable instrument such as a dew point hygrometer (Pragnell, 1989). This service should be available from the supplier of the instrument but failing this can be obtained from an independent laboratory such as SIRA Test and Certification Ltd. A range of instruments is also available capable of recording RH and temperature continuously over several days, weeks or months (Child, 1993). Such measurements are a valuable guide when assessing the suitability of an environment for display or storage of wooden objects. For extensive general discussion of moisture and humidity and their measurement see Wexler (1965) and the Instrument Society of America (1985). Measurement of moisture in wood is discussed in Chapter 2.

### RH and damage

Relative humidity influences deterioration in three main ways: first through high levels or excessive wetness of the air, secondly by excessive dryness and thirdly by changes, particularly rapid changes. Rhythmical daily changes such as those caused by turning lights on and off or seasonal changes such as those caused by winter heating are hard to evaluate but it is accepted that they are responsible for stresses that are damaging in the long term. Damage may be due to dimensional change, biological activity or chemical reaction. Constancy of RH around a predetermined optimum value is the aim in museums and other institutional collections but before examining ways in which this may be realized the major classes of objects affected will be briefly reviewed.

All moisture-absorbent materials including leather, parchment, textiles, wood, animal glue and some other adhesives, bone, ivory, paper and easel paintings are affected. Skin products, whether cured or uncured, become very dry and brittle in excessively dry conditions (RH <40%) since water acts as a plasticizer for most organic materials. Although in some cases flexibility can be restored, dimensional change in the support may cause irreversible flaking of surface decoration.

Wood is anisotropic. Moisture induced dimensional changes in wood take place mainly across the grain and very little along the grain. Tangential shrinkage is usually about twice radial shrinkage though in some species it may be much more. These differences account for much of the warping, dislocation of parts, splitting, loosening of joints and breaking of fibres that can occur in complex wooden structures exposed to wide fluctuations in RH. The nature of wood and its deterioration are further discussed in Chapters 2 and 7. Bone and ivory are also anisotropic and where these and other materials are used in conjunction with a solid wooden ground or support the different rates of expansion and contraction under conditions of changing RH can result in splitting and lifting.

Biological activity is mostly encouraged at high relative humidity. The growth of bacteria and moulds on leather is encouraged when RH is in excess of 68% at 20 °C and uncured skins may putrefy in damp conditions. All forms of paper can support the growth of micro-organisms under conditions of high RH and these can cause staining. Cellulose and gelatin sizes and various flour pastes and dextrin adhesives used on paper are excellent nutrient materials for fungi which may become active when RH exceeds 70%. Some micro-organisms live on size and others on cellulose. Where sizing material is destroyed affected areas become highly moisture absorbent. When cellulytic micro-organisms are present the surface of the paper will be eroded and the paper may become very brittle. In either case, iron salts tend to be accumulated in damaged areas where they give rise to rusty brown spots. This is one form of a problem known as foxing. The breakdown of size and cellulose may additionally provide food for book lice and silverfish which may cause staining by leaving their excrement. Textiles may be similarly attacked by insects accompanying fungal attack. Animal fibres, mainly wool and silk, provide foodstuffs for several varieties of insects. The optimum RH for clothes moths is 65–75% and for the brown house moth about 90%, though even very low levels of humidity may not deter them completely. Some paint media, particularly water colour used on ivory or vellum, may contain a proportion of honey or glycerine which can make them very sticky in damp conditions. This provides food for micro-organisms and may cause the paint layer to adhere to adjacent surfaces. The sapwood of many timbers is also a good source of nutrients for micro-organisms and fungi and may also be attacked preferentially by several wood-boring insects including powder post beetle, death watch beetle, common furniture beetle and longhorn beetle. Any type of object which contains any of these materials in its composition may be liable to attack.

Humidity is an important factor in the corrosion of metals, in the fading and tendering of textiles, in the movement of salts into and out of ceramics and stone and in the phenomenon known as glass disease. The consequences and mechanisms of deterioration of these materials are discussed in Chapter 8.

The mechanism of fading and tendering of textiles is still not perfectly understood but the photochemical degradation of textiles and water colours requires oxygen and water without which very little action takes place, as demonstrated by the early work of Russell and Abney on water colours (Brommelle, 1964). The influence of humidity may possibly be explained on the basis that most fading reactions are bi-molecular and are diffusion controlled. At higher levels of humidity, diffusion of the reaction partners towards each other becomes increasingly facilitated. The excited species formed by absorption of light then gets less time to dissipate its energy and return to the ground state before reaction occurs. In general, diffusion of the participants in a chemical reaction will be increased at higher RH and a film of moisture on surfaces will provide an ideal medium for reaction between objects and pollutant gases in the air.

### Control of RH

Criteria for moisture control are discussed by Brundrett (1990). Where water is an agent of deterioration, the humidity should be kept to a minimum. Where the water content of an object affects its physical properties, the humidity should be kept stable. Based on a compromise of the requirements of the different types of materials encountered in a mixed collection, a point in the range 50–60%, usually 55%, with a variation of ±5% has been chosen by many museums in the United Kingdom. Specially sensitive items may have to be isolated and treated individually if their requirements cannot be met in this range. For a collection of only one type of object a figure can be chosen which best suits that type of object. These set limits for variation do not necessarily represent the best that could be done for the sake of the objects. This is partly because the complexity of possible interactions mitigates against a single simple statement of 'ideal' conditions for all objects and partly because it is anything but easy to keep relative humidity constant (even within the above limits) in a building that is actually being used.

Having decided on a desirable level of RH, however, the question next arises as to how this is to be maintained throughout the day and throughout the year. There is no perfect answer to this question but it is certainly influenced by the resources available – especially money. Probably the most complete answer to humidity control is provided by air conditioning (Chadderton, 1993). Air conditioning should ensure that air in galleries is kept clean and free from pollutant gases and micro-organisms and is maintained at a near constant temperature and relative humidity. Before this can be installed it is necessary to have at least one and preferably two years readings for temperature and relative humidity in those buildings or parts of buildings which it is proposed should be air conditioned. The variables which most affect the system include the requirement for filtration, the movement of people in and out of the space, the lighting, climate and daily and seasonal variations. The heating and cooling requirements for the least, mean and greatest situations must then be worked out before air conditioning can be installed. Once installed, an air conditioning plant requires skilled attention to maintain it in good working order and emergency backup facilities in case any part of it breaks down.

Full air conditioning requires considerable space for plant and duct work, is expensive and disruptive to install and costly to run, the most expensive item being the electricity to power fans, for air movement and refrigeration plant. In addition it may not be suitable for some buildings. For these reasons and where action has to be taken quickly, air conditioning is not always the perfect answer and alternatives to full air conditioning have to be considered. Partial air conditioning, the provision of ventilation, heating and humidification is one such alternative. Where heat builds up under a glass roof, for example, it is possible to use internal blinds to shade areas below and to have these arranged at a suitable distance away from the glass (say 30 cm) so that the space between the glazing and the blinds can be ventilated. This will help to dissipate most of the heat before it can affect the major part of the environment. This technique can also be used as an adjunct to full air conditioning to help avoid overloading the main plant. Whether or not air conditioning is being used double or triple glazing is a good idea. In fact for an air conditioned room it is almost an essential requirement since air at 55% RH and 20 °C will lead to quite heavy condensation on cold glass in winter.

One may be able to eliminate dangerous extremes in RH by using equipment to provide extra water in dry conditions or to remove it in damp conditions. It is usually only one of these that is pertinent in any given environment. A humidistat can be used to control either a humidifier or a dehumidifier so that when the RH exceeds or drops below the desired level a machine is automatically switched on to correct the situation. Winter dryness in buildings, caused by heating cold air with a low absolute humidity, is a problem that can at least partially be overcome by keeping the heating at the lowest level commensurate with acceptable conditions of human comfort. If a humidistat and a thermostat are connected in series with the humidistat set to the lowest permissible limit of RH this will maintain the RH in the normal way. Thermostatic control of heaters can be used to ensure that they can only operate when the temperature falls below the thermostatic lower limit and only if the RH is in excess of the minimum.

*Humidifiers* Humidifying equipment is available in three basic types: atomizing, heated evaporative and unheated evaporative. The atomizing humidifier literally breaks water up into tiny droplets and flings them into the air together with whatever else in the way of salts or impurities the water may have contained. A variation on this theme uses ultrasonic waves to break up the water to a very fine mist. This machine can be controlled from a humidistat and is capable of achieving high humidity levels when required. Should the control fail, however, the atomizer carries on working even when the RH has reached 100%. The heated evaporative type consists of a container of water heated electrically which functions like a large kettle. This type is usually found in air conditioning systems. The type of humidifier most commonly seen in furniture conservation studios and museum display areas is the unheated evaporative type in which the water is evaporated from an absorbent material by a current of air blown through that material. A commonly used type consists of a drum, with an outer layer of plastic foam material, which revolves through a large reservoir of water in the base of the machine. A fan then blows room air through the plastic foam thereby evaporating the water (and slightly cooling the air). This type leaves salts behind in the water and requires regular and frequent cleaning. The instrument largely fails safe and is not capable of giving an RH much above 70%. Unless plumbed in the machine has to be filled more or less every day, depending on the conditions.

*Dehumidifiers* Dehumidifying equipment can be divided into desiccant and refrigerant types. The former is generally used in colder conditions and the latter in warmer conditions. In the desiccant type, air is blown through a desiccant material, for example lithium fluoride and then returned to the room. Usually the drying material is arranged in a drum so that only part of it is actually conditioning the air at any one time. The rest is simultaneously reconditioned by having hot air from another source blown through it. The moisture laden air is then ducted away. The refrigerant type of dehumidifier is basically a rearrangement of the ordinary refrigerator. A gas which liquefies under pressure alone is allowed to expand in one part of the machine where it picks up heat from its surroundings. This cools the air around that part of the machine below its dew point so that it loses moisture which is drained away. The air is then circulated to the other side of the machine where the gas inside is re-compressed. The gas gives out heat thus rewarming the air outside to its original temperature so that the net result is a lowering of the RH of the air.

In calculating the requirements for humidification control, the amount of ventilation is of prime importance, since each room change of air will need to be either moistened or dried. This is usually calculated as the amount of water which has to be added or removed per hour and capacity arranged accordingly. It is also necessary to ensure that local variations do not arise through inadequate mixing. The creation of buffer zones around doors can help in this respect. It has been observed in rooms with permanent exterior sources of dampness that dehumidifiers cannot eliminate this but merely create a gradient that will encourage damp to flow into the room. Such sources of dampness obviously need to be eliminated.

*Case control of RH using buffers* Rather than conditioning the very large volumes in the whole, or part of, a building, it is possible to condition the much smaller volume of air inside a display case. This can be done by piping conditioned air into cases or by conditioning the air in situ inside the case. Certain salts in saturated solution will produce a particular RH in their immediate environment. At 20 °C, magnesium nitrate gives, in practice, about 50% RH and sodium bromide about 58% RH. Trays can be used to provide a large surface area and a good degree of uniformity of RH can be maintained provided that cases are well sealed. Great care is needed to prevent migration of salt crystals out of their container and into the general environment of the case. If this happens there is a significant danger that corrosion will quickly get under way and may do considerable damage before it is detected. Dried salts may constitute a fire hazard. To prevent this problem, a barrier of some kind may be used to prevent the escape of salt crystals but as soon as this is done, the primary advantage of the use of salt solutions, that of rapid response, is neutralized. Rates of response may then be slowed down to those obtainable with silica gel. Silica gel (at approximately 20 kg per cubic metre of space) can be used as an RH buffer if it is first kept for a period of time (usually between four and fourteen days) at the same RH that is to be maintained in the showcase. It is then put in a tray and positioned in the showcase under a perforated base board upon which the object is supported. The silica gel tends to absorb water if the RH exceeds the conditioned humidity and to give up moisture if the air becomes too dry. There is a danger that changes in RH, larger and faster than silica gel can handle, will occur if lighting is not chosen carefully to minimize heating effects. Silica gel can be used both for display and for transit but the cabinet or container used should be well sealed because silica gel is not able to react to RH changes very quickly.

Many older buildings have thick walls which help to minimize solar gain and contain a great deal of hygroscopic material such as plaster, wood cladding, timbered floors and beams in their construction. Such buildings behave as good buffers and show great resistance to changes in temperature and relative humidity, especially when undisturbed by human visitors. Victorian timber show cases behave as good buffers if well sealed, providing the external temperature remains reasonably constant. Providing RH is carefully monitored, these principles can be extended to allow objects themselves to buffer their own environment. This does, however, require very well sealed cases with good temperature control and an understanding of the parameters of moisture content, RH, temperature change and case volumes involved. The efficacy of the sealing in a showcase may be determined from the number of times in one day the air in the case is completely exchanged by normal air movement between the case and the outside. A case in which 0.1 (i.e. one-tenth) of an air exchange takes place each day may be considered well sealed.

The concept of hygrometric half-time, that is the time taken for the difference between (show)case RH and room RH to drop to half its starting value, is useful in attempting to design stable environments. A continuing goal for many institutions is to arrive at hygrometric half times which are sufficiently long for the showcase RH to remain stable through a whole season without maintenance or mechanical aids. In any case, buffers can be a useful adjunct to other control techniques and as a back up in case these break down. Current thinking suggests that rather than attempting to maintain an absolutely stable and constant environment throughout the year irrespective of external conditions, it may be better to adjust RH over a season, following natural seasonal changes but in a gradual and controlled manner. An example would be to allow RH to change by 2% per month so that the mid winter RH (in northern temperate climates) would be 12% below the mid summer RH, to which it is gradually allowed to return over the intervening six months. For further discussion of RH see Thomson (1986) and the references given at the end of section 6.2.

## 6.2.5  Pollution

Pollution is defined by the *Oxford English Dictionary* as 'that which makes physically impure, foul or filthy, dirties, stains, taints or befouls'. Unlike the previously discussed agents of deterioration, pollution can take many forms. The problem may be considered under the headings of particulate pollution and gaseous pollution.

### *Particulate pollution*

The size of particulates – solid particles suspended in air – ranges from about 0.01 μm to about 100 μm and is of great importance. Some examples of the sizes of different particulates are as follows:

| | |
|---|---|
| Polymerized plant material, automobile exhaust and tobacco smoke | 0.01–0.1 μm |
| Soot, oil smoke | 0.1–1 μm |
| Sea salt | 1–10 μm |
| Coal dust, ash, pollens | 1–100 μm |

Particles from about 1 μm upwards are sometimes called *primary particulates* or *mechanical particulates* because they have all been formed by direct mechanical action or sent directly into the air as particles. Those below 1 μm are known as *secondary particulates* as they are formed by chemical processes between gases and vapours which have been introduced into the air.

The burning of fossil fuels in power stations, internal combustion engines and elsewhere produces a great deal of sooty and tarry material. This will usually have become acidic through adsorption of sulphur dioxide and may contain iron and other heavy metals in varying proportions. The continuous process of erosion, brought about by rain, wind, temperature changes and mechanical action, of all exposed material is another source of particulate materials. Areas near the sea may be affected by salt crystals blown into the air as spray. Inside buildings, the breakdown of the fabric of the building itself gives rise to a wide range of particulates, including very fine (0.01 μm) alkaline cement dust, plaster dusts and fibres from furnishing fabrics. People in buildings also give rise to very significant levels of particulate pollution in the form of dead skin, hair and textile fibres from clothing.

The Clean Air Act (1956) did much to reduce levels of particulate pollution in London from around 1000 μg/m$^3$ in the early 1950s to around 40 μg/m$^3$ in the late 1980s. Background levels over the whole of the industrialized countries may be expected to be in the region of 20 μg/m$^3$. The natural particulates produced from plants and from aromatic materials of plant origin which have been polymerized by sunlight could account for about half this figure.

All particulate material which settles on an object will make it dirty and impair the visual qualities of the surface thus making cleaning necessary. However carefully cleaning is carried out, the possibility of damage cannot be excluded; removal of some of the object along with the dirt is almost inevitable and repeated cleaning will cause deterioration to a varied but certain extent. Sea air laden with salt spray may find its way indoors in coastal areas where it will deposit small amounts of salt which can maintain a high local RH. This can greatly accelerate the corrosion of metals, especially bronze, and may find its way into ceramics and stone, storing up trouble for the future when it may recrystallize in a lower RH and damage the surface of the object. Acidic particulate matter attacks many materials, including all forms of cellulose. The alkaline dust from cement may cause damage to oil paint, silk and some dyes and pigments, notably Prussian blue. Moisture trapped on the surface of an object by particulate matter will speed certain reactions and fine particles of skin, textile fibres and plant materials will encourage the growth of micro-organisms. Some of these may produce ammonia, which has been implicated in the stress-corrosion cracking of copper alloys. Particulate matter on metals can give rise to differential aeration cells in situations where the predominant cathodic reaction is oxygen absorption and where one part of the metal surface is more readily attacked than another part.

*Control of particulate pollution* These few examples should serve to illustrate that mechanisms for deterioration exist as a result of the accumulation of particulate material which should therefore be prevented wherever possible. Although dirt covered surfaces can appear to survive unharmed it is not sensible to wait until proven damage has occurred before taking action to prevent it. One approach to this, in museums at least, is for all exhibits to be kept in well-sealed showcases and for all two-dimensional objects to be glazed in frames. All material in stores should be similarly well protected. This is, however, still an incomplete solution and it is desirable wherever possible to try to prevent the entry of particulates into the building in the first place. This can best be done by filtering the air circulating through the building from the moment it gains entry to the building. Good seals on windows and on doors are also very important, particularly when not in use. The process of removing particulates by filtration necessarily implies some form of air conditioning plant.

Various types and grades of filters are available to remove particles from 10 m or larger down to the very small particles in the 0.01 m range. The efficiency of these filters is variously quoted on the basis of the proportion by number of particles removed or as a percentage removed down to a certain size limit. To make use of the latter principle, one needs to know the size distribution of particles that one is likely to be dealing with. It should also be remembered that the volume of a sphere is determined by the expression $4r^3$ from which it can be shown that a 10 μm

particle weighs a billion ($10^9$) times as much as a 0.01 μm particle of the same density. Additionally there may be some difference in the ability of particles of different sizes to cover a surface: within certain limits, which do not define the whole range of particulate pollution, the smaller the particle the greater the covering power (see section 5.8.2). On balance, the best guide to the efficiency of a filter is probably the percentage by weight of the total particulate matter removed.

The smallest particles likely to be encountered are about 0.01 μm and from this size up to about 0.1 μm are unstable, tending to aggregate within a very short period of time to form particles in the range 0.1–1 μm. These latter particles can remain indefinitely suspended in the air until they hit something to which they may stick. The larger particles, over about 15 μm, tend to settle in still air. Although much larger particles may be blown some distance from their source of origin in a strong wind, they will not penetrate very far inside a building. In a selection of samples taken in London (Waller, 1968), about 50% of the total mass of particulates was under 1 μm in diameter. While this figure may be lower in some areas, it is clear that a suitable filter must have a high efficiency in this 1 μm region since all filters tend to become less efficient as the particle size decreases.

A convenient material which can be used to test whether a filter material can remove particulates in the range likely to be encountered in a museum or similar building is methylene blue dye. The test dust is made by spraying a solution of the dye into a stream of air, allowing the water to evaporate from the droplets and passing the resulting dust through the test material. The staining produced by particles which have passed the filter can then be measured colorimetrically. All the particles obtained in this way are under 2 μm in diameter, about 50% by weight being 0.5 μm or less and about 5% being less than 0.2 μm. The figures quoted for a filter material in terms of its efficiency in removing methylene blue are based on a single passage of the dye through the filter material. Thus a filter with a methylene blue efficiency of 60% will remove 60% of the total mass of methylene blue particles at a single pass. In general, at least 80% of the air in an air-conditioning system is re-circulated and under these conditions of recirculation the actual efficiency increases to about 90%. A filter material with a methylene blue efficiency of 80% used with a 90% recirculation of air would give about 97% by weight removal of all particulates. Although 'absolute' filters with a methylene blue efficiency of 99.99% are available, their use is not often considered justified in buildings with open doors and people wandering in and out. Instead, filters with an efficiency between 60% and 80% are generally recommended.

Fibre glass wool is one type of material commonly found in these filters and in general this becomes more efficient with use. The greater the efficiency of a filter material the greater is the pressure required to force air through it. The pressure drop across the filters should be monitored and when it becomes too great the filters must be changed. More efficient filters tend to be more expensive in installation, running costs and maintenance partly because they must be changed more often but also because more energy is required to move air through them and more heat is built up in the process and must be removed. It is sensible to have a relatively coarse pre-filter of some kind to remove the larger particles and thus extend the life of the finer filters. When filters are changed, there is a risk that some accumulated dirt may drop into the air ducts where it will be recirculated and care should be taken to avoid this. A check should be kept on the level of particulate material in galleries and small 'absolute' filters may be used for this purpose, the increase in weight of the filter being checked after a known amount of air has passed through them.

For some objects, particularly where open display is desired, removal of particulate pollution is of paramount importance. The greatest single risk to fragile textiles is cleaning. It is very important to protect such material, once cleaned, from deposition of further particulate matter which is likely to occur on horizontal surfaces on open display. A substantial quantity of dirt is actually produced inside buildings, particularly fibrous dirt from human occupants and visitors, hence the importance of filtering the air circulating inside the building. Ideally, objects not on display can and should be protected by means of Tyvek® or other suitable dust-proof covers. One way to deal with dirt produced inside the building is to arrange for air flow to move away from objects rather than towards them. Air at low velocity can be delivered near floor level and extracted close to the ceiling. In this way particulates generated inside the building are swept up away from object surfaces and can then be filtered out. Air velocity must be such that it does not cause damage to textiles and other fragile surfaces situated near air streams. Special care must be taken in siting filters in relation to displays so that dirt collected on the filters does not drop onto objects during maintenance. The effect of recirculating air to achieve improved dust control is that heat builds up in the system and must be removed. This cannot easily be achieved without drastic effects on RH unless full air conditioning is adopted.

Where filtration is in use, a buffer zone between entrances and exhibits is desirable to minimize the amount of particulate pollution introduced at the interfaces to the clean space. One way in which this might be achieved is to use the water aerosol principle, found in some coal mines. An aerosol generator of the Dautrebande type produces a sub-micron water aerosol which promotes the aggregation of smaller particles into larger ones. The larger particles tend to settle more readily and can then be removed by suction or by the familiar damp-mopping procedure. The amount of water involved in this process is quite small but interrelationships with humidity control have to be considered and checked.

Electrostatic dust precipitators are available which, by means of very high voltage confer a nett charge to particles passing through them. The charged particles are then collected on oppositely charged plates further down the air stream in the precipitator. These can be very efficient but the high voltage used causes ionization of the air and with it the production of ozone and an increased conversion of sulphur dioxide to sulphuric acid. For these reasons, electrostatic precipitators cannot generally be used in museums although it may be possible to produce charged particles by other methods that do not carry these risks. For a more extensive discussion of particulate pollution see Cass *et al.* (1991) and the references listed at the end of the following section on gaseous pollution.

### Gaseous pollution

There are many pollutants to be found in the museum in the gaseous or vapour states. Two of the most important of these, sulphur dioxide and ozone, are generated mainly outside the museum and these will be dealt with first.

*Sulphur dioxide* Although about half of all the sulphur dioxide ($SO_2$) on the surface of the earth comes from natural sources, this represents a concentration of only about $1-5 \text{ g/m}^3$. Levels in industrialized countries are much higher than this. Various European cities have concentrations of $SO_2$ up to a hundred times this amount. About 2.5% by weight of fuel oils is comprised of sulphur. Coal has up to 1.5% sulphur and diesel and petrol fuels also contain a proportion of this element. When these fuels are burnt in the presence of air, the sulphur combines with oxygen to produce sulphur dioxide. Sulphur dioxide in the presence of sunlight can form sulphur trioxide which combines with water vapour to form sulphuric acid. Alternatively, sulphur dioxide may combine with water to form sulphurous acid which is then converted by oxidation to sulphuric acid. In either case, the outcome is the same. Fine droplets of sulphuric acid thus formed are hygroscopic and continue to grow and absorb $SO_2$ until the pH may fall to about 4. This will then eventually be precipitated as rain. Some of the sulphuric acid may be at least partly converted to ammonium sulphate and precipitated in this form or be deposited as particulate material. Most of the $SO_2$, however, remains unchanged and finds its way into the museum where it may be converted into sulphuric acid directly on the surface of objects. It is generally found that the concentration of $SO_2$ in buildings is lower than outside, even without air conditioning, because of the tendency of $SO_2$ to be absorbed on plaster and similar surfaces.

Sixty-four micrograms of $SO_2$ will form 98 µg of sulphuric acid. In a room of one hundred cubic metres with a ventilation rate of twenty air changes per day and a sulphur dioxide concentration of 64 µg/m³ approximately 200 mg of sulphuric acid per day can be formed. This works out to about 6 g per month, at least some of which will stick to and react with many types of object materials, particularly those made of cellulose, stone or metal. Sulphuric acid is hygroscopic and may encourage glass disease.

All forms of cellulose are subject to attack by the sulphuric acid formed from $SO_2$. Wood, apart from its surface, is not greatly affected but cotton, linen and paper are all noticeably weakened and stained. Rayon, a reconstituted vegetable fibre, is also affected. Paper made from wood pulp contains a relatively high proportion of lignin, the breakdown products of which favour the conversion of sulphur dioxide to sulphuric acid. Iron and other heavy metals, particles of which are often found in paper, catalyse this reaction. The brown stain which is sometimes found on the outer edges of the pages of a book and which may extend some distance in towards the centre, particularly of those printed on cheap paper, is due to the action of $SO_2$. A combination of light and $SO_2$ has a super-additive effect on textiles and many of the dyes on silk and wool may be reduced to colourless leuco compounds by sulphurous acid, especially in high RH. The fading of ultramarine is also brought about in this way. The protein of animal fibres may be denatured by sulphuric acid and vegetable tanned leather is particularly vulnerable to a form of deterioration known as *red rot* in which the leather is reduced to a crumbly or powdery texture. Damage to stone and metal caused by sulphuric acid is discussed in Chapter 8.

*Ozone* Oxygen itself can hardly be considered a pollutant since it is essential for life on the planet. None the less, it is involved in many undesirable changes that take place in objects over time. In most cases there is not much that can be done about this besides reducing the energy available for activation of oxidation reactions. However, in certain cases, an oxygen absorber such as Ageless® can be placed with the object inside an oxygen impermeable bag to create a more or less inert low oxygen environment.

The powerful oxidant gas ozone ($O_3$) is formed from oxygen with considerable absorption of energy. This can occur through the action of silent electrical discharges or the ultra-short wave length UV radiation which penetrates from space to a height of 20–30 km above the earth (this explains the absence of UV radiation of wavelength shorter than 300 nm at ground level). Some of the ozone formed in these ways diffuses down to ground level to give a background concentration of 20–80 g/m$^3$. Much higher levels of ozone may be formed at ground level in a complex cycle of reactions involving oxygen, the NO$_2$ and NO oxides of nitrogen and sunlight. In the course of these reactions various reactive organic radicals may also be formed, one of which, peroxy acyl nitrate (PAN), is certainly damaging to health and perhaps to some object materials. The process, which is responsible for the infamous chemical smogs of Los Angeles can produce levels of ozone in excess of 1000 µg/m$^3$. Certain forms of electrical equipment may also produce ozone and nitrogen dioxide inside buildings. The strong electrical fields of electrostatic precipitators have been cited but mercury vapour lamps with quartz envelopes can also emit UV radiation shorter than 300 nm. The characteristic smell of ozone and NO$_2$ in the vicinity of photocopying machines, in which this type of lamp is used, is often quite marked, indicating a high concentration. The siting of photocopying machines should therefore be carefully considered.

Ozone (O$_3$) is one of the most powerful oxidizing agents. The usual reaction occurs when one atom of oxygen combines chemically with a reactant (X) and one molecule of oxygen is liberated as represented by the equation:

$$O_3 + X = O_2 + XO$$

All metals except gold and platinum can be oxidized by ozone. Paint, textiles, leather, furniture and almost all other materials which are wholly or partly organic may also be attacked. Those organic materials which are unsaturated absorb ozone completely, that is it breaks down all the double bonds with which it is in contact. Cellulose is rapidly degraded becoming brittle and cracking very easily when bent or strained. The partial conversion of ozone to hydrogen peroxide may also be involved in this. The oxidative degradation of organic materials and its im-

portance in the deterioration of artefacts is discussed by Grattan (1978). Protection of works of art from atmospheric ozone is discussed by Cass *et al.* (1991).

*Nitrogen oxides* Two of the oxides of nitrogen were mentioned in connection with the formation of ozone, but one of these, nitrogen dioxide, is also a considerable hazard in its own right. It is an oxidizing gas which reacts with an excess of water to form nitric acid – an exceedingly strong acid and an oxidizing agent. It reacts with most metals to produce the metallic nitrate and nascent hydrogen (the latter then reacting with the remaining acid to form some reduction product, e.g. NO$_2$ or NO). The salts formed will promote corrosion processes and, as in other cases of acid attack, may find their way into stone and ceramics. Many organic materials including cellulose and dyestuffs are also attacked, with the duel hazard of acid and oxidizing actions. To date, sulphates rather than nitrates have tended to accumulate on objects but as the concentration of nitrogen dioxide in the air is rising this may come to play a more significant role. Unlike sulphuric acid, nitric acid is not hygroscopic and is considerably more volatile. It does not therefore tend to sit on surfaces to the same extent but reacts on contact. The natural level of NO$_2$ is low, probably around 2–3 µg/m$^3$ although in towns with a heavy burden of traffic the figure may be nearer 100–300 µg/m$^3$.

*Hydrogen sulphide* Hydrogen sulphide (H$_2$S), which is found in the air in variable concentrations (5–30 µg/m$^3$), may be present as a natural product of decay, as well as from some industrial processes and it is in this form and as dimethyl sulphide that naturally occurring sulphur dioxide originates. Since hydrogen sulphide is extremely poisonous, rigorous controls are exercised by industry to prevent its release into the air. Hydrogen sulphide slowly brings about the tarnishing of silver by the formation of a brownish-black layer of silver sulphide on the surface. It is also well known for blackening lead pigments, particularly basic white carbonate, due to the formation of lead sulphide. The blackening of materials susceptible to hydrogen sulphide and also to certain other vapours may be brought about by localized conditions such as those found in display cases, packing cases or stores. Hydrogen sulphide is oxidized by ozone to sulphuric acid.

*Other pollutant gases and vapours*  All timbers may give off organic acid vapours (particularly acetic acid) that can be damaging to certain metals, particularly lead and its alloys, zinc and some copper alloys. This effect is more pronounced with some species such as oak and Douglas fir. Formic acid, used in the tanning of some leathers, in the coagulation of rubber latex and as a catalyst for certain adhesives, also gives rise to organic acid vapours and hence to damage. Marine animal shells containing carbonates and paper items are among other classes of material that may be damaged in this way. A great variety of materials including rubber, wool (especially felt) and adhesives used in particle boards and plywood may give off volatile sulphides, possibly encouraged by sulphur metabolizing bacteria. These can bring about the rapid tarnishing of silver including that found in photographic images. PVA emulsions may initially give off acetic acid vapours and the degradation of PVC may result in locally high concentrations of hydrogen chloride and hence hydrochloric acid, an extremely strong acid. Although the major problem in museums may be the removal of sulphur dioxide, nitrogen oxides and ozone, there are some recorded cases of really serious damage having been caused by local pollution of this sort. In addition, many hundreds of volatile organic compounds have been detected in show case environments (Martin and Blades, 1994) of which little is known concerning the damage they may cause. A general rule is to avoid organic materials in the construction and furnishing of cases for objects containing sensitive materials and, where this is not possible, to test such display materials carefully before use. However, if the objects being displayed are themselves predominantly of wooden construction this rule can be applied with far greater discretion. In a few cases, the materials combined in a single object may markedly react with each other. Testing of materials for short-term prediction of long-term effect is notoriously difficult but several materials testing services are available, including the

Oddy test offered by the British Museum and the Purafil coupon service.

*Control of gaseous pollutants*  A lesson that can be learned from the second law of thermodynamics (see section 6.2.1) is that pollutants should be trapped at source. If the randomization process is allowed to take over, by which pollutants are widely dispersed, then any process used in an attempt to reduce this disorder will itself result in the creation of even more disorder.

Two methods of removing pollutants are commonly used in museums. The first of these is a water spray, which is routinely used in air conditioning systems as part of the RH control. Since both sulphur dioxide and nitrogen dioxide are freely soluble in water, it will effectively remove these gases, provided that the water does not become too acidic. An alkali could be used provided it was not volatile but there are technical problems, such as the possibility of spray blockage, with this technique. Caustic alkalis would not be a good choice with $NO_2$ since NO is produced in the reaction and this is not very soluble in water but can recombine with oxygen to reform $NO_2$. Ozone is soluble in water but the solution formed is unstable, hence water spray is not satisfactory for ozone removal. In addition to the above mentioned gases, water spray should be very effective in removing hydrochloric acid and chlorides where these are present. Some volatile pollutants in cases can be absorbed on to materials such as activated charcoal or other, pollutant-specific, scavengers.

All substances are capable of retaining a film of gas on their surfaces but the amount retained is usually very small. Charcoal, having an enormous surface area absorbs gases in a remarkable manner. Specially prepared activated carbon filters can be obtained with surface areas of up to 700–1000 square metres per gram. The carbon granules are held in a mesh frame which is obliquely presented to the air flow. This type of filter is capable of removing up to about 95% of the sulphur dioxide in a typical industrial air sample at a single pass. Efficiency with nitrogen dioxide removal is more variable but can be up to 90% under similar conditions. The material is also very effective in reducing ozone to trace levels though this is not brought about by adsorption but by destruction of the ozone through reaction with traces of organic matter on the filter material. Charcoal filters are also capable of removing organic free radicals such as peroxy acyl nitrate. As with particulate removal, this type of filter improves in efficiency with recirculation of the air and there should be no difficulty in reducing $SO_2$ and $NO_2$ levels to below $10\,\mu g/m^3$ and ozone to trace levels (below $2\,\mu g/m^3$). Activated carbon filters need to be changed when their ability to absorb gases becomes diminished. This has to be determined by experiment in the first instance and a routine must then be established for their renewal. Where air conditioning is not available, the problem of air treatment becomes rather difficult as show cases have to be treated individually. Possibly a carefully chosen alkaline reagent might be useful in this respect. Although activated carbon filters may lose much of their efficacy unless air can be circulated through them, experience has shown that charcoal cloth can be effective in removing low levels of volatile organic substances produced inside show cases by the materials used in the construction of the case. For more detailed discussion of the causes, effects and control of air pollution see Calabrese and Kenyon (1990), Goodish (1990), Harrison (1992a, 1992b), Strauss and Mainwaring (1984) and Thomson (1986).

### 6.2.6   Biological agents

Many biological hazards, ranging from very small micro-biological agents such as bacteria, through mildew, moulds, fungi and insects to birds, rodents and other small mammals, have the potential to affect furniture collections. Damage between them may be interrelated. Surface dirt may allow creation of locally high RH that encourages mould growth which in turn may promote insect attack. The detritus that accumulates around pigeon nests on the outside of a building may encourage the growth and multiplication of insect pests such as carpet beetle which then find their way inside. Similarly, birds and small mammals may die in chimneys or roof spaces forming a source for insect infestation. Although it is not possible to fully investigate these interre-

lationships here, having proper regard to the principles of good housekeeping and some understanding of the needs of the various agents to flourish should enable them to be kept under control (Pinniger 1994, 2001; Sandwith and Stainton, 1991). For a general review of biological agents of deterioration see St George *et al.* (1954).

### *Fungi*

Damage to free-standing objects from fungi inside buildings has been known to occur in museums and country houses where some source of dampness has allowed locally high humidity to occur or where ventilation is poor. When it does occur it can quickly become deep-rooted. Fungi constitute a large and heterogeneous group of organisms within the plant kingdom, all of which lack chlorophyll and therefore cannot directly use energy from sunlight. Fungi are more complex in organization than bacteria but less so than mosses, ferns and flowering plants. Those responsible for deterioration of objects are mostly either moulds or wood-destroying fungi. Wood-destroying fungi are further discussed in Chapter 7. The term mould, although not very exactly defined in a biological sense, refers to the small non-parasitic fungi and the term mildew is generally used synonymously with it.

Fungi are found widely distributed in soil, water and air over much of the earth's surface with soil being the richest source. Fungi found in the air are primarily present in the form of spores. Fungi can utilize many different organic substrates. *Stachybotrys* is a common temperate climate form of fungus that attacks paper and textiles and *Pullularia* is common on paint films. Contact with soil is a good test for the resistance of a material to degradation and of the efficacy of fungicidal action. However, it is equally clear that the presence of soils (as may occur in old buildings and outhouses) is to be avoided as a potential source of deterioration.

Although wood-rotting fungi can be quite large, the vast majority of fungi are small enough that their characteristic structure can be made out only with the aid of a microscope, their largest parts being mostly less than 5 mm across. A large fungal spore measures about 20 μm in diameter, which is about the same size as the width of a cotton fibre, or of a very large bacterial cell.

Fungi have two basic kinds of structures, specialized for growth and for reproduction. The vegetative structure responsible for growth is the threadlike filament called the hypha. Collectively, hyphae are referred to as the mycelium. The diameter of the hyphae varies considerably but mostly falls in the range 2–20 μm. The principal reproductive unit is the spore. The relationship between the spores and the hyphae varies. In the simplest cases, the spore is formed from cells of the hyphae that separate at maturity. In other cases, more complex relationships exist. Spores may arise for example from specialized stalks or branches borne by the hyphae rather than directly from the hyphae themselves. Spores may be of two types. Under ideal growing conditions a type of spore may be formed rapidly and in large numbers that is suitable for rapid multiplication but has little resistance to adverse conditions. Another type of spore, suited to tiding the organism over periods unfavourable for growth, is produced under appropriate conditions. These may live for many years and can become widely distributed. Some of the fungi that cause deterioration reproduce by sexual methods while others do so asexually.

*Control of fungi* Factors that influence the growth of fungi include temperature, humidity, light, oxygen and the food source. The temperature range inhabited by various different fungi goes from just above freezing to about 50 °C. For each species there is a preferred temperature range at which growth rate is optimum, a temperature below which growth will not occur and a temperature above which growth will not occur. The optimum for many fungi lies in the range 15–30 °C. Many fungi will survive continuous freezing for several months but are less tolerant of repeated freeze–thaw cycles. Moist heat kills them more readily than dry heat. The critical average moisture content of a material for fungal growth is 20%. The corresponding RH is unlikely to be much below 70%. In conditions much drier than this fungi will not grow. Most fungi require a supply a supply of oxygen for growth but will operate independently of lighting conditions, although they may be damaged or killed by UV radiation. Fungi require sources of carbon, hydrogen, oxygen, nitrogen, sulphur, potassium, magnesium and phosphorous for growth. They may also require traces of iron, zinc, copper, calcium and manganese. Many naturally occurring compounds may be used by fungi as a source of carbon and energy. Glucose, sucrose, animal and vegetable fats and their component acids and glycerine can generally be used and some, but not all, fungi are able to utilize cellulose. Nitrogen may be assimilated as nitrates, ammonium salts, amino acids or proteins. Since the absence of any of these requirements will prevent or greatly inhibit growth, methods for control are based on eliminating or modifying one or more of these conditions by keeping objects clean and under suitable conditions of RH. Alternatively, poison, as used in wood preservatives, offers an effective and reliable means of protection in high risk situations. Methods of controlling fungal problems are further discussed by Strang and Dawson in Canadian Conservation Institute Technical Bulletin No. 12.

The chief products of fungal metabolism are carbon dioxide and water. However, other products are also formed that themselves have a deleterious effect on objects. These include various organic acids, alcohols and esters. The formation of coloured material is also frequently conspicuous.

### Insects

All insects are members of the class Insecta belonging to the vast phylum Arthropoda, the most complex and specialized group of invertebrates in the animal kingdom. About one million different insect species have been recorded to date though no one really knows how many species there are on the earth today. Between them, insects will eat virtually anything organic, including many of the materials used in the construction of furniture and wooden objects. They may also cause incidental damage, for example by their excreta. This causes them to be regarded as pests and for man to seek to eliminate them at least from environments in which valuable furniture is being maintained. Insect damage needs to be understood in relation to the habits of insects, their life cycle, the nature and distribution of the collections and the building. This chapter includes a brief general review that is complemented by more specific information on wood-boring insects in Chapter 7 and by a discussion of insect pests specific to textiles and other upholstery materials in Chapter 8. The steps needed to control insect infestation are broadly the same whether dealing with wood-boring insects or those which normally attack textiles and are dealt with in this chapter.

*Insect life cycles*   All insects have a segmented body, consisting of the head, thorax and abdomen, six legs and an exoskeleton made of a hard material called chitin. Insects cannot grow continuously in the way that vertebrates do, because of the hard exoskeleton, but instead grow in a series of steps made possible by moulting of the old hard skin. This occurs in one of two quite different ways. In *incomplete* or *gradual metamorphosis*, the eggs hatch to resemble miniature adults lacking only wings and the sex organs. Periodically, they form a new soft skin under the old hard one and when the old one is shed the insect swells to expand the skin which then sets hard. At the last moult the insect acquires wings and the organs of reproduction. Cockroaches, book lice and silverfish develop in this way. In the alternative process of *complete metamorphosis* the eggs hatch into *larvae* which do not resemble the adult at all and which normally have a completely different lifestyle and even different diet from it. The larvae grow by a series of moults but at the end of the larval stage they go through a *pupation* stage during which they change completely before emerging as the adult form. This process is used by many of the beetles and moths. It is most frequently the larval stage that causes damage to furniture collections, as is the case for example with carpet beetle and furniture beetle.

*Control of insects*   The growth and reproduction of insects are affected by temperature, humidity, light, oxygen and the food source. Insects are unable to maintain their body temperature independently of their environment and their metabolic processes therefore speed up as temperature increases and slow down as it falls. Most insect will not develop or breed below 10 °C and will breed only

slowly between 15 and 20 °C but will breed and develop rapidly above 25 °C. Insects require water but their sensitivity to moisture varies considerably. Some can obtain all they need from food but others require relatively high levels of moisture to sustain much activity. Insects need oxygen but they do not have lungs. Instead, they use a system of tubes called tracheae which branch from openings called spiracles on the side of the body. Oxygen exchange occurs by diffusion and this sets an upper limit on the size to which insects can grow. Insects are attracted to food sources in dark, warm, unventilated, undisturbed environments. Food sources include wood, textiles, upholstery stuffing, glues and storage and display materials. Soiled or dusty materials are most attractive. Insects can be classified as conveniently by what they eat (and therefore the type of damage they cause) as by their taxonomy. The most commonly occurring insect problems fall into three categories. The first of these is the wood-boring insects including furniture beetle and termites. Insects in the second category, which includes pests such as moth, carpet beetle and hide beetle that attack wool fur, feathers and textiles, are important to furniture because of the damage they cause to upholstery covers and fillings. The third category includes general detritus feeders, mould feeders and scavengers such as spider beetles, silverfish, book lice, cockroaches and ants that generally cause a nuisance and low levels of damage but which occasionally build up to levels sufficient to cause serious damage. In addition to these, problems may occasionally be experienced by parasites such as bed bugs (order Hemiptera, family Cimicidae) and fleas (order Siphonaptera) that are usually a domestic problem but which may be transferred to institutional collections with newly acquired objects.

Insects may arrive in various ways: via doors and windows, through air conditioning ducting from outside the building, from another area within the building, through the entry of an infested artefact, packing, storage or display material (e.g. floral displays or firewood), on the clothing of an employee during the normal performance of duties in storage areas, or on passing air flow, materials, or personal clothing in the display area. Insect pests may have been active in the building for some time before they are noticed. Infestations can build up on birds nests or dead animals in roof spaces and elsewhere and it is not until the balance of population exceeds the available food supply and the insects move out in search of food that they become noticed. Infestations may also go unnoticed for long periods as the larvae may live within the filling layers of upholstery undetected until physical evidence is observed at the surface or a structural failure occurs.

The ubiquitous nature of insects means that it is impossible completely to prevent their ingress into buildings. Good housekeeping, however, will ensure that the environment they find is inhospitable and does not promote rapid reproduction and infestation. An infestation will require a two stage response of treating individual objects and addressing the environmental conditions in which the object/s have been displayed. The steps which may be taken to identify and control an insect infestation can be summarized as monitoring, identification, assessment, treatment and, if necessary, conservation treatment of damaged object.

*Monitoring* Although it is not practicable entirely to prevent entry by all the above means, nevertheless some measures can be taken. It may be possible to reduce the numbers of doors and windows in stores or, if not, to provide more effective seals on doors, for example by means of draught excluder strips. Fine mesh screens can be fitted to windows and vulnerable objects can be stored in clear plastic bags provided that the environment created by the bag is suitable in other ways. Beyond this, prevention and control depend on regular and frequent inspection of the whole environment, especially of high risk items and areas and on good hygiene. All newly acquired material should be similarly inspected. Any active material found should be put into quarantine immediately and treated as soon as possible thereafter. To minimize the impact prior to detection of any insect damage that may occur, it is helpful to keep temperatures low, especially in stores where this is more readily achieved and to keep RH low, compatible with other physical needs of the collection. Good hygiene is especially important since

debris and rubbish, wherever they may be present in the environment, provide food and shelter for insects and can allow large populations to build up undetected. It is also helpful if textile objects themselves are clean since insect damage is then greatly reduced. All items loaned or acquired should be checked and surface cleaned. This may be undertaken ideally in a separate holding area over polythene sheeting which is destroyed at the end of the process. At the end of an installation checking should take place in the display area before removal to the storeroom. Use of residual insecticides in dead spaces in buildings and in cupboards can form part of the control strategy provided that they are used entirely in accordance with the manufacturers instructions and with proper regard for health and safety. Examples include pyrethrins (e.g. Drione, Lanasol), synthetic pyrethroids (e.g. Coopex), carbamate insecticides (Bendiocarb, Ficam) for use in dead spaces and dichlorvos (e.g. Vapona), a vapour phase insecticide, for use in cupboards. For further information on these materials see Pinniger (1994, 2001).

Despite the small size of most insect species and life stages, visual inspection is most important and enables a close check to be maintained on hygiene as well as on the actual physical presence of insects. Ideally all material on display and in store should be inspected regularly and frequently but this can become very demanding of resources, which may be scarce. It then becomes sensible to prioritize inspections and to put the greater part of the resources available into monitoring material at greatest risk, material of greatest value and parts of the building which have the greatest potential for, or historical record of, infestation. Places to look with extra care include dark corners and dead spaces, window sills and in among objects that might constitute potential food sources. Damage is often easier to see than insects themselves but dead insects and cast off skins may indicate activity as may fresh holes in wood or piles of dust or frass. Various kinds of insect traps are available, including sticky traps for carpet beetles and pheromone traps for furniture beetle. Traps may be placed in storage areas, or discretely in display areas, to help build up a picture of activity in the building. Regular inspection of traps can suggest when activity is reaching a level that gives serious cause for concern but traps must be periodically replaced to retain their efficiency. A regular 'insect sighting' reporting procedure for all staff together with specimen collection is useful. When insect activity of any sort is observed, it should be reported to the curator and to relevant conservation staff. Regular (twice yearly) cleaning of storerooms will disturb possible habitats and give occasion to check traps. It is most efficient to assign overall responsibility for scheduling the work and delegating the various duties to one person.

A powerful torch is an essential item of equipment as is a good plan of the building on all floors and a log book into which all information is recorded. If the numbers can be transferred to a spreadsheet this is even better. If damage is found it is helpful to photograph it so that future inspections can detect any change that might have occurred. Adult carpet beetles and furniture beetles are most likely to be seen in late spring and early summer, especially in June. If live insects are found on freshly damaged material, it is likely that the two events are connected. However, it is still desirable to get a positive identification to establish that the insect species that has been found is responsible for the damage seen. If doubt exists then an experienced entomologist should be consulted. The control measures to be adopted will depend on the nature and extent of the damage, the presence or absence of other objects at risk and the ease with which the affected area or object can be isolated or removed. No single control method is appropriate to all circumstances, it is therefore important to consider carefully how effective control of the insect can best be achieved without causing damage to objects or harm to personnel.

*Identification* Identification usually requires careful examination of an intact adult specimen cross-referenced with a suitable text such as Mourier and Winding (1986) or Pinniger (1994, 2001). Some larvae, for example that of the Guernsey carpet beetle (*Anthrenus sarnicus*), may be distinctive enough to allow a positive identification. Some beetles, such as the common furniture beetle, biscuit beetle (*Stegobium paniceum*) and the brown carpet beetle (*Attagenus smirnovi*) may be confused

by the untrained eye. Exit holes and frass may be used to identify many wood-boring insects (Hickin, 1975). Identifying the insect will allow likely habitats and food sources to be identified. The presence of large numbers of live insects usually indicate a serious infestation. The extent and level of activity of the infestation is often monitored, but cannot be controlled, by the use of adhesive 'blunder' traps which may incorporate pheromones. It is usually necessary to examine individual objects, displays, rooms or the building itself in order to establish the likely route/s of ingress, sources of food and environmental conditions such as elevated local temperature or relative humidity which contribute to insect activity (Child, 1997). Measures such as screens on windows, regular cleaning or elimination of 'dead' spaces, or, for example, treatment of unused ducting with a residual pesticide, will help prevent or limit the spread of insect infestation.

*Treatment* The principal aspects of treating active woodworm infestation and damage are to quarantine the affected object/s, to kill all stages of the life cycle of the insect present in the object, to repair structural damage, to disguise the disfigurement caused by flight holes if necessary (discussed in Chapters 13 and 14) and to reduce the likelihood of reinfestation.

The first stage of treatment is to isolate or enclose the affected object/s. Individual items may be sealed into a polythene plastic bubble. Although furniture beetle will chew through materials applied to wood, such as leather and lead foil, in order to exit the object, they are unlikely to bore through isolating material once they have emerged from the object.

Treatment for insect infestation can be broadly characterized by three strategies – insecticidal treatments, temperature-based treatments and low oxygen atmospheres. Insecticides may be applied directly to the object, usually dissolved in a hydrocarbon solvent, or by fumigation. Water-based formulations, developed as an alternative to solvent-carried insecticides, are unsuitable for finished domestic furniture because they penetrate wood poorly whilst causing the fibres to swell and stain (Pinniger and Child, 1996). Care should be taken when a painted or decorated surface is being treated as some formulations may cause irreparable damage. Applications which result in a deposit on the surface of an object will kill adults as they emerge, whilst insecticide in solution may be injected into wormholes to kill larvae and act as a residual treatment. It has been suggested that such contact or ingestion poisons provide protection for an extended time and therefore are more desirable than curative methods. This may not be true and it may not be desirable. The effectiveness of these liquid toxic materials largely depends upon the penetration rate of the liquid and on whether the entire piece is being treated or just a part of it.

*When using insecticides it is the responsibility of the conservator to be fully aware of the hazard presented and to take adequate precautionary measures.* These may include the use of suitable gloves, mask and coat and maintaining a high standard of personal and workshop hygiene. It is essential when using insecticides to follow the guidelines for safe use set out by the manufacturer. Ware (1988) and CCI Technical Bulletin 15 (1992) list numerous insecticides and pesticides which have been used to treat organic materials.

Insecticidal treatments have been used since the nineteenth century to control insect infestation. An overview of historical materials and methods is given by Unger *et al.* (2001) and Schiessl (1984). As side effects which are harmful to humans become known, insecticides are taken off the domestic market. An example of this was the insecticide lindane (hexachlorocyclohexane), which was widely used from the 1950s through to the early 1980s. Although an effective insecticide, its high vapour pressure resulted in it subliming off treated material over time. Concerns over long-term toxic and carcinogenic effects resulted in its withdrawal. Synthetic pyrethroids have been widely used to treat *anobium* infestations since the mid 1980s because they combine low mammalian toxicity, highly insecticidal properties which allow low dosage treatments, are odourless and do not stain (Pinniger and Child, 1996). However some research has connected their use with increased incidence of cancer (Nicholson, 1997). It may be necessary to label objects which have been treated with a residual pesticide to avoid any potential health and safety hazards for future handlers or conservators.

Dichlorvos vapour (2,2, dimethyl dichloro-vinyl phosphate) from insecticidal strips has proven to be effective against emerging adults. Such strips are particularly suitable for storage or display areas which are comparatively undisturbed and allow the slow and sustained release necessary for pesticidal effectiveness. Strips should not be placed in contact with objects. In the presence of moisture dichlorvos hydrolyses readily to form acidic compounds. At high RH (>70%) it is potentially damaging to metals and may cause natural resins, glues and plastics to become tacky and acid and disperse red dyes are also vulnerable to damage. Dichlorvos has a short term exposure limit (STEL).

Rentokil plc have developed a method which deposits a very low concentration of boric acid on exposed timber. This treatment is usually effective over a period of several years but will not prevent damage by larvae which will remain active until they emerge as adults and are killed.

*Fumigants* Toxic gases that have most commonly been used as fumigants for insect infestations in furniture include methyl bromide, ethylene oxide and phosphine, although sulphuryl fluoride, hydrogen cyanide, carbon disulphide and ethylene chloride have also been used. These materials have good penetration and are effective in treating complex furniture constructions and upholstery. They are not persistent, that is they do not prevent reinfestation, but they act quickly and have a high kill rate on all stages of the insect life cycle. The risk of staining is low compared to the use of solvent-based insecticidal formulations and the use of adhesives and coatings can proceed immediately after use. They have provided good results as a first line attack. However, they are highly toxic to other organisms, including people, and require special apparatus and fully trained and qualified personnel to be used safely.

There is a growing body of evidence that such materials are damaging to the environment and in some case to the objects being fumigated (Burgess and Binnie, 1991; Dow, undated; Florian, 1987; Koestler 1993). Methyl bromide for example has contributed to the destruction of the ozone layer and may damage some materials as it weakens chemical bonds in keratin found in hair, horn and turtleshell and sulphur bonds in rubber and some leathers. While some commercial fumigators today are still using materials such as methyl bromide, hydrogen cyanide and sulphuryl fluoride on common household furniture and on museum objects there is a growing movement towards the use of safer alternatives based on control of temperature and oxygen levels. Furniture conservators will need to be well informed about the side effects of each fumigant on a wide range of materials, since furniture often incorporates other materials such as upholstery fabric, leather, proteinous glues, varnishes, paints, metals, plastics, etc.

Treatments based on raising or lowering temperature must take into account the effect on RH and the possibility of dimensional change in wood and other materials, such as metals, incorporated into the object. Temperature treatments may be problematic for wooden components of large dimension since wood is an effective insulator and may protect larvae in the core. Temperatures of −25 °C to −30 °C maintained for two to three days will kill all stages of the insect infestation. Living tissue contains 90% or more water. The effects of freezing include dehydration, osmotic swelling, loss of bound water and ice formation within the insect's system, all of which are lethal. Objects with stratified layers, such as decorative surfaces, inlaid or veneered surfaces may not be suitable for freezing. Objects are often placed into plastic bags which may be aspirated using a vacuum or buffered to prevent potential damage from condensation in the bag as the temperature falls. Freezing treatments are widely used for textiles (Blyth, 1997). Raising the temperature above 50 °C is reported to kill all stages of the insect life cycle in less than an hour (Nicholson, 1997). The relative humidity must be kept constant to avoid the risk of damage to organic materials. The effect on adhesives and surface coatings of raising the temperature has not yet been fully investigated.

Low oxygen environments offer an alternative to insecticides. Gilberg (1989, 1990, 1991), Hanlon *et al.* (1992), Koestler (1992) and Rust *et al.* (1992) have experimented with replacing the air in a closed container with the inert gases nitrogen or argon. It has been demonstrated that stages of the insect life cycle are killed by lack of oxygen after a fourteen to twenty-one day cycle, depending on the type of gas, the tolerance of the insect species, temperature, relative humidity and oxygen concentration. Objects are usually placed in a gas-tight bag and the air replaced by flushing it with an inert gas such as nitrogen, argon or carbon dioxide. It is essential that the relative humidity is maintained at an appropriate level for the object being treated. The oxygen level can vary depending on the gas used and is measured with an oxygen meter. Oxygen scavengers may be placed in the bag to further reduce the oxygen level, but should not be placed in contact with the object as they produce heat. The system may be active, in which the flow of gas is maintained throughout the fumigation cycle to compensate for leakage, or passive, in which gas flow is stopped and the bag sealed with an oxygen absorber inside. When the cycle is completed the bag is vented and the object removed.

The advantages and disadvantages of a wide range of the methods available, including heating, freezing, low oxygen atmospheres, radiation and chemical agents, are further discussed by Pinniger (1994, 2001) and by Umney (1997). The use of inert gases in the control of museum insect pests is the subject of an extensive recent publication by Selwitz and Maekawa (1998).

When all the stages of dealing with an insect infestation have been completed, it is usually necessary to institute a monitoring programme, usually incorporating the use of blunder traps, to ensure that the treatment procedure has been successful and to identify any fresh outbreaks before substantial damage can be caused to objects. Fresh woodworm exit holes are usually light coloured and may need to be toned to a darker colour in order to be able to monitor for possible re-infestation.

An essential corollary to treating individual objects is addressing the environmental conditions which may have fostered the initial outbreak. This may include surveying the building in which the outbreak occurred and identifying vulnerable materials or objects, areas with high temperature or relative humidity and dead spaces, both in display and storage areas and those, such as chimneys or attics, incorporated into the architecture of the building. A high standard of housekeeping will ensure that the chance of further infestation is reduced and that, should it occur, biodeterioration is recognized before it can become established and serious damage results.

*Dealing with the effects of infestation* If *Anobium* infestation has caused severe structural damage it may be necessary to impart additional strength to structural components by consolidation, reinforcing the structure by introducing dowels or loose tenons, or in severe cases, replacing the entire component or, if the surface is valued, its core. The extent of reinforcement or replacement may be determined by balancing the loss of original material against the risk of further damage to the object or injury to people. In some cases an independent support for the structure of the object may obviate the need for interventive conservation.

## 6.2.7   Mechanical handling, packing and moving

Handling and movement are essential in the lives of objects but all object movements carry risk and take time and other resources to complete. Many of the most serious and obvious kinds of damage arise as a direct result of handling and moving objects. Conservators often need to move objects for examination, treatment, or photography but before moving an object it is important to consider the benefits the risks and the resources required. This may help to show that a move can be avoided, for example by carrying out work in situ rather than moving the object to a studio, or by photographing an object in the conservation studio rather than moving it to a separate photographic studio.

Some general principles for handling works of art are listed below:

- Always think first
- Be careful
- Take your time, irrespective of the financial value of the object
- Do one thing at a time
- Have enough people but only one leader – it is advisable to always have at least two people involved in any move, including one person not responsible for the object who will open and close doors etc.

- Restrict access – keep those who are not involved in the move away from the area
- Restrict handling to that which is essential
- Do not mix operations
- Keep everything clean
- Prohibit smoking, eating and drinking anywhere in the vicinity
- Put like works together and tie before moving
- During the move, avoid straining yourself or the object
- Report the full circumstances and extent of any damage as soon as possible.

The aim of every move should to be to accomplish transfer of the object(s) from one place to another without loss or damage to the object and without injury to people or damage to buildings or vehicles. Taking time to think through the complete sequence of a move before starting can help to make sure that these aims are achieved.

The complete sequence of a move can conveniently be considered as consisting of four phases. These are touching, lifting, moving, placing and leaving. Each of these carries its own risks which need to be managed. It is helpful to think through the sequence of these operations from beginning to end before starting the move to make sure that all important aspects have been considered before becoming committed to a course of action that might end in damage, injury or loss. A useful basic principle is to try to imagine what could possibly go wrong and then take steps to prevent it going wrong. This simple but powerful notion has been called 'Failure Mode and Effect Analysis' (Gilbert, 1992). The following paragraphs review the risks, preparation and protection for each stage in the moving process. Some points are applicable to more than one stage. Before an object is moved it should be examined carefully to determine inherent problems or weaknesses and characteristics, such as size, shape, weight, type of surface and fragility, that might affect handling or movement.

### *Touch*

The surface of an object often contains most of its relevant information, yet is the most vulnerable part. It may not be possible to detect new damage if the object has suffered previously. Conservation treatments are expensive, involve further risk to the object and do not replace lost information. Direct contact with an object can result in transfer of material between the handler and the object. Corrosion or other chemical reaction of the object may be caused or made worse by contact with moisture, salts, acids and dirt present on skin. Vulnerable surfaces include gilding, lacquer, metalwork and 'sick' glass. Staining and marking of objects containing materials such as paper, card and unglazed ceramics may be caused by skin contact. Contact with jewellery or other hard metal items worn by the handler may snag or damage delicate surfaces. Contact with soiled material present on the surface of an object, for example fumigant or pesticide residues or toxic pigments, may be hazardous to people.

### Clothing

It is advisable to wear clothing that allows free movement, offers protection to the wearer and does not pose a risk of getting caught up with the object. Footwear should offer a good grip and an appropriate level of protection. Assuming that direct contact with an object is necessary, then the decision as to whether gloves should be worn or not can be made on the basis of the likely advantages and disadvantages of wearing or not wearing them, bearing in mind the risks outlined above. The wearing of gloves is strongly recommended when handling unfinished wood, lacquered surfaces, upholstery textiles, metal furniture and hardware. Different gloves are available for different purposes. Plain cotton gloves, for general purposes, do not provide a secure grip and may cause snagging. They provide only a partial barrier to the effects of moisture and salts. Most vinyl and rubber gloves provide very secure grip and an excellent barrier to moisture and salts but the heavier ones may reduce sensitivity to an unacceptable degree. These gloves are uncomfortable to wear for long periods. Risk of snagging with the surgical type is minimal but many people find them uncomfortable to wear. At the cost of some additional loss in sensitivity, they can be made more comfortable by wearing a thin cotton or silk pair underneath. The advantages of wearing gloves are only obtained if the gloves themselves are clean and in good condition.

If gloves are not worn then hands should be clean.

### Forces applied to objects (lifting, moving and placing)

Before moving an object, it is important to think about the method of lifting it. This will be influenced by the nature of the surface, type of structure, centre of gravity and weight. A few principles intelligently applied can help to reduce the risk of damage. Most structures are designed to withstand forces of compression rather than tension. Many materials are weaker in tension than in compression. Most furniture objects are not designed to withstand the tension caused by lifting or the sideways force necessary to move the object from one place to another. A golden rule is to *never put a point of weakness under tension.* Furniture objects are normally best lifted from their lowest load-bearing member. Holding objects at the top will put them under tension and may open up cracks. Similarly, the use of protrusions as handles carries a high risk of damage because there is a point of weakness where the protrusion meets the main body of the object and leverage will put this point of weakness under tension. A joined wooden chair, for example, is usually lifted from the lower edge of the seat rail, never by the arms, unless covered in deep fringing in which case it is better to hold it by the legs. Maximizing the area of contact will help to reduce the pressure on the surface. Pressure = force/unit area and therefore increases as the area of contact becomes less. The centre of gravity of a supported object should be on an axis vertically above its base. A high centre of gravity or a narrow base mean that a small tilt could make the object unstable. If an object is suspended it will slip until its centre of gravity is vertically under the point of suspension. Movement of objects is best done slowly. The more force used the faster an object will move or deform. If the speed of an object doubles the amount of damage that could occur quadruples. A weak force at the end of a long lever can do as much damage as a strong force at the end of a short lever. Detachable parts should be secured or treated separately. The weight of an object can be estimated by treating it as a collection of boxes or cylinders. The total volume of boxes or cylinders multiplied by the density of the material gives the overall weight.

Having examined the object it is important to inspect the route that will be taken to determine suitable modes of transport and packing. An initial survey and consultation with those affected by the move will help in the selection of a route. Always walk the route first, preferably in both directions, even for a very short move. This will ensure that the receiving store, gallery, case, or rack is ready and can accommodate the load and that the destination will provide a clean, stable environment, similar to the one from which the object was moved. If it is necessary or desirable for the environment to be different then changes should be allowed to take place slowly. It should be possible to put the object down in a manner which will allow it to be moved again easily when necessary. Check that the weight of the object plus associated packing and handling equipment will not exceed the recommended load-bearing capacity of floors to be travelled over. Also check the size of the object plus the equipment and packing in relation to the size of doorways and other width restrictions. Other access issues to check when walking the route include the location of lifts, routes to them and their carrying capacity, the location of steps and stairs, the means of negotiating these and alternative access via ramps. Possible turning problems which might occur due to the length of an object also need to be considered. The route should be adequately lit and free from obstructions. Items en route that cannot be moved but may be at risk may need protection, as may the floors. It is advisable to check the route again immediately before use.

Packing may be necessary to prevent contact with people, other objects or the building, to maintain a stable environment, or to minimize vibration and shock. Packing should avoid awkward stresses and surface damage and prevent movement of objects when transporting them (see Williams and Baker, 1988). For short moves within a building most objects are best kept visible. For longer journeys, small, valuable objects are normally packed in a closed container. Larger objects, if travelling any distance, may be placed upright on a platform trolley or truck with the storage cover in place. A light-weight padded cover such as polyester batting can be used as a cover for the object to provide protection. To make the object easier and in some instances safer to handle, it is helpful to wrap the legs and arms separately using a soft, smooth packing materials so as not to damage surfaces. If a water resistant material has not been used for the storage cover, it is advisable to include one for packing. These layers will also act to a certain degree as buffers to changing levels of RH. Screens and textile insets in tables may be protected with light-weight rigid materials such as acid free foam core board or corrugated acid-free cardboard. Keys, pens and other hard or sharp objects that may be required for access and documentation during a move should be kept completely separate from objects.

For short distances by van or truck, objects can be placed in a well cushioned area such as quilted movers blankets or Bubblewrap® to absorb vibrations and then strapped, with webbing or other strong tape, to a stationary point within the vehicle. Points where the straps come into contact with the object need to be well padded. For long distance travel objects can be wrapped as above and then placed in a custom-made crate. If the crate is not climatically controlled then steps should be taken to maintain a stable environment. If moving to completely different climatic conditions the object will need to be gently acclimatized before removing from the packing case. Ideally, packing and unpacking should be carried out by the conservator in charge of the object. If not, clear instructions from the conservator should accompany the object. If a return journey is envisaged, it is a good idea to keep all packing materials and instructions with the crate or other container, preferably in conditions similar to those in which the object is held. After checking the condition of an object at its destination, the storage cover should be repositioned to maintain protection from dust and light and not removed until the object is required for display, e.g. just before the opening of an exhibition.

### The actual move

Once the object is ready to be moved, a run through the sequence of events by the leader will help to make sure that everyone understands and agrees what is to happen.

Thereafter, each stage should be clearly and concisely communicated to the team by the leader to ensure that the whole team is ready for each stage as it occurs. Before picking an object up it is very important that you know where and how to put it down.

### Protection of objects

Under certain circumstances it may be necessary to carry out work with objects in display areas or to work on exhibition fit-out in areas where objects are on display. In offices, stores and studios a clean, clear hazard-free space should be chosen to examine objects. In galleries, security staff should be informed before work begins and the area surrounded with No Entry signs. The best time to work in galleries is when there are no other activities going on; it may be necessary to abandon planned work if there is a distraction in the gallery.

Objects should always be removed from the immediate vicinity of building work of any kind but there may be a further zone in which objects are at risk unless protected. The decision whether to leave objects in the work area has to be balanced against the risks of moving them. An alternative may be to leave objects in the space suitably protected. Although dust and dirt from light building and fit-out work would normally be controlled at source, it is advisable to protect objects that are at all likely to be affected with polythene sheet. The same applies to paint and water splashes from redecoration and window cleaning. Use of percussive tools over 8 mm in diameter is best avoided. It may be necessary to remove objects if a part of the building that they are in is likely to be subjected to shock or vibration greater than 4 mm/s. If objects cannot be removed an adequate distance away from the work then it may be necessary to specify and monitor the tools to be used. To minimize the risk of a direct hit from scaffolding or roof works, for example, objects should be removed or contained in boxing. Nineteen millimetre ply on a 50×50 mm framework is suggested for the work area and 12 mm ply on a 50×50 mm framework is recommended along transit routes. Objects should be protected with Bubblewrap® or polythene before being boxed. Power drills rather than hammers should be used for the application of the necessary fastenings.

When an object is being delivered to an offsite exhibition, the venue should be well prepared and all building work and showcase construction complete before unpacking and installation of objects begins. The object should be prepared and packed into a suitable container bearing in mind the nature of the journey, the climatic variation likely to be encountered, the transport and insurance. It is very desirable that cases be stored under conditions similar to those in which the object will be displayed ready for the return journey.

### Damage

Action to be taken in case of damage to an object depends on the seriousness and circumstances of damage. In the event of an accident, injury to personnel should be dealt with first. After that it is best to take action on the object(s) as soon as possible to prevent the situation getting worse. There should always be at least two people with any object. One should stay with the object to isolate the area and prevent further damage occurring while the other acts as a runner. The situation should then be assessed and photographed and the circumstances of the accident recorded before the object is touched. The pieces can then be gathered together, using gloves if necessary, while recording information about them that may be useful during repair. Small fragments may be counted into a labelled container and preferably protected from contact with each other. Larger pieces should also be labelled. Where there is a clear risk of further damage this should be indicated by means of clear labelling or other forms of written advice attached to or placed near the object. Some form of additional support may be advisable to eliminate the need for direct handling and to reduce the risk of further damage and it can also help if such objects are placed in an area away from other objects to help minimize the risk of further handling. This applies as much to objects damaged in routine use as to those damaged in transit or on loan. For further information on the history, problems, potential solutions and standards of cultural materials in transit see Mecklenburg (1991), Merrill (1988), Richard *et al.* (1991), Shelley (1987) and Stolow (1979, 1987). Useful guidelines for couriers are provided by Rose (1993).

## 6.2.8 Environmental management for preventive conservation

Although practical intervention has traditionally been the essential role of the furniture conservator, the overall balance of effort in managing a collection should be towards prevention of damage rather than on repair once this has taken place. Ordinary, everyday conditions of light, heat, RH and pollution will mostly cause slow but steady erosion of collections. Accidents in handling will occasionally precipitate more sudden changes in condition. Catastrophic accidents may occur quite suddenly that cause far more severe damage to, or total loss of objects. Occasionally, as with a major fire, flood, or earthquake loss of whole parts of a collection can occur.

Control of individual elements of environment that promote deterioration does not add up to a complete system for display and control. Resources are under pressure everywhere and collections are made to work harder to justify the resources expended. Levels of accountability required by funding organizations and therefore by managers have also tended to increase. In this climate it is important to understand more fully the risks to which a collection may be exposed in order to optimize the control of such risks. Risk assessment and risk analysis seek to identify what risks exist and to estimate both their probability and their severity. The process then examines the controls that are in place for management of those risks to determine whether or not they are adequate and if not what improvements are required. This process balances the likelihood and severity of an outcome against the cost of control in determining the measures to be taken. Control systems that have a low management overhead may ultimately be preferred. Examples of the use of this approach to support decision-making in preventive conservation are given by Marcon (1996), Keene (1996) and Ashley Smith (1999). Health and safety management also provides a useful model for this activity (see Chapter 9).

As part of the process of managing risk it is essential to have good information. This includes knowing what is in the collection, where it is and what condition it is in.

Information about the relationship between the condition of objects and their environment, use, materials, age and so on can be used to make predictions and to monitor and evaluate change as it occurs. Having decided what controls are needed it is essential to ensure that they are put in place and that they are working. Further monitoring and evaluation will then be required to determine whether the controls are having the desired effect or whether more action is needed. A periodic audit of collection condition, environmental standards, procedures and documentation can help to reveal the extent to which the process of risk management is working. To be fully effective, everyone in the institution needs to understand the process and their part in it.

Control can be achieved at four different levels: the building; the individual rooms; the cases; and the objects. Although it is easy to forget the building it is the first line of defence against the elements and against gross changes in the weather. A well designed and maintained building can provide significant protection against a wide range of hazards. A poorly designed and maintained one can contribute significantly to deterioration. If the building itself is inadequate it is very hard indeed to overcome its shortcomings by lower level controls. Control implies both a reactive and proactive approach. The first approach must be at the design stage where bad practices and inappropriate materials can be eliminated.

Limiting factors in our ability to satisfactorily control the environment include the siting of collections in historic buildings, the siting of the buildings in urban environments, the varied nature of collections and a restricted budget. These constraints frequently force museums to take a pragmatic approach. Reference to some aspects of control measures has been made in this chapter. For a further discussion of environmental management see Cassar (1995).

### Stores and storage

Storage is traditionally an area that has been somewhat neglected, especially for furniture, since out of sight all too frequently means out of mind. Conditions for storage are as important as those for display, in some ways even more so since damage, if it does occur, may remain undetected for longer. Furniture in store should be easily accessible to reduce the likelihood of damage to artefacts and staff. To help achieve this, lighter weight furniture can be placed in single rows on metal shelf units with heavier pieces on lower levels or raised slightly off the floor on portable platforms or pallets. Oversized items (such as panels, woodwork elements and chandeliers) may require racks or customized shelving. Small items, including removed upholstery and fabric samples, can be stored in furnishing textile storage cabinets or in conservation grade boxes with lids on shelves. Good labelling of both objects and storage locations is important for efficient retrieval and to help avoid unnecessary handling of objects. The use of (Polaroid®) photo-labels on the shelves assists in locating and replacing pieces within the storeroom and provides a back-up system to main location records. Application of adhesive labels directly to objects is not recommended since they may be impossible to remove without damage. Painted accession numbers in an agreed, consistent location are preferable. For further information on labelling see the MDA fact sheets listed in the bibliography or at www.mda.org.uk/facts.htm.

Floors and work surfaces should be kept clear and dust-free and the rubbish bin should be emptied regularly and frequently. A ready supply of wipes and a vacuum cleaner within the store assist the regular cleaning of floors and surfaces and the habitual cleaning of shelving below artefacts whenever items are removed, for example for photography, conservation, or display. It is useful to have an area of floor reserved in the store with a table and trestles, large enough to allow for storeroom examination of objects.

To keep out light and dust, it is desirable to keep objects covered whenever practicable, especially in storage and after cleaning. Factors that need to be considered when selecting materials for storage and packing include the possibility of reaction with objects, ease of working, air exchange, flammability, protection from water damage, ease of cleaning and cost. Conservation grade materials are generally the safest and offer the best performance. Materials used to make covers that will require to be washed should be pre-shrunk. Covers of down proof cotton, Gortex®,

Kevlar®, Nomex® or Tyvek® can be used to protect from light and dust while allowing ventilation round the object. Polyethylene sheeting is often used to cover furniture in storage but it has some disadvantages. Static may cause the dust to cling to the covers and this is easily transferred to the object. However, anti-static treatments are available. In theory condensation can also occur, although this does not normally happen if temperatures are maintained within reasonable limits. In the event of fire, heat may melt the plastic onto the object before other damage occurs. However a fire retardant polythene is now available.

A programme of producing cloth covers for use on objects in storage, especially for upholstered items, can be planned and budgeted for. Storage covers that are loose fitting and of simple construction with simple closures (e.g. tape ties) help to minimize handling by allowing simple fitting and removal. To protect delicate surfaces from abrasion storage covers may be lined with a material with a smooth slippery surface such as undyed, de-gummed silk or scoured rayon. Very fragile pieces may require a self-supporting armature to prevent the storage cover from touching the object surfaces. These can be made quite simply of acid free card, acrylic sheet material or of polypropylene plumbing pipe and joints; all of these materials can be worked with simple hand tools. Each cover should be clearly labelled to uniquely identify the object underneath. If desired the object name, institution name, front, back, fragility and if necessary instructions on the application of the cover and the handling of the object can be included in the label. Machine embroidered labels are preferred as these allow the covers to be either laundered or solvent cleaned without the loss of the information – extremely important when bulk cleaning of covers is undertaken. When large numbers of covers are handled, for example for closed seasons in historic houses, a system of colour coding using either fast dyed threads to make the labels or fast dyed tapes may be found helpful.

Covers should be dry cleaned or laundered regularly, perhaps twice a year as part of a regular storeroom cleaning programme. Where polyethylene bags are used as covers these are best changed at the same intervals. During periods when objects are on open display, their covers can be cleaned and carefully stored so that they are ready to be replaced on the pieces after exhibition.

Many publications exist that cover various aspects of environmental management, of which the following may be recommended: Appelbaum (1992), ARAAFU (1992), Cane (1996), Cassar (1995), De Guichen (1984), Paine (various dates), Roy and Smith (1994), Sandwith and Stainton (1991), Schweizer (1989), Sneyers (1960), SSCR (1989), Thomson (1986). Storage is discussed at greater length by Norman and Todd (1991).

## 6.3   Disaster preparation

### 6.3.1   Disaster planning

Planning for disaster is an activity that is equally relevant to private conservators and to those working in institutions. Private conservators need to protect their own premises, may be required to provide help for a client and may be called upon to help with institutional disasters. Emergencies can arise through natural causes, acts of war, civil strife, failure in museum systems and as a consequence of work in progress on the building. They include fire, flood, explosions, strong winds, earthquakes, subsidence, riots, bombs and vandalism. Emergencies are likely to lead to damage to objects and injury to both staff and public. Emergencies are never expected but are logically foreseeable and predictable. They remain always possible, happen very quickly and at short notice. Emergencies can quickly become disasters which overwhelm the day to day running of the institution, unless the right action is taken at the right time. This is unlikely without previous planning, organization and training. Nobody wants a disaster to occur but pretending it can't happen is foolhardy. It is necessary to identify potential problems which if addressed will not only reduce the risk of disaster but will also increase the efficiency of normal operations. Being prepared brings increased peace of mind – if you have done everything possible, no one can point the finger or say 'if only'. Disaster planning involves prevention, pre-

paration ahead of disaster; response during disaster; action following disaster.

### Prevention

An assessment of risk will identify events that could lead to disaster and provide information about the likelihood and potential consequences of undesirable events from which it will be possible to formulate avoidance and reduction strategies. There is obviously more risk of some disasters in some areas than others. Earthquake, civil unrest, war and crime are examples where local factors may be important. Security, heating, lighting, power, drainage and use of flammable materials are all areas that suggest the need for thorough examination. Behaviour in a fire of the materials used for building, storage and display should be carefully considered at the time of their selection and is also an important consideration in workshop design. The best form of control is to eliminate high risk enterprises altogether but if this is not possible then it may be possible to substitute something less hazardous or to reduce the size, frequency, or location of the risk. In the case of flammable solvents, for example, it may be possible to use something safer, remove the activity or storage facility to a remote site, or reduce the quantities used. For security risks it may be possible to fit or upgrade doors, window locks, alarms etc., and to provide training. Better results are usually achieved by employing specialists in fire prevention, security, insurance and so on. Once risks are identified and controls have been improved it is important to have good housekeeping, training and documentation and regular inspection and maintenance. Inspection and maintenance are required to ensure that electrical systems, services and machinery are operating safely and correctly and also to ensure that the control measures, such as fire fighting equipment, security procedures and devices remain effective and in good working order. As well as the assessment of risks that might lead to disaster there are specific risks (for example, heat, flame, soot, water, impact) related to each type of object material and structure type (wood, metal, textile, ceramic etc.) that need to be assessed. Setting furniture on exhibition on plinths can help to keep the pieces above low water levels and above the level hoses may run during the course of fire fighting. Siting storage areas and shelving as far as possible away from pipelines, drains, waste lines and known sources of leaks helps to eliminate or reduce another major source of potential damage. It is preferable for objects to be covered while in storage. Materials used for storage and display should be selected which are unlikely to leach contaminants into the objects when the materials themselves become wet. For example, buffered cards and tissues are not recommended. Having supplies of waterproof covers available in areas close to objects will help to ensure that they can be quickly protected in an emergency. Although transferring risk to an insurer is designed to make recovery possible rather than to prevent disaster it may play a part in prevention since the insurer is likely to be a competent assessor of risk able to suggest measures that will be required before accepting the risk.

### Preparation

Preparation should aim to minimize the potential risk to people and ensure that the organization is able to adapt rapidly to any potential new situation. This includes the development of robust systems for normal day to day use, particularly those for communication and control. A regular maintenance schedule will help to ensure that all heating, lighting, ventilating and drainage systems are in excellent working order and that auxiliary systems are available for communication, lighting and power. In addition, good systems should be in place to deliver information about people, the building, other organizations, objects, materials, equipment and so forth. An emergency control centre should be established that has its own phone, the number of which is widely known. This needs to be big enough to contain the people and equipment needed in dealing with an emergency and furnished with access to all the necessary information.

Control centre staff should hold a list of the names, addresses, telephone numbers and roles of all those who might be required in the event of disaster either in or out of working hours. For larger organizations this may best be held in machine-readable form so that a single central up-to-date copy can be

maintained and identical printed copies circulated – normally in the form of a tree in which one person calls two other people who each call two more and so on. The list would normally include the fire service, police, ambulance, clients, gas technicians, plumbers, security specialists, electricians, conservators, curators, the engineering team responsible for the building and all senior staff. The list needs to be kept fully up-to-date with the home and work numbers of all relevant personnel. The control centre would also be expected to hold the numbers of first-aiders; if there is injury to personnel then they will contact them and direct them to the injured personnel. Within the disaster team responsibility for planning, training, co-ordinating recovery, decision-making and call-out must have been clearly defined to avoid confusion and duplication. All these people need to know the building and the collection and have rehearsed their strategy for response to fire, flood and storm under conditions that are as realistic as possible and preferably in the dark. They should know which objects to save, how and where to move them and what to do if time is very short or if only the fire brigade has access. As a conservator you should not feel comfortable unless this plan exists and that it has been rehearsed and shown to work.

The local fire prevention officer will be required to assist with prevention, fire fighting, salvage and rehearsal. The local crime prevention officer may assist with surveillance of premises and rescued objects. Both the police and fire service representatives need to be familiar with the layout of the building and the vulnerable and valuable nature of collections.

In any institution, it is essential that all staff are familiar with staff emergency procedures, copies of which should be freely available to staff throughout the building. Staff can help by being constantly on the look-out for potential hazards (not only within their own areas). Staff involved with collections should be aware of the location and contents of their stores and galleries and potential hazards within these areas such as water pipes and electrical supplies. Emergency equipment, including, tools, materials equipment and means of easily transporting these to areas where they may be required, should be ready on constant standby in locations familiar to all to save time in emergency.

Marked plans of the site and buildings should identify service points and the location of control valves and switches for gas, electricity, oil and mains water. Regular checks of stopcocks, gas, electricity, telephone lines and fuel tanks should be made to ensure that these are secure but accessible to emergency services. Lists of objects in each location should indicate priorities for removal and whether they are retrievable in the dark or in smoke. For all objects, unique identifiers and location records are vitally important. Information about objects that should be maintained, with secure up-to-date offsite copies, includes details of acquisition, provenance, current value, detailed description, measurements, photographs and condition. This information may be required soon after a disaster but may not be accessible in its usual location. Temporary accommodation and transport to it should be available together with an evacuation plan describing the circumstances and method of evacuation.

It may be possible to ensure against certain risks but the complexity of recovering from disaster should not be underestimated. There are many secondary issues that will arise that will require funding in addition to the cost of rebuilding. Disaster also entails considerable loss of face. Insurance cover may include the building, its furnishings, the cost of conservation of damaged objects, first aid to objects, compensation for loss or injury, cost of relocation, temporary storage and documentation.

### 6.3.2   When a disaster occurs

The first priority is the safety of all people in the building. All responses to emergency should be co-ordinated through the control centre, which will contact the emergency services as their first priority. In the event of advanced warning, it may be possible to move, protect or secure items at risk. If there is any hazard to human life, access for conservators will be delayed until the situation is controlled and safe. The protection and preservation of objects is then of major importance. The next priority is to prevent further damage. A salvage team will need to be assembled, a secure salvage area created and service providers contacted for necessary transport and equipment (e.g. freeze drying). The whole of the affected area and access routes immediately surrounding it should be isolated and steps taken to stabilize the building and its environment. This will include reducing temperature and RH to reasonable levels and removal of standing water. Once it is safe for the salvage team to enter the building (wearing suitable protective clothing if necessary), the location and condition of objects can be inspected to establish priorities. It is important that objects are not moved until their condition has been documented to provide evidence that may be required later. Satisfactory documentation may be achieved by means of photography supported by concise written notes or recorded verbal commentary. Depending on circumstances, fire, water, chemical and mechanical damage may be present.

Thermal damage may include charring, distortion, melting of paint and varnish and contamination with smoke and soot deposits. The long-term effect of smoke impregnation is difficult to assess. Smoke consists of small solid particles (less than 0.1 μm) which vacuum cleaning will not remove. Fumes, gases and vapours generated by the combustion of materials may cause degradation; for example, hydrogen chloride created by burning floor tiles may corrode metal elements and trimmings. Absorbent materials are particularly susceptible. When necessary, objects should be removed from a smoke filled environment in accordance with a list of curatorial priorities. If smoke damage is threatened objects can be covered with thermal barrier sheeting and polyethylene sheeting, but not if the area is threatened by heat or fire. Covers made from Dupont products Kevlar and Nomex can form part of an emergency response cart with a few kept close at hand. The use of protective case covers in storage obviates the need for staff to find and place covers during an emergency. The covers may absorb the worst of the smoke and be laundered or changed after the incident.

Thermal damage is usually followed by water damage sustained as a result of containing any fire. Above 70% RH, materials swell, adhesives soften, inlay, veneer, paint and lacquer may cleave, metallic elements corrode, finishes bloom and mould grows. Upholstered materials may stain, shrink or cockle and dyes may run. Water may also be soiled with contaminants which cause degradation. Painted surfaces, gilding, papier mâché and textile or parchment upholstered furniture are particularly susceptible. Water may be retained in the structure of the object leading to increase in weight, weakening or collapse. Water saturated objects may require additional support before it is safe to move them. Delayed effects of water include mould growth, corrosion of metals, distortion and bits of objects sticking together as they dry. Chemical damage may be caused by smoke and soot, by breakdown products of objects depending on the object material and the temperature reached, by chemicals used in fire fighting or by associated spills of oil or other chemicals held in the building. Mechanical damage may have occurred through translation of objects in space or by impact from falling masonry cased by a fire or by the weight of water used to fight it.

Decisions as to the priorities for action to be taken in each of these events is best assessed by groups of material rather than item by item. They will be influenced by the timescale of likely further damage under the circumstances, by previously agreed criteria of value to the institution and by the likelihood of successful salvage. Before moving anything it is important to take a little time to plan. Consideration must always be given to the safety of both personnel and objects. It must be decided which objects have to be moved and which should not. The risk of damage to some objects may be greater by moving them than by leaving them. Consideration has also to be given to the medium of the objects: some objects will not be particularly sensitive to increased humidity levels whilst others would suffer severe damage if left even for a short period of time in a humid atmosphere. Generally, after photography, retrieval and protection should proceed from the outside in towards centre. If the environment is stable and the area secure, items can be left in place. Otherwise items need to be labelled and removed to a suitable safe environment and protected, giving priority to the removal of undamaged objects and the separation of undamaged from damaged items. If no part of the building is dry, objects can be protected with loose plastic sheeting. Contact with broken surfaces should be avoided and pieces prevented from knocking about against one another. At all times the transit routes must be kept clear and security for objects maintained both in transit and in their new location. In case of damage involving water, it is critical that the appropriate salvage steps are taken within forty-eight hours of the emergency. Specific advice on first aid for individual materials and structures is given in the 'Emergency Response Wheel' published in the United States by the Heritage Preservation (see Bibliography).

### 6.3.3 After a disaster

A list and an assessment of the condition of all damaged items should be prepared as quickly as possible following thorough examination and documentation. Contact with insurers, loss adjusters, the owners of affected objects and with lawyers should also be made as soon as possible. It will then be necessary to agree priorities with all concerned and to plan the ensuing work programmes, bearing in mind that it may be necessary to recruit additional staff.

As soon as is practicable after the event debriefing sessions should be held to determine why the incident occurred and to explain what must be done to make sure it is less likely to happen again. It is very important at the same time to establish responsibility for who will carry out any improvements in disaster preparation and when will it be completed. Essentially the next step after the event is to go back to the beginning of the cycle of preparation. Various aspects of the avoidance, control of and recovery from disasters are discussed by Fishlock (1992), Manuele (1997), Meister (1991) and Nelson (1989) among many others.

## Bibliography

Ambrose, T. and Paine, C. (1993) *Museum Basics*, ICOM and Routledge

Ambrose, T. and Runyard, S. (1991) *Forward Planning: a Handbook of Business, Corporate and Development Planning for Museums and Galleries*, Museums and Galleries Commission in conjunction with Routledge

Appelbaum, B. (1992) *Guide to Environmental Protection of Collections*, AIC

ARAAFU (Association des restaurateurs d'art et d'archéologie de formation universitaire) (1992) *Third International Symposium on Preventive Conservation*, Paris, CCI, ICCROM

Ashley Smith, J. (1997) Risk analysis, in *The Interface Between Science and Conservation*, British Museum Occasional Paper No. 116, British Museum Press, pp. 123–32

Ashley Smith, J. (1999) *Risk Assessment for Object Conservation*, Butterworth–Heinemann

Bachmann, K. (1992) *Conservation Concerns: A Guide for Collectors and Curators*, Smithsonian Institution Press

Blyth, V.J. (1997) Pest management at the Victoria and Albert Museum, in *Pest Attack and Pest Control in Organic Materials*, UKIC, pp. 7–12

Brill, T.B. (1980) *Light: Its Interaction With Art and Antiquities*, Plenum: New York

Brommelle, N.S. (1964) The Russell and Abney report on the action of light on water colours, *Studies in Conservation*, 9, 140–52

Brown, G.I. (1964) *Introduction to Physical Chemistry*, Longmans

Brundrett, G.W. (1990) *Criteria for Moisture Control*, Butterworths

Burgess, H.D. and Binnie, N.E. (1991) The effect of Vikane TM on the stability of cellulosic and ligneous materials – measurement of deterioration by chemical and physical methods, *Materials Issues in Art and Archaeology II*, Materials Research Society, Pittsburgh, pp. 791–8

Calabrese, E. and Kenyon, E. (1990) *Air Toxics and Risk Assessment*, Royal Society of Chemistry

Cane, S.F. (1996) The introduction of preventative conservation at the Museum of Science and Industry in Manchester, in ICOM Committee for Conservation, Preprints 11th Triennial Meeting, Edinburgh, Vol. 1, pp. 14–18

Cass, G. and Nazaroff, W.W. (1993) *Airborne Particles in Museums*, Getty Conservation Institute, Marina del Ray

Cass, G.R., Druzik, J.R., Grosjean, D., Nazaroff, W.W., Whitmore, P.M. and Whittman, C.L. (1991) *Protection of Works of Art from Atmospheric Ozone*, Getty Conservation Institute, Marina del Ray

Cassar, M. (1995) *Environmental Management: Guidelines for Museums and Galleries*, Museums and Galleries Commission in association with Routledge

CCI (1994) Framework for the Preservation of Museum Collections (poster), Canadian Conservation Institute

Chadderton, D.V. (1993) *Air Conditioning*, Chapman and Hall

Child, R.E. (ed.) (1993) *Electronic Environmental Monitoring in Museums*, Archetype

Child, R.E. (1997) Detection, monitoring and control of insect pests, *Pest Attack and Pest Control in Organic Materials*, UKIC, pp. 1–3

De Guichen, G. (1984) *Climate in Museums*, UNESCO

Department of National Heritage (1996) *Treasures in Trust*, Department of National Heritage: London

Dow (undated) *Commodities Unsuited for Methyl Bromide Fumigation*, Form No. 132-141-76, Dow Chemical USA, Agricultural Products Department, Midland, Michigan

Fishlock, M. (1992) *The Great Fire at Hampton Court*, Herbert Press

Florian, M. (1987) The effect on artifact materials of the fumigant ethylene oxide and freezing used in insect control, in ICOM Committee for Conservation, Preprints 8th Triennial Meeting, Sydney, 1, pp. 199–208

George, G. and Sherrell-Leo, C. (1986) *Starting Right: Basic Guide to Museum Planning*, American Association for State and Local History (AASLH)

Gilberg, M. (1989) Inert atmosphere fumigation of museum objects, *Studies in Conservation*, 34, 80–4

Gilberg, M. (1990) Inert atmosphere disinfestation using Ageless® Oxygen Scavenger, in ICOM Committee for Conservation, Preprints 9th Triennial Meeting, Dresden, Vol. II, pp. 812–16

Gilberg, M. (1991) The effects of low oxygen atmospheres on museum pests, *Studies in Conservation*, 36, 93–8

Gilbert, J. (1992) *How to Eat and Elephant – a Slice by Slice Guide to Total Quality Management*, Tudor

Goodish, T. (1990) *Indoor Pollution Control*, Royal Society of Chemistry

Grattan, D.W. (1978) The oxidative degradation of organic materials and its importance in deterioration of artifacts, *Journal of the International Institute for Conservation – Canadian Group*, Autumn

Hanlon, G., Daniel, V., Ravenel, N. and Maekawa, S. (1992) A dynamic system for nitrogen anoxia of large museum objects: a pest eradication case study, *Proceedings of the Second International Conference on Biodeterioration of Cultural Property*, October, Yokohama, Japan, pp. 89–90

Harrison, R.M. (ed.) (1992a) *Understanding our Environment: An Introduction to Environmental Chemistry and Pollution*, Royal Society of Chemistry

Harrison, R. (ed.) (1992b) *Pollution: Causes, Effects and Control*, Royal Society of Chemistry

Heritage Preservation Emergency Response and Salvage Wheel, Heritage Preservation (formerly National Institute for Conservation of Cultural Property), 1625 K St, NW, Suite 700, Washington, DC 2006. See www.heritagepreservation.org/PROGRAMS/wheel1.htm

Hickin, N.E. (1975) *The Insect Factor in Wood Decay*, Associated Business Programmes

Instrument Society of America (1985) Moisture and humidity: measurement and control in science and industry, in *Proceedings of the International Symposium on Moisture and Humidity*, Washington, DC, 15–18 April 1985, Instrument Society of America, North Carolina

Johnstone, A.H. and Webb, G. (1977) *Energy, Chaos and Chemical Change*, Heinemann

Keene, S. (1996) *Managing Conservation in Museums*, Butterworth–Heinemann (in association with the Science Museum)

Knell, S. (ed.) (1994) *Care of Collections*, Routledge

Koestler, R.J. (1992) Practical application of nitrogen and argon fumigation procedures for insect control in museum objects, in *Proceedings of the Second International Conference on Biodeterioration of Cultural Property*, Yokohama, Japan, pp. 94–6

Koestler, R.J. (1993) Insect eradication using controlled atmospheres and FTIR measurement for insect activity, in ICOM Committee for Conservation, Preprints Tenth Triennial Meeting, Washington, DC, Vol. 2, pp. 882–6

Landi, S. (1998) *Textile Conservators Manual*, 2nd edn, Butterworth-Heinemann

Manuele, F. (1997) *On the Practice of Safety*, Van Nostrand Reinhold

Marcon, P.J. (1997) Decision support models for preventive conservation, in *The Interface Between Science and Conservation*, British Museum Occasional Paper No. 116, British Museum Press, pp. 143–51

Martin, G. and Blades, N. (1994) Cultural property environmental monitoring, *Preventive Conservation: Practice, Theory and Research*, Preprints of the contributions to the Ottawa Congress, IIC

McGiffin, R.F. Jr (1983) *Furniture Care and Conservation*, AASLH

MDA Fact Sheet No. 19 *Suggested marking positions*

MDA Fact Sheet No. 23 *Labelling and marking methods – Varnished drawing ink on a base coat*

MDA Fact Sheet No. 24 *Labelling and marking methods – Tacked on cloth tag*

MDA Fact Sheet No. 26 *Labelling and marking methods – Duplicated pencil marks*

MDA Fact Sheet No. 27 *Labelling and marking methods – Number applied directly with paint*

MDA Fact Sheet No. 30 *Labelling and marking – Surface preparation*

Mecklenburg, M.F. (1991) Art in transit: studies in the transport of paintings, in *International Conference on the Packing and Transportation of Paintings*, National Gallery of Art, Washington

Meister, P. (ed.) (1991) *Disaster Preparedness Seminar Proceedings*, American Association of Museums

Merrill, R M (1988) In the service of exhibitions: the history, problems and potential solutions of cultural materials in transit, in Preprints, AIC 16th annual meeting, New Orleans

Moncrieff, A. and Weaver, G. (1992) *Science for Conservators*, Crafts Council Conservation Teaching Series, Routledge

Mourier, H. and Winding, O. (1986) *Collins Guide to Wildlife in the House and Home*, Collins

Nelson, C.L. (1989) *Protecting the Past from Natural Disasters*, Preservation Press

Nicholson, M. (1997) The Thermolignum® controlled heating/constant humidity treatment' in *Pest Attack and Pest Control in Organic Materials*, UKIC, pp. 13–19

Norman, M. and Todd, V. (1991) *Storage*, UKIC

Paine, C. (various dates) (ed.) *Standards in the Museum Care of Collections* (various specialist subjects), Museums and Galleries Commission, London

Pinniger, D. (1994) *Insect Pests in Museums*, 3rd edn, Archetype

Pinniger, D. (2001) *Pest Management in Museums, Archives and Historic Houses*, Archetype

Pinniger, D. and Child, R.E. (1996) Synthetic pyrethroids, in *Insecticides: Optimising Their Performance and Targeting Their Use in Museums*, Conference Postprints, 3rd International Conference on Biodeterioration of Cultural Property, Bangkok

Pragnell, R.F. (1989) The modern condensation dewpoint hygrometer, *Measurement and Control*, 22, April, 74–7

Richard, M., Mecklenburg, M.F. and Merrill, R.M. (eds) (1991) *Art in Transit: Handbook for Packing and Transporting Paintings*, National Gallery of Art, Washington

Roberts, D. (ed.) (1988) *Collections Management for Museums*, Museum Documentation Association

Rose, C. (1993) *Courierspeak: A Phrase Book for Couriers of Museum Objects*, Smithsonian Institute

Roy, A. and Smith, P. (eds) (1994) *Preventive Conservation: Practice, Theory and Research*, Proceedings of the 15th IIC Congress, Ottawa 12–16 September 1994, IIC, London

Rust, M., Kennedy, J.M., Daniel, V., Druzik, J.R. and Preusser, F.D. (1992) *The Feasibility of Using Modified Atmospheres to Control Insect Pests in Museums*, Getty Conservation Institute Scientific Programme Report

Sandwith, H. and Stainton, S. (1991) *The National Trust Manual of Housekeeping*, Viking, revised edition

Schiessl, U. (1984) An historical survey of the materials used in pesticidal and strength increasing wood preservation, *Maltechnik restauro*, 90 (2), 9–40

Schweizer, F. (ed.). (1989) *Methods for Preservation of Cultural Property*, Haupt Bern

Selwitz, C. and Maekawa, S. (1998) *Inert Gases in the Control of Museum Insect Pests*, Getty Trust Publications, Los Angeles

Shelley, M. (1987) *The Care and Handling of Art Objects: Practices in the Metropolitan Museum of Art*, Abrams

Sneyers, R. (1960) *Climatology and Conservation in Museums*, UNESCO

SSCR (Scottish Society for Conservation and Restoration) (1989) *Environmental Monitoring and Control*, SSCR Symposium, Dundee, 15–16 March

St George, R.A., Snyder, T.E., Dykstra, W.W. and Henderson, L.S. (1954) Biological agents of deterioration, in G.A. Greathouse and C.J. Wessel (eds), *Deterioration of Materials. Causes and Preventive Techniques*, Reinhold, pp. 175–233

Stolow, N. (1979) *Conservation Standards for Works of Art in Transit*, UNESCO

Stolow, N. (1987) *Conservation and Exhibitions*, Butterworths

Storey, K.O. (1985) *Approaches to Pest Management in Museums*, Smithsonian Institution

Strauss, W. and Mainwaring, S.J. (1984) *Air Pollution*, Edward Arnold

Thompson, J.M.A. (1984) *Manual of Curatorship*, Butterworths/Museums Association

Thomson, G. (1986) *The Museum Environment*, 2nd edn, Butterworths

Umney, N.D. (1997) Low oxygen atmospheres for insect pest control in furniture: selection, investigation, application, in *Pest Attack and Pest Control in Organic Materials*, UKIC, pp. 20–33

Unger, A., Schniewind, A.P. and Unger, W. (2001) *Conservation of Wood Artifacts*, Springer-Verlag

Uzzell, D. (ed.) (1989) *Heritage Interpretation – Vol. 1: The Natural and Built Environment*, Belhaven

Van Emden, H.F. (1989) *Pest Control*, Cambridge University Press

Waller, R.E. (1968) Studies on the nature of urban air pollution, in *London Conference on Museum Climatology*, 2nd edn, IIC, pp. 65–9

Ware, G. (1988) *Complete Guide to Pest Control with and without Chemicals*, Thomson Publications

Wexler, A. (editor in chief) (1965) *Humidity and Moisture: Measurement and Control in Science and Industry*, 4 Vols, Reinhold

Williams, D. and Baker, M.T. (1988) Abrasiveness of packing materials: a preliminary research project report, in AIC Wooden Artifacts Group, Conference Papers, New Orleans

Zycherman, L.A. and Schrock, J.R. (1988) *A Guide to Museum Pest Control*, Foundation of the AIC: Association of Systematic Collections, Washington DC

# 7

# Deterioration of wood and wooden structures

Much of the deterioration of furniture is inherent in the compromises that are made in satisfying the original design requirements. Furniture is not usually made to be placed in a museum or even to last for ever but rather for practical use and ornament. Suitability for these purposes requires the appropriate qualities such as comfort, strength, appearance and economy. In its original form as part of a living tree, wood supports the crown and conducts water and nutrients between the roots and the leaves. That wood is able to meet so many of the requirements for the construction of furniture is a miracle of serendipity. Wood is, or can be, relatively stable, durable, strong, easy to work, light, beautiful and inexpensive. However, conflicts can arise in wooden structures between appearance, strength, stability, durability and cost. Deterioration results from a combination of elements including materials, structure, environment and usage but can often be seen to originate in the need to compromise different qualities of the material in order to get the desired qualities into the structure.

An understanding of the properties of wood and wooden structures is essential for minimizing deterioration and for producing aesthetically acceptable, strong and stable repairs. The purpose of this chapter is to review the main agents of deterioration of wood and wooden structures. The chapter begins by reviewing the deterioration of wood as material. Attention is then turned to the structural aspects of deterioration, first to review the causes of structural deterioration and then to examine its consequences.

## 7.1 Deterioration of wood as material

There are various irregularities or defects in or on timber which may lower its strength, durability or utility value. These may be natural defects present in the growing tree or artificial defects arising from careless handling, seasoning and so forth. Apart from any defects which may be present, deterioration of normal seasoned wood may proceed through the action of light, heat, relative humidity, biological and other factors.

### 7.1.1 Natural defects in wood in living trees

Included phloem affects seasoning, machining and subsequent treatment of timber. If it is softer than the surrounding wood it may tear out during machining, if harder it may lead to splits and may impede the penetration of stains or other treatments. Brittle heart is a form of abnormally brittle wood caused by compression failure in the fibres in many hardwoods. It occurs near the centre or heart and is difficult to detect. Affected wood has low impact strength and breaks with a carroty fracture. Compression wood, formed in softwoods (under branches) has abnormally high longitudinal shrinkage and this frequently causes boards to bow in seasoning. Compression wood is abnormally dense but is not stronger than normal wood and lacks toughness, possibly due to abnormally high lignin content. Tension wood in hardwood is paler than normal and exceptionally weak in compression parallel to the grain, though it may be stronger in tension and tougher than normal wood of the same density. Compared to normal wood it has abnormally high longitudinal shrinkage and slightly increased tangential shrinkage but normal radial shrinkage. The lignin content is deficient and gelatinous fibres may be present. Reaction wood is a generic term used to refer to both compression and tension wood. Heart rot, a form of decay caused by fungal activity near the heart of the tree, attacks the pith and heart wood and may lead to the production of a completely rotten core or pipe running down the centre of the tree. This is not normally active after seasoning.

Various wood-boring insects attack trees and green timber. These include wood wasps (Sirex wasps), Ambrosia beetles, pin hole borers, various longhorn beetles and jewel beetles – depending on country of origin. Although the wood may contain holes, attack by these insects usually stops when the timber dries (kiln drying kills eggs and larvae).

Ambrosia beetles and pin hole borers, belonging to the families Platypodidae and Scolytidae, are most common in tropical woods, but almost every species of wood is liable to attack and both heartwood and sapwood are affected. The larval stage of these insects feeds not on the wood itself but on a mould fungus (ambrosia fungus) which is introduced into the wood by the adult beetles. The fungus grows on the walls of the many small circular tunnels, which are created by the adult and which are 1–3 mm in diameter depending on species. Infestation can occur in the standing tree but is more likely to occur between felling and seasoning. Circular holes are evident on the outside of the wood corresponding to the diameter of the tunnels but the extent of damage is not fully apparent until the log has been converted. The infestation is terminated when the timber is dried during seasoning and cannot then recur or spread to other converted timber. The timber is safe for structural use but may be unacceptably marred by the holes and tunnels and by the dark discoloration that often surrounds them.

There are many species of longhorn beetles (Cerambycidae) and jewel beetles (Buprestidae) widely distributed in tropical and temperate forests, most of which are major forest and mill-yard pests but attack only trees and logs, the infestation dying out during seasoning to leave large oval shaped tunnels (3–25 mm in diameter) packed with bore dust. The damage is not normally significant from a structural point of view and can usually be eliminated during manufacture. An exception to this rule, the house longhorn beetle (*Hylotrupes bajulus*), is further discussed in the sub-section on insects below.

Knots are formed by the inclusion of lateral branches in the main stem or trunk and may influence the strength properties of wood depending on their size, position and type. Irregular grain which occurs around knots may constitute an area of weakness and for this reason they are often regarded as a defect. However, when imaginatively used they can contribute to the decorative potential of wood surfaces. Types include intergrown, spike knots, tight knots and loose knots (*Figure 7.1*). Burrs are abnormal outgrowths or protuberances formed by growth around groups of dormant buds or wounds. Burrs constitute areas of instability and weakness in furniture but have important decorative value when used in veneer form. Shakes are partial or complete separations between adjoining layers of wood and may be due to causes other than seasoning. They may be caused by relief of growing stresses or by impact when a tree hits the ground after felling. Shakes caused by felling are also known as thunder shakes. Occasionally shakes are caused by lightning. Compression shakes are seen as fine crinkled lines across the grain due to stresses set up by weight of rain, snow winds, and unequal growth. Heart shakes, splits that extend from the pith may be present before conversion. Other types include star shakes (several heart shakes together in shape of a star), cup or ring shakes (which follow the line of growth rings) and radial shakes (along the rays). Pitch pockets, resin canals, gum ducts and latex tubes may be a normal feature of the wood or a response to injury of the cambium. They affect the finishing process and may bleed through finishes, or they may be revealed at inconvenient moments during the processing of wood.

Within a species there is considerable variation in density and strength and the strongest

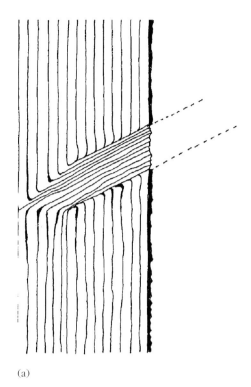

(a)

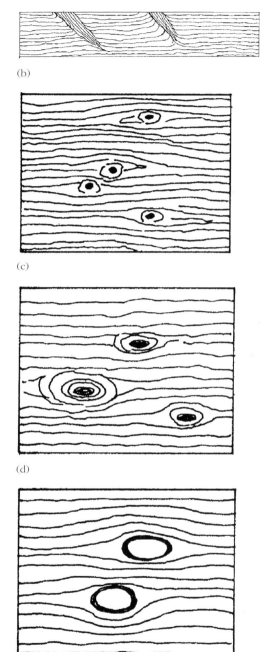

(b)

(c)

(d)

(e)

**Figure 7.1** A knot is a portion of a branch that has been surrounded by the structure of the tree trunk as it continues to grow
(*a*) Diagrammatic representation of a tree trunk where a branch has died and broken off. The tree will eventually encase the dead branch as it continues to grow, forming (in this case) an intergrown knot (intergrown knots have growth rings that are partly or completely intergrown with the growth rings of the tree trunk)
(*b–e*) The appearance of the knot is dependent on how the tree trunk is converted into boards of wood.
(*b*) Shows a spike knot, whose shape is a result of radial conversion of the log. Radial conversion cuts lengthwise or diagonally through the long axis of the original branch to produce a 'spike' shape that extends across the face of the board. When a log is converted by flat sawing (i.e. through and through conversion that produces mostly tangential boards) the knots are round or oval in shape and are called pin knots (*c*) or round knots (*d*) depending on their size. Tight knots are fixed in place by growth characteristics, shape, or position. Knots that are not held firmly in place by their growth ring structure or their position in the board are called loose knots: (*e*) shows the knothole formed when a loose knot is lost

wood, among straight-grained and defect-free samples, may have twice the strength of the weakest. Most of this strength range is associated with a density variation and can therefore be sensed by the weight of the piece.

However some is due to subtle variations in cell structure and cannot be predicted. Extremely narrow or extremely wide growth rings lead to weaker timber. In ring-porous hardwoods, increasing rate of growth (ring width) results in an increase in the percentage of the late-wood, which contains most of the thick-walled fibres. Density will therefore increase and so will strength. However, there is an upper limit beyond which the tree is unable to produce the requisite thickness of wall in every cell. Among diffuse porous hardwoods there is no clear relationship between growth rate and strength unless the growth rate becomes excessive. In the softwoods, increasing rate of growth results in an increase in the percentage of low density early-wood as a result of which both density and strength decrease as ring width increases. The optimum growth ring rate for softwoods is 7–20 rings per inch and for hardwoods 6–10 rings per inch. For some purposes, working qualities may be of greater importance than absolute strength and in this respect timber produced under other than optimum growth conditions for strength may be deemed superior. Mildness in working is usually associated with narrow-ringed material.

Grain direction is an important determinant of strength, stability, appearance and ease of working. It has a major bearing on the behaviour of wood in service and affects environmental response and structural integrity. For many purposes grain directions other than straight are regarded as defects. Straight grain timber, having the fibres parallel to the long axis of the wood, is strong and easy to work, but not usually ornamental. Irregular grain, with the fibres inclined at varying and irregular angles to the vertical axis in the log, has reduced strength and is more difficult to work but produces attractive figure – e.g. blister figure and birds eye. Diagonal grain, regarded as a defect of conversion, has reduced strength and stiffness. A 1:25 slope reduces bending strength by 4%, a 1:5 slope reduces bending strength by up to 45%. In spiral grain the fibres follow a left- or right-handed spiral course in the living tree. This is not always readily apparent but may be detected from the pattern of surface checks during seasoning and is a serious defect in timber intended for structural work. Interlocked grain, in which fibres of successive growth layers inclined in opposite directions producing a ribbon or stripe figure, is very common in tropical woods. It may not affect strength but can cause serious twisting during seasoning and

severe difficulties in working, especially planing. Interlocked grain is virtually impossible to split and may be very hard to saw. In wavy grain the direction of the fibres changes constantly so that a line drawn parallel with them appears as a wavy line on a longitudinal surface. Wavy grain produces fiddle-back figure, exploited entirely for its decorative potential. Wavy grain and interlocked grain may occur together to give a broken ripple called roe figure on quarter-sawn surfaces. For further information on natural defects in wood see Desch (1973) and Panshin and de Zeeuw (1980).

## 7.1.2   Artificial defects – conversion and seasoning

Green wood may contain up to 200% of its dry weight as water. It is therefore heavy, liable to rot and cannot be finished. Before use it must be seasoned and to do this effectively it has to be converted into smaller pieces.

### Conversion

Conversion has a critical effect on the strength, appearance and drying of wood and therefore profoundly influences subsequent behaviour. Key decisions during conversion include whether to remove sapwood and how best to cut up the log to fully exploit its potential. Sapwood is more susceptible to insect attack due to stored food materials. Starch, which only occurs in any quantity in sapwood, is food for powder post beetle and sap stain fungi. In contrast, some of the materials present in the heartwood of some timbers are toxic to fungi and insects and act as natural preservatives (e.g. in cedar). The average commercial log is 25–30% sapwood but in smaller logs this figure may rise to 50% or more. Removing sapwood may therefore have significant cost implications.

Various methods of conversion are used to provide economy, to select figure, to achieve good mechanical properties, to improve behaviour during seasoning, to work around defects in the log and to optimize performance in service. There is usually some trade-off between these various considerations. Live sawing (also called through and through) is economical but does not produce optimum figure or behaviour. Tangential (flat or slash cut) sawing is used to obtain growth ring figure in timbers such as cedar, Douglas fir, ash and pine with distinct growth rings. The timber seasons quickly but does not retain its shape well. Quarter-sawing (radial or rift cutting) is used to reveal medullary ray figure in oaks, beech and mahogany, and ribbon grain figure in Queensland maple and walnut. For a given surface area to volume ratio, it seasons slowly but retains its shape well. Rays constitute planes of structural weakness in wood which may lead to checking and splitting during drying. Areas of weaker ray tissue may also tear out during planing. Sapwood has a higher moisture content than heartwood. If left to dry out naturally, the sapwood will shrink more than the heartwood and planks will warp accordingly. Controlled drying or seasoning is therefore used to promote even drying.

## Seasoning defects

The idea of seasoning is to create a controlled moisture gradient steep enough to cause moisture to be lost but not so steep that damage occurs. However, during seasoning, differential shrinkage across the radial and tangential dimensions causes boards to cup away from the heart, rounds to become ovals and squares to become diamonds. Drying begins immediately after felling so care needs to be taken to prevent damage by uncontrolled drying due to wind or sun. Case hardening (usually associated with kiln drying) may occur in which the outside dries out before the inside so that the case or outside sets hard while the core becomes honeycombed with shrinkage checks. Case hardening causes re-sawing difficulties and leads to warping. Collapse is the term used to describe flattening or distortion of cells during drying showing excessive and uneven shrinkage on the surface of the timber. Checks, in which separation of wood along the grain occurs, usually in the direction of the rays, are generally the results of shrinkage stresses set up by the drying effect of the wind or hot sun on freshly sawn surfaces or during seasoning. Checks are measured in inches, shakes are much larger – both reduce shear strength of the timber. Types of checks include: end checks, heart checks, internal checks, ray checks, surface checks, through

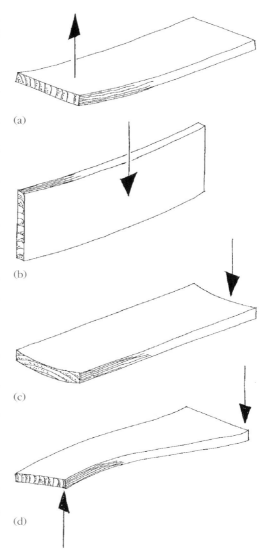

**Figure 7.2** Warping describes any deviation of converted timber from a flat surface. Common types include: (*a*) bow; (*b*) crook; (*c*) cup and (*d*) twist (arrows indicate direction of planar deviation). A warped board may have a combination of these faults

checks. Stresses which build up during seasoning and which exceed the strength of the material may also result in splits. A split is a separation of the wood fibres from face to face in a piece of wood while a check is a longitudinal shake (cleavage or split) that does not go through the whole of the cross section. Sap stain is a fungal infestation of sap wood common in pines resulting from poor hygiene in timber yards and leading to blue stain. Any deviation of converted timber from a flat surface is referred to as warping. The tendency to warp varies according to species, the way in which the piece is cut from the log, its size and the presence of other defects and internal stresses in the tree from which the timber is cut. Warping occurs particularly during seasoning when unevenness of shrinkage (caused by grain irregularities) is most likely and by incorrect stacking for drying. The same result can be seen at other times. *Figure 7.2* illustrates the various forms of warping. Bow is deviation from lengthwise flatness. Spring or crook is departure from end to end straightness along the edge of a board. Cup is deviation from flatness across the width of a board. Twist describes the situation in which the four corners of a flat face do not lie in the same plane. Defects arising from conversion and seasoning are further discussed by Brown (1988), Desch (1973) and Panshin and de Zeeuw (1980).

### 7.1.3 Deterioration of 'normal' seasoned wood

Wood is a durable material but its deterioration can be brought about by the environment, chemical decomposition and mechanical wear

**Figure 7.3** Wood will be altered, damaged or partly destroyed by weathering, in particular the alternate shrinkage and swelling due to exposure to rain and fluctuating relative humidity, rapid changes in temperature and the action of sunlight. Physical changes include colour changes, surface roughening and the development of surface checking and cracks. Chemical changes include the breakdown of cellulose and lignin. Shown here is a piece of weathered oak, with the characteristic grey colour associated with weathering. Surface checking and associated discoloration may extend a considerable distance into the wood, as can be seen in this example, where part of the surface has been planed to a depth of several millimetres

in use. Outdoors, above ground, a complex combination of light energy, chemical and mechanical factors contribute to the discoloration and disintegration of wood, a phenomenon known as weathering (*Figure 7.3*) (Feist and Hon, 1984; Hon and Feist, 1986). Wood kept in permanently wet conditions is susceptible to fungal decay or rot and can deteriorate rapidly. Indoors, wood is susceptible to the factors causing weathering but the effects are less severe.

### *Light*

Wood is an excellent light absorber, although cellulose itself is not, it is thus capable of absorbing sufficient visible and UV radiation to undergo photochemical reactions leading to discoloration and degradation of wood surfaces. Chang *et al.* (1982) and Hon (Hon and Chang, 1984; Hon and Feist, 1986) have demonstrated that the surface of wood severely degrades after exposure to UV radiation. Lignin components especially are broken down rapidly (Feller, 1971). However, because of the wide range of chromophoric groups associated with its surface components, wood cannot easily be penetrated by light and the discoloration observed is essentially a surface phenomenon extending up to a maximum of about 250 µm into the wood (Feist and Hon, 1984; Hon and Ifju, 1978). The initial colour change is yellowing or browning due to photo-oxidation of cellulose, lignin and wood extractives. Woods rich in extractives may become bleached before other colour changes become observable. With increased exposure, the surface may eventually change to a greyish colour that extends up to about 0.25 mm into the surface. The original coloration of marquetry woods may change substantially with excessive exposure to light. This change is exacerbated if individual components were stained as was common practice (Godla and Hanlon, 1995). The colorants used were rarely light-fast resulting in a muted visual quality after exposure to light. If parts of a wood surface are masked, by objects placed on top of them for example, marked differential colour changes may occur that are hard to reverse or obscure. Changes in the chemistry of wood surfaces due to exposure to light are rather complicated and depend upon the wavelength and intensity of light, temperature, time of exposure, moisture content of the wood, atmospheric composition and presence of light-absorbing substances. The surface changes include formation of free radicals, chain scission, dehydrogenation and de-hydroxymethylation of cellulose and splitting of double bonds, formation of phenoxy radicals and quinone structures and polymerization of lignin (Zavarin, 1984). Radiant light energy may lead to heating of the surface resulting in further damage to the surface associated with restrained dimensional change.

Much old furniture may already have succumbed to the effects of light since it has not traditionally been regarded as a particularly light sensitive class of material and may therefore have been exposed to relatively high light levels for considerable periods of time. However, light sources should still be filtered to remove UV and visible light should be kept at, or below 150 lux for wood furniture. Furniture decorated with distinctively coloured or stained woods, particularly those still showing good colour may benefit from a reduction of the intensity of exposure to about 50 lux. Reduction in the duration of exposure to light will also benefit such furniture. Since the most highly coloured parts of furniture are frequently those on inside surfaces it will help to preserve them if items such as doors, drawers and flaps are kept closed as much as possible.

### Heat

The strength of wood is inversely proportional to temperature. A nearly linear two- to three-fold reduction in strength occurs as temperature rises from −200 °C to +160 °C. The direct effects of heat on wood are of two types. Those effects that are maintained only as long as the change in temperature is maintained, and those that are permanent. The initial effect of heating wood without adequate compensation in RH is to reduce its moisture content. The nature of any further effects depends on such factors as species, moisture content, the heat source and the level and duration of heating. If a temperature of 55–65 °C is maintained for long periods (2–3 months) depolymerization of cellulose and hemicelluloses begins. At about 250 °C pyrolysis and volatilization of cell wall components occurs, followed by combustion in the presence of air or charring in its absence. Winandy and

Rowell (1984) reported that heating Douglas-fir in an oven at 102 °C for 335 days reduced modulus of elasticity by 17% modulus of rupture by 45% and fibre stress at proportional limit by 33%. The same losses might be observed in one week at 160 °C. Heating softwood at 210 °C for 10 minutes in the absence of air reduced modulus of rupture by 2%, hardness by 5% and toughness also by 5%. Under the same conditions at 280 °C modulus of rupture is reduced by 17%, hardness is reduced by 21% and toughness is reduced by 40%. Most of these effects are outside the range that would normally be experienced by furniture in most collections. Although the lower temperature ranges quoted could possibly apply to radiant heating of wood surfaces these effects would probably normally arise only as a result of a fire.

Like other materials, wood expands when heated and contracts when cooled. The unit amount by which a material expands (per unit of original length per degree rise in temperature) is called its coefficient of linear thermal expansion. For wood in the direction of the grain in the range −50 °C to +50 °C this averages $3.39 \times 10^{-6}$ per degree centigrade irrespective of wood species and specific gravity. This is small in comparison with other common solids. For example, the coefficient of linear thermal expansion per degree centigrade for flint glass is $7.9 \times 10^{-6}$, for steel is $10 \times 10^{-6}$ and for aluminium is $24 \times 10^{-6}$. However, across the grain the coefficient of linear thermal expansion for wood (for an average specific gravity of 0.46) in the radial direction is $25.7 \times 10^{-6}$ while in the tangential direction it is $34.8 \times 10^{-6}$. Values of thermal coefficients for wood in the radial and tangential direction vary directly in a straight line relationship with the specific gravity of the wood. The reasons that thermal changes are not more commonly recognized in wood are first that wood is usually used within a narrow range of temperatures and secondly that changes due to temperature are normally masked by changes brought about through fluctuations in RH and moisture content which are usually much larger and in the opposite direction. Heating a wood surface will tend to reduce the moisture content and the resultant shrinkage will outweigh expansion as an effect of heating.

Changes in temperature at constant RH also have an influence on the equilibrium moisture content (EMC) of wood. However, any resulting dimensional changes are relatively small (Skaar, 1988). It takes, for example, a temperature increase of about 25 °F to 30 °F (13.8 °C to 16.7 °C) to cause an approximately 1% drop in EMC (Hoadley, 1980).

### Moisture

Basic wood–water relations are discussed in Chapter 2 but, because they contribute so much to the deterioration of wooden structures, aspects of this topic important for an understanding of deterioration are briefly reviewed here. Damage may be caused under conditions of excessive dryness, excessive wetness or when change in moisture content takes place too rapidly. Damage may be caused by dimensional change, or through increased chemical or biological activity with consequences at both the material and the structural levels of organization. Deterioration starts before felling and continues before, during and after seasoning.

Wood is hygroscopic, that is, it has an affinity for water in both liquid and vapour form. Whether wood absorbs or loses water depends on the humidity and temperature of the surrounding atmosphere and the amount of water in the wood. Consequently, the moisture content of wood fluctuates. Moisture contents above about 20% are associated with fungal decay. The properties of wood are profoundly affected by its moisture content. Changes in the moisture content of wood below the fibre saturation point (about 30%) are associated with dimensional changes as the micro fibrillar network expands in response to entry of polar molecules. Wood is anisotropic, that is, movement, the dimensional changes of wood after seasoning, is unequal in the three structural dimensions. The ratio of tangential to radial shrinkage is called the differential shrinkage. Longitudinal dimensional change from the green to the oven dry condition is only about 0.1–0.3%. Change in the radial dimension from the fibre saturation point to the dry condition is about 2–3% and tangential shrinkage varies from about 1.4 × –2 × the radial change. A change in RH from 50–60% will cause approximate dimensional changes of 0.45–0.9% tangentially and 0.3–0.6% radially (0.03% longitudinally).

Differential shrinkage is probably the commonest source of uneven dimensional change – but not the only one. Understanding the ways in which uneven dimensional response may occur is of the utmost importance in understanding deterioration of furniture and of avoiding mistakes in conservation. Although this section is concerned with the behaviour of wood as material, ultimately it is aimed at understanding the behaviour of wooden structures. Differences in rate or extent of response ultimately lead to damaging stresses. Several factors may contribute to an uneven response to a given moisture change. Differences in hygroscopic behaviour occur between and within species, and even between different parts of a single tree. The dimensional changes in beech (*Fagus* spp.) are greater than those in mahogany (*Swietenia* spp.) under similar conditions (Dinwoodie, 1981; Thomson, 1986). Even within one species there can be differences in hygroscopic behaviour caused by variations in density or by the quality and means of seasoning the wood after the tree has been cut (Klein and Bröker, 1990). The selection of wood with regard to quality also plays a role as to how it will respond dimensionally. Boards selected near the pith are dimensionally more unstable than boards from the middle between the pith and the cambium. Boards selected from reaction wood, juvenile wood, or from trees with spiral grain will shrink unevenly, and cause warps or twists (Hoadley, 1980; Panshin and de Zeeuw, 1980). Some of the variables that might affect dimensional response include changes in the thickness of the cell walls and in the average micro-fibrillar angle in the cell walls (in early- and late-wood for example), variations in the chemical composition of the cell walls, particularly the extent of lignification of the cell wall (higher lignin content in radial than tangential walls) and stresses applied to wood in use (Skaar, 1988; Panshin and de Zeeuw, 1980). The action of the rays in restraining wood in the radial dimension are also important. Measurable variables in wood are influenced by several factors including changes in cambium as it ages, genetic controls that govern the form and growth of the tree, and environmental influences. Differences in response can be due to differences in the distribution of moisture as well as to the actual hygroscopic sensitivity.

RH changes lead to changes in moisture content which result in dimensional change. Eventually all parts come to equilibrium but parts, even of a single piece of wood, equilibrate at different rates due to differential moisture access in a single piece of wood. Buck (1961) demonstrated that yellow poplar (*Liriodendron tulipifera*) responded more rapidly to changes in RH than chestnut (*Castanea dentata*). He observed that at 24 °C the EMC will be reached about twice as fast as at 12 °C and that the greater the change in RH the faster the wood reacts. Because of the thickness of a piece of wood it may be some time before the inside reaches equilibrium whereas changes in the outer layers begin almost immediately. Similarly, access via the end grain of a piece of wood is usually very much quicker than side grain access. In a large piece of timber, say a life-sized sculpture, the changes in response to a fixed change in RH may take months to complete whereas a thin veneer would do so in hours and a sheet of paper begins to react in minutes. In fact, using very sensitive linear displacement transducers, tiny movement of surface layers of wood can be detected almost immediately (if the surface is wetted for example). Areas of defective wood may also respond differently and coated areas will respond differently to uncoated areas. The situation in wooden structure is correspondingly more complicated. Differences in response times and grain directions between components of wooden structures leads to movement in different directions and at different rates. These differences may result in warping, dislocation of parts, splitting and breakage of fibres. For example, the stress on a large panel, even when coated, will be greater at the ends than in the middle, possibly leading to propagation of cracks/splits. This is because moisture exchange is faster from exposed end grain. When seasoning timber, end grain is often sealed with wax to reduce this problem. If movement has not been allowed for in construction, damage will result. If wood is prevented from moving in response to changes in relative humidity, plastic compression (see section 7.3.4) can take place leading to permanent reduction in the maximum dimensions of the piece. This is typically seen in large panels, floor boards, hammer heads, and mortise and tenon joints but can also occur in a single piece

of wood in which one part of a board is restrained by another part of the same board. Frequent changes in moisture content are a principal cause of weathering. Stresses are set up in the wood as it swells and shrinks due to moisture gradients between the surface and the interior. Stresses are greater the steeper the moisture gradient and are usually largest near the surface of the wood. Unbalanced stresses may result in warping and surface checks along the grain.

With time, the dimensional response of wood may lessen, in part because hygroscopicity of the wood may decrease, or because of mechanical effects of repeated shrinkage/swelling cycles, or stress-setting of the wood. However, experiments with wood taken from artefacts thousands of years old have shown the wood to have retained its hygroscopicity and its capacity to respond dimensionally to changes in moisture content. Klein and Bröker (1990) demonstrated that dimensional changes were almost equal between a seventeenth-century oak panel and a newly made oak panel, after exposing them to fluctuating RH cycles. The assumption should therefore prevail that wooden objects, regardless of age, can demonstrate dimensional movement when subjected to variable relative humidity conditions.

Moisture content of wood can also affect mechanical, chemical and biological aspects of deterioration. As wood dries below the fibre saturation point the strength increases with the loss of bound water. For example, the compressive strength parallel to the grain is doubled when wood is dried from green to 12% and tripled when oven dried. Production of acetic acid by hydrolysis of acetyl groups on acetylated hemicelluloses increases in damp conditions. Excessively high moisture levels are associated with staining and damage to wood surfaces and finishes. High moisture contents also support the growth of fungi and moulds and favour the establishment of insect pests.

For internal woodwork, a theoretical ideal is for RH to be kept constant at a level of 50% with no more than ±5% variation. In practice the set point depends on the previous history of the piece. Objects which have spent most of their lives in unheated churches at RH 50–70% or more are likely to crack and split if suddenly introduced into a much drier environment. Objects may be able to tolerate larger variations if these are achieved slowly. Many objects seem to be able to accommodate ±10% RH on a seasonal basis with little readily apparent damage. Control of heating represents an important step in RH control.

### Pollution

Pollution is not a major source of structural deterioration in wood but is more likely to affect its surface qualities, particularly colour, and other non-wood materials present in furniture, for example textiles and coatings. Both sulphur dioxide and ozone are implicated in the fading of dyes present in many decorative timbers. Particulate pollution is more likely to cause concern than to cause damage though repeated careless removal of particulates can damage high gloss surfaces. Wood itself is a source of organic acid pollution, particularly acetic acid produced by hydrolysis of acetylated hemicelluloses that can lead to corrosion of lead and its alloys and damage to materials that contain calcium carbonate, such as marine animal shells for example (Farmer, 1962). This type of damage to objects can occur where wood is used in showcase construction (Padfield *et al.*, 1982). Other wood and metal combinations may cause degradation and staining of wood (Forest Products Research Laboratory, 1970; Pinion, 1973). Interaction of oak, and other timbers with a significant content of tannins, with iron causes a blue black stain to be produced.

### Fungi

Although fungal decay occurs in wood under appropriate conditions, in fact accounting for about 90% of all timber losses in the world, it is rare in furniture. The comparative durability and resistance of wood to decay by microorganisms is explained by its sub-cellular organization. Highly complex, insoluble polymers which make up the cell wall require enzymatic breakdown before they can be assimilated by micro-organisms. However, enzyme action is mainly restricted to non-crystalline regions of the cellulose and since wood is more crystalline than most other plant tissues it provides greater resistance to fungal and bacterial degradation. Lignification also creates a physical barrier to enzymatic attack on the polysaccharides so that only those organisms that possess enzymes capable of

altering the protective association of lignin are capable of destroying wood. The low nitrogen content of wood (only about 0.03–0.1% compared to the 1–5% in herbaceous tissues) further reduces susceptibility to decay. Also, for reasons which are not fully understood, a higher moisture content is required for the initiation of deterioration in wood than in other plant tissues. Finally, substances toxic to such organisms are present in the heartwood of many timbers.

Fungi are broadly classified into the sap stain fungi which eat only the cell contents and the wood-destroying fungi and soft rots which cause decay in wood by disintegrating cell walls to obtain food for growth and reproduction. Based on physical and chemical changes produced in wood and the resulting alterations in colour of decaying wood, wood destroying fungi are classified as brown rots, white rots and soft rots (Panshin and de Zeeuw, 1980). Brown rots break down cellulose components leaving brown powdery residues of lignin which make the wood appear darker in colour. The wood surface displays small cracks across the grain and in an advanced state of decay rectangular pockets of degraded wood may fall out. Brown rots are more commonly associated with softwoods. They are the commonest form of fungal decay in the UK accounting for the great majority of damage to wood in buildings. White rots break down both the cellulose and lignin content of wood causing the wood to become lighter in colour, softer and somewhat fibrous and result in up to 90% weight loss in affected timber (Otjen and Blanchette, 1987). White rots are more commonly associated with hardwoods. Soft rots are further classified as cubical, spongy, pocket, or stringy according to the pattern of deterioration they cause. Soft-rots occur under special circumstances where extremely high moisture levels are found, or when no other rots can prevail (Blanchette and Simpson, 1992; Caneva *et al.*, 1991). The terms dry rot and wet rot are somewhat misleading, as all fungi require a minimum moisture content in wood of 20% and will not grow below this level whilst a level of 35–50% or more is preferred by many. However, once growth has started certain fungi are able to transport the necessary moisture considerable distances via

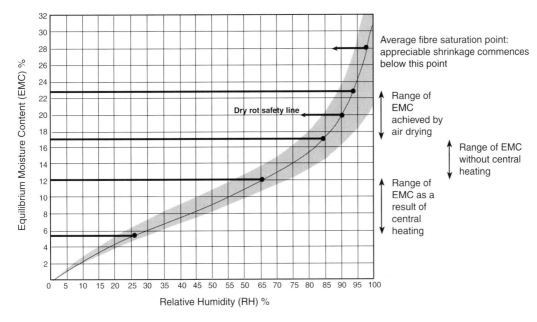

**Figure 7.4** Graph of the average relationship between the equilibrium moisture content of wood and relative humidity (figures for different species vary). In terms of decay potential, important positions on this graph are the fibre saturation point (average 28%) and the dry rot safety line (20%). Note also the range of EMC for air dried timber (17–23%), the range of EMC without central heating and the range of EMC as a result of central heating (figures for London, UK, derived from *Figure 7.15*)

tubelike conducting veins in the mycelium. In the final stages of decay caused by those fungi that continue active in wood near the critical moisture content the wood itself may be dry and friable and this has led to the use of the term dry rot. In the final stages of decay of wood caused by fungi that require wood to be comparatively wet for attack to continue the affected area is itself often wet, hence the term wet rot (Dawson, 1980; Sutter, 1986).

Requirements for fungal decay have been reviewed in Chapter 6. As long as wood is below the fibre saturation point it is immune from fungal decay; only when liquid water is available can fungi start to grow. However, it must be remembered that condensation in the region of the fibre saturation point may lead to the availability of free water, and that water itself is a product of decay. Therefore, 20% moisture content (typically in excess of 85% RH) is taken as a stable limit even though the fibre saturation point is generally around 28% (*Figure 7.4*). Suitable temperatures (10–30 °C), oxygen and a food source (the wood itself or, in some cases wood finishes) are also

required. Fungal infestation is not frequently encountered in furniture collections which are appropriately housed and well maintained but may occur in furniture in poor storage conditions especially when in contact with the ground (*Figure 7.5*). Prevention and control

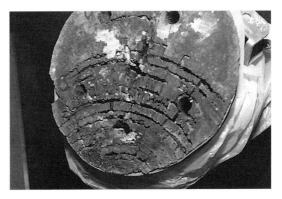

**Figure 7.5** The base of a sculpture by Brancusi showing evidence of fungal decay and insect infestation. Fungal attack has proceeded along the early-wood growth. Subsequent death watch beetle infestation has followed the lines of fungal infestation

can be achieved by eliminating or modifying one or more of conditions required for growth or poisoning wood with preservatives (see Canadian Conservation Institute Technical Bulletin No. 12).

Bacterial infestation is rarely found in furniture and mostly is encountered on wet archaeological wooden objects. Certain bacteria, however, are able to break down cellulose, hemicellulose and lignin under aerobic condition but this is not a concern for furniture. Staining from fungal and bacterial activity may be a concern for decorative surfaces.

### Insects

Insect infestation of wood may result in damage to both structural components and decorative surfaces. Structural damage in furniture is particularly prevalent at joints where the presence of animal glue provides a rich source of the nitrogen necessary for insect development. For the same reason woodworm are commonly found in houses in floor boards around the lavatory. Decoration may suffer as a result of collapse of the surface caused by the tunnelling underneath. When insects encounter a paint or other opaque decorative surface layer they may tunnel parallel to it. The result will be a diminished substrate and potentially inadequate support for paint, gesso or veneer.

Many different species of insects may attack wood during its life from living tree to seasoned timber. Insect pests are often specific to particular types and states of wood. Some will only attack living timber while others require seasoned or decaying wood. Some insects cause damage even though their use of wood as a food source is not significant. Insects that attack living trees and unseasoned logs are discussed above (section 7.1.1) Those that attack seasoned timber present the greatest hazard to furniture. Many of the most destructive are beetles (Coleoptera), among which it is the larvae which do the damage, feeding in the wood. In countries with warm temperate or tropical climates the most destructive pests of structural timber are termites (Isoptera). Wood-boring weevils can accompany wet rot. Important species of beetles which affect furniture and interior joinery in temperate regions include the common furniture beetle, death watch beetle, powder post beetle and house longhorn beetle.

***Common furniture beetle (Anobium punctatum)*** The common furniture beetle, often referred to simply as woodworm, is shown in *Figure 7.6*. It is the chief insect pest of wooden furniture in the UK, Europe and North America and is widespread in most temperate countries, being present in many houses, buildings and furniture. It attacks furniture, structural timber and joinery, certain types of plywood and wicker. Like all beetles, *Anobium* has a life cycle consisting of four successive stages: egg, larva, pupa and adult. The adult female lays eggs, which are just visible to the naked eye, in cracks or joints of suitable timber, on rough sawn surfaces, in end grain or in old flight holes. The larvae hatch in about four weeks and bore into wood where they may tunnel for two to five years depending on climate and type of wood infested, until fully grown. The refuse left behind the larvae as they tunnel through the wood is commonly known as frass. The entrance tunnels are too small to be seen without a lens. At the end of its development period, the larva excavates a small frass-free cavity just under the surface of the wood before pupating and then emerging 6–8 weeks later as the adult beetle, generally on the dark side of the infested object, through a circular exit hole 1.5–2 mm in diameter. A similar pattern of complete metamorphosis is followed by the other wood-boring beetles. Adult furniture beetles usually emerge between May and August, chiefly in June and July, when they may be seen crawling on walls, ceilings and windows, or actively in flight. They survive for only three to four weeks but the female can lay up to eighty eggs, some of which are deposited on the wood from which the adult emerged, but not all of which will survive. Adult beetles measure 2.5–5 mm in length and are reddish to blackish brown. The female is generally larger than the male. The prothorax is hood shaped and when viewed from above almost completely hides the head. The upper parts of the body are covered with fine, short, yellow hairs and rows of small pits or puncture marks are clearly visible on the wing covers (*Figure 7.6*). The seasoned sapwood of most softwoods may be attacked but some species (including spruces and pines) are more susceptible than others (Building Research

(a)

(b)

**Figure 7.6** The common furniture beetle, *Anobium punctatum* seen from above (*a*) and from the side, emerging from a flight hole (*b*) (© Crown Copyright)

(a)

(b)

(c)

**Figure 7.7** Examples of frass: the faecal pellets of (*a*) the common furniture beetle (*Anobium punctatum*) are cigar-shaped and approximately 0.5 mm long; those of (*b*) the death watch beetle (*Xestobium rufovillosum*) are bun-shaped; those of (*c*) the house longhorn beetle (*Hyloptrupes bajulus*) are sausage-shaped with flat ends (© Crown Copyright)

Establishment, 1977. Heartwood is not immune, especially if any fungal decay is present. Hardwoods including beech, birch, elm, oak, walnut, lime and birch are commonly found to have been attacked and few if any of the traditional temperate hardwoods are immune but some tropical hardwoods do seem to be (Farmer, 1972). Frequently only the sapwood is attacked. Furniture beetle often attack hidden rails of upholstered furniture. Plywoods made from glues of natural origin (e.g. blood, casein, or soya) are particularly susceptible to attack, since they provide a rich source of protein, but damage in plywoods prepared with synthetic adhesives seems to be rare.

Signs of attack include the presence of tunnels, containing bore-dust (frass), within the wood and circular flight (exit) holes on the surface. Fresh light coloured frass and clean holes with sharp edges are signs of active workings, though the larval stage may last up to 5 years before adults emerge. Different species of insect produce frass of characteristically different sizes and shapes (*Figure 7.7*). In some cases, it can be difficult to properly assess whether an object is currently infested,

**Figure 7.8** Cones of frass produced by the common furniture beetle *Anobium punctatum* from heavily infested wood

or whether it shows signs of previous attack. It is also possible to confuse insect frass with wood dust from other sources such as worn drawer runners. In case of doubt the suspect

object can be thoroughly vacuumed to remove existing dust and stood upon black paper undisturbed in a warm and darkened room free of vibration to monitor production of frass (*Figure 7.8*). If frass continues to be produced, which will be clearly visible on the black paper, it is likely that the object is infested. Moderate increase of temperature (5 °C) makes larvae more active, and may shorten the pupal stage, for faster results. However in most cases it would not be desirable to wait for damage to occur. Soft (i.e. low energy) X-rays can be used to diagnose presence of larvae within the wood and this technique can distinguish between live and dead larvae (*Figure 7.9*). A modified $CO_2$-FTIR system is being developed and tested by Koestler (1993) that measures the $CO_2$ produced by respiration of live insects in a closed environment. When elevated levels of $CO_2$ are detected in a closed bag, in comparison with $CO_2$ levels in a control bag,

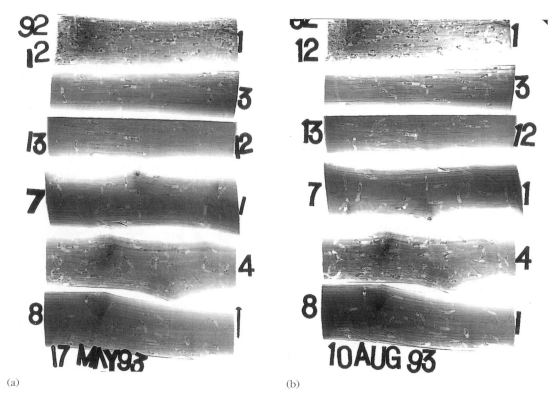

(a)                                                              (b)

**Figure 7.9** (*a*) X-ray photograph of hazel twigs infested with the common furniture beetle *Anobium punctatum*. (*b*) Twigs after exposure to a nitrogen-based anoxic fumigation treatment (from top to bottom, after exposures of one week, two weeks, four weeks, three weeks, control and five weeks). X-ray photography has captured the shrivelled appearance of the dead larvae

one has proof of active infestation. Exit-holes, frass and, when possible, larvae or adult beetles should be examined to identify the species (Dawson, 1980; Kingsolver, 1988; Mallis, 1982; Pinniger, 1994; Sutter, 1986).

The probability, severity and rate of attack by woodworm are influenced by moisture content, temperature, width of sapwood, resin content and presence of fungal decay. Woodworm prefer timber with high moisture content and comparatively low maximum temperatures. For this reason they are more prevalent in temperate regions and less common in centrally heated accommodation where they are discouraged by reduced moisture content of wood. Larvae also prefer sapwood wood and wood with a low resin content. They grow more rapidly in wood decayed by soft and white rots. Appropriate storage and display conditions therefore play an important role in preventive conservation. Avoidance of high moisture levels, clean secure environments and programmes of monitoring are key elements of the general control strategy for insects. When infestation is suspected the affected objects should be isolated, and the surrounding objects and environment should be carefully inspected. Quarantine can effectively be achieved by placing the object in a bag, made of poly-ethylene or similar material, which can be securely sealed. For practical purposes, separate bags may be more secure than a quarantine room. Sticky-traps placed in an area of suspected infestation can be helpful in trapping adult beetles and a pheromone trap is now available for *Anobium*. An entomologist should be consulted when there is doubt about the insect species. Methods available for the elimination of an active infestation, including chemical treatments, freezing and low oxygen environments, are discussed in Chapter 6.

### Death watch beetle (Xestobium rufovillosum)

A member of the same family (the Anobiidae) as the common furniture beetle, the death watch beetle, is well known for the damage it causes to the woodwork of historic buildings, especially churches. It is widely distributed in England, Wales and Ireland but occurs less frequently in the North and is not recorded in Scotland. The name is derived from the tapping sound produced by both sexes during the mating season (between June and March), a series of six to eight rapid taps repeated at short intervals.

The life cycle of this beetle is similar to that of the common furniture beetle but, under normal conditions, may vary in length from 5–10 years or more largely depending on the extent of fungal decay in the wood but also on temperature, moisture content and the amount of sapwood present. The white, lemon shaped eggs, usually 40–60 but occasionally up to 200 in number, are laid between March and June and normally hatch in about five weeks. The larvae wander over the surface before boring deeply into the wood where they may cause severe damage. When the larvae are fully grown they change into pupae, during July and August, and two to three weeks later the pupae change into beetles which then remain within the wood until the following spring. Adult beetles emerge between March and June through a round flight hole about 3 mm in diameter. The adult beetle, the largest of the British Anobiids, is 6–9 mm long, chocolate brown in colour and covered with patches of short yellow hairs giving it a variegated appearance which makes it somewhat difficult to spot on the surface of old wood (*Figure 7.10*).

Recent research has demonstrated that, contrary to previous belief, infestation of wood by the fungus *Donkioporia expansia* is not critical for beetle development although

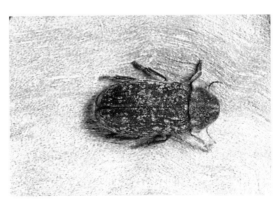

**Figure 7.10** The death watch beetle (*Xestobium rufovillosum*) seen from above (© Crown Copyright)

beetles may develop faster in fungal infested wood (Simmonds, 1997). The timber most frequently attacked in buildings is oak although damage has also been recorded in alder, beech, chestnut, elm and walnut. In its wild habitat the beetle also attacks a variety of other hardwood trees. Tropical hardwoods, by virtue of their generally greater resistance to fungal decay, may be less susceptible to attack. Softwoods appear to be attacked only when they are in close proximity to infested hardwoods. Attack mostly occurs in timber which was installed in an unseasoned condition or which has subsequently become wet for prolonged periods. Damage to installed items such as pews and screens occurs but damage to free-standing furniture is rare, although not unknown (see *Figure 7.5*).

The frass from the death watch beetle is coarser than that from common furniture beetle and contains bun-shaped faecal pellets in contrast to the finer dust and ellipsoid pellets produced by the common furniture beetle (see *Figure 7.7*). Presence of frass, clean sharp holes and the presence of living beetles on or near damaged timbers or on the floor underneath affected timbers are good indications of active infestation. The severity of attack can be judged up to a point by the number of flight holes present but because death watch beetle can bore deeply into timbers it may be necessary to carry out exploratory drilling to determine the full extent of the infestation and hence the structural implications of the attack and the remedial measures to be taken.

Preventive measures chiefly consist of elimination of conditions favourable to attack, that is of maintaining the building or other wooden structure in good condition free from damp (Melville and Gordon, 1984). Particular attention should be paid to roof coverings, gutters, rain-water pipes, damp-proof courses, broken or badly sealed windows and other structural defects which could allow the penetration of damp and the creation of conditions from which an attack could proceed. Regular inspections inside and outside can help to ensure the integrity of the building and freedom from damp. Determination of the extent and distribution of attack and of the structural condition of the timber are essential precursors to any remedial treatment.

*Powder post beetle (Lyctus spp.)*   Powder post beetle larvae are so called because they reduce the sapwood of many partially or fully seasoned timbers to a fine flour-like powder. Powder post beetles are found in several different families, of which two of the most common are the Lyctidae and the Bostrychidae, and are distributed world wide. The commonest species in the United Kingdom is *Lyctus brunneus*, a small reddish brown or black beetle about 5 mm long and of somewhat flattened appearance. The curved white larva of this species are 5–6 mm long when fully grown and are distinguished by a pair of oval brown spots (spiracles) near their posterior end, which are visible with a ×10 hand lens.

Development from egg laying to emergence normally takes one to two years. It may take longer under unfavourable conditions but in heated buildings may take only eight to ten months. Emergence mostly occurs from late May to early September with a peak in July. The larvae feed mainly on the cell contents (starch) of sapwood although they may emerge through adjacent hardwood, leaving a circular exit hole approximately 1.5 mm in diameter. The small thread-like larval tunnels running mainly parallel to the grain which are characteristic of the early stages of attack may be revealed when wood is machined but are easily overlooked. In its later stages, the sapwood may be almost completely disintegrated although a thin skin is usually left on the surface. The frass is extremely fine, like talc.

Most commercial hardwoods, including oak, ash, elm, walnut, hickory and mahogany which contain a normal amount of starch are attacked, those with large pores are preferred. Veneers and plywoods are also susceptible. Fine textured timbers such as beech and birch, in which the vessels are less than 0.1 mm in diameter are normally too small to admit the ovipositor of the female and are therefore immune. Most softwoods are also normally immune since vessels are absent. Lyctus is a pest mainly of sawmills, timber yards and wood manufacturing premises and strenuous efforts are needed in these environments to prevent Lyctus infestation. Good hygiene and regular inspection are essential but not normally sufficient. Active control methods including starch depletion of timber, heat sterilization and chemical treatments for control of infestation both pre and post manufacturing are discussed by Desch (1973) and in a wide range of publications available through the Building Research Establishment (bre.co.uk). Preservative treatment of hardwoods in service is rarely necessary since the are usually removed from sources of infestation and are protected by surface finishes against the risk of egg laying.

*House longhorn beetle (Hylotrupes bajulus)*
Longhorn beetles (of the family Cerambycidae) are normally pests of forest trees and freshly felled logs. However, the house longhorn beetle is an exception to this in that it attacks seasoned sapwood of softwoods and may cause serious structural damage.

The beetle is 10–20 mm long and flattened in shape. The head and prothorax are thickly covered with grey hairs except for a smooth central line on the prothorax. When fully grown, the white, straight-bodied larva is about 30 mm long. The lifecycle, which is similar to that of the other wood-boring beetles already described, may take from three to eleven or more years to complete. The adult beetles emerge during warm periods in July, August and September through oval exit holes, the major diameter of which varies from about 6 to 9 mm.

Since the beginning of the twentieth century, the status of this insect in continental Europe has changed from that of comparative rarity to being a widespread pest, causing serious structural damage to timbers in buildings. Although the species has been known in Britain at least since 1795 it is only since the early 1940s that numerous instances of infestation have been detected. These have occurred chiefly in an area to the south west of London but also in Essex and elsewhere round the perimeter of Greater London. Attack has also been observed in packing crates from which it is conceivable that it could spread.

Damage occurs in seasoned softwood timbers such as fence posts, fences and structural woodwork in outbuildings and homes. Only the sapwood is affected. Where damage is severe, structural integrity may be completely undermined. Because of the long development period before the adults emerge,

great damage can be done before infestation is detected. Relatively little bore dust is produced and there may be comparatively little evidence that an attack is in progress. Slight corrugations may be present in the surface of the wood indicating the presence of dust-filled larval tunnels. When broken open these will reveal the powdery condition of the underlying timber. When active, under warm conditions, the larvae give rise to a faint and intermittent but clearly audible sound as they move through the wood.

In an attempt to prevent the potentially very serious consequences of this insect pest spreading, it has become a notifiable pest in the UK. If house longhorn beetle infestation is detected it should be notified to the local authority who will then be able to confirm what measures are to be taken. Provided the attack is detected before damage becomes severe, the treatment is comparatively simple and relatively inexpensive. However, severe cases may involve removal and replacement of all affected timber.

In contrast to the situation created by house longhorn beetle, the presence of oval tunnels and flight holes unaccompanied by disintegrated wood is frequently noted in buildings. This is a sign of attack by forest longhorn beetles which does not normally persist for long and does not spread in seasoned wood. Further information on house longhorn beetle is available in the UK through the Building Research Establishment.

Wood microbiology and the prevention of decay are discussed by Zabel and Morrell (1992). An excellent bibliography on biodeterioration of cultural property is given by Koestler (1991). The mechanisms of biodegradation of wood are described by Blanchette *et al*. (1990, 1991), Caneva *et al*. (1991), Dawson (1980), Eriksson *et al*. (1990) and Koestler (1991). For further discussion of the habits and life cycles of wood destroying insects see Kingsolver (1988), Mallis (1982), Pinniger (1994), Schippers-Lammertse (1988) and Sutter (1986). Recognition of wood rot and insect damage in buildings is discussed by Bravery *et al*. (1987).

**Mechanical deterioration of wood**
Mechanics is the branch of physical science dealing with the behaviour of matter under the

action of force. Forces are applied to furniture as a consequence of use and of environmentally induced dimensional changes. The major factors that influence mechanical performance in relation to furniture are the structural dimension (Radial, Tangential etc.), loading (Tension, Compression, Shear, Bending), environment and defects.

The mechanical properties of wood are anisotropic. It is not uniform in composition and its properties are not equal in the three structural dimensions. Some properties of wood which developed to meet the needs of the tree also suit its use in furniture. Wood is strongest in compression parallel to the grain (axial compression), has excellent bending strength characteristics, and for its weight, wood demonstrates amazing stiffness and fracture resistance. However, its comparative weakness in tension and in compression at right-angles to the grain define limits to its performance with respect to surface indentation, splitting, and the failure of joints. The strength can be assessed by specific gravity, grain orientation and the absence of defects.

In furniture, strength of wood plays a critical role in various ways. Bending strength may determine the integrity of legs and stretchers in chairs and tables, the rails or posts of beds, or the planks of benches and leaves of tables. Hardness usually predicts how well surfaces resist indentation under practical use or abuse. The strength of wood in compression across the grain – in particular, the elastic strain limit – is important to the performance of joints such as mortise and tenon and dowel joints. Racking loads may concentrate excessive compression loads on mating parts of joints and compression set resulting from restrained swelling under variable moisture conditions is a major cause of joint failure. Components rarely break in two, usually objects simply 'fall apart' – indicating that the limiting strength was related to joints. Understanding the nature and properties of various forms of furniture construction is therefore an important precursor to any discussion of structural deterioration. The main types of joints, the critical factors that determine the success of joints, a detailed analysis of some representative joint types and a review of the main types of construction is given in Chapter 2.

## 7.2  Deterioration of wooden structures – causes

Well-made pieces of furniture, employing good quality materials (fine straight grained wood free of defects), good principles of construction and closely fitting joints, properly glued together using fresh glue, are likely to maintain a good state of preservation (Brachert, 1986; Michaelsen, 1978). When compromises were made in the past, for example, with the selection of poor quality secondary woods, or when pieces were poorly constructed, damage may have occurred due to those initial decisions (Baarsen and Folkers, 1992; Gustler, 1988; Hlopoff, 1978; Schnepper, 1985; Smith, 1975). Deterioration of structures arises where there is some interaction between two parts or where the deterioration of materials has structural consequences. Structural problems may arise through faulty construction or conservation, through fair wear and tear in use, through normal environmental interaction, or through catastrophe, though even well-constructed and carefully used pieces will deteriorate eventually. Depending on the strengths and weaknesses of the design and construction of the artefact these translate into various kinds of failures, some of which are general and some of which apply to specific kinds of structures only. Common problems in furniture and wooden objects include broken and damaged parts and losses, loose and lifting veneer, loose and broken joints, shrinkage splitting and warping. Specific damage types of non-wood materials, decorative structures (surface finishes), upholstery are discussed in Chapter 8. The purpose of this section is to briefly draw attention to the structural implications of aspects of the behaviour of wood. It attempts to provide a framework within which to illustrate examples of the general types of problems. It is not exhaustive and readers are encouraged to develop their own checklist of things to look out for and things to avoid in their own work. In practice, many of the categories of deterioration of structures are closely interrelated and failure is unlikely to be due to a single cause.

### 7.2.1  General – dimensional response of wooden structures

The fact that wood is anisotropic in both hygroscopic and mechanical behaviour gives rise, when making wooden structures, to the need to use wooden members with the grain at right-angles to each other. The creation of strong structures frequently leads to restricted movement which then leads to damage. Differences in both the extent and rate of dimensional response of different components in the structure sets up stresses that lead to various kinds of damage. The different hygroscopic sensitivities of different components of a structure may be due to the presence of different materials (e.g. wood, ivory, metal in a mixed media object), to different species having been used together, to defects in the wood or to the way the wood has been cut or arranged in the structure. Rate of response to RH changes is also affected by finishes (e.g. varnish, paint) and by veneers. Compression set can lead to damage in both large panels and in joints and all of these factors can contribute to the damage caused to decorative structures through differences in the dimensional response of the support, ground, paint or other layers. Moisture-induced dimensional change contributes to adhesive failure and is frequently a precursor to mechanical damage.

In the absence of stable RH, damage such as loose joints, splits, checks, and warping may develop (von Reventlow, 1978; Wright, 1978). The introduction of central heating systems has caused damage to furniture and other woodwork due to the extreme fluctuations in RH that accompany its use. Before any attempt is made to treat such damage, however, the conservator should thoroughly understand the cause of the problem (Baumeister and Müller-Amecke, 1989). Splits caused by compression set, for example, may re-occur if treated by simply filling the split and assuming that this will hold the panel together.

## 7.2.2 Faulty construction and conservation

Most errors in construction reflect a lack of understanding of the dimensional behaviour of wood or occur when such issues were deliberately subjugated to realize the design. What may be considered as faulty construction or conservation may arise because the design was faulty, or because the execution was faulty or because poor quality materials were used. Inappropriate use of material and the

role of fashion in design and construction are two other factors to be considered. Conservation treatment offers the scope to repeat many of these errors and to introduce many new ones.

### *Design faults*

Some examples of different types of design faults include designs that are not suited to bear the applied loads, those not suited to accommodate the movement that would occur in service and those in which incompatible materials have been specified in the design.

An example of a design that may not be suited to bear the loads to which an object would be exposed in use can be observed in the short grain of the Regency sabre leg and scrolled arm. Where such curved structures are formed by cutting from straight grained timber there is a section of so-called short grain at the curve which may be exposed under load to high shearing forces with a corresponding tendency to break at that point. Another example is the architect's table illustrated in *Figure 7.11* in which the legs have been tenoned to the drawer front. Dovetail housings used to attach the drawer sides coincide with the mortise and tenon joint, exacerbating its inherent weakness.

Forces acting on the joints of furniture made with long cabriole legs, where typically no stretcher is used, may be multiplied by the effect of leverage and the joint may thereby be subjected to forces greater than it can withstand. This is particularly the case when furniture with this type of leg is dragged along the floor thereby imposing a sideways force on the leg which is transferred to the joint. Deformation of wood can occur through plastic flow or creep, for example book shelves can sag under the weight of books, where the parameters of the design are not carefully considered.

Well-designed furniture allows for the dimensional response of wood to occur without damage. In a frame and panel construction, the panel should be able to move freely within the frame, or the panel may develop splits (*Figure 7.12*). Thinner elements, e.g. sides of case furniture, react more rapidly to changes in RH than thicker cut sections, such as stile and frame work (Buck, 1961; Stevens, 1961). Cleats, also

(a)

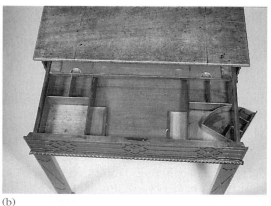

(b)

**Figure 7.11**  A mid-eighteenth century mahogany architect's table, English
(*a*) Table open (after conservation)
(*b*) Detail of the open drawer (after conservation)
(*c*) Detail of the jointing of drawer front to front leg (mortise and tenoned) and drawer front to drawer side (dovetail housing) before conservation

(c)

known as end clamps, restrict the movement of panels or boards and often result in splits caused by compression set when the RH fluctuates (Stürmer and Werwein, 1986). Many examples of design not suited to accommodate movement that would occur in service are found in the early use of walnut in English furniture, where mouldings are extensively applied across the grain and veneers are laid over both frame and panel of framed components such as doors. The nailing or screwing of drawer bottoms is another example. Splits along the grain of wood near the ends of panels are typical of the damage that may occur through the use of cleats or battens fixed across the grain of the wood in the construction of doors and fall-fronts in furniture. *Figure 7.13* shows a detail of the use of cleats and typical damage that may result when the two components are fixed in relation to each other instead of being allowed to move (as could occur for example if a dovetail housing were used).

The use of metals with wood is one of the commonest examples of the use of incompatible materials. Strap hinges running across the grain and boulle marquetry are two instances of this. The furniture designed by Carlo Bugatti (1856–1940) often develops problems in the vellum or parchment coverings that decorate the furniture as the amount of expansion and contraction of the skin material is different from the substrate wood. Similar problems have occurred with furniture decorated in the style of Andres Charles Boulle in which veneers of brass and tortoiseshell are frequently combined with pewter, horn and exotic woods. This is nearly always found to have suffered tremendous problems of loose and lifting veneers requiring elaborate and time-consuming treatments (Alcouffe, 1977; Considine *et al.*, 1990; Eames, 1980; Michaelsen, 1978; Ramond, 1989; Wackernagel 1978).

It is actually very difficult to overcome all these potential design faults and still produce something interesting and usable.

(a)

(b)

**Figure 7.12** A seventeenth century oak panelled doorway, English
(*a*) The doorway
(*b*) Detail of panels on door. Where movement was unrestricted, the panels remain intact, whilst split upper panels have resulted when movement was restricted (in this case free movement of the panels within their grooves was prevented by accretions of paint, now removed)

(a)

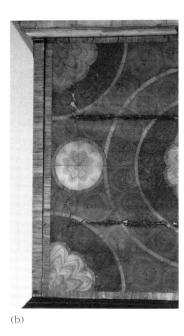

(b)

**Figure 7.13** Damage in a cabinet of cleated construction
(*a*) Cabinet on stand, oyster veneered in kingwood and East Indian rosewood
(*b*) Detail of the fall front, which has cleated construction. Splits between the horizontal boards have been filled with wooden fillets in the past and then retouched. This old retouching is now markedly darker than the original veneered decoration. Cycling relative humidity in combination with compression set caused by the use of wooden fillets has resulted in the recurrence of splits and loss of original veneer

## Faults in execution of the design

However good or bad the design, its performance in service will be markedly influenced by how well it was put together. Ideally, carefully selected materials will have been assembled using well fitting joints correctly aligned and appropriate and well-used fixings, fastenings and adhesives. In some cases, however, joints may not fit properly due to the use of blunt or otherwise badly prepared, or badly used, tools or poor marking out. The geometry of the piece may be incorrect, because components were cut or glued out of alignment, causing loads to be transferred to parts of the structure which are not fully able to support them. Adhesives may have been correctly chosen but may have been used incorrectly. Glue may have been allowed to chill off during assembly or surfaces may have been inadequately prepared before use or quality control of materials may have been inadequate. Inappropriate use may have been made of screws, nails, or other hardware such as metal straps and brackets or the wrong adhesive may have been selected for the intended service conditions. Even in high-quality pieces, unbalanced construction, for example the use of veneer or decorative surface on one side only of a panel, is a common cause of degradation and failure. Panels veneered on one side often have a tendency to develop a concave warp opposite the veneered surface (Hlopoff, 1978). Applying gesso or veneer on only one side of a panel will result in an unequal dimensional response to changes in moisture content (Buck, 1961). This is a well-known phenomenon in the field of panel paintings conservation (Kuhn, 1986). The same principles apply to decorative surfaces on wood in furniture where one side of a panel is treated differently than the other. Conversely, wooden structures that are veneered on both sides tend to be less prone to planar distortion. The benefits of coatings on both sides of a substrate is illustrated by the outer panels of triptychs where increased stability is attributed to sympathetic layering since both sides are painted.

### Poor quality materials used
Wood with one or more of the defects discussed earlier in this chapter may still have been included because it was considered too expensive to eliminate them or because the user was not aware of them. Animal glue may have been overheated before use or reheated too often. Other materials, particularly adhesives, may have been used past their shelf life or cheaper, inferior grades may have been selected.

### Inappropriate use of material
There may be nothing 'wrong' as such with a material that has been used, it may just be that it was not the best material to have chosen for the particular application. An example might be the use of a timber with large movement in wide boards. Other examples might relate to hardness, resistance to splitting, or other aspects of strength. Traditionally animal glue has been the furniture adhesive of choice but with the development of polymer science has come many new adhesives some of which are particularly suited to new materials and new construction methods. Choice of adhesive is discussed elsewhere but, by way of example, needs to take account of service conditions, strength, loading and gap filling ability.

### Role of fashion and technical innovation
As new materials, types of construction and design have been introduced, artists, designers and makers have had to experiment and learn how to exploit the strengths and minimize the weaknesses of a new material or technique. There is always a learning curve and mistakes are frequently made during the initial period of use. This applies to the construction of early chests, to the introduction of kiln drying, to the introduction of veneers and to the manufacture and use of plyform constructions, for example. In a different sense, fashion plays an important part in whether things are accorded a status that helps them to survive.

### Conservation treatment errors
The potential for error in conservation is large. It includes unnecessary additions and removals, the use of inappropriate or unstable materials, the use of repairs in which the grain direction of the wood is wrongly oriented, and the inadvertent transfer of stress to a weak member or component of a structure. Treatments such as butterfly keys, long dowels or hardware where the intervention restrains the original wood or other furniture material from expanding and contracting are a major cause of failure. Furniture restorers have tried to reinforce wooden panels by inserting long dowels perpendicular to the wood grain in the hope that the panel will not shrink, split or warp (Sutter, 1986). Another method of reinforcing repaired splits is to insert cross-grain 'butterfly' or dovetail keys (*Figure 7.14*). Although the use of butterfly or dovetail keys dates back as far as the twelfth century, these inserts cause partial restraint of movement of

**Figure 7.14** Rear door of a boulle bracket clock, French, seventeenth century, showing the use of dovetail keys to reinforce a repair

the wood in which they are introduced, and may cause additional damage. All of these restoration methods will restrain the natural movement of the wood and have the potential to cause further splitting in areas that previously were sound. In addition, wood fillets themselves shrink over the years due to compression set and cease to function as intended (see *Figure 7.13*). The use of screws, nails, brackets and straps to reinforce parts that are already mechanically weak and failing may be successful in the short term but, in the long term may stain the wood and usually leads to significantly more damage and, as a result, more complicated repairs.

## 7.3  Deterioration of wooden structures – consequences

The general consequences of deterioration of wooden structures include broken and damaged parts and losses, loose and lifting veneers, shrinkage splitting and warping, accretions and surface disfigurement. Other specific consequences apply to particular structural types and to the ways they are used and typically abused.

### 7.3.1  Broken and damaged parts and losses

Direct mechanical damage caused by accidental impact can occur at any time but is frequently preceded by moisture-induced dimensional changes, biological damage or structural weakness caused by adhesive failure. Such changes may follow a more or less prolonged period of moisture cycling or lengthy exposure to excessively high or low RH. Corners, mouldings and other applied decoration, inlay, fine detailed projections and carvings are frequently the first casualties. Carved figures and ornament that are easily detached are frequent targets of petty theft in public collections. As joints become progressively weaker or splits open up any applied force tends to be concentrated in areas of weakness and to do proportionately and progressively more damage.

### 7.3.2  Loose and lifting veneer

Veneer on a stable substrate in the absence of environmental extremes can remain secure for prolonged periods. However, problems with veneer are by no means uncommon. Veneered decoration almost invariably implies the juxtaposition of different timbers with different grain directions, different hygroscopic sensitivities and different rates of response. Veneer also implies adhesive and hence adhesive failure. Commonly experienced problems with veneer include blisters, splits and glue failure. The effects of movement of wood with opposing grain directions may be to leave veneers and banding oversized with respect to the carcase and therefore vulnerable to mechanical damage during routine cleaning and handling. Splits and cracks in veneers are frequently observed when the underlying support is a frame and panel type of construction, a board with end cleats, or solid timber with the grain at right-angels to the veneer. Although it is not always easy to ascertain the treatment history of veneered objects from the eighteenth century and earlier there is reason to believe that traditional adhesives such as hide glue can continue to function for very long periods of time. Incompatibilities between substrate and veneer or problems with high humidity can lead to failure on a much shorter time scale. Inlay will normally remain intact unless it is at right-angles to the grain of the substrate. Popping and subsequent losses occur routinely when the primary wood support contracts while the longitudinally oriented inlay does not. The solutions are problematic since the primary wood has reduced dimension in comparison to the unchanged inlay.

### 7.3.3    Loose and broken joints

Loose and broken joints can occur when joints are overloaded or are forced to take loads for which they were not intended, for example tension or racking, especially in chairs. Mortise and tenon, and dowel joints in chairs are among the most common joint failures while joint failure in carcases is much less common. Moisture cycling of joints, especially those of the mortise and tenon type, is a well-recognized form of failure that both contributes to and is exacerbated by glue failure (Hoadley, 1980). Although glue failure can cause joints to become loose it should be remembered that not all joints will have been glued originally. Glue failure may be the result of old or overcooked glue in the original assembly or the result of glue being allowed to gel on the surface of the wood before the joint was closed. Glue also can be broken down by biological degradation of the proteins, or by extreme dry conditions causing the glue to become brittle. The nitrogen in animal adhesives provides a source of food for woodworm and attack by this insect is frequently concentrated in the region of joints. The initial quality of fabrication of the joint will contribute to the speed at which it deteriorates. A joint that was poorly fitted in the first place, and therefore required a thicker glue layer, will lose its strength faster than a tightly cut joint with a thin glue line.

### 7.3.4    Shrinkage splitting and warping

Factors that contribute to splits and checks include rapid changes of RH, compression set and subsequent shrinkage of wood, faulty construction and removal of an item from its established environment to a radically different environment. Modern heating systems producing excessively dry air are a prime cause of damage. Air outside in northern temperate climates in winter is typically at a temperature where it is able to hold only small amounts of moisture (absolute humidity). Although the relative humidity of this outside air may still be quite high, when the air enters a building its temperature may be raised 15–20 °C or more. The absolute humidity remains the same but the amount of water that air at the new temperature is capable of holding is now greatly increased so the relative humidity drops drastically. Figures of 30% RH are common and RH as low as 20% may be encountered. This is graphically illustrated in *Figure 7.15*. The general relationship between temperature and relative humidity is illustrated in *Figure 6.3b*. Splits and checks will occur in most pieces of furniture under extreme dry conditions. Especially vulnerable are those pieces in which the construction prevents expansion or contraction of the furniture materials and pieces which are moved too quickly from a cool damp environment such as an unheated church into a hot dry environment such as a normal domestic interior or museum exhibition hall. In sound wood, splits and checks always occur parallel to the grain of the wood because wood is weakest in tension across the grain. Movement of water is greater through end-grain than through side-grain and splits commonly occur at the ends of boards, especially where these are unsealed. When two or more layers of wood are joined together, such as on veneered surfaces or with plywood, the dimensional forces can be complex. The shrinkage or expansion causes stress in any of the wood layers, decreasing from the outer layers inward. Substrate wood and solid wood panels frequently develop splits, while checks are more common in veneer. Dimensional forces may also cause checks in plywood. Minor (1993) demonstrated that lathe-checks are introduced in the individual veneer layers when they are rotary cut and that these checks open further when the outer veneer layers shrink relative to the core of the plywood.

Frame and panel construction is designed to provide strength and rigidity while allowing for movement of the panel. However, under some circumstances splits may still be observed in the panel due to differences in speed of reaction of bulky frames and thin panels. Under conditions of high relative humidity, both the frame and the panel will pick up moisture and swell. This can result in the panel being pinched around its edges so that it is no longer able to move freely. In a subsequent period of low RH, the thinner

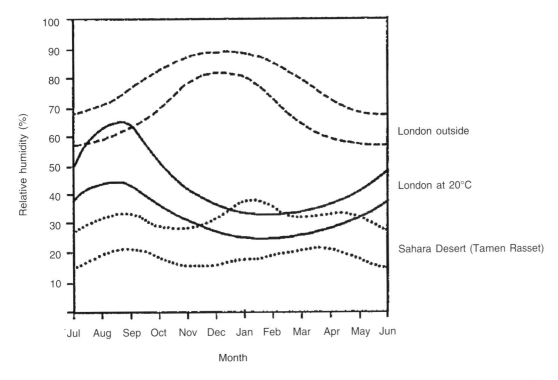

**Figure 7.15** Effect of winter heating on relative humidity in temperate climates. The relative humidity in London, UK ranges from around 65% in summer to 85% in winter (indicated by broken lines). The use of heating reduces the RH in winter, so that the annual RH ranges from around 65% in summer to 30% in winter (indicated by unbroken lines). The RH range in the Sahara desert (Tamen Rasset) ranges between 20% and 40% (indicated by dotted lines). It can be seen from the graph that winter heating in London can reduce relative humidity to levels comparable to an arid desert climate

panel may dry out before the framing and, being thus prevented from moving, may split from top to bottom.

Warping results from non-uniform moisture-induced dimensional change. One reason for this might be because the amount of moisture getting to the piece of wood was different in different parts, for example because one side is painted or veneered and the other side is not. Another reason for non-uniform response might be that the reaction to a given amount of moisture was different in different parts. This could occur because the piece of wood was part of a structure that prevented an equal response or because of variations within a single piece of wood. Variations within a single piece of wood that might account for non-uniform response could include defects such as reaction wood or variations in microfibrillar angle.

Wooden panels on which there is an effective moisture barrier on one side only (e.g. paint) are often subject to compression set. If there is a moisture barrier on only one side (the front) of the panel then the movement of moisture in and out is restricted on that side. If the RH falls, moisture leaves more rapidly through the back than through the front and shrinkage will be greater at the back. The panel will take on a convex warp and this may cause a painted or gilded layer to crack. If no further change in RH occurs the panel may even out. In many cases, however, panels of this type have a permanent convex warp as a result of the following process. During periods of high RH, moisture entering through the back of the panel causes expansion of the wood at the back. This should result in a concave warp but wood in a damp condition is weaker than and more plastic than dry wood. Part of the movement is therefore restrained by the drier wood at the front of the panel as a result of which wood at the back of the panel swells against itself and a certain amount of permanent plastic compression takes place. When the RH falls and the timber becomes drier, the back layers shrink in the normal way but since they will now be permanently smaller, the panel assumes a convex shape. This effect can be reinforced through several cycles and is known as compression shrinkage, or compression set. In fact, because converted timber rarely dries uniformly throughout, stress set (either compression set or tension set) is the rule rather than the exception.

### 7.3.5   Accretions, and other surface disfigurement

Surface disfigurement occurs by accretion of additional material, by removal of original material and by changes in form of the surface. Accretions can include practically anything accidentally or deliberately applied to or deposited on the surface. Examples include wax, food, drink, fly specks, dust, grease and salts from skin contact. These may cause damage to coatings, stain the wood, or build up to the point where the surface or other detail such as carving is obscured. Removal of original material from surfaces which occurs by a slow process of abrasion depends on the type of object, the uses to which it is put, the hardness of the wood and on coatings that may be present. More acute damage in the form of scratches and score marks may be sustained in accidental contact with sharp edges of other objects (e.g. ceramics) or through the action of large sharp particles (grit) between the object and another object placed on top. They may also result during a move when the object is more likely to come into contact with other objects, buildings or vehicles, or by deliberate acts of vandalism. Bruises and dents constitute two common forms of change in the surface through mechanical means. Fire and flood are two other means by which the original form of a surface may be drastically altered, stains caused by water spills from plant containers or drinks cause less extreme but often serious disfigurement.

### 7.3.6   Review of damage by structure

The way in which objects are used clearly plays an important part in the types of damage that they sustain. Certain types of structures have particular uses and are most likely to sustain damage because of this, although the issues of materials, construction and environment which have already been discussed remain important. An obvious example of a specific type of damage would be drawers, where various surfaces, but particularly the runners and the bottom edge of the drawer sides, wear against each other. This section provides a very brief review of some examples of the kinds of damage from all causes which are likely to be found in particular wooden furniture structures. The frequency of occurrence of various kinds of damage in a sample of two thousand treatments on three different furniture types carried out in the Victoria and Albert Museum furniture conservation studio from the beginning of 1975 to the end of 1985 has been tabulated in *Figure 7.16*.

Chairs have generally to be relatively light to be portable, they are generally of framed construction and often of quite slender members yet have to support considerable loads. In use they are probably the most abused type of furniture and are frequently subjected to racking loads that concentrate forces at joints which may already have become loose through compression set. Even when reprieved from active service, pieces will not be entirely free from accidental damage in handling and transit and the more elaborate and delicate types of carved and turned decoration common in museum pieces are particularly vulnerable to knocks, sharp blows and other mechanical damage. The early type of relatively heavy construction of oak with pegged joints was replaced towards the end of the seventeenth century by lighter constructions, often of walnut, with increasing reliance being placed on glued joints. In many cases the very tall, heavily canted backs provide enormous leverage by which the whole of the back frame may be separated from the remainder. Some of the elaborately carved riband backs and similar splats of the eighteenth century contain similarly vulnerable material in which stresses induced by loads on the wood do not develop parallel with the grain. Often,

**Figure 7.16** Frequency of occurrence of various kinds of damage in a sample of two thousand treatments on three different furniture types carried out in the Victoria and Albert Museum furniture conservation studio from the beginning of 1975 to the end of 1985. A: Chipped/scratched or dirty/discoloured finish or decoration including paint, japan, gilding, varnish, including baize and leather on tables; B: Damaged, broken or partially broken or loose and weakened joints, broken rails and stretchers, arms and legs (internal breaks) and delaminations (e.g. splats); C: Chipped or loose/missing decoration including applied mouldings and integral and applied carving, fretwork and turning; D: Woodworm damage (generally involved with one or other of the preceding categories); E: Damaged upholstery (including deterioration of leather, cane or rush seating or degradation of webbing leading to collapse of seat but excluding problems of silk damask, needlework, velvet, horsehair, etc.); F: Loose, lifting, missing and buckled veneers and inlays; G: Metalwork: loose or missing fittings and fastenings. Misalignment due to shrinkage. Dirty, loose, or missing decoration (mounts); H: Missing and loose components, other than decorative moulding and carving, requiring refitting or

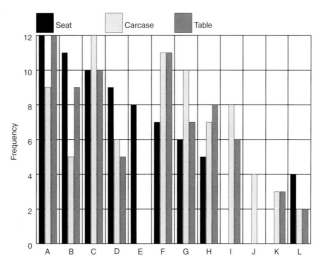

replacement of whole or substantial part, e.g. drawer fronts, legs, arms, rails, knobs; I: Shrinkage splits and warps and repairs to panelling; J: Assembly and disassembly for exhibition; K: Ensuring object security on display; L: Historical restorations and other problems. It can be seen that minor damage, such as accretions of dirt and scratches on chairs, chipped and loose decoration on carcase furniture, or lifting problems with veneer on carcase furniture were the most frequently encountered types of damage. Whilst all types of wooden furniture are equally susceptible to woodworm infestation, chairs are far more likely to require conservation treatment as a result of infestation than carcase or table types

woodworm damage is accompanied by secondary damage arising as a consequence of combination with mechanical damage: partial or complete breaks in rails, stretchers arms and legs, sometimes at joints and sometimes within their lengths. In addition to the basic wood structure and its integral and applied carving, moulding and other ornamentation, lacquer, paint, varnish, japanning and gilding are especially susceptible to damage due to the very nature of their surface qualities and by the additional handling afforded to chairs in comparison to carcase furniture.

### Carcase furniture
Although shrinkage in chairs, besides that associated with joints, can sometimes be a serious problem, it is generally less of a problem than in carcase construction where allowance must be made for the greater movement associated with wider boards. Certain allowances for this movement can be and were made in carcase construction. For example, drawer runners and other members which run across the sides of carcases can be slotted into a groove in the sides and only glued into the rails at the front. Problems arise with mouldings and inlays commonly applied

round the sides and edges of chests of drawers, bureaux and cabinets. Movement across drawer fronts will tend to loosen and detach mouldings applied at right-angles to the grain and brass inlay running at right angles to the grain will be forced out of its groove. It is fortunate that traditional animal glues tend to break before the wood. Compression set, which may arise in service, leaves the drawer fronts slightly smaller than the moulding, which will then tend to become dislodged by knocking against the drawer rails or by overzealous dusting. Loosening of mouldings is a common defect associated with this class of furniture and is again compounded by simple mechanical actions. Mouldings and carvings project and present irregular outlines and are therefore likely to be among the parts first damaged.

Splits are likely to occur in carcase construction as a consequence of different rates of response to changes in relative humidity. Splits are also likely to occur on drying following compression set in boards which have been restrained during periods of high relative humidity. As a result of compression set, panels, especially those which have been painted or veneered on one side only, are

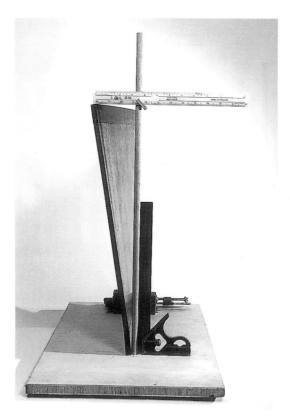

**Figure 7.17** Compound warp of approximately 90 mm (3½ in) in a door from a piece of early twentieth-century furniture

commonly found to have warped. Depending on the grain patterns involved this may be a simple convex warp or a compound twist, as shown in *Figure 7.17*.

The larger flat or gently curved surfaces of carcases are ideal grounds for the execution of decorative marquetry designs in rare and exotic veneers. Decorative timbers unavailable in large sizes, or unsuitable by virtue of grain patterns for use in solid form, have been employed to dazzling effect, especially in continental furniture. Veneer in general, by virtue of its thinness and often wildly variable grain, may give rise to problems which are compounded where many different materials are found in close juxtaposition. Loose, lifting and missing veneer provides a substantial part of the conservation and restoration work associated with carcase furniture.

Metalwork is a common feature of carcase furniture, both as fittings and fastenings and in

the form of decorative mounts, beadings and inlays and these are often found to be loose or out of alignment. Quality carcase furniture was probably much less susceptible than chairs to ill-treatment during its useful lifetime, often being tucked away against a wall and much less likely to be subjected routinely to rigours of movement than other pieces. The fact that loading is generally less in relation to construction than with chairs is reflected in a smaller number of major carcase restorations. Minor scratches, dents and chips to wood and surface finishes and dirty or damaged varnish and staining still occur and regrettably sometimes while in storage or transit. By virtue of its size, much furniture of this type which is either borrowed or loaned for exhibition purposes has to be assembled and disassembled for transport. Despite rigorous precautions and the utmost care in packing and handling taken to minimize the risk of accidents, these do regrettably sometimes still occur and an occasional piece with shattered glass door, or similar, requires attention. Other problems with doors include sagging, distortion, swelling (in which the door appears not to fit the opening in the carcase), misalignment of joints, and damage to, or poor alignment of hinges.

Problems with drawers typically include worn runners, loose joints, damage to mouldings and the loosening and splitting of the bottom. For some people unlocked drawers have an irresistible fascination. Large doors on some cabinets will, if opened together to their full extent, cause the whole piece to over balance. Some of the work of the museum conservator is therefore associated with security. Although ordinarily simple, it can be taxing to the ingenuity to devise methods of securing unlockable drawers by an easily reversible method which is not harmful to the object. On the rare occasions when an attempted theft is successful it may be necessary to replace parts in order to safeguard the aesthetic integrity of the object.

### Tables

Tables range from the most massive early oak dining tables through delicate inlaid Sheraton satinwood tea-tables to the chromed-steel and glass coffee tables and plastic-finished stacking plywood dining tables of the twentieth century. In between these examples there is a wide variety of combinations and styles enriched with all forms of turned, carved and applied ornament. It seems that there is, or has been at some time, a separate table for almost all human activities and situations. These include card, games, tea, occasional, sutherland, pembroke, sofa and night tables, side, reading and writing and artists' and library tables, refectory, gateleg, single and multi-pedestal dining tables and others such as fantastically carved and gilded pier or console tables which have sometimes been supporting weights of many hundreds of pounds of marble for two hundred years or more. Table tops are often warped or split and flaps are often prevented from hanging properly because of misalignment due to shrinkage between the framing and the joints in the top. Legs and feet are vulnerable to leverage forces from kicking and dragging over floors and to contact with floor cleaning materials.

This chapter has indicated some of the ways in which furniture and wooden objects deteriorate through a combination of issues of material, structure environment and usage. Practical methods of treatment of these problems are discussed in Part 4. Further information on the care and preservation of furniture and woodwork can be found in Guldbeck and MacLeish (1985), McGiffin (1992), Richardson (1993), Sandwith and Stainton (1993) and Williams (1988).

## Bibliography

Alcouffe, D. (1977) *The Restorers Handbook of Furniture*, Van Nostrand Reinhold

Baarsen, R.J. and Folkers, J.P. (1992) De restauratie van een ensemble Nederlandse marqueterie-meubelen uit de late achttiende eeuw, *Bulletin van het Rijksmuseum*, 40 (2), 140–57

Baumeister, M. and Müller-Arnecke, S. (1989) Die Veränderung eines barocken Chorgestühldorsals aus der ehemaligen Kartause zu Mainz, *Zeitschrift für Kunsttechnologie und Konservierung*, 3 (2), 378–93

Blanchette, R.A. and Simpson, E. (1992) Soft rot and wood pseudomorphs in an ancient coffin (700 BC) from Tumulus MM at Gordion, Turkey, *IAWA Bulletin*, 13 (2), 201–13

Blanchette, R.A., Cease, K.R., Abad, A.R., Koestler, R.J., Simpson, E. and Sams, G.K. (1991) An evaluation of different forms of deterioration found in archaeological wood, in *Biodeterioration of Cultural Property*, reprint from *International Biodeterioration*, 28, 1–4, Elsevier Applied Science, pp. 3–22

Blanchette, R.A., Nilsson, T., Daniel, G. and Abad, A. (1990) Biological degradation of wood, in *Archaeological Wood Properties, Chemistry, and Preservation*, Advances in Chemistry Series, No. 225, American Chemical Society, Washington, DC, pp. 141–74

Brachert, T. (1986) Technische Innovationen der Roentgenwerkstatt, *Beiträge zur Konstruktion und Restaurierung alter Möbel*, Callwey, pp. 115–29

Bravery, A.F., Berry, R.W., Carey, J.K. and Cooper, D.E. (1987) *Recognizing Wood Rot and Insect Damage in Buildings*, Building Research Establishment

Brown, W.H. (1988) *The Conversion and Seasoning of Wood*, Stobart

Buchanan, G. (1985) *The Illustrated Handbook of Furniture Restoration*, Batsford

Buck, R.D. (1961) The use of moisture barriers on panel paintings, *Studies in Conservation*, 6 (1), 9–19

Building Research Establishment (1977) *A Handbook of Softwood*, HMSO

Caneva, G., Nugari, M.P. and Salvadori, O. (1991) *Biology in the Conservation of Works of Art*, ICCROM, Rome

Chang, S-T., Hon, D.N.-S. and Feist, W.C. (1982) Photodegradation and photoprotection of wood surfaces, *Wood and Fiber*, April

Considine, B.B., Jamet, M. and Østrup, A. (1990) The conservation of two pieces of boulle marquetry furniture in the collection of the J. Paul Getty Museum, in ICOM Committee for Conservation, Preprints 9th Triennial Meeting, Dresden, Vol. II, pp. 831–4

Dawson, J.E. (1980) Biodegradation of wood, in *Proceedings of the Furniture and Wooden Objects Symposium*, Canadian Conservation Institute

Desch, H.E. (1973) *Timber, Its Structure and Properties*, 5th edn, Macmillan

Dinwoodie, J.M. (1981) *Timber, Its Nature and Behaviour*, Van Nostrand Reinhold

Eames, R. (1980) Conservation of a clock in the style of Boulle, in *Proceedings of the Furniture and Wooden Objects Symposium*, CCI, pp. 117–19

Eriksson, K.-E.L., Blanchette, R.A. and Ander, P. (1990) *Microbial and Enzymatic Degradation of Wood and Wood Components*, Springer-Verlag

Farmer, R.H. (1962) Corrosion of metals in association with wood, *Wood*, 27, 326–8 and 443–6

Farmer, R.H. (1972) *Handbook of Hardwoods*, HMSO

Feist, W.C. and Hon, D.N.-S. (1984) Chemistry of weathering and protection, in R. Rowell (ed.), *The Chemistry of Solid Wood*, Advances in Chemistry Series, No. 207, American Chemical Society, Washington, pp. 401–51

Feller, R.L. (1971) Notes on the chemistry of bleaching, *Bulletin IIC-AG*, 11 (2), 47

Fielden, B.M. (1982) *The Conservation of Historic Buildings*, Butterworths

Forest Products Research Laboratory (1970) *The Degradation of Wood by Metal Fasteners and Fittings*, Timberlab Paper, FPRL, Princes Risborough

Godla, J. and Hanlon, G. (1995) Some applications of Adobe Photoshop for the documentation of furniture conservation, *JAIC*, 34 (3), 157–72

Guldbeck, P.E. and MacLeish, A.B. (1985) *Care of Antiques and Historical Collections*, 2nd edn, American Association for State and Local History, Nashville, TN

Gustler, W.B. (1988) Eighteenth century case furniture analysis and treatments, in AIC Wooden Artifacts Group, Conference Papers, New Orleans

Hayward, C.H. (1969) *Furniture Repairs*, Evans Brothers Ltd

Henderson, F.Y. (1977) *Handbook of Softwoods*, HMSO

Hlopoff, S.N. (1978) On the straightening of a warped mahogany-veneered panel, in *Conservation of Wood in Painting and the Decorative Arts*, Conference Preprints, IIC, pp. 33–6

Hoadley, B.R. (1980) *Understanding Wood: A Craftsman's Guide to Wood Technology*, Taunton Press

Hon, D.N.-S. and Chang, S.-T. (1984) Surface degradation of wood by ultraviolet light, *Journal of Polymer Science*, 22, 2227–2241

Hon, D.N.-S. and Feist, W.C. (1986) Weathering characteristics of hardwood surfaces, *Wood Science and Technology*, 20, 169–83

Hon, David N.S. and Ifju, G. (1978) Measuring penetration of light into wood by detection of photo-induced free radicals, *Wood Science*, 11 (2), 118–27

Kingsolver, J.M. (1988) *Illustrated Guide to Common Insect Pests in Museums, A Guide to Museum Pest Control*, Foundation of the American Institute for Conservation of Historic and Artistic Works and the Association of Systematic Collections, Washington, DC, pp. 53–81

Klein, P. and Bröker, F.W. (1990) Investigation on swelling and shrinkage of panels with wooden support, in ICOM Committee for Conservation, Preprints 9th Triennial Meeting, Dresden, pp. 41–3

Klim, S. (1990) Composite wood materials in twentieth century furniture, in AIC Wooden Artifacts Group, Conference Papers, Richmond, Virginia

Koestler, R.J. (ed.) (1991) *Biodeterioration of Cultural Property*, reprinted from *International Biodeterioration* 28, 1–4, Elsevier Applied Science

Koestler, R.J. (1993) Insect eradication using controlled atmospheres, and FTIR measurement for insect activity, in ICOM Committee for Conservation Preprints from the 10th Triennial Conference

Kuhn, H. (1986) *Conservation and Restoration of Works of Art and Antiquities*, Butterworths

Mallis, A. (1982) *Handbook of Pest Control*, 6th edn, Franzak & Foster

McGiffin, R. (1992) *Furniture Care and Conservation*, 2nd edn, American Association for State and Local History Press, Nashville, TN

Melville, I.A. and Gordon, I.A. (1984) *The Repair and Maintenance of Houses*, Estates Gazette Ltd

Michaelsen, H. (1978) Restaurierung eines intarsierten Prunktisches von Johann Daniel Sommer, *Neue Musemskunde*, 21 (2), 125–9

Minor, M. (1993) The nature and origin of surface veneer checking in plywood, in *Symposium '91, Saving the Twentieth Century, The Degradation and Conservation of Modern Materials,* Canadian Conservation Institute, pp. 155–65

Otjen, L. and Blanchette, R.A. (1987) Assessment of 30 white rot basidiomucetes for selective lignin degradation, *Holzforschung*, 41, 343–9

Padfield, T., Erhardt, D. and Hopwood, W. (1982) Trouble in store, in *Science and Technology in the Service of Conservation,* IIC, pp. 24–7

Panshin, A.J. and de Zeeuw, C. (1980) *Textbook of Wood Technology*, 4th edn, McGraw-Hill

Pinion, L.C. (1973) *Chemical Staining in Wood*, Building Research Establishment, Princes Risborough

Pinniger, D. (1994) *Insect Pests in Museums*, Archetype

Ramond, P. (1989) *Marquetry*, Taunton Press

von Reventlow, V. (1978) Use of B72 in the restoration of a marquetry surface – case history, in *Conservation of Wood in Painting and the Decorative Arts*, IIC, pp. 37–40

Richardson, B.A. (1993) *Wood Preservation*, Chapman and Hall

Rodd, J. (1976) *Repairing and Restoring Antique Furniture*, David & Charles, Newton Abbot

Salazar, T. (1980) *The Complete Book of Furniture Restoration*, Tiger

Sandwith, H. and Stainton, S. (1993) *National Trust Manual of Housekeeping*, rev. edn, Penguin Books

Schippers-Lammertse, A.F. (1988) Wann droht Insekten- und Schimmelbefall, *Restauro*, 94 (1), 44–9

Schnepper, G. (1985) Merkmale der Konstruktion und Gedanken zur Restaurierung, Barockmöbel aus Württemberg und Hohenlohe 1700–1750, in *Geschichte, Konstruktion, Restaurierung*, Württembergisches Landesmuseum, Stuttgart, pp. 19–27

Simmonds, M. (1997) Wood care project, *Kew Scientist*, 12, October

Skaar, C. (1988) *Wood–Water Relations*, Springer Series in Wood Science, Springer-Verlag

Smith, N.A. (1975) *Old Furniture, Understanding the Craftsman's Art*, Bobbs-Merrill, p. 191

Stevens, W.C. (1961) Rates of change in the dimensions and moisture contents of wooden panels resulting from changes in the ambient air conditions, *Studies in Conservation*, 6 (1), 21–5

Stürmer, M. and Werwein, E. (1986) Zwei Eckschränke von Abraham Roentgen aus den 1760er Jahren, in *Beiträge zur Konstruktion und Restaurierung alter Möbel*, Callwey, pp. 72–88

Sutter, H.P. (1986) *Holzschädlinge an Kulturgütern erkennen und bekämpfen*, Haupt, p. 167

Thomson, G. (1986) *The Museum Environment*, 2nd edn, Butterworths

Wackernagel, R. (1978) The restoration of boulle marquetry at the Bavarian National Museum, in *Conservation of Wood in Painting and the Decorative Arts*, IIC, pp. 41–4

Williams, M.A. (1988) *Keeping It All Together: The Preservation and Care of Historic Furniture*, American Association of Museums

Winandy, J.E. and Rowell, R.M. (1984) The chemistry of wood strength, in R. Rowell (ed.), *The Chemistry of Solid Wood* (Advances in Chemistry Series No. 207), American Chemical Society, Washington, pp. 211–55

Wright, C.D. (1978) Restoring an Italian commode, in *Conservation of Wood in Painting and the Decorative Arts*, IIC, pp. 27–31

Zabel and Morrell (1992) *Wood Microbiology: Decay and its Prevention*, Academic Press

Zavarin, E. (1984) Activation of wood surfaces and nonconventional bonding, in R. Rowell (ed.), *The Chemistry of Solid Wood*, Advances in Chemistry Series, No. 207, American Chemical Society, Washington, p. 357

# 8

# Deterioration of other materials and structures

## 8.1 Ivory, ivory-like teeth, bone and antler, horn and turtleshell

Many aspects of the deterioration of ivory, bone, antler, horn and turtleshell are similar and may be discussed together.

Although ivory and other animal derived materials are made up of both organic and inorganic constituents, most processes of deterioration involve the organic, protein-aceous component alone. Proteins are highly polar due to the presence of hydrogen and oxygen in their molecular structures. This means that water is readily absorbed during periods of high relative humidity causing them to swell. During low RH cycles water may also be lost causing the material to shrink, often with disastrous results. As with wood, the moisture content of proteinaceous materials is in dynamic equilibrium with moisture in the air. As relative humidity changes they take up or give off moisture and change shape.

Organic coatings slow down, but do not stop, this behaviour. Ivory is particularly quick to respond to changes in humidity and the application of water and solvents due to the fine tubes (tubules) which penetrate it throughout. Thin pieces of ivory are much more sensitive to humidity changes than thick pieces and even the moisture from handling can be enough to cause them to warp.

While heat as such does not have a dele-terious effect on these materials (except at temperatures high enough to burn or char them) it will have an effect on relative humidity and this remains the chief concern. Relative humidity guidelines for wood apply to most organic materials and will prevent destructive dehydration. Drying out is simply loss of water adsorbed on polar protein (collagen) by hydrogen bonding. As with wood, moisture content profoundly affects mechanical properties. Ivory and other teeth, tusks and bone exhibit directional or anisotropic shrinkage

(a)

(b)

**Figure 8.1** Cracking in ivory: (*a*) mammoth ivory sample exhibiting circumferential cracking; (*b*) weathered elephant ivory sample showing radial cracks and circumferential flaking and delamination

315

characteristics, which causes them to check or crack as they dry. In bulk specimens or large objects, the cracking pattern can be material specific. Ivory, for example, cracks in both a circumferential cone-within-a-cone pattern as well as developing longitudinal splits in the radial plane (*Figure 8.1*). In veneers both types of cracking will show up as small parallel cracks. Horn exhibits a fine parallel surface cracking or, depending on its orientation, may delaminate in fine layers much like the mineral mica, or like one's own fingernails. The most common moisture-related conservation problems involving ivory, horn and turtleshell veneers are due to differential movement of the wood, glue and covering material and must be seen as systems rather than isolated reactions.

Proteinaceous materials are attractive to a variety of animal pests including rats and mice and protein-loving insects such as cockroaches, silver fish, dermestid beetle larvae and clothes moths. In some cases, veneers of ivory and horn are perforated by adult powder post beetles or *Anobium* exiting from the wood substrate.

These materials do not normally support fungal activity unless they are very wet. However, the application of oils will often furnish a more attractive culture medium that will support mould at lower RH levels. While ivory has often been described as 'oily' this is usually due to its having been oiled. The natural lipid content of ivory is quite low, certainly less than 2% and normally, much less. A figure of 0.24–0.34% is given by Thorpe and Whiteley (1946). However, people have often oiled ivory (as they have done with wood) in an attempt to prevent drying cracks. Although no organic coating will prevent drying and cracking, oils are particularly undesirable because they remain soft and entrap atmospheric particles and because they are nourishing to fungi.

All of the animal-derived organics are fairly tough when fresh and hydrated, but will become progressively more brittle with age due to degradation of the constituent proteins and loss of water. Drying out is one form of degradation but there appear to be many others (Mills and White, 1987). Scission of polymer chains can occur, usually due to extreme low or high pH. Stability is also

affected by electromagnetic radiation, especially in the UV range. Ivory yellows in the dark but stays white in the light. All of these materials are relatively soft and susceptible to mechanical damage (e.g. scratching), especially when aged. Horn and turtleshell may also lose their translucency as a result of internal degradation leading to microscopic cracks.

Ivory objects should be wrapped in acid-free tissue paper for storage. Cotton wool, soft paper and similar materials should be avoided as they are more hygroscopic and could hold moisture that would cause warping of the ivory. The hydroxy apatite mineral component of ivory readily absorbs a variety of ions, particularly metal ions, on to its surface that may lead to discoloration and staining. Ivory must therefore not be left in contact with iron, copper, brass, or any coloured material. Rubber containing materials should also not be used as sulphur from the rubber can cause ivories to become stained a disagreeable yellow colour. Ivory should not be allowed to get damp and whenever possible, air circulation should be encouraged to inhibit the growth of mould on the surface of the ivory or the packing material, as this can cause pitting and staining of the surface. The results of studies by Matienzo and Snow (1986) indicate that solvents commonly used in conservation treatments may affect the surface composition and morphology of ivory.

## 8.2  Mollusc shell – mother-of-pearl and related materials

Shell materials are prone to deterioration by acid fumes. Volatile organic acids, such as acetic acid and formic acid, given off by wood (particularly oak) and other materials can react with calcium carbonate to form hydrated calcium acetate and formate salts. Acetic acid comes from hydrolysis of acetylated hemicelluloses in wood and formic acid can be formed by the decomposition of formaldehyde to formic acid and methanol (a thermodynamically easy reaction). White powdery water-soluble salt efflorescence appear on the surfaces which are etched as a result. This condition, called Byne's disease, has been observed on mollusc and egg shell collections

(Tennent and Baird, 1985). Coatings appear to prevent or retard this acid attack on shell and since most shell inlay and marquetry on furniture has been coated, the incidence of this condition on mother-of-pearl may be uncommon. Nevertheless it is only prudent that objects including shell material should be isolated from acid- and formaldehyde-producing materials and that good ventilation be provided where this cannot be done.

## 8.3 Paper and paper products

The chief enemy of paper is acid. Acids can be produced internally by the oxidation of sizing agents or, as is the case with wood pulp papers, from the breakdown of lignin and residual chemicals from processing. Papers made from pure cellulose sources such as rags can be remarkably durable but are still degraded by acidity from external sources such as the wood under furniture labels, from deteriorating adhesives and media and atmospheric pollution. Papier mâché may be rotted by the increasing acidity of the glues and oils used in manufacture. Heat serves to speed up all chemical reactions, including those of degradation and elevated temperatures are also favourable to micro-biological deterioration. The acid in wood substrates is likely to accelerate the degradation of paper products, particularly in the presence of a high enough relative humidity to make acidity a factor.

Paper, like all cellulosics, is a polar material that responds rapidly to changes in relative humidity by changing dimension. Where it is prevented from moving (by a partial adhesive layer on a label for example) it will wrinkle and cockle and eventually lose strength and break as the fluctuations continue to flex it.

Few biological pests can digest cellulose (with the exception of termites) but most papers are composite materials which may be sized with animal glues and starches and penetrated with adhesives and media that are attractive to insects and fungi. Mould generally requires high temperatures (above 21 °C) and high RH (above 70%) to colonize organic materials, but may persist, once established, at much lower temperature and humidity levels, particularly in still air. Most insect pests also require a certain level of absorbed water in their food source and will become inactive at low RH (below 55%).

The chemical processes of paper degradation cause the cellulose polymer chains to break into smaller fragments leading to embrittlement as time goes on. All paper associated with furniture should be regarded as highly degraded and fragile. Care of paper is further discussed by Baynes Cope (1989) and Clapp (1987).

## 8.4 Metals

The most important cause of deterioration in metals is corrosion – the unwanted chemical attack of a metal by its environment. The most immediately familiar example of this is the formation of rust (hydrated ferric oxide) on iron and other ferrous metals.

Most pure metals and mixtures of metals are thermodynamically unstable and are very prone to form compounds with other elements. This process, called corrosion, can be thought of as the reverse of what occurs when metals are smelted from their combined compounds or ores. In the simplest terms electrons are given up by metals in corroding, while during smelting, electrons are given to the metal by the combustion of a fuel source, thereby reducing the metallic compound to metal.

Stable corrosion layers form a protective barrier that slows or prevents further reaction in the underlying metal. Such layers are in a state of thermodynamic equilibrium and will not convert to another compound under normal circumstances. However this does not mean that more of the same product will not be formed if conditions are favourable. In many cases, however, the rate will slow due to the somewhat protective presence of a stable corrosion layer. The formation of stable aluminium oxide on freshly exposed aluminium, a highly reactive metal, is an example of a stable corrosion layer. The aluminium oxide layer virtually stops further oxidation under most conditions of use. Stable corrosion layers are usually uniform, well adhered and smooth.

Unstable corrosion layers either do not inhibit, or may actively cause, further corrosion of the underlying metal. Active corrosion products are those that are not at equilibrium and may convert to other products or release

**Table 8.1** Ferrous corrosion products

| Name | Formula | Colour |
|---|---|---|
| Goethite (alpha ferric oxyhydroxide) | $\alpha$-FeO(OH) | Yellow ochre |
| Akaganeite (beta ferric oxyhydroxide) | $\beta$-FeO(OH) | Dark red-brown (burnt sienna) |
| Lepidocrocite (gamma ferric oxyhydroxide) | $\gamma$-FeO(OH) | Bright orange-red |
| Haematite | $\alpha$-Fe$_2$O$_3$ | Red ochre |
| Magnetite (ferrosoferric oxide) | FeO.Fe$_2$O$_3$ | Shiny dark-grey |
| (also called fire scale, mill scale) | or 8[Fe$_3$O$_4$] | |
| Ferric chloride | FeCl$_3$ | Red-brown |
| Ferric oxy-chloride | FeOCl | Red-brown |
| Vivianite (basic iron phosphate) | Fe$_3$(PO$_4$)$_2$.8[H$_2$O] | Blue |
| Jarosite | KFe$_3$(OH)$_6$(SO$_4$)$_2$ | Lemon yellow |
| Natrojarosite | NaFe$_3$(OH)$_6$(SO$_4$)$_2$ | |

**Goethite** is common but non-destructive. The other oxyhydroxides will sometimes convert to this under natural conditions. **Akaganeite** occurs only on chloride-contaminated objects and is unstable and destructive. Its lattice structure randomly incorporates Cl ions. As it converts to goethite and lepidocrocite it releases Cl ions to catalyse further corrosion. Akaganeite often forms column-like structures that exert great pressure on overlying iron layers or coatings. **Lepidocrocite** is common and ubiquitous on terrestrial site artefacts, but uncommon on artefacts from a marine environment. **Haematite** is a very common ore, but is uncommon on artefacts, forming only under anaerobic conditions. The oxyhydroxides convert to haematite when strongly heated, and the presence of haematite on an object can usually be taken as a sign that it was heated after it had rusted. **Magnetite** is a mixture of ferric and ferrous oxidation state oxides. It is the product which gives rise to temper colours and mill scale when iron and steel are heated. It can also be formed by the reduction of other corrosion products. It is stable, and when present in compact and even layers is protective and even decorative (fire blue). Large pieces of naturally magnetic magnetite were known as lodestones. When chloride contaminated ferrous objects are subjected to high humidity, **ferric chloride** hydrates and forms tears of highly acidic ferric chloride (known as weeping iron). When the tears dry out they resemble hollow spheroidal 'insect eggs' under the microscope. **Ferric oxy-chloride** has been reported as a major component of corrosion layers on iron objects from a marine environment. **Vivianite** forms on iron artefacts that have corroded in anaerobic conditions in contact with phosphorus containing materials such as bone and leather. It can easily be mistaken for traces of blue paint. **Jarosite** and **natrojarosite** are stable brightly coloured products that do not present a danger to artefacts.

corrosive species. Active corrosion layers are often visible as powder or flakes on the surface of the object. Examples of active corrosion may be found on ferrous metals in the presence of salts and lead in the presence of organic acids. Guidelines for identifying active corrosion have been published by the CCI (1989). Active corrosion will lead to further loss of material and damage to the object and should be removed where possible. The treatment of corrosion is in part dependent on the relative molar volume of the corrosion products in comparison to the original metal. In the case of ferrous metals and lead, the corrosion products are larger in volume. Once corrosion has occurred there will be disruption of the surface and a loss of metal where the surface has corroded. In some cases, metal ions migrate beyond the original surface to form an overlying corrosion crust, which can in some instances be safely removed to expose original detail. Some copper corrosion products are smaller in volume than the metal and can retain decorative detail in the corro-

sion layer. In such cases, aesthetic considerations aside, it is usually acceptable to stabilize and coat the corroded surface.

The majority of metals are reactive and tend to combine with other elements such as oxygen, sulphur and chlorine to form metal corrosion compounds (Brown, 1991). Common corrosion products for iron, copper, silver and lead are listed in *Tables 8.1–8.4*. Metallurgists use the term oxidation to describe corrosion reactions even where other elements are involved because oxygen from air or water is so often involved in corrosion of metals. It is interesting to note that since virtually all of the oxygen in our atmosphere is the result of photosynthesis, trees have been at war with metals since they first evolved! In oxidation, surface metal ions combine with oxygen or another reactive species to form corrosion products. Moisture is usually present in the form of an adsorbed layer from water vapour in the ambient atmosphere, forming an electrolyte in which charges can be easily transferred.

**Table 8.2** Copper corrosion products

| Name | Formula | Colour |
|------|---------|--------|
| Nantokite (cuprous chloride) | CuCl or $Cu_2Cl_2$ or 4[CuCl] | Greyish-white |
| Atacamite | $4[Cu_2Cl(OH)_3]$ or $4[Cu_2Cl_2.2H_2O]$ | White |
| Paratacamite | $8[Cu_2(OH_3)Cl]$ or $Cu_2Cl(OH)_3$ | Light lime-green |
| Cuprite (cuprous or copper (I) oxide) | $Cu_2O$ or $2[Cu_2O]$ | Pink, red or purplish-brown |
| Melaconite (cupric or copper (II) oxide) | 4[CuO] (tetrahedral cubic crystals) | Black |
| Tenorite (cupric or copper (II) oxide) | CuO (triclinic crystals) | Black |
| Malachite (basic cupric carbonate) | $CuCO_3.Cu(OH)_2$ or $Cu_2CO_3(OH)_2$ | Malachite-green |
| Azurite (basic cupric carbonate) | $2CuCO_3.Cu(OH)_2$ or $Cu(CO_3)_2(OH)_2$ | Azure-blue |
| Covellite (covelline) (cupric sulphide) | CuS or 6[CuS] | Indigo to dark blue-black |
| Chalcocite (cuprous sulphide) | $96[Cu_2S]$ | Blue-green, black, grey (violet single crystals) |
| Chalcopyrite (copper-iron sulphide) | $4[CuFeS_2]$ | Metallic gold |
| Bornite | $Cu_3FeS_3$ | Bronze-brown to purple-brown |
| Chalconatronite | $Na_2Cu(CO_3)_2.3H_2O$ | Light blue |
| Antlerite (copper sulphate dibasic) | $Cu_3H_4O_8S$ or $CuSO_4.2Cu(OH)_2$ | Light green |
| Brochantite (copper sulphate tribasic) | $Cu_4H_6O_{10}S$ or $CuSO_4.Cu(OH)_2$ | Emerald to blackish-green |
| Chalcanthite (cupric sulphate pentahydrate) | $CuSO_4.5H_2O$ (triclinic crystals) | Bright blue to ultramarine |

Cuprous (copper (I)) products will be found closer to the metal surface, and cupric (copper (II)) will be found closer to the environment. The first seven corrosion products listed (with the exception of paratacamite) occur in layers more or less in this order from the metal surface outwards. Alternate formulas are given in cases where there is disagreement in the literature. The listed colours are an approximation because colours of corrosion products can vary greatly due to particle size and impurity compounds. **Nantokite** forms close to the metal surface in chloride contaminated objects, and has a waxy texture when probed. It is the most damaging of the copper corrosion products. **Atacamite** is a white granular (orthorhombic crystalline) product that occurs on very dry objects, or where the chloride layers have been protected by other overlying corrosion products. **Paratacamite** forms when atacamite hydrates due to high RH or cracks in the overlying stable corrosion products. Intergranular corrosion can cause destructive damage due to paratacamite's voluminous rhombohedral structure. It is common to find a mixture of atacamite and paratacamite on objects suffering from bronze disease. **Cuprite** is one of the most common corrosion products on copper. The colour can vary considerably due to crystalline size. Cuprite is completely stable but may be considered unsightly, particularly on ormolu. **Melaconite** and **tenorite** are impossible to distinguish by eye. They usually occur together, though tenorite is more common. Copper may also react with carbon dioxide in the presence of water to form copper (II) carbonates such as **malachite** and **azurite**. Azurite and **malachite** are often mixed, but azurite may occur somewhat closer to the environment (outermost layer) than malachite. **Covellite** and **chalcocite** are found on buried bronzes where sulphur has been available. Covellite has also been identified as a component of the patina on copper roofs and outdoor bronzes. **Chalcopyrite** has been found on bronze artefacts recovered from wet sites and can look very much like gilding. **Chalconatronite** has been identified on objects from arid areas of Egypt, but may also result from some conservation treatments such as soaking in sodium sesquicarbonate. In the presence of water copper may react with sulphur dioxide ($SO_2$), nitrogen oxides (e.g. $N_2O$, $NO_2$) and other air pollutants to form green-coloured basic copper (II) salts such as **antlerite** and **brochantite**, which are common on outdoor copper and bronze surfaces in polluted urban environments. **Chalcanthite** has been identified as a component of the patina on outdoor bronzes, but it is highly soluble in water. Bronze disease refers to the formation of corrosion spots on bronzes, often whilst in storage. It is caused by chloride contamination. Black spot disease, also found on bronzes, is caused by the formation of copper (II) sulphide as a result of exposure to atmospheric pollutants.

**Table 8.3** Silver corrosion products

| Name | Formula | Colour |
|------|---------|--------|
| Acanthite (silver sulphide) | $4[Ag_2S]$ | Black, lustrous |
| Argentite (silver sulphide) | $2[Ag_2S]$ | Black, lustrous |
| Stromeyerite (copper/silver sulphide) | AgCuS | Black |
| Cerargyrite (silver chloride fluoride, bromide (halides)) | AgCl, AgFl, AgBr (or all) | Grey-lavender |

*Hey's Chemical Index of Minerals* (Hey, 1975) states that most if not all natural **silver sulphide** consists of **acanthite** pseudomorphic after the first-formed **argentite**, and most writers on the subject give **acanthite** as being the usual silver sulphide. Pure samples of **cerargyrite** are white and translucent, but on objects it is always coloured by copper (particularly cuprite, which is reddish-purple) and other trace metals, and by included dirt.

**Table 8.4**  Lead corrosion products

| Name | Formula | Colour |
|---|---|---|
| Lead formate | $Pb(CHO_2)_2$ | 'White fuzzies' |
| Cerussite (lead carbonate) | $PbCO_3$ | |
| Hydrocerussite (basic lead carbonate) | $Pb_3(OH)_2(CO_3)_2$ | Lead white |
| Anglesite (lead sulphate) | $PbSO_4$ | |
| Cotunnite (lead chloride) | $PbCl_2$ | |
| Phosgenite (lead carbonate chloride) | $Pb_2CO_3Cl_2$ | |
| Leadhillite (lead sulphate carbonate hydroxide) | $PbSO_4(CO_3)_2(OH)_2$ | |
| Penfieldite (basic lead chloride) | $Pb_2(OH)Cl_3$ | |
| Lead monoxide (litharge, massicot) | $PbO$ | |
| Plattnerite (lead dioxide) | $PbO_2$ | |
| Galena (lead sulphide) | $PbS$ | |

Corrosion in many metals takes place on both sides of the original surface, with ions moving out into the environment in more or less straight lines. This means that a lump of corrosion on the surface is likely to be matched by an area of depleted spongy metal mixed with corrosion below the surface that is similar in shape and extent (mirror imaging).

Corrosion is an electrolytic form of decomposition which results when different electric potentials are established either between metals or between different points on a metal surface. For this to occur one part of an object must behave as an anode and another part as a cathode and these must be connected together so that electrons flow into the cathode out of the anode. In addition an electrolyte, forming a continuous link between the substances which react at each electrode, is required (*Figure 8.2a*). There are several ways in which corrosion cells may be set up in practice (*Figure 8.2b*). The presence of particles of an impurity or contact with another metal allows a difference of voltage to be set up. In the presence of moisture containing air, or some dissolved chemical substance that will conduct electricity, an electric current will flow and corrosive attack will begin.

Electrochemical corrosion occurs wherever different electric potentials are established either between metals or between different points on a metal surface. Such different electric potentials are normally due to local areas of differing composition known as

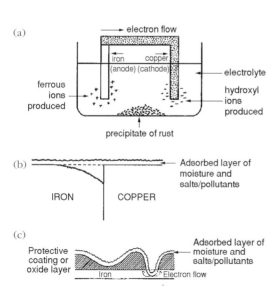

(a)
electron flow
iron   copper
(anode)   (cathode)
ferrous ions produced
electrolyte
hydroxyl ions produced
precipitate of rust

(b)
Adsorbed layer of moisture and salts/pollutants
IRON   COPPER

(c)
Protective coating or oxide layer
Adsorbed layer of moisture and salts/pollutants
Iron   Electron flow

**Figure 8.2**  Corrosion cells
(*a*) A simple corrosion cell consisting of iron in contact with copper in the presence of an electrolyte (e.g. acid). Positively charged ferrous ions form around the iron electrode, whilst negatively charged hydroxyl ions are produced around the copper electrode. (This is the principle behind the construction of batteries)
(*b*) Galvanic corrosion occurs where two dissimilar metals are in contact in the presence of an electrolyte. In this example, the iron adjacent to the copper will be most severely corroded
(*c*) Pitting corrosion describes very localized corrosion at points where there are cracks in a protective coating or oxide film or where the protective layer is thin. The area where the protective later has been disrupted acts as an anode, whilst the adjacent (still protected) metal acts as a cathode causing corrosion pits to develop

**Table 8.5** Galvanic series in seawater

DIRECTION OF ELECTRON FLOW

| Most anodic, active or base |
| --- |
| Magnesium/magnesium alloys |
| Zinc |
| Aluminium |
| Mild steel |
| Wrought iron |
| Cast iron |
| Chromium stainless steel (most stainless steel fittings) |
| Lead–tin solder (50:50) |
| Lead |
| Tin |
| Brasses |
| Nickel (active) |
| Copper |
| Bronze |
| Silver solder |
| Nickel (passive) |
| Silver |
| Gold |
| Platinum |
| **Most cathodic, passive, or noble** |

*Source:* LaQue, 1948

phases in metals of mixed composition (alloys). This may be a result of the presence of salts or the interaction of alloyed metals. Salts function as electrolyte formers, or by creating local areas of aggressive corrosion. Two arrangements of metals are used to predict the potential for corrosion between metals – the electromotive force (EMF) series and the galvanic series. The EMF series ranks metals according to their standard oxidation or reduction potentials but is of limited use for predicting interactions between metals because this varies with environment (Uhlig and Revie, 1985). A galvanic series ranks the measured oxidation or reduction potential of metals (their corrosion tendencies) in a specific environment (*Table 8.5*).

The galvanic series for seawater is often used as a general approximation of how metals will inter-react. Metals may occupy two positions in the galvanic series – in the passive state a layer has formed on the metal and it is therefore less prone to corrosion. Galvanic corrosion is a type of electrochemical corrosion that occurs when two dissimilar metals form a galvanic couple in the presence of an electrolyte such as water or moisture from high RH. Electrons flow from the anodic metal to the cathodic metal, causing corrosion of the

anodic metal. The intensity of the electron exchange and hence corrosion, is determined by the metals' ranking in the galvanic series, although factors, such as pH and the nature of the electrolyte, can complicate this picture. The metal that is ranked lower on the galvanic scale will corrode before the metal which is higher on the scale. The further apart on this scale the alloyed metals are, the greater the corrosion potential will be. The electron exchange protects the more cathodic metal (traditionally called more noble) whilst causing the more anodic metal (traditionally called more base) to corrode faster.

Galvanic corrosion has important implications for the conservation of historical metal alloys such as pewter and brass. Chemical removal of corrosion products of metal, for example, may cause the preferential attack of one component of an alloy. The presence of impurities in a metal that was not intentionally alloyed can cause galvanic corrosion, particularly if the impurity metal is lower on the electromotive (EMF) scale. Heath and Martin (1988) found the corrosion of lead inlay on urushi objects exposed to acetic acid vapour in storage was inhibited by the presence of tin and copper in lead inlay but accelerated by the presence of ferrous impurities.

### Role of moisture

It is easy to see that when a metal surface is exposed to rain or mist it will become wet and therefore it is possible for a corrosion cell to be set up on its surface. The atmosphere under these conditions is at 100% RH, that is the air is saturated with water vapour. Metal surfaces can suffer corrosion even when exposed to RH of less then 100%. Even though a metal surface may not be visibly wet, a thin film of moisture can still be present that can support a corrosion cell. At very low RH this film becomes very thin and corrosion effects diminish and become negligible. Whilst there are various contaminants that occur in polluted air which greatly accelerate corrosion and while water on its own does not usually give rise to very serious damage, it is essential for corrosion that enough moisture should be present. The tarnishing of silver is accelerated by high relative humidity, whilst that of lead, tin and pewter is not much affected.

### Chlorides

Next to oxygen, chloride ions, usually from sodium chloride (common salt), are probably the most important agent of deterioration. Chloride ions in particular are aggressive agents of corrosion on virtually all metals. In combination with water, salt forms an effective electrolyte in which corrosion reactions can readily occur. Many chloride-containing corrosion products are dimensionally and chemically unstable and will continue to cause deterioration especially at high RH levels. Although chlorides are particularly associated with archaeological material, chloride corrosion products may be found on furniture hardware as a result of handling. In addition, aerosol droplets of salt water are present near sea coasts. In some instances, chloride ions and associated degradation have been associated with the metal fabrication process itself rather than contamination from the environment (Flotte and Dommermuth, 1995).

The upper permissible limit of RH for bronzes containing chlorides is 40–45%, which is near the lower limit normally recommended for moisture absorbent materials. Good quality iron in clean condition and suitably protected and bronzes with stable patinas may be permanently safe at 55% RH. However, iron containing chlorides may be unstable even at very low levels of RH (> 5%).

### Light

Light may play a small role in metal corrosion by exciting the atoms and making them more reactive. Indeed, the photosensitivity of silver and its compounds is the basis for most photographic processes. Light may also damage coatings applied to metals to prevent corrosion or for decoration. Partial failure of coatings on the metals can lead to preferential oxidation and the development of local corrosion cells.

### Heat

Heat plays the same role that it does in all chemical reactions by speeding up the reaction rate. Cans discarded by Arctic explorers remain virtually unchanged over ensuing decades since they are protected by slow reaction rates due to low temperatures and the unavailability of liquid water as an electrolyte. Woods and metals have different coefficients of expansion and contraction which can cause lifting of metals attached to wood, as occurs with boulle marquetry. Adhering non-porous metal to a porous wood can be problematic and can lead to premature failure.

### Pollutants

Airborne pollutants can damage many metals. Notable examples are the black sulphides formed on silver by sulphur containing pollutants such as hydrogen sulphide and sulphur dioxide. Silver tarnishes quickly on contact with air but if protected with a lacquer may retain its lustre for many years. Because of its greater thickness, silver leaf is very resilient and is less prone to abrasions than gold leaf and, underneath the discoloured protective lacquer, will look much the same as it did when it was first laid. Below 22 ct, gold leaf will also tarnish with time, the greatest danger coming from atmospheric sulphur. Dilute sulphuric acid reacts with all metals except antimony, bismuth, copper, lead and the noble metals to form hydrogen and the sulphate of the metal. The corrosion of iron may be greatly accelerated by the presence of sulphur dioxide. Both sulphuric acid and ammonium sulphate are good electrolytes, both attract moisture and both remain on the surface thus encouraging the development of corrosion. The corrosion of copper alloys may also be encouraged by airborne pollutants, particularly where these have a high lead content. However, this will not usually occur inside buildings unless the RH rises much above 60%. Formaldehyde given off by wood products and textiles as well as organic acids given off by many timbers are particularly deleterious to lead and its alloys, forming expansive and powdery lead formate, acetate and carbonate. Because lead does not go into solution with most metals but instead segregates out into pockets of lead within an alloy, this form of attack may even form on cast copper alloys which contain lead (as many historic examples do).

Corrosion of metals may be caused by the evolution of organic acids, particularly acetic acid, from wooden components of the furniture or due to the common traditional practice of cleaning copper alloy mounts with a mixture of vinegar and water. The corrosive effect is exacerbated by micro-climates that occur either as a result of the design of the furniture itself (e.g. drawer interiors) or storage (Thickett *et al.*, 1998). Evidence of general wood and metal reactions can be found at the interface of unprotected metal parts and raw wood. Tannin in oak (*Quercus* spp.) can readily corrode metals, particularly iron and other specific wood-metal interactions have been described (Pinion, 1973). The relative acidities of some woods and the risk of damage from the evolution of organic acids can be found in *Table 10.1*. Carbon and low alloy steels, lead, zinc and magnesium and their alloys are highly susceptible to corrosion as a result of exposure to acetic acid in a microclimate. Copper and brass are only moderately susceptible to such corrosion, whilst the corrosion of gold, silver and tin in such conditions has been described as insignificant (*Corrosion of Metals by Woods*, HMSO, 1985). Studies of the corrosion of metals caused by organic acids present in various woods are discussed by Umney (1992) and Werner (1987).

Tanning materials used in leather and the subsequent polishes can cause degradation products on metals. Depending on the prevailing conditions, a variety of corrosion products may form on copper alloys including cuprous and cupric oxides, cupric sulphide, cupric sulphate and cupric nitrate. Corrosion products that form on brass upholstery nails from atmospheric pollution or contact with wood textiles or leather may in turn stain other materials with which they are in contact. Corrosion of metals can also be caused, influenced, or accelerated by bacteria (Korbin, 1993). For further information on corrosion see Trethewey and Chamberlain (1988), Stambolov (1985) and Jones (1996).

### Mechanical damage

Mechanical damage will cause most metals to bend or dent due to their plasticity. Many cast alloys, however, are inherently brittle and even metals that are flexible when new will often become brittle with age, a phenomenon known as precipitation hardening. Anyone who has broken a wire by repeatedly flexing it knows that metals will become harder and eventually fail if bent repeatedly (cold working leading to metal fatigue). Metals that have been highly stressed by cold working during

forming, such as stamped brass furniture, hardware or lathe spun sheet metal elements, may spontaneously crack with age or as a result of chemical cleaning (stress cracking). The effect of continual movement caused by expansion and contraction due to changes in temperature, or vibration caused by playing on musical instruments, will eventually lead to stress cracking.

## 8.5   Ceramics and glass

Because of the inherent fragility of glass and ceramics, mechanical damage is the most common cause of deterioration, or at least the most commonly noticed. Ceramics also have low resistance to thermal shock. The softness of some glazes and decorative applications makes them liable to scratching and wear. Defects of manufacture may cause cracking of the body or a tendency for glazes or enamels to flake off. Ceramic bodies can be roughly divided into two groups: low-fired bodies such as earthen wares and high-fired bodies including stoneware and hard paste porcelain. Unlike high-fired bodies which become highly vitrified during firing, low-fired bodies are porous and are vulnerable to staining and to the absorption of soluble substances. Both ceramics and stone may contain various salts, for example nitrates and chlorides, which they have picked up from contact with other salt-containing material or from the air. Stone and tiles which have been in contact with Portland cement are examples. When the RH falls, the salts may crystallize and this can lead to powdering and cracking of the surface and even complete disintegration of the outer layers. Ceramics may have their glazes pushed off and sculptures which have been made or previously repaired with an iron dowel may split because of internal pressure from corrosion products. The extent to which ceramics are affected by these problems depends on their composition, design and firing conditions. The higher porosity of low-fired materials causes them to be weaker and they are therefore potted more thickly. They are softer, coarser and more crumbly than higher fired bodies.

Glass is hard and brittle, causing it to be susceptible to mechanical impact and stress.

Sudden changes in temperature, especially sudden rapid cooling, may cause glass to crack. It can be resistant to many chemicals but water is an enemy of most common glass and vitreous glazes. Glass, which is a network of negatively charged polysilicate ions containing positively charged $Al^{+++}$, $Ca^{++}$, $Mg^{++}$, $Na^+$ and $K^+$ ions, is 'corroded' by the penetration of water which replaces oxygen in the silicondioxide matrix with hydroxyl (OH) groups thereby hydrating the glass. This hydration layer is always present on glass causing a range of effects depending on the stability of the glass composition. The more noticeable manifestations of this layer on less stable types of glass range from surface opalescence through crazing to deep pitting and opacity. If the proportion of $Ca^{++}$, $Mg^{++}$ and $Al^{+++}$ ions is low, a potential exists for the migration of $Na^+$ and $K^+$ ions. $Na^+$ and $K^+$ ions are replaced by $H^+$ ions from water leading to the formation of highly alkaline, hygroscopic and damaging sodium and potassium hydroxides on the surface which then react with carbon dioxide in the air to form sodium and potassium carbonates. The resulting film absorbs moisture from the air producing droplets of moisture in a process called weeping or sweating. Calcium migrates to the surface forming opaque calcium sulphate (gypsum) crusts. If left untreated, this can continue to the point where the glass becomes opaque and badly crizzled, with tiny scales of glass flaking off when the glass is touched. To avoid the risk of this type of *glass disease* a constant RH of about 40% is recommended, but care should be exercised since it is possible that a very low humidity may also be damaging to certain types of glass. The more severe forms of glass disease are found on vessel glass and are unlikely to be encountered in furniture. The softness of some glass and glazes makes them surprisingly liable to scratching and wear.

For further information on the deterioration of ceramics and glass see Buys and Oakley (1994) and Newton and Davison (1989).

gaseous sulphur pollution to produce calcium sulphate, carbon dioxide and water. The calcium sulphate is left behind in a loose and finely divided state where it is easily eroded away, exposing a fresh surface to attack. This process also tends to create a finely pitted surface, thus not only vastly increasing the surface area for fresh attack but also providing pockets for the collection of acid which then begins to tunnel into the stone. Carbon dioxide ($CO_2$) which is present in the air in concentrations of around 600 000 $\mu g/m^3$ (much higher than $SO_2$) is also capable of attacking calcium carbonate in all its forms. Calcium carbonate is almost insoluble in water (solubility 0.018 g/l). Carbon dioxide dissolves in water approximately 1:1 by volume at 15 °C (cf 40 parts of $SO_2$ will dissolve in 1 part of water) to form carbonic acid ($H_2CO_3$) which ionizes to a small extent and is a weak acid. This can react with calcium carbonate to form the bicarbonate which is soluble in water and in this way as much as 2.29 g of calcium carbonate can be dissolved in a litre of water. Although sulphuric acid is a more strongly ionized and much more powerful acid than carbonic acid, there is a correspondingly larger amount of $CO_2$ in the air. However, $CO_2$ mainly presents a problem in outside environments. Calcareous stone is also attacked by nitric acid. These types of reactions present serious problems for stone in the open but normally proceed only very slowly inside buildings.

Besides pollution, a major risk to stone (and to those handling it) comes from inappropriate handling. Natural planes of weakness and fault lines in stone can easily be stressed beyond breaking point if large heavy but relatively thin flat slabs are picked up by their ends in a horizontal position. Table tops should *always* be supported by carefully easing them off on to a wooden support that should extend over the full area of the stone slab. They should then be carried on edge, vertical rather than flat. For further information see Amoroso and Fassina (1983).

## 8.6   Stone and related materials

Any kind of stone which contains calcium carbonate, for example marble and limestone, will react with sulphuric acid formed from

## 8.7   Colorants – pigments, dyes and stains

Many pigments are extremely stable and remain unchanged for centuries. However, the colour of a decorative paint surface may no longer be as the artist intended due to the chemical change of the pigments, lakes or dyes that were used. This change can be driven by the effects of light and oxygen or through chemical reactions with other materials in the paint layer. In general, dyes are far less stable than pigments. Dyes are particularly prone to fading by light and may be subtly altered or in extreme cases, completely decolourized by long exposure. Furniture restorers have been startled by the brilliant colours present on the underside of marquetry veneers. The use of dyes and coloured varnishes in wood polychromy has been reviewed by Thornton (1998). Deterioration of dyes is discussed in section 8.12.1 in the context of textiles. In principle there is little difference between the behaviour of dyes on cotton or wool substrates and their behaviour on wood or ivory.

Pigments are simply coloured chemical compounds and, not surprisingly, they can participate in a wide variety of alteration reactions. Some of these reactions occur more or less immediately with the admixture of incompatible pigments or media whilst others may only become apparent after many years. It might be expected that reactions occurring within a short time scale would be familiar to many artisans and that there would be a tendency to avoid the worst types of incompatibility. Equally, it might be expected that the reactions that occur over longer periods of time would be less likely to enter the traditional canon of knowledge. Many of these reactions are very complex, difficult to predict and poorly understood, even now. In this discussion it is possible to list only the most notorious pigments prone to alteration reactions and the agents responsible. Some examples of the types of reactions in which pigments may participate were also given in Chapter 5 to illustrate their chemical and physical properties. Further information may be obtained from Gettens and Stout (1966), Harley (1982), Mayer (1982) and McLaren (1983).

Lead pigments including lead carbonate ($PbCO_3$ white lead) and the oxides of lead (yellow: litharge and massicot and red: red lead and minium) can all be darkened by sulphur to form lead sulphide. The black lead dioxide ($PbO_2$) has also been encountered as an alteration product. The darkening effects are particularly apparent where these pigments have been used as water colours or pastels. In oil films they are not only better protected from atmospheric pollutants but form stable lead soaps with the fatty acids present in the oil. Red lead may also convert under acidic conditions to white lead carbonate. Chrome green, a form of lead chromate, can be photochemically altered to a brown or greenish-brown colour. Older types of this pigment based on the rhombic form were more prone to darkening by hydrogen sulphide or by conversion to a red colour under alkaline conditions than the currently produced monoclinic crystalline form. Ultramarine can darken under acidic conditions (ultramarine disease). Ultramarine contains sulphur and for this reason should not be used with lead pigments. Smalt is the name given to blue cobalt glass when it is powdered and used as a pigment. Because it is often a highly fluxed glass it is prone to corrosion by water, causing an optical greying of the pigment. Because it had a brighter colour if coarsely ground it did not form a very smooth paint when mixed with a medium. Decorative painters could overcome this problem, as well as exploit its sparkling glassy qualities, by strewing it onto the surface of a tacky medium, but this left it unprotected from attack by moisture. Prussian blue, a synthetic blue pigment available after 1704, is decolourized under alkaline conditions but is stable to light and acidity. Verdigris, a form of copper acetate, is one of the most reactive and unstable of pigments turning brown or black when mixed with sulphur containing pigments or when exposed to the air. Beautiful green glazes composed of metallic soaps (copper oleate and resinate) could be made by heating oils and resins with verdigris. However, the original colour of such glazes can only be imagined due to their browning over time. Vermilion, a red mercuric sulphide pigment, can be ground from the natural mineral called cinnabar or prepared synthetically. It undergoes a photochemical alteration to black, particularly when used in water colour or tempera mediums. The bright blue and green copper carbonates, azurite and malachite, are, like all carbonates, sensitive to acids which cause them to become lighter in colour. The synthetic azurite called blue verditer or blue bice has been regarded as an unstable pigment due to its conversion to green, or its darkening in the presence of hydrogen sulphide.

Lakes, which are pigments made from dyes by precipitation, are particularly prone to light fading. Commonly encountered lakes are the bright reds produced from various scale insects: including carmine from cochineal (new world) and kermes (old world) and lac lake from raw shellac resin. Alizarin red was derived from madder root and indigo blue from plants of the genus Indigotifera. Of the naturally derived lakes, madder and indigo are the most permanent, but modern synthetic organic pigments are now available that far surpass these in stability.

It should be emphasized that the behaviour of pigments may differ significantly in different media. Some illustrations of this have been given above with respect to oil and water colour media. Further differences can be expected with other media such as shellac, animal glue, casein, urushi and japanning.

## 8.8   Plastics and polymers

The use of polymers in furniture, including upholstery materials and composites and indeed as materials for conservation, continues to grow. Recent collection condition audits have shown that the problems of modern materials are becoming increasingly serious and demanding of urgent attention (Then and Oakley, 1993; Griffith, 1997). From the point of view of degradation, polymers will behave similarly whether they are used as bulk materials (plastics) or function as adhesives, paint media or coatings. Obviously, however, the life expectancy of a polymer material is influenced by the nature of the application for which it is used and the type of object in which it is incorporated and is therefore not precisely defined. The form of degradation also depends on the material, its history, including manufacturing process and the environment to which it has been exposed. There is considerable variation between polymers. Polymers encompass such a chemically diverse range of materials that it can be said that as a category they may be degraded by every known agent of deterioration. Most

polymers are far from inert and are prone to a host of ills.

Physical causes may be responsible for distortion or dimensional change, crazing or cracking, surface deposits, which are often tacky and changes in flexibility. Migration of plasticizers in materials such as polyurethanes (PU) and poly(vinyl chloride) (PVC) results in these materials becoming rigid which in turn may lead to distortion and cracking. Chemical effects are more serious than physical effects and are nearly always progressive and irreversible. Degradation resulting from reaction with oxygen is the most important reaction leading to polymer failure. Evidence for chemical effects includes: colour change, chalkiness or surface bloom, crazing, embrittlement with loss of strength and evolution of degradation products (often acidic). Major factors involved in bringing about chemical change include light and UV radiation, heat, stress, oxygen and ozone, contact with other substances such as moisture and pollutants and some forms of biological attack. Chemical changes in polymers may also be produced by ionizing radiations.

Almost all polymers age at a significant rate unless steps are taken to stabilize them. Degradation is a major factor limiting the application of these otherwise remarkable and versatile materials. Even the mildest of human environments may be extremely aggressive to synthetic materials and in some cases the rate of deterioration of commercial formulations may set surprisingly short limits to the expected lifetime. Unacceptable aesthetic changes frequently occur long before the component becomes functionally unserviceable due to loss of mechanical strength. Weathering is the result of exposure of polymers to conditions under which thermal oxidation and photo oxidation may occur together with the effects of water, abrasion and atmospheric pollution. The extent of weathering varies with surface to volume ratio and is sensitive to small variations in conditions that may quite easily become established even over small distances on the surface of an object due to the aspect of the object in relation to light exposure, dirt accumulation or mechanical stress etc. The chemistry of polymers is highly complex and these materials contain more than a few surprises in comparison to some of the more traditional furniture materials. Polyethylene (PE) for example is unaffected by prolonged contact with strong acids (including hydrofluoric acid), highly caustic alkalis and most organic solvents and yet weathers rapidly when exposed to outdoor atmospheres, burns readily and may be damaged by common detergents.

There are four main types of structural changes of polymers. These are chain scission, crosslinking, the development of chromophoric groups and the development of polar groups. Chain scission or breaking of chains can lead to catastrophic reduction in the average molecular weight of a polymer, resulting in loss of strength and toughness. Crosslinking in a linear polymer, or an increase in the degree of crosslinking in a network polymer, may lead to hardening and brittleness. In linear polymers, marked solubility changes often occur. In polymers used as conservation materials this leads to a reduction in ease of reversibility. The development of chromophoric groups leads to colour formation and change in appearance referred to as yellowing. In conservation, previously invisible repairs may become visible for example, or the appearance of paint under a varnish may change. The development of polar groups may lead to a change in chemical reactivity, altering the solubility characteristics of the material and making it more susceptible to attack by atmospheric gases and pollution. Yellowing is a visual phenomenon that is a result of the changing chemistry of an ageing resin. Some coatings are more photochemically reactive, meaning that light energy will alter the structure of the polymer more readily. Natural resins are more prone to bond breaking or the formation of double bonds which can result in the formation of light absorbing chromophores. The viewer sees this as yellowing. Ideally, wood coatings that are less photochemically reactive should be used in treatment.

### Environmental stress cracking and crazing

Some polymers when stressed are adversely affected by contact with certain chemicals. For example aqueous solutions of surface active agents such as detergents can slowly produce large brittle cracking in polyethylene. This phenomenon, called environmental stress cracking, is also seen in PVC. The phenomenon of crazing, distinguished by a network of fine voids, is observed in amorphous polymers such as polystyrene (PS) in response to the action of organic liquids and gases. Crazed material may retain considerable strength but crazing may be visually disruptive and small cracks at the surface may propagate through the material and cause fracture or complete failure of the polymer material. In both stress cracking and crazing it appears that the substance is adsorbed or locally dissolved in the region of defects in the polymer structure and that it assists failure, perhaps by modifying surface energy or by plasticizing highly stressed materials at crack tips thereby promoting crack propagation. Susceptibility to these phenomena depends on various structural factors such as density, chain length and crystallinity.

### Oxidation

Polymers, in common with all other organic compounds, are vulnerable to oxidation involving free radical chain reactions. Unstabilized polymers undergo slow ageing in contact with air and even substances such as PE, which are expected to be inert at moderate temperatures in the absence of light, react quite rapidly with oxygen unless stabilized. Oxidation reactions are frequently strongly promoted by UV and heat is an agent of polymer deterioration both in the presence and in the absence of oxygen. The higher the temperature the more rapidly degradation of primary chains occurs. The rate of oxidation is closely related to the degree of chain branching. Saturation (absence of double bonds) improves resistance to oxidation. Because of differences in oxygen permeability, crystalline polymers are much more resistant to oxidation than amorphous structures. Ozone is also responsible for oxidation reactions (see below).

In addition to the action of oxygen, such changes as those described above are brought about by various agents acting alone or in combination. These include heat, light and chemicals present in the environment. Among the latter are ozone, sulphur oxides, nitrogen oxides, organic acid vapours and water. Like a chain, the chemical resistance of a plastic is

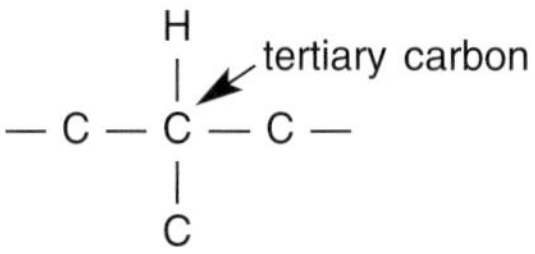

H
|  ← tertiary carbon
— C — C — C —
|
C

**Figure 8.3** A tertiary carbon atom is a carbon atom attached to three other carbon atoms with single bonds. Tertiary carbons are slightly electronegative in comparison to the rest of the carbon chain and react more easily with electro-positive molecules (e.g. oxygen) (Torraca, 1990)

only as good as its weakest link. Although the chemical reactivity of polymers is not directly reflected by that of small molecules, the nature of the chemical groups present will still influence it considerably. Polymers containing only C—C and C—H bonds (e.g. polyethylene and polypropylene) are somewhat inert. However, branched chains containing tertiary carbon atoms (*Figure 8.3*) are reactive sites for oxidation and, in the presence of peroxides, may crosslink. A limited degree of chain branching is commonly found in linear thermoplastic materials as an accident of manufacture. Polymers containing double bonds will react with many agents including oxygen and ozone, leading to scission of the main chain at the site of the double bond. Ester, amide and carbonate groups are susceptible to hydrolysis. When these groups are present in the main chain hydrolysis will result in a reduction in molecular weight.

### The effect of light on polymers

In the absence of light, most polymers are stable for very long periods at ambient temperatures. Most polymers are profoundly affected by exposure to light, particularly sunlight. Generally, they either degrade (e.g. poly(methyl methacrylate) and cellulose) or crosslink (e.g. poly(methyl acrylate)), though some may do both. Damage results from absorption of radiant light energy by chemical structures. Light will fade dyes and colorants and cause many polymers to become yellow, although some will yellow more in the dark. Light, particularly the high energy blue-visible and ultra violet ends of the spectrum, will initiate other chemical processes of degradation and accelerate the rate of oxidation of polymers. Chemically active free radicals liber-

ated by the high energy photons of blue light and UV radiation may act internally to promote further oxidative breakdown in a process known as autoxidation. PVC is prone to breakdown when exposed to light for very long periods resulting in production of free hydrochloric acid. Photo-oxidation leads generally to discoloration, surface cracking and deterioration of mechanical and electrical properties.

The mechanisms of oxidative photo degradation are potentially very diverse. In the absence of other active substances such as oxygen, the photochemical and heat stability of a polymer is related to the bond energy of the chemical linkages present. It is possible, in theory, to calculate the potential stability of a polymer from values of bond dissociation energies. Most damage is done by ultra violet radiation in the range of wavelength of 300–400 nm. At 350 nm the light energy is equivalent to a bond dissociation energy of 82 kcal/mole and this is greater than that of many bonds. Whether or not damage is done to a polymer also depends on the absorption frequency of the bonds present. The C=O bond, which occurs in shellac and other natural resins, polyesters, polyurethanes and polyamides, strongly absorbs short wavelength radiation and is important in initiating photo-oxidation in these polymers. In practice, stability is influenced by the interaction between linkages and by the presence of weak links. Weak links may arise at chain ends because of the mechanism of chain termination used during the polymerization reaction. Aberrations in the polymerization reaction may result in weak links at non-terminal positions. Weak links, especially at terminal positions, can be the site of a chain 'unzipping' reaction. A monomer unit or other simple molecule may be removed by a reaction at the chain end in a way that leaves the new chain end also unstable. The reaction repeats itself and the polymer depolymerizes or otherwise degrades. This can occur to a serious extent with poly acetals, poly(methyl methacrylate) (PMMA) and with PVC.

Whenever possible, UV radiation should be eliminated and the intensity and duration of visible light exposure reduced to a minimum. The light stability of polymers may be improved by incorporation of additives that preferentially absorb energy at wavelengths that damage susceptible linkages. As these materials filter out more of the blue component of light they may take on a yellow cast. Other steps can be taken to improve performance, especially to prevent unzipping reactions. Rigorous purification of monomer helps to eliminate the formation of weak links during manufacture but is expensive. Additives may be used to divert or moderate degradation reactions and this is less expensive. Chain ends can be capped with a stable group (e.g. poly acetals) to prevent degradation initiated at the terminal group. Co-polymerization with another monomer can help to obstruct unzipping reactions that have started. Methyl methacrylate is sometimes co-polymerized with a small amount of ethyl acrylate for this reason.

## The effect of heat on polymers

Heat has the effect of accelerating all chemical reactions and will speed up deterioration of polymers. Oxidation reactions proceed more rapidly at higher temperatures and heat may be partly responsible for the unzipping reactions of PMMA and PVC mentioned above. In the case of other polymers such as the polyolefins, scission occurs at random locations on the chain and the number of monomer units released is small. The degradation reduces chain length thereby affecting mechanical properties and secondary reactions may produce more or less complex mixtures of volatile degradation products. It is appropriate to keep temperatures as low as possible and for some polymer materials, such as cellulose nitrate film stock, low temperature storage is an important method of preservation.

The thermal stability of most polymers is severely restricted in comparison to many other materials. Most polymers will expand and contract a great deal with changes in temperature and the rate of purely physical processes such as diffusion is greatly increased with increasing temperature. Compared to wood, polymers will exhibit more dimensional instability with regard to temperature than with humidity. Change in temperature around Tg has a profound effect on the mechanical properties of plastics materials (see section 4.1). Most thermoplastic polymers will permanently change shape under their own weight or by any other stress exerted on them, a phenomenon known as creep. The rate at which this will occur is dependent on temperature. At temperatures above about 400 °C the rate of degradation of the common polymers is rapid with pyrolysis largely complete in a few minutes All polymer materials are regarded as combustible although the range of behaviour observed is very wide and the assessment of fire properties extremely complicated. For further information see Fabris and Sommer (1977), Fenimore and Martin (1972) and Kuryla and Papa (1973). Thermal stability is more likely to be observed in highly crosslinked and structurally rigid polymers such as the polyamides.

## The effect of RH on polymers

Some polymers are moisture-sensitive and will react to changes in RH by swelling or contracting. Hydroxyl groups, found attached to the backbone of the cellulose molecule and to poly(vinyl alcohol) (PVAL), are extremely reactive and make the polymer very susceptible to changes in the relative humidity of its environment. This behaviour will often increase as they degrade due to the greater polarity that comes about as a result of oxidation. The surfaces of some polymers may be swelled during aqueous cleaning, resulting in surface cracking as they dry. A polymer such as oriental lacquer (urushi) which is quite impervious to moisture when new will become increasingly water sensitive due to oxidation following exposure to light.

## The effect of pollution on polymers

A wide variety of air-borne pollutants can degrade polymers. Particularly deleterious are ozone, sulphur oxides, nitrogen oxides and formaldehyde. Many pollutants act with atmospheric moisture to create acids which help to promote hydrolysis – the breakage of polymer chains by water molecules. Specific chemical reactions may also occur. For example, polystyrene may be sulphonated by reaction of sulphuric acid with phenyl groups and polyethylene may become partially chlorinated by a similar type of reaction. Polymers may themselves be potent sources of pollutants as formaldehyde is released from urea and phenol-formaldehyde adhesives used in plywood, particle board and Formica®, nitric acid from degrading cellulose nitrate, or hydrochloric acid from poly(vinyl chloride). Both natural rubbers and synthetic elastomers are attacked by ozone ($O_3$). The ozone content of air is usually in the range 0.01–1.0 mg/kg (1 part in $10^8$ – $1:10^6$). Even at such low ozone levels as these rubbers require stabilization against ozone attack to achieve acceptable service lives. The $O_3$ molecule attacks C=C bonds (not a free radical reaction) and can cause scission of the main chain. The effects of solvents on polymer molecules are usually physical rather than chemical. The primary chains remain intact and the polymer can usually be recovered chemically unchanged though the microstructure (morphology) may be very different from that of the original.

### Biological damage to polymers

Synthetic polymers are not attractive to most biological pests but may sustain damage due to association with other target food stuffs such as wood, glue or coatings. Oil, that universal folk panacea for all observed problems, will provide a nutritious medium for mould growth. Mould has even been observed on acrylic sheet, probably due to oil residues present from handling. In some environmental conditions polymers based on cellulose, protein and latex may support bacterial and fungal life resulting in loss of strength.

### Prevention and care

In the conservation of polymeric materials good handling and environmental control are of primary importance. Many physical effects can be controlled by maintaining stable conditions of temperature and relative humidity, by avoiding mechanical stress, by avoiding contact with liquids and vapours that might be absorbed by the polymer material. Low light levels or dark storage, cool temperatures and average (40–55%) relative humidity are useful general guidelines. Conditions should be kept constant to avoid the imposition of thermal stress. Objects should be protected from dust by Tyvek® dust covers or other means. Storage in low oxygen environments may be appropriate for some materials. Work on the use of low oxygen environments has been published by Shashoua (Shashoua and Thomsen, 1993; Shashoua and Ward, 1993) and Gilberg and Grattan (1994). For materials such as PVC and

cellulose nitrate, which produce auto-catalytic degradation products, good ventilation is essential unless degradation can be otherwise prevented.

The fact that objects made of plastic look modern devalues them in the eyes of many. There is a misplaced perception that they are new, cheap and strong. A careful educational campaign (even in museums) is required to impress upon those handling these objects that they are both important documents of technological history and fragile. When objects of this type are moved every effort should be made to avoid touching the material, which may be tacky or very brittle. Trays placed under pieces of furniture in storage may be used to help lift the object onto wheeled transport to display or treatment. Display should be short term if possible as the materials are highly light-sensitive. Early detection of degradation and its likely causes is most important but can only be achieved if objects are examined regularly Frequent condition checks are advocated so that adequate treatment responses are made.

The first step in identifying a particular cause of damage must be identification of the polymer and investigation of the specific literature to provide appropriate conditions for display or storage. Polymer materials and their degradation products can be identified using various techniques (see Chapter 4). Among these FTIR and various forms of GC MS are the most useful (Learner, 1995; Shearer and Doyal, 1991). FTIR is suitable for identification of base polymers but not suitable for identification of additives and plasticizers.

Ultimately the best means of control of some of the problems of plastic materials outlined above is to develop more durable materials. However, a serious current problem is the prediction of the ageing and weathering properties of a polymer over a long period of time. Accelerated tests are potentially an invaluable way to get this information while there is still time to act on it, but there are several problems with such tests that complicate their interpretation. Several agents of deterioration acting together may produce an overall effect that is different from the sum of their individual effects. Higher temperatures and higher light levels may lead to fundamentally different kinds of reactions taking place than would normally occur. Rates of reactions may not be directly proportional to light level over a very wide range of light levels.

The changes in solubility that occur over time in various thermoplastic materials used as coatings are discussed below in the section on coatings. Information on specific polymers is given in *Table 4.1* and on four polymers used in upholstery (PVC, polyurethanes, rubber and cellulose nitrate) in section 8.12.1. Further information on the deterioration of polymers and plastics is given by Jellinek (1978), Davis and Sims (1983), Blank (1990), Crighton (1988), Hamid *et al.* (1992) and McGlinchey (1993) and in the bibliography cited in Chapter 4.

## 8.9  Coatings – deterioration of some common systems of surface decoration

Decorative surfaces on furniture are particularly important to the conservator. These surfaces may contain much of the expression and design of the object while the substrate and structure is clearly subordinate. However, the decorative surfaces of joined wooden objects can be the most degraded part of the object due to their complexity, exposure, wear and materials. Changes in the appearance of coatings may be due to both chemical and physical processes. These may occur at the interface between the coating and the air, within the coating itself or in layers of ground and support beneath the coating. Such changes are uniformly referred to here as deterioration even though some types and degrees of this process of change may be considered desirable in adding to the character or aesthetic quality of the piece.

Surface coatings consist primarily of organic materials which have a natural tendency to slowly break down, eventually to carbon dioxide and water. This phenomenon of oxidation of coatings is exothermic but does not take place spontaneously. It requires an initial input of energy (activation energy) to occur. The thermodynamics of these reactions and the influence of light, heat and moisture upon them are discussed by Mills and White (1987).

Light is a primary source of the activation energy that is needed to initiate the chemical reactions that result in the deterioration of coating materials. Light energy is absorbed to varying degrees by coatings and colorants with that energy being released through electron excitation or heat. The energy absorbed may cause bonds to break resulting in the degradation of the surface coating material. The process that is responsible for the appearance of a material may also result in the breakdown of the electron arrangement. The result of bond breakage is that the material is no longer capable of the electron excitement that gives it the colour first observed. This is observed as a colour change or fading and is permanent.

The study of chemical processes that take place only under the influence of light is called photochemistry (Brill, 1980; Suppan, 1972). The consequences of photochemistry may manifest themselves in the yellowing of surface coatings. A material such as a fresh resin coating that absorbs very little visible light will tend to be essentially transparent. A resinous coating will tend to become less transparent, or yellowed, as a coating ages due in part to the effect of light energy on the organic structure. This change is a function of chromophores which can form in a resinous coating as it ages. As a result, an aged resin will absorb more light and allow less to pass through it. Degraded finishes are often described as seeming to be dry and cracked like one's skin on a dry winter's day. This is not due to the loss of inherent moisture that needs to be replenished. Instead, an old coating with such an appearance has usually changed physically and chemically in a way that cannot be reversed and photochemical reactions play a large part in this process.

Oxygen plays a key role in many deterioration reactions. The crosslinking of linseed oil and its eventual transformation into linoxyn is a good example. Gases can only affect materials that they come in contact with. The outermost portion of a surface coating is more susceptible to chemical changes from gases such as oxygen than are the inner zones of the same material. Darkening of surfaces may be due to oxidation reactions in the resin (or oil) present in surface layers but it may also be due to layers of toning deliberately applied to hide breaks or irregularities in the surface. It is important to understand the nature of the altered state of aged surfaces in order to properly select and complete effective and responsible treatments.

It is easy to overlook the most obvious and mundane types of damage in favour of the more esoteric chemical deterioration but surface coating materials are also subject to deterioration through wear and tear, physical abrasion and biological causes. Chemical and mechanical changes may be seen as two aspects of deterioration that are closely connected. Changes that occur through exposure to light and oxygen, for example, cause changes in the physical properties of coatings (e.g. modulus of elasticity) that make them more sensitive to abrasion, contusion and other forms of mechanical damage. The dirt and grime that are a part of use may also contribute to the process of chemical degradation.

Most furniture items were intended to be used and this has an impact on the condition and the treatment of the object. Surface coatings will naturally deteriorate through the wear of regular use. The finish that has been rubbed away from the arms of chairs is a common example. This mechanical deterioration of the surface coating may or may not be deemed a desirable aspect of the object when treatment choices are made. It is useful to distinguish between damage and 'fair wear and tear'. The condition of a surface coating and its substrate are closely interlinked. This is emphasized as problems with the substrate will inevitably transfer to the surface. Expansion and contraction of wood in an unequal manner, due to the anisotropic nature of the material, causes surface coatings to deform or even cleave from the surface.

Another obvious change at surfaces is the accumulation of atmospheric dirt and grime. Specks of dust once adhered to the surface can become the focal point for condensation of moisture thus becoming more tightly adhered. The hygroscopic nature of dirt allows it to serve as a reservoir for water furthering its negative impact on coatings, particularly in instances of high humidity. Dirt can also be acidic, presenting free H+ ions which will accelerate degradation. Nitrous oxides, ozone, sulphur and other common gaseous pollutants have long been known for their negative impact on art objects in general.

There are many steps that can be taken to prevent damage and deterioration and mostly they are of the common sense variety.

However the complete elimination between such problems is not easy. Deterioration of coatings affects the data produced in the course of characterization and analysis (Bentsen *et al.*, 1990; Birstein and Tul'Chinsky, 1981). The deterioration of coatings and adhesives is discussed in two parts; the first part discusses the interaction of the components of commonly encountered systems of surface decoration under the influence of different environmental factors; the second discusses the materials in more detail as members of their chemical class.

### 8.9.1   The support

The nature and behaviour of supports can profoundly affect the performance of coatings and it is important to consider the support structure before carrying out treatment. Supports used for decorative surfaces on furniture include leather, textile, glass and metal but wood is the most common. Wood as a physical surface for paint application is discussed by Hoadley (1998). Differences in the dimensional response of wooden supports and of grounds applied to them can have profound deleterious effects on the ground and on decorative layers applied to it. As an example, a gesso and gilt surface on a turned chair leg may de-laminate due to the shrinkage of the wood. The volume of the leg has decreased while the surface area of the gesso and gilt has not. The majority of the factors discussed in Chapter 7 are relevant to the interaction between wooden supports and coatings applied to them. These include natural and artificially induced defects in the material, differential shrinkage, differences in hygroscopic sensitivity and rate of response of different structural components, the type of construction employed, poor quality materials, poor workmanship and biodeterioration.

Any distortion in the support will be reflected in stress applied to the decorative layers of ground and paint applied to it. Differential responses to moisture content changes commonly cause some distortion of design and may cause splits. Compression set in wooden supports leads to slight reduction in width of wooden panels over time. Various construction techniques were used to minimize distortion or weaknesses in the substrate.

**Figure 8.4**  Detail of a pine panel from the David Hottenstein House, Berks County, PA, 1783. Woodwork installed as the 'Fraktur Room' at Winterthur Museum in 1952. Poor absorption properties can cause paint loss along the lines of late wood growth, seen here as lighter lines of paint loss contrasting with darker areas where paint remains

Battens on the ends of a board or a flush frame and panel were employed by cabinet-makers as a base for painted, veneered or otherwise decorated surfaces. Another common cause for distortion or deterioration of a decorative surface is the result of non-parallel construction. Applying gesso or veneer on only one side of a panel will result in an unequal dimensional response to changes in moisture content (Buck, 1961). The benefit of applying coatings on both sides of a substrate is illustrated by the outer panels of triptychs where increased stability is attributed to sympathetic layering since both sides are painted (Kuhn, 1986).

The surfaces of some woods can vary in their physical properties creating a difference in suitability as a substrate for decorative surfaces. A common example of this is the nature of early and late wood in some pines (*Pinus* spp.). The less dense early wood absorbs the glue, ground or paint creating a long-term bond while the denser late wood absorbs less satisfactorily causing premature failure of the ground or paint (*Figure 8.4*). A paint, ground or adhesive may be less able to wet into a burnished or compressed wood substrate causing premature failure of the glue, ground or paint.

Identifying such issues plays an important part in assessing the health of an object's decorative surface and in making proposals for care or treatment. The conservator may be in a unique position to recognize deliberate choices made by the maker to enhance the longevity of decorative surfaces.

### 8.9.2  The ground

Grounds vary tremendously in their composition and complexity (Massey, 1967). Grounds for paint and gilding may be made primarily of a protein binder such as hide glue or casein and gypsum, chalk or other inert base material. Sometimes, the ground may itself be a simple paint layer. Although the ground is rarely seen unless damage to surface layers is substantial it is subject to stresses from the support below and the paint and varnish layers above and is subject to both adhesive and cohesive failure (Emile-Male, 1976). The main source of damage is incompatibility between the ground and the support. The shrinkage and swelling of glues with changes in RH and the activity of micro-organisms at high RH are important causes of failure in aqueous grounds such as gesso. Stains, discolorations and scars are defects in the ground which may telegraph through to the paint. Movement of the support transmitted upwards through the ground into the paint will result in cracks in the paint, but cracks which originate in the paint layer are unlikely to penetrate the ground. The failure of a ground can progress over a long period of time as exposure causes a slow reduction in performance. This change is rarely linear, being likely to occur more rapidly in certain stages than in others (Feller, 1994). Deterioration of the ground can be difficult or impossible to treat because of limited access, particularly on a wooden substrate.

Organic binding materials in the ground progressively deteriorate, losing adhesive strength, tensile strength and flexibility. In order that grounds can relatively easily be prepared to a smooth flat condition for taking paint, gilding, or other decorative layer, they normally contain relatively small amounts of medium in proportion to the quantity of inert filler. Where wood is the support, this thin, weak rather brittle 'crust' lies next to a tough, fibrous, active support. In addition to this, grounds are generally unbalanced, being applied to only one side of the support. This makes it easier for moisture changes, and hence movement, in the support to occur and more likely that distortion will result. Differential movement of the ground and support leads to shear forces at the interface that cause loss of attachment or cleavage of the ground from the support. This is adhesive failure (*Figure 8.5*). When these detached areas of the ground are subsequently placed in tension by further movement of the support they break at right-angles to the support and cracks are formed. Further movement leads to damage at the break edges and enlargement of the cracks with penetration of dirt and further ingress and egress of moisture. These cracks do provide some relief from stress in the ground and allow movement in the support to be more readily accommodated. Eventually, however, the break edges become pushed upwards slightly away from the support. The slight but noticeable loss in width of wide panels of wood across the grain that occurs in time through compression set in wood contributes to this process. Parts of the ground eventually become completely surrounded by cracks and cup upwards at their edges like saucers. They may become fully detached from the support, only held in place by sideways pressure from the surrounding areas and therefore very vulnerable to mechanical damage. In aqueous grounds, condensation in cracks may cause swelling and further damage at break edges. Examination of a painted surface in raking light will reveal the slight difference in contours of the surface caused by buckling of the cleaved paint layers as these are pushed upwards along the edges of cracks (see *Figure 9.3*). Eventually some of the pieces of the ground may become sufficiently loose to fall out. Once this occurs, the exposed areas become the focus for more rapid deterioration and loss to occur.

Cleavage of paint on metal or stone may also occur, partly because of the effects of temperature but more importantly because of the stresses imposed by embrittlement of surface coatings. Although paints and grounds do shrink, this effect is generally most noticeable with clear resin coatings, partly because resins shrink more than the oil and glue media commonly used in paints and grounds but also because pigments and fillers reduce shrinkage. The greater shrinkage of a resin varnish layer

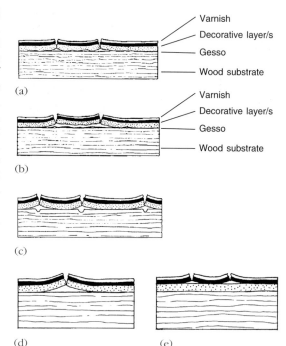

**Figure 8.5** Cleavage of ground from substrate
(*a*) Movement of the wooden substrate may cause cracks and loss of adhesion in the gesso ground
(*b*) In cases where flakes are completely detached, they may be held in position by adjacent layers only
(*c*) Cracks and cleavage in the decorative layers may develop at points where woodworm larval tunnels have affected the surface of the wood substrate
(*d*) Adhesive failure between substrate wood and ground
(*e*) Adhesive failure between decorative layers and ground

may eventually literally pull the paint off the support (*Figure 8.6*). It is often much more difficult to obtain satisfactory adhesion between metals and paint films and certain pigments show specific reactions with metal substrates (Cowling and Merritt, 1954). Ineffective preparation of the support or defects in it that may resist proper saturation of the ground by the medium can readily lead to flaking and blistering of the ground and decorative layers associated with it on a much shorter time scale than those caused by progressive failure of the ground. Similarly improperly prepared grounds, for example those that are overbound or underbound or gesso grounds that were overcooked in pre-

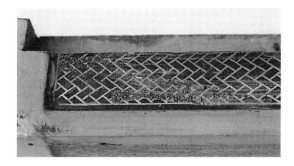

**Figure 8.6** Detail of the lower part of a bedpost from the Badminton Bed (*c*.1754), before conservation. The shrinkage stress exerted by a degraded restoration varnish has caused the loss of areas of japanned decoration

paration, may fail much more quickly than those that were correctly prepared.

Where paint has come loose due to loss of adhesion between the ground and the support, the obvious remedy is to introduce fresh adhesive. However, further damage may easily be caused in attempting to correct the situation. Damage may be done in the attempt to introduce adhesive into the inaccessible areas where it is required and if too much adhesive is introduced it may subsequently make the whole structure extremely brittle and cause further damage.

### 8.9.3 The paint

Painted surfaces represent some of the most artistic yet perishable decorative surfaces on furniture. Paints are essentially colour-bearing pigments, lakes or dyes and a binding medium delivered in a vehicle (see section 4.4.3). While the vehicle, or solvent, usually dissipates, the binding media remains to provide structural integrity to the paint film. The binding medium in a paint can cease to serve its function as it ages, causing similar failures as noted above for grounds. This is often a result of a resin, gum, tempera, oil, casein or other substance that has changed to the point that it is no longer able to keep the paint layer intact. Water-soluble media remain susceptible to RH change, the action of liquid water and mould growth while oil media, although less susceptible to these changes, follow a constant course of oxidation becoming progressively

more brittle, more translucent and more yellow as time goes on. Oriental lacquer and wax are generally more permanent. Paint media may darken with age or degrade on the surface causing a perceived lightening of colour due to minute cracks (blanching) or increased light scattering of unbound surface pigment (chalking). Media will often show a rise in refractive index as they age, causing paint layers to become more transparent as the refractive index of the medium approaches those of the pigments. This may cause more of the base colour, ground or substrate to show through, leading to the effect in painting called pentimenti. Typically, the effect of an increase in the transparency of a paint film is a darker decorative surface (Rees Jones, 1991). Paints may also fail because of inadequate preparation (Emile-Male, 1976).

Whether a function of age or inadequate fabrication techniques, painted surfaces eventually undergo chemical and physical changes which alter them both structurally and visually. Deterioration of painted surfaces may occur through changes in the support, ground or varnish layer as well as through changes in the paint itself. Deterioration of specific media is further discussed in section 8.11.

Chalking, sometimes called skinning is a common failing of paint exposed to the weather but is not confined to this cause. Loss of binding medium results in exposure and eventual loss of pigment particles. A contributory cause to chalking may be abrasion during varnish removal or during routine household cleaning. Chalking is particularly likely to occur with pigments that were coarsely ground and under bound in order to get the maximum strength of colour. Also, binding media may be consumed by insects, moulds or other micro-organisms. Chalking leads to an overall thinning of the paint, often with exposure of the ground or support underneath. Chalked paint does not retain brush marks, a fact that may distinguish it from paint that was originally applied in a very thin layer.

Paint which is more generously bound tends to become brittle and form cracks rather than chalking. The nature of the cracks formed has to do with the nature of the medium (egg, aqueous, oil etc.), the relative drying rates of the different layers in the paint and the way they were applied, the thickness of the paint and the strains caused by the support and any coating that may be present. All binding media that become hard enough to act as a paint film also, eventually, become sufficiently brittle that they are unable to withstand these stresses and therefore crack. Cracks in paint and ground arising from movement of wooden supports are thin and fine and tend to reflect the pattern of movement and hence the underlying grain direction and construction, of the support. A different kind of crack arises from forces acting within and between the layers of paint. Paint films have a smaller volume when dry than when wet and hence can be considered to shrink on drying. If the rate or extent of drying is too great, the ability of the paint film to resist the stresses imposed by drying will be exceeded and it will crack. The time taken for a paint film to dry can be considerable but will vary according to the type of medium (e.g. different oils), the amount of thinners or diluent used, the amount and type of drier added to the medium, the pigment(s) present and the state of the underlying layers. The rule in painting has been to apply fat over lean, that is slow-drying layers over quick-drying ones. If quick-drying layers are applied over slow-drying layers they are very likely to crack. This has been used in the deliberate creation of age-imitating craquelure. The pigment to medium ratio is also important since the pigment acts as a filler to increase the modulus of the coating. If too little pigment is present the film will be more brittle and more likely to crack. Problems can also arise if a paint layer was not dry before the next one was applied or even in some cases where a mistake was made and retouching varnish was applied over soft paint so that corrections could be made before the paint was dry. Paint applied over an unstable film such as bitumen for example and covered over with a thick layer of varnish often splits open into wide rifts from the pull of drying. This has been called alligator crackle or alligatoring (Stout, 1975). Cracks caused by the inability of the paint film to hold together as it dries are characteristically wider than those caused by movement in the support and have more of the appearance of cracks in a dry clay soil with the paint in between having a somewhat lumpy appearance.

Surface deterioration of paint films can take many forms, some of which are shared with degradation seen in clear varnish coatings. Spots on paint can be caused by mould growth which will cause pitting or staining if allowed to persist for any length of time. Fly excrement causes small brown marks on the surface of paint which by their acidic nature may also be etched deep into the surface. Woodworm larval tunnels under a painted surface may leave only a thin skin that will tend to sink or collapse in time and mature insects leaving an underlying wooden support through the paint are further examples of biological mechanisms of deterioration. Discoloration (yellowing and darkening etc.) of paint films may arise through changes in the medium caused by light but may also be due to, or made worse by, previous treatments. Retouching may discolour due

**Figure 8.7** Detail of the Garrick wardrobe (*c*.1772–1778, made by Thomas Chippendale), before conservation. Old restoration retouching extends beyond the area of loss, covering original paint

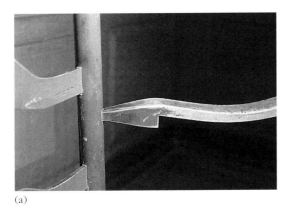

(a)                                                    (b)

**Figure 8.8**  Old wear and natural abrasion: (*a*) detail of natural wear on the arm of a painted chair, Pennsylvania, *c.*1750; (*b*) detail of natural wear on a painted blanket chest, Pennsylvania, *c.*1788

to changes in the medium used that are different from the original medium and may extend considerably beyond the original areas of loss (*Figure 8.7*). When varnish is removed from a surface during cleaning it may be left in the hollows of the texture of a paint film and may show up later as a mottled darkening of the surface. Such varnish may prove difficult to remove without causing damage to the paint. Previous treatments to improve clarity of a surface may have included rubbing with oil, leaving a sticky film which collects dirt. Mechanical deterioration of paint includes scratches, dents and abrasion. Old wear and natural abrasion of a painted decorative surface through use is common in furniture and often considered appropriate and part of its history (*Figure 8.8*). The degree to which this sort of deterioration of a decorative surface is considered acceptable and what sort of treatment is in order may vary from collection to collection. However, the evidence found in a surface coating about an objects history is valuable and should not be discarded simply to obtain an ideal appearance for display. For further information on historic binding media, the technology of paints and the defects of paint films see Masschelein-Kleiner (1985), Martens (1968) and Hess (1965).

### 8.9.4  Transparent top coatings – varnishes

Changes in the appearance, mechanical properties and solubility of coatings result from a combination of chemical and physical interactions between the coating and its environment. Coatings are usually readily oxidized. Light, heat and moisture are important contributing factors. The most common visual change is a reduction in transparency. This is particularly true with natural resins. Changes in the optical qualities of the coating may include colour changes such as yellowing and darkening, changes in gloss and loss in transparency. Cracking, checking and crystallization may contribute to these changes. The adhesion of transparent coatings to the underlying decorative surface may fail causing it to de-laminate and flake off. This can also cause a significant change in the visual properties of the surface and leave portions of it exposed to the environment. SEM photographs of aged resin coatings on wood are shown in *Figure 12.8c,d*. As coatings age, the molecular structure is likely to be altered chemically, particularly due to photochemical reactions involving oxygen. Reduction in molecular weight and average length of polymer chains are common consequences of this process. Crazing or craquelure is a common manifestation of oxidation, and will cause the varnish to refract or bend light differently than when fresh, causing a visual change. While an aged coating may appeared to have 'dried out', it is actually a much more complicated combination of non-reversible physical and chemical changes. The notion of 'feeding' such a dried out surface to restore its vitality is inappropriate and misinformed.

338 Conservation of Furniture

Coatings do not require nourishment. Transparent coatings have long been known to become brittle and to require progressively more polar solvents for their removal. This change in properties has been attributed to oxidative changes resulting in the formation of more polar groups in the polymer. However, polymerization as well as chain breaking and weight loss of the molecule may occur. This can both accelerate delamination of the coating and complicate solvent based treatments as the polarity of the solvent required for removal of varnish may approach that of the underlying paint film.

Many of the deterioration processes that occur are due to chemical reaction but some may be purely physical. Shrinking, cracking and some types of blooming may be primarily physical in nature. However, some of the root causes of physical change can be traced to chemical reactions, particularly oxidation reactions, occurring within the coating. Embrittlement, hardening and discoloration (yellowing) have been linked to oxidation (Feller et al., 1985). Oxidation is not limited to reactions involving oxygen. It may also result from reactions involving ozone, sulphur dioxide, chlorine or other gases.

Bloom, a general term used to describe a whitish, foggy, or cloudy appearance is characterized by breakdown of the smooth uniform consistency of the coating resulting in scattering of light at the surface. Two among many possible causes are the presence of moisture in the film and the presence of fine cracks caused by long-term drying.

Wear and abrasion are common to transparent coatings which may alter the visual properties of the decorative surface they cover. Such evidence of use may be a significant part of the history of the object. The importance of this mechanical change in the transparent coating needs to be weighed before the wear and abrasion is considered a negative aspect of the condition of the object.

The damaging effects of water on a varnished wooden surface are demonstrated by rings or water marks. Water marks are a common and difficult problem. Since resinous coatings are not water-soluble, it may seem odd that such materials are unable to fully protect wood from water. While water does not dissolve true resins it can permeate through resin films into the substrate below. The result is either a loss of adhesion between the coating and the wood (a white water mark), a staining of the wood below (a black water mark) or both. Water containing dissolved salts or alcohol may cause considerable damage to the coating itself. The presence of high levels of moisture in coatings can significantly increase the rate at which chemical reactions occur following absorption of light. A surface coating that exists for an extended period of time in a high moisture environment is likely to degrade more rapidly than is a surface coating that has had a lower exposure to moisture over a similar period of time.

Solvent marks may disfigure an object and so need to be reworked. Abrasion, mechanical polishing or solvent/resin polishing in the affected area may be required (see Chapter 12). Some marks may be intentionally retained as part of the object's history of use as a functional object.

Many of the changes that occur in transparent coatings are essentially the same as those that would occur in a paint medium if it were being used as a coating. The presence of inorganic material such as pigment in paint films normally makes paint films more durable than transparent films. One effect of a pigment, for example, is to reduce the amount of light entering a coating. Changes in the chemistry of coating materials that occur with time are, for all practical purposes, irreversible.

The exact nature of the changes observed depends on the nature of the polymer material from which the coating is made. The main distinction that has been made is between solvent-release varnishes based on simple solution thermoplastic polymer materials and reactive varnishes. Simple thermoplastic polymers may be altered in at least three ways. First the polymer chains may break up into smaller units, a process of depolymerization; secondly, there may be alteration of chemical groups within the polymer (e.g. the formation of ketonic and acidic groups); and thirdly, crosslinking may occur.

Three stages can be recognized in the life of a simple solution thermoplastic film: first, after initial drying when solvent is still present and its concentration is rapidly changing; second, when there are no measurable processes of solvent loss or deterioration; and the third in which property changes become apparent due to progressive degradation of the film. In the first stage, when solvent is still present, the film is still flexible and has not yet come to a solvent/environment equilibrium. The solvent will diffuse through the body of the coating to the upper portion of the film and evaporate from the surface, a process that may take months to complete (Martens, 1968). Solvent may also diffuse into the layers below the coating and begin to dissolve soluble low molecular weight components into the varnish layer itself. Also, a small amount of some solvents may be permanently retained. Physical stress caused by solvent evaporation may result in fissures which may appear as a very pronounced craquelure or small fault lines only visible with magnification. The second stage (solvent dissipated), when the film has lost all of the free solvent and is set into a fairly stable coating is usually the longest stage in the life of the coating. In the third stage, physical and chemical changes occur yielding an oxidized film which may be crazed, brittle, opaque, discoloured or otherwise altered in properties. This aged coating is likely to be chemically quite different from the initial state. Materials which are substantially changed during this process would be considered less stable. Some coatings such as beeswax may change very little over an extended period of time.

### Development of insoluble matter

The tendency for thermoplastic polymers to develop insoluble matter with time is the rule rather than the exception. This is generally due to crosslinking but the formation of ketonic and acidic groups, which also takes place in the process of oxidation, tends to make polymers more polar. For example, the decreasing solubility in toluene of Acryloid B82 and Rhoplex AC33 that occurs with time is apparently not due to crosslinking but rather to a change in polarity. This is also the case with the natural resins dammar and mastic and with the cyclohexanone based coatings AW2, MS2, MS2A and Ketone N. When fresh these are soluble in white spirit but require more polar solvents for their removal as time goes on. They may eventually require ethyl alcohol or similar solvent for their removal.

While poly vinyl acetate is highly resistant to crosslinking, many of the methacrylate polymers of interest in conservation are highly prone to becoming insoluble through this mechanism. These include iso amyl, iso butyl and n-butyl methacrylates. However, there are others, including poly (n propyl methacrylate) and Paraloid B72 (co-polymer of methyl methacrylate and ethyl acrylate), which are highly resistant to crosslinking. The most sensitive materials tend to be those polymers based on methacrylic esters which have a tertiary hydrogen atom in the alkyl radical of the alcohol group.

The development of insolubility seems to proceed in four stages for polymers that crosslink on ageing. There is generally an induction period during which the development of insoluble material is not noticed. This may be because the polymer contains substances (either intentionally or accidentally) which are attacked more readily than the polymer itself and therefore protect it. It is also a consequence of the growth of molecules by crosslinking to a size sufficient to become insoluble. It does not need many crosslinks to form before a high molecular weight material becomes insoluble. Low molecular weight materials require many more reactions before insoluble material is formed. That part of the induction time that is the result of the growth of molecules to a sufficient size to become insoluble is thus inversely proportional to molecular weight. The exposure necessary before the first insoluble matter is formed is sometimes referred to as the gel dose.

In the second stage, following the point of initial appearance of insoluble polymeric material but before a high degree of crosslinking has occurred, most films can be removed as a mixture of highly swollen gel and dispersible sol. This relative ease of removal appears to last up to about five times the gel dose. The rate at which insoluble matter builds up follows a regular mathematical law usually becoming approximately 90% insoluble after five times the gel dose. If chain breaking and crosslinking occur simultaneously this will effectively reduce the percentage of insoluble material. Nevertheless, the density of crosslinks in the insoluble portion will steadily increase and this will therefore become less able to swell and hence more difficult to remove. During this period, polymers such as poly (n-butyl methacrylate) and poly (iso-amyl methacrylate) can usually be removed in their original solvents as a mixture of swollen gel and sol up to the point at which the film becomes 90% insoluble.

The third stage in the ageing of a polymer that exclusively crosslinks occurs when the film is almost completely insoluble but is able to swell with solvents. With increasing crosslink density and possible accompanying changes in polarity progressively more polar solvents are required to cause swelling. Eventually a polymer may become so highly crosslinked that it is not effectively swollen by solvents.

The crosslinking of n-butyl and others of the methacrylate series is a phenomenon that can take place under ordinary gallery conditions. Under conditions where precautions are taken to reduce the light intensity below 150 lux and to remove the UV component these films will perhaps become about 50% insoluble in about twenty-five years. Tests are available to detect the presence of insoluble material and to monitor the course of such changes with a fair degree of confidence. It is possible to inhibit the crosslinking tendencies of some methacrylates (e.g. iso amyl methacrylate) but once the inhibitor has been used up through preferential reaction with light or oxygen the polymer material itself again becomes susceptible. Co-polymerization techniques may be more effective. The deterioration of surface coatings is further discussed by Feller (1994; Feller *et al.*, 1985), Horie (1987), Koller and Mairinger (1975) and Masschelein-Kleiner (1985).

### 8.9.5  Gilding

Gilded surfaces employ gold or imitations of gold adhered to a suitable ground or support. Supports are commonly wood but may also be metal, ivory, stone, glass, ceramic or other material. Gilding can be applied directly to the support but frequently a ground is present, especially where wooden supports are used. This may be a simple paint or a more complex preparation of gesso and bole. The metal leaf can be attached with an oil-based gold size or with a protein based adhesive such as an animal glue or egg white. Deterioration of gilded surfaces can occur through changes in the support, the ground, the mordant or the metal itself and is commonplace with furniture

and related objects. Indeed, it is rare and pleasing to find an intact gilded surface on any object of substantial age. Factors that may contribute to the process of deterioration have their origins in the materials and techniques used in the original construction, in the pattern of usage of the gilded object and in the nature of the environment to which it has been exposed. The process of gilding is not actually difficult but requires considerable skill and judgement by the practitioner to ensure the longevity of the surface.

Failure in wooden supports is discussed in Chapter 7. Unbalanced construction, poor selection and preparation of materials predispose gilded surfaces to failure. Gesso adheres much better to most softwoods than to hardwoods, though non-resinous softwoods are preferable. Examples of gilding on birch, maple, oak and mahogany may be found in good condition but gilding on beech is frequently found to have flaked off to a marked degree. Gilded objects placed in centrally heated environments are especially prone to damage caused by movement in the support. This is made worse by unbalanced construction and by placing objects against cold (and possibly damp) exterior walls when a notable difference may result in the RH of the air trapped behind the piece as compared to general room RH. Inadequate preparation of wooden supports to receive gesso grounds can cause premature delamination of the ground.

The ground, usually a gesso, can lose its properties of adhesion and cohesion and separate from the substrate (see section 8.9.2). The commonly observed cracking of the gesso/gilded structure perpendicular to the grain of the wood is a complex phenomenon. It may occur in part because the gesso is under the most stress under low humidity conditions with fractures occurring as the gesso contracts more or less equally in all directions while the wood does not (Mecklenburg, 1991). The characteristics of a good gesso and the means of applying it to wood to create a ground are described by Thompson (1962) and in Chapter 14. Several things can go wrong during preparation or application. Glue size may chill too quickly during preliminary sizing of the wood thus leading to the creation of a relatively weak bond with the support. Uneven drying of gesso, which may occur for example through direct heating by the sun or by too rapid drying, may lead to the formation of a hard dry layer over a softer wetter layer during the build up of the ground and cause premature cracking. Overheating the gesso will denature the protein in the animal glue binder and cause loss of strength in the ground and is a frequent cause of air bubbles in gesso. Changes in strength of gesso in the ground layers should be gradual with the strongest layers next to the support. Slightly weaker layers may be applied satisfactorily over the first layer but application of stronger layers over weaker layers may cause the top coat to curl up and pull off the layers beneath. This can happen if too much water is allowed to evaporate from the gesso mix during the application of the ground. Size that is too strong will lead to the ground flaking and cracking off while gesso grounds that are too weak will tend to chalk and burnish poorly. With the exception of the application of the initial size layer, it is important that the gesso ground should be completed from a single batch of gesso and that the ground is not allowed to dry out completely once the process of applying gesso has started. Faults can also occur in the application of both gesso and bole layers. Bridges, which may form over recessed parts, may later break. Attempts to rectify imperfections in wet bole during its application may lead to later failure where the ground has been unduly disturbed. Gilders composition, frequently used for imitating carved ornament, is prone to shrinkage, cracking and embrittlement on drying. Dirt and cleaning materials penetrate the cracks and weaken the bond with the substrate.

Oil gilding, though easier to do than water gilding, still requires skill and judgement. Dust allowed to settle over a slow drying oil size will spoil the surface and render it more liable to subsequent tearing and abrasion (e.g. during cleaning). If oil size is applied over too large an area at one time it will not be possible to complete the gilding while the mordant is in the correct state to receive the gold and this will lead to uneven brightness. Gold that is applied while the oil is still too wet will not give a good lustre, whilst that applied when the size is too dry will not adhere properly. If

the oil size layer is too thick or if too much oil is added to it a soft film will remain under the gold which will cause it to mark easily and wrinkle. Oil gilding is easily damaged by polar organic solvents but is resistant to water. Water gilding is very easily damaged by water but is resistant to non-polar organic solvents.

The gilding itself can corrode, particularly when it has been alloyed with other metals or when its primary component is a metal other than gold. Gold leaf alloys below 22 ct may be subject to sulphide tarnishing (Linns, 1991). High purity gold is resistant to corrosion but leaf alloyed with silver and copper is susceptible to tarnish from pollution in various forms. Skin salts and acids will frequently cause finger prints to appear on the gilded surface shortly after handling and these will be permanently etched into the surface. Silver leaf

**Figure 8.9** Spirit gilding that has taken on the craquelure of aged varnish can be seen in this detail of a dressing bureau, rosewood (*Dalbergia latifolia*), Philadelphia, Pennsylvania, *c*.1830. Part of the 'Empire Bedroom Suite, Winterthur Museum

may tarnish in the presence of egg mordant. Partial loss of a coating over a gilded surface may result in preferential corrosion of the exposed metal leaf. Metal leaf surfaces are exceedingly thin and easily scratched or abraded by handling and cleaning. Surface coatings applied to gilding for protection or toning are prone to the changes noted previously (section 8.9.4), including damage by light and moisture. Gilding suspended in a varnish, often referred to as 'spirit gilding', differs from gilding applied on top of an oil varnish size. Spirit gilded structures are affected by changes which occur in the varnish layers. As an example, such gilding may take on the craquelure properties of an aged varnish (*Figure 8.9*).

According to Green (1991), previous repairs, alterations and restorations probably pose more problems than anything else. Previous cleaning, especially of water gilding, without replacement of the protective size may make future cleaning without causing irreparable damage to the gold, difficult if not impossible. Original surfaces are frequently found to have been overgilded, sometimes with the addition of a new ground, or repaired with a wide range of different types and strengths of material ranging from the traditional to more modern synthetic media. These frequently delaminate or cause adverse reactions in the original but rarely do so sufficiently completely to make removal a simple matter. Dealing with such problems is frequently both problematic and exceedingly time consuming.

### 8.9.6   Oriental lacquer

Despite the description of oriental lacquer as a 'super-durable material' (Kumanotani *et al.*, 1980, Kumanotani, 1983), it is well known that lacquered wares placed on exhibition in museums and elsewhere lose their lustre and/or become discoloured (Araki and Sato, 1978). It appears that the main factors in the discoloration caused by lighting are ultra-violet radiation of 365 nm or less and heat. Unfiltered light from fluorescent lamps may have played an important part in this process. The test results of Araki showed that it is particularly desirable to use filters with fluorescent lamps or to use incandescent lamps so arranged as to avoid heating effects. Direct

exposure to sunlight should be avoided in all cases. Araki and Sato (1978) claim to have calculated the maximum 'safe dose' of illumination as follows:

| | | |
|---|---|---|
| Black lacquer | 900 lux | 3.5 years |
| Red (HgS) | 900 lux | 8 months |
| Red (CDs) | 900 lux | 1 year |

Urushiol shows strong absorption for light of wavelength less than 360 nm but visible light may also be damaging. Kumanotani has suggested that the 365 nm cut off should be extended to 400 nm, which may begin to exceed the filtering capability of some materials commonly used for this purpose. He also points out that exposure to light of short wavelengths causes the lacquer surface to become hydrophilic, a phenomenon confirmed in practice by a radical change in the susceptibility to damage by aqueous cleaning media. The effect of ultra violet radiation on hardened urushi films is well illustrated by Kenjo (1988). Absorption of light of short wavelengths leads to photo-oxidative degradation of the urushiol moiety binding each of the lacquer grains in the surface. The first row of grains in the film disappears as powdery efflorescence and the second row appears as a new surface. Due to the limited thickness and heterogeneity of the film this process can only be allowed to proceed to a limited extent before serious harm is evident. Damage caused by the heating effect of radiation of longer wavelengths and spotlights may have been underestimated (Franke, 1976). While display lighting in museum galleries is normally carefully controlled, great vigilance is needed to ensure that lacquer objects are not irreversibly damaged by needless exposure to light in workshops, auction houses, shop windows, stores and elsewhere.

One very serious consequence of the heating effect of lighting is on the moisture relationships of lacquer films. In particular, it will tend to reduce the RH of the object's immediate environment, possibly to extremely low levels. According to Franke (1978), most damage done to East Asian works made of lacquer is caused by changes in relative humidity and the varying shrinkage of wood and lacquer. Kumanotani (Kumanotani *et al.*, 1985, Kumanotani, 1988) has observed that water is an essential part of the structure of the lacquer film and that internal stress develops in the film on water desorption. Loss of bound water leads to progressive deterioration of the lacquer film including loss of flexibility and toughness (hence an increase in brittleness) and changes in the barrier properties to water and oxygen. However, excessively high levels of RH may actually promote oxidative degradation of the film by enhancing oxygen transport. This highlights the need to know what is happening to both objects themselves and to their environments. In the typical case of lacquer on a wooden core, RH changes could lead to a variety of different types of loss of structural integrity of the film including cracking, splitting, delamination, or warping. The outcome depends on various factors such as the moisture vapour transmission rate of the lacquer, the strength and elasticity of the lacquer film, the moisture content and plasticity of the core, the adhesion between the various layers and the different types and amounts of movement. Once the structural integrity of a lacquer film is disrupted there is greater potential for much more rapid deterioration. This is recognized in Japan where great concern is shown to preserve the structural integrity of lacquer films at all costs and to maintain appropriate levels of RH to do so. When an object has been made and subsequently kept under particular conditions this may seem the best course of action. It is less clear for objects that have been in much lower average relative humidity conditions in Western collections for many years whether it would now be appropriate to significantly raise the RH of their environment. This needs to be approached cautiously beginning when RH indoors is naturally high (i.e. the summer) and aiming to reduce the extent of winter heating and the accompanying drop in RH.

The best lacquer prepared from the best quality materials, carefully crafted and well cared for, will survive for centuries. On the other hand examples of export lacquer hastily prepared from inferior quality materials may exhibit the most horrendous problems of cupping, delamination and embrittlement. From measurements of the dynamechanical properties of sap and lacquer films it has been demonstrated that films prepared from sap undergo a large degree of crosslinking during their first three years but that carefully prepared lacquer films keep almost the same degree of crosslinking during this period (Kuwata *et al.*, 1961). Moreover, further work by Kumanotani (1981, 1983) shows that lacquer films stored over twenty years change very little. Comparison of the density of sap and lacquer films stored for nineteen years shows almost no variation in density for lacquer films but a remarkable change for sap films.

Some very real practical measures can be adopted to help reduce the risk of handling damage to which lacquer is likely to succumb following the damage caused by exposure to light and low RH. In general this means following carefully the precautions outlined in Chapter 6 (section 6.2.7). In particular, lacquer objects should not be stored close together unless individually protected to prevent accidental contact with other objects during handling. Always remove jewellery before handling lacquer, wear moisture-proof gloves when handling it and use both hands. Most important Japanese lacquer objects were supplied from the maker wrapped in a suitable cloth inside a (wooden) box for protection. This is how objects are generally stored in Japanese museums. There are many advantages to this system in reducing exposure to light, handling and RH changes. However, there may be some disadvantages that it would be wise to consider before adopting this system. Lacquer objects decorated with lead (or alloys high in lead and low in tin) are susceptible to damage by organic acid vapours from wood. Boxing in acid free card may be an alternative for such pieces (Umney and Winness, 1994).

A good source of practical illustration of a wide range of the problems that may affect lacquer objects is provided by Chase (1988). A good bibliography of scientific research on urushi is provided by Sano (1993). The proceedings of the 1993 International Symposium on the Conservation and Restoration of Cultural Property, in which Sano's paper is published, are an excellent source of further information on all aspects of the conservation of oriental lacquer.

### 8.9.7 Japanning

Japanned surfaces were originally intended to imitate oriental lacquer (urushi). The term japanning is usually applied to designs that use a contrast between a monochrome background (black, red, green, blue etc.) and decorative designs, often picked out in gold, that have an 'oriental' influence or feel (chinoiserie). Japanning describes the decorative effect rather than the materials used and thus the term spans several centuries and encompasses surfaces based on alcohol soluble ('spirit') resins, oil paint, oil soluble fossilized resins and stoved linseed oil.

Treatises describing the techniques used in japanning furniture in seventeenth and early eighteenth century England provide a comprehensive picture of a complex laminate structure which may include priming, up to twenty-four layers of varnish which may be decorated with pigments, metal and raised detail which are in turn secured to the body of the work with up to ten further coats of varnish (see section 4.4.7). The materials are not as durable as those used for the preparation of oriental lacquer and the layered structure is composed of materials whose properties are not always compatible. Most of the problems outlined within this section (8.9) are well represented in japanned objects.

Delamination and loss of the japanned surface through moisture induced movement of the wooden support is a common problem though some woods are noticeably worse than others. Japanning does not survive as well on beech or oak, where it is often found to split, crack and flake off, as it does on pear, walnut or lime, for example. The use of veneer may also prove problematic because adhesive failure leads to lifting which results in cracking of the surface decoration and loss of raised work.

Gum lac and many other natural resins have a tendency to yellow, darken and become insoluble (more polar) with age. Some resins, such as sandarac, are very brittle and films containing them become more so with age and tend to crack in service. Oleoresins, added to varnish films to increase their elasticity, also tend to become rather brittle once dry. Despite the attempt by japanners to balance the properties of the ingredients in their varnish formulations to achieve a result that would be as transparent and long-lasting as possible, varnishes do discolour and therefore alter the appearance of the pigment underneath. The collagen-based isinglass medium that was adopted for the production of blue and white grounds in recognition of this problem was itself apt to 'crack and fly off' if used too strong. If used too weak it is liable to adhesive failure. Some materials, particularly shellac (as opposed to seed lac), may have been adulterated or otherwise impaired in performance by the refinement process. Carbon blacks are very poor driers in oil paint due to the large amount of oil they absorb. A film of any other pigment laid over them is therefore very likely to crack as a result. Verdigris, a reactive and unstable pigment, was sometimes added to improve the drying quality of oils containing carbon black. Shellac films are sensitive to moisture and may bloom in high RH and on contact with liquid water. The use of spirit-based varnishes in japanning renders the entire finish vulnerable to damage from alcohol and moisture. The combined use of spirit soluble resins as medium and as varnish makes this type of decoration particularly difficult to clean and treat since the decoration is essentially locked up in the varnish. It is also very easily damaged during removal of layers of varnish applied in old restoration treatments.

The base colour was decorated after it had been varnished and rubbed down with an abrasive lubricated with oil. Despite subsequent efforts to degrease the surface it is probable that small amounts of oil would sometimes remain to impair the adhesion of applied raised decoration. Both silver and the base metals used to decorate surfaces are subject to tarnish by sulphur-containing gases present in the atmosphere and by the acidic nature of resins used as media and varnishes. Weak gum arabic water, recommended for attaching painted decoration, has been a factor in the deterioration of both pigment and metal powder decoration. Raised detail is especially vulnerable to damage and loss as a result of both wear and tear and adhesive failure caused by differential expansion between the detail and the substrate.

Nineteenth century oil-based japanning may be prone to delamination, particularly from papier mâché substrates.

Japanned objects are frequently found to have been overpainted, revarnished and restored. Examples of deteriorated japanned surfaces are illustrated in case studies by Ballardie (1994), Beale (1994) and Wachowiak and Williams (1994).

## 8.10   Adhesives

In practice, adhesives and adherends often fail long before theoretical calculations of bond strengths predict that they should. In theory, failure can occur within the adherend, along the adhesive interface or within the adhesive. In practice it will occur at the weakest point in the system. This normally involves cohesive failure in the adhesive layer (Kinloch, 1987). In the case of surface coatings with a layer structure (support, ground, paint, varnish etc.) each component of the laminate may potentially fail adhesively or cohesively.

It has been argued that all joint failure is actually cohesive and that even where failure has apparently occurred at the interface there is still a very thin layer of adhesive on the surface of the adherend (or, conversely, a thin layer of adherend on the surface of the adhesive). This suggests that the bulk properties of an adhesive can be different from those at the boundary layer of the interface and that it is the formation of a weak boundary layer which leads to adhesive failure. The theory of the weak boundary layer suggests that if a region of low cohesive strength exists at the interface between a substrate and a hardened adhesive, failure will occur at a lower stress level than predicted. High surface energy solids attract low surface energy contaminants and these may prevent a strong adhesive bond from forming if they are not displaced before joint formation. Weak boundary layers may also form in situ after the adhesive joint has been assembled.

Delollis (1973) has argued that this is an oversimplified generalization and has proposed an alternative mechanism of desorption of adhesive caused by contamination of the interface by water. This desorption may occur either through absorption of water by the adhesive followed by migration to the interface or by water diffusing along the adhesive-adherend interface.

Other factors which may contribute to adhesive joint failure include inherent differences between adhesive and adherend (e.g. density, coefficient of linear thermal expansion, modulus of elasticity etc.) air bubbles trapped at the interface or in the adhesive, swelling in response to exposure to polar molecules such as water, stress concentrations (e.g. caused by the geometry of the joint), contamination of the adherend surfaces, improper preparation of the adhesive (e.g. inadequate mixing of two pack adhesives or overcooking of animal glue) and deterioration of the adhesive in storage. The effects of inherent differences between materials are most likely to be concentrated at the interface and to produce stress concentrations in the boundary layer that may predispose to failure in this region.

## 8.11   Deterioration of specific materials

### 8.11.1   Oils and fats

The high susceptibility of fatty acids containing two or more double bonds to oxidation is the basis of their use as drying oils, the gradual conversion of liquid oil through soft gel to rubbery solid occurring as a result of free radical chain reactions (Mills and White, 1987). Oxidation, which at first is necessary for drying continues throughout the life of the film which becomes more oxidized and crosslinked and consequently more brittle and less soluble with time, especially under the influence of UV radiation. At the same time, oxidation reactions may occur that are degradative in nature leading to the formation of small molecules such as carboxylic acids. The influence of pigments (and other additions) on the behaviour of linseed oil films is very profound. As a clear exterior finish, linseed oil would fail under the influence of UV radiation in a matter of weeks but when used in pigmented finishes it is very satisfactory. Besides light, the influence of metal ions and the availability of oxygen, as determined by the thickness of the film, are of great importance. Yellowing is most marked in oils containing appreciable amounts of linolenic acid (e.g. linseed oil). The ester groups of fatty acid esters may be broken down by saponification or hydrolysis to yield glycerol and free fatty acids. Under appropriate conditions this form of degradation of fats can be achieved by micro-organisms such as *Staphylococcus* spp. and *Proteus* spp. The probable mechanisms involved in these reactions are outlined by Mills and White (1987). The behaviour of different oils and the influence of the refining process on their subsequent behaviour are discussed by Mayer (1982).

### 8.11.2 Waxes

Although waxes do not form a single chemical class the fact that they are fully saturated materials helps to explain their considerable chemical stability. The low melting point of many waxes renders them somewhat susceptible to loss of form through softening by heat from spotlights or direct sunlight penetration into buildings. Softer waxes will tend to retain dust on their surfaces and become grimy. Waxes become hard and brittle at low temperatures. Although waxes are susceptible to damage by micro-organisms, this is only likely to occur in practice in tropical climates, where other deterioration processes may be much more serious. Waxes have been shown to be remarkably resistant to tests of endurance that should be considered extreme in relation to normal exposure of furniture and related art objects indoors (Plenderleith and Cursiter, 1934).

### 8.11.3 Carbohydrates: sugars and polysaccharides

Starch has good resistance to autoxidation although starch paste films do become brittle with age, probably from gradual loss of moisture or as a result of mould growth to which starch is highly susceptible in damp conditions. Plant gums and mucilages are subject to dimensional change with changing RH.

### 8.11.4 Proteins

Proteins form a large group of huge diversity including materials such as bone, ivory, horn and tortoiseshell. This discussion focuses on the deterioration of proteins used as binding media and adhesives. It will be recalled from Chapter 4 that proteins have highly complex ordered structures. Following a change in this ordered structure the protein is said to be denatured and this results in altered physical and chemical properties.

Air-dry gelatine contains 8–15% moisture. Over-dry gelatine is brittle and probably somewhat denatured whilst damp gelatine may be readily attacked by moulds and putrefactive bacteria. These secrete proteolytic enzymes which break down the protein structure into constituent amino acids can be digested by the organism. Enzymatic hydrolysis is greatly affected by conditions of moisture, temperature and pH. Proteins are also slowly hydrolysed in the presence of moisture and more rapidly by acids and alkalis. Alkaline hydrolysis results in scission of peptide bonds and therefore strong alkalis should be avoided when cleaning protein based paint media, especially casein. Acid hydrolysis may be promoted by pollution from acidic gases. Low molecular weight alcohols tend to remove water structurally bound with proteins and may therefore change the chemical and physical properties of proteins making them more susceptible to other chemical agents present in the environment or in treatment materials. Certain organic solvents may react chemically with particular amino acids, cysteine for example reacts with trichloroethylene and even non-polar organic solvents can denature some proteins.

Proteins are not greatly susceptible to oxidative degradation. Oxidation of irradiated proteins probably only occurs in the presence of a photosensitizer which is able to pass its energy of excitation on to the protein molecule and thereby initiate the production of protein hydro peroxides and free radicals. Some natural organic dyestuffs found in native proteins and some artificial dyes used as pigments may function in this way. There may be some interaction of proteins with oxidizing lipids and protein-carbohydrate condensation reactions may also occur.

Because protein media are relatively very stable their interaction with light, heat, moisture, oxygen and pollutant gases has been much less extensively studied than that of the less stable resins and oils. However, further information on this topic is given by Birstein and Tul'Chinsky (1981), Grattan (1978) and Karpowicz (1981).

### 8.11.5 Natural resins and lacquers

Most natural resins yellow and degrade in ultraviolet light though they are by no means universally inferior in this respect to synthetic

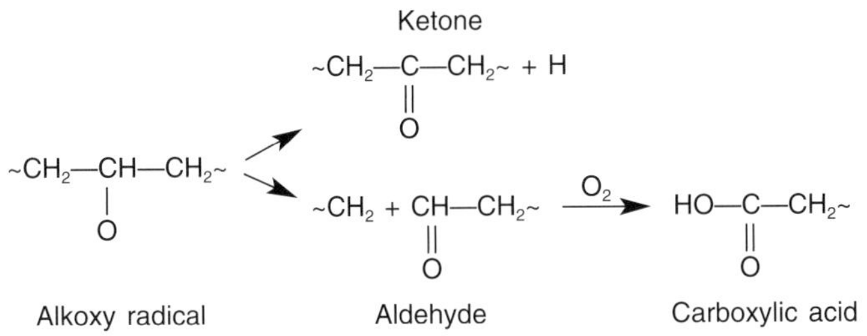

Ketone

~CH₂—C—CH₂~ + H

$$\sim CH_2-C-CH_2\sim \ + \ H$$
$$\quad\quad \parallel$$
$$\quad\quad O$$

~CH₂—CH—CH₂~
|
O

Alkoxy radical

~CH₂ + CH—CH₂~ $\xrightarrow{O_2}$ HO—C—CH₂~

Aldehyde                    Carboxylic acid

**Figure 8.10** Degradation of natural resins: alkoxy radicals may produce ketones or undergo scission to form aldehydes, which easily oxidize further to carboxylic acids

resins. All true resins are insoluble in water but their solubility in organic solvents may change on ageing due to crosslinking, degradation (chain scission) or the development of polar groups, accompanied by the absorption of oxygen. These changes are more fully explained by Copestake (1992) as follows.

Degradation of films of natural resins involves photochemically initiated autoxidation reactions followed by non-oxidative thermal processes leading to the familiar degradation phenomena such as yellowing, cracking, hazing, loss of gloss, change in solubility and fluorescence. The process involves homolytic bond cleavage (the breaking of chemical bonds so that neutral atoms or radicals are formed) during which free radicals are produced and a subsequent chain mechanism which leads to new free radicals (i.e. the autoxidation process is auto-catalytic). A variety of secondary autoxidation reactions can occur leading to products containing hydroxyl, carbonyl and carboxylic acid groups and carbon–carbon double bonds with consequent increase in polarity. Alkoxy radicals, for example, can produce ketones or undergo scission to form aldehydes which easily oxidize further to carboxylic acids (*Figure 8.10*). Certain functional groups (e.g. carbonyls, ether oxygens, carbon–carbon double bonds and tertiary carbon atoms) are more susceptible to autoxidation reactions than others and are subject to scission reactions under UV.

The chemical constituents of natural resins have high levels of unsaturation and contain many susceptible functional groups. The presence of hydro-peroxides also plays an important part in photo-oxidation and these are a large source of free radicals. Photo-oxidation leads to the production of acid groups, to the destruction of the original carbonyl species (probably the groups primarily responsible for absorption of UV radiation) present in the resin, to a considerable change in solubility and to increase in molecular weight in some cases. These changes occur to a much lesser extent under non-oxidative thermal ageing alone.

Attempts to slow down the degradation process should therefore focus on the beginning of the degradation chain. Reductions in light levels and elimination of UV radiation are thus primary concerns. Stabilizing additives such as the very powerful HALs (hindered amine light stabilizers) and UV absorbers are also useful in reducing the effects of degradation although due to the abundance of reactive functional groups it is not so easy to stabilize natural resins as it is to stabilize synthetic resins.

The polarity of dammar increases on exposure but no crosslinking or degradation seems to occur. Dammar films hold on to solvent and dry relatively slowly which may help to explain the formation of surface wrinkles during drying. Also, they may form an ammonium sulphate bloom if dried in humid environments. Dammar becomes more brittle and yellow with age though the yellowing and the polarity change can be reduced by the incorporation of an antioxidant (Horie, 1987). Mastic also shows changes in polarity, yellowing and embrittlement. It is more brittle than dammar and the effects of the changes in polarity are more profound. This led to its replacement by dammar as the picture varnish of choice prior to the adoption of newer synthetic materials. However, mastic remains easy to remove when this becomes necessary. Rosin oxidizes rapidly becoming yellow and increasingly sensitive to water and losing its initial high gloss.

Although shellac forms a hard, transparent film which is easily applied to give a smooth, durable and aesthetically pleasing finish which is easily repairable, it lacks resistance to damage by water and alcohol and deteriorates under conditions of high humidity. Commercially produced bleached and decolourized grades of shellac are altogether much less stable than their less refined coloured counterparts (e.g. garnet, button). Bleached shellac is notoriously unstable in solid form, as solutions and in varnish films. It is adequate for short-term use but is not considered suitable for long-term use. Solid bleached shellac should be stored below 15 °C. Decolourized shellac is unstable in solution and varnish films prepared from solutions which have been stored for more than six months are often found not to dry to a hard film but to remain tacky for prolonged periods. It is likely that at least some of the problems of stability of bleached and decolourized shellac arise from extended exposure to excessively high processing temperatures. Copestake (1992) demonstrated that heat ageing at 50 °C produced extensive crosslinking and insolubility in these materials.

Changes in films of shellac and other natural resins can be monitored by means of infra red and ultra violet spectroscopy and by differential scanning calorimetry as well as by visual observation of various physical and mechanical properties and simple solubility tests (Copestake, 1992). Additional general information on deterioration of resins is given in section 8.9.4. Further information can be found in Mantell *et al.* (1942) and Newman (1972).

### 8.11.6   Synthetic materials

The general mechanisms of deterioration of plastics and polymers have been briefly explored in section 8.8. The reader is referred to Horie (1987) for details of the deterioration of specific materials.

## 8.12   Deterioration of upholstery materials and structures

### *Preventive conservation*

Upholstered objects are multi-media pieces, each material reacting in different ways to the environment and to other materials. In theory, a constant ('set point') temperature and humidity level of 18 °C, 50% RH under UV filtered light (less than 75 micro watts per lumen) of around 50 lux is recommended for most upholstered pieces. In practice, recommended 'ideal' conditions are sometimes undesirable or unachievable and may need to be revised depending on the number, type, location and quantity of each individual material making up the unit, on previous exposure on the use to which a piece is to be put and on the resources available. Within a historic building, the conditions must take into account the needs of the building as well as those of the collection. The risk to an object will increase as conditions become more extreme in set point or in variation about that set point but it is difficult to be absolutely precise about the rate of change in damage with change in conditions. Nevertheless, target figures have been offered for guidance in the following text.

### 8.12.1   Top surface/simple structures

#### *Leather, skin and parchment*

The deterioration of leather, skin and parchment is due to a combination of chemical, physical, mechanical, environmental, insect and microbiological factors.

The main chemical factors that affect leather seat furniture concern the tanning processes used and environmental conditions. The tanning process may contribute to or may inhibit deterioration. Parchment and vellum (non-tanned skin) remain alkaline due to chemical traces that persist after processing. This may confer some protection against acid environments and biopredation. However, collagen may be degraded by pH levels above 9.5. Some nineteenth century vegetable tanned leathers, especially those which have been processed with sulphuric acid, are vulnerable to acid decay commonly known as 'red rot' (*Plate 1*). A pH of 3 or less is an indication of serious problems. Oxidation of the condensed tannins brings about a reddish coloration of the leather fibres, excessive dryness and brittleness and loss of strength. Absorption of sulphur dioxide and other acidic gases by vegetable tanned leathers from polluted air and their conversion to acids within the leather leads to a reaction in which the breakdown of the polypeptide chains occurs. Some leathers are much more prone than others to this phenomenon and this is further discussed by Calnan (1991) and by Hua and Haslam (1992). Red rotted leather will hydrolyse very rapidly on contact with water and aqueous treatments should therefore be avoided.

'Black rot', another form of leather deterioration, is caused by iron-catalysed oxidative attack that leads to symptoms very similar to those of red rot, except for colour. This can be caused by contact between leather and iron fasteners on upholstery (see Calnan, 1991). Attempts should be considered to slow down collagen deterioration by stabilization of leather which has a pH of 3.0 or less (or pH 3.5–5.0 for leather with black rot deterioration). Over-acidic leather may be stabilized and in some instances protected against further deterioration, by re-tanning with alum salts (see Calnan, 1989).

By definition, true leathers are resistant to bacterial action but may crack, lose strength and show other signs of physical deterioration associated with mould growth. Fungal enzymes can digest fats and carbohydrates present in leather and these may react with vegetable tannins to break down the tannin–protein complexes. Once tanned, collagen is resistant to insect attack but may be damaged incidentally as insects pass through or across the leather surface in search of other food.

The main physical factors that affect skin and leather seat furniture are stresses, mechanical abrasion and maintenance incurred when the object was a functional piece of furniture. Leather upholstery panels are particularly susceptible to overstretching, cracking, splitting at folds, stitched and glued seams and tack lines due to the weight of the sitter. Body oils, waxes, polishes and over-application of dressing render leather dark and brittle. As with chemical factors, the rate and type of physical deterioration is directly affected by fluctuations in environmental conditions.

Skin and leather are both anisotropic and hygroscopic. Different rates of expansion and contraction between leather and seat frame, due to fluctuations in RH, will create areas of stress, and perhaps tearing, in the leather at

the point of attachment with metal fasteners. Different animal skins and leathers may respond differently to these factors. For example, parchment and vellum are considerably more sensitive to changes in RH than leather. Prolonged exposure to high levels of RH may cause buckling, staining and mould growth; low levels may lead to embrittlement. Temperature influences the rate of chemical reactions and fluctuating temperatures may cause structural damage as the leather expands and contracts.

RH should preferably be maintained within the range 45–55% with fluctuations kept as small as possible and temperature in the range 18–24 °C. High light levels and UV radiation will cause leather to fade. Light will also damage the physical structure of leather, by breaking chemical bonds in the collagen polymers, causing it to become more brittle and light levels should therefore be kept low (50–100 lux). For further information on the deterioration of these materials, see Calnan (1991).

### Rush, reed and cane

As for all organic materials, the useful life of these materials will depend on their original quality, usage and environment. The authors' personal observations lead to the view that most objects do not retain their original rush or cane and that a 10–25 year life is fairly typical. However, Egyptian examples do survive as grave goods. These materials are prone to embrittlement, yellowing and darkening. Loss of elasticity is due to physical and chemical processes including loss of moisture from the material and chemical degradation by oxidation and acid hydrolysis (Florian *et al.*, 1990). Acidity may come from the breakdown of the material itself or from acid contamination in the environment. Light causes fading of many coloured materials and degradation of lignin and related material causing it to become more water-soluble and yellowed. Both yellowing and darkening are a result of oxidative reactions. Dry cellulose is inflexible or brittle, but cellulose with 12% moisture content at 60–80% RH is quite flexible. Water therefore acts as a plasticizer for cellulose (Florian *et al.*, 1990). High moisture levels may cause excessive swelling leading to irreversible bond breakage and deformation of cellulose fibres and also contribute to other degradation reactions, such as acid hydrolysis, in which water is involved. Particulate soiling lodges easily in interwoven structures which may then abrade the material, contributing to loss of strength or the destruction of a surface. Acidic pollutants in both gaseous and particulate forms may also contribute to degradation processes (Florian *et al.*, 1990).

Cellulose is prone to enzymatic degradation caused by cellulytic bacteria and fungi in damp conditions, which can result in pitting of the surface (visible under magnification) and staining. Fibrous materials interwoven in furniture are subject to biopredation by a variety of insects which may feed on the material or on coatings or dressings applied to it. Wicker work seems to be highly susceptible to attack by wood boring insects, both furniture beetle and wood boring weevil. This damage is evident because of flight holes in the surface of the material and frass left behind by the feeding larvae. The material may be very much weakened by the attack and may seem unnaturally light in weight if the attack has been severe. The susceptibility of this type of material may be due to the high water content as the materials are soaked before and during construction. Also, water soaking or spraying was often advocated as a renovative/restorative treatment during the life of these materials. Good environmental control is advocated as a preventive measure. Rush-bottomed seats are more likely to harbour vermin than cane and rodents are a risk to straw-work furnishings (Doussy, 1990).

Over a period of use the materials lose the ability to recover shape and may become 'seated'; that is the seat takes up a curve below the rails. This puts extra stress on the material in use causing rubbing along the rail edges which may eventually become breaks. Sometimes an area of weaving may break, which leads to a rapid loss in strength of the structure.

When in use, objects may be subject to restorative or maintenance treatments. Some such treatments might be described as popular myths. For example, over-dry or embrittled wood, leather and plant materials are each popularly supposed to benefit from 'feeding' with oils or waxes. In fact, these treatments are unnecessary and may inhibit moisture regain and contribute to degradation reactions. Alternatively oils, waxes, varnishes, dyes, or paints may be applied to 'revive' colour or to consolidate friable or delaminating materials. Colouring does nothing to improve mechanical strength and may lead to the impression that material is stronger than it really is. Attempts to repair an existing structure with new material may result in additional and unbearable stress being imposed on the existing dry and brittle deteriorated original.

The recommended environment for rush, reed and cane is a steady relative humidity between 40% and 60%. In low humidity these materials become brittle and at high humidity are subject to bio-predation. A temperature below 25 °C is recommended to avoid embrittlement. Exhibition light levels of 50–100 lux combined with the elimination of ultra violet radiation are suggested. Acid-free, unbuffered storage materials are preferred. Dust protection is advocated as the structures are liable to trap surface dust. Material should be checked twice a year for pest infestation. For further information on these materials see Florian *et al.* (1990) and Doussy (1990).

### Textiles

Textiles are under a variety of physical stresses related to manufacture or construction, including stretching and flexing. How well the textile fibre responds and recovers from these applied forces largely depends on the fibre type, construction and condition. For example, webbing constructed in reverse twill weave with jute thread is most resistant to stretching, an essential feature of seat webbing. This is due to a combination of the fibre and weave types. However, jute degrades very quickly compared, for example, to linen. Therefore in the long term, in the same environment, linen webbing of identical construction would be less resistant to stretching but more resistant to deterioration. Either fibre in a plain weave would be less resistant to stretching. The two fibre types combined together in a plain weave or reverse twill would possess a combination of qualities. On ageing, stretched textiles may no longer have the strength to be re-stretched to the same dimensions (particularly after wet cleaning). This is most relevant if the intention is to remove and re-apply a top cover to its upholstered frame. A fold or crease at corners of upholstery, or pleats in curtains may eventually become a crack. Fibres are difficult to identify when degraded, for example the scales on hair fibres, an identifying characteristic, wear away.

### Chemical degradation

Light, particularly ultra violet radiation, acts as a source of energy for photochemical reactions that occur in the presence of oxygen and moisture. The cellulose molecules which are the main constituent of vegetable fibres in cotton, linen and paper and the protein fibres in wool and silk are colourless. They absorb electromagnetic radiation in the ultra violet range. These fibres are not found in their pure state in objects but are nearly always combined with dyes, mordants, various kinds of dirt, residual chemical treatments and other impurities which may promote degradation reactions. When one or other of the component molecules of these systems absorbs a photon of light energy, a number of things may happen. First, the energy absorbed may be dissipated as heat when the excited molecule returns to its ground state, without chemical reaction occurring. Secondly, the energy may be transferred to another molecule which itself does not absorb light. The water vapour and oxygen in the air may be energized in this way and the activated oxygen and hydrogen peroxide thus formed are capable of oxidizing both the fibre and its dye. Another possibility is that the absorbed light energy may cause a direct reaction of a dye with its fibre (the dyes concerned would contain carbonyl groups, quinoid configurations or azine groups). Dyes on wool in particular may fade by oxidizing the fibre, by removal of hydrogen atoms from reactive methyl, methylene and methine groups on keratin, being themselves reduced in the process. The same principle applies to the cellulose in cotton.

As a result of reactions of the type outlined above areas of textile exposed to light become brittle. Fibres are weakened by the breaking of the long molecules to which they owe their strength, with broken fibres leading to tears and loss of textile. Coloured decomposition products stain fibres yellow and the dyes fade or darken. A further complication that may arise is that the degradation may increase the danger of damage through conservation procedures such as vacuuming and washing, particularly in the case of alkaline washing of degraded cellulose.

Heat or low levels of relative humidity cause embrittlement of fibres. Extremely low moisture content may render fibres permanently inflexible (Cooke, 1988), for example due to denaturing of proteins. High moisture content accelerates the rate of photo-degradation and in warm conditions may induce mould growth. Rapid fluctuations in relative humidity levels will cause temporary stresses to be set up in the fibres as they swell and contract within the twisted, interlaced textile structures. These tensions and stresses may cause permanent structural damage and breakage of degraded fibres.

Generally speaking, cellulose materials are very sensitive to acid attack but more resistant to alkaline environments whilst proteins are resistant to acids but more susceptible to attack by alkalis. However, strong acids can destroy both cellulose and protein, silk being the most vulnerable protein fibre (Landi, 1992/1985). In cellulose, hydroxyl groups become transformed to acidic groups as a result of photochemical reactions. Degraded textiles are more sensitive to alkaline and acidic conditions than new textiles. One major source of acid is polluted air. In particular, sulphur dioxide combined with moisture may generate sulphuric acid. This reaction occurs in air, on surfaces and with objects containing a layer of adsorbed moisture Also, the materials making up the upholstered unit may themselves be a source of pollution. For example, most woods produce acetic acid as a result of gradual hydrolysis of acetyl groups (esters) in the hemicellulose fraction. Sugar acids are also present in wood. Proteinaceous upholstery materials such as horsehair and wool (especially felted wool) may produce sulphur-containing gases such as hydrogen sulphide as sulphur-containing amino acids (cysteine and cystine), present in these materials, breakdown. These may in turn interact with other materials, contributing to the overall degradation of the composite upholstered unit. For example, sulphuric acid may assist in the corrosion of iron tacks anchoring under-structure materials. In turn, these corrosion products may stain the textile (usually orange brown coloration) and may also promote tendering reactions caused by light.

### Biodeterioration

The major insect pests of textiles are carpet beetles and clothes moths which attack mainly wool, silk and other proteinaceous materials. Cotton materials are not normally at risk of attack by carpet beetles or clothes moths.

Several species of the family Dermestidae are widespread in museums and may cause serious damage to proteinaceous materials such as silk, wool and leather used in upholstery. The most common species of carpet beetle is the variegated carpet beetle (*Anthrenus verbasci*) but others such as the Guernsey carpet beetle (*Anthrenus sarnicus*) are similar in habits and appearance. Damage to textiles is caused by the short, fat hairy larvae of these insects, which are often referred to as 'woolly bear'. The larvae rapidly destroy proteinaceous textiles, fur and feathers and develop by a series of larval moults, leaving behind their empty cast skins which frequently provide the first sign of an attack. Six to eight moults is normal but in adverse conditions the number of moults may be much higher. The insect pupates in the last larval skin which is left behind when the adult emerges. These large moults may be found in places which are some distance from infestation centres because the larvae have moved away to find a safe pupation site. Because carpet beetle larvae are small and can exist on dust, hair, fibres from clothing and dead insects, they do not normally have to move far for food. However, larvae are highly mobile, gaining access through cracks and crevices to store rooms, display cases and other vulnerable areas containing food sources to which they are attracted. Within a major infestation, larvae may be found at several different developmental stages. A characteristic of new local infestations is the predominance of small larvae. *Anthrenus* spp. are able to tolerate humidities as low as 20%–30%. The small round adult beetle are 2–3 mm long and have patterned markings of grey and gold. Adult beetles are phototropic and are attracted to short wavelength ultra violet radiation. They fly from the safety of a dark area where pupation has taken place towards the light in order to leave the building to mate. Thus adults may be found on window sills, particularly of north facing windows, during peak emergence months of June, July and August. Mating frequently occurs on flowers (especially *Spirea* spp.) and adult females then re-enter the building through chimneys, air vents and cracks to lay their eggs. However, adults do not always have to leave the building to mate and it is thus possible for an infestation to become established and spread despite meticulous sealing of entry and exit points. Eggs are laid in dark crevices, usually close to a food source for the newly emerging larvae. Breeding reservoirs inside buildings are usually associated with poor hygiene, although objects may also become breeding reservoirs. Birds nests, feathers, bird droppings and broken birds' eggs provide a rich source of food for larvae and are typical external reservoirs. For further information on carpet beetle and its control see Blyth (1997), Hillyer and Blyth (1992), Tímár-Balázsy and Eastop (1998).

Several species of clothes moth attack and damage textiles of which the webbing clothes moth (*Tineola bissellielia*) and the case bearing clothes moth (*Tinea pellionella*) are the most common. Clothes moths prefer vitamin B, sulphur and salts found in sweat and urine and are attracted to dark humid, dirty surroundings and soiled and degraded proteinaceous materials, particularly wool based textiles which are rich in sulphur containing amino acids. The adults are small dull grey-brown moths which scuttle around rather than fly and which fold their wings along their backs when at rest. Eggs may be laid on fur, feathers, wool, or soiled silk. The complete life cycle generally takes a year but may be shorter under favourable conditions. The case bearing clothes moth spins an open fronted silk case around itself which it then carries with it as it moves across the textile, leaving a trail of partially eaten material and fragments of excreta or frass. The larva moults within the case and on maturity pupates before emerging as the adult moth. The webbing clothes moth also spins silk but produces a sheet or tunnel of silk under which it feeds on the textiles surface. Damage from this source is evident by the large amount of silk webbing and frass present. Adult moths can fly in from outside and birds' nests under eaves of buildings are a source from which infestation may arise. Other moths that may cause damage to textiles include the brown clothes moth (*Hofmannophila pseudospretella*) the tapestry moth (*Trichophaga tapetzella*) and the white shouldered house moth (*Endrosis sarcitrella*). As with other insects the best chance of prevention and treatment is provided by correct identification of the insect(s) causing the problem.

Mould can also damage textiles. The dark stains, a by product of enzymes produced by the organisms to breakdown the fibres, may degrade the fibres.

Chemicals used for remedial and preventive treatments of textiles against insect attack are discussed in Chapters 6 and 7 but it is worth mentioning here that some of these chemicals may themselves cause damage to textiles as well as being hazardous to those carrying out the treatment or subsequently handling treated material. Methyl bromide may attack proteins such as keratin that contain sulphur bridges, accelerating their deterioration. It may also damage rubber and imparts an unpleasant smell to leather. Ethylene oxide is a suspected carcinogen. It can soften glues and reacts with cellulose causing permanent alterations. It also reacts with protein causing premature ageing. Naphthalene is alkaline. It may affect dyes, soften varnishes and promote the corrosion of some metals. Paradichlorobenzene can damage dyes, feathers and leather. Sulphuryl fluoride ($SO_2F_2$), registered in the USA as Vikane, though thought to be one of the least reactive fumigants, may react with metals and if mixed with water vapour may form sulphuric acid ($H_2SO_4$). Further information on these interactions may be obtained from Peltz and Rossal (1983). Because of these specific reactions and concern for the health, safety and welfare of personnel and the environment, chemical insecticides are much less commonly employed than they once were. For textiles, treatment by freezing or by prolonged exposure to inert gases is now generally preferred to active chemical methods the use of which is now generally confined to sanitizing the built environments where textiles may be stored or displayed. Further information on disinfestation and disinfection may be obtained from Tímár-Balázsy and Eastop (1998).

## Structure of textiles

The very structure of a textile may assist in its degradation. For example, the pile on velvet or plush may be less resistant to mechanical abrasion than the ground weave, resulting in pile loss, particularly if the ground weave has weakened, reducing its ability to hold pile yarn in place. Thread floats from satin weave and warp faced braids are more vulnerable to wear than the heavier and more protected weft threads. In combination weaves, for example silk warp and wool weft, one fibre may degrade more quickly than the other rendering the cloth weaker in one direction.

Other examples include failure of adhesive in bonded textiles. An example of an adhesive bonded textile is an open weave cloth which has been adhered to a second layer of cloth to give the decorative top layer the extra body required to make it sufficiently robust to be used as an upholstery covering. After wet cleaning, canvas work panels, particularly those which have been tent stitched, may become distorted and stamped designs may loose some definition. In moist conditions glazed fabrics are prone to mould attack because some dressings and glazes, such as starch and gelatine, are hygroscopic and therefore retain moisture and contain nutrients which may support fungal life.

## Dyes and finishes

Following the absorption of light energy by a dye molecule various photo-physical processes may occur which result in the absorbed energy being converted harmlessly to heat (McLaren, 1983). Alternatively, in the presence of oxygen and moisture chemical reactions can occur which result in a shift in the wavelength at which they absorb light, a phenomenon known as fading. A slight shift will result in some loss of colour, a large shift will result in total loss of perceived colour. Many dyes of moderate resistance to light are faded primarily by the visible light they absorb (McLaren, 1956). The mechanisms of fading, which are both highly specific and highly complex, have been reviewed by Bentley *et al.* (1974), Egerton and Morgan (1970), Griffiths (1972), Leaver (1980) and Meier (1977). Some dyes are pH-sensitive and their colour may change as the textile becomes acidic on ageing, or is neutralized or made alkaline by wet cleaning.

Paper pH testing strips make use of this property. The iron mordants used in the printing and dyeing of dark colours accelerate degradation of the fibre (Storey, 1978). Iron acts as a catalyst for the conversion of sulphur dioxide to sulphuric acid. The acidic conditions combined with the energy from light cause degradation. Dyes may bleed either in wet cleaning or in high humidities. Sulphur dyes contribute to sulphur reactions.

Another type of reaction that may occur is the photochemical degradation of textile fibres catalysed by the presence of certain dyes of high light fastness, a phenomenon known as tendering. Various direct, acid, basic, sulphur, vat and disperse dyes of many different colours sensitize the photochemical degradation of cotton, viscose, rayon, silk, nylon and acetate fibres, providing oxygen is present. When cotton dyed with a tendering dye is exposed to light under moist conditions hydrogen peroxide is formed. The complex mechanisms by which this may occur are discussed by McLaren (1983). Some of the energy of the excited molecules may be transferred to oxygen molecules promoting them to an excited state in which they may react with water present in moist air to form hydrogen peroxide. Alternatively, the dye in an excited state may react with the substrate by a process of hydrogen abstraction to create a 'free radical centre' which is then attacked by molecular oxygen. In both mechanisms, the dye behaves as a catalyst for photo-tendering by oxygen in the air. The relative importance of the two mechanisms remains unclear but in any case it is not necessary to propose an exclusive mechanism. For further information on this subject see Tímár-Balázsy and Eastop (1998).

Finishes also affect the textile and its degradation. Starches are foodstuffs for moulds which may stain textiles during their digestive process. Formaldehyde is used in finishing some textiles and in some leather tanning processes. It is often used in the manufacture of 'permanent press' fabrics, as the primary crosslinking agent. Exposure of proteinaceous materials to formaldehyde may result in loss of elasticity (Carpenter and Hatchfield, 1986). Animal glue, for example, is crosslinked by formaldehyde. Formaldehyde is a reducing agent that can discolour metal oxide pigments

and make cotton, wool and leather brittle by linking two alcohol or amino groups in the polymers making up those materials (Berndt, 1987). Formaldehyde can also be transformed in the presence of oxygen to formic acid which can react with a variety of materials in a similar manner to acetic acid. For further information on this subject refer to Tímár-Balázsy and Eastop (1998).

### Preventive conservation of textiles

The recommended environment for textiles is a constant relative humidity within the range 50–60%. In conditions of low relative humidity these materials are prone to embrittlement whilst in high RH levels they are subject to bio-predation. A temperature of 18 °C is recommended as a reasonable compromise between the needs of objects, people and effective RH control. Exposure to light should be as low as possible. Light should be filtered to remove UV radiation and should be kept to the minimum needed for the purpose, preferably not exceeding 50–100 lux for continuous exposure. Air should be filtered to remove particulate pollutants and gases such as oxides of sulphur and nitrogen if possible. Removal of particulate pollution is probably the greatest single cause of damage and it is therefore most important to reduce the frequency with which this needs to be done, particularly for textiles with degraded fibres. In storage, materials in contact with textiles or in close vicinity to them should be acid-free. Unbuffered materials are recommended. However, buffered materials can be used next to most cellulosic materials. When handling textiles, gloves should be worn to protect them from acidic and oily skin deposits. Alternatively, where gloves themselves might pose a risk, hands should be washed and thoroughly dried as required during handling. For further information see Landi (1992/1985), Flury-Lemberg (1988) and Tímár-Balázsy and Eastop (1998).

### Plastics

Plastics and rubbers, whether synthetic or natural, deteriorate continuously from the time of manufacture. Deterioration of plastics and polymers is discussed in general terms in section 8.8. At the molecular level, polymer chain sizes, structural organization and other inter-chain interactions are the main features that determine mechanical properties. Moisture, heat, light, oxygen and chemical pollutants are the main sources of chemical actions from which changes result. Variations in polymer morphology can also arise from purely physical causes (Crighton, 1988). The deterioration of many of the synthetic materials in early use in upholstery is clearly apparent in artefacts already too fragile to display. The most problematic deterioration is usually the collapse of the structure. Latex foam is frequently found to be so embrittled as to crumble at the touch so that a grip on an edge is sufficient to crush it. Polyurethane foam becomes soft and tacky so that a gripped edge collapses, sticks to itself and does not regain its shape (Gill and Eastop, 2001). Chemical degradation of polymers is affected by such factors as conformational stress, points of adhesion, storage and climatic history; that is, physical factors may make chemical degradation critical in one object over another. This is further discussed below. This section, based mainly on the work of Griffith (1997) will explore the deterioration of rubber, polyurethane, PVC and cellulose nitrate.

### Rubber

Rubber components are relatively common in furniture especially in foam fillings of the 1950s and 1960s. Natural rubber contains 95% cis-1,4-polyisoprene and 5% resins, gums and protein. Latex foam rubber contains in addition organic accelerators, antioxidants, loading materials and softeners. The most basic mechanism of degradation of rubber is by oxidation, a free radical chain reaction which causes embrittlement, loss of strength and discoloration (Kelen, 1983). The effects of this process can be seen in *Figure 8.11*. This is greatly accelerated by elevated temperature and by exposure to short wavelength radiation but relative humidity does not appear to be an important factor at room temperature (Shashoua and Thomsen, 1993). In upholstered furniture, light damage has been observed on the undersurface of rubber webbing caused by reflected light from a polished floor or through a textile covering. These materials should therefore be protected from light even during production. Ozone, sulphur dioxide and nitrogen dioxide air

**Figure 8.11** Detail of degraded latex rubber cushion for 'Mambo Chair' designed by Michael Inchbald in 1954

pollutants are also damaging. Stress cracks caused by flexing of these materials allows air to penetrate deeper into the material allowing oxidation to occur beyond the surface.

Latex rubber foams used in upholstery are susceptible to mechanical deterioration caused by stress and tension imposed by the weight load of the sitter and by mechanical abrasion. These effects are much more noticeable in oxidized material. In the Lady Chair of 1951, designed by Zanuso, the structural upholstery is of foamed rubber laid over a support of Pirelli rubber webbing (Gill, 1990). Chemically the upholstery and webbing were very similar but the way the material was expected to perform is different. The foam is under compression below a taut top covering, the webbing is under tension when applied and subject to further tension in use. When degraded, the foam loses its ability to recover after compression and the webbing loses the ability to stretch further when weight is applied. The chair then loses its ability to perform its designed functions because of the physical consequences of chemical degradation (see also Gill and Eastop, 2001).

Two important types of ageing of rubbers are shelf ageing and atmospheric cracking. Shelf ageing occurs at ambient temperatures in the dark and is due to autoxidation. Atmospheric cracking is the term given to the reaction which occurs when rubber artefacts are exposed to UV. In addition to the oxidation mechanism, attack by ozone (ozonolysis) may take place (Shashoua and Thomsen,

1993). This is a process in which ozone reacts with non-stretched rubber by adding to double bonds to form ozonides. When all the surface double bonds are consumed, the reaction stops but when mechanical stresses are applied and more unsaturated molecules are exposed, the process continues. Cracks propagate and eventually cause complete failure (see *Figure 8.11*).

Rubber is best stored in cool, dry, dark, well ventilated, dust-free environments. Rubber could be stored to advantage in a low oxygen environment (see Chapter 6) or failing this, in well ventilated conditions.

### *Polyurethanes*

Polyurethanes (PUs) are extremely versatile. It is possible to make a variety of different PUs with different physical and mechanical properties suitable for different applications. They are generally synthesized by a two-step reaction (*Figure 8.12*). The starting material is usually a short chain polyester or polyether with hydroxyl groups at each end (a polyol) which is reacted with an excess of a diisocyanate to form a prepolymer. In the second stage the prepolymer units are linked into a long chain polymer by reaction with a chain extender, usually a diol or diamine (Hepburn, 1982; Kerr and Batcheller, 1993). When the chain extender is a diol the polyurethane polymer contains urethane links; when an amine is used, urea links are formed. If carbon dioxide is released during the reaction a foam is produced.

Polyurethanes are degraded by exposure to light and heat and are inherently susceptible to hydrolytic degradation (Crighton, 1988). Photo-degradation by UV radiation and visible light, the main cause of deterioration, may be accelerated by moisture and ammonia and produces a variety of breakdown products. It is possible to stabilize PU to light degradation and provide some resistance to UV by incorporating antioxidants. Polyurethanes do not usually tear or crumble in service but they soften and loose height and the shape distorts, especially initially. The coated fabrics and imitation leathers made with PUs commonly crack, peel away from the substrate or become tacky so that folds stick to each other. The yellowing of PU is an inherent problem particularly with foams made from aromatic diiso-

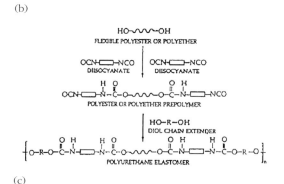

(a)

(b)

the urethane linkages in a polyurethane

(c)

**Figure 8.12** Polyurethanes
(*a*) A urethane group
(*b*) The urethane linkages in a polyurethane
(*c*) Polyurethanes are synthesized in a two-step reaction. For convenience, the functional groups of the generic monomer types are shown, whilst the parts of the molecules that do not participate in polymerization are indicated with wavy lines (di-alcohol, or diol components) or rectangular boxes (diisocyanate components) (Hepburn, 1982)

cyanates. The weak points on the molecule are the various reactive bonds in the main polymer chain such as urethane, ester, ether, amide urea and biuret, though these bonds vary in their resistance to hydrolysis and oxidation (*Figure 8.13*) (Kerr and Batcheller, 1993). PUs based on polyesters are much more susceptible to hydrolysis than those based on polyethers. Catalysts, such as tertiary amines which remain from the polymerization of PU foams, appear to accelerate degradation by light causing both chain scission and crosslinking to occur. When scission of the urethane link occurs new, polar, amino groups and

(a)

ESTER HYDROLYSIS

NO HYDROLYTICALLY-SUSCEPTIBLE GROUPS IN POLYETHER

(b)

URETHANE CHAIN SCISSION

**Figure 8.13** Degradation of polyurethanes: (*a*) degradation by hydrolysis; (*b*) degradation by oxidation

carboxyl groups are formed in the polymer. Over a period of time, crosslinking continues and the polymer becomes weak and brittle. Mechanical stress, such as stretching and flexing, then causes the material to break down completely (*Figure 8.14*).

PU objects should be kept in a cool, dry, dark, dust-free environment in conditions of stable RH and temperature with RH in the range 40–55%. The use of dust covers made from Tyvek®, a non-woven, bonded polyethylene sheet material, is recommended. Removal of the antistatic finish from Tyvek® before use with artefacts containing metal components is also recommended (Tímár-Balázsy and Eastop, 1998). The progress of oxidation of PU could be delayed by storage in low oxygen environments (see Chapter 6).

### Polyvinyl chloride (PVC)

The degradation of PVC is caused by both crosslinking and chain scission. Degradation may be initiated by heat or light energy leading to thermal or photo oxidation. Colour changes are due to photo oxidation. A chain unzipping reaction (*Figure 8.15a*) that leads to sequential loss of hydrogen chloride (HCl) molecules along the backbone of the polymer is accompanied by discoloration and by unfavourable changes in mechanical and electrical properties (*Figure 8.15b*). The HCl produced is auto-catalytic and once dehydrochlorination is initiated the reaction will proceed quite quickly if the HCl liberated remains in the vicinity of the object. The mechanism of this reaction and the use of Zeolite pellets as adsorbents to remove the HCl produced from storage and display environments are discussed by Shashoua

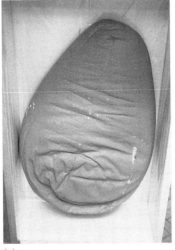

(a)

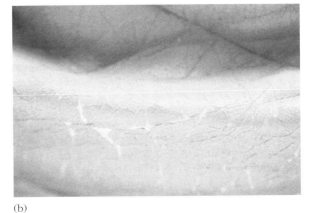

(b)

**Figure 8.14** Sacco (bean bag or bean sack chair), designed by Design Studi, Turin, Italy, 1969: (*a*) in storage; (*b*) breakdown of polymer structure in the polyurethane textile of Sacco

~CH$_2$ – CHCl – CH$_2$ – CHCl~
→ ~CH = CH – CH = CH~ + HCl

(a)

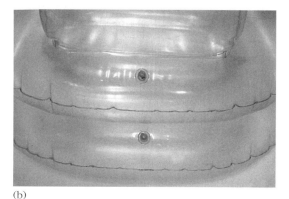

(b)

**Figure 8.15** A chain unzipping reaction
(*a*) Degradation of polyvinyl chloride – the splitting off of one hydrogen chloride (HCl) molecule from the polymer backbone encourages adjacent (HCl) molecules to split off, 'unzipping' the polymer chain. As the HCl molecules break, a series of conjugated double bonds form within the polymer chain. As the length of these sequences increases, the colour of the polymer shifts from white to yellow, red, brown and black (Shashoua, 1996)
(*b*) Detail of 'Blow', an inflatable chair designed by Design Studio, Milan (1967) and manufactured by Zanotta Poltrone from PVC. Yellowing is evidence of the process of polymer degradation

(1996). PVC should be stored in stable conditions of temperature, free from dust and as cool as possible between 40–55% RH.

### Cellulose nitrate

Cellulose nitrate has been used in upholstery components but is also important to furniture in the form of lacquer finishes and continues to be used as a conservation material for the coating of metals and as an adhesive used with stone, metal, ceramics and glass despite the fact that it is potentially a very unstable material (Selwitz, 1988). It degrades at room temperature by a combination of oxidation and hydrolysis which are catalysed by the presence of acid impurities and accelerated by light. These reactions result in a reduction of molecular weight and in the production of nitric oxide and nitric acid. Progressive yellowing to dark brown occurs and the changes are accompanied by foul odours of nitrogen

oxides. Moisture causes hydrolysis which leads to the emission of nitric acid (HNO$_3$), thus accelerating degradation. Cellulose nitrate is inherently brittle in the absence of a plasticizer and camphor is commonly found to have been used for this purpose. Loss of plasticizer, frequently evident from the odour of camphor which has migrated to the surface, is a common form of deterioration for this material. Degraded cellulose nitrate may be discoloured, cracked, warped, crazed, sweating or sticky with droplets of acid and can disintegrate into a heap of crystalline material. Objects which contain cellulose nitrate should not be enclosed but should be stored in cool, dark, generally dry, well-ventilated conditions to allow air to circulate freely and to vent gases formed by decomposition. Williams (1988) and Reilly (1991) have both published excellent guidelines for the storage of this material. For further information on the degradation of cellulose nitrate lacquers used on furniture see Calhoun (1953), Hagar (1983), Johnson (1976), Koob 1982, Selwitz (1988) and Shashoua *et al.* (1992).

### Trimmings

Textile trimmings are vulnerable to mechanical abrasion when furniture is in use, particularly along front seat rails and crest rails. Textile trimmings which are part of window furnishings, for example pelmets and curtains, are particularly vulnerable to light damage, the results of which can be seen in tendering and weakness. The stresses between the different materials constituting the trim may accelerate deterioration, for example stress on the threads from which a heavy tassel or bead hangs. Threads such as silk floss wrapped around thin strips of vellum or wood moulds often wear away along protruding or sharp edges. The rate of degradation of the thread may be accelerated by the nature of the material which it surrounds (the alkalinity of vellum, the acidity of wood). Insect infestation can be a problem as deep fringes provide an ideal breeding and feeding ground. Additionally, the wooden moulds which are a basis for many trimmings are prone to furniture beetle attack. The larval feeding activity may cause the mould to collapse. The emerging adults cut holes through textile coverings which may lead to rapid unravelling. Adhesives holding trims to the frame may render fibres weak and brittle or discolour on aging. Gimp pins, tacks and nails damage trim physically when driven through the trim and chemically when they corrode. Brass nails are susceptible to corrosion in the presence of various acidic gases and vapours. This may weaken the nail, particularly where the shank meets the head. The nail shanks may become bent and twisted when they are hammered into a wooden frame. Both types of damage are problematic only when removal and reapplication to the frame is required. Nails may be finished with lacquers or gilding. This may be abraded in use or easily damaged in removal and replacement during treatments. For further information see Berkhouwer (1990) and Westerman Bulgarella (1987).

### Understructures

Upholstery understructure materials are susceptible to biopredation and the same physical, mechanical and chemical degradation as outlined in the sections on textiles, elastomerics and hardware. Light is less of an issue with the inner-most concealed layers, however, photochemical degradation has been observed on exposed webbing, base cloth and bottom linings as a result light reflecting up from a polished floor onto the underside of seat furniture. The fibres of loose fillings such as horsehair and coir fibre often break as a result of degradation. Denser fillings such as straw, ulva marina and tow become embrittled and also break down. The rubber in rubber-ized fillings crumbles and polyurethane becomes soft and sticky. In all cases the fillings become less resilient, distorting the profile of the upholstery under-structure.

There are three major contributing factors which accelerate the degradation process of these structures which relate broadly to manufacture, usage and intervention. The first is the interrelated stresses occurring between the materials due to the way they are built up on the frame. For example springs pushing against the adjacent upholstery layers may cause the webbing to break and consequently, the springs to drop. Similarly, the twine holding the springs under compression may deteriorate, causing the springs to rip through the overlying upholstery layers, resulting in a deformed profile. Additional stresses occur

between tensioned upholstery material and frame as they respond to fluctuating humidity levels. For example, tensioned vellum may split, a leather panel may pull away from point of attachment or a textile glued to a table top may buckle, lift or tear as the wood substrate responds to RH fluctuations. The second factor is the mechanical damage created while the object was a functional piece of seat furniture. The weight load of the sitter imposes tension, stress and mechanical abrasion upon the upholstered frame. Sweat and accidentally spilled drinks do affect top covers but are not usually in contact with understructures. The third factor is a result of later upholstery interventions. As a result part of the original understructure may be replaced with new materials causing additional strain and damage to the remaining upholstery and frame. Further information on this topic is provided by French (1990), Gill and Eastop (2001) and Williams (1990).

### Hardware

The main chemical factors that effect the metals fasteners are environmental. High levels of relative humidity, the acidity of the surrounding wood and the sulphur compounds in rubber, leather, wool and certain textile finishes will cause some metals, particularly iron and copper alloys (brass and bronze), to corrode. Tack and nail heads and staple bars become weakened and eventually the corrosion products (copper carbonates from copper and its alloys, rust from iron) bond with the surrounding upholstery making removal difficult. Similarly the shanks become locked into the wood. In this condition it is quite difficult to remove the tack or staple without the head or bar snapping off. Fibres become acidic as they degrade. Metal ions catalyse the degradation of cellulose in the presence of oxygen and moisture. Carbohydrates present in cellulose base polymers may be a contributing factor in corrosion reactions with copper ions. Sulphuric acid produced by degradation processes and the burning of fossil fuels corrodes metals which in turn act as catalysts for further degradation. Wood produces organic acids which attack metals and textile fibres. Metal support systems (compression and tension springs) are vulnerable to corrosion attack and metal fatigue which may result in permanent distortion or complete breakage of the metal at the weakest point, that is the point under most pressure. Environmental conditions for the care of metals in general have been discussed above (section 8.4). Since metals are subject to corrosion at high relative humidities it is recommended that a constant RH of not more than 55% is maintained. If the metal is already in a corroded state the RH should be at least 10% lower provided that this is not detrimental to the other materials of which the object is composed, bearing in mind the balance of risk. Where possible the air should be free of sulphur and other acid gases. To protect metal surfaces from corrosion by skin salts and acids, gloves should be worn when handling metal surfaces. Surface coatings are sometimes applied to metals as corrosion inhibitors, however due to the size and function of the metal fastener this would not be a viable solution since the protective film could easily be scratched when the metal fastener is re-applied to the upholstered frame. Pin beading has been discussed in an unattributed article published in the BAFRA section of UKIC Conservation News No. 50 (March 1993).

# Bibliography

Amoroso, G.G. and Fassina, V. (1983) *Stone Decay and Conservation*, Elsevier

Araki, T. and Sato, H. (1978) Relationships between exhibition lighting and discoloration of lacquered wares, in *Scientific Papers on Japanese Antiquities and Art Crafts* (Kobunkazai no Kagaku) 23, December, pp. 1–24

Ballardie, M. (1994) Conservation of an 18th century chest, lacquered and japanned, in *Lacquerwork and Japanning*, Conference Postprints, UKIC, pp. 11–13

Baynes Cope, A.D. (1989) *Caring for Books and Documents*, 2nd edn, British Library

Beale, R. (1994) Restoration of a late 17th century japanned longcase clock, in *Lacquerwork and Japanning*, Conference Postprints, UKIC, pp. 45–50

Bentley, P., McKellar, J.F. and Phillips, G.O. (1974) *Review of Progress in Coloration and Related Topics* 5, Society of Dyers and Colorists

Bentsen, J.G., Meilunas, R.J. and Steinberg, A. (1990) Analysis of aged paint binders by FTIR spectroscopy, *Studies in Conservation*, 35

Berkouwer, M. (1990) The conservation of tassels and trimmings from Castle Coole, in A. French (ed.), *Conservation of Furnishing Textiles*, Postprints of the Conference held at the Burrell Collection, Glasgow, 30–31 March 1991, Scottish Society for Conservation and Restoration, Edinburgh

Berndt, H. (1987) Assessing the detrimental effects of wood and wood products on the environment inside display cases, in AIC Conference Preprints, Vancouver, BC

Birstein, V.J. and Tul'Chinsky, V.M. (1981) IR-spectroscopic analysis of aged gelatins, in ICOM Committee for Conservation, Preprints 6th Triennial Meeting, Ottawa, p. 81/1/9

Blank, S. (1990) An introduction to plastics and rubbers in collections, *Studies in Conservation*, 35, 2

Blyth, V. (1997) Pest management at the Victoria and Albert Museum, *Pest Attack and Pest Control in Organic Materials*, Conference Postprints, UKIC, pp. 7–12

Brill, T.B. (1980) *Light, Its Interaction with Art and Antiquities*, Plenum Press

Brommelle, N.S., Moncrieff, A. and Smith, P. (eds) *Conservation of Wood in Painting and the Decorative Arts*, Conference Preprints, IIC

Brown, B.F. (1991) *Corrosion and Metal Artifacts: A Dialogue Between Conservators and Archaeologists and Corrosion Scientists*, National Association of Corrosion Engineers, Houston

Buck, R.D. (1961) The use of moisture barriers on panel paintings, *Studies in Conservation*, 6, 1, 9–19

Buys, S. and Oakley, V. (1994) *Conservation and Restoration of Ceramics*, Butterworths

Calhoun, J.M. (1953) Storage of nitrate amateur still-camera film negatives, *Journal of the Biological Photographic Association*, 21, 3, pp. 1–13

Calnan, C.N. (1989) Re-tannage with aluminium alkoxides – a stabilizing treatment for acid deteriorated leather, *ICOM International Leather and Parchment Symposium Preprints*, Deutsche Ledermuseum, Offenbach, pp. 9–25

Calnan, C. (ed.) (1991) *Conservation of Leather in Transport Collections*, Conference Postprints, UKIC

Calnan, C.N. and Haines, B.M. (eds) (1991) *Leather Its Composition and Changes With Time*, Leather Conservation Centre

Calnan, C., Selm, R. and Haines, B. (1990) Conservation of automobile and carriage leathers, *Leather Conservation News*, 7, 1, 7–8

Carpenter, J. and Hatchfield, P. (1986) The problem of formaldehyde in museum collections, *International Journal of Museum Management and Curatorship*, 5, 2, 183–8

Carthy, D. and McWilliam, C. (eds) (1984) *Proceedings of the Symposium: Decorative Wood*, Scottish Society for Conservation and Restoration (SSCR)

CCI Notes (1989) *9/1 Recognising Active Corrosion*, Canadian Conservation Institute

Chase, W.T. (1988) Lacquer examination and treatment at the Freer Gallery of Art: some case histories, in N.S. Brommelle and P. Smith (eds), *Urushi*, The Getty Conservation Institute, pp. 95–112

Clapp, A. (1987) *Curatorial Care of Works of Art on Paper*, 3rd edn, Lyons and Burford

Cooke, B. (1988). Creasing in ancient textiles, in Textile Section of *Conservation News*, No. 35 (March)

Copestake, S. (1992) The ageing and stabilization of shellac varnish resin, Third Year Undergraduate Research Project Report, Dept. of Chemistry, Imperial College, London

Cowling, J.E. and Merritt, E.R. (1954) Paints, varnishes, enamels and lacquers, in G.A. Greathouse and C.J.

Wessell (eds), *Deterioration of Materials, Causes and Preventive Techniques*, Reinhold

Crighton, J.S. (1988) Degradation of polymeric materials, in Preprints of Contributions to the Modern Organic Materials Meeting, SSCR, pp. 11–19

Davis, A. and Sims, D. (1983) *Weathering of Polymers*, Applied Science

Delollis, N.J. (1973) Adhesive theory and review, in *Handbook of Adhesive Bonding* (ed C.V. Cagle), McGraw-Hill

Doussy, M. (1990) *Antiques Professional Secrets for the Amateur*, Book Club Associates

Ecker, H.L. (1989) The characterization of weathering effects and the conservation of a mammoth tusk from Roxton, Bedfordshire, reprint from *Institute of Archaeology Bulletin*, 26, 183–223

Egerton, G.S. and Morgan, A.G. (1970) *Journal of the Society of Dyers and Colorists*, 86, 242

Emile-Male, G. (1976) *The Restorer's Handbook of Easel Painting*, Van Nostrand Reinhold, pp. 58–61

Fabris, H.J. and Sommer, J.G. (1977) Flammability of elastomeric materials, *Rubber Chemistry and Technology*, 50, 523–69

Feller, R.L. (1994) Aspects of chemical research in conservation: the deterioration process, *JAIC*, 33, 2, 91–9

Feller, R.L., Stolow, N. and Jones, E. (1985) *On Picture Varnishes and their Solvents*, National Gallery of Art, Washington, DC

Fenimore, C.P. and Martin, F.J. (1972) Burning of polymers, in *The Mechanisms of Pyrolysis, Oxidation and Burning of Organic Materials*, National Bureau of Standards Special Publication No. 357, Washington, DC, pp 159–70

Fink, C.G. (1933) The care and treatment of outdoor bronze statues, *Technical Studies*, II, 34

Florian, M.E., Norton, R. and Kronkright, D. (1990) *The Conservation of Artefacts Made from Plant Materials*, Getty Conservation Institute

Flotte, J. and Dommermuth, J. (1995) Richard Lippold's *The Sun*: investigation and treatment, in T. Drayman-Weisser (ed.) (2000), *Gilded Metals: History, Technology and Conservation*, Archetype

Flury-Lemberg, M. (1988) *Textile Conservation and Research*, Abegg-Stiftung

Franke, A. (1976) Ostasiatische Lackarbeiten und das Problem ihrer Konservierung (East Asian lacquer work and the problem of its conservation), in *Arbeitsblatter fur Restauratoren*, 1(11), 1–10

Franke, A. (1978) The use of beeswax and resin in the restoration of East Asian lacquer work, in *Conservation of Wood in Painting and the Decorative Arts* (N.S. Brommelle, A. Moncrieff and P. Smith, eds) IIC, London, pp. 45–7

French, A. (ed.) (1990) *Conservation of Furnishing Textiles*, Postprints of the Conference held at the Burrell Collection, Glasgow, 30–31 March 1991, Scottish Society for Conservation and Restoration

Gettens, R.J. and Stout, G.L. (1966) *Painting Materials: a Short Encyclopaedia*, Dover

Gilberg, M. and Grattan, D.W. (1994) Oxygen-free storage using Ageless® oxygen absorber, in *Preventive Conservation: Practice, Theory and Research*, Conference Preprints, IIC, pp. 177–80

Gill, K. (1990) Approaches in the treatment of 20th Century upholstered furniture, In Williams, M.A. (ed.) *Upholstery Conservation Symposium Pre-prints*. New Hampshire: American Conservation Consortium Ltd., pp. 305–322

Gill, K. and Eastop, D. (2001) *Upholstery Conservation: Principles and Practice*, Butterworth–Heinemann

Grattan, D.W. (1978) The oxidative degradation of organic materials and its importance in deterioration of artifacts, *J. IIC-Canadian Group*, 4(1), 17–26

Grattan, D.W. (1987) Rubber deterioration: can antioxidants help save artifacts?, *J-IIC Canadian Group Newsletter*

Green, M. (1991) Thirty years of gilding conservation at the Victoria and Albert Museum, in D. Bigelow (ed.), *Gilded Wood Conservation and History*, Sound View Press

Griffith, R. (1997) Storage: not so simple – improved storage specifications for modern furniture collections, RCA V&A Joint Conservation Course, MA Final Degree Project

Griffiths, J. (1972) *Chemical Society Review* 1, 481

Hagar, M. (1983) Saving the image: the deterioration of nitrate film, *Image*, 26(4), 1–18

Hamid, S.H., Mohamed, B.A. and Ali, G.M. (1992) *Handbook of Polymer Degradation*, Research Institute, King Fahd University of Petroleum and Minerals, Dhahran, Saudi Arabia/Marcel Dekker

Harley, R.D. (1982) *Artists' Pigments c.1600–1835*, 2nd edn, Butterworth

Heath, D. and Martin, G. (1988) The corrosion of lead and lead/tin alloys occurring on Japanese lacquer objects, in *The Conservation of Far Eastern Art*, IIC

Hepburn, C. (1982) *Polyurethane Elastomers*, Applied Science Publishers

Hess, M. (1965) *Paint Film Defects – Their Causes and Cures*, W & J MacKay

Hey, M.H. (1975) *Chemical Index of Minerals*, British Museum of Natural History

Hillyer, L. and Blyth, V. (1992) Carpet beetle: a study in detection and control, *The Conservator*, 16, 65–77

Hoadley, R.B. (1998) Wood as a physical surface for paint application, in *Painted Wood: History and Conservation*, Getty Conservation Institute, pp. 2–16

Horie, C.V. (1987) *Materials for Conservation*, Butterworth

Hua, L. and Haslam, E. (1992) Vegetable tannins and the durability of leathers, in *Conservation of Leather Craft and Related Objects*, ICOM Committee for Conservation Interim Symposium held at the Victoria and Albert Museum, London, pp. 24–7

Jellinek, H.H.G. (ed.) (1978) *Aspects of Degradation and Stabilisation of Polymers*, Elsevier

Johnson, M. (1976) Nitrocellulose as a conservation hazard, in AIC Conference Preprints, pp. 66–75

Jones, D.A. (1996) *Principles and Prevention of Corrosion*, 2nd edn, Macmillan

Karpowicz, A. (1981) Ageing and deterioration of proteinaceous media, *Studies in Conservation*, 26, 153–60

Kelen, T. (1983) *Polymer Degradation*, Van Nostrand Reinhold, pp. 107–36

Kenjo, T. (1988) Scientific approach to traditional lacquer art, in N.S. Brommelle and P. Smith (eds), *Urushi*, The Getty Conservation Institute, p. 162

Kerr, N. and Batcheller, J. (1993) Degradation of polyurethanes in 20th century museum textiles, in *Saving the Twentieth Century: The Conservation of*

*Modern Material*, Canadian Conservation Institute, pp. 189–206

Kinloch, A.J. (1987) *Adhesion and Adhesives*, Chapman and Hall

Koller, M. and Mairinger, F. (1975) Problems of varnishes: use appearance and possibilities of examination, in ICOM Committee for Conservation, 4th Triennial Meeting, Report No. 75/22/9, pp. 1–9

Koob, S.P. (1982) The instability of cellulose nitrate adhesives, *The Conservator*, 6, 31–44

Korbin, G. (ed.) (1993) *Microbiologically Influenced Corrosion*, NACE

Kuhn, H. (1986) *Conservation and Restoration of Works of Art and Antiquities*, Butterworths, p. 5

Kumanotani, J.S. (1981) High durability and structure of Japanese lac and attempts to synthesize it, *American Chemical Society, Division of Organic Coatings and Plastics Chemistry*, 45, pp. 643–8

Kumanotani, J.S. (1983) Japanese lacquer – a super durable coating, in C.E. Carraher and L.H. Sperling (eds), *Polymer Application of Renewable-Resource Materials*, Plenum, p. 225

Kumanotani, J. (1988) The chemistry of Oriental lacquer (*Rhus verniciflua*), in N.S. Brommelle and P. Smith (eds), *Urushi*, The Getty Conservation Institute, pp. 243–51

Kumanotani, J., Achiwa, M., Oshima, R. and Adachi, K. (1980) Attempts to understand Japanese lacquer as a superdurable material, in *Cultural Property and Analytical Chemistry* 2, Proceedings of 2nd ISCRP, Tokyo, pp. 51–62

Kumanotani, J., Inoue, K. and Chen, L.W. (1985) The behaviour of water in the surface of Oriental lacquers and analogues, *Polymeric Materials Science and Engineering*, 52, 163–7

Kuryla, W.C. and Papa, A.J. (eds) (1973) *Flame Retardancy of Polymeric Materials*, 5 vols, Dekker

Kuwata, T.J., Kumanotani, J.S. and Kazama, S. (1961) Physical and chemical properties of coating films of Japanese lac (urushi) (rigidity modulus–temperature relations measured by torsional pendulum method), *Bulletin of the Chemical Society of Japan*, 34, 1678–85

Landi, S. (1992/1985) *The Textile Conservator's Manual*, Butterworth-Heinemann

Lang, S. (1997) English Japanning: 1660–1700 (An essay on the materials and techniques of English Japanning), Royal College of Art/Victoria and Albert Museum, unpublished

LaQue, F.L. in Uhlig, H. (1948) *Corrosion Handbook*, Wiley

Learner, T. (1995) The analysis of synthetic resins found in 20th century paint media, in *Resins Ancient and Modern*, Conference Preprints (M.M. Wright and J. Townsend, eds), Scottish Society for Conservation and Restoration, pp. 76–84

Leaver, I.H. (1980) Chapter 4 in N.S. Allen and J.K. McKellar (eds), *Photochemistry of Dyed and Pigmented Polymers*, Applied Science

Linns, A. (1991) Basic properties of gold leaf, in D. Bigelow (ed.), *Gilded Wood Conservation and History*, Sound View Press, p. 22

Lomax, S.Q. and Fisher S.L. (1990) An investigation of the removability of naturally aged synthetic picture varnishes, *JAIC*, 29, 181–91

Mantell, C.L., Kopf, C.W., Curtis, J.L. and Rogers, E.M. (1942) *The Technology of Natural Resins*, Wiley

Martens, C.E. (1968) *Technology of Paints, Varnishes and Lacquers*, Robert E. Krieger

Masschelein-Kleiner, L. (1985) *Ancient Binding Media, Varnishes and Adhesives*, ICCROM: Rome

Massey, R. (1967) *Formulas for Painters*, Watson Guptill

Matienzo, L.J. and Snow, C.E. (1986) The chemical effects of hydrochloric acid and organic solvent molecules on the surface of ivory, *Studies in Conservation*, 31, 133–9

Mayer, R. (1982) *The Artist's Handbook of Materials and Techniques*, 4th edn (ed. E. Smith), Faber

McGlinchey, C.W. (1993) The physical ageing of polymeric materials, in D.W. Grattan (ed.), *Saving the Twentieth Century: The Conservation of Modern Material*, Conference Proceedings Canadian Conservation Institute, Ottawa, pp. 113–21

McLaren, K. (1956) The spectral regions of daylight which cause fading, *Journal of the Society of Dyers and Colorists*, 72, 86

McLaren, K. (1983) *The Colour Science of Dyes and Pigments*, Adam Hilger

Mecklenburg, M.F. (1991) Some mechanical and physical properties of gilding gesso, in D. Bigelow (ed.), *Gilded Wood Conservation and History*, Sound View Press, p. 171

Meier, A. (1977) Chapter 7 in K. Venkataraman, (ed.), *The Chemistry of Synthetic Dyes*, Vol. 4, Academic Press

Meilunas, R.J., Bentsen, J.G. and Steinberg, A. (1990) Analysis of aged paint binders by FTIR spectroscopy, *Studies in Conservation*, 35, 33–51

Mills, J.S. and White, R. (1987) *The Organic Chemistry of Museum Objects*, Butterworths

Newman, A.A. (ed.) (1972) *Chemistry of Terpenes and Terpenoids*, Academic Press

Newton, R. and Davison, S. (1989) *Conservation of Glass*, Butterworths (2nd edn, S. Davison, 2003)

Odegaard, N. and Kronkright, D. (1985) Giving your baskets a long, healthy life: a basic guide to basketry conservation, *Fiberarts Magazine*, March

Peltz, P. and Rossal, M. (1983) *Safe Pest Control Procedures for Museum Collections*, Center for Occupational Hazards, USA

Pinion, L.C. (1973) *Chemical Staining in Wood*, Building Research Establishment, Princes Risborough

Plenderleith, H.J. and Cursiter, S. (1934) The problem of lining adhesives for paintings – wax adhesives, *Technical Studies*, III, pp. 90–113

Rasti, F. (1980) The effects of some common pigments on the photo-oxidation of linseed oil-based paint media, *Studies in Conservation*, 25, 145–56

Rees Jones, S. (1991) The changed appearance of oil paintings due to increased transparency, *Studies in Conservation*, 36, 151–4

Reilly, J.M. (1991) Celluloid objects: their chemistry and preservation, *JAIC*, 30, 145–62

Sano, Y. (1993) Scientific research on *Urushi* in Japan, in *Proceedings of the 1993 International Symposium on the Conservation and Restoration of Cultural Property*, Tokyo National Research Institute of Cultural Properties, Japan

Selwitz, C. (1988) Cellulose nitrate in conservation, *Research in Conservation*, 2, Getty Conservation Institute

Shashoua, Y. (1996) A passive approach to the conservation of polyvinyl chloride, in ICOM Committee for Conservation, Preprints 11th Triennial Meeting, Edinburgh, pp. 961–6

Shashoua, Y. and Thomsen, S. (1993) A field trial for the use of Ageless® in the preservation of rubber in museum collections, in *Saving the Twentieth Century: The Conservation of Modern Material*, Conference Postprints (D.W. Grattan, ed.), Canadian Conservation Institute, Ottawa, pp. 363–72

Shashoua, Y. and Ward, C. (1993) Progress report on a field trial for the use of Ageless® in the preservation of rubber in the Department of Ethnography, in Conservation Research Section, British Museum, Report No. 1993/19

Shashoua, Y., Bradley, S.M. and Daniels, V.D. (1992) Degradation of cellulose nitrate adhesives, *Studies in Conservation*, 37(2), 113–19

Shearer, G.L. and Doyal, S. (1991) Use of FTIR in the conservation of twentieth century objects, in *Materials Issues in Art and Archaeology II*, Pittsburgh Materials Research Society, pp. 813–23

Stambolov, T. (1985) *The Corrosion and Conservation of Metallic Antiquities and Works of Art*, Central Research Laboratory for Objects of Art and Science, Amsterdam

Storey, J. (1978) *Thames and Hudson Manual of Dyes and Fabrics*, Thames and Hudson

Stout, G. (1975) *Care of Pictures*, Dover

Suppan, P. (1972) *Principles of Photochemists*, Monographs for teachers No. 22, The Chemical Society

Tennent, N.H. and Baird, T. (1985) The deterioration of mollusca collections: identification of shell efflorescence, *Studies in Conservation*, 30, 73–85

Then, E. and Oakley, V. (1993) A survey of plastic objects at the Victoria and Albert Museum, *V&A Conservation Journal*, 6, 11–14

Thickett, D., Bradley, S. and Lee, L. (1998) Assessment of the risks to metal artifacts posed by volatile carbonyl pollutants, in *Metal 98*, James and James, pp. 260–4

Thompson, D.V. (1962) *The Practice of Tempera Painting*, Dover

Thornton, J. (1998) The use of dyes and coloured varnishes in wood polychromy, in *Painted Wood: History and Conservation*, Getty Conservation Institute

Thorpe, J.F. and Whiteley, M.A. (1946) *Thorpe's Dictionary of Applied Chemistry*, 4th edn, Vol. 7, Longmans, p. 71

Tímár-Balázsy, A. and Eastop, D. (1998) *Chemical Principles of Textile Conservation*, Butterworth-Heinemann

Torraca, G. (1990) *Solubility and Solvents for Conservation Problems*, ICCROM: Rome

Trethewey, K. and Chamberlain, J. (1988) *Corrosion for Students of Science*, Longmans

Uhlig, H.H. and Revie, R.W. (1985) *Corrosion and Corrosion Control: An Introduction to Corrosion Science*, Wiley

Umney, N.D. (1992) Corrosion of metals associated with wood, *V&A Conservation Journal*, 9–12

Umney, N.D. and Winness, M. (1994) Prevention or cure, *Lacquerwork and Japanning*, Conference Postprints, UKIC, pp. 3–5

Wachowiak, M. and Williams, D. (1994) Conservation of an 18th century English japanned surface, *Lacquerwork and Japanning*, Conference Postprints, UKIC, pp. 27–9

Werner, G. (1987) Corrosion of metal caused by wood in closed spaces, in *Recent Advances in the Conservation and Analysis of Artifacts*, Summer School Press, University of London, pp. 185–7

Westerman Bulgarella, M. (1987) Gli interventi di conservazione sulle tappezzerie di Palazzo Pitti, in *Le tappezzerie Nelle Dimore Storiche Centro Italiano per lo Studio della Storia del Tessuto*, Umberto Allemandi, Florence

Williams, M.A. (ed.) (1990) *Upholstery Conservation*, Preprints of a Symposium held at Colonial Williamsburg, 2–4 February 1990, American Conservation Consortium Ltd, Kingston, NH

Williams, R.S. (1988) *Display and Storage of Museum Objects Containing Cellulose Nitrate*, CCI, Ottawa

Williston, S.S. (1982) Preliminary findings of the reactions of coatings and adhesives with metals, *Science and Technology in the Service of Conservation*, IIC

# Part 4

# Conservation

# 9

# Conservation preliminaries

This chapter covers some of the general issues that affect the approaches to, and execution of, furniture conservation. These include the context in which conservation takes place, the ethical principles that guide our work and the importance of documentation as a tool in conservation. Information is also given on aspects of setting up a workshop, the tools, machinery and equipment required and the health and safety implications of the work. The outline presented of the practical processes typically involved in furniture conservation provides a framework for discussion in subsequent chapters. In most cases the principles underlying the discussion will be the same throughout the English-speaking world. However, the international nature of the audience and rapidly changing nature of law mitigate against specific instruction, though in some cases examples have been given from the UK and European perspectives.

## 9.1 Context

This section briefly addresses the historical context of conservation, seeks to define the profession, elucidate the role of some important professional organizations and outline what is involved in the business side of delivering conservation services.

### 9.1.1 Historical background

Although there would always have been people whose function was to repair furniture in use, the rise of furniture conservation has been closely associated with the development of museums. Private, royal and ecclesiastical collections existed from early times but the earliest public collections in the UK date mainly from the eighteenth century, though the Ashmolean Museum in Oxford was established in 1683. Steady growth of museums continued until there were some 900 museums in Britain in 1963. From this point growth in numbers was nearly explosive, rising to 2300 establishments in 1988. Corfield (1988) has traced the emergence of conservation as a profession.

Traditionally, remedial work on furniture was the province of the furniture restorer, a person (most likely male) who, until recently, was very likely to have trained as a cabinet-maker or joiner and who would use very much the same skills of making and finishing. The same would be largely true of upholstery and gilding. The last forty or so years have seen both diversification and systematization of approach and greater awareness of and concern for the historic value of original material. There are probably several reasons for this, including changes in training and routes into conservation, the influence of conservation professional bodies and an increase in accountability. All this has been underpinned by the far greater interest in and expenditure on, the heritage implied by the expansion noted above.

Diploma and degree courses in conservation of paintings were introduced at the Courtauld Institute in London in 1932. Archaeological conservation, for which there is no trade equivalent and for which more emphasis is placed on the verity of the historic record, was also one of the first to be taught at degree level. Opportunities then became available in other National Museums and Galleries, to people with backgrounds in the sciences as well as those educated and trained in art history and the practical arts, though evidence of interest and ability in these areas was required. The application of scientific thinking in these subject areas has influenced approaches to conservation in the major museums and galleries in all disciplines. There has been a gradual move away from the traditional apprenticeship training towards the teaching of furniture conservation (and related topics) as a more academic discipline. This has broadened the existing base of furniture conservation as people with widely different educational backgrounds and experiences have come into the profession through graduate and postgraduate courses. Furniture conservation has been enriched by this development and by the environment in which people with widely different educational backgrounds and approaches can interact and learn from each other. An international index on training in conservation of cultural property was co-published by the Getty Conservation Institute and the International Centre for the Study of the Preservation and Restoration of Cultural Property (ICCROM) in 1987.

### 9.1.2  Definition of the profession

In most countries, the profession of conservator–restorer was until relatively recently undefined. Whoever conserved or restored was called a conservator or restorer regardless of the extent and depth of their training. Concern for professional ethics and standards for the objects being treated and for the owners of these objects led to various attempts to define the profession to distinguish it from related professions and to establish proper training requirements. In response to this need, ICOM (1984) defined the activity of the conservator–restorer as consisting of technical examination, preservation and conservation/restoration of cultural property. According to this account, *examination* is the preliminary procedure performed to determine the documentary significance of an artefact, original structure and materials, extent of deterioration, alteration and loss and the documentation of these findings. *Preservation* is action taken to retard or prevent deterioration of or damage to cultural properties by control of their environment and/or treatment of their structure in order to maintain them as nearly as possible in an unchanging state. *Restoration* is action taken to make a

deteriorated or damaged artefact understandable with minimal sacrifice of aesthetic and historic integrity. The ICOM definition of the profession, from which this account is taken, goes on to consider the impact and ranking of the activities of the conservator–restorer, the distinction from related professions and the training and education of the conservator–restorer.

The essential elements of the ICOM definition of the profession have been developed by conservation bodies such as the American Institute for Conservation of Historic and Artistic Works (AIC) and the United Kingdom Institute for Conservation of Historic and Artistic Works (UKIC), among others. The nature of conservation, the role of science in conservation and the ethical issues faced by conservators are among issues discussed in a seminal work by Ward (1989).

The conservator–restorer has a particular responsibility in that treatment is performed on irreplaceable originals that are often unique and of great artistic, religious, historic, scientific, cultural, social or economic value. The value of such objects lies in the character of their fabrication, in their evidence as historical documents and consequently in their authenticity. Objects are a significant expression of the spiritual, religious and artistic life of the past, often documents of a historical situation, whether they are fine art or simply objects of everyday life. Preservation of their physical integrity is important because they form the basis for further research.

Interdisciplinary cooperation is of paramount importance. The conservator–restorer must work as part of a team in close collaboration with curators, historians, conservation scientists and others who are able to assist in the necessary dialogue with the object. All interventions should be preceded by methodical and scientific examination aimed at understanding the object in all its aspects and the implications of any treatment proposed. To ensure that treatment preserves the integrity of the object and makes its significance accessible, the intervention itself should follow the sequence common to all scientific methodology: investigation of source, analysis, interpretation and synthesis.

Training should involve the development of sensitivity and manual skills, the acquisition of theoretical knowledge about materials and techniques and rigorous grounding in scientific methodology to foster the capacity to solve conservation problems by following a systematic approach, using precise research and critically interpreting the results.

### 9.1.3 Professional organizations

The professional bodies for conservation and for museums have done a great deal to carry the conservation message and to promote the development of conservation from a craft-based activity to a profession in which there is an accepted corpus of principles and methods. They have worked hard to define acceptable standards of behaviour for those wishing to call themselves conservators, have lobbied to achieve greater recognition for the profession, have done much to reconcile the different perspectives of those in the trade and those in institutions and are working hard towards professional accreditation. They can only do this however with support from individual members of the profession.

The International Institute for the Conservation of Museum Objects was founded in 1950 as a result of a series of international discussions between 1946 and 1948. This organization has been known as the International Institute for Conservation of Historic and Artistic Works (IIC) since 1959. It was incorporated as a limited company in the United Kingdom and its aims were 'to improve the state of knowledge and standards of practice and to provide a common meeting ground and publishing body for all who are interested in and professionally skilled in the conservation of museum objects'. IIC has over 3000 members in around 65 countries drawn both from museum personnel and from professional conservators working independently. Members are enabled to keep abreast of technical advances and in personal contact with their colleagues world-wide through IIC's publications (*Studies in Conservation* and the *Bulletin*), international congresses (held every two years) and groups. IIC gave rise to independent national groups in USA (AIC), Canada (IIC-CG) and the United Kingdom (UKIC). Specialist groups exist for furniture and wooden objects within both AIC and UKIC. Regional groups, with their own structure and

by-laws, operate autonomously with the approval of the Council of IIC, in Austria, France, Holland, Scandinavia and Japan.

ICOM, the International Council of Museums, is a non-profit organization dedicated to the improvement and advancement of museums and of the museum profession. It provides a world-wide communication network for museum people and counts over 8000 members in some 120 countries. Its National Committees coordinate a vast international effort aimed at continuing improvement of museums in their scientific, educational and conservation roles. Its International specialized committees and Affiliated Organizations group together professionals representing the leading authorities on a given type of museum and are subdivided into working groups which study various specific aspects of the overall discipline. These include Scientific Examination of Works of Art, Lighting and Climate Control, Training in Conservation and Restoration and many others including, more recently, a group specializing in furniture and lacquer conservation. All the international committees meet together regularly to discuss new developments, familiarize themselves with the latest techniques and make recommendations which are made available to ICOM members throughout the world. ICOM is associated with UNESCO as a category 'A' Non-Governmental Organization and has been granted advisory status by the United Nations Economic and Social Council. It provides services and technical assistance to UNESCO and to its Member States through expert missions, the planning of museums, the organization of meetings and the preparation of publications. ICOM organizes numerous expert meetings through the intermediary of its National and International Committees and every three years holds a General Assembly and General Conference, the proceedings of which are published. Membership is open to those whose work is directly linked to museums as well as to museum professionals themselves.

The Canadian based Association for Preservation Technology (APT) was first organized in 1968, formally constituted in 1969 and incorporated in 1975. It is an association of preservationists, restoration architects, furnishings consultants, museum curators, architectural educators, archaeologists, craftspeople and other persons directly or indirectly involved in preservation activities.

### 9.1.4   The business of conservation

What might be termed the business of conservation covers a wide range of issues. A partial list includes:

- Accommodation and space – setting up and maintenance of premises
- Establishing terms and conditions, writing contracts
- Costing, estimating and planning work
- The organization, planning, control and execution of conservation treatments
- Handling packing and transport
- Financial issues including the keeping of accounts and tax records
- Presentation, advertising and negotiation
- Staff issues including recruiting, training, pensions, insurance, sickness and injury
- Health and safety.

All of these issues are capable of influencing the life of the conservator, whether institutional or private and need to be considered as part of the job. They can all affect the outcomes of conservation. The legislative framework within which we operate is ever expanding and the requirement for accountability continually growing, whether in providing value for money, health and safety, or in demonstrating ethical behaviour. A range of publications on general management issues is available and it is superfluous to specify particular sources. Information of specific relevance to conservation can be found in Keene (1996). Advice and help with finding services is available from the professional bodies.

## 9.2   Ethics

Ethics provide a conceptual framework for conservation treatment. This section begins with the broadly accepted principles found in the codes of ethics of the conservation profession. It discusses the historical conflict between restoration and preservation and the implications of this conflict for conservation. Finally, it offers some tools for making well-considered ethical judgements for conservation treatments.

### 9.2.1   Codes of ethics and practice

Conservators should always remember their responsibility for the material preservation of furniture and the impact they can have on the aesthetics of the treated objects. Owners and curators should have a major input in the decision-making of the treatment options of the object and with the conservator, arrive at a responsible treatment proposal (Van Horne, 1991a). In the end, however, it is the 'hands-on' work, choice of materials and manual dexterity, combined with (art-)historical understanding, appropriate research and sense of aesthetic evaluation and balance, which makes the conservator accountable for the quality of the treatment (Price *et al.*, 1996). It has been widely published and accepted among museum professionals that the overall integrity of works of art should be respected and that any conservation treatment should be guided by this principle. It is not always easy to define the integrity of an object because this involves value judgements and therefore is subjective. Views on the integrity of an object may also change with time. Choice of construction and decoration material, proportions and volume of the object, shape and ornamentation, colour and texture of materials, natural ageing of the object and sometimes alterations to the object are important to this concept. There are several generally accepted (ideal) ethical principles and codes of practice to guide the conservation of works of art. These include, but are not limited to:

- An emphasis on preservation for the future (stewardship for future generations), though often a balance must be found between preservation and the demands of use
- Understanding and appreciation
- An emphasis on preventive conservation
- A responsibility to owners, custodians or an object's creator/s
- The application of high standards to conservation practice
- The recognition of the limits of one's skills
- Documentation of the nature and extent of conservation work
- The principle that work need not be obtrusive but should be detectable without reference to documentation (the 'six foot–six inch rule')
- The keeping of intervention to a minimum to achieve an agreed goal

- The retention of as much original material as possible
- The addition of as little new material as possible
- The avoidance of irreversible alterations, though cleaning may be an exception to this
- The use of techniques that allow future retreatment wherever possible
- The use of materials that are durable and fit for the purpose intended
- The use of materials should not pose a threat to endangered species
- The use of procedures that conform to best practices of health and safety.

The American Group of IIC was the first group of conservators in any country to formulate its standards of practice in an explicit document. This was based on the work of a Committee on Professional Standards and Procedures under the direction of the late Mr Murray Pease and was adopted by American Group members at a meeting in New York in June 1963. This has been refined and developed into an extensive document covering all aspects of professional behaviour, standards and principles governing the work of the profession (Pease *et al.*, 1968). Similar documents have been developed by conservation professional bodies in other countries and form part of the documentation supplied to every member upon joining and subsequently as revisions occur. The codes of practice of the conservation professional bodies (e.g. AIC and UKIC) are generally prescriptive and may sometimes be found difficult to interpret and apply, although an increasing body of 'case law' with commentaries is being built up, especially by AIC. There is in fact still considerable confusion about conservation ethics. It may therefore be helpful to examine some aspects of the inherently contradictory nature of conservation, the values that determine what we do to objects and the historical development of ideas related to conservation before offering some further specific practical guidelines for coping with conservation decision-making.

### 9.2.2 Historical conflict between restoration and preservation

The principle of restoration, i.e. the modification of objects in order to return them to some former, more perfect state, was widely accepted from the Renaissance. However, in the nineteenth century, changes in attitudes to the past were reflected in public debate about how the past was to be represented. Preservation, i.e. the maintenance of objects in an unchanged and unchanging state, was proposed as an alternative to restoration. Proponents of each approach were vociferous and debate was polarized between these two, mutually exclusive, concepts. The shift in cultural values expressed in this debate gave rise to the concept of conservation in the twentieth century.

The debate between restoration and preservation first took place in the context of the treatment of historic buildings. One of the most well known proponents of restoration was Eugene Emmanuel Viollet-le-Duc, who believed that the long-term well-being of buildings stemmed from their continued use. He supported restoration in which poor quality later material was stripped away and the building restored 'in the style of the original'. Restoration was based on meticulous, detailed and accurate documentation of the building, its principle style and original construction methods. In cases where past changes were deemed important or had been substantial, Viollet-le-Duc favoured their retention (Price *et al.*, 1996).

One of the first decisions to preserve rather than restore was taken when the British Museum acquired the Elgin marbles in 1816. In 1855 the Committee of the Society of Antiquaries stated:

> ... *no restoration should ever be attempted, otherwise than the word 'restoration' may be understood in the sense of preservation from further injuries by time or negligence: they contend that anything beyond this is untrue in art, unjustifiable in taste, destructive in practise and wholly opposed to the judgement of the best archaeologists.* (Cook and Wedderburn, 1903–10)

Examination of this statement reveals a sophisticated understanding of what would today be called 'ethics', now applied in all fields of conservation. The Committee was concerned about authenticity, about preservation for posterity, about the danger of restoration that reinterpreted an object according to the fashion of the day and about the destruction of original material in the restoration process.

In 1877 William Morris put forward his view that in the past change had been an organic process and that restoration, destructive by its very nature, conflicted with this:

> *if repairs were needed, if ambition or piety pricked on to change, that change was of necessity wrought in the unmistakable fashion of the time; a church of the eleventh century might be added to or altered in the twelfth, thirteenth, fourteenth, sixteenth, or even the seventeenth and eighteenth centuries; but every change, whatever history it destroyed, left history in the gap and was alive with the spirit of the deeds done midst its fashion.* (Harvey, 1972)

Morris was opposed to the very idea of restoration. He described restoration as:

> *... the strange idea which by its very name implies that it is possible to strip away ... this, that and the other part of history – of its life that IS and then to stay the hand at some arbitrary point and leave it still historical, living and even as it once was ...* (Thompson, 1967)

He was sceptical that restoration could make a building and by extension any object, 'as it once was' and he labelled such attempts forgery. Morris shared John Ruskin's conviction that it was:

> *no question of expediency or feeling whether we shall preserve the buildings of past times or not. We have no right whatever to touch them. They are not ours. They belong, partly to those who build them and partly to all the generations of mankind who are to follow us.* (Ruskin, 1849)

Although the dichotomy between preservation and restoration may seem a distant relic of the nineteenth century, it is part of the tradition that Western conservators draw on when grappling with ethics. The continuing polarization between preservation and restoration was evident at the 1994 conference 'Restoration – Is it Acceptable', held at the British Museum, London.

Even though preservation and restoration are often conceptualized as opposites, conservation draws on both traditions and attempts to balance these conflicting demands. Furniture conservation strives to preserve for the future, to balance historical accuracy and aesthetics and to accommodate continuing fitness for purpose, such as museum display or domestic use. As a result, there may be some overlap between conservation and restoration. Replacing missing components of furniture, for example, may enable remaining original material to survive intact where it would otherwise not have done so, or enhance the 'legibility' of an object. The differences and similarities between conservation and restoration are the subject of ongoing discussion in the furniture conservation profession.

### 9.2.3    Conservation as a cultural discipline

Conservation is both a practical discipline and a cultural discipline. Conservation does not occur in isolation but is shaped by social and cultural forces. Any society sees objects as more or less precious according to the values they are deemed to embody. Whilst Western culture places value on material objects, other cultures do not. In Japan, the traditional techniques of the applied arts and the performing arts are regarded as 'intangible cultural property' (Yagihashi, 1988). Understanding and replicating traditional techniques, on the object itself or by making a copy, may be considered part of the process of preservation (Kitamura, 1988).

Conservators act on the basis of their cultural values, preserving objects that are believed to be significant. It is tempting to think that the nature and extent of a conservation treatment is dictated by economics. However, it is cultural values that set the economic agenda, not the other way round. The more something is valued, the more we are prepared to pay for it or spend on maintaining it. Cultural values may change over time.

Cultures and the people in them, may simultaneously hold a multitude of contradictory beliefs. For example, many people believe that murder is bad and at the same time that the death penalty is good. Holding conflicting beliefs is not necessarily a bad thing – there is considerable danger in inflexible and absolute answers to fundamental moral questions. A key aspect of conservation practice is the exercise of judgement. Good judgement requires that a balance be found between the conflicting values expressed in the codes of ethics.

(a)

(b)

(c)

(d)

(e)

**Figure 9.1** French (Paris) cabinet, nineteenth century, stamped Vitel (active 1838–64). (*a*) Front and sides decorated with Japanese lacquer panels dating from *c.*1630, these panels framed by marquetry elements in turtleshell, brass, ebony, satinwood and purpleheart, with ormolu mounts and a Brescia marble slab top. (*b*) Lacquer panel removed from the front of the cabinet, showing where wood was removed to allow a lock to be fitted to the cabinet, and a strip of overpaint applied around the edges. (*c*) Lacquer panel from the side of the cabinet. The decoration on the two side panels aligns, suggesting they were originally one integrated piece that has been sawn in two. It is likely that the side panels were part of a chest at some time. The side panels have been patched in positions corresponding to where handles would have been fitted on a chest. (*d*) Rear view of side panel showing nashiji decoration on the patch. (*e*) Side panel viewed under UV, showing patchy varnish layer/s

The complexity of dealing with an object that has multi-layed values and a multi-cultural history is demonstrated by a piece of furniture found in the collection of the Victoria and Albert Museum, London. *Figure 9.1a* shows an early nineteenth century French cabinet (accession number 1084-1882). The front and side panels are high quality Japanese export lacquer dating from the 1630s (*Figure 9.1b*). The panels originally formed part of a chest, as evidenced by lacquer inserts in the side panels. Both front and side panels are constructed using a single softwood board onto which the urushi decoration has been applied. The panels are framed by ormolu mouldings. Nails have been driven through the mouldings and panels to fix them to the cabinet.

The side panels have a patch visible at the top of the panel in a position that corresponds to the position of a handle on the original chest (*Figure 9.1c*). The patch is comprised of urushi and wood and has nashiji decoration on the back (*Figure 9.1d*). The patch, once fitted, was integrated into the panel decoration using japanning techniques. Varnish was then applied over the whole panel. The decoration on the side panels is now somewhat obscured under normal viewing conditions by a cloudy effect caused by degradation of later varnish layers. *Figure 9.1e* shows patchy varnish on one of the side panels, under UV.

Various approaches could be suggested for the conservation of the cabinet and the lacquer panels:

- The panels are single wide boards, prone to expand and contract with fluctuations in RH. In the absence of a stable environment, it could be argued that the panels, aesthetically and historically important in their own right, should be removed to facilitate their *preservation* in an undamaged state.
- The panels form part of a greater whole and should not be separated from the cabinet. Removing the panels would disrupt the aesthetic, historical and functional aspects of the cabinet. The cabinet should be *preserved as an integrated whole.*
- The history of the panels spans 350 years. To remove the varnish would be to disrupt that historical continuity and diminish the *historical value* of the object as a whole.
- *Technical understanding* of the materials

and techniques of japanning found in combination with oriental lacquer would be facilitated by retaining the varnish.
- *Technical understanding* of export lacquer techniques would be facilitated by removing the varnish.
- The *aesthetic value* of the panels is compromised by the cloudy appearance of the old varnish, so the varnish should be removed.
- One of the characteristics Europeans found desirable about Oriental lacquer its lustre and sheen, the translucent quality of the finish. The *original intent* of both the Japanese maker of the panels and the Europeans who fixed them into the cabinet should be respected.

The conservation treatment of this cabinet and the lacquer panels would be determined by which aspect/s are most highly valued at the present time. A good case could be made for removing the panels or for leaving them fixed to the cabinet. Similarly, a persuasive argument could be made for retaining or removing varnish.

The conclusion that there are no absolutely right answers should also lead us to the possibility that there are no absolutely wrong answers. Rather than abdicating responsibility, however, we are required to exercise judgement. Conservators are required to find a course of action that balances conflicting values and is ethically defensible.

### 9.2.4 Tools for balanced ethical judgement

Balanced ethical decision-making is a three-stage process. First, agree a clearly defined treatment goal with interested parties (e.g. curator, owner, artist etc.). Secondly, establish the relative importance of the values embodied in the object (aesthetic, historical, spiritual etc.), undertaking further research about the object if necessary. Thirdly, establish a treatment that provides the best balance between the most important values. The following two approaches have been proposed to assist conservators in finding the right balance.

Caple (2000) suggested that any conservation activity required a compromise between the three absolutes of revelation, investigation and preservation. He proposed a model in which each of these absolutes occupies the corner of a triangle. Plotting a conservation activity within this triangle can help the conservator visualize the compromises involved in a conservation treatment.

Others have suggested an approach based on a series of questions. The Conservation Department at the Victoria and Albert Museum developed an *Ethics Checklist* to help conservators engage in a clear decision-making process.

### The V&A ethics checklist

*Why is action needed?* This question should be asked to determine whether work is necessary and what would happen if the work were not carried out. There could be many reasons for an action, such as stabilizing the object or aesthetics. Often, some intervention is necessary, to render the object stable for its end use. No matter how minimal, this intervention will change or may even destroy the original construction of the artefact. However, if the artefact is left untreated the process of degradation may be at least equally damaging. Sometimes very difficult decisions have to be made. In assessing the damages to a piece of furniture and in evaluating the treatment options, there is always the alternative not to treat them. This may be the best solution for the object. This conclusion may be reached after considering stability, likelihood of future change and the damage likely to occur from treatment. Damage may be a result of a historic event and should perhaps be respected as such. The construction of a piece of furniture may impede restoration or the restoration may cause additional problems. When there are no clear examples available for reconstructing missing elements, it may be best not to restore the object, or to leave parts untreated. Finally, when the conservator does not feel competent to handle a certain problem, he or she should either consult with a colleague or a specialist, or leave the object untreated. If there is no specific reason against treatment, however, a number of options may present themselves from which the conservator should select the most suitable one. The conservator should always seek to preserve without disturbing or obliterating evidence. Factors to consider before treatment of upholstery are discussed by Bergen (1952).

*Have I consulted all available records?* At the most fundamental level, records can show that the object is in fact the one we suppose it to be. Most institutional owners will uniquely identify their objects by some form of numbering system and record important information about them in a catalogue. It is an obvious step to check that the number and the description match the object. Such documentation may also reveal that an item is one of a set, which may be an important consideration. Records may show whether an object has previously been conserved/restored, may reveal the intention of the artist (or designer or maker) and may show whether any copyright exists in the work. Photographs of the object may be available that provide evidence of an earlier state, for example the appearance of a component that has subsequently been lost. This question was designed to be very open so that nothing is excluded. Of course it is rarely possible to answer 'yes', but the words 'necessary' or 'relevant' were deliberately left out. The conservation professional should be able to judge what is necessary or relevant, but only after thinking about everything that might be available.

*Do I need to consult clients, peers or other specialists?* This question is intended to ensure that the owner, curator, or other persons responsible for the object have been informed of the intended action. It is important to be clear for whom one is working and to ensure that the need for treatment has been discussed and agreed with the owner or curator. There may also be other stakeholders and sources to be consulted. It may be helpful to discuss the need for treatment with other conservators. Scientific input may also be required before treatment can be fully informed or safely carried out.

*What are the factors contributing to the identity and significance of the object?* For example, these may include historical and technical factors, the maker's intentions, the sacred nature of the object or any associations with people or events. A fundamental aspect of this question is to determine what effect any proposed actions might have on the evidence for these factors. The essence of this question is an attempt to determine the significance of the work in its cultural context and where the identity of the object resides. The 'value' or importance of the object may be artefactual or informational. The object may have religious or fetishist significance. If so this may be one reason why an object should perhaps not be treated. It may be that the deterioration of the object is wholly or partly of historical significance. The object may contain or provide important evidence manifested in the form of certain accretions or patterns of use which, if disturbed, will reduce the amount of information that can be obtained from the object in future. It is frequently not possible to preserve equally the historical integrity, physical integrity and aesthetic integrity it is therefore important to try to determine the relative importance of these factors. If possible, the artist (or designer or maker) should be consulted. Most of these points are self-explanatory, but the issue of the maker's intentions is more contentious. The maker's intentions are important and if the maker is still living his/her views should be sought. The group who compiled the checklist believed that that if these views can be respected they should be. If not, there should be reasonable justification why not.

*Do I have sufficient information and skill to assess and implement actions?* Some important questions for the individual to address focus on whether he or she has sufficient knowledge and experience to make an assessment and enough knowledge and skill to do the work.

*What options are available for actions that will produce an acceptable result with minimum intervention?* The condition of the various parts of the object, budget and time constraints, availability of treatment, materials, facilities and expertise are important considerations. Preventive measures may be available as an alternative to intervention.

*What are the advantages and disadvantages of each course of action?* It can be helpful to record in writing the alternatives that have been considered and to formally review the advantages and disadvantages of each option, including that of doing nothing. Options where the disadvantages outweigh the advantages may be seen as prime candidates for rejection. Changes produced by the treatment should be

acceptable to the client (or to the artist, designer or maker). Whether or not a proposed method of treatment has been tested/proven and whether it has been generally accepted by the profession as suitable are also important considerations. Some treatments are generally accepted and the conservator decides in each case whether or not they are suitable or adequate, others can only be proposed on an individual basis. If the treatment proposed goes beyond the minimum compatible with the agreed use of the object, it should be clear to everyone why this is, how the object will benefit from the actions proposed and what would happen if some or all of this work were not done. Following up published case studies may help the conservator to decide on the long-term value of a treatment method. If there is currently doubt about a treatment it may be better to wait for resolution of a potential problem rather than treat the object, even if it is somewhat unstable. The circumstances under which it is acceptable to be experimental need to be very carefully considered. When a treatment has been decided upon it may be helpful to test the decision by asking what are the pluses, minuses and interesting features of the proposed treatment and what arguments count to your mind most strongly against what you propose to do.

*Rather than intervening with an object, can use or environment be modified?* It may sometimes be possible to prevent damage or improve stability by non-intrusive methods, such as improving the environment to which an object will be returned. In any case it may not be sensible to carry out remedial work unless the causes of further deterioration in the environment to which the object will be returned have been eliminated or reduced. Elements of preventive conservation, for example coatings, covers and mounts, may be applicable to the object as well as to the environment.

*What are the resource implications of my actions and does my intended action constitute the best use of resources?* Resources include time, money, people, space, equipment and materials. They are only included among ethical considerations in so much as they may affect the object, but they do constitute a constraint in the amount and type of work that can realistically be undertaken. Before embarking on a treatment it is important to have a good idea of the amount of time it will take to complete each phase of the work, for example stabilizing and aesthetic aspects of the treatment, and how much time is available. A deadline may influence the action taken. It should not influence the quality of the action though it may affect the quantity or extent of the work. If acceptable work cannot be done with the resources available then there are, for the institutional conservator at least, various options. The conservator could either use institutional mechanisms to bid for additional resources, or not do the work at all, or do the work to the best possible standard ensuring that everyone concerned understands the implications of the resource constraint. Not all conservation professionals, especially those at junior grades, will be able to control the availability of resources but all have a role to play influencing their allocation. Also all conservators have a duty to develop more efficient processes and to look for the best ways of using their time. In the ethical context, the balance between activities such as surveys, preventive conservation and interventive conservation is important. A question that can be revealing is what am I not doing during the time it takes to treat this object? Cost parameters in the conservation of works of art are discussed by Farancz *et al.* (1985).

When treating sets of objects, time may influence treatment in other ways. Treatments may spread over a period which is long enough to include changes in approach to treatments, conservation materials, or changes in staff. The authors have personal experience of a treatment spread over twelve years and seven conservators each with a slightly different approach. This can result in significant differences in appearance. Even if the materials and methods stay the same, the objects or early treatments may have changed during the treatment period. Multiple treatments spread over a period may also result in an escalation of costs that may no longer represent value for money to the client. It would be naive to ignore the fact that for some clients there is a correlation between the financial value of an object and conservation investment. Availability of space for display also has a profound influence on how resources are allocated. If there is insufficient space for display, even very important

pieces may be retired to storage and be low on conservation priority lists.

*Do established courses of action need to be adapted or new ones established?* This raises the question of whether and when it is acceptable to be experimental. The profession can only advance through experiment and innovation and every practitioner has some responsibility to contribute towards this. There are few perfect treatments, there are always 'problem' objects and materials may be withdrawn for health and safety reasons or be discredited for use in particular applications. These are all reasons why the profession must constantly look to the future and think about improvements.

*Are all my actions fully documented to a known and accepted standard?* While most people agree that documentation is a necessary and important part of conservation, it is arguable whether there is a 'known and accepted standard' even within most large practices let alone within the profession. Although there is evidence that such a standard is beginning to emerge it has yet to be fully documented and accepted as such. It is very important that conservation professionals should know what is appropriate for themselves, for their clients and for those who may need access to information about objects in the future. Typically, documentation will include the condition of objects before treatment, the materials and processes of treatment, the condition afterwards and the presence and location of potential or actual instabilities. The methods by which assessments, actions and outcomes should be documented and the means by which the viewer is to distinguish between original and conserved parts need to be carefully considered. Object-based documentation typically includes photographs and drawings, written descriptions, marking on the object and technical information in the form of samples and so forth. A fundamental ancillary question is whether our records are accessible to appropriate users and what steps we can take to ensure that this is the case. Documentation is further discussed below.

*How will my action(s) affect subsequent action(s)?* A concern among conservators for many years has been whether a treatment could be reversed without causing damage to original materials or structures. In recognition of the practical limits of reversibility in many circumstances the balance of emphasis may now have shifted to another fundamental issue which is whether re-treatment will be possible or whether the current treatment will inhibit future work. This may include simple questions such as whether the object should be protected to make cleaning easier or less damaging in future as well as addressing major intervention. It is very important to think about what follow-up treatment may be required in future, how this might be achieved and how the treatment affects what could be done if it were required again – of the options available now, how many would still be available after treatment? This can be related to the statistical concept of the number of *degrees of freedom* preserved. As with other items on the checklist, this question is phrased to prompt questioning by the conservation professional. If an action might prevent a future action (e.g. sampling), it does not necessarily mean that the action should not be taken, but it should mean that the decision to proceed is only taken after the implications have been carefully considered.

*Have I taken into account the future use and location of the object(s)?* The proposed location and purpose for which an object or collection is to be used are factors which a conservator may feel should influence a treatment proposal. Objects may require different actions to be taken if they are being returned to fully functional use or being sent on a lengthy touring exhibition than if being returned to storage for occasional study. Different individuals and organizations have legitimately different purposes that will have a profound influence on what is an appropriate goal for any related conservation treatment. Use may include temporary or permanent display, long- or short-term loan (perhaps to multiple venues), frequent study, storage, partial or full functional use. An object retired from functional use and intended for display can be treated as any museum object; that is the piece can be treated with full regard to preservation ignoring the needs of its original function. An object that is being used as a functional piece may be treated with regard to function first

with preservation as an artefact of cultural significance as a secondary consideration. This may mean that materials that might be entirely appropriate for conservation are quite simply impractical. A functional piece of upholstered seat furniture, for example, has to withstand mechanical abrasion and the weight of the sitter. Ceremonial pieces such as thrones, Masonic chairs and religious furnishings may be venerated and preserved for their historic significance but expected to perform functionally from time to time. This may necessitate treatment concessions (Rendall, 1990).

The public has a right to expect certain standards of behaviour from publicly funded organizations and in many cases what museums and similar cultural heritage organizations may do is governed by law. Private owners operate under far fewer constraints though not entirely without them. In every case, independently of any conservation considerations, behaviour should remain within what is appropriate for a particular purpose and in every case where conservation is an issue, the questions posed by the checklist should be applied. However, one should not be surprised or upset to obtain different answers in different cases. In the authors' view the application of the process of questioning and agreement between the relevant stakeholders plays a far greater part in determining whether the treatment can be considered ethical than the actual nature of the treatment itself.

Within the museum context, an object may or may not be in environmentally controlled space, on constant display or part of a rotated display or subject to loan or travelling display agreements. Large sets are often split between institutions wishing to represent a particularly fine example of type rather than several examples of the same piece. This may lead to treatments being devised based on an incomplete understanding of the whole significance of a piece within a set. Collaborative treatments between institutions are possible but are subject to planning difficulties – for example, the year one institution wishes to treat an object may be financially impossible for another.

There are advantages and constraints in displaying furniture within the historic interior. The most obvious difficulty to be faced is that of controlling the environment. Where environmental control of a whole space is impractical, solutions include enclosing the object in a 'Museum Room' where tighter control of environmental parameters is possible. Such spaces may limit the display to containing one piece from each of several sets. Alternatively, the viewer can be enclosed. A less obvious difficulty may be one of public access. The benefits of allowing the public to see the furniture in a room setting may be at odds with keeping the furnishings out of reach. This is particularly the case with textile hangings and coverings where the tactile qualities are part of the appeal. Large sets of furniture, not unusual in the historic house setting, are less likely to be acquired by museums as they lose some meaning outside the context of the type of room for which they are designed and take up valuable space. The period room setting is an exception. Museum conservation solutions designed for single pieces may be inappropriate or impractical applied to a set. The treatment of large sets of upholstered furniture may be approached differently than an individual item for reasons of uniqueness, time, cost or space. The existence of a set means, in a sense, that the object is not unique. The client may therefore have options available such as rotation on exhibition or may decide that the item is not exceptional and therefore not deserving of treatment. Where normally one option only can be chosen from a range of possibilities for treatment, in the case of sets, there may be more flexibility. Different members can be treated differently to allow different points to be made. For example, one might be left untreated, one conserved and one restored to show how it might have appeared originally.

When an object is to be conserved for a private collection it is important to assess the degree to which an item will be used. It is a simple matter to persuade the owner of a work of fine art that these items confer a degree of privilege of ownership and responsibility to posterity. It is less simple to persuade the owner of a rare piece of furniture upholstery that they should not sit or lie upon it! When an upholstered object has a high degree of decorative merit, embroidered top covers for example, it is easy to persuade a client that the object can be put to good decorative effect without use. It is the utilitarian which is most at risk; the understructure of such an upholstered object, for example, which may be renewed for cleanliness or comfort. In the context of upholstered furniture, essential reading on considerations of whether to conserve or reupholster and on the costing and estimating of work is provided by Florian *et al.* (1990), French (1990), Landi (1985) and Williams (1990). The ethics and aesthetics of upholstery conservation are further discussed by Cornforth (1981, 1988), Lahikainen (1990), Montgomery (1984), Nylander (1990) and Pilgrim (1983).

*How will I assess the success of the action(s) and how will I get feedback from clients and peers?* It is important to have some measure of the quality of the work which a client can expect as well as the time and cost. Working to a known, accepted and agreed quality standard may require specific arrangements to be made such as the provision of sketches, samples, access to previous work or other evidence of what the client can reasonably expect. It is then important to identify the stages at which feedback will be obtained from the client, the form that this will take and the actions that can arise from it. It is also important that discoveries, whether of an historical or technical nature should be communicated.

The dictionary definition of quality (as a noun) is 'the degree of excellence of a thing' and (as an adjective) of high grade of excellence'. A more illuminating definition can be found in BS4478 'Quality Vocabulary' (equivalent to ISO 8402). Quality is 'the totality of features and characteristics of a product or service that bears on its ability to satisfy stated or implied needs'. This definition is followed by three notes:

(1) In a contractual environment, needs are specified, whereas in other environments, implied needs should be identified and defined.
(2) In many instances, needs can change with time; this implies periodic revision of specifications.
(3) Needs are usually translated into features and characteristics with specified criteria. Needs may include aspects of usability, safety, availability, reliability, maintainability, economics and environment.

Three important elements of quality to remember are fitness for purpose, value for money and customer satisfaction. Use of the checklist outlined above can go a long way to assuring quality. For those who would like to pursue this further, the literature on quality is vast but most of it is linked in one way or another to various published quality standards. There are many American, British and International standards covering all aspects of quality. Standards for quality assurance were originally published as British Standards in 1979 and have been known as the BS5750 series. With a little modification this standard was adopted internationally by the International Organization for Standardization (ISO) in 1987 as ISO 9000. The European Standards body also adopted the standard that became known as EN29000. To remove the confusion caused by the different numbering systems, the British Standards Institution (BSI) announced in July 1994, as part of a review of quality management standards, that BS5750 would be phased out and replaced by a new number BS EN ISO 9000. For further information see Ashwood (1996).

Regrettably there is no guide to the process by which these questions are to be used – just questions which, if answered honestly, may at least promote integrity. It is important to remember that issues of ethical behaviour in conservation are not confined to intervention but apply to all aspects of the work of the conservation professional. For further discussion on general philosophical issues, on the understanding and interpretation of works of art and the potential impact of conservation the reader is referred to works by Angst (1980), Beck and Daly (1994), Dorge (1987), Elwood (1980), Ground (1989), Mackie (1977), Oddy (1992, 1994), Price *et al.* (1996), Sheppard (1987), Singer (1979). De Bono (1996) provides an excellent introduction to some tools and structures useful in the context of making conservation decisions.

## 9.3   Examination

Examination is required for many reasons. In each case, the *purpose* of the examination determines *what* we need to look for, which in turn determines *how* we might best go about looking. Furniture conservators should be aware of the general principles of examination and the techniques available so that they are able to select the most appropriate techniques

and carry them out, or have them carried out, in a competent manner. This section shows some of the choices available and provides some background information relevant to any type of investigation. The emphasis is on simpler methods in day-to-day use by a typical conservation studio.

### 9.3.1   Purpose of examination

Thorough examination of objects should always be undertaken before treatment but may also be required for one or another of the following reasons:

- To determine the suitability of object for collections management activities – acquisition, display, loan etc.
- To establish or refute authenticity, age, date of manufacture
- To record condition before or after loan or transportation
- To determine the need for active or passive conservation
- To determine the nature and extent of previous restoration and the success or failure of previous conservation techniques
- To increase understanding of the causes of deterioration
- To determine appropriate courses of treatment
- To estimate the cost of work required
- To provide a reference point before making changes
- To provide knowledge about the materials and techniques of artists and craftspeople.

The careful examination of furniture directed towards materials and construction can reveal the object's condition and authenticity. This investigation is essential in order to develop a responsible concept for conservation treatment. The preliminary stages of examination lead the conservator to a better understanding of the object and to the formulation of specific questions that prompt further investigation.

Examination and documentation of the results of examination provide reference for materials, structure (dimensions, angles, methods of construction), condition, which it is essential to have before consideration of specific treatments or conservation.

Characterization sets out to increase understanding of the arrangement and properties of various materials that make up the object rather than specifically identifying each component. Characterization seeks to determine, for example, the appearance, condition, layer structure, solubility and fluorescence characteristics of a coating to help uncover the history of the piece and to determine treatment needs and options. It is somewhat distinct from the process of analysis that is used to confirm the specific identities of particular materials.

### 9.3.2 What to look for

In general terms there are two kinds of evidence: evidence from the object itself and related evidence which comes from the previous environment, from documentation, from other members of sets or from related objects. Evidence from the object itself includes the materials, construction and condition of the object and the overall quality and variations in quality of these things. An essential aspect of knowing what to look for is to know the kinds of materials and structures that were used in furniture at different times and places. It is also essential to become familiar with the properties and characteristics of materials and their modes of deterioration and failure. The more complete one's knowledge of the macroscopic and microscopic features of materials and of their physical, chemical, optical and other properties the better one is able to lead an examination and the better one is able to attach significance to what is observed. The fact that a certain pattern of cracks may be observed in a surface coating may not mean anything by itself. It is essential that the observer has the knowledge to interpret the observation.

The most obvious question about furniture during examination is: what wood is it made of? However, attention should also be paid to any metal fixtures, fittings or fastenings, ceramics, upholstery materials, adhesives, coatings and other materials that may be present, either as part of the original structure or as repair materials. The use of certain materials and certain processes was developed at certain times in the past and this may provide a guide to age and authenticity (Bowman, 1990; Kaye, 1991). Whether the materials and techniques of construction (both original construction and signs of alteration) are consistent with what would be expected for a piece of the supposed age,

origin or maker are frequently asked questions. Usually, if a material or technique turns up in an object at a date earlier than expected it will throw suspicion on the piece. However, where supporting evidence for the age of the piece is irrefutable it may point towards the need for revision of the chronology for that material or technique.

The overall shape of the piece, its structure and evidence of methods of construction may help to support the authenticity of the object, add to our knowledge of the type and contribute to our understanding of how the piece should be treated in the context of present condition and desired end use. Hidden elements of construction may, under appropriate lighting conditions, be read in the surface where they 'telegraph' their way through to the surface as undulations revealed in the pattern of light reflected at the surface. This is particularly useful for elucidating the structure of objects which have been veneered or in which the method of construction is otherwise hidden by paint or gilding. These patterns may be revealed even through very slight differences in thickness that arise through moisture induced-dimensional change of components with differing grain orientations.

Various properties of different materials that vary in some predictable way with time or which have changed radically at a particular point in time have been used to determine the age of materials. The techniques of radio carbon dating and dendrochronology that can sometimes be used with wood may be helpful in resolving its age and are further discussed below. It should be remembered, however, with all such techniques that what is being measured is the age of the material or component. This does not necessarily confirm the age for the entire structure. An object made from a tree that was felled in 1920 cannot have been made in the seventeenth century but wood from a tree that was felled in 1620 could have been used at any subsequent date. Similarly old screws could have been used in new locations or those in an old structure replaced with new ones, although some clues to what has actually happened usually remain.

The presence of various kinds of marks, inscriptions and labels can also provide valuable information about provenance and methods of construction. Occasionally stamped marks, labels, or signatures may indicate the origin, workshop or actual maker of a piece (Brandner, 1976; Kisluk-Grosheide, 1991; Stratmann, 1975; Van Duin, 1989). Since this would add considerably to the value of an object, further examination might then be required to substantiate the authenticity of this evidence. Labels may provide information about manufacturer, owner, or auction houses that have been involved in previous transactions, for example. Patterns of tool marks such as those from adze, pit saw or frame saw, circular saw and bandsaw are quite distinctive and can help to resolve questions of authenticity and later alteration (Hayward, 1970). Similarly, patterns of marks may suggest carving or sanding. Concentric scratches may suggest turning. The presence at joints of double lines from a mortise gauge would indicate mortise and tenon construction whereas the presence of a single line running through the centre would normally indicate dowel joint construction. The absence of gauge lines at dovetails would suggest a machine-made joint, though in any case the pattern of hand cut dovetails is usually quite distinctive and in English furniture follows a certain development with time (Hayward, 1970). Knife marks in the surface of a support under a veneered surface may also shed valuable light on the techniques that were used (Hawkins, 1986). Metals may show mould marks from casting, incised grooves from engraving, or compressed channels from chasing (Larsen, 1987; Watts, 1982).

The nature of any coatings, patination, corrosion or dirt also needs to be considered. The gloss, thickness and clarity of a coating are important characteristics. Thinness and a low sheen suggest a wax or oil film while a thicker, reflective coating indicates a resinous surface. A less than fully transparent coating can be a result of ageing, dirt or an intentional toner layer. The condition and visual qualities of the coating may suggest a particular class of finish, age and exposure and should be noted. A fine or dramatic craquelure (fissuring), for example, is suggestive of a resinous coating. An exaggerated craquelure indicates that the coating is quite thick. The lack of a craquelure in an isolated area may indicate lack of exposure to light and other agents of deterioration, on that part. A coating that is discontinuous with significant areas of substrate exposed may present a

greater level of difficulty in treatment than a film that is continuous over the whole surface. The coating–substrate adherence properties are important to consider. Pressing the finish with a finger nail can determine how secure the finish is. A coating that turns white or flakes off under the pressure of a finger nail is poorly adhered and presents some significant problems. Similarly, the presence of certain kinds of corrosion or dirt may give important clues about the previous environment and sometimes about the composition of the material from which the object is made. The stratigraphy or layer structure of surface decoration is an essential element of investigation for all but the simplest kind of surface decoration that can be used to discover the numbers and types of layers of decoration, the extent of wear, damage and soiling to successive layers and by further analysis shed light on the detailed composition of the layers.

Variations within and between elements of a structure can also be revealing. Whether the object is 'all of a piece' or has variations in quality of materials or workmanship can suggest reconstruction, removal or addition of parts of the structure and sometimes indicate the circumstances of and motivation for the alteration. For example this might be an 'honest repair' or it might be a modification intended to enhance the value of an object by adding ornamental detail or by changing one kind of structure to another. Two common kinds of structural alteration of furniture are 'marriage' of two or more elements from different pieces and 'divorce' of one structure into several parts. This is frequently associated with discrepancies in materials, construction technique or quality of workmanship, fittings, markings, colour, texture, sharpness of edges and so forth. Patterns of the quantity, quality and location of damage and wear can also be very revealing as to whether they are what would reasonably be expected or not. The presence of outlines, marks, holes and plugs can indicate previous attachments (hardware). Investigations into the authenticity of furniture are discussed by Cescinsky (1967), Crawley (1971) and Hayward (1970).

Accurate determination of the condition of objects is important to determine the nature of the intervention that may be required but also to determine the need for improved storage and to estimate the cost of work. This requires

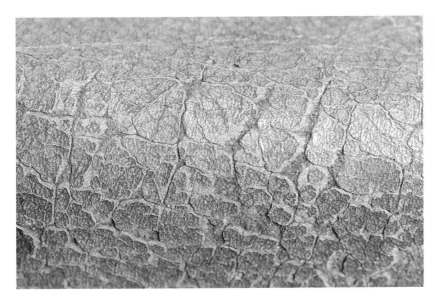

**Plate 1** Detail of leather upholstery on a chair, showing the characteristic red powdery appearance of 'red rot'

(a)

(b)

(c)

**Plate 2** Examination of surfaces under ultra violet light
(*a*) Marquetry cabinet, German, late fifteenth or early sixteenth century, viewed under visible light
(*b*) Cabinet viewed under UV. There is an orange tone to the auto-fluorescence that suggests restoration coatings based on shellac
(*c*) Two drawers from the cabinet, under UV. The drawer on the left has a greenish white auto-fluoresence typical of a natural resin varnish. The drawer on the right has been restored. The lack of yellow auto-fluorescence, present on the original, makes replacement stringing easy to identify

*continued*

(d)

(e)

**Plate 2** *continued*
(*d*) Nineteenth century Japanese stacking cabinet, viewed under visible light
(*e*) Stacking cabinet viewed under UV. Small areas of retouching appear as black spots. The bright orange fluorescence of some Oriental lacquer may be mistaken for shellac by the unwary
(*f*) Cabinet with top removed. One effect of light degradation on lacquer can be a change in its appearance when viewed under UV. In this case, the original bright orange auto-fluoresence of the lacquer has been lost where the cabinet has suffered long exposure to light, but remains where the surface has been protected by the top

(f)

**Plate 3** Side table (*c*.1775) designed by William Chambers. Detail of the painted table top during removal of varnish. The low glass transition temperature of the varnish meant that, as dirt was deposited from the ambient environment, it sank into the coating and became integral to it

**Plate 4** Rear view of a fancy painted chair, Baltimore, early nineteenth century, during conservation treatment. A discoloured oil coating was removed with a lipase gel to reveal the original green decoration and gilt highlights

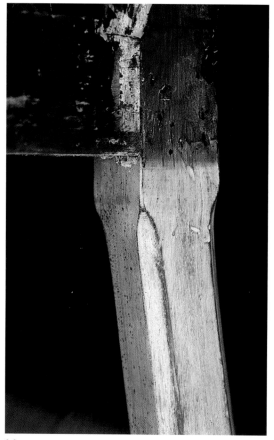

(a)

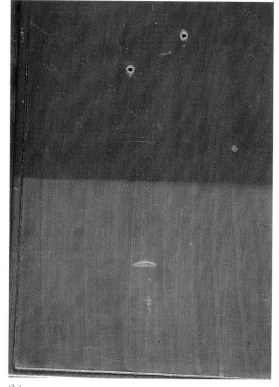

(b)

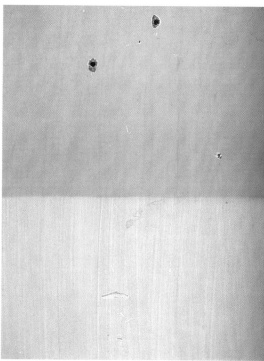

(c)

**Plate 5** Shifts in the colour of auto-fluorescence
(*a*) Detail of the leg of a chair (*c*.1800) viewed under
UV. The bright orange auto-fluorescence is typically
associated with shellac whilst the green auto-
fluorescence is normally associated with natural resins
such as dammar or mastic. In this case, however, both
colours are emitted by a shellac coating. The greenish
areas of auto-fluorescence were observed wherever the
surface of the chair had been exposed to sunlight,
whilst the orange auto-fluorescence was found wherever
the surface had been protected from light. Areas that
had received graded exposure to light exhibited a
corresponding gradual shift in the colour of the auto-
fluorescence. (*b*) A cellulose nitrate coating viewed
under normal light. The top was protected from
exposure to light, whilst the bottom had two years'
exposure to daylight in a south facing window (approx.
39th parallel, northern hemisphere)
(*c*) Cellulose nitrate coating as in (*b*) viewed under UV.
The protected surface has a bluish auto-fluorescence,
whilst the surface exposed to sunlight exhibits a
greenish auto-fluorescence. Unaged shellac and cellulose
nitrate are chemically very different and have distinctly
different appearances when viewed under UV. In
contrast, light ageing can produce very similar auto-
fluorescence under a UV light source

(a)                                                                                    (b)

**Plate 6**  A tall case japanned clock, attributed to Gawen Brown, Boston, late eighteenth century
(*a*) Detail before conservation: the elaborate oil based japanned decoration was completely obscured by restoration
varnishes that had darkened
(*b*) Detail during conservation: solvent gels were used to remove the restoration varnish layers, revealing the
original japanned decoration

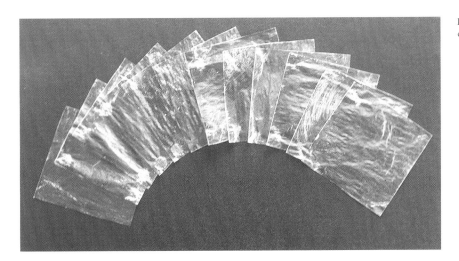

**Plate 7**  Some of the
colours of gold leaf

(a)

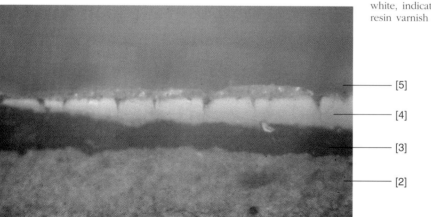

(b)

(c)

**Plate 8** Lacquer sections viewed in cross-section

(*a*) Photomicrograph of a cross-section of a Japanese export lacquer surface (*c*.1600) viewed under visible light. Two ground layers are apparent, the first (1) characterized by the use of coarse unevenly sized particles, the second (2) by fine evenly sized particles. The lacquer layers (3) above the ground appear black. Layer (4) is dark brown and has a translucent appearance, whilst layer (5) is grey

(*b*) Cross-section from an early eighteenth century Coromandel screen viewed under near UV. An example of the orange auto-fluorescence that can be seen in some black lacquers

(*c*) Photomicrograph of (*a*) viewed under UV. Layer (3) comprises non-fluorescent lacquer layers. Layer (4) can be seen auto-fluorescing bright white, indicating that it is a natural resin varnish

the nature, extent, severity and location of each kind of damage, wear or loss to be observed and recorded and may require various kinds of analysis to be carried out to determine the nature or properties of the object materials. Examination of condition should also consider the age and type of the object, whether damage or loss is recent, the likelihood of further damage or loss, the potential effect on other items in a collection and the likelihood of injury to people or damage to the fabric of the building. There are advantages in developing a recording system, as many museums have done, that uses standard headings for the categories of damage and a standard grading system for their severity (Keene, 1996).

Commonly used *categories of damage* include: structural damage (major and minor); surface effects; old repairs; biological damage; chemical damage. This can be used in conjunction with an overall grading system of 1–4 for condition representing object condition as good (1), fair (2), poor (3) or unacceptable (4). *Good* means that the object in its context is in good conservation condition or is stable. In this category different absolute degrees of change might be expected between a sixteenth century oak table and a similar object from the late twentieth century. *Fair* indicates that an object is disfigured or damaged but stable and not in need of immediate attention. *Poor* means that the object is probably unstable, its use should be restricted or stopped and that remedial action is desirable. *Unacceptable* indicates that immediate action should be taken as the object is severely weakened or highly unstable or is affecting (or likely to affect) other objects in the vicinity.

### Structural damage

Examples of structural damage include separation or loss of components and shrinkage, splitting or distortion. Objects in good condition should be complete. Some loosening of metal fittings such as mounts, locks and hinges is normally acceptable provided that these are not major load-bearing components of the structure. Loss, detachment or severe loosening of major structural components is unacceptable. Objects in fair to poor condition may exhibit varying degrees of loss or detachment of applied elements such as mouldings, carvings and glue blocks that are not jointed parts

of the structure. Greater than about 10% losses would place an object condition as poor or worse. Similarly, objects in good condition should be free of distortion, splitting or other evidence of excessive movement. Objects in good to fair condition may exhibit fine, thin, short cracks that are not readily visible from normal viewing distance. Progressing by stages, distortion or open splits and cracks that are not sufficient to impair function but are visible from normal viewing distances may eventually reach a stage where they are liable to cause loss of mouldings, veneers, inlays or painted and gilded surface decoration and eventually to impair the function of moving parts such as drawers, doors and falls.

### Surface effects

Surface effects include surface accretions and losses from the surface of substance or of form. Surface accretions may include loose deposits, greasy dirt or mould, stains, exudations and firmly adhered surface dirt and deposits. Surface losses may include bruises, dents, scratches, abrasions, loss of colour (especially non-uniform fading and oxidation) and small losses of paint, gesso or veneer. It is important to observe whether such areas are stable or unstable as a guide to whether further losses are likely to occur or not. As with many other aspects of condition, the age and type of the item being examined as well as the extent and location of the accretion or loss will affect judgement of the degree of seriousness of the condition and the action to be taken. As part of the process of examination it is important to consider whether the line or form of the object has been or is likely to become obscured by damage and the extent to which other vital information has been lost or is at risk.

Old repairs may be sound, intact, correctly aligned or not visible under normal viewing conditions. They may be more extensive or obvious, misaligned, unsound or constituting a major visual distraction. Structurally weak or unstable old repairs and those causing, or likely to cause, (further) damage to original material should be carefully noted during examination. The materials used in old repairs may have a bearing on subsequent courses of treatment if they do not behave in the same way as original material. It is therefore important to consider this during examination.

Signs of structural damage include shrinkage, distortion, splits, cracks and separation or loss of components. Structural damage is not always as readily apparent as the term might suggest. It may include fine, thin, short, closed cracks which will open under load but are not easily seen from normal viewing angles or distances. It is therefore advisable to check objects from different angles under varying degrees of (moderate) applied loads, especially at or near joints to determine whether the condition is sufficient to impair function or cause damage in future. More serious splits, cracks or distortion may cause varying degrees of impairment of function, such as preventing drawers, doors, or falls from working properly. It is therefore important to check during examination to see that the object does function as intended. Since the state of wood is affected by the prevailing conditions of humidity, this may be a factor that needs to be considered in relation to any functional checks. Splits, cracks or distortion not sufficient to impair function but liable to cause loss are commonly found in areas where wood grain of adjacent components changes direction. This may affect mouldings on drawers, cross-grained inlay or other veneer, paint, gilding or other surface decoration present. Evidence of structural damage and loss may also include loose, detached or missing mouldings, (carved) ornament, glue blocks and metal fittings and fastenings such as mounts, hinges and locks.

Biological damage includes fungal and insect attack of various kinds. Absence of flight holes is not necessarily conclusive evidence of the absence of an active infestation of wood-boring insects. Similarly, the presence of exit holes does not constitute proof of an active infestation. Ways in which an active infestation can be recognized and identified have been discussed in Chapter 7. The condition of the surface in the vicinity of any holes should be carefully checked to ascertain the likely extent of damage and the nature of the treatment required. Some obvious flight holes but not sufficient to cause structural weakness or surface collapse would normally be regarded as acceptable in older objects containing susceptible woods such as lime, walnut and elm, particularly in the sapwood. Surface mould which could easily be wiped off would also not be considered serious. More extensive flight holes,

damage round joints or collapse of the surface might be considered to indicate poor condition. Active infestation of wood-boring insects indicated by clean fresh flight holes and fresh frass or a soft rotten powdery surface with damage extending below the surface should be regarded as unacceptable and should lead to the object being isolated and treated straight away. The environment in which the object has been kept should also be thoroughly examined to determine the source and extent of any insect or fungal infestation that may be present.

Damages due to chemical reactions in wood are not commonly observed but some types of blue–black staining may be caused by interaction of tannin in wood with ferrous metals or their salts. Chemical damage to other types of material, particularly metals and plastics, is relatively common. Irregular powdery and/or hard nodular deposits standing proud from the metal surface are corrosion products. They may vary from the familiar bright orange rust of ferrous materials to bright green, turquoise blue, or dark green powdery spots or patches of copper alloys. Light grey to white powdery fils or nodules may be found on lead, zinc, tin alloys and aluminium and black to blue–brown deposits are found on silver. Closer analysis of corrosion products in metals can be very revealing of the nature of the corrosion process and the action that needs to be taken to prevent or reduce further damage.

### 9.3.3   Methods of examination

It is convenient to distinguish between *characterization* and *analysis*. Characterization relies on techniques such as gross examination, solvent testing, examination under low power magnification, various forms of light microscopy and alternative light sources. Analysis is concerned primarily with the identification of materials. The techniques used to identify non-homogeneous and sometimes complex mixtures fall into two broad classes, spectrometric methods and separation techniques, principally chromatography. Together, they provide powerful tools for the identification and structural analysis of organic compounds and the qualitative and quantitative determination of metals and other elements. The information obtained can contribute to our understanding of such things as an object's age, condition, authenticity and treatment needs. Reliable identification of many materials requires the services of conservation scientists with the special competencies and equipment needed. For those materials that are not frequently encountered in furniture it is advisable to consult with conservators in other disciplines.

No matter what optical, chemical, instrumental, or other technique is used, examination should proceed by certain principles so that we can have confidence that our conclusions are properly supported by evidence. This has to do with the nature of the reasoning process, with objectivity, standards of comparison, controls, accuracy, precision and other components of the scientific method. Careful observation and reasoning should characterize both low-tech and hi-tech approaches (Sibilia, 1996).

### General aspects of characterization

It is very important to examine the whole object and not to be satisfied with limited information from just one part. It is also useful to examine objects in a systematic fashion. The order in which parts of an object are examined is an important factor in ensuring that nothing is missed. There is no, one, absolute method for all purposes but rather individual conservators should develop their own preferences. Examples might be to examine from the outside towards the inside, from front to back, from top to bottom. For seat furniture one might develop a rule to examine backs, sides, front and underside in that order or for carcase furniture to examine top, front, sides, base, back, base, interior. It may also be helpful to consider separately *structure, ornament, surface decoration and finish* or to look for say biological damage, structural damage and so on in a particular order. The process of examination can usefully continue through several iterations with each look producing fresh ideas which prompt further examination with a different view in mind. When examining metalwork, it is especially important to look under platings, around catches and rivets and at the contact points with other metals and materials. Appropriate clothing should be worn during this process. For example, when handling intricately cut metalwork fine rubber gloves should be worn rather than cotton to avoid catching delicate strands or claws on glove fibres.

The essence of examination is comparison of the characteristics, properties or qualities of the 'unknown' object/component/material with something which is known. In terms of analytical techniques, a standard is a pure substance which reacts in a characteristic, quantitative and known way under specific conditions in a given test. By comparison of an unknown sample with various known standards it becomes possible to identify the unknown. In the most highly formalized types of comparison, strenuous efforts are made to ensure that the comparison between the unknown and the sample is valid. This involves, for example, demonstrating that the response to a given test is unique for a material or class of materials, that the unknown and standard were compared under identical conditions and that the response of the unknown was identical to that of the known sample. This type of highly formalized comparison is possible for many chemical substances and frequently it is possible to extend the comparison to a quantitative as well as qualitative comparison because there is a known relationship between the amount of the material present and the size of the response obtained.

Comparison between an unknown and a standard need not rely on a single property or reaction. The identification of timbers, discussed in Chapter 2 can be based on systematic criteria related to the type, number, size and distribution of different cellular elements. As wood is a biological material there is more variation so it becomes more difficult to define and apply a standard but it is still perfectly possible to do so in a meaningful way and to obtain a very high percentage of correct identifications. Many keys for the identification of biological material have been developed in this way.

For other types of comparison formal standards of comparison may not exist, for example, because it is difficult or impossible to create them or because they have not been recorded as such. Certain characteristics of furniture can act as a guide to when that piece was created but not as defined standards. These include the type of furniture (for example tea tables did not exist before tea drinking became fashionable), the materials used, the pattern and arrangement of structural, or decorative elements, the nature of the finish and so forth.

The number and arrangement of pins in a drawer dovetail and the direction of the grain in drawer bottoms may follow a distinct trend in English furniture in relation to date. However, it would be unwise to assert because of a certain arrangement of these elements that a drawer, still less the whole piece of furniture must have been made at a particular date. In this territory, there may be several alternative explanations or possibilities and the development of standards becomes to a large extent something that each individual has to do for themselves from the available information.

The development of this 'connoisseurship' can be assisted by several things, first among which is the opportunity to examine primary standards. In furniture terms this means looking at objects for which it is known who made them, where they were made, when they were made, where they have been since and what has been done to them since they were made. The best of these are items that were sold by the maker to the present owner who has never done anything to them. Such items are rare. Careful observation, accurate recording and comparison with other items to establish similarities and differences then provides a reference standard for future comparison.

### Estimating

A similar approach to that described in the foregoing paragraph can be adopted as a means to the end of producing accurate estimates of the timing and cost of conservation work. Estimates are more likely to be accurate if they are based on a fairly detailed breakdown of any problem and its likely method of solution and also if they are based on a rate for each aspect of the work which has been developed from previous work. The systematic breakdown (functional decomposition) of conservation condition provides the basis for proposal of treatment and hence for estimating based on the type, rate and amount of work. The guides for estimating for antique furniture repairs and for estimating for cabinetmakers that were produced by CoSIRA (the Council for Small Industries in Rural Areas) were based on a rate for each element of a job that was calculated according to the type of work and the number and size of the elements required. For example laying patches of loose veneer might be calculated at so much per square inch per

patch. Such figures may be useful as a guide in the first instance but there is no substitute for keeping accurate records of one's own work to use as a basis for estimating future work. However, in a competitive world, bench marking (in this case, comparison with other people's rates and times) is obviously important. Conservators seeking to develop good estimating skills should find much of interest in Brook (1998), Paxton (1999) and in the code of estimating practice of the Procurement Committee of the Chartered Institute of Building (1997).

### Gross examination

Gross examination often concentrates on low power optical methods using different light sources but should also make use of the other senses, of touch, smell, taste and hearing.

Gross examination with the naked eye is usually a helpful first step in revealing details of materials, structure, techniques and condition. There is much that can be determined without the aid of sophisticated equipment and it is important to establish the general character of materials before any attempt is made to establish their more exact identities. The construction techniques of furniture can be examined visually, under normal or raking light, for evidence of tool marks and joinery techniques (Kaye, 1991; Smith, 1975; Van Horne, 1991b). The enormous variety of surface decorations on furniture can be examined by eye and when necessary under magnification, to help determine manufacture techniques, methods of application and the nature of materials and their condition (Brachert, 1986; Buchholz, 1991; Burek, 1989; Hulbert, 1987; Michaelsen, 1989, 1992; Van Duin, 1989; Young *et al.*, 1991). Rather vague problems such as surface haziness may become visible as specific surface deterioration phenomena and previous restorations may be revealed by slight differences in opacity, colour or gloss of the surface finish. Features such as dirt particles and craquelure details and an increased sense of depth, are revealed through low magnification techniques. Changing the type and angle of the light, the position of the object or one's own viewpoint may reveal new information each time. Raking light (light shone across the surface at a low angle to it) may reveal fine surface detail such as engraved or incised marks arising from the use of particular tools and may

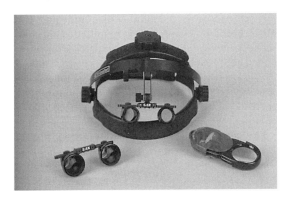

**Figure 9.2** A good quality loupe (right) is invaluable for examination, whist optivisors (stereoscopic magnifiers mounted on a headband – magnification 2.5× and 5.5× (shown centre and left) can be used to provide low-level magnification for examination or during treatment

also reveal in the surface the pattern of the underlying structure. Silicon rubber moulds of the surface, which provide a reversed pattern in relief may also help to show up tool marks.

Low-level magnification by means of simple low power (5–10× power) magnifiers such as a good quality hand lens (as recommended by Hoadley (1990) for the purpose of wood identification), traditional jewellers loupes, linen testers, 'opti-visors', or surgical loupes (see *Figure 9.2*) can quickly provide information about a surface that would not easily be seen with the unaided eye. Inexpensive box like magnifiers, which often include a light source and stereo binocular microscopes can usefully extend the range up to about 30× magnification or more and video microscopes can extend the magnification range up to about 200×, though the field of view and depth of field are often unhelpfully small at such large magnifications. Linen testers have the advantage of letting in plenty of light and of maintaining the correct focal length and thereby providing a sharp image when in contact with the surface being viewed, something that may not be possible, however, if the surface is severely degraded.

As magnification increases, depth of field and field of view tend to be reduced. The focal length of instruments such as surgical loupes and stereo binocular microscopes is of particular importance in determining the working distance and amount of room that the conservator has available to manipulate tools and equipment in the space between the magnifying instrument and the object being examined. A zoom facility is especially useful on instruments with higher magnification as it makes the process of moving from inspection of one area to another easier and safer if one can quickly zoom out to establish position and then zoom in to view detail. The ability to maintain a fixed position also becomes more important as magnification increases. To enable a stereo binocular microscope to reach across the surface of a large piece of furniture, a large, heavy, rigid stand becomes necessary. Such stands may cost several times the price of the original instrument. Even the most expensive surgical loupes (which are fixed to the operator rather than to the bench or the floor) can seem like a bargain in comparison. Nevertheless the stereo binocular microscope is a most useful item of equipment especially when provided, as it should be, with the means to attach a 35 mm SLR type camera. Also, as larger magnifications are used, it becomes necessary to augment the supply of natural light. Fibre optic lighting is most convenient because it is unobtrusive in the working area, is 'cool' (i.e. does not greatly heat the surface) and readily puts the light where it is needed as it allows the light to be varied in direction, angle and intensity.

Access to view the internal condition of wood is frequently denied although it may often be possible to infer this from external signs, such as the presence of flight holes. Access at joints, breaks and gaps in the surface may help and further information can be obtained by probing with a mounted needle or dental tool. For viewing inside larger inaccessible structures an endoscope may sometimes be useful.

Natural, incandescent, halogen and other visible light sources will give useful information under both raking and reflected light conditions on the visual qualities of a finish (*Figure 9.3*). However, no gross examination of a surface is complete without studying it under ultra violet light. Examination of surfaces under UV can be most useful in discovering the presence of fluorescent materials in the finish, particularly natural resins (*Plate 2*). UV can be useful for identification of a variety of adhesives coatings and media, ivory, bone, antler and wood.

**Figure 9.3** Detail of a the leg of a painted side chair, Baltimore, Maryland, *c.*1810, before treatment. Examination under raking light reveals the fragile condition of the paint

It can be used to particular advantage in the examination of surface coatings to reveal evidence of the type of coating used, imperfections in the coating and manipulations that may have been carried out on it. A good high intensity UV-A light (315 nm to 400 nm) will enable examination of surfaces wherever required even under normal lighting conditions, though some less powerful lamps do require black out conditions. This 'long wavelength' UV-A can be augmented by shorter wavelength UV-B (280 nm to 315 nm). The fluorescence colour typically obtained from different coatings is discussed in section 13.3.

Although fluorescence is useful, it needs to be carefully interpreted or it may easily mislead. It is primarily the outermost molecules of a coating that are excited by ultra violet light. Materials located in the middle or lower layers of a coating are not normally discernible with UV. Therefore, a finish that includes layers of distinctly different resins will most often only fluoresce the colour of the outer most finish. The layers below will not normally be discerned with this light source. Non-fluorescing materials such as dirt, grime and oil will obscure fluorescing materials underneath. Synthetic materials such as acrylics or cellulose nitrates are less prone to fluoresce since their chemical structure is not easily excited by ultra violet radiation. Aged synthetic materials do tend to become more fluorescent over time making it difficult to distinguish them from natural resins. It may be possible to excite a natural resin that is under a synthetic coating that

can pass most of the ultra violet light and the subsequent emission. As a result, the fluorescence detected may be misread as indicating only the presence of a natural resin. Solvent tests can be used in conjunction with UV to help reveal the fluorescence of different layers, or this can be done using fluorescence microscopy.

Fluorescence is best viewed with all visible light filtered from the surroundings. Also, when comparing results with other laboratories it is important to verify that the different UV sources have the same excitation wavelength. For more accurate interpretation of the emission colour of the fluorescence, a spectrophotometer can be used to supplement visual inspection.

It is important to minimize exposure times of objects to UV and possibly avoid it when examining highly UV sensitive artefacts. Eye protection specifically designed to remove UV must be worn while examining fluorescence since high intensity UV sources can cause irreparable damage to the eye. It is also sensible to minimize UV exposure to unprotected skin in order to minimize the risk of skin cancer from this source.

Infra red reflectography takes advantage of differences in heat reflected back to the viewer from different parts of a surface and can therefore be useful in identifying contrasting materials. Outlines of pre-existing designs or attachments may be visible with this light source that otherwise would be left unnoticed. This may help when viewing decorated surfaces where a design is difficult to decipher. Infra red units vary in type from simple hand-held equipment that is both inexpensive and portable to extremely sophisticated and expensive.

### Simple mechanical tests
Handling is a most necessary part of the process of examination that when carried out with sensitivity and care can give further information about the overall structural integrity and condition of objects without causing noticeable harm. At the same time, careful probing into joints with very thin steel blades, such as feeler gauges or spatulas and measurement of components using steel tapes, thin accurate metal rules and vernier gauges can help to elucidate means of construction. Such

information should always be carefully recorded before an object is taken to pieces. A hand-held metal detector is also useful for finding concealed metal fittings and fastenings.

The overall weight and balance of an object can help to confirm visual clues about the nature of materials used in construction and give a rough preliminary indication of anything out of the ordinary. If the object seems much heavier or lighter than might have been expected from the overall size, shape, construction and visual clues about materials, it is important to follow this up to find out why. For example if the object seems very heavy or out of balance then perhaps this is accounted for by an unusually dense timber, or by some hidden mechanism or structural element of another, denser material. If the object seems lighter than one might have expected this might indicate the use of lower density timbers (e.g. beech in place of rosewood or veneers over low density substrates), or of (possibly concealed) severe insect damage.

It is difficult to use the density of structures in a precise way but this can provide a useful means of estimating reduction in strength. Since for wood specific gravity is the best single predictor of strength, reduction in density is a measure of reduction in strength. Density is calculated as mass per unit volume. Mass can often be measured with great precision but volume less so. For some structures it is possible to calculate volume but for many this is difficult to do. Measurement of the volumes or masses of individual components of a structure is best achieved when objects are disassembled. One method of obtaining the volume of components is by immersion (in a suitably protected state) in a suitable fluid. It should be possible to demonstrate reduced density of one component compared to another similar component by its greater porosity and therefore by increased fluid penetration and wettability (e.g. by aliphatic solvents). Reduced density also leads to more marked deformation under pressure.

The feel of parts moving in relation to one another under very gentle pressure can provide useful information about the condition of joints and in some case even how the piece is put together. With care some idea can be gained of stiffness or rigidity and of the strength of structure while gently testing each area under compression, tension, bending and

shear, a watchful eye should be kept for signs of any opening of joints and closed splits. Particularly when located close to joints, splits may constitute points of weakness that could subsequently fail under tension. The object should be given an all over examination in which it is subjected to very light loads before more robust application of any testing loads is made to determine whether the structure is strong enough overall for its intended purpose. This process may sound rather crude and subjective but with practice it is amazing how refined a measuring instrument the conservator can become, applying just enough force to experience useful feedback about the state of the object without causing damage. Such techniques partly seem crude because the measuring units are not rigorously defined and are therefore not transferable from one measuring system (conservator) to another.

During this process of mechanical testing by the conservator there are other properties it may be possible to detect. Loose and lifting veneer and other elements of partially detached applied decoration will move slightly under pressure. Lifting areas of veneer also sound hollow when tapped with a finger nail. The feel of the surface can also provide important clues about the types of tools used and the processes carried out with them. Regular undulations along or across the grain may indicate plane marks or turning marks respectively and it may be possible to pick up by touch other information about dimensional change and surface finish.

The hardness (ability to resist indentation and scratching) and toughness (ability to deform somewhat without breaking) are interrelated ideas that can give useful indications of durability and resistance to wear and hence about susceptibility to damage from handling and treatment. Whether or not the surface is indented by a finger nail can give a rough indication of hardness. A finger nail will mark between 3 and 4 Mohs, a needle between 6 and 7 Mohs (for an explanation of the Mohs scale of hardness see Chapter 10). Probing with dental tools and the feel of the surface under gentle pressure may help to indicate condition of worm damaged timber.

The use of other senses should not be neglected. Certain materials leave behind characteristic odours, for example the smell of wood preservative treatments on furniture is highly recognizable. Certain timbers such as cedar, rosewood and sandalwood have characteristic odours as do certain finishing materials (e.g. turpentine). The taste of true oriental lacquer on the tip of the tongue, once learned, is also unmistakable.

Techniques such as those described above can help to give a sense of the object and especially its surface as something that may contain a wide variety of finish materials, dirt and grime rather than a singular material and this is important.

### Microscopic examination

The basic principles of microscope optics set up for transmitted light operation have been described by Catling (1981) and McCrone (1987). For a detailed explanation of special methods in light microscopy see McLaughlin (1977). A useful introduction to some of the many applications of light microscopy is given by Simpson and Simpson (1988). An introduction to microscopy using electrons, X-rays and acoustics is given by Rochow and Tucker (1994).

*Stereo microscopy*   Stereo light microscopy is a useful and powerful technique that can be used to examine surfaces in detail, to monitor the results of solvency tests and to assist the removal of samples for analysis or other forms of microscopy. The most useful type is one that will swing out over the surface being studied. It is not necessary to take samples so the surface remains in context, unlike most forms of microscopy where sample removal is required. The addition of photographic equipment and zoom lens can make this an extremely powerful examination, documentation and treatment tool.

*Incident light microscopy*   Understanding the nature of a finish and problems associated with it can often be achieved through incident light microscopy, also referred to as reflected light microscopy. This usually requires the extraction of a sample but video microscope techniques can be used directly on the surface without sampling. Rather than transmitting light through a thin section on a microscope slide, incident light microscopy uses a 'thick section' that is illuminated from above with the light

being reflected back into the objective. Viewing a sample under the microscope with incident light does take some getting used to, whether it be normal or fluorescent light. A properly sectioned sample will reveal the stratification of a surface, showing its history the way a road cut through a mountain side will reveal geological strata.

Except for the video microscope, which is relatively expensive, the technology required is within reach of the average conservator. A fairly basic microscope is all that is needed to use this technique in one's every day work. Used equipment from universities or the biomedical industry is inexpensive and satisfactory. The results observed with incident light microscopy can be a compelling component of examination that will give a more objective basis to an evaluation than would otherwise be possible.

In incident microscopy using normal light, illumination is generally achieved through external lighting such as fibre optics or an internal source that transmits light down the objective's cylinder. An external source is most effective when positioned at a 45° angle to the sample. The fibre optic system allows the viewer to manipulate the angle of the light which can help make components like metals or pigments stand out. However, an internal source has an advantage of being out of the operator's way and giving consistent lighting. Normal light shows up pigments, metallic particles, gold leaf and other parts of a decorative surface but varnishes can be difficult to detect with normal light microscopy since they appear amber in colour, creating insufficient contrast with the wood part of a sample. It is useful to move back and forth between normal and fluorescent light sources to help bring out and interpret information.

Incident light fluorescence microscopy uses a specialized light and filtering system to render visible the components of a coating that would otherwise go unnoticed. Resinous surface coatings absorb light at different frequencies across the spectrum. For example, light typically passes through resins with minimal absorbency. As a result, layers of resins in cross section will look fairly clear with a normal, or white, light source. However, enough of the ultra violet light spectrum is absorbed by natural resins to cause emission in the visible range immediately upon excitation. This phenomena is known as fluorescence. Most synthetic resins do not significantly absorb ultra violet light and this can help to distinguish them from natural resin coatings. A properly equipped microscope can be used to distinguish various coatings on the basis of their fluorescence under UV. A light source, commonly mercury or xenon, with a strong emission in the ultra violet range is coupled to the microscope. This light is filtered with a three part glass cube to irradiate the sample within a specific wave length range.

It is important to distinguish between primary and secondary fluorescence observed with the microscope. A material capable of primary fluorescence can be excited by ultra violet light and emit light in the visible range without the addition of any 'enhancer'. Natural resins are examples of materials capable of primary fluorescence. Secondary fluorescence occurs when a dye, or fluorochrome, is added that will cause a particular component within a sample to fluoresce. This technique of characterization, referred to as immunofluorescence in the biomedical field, is the most common application of fluorescence microscopy. It is used to help identify specific organic structures such as lipids, carbohydrates and proteins (Wolbers and Landrey, 1987; Baumeister, 1988; Landrey, 1990; Becker, 1985; Ploem and Tanke, 1987). Immunofluorescence requires exacting skill in the application of fluorochrome and interpretation of the reactions. Immunofluorescence is particularly useful in helping to identify certain structures within a coating that can be used in selecting treatment options. Primary, or autofluorescence, is directly applicable to the study of surface coating stratification. Observing the character of a surface coating sample with primary fluorescence makes the surface layering more distinct.

Some cautions are in order when applying fluorescence microscopy to the study of historic surface coatings. Much of the literature from the biomedical field is focused on secondary fluorescence and the use of fluorochromes. This can be confusing for a conservator trying first to master primary fluorescence. Careful reading of manufacturer's brochures and publications may help. It is important to use a filter cube with a combination of excitation, dichroic and barrier filters that meet the needs of the characterization being performed. While there are countless variations of filter cube combinations, some general guidelines for application can be given. For primary fluorescence studies, ultra violet (excitation *c.*330–380 nm) or violet (excitation *c.*380–430 nm) filter cubes are the most useful. For secondary fluorescence, other filter cubes such as blue (excitation *c.*450–500 nm), green (excitation *c.*510–560 nm), red (excitation *c.*560–610 nm) are normally employed.

*Transmitted light microscopy* For transmitted light microscopy, a thin, transparent sample, is necessary. Creating a thin section sample of a surface coating can be done by processing an encapsulated sample with a microtome (Derrick *et al.*, 1994). It may be difficult to keep a finish sample fully intact because of the thinness required for light to pass through the sample. Transmitted light microscopy allows for more specialized examination, including polarized and fluorescent light microscopy (McCrone, 1987). Thin sections are also sometimes amenable to Fourier Transform Infra Red spectroscopy (FTIR) analysis. This type of microscopy requires a sample to be taken. Specific sample preparation methods depend on the material being sampled and the purpose of the examination but sampling in general is reviewed below.

### Sampling

All examinations can be said to look at a sample even when this is a whole object sample but it is convenient to use this term to refer to techniques that actually remove part of the object as a necessary precursor to some kind of analysis. From the point of view of the object, it is always preferable to choose non-destructive techniques for analysis, when suitable methods are available. Any technique that requires sample removal is necessarily destructive. Once removed, the sample can never be properly returned to the object. Careful consideration of the potential information to be drawn from the examination should be weighed against the loss of material and the resulting interference with the artistic and structural integrity of the object no matter how small. Frequently, the information gained from a sample is so useful to one's understanding and interpretation of the object and to the development of a course of treatment, that the small loss of material is considered worthwhile. Before taking a sample it is also important to check that someone else has not done so previously. Samples properly extracted, encapsulated and stored can be kept for an extended period of time for later reference. They are rarely consumed in the microscopy process.

Sampling technique includes choosing a site and method of extraction and subsequent preparation. Proper locations must be chosen. It is rare that just one sample will suffice to confidently represent the area being studied. It may take several samples to establish a representative cross-section of an object's surface history. Generally, samples should be drawn from areas that are not prominent. However, care is needed to ensure that the area selected is complete and representative of the whole, unless there are good reasons otherwise. Existing cracks or fissures make sample removal easier and less disruptive and are therefore often chosen as sites for sample removal. Samples of transparent coatings often need to have a small portion of wood included in the sample in order to establish the base of the finish. The first coating applied to wood can easily penetrate twelve or so cells deep. Some decorated surfaces can be satisfactorily sampled without wood substrate. A fine-bladed knife or scalpel is usually employed for sample extraction. Cleavage is a common problem in extracting a complete sample. It may be necessary to accept several parts to a sample when it is impossible to keep all fragments together during sampling. In some instances a sample can be consolidated during the sampling process in order to hold the layers together. This consolidant needs to be noted and accounted for when 'reading' the cross section. It is important to consider before removal the amount and orientation of the sample required and upon taking the sample to record carefully the location from which it was taken. Some pitfalls to be avoided are excessively worn areas such as feet or arms on a chair, repaired areas and sections that have been distorted through damage. Extracting a sample can be a tedious process. It is advisable to practice sampling on discarded furniture parts before carrying out the technique on valuable objects.

After removal, samples need to be prepared according to the needs of the examination technique for which they are required. Paint samples and other surface coatings for microscopical examination are commonly encapsulated in a support material before further preparation (Derrick *et al.*, 1994). Waxes and synthetic resins are the most common encapsulating materials with enough hardness for cutting and polishing being important. It is necessary for the embedding material to disturb the sample as little as possible. It is important to locate the sample in a known orientation that will permit expedient grinding to a cross-section view. The preferred orientation for grinding/polishing should be considered as a sample is placed on the binding media substrate. Generally, the end-grain view of samples gives the clearest information.

Samples can be expediently processed for incident light microscopy using a variety of procedures of which slicing or grinding are the most common. Slicing (e.g. using a microtome) is used for transmitted light microscopy and can also be used to create a level surface for incident microscopy. For further discussion of microtome procedures see Walter (1980) and Sanderson (1994).

Grinding and polishing, to create a satisfactory surface on cross-section samples to be examined with incident light microscopy, can be done with minimal equipment and materials. A small grinder and abrasives are commonly used, but is not applicable to transmitted light microscopy. With a little practice, samples in a cube of encapsulating medium can be made microscope ready in a matter of a few minutes. In general there are three stages to sample preparation which are:

(1) Coarse grinding to the approximate point in the sample cube.
(2) Medium polishing (e.g. with fine abrasive paper) to remove the coarse grinding marks.
(3) Polishing with an extra fine abrasive paper or powder.

For most applications of incident light microscopy, it is not normally necessary for a sample to be highly polished. It is important to keep the viewing surface as flat as possible or the sample may be difficult to keep in focus on the microscope. Minimizing the polishing procedure helps to keep the sample in plane. Special attention to polishing is necessary when dyes are being used to achieve secondary fluorescence. The clarity needed for an accurate reading of a fluorochrome may be compromised if the dye puddles in abrasion and polishing marks that were not removed from the face of the sample.

Samples can be polished wet or dry. Many of the ultra fine abrasive papers can be used dry. Sheet abrasives with a US mesh grade of 8000 with 1 micron particle size are available for sample preparation. Useful information is available from the 3M Corporation's Super Abrasives and Microfinishing Department. Water can be used to facilitate the use of abrasive papers or powders with materials that are not easily dissolved in water. Mineral spirits (white spirits) can be used for water-sensitive coatings.

Samples are only of value if clearly labelled with enough information to uniquely identify their source and details of the location from which they were removed. Archival quality transparent bags and slide protector sheets are recommended for the long-term storage of small samples of upholstery under structures removed during conservation. A line of machine stitching is a simple, quick method of keeping the samples in place in slide sheets. The identification, interpretation and preservation of textile evidence on upholstery tacks and frames is discussed by Francis (1990).

Wood samples are ideally taken during conservation treatment when the object is disassembled and the conservator has access to inconspicuous areas. Independent wood scientists should be guided by conservators in determining the location from where samples can be taken. A small hollow drill with an inside diameter of 2 or 3 mm which can be made in any machine shop is useful in taking samples, for example from underneath the foot of a chair. Veneer can be sampled when it is lifting or loose from the substrate wood. Obviously, samples are not taken when this would damage the integrity of the object. There are essentially two ways to obtain a sample from furniture: a small three-dimensional sample can be taken and sectioned by hand or on a microtome, or sections can be shaved directly from the object in transverse, radial and tangential orientations. It is important to cut these orientations precisely, otherwise the identifying features cannot be observed accurately.

## General aspects of analytical methods

Analytical techniques, including traditional wet chemical tests and instrumental analysis, are concerned primarily with the identification of materials. There are many types of chromatography, spectrography and imaging systems being used by conservation analytical laboratories for doing organic analysis and the technology is continually changing with new equipment and techniques being added all the time. It is useful for the conservator to stay abreast of what technologies are available, how they can be accessed and the type of information that can be provided. However, it is equally important to realize that the solution of all analytical problems both qualitative and quantitative follows the same basic pattern (Fifield and Keeley, 1995). From our observations of the object and related documentation we may have some idea about the object that we wish to confirm or reject and therefore seek a method to do this. If the idea is correct, some testable hypothesis must prove true or false. The trick is to formulate the problem in a way that can be tested. The proposed test method needs to be formulated appropriately to test the idea, the whole idea and nothing but the idea. It is very important to be clear what the results of any analysis actually show and equally to be clear about what the actual result achieved means in the context of the original question. Selection of the proper technique requires an understanding of the material under investigation. The factors determining the method of choice include: destructiveness versus non-destructiveness, sample size, sensitivity of method to specific elements, surface versus interior analysis and quantitative versus qualitative results.

Texts on microchemical analysis either focus on identifying organic materials through their functional groups (Stevens, 1980), or identify inorganic materials according to their specific group chemistry based on the periodic chart (Chamot and Mason, 1958, 1960; Feigl and Anger, 1972; Svehla, 1979). Qualitative microchemical tests can be used for the identification of metals and their alloys (Laver, 1978), pigments (Plesters, 1956) and have limited use for wood (e.g. Kukachka and Miller, 1980). Even simple solubility tests can be most revealing. The fact that different coatings materials are soluble in different solvents has been used traditionally as a way of identifying resins. The Teas diagram, developed by J.P. Teas as a tool to explain and predict solubility, can be used as a guide here. This is further discussed in Chapter 11 and in Gordon and Teas (1976) and Headley (1980). Resins become increasingly polar as they age causing a shift in solubility properties. The outer zone of an aged coating may be more resistant to various solvents than the inner zone of the same layer because of more rapid ageing on a coating's exterior. A finish containing a combination of resins will have a complex solubility plotting on the Teas' diagram. It may be possible to take advantage of this phenomena in developing cleaning systems.

Solvent applied with a cotton swab to a small test area can be used to help characterize coatings. Resistance to ethanol suggests a fossil resin, a synthetic coating or a finish that has aged to the point of being insoluble and very polar. Conversely, a finish easily soluble in ethanol suggests the presence of natural non-fossil resins. A finish that can quickly be picked up in a petroleum distillate may be a wax without any resin component.

Advanced analytical techniques can be classified into separation techniques and spectroscopic techniques. Sophisticated hybrid techniques combining separation and spectroscopic techniques provide valuable spectroscopic information on separated components of a heterogeneous mixture. The most notable example in this case is gas chromatography-mass spectrometry (GC-MS); the GC can separate a heterogeneous composition while the MS provides spectral information that helps to precisely identify the separated elements. Spectroscopic techniques have also been fitted to both optical and electron microscopes. Infra red microscopy and laser micro probe are optical microscope-assisted methods and Energy Dispersive X-ray analysis can be placed in the chamber of the scanning electron microscope. The underlying principles of many of these techniques commonly employed in conservation research are discussed by Mills and White (1987). For an account of all techniques available to sophisticated materials science facilities consult Sibilia (1996).

### Dating methods

The materials and methods used in the manufacture of a piece of furniture provide evidence for its dating. The age of some natural materials can be determined by scientific methods. Man-made materials as well as workshop practices can sometimes be dated by comparison to documentary sources and references. Maker stamps or signatures can be useful in further assessing the date of an object. In evaluating the authenticity of a piece of furniture all information obtained from the examination methods above is assembled. However, it must be taken into consideration that forgers often make use of the available knowledge about historic materials and techniques and may understand systematic methods of examination.

There are two methods – carbon-14 dating and dendrochronology – that can be used in determining the age of wood. These methods, which have been primarily developed for dating archaeological wood, historical building materials and panel paintings, can occasionally be useful in dating furniture woods and organic decorative elements.

*Carbon-14 dating*   All living organisms that absorb carbon dioxide through photosynthesis (e.g. trees) or subsequently carbon through the food chain, also absorb the unstable radioactive isotope of carbon, carbon-14. Carbon-14 is formed in the upper atmosphere and decays slowly to nitrogen-14 from which it originated. The formation and decay of carbon-14 are in equilibrium and because of this equilibrium almost all living organisms contain the same level of carbon-14. From the moment an organism dies the intake of carbon-14 stops, however, the carbon-14 that is already present continues to decay with a half-life of 5730 years (Aitken, 1990; Bowman, 1990). By measuring the level of radioactivity, or by counting the number of carbon-14 atoms remaining, the age of a sample can be calculated. The level of decay was measured first with modified Geiger counters and other detectors for beta activity, which required sizeable samples of up to 20 g of sound wood. Modern techniques require no more than 50 g of sound furniture wood. Accelerator Mass Spectrometry (AMS) is used to directly count the number of carbon-14 atoms in a sample. This technique has been used for the radiocarbon dating of iron artefacts (Creswell, 1991) as well as wood. Degraded wood should not be sampled since fungi introduce new carbon-14 and therefore cause inaccurate readings. Wood that has been treated with any carbon containing material, e.g. consolidants, hydrocarbons etc., is also not suitable for carbon-14 dating. Samples can be taken by drilling a small hole ¼ inch deep into the object to clear the surface, followed by a smaller drill into the clean area. The frass from the second drilling can be collected on cleaned aluminium foil which can be folded into a small envelope. All equipment should be carefully cleaned with distilled water. Carbon-containing solvents should be avoided. The wood dating institution should be supplied with all relevant information relating to the object and how the sample was obtained.

Carbon-14 dating can be used in determining the age of furniture woods, however, there are some limitations to the processes. In dating a 50 mg sample only those 50 mg of material will be dated and not the entire object (Weaver, 1982). A longitudinal sample, for example, taken from furniture made of a tree that lived from 1200 to 1600, can provide a date in the direction of any of those 400 years. Only sapwood samples can provide more accurate dating about when the wood may have been used, since the intake of carbon-14 stops when a tree is felled. The intake of carbon-14 of the heartwood, of course, stops when it is being formed in the still living tree. Even when a carbon-14 date is provided for furniture wood, it does not necessarily provide an answer about when the piece was made (Hall, 1987; Pearson, 1987).

Carbon-14 dating, however, can be a useful tool in dating organic furniture material despite the destructive nature of the method. Interpretation of data should be carried out with the greatest care by scientists, conservators and curators alike (Aitchison and Scott, 1987; Bowman, 1990; Chase, 1972; Coles and Jones, 1975; Stenhouse and Baxter, 1983).

*Dendrochronology*  Dendrochronology is literally the dating of wood. Trees which grow in temperate climates grow in the summer, adding a layer of new wood to the outside of the trunk each year. In autumn growth slows down and in winter stops altogether. In many cases this leads to an obvious annual ring due to the difference in size and/or wall thickness of cells in the autumn and spring wood. Trees grown in the tropics do not have annual rings.

Some may have growth rings but these are caused by spurts of growth in the wet season which may occur only once every few years or several times in one year. The annual rings of temperate trees may be counted to ascertain the age of the tree. In some species it was found that regular patterns of ring widths occur in certain years in each tree examined. It was then realized that this could be used to date wood which had been converted in buildings, furniture, paintings and archaeological material. The trees which give these definite patterns are those which respond to some limiting factor in their environment such as rainfall or temperature. In oak, for example, a dry summer will give a narrow ring, a wet one a wide ring. Growth rings may also vary in dimension under influence of altitude, soil fertility, volcanic eruptions, fungal or insect attack and pollution (Schweingruber, 1983). Obviously, if the ring widths depend on rain fall they will not be same in, for example, England, Germany and Italy. Chronologies are therefore worked out for particular trees for particular areas. Master curves exist for most main wood producing regions (Baillie, 1984; Fletcher, 1977; Fletcher and Tapper, 1984; Klein *et al.*, 1987). Wood sections with sufficient annual growth rings are compared against master curves, climatological time charts, compiled from past and present growth-ring-forming trees. About thirty tree rings are minimally required for dating a characteristic sequence, however, accuracy increases with increase of growth rings. In general an average of 120 tree rings are considered to provide reliable results (Schweingruber, 1983). A smooth end-grain surface has to be prepared with a sharp knife, rather than by sanding. The wood surface can be examined and measured directly under low power magnification of a binocular microscope. X-ray radiography of coniferous wood samples enhances the contrast between early- and late-wood considerably by recording the variety in their density on X-ray film (Schweingruber, 1983). These filmstrips then can be analysed by a micro-densitometer which feeds information into a computer. The computer averages and compares the pattern against master curves resulting in dating of the sample. Other X-ray radiography techniques such as computer tomography (CT) also record density variations (Reimers *et al.*, 1989).

Computer tomography is a non-destructive technique, especially suitable for reading the growth-ring patterns in softwoods, even when the wood surface is not exposed. The technique may prove to be valuable in reading tree ring patterns of coniferous substrate wood of painted or veneered furniture.

There are some limitations to dendrochronological dating in conjunction with furniture. The method of taking the sample, or preparing the surface of a board for examination is destructive. Since furniture mostly is constructed of smaller elements it will often be difficult, if not impossible, to find radially cut elements with a sufficient number of growthrings. When no sapwood is included in a sample there can be no certainty about the felling date of the tree. The interpretation of such samples should be carried out with the greatest care and the data should not be confused with the possible age of the furniture. Wood from a three hundred year old tree felled in 1999 could be used to make a copy of a piece of two hundred year old furniture. It would not be possible to distinguish the lack of authenticity of such a piece by dendrochronology alone. Dendrochronology is mostly applied, and limited, to medieval and earlier furniture (Fletcher, 1977; Fletcher *et al.*, 1974; Weaver, 1982). Problems of dating and interpreting results from archaeological timbers have been discussed by Hillam (1987).

All aspects of examination such as where samples were taken, how they were analysed and what results were obtained should be documented.

## 9.4   Documentation

This section examines the nature and importance of documentation, some information needs of conservators in both private practice and institutions, some aspects of documentation practice and what is involved in setting up a documentation system. The section concludes with a discussion of photography.

### 9.4.1   What is documentation and why is it important?

Documentation in its broadest sense is the information needed to run a business. It includes facts about people and organizations, buildings, finance, objects, goods and services, transactions and other concerns of management for businesses large and small and not just information about conservation treatments and object condition. This information is needed for all aspects of managing an enterprise for planning, assessment, co-ordination, selection, monitoring, controlling, decision-making, directing, research and publication.

Accountability is increasingly important to the client, to the tax collector, to the taxpayer (for the use of resources in publicly funded institutions), to posterity for actions taken that may change the qualities by which the significance or intention of a work is judged and for health and safety purposes. Most successful businesses set out objectives and performance plans and record actual performance against the plan as a guide to future action that might be taken to improve business performance. Conservators in business need to know how they are performing and how they compare to other conservation practices. They need to be aware that their clients will almost certainly be looking at their performance and it is therefore very much in the conservator's interest to keep tabs on their business.

### 9.4.2   Information needs

It is fundamental to know what objects are in our care, where they are and what condition they are in. Relevant information for conservation documentation for the practical conservator working at the bench includes the nature, extent, severity and location of damage, treatment options and concept, actual action of treatment, results of material analyses (if any) and materials used during treatment. The practical conservator responsible for the treatment of an object needs to know something of what the piece is, how it is uniquely identified, the work that is to be carried out and any specific client requirements, the amount of time allowed for the job and the date by which it has to be ready. Information discussed in the previous section may be relevant in coming to a treatment decision. Actions taken to identify materials or to assess condition should be recorded together with reasons, methods, results and conclusions. As work progresses the identity and location within the overall structure of elements that have been removed should be recorded, both on the component removed and as part of the ongoing treatment record. Everyone in a workshop should be able to identify at all times what objects are in stock and where they (and all their bits) are. As treatment progresses the actions taken, the part(s) of the object affected, the materials used and the result should be recorded together with dates and times. Analysis and treatment, particularly of upholstered objects, may reveal information on history and technology. Recording of this information is especially important when survival of the object cannot be assured (for example objects in private use or those made of unstable materials). The information may also be useful in interpreting the object or other similar objects.

In order to plan and to balance present and future needs with available resources, institutions may ask conservators to assess the condition of a whole collection. One measure both of need and of success is the state of the collections. An overall measure of object condition at one point in time is a measure of need. At two points in time this can become a measure of change. A numbering system from one (best) to four (worst) is recommended to describe overall conservation condition (Keene, 1996). It should therefore be possible to state the percentage of each collection in each condition category. In practice, it is unlikely that the condition of all the objects in the collections will be known accurately at any one point in time. In the time it takes to find out the answer it may change. However, it is generally possible to get a sufficiently accurate picture of the condition of a whole collection by surveying part of it. In thinking about how resources should be targeted it may also be important to consider the curatorial view of the relative importance of the objects in a collection. Also, before dedicating extensive conservation resources we should ensure that objects are in satisfactory environmental conditions. The percentage of collections that can be so described is another important indicator.

A single indicator for condition is complemented by further information as to what is wrong with an object and what is required to put it right. The approach to this is to describe eight categories of damage that can be universally applied (Keene, 1996). These include major and minor structural damage, surface damage, biological damage, chemical damage, accretions and old repairs. Together with an estimate of the time resources required these can give a useful estimate of conservation condition, risk and priority. In particular this system allows comparison of one collection with another.

In theory the assessment of the environment should precede the recording of object condition. In practice the two are often linked. Many survey programmes identify very obvious deficiencies in environmental conditions particularly in the way objects are stored. These have formed the basis of important preventive conservation programmes. They also lend perspective to programmes of interventive conservation. When such a comprehensive assessment of conservation priorities is documented it should contribute to the highest levels of decision-making.

In an increasingly competitive world, it is important for conservators to be able to estimate the resources a proposed project will require. Information collected from previous treatments can be used for estimating the conservation resources needed for future work. The documented incidence of damage arising from different collections' management activities can pinpoint the need for better training, policy and procedures. If this information is properly recorded it can tell us a lot about how resources are currently being used and how effective this use of resources is in achieving our primary objectives and how the allocation of resources might be changed.

The process of active interventive conservation is seldom unattended by risk. Conservators can not only make discoveries that change the way an object is perceived but can also change objects in a way which may be unacceptable. There is accordingly a huge burden of responsibility of decision-making. It seems that there are no right answers but there are good and bad processes of decision-making. The decision-making process should begin with a clear understanding of purpose. It is of paramount importance that consultation of all available records and discussion with stakeholders takes place to consider the significance of the object to be treated and the effect of various possible alternatives on significant factors. All the options are then considered in relation to the resources available to predict the likely out-comes of each alternative. The methods by which the success of the treatment are to be judged are worked out before the treatment is undertaken. The documentation components of this decision-making process are consider-able. Some of the questions which should be asked have been reviewed above.

Everything the conservator finds out about the object during examination or treatment becomes part of the new identity of the object and must be recorded and communicated to relevant parties. This includes everything added or removed, the results of analysis, the nature, location and extent of treatment and all drawings, photographs and measurements. Evidence left intentionally on the object as a guide to those who follow should also be noted. Only in this way can those who follow have satisfactory documented evidence on which to base their own decision-making and the continued survival of the object.

Individual records over a long period enable patterns and trends to be recognized and sta-tistics to be generated. They also form a resource for further research and development, education and training and communication with the profession. On large projects, conser-vators may also need to work in a team with curators, scientists, architects, designers, engi-neers, educators, researchers and others to make decisions to meet the overall needs of the project. The basis of good decision-making is good information and good communication.

### 9.4.3   Documentation methods

In thinking about what constitutes good prac-tice and what methods to use it is most import-ant to consider in the first place the primary purpose of documentation and secondly what other value the documentation may have. Conservation documentation can carry infor-mation through time and space from one per-son or group to another. It may therefore be helpful to think about who these persons or groups are and what they might need or want to know. For example, the client may wish to see an assessment of condition to approve a course of action or cost and to see a final bill of work. The client may also wish to retain a copy of any treatment documentation as a record of honest work performed. The conser-vator may need, among numerous other possi-bilities, a record of how to put the object back together, a record of what to charge the client and a reference to future work of the same type. Other stakeholder requirements may be identified in individual cases. The form that the documentation should take should perhaps reflect the need. Although this is not always possible it may at least be a guide to thinking about setting up a system. It would obviously be helpful if the requirements of different stakeholders could be integrated into a single system rather than having to maintain com-pletely separate systems. This hints at the pos-sibility of computerization which is discussed below. It may also be helpful to distinguish between object-based documentation and paper-based documentation.

When a piece of furniture needs to be dis-mantled it is strongly recommended to mark each individual element to ensure that precise re-assembly is possible after treatment. Preferably, each element should be marked with a label tied around it. When this is not possible chalk or other soft writing material such as a grease pencil can be used to write directly on the individual pieces. Whatever writing material is used it should be removable without leaving traces or an impression. One should only write on surfaces that will be hid-den from the eye once the piece is assembled. Self-adhesive-tape should be avoided because the tape may leave stains on the surface which can be difficult to remove. A drawing of an object can be helpful to identify where each element is located. Such a drawing can also be stuck on Fome-cor®, or other soft material, for cataloguing hardware such as screws that need to find their exact placing back into the object (*Figure 9.4*). When large elements need to be replaced conservators should consider marking the pieces in a way that they easily can be dis-tinguished by the untrained eye. One can, for example, stamp newly made pieces with a place and date, or add to gesso or glue X-ray dense material such as barium sulphate, so that the restored elements show up on X-radi-ographs (Thornton, 1991). It may be possible to stamp replacement elements to prevent con-fusion about which elements are original and which have been added during restoration (see *Figure 15.6*). Such stamps can be very small yet clearly visible without interfering with the

(a)

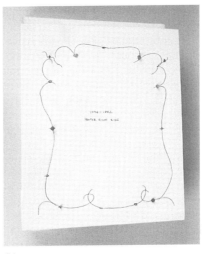

(b)

**Figure 9.4** Eighteenth century French commode, *c*.1740, stamped BVRB for Bernard II Van Risenburgh, which incorporates Japanese lacquer panels and elaborate ormolu mounts
(*a*) Side view
(*b*) Rough outlined line drawing of the mounts, on foam, that ensures that each screw or pin that is removed can be returned to its original position on the object

'reading' of the object. For example, in 1884/5 the New York-based Herter Brothers restored a seventeenth century French ebony cabinet by completely rebuilding its structure. If the cabinet had not been stamped, it could easily have been mistaken for a nineteenth century piece because of its fine, typically nineteenth century cabinet work.

Paper-based documentation includes all forms, letters, free text, drawings, sketches, photographs, charts and related material that accrue from the first enquiry to the completion of treatment. Such documentation should be kept with the furniture until the treatment is completed. It is suggested that one suitably presented copy of the documentation should be submitted to the owner or curator and one copy should stay with the conservator.

Information contained within any conservation documentation system will generally have the greatest value if it can be shared. For example, engineers and scientists communicate information about the built environment to conservators. Information about the conserva-

tion condition of the collections is obtained by conservators and used by curators and conservators to determine priorities. Technical information from conservation scientists and historical information from curators is used by conservators in formulating treatment proposals. However, much documentation is still held in the form of day books, paper forms, diaries, card indexes, files and ledgers. These paper systems have several inherent disadvantages. First, access is restricted. If only one copy is available access is physically restricted to those close to it. The creation of multiple copies risks the introduction of inconsistencies and errors as each owner makes small alterations to the record. In paper form the logical order is also the physical order. To find information by other search criteria involves cross-referencing. This also introduces redundancy and risk of errors. The format of the paper system is unlikely to be suitable for all applications for which data are required. Paper systems are physically bulky and have limited durability and security. It is virtually impossible to maintain an adequate backup to cover the event of loss. Calculations and statistics based on paper systems are prohibitively labour-intensive. Such systems have not been properly planned, coordinated or controlled and do not permit the kind of shared use that is essential to ensure the required flow of data around or between organizations. Information systems should therefore be developed with automation in mind.

A good documentation system will be maintained in an accurate, complete, concise and up-to-date condition to provide the right information to the right people in timely fashion. Institutional systems should conform to institution-wide data standards and allow monitoring and control of terminology and validation of items such as dates and codes at the point of entry of data into the system.

In an automated system, periodic audits can be undertaken to ensure the integrity of the data. Conflicting requirements of different users can be met and many different logical views of the data allowed, enabling us to search freely, to select the items we wish to see and decide how these should be presented. At the same time, only one physical record is maintained. This control of redundancy not only leads to greater consistency but achieves economy since data are entered and stored only once. Much conservation information has an inherently regular structure and is particularly suited to automated procedures. The disadvantages of automated systems are their size, complexity and cost, the additional hardware requirement and the higher impact of failure.

### 9.4.4   Setting up a documentation system

The goal, which is the same for manual and automated systems, is to meet organizational requirements, to solve problems and make decisions. It is therefore important to clarify what is to be achieved and what problems are to be solved.

The real world situation then has to be mapped on to the computer and it is therefore necessary to understand the concept behind the software. A simple view of events is that, data are input, processed, stored, processed again and then output. Analysis of require-

ments should be principally concerned with the output that is required and then with the storage, processing and input required to achieve that output. In more complex situations, formal methodologies can be used to define what has to be done, when and to what standard to create the system. For larger projects, a feasibility study is generally recommended to define the problem to be addressed and the scope of the project intended.

Analysis of the problem begins with a statement of the physical reality of what is actually done now. To whom is information sent and from whom is it received? In what form is it sent and received? What are the processes that act on it or in which it is involved (e.g. condition reporting, acquisition, loan). From this statement of present physical reality a specification of logical requirements can be developed that is removed from physical considerations of individuals, forms or files. The next step is to produce a design that will turn the desired logical system into a physical reality.

Data design requires decisions to be made about the sort of information that is to be processed, the amount of space that should be allocated for each type and how information should be grouped into files, fields and records. Examples of data types include free text, structured text, numbers, dates and images. Data design is often referred to as leading the design because *what* we do is much less likely to change than *how* we do it.

Detailed process design is concerned with such issues as validation of data on entry, batch versus individual updating of records and the need for calculations on the data (e.g. volume from dimensions, total costs from hours worked and rates). Retrieval is of paramount importance and the keys for data indexing and selection, sequencing, formatting and types of device required for output all need to be carefully considered. At this stage, it is also necessary to consider how much information will be processed, how often this will occur and how fast it should be done. Also, who will process it, who will share it, what kinds of access controls and security are required and most importantly what it will look like to those who will use it.

Armed with this information, a package or system is chosen with which to implement the design. This can be specially commissioned, though this is likely to be expensive, error-prone and time-consuming. Alternatively, an off-the-shelf package can be purchased or a general purpose data management system adapted to our requirements. Off-the-shelf packages have for some time been available to libraries because they have sufficiently common purpose and clearly defined standards. The general lack of standards, until recently, has hindered the commercial development of systems for conservation and collections management. However, such systems are now advertised in the professional literature and there are many small business packages and business consultancies available to help with this task.

### 9.4.5 Photography

Photography is a very important method of recording that is generally used to complement written documentation but is frequently done less well than it might be. Where the very best results are needed it may be better to employ the services of a professional photographer. On the other hand, with an understanding of the basic principles, appropriate equipment and care good results can be obtained by conservators themselves. A basic decision that needs to be made is whether to use black and white or colour and whether to use prints or transparencies. Among the issues that need to be considered are durability, accuracy of colour rendition, ease of access and reproduction. Black and white photographs have been preferred to colour for their archival qualities, however very long life is now claimed for modern colour processes. Colour clearly does add another dimension in many cases. Prints are very convenient for immediate reference, for reports and for access by small numbers of people. Slides are generally preferred for lectures and publications. Cost is another issue. Virtually any requirement can be met from large format colour transparencies but these are expensive.

The basic process of traditional black and white photography is as follows. Light-sensitive film or plate is contained in a light-proof chamber in the body of the camera at the back. By manipulation of a shutter light is allowed on to the film for a definite amount of time. A sys-

tem of lenses at the front of the camera is used to focus light rays on to the film and a shutter placed somewhere in front of the film is used to control the amount of light reaching the film. This can be achieved by changing the size of the opening or the duration of time for which the shutter is open, both of which can have different results. Light-sensitive material consists of silver halide crystals in gelatin coated on to the support. Silver halide crystals exposed to light undergo chemical change by means of which a latent image is formed. When the film is exposed to the chemical action of a *developer,* a black deposit of fine particles of metallic silver is produced on the film in those areas which were struck by light. By the action of a chemical *fixative* following development, areas that were not affected by light are removed to give a *negative* that is free of unreacted light-sensitive silver salts. By shining light through the negative on to an area of light sensitive paper (similar to film), the silver salts in the paper are affected in a similar way to those in the original film. Those portions of the negative that were lightest let through the most light on to the paper and those portions that were darkest let through the least. Following development and fixing, a *positive* image is created on the paper.

Colour negative films consist effectively of three types of black and white emulsion sensitive to blue, green and red wavelengths of light respectively. They reproduce a negative image in complementary colours. Cyan, magenta and yellow are the respective complementary colours of red, green and blue light. Each emulsion layer also contains a colour coupler chemical – a yellow dye former in the blue-sensitive layer, a magenta dye former in the green-sensitive layer and cyan in the red-sensitive layer. Couplers turn into their designated colour dye upon development in colour developer only where they have been affected by light. Colour films designed to produce a negative image for subsequent printing on paper carry the suffix *colour.* Colour films which are designed to give a positive image direct carry the suffix *chrome.* Chrome films are collectively known as colour reversal films because of the special reversal process they must undergo during development to give a positive image. All reversal films have a multi-layer structure including red-, green- and blue-sensitive emulsions and most have cyan, magenta and yellow dye forming couplers similar to those used in colour negative film.

The key components of the photographic system are the film, the light source and the camera. Each of these is briefly explored below.

### The film

Films vary in their sensitivity to light, both in the quality of the light in which they have been designed to be used and in their sensitivity – the amount of light required to form a usable image. The majority of black and white films are *panchromatic,* that is they respond, in monochrome, to virtually the whole of the visual spectrum. Their sensitivity also continues some way beyond blue into the ultraviolet. There are, however, some differences in response to light as compared to the human eye. Orange-red, blue and violet are reproduced somewhat lighter in tone and greens darker in tone than we would judge them to be. A yellow filter on the camera can be used to give a closer match if desired. A few black and white films are made insensitive to the red end of the spectrum beyond about 590 nm. These *orthochromatic* films are useful for photographing black and white photographs or drawings not involving colour. In addition to these types, films are also made for special applications that are insensitive to virtually the whole of the visual spectrum but respond to infra red and ultra violet.

The balance of sensitivity of the different layers in colour films is adjusted during manufacture to render the film suitable for use in particular lighting conditions. Most colour films are balanced to give accurate colour reproduction when the subject is exposed to daylight or flash. This corresponds to light of colour temperature 5000–6000 K. Film which is balanced to give correct colour rendition under tungsten lighting (3200 K) is also available.

All types of films vary in the amount of light required to give a satisfactory image under standard conditions of lighting, exposure time and processing. The sensitivity of film to light is denoted by an emulsion speed rating. The most commonly used system for rating film speed is the ISO (International Standards Organization) system. Low numbers correspond to slow films, in other words films

requiring more light to give a satisfactory image. The ISO rating consists of two figures, the first number corresponding to the ASA (American Standards Association) rating doubles with each doubling of light sensitivity, the second number (marked with a degree sign and corresponding to the European DIN standard) increases by 3 with each doubling of sensitivity. Slow films are typically rated ISO 25/15 to 64/19, medium films 100/21 to 400/27, fast films 640/29 to 1000/31 and ultra-fast films 1600/33 to 3200/36. There is a trade off between speed, graininess and sharpness of the image. Graininess is the pattern of clumps of silver grains that can be seen in the processed image. If this is coarse it will give a mealy or powdery appearance to the image, especially when enlarged. Sharpness of the image is concerned with the degree of fine image detail the film can record. It is difficult to increase film speed without increasing the size of the silver halide particles and therefore coarsening the grain. If the emulsion is made thicker to increase speed by increasing the number of silver halide particles then sharpness will decrease as a result of light scattering within the emulsion layer. Consequently, slower films are generally preferred where the sharpest images are required and faster films are preferred for use in low light conditions.

All film compresses tones. That is, it will not see the same amount of detail in both highlights and shadows. If importance of detail is in highlights then exposure should be reduced. If important detail is in shadow more exposure should be given. Kodachrome is relatively inexpensive but gives good results. It is generally slow but gives good colour rendering with satisfactory grain and good definition. It is intended for daylight use but will give good results with other light sources if a suitable conversion filter is used.

### The light source

To obtain good shots light needs to be of the right quality for the film. To a marked degree, the eye is able to make corrections for the colour of light so that objects are still seen at their 'correct' colour for a range of different light sources. Film is not able to do this and works best with a particular light source. The colour temperature of some common light sources are as follows:

| candle | 1900 K |
| Household electric light bulb | 2800 K |
| Tungsten photographic studio lamps | 3200 K |
| Tungsten halogen lamp | up to 3500 K |
| Sun 10° above horizon in clear sky | 4100 K |
| Mean noon daylight | 5500 K |
| Electronic flash | 5600 K |
| Zenith sun (in clear sky) | 6200 K |
| Overcast sky | 6500 K |
| Clear blue sky | 15 000– 30 000 K |

As far as possible light should be of single colour temperature as films do not cope well with light of mixed colour temperature. Museum galleries are bad in this respect because of mixed lights and glass (unwanted reflections) and lack of possibility for control. Colour temperature meters exist but not for mixed light sources. Films are available for daylight, for tungsten and for fluorescent lighting. Colour correction filters are available and are especially useful for daylight/tungsten conversion when moving between indoor and outdoor shots on one film. When it is necessary to work in daylight with film intended for artificial (tungsten) light, an 85B filter can be used to prevent the pictures coming out blue.

Diffuse lighting such as that from an overcast sky or fluorescent tubes will illuminate the surface of an object more evenly than light which comes from a single point such as spotlight, rising or setting sun. It is from the contrast of shadows and highlights that detail is perceived. Hence diffuse light sources will usually not show detail as well as light that has a more directional component. On the other hand light that comes from a spot source may give rise to reflections on certain types of surface. It is therefore necessary to select the type of lighting appropriate to the type of object and record required. If an object is illuminated slightly more strongly from one side than the other slight shadows will be cast that will give a more three-dimensional quality to the surface and allow elements of form or surface detail to be more readily appreciated. Any difference in the intensity of illumination from one side or the other can be judged by the length and direction of the shadow cast by a pencil held upright with its base in contact with the surface. This is particularly useful when setting up copy stand photography for flat objects. It may be difficult to illuminate some objects, e.g. carving with deep hollows as evenly as one would like, and though there are ways of reducing contrast through selection of film and aperture settings, it may sometimes be necessary to deliberately select shadow or highlight areas and expose accordingly. When lit directly from above, the hills and valleys of a surface will be illuminated more or less evenly (hence the flat appearance of landscapes taken at noon). As the angle of the light is lowered the degree of contrast between low and high spots increases (e.g. autumn afternoon light picks out details of every pebble on a beach or stone on a ploughed field). To get the desired result, lighting may therefore need to be adjusted both for intensity and direction (and hence also position). It is useful to remember that intensity varies inversely with the square of distance. In other words, halving the distance from light source to object will reduce illumination to a quarter.

Daylight is the best light source but if the object cannot be taken outside there may be a problem getting enough of it. Electronic flash or floodlight of correct colour is good choice. Electronic flash is about right for daylight film. It corresponds closely in characteristics to daylight at least as far as daylight films are concerned. The length and hazard potential of cable runs should be considered when using floodlights. Indoors, use of daylight will result in long exposures (e.g. of ½–1 second) given the small apertures that are often necessary to obtain the required depth of field when taking photographs of objects at close range. Preferably the camera should not be hand held for exposures under 1/60th sec though it may be possible to get away with 1/30th sec exposures if desperate. The ideal solution to keeping the camera steady is to use tripod – which should have pan, tilt and swivel head. This should be available in the studio or workshop. In other circumstances exposures of several seconds can be managed (assuming a small format camera is being used) with the uncased camera held flat against some solid and flat part of a building, radiator, table or floor. If nothing else is available squatting with elbows on knees, heels firmly planted on floor can be good for exposures up to ½ second. When using a camera hand-held it also helps to take shot just at the end of exhalation of a deep breath. The shutter release mechanism should be gently squeezed rather than suddenly pressed.

When photographing shiny objects or those behind glass, reflections of equipment such as camera, tripod, or light or other objects in the room may interfere with the shot. This may be difficult to resolve. Steps to take include looking to see where the reflections are, moving slightly to right or left. When using flash, taking the shot at a slight angle from one side or the other, rather than straight on, helps to prevent unwanted reflections. It may be possible to cover objects causing unwanted reflections with a large piece of matt black cloth (e.g. felt). While the photographer looks through the lens, the cloth should be moved around until the reflections disappear. This could take the form of a huge sheet of black with just a tiny hole cut in it through which the camera lens projects. Under circumstances where room for manoeuvre is restricted, it may be possible to use a polarizing filter on the camera which can be rotated until unwanted reflections disappear. This works best at angles up to about 40 degrees. Under very demanding circumstances it may be necessary to use only controlled light sources with a polarizing sheet placed over each light source and another over the camera lens. In this way, it is possible to suppress unwanted specular reflections from any surface at any angle. The use of such tricks requires an increase in exposure of 2–4 times.

Two advantages of flash are that colour rendering is good and a tripod is not necessary. However, pictures should not be taken head on when using flash. It is better to move over to one side or to move the flash gun over to one side – the flash doesn't have to be on the camera and doesn't have to be a single unit. Flash can be mounted on a tripod, on a pole, or on an assistant instead of, or as well as, on the camera. When using flash close to glass it is advisable to poke the camera through black felt as described above. It is also possible to bounce flash using, for example, white card or a white ceiling, but over long distances there may be too little light to do this successfully. It is better when possible to arrange to have objects illuminated from above, as most often seen in natural light. In calculating the exposure it is necessary to measure the total distance travelled by the light rather than the distance of the object from the camera. It is necessary to watch colours of reflected light and light filtered through window blinds when using flash especially when deliberately using surfaces to bounce the light. A consistent way to modify flash exposure is to adjust the setting of the speed of the film. Flash can provide useful augmentation of daylight. For example, 'telling' a flash unit that the speed of the film being used is ISO 400/27 when in fact the film is actually ISO 100/21 rated allows the flash to effectively provide ¼ of the exposure necessary.

Other light sources include floods, spots and soft lights. Photoflood units with approximately 1000 watt bulbs give soft, even light balanced over a 60° arc that is appropriate for artificial light films. However, these do not give a good result when there is a lot of daylight about as the latter then spoils colour rendering. They also have a short life. Photo lamps give a longer life but are more expensive. By using a very small aperture and long exposure, it is possible to 'paint' with this type of light waving it round to illuminate each part in turn of a large area. If a shadow is required this can be achieved by holding the light in one position for the last part of the exposure. The use of reflectors such as white card or large sheets of expanded polystyrene round the camera and object to be photographed to throw light back on to the subject can be very useful for reducing shadow density but attention must be paid to the colour of the reflected light. Softer, more diffuse lighting can be obtained from floodlights with capped bulbs. Diffusion of light source can also be achieved by placing translucent material between the light source and the object to be illuminated. Too much diffusion of the light can lead to loss of shadow, thereby rendering the object dull and flat but just enough can sometimes lead to reduction of unwanted shadows and highlights that may allow a greater degree of surface detail to be observed. It is a good idea always to use a lens hood to cut down stray light reflections.

It is very desirable to maintain consistency of both lighting effect and background throughout a series of shots illustrating a conservation process or treatment episode. Backgrounds or sets are a most important part of achieving professional quality shots in conservation. More than anything else the lack of proper background betrays the amateur effort and interferes with the main purpose of the record. It is very useful to incorporate a scale and colour patch and a 'slate' showing object identification, date and state (before, during and after conservation).

A one piece background, suitable for larger, floor standing objects, can be simply made from a large sheet of plain paper or fabric unwound from a roll mounted at high level and gently curving from vertical to horizontal. The object is placed directly on the background, well in front to avoid too harsh shadows. Colour and tone of background should take into consideration the nature and especially the colour of the object. Shots taken on highly coloured backgrounds tend to date more rapidly and the colour of the background may lend more of a colour caste to the object than when black, white or neutral grey is used. The background should be protected, using old background paper for example, when positioning objects on it to avoid footprints and other marks showing up in the photograph. The protection should only be removed just before the photograph is to be taken.

An effective two-piece background suitable for smaller objects can be formed by placing the object on a table covered with coloured paper or cloth at a little distance in front of a vertical screen of coloured paper. A copy stand can be used for small three-dimensional objects. Sets can be lit in various ways. Perhaps the easiest one is with the camera straight on and lights coming at an angle from either side of the camera. Another way is with one light illuminating background and one at an angle on the object with the camera at an angle to the second light.

When even simple background sets are not feasible it is possible to secure acceptable results by arranging for the depth of field to be such that the background is well out of focus.

### Alternative light sources

By the selection of appropriate light sources and equipment, the photographic process can be extended to reveal elements of both surfaces and structure not ordinarily visible to the naked eye. Furthermore, the images obtained may be subjected to analysis to enable counting or measurement of particular features and can be digitized in a manner that enables the image to be manipulated in ways far beyond those available in the traditional darkroom.

Discrete portions of the electromagnetic spectrum are subdivided according to their interaction with atomic and molecular matter. For example: ultraviolet, visible and infrared radiation all involve distinct aspects of outer orbital electrons, X-rays excite inner-shell electrons and gamma-rays are higher energy emissions from atomic nuclei. Different energies within each portion of the spectrum will modify the results of the imaging processes.

Film or imaging techniques sensitive to these specific energy domains make it possible to visualize such characteristic phenomena when 'illuminated' by the proper energy source. This evidence will reveal materials and construction techniques hitherto concealed from the unaided eye of the examiner. In general, these techniques operate on the principle of contrast between areas of absorption and: reflection (infrared reflectography), transmission (X-ray radiography) and emission (ultraviolet illumination). The five techniques which have the most widespread application are photography by reflected UV, photography by reflected IR, fluorescence excited by UV, fluorescence excited by IR and X-ray radiography.

When attempting photography by either reflected UV or reflected IR, the subject must be lit with lights which emit the wavelengths by which we wish to photograph. A filter must then be placed in front of the film (usually over the camera lens) which passes only those wavelengths. Electronic flash is a good source of both UV and IR wavelengths. For UV, an 18A filter is required on the camera and for IR the filter required is an 87 or 87C. Almost any black and white film, especially those with lower film speeds, is suitable for reflected UV. For reflected IR, Kodak High Speed Infrared film is recommended.

When some subjects are illuminated by certain wavelengths they may transform some of the incident radiation into other, usually longer wavelengths which are then reflected back along with the same wavelengths that they were illuminated by. When a subject behaves in this way it is said to fluoresce. Some subjects change short, ultraviolet, wavelengths into longer visible wavelengths. Others may change visible rays into yet longer infrared wave-lengths. The former effect is of course visible while the latter is not. Fluorescence photography starts with a source that contains the wavelengths which the subject will transform into longer wavelengths and usually an exciter filter is placed over the source that will allow through only those wavelengths which will cause fluorescence. For UV fluorescence a Wratten 18A filter can be used and for IR fluorescence a Corning 9788 filter is suitable. For UV fluorescence photography a Wratten 2A or 2E filter is placed over the camera lens to block reflected UV and colour reversal daylight film used to record the results. The barrier filters suggested for IR fluorescence photography are Wratten 87, 87C or 88A with Kodak High Speed Infrared film.

Silver halide emulsions are also sensitive to X-rays, gamma rays and charged particles emitted by radioactive substances. Some of these rays penetrate visually opaque materials to varying degrees to show up internal structures. Radiography covers techniques of recording the subsurface features of objects. X-rays, which have wavelengths 1/100th to 1/100 000th that of visible light, are produced by bombarding an electrode with a high voltage stream of electrons. For radiography, the object to be recorded is placed between the X-ray tube and the film. The differential absorption of X rays by the object's internal structure is recorded on the film as a projection shadow graph. The energy of X rays, which is quoted in Kilo volts, can be adjusted according to the density and thickness of the structures being examined. Generally higher energies are used for thick and dense materials and lower energy 'soft' X-rays are used for thinner low density materials. Good contrast can be achieved with wooden structures by selecting the proper X-ray kilovoltage and exposure time (Gilardoni *et al.*, 1994). Xeroradiography which uses an X-ray source employs a recording process similar to the photocopying process. The technique requires a selenium developing plate which provides a wider latitude in a single exposure. In addition, it offers enhanced contrast and can either be printed in positive or negative. Magliano and Boesmis (1988) have demonstrated this technique for panel paintings and Willisch (1989) has examined among other materials wooden and ivory objects. Advanced

X-ray computer tomography provides the synchronized movement of a focused X-ray beam around the object to be examined. Electronic images, corrected for overlaps and distortions, of transverse or longitudinal sections of the objects are created (Martius, 1992). Because radiographs show a limited indication of depth, stereoradiography may be useful in determining the location of a specific feature in three dimensions (Gilardoni *et al.*, 1994).

Bernstein (1991), Brachert (1986), Gill *et al.* (1990), Levitan (1987), Van Der Reyden and Williams (1992) and others have shown the value of X-ray radiographs in revealing construction and other information such as the extent of damage caused by insect infestation that is not otherwise readily accessible.

### The camera

There are many different cameras available for different purposes and no one camera is ideal. Some are specialized to perform a small range of tasks that would be impossible with other types of equipment. Others are very versatile and can cover a wide range of photographic assignments without being ideal for any. The four main types of camera are the view camera, the direct viewfinder camera, the twin lens reflex and the single lens reflex. The advantages and disadvantages of each type are comprehensively and concisely reviewed by Langford (1997). A list of some factors to consider when choosing a camera is given below.

- Purposes for which the camera is required. Would it be better to have one camera for everything or to use more than one type depending on need?
- The format – large format gives better definition and enlargement, wide range of camera movements for image control availability of specialist film and easy film change. Small format cameras are less intrusive, quicker to use, have greater depth of field and generally faster lenses.
- Film types available.
- Focal length of lens, means of focusing and availability of other lenses and filters. Whether the camera sees what the eye sees should also be considered.
- Shutter speed and aperture control and means of metering and controlling exposure.

- Availability of adaptors for close-up work and attachment to microscope if required.
- Cost.

Control of the amount of light falling on the film can be effected by changing the lens aperture and by changing shutter speed. To achieve a given exposure, as the shutter speed increases the size of the aperture will need to be increased. Conversely, a reduction in shutter speed allows the lens aperture to be reduced or 'stopped down'. Reducing the shutter speed affects the sharpness of objects in motion and renders the effects of camera shake more likely. Changing the lens aperture affects depth of field, contrast and definition. The depth of field, the distance in front and behind the subject that will be in focus, increases with smaller apertures. Since depth of field increases as we move further away from the object, a useful guide is to focus slightly behind the near parts of object. Using small apertures gives sharper definition as this effectively makes use of the centre of the lens. As more of the lens is used, picture quality may begin to degrade.

Single lens reflex cameras and other through-the-lens metering systems have advantages for routine determination of correct exposures but are not infallible under all circumstances. For very long exposures a TTL meter will not work satisfactorily and a separate light meter needs to be used. The colour of the background has an important effect on the exposure determined by a TTL meter of an object placed against it. An object placed against a white background will tend to come out underexposed if the meter reading is followed (therefore have to give more exposure, ½ to 2 stops). A light object on a dark background will tend to come out overexposed and should therefore be given less exposure. It is a good idea to work out two positions of compensation – one moderate and one more extreme and to record all such experiments while becoming familiar with equipment and circumstances. The technique of taking the same shot using a range of different exposures above and below the theoretically correct exposure is referred to as bracketing.

The Reciprocity law (Chapter 6) applies especially to colour films. For example, for Kodak Ektachrome, over the range 1/1000 second to 1/100 second the relationship between light level and response of the film is linear. At 1/20 second response is within an acceptable range but at light levels theoretically requiring a 1 second exposure it is necessary to increase aperture by one stop and use a 15B filter to obtain a correct result. At 10 seconds a 1½ stop compensation and use of 20B filter are required.

Close-ups can be taken using close up lenses, macro lens, extension tubes or bellows. A 100 mm lens on bellows will go from infinity to extreme close up and is therefore potentially a very useful set up. It is the viewpoint that determines perspective but the lens that determines the viewpoint. Viewpoint governing perspective becomes weird if too close to objects. A long focus lens (say 100 mm on a 35 mm SLR camera), though it may have limited actual close focusing, may be preferable in achieving the effect of making the chosen subject appear larger on film without the apparent distortion that can occur by actually going in close to an object. Alternatively, adjustable tilt and swing lenses available for some cameras (view cameras especially – 35 mm cameras are rather limited in this respect) can be used to compensate for the apparent distortion caused by taking shots close up. Some close-up equipment, such as bellows and extension tubes, has a marked effect on exposure. The square of the distance from the film to the nodal point of the lens system (approximately the centre of the lens barrel) divided by the focal length of the lens gives the factor by which exposure must be increased (unless using TTL).

## 9.5 Studio organization and layout

The basic requirements of any furniture conservation studio or workshop space are to provide a safe and secure environment for the objects being worked on, to provide a safe and comfortable environment for the conservators doing the work and to provide a space that is suitable to effectively and efficiently carry out the work required. To achieve this, a great deal of careful thought and planning is needed, every aspect of which should be driven by the work that will be carried out and by the needs of people to carry it out. This section therefore starts with a basic outline of the main processes and procedures generally involved in a furniture conservation commission. Useful sources of information on setting up a business include: the conservation professional bodies (see above); local contacts such as banks, accountants, insurance brokers and solicitors; local and national government organizations connected with trade, industry, employment, welfare, taxation and so forth. Help with the planning process can be obtained from architects, structural engineers, quantity surveyors and specialist consultants. There are many other organizations concerned with specific aspects of setting up and running a business, such as fire, safety and security, that can be identified through directories of organizations held by the reference libraries of larger towns and cities. Comprehensive works by Kingshott (1993) and by Landis (1999) are devoted to designing, planning and equipping the workshop and useful ideas are provided by Peters (1984) and by Deasy (1985) among others. However, final decisions should only be taken once you are satisfied that the design will work. It is unwise to place undue reliance on people who ultimately are much less affected by the outcome than you are. To this end, rehearse the work using drawings, models, full-size floor layouts (in the garden) and even mock-ups of bits of studio to 'walk through' the processes that need to be carried out from arrival of objects to their despatch and think through the best overall arrangement that will work for you and that you can afford. Fire safety is an essential component that must be built in at the design stage.

### 9.5.1   Workshop processes and procedures

Furniture conservation cannot be reduced to a formula but it is possible to trace certain patterns in the work that provide a useful framework for thinking about the studio and flow of work.

#### Examination and recording of condition

In every case it is necessary to examine the object to determine its condition, to be able to propose possible treatments and to estimate the time and cost of carrying them out. This process requires a well-lit uncluttered space with the necessary equipment close to hand to complete the examination and record the result.

#### Dismantling the object

It is by no means always necessary to dismantle the object and this should certainly not be done unnecessarily. However, when required it is usually the next step after examination. This requires a clear space with good access to the appropriate equipment and plenty of clear softened surface area to lay out parts in safety after they have been dismantled. This process often uses a lot of equipment, which should be kept separate from parts of objects. After parts have been dismantled, examined, recorded and labelled they will need to be put somewhere conveniently close to hand but out of harm's way.

#### Repair of existing components and making of new ones

This covers a whole range of processes and procedures discussed in the following chapters. Once suitable materials and methods of fabrication have been decided, the materials must be retrieved from storage and selected for quality and quantity then converted to the size and shape required. This includes all the basic woodworking techniques and may also include consolidation of existing material or moulding and casting of new parts. Once prepared, new parts need to be fitted, adhered to existing parts and then set aside undisturbed for the adhesive to solidify. Once set, further shaping may be required. The way that the workshop is laid out, the organization of work surfaces and the storage of tools, materials, equipment and object parts can have a profound influence on the ease with which these processes can be carried out.

#### Re-assembly

All parts of the object are brought back together at this stage, trial fitted and prepared for assembly. Large surface areas are often needed to have everything to hand, systematically organized and uncluttered with easy access to cramps once the final process of assembly starts.

#### Finishing and colouring

In many workshops this is considered as two distinct processes. First the rather dusty operation of finishing the wood itself and second the colouring, polishing and related operations.

### *Recording and reporting treatment*

Once the work is completed the object should be photographed, final details of the processes carried out and the result recorded. It is also important to think where the object will go once the final process has been complete. It may be that the object will be mounted, installed, packed for transport or stored pending further action. These processes may also affect the choice, design and layout of a workshop or studio.

### 9.5.2    The location

Factors that will affect the choice of location include access to clients, access to other professional services, proximity to home, economics, availability of suitable premises, planning controls, convenience and psychological factors. The latter for example come into play when working from home. This can be a very good way to start off a small business since it is very convenient and initial costs are lower. However the feeling of pressure or stress that can arise later from living at work should not be underestimated. As the business expands more space may be required which is not available at home. This may lead to considerable disruption while the business is relocated to new premises. When choosing a location, consideration should also be given to ease of access, security and environment. Ease of access is partly determined by the surrounding road and rail networks and by ease of access to the actual site on which the building is situated. Is it straightforward to load and unload large pieces of furniture, timber and so on and can staff get to work? If by car can they park when they get there? Different areas do definitely have different crime rates and incidence of vandalism and security is more easily maintained to some premises than others by nature of the perimeter. Improving perimeter security can be expensive. The location of a building can affect the environment through likelihood of flooding, exposure and prevailing wind conditions and also by pollution levels.

### 9.5.3    The building/space

Once a suitable location has been determined a site may be selected on the basis of its suitability for a new building or for modification of an existing one. Factors to consider when assessing the space include the title to the property, structural strength and condition of the building, access, floor loadings, quality of light, security, services provision, other activities being pursued in the immediate vicinity and any plans for development in the surrounding area.

It is not possible to review in detail all the processes that one might wish to carry out but some of the main functional areas into which the space might need to be divided include: loading and unloading bay for objects, storage area for objects, reception area for clients, timber storage, machine shop, main woodwork conservation studio area, surface finishing area, upholstery workshop, metalworking area with hearth, rest area for staff. The processes that will go on in support of these functions have different and somewhat incompatible requirements. They may be clean/dirty, wet/dry, noisy/quiet and may require different levels of light, security, power supply and so on. These requirements may change from time to time in relation to such matters as health and safety legislation. Object storage requires the highest security whereas timber storage is less demanding in this respect. Polishing and other finishing work requires a clean, dust-free environment that is therefore best situated away from dust-producing machinery. As many of the materials used in finishing processes are flammable, sources of ignition such as a metalworking hearth should not be situated nearby. Machinery might be best situated close to where timber is stored and to where the semi-prepared timber is used. Eating and drinking in work areas, always unwise, now contravenes health and safety legislation in many countries. A separate rest area is therefore required for consumption of food and drink on premises employing more than a few people.

Access between adjacent areas also needs to be carefully considered in terms of the processes and flow of work between them. The layout of the workshop should then reflect this flow. For example a typical order of work might include arrival of object, logging in, storage, examination, photography, structural work, finishing, photography, storage, logging out. One does not want to have to routinely carry objects through areas where people are working to get from one part of the building to another especially not through areas where machinery is situated. Clear separation between activities with ease of access can be achieved by having large corridors between all rooms but this may not be possible where space is at a premium.

### Entrance/loading bay

It should be possible for arriving and departing vehicles to load and unload objects so that their journey between the vehicle and the store, studio or examination room is short, secure and under cover. This can be a covered area open at the sides or an enclosed space that forms part of the workshop complex. For large objects, handling equipment may be necessary and the space should allow such equipment both to be used and to be stored out of the way when not required. There should be space around the building for the appropriate number of vehicles to arrive, unload, park, turn round and depart with adequate freedom. A convenient layout allows easy access from the loading bay/entrance to object stores, main woodworking area and office.

### Client reception and administration area

These need not necessarily be combined but it is essential to have somewhere to 'do the paperwork' and useful to have somewhere that clients and other visitors can be invited to sit down in a quiet and safe environment to discuss business. In addition to these activities the business might sell from this area a range of finishing materials, fixtures and fittings appropriate to the clients' own uses. In this area one might expect to find the normal range of office equipment supporting well-oiled procedures that not only make the business run smoothly but create a favourable impression to the client. Preliminary discussion with the client may have taken place off site but visits to view work in progress or to inspect the finished work before its return to the client are likely. In order to maximize business opportunities and minimize the time spent on administrative overheads it is important to give thought to this side of the business to make it as efficient as possible. A larger business may employ a full- or part-time administrator while a smaller one might simply provide the administrative tools and equipment for a conservator to use as and when necessary. It is a good idea at least to

seek advice from a well-organized and experienced administrator or secretary on how to set this up.

Good communications are vital and should include, if possible, separate lines for telephone (with voice mail and message management facilities) and facsimile transmission, mobile telephone and e-mail. Since any caller represents potential business it is very desirable that every call should be answered personally. If this is not possible then the caller should be given a clear indication of when they can expect a return call and any other information that might be helpful. Callers can be referred to a mobile phone number. Appropriately placed and used extensions can allow the telephone to be answered if necessary by conservation staff without undue loss of time or concentration. The way that the communications system is best set up depends on the size of the business, the likely volume of calls and the individuals involved but it should be thought of as a system that provides the best possible response to the client with the least loss of productive conservation time.

Huge rewards can accrue from having information well organized and readily available to everyone who might need it. Conversely there are huge penalties in time, morale and client satisfaction for poor management of information. The range of information that may be required is considerable including contact details for clients and suppliers, financial records of income and expenditure for accounting and tax purposes and the documentation of work in progress. A lot of this is best managed using modern information technology.

### Object storage

There should be a secure area into which objects can be safely and securely decanted on arrival at the premises and to which they can be returned on completion prior to their return to the client. This will need to allow for a range of different sizes and types of object and one arrangement that can be successful is to have larger objects on pallets or racks at ground level and smaller objects in cupboards or on shelves above. It is highly desirable that the store should be arranged to provide access to any object without having to move others. A space should also be provided in or close to the store for handling equipment and perhaps also for packing materials. It is not necessary that the store itself should be provided with daylight but there should be enough space adjacent to this store to allow the client to view the conserved object in good light; this might be the inward end of the loading bay for example.

### Examination and photography

In setting up a workshop, consideration needs to be given to the scope of examination and photography that the business is able to undertake and where this is best carried out. Every object will require, at the least, careful examination in good light and basic photography as part of the process of recording condition and developing a treatment proposal. More advanced techniques, such as microscopy, that require specialized and delicate equipment are best separated from the area where practical conservation is carried out. It might be that different techniques would best be carried out in different locations. Some techniques will require very good lighting others may require an area that can be blacked out (e.g. UV fluorescence). Photography needs to take place against a suitable and uncluttered background. This might be a roll of photographic backing paper, especially produced for the purpose, or it might be a plain wall, but there needs to be enough space in front to display and light the object and set up the camera without interfering with other work. Also this area should be situated to avoid excessive handling which is bad for the objects and staff and wastes time. This space might be situated at one end of the main workshop.

### The main work area

The area where practical interventive structural conservation and restoration is done can be set up in various ways. Probably the most usual way for this to be done is what might be termed 'conservator centred'. Each conservator has a fixed personal work space containing personal tools, equipment and a certain amount of commonly used materials to which is brought the object or objects on which that conservator will work. Space needs to be allowed in this work area for a solid bench for preparation of repair material, space to put dismantled parts of objects and space for a work

surface such as a lightweight (possibly portable) bench that can be used for assembly and for lighter duty operations such as cleaning. Paperwork in the workshop should be kept to an absolute minimum but some space to record observations, treatment details and time spent is also required. The position of the personal work space with respect to access routes needs to be carefully considered. In smaller workshops personal spaces can be distributed along one or more edges of the room. In larger establishments floor markings can be used to help delineate space. The arrangement adopted needs to take into account access to available natural light and to adjacent communal spaces that will contain shared equipment. An alternative arrangement to the purely conservator-centred approach is to allot spaces to objects and to have the conservator move to the object rather than having the object brought to the conservator. This allows more objects to be worked on in parallel and is useful for jobs such as picture frame repairs where a more or less identical sequence of operations can be carried out on several objects with some economy of scale. The type of arrangement that will find favour depends on the type of work, the size of space, the availability of facilities such as extraction and the number and preferences of the individuals concerned. It is worth spending some time working out the advantages and disadvantages of a particular set up, rather than simply reproducing a previous environment. It is very desirable to maintain as much flexibility as possible in the working environment to be able to accommodate unusual objects or work patterns if the need arises. It is also desirable to have control of the space to be able to choose conditions of illumination, ventilation, temperature and humidity as well as spatial layout.

### Machine room

Different conservators vary greatly in the extent to which they use woodworking machinery and therefore in the nature, size and organization of the space required. Whatever the size of the business or disposition of the conservator it is likely that some machinery will be used in basic re-sawing of large boards to suitable sized blanks for further processing by hand. Whether a completely separate space is justified or whether the necessary operations can be performed within either the dry timber store or the workshop itself is a matter for individual consideration. A small- to medium-sized bandsaw can, with the right kind of dust extraction equipment, be accommodated in the main workshop and can greatly speed up rough shaping and removal of waste wood. It is very inconvenient to have to go into a separate space to perform such simple light-duty operations but very distracting, dangerous and unhealthy to have a lot of power tools or machinery in a shared workshop space. Increasingly, health and safety legislation determines the conditions under which woodworking machinery is to be used and it is essential to consult both the relevant legislation and approved codes of practice before proceeding. A logical place to put a separate machine shop is between the dry timber store and the main studio.

### Retouching area/clean room

Traditionally, polishing has been a separate activity carried out in a separate part of the workshop by a specialist. This good idea is worth extending to a wider range of conservation finishing processes for various reasons, the most obvious being that of dust control. Such work may also require specialist equipment such as that used for spraying coatings and may therefore also need compressed air and more sophisticated extraction facilities. In terms of location in the overall plan of the building there is much to argue for the finishing area to be located between the main studio and the store into which the finished object will be transferred to await collection. The finishing area itself might be subdivided into an ultra clean room where application of surface coatings is done and a preparation area for other tasks to be completed. Alternatively, this might be achieved by more traditional dust management techniques. Where there is much gilding to be done it is worth considering whether the preparation of the gesso and bole foundations should be separated from the application of the gold and where each of these operations should be performed. Rubbing down of gesso makes a good deal of dust which needs to be excluded from the final stages of the gilding process. Application of gold leaf benefits from a clean, dust- and draft-free environment.

### The wood store

Wood is a highly variable material and many of the woods and other materials used by furniture conservators are in short supply. Accordingly, few furniture conservators will pass up the opportunity to acquire potentially useful material, sometimes at considerable financial cost. There is no point in having this if it is not maintained in good condition or cannot be found or got out when required. Large heavy boards must be properly stacked if they are not to constitute a hazard. Therefore the store should be well set out with sturdy racks that allow related material to be kept together with good access and suitable environmental conditions that will prevent deterioration. It is advisable to label each storage location with a code and to keep a separate hand list of the woods at each coded location since this makes it easier to maintain an up-to-date stock list. The authors' own timber stocks are divided into large boards, offcuts (including short lengths) and veneers. The large boards are kept on a heavy duty, double-sided rack in the centre of the store, each timber being identified by a chalk mark on the end of the board. Veneers are kept in presses on one side wall and offcuts are kept in metal bins which allow the suitably marked cut ends to be viewed. Within these groupings, storage is subdivided by timber type into temperate hardwoods, tropical hardwoods and softwoods. Man-made boards and composites are kept in a rack on the other end wall. Space is provided in the store that allows timber to be manipulated for selection.

### Upholstery workshop

The range of treatments an upholstery conservator might expect to undertake on upholstered objects would include technical examination, removal and replacement of upholstery (with facilities for full re-upholstery), simple frame repairs, cleaning, conservation and preparation of materials. One main space, sub-divided into three separate areas – a dust area, a clean area and a wet area – would provide an ideal foundation to satisfactorily undertake the different stages of work. When conserving upholstered objects, close collaboration with textile and furniture conservators is desirable. When located in close proximity to each other (ideally in adjacent rooms) it is possible to share some facilities. The workshop described assumes that the upholstery conservator is working with no access to a textile conservation facility.

The space required is determined, to a degree, by the largest piece of upholstered furniture it is envisaged that the workshop is likely to undertake; if beds and hangings are to be treated, height will be a priority. There should be sufficient access to the object to approach it from all angles for treatment. The doors and work spaces should be large enough for easy manoeuvrability of the objects. Some consideration should be given to the necessity of treating suites of furniture rather than pieces in isolation. Sufficient space for essential equipment and materials storage should be allowed since upholstery materials are often bulky. Frames may also require storage and dust covering while upholstery elements are being treated. As a guide, 75 square metres (approximately 800 square feet) has been found to be sufficient for two full-time upholstery conservators with occasional student projects being included in the space. Equipment should be as versatile as possible to keep the space fluid and adaptable to purpose. Floors should be tiled throughout with a solvent-resistant, non-slip material. Lighting requirements are discussed below.

*The dust area*  Work undertaken in this area includes all dust-creating operations:

- Preliminary investigation of objects before treatment
- Removal of covers
- Vacuum cleaning of covers and upholstery under-structures
- Conservation of existing upholstery under-structure and complete re-upholstery
- Preparation of substructures (e.g. machine tooling expanded polyethylene forms, wood sub-frames).

The area should be partitioned off and have a separate entrance from the adjacent areas. A suitable dust extraction system will reduce the risk of dust migration into clean areas.

*The clean area*  This area is primarily used for the conservation of extant upholstery removed from its frame and 'top cover' work. Work undertaken in this area includes:

- Preparation of removed materials for wet and dry cleaning treatments, e.g. dye and fibre tests, sandwiching textiles in net and making templates of covers.
- Actual conservation work of removed textiles, e.g. re-attaching loose areas.
- Re-applying conserved covers to the prepared upholstery.
- Preparing documentation reports and photography.
- Storage of conservation materials and tools.

*The wet area*  This area to be used for the wet cleaning and drying of covers, foundation materials and fillings and for cane and rush seating. An isolated area with fume/moisture extraction is needed for dyeing support fabrics and threads. It is also useful for scouring fabrics used in conservation (support fabrics or replacement/additional upholstery layers). If no access to a laboratory is available, space within this area may be reserved for wet chemical work.

### Metalworking area

It is possible to get away with very small amounts of work on non-ferrous metals in the environment described for woodwork but it is inadvisable and unsafe to undertake more than this amount of work unless a separate metalworking area is available. In particular, ferrous metalwork and woodwork do not mix well. Sparks from metalworking operations and from metal swarf may ignite wood dusts and the two are not permitted to share extraction facilities. Finely divided iron and steel interact with some timbers to stain them a blue–black colour.

Metalworking activities that may be required in support of furniture conservation include tool-making and repair or replacement of furniture fixtures and fittings. A forge for soldering, brazing, annealing and tempering metal items is needed if this kind of work is to be undertaken. An acid bath will also be needed for removal of fire scale. A metal-turning lathe, drill press, grindstone and buffing wheel are also very commonly used items of equipment that should be accommodated. For sheet metalwork, a range of dollies and stakes and a firm bench in which to fix them is desirable. Metal casting is a more specialist activity that is nevertheless undertaken by a few furniture conservators who have found it worthwhile to invest in the necessary (centrifugal) casting equipment and who may carry on this work for others as a sideline. In this case space is also needed for the mould-making processes and possibly for metal-plating equipment for gilding finished castings. Separate extraction facilities are required for fumes from processes involving hot metals and those involving chemical processes such as electroplating.

### Recreational areas

Eating and drinking, and smoking should not be allowed in working spaces and therefore an area will need to be provided for these activities, along with lavatories and hand washing facilities and space for changing into work clothes and storing outer garments. Food storage facilities should be kept completely separate from those used to store conservation chemicals and other potentially hazardous materials.

### 9.5.4   Detailed requirements

This section includes discussion of furnishings, fittings and fixtures, with reference to floors, walls, doors, storage, heating, lighting, power and ventilation.

All furnishings should be practical and easily maintained. Colour of surfaces should be chosen to avoid interfering with colour matching. A light neutral colour is suggested rather than pure white, which may lead to excessive glare. Floors should be non-slip, solvent-resistant and easily cleaned. Entrance doors should be wide with reinforced glass windows for good vision beyond the door and a mechanism to hold the doors back for safe access for large objects.

### Storage

Careful consideration needs to be given throughout the space to storage. Storage will be required for objects before treatment, objects after treatment, work in progress, materials, tools and equipment, solvents, corrosive chemicals, waste, perishable materials – in cool store or deep freeze but not with food, personal possessions, stationery, special items of high value and portability (e.g. cameras, gold leaf), maintenance and cleaning materials and equipment. In general, careful consideration should be given to personal versus communal storage.

(a)

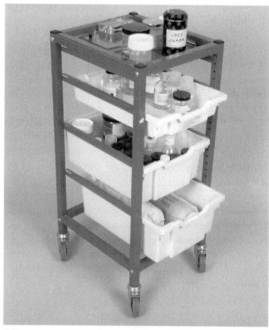

(b)

(c)

**Figure 9.5**  A solvent storage system
(*a*) Small quantities of solvents used in day-to-day conservation treatments stored in a tray
(*b*) Several trays can be accommodated on a trolley
(*c*) Storage of trays in a solvent cabinet when solvents not in use

*Solvent storage*  Solvents should be stored in fire-proof stores in limited quantities. Corrosive and flammable materials should be stored separately, preferably in different rooms and certainly not in the same cupboard. Bench storage of solvent should not exceed about 250 ml of each of the four most commonly used solvents. Reserves of up to 50 l may be kept in the studio in lockable fire-resistant steel cabinets. Bulk storage of flammable solvents should be in a separate building away from the main site provided with adequate ventilation and decanting facilities. Solvent storage is usefully developed as a system that includes fully labelled bottles and dispensers containing small quantities of the solvents most commonly used together with those required for the job kept together in a tray. During the working day the tray can be accommodated on a suitable trolley and at night can be put away into a suitable solvent cabinet. The components of this system are shown in *Figure 9.5*. Flammable solvents must be kept away from sources of ignition. Swabs and solvent impregnated waste should be stored in metal safety bins and emptied regularly at the end of each working day.

*Tool storage*  Tool storage needs to keep tools in good condition, close at hand, safely stored, easily accessed and easily put away. Tool storage needs to be flexible to adapt to different patterns of usage and to accommodate new tools as they are acquired and to be a good advertisement to any one who comes into the workshop. A range of tool cabinets based on removable trays, developed after long experience, is illustrated and described by Frid (1980). An excellent range of under-bench tool storage options is available from the German bench-maker Ulmia.

## Wet areas

Wet areas may be required in the main workshop, the finishing shop and the recreational area. Consideration of the processes that will be carried out in each area will enable the right type and size of sink, taps and adjacent working and storage spaces to be achieved. It may be necessary to have fume extraction in some wet areas and in particular to have one wet work area with fume hood where potentially hazardous wet chemical preparations (e.g. diluting commercial strength ammonium

hydroxide solutions) can be completed safely. It is very helpful if risk assessments on the processes that will be performed in the workshop can be carried out before finalizing these arrangements. Purified water from a distillation apparatus, deionizer or reverse osmosis device can be provided on demand but may require a storage vessel if large quantities are likely to be required at short notice.

## Electrical power supply

Consideration should be given, with a qualified electrician, to the types of loads and usage patterns that will be sustained to determine the number of phases of the supply and the cabling requirements. Before installing sockets, thought should be given to how the supply will be used to avoid leads trailing over work. In the UK, regulations for site work require a 110 volt supply to be used. If the possibility of much off-site work is envisaged it may be worth setting up a 110 volt supply in the studio that can be used with the same portable equipment that will be used off site. There are also regulations on the protection of power supplies where solvents are in use and only spark-proof equipment should be used when working with solvents. This includes extraction equipment and refrigeration plant. For safety reasons, power supplies should be protected by earth leakage circuit breakers.

## Lighting and heating

It should be possible to achieve the right quality and quantity of light when and where it is wanted. UV radiation is not normally wanted and should be eliminated. In studios where daylight makes an important contribution to the overall lighting, there should be UV retarding film on the windows. Both quartz halogen and fluorescent lamps should also be fitted with UV filters. While a good overall light level is desirable it is usually necessary to supplement this locally by task lighting. This will require different apparatus for different tasks and careful consideration should be given to the number and type of different light sources that will be used. For good colour rendering the available light sources include daylight, tungsten (including quartz halogen) and *some* fluorescent lamps specifically prepared to have good colour rendering. Some colours which match under one light source will not match under another light source. This is called *metamerism*. It is possible to calculate whether a lamp will distort colours by one of two methods. The first of these is the CIE colour shift method (CIE, 1974) and the second is the NPL Crawford Spectral band method (Crawford, 1959, 1960). In the CIE method the test lamp is compared with a reference lamp of the same correlated colour temperature to determine the (average) shift in position in colour space of eight test colours. A lamp with a *colour rendering index* ($R_a$) of 100 has perfect colour rendering. The lower the colour rendering index the worse the shift in colour that is observed. Pure, unfiltered daylight has a colour rendering index of 100.

Although lamps of both high and low colour temperature can have good colour rendering, if they are used together the eye will adapt to one or other of them making the other(s) appear wrong. Tungsten lights appear to give a yellow cast and fluorescent lights a blue cast whereas on their own any of these sources (provided it had good colour rendering) could give satisfactory viewing. It will make matters simpler in the long run to decide on a restricted range of light sources of known qualities for use in the studio. Issues that should be considered in relation to lamp choice besides colour rendering and colour temperature are ease of control, the extent of radiant heating produced by the lamp, cost of installation and maintenance and personal preference.

The temperature of the work space needs to be regulated for comfortable working, and for the safety of the objects and for the success of many conservation operations temperature needs to be maintained fairly constant in the range suggested in Chapter 6. An architect should be consulted for advice on how best to deal with the building to achieve efficient control of temperature. This will involve some calculations on the thermal mass of the building, the probability of overheating in summer months and the need for heating in winter. In an environment where flammable solvents may be in use, safety is paramount and no naked flames should be used for heating the space or for heating water. Electrical convection heaters tend to stir up any solvent vapours that may be present and are therefore not a good choice. Central heating radiators are a good choice as long as the boiler is remote. Electric oil-filled radiators are also satisfactory. Thermometers and hygrometers (or thermohygrographs) should be installed to monitor the space to ensure that satisfactory conditions are being maintained.

### Extraction

Extraction may be of two types, the dilution type and the local exhaust ventilation (LEV) type. Dilution extraction removes stale air and provides a supply of fresh air but allows any contamination, although diluted, to become mixed into the general room air supply. For efficient removal of noxious vapours removal at source using local exhaust ventilation is necessary. Using this system a hood and duct are situated close to the work and noxious vapours can be extracted away from the person using hazardous materials. Flow rates measured in cubic metres per second or cubic metres per hour give a good guide to the efficacy of such systems. Low level solvent use, such as occurs in retouching for example, requires extraction of 0.5 cubic metres per second extraction at source (Hughes, 1987). Other processes, such as the use of an air brush, may need 0.6–1.0 m/s and may require work to be done in a spray booth or fume cupboard, for which well defined standards (e.g. BS DD80) exist. Systems to achieve this can be portable, free-standing or fixed. Systems that are fixed in space are obviously less flexible than portable systems (*Figure 9.6*). Such systems are noisy, as is any system in which a large volume of air is being moved at speed although devices to reduce the noise level can be fitted. With any such system careful thought needs to be given to where the air is going to and where it is coming from. Contaminated air should be vented well clear of the building and away from areas where people may be working. In the long run we should be working to avoid the need for such systems by using less hostile materials in our work. A disadvantage of fixed systems is that not only contaminants but also warm and possibly humidified air is extracted out of the building causing air to be replaced with (possibly) cold dry air. If air is being extracted out of the building, the volume of air extracted has to be balanced by a similar volume of fresh air coming in to the room. It is therefore important when installing such systems to think very carefully about the source

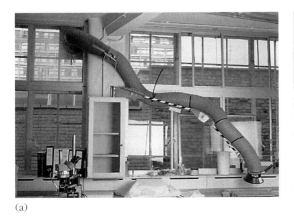 

(a)                                                    (b)

**Figure 9.6** Fume extraction
(*a*) Fixed local exhaust ventilation trunking (LEV) system that discharges fumes to the external atmosphere
(*b*) LEV extraction must be close to the source of fumes to be effective. A useful rule of thumb is that the extractor
hood should be within six inches of the solvent source

and condition of incoming air. An alternative to fixed or free-standing systems venting air out of the building is to use portable equipment that passes contaminated air over an active carbon filter and returns the filtered air back into the room. These machines, which have disposable filters, have some advantages *for light use* in that they do not alter the balance of air in the room and can be used anywhere. However, the filters are expensive and must be checked carefully to ensure that they are working. Such machines should have a spark-proof motor if they are to be safely used with a range of solvents and it is very important to check that this is in fact the case. Whatever system is chosen, regular maintenance is required. Fixed extraction should be properly tested at least every fourteen months. Portable units should be fully tested much more frequently.

The dust of many hardwood timbers is harmful and is classified with a maximum exposure limit ($5 \, \mathrm{mg/m^3}$). Fine dust is both extremely harmful to the operator and may form an explosive mixture that is capable of flashing over large areas under certain conditions. It is therefore extremely important to have efficient dust extraction. It is advisable to consult specialists in this area to ensure that any equipment installed will be safe and meet current legislation and always advisable to obtain at least three quotes. The type of installation used will depend on the number, size

and distribution of machines, the frequency of use, the number of machines it is necessary to have running together and the budget available. A damper-controlled dust collection system for small workshop use is described by Johnson (1980).

## 9.6 Tools and equipment

The list of things that one might like to have to hand in a furniture conservation studio seems never ending. In addition to a full range of woodworking tools, equipment may be required for the following activities: metalworking; upholstery; monitoring and control of the environment; fire detection and control; object handling and transport; examination and recording; dismantling; cleaning and conservation of surfaces; weighing and measuring.

### 9.6.1 Woodworking tools and equipment

Potential use may be found for a vast range of woodworking tools and equipment and yet a considerable amount of work can be achieved with a surprisingly modest selection. The range of tools and equipment employed in practice has as much to do with the outlook and personal preferences of the individual as with the nature of the work being undertaken. For

**Figure 9.7** A work bench fitted with a pattern maker's vice and end vice

those who love tools, conservation provides a fair excuse to collect just about everything going and then to make some more along the way. There are many fine publications on this subject, a selection of which are cited below as an alternative to a lengthy discourse here.

One item of equipment that deserves special mention is the bench. A firm and solid work bench allows work to be firmly held during various work processes of cutting, shaping, sanding and so forth (*Figure 9.7*). A wide range of different types and sizes of bench is available commercially or can be made by the conservator to suit personal requirements and preferences (Hoadley, 1980; Landis, 1998). The authors' preference include a pattern-maker's vice and a bench vice adapted to fulfil the function of a full-width end vice. Using the end vice in conjunction with circular bench dogs, each with one face squared off, it is possible to safely and securely hold a very wide range of different sizes and shape of material. The traditional tool-well has been deliberately omitted. Experience shows that this is often more of a hazard than a benefit and because workshop space is limited the bench has been chosen to provide a large clear flat surface that can be used for a wide range of jobs besides timber preparation.

Many woodworkers prefer to use old woodworking tools, particularly planes, many of which will give a superior performance to their modern counterparts. The quality of furniture produced by some of these tools stands witness to their performance in capable hands. A large number of tool manufacturers, many of whom

were using labour-intensive methods of production, went out of business between 1914 and 1960 as a consequence of which the range, diversity and perhaps also quality, decreased. Many of these older items are now highly prized by collectors and extremely expensive. An introduction to this subject is provided by Proudfoot and Walker (1984). Further treatments are given by Dunbar (1979), Goodman (1964, 1993), Roberts (1980, 1982), Sellens (1975a,b) and Smith (1981). The most comprehensive reference work, containing some 2600 entries and 2000 illustrations of traditional hand tools, is that by Salaman (1997). For a more recent collector's guide see Rees and Rees (1996). Comprehensive information on restoring older woodworking tools for use is given by Dunbar (1989). In addition, many woodworkers traditionally made at least some of their own tools, a subject on which *Fine Woodworking* magazine has carried many excellent articles.

### 9.6.2   Other tools and equipment

Tools for metalworking are described by Love (1983), McCreight (1991) and Untracht (1969). Those for upholstery are described by Gill and Eastop (2001), James (1994, 1999) and Thomerson (1996).

Equipment required for environmental monitoring and control includes apparatus for making spot checks on temperature, humidity, light and UV radiation and for providing permanent record of variation in these parameters with time. Equipment that may be required to maintain workshop conditions within an appropriate range include heaters, chillers, humidifiers and dehumidifiers. Refrigerators and ovens may be required to provide locally reduced or elevated temperatures. Cool storage is advantageous for epoxy resins, hydrogen peroxide, silicone rubber and film and low temperature storage can be used (–18 °C) for gilders composition. Refrigerators used for storage of flammable materials must be spark-proof. Refrigerated storage for foodstuffs should be completely separate from chemicals storage.

An adequate number and range of extinguishers, sand buckets and fire blankets, as recommended by the local fire prevention service, should be installed and regularly maintained. Smoke detectors should be fitted and wired together so that if one goes off, they all do.

Wherever possible, manual handling should be avoided. Larger and heavier objects benefit from being palletized, after which they can be manipulated using the appropriate types of trolleys and hydraulic lifting equipment. This approach minimizes risk to objects as well as to those who need to handle them, cuts down the number of people required and therefore the disruption to the work of the studio and helps to make the best use of available storage space.

Two examples of specialist equipment available to assist the process of dismantling are the Solomons steam generator and the Wood Welder radio frequency glue line heater. A supply of disposable hypodermic syringes and different-sized needles is invaluable for injecting water or industrial methylated spirits into joints to help in the dismantling process. A foot-operated dental drill can be put to many uses, including drilling out small broken metal parts.

Apparatus used for cleaning and conservation of surfaces includes vacuum cleaners, deionizer, still or reverse osmosis plant for the production of purified water, pH meter for checking purity of water and the pH of solutions for enzyme cleaning applications and ultrasonic cleaning tank for metals. Storage and dispensing of solvents also requires a range of containers for the solvent and suitable metal storage cupboards. Cupboards fitted with air extraction are available. To prevent unnecessary evaporation of solvent into the air, dispensing devices of the type illustrated in *Figure 9.8* are available which allow small quantities of solvent to be dispensed directly onto a cotton wool applicator as required. Heated spatulas for laying loose veneer and for consolidation of surfaces have a calibrated and thermostatically controlled power unit, adjustable up to about 150 °C, into which the heated spatula iron is plugged. Irons may have fixed or removable heads. In the removable head type a variety of different sized and shaped heads is available to suit different applications (*Figure 9.9*).

Hot-air guns range from low temperature hair dryers through domestic and professional high temperature guns designed for paint stripping and low temperature soldering of metals. The Leister Labor unit, illustrated in *Figure 9.10*, has independent air flow and heating

**Figure 9.8** A solvent dispenser that allows small quantities of solvent to be dispensed as required

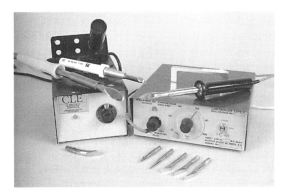

**Figure 9.9** Examples of heated spatulas that may be used for laying loose veneer or consolidation of decorated surfaces

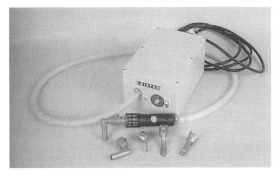

**Figure 9.10** The Leister Labor hot air gun is well suited to furniture conservation, with separate air flow and heating controls and attachments that allow it to be used as a heated spatula

controls and can achieve a wide range of temperatures. A variety of attachments can be placed over the hot air outlet to adapt the unit to small scale work and to allow it to be used as a heated spatula.

Surface finishing and retouching equipment includes the airbrush, paintbrushes of various types and sizes, mixing pallets and containers for pigments, resins, waxes and so forth. Spray finishing equipment requires a source of compressed air which may come from a compressor, foot pump, aerosol can, or cylinder of compressed air. The recommended type of compressor is capable of reaching a pressure of 40 psi and is fitted with a pressure gauge, regulator, reserve tank, air filter and water trap. Other factors to consider include the size and weight of the machine and noise levels in use. Compressed air may also be used for powering air tools, which are favoured in some workshops for economic and safety reasons. Since the risk of electrical arcing is eliminated, air stirrers are useful for stirring the solvent gels used in Wolbers cleaning methods. An air abrasive unit may occasionally be found useful. Tools and equipment for gilding are illustrated in Chapter 14.

Other miscellaneous items of general equipment include seating, weighing and measuring equipment, hot plate, glue pot (or baby's bottle warmer) and modelling tools. Equipment used for examination and photographic recording has been discussed previously in this chapter.

The extent to which work will be carried out from a sitting position depends very much on the type of work and on personal preference. Some practical conservation work such as cutting fine parts or detailed finishing or cleaning work may be better done seated. Chairs should be carefully selected for the purpose in mind. Chairs for work, as opposed to relaxation, should generally have well-padded backs and seats, have back height and tilt adjustment to provide support for the sitter's back, be height-adjustable while in use and should also provide support for the sitter's feet. The ability to revolve easily through 360 degrees while seated may be an advantage.

In many operations in furniture conservation better results are obtained if materials are accurately weighed and measured. Scales for weighing out reagents are needed to cover the range from a few hundredths of a gram of

enzyme for cleaning to perhaps several kilograms of whiting to make composition. This range will not be covered by one piece of apparatus. Equipment to suit a range of loads, accuracy and price is available from scientific supply houses.

For measuring volume, a range of glassware including beakers, measuring cylinders and pipettes is needed. Stirring rods and glass bottles are useful for making up and storing solutions at the required strength. For many purposes glass can be substituted by the less expensive disposable polythene equivalent, particularly for resins which otherwise require difficult cleaning to be done. Pasteur pipettes are invaluable for such tasks as drop-wise application of consolidant, decanting small quantities of stains and making working dilutions of strong materials for cleaning. A range of different sizes of disposable syringes from 1 ml up to about 50 ml with needles of various diameters and lengths (and a proper 'sharps' bin for disposal) is invaluable.

## 9.7   Health and safety

Most accidents happen through four interlinked causes: *ignorance* of the hazards through lack of communication; *horseplay* – ignorance of risks arising from the joke; *complacency* – 'It won't happen to me' arising from ignorance of the risks; *poor planning* – as a consequence of which hazards go unnoticed. By being aware of hazards around one, taking steps to eliminate or avoid them and warning others, around 70% of all accidents could be prevented.

Conservators should aim to create in the workplace robust systems for the management of health and safety that comply with the law and allow for and encourage continuous improvements in health, safety and welfare at work for all. Health and safety management is very much a matter of common sense put into a formal context, but although the aims may be the same anywhere in the world, the specific legislation to be complied with may vary from one place to another. This brief guide is based on the requirements of the relevant United Kingdom and European Community legislation. It covers health and safety requirements and the process of managing health and safety with some specific details of that process used by way of illustration. Further discussion of specific aspects of health and safety practice has been included at the relevant point in the text.

### 9.7.1 Health and safety requirements

#### *Principal legal requirements*

United Kingdom law on health and safety at work has developed in a fragmented way over the last two hundred years. Modern health and safety legislation began with the Factories Act 1937, the predecessor of the current Factories Act 1961. Similar legislation came into operation at about this time, dealing with mines and quarries, offices, shops and railway premises and agriculture. The Report of the Committee on Safety and Health at Work, published in July 1972, proposed substantial changes in the law and administration of occupational health and safety and was instrumental in the passing of the Health and Safety at Work Act 1974. Since 1993, European Directives have had a significant effect on UK health and safety legislation. Conservators with management responsibility should be aware of the following legislation:

- The Health and Safety at Work Act 1974
- The Management of Health and Safety at Work Regulations 1992
- The Control of Substances Hazardous to Health 1988 and 1994
- The Chemicals Hazard Information and Packaging (CHIP) Regulations 1993
- The EEC 'Six Pack' of regulations effective from 1 January 1993
- Management responsibilities
- Workplace conditions
- Provision and use of work equipment
- Personal protective equipment
- Manual handling
- Display screen equipment
- The Factories Act 1961
- The Offices Shops and Railway Premises Act 1963
- The Fire Precautions Act 1971.

#### *What you should know about health and safety law*

Your health, safety and welfare at work are protected by law. In general terms, we all owe a common duty of care to each other.

Employers have a duty to ensure that their staff, visitors to their premises or the public are not put at risk through their activities and employees have a responsibility to take reasonable care of themselves and others who may be affected by what they do, or fail to do. Specifically, in the UK, the following applies:

- The employer has a duty under the law to ensure so far as is reasonably practicable the employees health, safety and welfare at work. In general, the employers duties include:
  - making the workplace safe and without risks to health
  - keeping dust, fume and noise under control
  - ensuring plant and machinery are safe and that safe systems of work are set and followed
  - ensuring articles and substances are moved, stored and used safely
  - providing adequate welfare facilities
  - providing the information, instruction, training and supervision necessary for health and safety.
- The employer must make a suitable and sufficient assessment of:
  - the risks to the health and safety of their employees to which they are exposed whilst they are at work
  - the risks to the health and safety of persons not in their employment arising out of or in connection with the conduct of their undertaking.
- The employer must also:
  - draw up a health and safety policy statement, including the health and safety organization and arrangements in force and bring it to the attention of employees
  - provide free, any protective clothing or equipment specifically required by health and safety law
  - report certain injuries, diseases and dangerous occurrences to the enforcing authority (the Health and Safety Executive or the Local Authority Environmental Health Department)
  - provide adequate first aid facilities
  - consult a safety representative, if one is appointed by a recognized trade union, about matters affecting health and safety

- set up a safety committee if asked in writing by two or more safety representatives.
- The employer has duties to take precautions against fire, provide adequate means of escape and means for fighting fire.
- Other specific duties of the employer arise out of the legislation listed above.

Employees, also have duties under the law. They include:

- Taking reasonable care for their own health and safety and that of others who may be affected by what they do or do not do
- Co-operating with managers on health and safety
- Not interfering with or misusing anything provided for health, safety and welfare.

### 9.7.2   The process of managing health and safety

The emphasis of good health and safety management is on a forward-looking, proactive approach. The systems needed for good health and safety management are the same as those needed to perform well in every other aspect of our work: first it is necessary to know what the current situation is; second we need to set targets; third we need to monitor and review to see that we are meeting targets. If we are not we must respond in away that enables us to do so. If the review process shows that we are improving then we will set new, more challenging targets and in this way we will obtain continuous improvement. We also need to respond to events as they arise, to take notice of incidents that may occur and to put into practice the lessons that can be learned from them. Documentation is vitally important in this process. Under European Economic Community Directives there is a common ethos for the management of Health and Safety – a common process for meeting the requirements of all health and safety legislation which consists of the activities listed below:

- Assess the hazards/risks to staff and others
- Identify measures to control those hazards
- Involve staff and union representatives in the assessment and control process
- Inform staff of the hazards and risks

- Inform staff of the control measures introduced and how to make them work
- Train staff to do their tasks safely
- Record any actions taken
- Monitor the effectiveness of the control measures
- Review and re-assess as necessary.

The practical steps to be taken to achieve each of these steps are detailed below. Further information is given by Stranks (1999).

### 9.7.3   Documentation for health and safety management

Documentation is an essential component of good health and safety management. You must record what you do and what you find. This provides the accountability and audit that is an essential part of Health and Safety management. The first step is therefore to set up the necessary documentation. How you do this is up to you but what needs to be accomplished is described below. The main documents required to support health risk control are:

- Health and safety information from suppliers and independent sources
- Risk assessments file
- Manual of policy and procedures
- Log book to record plans and all actions taken.
- Personal safety file – substances used, accidents/incidents, training received.

These components provide the inputs to and outputs from the various processes required to manage health and safety. Sources of general information for health and safety are listed below. Further specific information on particular products can be obtained from manufacturers and suppliers. To be of use the various bits of information need to be collated in an indexed file or database for ease of access. This information provides much of the basis for making an assessment of risk and deciding on the control measures that need to be adopted. For chemical hazards, typical information that might be needed would include: substance/chemical name; supplier name; catalogue number; physical form (liquid/solid etc.); Maximum Exposure Limit (MEL); Occupational Exposure Standard (OES); Category of Danger;

routes of entry to the body; risk phrases; safety phrases; first aid information; storage requirements; spillage information. Some of these are further explained below.

*Risk assessments* should be kept in clearly labelled folders in a convenient place where everyone can easily consult them. It may be helpful to separate assessments for different classes of risk, for example chemical separate from manual handling and other physical risks.

Any organization employing more than a few people would be well advised to develop a simple *manual* explaining company health and safety policy and giving instructions on how to carry out the required procedures. A copy should be available in each work area.

The purpose of a *log book* is to keep a complete record of health and safety plans and transactions for the business. It is useful in monitoring and improving health and safety performance and can be produced if required to demonstrate compliance with health and safety legislation. Typically, the log would include the following components: an action plan; record of accidents and incidents; a record of independent health and safety audits; communications log (containing memos, minutes of meetings and a record of reports); health surveillance records; a list of improvements made; a record of regular inspections carried out in the workplace; maintenance record of machinery and equipment, including that required for provision of a safe working environment; training record; work place monitoring records.

The *personal health and safety folder* could be one folder subdivided into: record of exposure to risks having potential long-term consequences (e.g. substances used); personal training record; accident record; incident record; health record. This information can be used for epidemiological studies, analysis of specific adverse reactions, usage levels (purchasing) and for monitoring to provide feedback on the effectiveness of controls.

### 9.7.4 Risk assessment

Risk assessment is a vital element in health and safety provision to make sure that no one gets hurt or becomes ill. However it need not be overcomplicated. Assessment of risk is nothing more than a careful examination of what, in your work, could cause harm to people, so that you can decide whether you have taken enough precautions or should do more to prevent harm.

*Hazard* and *risk* are two important terms used in making risk assessments. A hazard is a source of possible harm. A risk is the likelihood of that harm being realized. The important things to decide are first whether a hazard is significant and secondly whether it is covered by satisfactory precautions so that the risk is small. For example, electricity can kill but the risk of it doing so in the office is very small provided that live components are insulated and metal casings are properly earthed.

To make an assessment of risk that is 'suitable and sufficient' and complies with legal requirements, Stranks (1994) advises that you must:

- Identify all hazards associated with the business and evaluate the risks arising from them taking into account current legal requirements
- Identify any employee, or group(s) of employees who are especially at risk (e.g. asthmatics, pregnant women)
- Identify others who may be specially at risk (e.g. visitors, contractors, members of the public)
- Evaluate existing controls, stating whether or not they are satisfactory and, if not, what action should be taken
- Record the significant findings (electronic methods may be used)
- Evaluate the need for information, instruction, training and supervision
- Judge and record the likelihood of an accident occurring as a result of uncontrolled risk, including the worst case likely outcome
- Record any circumstances arising from the assessment where serious and imminent danger could arise
- Provide an action plan giving information on implementation of additional controls, in order of priority and with realistic time scales.

However, this should not be overcomplicated. Assessments need to be suitable and sufficient not perfect. The real points are: first, are the precautions reasonable? and second, is there something to show that a proper check was made?

### Generic assessments

In many cases, where the same activity is undertaken repeatedly, it is possible to undertake a single generic assessment for that specific type of activity or workplace. For generic assessments to be effective, they need to consider 'worst case' situations. In some cases there may be risks which are specific to one situation only and these risks may need to be incorporated in a separate part of the generic risk assessment.

### Five steps to risk assessment

Several different approaches can be adopted in the workplace to the assessment of risk. For example, examination of each activity that could cause injury, examinations of hazards and risks in groups, or examination of specific work groups. Whichever approach is adopted, risk assessment is essentially a five-stage process. But before you start from scratch to do an assessment you should take one extra step – check to see if this risk has already been assessed, and if it has, whether that assessment still holds for your purposes. The United Kingdom Health and Safety Executive recommends five steps to risk assessment.

### Step 1: Look for the hazards

Potential hazards in the workplace include: fire; machinery, tools and equipment; chemicals; manual handling; display screen equipment; noise; ionizing radiation; extremes of temperature, pressure and relative humidity; stress; hazardous micro-organisms; poor lighting; dust (e.g. from sanding, grinding); fume (e.g. from welding); electricity, e.g. poor wiring; vehicles; pressure systems; ejection of material; work at height (e.g. from mezzanine floor or scaffolding); slipping/tripping hazards (e.g. poorly maintained floor or stairs).

*Chemical hazards* Many different chemicals are used in conservation, including pigments, hardwoods that produce toxic dust, consolidants and their solvents and fumigants or pesticides that may remain on the surface of treated objects. Such material may enter the body by ingestion through the mouth (including transfer from hand to mouth), by skin con-

tact including entry through the eye, or by inhalation. Because of the large surface area and rich blood supply of the lungs, toxic materials that are inhaled are quickly transferred to the bloodstream and rapidly circulated round the body. Information on routes of entry is available in Croners Substances Guide and in the publication EH40 which contains notes indicating whether a substance can enter the body through unbroken skin and whether or not it is a respiratory sensitizer and therefore liable to cause occupational asthma. Hazardous substances may affect the nervous system, respiratory system or cardiovascular system (Pascoe, 1980; Rodricks, 1994). Substances may have more than one kind of action and may lead to various kinds of interaction with other substances. For example, by removing natural oils from skin, solvents render the body more susceptible to damage by other agents. Many hazardous substances are fat-soluble. Because of this and because of the generally higher fat content of women's bodies than men's, women are more at risk from such materials. In addition the susceptibility of women to substances affecting fertility and reproduction needs to be carefully considered during the risk assessment process.

The *Category of Danger* describes the essential nature of the hazards presented by the substance. Chemical hazards in the UK are classified as explosive, oxidizing, extremely flammable, highly flammable, very toxic, toxic, corrosive, harmful, irritant and dangerous for the environment (*Figure 9.11a*). Other categories include sensitizing, carcinogenic, mutagenic and teratogenic. This information is available from a variety of sources including the Health and Safety Data Sheet for the material and Croners Substances Guide. It is the symbol in orange that must be used in the labelling of the material. It is possible for a substance to be described by risk phrases for which it is not required to carry an orange sticker. For example, a substance may be an irritant and highly flammable but may only be required to carry the highly flammable label. Substances must not be over-labelled and only the label appropriate to the classified category of danger should be used (*Figure 9.11b*).

Risk phrases are standard phrases set out in the Chemical Handling Information and Packaging (CHIP) Regulations. Risk phrases

| **Figure 9.12a CHIP labelling of chemical hazards (UK)** | | |
|---|---|---|
| Category of danger | Symbol letter | Indication of danger (label) |
| Explosive | E | 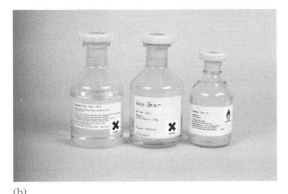 EXPLOSIVE |
| Oxidising | O | OXIDIZING |
| Extremely flammable | F+ | EXTREMELY FLAMMABLE |
| Highly flammable | F | HIGHLY FLAMMABLE |
| Very toxic | T+ | VERY TOXIC |
| Toxic | T | TOXIC |
| Corrosive | C | CORROSIVE |
| Harmful | Xn | HARMFUL |
| Irritant | Xi | IRRITANT |
| Dangerous for the environment | N | Dangerous for the environment |

(a)

(b)

**Figure 9.11** Examples of appropriately labelled solvents

describe the dangers of the chemicals in more detail, e.g. 'May cause cancer' or 'Toxic by inhalation'. Risk phrases can be found in Croners Substances Guide. Each risk phrase has a number, e.g. '27 Harmful by Inhalation', with higher numbers generally indicating higher risk. Risk phrase numbers are also given in some suppliers catalogues.

Safety phrases are standard phrases, also set out in the CHIP Regulations, that tell the user what to do or what not to do with the chemical, e.g. 'Keep away from children' or ' Do not empty into drains'. Safety phrases are also numbered and can be obtained from the same sources as risk phrases.

The Maximum Exposure Limit (MEL) is one of two types of Occupational Exposure Limit (OEL), the other being the Occupational Exposure Standard (OES). The MEL is the *maximum* concentration, measured in $mg/m^3$ or parts per million (ppm), of an airborne substance, averaged over a reference period (LTEL 8 hours, STEL 10 minutes) to which employees may be exposed through inhalation under any circumstances. CoSHH legislation requires employers and managers to keep exposure to MEL assigned substances to as low a level as reasonably practicable. It is an offence to exceed an MEL. If a substance has an MEL (substances with MELs are listed in EH40 Occupational Exposure Limits) then work *must* be contained to the lowest level possible of that substance. It is a criminal offence to go over the limit.

The OES is the concentration of an airborne substance at which, according to current knowledge, there is no evidence that there is a risk to health if exposed to that level of concentration day after day. Employers and managers are required to keep levels of exposure to such substances at, or below, the limit set. Substances with an OES are listed in EH40 Occupational Exposure Limits.

Both OES and MEL may be quoted as a long-term exposure limit or as short-term exposure limit. Long-term exposure limit (LTEL 8 hour time-weighted average) is the level of exposure averaged out over the typical working period of 8 hours. Short-term exposure limit (STEL, e.g. 10 minute reference period) is the level of exposure in any 10 minute reference period. Short term exposure limits are listed for those substances for which there is evidence of a risk of acute effects occurring as a result of brief exposure. It follows that the lower the MEL/OES, the more toxic the chemical.

In the United States, TLV (Threshold Limit Value) is the recommended maximum average concentration in air of the chemical that may be considered to be without risk in a normal person's working life. The lower the TLV the more toxic the chemical. TWA (Time Weighted Average) is exposure averaged out over an 8 hour, 5-day week. TLV/STEL (Short Term Exposure Limit) is the maximum concentration of that chemical in the air for a maximum exposure of 10 minutes – there should be at least 60 minutes between each exposure and no more than four exposures per day. It should be noted that American and British/European standards are not interchangeable.

Further information on conservation chemical hazards is given by Clydesdale (1990). For information on toxicity of wood dusts see Tinkler *et al.* (1986).

### Step 2: Decide who or what might be harmed and how

There is no need to list individuals by name – just think about (groups of) people doing similar work or who may be affected. Think about people who may not be in the workplace all the time. Anyone who could be harmed by your activities should be included. Examples include: people sharing your work space; office staff; security staff on patrol; contractors; maintenance personnel; cleaners; the building itself – e.g. by fire; objects – e.g. by fire or by poor manual handling. When deciding who or what might be harmed, pay particular attention to groups and individuals who may be more vulnerable, such as: staff with disabilities; visitors; inexperienced staff; lone workers; pregnant women. *What is good for people is often good for objects too!*

### Step 3: Evaluate the risks

Evaluating the risks arising from the hazards and deciding whether existing precautions are adequate or more should be done can result in one of three main conclusions. First, that risk is adequately controlled, secondly that risk is controlled but the controls could be improved; and thirdly that risk is not adequately controlled. Where risk is not adequately controlled, it is essential to inform the line

manager and *stop* the activity or process until improvements are made. Record the nature of improvements required and the date and responsibility for carrying them out on the form then transfer the information about further action necessary to control risk to the action plan in your Health and Safety Log. In the event that several risks are found to be inadequately controlled, priority should be given to those risks that affect large numbers of people and/or could result in serious harm. Information on the control of risk is given below.

Although we all live with risk management in our everyday lives, coming to a decision about whether risks in the workplace are adequately controlled is something that many people find difficult. When trying to decide whether controls are adequate it is helpful to consider the precautions you have already taken against the risks from the hazards listed in step 1. For example, have you provided adequate information, instruction or training and adequate systems or procedures of work? It is also helpful to ask whether the precautions meet the standard set by a legal requirement, whether they comply with a recognized industry standard, whether they represent good practice and whether they reduce risk as far as reasonably practicable. If the answer to these questions is 'yes' then the risks are adequately controlled, but you need to indicate (on your risk assessment form) the precautions you have in place. You may refer to procedures, manuals, company rules etc., giving this information.

Even after all precautions have been taken, usually some risk remains. What you have to decide *for each significant hazard* is whether this remaining risk is high, medium or low. First ask yourself whether you have done all the things that the law says you have got to do. For example, there are legal requirements on prevention of access to dangerous parts of machinery. Then ask yourself whether generally accepted industry standards are in place. But don't stop there – think for yourself, because the law also says that you must do what is reasonably practicable to keep your workplace safe. Your real aim is to make all risks small by adding to your precautions if necessary. If you find that something needs to be done, ask yourself can I get rid of the hazard altogether? If not, how can I control the risks so that harm is unlikely? Only use personal protective equipment when there is nothing else that you can reasonably do. When sharing a workplace, tell the other people using the space about risks your work could cause them and what precautions you are taking. Also think about the risks to yourself and/or your workforce from those who share your workplace. Useful guidelines on how to assess the risks and containment regime for chemical hazards are available from the Royal Society of Chemistry booklet *CoSHH in Laboratories* (2nd edn, 1996).

### Step 4: Record your findings

In the United Kingdom, an organization with five or more employees must record the significant findings of the risk assessments. This means writing down the more significant hazards and recording the most important conclusions. Irrespective of any legal obligation, these are sensible and useful steps to take. There is no need to show how the assessment was done provided that you can show that a proper check was made, that you asked who might be affected, that you dealt with all the obvious significant hazards taking into account the *number* of people who could be involved, that the precautions are reasonable and the remaining risk is low.

Keep the written document for future use and reference, it can help you if an inspector questions your precautions or if you become involved in any action for civil liability. It can also remind you to keep an eye on particular matters and it helps to show that you have done what the law requires. It can be used by staff to ensure that they know what the controls are that should be used with particular processes or materials.

How you record the list of hazards is up to you but various standard forms are available for this purpose from organizations such as Croners. To make things simpler, you can refer to other documents, such as manuals, company rules, manufacturers' instructions and your own health and safety procedures. These will probably already list much relevant information. You don't need to repeat all that and it is up to you whether you combine all the documents or keep them separately. Use team briefing sessions and staff meetings to regularly raise health and safety issues and assessments.

### Step 5: Review your assessment

All conservators should ensure that they are familiar with the contents of the risk assessments for their workplace. Before undertaking any process, you should check to see that the risks to health and safety have already been assessed and that the assessment still holds for your purposes.

The risk assessment must be maintained. Sooner or later, new machines, substances and procedures will be introduced that could lead to new hazards. If there is a significant change, to a workplace, process or activity, or the introduction of any new process, activity or operation, it must be added to the assessment to take account of the new hazard. In any case it is good practice to review the assessment from time to time. Do not amend the assessment for every trivial change or each new job but if a new job introduces significant new hazards of its own, you should consider them in their own right and do whatever you need to do to keep the risk down.

Reviewing and updating of the risk assessment is best achieved by a combination of safety inspections and monitoring techniques, which require corrective and/or additional action where the need is identified. The frequency of review depends on the level of risk in the operation and should not normally exceed ten years. Further, a review is necessary if an accident, or near miss, occurs in the organization or elsewhere, or a check on the risk assessment shows a gap in assessment procedures. The process for monitoring, review and corrective action is further discussed below.

### 9.7.5 Control risk

Once a hazard or risk has been identified and assessed employers must either prevent the risk arising or control it. Most hazards can be considered as having a *life cycle* from acquisition to disposal. In each case a range of control methods (*hierarchy of control*) appropriate for different kinds of risk is available. These will not be effective unless they are actually used, and in some cases, the level of competence of operators may need to be assessed before they do certain work. People must know what the controls are and how they should be applied before they can use them. Therefore written procedures are very important. Before any work activity, *think* first about risks to your colleagues, visitors, yourself and the objects. *Check* whether you need to take precautions to avoid hazards. *Inform* others of your actions for future reference.

### The hierarchy of control

The amount of time and management effort needed to ensure the effectiveness of control measures increases greatly for the controls lower down this list. The first item on the list, once implemented, requires no further effort whereas the last item requires a high degree of control. The preferred controls are those requiring the least amount of management control though in many cases a combination of control methods may be necessary. The recommended means of control should be recorded in the written assessment.

- *Eliminate* the risk completely, e.g. prohibit certain practices or the use of certain hazardous substances
- *Substitute* with something less hazardous or risky
- *Enclose* the risk so that access is denied
- *Fit guards or install safety devices* (e.g. extraction) to prevent access to danger points or zones on work equipment and machinery
- Adopt *safe systems of work* that reduce the risk to an acceptable level
- *Write procedures*
- Provide *adequate supervision*, particularly in the case of young or inexperienced persons
- *Train* staff to appreciate the risks and hazards
- *Inform* – provide adequate labelling for chemical substances, safety signs and warning notices
- Provide and use *personal protective equipment*, e.g. eye, hand, head and other forms of body protection.

Although personal protective equipment is a non-preferred means of protection it should be stressed that eye protection, gloves and overalls should *always* be worn when using materials classified as *irritant*. Other methods of keeping the hazard at a distance from the body include swab sticks and brushes.

### The life cycle of control

The most effective way to control risks to health and safety in our work as conservators

is to think before we act – in effect to carry out a risk assessment – *before* we conserve, *before* we move an object, *before* we order new materials or equipment. This process of thinking of the possible consequences of our actions before carrying them out will help us to choose the safest and best alternatives in what we do and avoid the worst possible things that can go wrong if we don't think things through first. It will also improve the quality of our planning generally with the extra benefits that brings. Every stage in the completion of an activity, or process, is amenable to this approach, for example:

- Before acquiring any new work space, substance or piece of equipment
- When new equipment or dangerous substances arrive
- At point of use before starting work
- Maintenance and repair of machinery, equipment and work spaces
- Disposal of chemicals, sharps, swabs, equipment
- Accidents or emergencies involving hazardous substances.

To help reinforce this approach, in larger organizations, written procedures can be provided for each of these activities. The following guidelines for lifting are an example.

*Guidelines for lifting*
- Keep your back straight, using your legs or arms as leverage – keeping a straight back prevents uneven stress on the discs and back muscles and reduces overall strain by 25%
- Distribute the weight evenly
- Support items on the bone structure of the body
- Hold items close to the body
- Use devices provided for assistance, making sure they have been thoroughly checked beforehand.

### 9.7.6   Maintain controls

Two kinds of maintenance are required for good health and safety. First, maintenance of health and safety controls of all types is necessary to ensure that they continue to be effective; controls are of no use if they are not maintained in good working order. Secondly, general maintenance of the workshop and of the materials and equipment it contains is required. All machinery, equipment and work spaces require maintenance (and probably occasional repair) to ensure that they operate correctly and in a safe manner. The specific safety controls in use in the workplace should be recorded in a maintenance log along with the maintenance requirements for other items like microscopes and machines. In your health and safety documentation you should show what is required, who is responsible, when action is due, when action was last taken and by whom.

### 9.7.7   Monitor exposure

Once risks have been assessed and properly maintained control measures introduced, it is important to ensure that the measures in place are actually effective in providing the required degree of control. This is especially true of substances hazardous to health. Typical monitoring systems include: preventive maintenance inspections; safety representative/committee inspections; statutory and maintenance scheme inspections, tests and examinations; safety tours and inspections by management; occupational health surveys by a safety adviser and occupational health service agencies; air monitoring by safety advisers and consultants; safety audits by safety advisers.

Useful information on checking performance against control standards can also be obtained reactively from accident and ill health investigations, from investigation of damage to plant, equipment and vehicles and from investigation of 'near-miss' situations (incidents).

Safety advisers can help to identify areas where monitoring is needed and to get it done. If monitoring shows levels of substances present in the environment likely to exceed the OES or MEL, *immediate* action must be taken to reduce airborne concentrations to acceptable levels. Otherwise, action that needs to be taken should be discussed with the relevant adviser and recorded in the action plan in the health and safety log.

### 9.7.8   Survey health

Individuals using certain substances require health surveillance. In the United Kingdom,

this will include certain specific substances listed in the General CoSHH Approved Code of Practice and substances for which an MEL has been assigned. In addition, everyone should look out for signs of ill health and adverse reactions in themselves, staff and colleagues. The employer should keep health surveillance records in the log. All other staff should keep a note in their personal health and safety file and should inform their manager if they feel unwell at work.

### 9.7.9   Inspect the workplace

Regular inspections are an important component of effective health and safety management.

Initially, inspection should be carried out as part of risk assessment to identify risks to health and safety at work. Those involved in this process should walk around looking at what could reasonably be expected to cause harm, at what people are doing, at what they work with and at what is already done to protect health. It is also helpful to talk to employees, to look at accident and sickness records. Advice can be obtained from suppliers of equipment, materials and chemicals in the form of guidance notes and data sheets. Remember, some health problems can be caused both at home and at work. Ignore the trivial and concentrate on significant hazards that could result in serious harm. The hazards identified must be recorded. Record the date of the inspection in the health and safety log. When compiling a list of hazards for the purpose of risk assessment, the hazards found can be listed at the beginning of the risk assessment folder as an index to the contents.

Having assessed risks to health and safety, introduced controls and made sure that the controls are working, everything should now be under control. To make sure that this is the case, those with management responsibility should undertake formal inspections of the work area. Dates should be set for this in advance in the action plan, preferably spaced at six month intervals. It may be useful to ask someone from another studio or organization to assist with this. Some suggestions for items to include on a checklist are given below. Any new hazards that are identified should be added to the list of risks to be assessed and a proper risk assessment made for them. Recurring hazards or short-falls in performance should be recorded along with the date of the inspection in the Health and Safety Log. Once you have decided what action to take, set a date for completion and transfer a record of your decision to your action plan. Every so often, it is very helpful to have independent checks made by others who can look at the situation with a fresh eye.

### Checklist for health and safety review

Items to include on a checklist for use during health and safety inspections can be grouped under headings of workplace, people, safety systems and environment. Workplace items include: cleaning and housekeeping; structural safety; machinery safety; fire protection; chemical safety; electrical safety; internal transport; access equipment; internal storage. Personnel issues include: personal protection; chemical handling; manual handling; information; training; safe behaviour. Safety systems should embrace: policy statement and plan; safe systems of work; accident reporting/costing; sickness absence reporting/costing; hazard reporting; cleaning schedules; emergency procedures; safety monitoring procedures and documentation. Environmental issues include: environmental control; noise control; welfare amenity provision.

### 9.7.10   Inform, instruct and train

Employers should provide their staff with *comprehensible and relevant* information on the risks to their health and safety identified by the assessment, the preventive and protective measures, the emergency procedures, the identity of people appointed to assist with health and safety matters and the risks associated with shared workplaces. In entrusting work to an employee, the line manager must take account of the individual's capability to do the job safely and must provide adequate health and safety training both on recruitment and on being exposed to new or increased risk because of change in responsibilities, introduction of new technology or equipment, or introduction of new or altered systems of work.

### Shared workplace and visiting workers

Where people from outside organizations are present to do work the manager must give them appropriate information on health risks and the precautions that are to be taken. In situations where the workplace is shared, every employer must co-operate with other employers, assist in the coordination of safety measures and inform other employers of risks arising out of the work. Temporary staff and those with fixed-term contracts must be supplied with health and safety information before starting work.

### Duties of employees

Every member of staff must use the machinery, equipment, dangerous substances, transport equipment, means of production and safety devices provided properly and in accordance with instructions and training. Staff must inform their line manager or any specially appointed person of any situation which represents a serious and immediate danger to health and safety and any matter which could be considered a shortcoming in the protection arrangements for health and safety. Managers should keep a record of information, instruction and training they have provided and their staff should keep a record of information, instruction and training they have received.

### Labelling and signage

Labelling and signage are vital aspects of providing health and safety information. All hazardous substances should be labelled with the name of the substance, the appropriate hazard warning symbol, the risk phrases, the safety phrases and information about the supplier.

### 9.7.11   Audit

Audit is the final step in closing the feedback loop that is the essence of improving performance in the management of risks to health and safety. At a predetermined fixed time interval (say once a year), an independent adviser should review the health and safety systems in the workplace and communicate the results to the employer or a senior person in the management line for appropriate action to be taken.

### 9.7.12   Accidents and emergencies

Procedures for first aid and medical emergencies, accidents and incidents, fire, chemical spills and other emergencies such as gas leaks, power failure, flooding and water damage, damage to building or display cases should be documented and thoroughly disseminated. Accidents and incidents that do occur must also be documented. Thinking about what may have caused an accident or incident and how could it have been prevented may help to reduce the risk of future occurrences. Write down your thoughts and decide what actions need to be taken now or in the future. Record what you have done and tell everyone else you work with.

### *Fire prevention*

For a fire to start there must be a supply of fuel, a supply of heat energy and oxygen. You can help to prevent fire from starting by checking the work area carefully before you leave:

- Turn off all heat sources that can be turned off
- Ensure that no heat source is left near combustible material
- Do not overload electrical wall sockets (one plug per socket)
- Unplug all electrical appliances
- Turn off lights
- Close all doors and windows.

### *Fire precautions*

It is important for everyone to know what to do if a fire breaks out. Each organization should develop its own procedures which will identify: how to prevent fire; the precautions to be taken in the event of fire; what to do in the event of fire; the alarm sequence and what to do on hearing the alarm; escape routes from the building; evacuation procedures; special responsibilities for particular individuals. In general, all staff should:

- Know the fire procedures
- Keep all fire doors closed
- Know the location of the nearest fire alarm call point
- Know the location of the nearest fire fighting equipment
- Know alternative escape routes.

On discovering a fire, staff should know how to:

- Raise the alarm – e.g. by breaking the glass of the nearest fire alarm call point and/or by shouting 'Fire' to summon assistance and warn others in the vicinity

- Attack the fire if possible to do so without danger but taking care to use the correct type of extinguisher. Dry powder extinguishers may be used on all types of fire. Water extinguishers are suitable for general use but must not be used on live electrical apparatus or solvent fires. Foam-based extinguishers must not be used on live electrical apparatus, solvent fires, paintings or textile objects. Carbon dioxide extinguishers are best used for flammable liquid and electrical fires
- Restrict the spread of fire and smoke by closing doors and windows
- Leave the vicinity of the fire or the building if necessary by the normal routes if usable or by the emergency fire exits which are marked.

### *Chemical spills*

Procedures for dealing with chemical spills are given for individual substances and chemicals in Croners Spillage Guide. The first step is normally to attempt to absorb the spill onto inert material. Spillage absorption granules should be kept wherever solvents are stored and decanted. For major spills the area should be evacuated immediately and management informed. In the presence of flammable spills, staff should know not to operate electrical equipment.

### 9.7.13 Further information on health and safety

In addition to references cited in the text, information is given in the following publications:

- *Essentials of Health and Safety at Work*, HSE Books, ISBN 0 7176 0716X
- *Management of Health and Safety at Work: Approved Codes of Practice*, HSE Books, L21, 1992, ISBN 0 7176 0412 8
- *General CoSHH ACOP (Control of Substances Hazardous to Health Regulations 1994)*, HSE Books, L5, ISBN 0 7176 0819 0
- *Workplace Health, Safety and Welfare: Approved Code of Practice*, HSE Books
- *Work Equipment: Guidance on Regulations*
- *Personal Protection Equipment at Work: Guidance on Regulations*, HSE Books, L25, 1992 ISBN 0 7176 0415 2

- *Manual Handling: Guidance on Regulations*
- *Display Screen Equipment Work: Guidance on Regulations*, HSE Books, L26, 1992, ISBN 0 7176 0410 1
- *Five Steps to Risk Assessment*, HSE Books

HSE Publications can be obtained from HSE Books, PO Box 1999, Sudbury, Suffolk, CO10 6FS (Tel: 01787 881165, Fax: 01787 313995).

## Bibliography

Aitchison, T.C. and Scott, E.M (1987) A review of the methodology of calibrating radiocarbon dates into historical ages, in Ward, R.G.M. (ed.), *Application of Tree-ring Studies in Current Research in Dendrochronology and Related Subjects*, BAR International Series 333, BAR, Oxford, pp. 187–201

Aitken, M.J.K. (1990) *Science-based Dating in Archaeology*, Longman Archaeology Series

Angst, W. (1980) Ethics in scientific furniture conservation, in *Proceedings of the Furniture and Wooden Objects Symposium*, Canadian Conservation Institute, pp. 123–35

Ashwood, B. (1996) *The Quality Standards Master Plan* (The Complete ISO 9000 Implementation Kit including ready drafted quality manual and procedures), 2nd edn, Wyvern Crest Publications

Baillie, M.G.L. (1984) Some thoughts on art-historical dendrochronology, *Journal of Archaeological Science*, 11, 371–93

Baumeister, M. (1988) Die Fluoreszenzmikroskopie als Untersuchungsmethode für historische Möbeloberflächen, *Maltechnic Restauro*, 94 (2), 100–4

Beck, J. and Daly, M. (1994) *Art Restoration – The Culture the Business and the Scandal*, Norton

Becker, E. (1985) *Fluorescence Microscopy*, Ernest Leitz Wetzlar

Bergen, J. (1952) *All About Upholstering*, Hawthorn/Dutton

Bernstein, J. (1991) Microscopy-based characterization of gilded decoration on furniture, in *Selected Student Papers of the Seventeenth Annual Conservation Training Programs Conference*, pp. 136–50

Bowman, S. (1990) *Radiocarbon Dating*, British Museum Publication, London

Brachert, T. (ed.) (1986) *Beiträge zur Konstruktion und Restaurierung alter Möbel*, Callwey

Brandner, W. (1976) Die Restaurierung einer Garnitur Augsburger Prunkmöbel, *Jahrbuch der Staatlichen Kunstsammlungen in Baden Württemberg*, 13, 55–64

Brook, M. (1998) *Estimating and Tendering for Construction*, Butterworth-Heinemann

Buchholz, R. (1991) Eingedrückte Streifen an Holzobjekten, *Restauro*, 97, 101–24

Burek, M. (1989) *Der Fiesole-Altar Im Domschatz Zu Hildesheim*, Institut für Museumskunde an der Staatlichen Akademie der Bildenden Kunste, Stuttgart, p. 108

Caple, C. (2000) *Conservation Skills: Judgement, Method and Decision Making*, Routledge

Catling, D. (1981) Guidance for the inexperienced microscopist, *The Conservator*, 5, 15–19

Cescinsky, H. (1967) *The Gentle Art of Faking Furniture*, Dover

Chamot, E.M. and Mason, C.W. (1958) *Handbook of Chemical Microscopy Vol. I: Principles and Use of Microscopes and Accessories; Physical Methods for the Study of Chemical Properties*, 3rd edn, John Wiley/Chapman and Hall

Chamot, E.M. and Mason, C.W. (1960) *Handbook of Chemical Microscopy Vol. 2: Chemical Methods and Inorganic Qualitative Analysis*, 2nd edn reprint of 1940 edition, John Wiley/Chapman and Hall

Chappell, V. (ed.) (1994) *Cambridge Companion to Locke*, Cambridge University Press

Chase, W.T. (1972) Science in art, in *The McGraw-Hill Yearbook of Science and Technology*, McGraw-Hill, pp. 10–23

CIE (Commission International de l'Eclairage) (1974) *Methods of Measuring and Specifying Colour Rendering Properties of Light Sources*, Publication No. 13.2 (TC-3.2)

Clydesdale, A. (1990) *Chemicals in Conservation: A Guide to Hazards and Safe Use*, 2nd edn, Scottish Society for Conservation and Restoration, Edinburgh

Coles, J. and Jones, R.A. (1975) Timber and radiocarbon dates, *Antiquity*, 49, 123–5

Conservation Unit (1993) *Conservation – Restoration: The Options*, Brochure published jointly by The Conservation Unit, Museums and Galleries Commission and Historic Scotland, Scottish Conservation Bureau

Cook, E.T. and Wedderburn, A. (1903–10) *The Complete Works of John Ruskin* (39 Vols), Vol. 8, George Allen, London

Corfield, M. (1988) Towards a conservation profession, in V. Todd (ed.), *Conservation Today*, Conference Preprints, UKIC

Cornforth, J. (1981) Ham House reinterpreted, *Country Life*, Jan/Feb

Cornforth, J. (1988) An uncertain climb, *Country Life*, March

Crawford, B.H. (1959) Measurement of color rendering tolerances, *Journal of the Optical Society of America*, 49, 1147–56

Crawford, B.H. (1960) Colour rendering and museum lighting, *Studies in Conservation*, 5, 41–51

Crawley, W. (1971) *Is It Genuine? A Guide to the Identification of Eighteenth Century English Furniture*, Eyre and Spottiswoode

Creswell, R.G. (1991) The radiocarbon dating of iron artefacts using accelerator mass spectrometry, *Historical Metallurgy*, 25, 78–85

Deasy, C.M. (1985) *Designing Places for People*, Whitney

De Bono, E. (1996) *Teach Yourself to Think*, Penguin

Derrick, M., Stulik, D., Landry, J.M. and Bouffard, S. (1992) Furniture finish layer identification by infrared linear mapping microspectrometry, *JAIC*, 31, 225–36

Derrick, M., Souza, L., Kieslich, T., Florsheim, H. and Stulik, D. (1994) Embedding paint cross-section samples in polyester resins: problems and solutions, *JAIC*, 33 (3), 227–45

Dorge, V. (1987) The furniture and wooden objects laboratory: the Canadian Conservation Institute – its practice and principles, in ICOM Committee for Conservation, Preprints 8th Triennial Meeting, Sydney

Dunbar, M. (1979) *Antique Woodworking Tools: a Guide to the Purchase, Restoration and Use of Old Tools for Today's Shop*, Stobart

Dunbar, M. (1989) *Restoring, Tuning and Using Classic Woodworking Tools*, Sterling/Cassell

Elwood, M. (1980) Historical and curatorial aspects of furniture conservation, in *Proceedings of the Furniture and Wooden Objects Symposium*, Canadian Conservation Institute, pp. 137–48

Farancz, A., Hutchins, J., Moon, T.P., Preusser, F.D. and Roberts, B.O. (1985) Cost parameters in the conservation of works of art in both museum and private sectors in the USA in 1984–85, AIC 13th Annual Meeting, Preprints

Feigl, F. and Anger, V. (1972) *Spot Tests in Inorganic Analysis*, 6th edn, Elsevier

Fifield, L.K. and Keeley, N. (1995) *Analytical Chemistry*, 4th edn. Chapman and Hall

Fletcher, J.M. (1977) Tree-ring chronologies for the 6th to 16th centuries for oaks of Southern and Eastern England, *Journal of Archaeological Science*, 4, 335–52

Fletcher, J.M. and Tapper, M.C. (1984) Medieval artefacts and structures dated by dendrochronology, *Medieval Archaeology*, 28, 112–32

Fletcher, J.M., Tapper, M.C. and Walker, F.S. (1974) Dendrochronology: a reference curve for slow grown oaks, AD 1230 to 1546, *Archaeometry*, 16 (1), 31–40

Florian, M.L., Norton, R. and Kronkright, D. (1990) *The Conservation of Artifacts Made from Plant Material*, The Getty Conservation Unit

Francis, K. (1990) Fiber and fabric remains on upholstery tacks and frames: identification, interpretation and preservation of textile evidence, in *Upholstery Conservation*, Preprints of a Symposium held at Colonial Williamsburg, East Kingston, pp. 63–5

French, A. (ed.) (1990) *The Conservation of Furnishing Textiles*, Conference Postprints, SSCR

Frid, T. (1980) Tool cabinets: removable trays are at the heart of them, *Fine Woodworking Techniques 2*, Taunton Press, pp. 26–7

Gilardoni, A., Gilardoni, M.T. and Taccani, S. (1994) *X-Rays in Art: Physics – Technique – Applications*, 2nd edn, Gilardoni, Mandello Lario

Gill, K. and Eastop, D. (2001) *Upholstery Conservation: Principles and Practice*, Butterworth-Heinemann

Gill, K., Soultanian, J. and Wilmering, A. (1990) The conservation of the Seehof furniture, *Metropolitan Museum Journal*, 25, 205

Goodman, W.L. (1964) *The History of Woodworking Tools*, London

Goodman, W.L. (1993) *British Plane Makers from 1700*, 3rd edition revised and enlarged by J. & M. Rees (eds)

Gordon, J.L. and Teas, J.P. (1976) Solubility parameters, in R.R. Myers and J.S. Long (eds), *Treatise on Coatings*, Edward Arnold

Ground, I. (1989) *Art or Bunk?*, Bristol Classical Press

Guyer, P. (ed.) (1992) *Cambridge Companion to Kant*, Cambridge University Press

Hall, E.T. (1987) The Courtrai Chest re-examined, *Antiquity*, 61, 104–7

Harvey, J. (1972) *Conservation of Buildings*, Appendix III, London

Hawkins, D. (1986) *The Techniques of Wood Surface Decoration: Intarsia to Boullework*, Batsford

Hayward, C.H. (1970) *Antique or Fake?* Evans

Hedley, G. (1980) Solubility parameters and varnish removal: a survey, *The Conservator*, 4, 13–24

Hillam, J. (1987) Problems of dating and interpreting results from archaeological timbers, in Ward, R.G.M.,

Application of Tree-ring Studies in Current Research in Dendrochronology and Related Subjects, BAR International Series 333, BAR, Oxford, pp. 141–55

Hoadley, R.B. (1980) Small workbench: a simple and versatile design, in *Fine Woodworking Techniques 2*, Taunton Press, p. 25

Hoadley, R.B. (1990) *Identifying Wood*, Taunton Press

Hughes, D. (1987) The containment and ventilation of hazardous fumes in laboratories, workshops and studios, in *Safety in Museums and Galleries* (ed. F. Howie), Butterworths

Hulbert, A. (1987) Notes on techniques of English medieval polychromy on church furnishings, in *Recent Advances in the Conservation and Analysis of Artifacts*, Summer Schools Press, pp. 277–9

ICOM (International Council of Museums) (1984) The conservator–restorer: a definition of the profession, in ICOM Committee for Conservation, Working Group for Training in Conservation and Restoration, Triennial Meeting Copenhagen

James, D. (1994) *Upholstery Techniques and Projects*, Guild of Master Craftsmen

James, D. (1999) *Upholstery: A Complete Course: Chairs, Sofas, Ottomans, Screens and Stools*, Sterling

Johnson, D. (1980) Dust collection system: damper-controlled setup keeps basement shop clean, *Fine Woodworking Techniques 2*, Taunton Press, pp. 22–4

Kaye, M. (1991) *Fake, Fraud, or Genuine? Identifying Authentic American Antique Furniture*, Bullfinch Press

Keene, S. (1996) *Managing Conservation in Museums*, Butterworth-Heinemann, published in association with the Science Museum, London

Kingshott, J. (1993) *The Workshop*, Guild of Master Craftsmen, Lewes

Kisluk-Grosheide, D. (1991) A group of early eighteenth-century 'Ausburg' mirrors, *Furniture History* (Journal of the Furniture History Society), 27, 1–18

Kitamura, K. (1988) Some thoughts about conserving urushi art objects in Japan, and an example of conservation work, in N. Brommelle and P. Smith (eds), *Urushi*, Getty Conservation Institute, pp. 113–20

Klein, P., Eckstein, D., Wazny, T. and Bauch, J. (1987) New findings for the dendrochronological dating of panel paintings of the 15th to 17th century, in ICOM Committee for Conservation, Preprints 8th Triennial Meeting, Sydney, pp. 51–4

Kukachka, B.F. and Miller, R.B. (1980) A chemical spot-test for aluminium and its value in wood identification, *IAWA Bulletin*, 1(3), 104–9

Lahikainen, E. (1990) Upholstery conservation: a review of the issues, in *Upholstery Conservation*, Preprints of a Symposium held at Colonial Williamsburg, East Kingston

Landi, S. (1985) *The Textile Conservator's Manual*, Butterworths

Landis, S. (1998) *The Workbench Book*, Taunton Press

Landis, S. (1999) *The Workshop Book*, Taunton Press

Landrey, G. (1990) The use of fluorescence microscopy in furniture conservation, in ICOM Committee for Conservation, Preprints 9th Triennial Meeting, Dresden, pp. 835–9

Langford, M. (1997) *Basic Photography*, Focal Press

Larsen, B.E. (1987) SEM-identification and documentation of tool marks and surface textures on the Gundestrup Cauldron, in *Recent Advances in the Conservation and Analysis of Artifacts*, Summer School Press, University of London, pp. 393–408

Laver, M. (1978) Spot-tests in conservation: metals and alloys, in ICOM Committee for Conservation, Preprints of 5th Triennial Meeting, Zagreb, pp. 78/23/8/1–11

Levitan, A. (1987) Conservation of furniture from Russia and Alaska, *CRM Bulletin*, 10 (2), 7–15, National Park Service, Washington

Love, G. (1983) *The Theory and Practice of Metalwork*, Addison-Wesley Longman Education

Mackie, J.L. (1977) *Ethics – Inventing Right and Wrong*, Penguin Books

Magliano, P. and Boesmi, B. (1988) Xeroradiography for paintings on canvas and wood, *Studies in Conservation*, 33, 41–7

Martius, K. (1992) Computertomographie und ihr Einsatz in der Dokumentation von Musikinstrumenten, *Arbeitsblätter für Restauratoren*, 25, 129–34

McCreight, T. (1991) *The Complete MetalSmith: An Illustrated Handbook*, Davis Publications

McCrone, W.C. (1987) *Polarized Light Microscopy*, sixth printing, McCrone Research Institute

McLaughlin, R.B. (1977) *Special Methods in Light Microscopy*, Microscope Publications

McMaster, M. (1996) *The Intelligence Advantage: Organising for Complexity*, Butterworth-Heinemann

Michaelsen, H. (1989) Ein frühes Möbelensemble aus der Werkstatt David Roentgens, *Restauro*, 95, 101–24

Michaelsen, H. (1992) Die Technik der Reliefintarsie, *Restauro*, 98, 293–303

Mill, J., Bentham, J. and Ryan, A. (1987) *Utilitarianism and Other Essays*, Penguin

Mills, J.S. and White, R. (1987) *The Organic Chemistry of Museum Objects*, Butterworths

Montgomery, F.M. (1984) *Textiles in America: A Dictionary Based on Original Documents, Published Prints and Paintings, Commercial Records, American Merchants' papers, Shopkeepers' Advertisements and Pattern Books with Original Swatches of Cloth*, Norton

Nylander, J.C. (1990) *Fabrics for Historic Buildings: a Guide to Selecting Reproduction Fabrics*, 4th edn, The Preservation Press: Washington

Oddy, A. (ed.) (1992) *The Art of the Conservator*, British Museum Press

Oddy, A. (ed.) (1994) *Restoration: Is It Acceptable?* British Museum Press

Pascoe, M. (1980) Toxic hazards from solvents in conservation, *The Conservator*, 4, 25–8

Paxton, A.S. (1999) *2000 National Repair and Remodelling Estimator*, 34th edn, Craftsman Book Group

Pearson, G.W. (1987) How to cope with calibration, *Antiquity*, 61, 98–103

Pease, M., Gettens, R.J., Keck, S.E and Coutais, H.G. (1968) *The Murray Pease Report: Standards of Practice and Professional Relationships for Conservators*, IIC-AG (also published in *Studies in Conservation*, 9 (4), 1964, pp. 116–21)

Peters, A. (1984) *Cabinetmaking, the Professional Approach*, Stobart

Pilgrim, D. (1983) The period room – an illusion of the past, in D.C. Peirce and H. Alswang (eds), *American Interiors: New England and The South*, St Martins Press

Plesters, J. (1956) Cross sections and chemical analysis of paint samples, *Studies in Conservation*, 3, 110–55

Ploem, J.S. and Tanke, H.J. (1987) *Introduction to Fluorescence Microscopy*, Oxford University Press/Royal Microscopical Society

Price, N.S., Talley, M.K. and Vaccaro, A.M. (eds) (1996) *Historical and Philosophical Issues in the Conservation of Cultural Heritage*, Getty Conservation Institute

Procurement Committee of the Chartered Institute of Building (1997) *Code of Estimating Practice*, Longman Higher Education

Proudfoot, C. and Walker, P. (1984) *Woodworking Tools, A Christies Collectors' Guide*, Phaidon/Christie's

Rees, J. and Rees, M. (1996) *Tools: A Collectors Guide*, Roy Arnold: Needham Market

Reimers, P., Riederer, J., Goebbels, J. and Kettschau, A. (1989) Dendrochronology by means of x-ray computed tomography (CT), *Archaeometry* (Proceedings of the 25th International Symposium), Elsevier, pp. 121–5

Rendall, C. (1990) The Archbishop's chair: York Minster, in Conservation of Furnishing Textiles Conference Postprints, Scottish Society for Conservation and Restoration, Edinburgh, pp. 14–20

Roberts, K.D. (1980) *Some 19th-Century English Woodworking Tools*, Ken Roberts Publishing Company, New Hampshire

Roberts, K.D. (1982) *Woodworking Planes in 19th Century America*, Ken Roberts Publishing Company, New Hampshire

Rochow, T.G. and Tucker, P.A. (1994) *An Introduction to Microscopy by Means of Light, Electrons, X-Rays and Acoustics*, Kluwer Academic/Plenum

Rodricks, J.V. (1994) *Calculated Risks: Understanding the Toxicity and Human Health Risks of Chemicals in Our Environment*, Cambridge University Press

Ruskin, J. (1849) *The Seven Lamps of Architecture*, Smith, Elder

Salaman, R.A. (1997) *Dictionary of Tools used in the Woodworking and Allied Trades, 1700–1900*, 2nd edn, Astragal Press

Sanderson, J. (1994) *Biological Microtechnique*, BIOS Scientific Publishers Ltd

Schniewind, A.P. (1987) What goes up must come down … but is it reversible?, in *AIC-WAG* 15th Annual Meeting, Preprints, pp. 107–17

Schweingruber, F.H. (1983) *Der jahrring: standort, methodik, zeit und klima in der dendrochronologie*, Paul Haupt

Sellens, A. (1975a) *The Stanley Plane*, The Early American Industries Association: South Burlington, VT

Sellens, A. (1975b) *Woodworking Planes*, published by the author, Augusta, KS

Sheppard, A. (1987) *Aesthetics – an Introduction to the Philosophy of Art*, Oxford University Press

Sibilia, J.P. (1996) *A Guide to Materials Characterization and Chemical Analysis*, VCH Publishers

Simpson, D. and Simpson, G.W. (1988) *An Introduction to Applications in Light Microscopy*, Royal Society of Chemistry, London

Singer, P. (1979) *Practical Ethics*, Cambridge University Press

Smith, N.A. (1975) *Old Furniture*, Bobbs–Merrill

Smith, R.K. (1981) *Patented Transitional and Metallic Planes in America*, 2 Vols, North Village Publishing, Massachusetts

Stenhouse, M.J. and Baxter, M.S. (1983) Carbon 14 dating reproducibility: evidence from routine dating of archaeological samples, in W.G. Mook and H.T. Waterbolk (eds), PACT 8, Proceedings of the First International Symposium held at Groningen 1981, Council of Europe, Strasbourg, pp. 147–61

Stevens, R.E. (1980) *Microscopical Identification of Organic Compounds*, 2nd edition, Microscope Publications

Stranks, J. (1994) *A Manager's Guide to Health and Safety at Work*, 3rd edn, Kogan Page

Stranks, J. (1999) *The Handbook of Health and Safety Practices*, Financial Times/Prentice Hall

Stratmann, R. (1975) Eine Garnitur Ausburger Prunkmöbel des frühen 18. Jahrhunderts, in *Jahrbuch der Staatlichen Kunstsammlungen in Baden Württemberg*, 12, 157–70

Svehla, G. (1979) *Vogel's Textbook of Macro and Semi-micro Qualitative Inorganic Analysis*, Longman

Thomerson, C. (1996) *The Complete Upholsterer*, Francis Lincoln

Thompson, P. (1967) *The Work of William Morris*, Heinemann

Thornton, J.T. (1991) Minding the gap: filling losses in gilded and decorated surfaces, in *Gilding and Surface Decoration*, Conference preprints, UKIC, pp. 12–17

Tinkler, J.J.B., Greenberg, M. and Illing, H.P.A. (1986) Carcinogenic hazards of wood dust, in *Toxicity Review 15*, HMSO, London

Untracht, O. (1969) *Metal Techniques for Craftsmen*, N.A.G. Press

Van Der Reyden, D. and Williams, D.C. (1992) A load to bear: papier-mâché furniture ... its conservation and care, *Antiques Show Magazine*, pp. 29–34

Van Duin, P. (1989) Two pairs of boulle caskets on stands by Thomas Parker, *Furniture History*, 25, 214–17

Van Horne, C.L. (1991a) Ethical considerations of the conservator in private practice, in AIC Wooden Artifacts Group, Conference Papers, Albuquerque

Van Horne, C. (1991b) The conservation of a suite of late eighteenth century seating furniture, in D. Bigelow, E. Cornu, G.J. Landrey and C. Van Horne (eds), *Gilded Wood, Conservation and History*, Sound View Press, pp. 309–18

Walter, F. (1980) *The Microtome: A Guide to Specimen Preparation and Section Cutting*, Leitz GMBH/Tecnisch-Paedagogischer Verlah Scharfes Druckerein K.G.

Ward, P. (1989) *The Nature of Conservation – A Race Against Time*, Getty Conservation Institute

Watts, S. (1982) Period furniture hardware, *Fine Woodworking*, 34, 86–91

Weaver, W. (1982) A seat for St Peter, *Connoisseur*, September, pp. 112–13

Williams, M. (ed.) (1990) *Upholstery Conservation*, Preprints of a Symposium held at Colonial Williamsburg, East Kingston, pp. 63–5

Willisch, S. (1989) Anwendung und Ergebnisse der Xero-radiographie bei der Untersuchung von Kunstwerken und historischen objekten, (Technique and application of xeroradiography for investigations into art and historic objects), *Zeitschrift für Kunsttechnologie*, 3 (1), 197–213

Wolbers, R. and Landrey, G. (1987) The use of reactive fluorescent dyes for the characterization of binding media in cross sectional examinations, in *AIC Preprints*, AIC, Washington, DC

Yagihashi, S. (1988) The preservation and handing down of traditional urushi art techniques in Japan, in N. Brommelle and P. Smith (eds), *Urushi*, Getty Conservation Institute, pp. 79–86

Young, P., Darrah, J., Pilc, J. and Yorke, J. (1991) A Sienese cassone at the Victoria and Albert Museum, *The Conservator*, 15, 45–52

# 10

# Principles of conserving and repairing wooden furniture

This chapter examines the principles and techniques that relate to the repair of wooden furniture. Although the emphasis is on wood, many of these principles and techniques may be applied to other materials found in furniture, such as ivory and turtleshell. The first part of this chapter is divided into three sections: general principles, general techniques and consideration of specific types of damage and their possible remedies. The second part considers the conservation of surfaces embellished with veneer, marquetry or boulle. Finally casting and moulding techniques for non-structural repairs are considered with particular emphasis on the conservation aspects of these processes.

The conservation techniques discussed below rely on familiarity with techniques for working wood, including the use and maintenance of tools, preparation of timber, jointing of wood, carving and turning. It is beyond the scope of this chapter to discuss basic woodworking techniques in detail. Excellent texts that elucidate the techniques involved in cabinetmaking and fine joinery include Hayward (1974), Joyce (1987) and Walton (1979). Texts written about furniture restoration that incorporate useful information on repairs to wooden furniture include Alcouffe (1977), Bennett (1990), Buchanan (1985), Hayward (1967) and Rodd (1976). Learoyd (1981), Rogers (1959) and others discuss and illustrate historical methods of jointing furniture. Related disciplines such as structural repair of panel paintings (Dardes and Roth, 1998) may offer additional insights.

There may be an overlap between the techniques used in the original manufacture of an object and those used for its repair. If it is necessary to replace an entire component it should be clearly labelled or marked as such – some conservators have signed and dated the reverse side of new panelling or chair rails, or dated a new component in an inconspicuous place. The replacement of entire components should be approached as a last resort, since an important part of the role of the conservator is to preserve as much original material as possible. This not only contributes to an understanding of the history and development of furniture but, as fewer objects survive in an unmolested state, may actually result in enhanced monetary value, particularly for those objects treated in the commercial environment.

The ethical principles that may guide a conservator undertaking structural repairs are discussed in Chapter 9. These principles have been accepted by the conservation profession and include minimum intervention, retention of as much original material as possible, adding as little new material as possible, avoiding irreversible alterations to the original, the use of materials of known properties and the use of materials and techniques that allow future reversibility/retreatability.

For any problem there are a range of solutions, some of which may be undesirable, but being aware of the possibilities may help in the analysis of a problem. It is essential to avoid a dogmatic approach. The treatment option that is chosen may be influenced by issues of stability, aesthetics, historical and physical integrity and evidence, or the time, skill and resources available for the treatment. Each of these issues carries with it inherent costs and benefits for the object, the implications of which will affect the conservation treatment. In museums, for example, extensive treatment on one object may mean many other objects are left untreated. Preventive conservation measures, including environmental control, disaster preparedness and high standards of housekeeping, will result in more long-term benefit to objects than the most skilled intervention.

## 10.1 General principles

When attaching new material to a wooden object there is usually a general procedure that is followed regardless of the specifics of the damage. First, the cause of failure should be diagnosed as this will inform the conservator's choice of treatment. If wood is to be used as a repair material, a suitable piece is selected and then shaped. It may be necessary to create a suitable surface on the object to receive a repair to ensure the repair will fit snugly or provide a clean surface for gluing. Two options are building up the surface with a carvable epoxy (isolated from the original with animal/hide glue) to allow a flat surface to be chiselled, or planing a broken surface flat. Thus preparation of the object and the repair piece often go hand in hand. A suitable adhesive and/or joint is selected and the repair secured in place after a dry run of the procedure is carried out. When the adhesive has cured the repair is shaped to its final dimensions. Finishing and colour matching of varnished wood is discussed in Chapter 13.

### 10.1.1 Diagnosing the cause of failure

Understanding the cause of structural failure is an essential prerequisite to a conservation treatment. It is important to understand why a structural failure has occurred in order to tailor a treatment that will address the problem rather than causing more extensive damage in the future. Analysing the cause of failure may make it very clear that in some cases no permanent or completely satisfactory treatment is possible due to original construction techniques or materials, or the environmental conditions in which the object is kept (e.g. fluctuating RH).

Common causes of structural failure in wood include insect infestation, misuse, the physical and mechanical properties of the wood itself, such as weakness in areas of 'short grain' or warping due to internal stress. Factors related to environmental conditions include loose joints or splits that result from compression set. It is unavoidable that wherever the movement of a component is restrained by a fixing or joint, fluctuations in relative humidity will result in differential shrinkage, compression set and splits (Hoadley, 1978, 1980). Other problems, such as warping, may be caused by post-construction treatments such as the application of veneer or a surface coating to one side only of a component. The deterioration of wood and wooden structures is discussed in detail in Chapter 7.

Where the object is kept in an environment with fluctuating RH, the conservator must allow for some inevitable movement of the wood, either by the selection of materials or repair technique. If such allowances are not made, the problem will reoccur and the area of damage will be extended. If the cause of the damage is inherent in the original construction of the object, for example splits arising as a result of cleated boards, a weak repair will break before failure occurs in an adjacent weak area and will thus prevent extension of the area of damage if the problem recurs in the future. It may be possible for the conservator to make use of techniques specifically developed to compensate for uneven movement, such as buttons or shrinkage plates (see *Figure 10.16*), to reattach a table top to an underframe after treatment. It may also prove necessary to resist demands for the impossible by those who do not understand the inherent properties and limitations of wood.

### 10.1.2 Selection of repair method and repair material

Once the nature and cause of failure is understood a repair method and suitable materials must be chosen. These two factors are interrelated and the conservator must often balance contradictory treatment priorities. Intended use after treatment will also define the repair method and material – for example a chair with a broken leg may require a different treatment if it is intended for museum display as opposed to regular domestic use. The aim is to select a repair material with appropriate properties and apply it in such a way as to achieve treatment objectives. It may be necessary for the conservator to make a prototype or mock up to establish the likely success of a repair.

Material dissimilar to the original may be used where a material cannot be identified or resources are not available for identification. In other cases the material is no longer available or there are aesthetic objections to the repair that would result from the use of original materials. The conservator may apply selection criteria (e.g. known strength, chemical stability or resistance to a particular agent of deterioration) and choose from materials that meet such requirements. They may also simply choose from easily available alternatives that have been tested for use in a given situation. The following discussion examines the criteria used to select a piece of replacement wood, but other materials may also be used where appropriate.

### 10.1.3   Selection of wood for a repair

There are both advantages and disadvantages to the use of wood as a material for structural repairs to wooden objects. Advantages include strength, appearance, compatible dimensional movement (if repairs are well executed) and working properties. Disadvantages may include the risk of damage or distortion of the original object, risk to other objects or materials in direct or indirect contact, or failure in a similar manner to that which occurred in the original object.

Appropriate selection of wood is a prerequisite for the successful matching of a repair. In selecting wood for a repair the conservator should consider whether it is possible or desirable to use timber from the same species. In some cases this may allow a repair to be quickly and effectively matched to the original, but in others, oxidation of the original and the resistance of the replacement to treatments used for colour matching may necessitate the use of a paler wood with a similar surface appearance. In either case the wood used in the repair should match the original as closely as possible in density, grain direction, pore size and the angle of the pores relative to the surface. Other visual features, such as texture and the size and distribution of rays, are also important. Careful choice will minimize retouching, reduce stress on both the repair

and object and help ensure the durability of the replacement component. Of particular importance is matching the tangential, radial or transverse orientation of the piece used for repair to that of the original – no amount of colour matching will successfully blend a radially cut repair into a tangentially cut original. Matching orientation is also important for matching the relative movement in service. Radially cut surfaces exhibit approximately double the movement in service of tangentially cut surfaces in response to changes in relative humidity.

The moisture content of the wood used for repair should be as close as possible to that of the original object. If it is not, differential movement may result in either splits opening up between the repair and original or, if the repair expands, crushing of wood fibres and the potential for compression set to exacerbate the damage. The moisture content of both the original object and the repair will move to equilibrium with the environment of the work space. If timber is not generally stored in the work space it should be moved there for sufficient time to allow equilibrium to be established before a repair is incorporated into the original piece. The time taken for equilibrium to be established increases with the thickness

**Table 10.1**   Relative acidities of wood

| Wood | pH values | Risk of damage from evolution of organic acids |
|---|---|---|
| Oak | 3.35–3.9 | High |
| Sweet chestnut | 3.4–3.65 | High |
| Steamed European beech | 3.85–4.2 | Fairly high |
| Birch | 4.85–5.35 | Fairly high |
| Douglas fir | 3.45–4.2 | Fairly high |
| Teak | 4.65–5.45 | Fairly high |
| Western red cedar | 3.45 | Fairly high |
| Parana pine | 5.2–8.8 | Moderate |
| Spruce | 4.4–4.45 | Moderate |
| Elm | 6.45–7.15 | Moderate |
| African mahogany | 5.1–6.65 | Moderate |
| Walnut | 4.4–5.2 | Moderate |
| Iroko | 5.4–7.25 | Moderate |
| Ramin | 5.25–5.35 | Moderate |
| Obeche | 4.75–6.75 | Moderate |

The pH values were derived using a standard quantity of five parts distilled water in contact with one part of wood raspings or sawdust.
*Source*: Department of Industry, *Corrosion of Metals by Wood*, HMSO, 1985

of the stock and a rule of thumb for seasoning converted timber is one year for each inch (25 mm) in thickness. End grain should be sealed with wax or a similar material to prevent splits.

Another criteria in the selection of wood for repairs may be the degree of off-gassing of volatile organic acids such as acetic acid. Many materials associated with wooden furniture, e.g. paper and metals, will be damaged by acidic conditions. As a general rule, unseasoned, kiln dried wood, and those woods with a pH lower than 5, should be avoided if adjacent material is susceptible to damage (*Table 10.1*).

### 10.1.4  Transferring shapes, profiles and measurements

As with cabinetmaking, it is essential that measurements are accurate. In addition, the conservator should be faithful to the tolerances of the original object. Screw lockable dividers can be used to transfer profile of carved or curved components quickly and easily and reduce the risk of inaccurate measurements (*Figure 10.1*). This will provide a working template for replacement of an irretrievably broken component.

### 10.1.5  Making the repair piece

Consideration must be given to the size, shape and orientation of the repair before shaping begins. In some cases the first step may be to make the surface that will be jointed before commencing general shaping – for example, when scarfing new wood to the broken leg of a tripod table. In other cases, such as preparing false tenons, the process is one of planing the wood to set dimensions. As is the case when joints are first manufactured, accurate measurements and good cabinetmaking skills are required. Repairs should closely mate with the original to provide a strong joint for the final repair. It may be necessary to incorporate excess material for shaping and cramping, which is cut away after the repair is fixed into place.

### 10.1.6  Fitting the repair to the object

A structural repair to an object should be securely attached and provide the best possi-

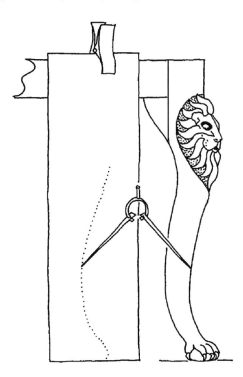

**Figure 10.1**  Transferring shapes, profiles and measurements. A piece of card is cramped so that it is parallel to the joint edge of the component. Dividers are used to transfer the profile of the component to the card. Once the first outline is completed, measurements of the thickness of the component can be taken with spring screw callipers and transferred to the card. A template made in this way is usually sufficient for both faces of a component such as a cabriole leg, but if in doubt both faces can be checked against the template

ble aesthetic and mechanical integration of new material with the old. This requires that the surface profile of new and old should match closely and gluing surfaces should be clean and sound. This is more readily achieved when the gluing surfaces are straight and flat although there may be situations where shaped surfaces are necessary.

The first stage of fitting a repair is to prepare the surfaces that are to be jointed or adhered. This may involve removing some original material to provide a level surface for the joint or matching the repair to an uneven surface. Rather than taking a dogmatic stance to either approach it is more realistic to consider each case within the constraints imposed by commonly accepted ethical guidelines. Whilst these generally assume a presumption against the removal of original material, factors such as the need for an uncontaminated gluing surface, the desire to preserve the maximum amount of original material, the strength of the adhesive bond and the time necessary to complete the repair may influence the decision whether to remove original material or not. The conservator may consider how much information, value or utility is lost by trimming the original. Most adhesives are sensitive to surface contaminants, and though they may initially adhere well, the service life of the adhesive bond may be greatly reduced if the bonded surfaces are contaminated by dirt or grease. Straight cuts across the grain may be difficult to disguise, and in many veneer or marquetry designs may be unacceptably obtrusive.

Consideration should be given to the size and shape of any missing areas, the tolerances to which the original has been worked, the stresses that are likely to be placed on the repaired area and the type of bonding that will be used. There are three possible approaches for fitting a repair and ensuring the surfaces are mated to each other to provide the best possible adhesive bond. The first, and traditional, method, was to prepare a repair piece, place it on the object, trace around it, and then cut away original material on the object to provide a clean surface. Whilst this may be necessary in some cases the removal of original material should be avoided wherever possible. The second method was to cut away material on the repair piece so that it matched the contours of the original. Carbon paper (carbon side to the repair piece) may be used between the two surfaces to mark high spots. Progressive removal of high spots will produce a well-mated joint. This process may be time-consuming. The third method uses a carvable epoxy resin as an alternative to chiselling original material away. A layer of thin animal glue is applied as an isolation layer. Once this is dry, carvable epoxy may be used as a gap filler, or to build up the original to allow a flat, true surface to be created without removing original material.

When the surfaces that are to be jointed and adhered have been cut, the next step is to carry out preliminary shaping for simple repairs, or to add decorative elements if necessary. In the case of wooden repairs there may be both a preliminary stage of shaping before repair is attached and a post-attachment phase. The balance between these will be defined by the repair itself, but the principle of reducing the risk of damage to the original should be paramount. It may be more convenient to do as much shaping as possible before attaching the repair, leaving a slight excess in case of movement during gluing up, and carrying out the final levelling to match the original surface afterwards.

It is essential when levelling a repair to direct cutting tools from old material to the new to avoid the risk of damaging the original. It may be necessary to protect the exposed parts of an object's original surface. A temporary, reversible coating with different solubility parameters to an original varnish/coating, or a physical barrier such as pressure-sensitive tape may be used. Applying tissue to a protective coating will serve as a visual alarm when adjacent work is putting the original surface at risk. It may be necessary to make a jig or support to prevent damage to original surfaces next to the repair.

The question of the extent of replacement of decorative elements remains somewhat unresolved. In general, conservators rely on establishing reliable evidence such as overall design intention, documentation, the symmetry of the object and the extrapolation of extant information. Thus mounts have been copied and mouldings replaced. Investigation of the original technique may help provide information for the reconstruction of lost elements. When there is no clear historical or material evidence, however, there is a risk that additions or replacements may be at best misleading or at worst entirely spurious. Some conservators have argued that it is better to leave an object untreated rather than introduce alterations that were never part of the original design (McGiffin, 1992; Rotter, 1979). The decision whether to reproduce tooling marks must be taken on a case by case basis and may be informed by the need to identify repairs or restorations in the future. All alterations and replacements should be clearly documented.

### 10.1.7   Adhesion and surface preparation

Careful preparation of the surfaces that are to be joined is critical for the creation of a durable

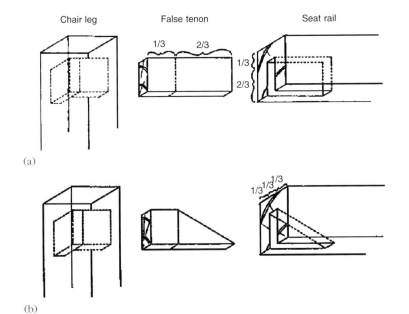

Chair leg     False tenon     Seat rail

(a)

(b)

**Figure 10.2** False tenons may be rectangular (*a*) or triangular (*b*). The principles that apply to making mortise and tenon joints also apply to their repair. Thus the width of the false tenon is usually one-third of the width of the rail and two-thirds of the height of the rail. The length of the false tenon is usually three times the depth of the mortise (one-third jointed into the stile, two-thirds jointed into the rail). False tenons may be visible or concealed. Inserting tenons into the lower part of a chair rail, as illustrated, combines mechanical and adhesive strength, and allows future identification of repairs

adhesive bond. The process of using an adhesive to joint two adherends together involves surface preparation, a dry run, assembly and cramping, followed by the removal of excess adhesive. Each step of the process should be planned so that potential problems can be identified. Apart from the adhesive properties of the joint itself, joint function, stress and loading, and environmental conditions will play a role in the durability of a repair.

The ability of the adhesive to wet onto and into the surface is critical in establishing a strong adhesive bond. Surface contaminants such as dirt, dust or oil, which repel most adhesives, will prevent good wetting of the surface and result in a weak adhesive bond. Surface dirt may be removed with a slightly damp cloth whilst white spirit, IMS or acetone may be used for degreasing the surfaces to be bonded. A rag should be used to wipe over the surface once solvent has been applied because applying solvent to the surface without removing the grease brought into solution may allow it to be carried into a porous surface such as wood. Many wood adhesives will not adhere to oily or greasy surfaces and some woods with a high oil content, such as teak, may require degreasing before application of an adhesive.

The strength of an adhesive joint is dependent on both the cohesive strength of the adhesive and the adhesive bond established between the surface(s) and the adhesive. Wood is composed of microscopic vessels and fibres, which can be conceptualized as long hollow straws aligned parallel to each other to create the grain of the wood. Adhesive bonds formed between the sides of the straws (side-grain to side-grain) are strongest. End-grain to end-grain joints are very weak because capillary action and the hydrophilic nature of the cell walls draw most of the adhesive away from the surface and down the fibres. In addition, the hollow fibres substantially reduce the surface area available for adsorption. Strong end-grain to end-grain adhesion is virtually impossible. A weak adhesive joint will occur whenever the wood is cut at an angle and the end-grain exposed. If there is no alternative to end-grain repairs for structural components, the joint must incorporate some form of side-grain to side-grain bonding, for example by introducing a dowel or false tenon (*Figure 10.2*). As a general rule the strength of an adhesive bond is proportional to the contact area – the larger the surface area of the side-grain to side-grain joint, the stronger the joint.

The overall moisture content of the wood will determine the glue line moisture content and will affect the depth of adhesive penetration and curing time of aqueous adhesives. If the moisture content of the wood is less than

5%, the wood will rapidly absorb most of the water from the adhesive. This may result in glue line starvation and subsequent joint failure.

As a result of the anatomy of wood and its fibrous nature, wood surfaces are inevitably rough. This may be compounded by the type of tooling used in timber preparation. A surface that has been prepared by a sharp plane or chisel is characterized by cleanly severed fibres and minimal dust contamination, whereas sawn or sanded surfaces result in torn or crushed fibres and dusty surfaces. Since a strong adhesive joint requires the least damaged surface, a planed surface is preferable to a sanded one. If sanding is unavoidable, then a finely sanded surface is preferable to a coarsely sanded surface. Deliberate roughening the surface, for example by toothing or scoring the wood, damages the fibres and creates voids that the adhesive must then fill. Adhesives traditionally used for veneering, such as hydrogen bonded animal/hide glue, have poor gap-filling properties, so this treatment may result in a weaker adhesive interface than would have resulted if the surfaces had been planed smooth. Adhesive penetration in hardwoods may be limited to one or two fibres deep, and the resulting adhesive joint may be compromised if these fibres have been damaged in the process of preparing the wood.

The gap-filling properties of an adhesive are determined by its cohesive strength, which in turn is dependent on the strength and type of intermolecular bonding. Adhesives that form a covalently crosslinked three-dimensional network within their bulk, such as epoxides and formaldehyde based glues, have sufficient cohesive strength to act as gap fillers. All the solids present are involved in bond formation, which results in minimal shrinkage on curing. The adhesive layer may be brittle as a result of crosslinking holding the molecules rigidly in place (Skeist, 1962). Gap-filling glues are unsuitable for many applications in cabinetmaking. In chair joints, for example, brittleness caused by the fixed crosslinked bonds means the adhesive cannot flex when the furniture is in use, the glue is liable to fracture and the adhesive fails. Adhesives that do not crosslink, such as animal/hide glue, are held together by secondary bonding only and are poor gap

fillers as a result. In order to form a strong adhesive bond the glue line for such adhesives must be as thin as possible – typically a maximum of 0.1 mm for joints in cabinetmaking (Tout, 1992). Thus the adhesive used in structural joints in furniture will be most durable when the joint is close-fitting and the adhesive has a degree of flexibility in use.

### 10.1.8   Selecting an adhesive

The material properties of adhesives are discussed in Chapter 4. The factors involved in selecting a suitable adhesive may include the following: the degree of surface preparation required, viscosity, bond strength, the loads and stresses that will be placed on the joint, durability in service in relation to relative humidity and temperature, retreatability or reversibility, open time, closed time, toxicity or other health hazards, characteristics of cured material, colour, chemical stability, water resistance, gap-filling ability, formulation, the nature of the substrate and the cost of the adhesive product. Adhesives that cure partially or wholly by loss of a volatile solvent, such as PVACs and animal/hide glue, are prone to shrinkage during curing although thin glue lines will minimize the resultant stress in the cured glue line. The effect of adding fillers to collagen glue has been examined by Von Endt and Baker (1991).

Animal/hide glue has proven to be very effective and continues to be used by the majority of furniture conservators for structural repairs. It should be freshly made and can be kept for several weeks provided that it is refrigerated. The protein chains slowly break down each time the glue is heated, especially when it is overheated, which reduces the strength of the glue. Whilst large restoration workshops may keep a continuous supply of hot animal/hide glue to hand, if use is intermittent it is better to make small fresh batches as required.

Although animal/hide glue is a poor gap filler, freshly prepared glue will provide an adhesive bond comparable in strength to an epoxy. It is usually sold in the form of pearls, which should be covered with water and pre-soaked overnight then warmed the following day at 55–60 °C. Water is added as necessary to produce the right working consistency,

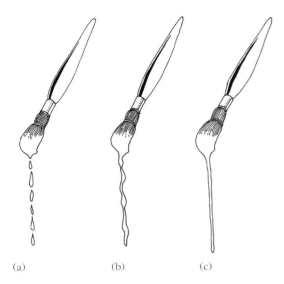

(a)                    (b)                    (c)

**Figure 10.3** Testing the consistency of hot animal glue
The brush is dipped into the hot glue and then held
8–10 inches (20–25 cm) above the pot. If the glue
breaks into droplets it is too thin and more glue must
be added (*a*). If the glue is thick and lumpy it is too
thick and more water must be added (*b*). Glue flow
from the brush should be even and continuous (*c*)

which can be judged by the flow of liquid from
a brush (*Figure 10.3*).

Glues based on PVAC may be more convenient than hot animal/hide glue but may be less
easily reversed. Some common proprietary
'white' wood glues, such as Resin W (UK), are
not soluble in organic solvents and may only
be slightly swollen by water. If a PVAC adhesive is to be used, current literature should be
consulted to select a suitable conservation
grade adhesive (see the discussion of materials
for consolidation of decorative surfaces in
section 12.2.4).

When the use of a cold setting glue is
desired, for example when assembling complex structures or joints, liquid animal/hide or
fish glues should be considered as an alternative over PVAC glues. These glues are based
on traditional protein glues and commonly
incorporate a liquifier or gel depressant (e.g.
urea) and preservatives. Liquid animal/hide
glues can provide a bond as strong as traditional protein glues (Buck, 1990). Podmaniczky
(1998) has reported that cold set animal/hide
glues may fail in conditions of elevated
temperature or humidity. Although they

provide a longer working time, some contain
additives such as urea, which may cause
unwanted side effects such as discoloration of
the wood. The long-term effects on bonding
strength and possible side-effects from any of
the additives such as urea, odour depressants
or fungicides are not yet known. Lee Valley
Tools' High Tack Fish Glue has very good
adhesive properties and is used by many
conservators.

In some cases the use of an epoxy resin may
be required for a break in a structural component. Epoxies have good wetting properties
and, as gap filling adhesives with a rigid three-
dimensional network structure, they do not
require strong cramping pressure. Viscous
formulations are more tolerant of slight greasy
contamination of the surface whereas low
viscosity formulations have better immediate
wetting properties. Although they do not
contain water, some moisture is evolved as a
result of condensation polymerization. Epoxies,
which are rigid and non-reversible, are not suitable for interlocking joints. Epoxy glues may be
appropriate for gluing small wooden elements
where it may be difficult to apply sufficient
pressure in order to get a strong bond or where
the water content of a traditional protein glue
would cause deformation. Epoxies are often
used in conjunction with a thin isolating layer
of animal/hide glue, particularly in cases where
gap filling is necessary, or to build up an area
of damage to allow a repair to be fitted without removing original material.

Urea formaldehyde is available as a one-part
adhesive, marketed under trade names such as
Cascamite, for joinery and general purpose
woodwork. It has a rigid three-dimensional
structure and is strong and durable, though
brittle. It is non-reversible and therefore inappropriate for conservation use.

Some conservators have argued that the
strength and longevity of a structural repair
should be paramount and have questioned
whether the criteria of reversibility is appropriate in all cases. Others have included a pre-
treatment of a reversible adhesive such as
animal/hide glue before the application of a
crosslinking thermoset. Reversibility is the
property of a system and not of a material.
Reversibility often exploits solubility difference
in the properties of component materials but if
the thermoset is insoluble and access cannot

be gained to the isolating layer, then the system as a whole may not be reversible.

Manufacturers' instructions regarding mixing or application should be followed. If the adhesive requires pre-mixing, care should be taken to avoid contamination with dirt or dust. Weighing the ingredients is usually the easiest way to ensure that the right proportions are used. Adhesives that may be appropriate for non-structural repairs, such as acrylics, conservation grade PVACs and methyl cellulose, are discussed in Chapter 12.

### 10.1.9   Assembly

It is essential to plan the assembly operation and to ensure it can be completed within the available working time of the adhesive. A warm draught-free working environment will facilitate the use of animal/hide glue. If the process is complex it may be necessary to pre-assemble subframes or several people may be required to assist in gluing up. Assembly must be completed within the open time of the adhesive and cramping must be completed within the closed time. Fish glues or cold set hide glues are often used for complex jobs.

The surfaces that are to be bonded should be clean and free from dust. The adhesive should be compatible with the ambient temperature and intended use. Pre-treatment with glue size may be necessary if the surface to be bonded is porous.

A dry run is essential for any gluing up process. This will clarify factors such as the order of cramping, numbers and types of cramps, and the likely assembly time. Cramps will then also be set to the right dimensions and softening blocks, jigs and templates pre-prepared. If the pressure from cramps is not perpendicular to the joint, the application of adhesive may reduce friction between the parts and may result in slippage and misalignment.

Although it is sometimes possible to reglue individual joints, as a general rule the best results are achieved by gluing up sub-units, such as the front two legs and seat rail of a chair or the back frame. It may help to assemble the whole chair but glue only sub-units, using the whole structure as a jig to preserve the original relationship between parts. If this is not possible it may be necessary to make use of pre-prepared templates, diagrams or measurements to reproduce the original geometry of the object, since many old pieces are not perfectly symmetrical.

Adhesive should be applied to a surface immediately before assembly as most have a limited working time. Glue should be applied in such a manner that the adhesive is deposited where it is required, in a thin and even glue line. Adjacent surfaces that may be damaged by contact should be protected. The surfaces are then brought into contact and held in the correct alignment until the adhesive has set. Excess adhesive should be removed before it has set. In some cases it may be necessary to cramp up, uncramp and remove excess adhesive before the final application of cramps.

When animal/hide glue is used, the surfaces to be bonded may be slightly warmed to delay the gelling time of the glue. The surrounding wood can be protected from the heat by covering it with a heat isolating material. When smaller broken parts need to be glued, a small hole may be cut in the isolating material for the heat to pass through. The glue should be applied in a thin layer to both surfaces, which are then pressed together. It may be necessary to apply moderate pressure with cramps, in which case the surface should be protected from bruising with a soft material, such as a thin sheet of cork. Excess glue should be removed with a slightly damp cloth and care taken that ferrous metal components of cramps are not in contact with the dampened surface.

### 10.1.10   Cramping/clamping

The purpose of cramping is to apply pressure to the right parts of an assembly to bring parts being adhered into close contact with the correct alignment. Further, cramping should hold the components under the required pressure, without causing damage or distortion, until the final cured properties of the adhesive are achieved.

In some instances, the adhesive itself can serve as a clamp, as is the case with a traditional rubbed joint using hot animal/hide glue. Pieces with small surface area and uncomplicated fit, such as glue blocks, are simply rubbed to squeeze out excess adhesive until gelling of the glue inhibits further movement.

Hammer veneering with animal/hide glue is another example, but in this case the veneer should be flexible enough to be fitted closely to the carcase as the glue cools and gels. Cyanoacrylates, which cure very rapidly, may also function as self clamping adhesives.

Distribution of clamping pressure is an important consideration in achieving optimum results. If a wide flat component is to be clamped, the clamps must be spaced closely enough together that the adherends cannot bow away from each other between pressure points. A rigid material shaped to the adherend surface, known as a caul, can be employed to distribute clamping pressure evenly on curved surfaces or components (*Figure 10.4*). Cauls can be as simple as a flat board or as complex as the inversely shaped and metal-covered heatable cauls used traditionally to veneer mouldings and complex surfaces. Some conservators make cauls for laying/flattening veneer from 18 mm (¾ in) chipboard lined with lead, zinc or brass sheet. Brass sheet (e.g. 16 SWG) may be screwed and countersunk into the board and can be warmed on a hot plate before use. It may be helpful to line a shaped caul with bandsawn veneers of varying thickness in order to facilitate adjustment of the final shape of the caul. Such linings may also be made from balsa or fibreboard depending on the desired compressibility. All these linings may be attached with a contact adhesive and faced with foam or Melinex/Mylar. Hot sand bags may also be used to veneer complex surfaces, functioning as self-shaping cauls. Small pieces of acrylic or polycarbonate sheet make excellent cauls for regluing small parts and veneers because the squeeze out of the glue can be observed through them, indicating the degree of conformity to the surfaces, and because they shear away cleanly from the surfaces after the glue is hard. They can also be pre-warmed by immersing them in hot water. Cauls have the additional important purpose of protecting show surfaces from damage by clamps. Cauls should be inspected before use to ensure they are free from old dried glue and the like, which would damage an original surface. Cauls that do not cover the entire surface may need to be softer than the surface of the object and have rounded edges to avoid denting the surface that is being veneered.

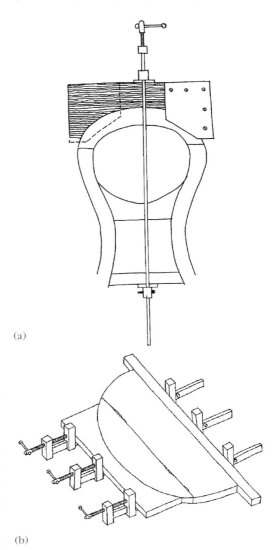

(a)

(b)

**Figure 10.4** Cramping curved surfaces
(*a*) Cramping a curved chair back. Scrap wood is shaped to fit the curved crest rail. Thin foam can be used as softening to prevent damage. Supports can be screwed to the shaped cramping block to prevent lateral movement when pressure is applied
(*b*) Cramping a semi-circular table top

The clamping pressure required will depend on the nature and porosity of the adherend, the viscosity and gap filling ability of the adhesive and the density of the wood. More pressure may be required for non-porous substrates, viscous adhesives and high density woods. Heavy cramping pressure is not necessary for a well made joint and the conservator should aim

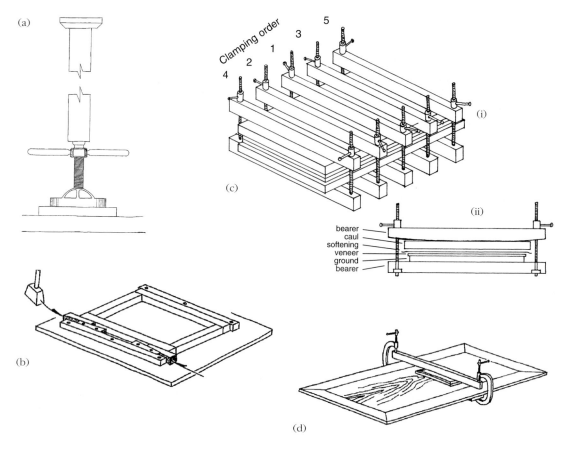

**Figure 10.5** Types of clamping/cramping system. (*a*) Screw jacks cab be braced against a wall or ceiling. (*b*) Folding wedges. Measurements across the diagonals of the frame should be taken to ensure it is square and true. (*c*) (i) Cramping/clamping system for veneering a board: the clamps should be tightened in the order indicated; (ii) cross-section of system illustrated in (i): the curve on the upper bearer has been exaggerated for illustrative purposes. (*d*) Cramping a small area in the centre of a wide board

to 'pinch' surfaces together rather than using brute force to compensate for poor workmanship. The goal is to apply the minimum pressure to the right area without damage to the surface or distortion of the object.

Inappropriate cramping can cause both minor and major damage to an object. Structural distortion may occur if the weight of the cramps pulls the objects out of true. Cramps that are large or heavy in relation to the object should be supported to prevent this. Over-tightening cramps may cause plastic compression of wood and, although reversible in some instances, in others the damage is permanent. Ferrous cramps may cause staining

if left in contact with tannic woods that have been dampened by the adhesive or removal of any excess. It may be possible to ameliorate this staining using an acidic solution (e.g. citric acid) but the damage cannot be completely reversed. A piece of scrap softwood or an isolating layer of Perspex will prevent such damage. An isolating layer of Melinex or silicone impregnated release paper may be used to prevent cramps or cauls from sticking to the surface. Loss of decoration or transparent coating may occur if excess adhesive is left on the surface. Kolbach (1998) has described the use of Peel Ply, a non-woven polyester release fabric that has been treated so that adhesives

**Figure 10.6**   Clamping/cramping set-ups
(*a*) Eighteenth century mahogany spiral fluted urn, attributed to John Cobb, catalogued in Gilbert (1978: 347). A tourniquet was used to apply pressure around the circumference of the urn. G-cramps (with softening blocks) were used to prevent the tourniquet slipping. (*b*) The flutes in the lid were aligned with the flutes on the urn. Thin plastic film protected vulnerable surfaces and allowed the use of adhesive tape to apply cramping pressure. (*c*) A damaged papier mâché globe. (*d*) Pressure applied evenly around the globe by tying together two pieces of rubber sheeting. (*e*) Jig to allow the application of cramping pressure to the curved stock of a gun

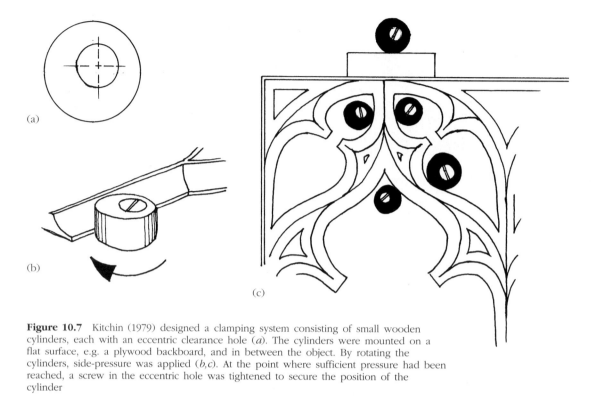

(a)

(b)

(c)

**Figure 10.7**   Kitchin (1979) designed a clamping system consisting of small wooden cylinders, each with an eccentric clearance hole (*a*). The cylinders were mounted on a flat surface, e.g. a plywood backboard, and in between the object. By rotating the cylinders, side-pressure was applied (*b,c*). At the point where sufficient pressure had been reached, a screw in the eccentric hole was tightened to secure the position of the cylinder

do not adhere to the material but wick through it. Peel Ply may be peeled from the surface after the adhesive has dried.

A wide variety of clamps are commercially available, and a great number of clamps and clamping set-ups can be made by the craftsperson or conservator to suit special requirements (*Figure 10.5*). Clamps and set-ups are limited only by the knowledge and imagination of the operator, and considerable ingenuity is often required (*Figure 10.6*). Books dealing with traditional furniture-making and repair, and modern tool catalogues, are good sources of information and ideas. In addition, a variety of cramps may be found in the surgical section of medical suppliers catalogues. Kolbach (1998) described the equipment and techniques used for localized application of vacuum pressure. Kitchin (1979) reported a useful clamping system for gluing delicate, irregularly carved flat ornaments of a German neo-gothic bookcase (*Figure 10.7*). *Table 10.2* lists cramping devices in approximate descending order of pressure exerted.

### 10.1.11   Levelling repairs

The process of levelling the repair should *never* result in the removal of finish or wood from the original surface next to the repair. Not only is such removal evidence of poor working practice but it will inevitably complicate colour matching by creating a fresh and distinct area of damage that will form a halo around the repair.

If the repair has been let into a flat surface, a sharp chisel may be inverted so that the blade functions as a plane. A small skewed carving chisel may also be used for this purpose. If the surface is irregular the corners of the chisel should be rounded off to prevent them from scratching the original surface. Careful abrasion may be possible using folded paper to provide a clearly defined corner or edge. Some sources recommend the use of angle cut dowels with abrasive paper glued to the end, though the preparation of such dowels is time-consuming.

Scrapers made from hand files may be useful in levelling repairs (*Figure 10.8*). The size of

**Table 10.2**   Cramping/clamping devices

| Type/principle | Examples |
| --- | --- |
| Screw action (spiral inclined plane) | C- or G-clamps, hand screws, Jorgensen clamps, bench vices, rods and screw-jacks from an overhead surface |
| Wedge action (inclined plane) | Wooden wedges, folding wedges used in opposition to each other, temporary or permanent staple-like iron 'pinch dogs' |
| Cam action (revolving wedge) | Eccentrically drilled spools fastened to a back-board, *Klemsia* cam clamps |
| Twist tensioning (shortening of a cord by twisting) | Tourniquets, toggle and rope, 'luthiers' clamp |
| Band clamps | Tensioned by screw, lever, ratchet etc. |
| Elastic (organic elastomeric polymers) | Rubber bands, surgical tubing, inner tube strips, rubber and cloth 'elastic' bands, old pantyhose etc. |
| Spring action (metal or wooden spring) | Spring clamps, *Ulmia* mitre clamps, old mattress or upholstery spring sections, clothespins, bulldog clips etc., springy sticks from an overhead surface or wall |
| Fasteners | Nails, screws, staples and rivets |
| Weight | Lead and iron weights, plastic bottles filled with lead shot, atmospheric weight (vacuum veneering) |
| Air pressure | Inflatable presses |
| Magnetism | Small magnets can be used on opposite surfaces of a board to exert gentle pressure |
| Adhesive | Rubbed joints, hammer veneering, cyanoacrylates and quick setting epoxies, pressure-sensitive tape |

the file may vary from 4 inches (100 mm) down to needle files, depending on the size of the repair. These tools give excellent control and allow good visibility of the levelling process.

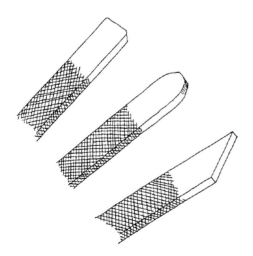

**Figure 10.8**   Files ground for levelling repairs
The surface of the file is ground smooth. The edge is then ground at 90° to the flat surface and shaped as required (e.g. flat, slightly rounded or skewed). Grinding the edge produces a burr

### 10.1.12   Preparation of repair for finishing

The repair is shaped using standard stock removal tools such as planes, spokeshaves and cabinetscrapers. Some shapes, such as barley twist legs, may have required the use of coarse rasps and files. A cabinetscraper may be used to execute final shaping and to prepare the wood for finishing. The wood should be tooled to the point that the shape is correct rather than relying on abrasion to complete the shaping process. As with levelling the repair, the process of surface preparation should *never* result in the removal of finish or wood from the original surface next to the repair. The pre-finishing process for a new part can be divided into two basic approaches: abrasion and burnishing.

A wide range of abrasive materials have been used to prepare wood in the past (*Figure 10.9*). Abrasive papers have been in use for nearly two centuries (Mussey, 1987). Commercially available abrasive papers can be used to smooth the wood. The degree of smoothness required will depend largely on the original surface. Abrasive papers will help to level out tooling marks and other irregularities in the wood. It may be necessary to use a cork or rubber block to support abrasive paper. A

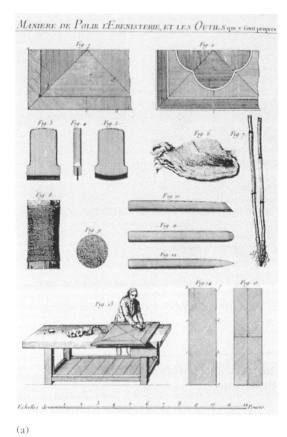

(a)

(b)

**Figure 10.9** Abrasives
(*a*) A plate from J.A. Roubo, *Le Menuisier ebeniste* (1772) illustrating eighteenth century abrasives, including scrapers, sharkskin, polishing sticks and Dutch rushes (obtained from members of the Equisitaceae, the horsetail family of jointed ferns, whose stems contain large amounts of silica). (*b*) Some traditional abrasives, including a bundle of Dutch rushes, emery, rottenstone, glass and pumice

variety of materials are used for the particles on abrasive papers and these vary in their hardness (see *Table 10.3*). Harder particle papers may be more appropriate for harder woods.

Abrasive papers vary in the nature of the material used to bond the particles (e.g. some are waterproof), how much abrasive is adhered to the paper, and the thickness or weight of the backing paper. Mesh sizes for abrasive particles refer to the number of openings per square inch in the wire screens used to grade them. Mesh sizes range from coarse (80) to fine (1000 or more). Those up to around 180 grit are used to level bare wood. After around 180 grit the scratches produced by the abrasive are smaller than already exist on the surface of the wood and thus they do not affect the overall appearance of roughness. Given that the lower the number the coarser the grit, an 80 grit paper will remove stock rapidly and is suitable for coarse work, whilst a final surface may be produced with 180 grit paper.

Abrasives work by a cutting or grinding action that scratches and removes a small amount of surface. Abrasives vary in hardness, particle size and the manner in which they are applied (powder, paste or adhered to a backing such as paper). Harder abrasive particles will remove more of the surface with each comparable motion, but particle size will determine whether the scratches produced will be visible. The abrasive effect of particles on a surface is ameliorated by the presence of a lubricant, such as solvent or wax. The conservator may need to take measures to control exposure to abrasive powders, the dust produced or solvents used as lubricants.

The Mohs Hardness Scale is a comparative scale using various minerals as standards:

| | |
|---|---|
| talc | 1 |
| gypsum | 2 |
| calcite | 3 |
| fluorite | 4 |
| apatite | 5 |
| orthoclase | 6 |
| quartz | 7 |
| topaz | 8 |
| corundum | 9 |
| diamond | 10 |

Materials of Mohs hardness 1–2 can be scratched by a finger nail, those of Mohs hard-

**Table 10.3**   Abrasives

| Group | Abrasive name and composition | Hardness Mobs | Knoop | Sizes available | Notes (names given in brackets are trade names) |
|---|---|---|---|---|---|
| Diamond | Synthetic diamond: Pure carbon | 10 | 5500–7000 | Coarse – v. fine | Hardest substance known. Used to cut, grind and polish all very hard materials including diamonds |
| | Natural diamond: Carbon + impurities | | | | Natural industrial grade or 'bort' is slightly softer than the synthetic variety because of impurities and inclusions |
| Carbides | Boron carbide: – $B_6C$ or $B_4C$ | | 2800 | Standard mesh | Synthetic. Second only to diamond in hardness. Used for similar applications |
| | Silicon carbide: – SiC | 9.3 | 2500 | Standard mesh | The most common abrasive available in granular form or bonded on paper (Wet or Dry) or in the form of oil stones and grinding wheels (Carborundum, Carbolon, Carbolite) |
| | Tungsten carbide: WC, $W_2C$, $W_3C$, $W_3C_4$ – the forms may be mixed | see notes | see notes | | Tungsten carbide crystals have Mohs hardness > 9.5, but when alloyed with cobalt and nickel and sintered at high temperature to produce pieces large enough for cutting tools (Widia Metal, Carboloy, Diamondite), the hardness is Knoop 1880 – softer than the aluminium oxides |
| Aluminium oxides | Alumina: $Al_2O_3$ (synthetic form) | | 2000 | Standard mesh | A very useful and common abrasive available in powder form and also bonded together to make India stones and Japanese water stones. Very fine particle sizes of two crystalline types for very fine polishing operations are also available: type A alpha alumina 0.3 (Mohs 9) and type B gamma alumina 0.1 (Mohs 8) (Aloxite, Lionite, Garnal) |
| | Corundum: – $Al_2O_3$+ various impurities | 8–9 | | | Natural varieties include sapphire and ruby. Grades containing iron oxide impurities that are softer than sapphire and ruby and are unsuitable for gems have been used as abrasives since antiquity. A fine synthetic corundum abrasive is available for gem and stone polishing (Linde A) |
| | Emery: (impure corundum) – 55–75% $Al_2O_3$ in an iron oxide matrix | 8 | | Standard meshes + fine flour grades F, FF and FFF | Once the most common abrasive material. Modern polishing emery is likely to be an artificial mixture of synthetic alumina and iron oxide. The most common use is emery paper |
| Garnets | Garnet: $3RO.R'_2O3.3SiO_2$ where R is Ca, Mg, Fe or Mn. R' is Al, Cr or Fe | 6–7.5 | | | A family of minerals with the general formula shown in column 2. Used extensively for abrasive paper coating. The twelve types are often mixed but the iron garnet, almandite, is the hardest and most useful for abrasives and is used on garnet paper |
| Metallic oxides | Cerium oxide: $CeO_2$ 'yellow rouge' but usually mixed with oxides of the Lanthanum series (elements 57–71) | | | Crystals 0.1–1 μm | Fine yellow powder useful for polishing glass and hard stones |
| | Chromium oxide: $CrO_2$ 'green rouge' | | | | Used for polishing stainless steel and hard plastics |

*continued*

**Table 10.3**   Abrasives – continued

| Group | Abrasive name and composition | Hardness Mohs   Knoop | Sizes available | Notes (names given in brackets are trade names) |
|-------|-------------------------------|------------------------|-----------------|-------------------------------------------------|
| | Iron oxide: 'Crocus' red ferric oxide and 'rouge' hydrated iron oxide | 5.5–6.5 | Particle size < 1 μm | Crocus has sharp-edged particles, used for faster cutting whilst rouge has rounded particles and is used for final polishing. The term 'rouge' is also applied to various other very fine metallic oxide polishing abrasives |
| | Tin oxide: $SnO_2$ stannic oxide | | | 'Mild polish' used as a final polish on a wide variety of materials, especially softer stones such as marble and alabaster. Mixtures with lead carbonate impurities used as 'putty powder' in glazing compounds |
| Silicon dioxide | $SiO_2$: Crystalline forms include quartz, sandstone, quartzite, flint | | | Crystalline forms of $SiO_2$ are harder than metallic oxides. The massive crystalline variety of quartz (Mohs 7) is sometimes crushed and graded for use as an abrasive. Natural whetstones and oilstones are usually composed of $SiO_2$ in the form of sandstone or quartzite (finely crystalline quartz). 'Novaculite', a finely crystalline version of quartzite used for oilstones, is known as Arkansas stone. Flint, a coloured $SiO_2$ variety, is crushed and graded for use on flint paper |
| | $SiO_2$: Vitreous (amorphous) forms include powdered glass and pumice | | | Vitreous forms of $SiO_2$ are softer than metallic oxides. Powdered glass is used as an abrasive on paper. Pumice, a volcanic glass frothed by gases at the time of formation, is porous and has numerous sharp edges. Washed and settled to remove larger particles, it is very useful as an intermediate finishing abrasive |
| | $SiO_2$: Opaline (amorphous) forms, with up to 10% water include various forms of diatomaceous earth | 1–1.5 | | Diatomaceous earth, or infusorial earth, is composed of exoskeletons of unicellular algae called diatoms of which there are several thousand species. Tripoli is a name sometimes given to impure diatomaceous earth and clay when used as an intermediate polishing abrasive. Kieselguhr is a pure white diatomaceous earth used for polishing (e.g. in admixture with petroleum distillates as Solvol Autosol) |
| Limestone and claystone | Claystone: very fine, argillaceous (clay like) silicates composed of silica, alumina, and iron oxides | | | As water lubricated honing and finishing stones it is known as Scotch, water of Ayr, and snake stone. As finely divided powder mixed with diatoms it forms the main or only constituent of Tripoli |
| | Rottenstone: weathered, silaceous, argillaceous limestone | | | Material in which the binding carbonates have been naturally washed away by water percolation. Used as final finishing abrasive on coated wood and on natural materials such as horn and turtleshell |
| Calcium carbonate | Cuttlefish bone: soft, porous, internal skeleton of a type of squid | 1–2 | | Used in small pieces as an intermediate polishing step |
| | Whiting: chemically precipitated or naturally occurring $CaCO_3$ | | | Used as final polishing abrasive for ivory, bone, and precious metals Charcoal sticks and powders have been |

**Table 10.3**  Abrasives – continued

| Group | Abrasive name and composition | Hardness<br>Mobs   Knoop | Sizes available | Notes (names given in brackets are trade names) |
|---|---|---|---|---|
| Charcoal and ash | | | | used as fine abrasives. Holzapffel stated that elder-wood charcoal was used by engravers to polish plates. Lamp black in brick form, called 'satin rouge', has been used to polish silverware. Fine ash of various types has been used as a final polish for gemstones. Rice chaff ash has been used as a final polish for Oriental lacquer |
| Organic abrasives | Horsetails: *Equisetum hyemale*, 'Dutch rush' or 'shave grass' is a hollow reed-like plant with nodes and a silaceous cuticle<br>Shark skin | | | Dried and tied up in bundles, horsetails have been used to polish scagliola, plasterwork and meerschaum. Small, flattened sections of the cuticle have been used by gilders to polish gesso and bole. The rough sandpaper-like skins have been used as an abrasive for wood, especially in Asia and Oceania, but also in Europe |

ness 3 or less by a copper coin. A harder material will scratch and wear away a softer one – the greater the difference between the two materials the more pronounced the effect will be. The properties of common abrasives can be found in *Table 10.3*. The Knoop Hardness Scale is a series of values arrived at by an indenting instrument. It is more accurate than the Mohs scale, but many abrasive particles are too small to be tested this way.

Abrasives work by scoring the surface – the larger and harder the particles the deeper are these score lines. On wood, it is essential to work abrasive papers along the grain so that the lines scored into the surface are parallel with the grain. Sanding marks across the grain will be visible on raw timber, through any transparent finish that is applied, and will take up a disproportionate amount of any stain that is applied directly to the wood. It is necessary to work through the grades of paper (i.e. 80, 100, 120, 150, 180) so that each removes the score lines left by the previous and replaces it with progressively shallower lines, parallel to the grain, which become imperceptible to the eye on a wooden surface at about 180 grit. Grit sizes of 240 and above are appropriate for denibbing or abrading transparent finishes. The score lines that may be present on original surfaces may be used to identify the abrasive material – the deep and parallel lines left by Dutch reeds, for example, are quite distinctive.

Hand sanding will be necessary for most conservation work but it is possible that there may be situations where machine sanding is appropriate. There are several types of power tool sanders available but the defining factor in both cabinetmaking and conservation is that the abrasive action is parallel to the grain. Belt sanders may produce a satisfactory finish but those with a circular motion, such as disc sanders and orbital sanders, will produce surface defects similar to those found when hand sanding across the grain.

All sanding involves generating fine particles of wood dust. Prolonged exposure to wood dust has been connected to nose and throat cancer as well as lung complaints. Measures should be taken to collect dust as it is generated and the use of personal protective equipment such as dust masks is essential. In some countries, for example in the UK, control of wood dust in the workplace is subject to government legislation. All dust must be removed from the surface of the wood before any finishing process commences.

The process of using abrasive papers compresses the grain. It may be necessary to raise the grain by wetting the surface and allowing it to dry before using 180 grit paper on the roughened surface. It may be necessary to repeat this process a second time if a bleach or water stain is to be applied directly to the timber.

Steel or wire wool is inappropriate for smoothing uncoated wood because it tends to leave metal particles behind. The combination of steel wool and moisture will cause staining on woods with any significant tannic acid content. Steel wool comes in a numerical grading from 4 (coarse) to 0000 (very fine) and is often coated with oil- or silicone-based lubricants by the manufacturer to retard rusting. Lubricant-free grades are generally used in furniture conservation. A range of nylon abrasive pads is available from 3M.

Burnishing the surface or exposed edges of a repair, which compresses the upper wood fibres, may assist blending it in with the surrounding original material. A wooden burnisher with a concave or convex shape may be useful. The inside curve of a gilder's dogtooth agate burnisher is particularly effective on arrises, where sanding will produce a crude and inaccurate approximation of historical wear. If the outer face of an agate burnisher is used, it will need professional repolishing before it can be used on gilded surfaces. Burnishing can result in a more reflective and faceted surface, a markedly different effect from a surface that has been abraded. The nature of the surface being matched will determine whether this is appropriate. Burnishing should be tested on a scrap piece of wood to see if it gives the desired effect and to ensure that it will not inhibit subsequent stain or finish. Although abrasion is often the most efficient and reliable way to prepare a new surface, burnishing may aid in rendering an appropriate surface texture and is particularly useful on arrises and irregular shapes. Burnishing creams, paste and powders should not be used on unfinished or open-grained timber because they will lodge in the grain, may be difficult to remove completely and may interfere with subsequent coatings.

## 10.2   General techniques

### 10.2.1   Dismantling furniture

Dismantling furniture may be quick and straightforward or very slow and complicated, depending on the looseness of the relevant joints, previous attempts to compensate for loose joints such as nails or screws, and the complexity of the joints used. Unless the joints in the object are already uniformly loose, it is possible that the process of dismantling may cause further damage. The decision whether to dismantle may take into consideration fitness for intended use, potential vs. actual damage both now and in the future, balancing minimum intervention against the need for a satisfactory repair or the need to separate components to achieve a satisfactory adhesive bond.

The first step is to assess which joints are loose, whether the object needs partial or total disassembly, or whether disassembly will be likely to cause excessive damage and an alternative must be found. Joints in chairs may be tested for soundness by grasping the base of chair legs attached by a single rail and flexing them slightly, towards each other and then apart. Loose joints are indicated by movement along the line of the joint. Each joint should be tested in the same manner. This technique can be applied to most objects with a frame construction (characterized by the use of mortise and tenon joints). Loose joints in box construction (characterized by the use of dovetail joints) will manifest itself in racking of a carcase or by flexing individual joints. A single slightly loose joint may be acceptable in a museum object but may present a hazard in domestic use.

If a decision is made to dismantle and there is any potential for confusion about the position of any component, each should be marked clearly before proceeding. Masking tape may be used on non-presentation surfaces to mark the parts of each joint with corresponding numbers. When working with circular components it may be necessary to use register marks or tape to ensure the pieces are returned to the correct position. It may also be necessary to record the original geometry of components using templates and diagrams. Whatever method is chosen the conservator should ensure marks can be removed after reassembly without damage to any surface finish that may be present.

Chairs can present problems when the shape of the seat has no 90° corner or the angle of each corner is slightly different. It is important to record these angles to ensure that the seat will return to its original shape when it is reassembled, especially if it incorporates a drop-in or slip-seat. A simple solution is to measure the diagonals across the seat area and ensure the same measurements are reintroduced when the chair is reassembled.

Furniture is generally dismantled in the opposite order in which it was constructed – upholstery may need to be removed from chairs or tops from tables before the major joints are accessible. Original screws that are removed during dismantling should be stored and labelled so that they can be returned to their original position (see *Figure 9.4*). Soft white foam may be used for this purpose, or a tag of masking tape that notes the original position may be attached to the thread

Each joint should be carefully examined for additions, such as pegs, screws or nails, that may prevent the joint being separated cleanly. Original through-pegs may be driven out whilst blind pegs may be sufficiently loose to be withdrawn with pliers. If this is not the case they can sometimes be removed by inserting a thin wood screw into a centred pilot hole and pulling them free. If all else fails they may be centre-punched and drilled out. Some pegs were tapered and in such cases the centre may be drilled out with a drill bit slightly smaller than the peg and remnants in the joint removed using pliers or a carving chisel.

It is essential for the removal of screws that rust and dirt are removed from the slot. The tip of the screwdriver should fit the width and length of the slot snugly. Hollow ground tips are used by some conservators because the sides of the screwdriver at the tip are parallel and therefore do not tend to 'cam' out of the slot. Screws in wood often become slightly loose as the wood expands and contracts around them due to changes in RH. Screws should always be tested for ease of removal by slightly tightening them. If any movement occurs, screws are usually easily removed. Tightening has the advantage that if the screw head is stripped inadvertently, the conservator has a second chance at unscrewing. Screws may have rusted tightly into position and it is not uncommon for glue to have been added when screws have been replaced in the past. If the screws do not move, several methods may be used to break the bond that holds them fast. If none of the following methods work, the screw must be drilled out.

It may be sufficient to place the tip of the screwdriver into the slot and strike the tool sharply with a hammer. Vibrating the screw with an engraving machine may also work. The most consistently successful method is to apply a heated soldering iron to the head of the screw for a time, which will cause the metal to expand slightly. When the iron is removed and the metal contracts this may be sufficient to allow first slight tightening, and then removal of the screw. A retort stand and cramps may be used to support the soldering iron if prolonged contact is necessary. Removal may be assisted by repeatedly tightening and then loosening the screw.

Screw extractors are another solution to the ever-present problem of removing screws with damaged or missing heads. Essentially, they are tapered, reversed-threaded bits in varying sizes. Select the appropriate size (usually the smallest) and then drill a hole down the centre of the screw using the drill size indicated on the extractor, making certain that the hole is deep enough to engage a reasonable portion of threads on the extractor. Place the extractor in the hole and, with a small (preferably brass or nylon faced) hammer, tap the extractor into place. The reversed threads have now bitten into the screw. Keep the extractor in line with the screw – any sideways pressure may snap the screw extractor. Attach a tap wrench to the top of the extractor and *gently* begin to turn anti-clockwise. The more force applied to the extractor, the more it bites into the screw. The extractor is quite brittle, so it is vital that even pressure is applied to the tap wrench. There will inevitably be resistance, but the extractor can only absorb so much before it breaks. Use the techniques described earlier to loosen the screw before attempting the use of the extractor.

Nails driven into loose joints *always* result in further damage. Furthermore, they are often punched below the surface making their removal difficult. It may be impossible to remove nails without damaging the surface of the wood. There are two methods commonly used to remove nails. If the head of the nail lies at the surface of the wood it may be levered out using pliers that form a point. Flush cutting wire pliers are useful because they are only bevelled on the inside of the jaws. Care should be taken not to damage or bruise the surrounding wood. A thin piece of scrap wood or steel, for example a hacksaw blade with the set removed, or thin steel 'shim stock' (available

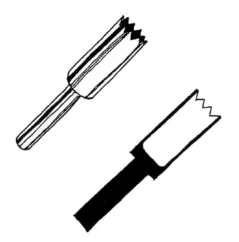

**Figure 10.10**   Home-made hollow drill for removing nails

through gunsmithing catalogues), may be used for this purpose. The second method requires a hollow drill fashioned from a piece of brass or silver steel of a suitable diameter. The centre is drilled out to a depth of about 25 mm and teeth are filed into the end (*Figure 10.10*). If the drill bit was made from silver steel, it is then tempered 'by the colours'. The surface is polished and the tool slowly heated from the non-tooled end. The temper colours (light straw through to blue) travel along the length and when the light straw colour reaches the saw teeth the tool is plunged again. Once cool, the saw teeth can be filed sharp. Information on hardening and tempering home made tools can be found in Weygers (1973). Proprietary hollow drills are manufactured by Holzer. A carving gouge is used to mark a circle around the nail to provide a secure start position for the drill bit. The drill should be withdrawn and waste cleared regularly and this can provide an opportunity to see if the nail can be removed.

Nails have often been used in a range of ill-conceived places. It may be possible to saw through the nail with a hacksaw to allow the components to be separated before removing the nail itself. If the space is narrow, a hacksaw blade may be used without the saw frame. Removing the set of the teeth, by working the hacksaw flat on an oilstone, will prevent damage to the wood. The small circular saw blades used with a flexible shaft machine or a Dremel tool are very thin and may also be

useful in this context. If a nail head is punched through from underneath the upper surface should be held firmly against a scrap piece of softwood to prevent breakout of the surrounding wood. Rivets holding metal brackets may be removed by drilling out the rivet heads to allow removal of the bracket. A flexible shaft machine with a burr or stone is often useful. Shanks may be removed in the same way as described for nails.

Once the joint has been cleared of obstructions it can be taken apart. If it is very loose a few blows by the joint with a white rubber mallet may suffice to separate the components. If a wooden or dark rubber mallet is used the surface of the component should always be protected from damage by a scrap piece of wood. Care should be taken that the force of the blow is directed through the joint and is not transmitted to thin or fragile components. Whenever force is applied to separate a joint, it should be directed so that the original geometry of the joint is maintained.

On occasion it is necessary to dismantle a joint that is sound in order to gain access to another that has been damaged or is loose. Joints that have been adhered with animal/hide glue may be loosened by injecting a small amount of water, isopropanol or ethanol through a pre-drilled hole into the joint to break the adhesive bond. Isopropanol is particularly effective. In some cases water injected into the joint may cause animal/hide glue and joint components to swell and may thus hinder rather than help dismantling the joint. It may be more effective to combine both heat and water by using a small steaming device, such as tubing with an attached syringe coupled to a pressure cooker (Rodd, 1976). Care must be taken to ensure that isopropanol or ethanol do not come into contact with the surface finish, which they are likely to damage. Some conservators have successfully experimented with portable radio frequency heating units. A small amount of water is injected from a syringe into the joint through a pre-drilled hole. The RF unit excites and heats the water, dissolving the glue and allowing the joint to be dismantled (Neher, 1996).

It may be possible to use wooden wedges to force a mortise and tenon joint apart. Such wedges should be wide and made from softwood to prevent crushing or bruising the

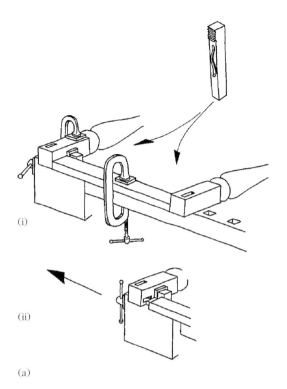

(a)

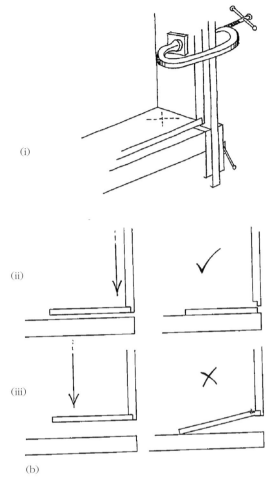

(b)

**Figure 10.11** Dismantling joints
(*a*) Bench dogs (one in the end vice or the work bench) are positioned next to the joints on the object (i). The end vice is then slowly opened to force the joints apart (ii). Softening blocks should be used to prevent bruising the surface of original components. Pressure should be applied gradually and it may help break the adhesive bond if the joint is alternately opened and then closed. (*b*) Dismantling dovetail joints. The component with the pins (e.g. a drawer front) is held vertically, leaving the component with the tails (e.g. the drawer side) parallel to, and just above the surface of, the workbench. A white rubber mallet may be used to strike the wood immediately adjacent to the joints so that the force of the blow is directed straight down the joint lines (ii). The further away from the joint such force is applied, the greater the risk of damage (iii)

shoulder of the joint. Small wedges may be inserted at the shoulder of the tenon from both sides. By carefully moving the wedges toward each other a shearing force is applied, which aids in separating the joint. Metal cramps, in which the direction of the heads can be reversed, may be used to provide continuous pressure at the joints. Similarly, bench dogs on a workbench may be used on the mortise and tenon joints of smaller objects, such as chairs (*Figure 10.11a*).

Where fox-wedged tenons are encountered, the joint should be drawn apart as far as possible and a saw used to cut down to the upper wedge. This will allow the joint to be dismantled, but will necessitate repair to the tenon before the joint can be reassembled.

Dovetail joints may be dismantled by hammering the joint apart (*Figure 10.11b*). Scoring the glue lines of the joint may prevent breakout as the components separate. Attempts to wiggle the joint apart should be avoided as this will crush the wood fibres and damage the joint.

Glue blocks may be removed using a chisel as a wedge. The chisel is placed onto the glue line and struck sharply with a mallet. Any clean splinters that remain glued to the surface may be left in place to help position the block when it is reglued into its original place.

### 10.2.2  Cleaning joints after dismantling

If the joint has come apart at the glue line and the components are intact, the old degraded glue must be removed to provide a clean surface for a new adhesive bond. The glue may be scraped or chiselled away but care should be taken to avoid removing wood because this will result in a loose joint.

Old animal/hide glue may be softened by the application of a water poultice using dampened newspaper, cotton wool, methyl cellulose or Laponite RD® (see section 11.7). Application of these materials should result in softened and easily removable glue within 10 minutes to half an hour. A 2% Laponite suspension has a pH of around 9.8, which will aid in breaking down the glue but will adversely affect many surface finishes such as shellac or oil paint. Care should be taken to prevent contact between finished surfaces and the poultice.

Reversal of many synthetic woodworking adhesives may present a hazard to the object or the conservator. For example, although epoxy resins can be softened by heating to 100–160 °C, by prolonged exposure to dichloromethane or hot dimethyl formamide, all these procedures entail a significant hazard to the object and/or the conservator. Casein adhesives that have not crosslinked by the inclusion of formaldehyde in the original application may be softened or dissolved by an aqueous solution with an elevated pH. If the pH required proves excessive or there is a risk of darkening the wood, enzymatic treatment with pepsin or trypsin may prove effective. White proprietary PVAC-based wood adhesives are often insoluble in organic solvents, though they may be softened by exposure to water and/or heat. Howells *et al.* (1984) has suggested that crosslinking of some white glues occurs after thermal ageing. Urea and resorcinol formaldehyde adhesives are insoluble in organic solvents and water and are not softened by heat.

### 10.2.3  Repairs after insect infestation

A component or object that has been infested by an insect, e.g. *Anobium punctatum*, will suffer a loss of strength proportional to the amount of wood destroyed by the larvae. If severe damage has occurred, it may be neces-sary to impart additional strength to structural components. Structural repairs may include consolidation (see section 12.2.3) and/or reinforcing the structure by introducing dowels or false tenons. Whilst a straight-grained wood such as beech has been the traditional choice for dowels, some have used more robust materials, such as stainless steel studs (threaded rods), glass fibre/epoxy dowels or Kevlar®/nylon dowels (Augerson, 1999). If such strong materials are used, it is important to consider how the object is used and where stress will be concentrated. Stress from gravity or normal use that runs parallel to the dowel (i.e. compression stress) may be unlikely to cause damage to the original in future. When stress is directed at an angle that differs from the direction of the dowel (i.e. shear stress), stress may concentrate in an adjacent weak area. This may eventually cause a second break that significantly extends the original area of damage. Where the material used is less compressive than the wood and fluctuations in RH are not controlled, the wood that encloses reinforcing dowels will be subject to compression set, weakening the adhesive bond in the long term. Thus whilst structural repairs should aim to combine durability with fitness for purpose, conservators should consider the potential for, and effects of, future failure of their repair.

In cases of severe structural damage, it may be necessary to replace the entire component or, if the surface is valued, its core. The extent of reinforcement or replacement may be determined by balancing the loss of original material against the risk of further damage to the object or injury to people. Glue blocks in a carcase or corner blocks in a chair seat may need to be provided or renewed. Where upholstery has been renewed many times in the past it may be necessary to build up or replace, in part or in total, some components (e.g. rails) to ensure new fixings are secure. In some cases fragile components may be reinforced by the additional of new material behind the original.

Where extensive support is required, this may be provided by an independent structure capable of being incorporated, and if necessary subsequently removed, with minimum damage to the object. The aesthetic impact of such structures should be minimized as far as possible.

## 10.2.4 Reinforcing joints

If a loose joint has been treated so that it is well adhered with closely mating surfaces, reinforcement with fixings such as nails, screws or metal brackets is unlikely to be necessary. Such fixings have often been employed by amateurs in an attempt to reinforce loose or weak joints. Some, such as screws and nails, inevitably lead to substantial further damage to loose joints, whilst the effect of others, such as obtrusive metal brackets, have met with varying success. If the underlying problem of the loose joint is not addressed all these methods will result in substantial further damage to the joint and the surrounding wood as leverage forces become concentrated on a small area of contact around the fixings. Fixings such as screws and nails are often difficult to remove without widening the area of damage.

If screws or nails are part of the original construction of the object, as a general rule they should be retained in their original positions. Adhering small blocks of wood along the grain may strengthen a joint when no other option exists. When applied with animal/hide glue they are readily removable without damage to the original.

## 10.2.5 Frames

The construction techniques used in frames are similar to those used in joinery and cabinet-making. Corner joints in frames may utilize mortise and tenon joints that may incorporate one mitred side or pegs, lap joints that sometimes have a mitred side, and simple mitres that may be reinforced with wooden splines cut into the corner or a wooden wedge at the back. Frames were usually integral to panel paintings until toward the middle of the fifteenth century, when the two forms were separated (Newberry *et al.*, 1990). Most mirror and picture frames utilize wood as a substrate. The decorative materials and techniques used to enhance them are similar to those found on furniture. The conservation problems that apply to frames are often analogous to those in the broader discipline of furniture conservation. Frames were usually made to enhance the presentation of a specific work of art, and often also functioned as an architectural element within the broader context of an interior

design. This symbiosis may be an important consideration for evaluating the degree of treatment necessary for the conservation of a framed painting or mirror. In the case where a painting or mirror and its frame are both to be treated, the aesthetic balance between them should be maintained. From the third quarter of the eighteenth century and onward, composition became a popular material for the surface decoration of gilded frames (see section 10.5.7). An introduction to the history and stylistic development of frames may be found in Jacob (1996), Newberry *et al.* (1990) and van Thiel and de Bruyn Kops (1995). Mendgen (1995) examines nineteenth and early twentieth century frames whilst Baldi *et al.* (1992) offer excellent illustrations, including profiles, and an introduction to the restoration of frames.

### *Handling mirror frames*

Structural factors and the condition of surface decoration should be considered before handling and moving mirror frames. Handling carved mirror frames may be problematic because there are often few, if any, handling points that do not involve applying pressure to fragile elements of the frame. The frame itself may not be structurally sound as a result of adhesive failure due to excessively low, high or fluctuating RH, insect infestation and minimal fixings that may have corroded. In addition, mirrors may contain multiple sheets of glass that are often not securely fixed to the frame. There is a danger of catastrophic failure if a mirror is moved, particularly as it is moved from a vertical to horizontal plane. Mirror plates are sometimes held in place with glue blocks, which may also be pinned. The glass may break if it shifts and comes into contact with these pins. The frame should not be relied on to hold the weight of the mirror if it is placed face down. Thus a frame should not be moved from a vertical to a horizontal position without taking into consideration the construction and stability of the frame, the change of weight distribution and pressure points, movement of panes and the way in which they have been secured. It may be necessary to provide support for glass and fragile decorative elements on the frame. Dowling (1999) describes a system for the removal and installation of mirrors, which ensures they are kept vertical throughout the process. This method may also be used to allow conservation of vulnerable mirrors, to transport frames, or to transfer a wall-mounted mirror onto a backboard if required.

## 10.3  Repair by damage type

### 10.3.1  Loose and broken joints

When joints are broken or loose, their structural function may be an important factor in deciding the appropriate level of intervention for a conservation treatment. Other factors include the loads or stresses they are subjected to in use and the accessibility of the joint for treatment.

Dismantling joints generally ensures the best repair is made by allowing the conservator to remove degraded glue, check the fit of the joint and tighten it if necessary, and provide a clean and well-prepared surface for adhesive bonding. Thin strips of veneer, preferably of the same species as the original, may be used to compensate for losses or gaps caused by compression set within a joint.

It is not always practicable to dismantle joints. Problems may arise where a single joint has failed but others that would have to be dismantled to allow access are sound, or when the process of disassembly might endanger a fragile decorative surface. When a loose joint cannot be taken apart without causing damage to the piece, it may be better to leave it untreated or seek an alternative such as injecting adhesive into the joint. It may be necessary to pre-drill a small diameter hole to allow adhesive to be syringed into the joint. A cold set collagen glue (e.g. fish glue) may provide the best chance of distributing the adhesive evenly within the joint. Moving the loose elements or adding a drop of surfactant will assist the glue to spread. In some cases it may be possible to stiffen the joint using wedges, but care must be taken not to add undue stress that may lead to further damage or joint failure. Additional support may be provided by improving external supports such as glue blocks or brackets, where these are already present.

There is generally a presumption against the use of wood swelling agents, such as Chair-

loc® or Bondex Wood Swell and Lock®, because of potential problems with reversibility (Howlett, 1988). The swelling action of such products is often a result of a polyethylene glycol (PEG) component. The presence of PEG on and in a wood joint may limit future conservation treatment options. Triboulot (1999a) suggested that PEGs are compatible with protein glue, though limited testing suggested a 50% failure rate of the glue line when samples were treated with PEG and then glued with animal/hide glue.

Joints in furniture were not always glued when the piece was originally constructed. Certain types of furniture, for example Windsor chairs made from unseasoned wood, were jointed together but relied on wedges and shrinkage as the wood dried to provide a tight joint. Medieval mortise and tenon joints may have been pegged rather than glued. In such cases it may be important to avoid introducing glue and losing evidence of original manufacturing techniques.

Butt joints are those in which two pieces of wood are glued together side-grain to side-grain. This type of joint requires intimate contact between the whole length of the edges that are to be glued because the strength of the joint relies on the quality of the adhesive bond. The edges must be straight and true over their entire length. In the past the edges of boards have often been re-planed to ensure a good joint, but repeated treatments may lead to a significant loss of material. This has proven a problem for some panel paintings where it has resulted in the loss of significant areas within portraits. In the case of furniture it has resulted in alterations in the shape or overall dimensions of components such as table tops. Where butt joints have failed, for example in a table top, they may be contaminated by wax, oily food residues and dirt. Planing does have the advantage of providing a clean surface for adhesive bonding. The alternative to removing material is to accept the gaps or to compensate for them by using wooden fillets or a gap filling glue (e.g. carvable epoxy). Such adhesives may be isolated from the original with a layer of animal/hide glue. Carvable epoxies, such as Bencon 22 (UK) or Araldite AV 1253/HV1253® (USA), were originally developed for pattern-makers, and usually have an equal proportion of resin and hardener bulked with phenolic microballoons. They may be levelled before the adhesive has completely cured using wetted tools, or simply carved after the epoxy has set.

Interventive restoration methods used in the past to reinforce butt joints or ensure a level surface have included loose tongues and dovetail keys. If the grain of the loose tongue runs parallel to the main components it offers no additional strength, unless the edges of the butt joint were in very poor contact. If plywood tongues, cross-grained tongues or dovetail keys are used there is the potential for further damage as a result of differential movement. Large dovetail keys may prove particularly problematic and may lead to the creation of new splits where wood movement is restrained (see Chapter 7).

When wooden elements within a joint are broken or have severely deteriorated it may be necessary to cut new parts, add new wood, or reinforce broken parts with veneer, splines, loose tongues or dowels. A common problem occurs as a result of woodworm attack that has concentrated on mortise and tenon joints. Severe damage necessitates the replacement of the original tenon with a false tenon that extends into the rail to provide adequate surface area for a strong adhesive bond (see *Figure 10.2*). The false tenon must be a tight fit to the mortise and the rail. Gaps that result from compression set in a mortise and tenon joint may be built up with veneer. In more severe cases, for example insect attack, it may be necessary to fit a patch and recut the mortise in fresh, undamaged wood.

Knuckle joints are used to attach fly rails or legs to the main carcase frame of drop-leaf tables. Fly rails or legs support the leaf when it is raised for use. Good cabinetmaking skills are required to produce a well-made knuckle joint and the critical process is drilling the pivot hole so that it is absolutely vertical and exactly centred in both sets of knuckles. Knuckle joints are prone to wear on the horizontal faces, which results in racking of the fly rail or leg and may lead to damage or breakage of the pivot pin. If the joint is in regular use it may be necessary to add veneer or thin fillets of wood to compensate for wear on the knuckles. The pivot pin was often made from steel or iron, approximately ³⁄₁₆ inch (4.5 mm) in diameter. If the pin is broken or has partially

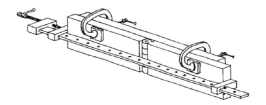

**Figure 10.12** Cramping a knuckle joint to redrill the pivot hole

seized it may be tapped out and a replacement fitted. It may be necessary to drill a larger hole, in which case the joint must be cramped up as illustrated in *Figure 10.12*. If wood is used for a replacement pivot pin it should be slightly softer than that in the knuckle joint itself so that wear is absorbed by this replaceable part rather than the knuckles. Screws are liable to snap as a result of shear and should not be used as pivot pins.

Many problems with rule joints are caused by faulty fitting of hinges (see section 10.3.3). Other problems may be caused by warping of a drop leaf or swelling that may result in the joint binding. The narrow lip of the cove moulding on the drop leaf is vulnerable to damage if the hinges are loose. Excess leverage applied when the leaf is lifted may also cause splits or breakage.

### 10.3.2 Shrinkage checks and splits

Surface checks are unusual in solid wood furniture in a well-maintained environment (*Figure 10.13*). Surface checks are often encountered in furniture that incorporates rotary cut veneer, for example the moulded plywood furniture associated with twentieth century designers such as Marcel Breuer or Charles Eames. Minor (1993) found that lathe checks, caused in the manufacture of rotary cut veneer, were exacerbated by fluctuations in relative humidity. Filling surface cracks in plywood will exacerbate the problem. Lathe checks and surface cracks in rotary cut plywood veneer are an inherent part of the ageing process of this material.

Shrinkage splits in furniture and wooden objects are caused by the dimensional change of wood in response to a reduction in relative humidity *in combination with* a fitting or joint

**Figure 10.13** Surface checks and splits in a carved oak panel. Such checks may be a result of the use of unseasoned wood or fluctuations in RH

**Figure 10.14** Differential shrinkage of the cleated substrate of the door of a marquetry longcase clock, *c.*1685. Splits in the marquetry decoration have collected dirt and wax

that restrains this movement. Shrinkage splits are often exacerbated by compression set caused by repeated cycles of fluctuating relative humidity (see Chapter 7). Any repair undertaken without addressing this environmental problem will be temporary and may lead to further damage. It is important to understand the cause of the split before any treatment is undertaken.

The dimensional response of wood to changes in RH will be influenced by the frequency, rate, size and duration of such fluctuations. Michalski (1994) suggested that, in some cases where environmental conditions are not stable, splits in carcase furniture could be minimized or prevented by storing textiles (preferably undyed cotton such as terry cloth) within the carcase structure, e.g. in drawers and compartments. The textiles act as a buffer

to fluctuations in RH and slow the rate of moisture content change within the wood. Slowing the rate of change means that the application of stress within the wood is gradual, and can be more easily absorbed by the inherent plastic and visco-elastic properties of the wood itself.

Shrinkage splits do not automatically require conservation treatment. Given that further damage may result from closing or filling a split, in many cases a strong argument can be made for leaving them untreated. The dictum of minimal intervention may suggest that treatment should be avoided unless further damage is likely to occur without it. Unless a split is comparatively fresh it may not be possible to disguise it without obscuring discoloured or darkened adjacent original surface with pigments, and in some cases fill treatments may be more obtrusive than the original split. In some cases shrinkage of a component may leave a moulding proud of an edge. In the past such mouldings have been pared to the smaller dimension but current ethics would usually preclude such removal of original material in favour of a reversible treatment or no treatment at all.

Although there is an argument that splits constitute an unacceptable aesthetic impairment and should be treated, this perspective may spring from a desire for perfection rather than acceptance of the inherent properties of the material from which the object is made. Where veneer has been laid over an inherently

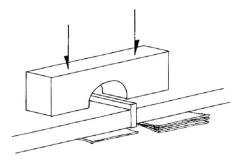

**Figure 10.15** Jig used to keep fills level. The jig spans the gap to be filled. G-cramps can be used to apply pressure as indicated by the arrows. In cases where the boards either side of the fillet are of uneven thickness, packing can be used to ensure the upper decorative face will be level

problematic substructure, such as cleated boards or a framed door with flush panels, an unobtrusive repair may be impossible without major intervention such as lifting the veneer and re-laying it on a different substrate (*Figure 10.14*). Since the original construction contributes historical and monetary value to the object, such treatment can offer an aesthetic improvement but may devalue the object in the long term.

The treatment options for shrinkage splits will depend on the construction of the substrate, the presence of a decorative surface, the position and width of the split, and, perhaps most importantly, the need to select a treatment that will not need to be repeated in the future and will not cause further damage.

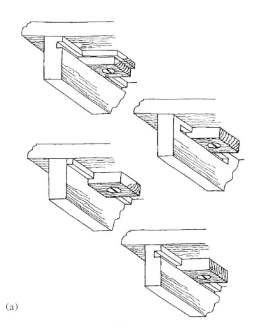

(a)

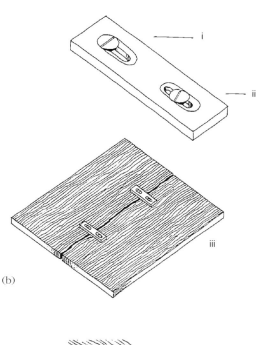

(b)

**Figure 10.16** Methods of fixing boards that do not restrain movement in response to fluctuations in RH. Note that in all cases, the fixing is positioned to allow movement *across* the grain
(*a*) Buttons. (*b*) Slot screwed supports applied to the rear of a split component. Screws are positioned in the middle of the slot (ii). Positioning the screws at the end of the slot (i) would restrain movement of the panel and could cause further damage. The slotted supports are positioned across the grain (iii) and ensure that the screws do not restrain movement of the component in response to fluctuations in RH. The split is shown for illustrative purposes, but would be closed before the screws were 'nip' tightened. The bevelled-edged slots can be made using a pillar drill. (*c*) Shrinkage plates

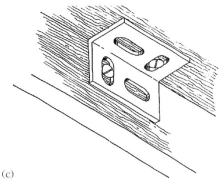

(c)

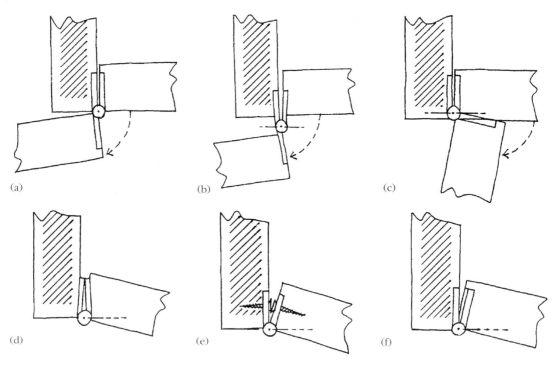

**Figure 10.17**   Diagnosing problems with hinges
(*a*) Correct alignment of butt hinge pivot pin (other methods of fitting butt hinges can be found in Joyce, 1987)
(*b*) Pivot too far forward – hinge protrudes
(*c*) Pivot too far back – door can't be opened properly
(*d*) Recess for hinge too shallow – door can't close properly
(*e*) Screw heads too large – door can't close properly
(*f*) Recess for hinge too deep – door can't close properly

Shrinkage may produce a clean separation between components as a result of adhesive failure, a ragged irregular crack as a result of cohesive failure of the wood itself or a combination of the two. It may be desirable in some cases, such as those with a pictorial or geometric symmetrical design, to close the gap and compensate for the change of dimension on one or both sides. Curved elements in a decorative veneered or painted design may be distorted or misaligned if splits are closed.

If shrinkage has occurred and the RH conditions in which the object is normally kept are stable, treatment options range from limiting treatment to stabilizing vulnerable edges through to closing the split and/or adding material to compensate for the gap. The focus of much research has been to develop methods that bridge the gap but which will not exacer-

bate compression set if RH should rise and the wood expands. Wherever possible, the surfaces either side of the fill should be level (*Figure 10.15*). Approaches to structural fills for wooden objects have been reviewed by Podmaniczky (1998). A variety of fill materials and fillers, including silicone/microballoons, epoxy/microballoons and wood, have been examined by Barclay and Grattan (1987), Grattan and Barclay (1988), and Barclay and Mathias (1989). Grattan and Barclay (1988) concluded that fillers with a low modulus of compression, such as waxes, balsawood and silicon rubber/microballoon mixtures, are least likely to cause damage if further movement as a result of fluctuating RH occurs. Silicone rubbers may stain and wood may need pretreatment to avoid this problem. Epoxy resin/microballoon mixtures may be appropriate as a gap filler in cases where a fairly stable RH can be maintained.

Splits in uncleated surfaces are the least problematic to treat as they can usually be closed under moderate cramping pressure. Such splits are often found in table tops where they result from the method used to fix the top to the underframe. The treatment decision may be based on whether to retain or adjust the original fixing method, for example whether to substitute buttons, slot screws or shrinkage plates (*Figure 10.16*). If original construction methods that are the cause of the break are retained, there may be little point in attempting to close a split. If a split has occurred in an unrestrained framed panel it may be possible to move one end of the panel toward the other rather than taking the panel out of the frame and risking further damage.

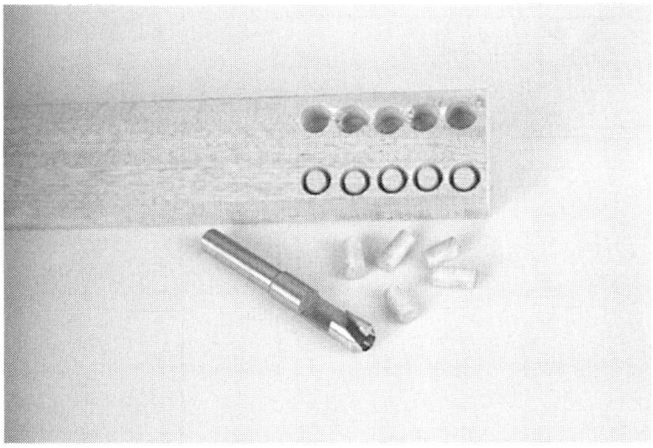

**Figure 10.18**  Parallel-sided plugs and the cutter used to produce them. Tapered plug cutters produce a very snug fit but in time, as the wood and plug expand and contract in response to fluctuations in RH, the pressure exerted by the taper can cause the plug to become proud of the surface

### 10.3.3   Hinges

Fitting traditional hinges to newly made furniture, in which all the components are straight and true, requires accurate measurements and good cabinetmaking skills. Repairs to antique furniture in which the components are no longer necessarily straight or parallel is doubly difficult. When diagnosing problems with hinges it is essential to understand where the pivot point/s should be located in relation to the component parts and to understand the effect that hinge recess depth has on the function of the hinge (*Figure 10.17*). In some cases, such as rule joints and doors, faulty fitting of hinges or timber swelling can result in damage to the joint. Other problems include replacement screws that are not flush with the hinge plate and cause screw binding, bent plates, or replacement hinges fitted in the past whose plates are too thin for the original recess.

Amateur repairs to loose and poorly aligned screws include pushing or gluing matchsticks into the screw hole, the use of replacement screws with a larger shank than the original (the heads of which may or may not fit the countersunk hole in the hinge plate), or wrapping thin string around the thread of the screw before gluing it back into place. The most durable repair will be effected by accurately drilling out the original hole and filling it with a plug of wood whose grain orientation matches the original. These may be cut using

a parallel-sided proprietary plug cutter (*Figure 10.18*). Dowels or matchsticks pushed into the hole will fail comparatively quickly because screwing into end grain is inherently weak.

It may be possible to compensate for a poorly fitted hinge by using veneer underneath or beside the edges of the hinge plates but in some cases it may be easier to fill the recess and refit the hinge from scratch. In some cases it will be necessary to replace damaged wood beneath the hinge before refitting the original hinge (*Figure 10.19*).

### 10.3.4   Warping

Distortion of wood out of plane is described as warping. It may take several forms including bowing, spring, cupping or twist (see *Figure 7.2*). Such uneven dimensional change may occur as a result of internal tension in the wood, poor seasoning or assembly techniques. It may also result from original construction methods, for example components that are veneered on one side only. Warping may also result in cases where the surface coating has not been applied to all surfaces of a wide component. The problem of warped wooden panel paintings has been considered by Dardes and Roth (1998) and by Klein and Bröker (1990).

Treatment options may be influenced by any decoration that may be present on the warped

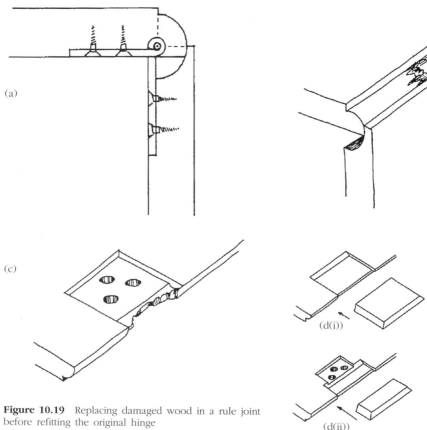

**Figure 10.19** Replacing damaged wood in a rule joint before refitting the original hinge
(*a*) Cross-section through a rule joint showing the layout of the hinge (after Joyce, 1987). Note the alignment of the pivot point of the hinge, indicated by dotted lines and the thin section of wood surrounding the knuckle which is easily damaged if the hinges are misaligned. (*b*) Loss of wood as a result of misaligned hinge. (*c*) Underside of table top, hinge removed. (*d*) Underside of table top. The size of the repair piece is dependent on the cause of the problem. The repair may be dovetailed for additional strength. If the hinge was misaligned in the past, a larger repair that allows the screw holes to be repositioned may be necessary (i). If the hinge was aligned properly and damage has occurred for some other reason, a smaller repair that compensates only for damaged wood may be all that is necessary (ii). In both cases, the repair must be recessed to accommodate the knuckle of the hinge (iii, iv). (*e*) Excess wood removed and the repair matched to the radius of the joint

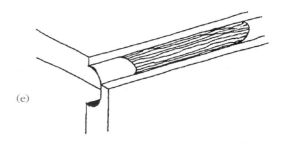

member, its position in the structure of the object, the instability created by the warped component/s, fitness for use and the potential for further damage to the object. Although it may be possible to compensate for warping, for example by adjusting the hinges on a warped door or adjusting the runners to better support a warped drawer, as a general rule correcting warped wood is difficult and involves major intervention. In many cases there is no truly satisfactory solution. The technical and aesthetic damage caused by warping should be critically evaluated before any treatment is undertaken. If the warpage is compatible with the age and character of the object, the piece may be best served by leaving it untreated. It is not always necessary to flatten each and every irregularity in a piece of furniture and often irregularities wrought by time may enhance appreciation of the object and the period in which it was created. In the past, furniture restorers have used a variety of extremely interventive methods to treat warped panels. Many of these techniques would be considered inappropriate within a modern ethical framework because they destroy original material and with it historical information, such as tools marks or construction techniques.

Warping caused by application of veneer to one face of a board may be corrected, where this is desirable, by counter-veneering. In some cases warping that has occurred as a result of poor assembly techniques may be corrected by dismantling and reassembly but in others compression set may have occurred and reassembly may be insufficient to remove the warp.

Saw kerfing is a traditional method for producing non-structural curved work such as mouldings (*Figure 10.20*). A series of saw cuts are made in the timber, perpendicular to the direction of the curve, to within 3 mm (⅛ in) of the show surface. Within the parameters set by the wood species itself, the closer the cuts the more the wood will bend. The wedge shaped

spaces left when the component has been curved could be filled with wood or left empty. There is a marked tendency for the cuts to telegraph through to the show surface of the wood and result in a series of flats, which are particularly visible in raking light or if the surface has a glossy finish.

The technique of kerfing has been used to straighten warped wooden panels in furniture. Parallel saw cuts or router grooves were cut into the concave side of a warped panel, having first removed any veneer. The panel was then cramped flat or into a reverse twist position before fillets were glued into the grooves (see, for example, Hlopoff, 1978; Rotter, 1979). This treatment attempts to address the underlying problem of warping by severing the wood fibres, releasing the tension that caused the warp. The wood is forced into a different, hopefully flatter, plane by inserting fillets. Veneer is relaid after the grooved and filled surface has been levelled. As is the case with traditional saw kerfing, there is a risk that the grooves will, in time, telegraph through to the presentation surface of the component. This risk can be minimized by limiting the depth of the cut to between half and two-thirds of the thickness of the warped component.

Other possible remedies for warped wood include removing of veneer from a warped substrate and relaying it. It was not uncommon for the old substrate to be discarded and a new substrate used, although in some cases the old substrate was flattened and reused (Considine *et al.*, 1990). Some conservators have counter-veneered components that were previously veneered on one side only. Attempts have been made to remove warp by introducing moisture into the concave face. Components almost always revert to their warped state on drying and such treatment may exacerbate the warp as a result of compression set.

Some conservators have used polyethylene glycol (PEG) to treat warped wood. PEG can be characterized as a water soluble artificial wax. In conservation, PEG has been widely used to impregnate waterlogged wooden artefacts that would otherwise warp, crack or disintegrate as they dried. PEG impregnation of waterlogged artefacts has been used in a two-stage process, during which the object is completely immersed. The first stage used a low molecular weight PEG (200–600) to

**Figure 10.20** View of the base of an English barometer, 1787, made by Benjamin Vulliamy. Kerfing has been used to create the curved moulding of the plinth

displace water bound to the cell wall. The second stage used a much higher molecular weight PEG (1500–4000), introduced in stages of increasing concentration and at an elevated temperature, which displaced water in the lumen of the wood fibres. Such treatment was often carried out over a period of several years. Factors that affect the uptake of PEG in such treatments include wood density, anatomical characteristics and the degree of degradation. In seasoned or dry wood, moisture content will have a significant effect on the uptake of PEG. The porosity of the cell wall varies from approximately 2% to 4% in dry cell walls to about 25% in water-swollen walls. It has been suggested that the pore size of a cell wall swollen with water is large enough to permit the passage of PEG molecules with a molecular weight of 3000 or less (Schneider, 1972). Potential problems discussed in the conservation literature have included long-term chemical stability and reversibility.

PEG can be used to stabilize unseasoned wood and has been used by wood turners for this purpose. Several articles that date from the 1960s and 1970s examined the use of PEGs to stabilize the dimensional movement of seasoned wood as a result of fluctuating RH (see, for example, Leslie, 1973; Sadoh, 1967). Seasoned wood offers comparatively limited opportunity for PEG diffusion into the cell wall and low molecular weight PEGs may be more successful (Wallstrim and Lindberg, 1995). The use of polyethylene glycol to treat warped furniture components has been considered by Boucher (1999), Howlett (1988, 1995), and Triboulot (1999a). Potential problems identified for the treatment of seasoned wood include controlling the swelling action of PEGs, colour changes caused by transportation of wood colorants by PEG, darkening of treated surfaces and compatibility with adhesives used in subsequent treatments. Rice (1990) suggested that PEGs may cause weak boundary layers between the adhesive and the wood. PEG may chemically interfere with the formation of the bond between adhesive and wood or further consolidation treatments with polymers (e.g. acrylics). PEG is mildly acidic and this may have implications for the corrosion of metal fixings. Florian (1982) found that PEGs could not overcome inherent dimensional instability that resulted from anomalous growth. None the

less in some cases treatment with PEG may offer an alternative to traditional kerfing techniques.

### 10.3.5 Breaks and losses

When possible, fresh breaks should be treated immediately to prevent loss of pieces or damage and contamination of break surfaces with dirt or grease. If this is not possible parts should be bagged, clearly labelled and preferably kept with the object until a repair is possible.

Major losses are those that result in a serious disruption of aesthetic or historical interpretation whilst minor losses, although they may be distracting, do not significantly impede the aesthetic or historical understanding of an object. The degree of intervention for both major and minor losses may be influenced by philosophical or ethical considerations, for example whether losses can be replaced whilst still retaining the historical integrity of the piece. Other factors include the nature and extent of evidence for replacements and how replacement parts should be finished, labelled and documented. There may be some debate about the degree of invisibility of the repair or the materials and techniques that may be used. The 'six foot–six inch' rule has been adopted by some conservators. This describes repairs or retouching that are unobtrusive at a normal viewing distance but easily identified on close inspection without reference to documentation.

In some cases wood may be so damaged that replacement of a section may be necessary. The position and type of damage will dictate the joint used. New wood may be scarfed on at an angle to reduce the aesthetic impact. In such cases the conservator may plane a flat surface on the original to mate the repair piece to it, or fill gaps with a carvable epoxy (isolated with a thin animal/hide glue) and plane a flat surface onto the cured epoxy. If the joint is composed primarily of end-grain it should be reinforced by the side-grain joint of a dowel or false tenon. This should be of a size and position consistent with general principles of jointing wood (Joyce, 1987). Dowels or false tenons may allow the removal of all excess wood from the repair before it is glued into position. Dowels may be positioned using dowel pins or by taping a pin to one face of the joint and striking or cramping the faces

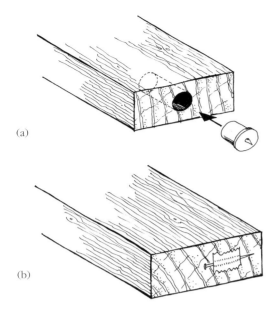

(a)

(b)

**Figure 10.21** Marking out dowel joints. Although only one joint is illustrated, it is usual to use a minimum of two dowels to prevent movement in the joint (*a*) Proprietary dowel pins. A hole is bored into one part of the joint, the dowel pin inserted. The second component is aligned and tapped lightly against the dowel pin. (*b*) The head of a metal pin used to mark both sides of a dowel joint simultaneously. A small dot of paint can be used in the same way

together so that each is marked (*Figure 10.21*). Small dots of paint, e.g. a red acrylic emulsion, may be used in a similar way. Alternatively, a fine pin may be tapped a few millimetres into one component, the end nipped off leaving about 3 mm of the pin protruding. The second component is then aligned with the first, and tapped lightly against the protruding pin.

Wood repairs let into the surface of wood usually rely solely on the adhesive bond. Selecting wood for repair has been outlined earlier in this chapter but the minimum requirement is that the piece used for repair should match the orientation of the original (i.e. transverse, radial), its appearance and reflective properties. In the case of a small or irregular loss that requires a new piece to be laid into the surface, acetate may be used to trace off the outline of the damage, which is then transferred to the surface of the wood to be used for the repair. Depending on the situation, the repair may be matched to the damage or made slightly oversize. In either case it is planed flat on the underside though it may be thicker than required and levelled after the repair has been glued into place. The shape of the repair piece may need to balance the best aesthetic integration with minimal loss of original material.

The traditional way of approaching this type of repair was to cut the repair piece so that it was slightly oversize. It was then laid over the area of damage and the outline marked onto the surface using a fine marking knife or scalpel. Unwanted material was pared away from the original. The scored line provided an exact position for the last stroke of the chisel. It is important that the area below the repair is absolutely level and a power or traditional hand router was often used for this purpose. Angles on the repair piece were compatible with the available tools – excessively acute angles are very difficult to level. The repair was then glued into place and levelled flush with the surrounding surface without damaging or removing adjacent original surface finish or wood. Although this method provides an excellent fit for a wood-in-wood repair, it is possible that future repairs to the same area can extend the loss of original material. Alternatives include the use of fills, or building up the edge of a loss with a carvable epoxy, to allow the patch to be let in without removing original material. Materials that may be suitable for non-structural repairs to wood are discussed in section 12.3.1. The range of materials used in the past has been reviewed by Thornton (1998a).

Mechanical wear caused by the action of moving furniture parts can be treated if necessary. The primary criterion for conservation is whether the object is stable and whether further damage will occur as a result of leaving it untreated. In the past drawer runners have been turned around or replaced in objects that were still in use. An alternative is to replace worn areas of runners and drawer sides with fresh wood, keeping as much of the original as possible. In contrast to domestic furniture, that in museum collections is not usually in use and this type of wear may remain untreated. Other mechanical parts, such as poorly fitting doors, may cause further wear or damage and therefore require treatment. When a door on a pivot hinge is worn out, for example, a washer may be sufficient to lift the door up.

### 10.3.6   Faulty construction

Furniture has been manufactured by a wide range of people. Workers in related fields such as carpenters, shipwrights and joiners often made furniture as a sideline. Such furniture, often made by non-specialists within a vernacular tradition, may incorporate quirks in construction that may lead to premature failure but can also offer an intriguing insight into social history. Treatment of such 'faulty' furniture must balance the object's survival against the need to respect its integrity and preserve the historical information and value carried within it. As a general rule conservators do not 'improve' objects. The emphasis with such pieces should be to retain original construction without interventive improvement. It may be possible to incorporate supports or add instructions such as 'Handle with care' or 'Do not open this drawer'. A similarly cautious approach may be necessary with the fit of joints or the geometry of an out of true seat. The definition of faulty construction carries with it an inherent value judgement and there is a danger that today's conservation treatment may be tomorrow's treatment error.

## 10.4   Veneer, marquetry and boulle

Veneer, marquetry and boulle are considered together because they all consist of thin sheet materials applied over a wooden substrate for decorative effect. The problems associated with these forms of decoration arise from differential movement between the surface and the substrate. This may be compounded by different orientation in the veneer itself (e.g. marquetry) or poor adhesion (boulle). Veneer, marquetry and boulle are vulnerable to damage and loss as a result of poor housekeeping practices (e.g. the use of feather dusters), substrate construction (e.g. cleated boards) and their proximity to edges (e.g. veneered drawer rails). Preventive conservation is essential to ensure the survival of veneered surfaces, which are likely to suffer adhesive failure if exposed to excessively low or cycling RH. Glass covers on tabletops will prevent damage from dusting and inadvertent spills. Such glass may need to be heat-treated or laminated to reduce the chance of injury in

the event of breakage and to conform to relevant legislative requirements. It is essential that the substrate is sound before treatment of surface layers commences.

Technical developments in the production of veneer are discussed in Chapter 1. Traditional techniques for repairing damaged veneer, marquetry and boulle may be found in general restoration texts, such as Bennett (1990), Hayward (1967) and Rodd (1976). Specialist texts on veneering and other related decorative techniques include Hawkins (1986), Hobbs (1953) and Ramond (1989). Wilson (1972) examined the work of Charles Andre Boulle and the historical techniques used to execute boullework. Pradere (1991) has reviewed the work of many significant eighteenth century French cabinetmakers. Callède and Ostrup (1984), Edwards (1997) and Kjelland (1997) have discussed the conservation of marquetry. ADEN, a group whose research has focused on developing new treatments for marquetry and boulle, can be accessed on the Internet at http://www.ucad.fr

The term 'boulle' describes furniture decorated with a veneer of brass and turtleshell. Other materials such as copper, pewter, horn and mother-of-pearl may also be incorporated into the design. Although Charles Andre Boulle is credited with popularizing this decorative form, it was previously known in Italy and was produced by other ebenistes such as Golle and Berain. Cutting brass and turtleshell in a sandwich creates both premier partie (brass design in a turtleshell ground) and contre partie (turtleshell design in a brass ground) designs simultaneously. Boulle furniture was produced throughout the eighteenth century and the style was revived in the mid nineteenth century. As a general rule the turtleshell found on eighteenth-century furniture is much thicker than that on nineteenth-century pieces, though there are occasional exceptions. Boullework is extremely time-consuming to conserve and repair – cutting six square inches (150 mm) of replacement may take up to eight hours. Case histories of the conservation of boullework include Considine *et al.* (1990) and Umney (1993). The metal elements of boulle designs were often elaborately engraved and filled with black or red mastic for added emphasis. Turtleshell and horn could be coloured by adding pigment to the glue used to adhere it to the substrate or by using paper to accentuate the colour of the tinted adhesive. Pigment analysis has identified the use of vermilion (mercuric sulphide), lamp black, smalt and copper resinate (Umney, 1993). Gold leaf may sometimes be found under turtleshell.

Differential movement between veneer and substrate or within the construction of the substrate can cause several problems. Some, such as loss of adhesion, may be relatively simple to fix whilst others, such as warping or stress cracks in the veneer over cleated joints, may have no completely satisfactory solution. Stress cracks are usually caused by low RH and if this problem cannot be addressed there is little to be done apart from consolidating the veneer as it is found. Checks and splits will reoccur unless fluctuations in RH are minimized. Attempting to prevent movement of the substrate using dowels or butterfly keys may result in merely extending the area of damage in the future and it is important to balance a desire for perfection against the inherent properties of the original material. Cracks caused by fluctuating RH and exacerbated by compression set may accumulate dirt, wax, and are vulnerable to discoloration from the oil component in traditional furniture revivers.

The use of decorative inlay in furniture has a rich and varied history. Inlaid furniture dating from the eighth century BC was excavated from Gordion, Turkey in the 1950s. Moorish craftsmen on the Iberian peninsula produced an array of inlaid objects in the tenth, eleventh and twelfth centuries. The Italian decorative form tarsie (plural of tarsia) developed in the fourteenth, fifteenth and sixteenth centuries. It was the source of the popular sixteenth and seventeenth century English decorative form now known as intarsia, although inventories from the period often refer to such decoration as 'markatree' (Edwards, 1987). The outline of an intarsia design was cut into the surface of the wood, waste removed to a depth of around ⅛ in (3 mm) before wood (holly, bog oak, fruitwoods etc.) or other materials (ivory, bone, turtleshell, mother-of-pearl) were inlaid into the surface to create a decorative effect. Replacement of losses uses the same techniques for creating a template described for marquetry and boulle, though the repair piece itself will be of a thicker dimension. Wilmering (1998) has described the conservation of fifteenth century intarsia panelling.

### 10.4.1 Laying veneer

There are several methods of laying veneer onto a wooden substrate. Hammer veneering can be used to lay knife-cut or rotary-peeled veneer on flat surfaces or those that curve in only one plane. Thick saw-cut veneer or complex curves were veneered using shaped cauls. Shrinkage as the glue dries will cause the substrate to bow unless it is firmly fixed to a frame or counter-veneered. The substrate should be level and free from defects. Traditionally the surface was scored with a toothing plane.

Hammer veneering requires a warm draught-free workspace, freshly made slightly thinned animal/hide glue, a supply of clean hot water, a clean undyed rag, a veneer hammer, veneer tape and pins, and an iron. Veneer hammers have a 4 or 5 inch (100–125 mm) non-ferrous tongue that is slightly rounded at the edges to prevent scoring the veneer as the glue is forced out. Smaller veneer hammers or a Warrington pattern hammer may be used for crossbanding and stringing.

Sheets of knife-cut veneer, which are usually around 0.7 mm thick, may be laid by hand, one at a time in a two-stage process. Firstly, hot animal/hide glue is brushed evenly over the substrate and the veneer placed on it. A little glue is brushed onto the surface of the veneer to lubricate the action of the hammer, which is worked in a zigzag pattern over the whole surface, working from the centre of the sheet to the edges, in the direction of the grain. This brings veneer and substrate into close contact and forces out some of the excess glue (*Figure 10.22a*). In the second step, a dampened rag is placed on the surface and a hot iron used to soften the glue. The iron should be hot enough to melt the glue under the veneer but not so hot that it scorches the wood. A workable area (maximum *c.*45 cm square) should be steamed and the veneer hammer used a second time, in the manner described above, working from the centre out the edge, with overlapping strokes, to force out the last of the excess glue. The hammer is worked along the grain of the veneer because the veneer will stretch and may break if force is applied directly across the

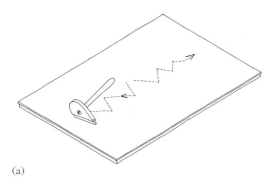

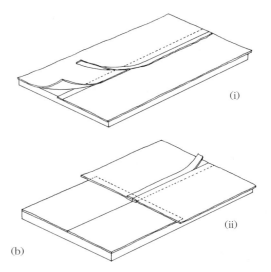

**Figure 10.22**  Laying veneer
(*a*) A zigzag action is used when using a veneer hammer to lay knife-cut veneer
(*b*) Removing overlapping waste veneer from (i) book-matched or (ii) quarter-matched veneer

grain. The pressure needed on the veneer hammer will vary with the type of veneer – some will require heavy pressure whilst for others medium pressure will suffice. If the sheets of veneer are less than *c.*45 cm square, the same procedure should be used, but only half the sheet worked in the second stage. This is to allow accurate positioning of the sheet, which would slip if the whole were steamed and ironed in one stage. The second step is then repeated for the other half of the sheet.

Where knife cut veneer is book-matched the second sheet is laid so that it overlaps the first by about half an inch (12 mm). When the second sheet has been laid, a line is scored using a straight edge and a sharp knife through both sheets. Removing the excess overlap from the upper sheet is straightforward. To remove overlapping veneer from underneath the joint, the veneer joint must be warmed using a damp rag and hot iron. The upper veneer is then lifted slightly and the excess removed (*Figure 10.22b*). When this has been done, a little extra glue must be added before hammering the veneer to a tight-fitting joint. The same process is used for quarter-matched veneer. Although it is possible to iron veneer more than once it is not usually necessary and repeated steaming may result in excess expansion followed by excess shrinkage as the veneer dries. This can exacerbate any tendency to warp and can also result in gaps opening up between book matched veneers. When the veneer has been

laid, excess gelled glue on the surface should be removed to facilitate later cleaning up and finishing. Veneer tape may be laid over joints to help prevent gaps opening up as the veneer dries. Edges may be carefully trimmed with a sharp chisel once the glue has gelled. If cross-banding or stringing is required, a cutting gauge may be used and the waste removed cleanly and rapidly before the glue has dried.

Cauls may be used to lay veneer when sheets are too thick to be successfully ironed (e.g. saw cut veneer) and for complex designs where movement or uneven swelling of the veneer would be problematic. A thin even layer of glue is applied to the substrate and allowed to gel. Gummed tape may be used to hold design elements in position. Pins, nipped off level with the surface, are sometimes used to prevent the veneer slipping, but these will interfere with cleaning up the surface when veneering is complete unless they are removed. A thin layer of paper is laid over the top and a sheet of heated lead or zinc may be laid on the paper (but is not essential) before the caul is placed on top. The surface of the caul may also be pre-heated. Finally bearers above and below are cramped up. The top bearer should be shaped slightly so that pressure is applied first to the centre of the veneered surface (see *Figure 10.5c(i)*). The cramps are pinch-tightened, working from the centre bearers outwards to the ends of the surface (see *Figure 10.5c(ii)*). The cramps may be progressively tightened over the next ten or fifteen minutes, gradually applying more pressure to the veneered board.

Veneer on components with a curve in one plane can be laid using a veneer hammer or by using negative formers made from wood or a plaster cast made for the purpose. If a cast is needed, an sandwich wrap or Teflon sheeting of the type used by plumbers to wrap pipes may be used as an isolating layer. Modelling clay (e.g. Plasticene) can be used to create walls for the plaster. Mix the plaster with water according to the manufacturer's instructions and pour. A loose woven material, such as upholsterer's scrim, may be used to reinforce the plaster. Allow it to set, then remove the mould and use it to cramp the veneer into place. An unreinforced cast will be brittle and it is advisable to use a piece of waste wood to spread the cramping load evenly on it. It is sometimes possible to compensate for curves by padding out a former that does not fit exactly. This may result in uneven pressure and when the glue has thoroughly dried out, unevenness may telegraph through the veneer. A quick and effective gluing caul can also be made using an oven hardened PVC gel such as Sculpey or Fimo to make a quick mould.

Complex curves may be cramped using heated sandbags. Woven cotton bags are filled with sand until about two-thirds full. The bags are then stitched closed. They need to be heated in an oven (c.70–80 °C) for several hours before use. The veneer is prepared as for caul veneering but the heated sandbags are pressed to conform to the shape of the ground before a board is placed over them and cramping pressure applied.

Whilst traditionally veneer was laid using glue from natural sources, modern furniture manufacturers utilize heated presses and synthetic adhesives such as urea formaldehyde. Small workshops may also have made use of modern adhesives. Some, for example, have used impact adhesive in an attempt to prevent warping when veneer is applied to one surface. Others have used PVAC wood adhesive for veneered furniture that was to be shipped to hot climates such as the Middle East. In the case of PVAC, traditional methods and modern materials were combined – the PVAC was applied to the surface, veneer placed on top and a hot iron applied until a hiss was heard, indicating evaporation of solvent. Although synthetic adhesives were used in the manufacture of twentieth century veneered furniture, problems of reversibility/retreatability usually preclude re-using such materials in conservation treatments.

### 10.4.2   Cleaning

Marquetry, boulle and complex designs executed in veneer may be dusted with a soft brush and the dust removed with a vacuum cleaner. Feather dusters should not be used as they may catch on loose edges and tear small fragments free or, in the case of boulle, bend brass up and crease it. White spirit or an aromatic hydrocarbon solvent will remove grease and finger marks. The presence of a natural resin varnish can be detected with the use of a hand-held UV light source (UV goggles should always be used).

Traditional furniture revivers that contain linseed oil are a significant source of damage to marquetry and veneer. As the surface ages small surface checks may form in the veneer and surface finish. Small gaps may also open up along saw cut lines. When reviver is applied linseed oil penetrates these cracks and is drawn by capillary action beneath the intact surface finish. Linseed oil traps dirt that is then incorporated into the macromolecular structure formed over the years the oil takes to dry. This accentuates the darkening associated with linseed oil films. Repeated applications of reviver often results in significant aesthetic disruption of the surface, which becomes blotchy and discoloured. In many cases reversing such damage completely may be impossible, although in some cases a selective cleaning treatment may be successful (see, for example, Philp, 1999).

Brass has often been selectively cleaned in the past with the result that varnish may be present only on the turtleshell. The wishes of the owner or curator should be discussed before any cleaning or polishing of the metal is undertaken. Metal polish should not be used for cleaning boulle. The ammonia present in many proprietary products may darken the substrate wood and cause irreversible staining. The traditional method of cleaning the brass has been to use a variety of abrasive materials (e.g. charcoal or pumice). Engraving on the best quality pieces was finely executed and is used for the decorative detail on large metal areas. Repeat treatment of engraved brass with abrasives can culminate in loss of detail. Without the engraving the overall design can become virtually unreadable. Options for the chemical cleaning of brass are discussed in the section on metals (section 15.3).

### 10.4.3  Consolidation

Loose veneer, marquetry or boulle may be detected by tapping a fingertip over the surface. A well adhered surface will sound dull when tapped lightly whereas loose veneer will produce a slight 'clicking' sound. Loose veneer may be marked with a small piece of masking tape, which is removed once the veneer has been glued down. Loose veneer and marquetry may be consolidated using fresh slightly thinned animal/hide glue, rabbit skin glue or fish glue. If pieces are sufficiently loose a warmed artist's palette knife may assist, otherwise it will be necessary to use a syringe or to gently massage the loose veneer to draw the adhesive underneath. An inert filler may be required to add bulk and prevent a dip in the veneer after the glue has dried. The gelling time of a hot setting animal/hide or rabbit skin glue may be delayed by gently heating the surface with a heat lamp or hot air gun, though care must be taken to avoid unwanted effects from an excessive localized drop in RH. Excess adhesive should be wiped away and a warmed block, isolated from the surface by silicone release paper or clear polyester sheet (e.g. Melinex or Mylar), cramped over the top. It may be necessary to apply cramping pressure and then release it to enable all excess adhesive to be removed and prevent damaging the adjacent surface finish. Kolbach (1998) has described the use of Peel Ply, a non-woven polyester release fabric which adhesives wick through rather than adhering to. The Peel Ply may be peeled from the surface after the adhesive has dried.

Blistered veneer was traditionally treated by cutting the veneer along the grain and squeezing glue underneath. Although this technique is reliable, the cut line may become visible in time and so should be kept as short as possible whilst allowing the glue to be forced underneath the whole of the blister. A thin sharp blade, such a single edged razor blade, should be used because a thick bevel edged blade will compress the wood fibres. The cut should follow the line of the grain to make it as unobtrusive as possible. Glue penetration may be aided by pre-wetting and massaging the blister once the glue has been applied. Fish glue may be used if there is a danger of the glue gelling before it has penetrated adequately under the blister. An alternative to cutting a blister is to pierce it and use a syringe to inject slightly diluted warmed glue or fish glue under the blister. A small amount of IMS may be added to reduce surface tension and increase the penetration of the glue.

Several cramping methods may be used if the loose veneer is too far from the edge to allow the use of a G-cramp. Weights may be useful or a cross bar, shaped as for use with caul veneering, may be cramped at either side of the surface (see *Figure 10.5d*). A screw jack or flexible rods from an overhead surface may also prove useful (see *Figure 10.5a*), though it may be necessary to support the surface from underneath to prevent it cracking as pressure is applied.

Veneer on complex curved surfaces, such as bombe commodes, may be consolidated by making use of heated flexible Perspex/ Plexiglass cauls or sandbags. Vacuum cramping, which uses atmospheric pressure to cramp loose veneer in place while the adhesive cures, may also be used to consolidate such surfaces. Whilst vacuum bags may be used to enclose an entire object, Kolbach (1998) has described a technique that allows localized application of vacuum pressure. This obviates the need to support a bagged object to prevent its collapse as vacuum pressure builds. This technique may be appropriate for consolidating the surface of degraded wood that would be in danger of structural collapse if traditional cramping tools were applied. Strong 'rare earth' magnets applied to both sides of a panel are also effective for clamping defects in veneer.

Shrinkage of the substrate may result in veneer or stringing that is proud of, and now larger than, the space on the surface and cannot simply be relaid. There are three options in such cases – support the raised area in place so that further damage does not result, lay it down so that it overlaps, or reduce its size so that it fits the present space.

Boucher (1995) described a technique that utilized cold set liquid animal/hide glue to consolidate marquetry in situ. Thin gauze or a similar fabric is dampened and placed over the surface until design elements begin to lift. The cloth and water are removed and a cold set animal/hide glue brushed onto the surface and worked under damaged or lifting veneer. A thin layer of plastic is placed over this gluey surface and the whole transferred to a press that has been pre-heated to 65 °C. The heat is turned off after five minutes and the marquetry left under pressure until the glue has dried (up to a week), after which excess adhesive on the surface is removed. This technique may be used for boulle but loose brass should be reglued with fish glue before treatment commences.

Fish glue is the traditional adhesive used for boullework, although it may be difficult to achieve a strong and lasting bond between wood and metal. The addition of garlic juice was reputed to improve adhesive properties and longevity, though it is not favoured by most conservators. Nagora *et al.* (1990) suggested the use of sturgeon glue with the addition of 5% glycerine, whilst Triboulot (1999b) suggested that the addition of 25% v/v alcohol and 25 g/l dextrin to collagen adhesives will increase the adhesion between the substrate wood and brass. Restoration books often recommend the use of irreversible adhesives such as epoxy, particularly if animal/hide or fish glue fails to stick metal down. This problem is caused by a contaminated surface rather than the use of a protein adhesive *per se*. Epoxies are sensitive to surface contaminants and though they may initially adhere well the service life of the adhesive bond may be greatly reduced if the bonded surfaces are contaminated by dirt or grease. Many epoxy hardeners contain amines, which can cause corrosion of copper alloys. Problems of future reversibility also weigh against the use of such adhesives.

The surface of the metal that is to be adhered must be clean and may be scored or sanded to provide a key. The metal should be cleaned immediately before adhesive is applied and care should be taken not to contaminate the surface by handling it. Some texts recommend the use of hot cauls to lay boulle, stating that if spit bounces straight off the metal of the caul it is too hot but if it sits and sizzles the temperature is right (Hawkins, 1986). Given the stress that will be placed on the adhesive bond as the metal cools and contracts, and the likelihood of destroying any surface finish on adjacent areas, such high temperatures are not recommended for conservation work. More recent sources have recommended temperatures in the range of 65–75 °C.

It may be possible to introduce fresh animal/hide or fish glue under loose areas before cramping them down. If a natural resin varnish is present, it may be necessary to remove excess adhesive by applying pressure and releasing it several times to prevent any excess from drying on the surface and damaging the surface finish. Often the metal surface is contaminated and it may be difficult to adhere. It may be necessary to lift a section of metal and clean the back before relaying it. Removal of old adhesive, especially from the ground, may result in differences in the level of treated and untreated areas. If only a small area has been treated, it may be necessary to apply a backing (e.g. a non-laminated paper) to compensate for the loss of thickness in the adhesive layer. A traditional treatment for laying metal in boullework was to place a flake of shellac underneath the loose end and apply heat. If metal has been treated in this way in the past it will require cleaning before it can be relaid. Repeating treatment with shellac will probably result in a repeated adhesive failure in the future.

If decorative elements are lifted, old glue and other contaminants must be removed before they are relaid. Turtleshell may become embrittled with age and it may be necessary to soften old glue with water or a Laponite gel to prevent fracturing of the edges of adjacent turtleshell when the glue is removed. Bubbles in turtleshell are particularly common in the thin shell used on nineteenth century pieces. Fresh glue may be worked under the bubble and then cramped up. In some cases a combination of water and methylated spirits (3:1) may be sufficient to reactivate the original glue if it is not severely degraded. In some cases the paper used under the turtleshell has delaminated and may be consolidated with isinglass.

Creased or buckled metal, that is not work-hardened or embrittled, may be straightened by careful hammering, or by putting it between two pieces of MDF or flat 6 mm (¼ in) mild steel and placing it in a vice. Hammering the brass directly will spread the metal and increase the size of the design element, which may then no longer fit into its place in the original decoration. The underside of the brass should be cleaned and degreased thoroughly before it is relayed. It is sometimes possible to straighten creases using pliers but there is a danger of work hardening, which will result in the metal snapping. If work hardening is suspected it will be necessary to anneal the brass by heating it on a fire brick surface until it is a uniform dull red colour then allowing it to cool naturally. Brass has a comparatively low melting point and care should be taken not to overheat small pieces.

Pins were sometimes used in the original manufacture to secure brass to the carcase. The holes drilled in the brass were accurately matched to the shank of the pin, the head planished so it was invisible and any engraving flowed over the pin. Pins were often used in past restoration treatments to secure loose brass but should not be used to relay brass in conservation treatments. Pins are unsuitable because they are often not round and thus do not give a good fit, ribbed shanks may pull the metal down and cause a dent, whilst tapered pins invariably cause denting. When brass has been lifted, restoration pins removed and the metal flattened and relayed, the old hole may be redrilled to match the exact diameter of a brass rod. Short lengths may be cut from the rod, sharpened to a point at one end (but not tapered) and tapped in flush to the surface. When brass is to be cleaned or polished to a high shine, holes may be filled using silver solder, which is levelled before the brass is relaid.

### 10.4.4    Transferring the outline of a loss

Losses in boullework occur more frequently from metal elements of decoration but on occasion whole design elements may have been lost. The first step in replacing a lost decorative element of marquetry or boulle is to create a paper template of the loss. In cases where a whole section of a design has been lost, it is sometimes possible to use acetate sheets to reconstruct the outline of a design from ridges of original adhesive.

In cases where a single component has been lost, any remnants of old glue should be removed. The most accurate method of producing a template for a restoration is to tape a thin paper (e.g. standard weight typing or copy paper) over the area of loss. Carbon paper is placed face down on the paper and a ball pein hammer rubbed over the surface. The carbon paper can be removed to check progress and to ensure that fine detail such as points, saw returns and tight curves have been reproduced. An acetate tracing of the loss with the grain direction marked on it can be used to select replacement wood veneer.

The paper template is glued onto the replacement material. It is important to minimize dimensional distortion of the paper template by selecting an appropriate adhesive. If animal/hide glue is used it should be applied very thinly and most of the moisture allowed to evaporate before the paper is glued down. A non-aqueous and easily removed contact adhesive such as Cow Gum, Thixofix or an aerosol photo mount are preferred by many because they will not cause dimensional distortion. These are applied to the repair material only and the paper pressed onto it. Metal should be degreased before the paper template is adhered to it.

### 10.4.5    Replacing losses

The location of replacements should be documented and repairs to the groundwork must be completed before treating the veneer. Most repairs to veneered surfaces may be undertaken with fairly simple equipment. It may be useful to make shaped punches for patching veneer when required. There are two alternatives when patching veneer – matching the repair to the loss, or cutting away original material to match the area of loss to the repair (*Figure 10.23*). Techniques for both options are set out in section 10.3.5.

Appropriate selection of material is a prerequisite for a successful repair. Wood is the usual material used to replace losses in veneer and marquetry but alternatives do exist: Dorge (1992), for example, used photographic reproductions as an alternative to replacing miniature geometric inlay with wood. In some cases it may be desirable to use wood from the same species as the original. In other cases, for

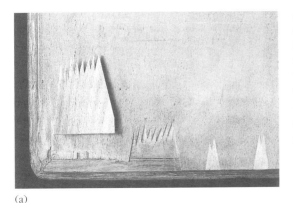

(a)

(b)

(c)

**Figure 10.23**  Repairing veneer
(*a*) The traditional method of letting in repairs to
damaged veneer relied on cutting away original material
to provide a clean edge for the new veneer. In this
case a tooth shape has been used to avoid a repair line
perpendicular to the grain. Patches that are
perpendicular to the grain draw the eye to the repair
and are difficult to colour match invisibly. Alternatives
to the tooth shape include boat shaped (for repairs
away from an edge) or mitred (for repairs abutting an
edge) patches. (*b*) Water damage on a veneered table
top, before repair. (*c*) Veneered table top, after repairs
to veneer, before colour matching

example, if an invisible repair is required,
oxidation of the original or the resistance of the
replacement to treatments used for colour
matching may necessitate the use of a paler
wood with a similar surface appearance. In
either case the wood used in the repair should
match the original as closely as possible in
grain direction, pore size and other visual
features such as texture and the size and distribution of rays. Careful choice will minimize
retouching, reduce stress on both the repair
and object and help ensure the durability of
the replacement. It is particularly important to
match the tangential, radial or transverse orientation of the piece used for repair to that of the
original – no amount of colour matching will
successfully blend a radially cut repair into a
tangentially cut original. Matching orientation is
also important for matching the relative movement in service as pieces cut on the tangent
(through and through) move approximately
twice as much in response to changes in relative humidity as those cut on the radius (quarter sawn).

It is common practice in furniture restoration
to make use of old polished and oxidized
surfaces to prepare patches for veneer. It
requires some skill to thickness a patch from
below to match the exact level of the original.
It is more time-consuming than levelling a
patch after it has been glued into place but this
may be compensated for by less (or no) time
spent colour matching. The use of old surface
wood can give an excellent match and is
viewed as particularly desirable in the commercial trade. Whilst it may be expedient to break
up furniture purely for this purpose it cannot
be considered ethical within current professional guidelines. As demand for antique furniture has grown, objects previously used as
breakers are now increasing in value. The
conservator must decide whether it is truly
necessary to achieve such an exact match. The
demand for such treatment may lessen in time,
as the supply of suitable breakers becomes
more limited and expensive.

Whether fresh timber or an old surface is
used, it is brought to thickness by machine or
hand sawing, planing, scraping and sanding.
Very thin or brittle materials, such as mother-
of-pearl, a single layer of veneer or oyster-cut
veneer, need to be glued to a support using
thinned animal/hide glue and a layer of paper

to facilitate removal. A non-aqueous contact adhesive such as Cow Gum or Thixofix, removed by soaking in acetone, is effective for sandwiches of brass and turtleshell. Marquetry may use a non-aqueous contact adhesive or animal/hide glue. The choice of adhesive is largely dependent on the ease of separating the layers after they have been cut. Thin short-grain veneer will break unless handled very gently and thus the traditional way of separating a veneer sandwich was to soak it in warm water until the layers separated, drying them thoroughly before reassembling the design, staining or sand-shading and laying it onto the original object. Soaking in methylated spirits will also release the adhesive but result in less dimensional swelling.

Cauls or sandbags are usually used to lay replacement boulle. The colour and thickness of the replacement should be matched as closely as possible to the original. Soft brass will prove easier to work than hard or half-hard sheets. Options for replacing turtleshell or horn losses are discussed in section 15.1.

Cutting replacement marquetry and boulle will require a vice-held fretsaw frame (*Figure 10.24*). The fit of the replacement to the original design should match the quality of the original. Whilst wood marquetry is often precisely fitted, much boulle incorporates a saw kerf gap between the turtleshell and the brass. The exact fit or gap can be replicated by sawing to the inner or outer edge of outline on the template. Whilst both piercing or fret saws may be used, depending on the size of the replacement, many conservators prefer to use jeweller's piercing saw blades in a fret-saw frame. The piercing saw blades should be very high quality. The teeth should be consistently sized and spaced. Faults will be immediately apparent if the blade is viewed with a hand lens – many hobbyists' blades are very poor quality and unsuitable for reproducing marquetry and boulle. A good source for good quality blades may be jeweller's or clock maker's suppliers. As with other saws, it will facilitate cutting if two to three teeth are in contact with the surface being cut. Marquetry and boulle usually require medium to fine saw blades. If boulle is cut in a 'sandwich' the saw kerf should be matched to the original.

As a general rule, when cutting a sandwich of veneer it is important to keep the blade

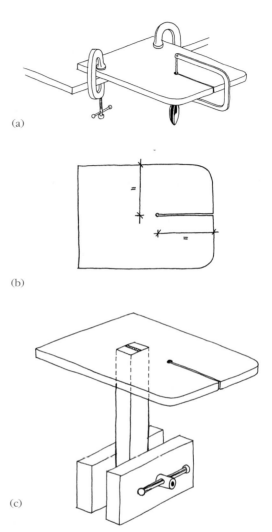

(a)

(b)

(c)

**Figure 10.24**   Using a fretsaw frame
(*a*) A fretsaw frame, made from 18 mm MDF or a similar material, cramped to a work surface
(*b*) Dimensions (=) should be slightly shorter than the full depth of the throat of the fretsaw frame
(*c*) The addition of an upright, with a through tenon into the MDF, allows working height to be adjusted in a vice

vertical. Any tendency to angle the blade will cause the parts of the design at the bottom (or top) of the sandwich to be smaller and result in a poor fit. Accuracy is essential – filing brass replacements for boulle, for example, will alter the shape and flow of the design and it is usually faster to recut an entire piece than try to file a poorly sawn replacement. Reproducing the curves on boulle and marquetry requires a relaxed and confident saw action. A blueprint for a full size marquetry donkey, usually used for cutting thick packs of veneer, can be found in Ramond (1989).

The underside of replacement brass should be cleaned, degreased and scored before it is laid. If large pieces are to be laid it may be helpful to warm them slightly before bringing into contact heat-setting animal/hide glue. Similarly sheet lead or zinc may be warmed to extend the contact time before the glue gels. More cramping pressure may be required if the metal has any undulations, whilst flat brass requires only medium pressure. After the glue has set any excess on the surface may be removed with a damp cloth. The metal elements of boullework were often finely engraved. In some cases it may be that not replacing the engraving allows the overall design to be read and easy identification of replacement areas. In other cases lack of engraving may be unacceptably obtrusive. Producing repairs to boulle work is very labour-intensive and the repair can be easily ruined by poor engraving.

Pewter was utilized in boullework and for metal stringing. Due to the toxicity of the lead in tin/lead pewter, antimony began to be substituted for lead in pewter in the eighteenth century. Modern pewter, or Britannia metal, is an alloy of tin (89%), copper (3.5%) and antimony (7.5%). Tin is amphoteric, corroding under both alkaline and acidic conditions. Care must be taken when treating pewter because it can corrode from underneath leaving a thin skin on top that abrasion will completely destroy. Replacement pewter can be cut accurately with a cutting gauge and will require a fine blade if sawn. It can be patinated with a strong solution of acetic acid, which is rinsed from the surface when the desired colour is achieved. Corbeil (1998) reported the presence of tin/mercury amalgam metal fillets on a boulle clock case. The corrosion process of such amalgams is discussed in the context of mirrors (see section 15.5).

The decorative effect of marquetry and veneer was often enhanced by the application of chemical stains or dyestuffs. Sycamore stained grey with ferrous sulphate, for example, was known as harewood. The materials used to stain wood have been considered by Baumeister *et al.* (1997), Blanchette *et al.* (1992), Roelofs (1994) and Thornton (1998b). Materials and techniques used for colour matching repairs to varnished wood are discussed in Chapter 13.

Sand shading can create a three-dimensional effect in marquetry designs. The original should be examined to determine what degree of shading is present and how far it extends on individual pieces of veneer. Fine sand is heated in a container deep enough to allow the degree of shading on the original to be reproduced without pieces of veneer touching the bottom of the pan. Experiments on a spare pieces of veneer will help gauge the right temperature, exposure time and whether the veneer should be pushed into the sand at an angle. Sand shading often results in shrinkage and it may be necessary to remoisten or soak veneer pieces to expand them. The moisture content of soaked pieces should be returned to equilibrium with ambient conditions before they are laid.

It may be helpful to lay a marquetry or boulle repair in a single operation if it consists of a discrete and complex design element, and several approaches may be used. The design element may be built up using gummed paper on the underside. When the design is complete a thin layer of glue may be applied to the upper surface and the marquetry secured in position with a thick paper placed between weighted boards and left to dry. The gummed paper can be removed by dampening the underside slightly and, when dry, gluing the repair into position. Excess glue that dries on the adjacent surface may damage the finish and it may be necessary to apply cramps, press out excess glue, release the cramps and clean up the glue before the final cramping operation, which leaves the repair cramped up for the glue to dry. Warmed glue blocks, slightly larger than the area of repair, may be isolated from the surface with Melinex/Mylar.

Alternatively, a design element may be built up using pressure-sensitive tape on the upper surface and, when complete, the repair applied straight to the substrate. This prevents slight movement that may result from the use of animal/hide glue and paper, allows slight repositioning if necessary and thus ensures a good fit. If movement within the design element may be a problem, a thin even layer of glue may be applied to the substrate and allowed to gel before the design element is applied, using hot blocks and cramps to secure it. Adhesive residue from the pressure-sensitive tape may be removed with white spirit.

The use of an isolating layer, cauls or cramps and softening blocks is essential when laying the replacement on to the original surface. Transparent Perspex/Plexiglass blocks will allow sight of the work should any adjustments be needed. A Melinex/Mylar isolating layer may result in a slightly longer curing time than if paper and wooden cauls are used. Once the glue has dried, the isolating layer and any excess glue are removed before the replacement is levelled and finished as necessary. The process of levelling the repair should *never* result in the removal of finish or material from the original surface next to the repair. Tools for levelling repairs are discussed in section 10.1.11 above.

### 10.4.6    Lifting original veneer

It may occasionally be necessary to lift an area of original veneer. One of the most common faults that causes such interventive treatment is shrinkage of the substrate (see *Figure 10.14*). It must be stressed that there is no long-term benefit, and a very real risk of causing further damage, if such treatment is undertaken without addressing the environmental conditions that caused the damage in the first place.

A traditional method of lifting marquetry or boulle involves removing the veneer piece by piece using a warm iron, sometimes in combination with a damp rag. A palette knife or other thin flat metal tool may be used to slide between substrate and veneer to help separate them. This requires patience because if an attempt is made to lift the veneer before the glue has sufficiently softened the veneer may split or break. Oyster veneers, composed entirely of end-grain, are particularly fragile. The surface finish is often irreparably damaged and in some cases varnish was removed to speed the process of veneer removal. A localized heat source, such as a heated spatula, may be useful for small areas. Once the veneer has been lifted the old glue is removed whilst still soft to prevent distortion and buckling of the veneer as it dries out. Lifted veneer is stored between flat weighted boards, with complex

design elements taped together if necessary, until needed for relaying. Plastic sheets encourage mould growth if the veneer remains damp for too long. If the veneer has been allowed to dry out and has buckled it may be necessary to spray it lightly with water, place it between two boards, gradually increasing the weight and respraying as necessary. Some restorers have resorted to complete removal of the substrate, planing or chiselling it from the back until the undersurface of the veneer was reached, before relaying the veneer onto a new substrate (see, for example, Hawkins, 1986).

Two methods that allow the removal of a marquetry or boulle surface in one piece are described by Ramond (1989) and Edwards (1997). The first, called the 'damp method', is particularly suited to boulle. It has also been used for marquetry, although the extended exposure to moisture may cause disruption of the design due to the expansion of individual elements. A wet cloth is applied to the surface, covered with plastic and left for about twelve hours, softening the adhesive and turtleshell elements, and beginning the process of separating the decorative surface from the substrate. The surface is then faced with Japanese paper and Paraloid B72, which holds the surface together whilst spatulas and alcohol are used to release areas that are still adhered to the substrate. Old glue is removed from both the underside of the boullework and the substrate. Kraft paper is stretched in the manner used to prepare paper for water colour painting. The paper is evenly wetted and taped to a rigid support board. It stretches as it dries and this prevents distortion during the next stage, when the underside of the boulle is glued to the paper. Boulle, paper and board are then placed in a press. When the boulle is flat and dry, the Japanese paper and Paraloid B72 are removed using an aromatic hydrocarbon solvent, allowing access to the boulle for replacement of losses. The boulle is removed from the rigid support board and then the upper face glued to paper as described above. Paper and glue are removed from the underside, minimizing as far as possible the length of exposure to water. The boulle may then be relaid onto a repaired substrate, glue and paper removed and the surface refinished as required.

The 'dry method' requires the removal of surface finish as the first step. Thin gauze or a similar fabric is stretched across the surface of the marquetry. A brush coat of neoprene (poly-chloroprene) glue is applied and allowed to dry for about twenty minutes. An iron or heat gun is used, at around 50–60 °C, to soften the original adhesive and, with the use of spatulas, the surface is removed in one piece. Old adhesive is removed from the underside of the marquetry and the substrate. The procedure outlined above for boulle is repeated and the neoprene glue removed using ethanol. This method may be adapted for boulle, in which case a pressure sensitive tape that resists deformation below 60 °C may be substituted for the neoprene. Care must be taken to use minimal heat as the turtleshell may otherwise be embrittled and damaged. When the boulle is transferred so that it is face down on the paper, a compressible card may be used to compensate for inherent differences in thickness of metal and turtleshell and ensure the upper surface is level.

### 10.4.7   Coatings for boulle work

The traditional coating material for boulle was a natural resin varnish, later shellac, sometimes followed by a pigmented wax polish. This slowed the diffusion of pollutants and moisture and saturated the surface of the turtleshell where it had become dull. Other surface finishes such as nitrocellulose and Paraloid B72 have also been used. A 7.5% w/v solution of Paraloid B72 in diacetone alcohol: ethanol 3:1 is suitable for brush application on boulle. Differential corrosion may become a problem where there are holidays in the coating or as it degrades. A clean and uncontaminated surface is essential for such coatings to be effective. Corrosion inhibitors and coatings are discussed more fully in the metals section (15.3).

### 10.4.8   Stringing and metal inlay

Stringing may be purchased from specialist veneer suppliers but may need thicknessing to match the original. A jig, such as that illustrated in *Figure 10.25*, may be used for the purpose. Stringing may be laid using pressure from above (e.g. with a small veneer or Warrington pattern hammer) and the side simultaneously (e.g. with the rounded end of a scalpel handle) working over a length until the glue has gelled.

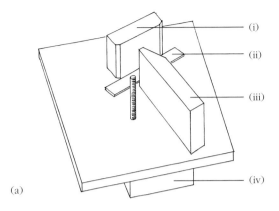

(a)

(b)

**Figure 10.25**  A jig for thicknessing replacement stringing
(*a*) A chisel plane is positioned against block (iii). The plane illustrated is a Record three-in-one plane with the bullnose removed. Block (i) functions as a fence when the stringing is pulled through the jig; (ii) is a thin piece of Formica or similar material; the block on the underside (iv) allows the jig to be held in a vice
(*b*) The plane blade is inverted and its depth adjusted to produce stringing of the required dimension. Stringing is pulled through the jig in the direction indicated by the arrow

Alternatively, veneer pins or gummed tape may be used to hold stringing tight to the adjacent veneer. Excess glue should be removed when gelled by running a chisel along the edge – this is far less time-consuming than trying to remove the excess once the glue has set. Some patterned bandings are still produced whilst others will have to be made up to match. Although they may initially appear complex they are usually fairly straightforward, if a little time-consuming, to make up from scratch. Bennett (1990) has described the use of a jig to set the angles and create the banding in stages.

There are several forms of metal inlay in furniture. Metal inlay was popular in England and the USA during the neo-classical revival at the beginning of the nineteenth century. Some designers and makers are particularly associated with inlaid metal decoration, including George Bullock and Charles Honore Lannuier. Thomas Hope (1807) referred to the early nineteenth century Parisian practice of stamping metal and wood together to produce repetitive designs that were then applied to furniture and small objects such as boxes. He noted 'The metal ornament, and the ground of stained wood into which it is inserted, being, there, stamped together, and cut out, through dint of the same single *mechanical* process, they are always sure of fitting each other to the greatest degree of nicety.' The use of lasers to reproduce such inlay is discussed by Minor (1996). The stamping process often left the edges on the underside slightly rounded over (Hawkins, 1986).

Brass may be inlaid into fluting. If the brass has been lost a replacement can be made by making a positive and negative mould and then cramping brass sheet between them to shape it to the fluting. Once the edges of the brass have been filed to fit the flute on the object, the negative mould may be used as a cramping jig.

Metal stringing often stands proud of the surface where the substrate has shrunk due to low RH. The traditional restoration treatment has been to remove original material so that the stringing fits the current dimensions. Other options are to support the stringing in place or to lay it with an overlap. Techniques for flattening creased metal, preparation and adhesives for laying it are discussed in the context of boulle (section 10.4.3).

## 10.5  Moulding and casting

In furniture conservation, moulding and casting is most commonly used to produce copies or replicas of existing objects, parts or surfaces. Moulds are negative matrices from which posi-

tive casts identical to the original may be produced. The materials used for casting positives may be more chemically and physically stable than the original and are often easily distinguished from them, thus fulfilling ethical criteria for conservation treatments. Casting materials used to replace components should be physically and chemically stable, compatible with original material and not impose additional stresses on the object. Information on techniques of moulding and casting is widely available and thus is considered only briefly here, whilst the conservation aspects of these processes and the range of materials available is emphasized. Information on casting and moulding can be found in specialist publications such as Clark (1971), Larsen (1981) or booklets produced by manufacturers or suppliers of casting materials such as Alec Tiranti Ltd (UK) (1990, 1995) or the Polytek Development Corporation (USA) (1992). References in the conservation literature include Chase and Zycherman (1981), Minney (1994), Newton and Davison (1989), Thornton (1991a) and Waters (1983).

Moulding and casting procedures are used extensively in restoration work for the replacement of missing elements because they are often easier and faster than using original materials and fabrication techniques, for example carving replacements for missing wooden or ivory elements. In addition to making repairs, conservators in museum practice are sometimes called upon to produce replicas of objects for study collections, or to oversee the production of replicas for sale in museum shops. In either case a working knowledge of moulding and casting is required to prevent damage to originals. Different materials and techniques may be required for these various applications.

### 10.5.1  General procedure

Moulding and casting can be thought of as the interaction between three categories of materials: moulding materials for the production of negatives, casting materials for the production of positives (including fillers and colorants) and release agents and coatings to allow pattern-to-mould and mould-to-cast separation without damage. The object to be copied is generally referred to as a pattern. The procedures involved in preparing a copy of an original via an intermediate mould will require the following steps: selection of moulding material, selection of casting material, preparation of object or pattern from which the replica is to be prepared, taking of mould impression, preparation of the mould for casting the replica, casting and finishing.

## 10.5.2   Selection of materials

Selection of materials for moulding and casting requires consideration of several inter-related factors. First the material of the original object – which materials would be compatible for casting a replacement? Secondly what type of mould is necessary – is the piece to be cast large or small, simple or complex, undercut or detailed? Will it be necessary to reproduce large flat areas, to use piece moulds or to cast replacements in situ? Finally, of the materials that are compatible with the original object, which are also compatible with the mould making material best suited to the job?

The method that is to be used to adhere or attach the replacement part to the original may also affect the selection of the casting material. There should be no deleterious chemical reaction between the moulding material and the artefact, pattern or casting material. Materials with a high water content, such as wet plaster, should not be used against moisture-sensitive surfaces unless an adequate moisture barrier can be provided. The variety of potential chemical or physical interactions between materials is great and it may be necessary to test procedures before using them on original artefacts or laboriously produced patterns.

Moulding and casting materials should conform well to, and retain shape and detail of, the surface whilst releasing easily from both the artefact and mould. The form in which the material is used influences these properties. Materials in liquid form are more difficult to confine in use than plastic solids such as dental impression compounds, oven-hardening PVC gels such as Fimo and Sculpey, Plasticene, or composition. The main advantage of semi-solid impression compounds is the short duration of exposure to an original surface. The graininess or particle size within the material will affect detail. Most thermoplastics shrink somewhat as they cool. In a given application it will be clear

whether the use of a liquid or semi-solid paste will be more convenient.

Moulding and casting materials should be usable at temperatures that do not damage the artefact, pattern or mould and should not generate excessive heat during cure, which might cause damage. Some thermoplastics polymers, including waxes and PVC, have to be melted and used hot. Clearly these cannot be used where the pattern cannot tolerate high temperatures, as is the case with many artefacts. Plaster, epoxies and unsaturated polyester resins may generate significant heat during cure depending on the exact formulation used, thickness, ambient temperature and other circumstances of use. If the final cast is required in metal then the moulding material must be chosen to withstand the pouring temperature of the metal.

Moulding and casting materials may present some health and safety hazards. These include the toxicity of thermosetting polymers, their catalysts and hardeners, risk of skin burns from exothermic reactions or hot melt materials, risk of fire from waxes, and risk of dust and fumes arising during processing. *It is the responsibility of the conservator to be fully aware of the hazards presented and to take adequate precautionary measures.*

There is a wide range of both thermoplastic and thermosetting materials available, some of which are listed in *Table 10.4*. The letters M and C in the table indicate that the material is used for moulding or casting respectively. No material is ideal in all respects and so one must be carefully chosen to suit the requirements of a particular job. Cost, for example, may be a factor for large volume jobs. In many cases the same material might be used to create a pattern, make a mould or cast a replica.

Wax has been used since antiquity for modelling, moulding and casting and various more or less complex recipes using natural waxes, resins and oils exist in historical literature. Synthetic microcrystalline waxes have largely replaced natural ingredients because they are available in hardness and melting ranges that will copy virtually any historic formula while being cheaper and more stable. Although waxes can be warmed and made pliable both for modelling and press-moulding purposes, they may also be used in fluid form. They can be painted or poured over a surface

**Table 10.4** Moulding and casting materials

| Material | Use | Temperature effects | Chemical effects | Health and safety | Dimensional change | Permanence | Cost | Notes |
|---|---|---|---|---|---|---|---|---|
| Alginates | M | Gel/liquefy at low temperatures c.40 °C | High water content | Non-toxic | None on gelling | Very low – shrink and warp on drying | Moderate | Often used for life moulding and architectural details; gives excellent detail but often requires a secondary plaster mould |
| Animal glue (gelatine) | M | Used warm. May form chill wrinkles | Moist during application and use | Non-toxic, safe in use | Little initial shrinkage | Low – shrink as they dry | Low | Has been used on sculptures that are to be cast in bronze |
| Hot melt PVC | M | Used at 120–170 °C | Avoid contact with metals | Burns, toxic gases | Some shrinkage | Moderate to good | Moderate | |
| Non-hardening clay Plasticene, Plastilene | M | Soften markedly as temperature increases | May contain sulphur; avoid metals, Si rubber | None | None | Poor | Low to moderate | |
| PVC gels | M | Used at room temperature but can be oven-hardened c.130 °C | None apparent | Toxic fumes. Skin absorption of vinyl monomer | < 1% on hardening | Good | Moderate to high | Good for squeeze impressions |
| Silicone rubber | M | Variable – some exothermic, some with high temperature resistance | Sulphur inhibits cure. Acetic acid may be produced | Catalyst components are toxic, harmful or irritant and may cause burns in contact with skin | Less than 0.6% shrinkage on cure | High | Very high | Release agent should be used between mould/object and may be necessary between mould/cast. RTV (room temperature vulcanizing) are cold cure; additives allow thixotropic non-drip mixtures to be formulated |
| Water clay | M | Very high temperature resistance when dry | Moist during application; inert when dry | Non-toxic, safe in use | 10–20% on drying | Green clay is fragile | Very low | |
| Plaster | M, C | Exothermic | Moisture evolved during setting; inert when dry | Burns, dust | Expands by up to 1% on hardening | Very good | Low | |
| Waxes | M, C | Used hot, temperature dependent on type of wax used | Mostly inert, especially microcrystalline types | Fire hazard, burns | Slight to moderate shrinkage on drying | Very good if kept cool | Moderate | Good release from oiled surfaces, wet water clay; plaster should be soaked in hot water before use |
| Epoxies | C | Exothermic cure | | Toxic | Less than 0.5% | Good when cured | High | Release agent essential |
| Polyesters | C | Exothermic cure | Cure inhibited by some metallic pigments, e.g. cobalt | Toxic by inhalation, ingestion and skin contact. Catalyst can cause blindness | 12% shrinkage, reduced with filler coat | | | Release agent essential |

and capture a high degree of detail. Waxes release well from oiled surfaces, wet water clay and thoroughly soaked gypsum plaster. If a plaster mould is to be used for a wax cast, it is best soaked in hot water before application of wax. The water will act as a release agent and heat will eliminate chill wrinkles. Waxes, especially microcrystalline types, are chemically inert but cannot be used in liquid form against temperature sensitive surfaces. Slight to moderate shrinkage occurs upon cooling. Permanence is very good if stored below softening temperatures and cost is moderate. They present few health hazards but melting waxes do pose a potential fire hazard.

Water clays are another ancient category of inexpensive moulding and casting materials. They are useful in modelling patterns and in taking quick squeeze impression moulds from patterns. They become progressively firmer as water is lost, which may be desirable when refining models to a high degree. The shrinkage of roughly 10–20% on drying can be exploited to scale down a model in size. Dried green clay is very fragile and water-soluble but otherwise inert. Clays cannot be used against water-sensitive surfaces but when thoroughly dry they will tolerate high temperatures, so molten metals and polymers can be poured against them. Health hazards resulting from breathing of clay and glaze dusts and breathing or ingestion of toxic metals in glazes have been reported but these problems are unlikely to be encountered in small-scale moulding and casting.

Non-hardening clays, also known as plastilene and Plasticene, have been mixed with oils, waxes and other non-drying materials to keep them permanently pliable. They are used in the same way as water clays for modelling patterns and taking impressions, but they do not dry or shrink. Various firmness grades are available and firmer clays should be chosen for more detailed work. These clays can be made softer or harder by manipulation of temperature. Some of them contain sulphur, which will interact with metal objects and inhibit the cure of silicone rubber, but sulphur-free varieties are also available. Oils present in these clays may stain porous objects. Though they have poor permanence, there are generally no known health risks associated with these materials. Cost is low to moderate.

Alginates are polysaccharides extracted from various species of marine algae (seaweed). They form hydro-colloidal gels in water that are similar to those formed by animal glues. Agar-agar is one such alginate and is also sometimes called 'Japanese isinglass'. Alginates have been used in moulding since about the mid-twentieth century, particularly in the formulation of dental moulding compounds. Most alginates are available as powders that gel rapidly when mixed with water. Agar is normally dissolved in hot water and allowed to cool and gel. It can then be reheated and will liquefy at around 42 °C. It is the principal ingredient in 'moulages', which are used to mould human flesh, because of its low gelling temperature. Alginates may be difficult to use because of rapid gelling and associated air bubbles and wrinkles. Alginate gels have a high water content and cannot be used against water-sensitive materials. Only plaster and low melting temperature waxes can be cast in alginate moulds. Dimensions do not change on gelling but alginate moulds shrink and warp radically as they dry. Alginate moulds must therefore be used immediately and cannot be kept for any length of time. They do not retain detail well and are not suited for multiple castings. Alginates are non toxic and their cost is moderate.

Animal/hide glues and gelatines were the first materials used to produce flexible moulds that could be stretched and released from undercuts. They were used for this purpose in the nineteenth and early twentieth centuries until largely replaced by synthetic elastomers. The properties of concentrated viscous glue solutions could be manipulated by the additions of materials such as glycerine to retard drying/shrinkage and sugar to plasticize the mixture. Glue moulds were poured at roughly body temperature. They cooled rapidly (depending on volume) and were prone to form chill wrinkles unless poured very smoothly. Glue moulds do not shrink appreciably upon gelling but do so as they dry out. They cannot be used in contact with water sensitive surfaces but are non-toxic and safe in all respects. Gelatine moulds were normally surface hardened with alum, formaldehyde (formalin) or tannic acid to prolong their usefulness that in any case was rather short due to surface blurring, contraction and distortion as they dried. Reproduction of detail is only fair due to rapid gelling, though cost is low.

Gypsum plaster is one of the most ancient moulding and casting materials. It generally consists of calcium sulphate hemihydrate ($CaSO_4.\frac{1}{2}H_2O$) prepared from gypsum (calcium sulphate dihydrate) by heating at about 145 °C. When mixed with water, the plaster rehydrates to $CaSO_4.2H_2O$ and recrystallizes, forming a dense network of interlocking needle-like crystals as it does so. This is an exothermic reaction resulting in a set plaster that hardens more fully as excess water evaporates. Gypsum plasters are actually a family of related materials because of the variety of ways they can be modified in manufacture and use to yield different setting rates, final hardness and other properties. This means that there is considerable choice in terms of working characteristics. Plasters with different setting times are available and those with faster setting times result in a greater temperature build up. Most plasters show expansion in setting between 0.05 to 1.0% by volume, though this may be reduced by the addition of a small quantity of ethanol before the plaster is poured. Plaster formulations can also be made to shrink slightly. Plaster is inexpensive and relatively safe in use but burns have resulted from very quick setting plasters and plaster dust should not be breathed, especially where silica has been used in the formulation. Optimum and reproducible results are only obtained if ingredients are carefully weighed, following the instructions in the manufacturer's literature. Plaster should be well sieved before being sprinkled into water until a cone has been formed. When this has become saturated with water the plaster mix is gently stirred to a creamy consistency, as free from air bubbles as possible. As with animal/hide glues and gelatines, additives such as glue, borax or dextrin have been used to manipulate the final working properties. Set and dried plaster is highly inert and may be considered permanent. The surface may be sealed with a coating such as shellac, followed by a suitable release agent, before the mould is used. Plaster cannot be used against moisture sensitive surfaces. There is a large body of literature on plaster and plaster casting techniques, including manufacturer's technical literature, which should be consulted when using this material.

Thermoplastic polymers have been used for various applications in moulding and casting. Historically they have been used to produce rigid moulds. Decorative plasterers have used mixtures of waxes, resins and fillers to produce moulds for repeat patterns. Many nineteenth-century moulds for composition ornaments were made of pitch mixtures enclosed in a strong frame and squeezed over an oiled carving while hot and pliable. Gutta percha was also used as a mould material. Modern synthetic resins can also be used in this way. Dental impression compounds have been used in picture frame restoration to make small squeeze moulds for the replacement of lost composition ornament.

Poly(vinyl chloride) hot-melt rubbers, which melt between 120 °C and 170 °C, have been used extensively by commercial mould makers for large flexible moulds. Their melting range means they cannot be used where the original artefact cannot tolerate such temperatures. Like most thermoplastics, they shrink somewhat as they cool but have moderate to good permanence and are relatively inexpensive. PVC hot melts release toxic gases when hot and fume extraction is essential. They should not be used in contact with metals.

PVC gels are available as modelling compounds in toy and hobby shops under trade names such as Fimo, Sculpey etc. They consist of colloidal particles of polyvinyl chloride mixed with a plasticizer. The plasticizer diffuses into the PVC when it is heated and fuses the mass together. These compounds are very useful for squeeze impressions because they have an unlimited working time and capture a high degree of detail. They may be used at room temperature, for high fidelity one-off castings in plaster, or oven-hardened at approximately 130 °C. There are no apparent chemical interactions, dimensional change is less than 1.0% upon hardening and permanence is good, but cost is moderate to high. Toxic gas is released if the material is overheated and fume extraction should be used whilst it is hardening. Unpolymerized vinyl monomer may be absorbed through the skin.

A wide variety of thermosetting polymers is available for moulding and casting including epoxies, polyesters and polyurethanes for rigid castings, and polysulphides, polyurethanes and silicone rubbers for flexible moulds. These materials, used extensively by sculptors and craftspeople, are highly variable both in chemistry and properties. Detailed general information on their chemistry and properties is available in a variety of published sources. However, new materials are developed and old formulations become unavailable with such regularity that current manufacturer's literature may be most useful and will generally yield an appropriate polymer for virtually any purpose. It may be necessary to pre-test to ensure good results. Generally, slight shrinkage occurs upon curing and all of these polymers are toxic to some degree by inhalation, ingestion or skin contact. Their successful use requires careful measuring and mixing of ingredients. Heat is generated by many of these materials as they cure. Slow curing polymers can dissipate this heat over a long period of time but faster curing ones may generate enough heat when used in large quantities to destroy both the polymers and the pattern. Epoxies and polyesters are particularly prone to such catastrophic 'meltdown'. A slow setting resin should be used for large pours. Alternatively, faster setting resins may be used in multiple thin layers or even chilled while they undergo initial cure to help dissipate the heat. Barrier layers and/or release agents must be used with thermosetting polymers to prevent damage to patterns and artefacts and to ensure clean release.

Most thermoset materials have limited shelf lives that may be prolonged by refrigeration. The cured polymers generally maintain their mechanical properties. Polysulphide rubbers are the least permanent of the elastomeric compounds and become sticky and unusable after a few years. In contrast, silicone rubbers, particularly those that utilize platinum catalysts, are essentially permanent. All these materials are several times more expensive than traditional materials such as clay, glue and plaster. Cost varies according to the specific compound and the quantity in which it is purchased.

Silicone rubbers have been used extensively by conservators for mould making because they are easy to use, reproduce very fine detail such as wood grain or fabric texture and can be reused for a large number of multiple casts. Silicone rubbers release easily from many surfaces, thus manufacturers' literature often suggests that the use of a release agent is

unnecessary. Silicone rubbers release low molecular weight silicone compounds, which will alter the appearance of porous or unsealed surfaces (Maish, 1994). In addition, residues of these compounds may prevent accurate material analysis in the future. Good conservation practice therefore requires the use of a barrier layer, such as wax, and in addition it may be necessary to seal porous materials. Brückle *et al.* (1999) have discussed the use of cyclododecane in combination with a layer of methyl cellulose or gum arabic for protecting sensitive surfaces during mould-making. Silicone rubbers will not cure in contact with sulphur-containing materials such as many non-hardening clays. They are expensive but the cost is often justified by their performance. The mould may be reinforced if desired by an open weave cloth such as mutton cloth or scrim. If necessary, silicone rubber can be coloured using acrylic/PVAC polymers such as the Maestro range, although adding fillers will reduce mechanical strength. Some flexible silicone rubbers may be appropriate for making moulds where the original has deep undercuts. Silicone rubbers with the consistency of a firm modelling clay are available from dental suppliers and are very useful for flexible press moulds.

A variety of silicone rubbers are available from suppliers to meet particular moulding needs (see, for example, *Table 10.5*). Although cheaper than platinum catalysts, tin catalysts are generally less archivally stable. RTV-11 is a good example of an easy to use, general purpose silicone rubber for mould-making. It is white, free-flowing and may be used for originals where there is no deep undercut. It is suitable for casting low melt metals, including pewter. Increasing the proportion of catalyst will shorten pot life and cure time. Additives are available that allow manipulation of the working properties of the rubber. One of these, called 'Thixo additive', may be used with T20 and T28 to give a rubber that may be applied with a brush, does not trap air and does not slump.

Polyester resins are often used as a casting material in conjunction with a silicone rubber mould. They can also be used as a moulding material that may be reinforced with glass fibre. There are usually three components: the resin, a catalyst such as methyl ethyl ketone peroxide, and an accelerator such as cobalt

**Table 10.5**   Comparative properties of four silicone rubbers

|  | T20 | T28 | RTV-11 | RTV-101 |
|---|---|---|---|---|
| Colour | Grey | Grey | White | Red |
| Grade | Medium soft | Standard | Firm | Hard |
| Specific gravity | 1.25 | 1.29 | 1.18 | 1.5 |
| Consistency | Pourable | Pourable | Very pourable | Pourable |
| Viscosity cps/sec | 26 000 ± 4000 | 27 000 ± 4000 | 11 000 | 25 000 |
| Shore A hardness | 16 ± 3 | 25 ± 2 | 41 | 55 |
| Elongation at break % | 650 ± 100 | 350 ± 100 | 186 | 150 |
| Linear shrinkage | 0.60% | 0.60% | 0.60% | 0.20% |
| Tear strength N/mm | 21 | 20 | 3 | 4.5 MPa |
| Catalyst | T6 catalyst 5% | T6 catalyst 5% | Dibutyl tin dilaurate 0.5% | Dibutyl tin dilaurate 0.5% |
| Pot life | 100 minutes | 100 minutes | 1.5 hours | 48 minutes |
| Demould | 24 hours | 24 hours | 24 hours | 5.5 hours |

These values are a guide only and are not specifications.
*Source:* Information courtesy of Alec Tiranti Ltd (UK)

napthenate, which in some cases is premixed into the supplied resin. Resins usually cure best at around 20 °C (68 °F). Temperatures above or below this will speed or slow curing respectively. The cure of polyesters is inhibited by many metallic elements such as cobalt and cadmium, found in some pigments (e.g. cobalt blue and cadmium red) or as a component in metallo-organic dyes (e.g. Orasol dyes). Shrinkage of up to 12% is common, though this can be reduced by up to half if fillers are used. Polyester catalyst can cause blindness by even brief eye contact. Fume extraction or personal respirators, gloves and goggles are recommended while mixing components and extraction may be needed until the resin has cured.

Epoxy resins are often used by conservators as a casting material in conjunction with a silicone rubber mould. They have the advantages of minimal shrinkage (0.5%), low odour and set at room temperature. Pattern-makers often use bulked or pigmented epoxies for casting. Air bubbles can be avoided by pre-wetting with unbulked adhesive. A small puddle of unbulked resin may be poured into the deepest part of the mould or pattern and then the bulked resin poured slowly and evenly into the puddle. The unbulked resin will pre-wet and avoid the formation of air bubbles. Unbulked resin will rise to the surface of the cast where it will provide the cast with a smooth finish. Low viscosity epoxies can be used in conjunction with silk ribbon or glass cloth to laminate repairs, build up or reinforce curved areas. The appearance and surface properties of epoxy

casts can be manipulated by the addition of pigments and fillers. A variety of formulations of epoxy resins are available and it may be useful to contact the manufacturer (e.g. Ciba Geigy) to match a product to a given requirement. Epoxies bulked with phenolic microballoons and foaming epoxies that generate bubbles as they cure both result in low weight casts with the general density of wood. As with polyester resins, the hardener or catalyst presents a health and safety hazard.

Other materials used for moulding and casting include latex, polyacrylate resin (Larsen, 1981), dental impression compounds (Chase and Zycherman, 1981) and Vinamold (Alec Tiranti Ltd, 1990). Small items may also be cast from materials such as Paraloid resins or PVACs with fillers such as whiting or microballoons, although such putties will exhibit shrinkage that is proportionate to the solvent carrier content.

### 10.5.3   Release agents

The nature and material of the original will define what preparation is needed before a mould can be taken. Most moulding and casting materials require a compatible release agent to allow clean separation from object or mould. Release agents should be compatible with, and removable from, the original and should not damage it or its surface coating. Porous surfaces may need to be sealed before a release agent is applied. Release agents must have a lower surface energy than the mould making material. Traditional release agents include non-drying oils such as almond oil, or a 2% wax mixture in a hydrocarbon solvent. Other parting agents are produced commercially and supplied for specific moulding materials.

### 10.5.4 Making a mould

The complexity of the piece being cast and the number of repeats required will determine the type of mould. It may be necessary to take a mould from another part of the object or surviving decorative elements. A simple low relief detail, such as a carved husk, may require only a simple press mould in Plasticene. The Plasticene mould may be chilled slightly to make it a little stiffer before pouring the casting material into it. Other shapes may require a one piece open sided mould whereas more complex or undercut shapes may require flexible moulds, closed piece moulds or both. Descriptions of these processes may be found in Larsen (1981), Thornton (1991c) and Alec Tiranti Ltd (1999) among others. When using very flexible moulding materials it may be necessary to support them with a rigid backing, such as plaster or epoxy, to prevent distortion. A support casing may be necessary to hold piece parts in position whilst casting.

### 10.5.5 Colorants and fillers

Colorants and fillers may be used to match the colour, density, physical or optical properties of the cast surface to the original. They may be applied in three ways – by dusting the surface of the mould, by mixing with the casting material or by applying to the cast once it has set. They may affect the cure if added to the casting material and it may be necessary to test first. Experimentation will also help determine which of these method/s will give the best results for matching a replacement to the original. Fillers reduce the volume of casting material and may thus reduce cost. They may be used to impart increased stiffness but may also reduce mechanical strength.

Mineral fillers such as fumed silica (e.g. Cab-O-Sil or Aerosil) are often used as thickening agents. They will increase the opacity of a clear casting material resulting in a translucent cast.

Dry pigments may be used to tint a casting material but often need to be sieved before use. The ability of a casting liquid to wet onto the pigment will affect their use. Some pigments are available pre-ground into a vehicle compatible with the casting liquid, such as polyester and Araldite epoxy colours. In either case the pigment should be mixed with a small amount of resin until a smooth paste is achieved, then further resin added. Dyes may be used to create transparency, though organo-metallic dyes that contain cobalt, e.g. some in the Orasol range by Ciba–Giegy, may inhibit the cure of polyester. Other dyes may be rendered colourless by components in the casting material (e.g. polyester).

Metal powders or flakes, such as aluminium, various alloys of brass, bronze and iron, allow the simulation of a metallic appearance for hardware components. The metal particles must be uncontaminated by oil or grease. The powder or flakes may be mixed into the casting liquid, used in a thin gel top coat or dusted onto the surface of the mould. Silicone rubber moulds retain a slightly tacky surface, so the metal particles adhere to the surface. Metal flakes have a high degree of metallic sheen, which spherical particles lack. When mixed into polyester resin, roughly equal volumes of resin and metal powder may be used. Aluminium powder should not be brought into contact with halogenated (chlorinated) hydrocarbons and should not be mixed with polyester hardener (organic peroxide). Thornton (1991c) has discussed the replication of stamped brasses using moulding and casting techniques.

### 10.5.6 Finishing

The materials used for finishing will depend on the material used for the cast. Porous cast materials, such as plaster, will require sizing or sealing before they can be finished. Texture not provided by the mould may be simulated in some cases by treating the surface of the cast with solvent. Low surface energy materials such as polyester will rule out the use of water colours, but acrylic emulsion paints stick very well. Materials used for general retouching work may be effective. These include acrylics, binding media such as Paraloid and conservation grade PVACs mixed with dry pigment. As is the case with retouching wood, the use of dry pigment colours can result in a surface that appears opaque and lifeless.

Gilding may be carried out using traditional methods where this is compatible with the substrate. In other cases a solvent or solvent mixture may be used to slightly soften the surface of the casting before applying gold leaf (Thornton, 1991a). Wrinkles may form if the solvent causes excessive softening. The solvent may be sprayed on to prevent physically disturbing the surface. The gilding may be toned once the resin has hardened again.

### 10.5.7   Gilders composition

Composition was made traditionally from a mixture of resin, linseed oil, animal/hide glue and whiting although other materials such as lead fillers, paper, starch pastes, pitch, eggs and varnish have also been incorporated on occasion. Freshly made composition is pliable when warm. It was forced into reverse carved wooden moulds and removed whilst still flexible. Although a recipe for composition is described below, there are many other recipes for this material, such as those published by Wetherall (1991) and Thornton (1985, 1991a).

#### Ingredients
130 g  (or millilitres) of water
 20 g  glycerol (glycerine is the same thing)
 20 g  Chardin rabbit skin glue (in plaque form, broken up with a hammer)
 70 g  ground animal/hide glue
 20 g  raw linseed oil
 50 g  crushed rosin
600 g  gilder's whiting (approximately)

The mix of glues has been determined by trial and error to yield the best 'gel strength' for good working characteristics. Different glues will have different gel strength and cannot be substituted without changing the properties of the mixture. Composition made entirely of rabbit skin glue will gel too quickly and be difficult to mix and work with, while composition made entirely of the weaker animal/hide glue will fail to set when it cools, staying soft in the middle and forming a wrinkled skin on the surface. Glycerol has a moisture buffering effect, and will tend to make the hardened composition a little softer and less flint-like

than it would be without it. The amount of linseed oil is barely sufficient to melt the rosin, and form a thick oil–resin varnish. Linseed oil oxidizes and shrinks with time, and this recipe limits this potential problem. Barium sulphate can be added to replace some of the whiting if the compo will be used on important pieces that might be radiographed in the future. This ingredient will add X-ray density and make fills distinguishable from original material.

#### Mixing
Soak and melt the glue in a container. The rabbit skin glue must be soaked overnight before the ground glue is added, or the ground glue will absorb all of the water while the rabbit skin glue fails to swell at all. Warm the swelled glues in a double boiler (e.g. a glass jar covered with foil) until the hot glue is completely smooth.

In another container (a disposable coffee can is ideal) melt the rosin into the oil. This cannot be done in a double boiler because it will not get hot enough, but it must be stirred and attended constantly on a hot-plate surface until the rosin has completely melted and dissolved into the oil.

The glue mixture and the oil–resin mixture are then mixed together by pouring a thin stream of the oil–resin into the glue while stirring vigorously. A few spoons of whiting can be added after the initial mixing to help the ingredients combine into a smooth 'batter'.

The batter is then poured into the cratered pile of whiting and mixed with a putty knife until the ingredients are well enough incorporated so that the mixture can be picked up and kneaded by hand. The compo should be kneaded vigorously and quickly to mix the ingredients well. The material will probably seem crumbly and unpromising before hand kneading is done, but will become smooth and pliable if mixed and kneaded vigorously. A warmed marble slab may be used for mixing but any smooth and cleanable surface can be used if the compo is put into the microwave oven periodically and taken back up to a good mixing temperature (about 45–50 °C/110–120 °F). There is no exact amount of whiting required, but the finished compo should be very smooth, pliable and non-sticky. A well-bulked compo will shrink less than one with insufficient whiting.

The compo can be rolled out into a long strip about a quarter of an inch thick (~6 mm), and 3–4 inches wide (75–100 mm), allowed to cool and cut into squares. These can be wrapped in damp paper towels and re-warmed in a microwave oven for immediate use. Glue that is kept wet and refrigerated will continue to hydrolyse and lose strength, altering properties as a result. If medium- or long-term storage is required, the squares can be wrapped in foil, dated, placed in a zip-lock bag and frozen for up to a year.

Compo was traditionally used in conjunction with a rigid mould. The mould was brushed with a little oil (e.g. almond or linseed oil) to act as a release agent. The warm soft compo was pressed into the mould. Sufficient compo was used to ensure that there was enough to fill the depths of the carving and some over to leave proud. A wetted board was placed over the top of the compo in the mould, and the board and mould placed under a screw press. Pressure was applied to push the compo into all the recesses of the mould. Excess compo was compressed between the mould and the board. The sandwich was then removed from the press, turned upside-down, and the mould carefully removed from the compo cast. The compo, still attached to the board, was left to harden for a few minutes and then the ornament sliced from the excess compo with a sharp knife. Excess compo on the board could be scraped off, melted down and re-used. Excess is trimmed away and the compo cast may be adhered to the support with a strong thin gesso or PVAC glue.

Compo ornament is very often gilded. Burnished water gilding will require the application of two or three coats of gesso and bole, though care must be taken not to clog detail of the ornament. Oil gilding requires the surface be sealed before the application of oil size. Highlights of the compo ornament were often picked out in burnished water gilding whilst other areas were oil gilded.

## Bibliography

Alcouffe, D. (1977) *The Restorer's Handbook of Furniture*, Van Nostrand Reinhold

Alec Tiranti Ltd (1990) *Vinamold: Flexible Mould Making*, Alec Tiranti Ltd

Alec Tiranti Ltd (1995) *The Polyester Resin Booklet*, Alec Tiranti Ltd

Alec Tiranti Ltd (1999) *The Silicone Rubber Booklet*, Alec Tiranti Ltd

Augerson, C. (1999) Hydlar ZF™, a nylon-Kevlar™ product suitable as a reinforcing material for wooden objects, in P. van Duin, D. van Loosdrecht and D. Wheeler (eds), *Proceedings of the Fourth International Symposium on Wood and Furniture Conservation*, Rijksmuseum/VeRes, Amsterdam, pp. 1–6

Baldi, R., Lisini, G.G., Martell, C. and Martell, S. (1992) *La Cornice Fiorentina E Senese: storia e techniche di restauro*, Alinea, Florence

Barclay, R.L. and Grattan, D.W. (1987) A silicone rubber/microballoon mixture for gap filling in wooden objects, in ICOM Committee for Conservation, Preprints 8th Triennial Meeting, Sydney

Barclay, R. and Mathias, C. (1989) An epoxy/microballoon mixture for gap filling in wooden objects, *JAIC*, 28, 31–42

Baumeister, M., Boonstra, J., Blanchette, R.A., Fischer, C-H. and Schorsch, D. (1997) Stained burl veneer on historic furniture, in K. Walch and J. Koller, *Baroque and Rococo Lacquers*, Arbeitshefte des Bayerischen Landesamtes für Denkmalpflege

Bennett, M. (1990) *Discovering and Restoring Antique Furniture*, Cassell

Blanchette, R.A., Wilmering, A.M. and Baumeister, M. (1992) The use of green stained wood caused by the fungus Chlorociboria in intarsia masterpieces from the 15th century, *Holzforschung*, 46 (3), 225–32

Boucher, N. (1995) La rehydration des colles anciennes, *L'Estampille l'objet d'art*, 296, Nov.

Boucher, N. (1999) Polyethylene glycol. (PEG) in furniture conservation, in P. van Duin, D. van Loosdrecht and D. Wheeler (eds), *Proceedings of the Fourth International Symposium on Wood and Furniture Conservation*, Rijksmuseum/VeRes, Amsterdam, pp. 13–21

Brückle, I., Thornton, J., Nichols K. and Strickler, G. (1999) Cyclododecane: Technical note on some uses in paper and objects conservation, *JAIC*, 38, 162–75

Buchanan, G. (1985) *The Illustrated Handbook of Furniture Restoration*, Batsford

Buck, S. (1990) A study of the properties of commercial liquid hide glue and traditional hot glue in response to changes in relative humidity and temperature, in AIC Wooden Artifacts Group, Conference Papers, Richmond, Virginia

Callède, B. and Ostrup, A. (1984) Study of adhesives for marquetry, in *Adhesives and Consolidants*, Conference Preprints, IIC, pp. 129–32

Chase, W.T. and Zycherman, L.A. (1981) Choosing dental plasters for use in the conservation workshop, *JAIC*, 21(1), 65–67

Clark, C.D. (1971) *Moulding and Casting*, Standard Arts Press

Considine, B.B., Jamet, M. and Østrup, A. (1990) The conservation of two pieces of boulle marquetry furniture in the collection of the J. Paul Getty Museum, in ICOM Committee for Conservation, Preprints 9th Triennial Meeting, Dresden, II, pp. 831–4

Corbeil, M-C. (1998) A note on the use of tin amalgams in marquetry, *Studies in Conservation*, 43, 265–9

Dardes, K. and Roth, A. (1998) *The Structural Conservation of Panel Paintings*, Symposium Proceedings, Getty Conservation Institute

Dorge, V. (1992) Photographic reproductions used to replace decorative veneer losses on a small sewing box, in AIC Wooden Artifacts Group, Conference Papers, Buffalo

Dowling, J. (1999) Removal and installation of mirrors for the British Galleries, *V&A Conservation Journal*, 33, 8–9

Edwards, R. (1987) *The Shorter Dictionary of English Furniture*, Spring Books/Hamlyn

Edwards, W.P. (1997) Current trends in conservation of marquetry surfaces, in AIC Wooden Artifacts Group, Conference Papers, San Diego

Florian, M. (1982) Anomalous wood structure: a reason for failure of peg from the ozette site, in *Proceedings of the ICOM Waterlogged Wood Working Group Conference*, Ottawa, 1981

Gilbert, C. (1978) *Furniture at Temple Newsam House and Lotherton Hall*, Vols I and II, Leeds Arts Collections Fund and the National Art Collections Fund

Gilbert, C. (1998) *Furniture at Temple Newsam House and Lotherton Hall*, Vol. III, Leeds Arts Collections Fund and the National Art Collections Fund

Grattan, D.W. and Barclay, R.L. (1988) A study of gap-fillers for wooden objects, *Studies in Conservation*, 33, 71–86

Hawkins, D. (1986) *The Technique of Wood Surface Decoration*, Batsford

Hayward, C.H. (1967) *Furniture Repairs*, Evans

Hayward, C.H. (1974) *The Complete Book of Woodwork*, Evans

Hlopoff, S.N. (1978) On the straightening of a warped mahogany-veneered panel, *Conservation of Wood in Painting and the Decorative Arts*, Conference Preprints, IIC, pp. 33–6

Hoadley, R.B. (1978) The dimensional response of wood to variation in relative humidity, in N.S. Brommelle, A. Moncrieff and P. Smith (eds), *Conservation of Wood in Painting and the Decorative Arts*, IIC Oxford Congress

Hoadley, R.B. (1980) *Understanding Wood: A Craftsman's Guide to Wood Technology*, Taunton Press

Hobbs, E.W. (1953) *Veneering*, Cassel

Hope, T. (1807/1971) *Regency Furniture and Interior Decoration*, Dover Facsimile Edition

Howells, R., Burnstock, A., Hedley, G. and Hackney, S. (1984) Polymer dispersions artificially aged, in *Adhesives and Consolidants*, Conference Preprints, IIC

Howlett, F.C. (1988) The potential for glycol treatments to counteract warpage in wooden objects, in AIC Wooden Artifacts Group, Conference Papers, New Orleans

Howlett, F.C. (1995) Counteracting warpage in wooden objects: two new approaches, in AIC Wooden Artifacts Group, Conference Papers, St Paul

Jacob, S. (1996) *The Art of the Picture Frame: Artists, Patrons and the Framing of Portraits in Britain*, National Portrait Gallery, London

Joyce, E. (1987) *The Technique of Furniture Making*, Batsford

Kitchin, J. (1979) Restoration of a 19th century Austrian bookcase, *The Conservator*, 3

Kjelland, J.R. (1997) Adhesive transfer of 24 520 square inches of marquetry, in AIC Wooden Artifacts Group, Conference Papers, San Diego

Klein, P. and Bröker, F.W. (1990) Investigation on swelling and shrinkage of panels with wooden support, in ICOM Committee for Conservation, Preprints 9th Triennial Meeting, Dresden

Kolbach, D. (1998) A note on the use of vacuum clamping to treat the damaged parquetry on a bombe writing desk, *Journal of the Canadian Association for Conservation*, 23, 15–19

Larsen, E.B. (1981) *Moulding and Casting of Museum Objects*, The Royal Danish Art Academy, Copenhagen

Learoyd, S. (1981) *English Furniture: Construction and Decoration, 1500–1910*, Evans Brothers

Leslie, H.Y.C. (1973) PEG of the woodworker's heart, in *Man/Society/Technology: A Journal of Industrial Arts Education*, 33 (1), 13–16

Maish, J.P. (1994) Silicone rubber staining of terracotta surfaces, *Studies in Conservation*, 39, 250–6

McGiffin, R. (1992) *Furniture Care and Conservation*, American Association for State and Local History

Mendgen, E. (1995) *In Perfect Harmony: Picture and Frame, 1850–1920*, Van Gogh Museum/Kunst Forum Wien, Waanders Uitgevers, Zwolle

Michalski, S. (1994) Relative humidity in museums, galleries and archives: specification and control, in B. Rose and A. Tenwolde (eds), *Bugs, Mold and Rot 3*, Conference Preprints, School of Architecture-Building Research Council, University of Illinois

Minney, F. (1994) The conservation of a Burmese dry lacquer statue of Buddha, *Studies in Conservation*, 39, 154–60

Minor, M. (1993) The nature and origin of surface veneer checking in plywood, in D. Grattan (ed.), *Saving the Twentieth Century: The Conservation of Modern Materials*, Conference Proceedings, CCI

Minor, M. (1996) Laser reproduction of brass/wood inlay in furniture by Charles Honore Lannuier, in AIC Wooden Artifacts Group, Conference Papers, Norfolk, Virginia

Mussey, R. (ed) (1987) *The First American Furniture Finisher's Manual*, Reprint of the 1827 edition of the Cabinet-Maker's Guide, Dover

Nagora, L., Fairbairn, G. and Manuel, J. (1990) Treatment of a boulle work bracket clock: a progress report, *CCI Newsletter*, 6, 1–3

Neher, A.L. (1996) Radio frequency heating and the reversibility of animal glue in furniture joinery, *Conservation News*, 59, 35–7

Newberry, T.J., Bisacca, G. and Kanter, L.B. (1990) *Italian Renaissance Frames*, Metropolitan Museum, New York

Newton, R.G. and Davison, S. (1989) *Conservation of Glass*, Butterworths

Philp, F. (1999) An alternative solution to an old problem: the conservation of an 18th century marquetry table, in P. van Duin, D. van Loosdrecht and D. Wheeler (eds), *Proceedings of the Fourth International Symposium on Wood and Furniture Conservation*, Rijksmuseum/VeRes, Amsterdam, pp. 41–5

Podmaniczky, M.S. (1998) Structural fills for large wood objects: contrasting and complimentary approaches, *JAIC*, 37, 111–16

Polytek Development Corporation (1992) *Moldmaking and Casting Methods and Materials: Manual and Catalog*, Polytek, Easton, PA

Pradere, A. (1991) *French Furniture Makers: the Art of the Ebeniste from Louis XIV to the Revolution*, Sothebys Publications

Ramond, P. (1989) *Marquetry*, Taunton Press

Rice, J.T. (1990) Gluing of archaeological wood, in R.M. Rowell and R.J. Barbour (eds), *Archaeological Wood:*

*Properties, Chemistry and Preservation*, Advances in Chemistry Series 225, American Chemical Society

Rodd, J. (1976) *Repairing and Restoring Antique Furniture*, David & Charles

Rodwell, D.F.G. (1984) Ageing of wood adhesives – loss in strength with time, in *Building Research Establishment Information Paper*, BRE

Roelofs, W. (1994) Coloured mordants on a set of Dutch marquetry furniture from the late 18th century, in *Contributions of the Central Research Laboratory to the Field of Conservation and Restoration*, Rijksmuseum, Amsterdam

Rogers, J.C. (1959) *English Furniture*, Country Life/Sterling

Rotter, M. (1979) *Alte Möbel Erkennen und Restaurieren*, Julius Hoffmann Verlag

Sadoh, T. (1967) The dimensional changes of wood during polyethylene glycol treatment and some elastic properties of the treated wood, *Journal of the Japan Wood Research Society*, 13 (2), April, 41–5

Schneider, M.H. (1972) Wood-coating interactions – a review, *Journal of Paint Technology*, 44 (564), 108–10

Skeist, I. (1962) *Handbook of Adhesives*, Van Nostrand Reinhold

Thornton, J. (1985) Compo: the history and technology of 'plastic' compositions, in AIC Wooden Artifacts Group, Conference Papers

Thornton, J. (1991a) Minding the gap: filling losses in gilded and decorated surfaces, in *Gilding and Surface Decoration*, Conference Postprints, UKIC

Thornton, J. (1991b) Replicating stamped brasses, *Fine Woodworking*, 86 (Jan/Feb), pp. 86–7

Thornton, J. (1998a) A brief history and review of the early practice and materials of gap-filling in the West, *JAIC*, 37, 3–22

Thornton, J. (1998b) The use of dyes and coloured varnishes in wood polychromy, *Painted Wood: History and Conservation*, Symposium Proceedings, Getty Conservation Institute, pp. 226–41

Tout, R.F. (1992) Wood adhesives – joints for furniture, in D.E. Packham (ed.) *Adhesion and Adhesives*, Longman

Triboulot, M-C. (1999a) Studies into the properties of polyethylene glycol. (PEG) in furniture conservation, in P. van Duin, D. van Loosdrecht and D. Wheeler (eds), *Proceedings of the Fourth International Symposium on Wood and Furniture Conservation*, Rijksmuseum/VeRes, Amsterdam, pp. 23–9

Triboulot, M-C. (1999b) Improving the adhesion between wood and brass, *Conservation News*, 69, UKIC, 30–32

Umney, N. (1993) The conservation of a Louis XIVth boulle marquetry bracket clock, *The Conservator*, 17, UKIC, 61–8

van Duin, P., Van Loosdrecht, D. and Wheeler, D. (eds) *Proceedings of the Fourth International Symposium on Wood and Furniture Conservation*, Rijksmuseum/VeRes, Amsterdam

van Thiel, P.J.J. and de Bruyn Kops, C.J. (1995, trans McCormick), *Framing in the Golden Age*, Rijksmuseum, Amsterdam/Waanders Uitgevers, Zwolle

Von Endt, D.W. and Baker, M.T. (1991) The chemistry of filled animal glue systems, in D. Bigelow *et al.* (eds), *Gilded Wood: Conservation and History*, Sound View Press

Wackernagel, R. (1978) The restoration of boulle marquetry at the Bavarian National Museum, in *Conservation of Wood in Painting and the Decorative Arts*, Conference Preprints, IIC

Wallstrim, L. and Lindberg, K.A.H. (1995) Wood surface stabilisation with polyethyleneglycol PEG, *Wood Science and Technology*, 29 (2), 109–19

Walton, H. (1976) *Home and Workshop Guide to Sharpening*, Popular Science/Harper and Row

Walton, J.A. (1979) *Woodwork in Theory and Practice*, 6th edn, Australasian Publishing Co.

Wang, Y. and Schniewind, A.P. (1985) Consolidation of deteriorated wood with soluble resins, *JAIC*, 24(2), 77–91

Ware, G.W. (1989) *The Pesticide Book*, Thomson

Waters, P.H. (1983) A review of the moulding and casting materials and techniques in use at the palaeontology laboratory, British Museum (Natural History), *The Conservator*, 7, 37–43

Wetherall, J. (1991) History and techniques of composition, in S. Budden (ed.), *Gilding and Surface Decoration*, Conference Preprints, UKIC

Weygers, A.G. (1973) *The Making of Tools*, Van Nostrand Reinhold

Wilmering, A.W. (1998) A renaissance *studiolo* from the ducal palace in Gubbio, in K. Dardes and A. Roth (eds), *The Structural Conservation of Panel Paintings*, Getty Conservation Institute

Wilson, G. (1972) Boulle, *The Journal of the Furniture History Society*, Vol. VIII

# 11

# Principles of cleaning

The cleaning of furniture has always been an important part of housekeeping and the restorer's trade (Hale, 1853). In the past, a variety of concoctions for cleaning furniture have been recommended, ranging from a dampened cloth to ground glass or stale beer and vinegar. Few were selected with any degree of specificity to the nature of a particular surface. The conservator's objective is to balance the removal of unwanted material from an object with the preservation of the varnish or decorated (e.g. painted, japanned, gilded or lacquered) surface.

This chapter identifies options for the cleaning of varnished and decorated surfaces on furniture and wooden objects. Although the theory of cleaning is discussed under four separate categories (mechanical, solvent, chemical and aqueous cleaning), in practice these approaches are often combined. The theory and practice of cleaning is central to much conservation research and it is essential to keep abreast of current developments.

The term cleaning often has a fluid meaning in conservation. The term cleaning refers to the removal of unwanted accretions, such as dirt, which obscure a surface. In the context of decorated surfaces, other treatments may also be called cleaning but it is more accurate to refer to them as 'removal of varnish' or 'removal of overpaint'.

Surfaces are important because they contain much of the value of the original object. This value may be aesthetic, historical, informational, spiritual, monetary or a combination of these. Varnished or decorated surfaces on furniture are very vulnerable to damage. They are usually thin, subject to the greatest wear and tear in use, and are at the front line of environmental change. It is convenient to

discuss surfaces separately from the wooden substrate because they are manufactured using different skills and techniques to those usually associated with cabinetmaking and because, although different in appearance, decorated surfaces share a similar fundamental structure. It must be remembered, however, that surface and substrate form an integrated whole and often in practice cannot be treated independently. Many defects such as flaking paint and gesso, for example, have their origin in the movement or chemistry of the underlying structure. Coatings can be responsible for unequal moisture movements in wood and can lead to warps, cracks and splits, which in turn result in damage to the varnish or decorative layers. Structural treatment of the wooden substrate is often constrained by the presence of coatings and vice versa.

Up until the twentieth century, the range of binding materials that were included in decorative surfaces was comparatively small. Materials used to create decorative surfaces on furniture include not only those found in other disciplines such as easel painting and polychrome sculpture but materials derived from a vernacular tradition, such as the use of beer as a binding media in simulated wood grain. The range of possible constituents of decorative surfaces has vastly increased in the twentieth century, particularly after 1945. Using painted surfaces as an example, not only have new materials such as alkyd resins and acrylics come into wide use but a huge range of materials such as thickeners and gelling agents, biocides, dispersion aids, UV absorbers, flame retardants and corrosion inhibitors may be added (see, for example, Rothenberg, 1978). These materials will complicate analysis and affect the solubility behaviour of twentieth and twenty-first century coatings.

Many of the materials used for cleaning are potentially dangerous. *It is the responsibility of the conservator to be fully aware of the hazards presented and to take adequate precautionary measures.*

## 11.1 Preliminaries

### 11.1.1 Cleaning objectives

Cleaning may be undertaken in preparation for further conservation treatment, to improve appearance or to prevent deterioration. A cleaning treatment should be as specific as possible and minimize unwanted side effects. It is important to understand the mechanism and potential impact of a cleaning technique or substance so that it can be used in a precise manner. If oily soot is to be removed, then a procedure should be chosen that will do just that and no more. Conservators have been criticized for over-cleaning painted surfaces and, more recently, varnished wood. Cleaning involves the irreversible removal of material from an object and the implications of such loss must be considered carefully before commencing any treatment.

The concept of over-cleaning is subjective and influenced by culture and fashion. In the past, cleaning controversies about paintings have been a result of varnish removal. The degree of removal of surface dirt may be an additional issue in furniture conservation (Jeffrey, 1999). This arises, in part, from the desire to maintain evidence of the passage of time. In cases where the removal of dirt is desirable, it may be impossible to remove all dirt from porous or textured surfaces without also removing material original to the object (*Figure 11.1*). The conservator should consult with the curator or owner and establish cleaning objectives before a treatment is undertaken. The measure of success of cleaning treatments should include not only how the object appears after treatment, but also how it was affected in the process and whether long-term preservation has been enhanced or diminished. Although an ideal cleaning treatment would remove undesirable dirt, leave original object material unaffected and leave

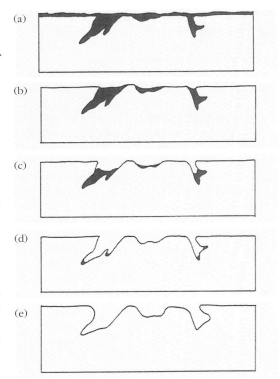

**Figure 11.1** Stages of removing unwanted material (dirt, varnish and/or degradation products) from a porous or textured surface
(*a*) Surface with accumulated dirt
(*b*) Unwanted material removed from surface only. This degree of cleaning may be unsatisfactory if there is a marked contrast between the cleaned surface and the dirt laden interstices
(*c*) Unwanted material removed from surface and partially removed from interstices. This degree of cleaning may represent a surface that retains a patina of age or use
(*d*) Almost all unwanted material has been removed, but as cleaning progresses, damage to, or erosion of the substrate may become more likely
(*e*) The surface has been eroded in an effort to remove all traces of unwanted material. This type of damage is particularly likely when both the unwanted material and the substrate share sensitivity to the cleaning treatment, e.g. the removal of varnish from painted, japanned or lacquered surfaces

no residue behind, it is rare to achieve such total selectivity in practice. Nevertheless, these goals should be kept in mind when undertaking cleaning treatments. Over-cleaning is irreversible and is often a result of a yearning for perfection. It is rare for furniture to be undamaged or in immaculate condition. Err on the side of caution and leave a doubtful or resistant film in place rather than risk damage to original material underneath.

Considerations that will motivate a conservator to accept the risks and proceed with cleaning can usually be reduced to improving the state of preservation of the surface decoration and/or enhancing the aesthetic qualities of the object. Deciding how much cleaning is necessary for an object can be difficult. It is important to consider the aesthetic qualities and the evidence of age and use that the condition of the present surface history may lend to an object. These may be irreversibly altered by removal of dirt and grime. The conservator should understand the historical materials and techniques used in creating the decorative surface they are considering cleaning. Cleaning is not just an exercise in craft or chemistry but often involves a reinterpretation of the aesthetics or design of an object.

### 11.1.2   Examination

Before beginning a conservation treatment it is important to examine the object thoroughly and to consider possible courses of action. It is helpful to understand as much as possible about the nature of the surface and the defects and deterioration to which it is susceptible. The conservator should identify fragile areas, surface losses, loose veneer, old repairs, retouches and previous treatments that might respond differently or reveal damage once removed. The historical significance that the dirt and grime on an object may have should be considered carefully before treatment is carried out.

Characterization sets out to determine the appearance, condition, layer structure, composition and solubility of a surface. This will help the conservator to uncover the history of the piece and to determine treatment needs and options. It may be distinct from the process of analysis, which is used to identify individual materials within layers.

### 11.1.3   Pre-cleaning checklist

The following checklist may help assess the potential risks and benefits of a cleaning treatment.

- What are the cleaning objectives?
- How will cleaning affect the object's functional, informational, aesthetic or other role/s?
- What risks are involved in cleaning and not cleaning? Which are greater?
- Is the structure and surface of the object sound?
- What is known about the materials to be used in cleaning, the surface to be cleaned and possible interactions between them? Is this knowledge sufficient to proceed?
- Can a suitable cleaning method (one that maximizes positive benefits for the object while minimizing intervention and risk) be identified?
- Have tests been successful (for example has dirt been removed and the original surface remained undisturbed)?
- Can a suitable post-treatment environment be provided?

### 11.1.4   General approach

The removal of dirt, unwanted varnish or overpaint share common principles. In each case, removal of unwanted material is undertaken in stages. Removal of dirt from furniture with a natural resin varnish, for example, may involve an aqueous solution followed by a hydrocarbon solvent. If varnish removal is undertaken, it is essential to remove surface grime first because it forms a layer with different solubility characteristics to the underlying varnish. Failing to remove surface dirt would lead to the use of more polar solvents and unnecessarily increase the chance of damaging underlying decorative layers. The final stage may be the removal of unwanted, inappropriate or discoloured overpaint. In cases where cleaning is problematic, the conservator may undertake partial or selective cleaning (*Figure 11.2*). A combination of partial and selective cleaning may be undertaken in an attempt to improve appearance without causing damage to a sensitive substrate.

When setting up photographs of an object during cleaning, or leaving an object partly cleaned for a time, care should be taken to halt the cleaning process along natural lines of the decorative elements within the design (see, for example, *Plate 3*). The edges of the

(a)

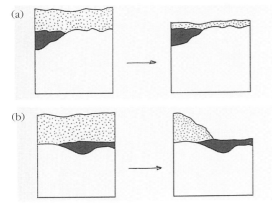

(b)

(c)

**Figure 11.2**　Partial and selective cleaning
(*a*) Partial cleaning to reduce the thickness of unwanted material
(*b*) Selective cleaning to remove unwanted material from some areas of the substrate, leaving others untouched
(*c*) Detail of a painted wardrobe, English, *c*.1775. The background is executed in oil paint, but the decorative details have been painted in a solvent sensitive medium. This surface has been cleaned in the past and small areas of loss attest to the solvent sensitivity of the green detail. Previous treatment involved selectively cleaning darkened varnish from the background, leaving the varnish on the green areas rather than risking further loss

**Figure 11.3**
Detail of a giltwood barometer *c*.1740. Repeated cleaning of the silver registration plate in the past has disfigured adjacent gilding

cleaned area should be feathered to avoid ridges of dissolved dirt or varnish because once hardened, they may be less readily soluble, more difficult to remove and will abut a clean and sensitive surface.

Unvarnished surfaces, such as bare wood or gesso, are more susceptible to damage during cleaning and may be contaminated by the cleaning material or displaced dirt (*Figure 11.3*). Exposed areas may be sealed before cleaning commences, for example if the wood was originally varnished or it is intended to seal exposed gesso as part of the conservation treatment. Pre-sealing will protect vulnerable areas from cleaning materials and reduce the possibility of cleaning solutions wicking under coatings, causing discoloration, delamination and other problems. The sealing material should be compatible with other potential treatments such as consolidation or recoating and may be temporary or permanent, as required. It may be possible to clean areas before a sealer is applied, though in some cases it will be necessary to consolidate and then clean.

### 11.1.5　Cleaning tests

Cleaning tests are an empirical method of determining the solubility of unwanted material and of establishing differences between the solubility of the unwanted material and the surface below. The aim is to establish which solvents will remove unwanted dirt, varnish or overpaint without affecting the materials below (*Figure 11.4*). It is helpful to have characterized the underlying surface and be familiar with its solubility parameters before conducting solvent tests to prevent damage that may not be immediately apparent, e.g. leaching or swelling of oil paint (see discussion of solvents in section 16.6.3 on removal of varnish).

(a)                                                      (b)

**Figure 11.4**   Varnish removal with a solvent gel
(*a*) Detail of the hood of a tall case japanned clock, attributed to Gawen Brown, Boston, late eighteenth century.
The elaborate japanned decoration was completely obscured by restoration varnishes that had darkened. The detail
shows the cleaning test using a solvent gel
(*b*) Faux turtleshell japanning revealed by removing discoloured restoration varnishes with a solvent gel

Testing a proposed cleaning system is an important step in establishing the risks and benefits of the treatment. A test area should be examined under low magnification, using a microscope or hand loupe, before and after cleaning, to assess the impact of treatment. Any swabs used in cleaning tests should also be examined for evidence of the type of material that is being removed (or not).

Tests should be undertaken in a systematic way. Materials and techniques should be tested on a small, inconspicuous part of an object, such as the back of a leg or the underside of a drawer front, to avoid damaging the object and wasting time. Uniform behaviour over a whole surface should not be assumed because tests in one area have been successful. A varnished or decorated surface may not respond uniformly to a cleaning system as a result of different treatments in the past, non-uniform thickness of varnish, differential degradation (for example parts of the object may have received more or less exposure to light), or the effect of different pigments on the binding media. Cleaning may result in components in a ground or other layer being deposited on the surface or in the craquelure, resulting in a whitish appearance. This will not be apparent by examining test swabs but viewing test areas under low magnification should identify this problem before cleaning begins.

Cleaning tests may embrace a wide range of techniques such as mechanical cleaning, dry cleaning, solvent and aqueous cleaning (including the manipulation of pH, conductivity, and/or the addition of chelating agents, enzymes, detergents or surfactants). A cotton swab or the corner of a lint-free cotton cloth may be a convenient way to apply test material. If cleaning solutions are used, the test should start with the application of a small amount for a very short time. The surface being tested should be allowed to dry completely before judging the full impact of cleaning. If there is no unfavourable reaction, longer times and larger amounts can be tried. If a test clean proves satisfactory in one area, several other small areas should also be tested to ensure uniformity of the result before committing to a course of action.

Ultraviolet light may highlight the degree of change caused by the cleaning test. For example, a brightly autofluorescing cleaned test area may contrast with muted fluorescence from the untreated coating. This suggests that non-fluorescing dirt, oil and grime have been removed and the naturally autofluorescent coating below has been retained and revealed through the cleaning process. Conversely, a total lack of autofluorescence in the test area may suggest that a coating has been removed rather than enhanced.

The basic principle behind all cleaning is to start with the least potentially damaging material or technique. If 'stronger' solvents or combinations are necessary, tests should progress in measured increments. Solvents may be combined with other cleaning methods or techniques, for example using dry cleaning materials in combination with hydrocarbon solvents. The wetting and cleaning properties of organic solvents may be enhanced by the addition of a small amount of a compatible detergent or surfactant.

### 11.1.6 Dirt

Dirt may be undesirable because it obscures the aesthetic, informational or other properties of an object, or accelerates the process of deterioration. Dirt is generally hygroscopic, often mildly acidic and may be characterized by source, size, chemical composition, or the mechanism by which it adheres to a surface.

Air filtered from urban environments may contain material such as industrial pollutants, brick dust, salts, oils, waxes, clay, protein, lint, pollen, mould spores and human skin. Surface dirt on decorative objects has been characterized as a combination of particulate material and greasy or oily material (Phenix and Burnstock, 1992). The particulate material varies in chemical composition, surface characteristics, size, shape and hardness and may include inorganic material and elemental carbon. Particles may be present in a range of sizes but are generally so finely divided that they exhibit colloidal properties. Carbon black and other solid particles can attract and absorb acid and alkaline agents, and oxidizing and reducing agents, from the surrounding atmosphere. This absorption can result in the formation of acid solutions where moisture is present and promote hydrolytic, oxidative or reductive breakdown of sensitive materials. Dirt that contains metal ions has a catalytic effect on the deterioration of some materials. Greasy or oily material composed of hydrocarbons and fats may contain free acids and also assist the adhesion of particulate matter to the surface. Dirt is discussed further in Chapter 6.

Surface grime may be a result of historical use and such dirt may have value in assisting in the interpretation of the object. Dirt can be separated into that which has been deposited on the object and that which is a result of the object's own degradation processes. To remove the latter is to take away some aspect of the object's original material and it is therefore essential to consider the nature of the object and how its surface relates to its history before any cleaning is undertaken.

The probability that dirt will be removed by a cleaning treatment depends on the type and strength of the adhesion between dirt and the surface of the object. Dirt may adhere to a surface coating mechanically by physical entrapment, as a result of static electricity, by hydrogen or dipole bonding or by van der Waals forces (Moncrieff and Weaver, 1992). It is usually a combination of these forces that results in dirt accumulating and remaining on a surface. The particle size of the dirt also affects how it is fixed to the surface. Larger particles of dirt (>1 μm) are held to a surface largely with electrostatic forces and can be dislodged from a surface with water alone (Wolbers *et al.*, 1990). Dirt may also be imbibed by varnish films or other materials (e.g. adhesives) with a glass transition temperature (Tg) that is the same as, or less than, the ambient temperature. The dirt becomes integral to the coating, rather than being attached to it by secondary bonding. Such dirt can only be displaced from the object by removing the varnish (*Plate 3*).

Dirt can be removed from a surface if the force of attraction between a cleaning system and dirt exceed the force of attraction that adheres the dirt to the surface. There are three general approaches to cleaning. Mechanical cleaning physically displaces dirt. In solvent or aqueous cleaning, dirt, unchanged in chemical form, is removed in solution. In chemical cleaning, the primary molecular bonds in the dirt itself are broken and it is converted into a different form during removal. In all cases the treatment should utilize the mildest available method.

### 11.1.7  Removal of varnish or overpaint

The most common reason for removing a varnish is that is has yellowed, discoloured and is obscuring or distorting the intended effect of the surface below. The removal of varnish is a potentially controversial treatment. In paintings conservation, criticisms of cleaning have been a result of shifting perceptions of how pictures *ought* to appear and debates about what has been removed. An aesthetic sensibility of the early nineteenth century was summarized by Sir George Beaumont (d.1827) who stated that 'A good painting, like a good violin, should be brown' (Keck, 1984). More recently, motivation for the cleaning of paintings has been ascribed to the twentieth century visual experience of television and advertising, cinema and modern art. Critics argue that this experience is characterized by bright colours and sharp contrast, and that this sensibility has often been inappropriately transposed onto works of art (Beck and Daley, 1993). Throughout the history of the removal of varnish from paintings, it has been the belief that subtle glazes and toning layers have been lost that has excited the most outrage. These delicate original layers are among the last to be applied and are the most vulnerable to damage or even complete

removal during cleaning. Thin resinous layers used to create decorative schemes on furniture are similarly vulnerable to damage during varnish removal.

Removal of layers involves judging the relative historical, material and aesthetic importance of each layer to the overall value of the object. When making treatment decisions that will permanently change the nature of a decorative surface, it is important to maintain a balance between original intent, history and current interpretative objectives of the object. It may be useful to review the considerations for ethical decision-making outlined in Chapter 9. The layer structure of an object should be understood in its entirety before treatment commences. Careful examination of a surface under low magnification, hand-held UV and raking light may reveal much useful information. It may be necessary to take samples in order to identify layer stratigraphy, characterize the binding media of each layer or identify pigments. It is essential that a treatment aimed at the removal of unwanted layers from an earlier surface should avoid damaging material that is to be retained. Although UV can be a useful tool, the appearance of a surface under normal viewing conditions should be the determining factor when assessing the progress of varnish removal.

It is common for a variety of surface histories to exist on a single piece of furniture. A table top, for example, may have been revarnished several times while the underframe has been left untouched. It is therefore likely that a variety of processes, rather than just one, may be necessary to complete a sensitive layer removal treatment. There are occasions when the removal of one or more layers may be considered desirable, for example if a later coating is seriously disfiguring an original decorative surface. In other instances, later coatings may represent an important part of the history of the object and should be retained. A small part of the surface (e.g. behind hardware or on the lower edge of a case piece) may be left untreated to serve as a physical document of a previous condition.

Although cleaning is potentially fraught with many difficulties, with careful consideration it is usually possible to select a cleaning method that will fulfil the demands of aesthetics and preservation.

**Figure 11.5** Removing dust from a painted and gilded leather panel using a soft bristle brush and low power vacuum cleaner

## 11.2   Mechanical cleaning

Mechanical cleaning relies on the physical displacement of dirt. It causes no shrinkage or swelling of the surface and, depending on the object, may present a low risk of displaced dirt being absorbed into a porous surface. It requires no toxic chemicals, although dust may be hazardous. Mechanical cleaning techniques include dusting, cleaving, abrasion and dry cleaning. Ultrasonics have been used to clean metal objects and lasers to remove corrosion products and dirt from metals, mineralized layers from stained glass and organic layers from terracotta but neither have found wide application to date in furniture conservation. Strictly speaking, laser cleaning is not mechanical but rather photothermal or photochemical, and affects both the physical and chemical properties of dirt (Cooper, 1998).

### 11.2.1   Dusting

Dust should be removed before undertaking further cleaning (Shelly, 1987). Dust is airborne particulate matter that collects on an object's surface and is not bound to the substrate or itself. Dust is an aesthetic problem as well as being potentially harmful to the object. Regular dust removal will increase the stability and longevity of objects and their coatings. In some cases the abrasive effect of repeated dusting on delicate decorative surfaces, such as gilded wood, may cause significant damage. Where possible environmental controls should be used to prevent the ingress and accumulation of dust.

Dusting should pick up and remove dust rather than merely displacing it within the same environment. Dust can be removed using a dusting cloth (e.g. varnished table tops), soft natural bristle brush (marquetry, boulle or gilded surfaces) or vacuum cleaner (thick deposits of dust). Feather dusters are not recommended. Dusting cloths can be evaluated using Perspex to assess whether, after numerous dustings, the dust has been removed, deposits left behind and if the Perspex remains free from scratches. Eighteenth century documents indicate that brushes were commonly used to dust furniture, frames and interior architecture (Balston, 1956). Dust dislodged in this way should be captured with a cloth or vacuum cleaner. A fine nylon mesh stretched over the nozzle can be used to prevent any loose parts being sucked into the vacuum cleaner (*Figure 11.5*). An established routine of dust removal should be part of general housekeeping practice.

### 11.2.2   Cleaving

Cleaving may be used to remove brittle dirt, metal corrosion products or an unwanted coating from an underlying surface that is undamaged and comparatively strong. Successful cleaving exploits the mechanism that causes layers to flake, that is, strong cohesive properties within a layer combined with weak adhesive properties between layers. This technique avoids the risks associated with solvent or aqueous cleaning.

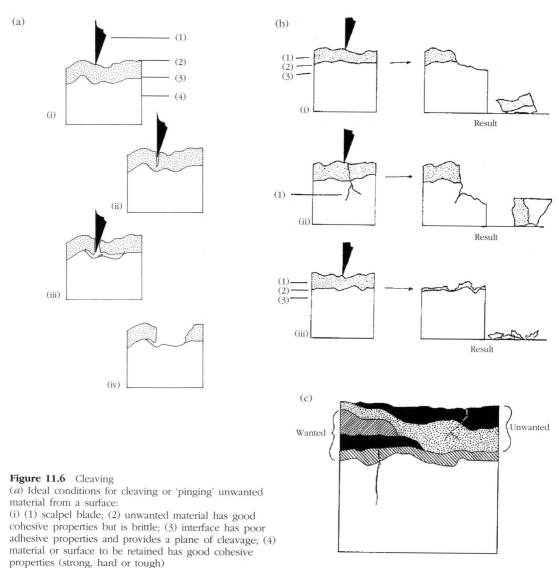

**Figure 11.6** Cleaving
(*a*) Ideal conditions for cleaving or 'pinging' unwanted material from a surface:
(i) (1) scalpel blade; (2) unwanted material has good cohesive properties but is brittle; (3) interface has poor adhesive properties and provides a plane of cleavage; (4) material or surface to be retained has good cohesive properties (strong, hard or tough)
(ii) As the scalpel enters, material either side of the blade is compressed and forced outward, whilst material in front of the blade is in tension. A crack develops ahead of the blade
(iii) Material either side of the blade is still under compression. The developing crack is diverted along the line of weakness caused by poor adhesion between the unwanted material and the substrate. Tension in the unwanted material is released as the crack develops
(iv) The stress caused by scalpel blade is released as a fragment of unwanted material breaks cleanly away from the substrate
(*b*) Unsatisfactory results from cleaving:
(i) (1) strong cohesive properties in the unwanted material; (2) strong adhesive interface; (3) weak cohesive properties in substrate; result – no plane of cleavage leads to damaged substrate
(ii) (1) lines of weakness in the substrate; result – unexpected damage
(iii) (1) weak cohesive properties in unwanted material; (2) strong adhesive interface; (3) strong cohesive properties in substrate; result – residues may leave an unsatisfactory appearance
(*c*) In practice, cleaving material is as complex as the surface itself. The stratigraphy may differ from place to place, the properties of a single layer may vary from place to place, there may be weaknesses at different points in different layers, or unwanted material may have been absorbed into a layer that is to be retained via cracks or porosity

When a scalpel is used to pick away dirt, the material either side of the blade is compressed and the material below the blade is in tension. A crack will develop ahead of the blade as this tension is released. When there is poor adhesion at the interface between the dirt and the surface, the crack will propagate along this interface, releasing stress and breaking a fragment of unwanted material away from the surface (*Figure 11.6a*). If there is strong adhesion at the interface however, there are two possible results. First, if the dirt layer is stronger than the surface, the crack will propagate into the substrate and damage it. Secondly, if the dirt layer is weaker than the substrate, the crack will propagate within the dirt layer, partially removing dirt, but also leaving some dirt behind on the surface (*Figure 11.6b*). If the surface is textured, rough or porous the result may be particularly unsightly. In practice the situation is more complicated, because the nature of both dirt and substrate may vary, resulting in changes in weakness and strength, adhesion and cohesion, at different places and in different layers (*Figure 11.6c*).

There is a risk that cleaving or picking unwanted material from a surface can scratch and damage the surface, and such damage is not always visible to the naked eye. In some cases such damage can be minimized or avoided by using tools made from ivory, bone, Perspex or Plexiglas. In some cases it may be possible to remove unwanted upper layers using pressure-sensitive tape (Webb, 1989).

### 11.2.3  Abrasives

Abrasives are not recommended for cleaning decorative surfaces because they are relatively indiscriminate and often damage the underlying surface. Abrasive techniques are occasionally used to reduce the thickness of an unwanted layer such as overpaint or transparent coatings on a flat surface. Fibreglass pens are unsuitable for, and will scratch, varnished and decorated surfaces. They may find occasional use for the mechanical removal of very hard accretions of surface dirt or corrosion products from metals. Gloves should be worn when using these pens as the glass fibres break off in minute pieces that cause painful irritation if lodged in the skin.

### 11.2.4  Dry cleaning methods

Dry cleaning methods have a long history in the cleaning of decorative surfaces. The term dry cleaning in the laundry industry refers to the use of solvent cleaning for textiles. In the context of the conservation of varnished and decorated surfaces, it refers to cleaning without the use of any liquid. When used correctly, dry cleaning methods are non-abrasive and rely on the adhesive properties of the dry cleaning material to pick up dirt and remove it from the surface. Cleaning does not require a rubbing action as these materials are usually rolled over the surface. Oil-free bread is a traditional dry cleaning material used for the removal of surface dirt but residues will support mould growth or pest attack. Specialized products are available that

**Figure 11.7**  Detail of painted decoration on a late eighteenth-century clock case, during conservation. Dirt was removed using a soft eraser

can be applied to a range of materials, including decorated surfaces, ivory and paper. Dry cleaning methods are particularly appropriate for porous surfaces. For information on individual products see Sterlini (1995).

Erasers have been used for cleaning of paper and painted surfaces (Hackney, 1990) (*Figure 11.7*). Most erasers are manufactured from rubber or polyvinyl chloride and some contain harsh abrasives. Vinyl erasers are less harsh than rubber but can contain up to 35% plasticizer. Two effective vinyl erasers are the Mars-Plastic (Staedtler) and Magic-Rub (Faber-Castell). These block erasers are soft, white and can be cut to a clean or angled edge if desired. Both contain calcium carbonate and a phthalate plasticizer that will dissolve in polar solvents such as alcohol, but can be used with water or a hydrocarbon solvent if desired. Sterlini (1995) reported minimal visible residues and changes to wetting properties when these products were used to clean paper.

Smoke or chemical sponges, made from vulcanised rubber and a very small amount of detergent, have been used for cleaning paper, textiles and plant fibres and are effective for large-scale cleaning of fairly flat surfaces. A gentle rolling action is used to press a piece of sponge onto the surface being cleaned.

Groomstick is a processed kneadable natural rubber product that contains titanium dioxide but is free from moisture, solvents or chemical additives. It is particularly useful for the accurate removal of small areas of surface dirt or for easily damaged surfaces such as water gilding. A small amount can be wrapped around the end of a bamboo stick and rolled very lightly over the surface. Groomstick is very tacky and should not be used on poorly adhered surfaces. No visible residues were found after cleaning paper with Groomstick but changes to wetting properties occurred (Sterlini, 1995).

Draft Clean granules are available in two grades. The standard grade is derived from vegetable oil fibre (soybean oil) ground into a powder, to which 5% or less talcum powder has been added. These contain no rubber but there is a small amount of sulphur present. The 'x' grade is a pH-neutral rubber material, free from sulphur. Both are applied by sprinkling the granules onto the surface and rolling them over with a brush. The granules spread out in use and should be brushed gently from the surface, taking care to remove any stray granules that may have lodged in crevices.

Traditional artist's gum, or Art Gum, is a polyvinyl compound loaded with factice, a vulcanized vegetable oil product. It has a tendency to crumble in use but leaves little visible residue.

The Canadian Conservation Institute (CCI) examined the Wishab sponge and reported an unidentified sticky yellow component, and as a result it is not recommended for conservation use. Skum-X (Dietzgen), a draughtsman's cleaning powder, may leave significant residues and is also not recommended.

## 11.3   Solvent cleaning

Solvents are used for many purposes in conservation, including cleaning and the application or removal of coatings, consolidants and adhesives. Making the most of solvents requires familiarity with basic principles of molecular bonding and an understanding of how the structure of solvents affects their physical and chemical properties. This information can be applied when choosing solvents for specific treatments or to solve cleaning problems. An introduction to the principles of solvents and solubility can be found in Torraca (1975). *Solvents included in the following discussion have been included for illustrative purposes and it should not be assumed that they are appropriate for use in conservation.*

All matter is made up of atoms that may be combined together in different arrangements to make molecules. The forces within a molecule (intramolecular) that hold it together may be ionic, covalent or metallic and are known as primary bonding. The forces that hold molecules to each other (intermolecular) are known as secondary bonding and may involve van der Waals forces, polar or hydrogen bonding. Molecular bonding is explained by Moncrieff and Weaver (1992). Primary bonds are usually stronger than secondary bonds and this is demonstrated by the approximate ratio of strength of different bond types e.g. van der Waals forces: hydrogen bonds: covalent bonds 1:10:100. Solvent cleaning involves breaking down secondary bonds that adhere the unwanted varnish or dirt to the surface and bringing these molecules into solution in order to remove them from a surface. An exception to this principle occurs when water is used to dissolve inorganic salts, in which case the primary ionic bonds of the 'dirt' are disrupted.

An ideal cleaning treatment would leave the primary and secondary bonding of the substrate intact. In order to do this the conservator needs to understand the forces at work in a solvent (e.g. degree of hydrogen/dipole/non-polar bonding, aromaticity) and the likely interactions between solvent and surface. Successful cleaning requires that the intermolecular forces within a solvent be matched to the intermolecular forces within the unwanted material ('like dissolves like').

Understanding the classification of solvents and the different contribution of polar and non-polar forces within them allows the conservator to tailor their cleaning treatment for a particular cleaning or layer removal problem. Ideally, the conservator should have a basic understanding of the chemistry of the unwanted material, the underlying surface, and the solvent/s that will be used to separate the two.

### 11.3.1 Classes of solvents that may be encountered in furniture conservation

Solvents are classified into broad groups that share common chemical characteristics. Although there are an enormous number of solvents available, a few solvents selected from different classes is sufficient for most cleaning problems. Understanding solvent classification will help the conservator to utilize the Teas chart to formulate test procedures and tailor their treatments. For example, if using solvents to test the solubility of an unknown coating, there is little point in selecting industrial methylated spirits, ethanol and isopropanol. Although they are different solvents, they are all in the same class (alcohols) and thus have similar intermolecular interactions. A sequence of solvents for cleaning tests to assess the general sensitivities and chemical character of the unwanted material may include a solvent from each class (e.g. aliphatic hydrocarbon, aromatic hydrocarbon, alcohol, ketone, water). On the basis of such tests, the conservator could then assess which solvents interact in a desirable way to remove unwanted material without damaging the substrate. If, using a sample solvent from each class, it had been established that alcohols were the most suitable for a cleaning treatment, it would be possible to exploit the subtle variations within this class to fine tune a cleaning treatment. Within the homologous series of alcohols, for example, the conservator could select a fast acting and fast evaporating solvent (ethanol), or a slower evaporating solvent whose branched structure also slows penetration (isopropanol, isobutanol).

A common solvent sequence in cleaning tests is an aliphatic hydrocarbon, followed by an aromatic hydrocarbon, an alcohol, a ketone and lastly water. It is important to understand that this does not represent a progression in solvent 'strength'. No solvent (or other cleaning method) is inherently strong or weak, but is more or less closely matched to the physical and chemical properties of the unwanted material and/or the substrate.

### *Hydrocarbon solvents*

Molecules that contain only hydrogen and carbon are called hydrocarbons. Differences in size and configuration alter their physical and chemical properties. Molecules that contain only single covalent bonds between carbon and hydrogen atoms are called alkanes and have the suffix -ane. In the past alkanes were called paraffins or iso-paraffins. 'Normal' (n-) alkanes have a straight chain structure. Hydrocarbons that contain a carbon atom connected to three other carbon atoms, giving a branched structure, are called isomers. Isomers have same number and types of atoms but in a different arrangement, which can lead to different chemical and physical properties. Hydrocarbons in which a carbon atom is connected to four other carbon atoms are given the prefix neo-.

Molecules that contain one or more double covalent bonds are called alkenes and have the suffix -ene. In the past alkenes were called olefins. Alkenes are often present as impurities in petroleum fractions. Molecules that contain one or more triple covalent bonds are called alkynes and have the suffix -yne. In the past alkynes were called acetylenes. Alkynes have no solvent usage. Five or six carbons may form a stable ring or cyclic structure (a

**Table 11.1** Hydrocarbon reference chart

| Class | Solvent | Manufacturer or supplier | Boiling range °C | Boiling range °F | Composition % Aliphatic (napthenic) | Composition % Aromatic | K-B value | Evaporation rate nBuAc = 100 | Evaporation rate Seconds to 90% evaporation | OEL ppm (8 hour) |
|---|---|---|---|---|---|---|---|---|---|---|
| **Isoparaffins** | **UK solvents** | | | | | | | | | |
| | Shellsol T | Shell | 187–213 | 369–415 | 100 | | 26 | 9 | 5000 | 150 |
| | Shellsol TD | Shell | 172–185 | 342–365 | 100 | | 26 | 18 | 2500 | 150 |
| | Isopar H | ExxonMobil | 182–192 | 360–378 | 100 | | 28 | 6 | 7600 | 180 |
| | Isopar G | ExxonMobil | 162–176 | 324–349 | 100 | | 29 | 16 | 2900 | 200 |
| **Dearomatized aliphatics** | Shellsol D60 | Shell | 187–211 | 369–410 | 100 (50) | | 30 | 4 | 11500 | 150 |
| | Shellsol D40 | Shell | 162–192 | 324–378 | 100 (45) | | 33 | 18 | 2500 | 150 |
| | Exxsol DSP 60/95 S | ExxonMobil | 65–99 | 149–210 | 100 | | 32 | 700 | 65 | 315 |
| | Exxsol DSP 145/160 | ExxonMobil | 147–159 | 297–318 | 100 | | 33 | 45 | 1000 | 300 |
| | Exxsol DSP 100/140 | ExxonMobil | 103–139 | 217–282 | 100 | | 34 | 125 | 370 | 303 |
| | Exxsol DSP 100/160 | ExxonMobil | 107–157 | 225–315 | 100 | | 34 | 95 | 480 | 295 |
| | Exxsol DSP 100/120 | ExxonMobil | 101–119 | 214–246 | 100 | | 36 | 210 | 220 | 326 |
| | Exxsol DSP 80/110 | ExxonMobil | 88–105 | 190–221 | 100 | | 36 | 300 | 150 | 299 |
| **Napthenics** | Cypar 9 | Shell | 138–164 | 280–328 | 100 (100) | | 41 | 67 | 700 | None assigned |
| | Nappar 10 | ExxonMobil | 163–186 | 325–367 | 100 (100) | | 41 | 13 | 3500 | 140 |
| | Cypar 7 | Shell | 98–114 | 209–237 | 100 (100) | | 46 | 380 | 120 | 400 |
| | cyclohexane | BDH | 81 | 178 | 100 (100) | | 54 | 260 | 176 | 100 |
| | turpentine (Winsor and Newton) | | 156–170 | 313–338 | 100 (turpenes) | | 61 | <100 | >458 | 100 |
| **White spirits** | Shellsol H | Shell | 187–210 | 369–410 | 80 (23) | 17 | 33 | 6 | 7400 | 100 |
| | Varsol 60 | ExxonMobil | 187–216 | 369–421 | 75 | 25 | 35 | 2.5 | 18000 | 110 |
| | low aromatic white spirit | Shell | 162–192 | 324–378 | 84 (33) | 18 | 36 | 16 | 2470 | 100 |
| | stoddard solvent (mineral spirits Type I) | | 150–210 | 302–410 | ~80 | ~20 | ~36 | 8 | 5725 | 100 |
| | Varsol 40 | ExxonMobil | 163–186 | 325–367 | 78 | 22 | 37 | 11 | 4200 | 110 |
| **Aromatics** | Solvesso 150 | ExxonMobil | 181–206 | 358–403 | | 100 | 86 | 5 | 9100 | 70 |
| | Solvesso 100 | ExxonMobil | 155–181 | 311–358 | | 100 | 90 | 15 | 3000 | 40 |
| | diethylbenzene (mixed isomers) | ExxonMobil | 180–182 | 356–360 | | 100 | Not available | <100 | >458 | None assigned |
| | xylene (mixed isomers) | Shell | 139–142 | 282–288 | | 100 | 90 | 76 | 600 | 100 |
| | Shellsol A100 (prev. Shellsol A) | Shell | 167–180 | 333–356 | | 100 | 90 | 20 | 2400 | 25 |
| | Shellsol A150 (prev. Shellsol NF) | Shell | 185–209 | 365–408 | | 100 | 95 | 7 | 6500 | 50 |
| | Shellsol A150 ND (prev. Shellsol AB) | Shell | 183–197 | 361–387 | | 100 | 95 | 10 | 4600 | 50 |
| | toluene | Shell | 110–111 | 230–232 | | 100 | 105 | 200 | 226 | 100 |

| | USA solvents (also known as) | | | | | | | | | TLV (ACGH) |
|---|---|---|---|---|---|---|---|---|---|---|
| **Mineral Spirits** | odorless mineral spirits (Shellsol OMS) | Shell | 174–204 | 346–400 | 100 | | 29 | 9 | 5100 | 100 |
| | mineral spirits 200 HT (Shellsol D43) | Shell | 162–206 | 324–402 | 100 (52) | | 32 | 13 | 3400 | 100 |
| | Sol 340 HT (Shellsol D38) | Shell | 159–176 | 319–349 | 100 (54) | | 32 | 27 | 1700 | 100 |
| | mineral spirits 150 EC (Shellsol 3 EC) | Shell | 163–199 | 326–390 | 97 (50) | 3 | 33 | 13 | 3400 | 100 |
| | mineral spirits 145 EC (Shellsol 7 EC) | Shell | 162–199 | 323–390 | 93 (48) | 7 | 35 | 14 | 3250 | 100 |
| | VM&P Naptha HT | Shell | 119–139 | 247–282 | 100 (46) | | 35 | 150 | 305 | 300 |
| | Sol 320 (obsolete) | Shell | 157–179 | 314–355 | 93 (50) | 7 | 38 | 28 | 1700 | 100 |
| | mineral spirits 135 (Shellsol 15) | Shell | 160–181 | 320–357 | 85 (43) | | 45 | 10 | 4700 | 100 |
| **Napthenics** | Cypar 9 | Shell | 138–164 | 280–328 | 100 (100) | 15 | 41 | 67 | 700 | None assigned |
| **Aromatics** | Cypar 7 | Shell | 98–114 | 209–237 | 100 (100) | | 46 | 380 | 120 | 400 |
| | Cyclo Sol 100 (Shellsol A100) | Shell | 160–176 | 320–348 | | 100 | 56 | 21 | 2200 | 25 |
| | Cyclo Sol 150 (Shellsol A150) | Shell | 182–215 | 359–419 | | 100 | 58 | 9 | 5000 | 50 |
| | TS28 | Shell | 161–198 | 322–388 | 25 | 75 | 73 | 14 | 3200 | 25 |
| | xylene (mixed isomers) | Shell | 139–142 | 282–288 | | 100 | 90 | 76 | 600 | 100 |
| | toluene | Shell | 110–111 | 230–232 | | 100 | 105 | 200 | 226 | 100 |

A wide range of hydrocarbon solvents is available through commercial distributors. Some important properties of hydrocarbon solvents are listed here. Most of the solvents have been mentioned in conservation literature, although some have been included for comparative purposes. Within each class, solvents are listed in increasing order of 'polarity' on the basis of their K-B value. Related information can be found under sections 11.3.1 (Hydrocarbon solvents), 11.3.2 (Evaporation rates, vapour pressure and density; Toxicity), and in Chapter 12. *Note that both exposure limits and product descriptions are subject to regular review: Conservators should consult current literature to ensure their information is up to date.*

In cases where individual solvents become obsolete (e.g. Sol 320), this chart can be used to select a replacement solvent with similar properties (e.g. Shellsol D38). The evaporation rate can be used in combination with the exposure limit to compare the relative risk to the conservator of different solvents, or to select a solvent suitable for a given application. For example, the evaporation rate or aromatic content of a solvent can significantly affect the process of cleaning, consolidation, retouching or varnishing.

The *Boiling range* describes the temperatures between which the solvent was distilled. Pure solvents have a narrow boiling range (e.g. xylene, toluene). A wide boiling range indicates the presence of a mixture of substances (e.g. turpentine).

*Aliphatic/aromatic* content can be useful for selecting a solvent with the required Teas solubility parameters for cleaning, retouching, consolidation or varnishing.

The *Kauri-butanol (K-B) value* is a shorthand measure of aromatic content and can be used to find the least aromatic hydrocarbon solvent that will dissolve a given substance. The K-B value is not particularly useful in judging comparative solubility properties of non-aromatic hydrocarbon solvents, which usually have a K-B value below 35.

The *nBuAc number* is a common measure of evaporation rate. Seconds to 90% evaporation is also a useful tool for comparison of evaporation rates. Not all manufacturers supply a figure for 'seconds to 90% evaporation'. This figure can be estimated by dividing the nBuAc number (e.g. 14, where nBuAc = 100) by 100 (14/100), inverting this fraction (100/14) and multiplying it by 458 (seconds to 90% evaporation of *nBuAc*). For example, for a solvent with an nBuAc (=100) number of 14:

$$\frac{100}{14} \times 458 = 3271 \text{ seconds to 90\% evaporation}$$

The *OEL/TLV* (ppm), in combination with the evaporation rate, is essential for choosing the least potentially harmful solvent for a given purpose. For example, Shellsol D40 and low aromatic white spirit have very similar K-B numbers and evaporation rates. The aromatic content in low aromatic white spirit, however, results in a lower OEL, indicting it is a potentially more harmful solvent than Shellsol D40. In contrast, xylene and Shellsol A100 have different OELs and evaporation rates but present a comparable risk to the conservator (see Toxicity under section 11.3.2). It is important to note that in the absence of an assigned OEL or TLV, conservators should identify the OEL/TLV of similar materials and use them as a guideline, always erring on the side of caution.

cycloalkane) although other atoms such as oxygen or nitrogen may also be substituted, creating a heterocyclic structure. The cyclic structure may include single (saturated) or double bonds (unsaturated) and side chains may be attached. In the past, saturated cyclic hydrocarbons (e.g. cyclohexane) were called napthas. In the solvent industry, the term naptha, e.g. VM&P naptha, is also applied to a solvent with a particular boiling range (see *Table 11.1*). Solvents with these structures, whether linear, branched or cyclic, are called aliphatics and are the most non-polar solvents.

Aromatic solvents contain a cyclic structure in which the electrons are delocalized over the entire ring and the structure is stabilized by this delocalization. The electrons are shared equally by the atoms that make up the ring structure. The delocalization of the electrons in the structure of aromatic solvents allows interactions with materials in a way that is different from van der Waals forces, dipole and hydrogen bonding. If a material is dominated by aromatic structures, then an aromatic solvent will be the most efficient way to bring it into solution.

The most common example of an aromatic structure is that of benzene, in which the cyclic structure is composed of six carbon atoms. Benzene ($C_6H_6$) is often represented by the symbol ⬡. When a methyl group ($CH_3$) is substituted for hydrogen on a benzene ring, the structure as a whole is called a phenyl group. The prefix for the $C_7H_7$ molecule is phenyl-, sometimes represented by the symbol Ph. Aromatics in which a different atom (e.g. nitrogen) is substituted for one of the carbons within the ring are called heteroaromatics, e.g. pyridine. Aliphatic structures do not contain a benzene or similar ring. Aromatics tend to have low OELs/TLVs and many can be absorbed through the skin. The use of aromatic solvents requires measures such as gloves and extraction to limit exposure.

Toluene (methyl benzene) and xylene (dimethyl benzene) are aromatic hydrocarbons. Toluene has one methyl group attached to a benzene ring whilst xylene has two, and therefore three possible isomers.

Hydrocarbons may have sub-units attached to them. If the sub-unit is saturated (i.e. contains only single bonds, e.g. —$CH_2$— or —$CH_3$) it is called an alkyl group. If the sub-

unit is an aromatic group it is called an aryl group.

Crude oil, from which most hydrocarbon solvents are derived, is a complex mixture of hydrocarbons along with traces of other substances. Shell and ExxonMobil produce a range of aliphatic and aromatic hydrocarbon solvents of varying composition and often attach trade names to their own products (e.g. Shellsol A100, Solvesso 100). The crude oil is distilled and as a result hydrocarbon solvents are often classified according to their boiling range. Pure substances have sharply defined physical properties and therefore a sharply defined boiling point. This means that unless the boiling point is within a 1 °C range, a mixture of materials is present. In the case of xylene, the fairly narrow boiling range indicates the presence of isomers with similar physical properties. In contrast, the wider boiling range for turpentine indicates the presence of a variety of substances.

The Kauri-butanol test is often used to classify the solvent properties of petroleum fractions. The test uses a solution of 100 grams of kauri gum dissolved in 500 grams of n-butyl alcohol at 25 °C. Kauri-butanol value is the volume in millilitres at 25 °C of the solvent required to produce a defined degree of turbidity when added to 20 g of the standard solution of Kauri resin in butan-1-ol. The Kauri-butanol number may be used to find the least aromatic hydrocarbon solvent that will dissolve a given substance. The K-B value has limitations, however, and is not particularly useful in judging comparative solubility properties of non-aromatic hydrocarbon solvents, which usually have a K-B number below 35.

Common names, such as petroleum distillates, petroleum benzine (note the -ine ending), naptha, white spirit, mineral spirits, petroleum ether and ligroine are often used to describe volatile hydrocarbons obtained from petroleum. These terms are non-specific and may be used to describe a variety of aliphatic solvent blends that vary in their constituents and properties.

In the UK, the term white spirit relates to boiling range and flash point and as a result the aromatic content may vary. Shell (UK) produces three grades of white spirit that vary in aromatic content, evaporation rate and Kauri-butanol value. Stoddard solvent is equivalent to low aromatic (*c.*17–20% aromatic) white spirit but has a slower evaporating rate.

A range of aliphatic petroleum spirits are available and vary in boiling range from around 30–40 °C to 120–160 °C. Petroleum spirit blends are not necessarily interchangeable. In the case of those supplied by Merck UK, the OEL varies according to the presence of n-hexane (40–60 °C – < 2%; 60–80 °C – 40%; 80–100 °C – < 0.1% n-hexane). Prolonged exposure to n-hexane can cause serious damage to health and carries a risk of impaired fertility. Thus the blends that contain any proportion of n-hexane have a significantly lower OEL than those without it.

Given the range of solvents included under generic names, it may be helpful to use and refer to named solvents whose properties can be specified (e.g. 'petroleum spirits 30–40 °C', rather than 'petroleum spirits' or 'ligroine'). Information such as boiling range, aromatic content and evaporation rate may be obtained from the manufacturer and can often be found in material safety data sheets. The properties of some common hydrocarbon solvents are listed in *Table 11.1.*

Turpentine is a volatile oil derived through the distillation of wood or resins from certain conifers. It is a naturally occurring cyclic hydrocarbon. Gum turpentine comes directly from processed pine sap, most often a species of an American southern pine, whilst wood turpentine is derived from extracts after the wood has been harvested. Turpentine has a boiling point range of around 154–170 °C, consists of unsaturated cyclic hydrocarbons (also called turpenes) and may also contain resin acids. Mills and White (1994) discuss and illustrate the structure of some of the components of turpentine. Many turpenes are reactive and oxidize with exposure to air, light or heat, leaving insoluble polymerized residues. As a result turpentine has been largely replaced by white spirit in most conservation studios, but there may be cleaning problems for which it is appropriate.

Hydrocarbon solvents such as petroleum distillates, white spirit, turpentine and xylene contain hydrocarbon structures similar to those in oily dirt, soot and waxes. They are good solvents for these materials and generally poor solvents for polar natural resins. The combination of varying proportions of alkanes,

**Figure 11.8** A japanned papier mâché tray *c.*1865. The inlaid mother-of-pearl is embellished with fine painted and gilded details. A natural resin varnish, visible under UV, was usually applied selectively to the decorated areas. The painted and varnished mother-of-pearl, inlaid into the black japanned background, was disfigured by a multitude of dirt spots. Solvent tests showed that an aromatic hydrocarbon solvent would remove these spots, but at considerable risk to the delicate paint layers on the mother-of-pearl. By mixing an aliphatic hydrocarbon solvent with an aromatic hydrocarbon solvent to give progressively increasing aromatic content, it was possible to find a mixture with sufficient aromatic content to dissolve to dirt without damaging the decoration

cycloalkanes and aromatic components within a hydrocarbon solvent determines its solubility parameters (see *Table 11.1* and *Figure 11.10*). Solvent tests for the removal of dirt from a surface varnished with a natural resin may start with an aliphatic hydrocarbon, progress through aliphatic/aromatic mixtures with an increasing aromatic content, to a pure aromatic hydrocarbon solvent if necessary (*Figure 11.8*).

### Chlorinated hydrocarbons

The non-symmetrical addition of chlorine to a hydrocarbon increases the contribution of dipole bonding to the solvent. A chlorinated solvent used in furniture conservation is dichloromethane.

$$Cl-CH_2-Cl \qquad \text{dichloromethane}$$

The solvent effect of dichloromethane is dominated by dipole bonding and as a result it is an effective solvent for many materials, including natural resins and oil-based layers. It is a major component in many paint strippers in the UK, though strippers based on this chemical are banned in many states in the USA. Dichloromethane is a poor solvent for materials that are predominantly hydrogen-bonded, thus it can be used on some water-sensitive surfaces, e.g. water gilding, without damaging them. Some chlorinated hydrocarbon solvents may form an explosive mixture with acetone and this solvent blend should be avoided. Non-polar chlorinated hydrocarbons (e.g. carbon tetrachloride) were used for large-scale industrial cleaning of textiles because they are non-flammable. Chlorinated hydrocarbons have been identified as contributing to damage to the ozone layer and their use, in large-scale industrial applications, has been curtailed.

### Alcohols

Alcohols contain an —OH or hydroxyl functional group, a permanent dipole that can form hydrogen bonds. They are usually identified by the suffix -ol, e.g. methanol. The presence of an alcohol group on an otherwise hydrophobic molecule such as benzene, e.g. phenol or benzyl alcohol, will impart a small degree of miscibility with hydrogen-bonded solvents. Ethanol is commonly used in conservation. The addition of unpalatable or poisonous substances to ethanol gives a solvent called methylated spirits (UK) or denatured alcohol (USA). Industrial methylated spirits (IMS) contains 95% ethanol and 5% methanol. Methylated spirits available for domestic use in the UK (mineralized methylated spirits, or MMS) contains 90% ethanol, 9.5% methanol and 0.5% pyridine, to which is added 0.375% petroleum spirits and methyl violet dye. In the USA, ethanol may be denatured by the addition of a range of materials including petroleum, aliphatic iso-alcohols and other solvents. With the exception of ethanol that is specified as anhydrous, these solvents also contain a small amount of water. Examples of alcohols used in furniture conservation are ethanol, benzyl alcohol and 1-methoxypropan-2-ol.

$$CH_3 - CH_2 - OH \qquad \text{ethanol}$$

Ethanol is a small linear molecule. It is fast-evaporating and a good solvent for natural resins and has a relatively fast swelling action on them. It is more polar than larger and branched alcohols. Methanol is slightly more polar, but it is more harmful and is too fast-evaporating and fast-acting for general use.

$$CH_2 - OH \qquad \text{benzyl alcohol}$$

Benzyl alcohol combines both aromatic and alcohol solvent properties. It is very effective on materials that combine both aromatic and hydrogen bonding, e.g. natural resins. It is not particularly selective for layer removal. If used either neat or as a large proportion in a solvent blend, it will damage substrates such as oil paint, japanning and oriental lacquer that has been exposed to UV. The addition of a small proportion of benzyl alcohol to solvent blends/gels and in resin and bile soaps has been reported in conservation literature. Such small proportions limit the potential for damage whilst exploiting its solvent properties.

$$CH_3 - \overset{\overset{\displaystyle OH}{|}}{CH} - CH_2 - O - CH_3 \qquad \text{1-methoxypropan-2-ol}$$

1-methoxypropan-2-ol (also known as methyl proxitol, glycol ether PM, Arcosolv® PM and propylene glycol monomethyl ether) can be used as a diluent for many resins used in retouching and varnishing. It is a less hazardous solvent in this context than xylene, toluene and cellosolve.

### Aldehydes and ketones

Aldehydes and ketones both contain the carbonyl group. Aldehydes are usually identified by the suffix -al, whilst ketones are usually identified by the suffix -one. In aldehydes the carbonyl group is bonded to at least one hydrogen atom whilst in ketones it is bonded to two carbon atoms.

$$C = O \qquad \text{a carbonyl group}$$

$$R - \overset{\overset{\displaystyle H}{|}}{C} = O \qquad \text{an aldehyde}$$

$$R - \overset{\overset{\displaystyle R'}{|}}{C} = O \qquad \text{a ketone (neither R can be H)}$$

The presence of the carbonyl group gives a permanent dipole with some potential for hydrogen bonding to H-donors such as water. The overall polarity of ketones and aldehydes depends on which groups are attached to the carbon, e.g. non-polar methyl groups will reduce the overall polarity of the solvent. Ketones are more common than aldehydes in conservation. Polar oxygenated solvents such as alcohols, ketones and aldehydes are effective solvents for many natural and synthetic resins but are relatively poor solvents for greasy dirt. Some common examples of ketones are acetone, methyl ethyl ketone and diacetone alcohol.

$$CH_3 - \overset{\overset{\displaystyle CH_3}{|}}{C} = O \qquad \text{acetone}$$

Acetone (propanone according to the IUPAC system) is a fast-evaporating solvent that rapidly swells and dissolves natural resins.

$$CH_3 - CH_2 - \overset{\overset{\displaystyle CH_3}{|}}{C} = O \qquad \text{methyl ethyl ketone}$$

Methyl ethyl ketone (butanone) has been used in furniture conservation but is not as common as acetone. The extra methylene group makes MEK slightly less polar than acetone.

$$CH_3 - \overset{\overset{\displaystyle CH_3}{|}}{\underset{\underset{\displaystyle OH}{|}}{C}} - CH_2 - \overset{\overset{\displaystyle O}{\|}}{C} - CH_3 \qquad \text{diacetone alcohol}$$

Diacetone alcohol combines both alcohol and ketone groups in a single solvent. The larger size of the molecule and its capacity for hydrogen bonding means that it evaporates slowly and the combination of functional groups makes it a good solvent for a wide range of resins.

## Ethers

Ethers have the general formula R—O—R or R—O—R$_1$. The functional group is an oxygen atom with two lone pairs of electrons, bonded to two alkyl groups, which may be different to each other. The structure of ethers is similar to that of water but although the oxygen atom is electronegative, the alkyl groups are only slightly positive, giving an overall weakly polar effect. They do not form hydrogen bonds, are very volatile, are immiscible or only slightly miscible with water and are not very reactive. Ethers have been used to clean some solvent-sensitive surfaces because their fast evaporation rate limits their solubility effect. They are not usually used in conservation because they are extremely flammable and have strong narcotic properties. Cellosolve ($C_2H_5OC_2H_4OH$) has been used in conservation. Its solvent properties are dominated by the alcohol group rather than the ether group. Less potentially harmful solvents (e.g. methoxypropan-2-ol) are usually substituted for it.

$$R - O - R'$$
Ether functional group

$$CH_3 - CH_2 - O - CH_2 - CH_2 - OH$$
Ethyl cellosolve

## Esters

Esters have the general formula RCOOR$_1$. The functional group is a carbon atom double-bonded to one oxygen atom and single-bonded to another, with alkyl groups at either end that may be different from each other. Although the lone pairs of electrons on both oxygens make esters polar, they do not hydrogen-bond themselves. Like aldehydes and ketones, esters hydrogen-bond with water. Esters are very good solvents for nitrocellulose and some are good solvents for polyvinyl acetate adhesives.

$$R' - \overset{\overset{\displaystyle O}{\|}}{C} - O - R$$
Ester functional group

$$CH_3 - \overset{\overset{\displaystyle O}{\|}}{C} - O - CH_2 - CH_3$$
Ethyl acetate

## Organic nitrogenous compounds

*Amines* Amines contain a nitrogen atom. They have the general formula R—NH$_2$ (the NH$_2$

group is also called an amino group). The exposed lone pair of electrons on the nitrogen makes them moderately polar. Amines are classified as primary, secondary or tertiary, depending on the number of organic groups that are attached to the nitrogen atom. Primary and secondary amines can form strong hydrogen bonds. Tertiary amines do not hydrogen-bond within themselves but do form hydrogen-bonds with water or other hydroxylic solvents. Amines are relatively weak bases and are sometimes used to combine solvent and reagent action to break down oil/resin films. Amines generally have a low vapour pressure and require a rinse procedure to remove residues. As bases, they have the potential to saponify fatty, oily or greasy materials. They should be used with care on pH-sensitive surfaces.

$$R - \overset{\overset{\displaystyle H}{|}}{N} - H$$

Amine functional group

$$OH - CH_2 - CH_2 - \overset{\overset{\displaystyle OH}{|}}{\underset{\underset{\displaystyle CH_2}{|}}{\overset{\overset{\displaystyle CH_2}{|}}{N}}} - CH_2 - CH_2 - OH$$

Triethanolamine

In conservation, triethanolamine is often referred to as TEA. It should be noted that in the broader world of organic chemistry, TEA is shorthand for triethylamine. These two solvents have different properties and are not interchangeable.

*Cyclic amines* All classes of solvents can have cyclic structures. Benzene rings that have an amino ($NH_2$) group attached are called arylamines. Heterocyclic amines contain one or more nitrogen atoms within the cyclic structure.

N-methyl-2-pyrrolidinone

N-methyl-2-pyrrolidinone is a heterocyclic amine. The *N* indicates that the methyl group is attached to the nitrogen atom. N-methyl-2-

pyrrolidone has a marked swelling action on oil-based varnishes and paint and is therefore sometimes used to remove oil based retouching. N-methyl-2-pyrrolidone is also an effective solvent for polysaccharides (Horie, 1992).

morpholine

Morpholine has both oxygen and nitrogen atoms substituted within the cyclic structure. It is an effective solvent for shellac, casein and linseed oil, all of which are sensitive to elevated pH. It has an unpleasant odour and with an OES LTEL of 20 ppm, it is not recommended for general use.

*Amides*

$$\overset{\overset{\displaystyle O}{\|}}{C-N} \quad \overset{\overset{\displaystyle O}{\|}}{R-C-N-H_2} \quad \overset{\overset{\displaystyle O}{\|}}{R-C-N(H,R_1)} \quad \overset{\overset{\displaystyle O}{\|}}{R-C-N(R_1,R_2)}$$

Amides contain a C—N group, as shown in the examples above, where R, $R_1$ and $R_2$ represent different alkyl groups. The lone pairs on the oxygen and nitrogen make amides very polar, although amides are essentially neutral in terms of acid/base reactions. Examples of amides are:

$$CH_3 - \overset{\overset{\displaystyle O}{\|}}{C} - NH_2$$

Acetamide

$$CH_3 - \overset{\overset{\displaystyle O}{\|}}{C} - NH - CH_3$$

N-methylacetamide

$$H - \overset{\overset{\displaystyle O}{\|}}{C} - N\overset{\displaystyle \diagup CH_3}{\diagdown CH_3}$$

Dimethyl formamide

Dimethyl formamide has been used for removing soot from water gilding but will swell oil-based layers. It is too harmful for general use.

## 11.3.2 Physical properties of solvents

A wide range of organic solvents with finely graded properties is available from chemical suppliers. Careful selection of solvent/s and delivery systems can greatly increase the specificity of a cleaning treatment and decrease the risk to the surface that is to be retained. By selecting solvents on the basis of, for example, volatility and relative compatibility to a surface, the speed and extent of action can be controlled. Solvents can be used on a wide range of dirt and surface types and can penetrate into otherwise inaccessible areas. Some of their disadvantages are their limited effect on very polar dirt, toxicity, flammability and expense. Factors influencing solvent choice include volatility, viscosity, surface tension (capillarity), toxicity, flammability and solubility parameters.

### Evaporation rates, vapour pressure and density

The evaporation rate describes the rate at which a material will change from liquid to vapour, at a standard temperature and pressure, in comparison to the evaporation rate of a specific known material. The evaporation rate of a solvent is dependent on the size of the solvent molecules and the forces of attraction between them. A homologous series of compounds only differs from the next compound in the sequence by the addition of a $CH_2$ group, e.g. methane ($CH_4$), ethane ($C_2H_6$), propane ($C_3H_8$) etc. The smaller the molecule in any given homologous series, the lower the boiling point, the higher the vapour pressure and the faster its evaporation rate. Van der Waals forces are the predominant attractive force in hydrocarbon solvents. These are weak and as a result low molecular weight hydrocarbons are very volatile (e.g. methane, ethane and propane). As the molecules become larger they evaporate more slowly and when very large, aliphatic hydrocarbons form solid substances called paraffin waxes. An aromatic structure induces slight polarity in otherwise non-polar molecules and results in a comparative increase in boiling point and vapour pressure. Alcohols are polar molecules that also have considerable hydrogen bonding between them. As a result they are less volatile than similar-sized hydrocarbons. Hydrogen bonding is the dominant intermolecular force in water. Thus even though water is a small molecule, stronger intermolecular forces mean that, comparatively, its boiling point is high

and its vapour pressure is low. Liquids that evaporate rapidly may be described as volatile. The evaporation rate of a single solvent is dependent on vapour pressure (in turn dependent on temperature and pressure), surface/volume ratio and the rate of air flow over the surface (Wicks *et al.*, 1992).

As a general rule, there is an inverse relationship between the boiling point of a solvent and its evaporation rate, i.e. the higher the boiling point, the lower the evaporation rate. Evaporation rates are usually expressed as a ratio and therefore do not have units of measurement. There are two widely used standard solvents, diethyl ether (ether) and n-butyl acetate (nBuAc), which are assigned a relative value of 1 or 100. Unfortunately, the scales are not interchangeable. A slow evaporation rate on the ether scale corresponds to a high number, i.e. the time a solvent takes to evaporate is many times that which ether takes. In contrast, a slow evaporation rate on the butyl scale corresponds to a low number, i.e. the evaporation rate is slower than that of butyl acetate. Evaporation rates may also be measured in 'seconds to 90% evaporation' (see *Table 11.1*).

The vapour pressure of a solvent is a measure of the pressure exerted by its vapour when the solvent and its vapour are in dynamic equilibrium, i.e. when the molecules leaving a liquid to form vapour and those rejoining it are in equilibrium. Vapour pressure is measured in a closed vessel and at a standard temperature and pressure. As a general rule, there is an inverse relationship between the boiling point of a solvent and its vapour pressure, i.e. the higher the vapour pressure, the lower the boiling point and the faster the evaporation rate.

Organic solvent vapours are heavier than air (i.e. their relative vapour density is higher than air). This is particularly important for ventilation and when dealing with spillages. Whilst extraction should draw solvent fumes away from the conservator, ventilation should be designed to draw from, and tests for toxic concentrations may need to be made at, floor level.

### Viscosity

Viscosity describes the resistance to flow of a liquid. It is a result of the size and shape (e.g.

branching) of molecules and the secondary bonding between them. Increasing temperature will reduce viscosity. Solvents commonly used in conservation are not very viscous and are sometimes gelled to increase their viscosity and hence application control. Viscosity is discussed in detail by Moncrieff and Weaver (1992).

### Surface tension and capillary action

Surface tension is a direct measure of inter-molecular forces and describes the strength of attraction between the molecules in a liquid. Whether a solvent wets onto a surface well and spreads out, or whether it wets poorly and forms droplets or beads, will depend on whether the liquid molecules are more strongly attracted to the surface or each other. Solvents that are predominantly bonded by van der Waals forces wet surfaces more effectively than those characterized by hydrogen bonding. Surface tension can be reduced by the addition of a surfactant (see section 11.5.4).

Capillary action occurs when liquids rise or spread spontaneously through very fine tubes or pores – a common example is water and blotting paper. Capillarity is important in solvent cleaning because fine pores in a decorated surface may trap solvents and delay evaporation, and because capillary action is the basis for cleaning using poultices.

### Toxicity

All organic solvents are potentially toxic, some are carcinogenic and some are teratogens and cause damage to fetuses. Manufacturers in the USA and UK are required to provide users with information about the physical and chemical properties of solvents (and other materials), the health and safety implications of their use and any special precautions that may be required. This information is provided in the form of Material Safety Data Sheets. *The relevant health and safety regulations should be read, understood and conformed with before any organic solvents are used.*

In the UK the Control of Substances Hazardous to Health (CoSHH) Regulations set out occupational exposure limits to solvents and other hazardous materials. The Health and Safety Executive publish an annual booklet (EH40), which lists occupational exposure limits (OEL) and maximum exposure limits

(MEL), both of which are legally enforceable under CoSHH (see section 9.7.4). Also included is a technical supplement on calculating exposure and, in the appendices, an ever-growing list of carcinogens. The maximum exposure limit is the maximum concentration of an airborne substance, averaged over a reference period (long-term exposure limit or LTEL is eight hours, short-term exposure limit or STEL is 15 minutes), to which employees may be exposed by inhalation under any circumstances. MELs are set for substances that may cause the most serious damage to health, such as cancer or occupational asthma, and for which safe levels of exposure cannot be determined or exposure cannot be practicably controlled. The occupational exposure standard (OES) is the concentration of an airborne substance, averaged over a reference period (LTEL 8 hours, STEL 15 minutes) at which, according to current knowledge, there is no evidence that it is likely to be injurious to employees if they are exposed by inhalation day after day at that concentration. Both are expressed in parts per million (ppm) or milligrams per cubic metre ($mg.m^{-3}$). As a general rule, the smaller the number the more harmful the substance. It is possible to convert $mg/m^3$ to ppm using the following formula (Health and Safety Executive, EH40):

$$OEL \text{ in ppm} = \frac{OEL \text{ in } mg/m^3 \times 24.05526}{\text{molecular weight}}$$

Similarly:

$$OEL \text{ in } mg/m^3 = \frac{OEL \text{ in ppm} \times \text{molecular weight}}{24.05526}$$

For example, the OEL for petroleum spirits 60–80 °C (Merck UK) is 70 $mg/m^3$. The constituent that is responsible for this comparatively low OEL is n-hexane (MW 86.18). To convert $mg/m^3$ to ppm:

$$\frac{70 \times 24.05526}{86.18} = 20 \text{ ppm (rounded up from 19.53)}$$

In the USA, permissible exposure limits (PELs) for toxic and hazardous substances are set by the Occupational Safety and Health Administration (OSHA), a federal government agency within the Department of Labor (www.osha.gov/). In addition, the National Institute for Occupational Safety and Health (NIOSH) produces recommended exposure limits (RELs), whilst the American Conference of Government Industrial Hygienists (ACGIH) produces threshold limit values (TLVs) (www.acgih.org). All three standards (PELs, RELs and TLVs) may be encountered in US material safety data sheets. The lower the PEL or TLV, the more toxic the chemical. Substances with an MEL, or an OEL or TLV lower than 200 ppm should be avoided where possible. Safety precautions, such as the use of a fume cupboard or portable solvent cabinet, should be taken if their use cannot be avoided.

Proper control of risks to health and safety is essential. The use of some solvents traditionally used in conservation and restoration has been curtailed because of acute and chronic health risks. Aromatic hydrocarbons such as xylene and toluene, for example, may clean some surfaces well but pose a health hazard. Whilst exposure limits or TLVs are useful, they must be considered alongside other factors such as evaporation rate to find the solvent that presents the least risk to the user.

Risk can be defined as hazard multiplied by exposure. Conservators wishing to assess the relative risk of different solvents must compare the hazard (represented by the OEL, PEL or TLV in ppm) in combination with exposure (evaporation rate, in this case using nBuAc as the standard). In the case of exposure limits, the hazard is inversely proportional to the limit, that is, the lower the OEL, the greater the hazard. Many people prefer to work in whole numbers rather than fractions, so for easier comparison, multiply the answer by 100.

$$\text{risk} = \frac{1}{\text{exposure limit (ppm)}}$$
$$\times \text{ evaporation rate (nBuAc)}$$
$$\times 100$$

The larger the resulting number, the greater the risk to the conservator from inhaling fumes.

*Example 1*
Compare two solvents with the same OEL (100 ppm). Solvent A has an evaporation rate of 8, whilst solvent B is a faster-evaporating solvent with an evaporation rate of 16 (nBuAc=100):

Comparative risk of Solvent A = 1/100 × 8 = 0.08 × 100 = 8

Comparative risk of Solvent B = 1/100 × 16 = 0.16 × 100 = 16

*Answer:* Solvent B presents twice the comparative risk.

*Example 2*
Compare two solvents with different OELs and different evaporation rates. Solvent C has an OEL of 100 ppm and an evaporation rate of 76 (nBuAc = 100), whilst solvent D has an OEL of 40 and an evaporation rate of 15 (nBuAc = 100):

Comparative risk of Solvent C = 1/100 × 76 = 0.76 × 100 = 76

Comparative risk of Solvent D = 1/40 × 15 = 0.375 × 100 = 37.5

*Answer:* Solvent C presents twice the comparative risk.

In most cases the main danger from solvents is from inhalation of fumes. It is worth noting that many commonly used solvents are absorbed through unbroken skin. In such cases appropriate gloves are essential, in addition to precautions such as good ventilation or extraction. General principles of the control of risks to health and safety are discussed in Chapter 9.

### Flammability

Flammability is defined in terms of flash point (FP). The flash point is the lowest temperature at which the concentration of vapour immediately above the surface of a liquid is sufficient to form an explosive mixture with air and be ignited by a flame. In the UK three grades of flammability are recognized – extremely flammable (FP 0 °C and less), highly flammable (FP 0 °C to 21 °C) and flammable (FP 21 to 55 °C), of which only the first two require hazard labels.

### 11.3.3  Solubility

### Process of dissolution

A true solution is a homogeneous molecular mixture of two or more substances of dissimilar molecular structure. The term is usually applied to solutions of solids in liquids but can equally well be applied to other systems.

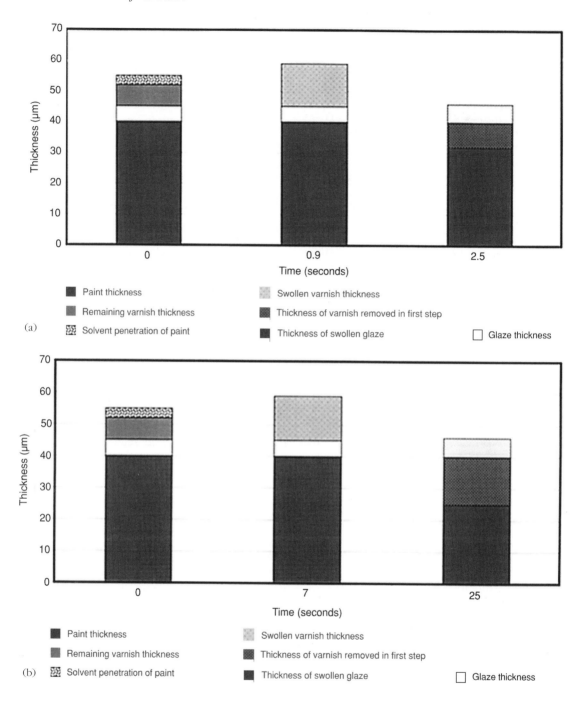

(a)

(b)

When a solid material has dissolved in a liquid, the molecules of the liquid separate all the molecules of the solid. The dissolved material, the solute, can be recovered in unaltered chemical form from the solvent. For example, if the liquid evaporates the solute molecules will coalesce into a solid material, unaltered in chemical form.

**Figure 11.9** Comparison of varnish removal from an oil paint substrate by fast-penetrating, fast-dissolving, fast-evaporating solvent and a medium-penetrating, slow-dissolving, slow-evaporating solvent

The two graphs illustrate varnish removal with a fast-penetrating, fast-dissolving (4 μm/s) solvent, for example acetone (*a*) and a medium-penetrating, slow-dissolving (0.4 μm/s) solvent, for example propan-2-ol (*b*) Fast-, medium- and slow-diffusing (and swelling) solvents diffuse into (and swell) varnish and paint at different rates and, within a given time, different amounts. During the process of varnish dissolution, solvent interacts with the varnish. The longer it takes the solvent to penetrate, swell and dissolve the varnish, the longer the solvent is in contact with the paint film and the greater the potential for the swelling of the paint layer(s). The effect of the solvent on the substrate is a result of the combination of the diffusion rate of the solvent into the paint layer, the rate of the swelling of the paint layer and the rate at which the solvent evaporates from the surface. Thus, during varnish removal, an ideal solvent is one that rapidly diffuses and dissolves the varnish layer, while not diffusing into or swelling the paint layer, and that rapidly evaporates from the paint film

Figure 11.9*a*

Time = 0 seconds: the initial thickness of each layer are oil paint = 40 μm, glaze = 5 μm and varnish = 10 μm. The paint thickness is arbitrary and was chosen for illustrative convenience. In this bar the total varnish thickness (10 μm) includes both the varnish that is dissolved after solvent application (3 μm) and the varnish that remains (7 μm)

Time = 0.9 seconds: once applied, the fast penetrating solvent front diffuses into the varnish layer within 0.9 seconds; 3 μm of the original varnish is dissolved and the remaining 7 μm is swollen to a thickness of 14 μm

Time = 2.5 seconds: within 2.5 seconds the fast-penetrating solvent dissolves the varnish layer completely and swabbing is stopped. The paint and glaze have been exposed to the solvent for 1.6 seconds resulting in the penetration of the solvent into the paint layer to a depth of 12 μm. The swab leaves a 1 μm thick layer of high volatility solvent on the paint surface; 50% evaporates, and the solvent front advances a further 2 μm (a total of 14 μm) into the paint layer. The glaze layer may exhibit some swelling as a result of this penetration. Because the thickness of the paint layer is arbitrary, this bar does not represent the percentage of penetration of the solvent into the paint layer, only the distance

Figure 11.9*b*

Time = 0 seconds: the initial thickness of each layer are oil paint = 40 μm, glaze = 5 μm and varnish = 10 μm. The paint thickness is arbitrary and was chosen for illustrative convenience. In this bar the total varnish thickness (10 μm) includes both the varnish that is dissolved after solvent application (3 μm) and the varnish that remains (7 μm)

Time = 7 seconds: once applied, the medium-penetrating solvent front penetrates the varnish layer within 7 seconds; 3 μm of the original varnish is dissolved and the remaining 7 μm is swollen to a thickness of 14 μm

Time = 25 seconds: within 25 seconds the medium-penetrating solvent dissolves the varnish layer completely and swabbing is stopped. The paint and glaze have been exposed to the solvent for 18 seconds, resulting in the penetration of the solvent into the paint layer to a depth of 17 μm. The swab leaves a 1 μm thick layer of low volatility solvent on the paint surface; most enters the paint, and the solvent front advances a further 4 μm (a total of 21 μm) into the paint layer. The glaze layer may exhibit some swelling as a result of this penetration. Because the thickness of the paint layer is arbitrary, this bar does not represent the percentage of penetration of the solvent into the paint layer, only the distance

There are four stages in the dissolution of a polymeric coating in a solvent. First the solvent molecules diffuse between the polymer chains. If there is a strong interaction between the solvent and the surface coating, the solvent will be absorbed into the outer layer of the polymer, causing it to swell. With continued solvent exposure, the outer layer of the polymer will continue to swell and become a rubbery gel. If the coating is not crosslinked it will dissolve, forming a solution that can be removed with a swab. If the varnish is substantially crosslinked it will reach a region of peak swelling and may be removed mechanically. The rate at which solvent molecules are lost from the surface is dependent on temperature, the vapour pressure of the solvent, and the rate of air flow over the surface. The surface/volume ratio of solvent over the surface as a whole will increase evaporation time, but solvent trapped in pores may take substantially longer to evaporate than that on the surface. Secondary bonding between solvent and substrate will also affect the evaporation rate. The evaporation rate of a given quantity of water from cotton or wood, which are hydrophilic, is slower than that from polyester, which is hydrophobic.

Ueberreiter (1968) has described the process of dissolution of polymers. Michalski (1990) has modelled the physical process of diffusion of a solvent into an oil paint layer. Solvent penetration of, and swelling interaction with, a decorative substrate will depend on several factors such as chemical compatibility and the surface area of the coating that is exposed to solvent. The presence of cracks, pores or cleavage between layers can significantly increase surface area, with a concomitant increase in solvent penetration and retention.

The amount of swelling that occurs in the substrate depends on the relative rates of solvent diffusion into the substrate and the dissolution of the varnish (*Figure 11.9*). Organic solvents that are able to remove varnish layers are also able to affect paint layers. The degree of effect depends on the chemical compatibility of the solvent with the paint medium. A slow diffusing solvent will swell a chemically compatible substrate layer if the solvent is also slow in penetrating and dissolving the overlying varnish. In contrast, a slow diffusing solvent that is chemically incompatible with the substrate will have little or no swelling effect during the short exposure of a varnish removal treatment. This is one reason for the development of aqueous solutions such as resin and bile soaps to remove degraded varnish from oil paint substrates.

### Solubility parameters

The principles of solubility are understood intuitively by most practitioners as 'like dissolves like'. This is an expression of the principle that the intermolecular bonding of the solvent should be similar to the intermolecular bonding within the material that is to be removed. Water, for example, characterized primarily by hydrogen bonding, is a good solvent for traditional furniture-maker's hide glue, the adhesive properties of which are also characterized by hydrogen bonding. Waxes, characterized by van der Waals forces, are insoluble in water but can be brought into solution by hydrocarbons such as white spirit or xylene. Thus understanding the composition of the materials to be removed will help in selecting a solvent with a similar chemistry. Conversely, knowing the nature of what is to be retained will aid the selection of a dissimilar solvent. The 'strength' of a solvent is not an intrinsic property but is relative to the chemical similarity of the solute and the solvent, the molecular weight of the material that is to be dissolved, duration of exposure and temperature.

### Predicting solubility

Several models that assign numbers to the intermolecular forces in liquids have been developed, primarily in response to the need of the coatings industry to match solvents with polymers. Three models are discussed here. Hildebrand solubility parameters ($\delta_s$) were the first to relate the solubility characteristics of a solvent to the intermolecular forces within a liquid:

$$\delta_s = \sqrt{(\text{cohesive energy dispersion, or CED})}$$

The cohesive energy dispersion was a measure of the energy required to vaporize one cubic centimetre of liquid solvent. The stronger the intermolecular forces, the higher the CED and $\delta_s$. Hildebrand and Scott (1948) predicted that solvents with a similar $\delta_s$ would be miscible. Hildebrand solubility parameters are not particularly effective for predicting the solubility of solids, though they have been used to predict the swelling effect of solvents on oil paint films (Feller *et al.*, 1985). They are still widely used in the industrial solvent and paint industries.

Hansen (1967) proposed a refinement of Hildebrand parameters by suggesting that the single solubility parameter $\delta_s$ could be divided according to the contribution of dispersion forces ($\delta_D$), polar forces ($\delta_P$) and hydrogen bonding ($\delta_H$):

$$\delta_s = \sqrt{(\delta_D{}^2 + \delta_P{}^2 + \delta_H{}^2)}$$

Teas (1968) proposed three parameters that were based on Hansen parameters but relative to each other as a proportion of 100:

dispersion forces   $f_d = 100 \; \delta_D/(\delta_D + \delta_P + \delta_H)$

polar forces   $f_p = 100 \; \delta_P/(\delta_D + \delta_P + \delta_H)$

hydrogen bonding   $f_h = 100 \; \delta_H/(\delta_D + \delta_P + \delta_H)$

Solvents that are predominantly characterized by dispersion forces are non-polar (e.g. mineral spirits). Polar solvents can be categorized according to whether hydrogen bonding predominates, in the past referred to as 'wet' polarity (e.g. water), and those in which dipole bonding predominates, previously known as 'dry' polarity (e.g. dichloromethane). Within these broad categories, subtle variations exist

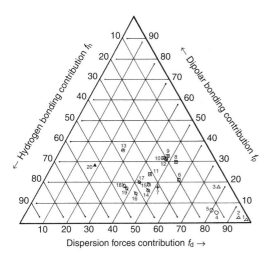

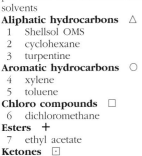

**Figure 11.10** The positions of some common solvents and reagents on the Teas diagram. Horie (1992) has plotted the Teas fractional solubility parameters of many solvents

**Aliphatic hydrocarbons** △
1    Shellsol OMS
2    cyclohexane
3    turpentine
**Aromatic hydrocarbons** ○
4    xylene
5    toluene
**Chloro compounds** □
6    dichloromethane
**Esters** +
7    ethyl acetate
**Ketones** ⊡
8    butan-2-one
9    acetyl acetone
10   acetone
11   diacetone alcohol
**Nitro compounds** ⊙
12   N-methyl-2-pyrrolidinone
13   triethanolamine (see notes for Table 11.2)
**Alcohols** ⊘
14   benzyl alcohol
15   1-methoxypropan-2-ol
16   n-butanol
17   2 ethoxyethanol
18   propan-2-ol
19   ethanol

20   water ▲

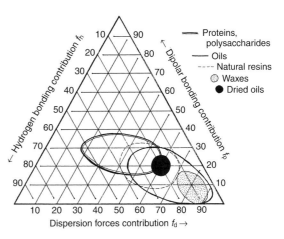

**Figure 11.11** The solubility regions of some common natural binding media (Banik and Krist, 1986)

graph, known as a Teas' chart. Solvents are assigned a single point according the contribution of dispersion/van der Waals forces ($f_d$), polar forces ($f_p$) and hydrogen bonding ($f_h$) to their overall intermolecular bonding. These three components may be expressed as a proportion of 100 (e.g. odourless mineral spirits 98, 1, 1) or as fractions that add up to 1 (e.g. 0.98, 0.01, 0.01).

The Teas' chart has found wide use as a conceptual tool in conservation. Horie (1992) lists the solubility parameters of many solvents used in conservation. Information can also be found on the Internet, for example the CoOL (Conservation Online) site. *Figure 11.10* shows the position of some common solvents on the Teas' diagram. *Table 11.2* lists some physical properties of these solvents. Polymeric materials such as resins are usually soluble in a range of solvents and therefore have solubility regions. *Figure 11.11* shows the solubility regions of some common classes of natural binding media. Comparing *Figures 11.10* and *11.11* allows the conservator to predict, for example, that the removal of waxes will probably require at least a proportion of an aromatic hydrocarbon in the solvent blend. Using a more specific example, *Figure 11.12* shows the solubility region of shellac. Comparison with *Figure 11.10* suggests that shellac will be sensitive to alcohols, ketones and esters.

that can be exploited by the conservator to achieve a degree of specificity for cleaning treatments.

The advantage of the Teas' system is that the three parameters ($f_d$, $f_p$, $f_h$) can be used to plot the position of a solvent on a triangular

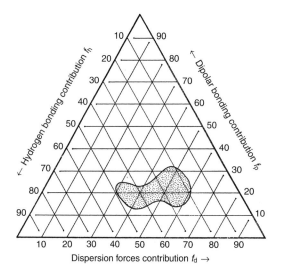

**Figure 11.12** Solubility region of shellac (Horie, 1992)

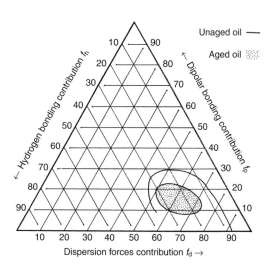

**Figure 11.13** Swelling characteristics of linseed oil (Horie, 1992). Unaged linseed oil is soluble in a range of solvents, including aromatic hydrocarbons, ketones and esters. As the polymer ages and crosslinks, it becomes insoluble. The swelling region of the polymerized oil contracts away from the non-polar corner of the Teas' chart

Materials that form crosslinked macromolecules, such as linseed oil, are often not soluble but their swelling characteristics can be plotted on a Teas' diagram (*Figure 11.13*). As natural binding media age their solubility or swelling region tends to contract and become more polar (*Figure 11.14*). Solubility and swelling regions for some common synthetic polymers can be found in Horie (1992).

Solvent cleaning or varnish removal involves breaking down the secondary bonds that adhere dirt or a varnish to a surface, preferably without affecting the primary or secondary bonds within the substrate. Using the solubility parameters of both an unwanted material and a decorative surface, the Teas chart can be used to formulate solvent tests. The solvent most likely to dissolve a particular type of dirt, varnish or adhesive (or paint) is one that matches its position (and therefore the type and balance of intermolecular bonding) on the Teas' chart. If the solubility parameters of the unwanted material and the substrate are sufficiently different, solvent cleaning can be undertaken (*Figure 11.15*). If solubility parameters are identical, an alternative to solvent cleaning must be found or the cleaning treatment abandoned. Even when the solubility parameters of a coating and a solvent overlap, the coating will not dissolve if the polymer molecules are sufficiently large

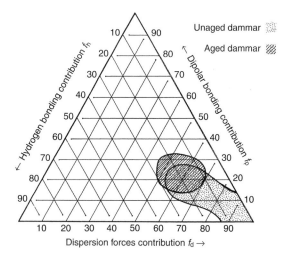

**Figure 11.14** Solubility region of dammar (Horie, 1992). Unaged dammar is soluble in a wide range of solvents, including aliphatic and aromatic hydrocarbons, esters and ketones. After ageing equivalent to one hundred years on a gallery wall, the solubility region has not only contracted, but has become more polar overall

**Table 11.2** Teas' solvent reference chart

| No. | Solvent or reagent | CAS No | Boiling point/range °C | °F | Fractional solubility parameters (100) $f_d$ | $f_p$ | $f_b$ | Vapour pressure, mmHg @20 °C (torr) | Evaporation rate nBuAc = 100 | seconds to 90% evaporation | Flash point °C | °F | OEL ppm (8 hour) |
|---|---|---|---|---|---|---|---|---|---|---|---|---|---|
| 1 | Shellsol OMS | 64741–65–7 | 174–204 | 346–400 | 98 | 1 | 1 | 0.5 | 9 | 5100 | 52 | 126 | 100 |
| 2 | cyclohexane | 110–82–7 | 81 | 178 | 94 | 2 | 4 | 95 | 260 | 176 | –18 | 0 | 100 |
| 3 | turpentine (wood distilled) | 8006–64–2 | 156–170 | 313–338 | 77 | 18 | 5 | 4 | <100 | >458 | 41 | 106 | 100 |
| 4 | xylene (mixed isomers) | 1330–20–7 | 139–142 | 282–288 | 83 | 5 | 12 | 8 | 76 | 600 | 25 | 77 | 100 |
| 5 | toluene | 108–88–3 | 110–111 | 230–232 | 80 | 7 | 13 | 22 | 200 | 226 | 7 | 45 | 50 |
| 6 | dichloromethane | 75–09–2 | 40 | 104 | 59 | 21 | 20 | 350 | 2750 | 17 | Not applicable | | 100 |
| 7 | ethyl acetate | 141–78–6 | 77 | 171 | 51 | 18 | 31 | 76 | 430 | 107 | –4 | 25 | 400 |
| 8 | methyl ethyl ketone (butan-2-one) | 78–93–3 | 80 | 176 | 53 | 30 | 17 | 78 | 460 | 100 | –1 | 30 | 200 |
| 9 | acetyl acetone (2,4,pentanedione) | 123–54–6 | 140 | 284 | 48 | 33 | 19 | 7 | Not available | Not available | 34 | 93 | None assigned |
| 10 | acetone (propanone) | 67–64–1 | 56 | 133 | 47 | 32 | 21 | 181 | 780 | 59 | –20 | –4 | 750 |
| 11 | diacetone alcohol | 123–42–2 | 168 | 334 | 45 | 24 | 31 | 0.95 | 14 | 3200 | 59 | 138 | 50 |
| 12 | N-methyl-2-pyrrolidinone | 872–50–4 | 202 | 396 | 48 | 32 | 20 | 0.3 | 6 | 7600 | 93 | 199 | 25 |
| 13 | triethanolamine | 102–71–6 | 360 | 680 | 27 | 36 | 37 | <0.01 | <1 | >45800 | 179 | 354 | None assigned |
| 14 | benzyl alcohol | 100–51–6 | 206 | 403 | 48 | 16 | 36 | 0.04 | Not available | Not available | 93 | 199 | None assigned |
| 15 | 1-methoxy-propan-2-ol | 107–98–2 | 120 | 248 | 46 | 19 | 35 | 10.9 | 71 | 645 | 35 | 95 | 100 |
| 16 | n-butanol | 71–36–3 | 118 | 244 | 43 | 15 | 42 | 4 | 46 | 1000 | 29 | 84 | no LTEL; STEL 50 |
| 17 | *ethyl cellosolve (2-ethoxyethanol)* | 100–80–5 | 135 | 275 | 42 | 20 | 38 | 3.8 | 35 | 1300 | 54 | 129 | 5 |
| 18 | isopropanol (propan-2-ol) | 67–63–0 | 82 | 180 | 38 | 17 | 45 | 33 | 220 | 208 | 12 | 54 | 400 |
| 19 | ethanol | 64–17–5 | 78 | 172 | 36 | 18 | 46 | 43 | 240 | 190 | 13 | 55 | 1000 |
| 20 | water | Not applicable | 100 | 212 | 18 | 28 | 54 | 18 | 27 | 1700 | Not applicable | | Not applicable |

Some important properties of solvents and reagents included in *Figure 11.10* are listed here. Although triethanolamine's three ethanol moieties give it solubility parameters in the alcohol region it is also an amine that is (weakly) basic. It is capable, therefore, of more than just simple solvation effects: it may also be involved in acid–base interactions, such as hydrolysis, that are promoted by bases.

Hansen (2000) and Barton (1983) list the Hansen solubility parameters for many other solvents, which can be converted to Teas fractional solubility parameters using the equation provided in section 11.3.3. Information on the physical properties of solvents, such as vapour pressure, evaporation rate, flash point and exposure limits can usually be found in manufacturers' or suppliers' Material Safety Data Sheets. These properties are discussed in section 11.3.2 and in *Table 11.1. Note that exposure limits are subject to regular review.*

*Conservators should consult current literature to ensure their information is up to date.*

Solvents may have different systematic, generic, proprietary and trivial names, though each refers to the same material (e.g. acetone, propanone etc.). The CAS (Chemical Abstracts Service) Registry Number assigns a unique number to substances and allows the conservator to accurately identify a solvent or reagent.

The vapour pressure of a solvent is a measure of the pressure exerted by its vapour when the solvent and its vapour are in dynamic equilibrium, i.e. when the molecules leaving a liquid to form vapour and those rejoining it are in equilibrium. There are several units in use for measuring vapour pressure, including pounds per square inch, atmospheres, torrs (mmHg), bars and pascals. mmHg (torr) is based on the original Torricelli barometer design. The pressure that causes the mercury column in a barometer to rise 1 mm is referred to as mmHg or torr. One atmosphere equals 760 torr, one bar equals 750 torr, one kilopascal equals 7.5 torr.

Those in italics have been superseded by safer solvents with similar chemical functionality.

These solvents may be referred to in conservation literature.

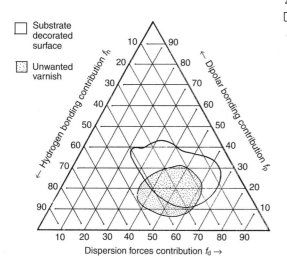

Key (right of figure):
△ Mineral spirits
▣ Acetone
✕ Position of a solvent blend containing one part acetone and three parts mineral spirits

**Figure 11.15** Using the Teas' chart to select a solvent for varnish removal. In a situation where it is desirable to remove an upper layer such as a varnish from a solvent sensitive layer, such as a painted surface, the solubility regions of both materials can be plotted on a Teas' chart. In this hypothetical example, the substrate is represented by the outlined area, whilst the varnish is represented by the dotted area. The area where the solubility region of the varnish does not overlap the solubility region of the lower layer can be used to formulate the least potentially damaging solvent blend for varnish removal. In this case, alcohols could be used to remove the varnish without damaging the substrate

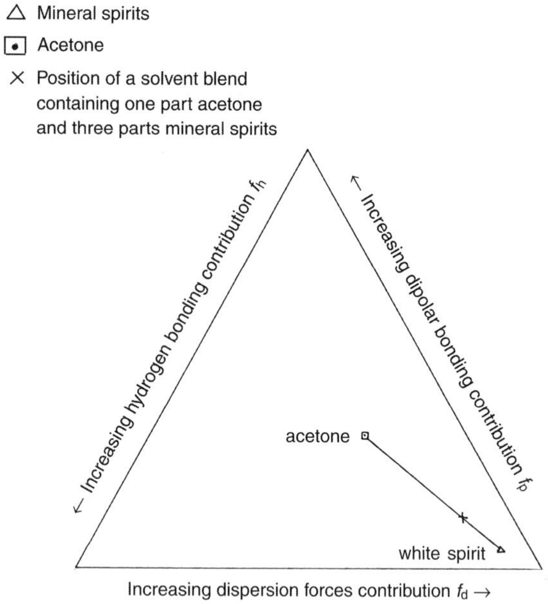

**Figure 11.16** Method for calculating the Teas' parameters of a two-part solvent blend. A mixture of three parts mineral spirits and one part acetone can be plotted on a Teas' chart by drawing a straight line between the two pure solvents and marking off a point ¼ of the way from mineral spirits. This represents the shift in polarity the addition of 25% acetone causes in the mixture. The positioning of the point that marks the new blend can be a little confusing, but it should be closest to the solvent present in the greatest proportion (in this case, mineral spirits)

or crosslinked, although the polymer may swell and soften enough to allow mechanical removal.

One of the main advantages of the Teas' chart is that it readily allows the solubility effect of mixing solvents to be predicted. The contribution of an individual solvent to the overall solubility parameter is equal to its proportion in the mix. The position of a solvent blend can be predicted mathematically or geometrically. The volume-wise contribution of the solubility parameters of the individual solvents is used for the mathematical method (see *Box 11.1*). The geometric method utilizes the Teas' chart itself. The solubility parameters of a mixture of three parts acetone and one part white spirit, for example, can be plotted geometrically by drawing a straight

line between the two pure solvents and marking off a point ¼ of the way from white spirit (*Figure 11.16*). Mixtures of more than two solvents can also be plotted using a Teas' chart (*Fig. 11.17*). In many cases the Teas' chart can allow the conservator to substitute a mixture of less harmful solvents for a more toxic one but still achieve the required solubility parameter.

It should be noted that whilst this approach can be useful as a rule of thumb, it does not take into account differences in evaporation rates or interactions between solvents. Since IMS evaporates faster than white spirit, the solubility parameters of the mix will be shifting back towards white spirit as the mix is used. In this way it is possible for a solvent mix that is on the edge of a solubility region

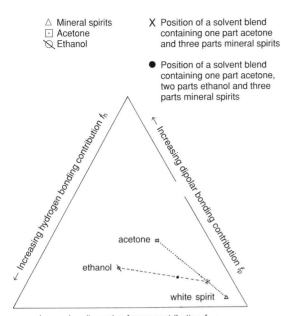

△ Mineral spirits
⊡ Acetone
⬿ Ethanol

X Position of a solvent blend containing one part acetone and three parts mineral spirits

● Position of a solvent blend containing one part acetone, two parts ethanol and three parts mineral spirits

**Figure 11.17** Geometric method for calculating the Teas parameters of a three-part solvent blend. Consider a mixture of one part acetone: two parts ethanol: three parts mineral spirits. Choose two of the solvents in the blend and plot a position between them according to the fraction of volume of those two solvents as described (represented by a dotted line). Plot the position for a third solvent by drawing a line between this point (marked x) and the position of the third solvent (represented by dashed line), plotting the position of the blend along this line according to the relative fraction of the total volume. As the total blend has six parts, the acetone/mineral spirits proportion is ¾ of the total volume, whilst the ethanol is ⅓ of the total volume. The contribution of any additional solvent can be plotted in the same way

to gradually shift and thereby enter the peak swelling region, damaging the substrate. The different rates of evaporation should be taken into account when mixing and using solvents.

Whilst Teas' solubility parameters have proven to be a useful tool for predicting the effect of solvent mixtures on a known substrate, the limitations of this system should be understood. Teas' solubility parameters describe only one aspect of the interaction of solvents and a surface. The Teas' chart cannot be used to predict the effect of solvents that

---

**Box 11.1 Mathematical method for calculating the Teas' parameters of solvent blends**

The mathematical method uses the volume-wise contribution of the solubility parameters of the individual solvents to estimate the overall solubility parameter of the mixture. The contribution of an individual solvent to the overall solubility parameter is equal to its proportion in the mix:

**Step 1:** Multiply the contribution of dispersion ($f_d$), polar ($f_p$) and hydrogen bonding forces ($f_h$) of the solvent by its proportion in the mix

**Step 2:** Add the proportional values of dispersion forces ($f_d$) of each solvent to find the overall $f_d$ of the mixture. Repeat this for polar ($f_p$) and hydrogen bonding forces ($f_h$)

**Step 3:** Plot the overall solubility parameters thus calculated onto a Teas' chart

*Example:* Calculate the overall solubility parameters of a 1:3 mixture of acetone ($f_d$ 47, $f_p$ 32, $f_h$ 21) and mineral spirits ($f_d$ 90, $f_p$ 4, $f_h$ 6). Teas' fractional solubility parameters are from Horie (1992):

**Step 1:** Multiply the $f_d$ of acetone (47) by its proportion in the mix (¼) = 11.75
Multiply the $f_d$ of white spirit (90) by its proportion in the mix (¾) = 67.5

**Step 2:** Add these two together (11.75 + 67.5) to get the $f_d$ of the 1:3 mixture of these solvents (79.25)

Repeat these steps to calculate the $f_p$ (11) and $f_h$ (9.75) of the mix

| | $f_d \times$ proportion | $f_p \times$ proportion | $f_h \times$ proportion |
|---|---|---|---|
| acetone (1 part) | 47 × ¼ = 11.75 | 32 × ¼ = 8 | 21 × ¼ = 5.25 |
| mineral spirits (3 parts) | 90 × ¾ = 67.5 | 4 × ¾ = 3 | 6 × ¾ = 4.5 |
| overall solubility parameter of a 3:1 mix | 79.25 | 11 | 9.75 |

The same procedure can be used to calculate the overall fractional solubility parameters of a mixture with multiple solvents, such as one part acetone, two parts ethanol and three parts white spirit:

| | $f_d \times$ proportion | $f_p \times$ proportion | $f_h \times$ proportion |
|---|---|---|---|
| acetone (1 part) | 47 × ⅙ = 7.83 | 32 × ⅙ = 5.3 | 21 × ⅙ = 3.5 |
| ethanol (2 parts) | 36 × ⅔ = 12 | 18 × ⅔ = 6 | 46 × ⅔ = 15.3 |
| mineral spirits (3 parts) | 90 × ½ = 45 | 4 × ½ = 2 | 6 × ½ = 3 |
| overall solubility parameter of a 1:2:3 mix | 64.83 | 13.3 | 21.8 |

have an acidic or basic character or the effect on solubility of acidic or basic conditions. Thus aqueous cleaning systems and those that utilize acid/base interactions cannot be evaluated using solubility parameters alone. The Teas' chart does not take into account the effect of aromaticity on a substrate. For example, when solvent testing, it may be observed that xylene, an aromatic hydrocarbon solvent, has the desired effect in removing dirt or an unwanted coating. The conservator may wish to substitute a less potentially harmful solvent blend, such as one part mineral spirits and six parts ethanol. Although this mixture matches the Teas solubility parameters of xylene, it is possible that it will not have the desired effect on the dirt or coating. In such cases it is likely that the dirt is characterized by the presence of aromatic groups or structures. It may be necessary to include a proportion of an aromatic solvent in the final solvent blend, or an aromatic solvent *per se* may be required to take into account the aromatic nature of the unwanted material. Michalski (1990) and Phenix (1998) have identified limitations of Teas' solubility parameters and proposed modifications and alternatives that may present a more complete description of solubility.

Other systems of describing solubility parameters also exist. The Edwards hydrogen bonding index is one of several solubility parameters used in industry and may be encountered in literature about solvents provided by the manufacturer. Hydrogen bonding in solvents is largely restricted to oxygenated solvents. Ketones and esters that contain oxygen atoms that are not immediately connected to hydrogen atoms act as acceptors and, by convention, are assigned positive hydrogen bonding indices. Alcohols, which usually act as donors but can occasionally act as acceptors, are assigned negative hydrogen bonding indices. Hydrocarbon solvents are non-hydrogen bonding, although aromatics have limited acceptor characteristics.

### Solvent removal of varnish

There are several important factors that should be considered when choosing a solvent for the removal of surface dirt or a varnish. These include the solubility parameters and compatibility of the solvent and dirt or varnish,

**Table 11.3**  Contribution of dispersion forces ($f_d$) to blends of cyclohexane, toluene and acetone

| Cyclohexane % volume | Toluene % volume | Acetone % volume | Approximate value of $f_d$ (Teas) | |
|---|---|---|---|---|
| 100 | 0 | | 96 | least polar |
| 75 | 25 | | 92 | |
| 50 | 50 | | 88 | |
| 25 | 75 | | 84 | |
| | 100 | | 80 | |
| | 87.5 | 12.5 | 76 | |
| | 75 | 25 | 72 | |
| | 62.5 | 37.5 | 68 | |
| | 50 | 50 | 64 | |
| | 25 | 75 | 56 | |
| | | 100 | 47 | most polar |

*Source:* Feller, 1976a

**Table 11.4**  Contribution of dispersion forces ($f_d$) to blends of mineral spirits, xylene and acetone

| Mineral spirits % volume | Xylene % volume | Acetone % volume | Approximate value of $f_d$ (Teas) | |
|---|---|---|---|---|
| 100 | 0 | | 90 | least polar |
| 75 | 25 | | 88 | |
| 50 | 50 | | 87 | |
| 25 | 75 | | 85 | |
| | 100 | | 83 | |
| | 87.5 | 12.5 | 78 | |
| | 75 | 25 | 74 | |
| | 62.5 | 37.5 | 70 | |
| | 50 | 50 | 65 | |
| | 25 | 75 | 56 | |
| | | 100 | 47 | most polar |

solubility parameters of the underlying decorative surface, the rate of dissolution of dirt or varnish in comparison to the rate of penetration into the substrate (see *Figure 11.9*), potential retention of solvent in the substrate, controllability of solvent application, solvent evaporation rate and the health and safety implications for the conservator.

Feller (1976a) proposed using three solvents of increasing polarity that were combined in graduated steps to identify the least polar solvent blend that would remove natural resin varnishes (*Table 11.3*). The mathematical method described in *Box 11.1* can be used in conjunction with Appendix 2.1 in Horie (1992) to formulate a similar table using solvents such as odourless mineral spirits or white spirits, xylene and IMS or acetone (*Table 11.4*).

The primary problem with using solvents to remove varnish is that both coatings and decorative layers are organic polymeric materials whose solubility parameters often overlap. This problem is often found where oil-resin paint media have been coated with a natural resin varnish. Underbound pigments are vulnerable during solvent cleaning, both from dissolution of the minimal binding medium and from the mechanical action of swabs. The interaction between pigment and binder should be understood before cleaning is attempted because some pigments may be removed by careless cleaning (e.g. carbon black and vermilion are poor driers in oil). Pigment–solvent interactions should also be taken into consideration, for example the affinity of zinc derived pigments for water and alcohol. Glaze layers are vulnerable to damage or inadvertent removal because they are usually the uppermost decorative layers, are very thin and the pigment is sparsely dispersed in binding medium. The belief that glaze layers have been lost as a result of varnish removal treatments has provoked significant criticism of painting conservators in the past (Keck, 1984).

A potential problem associated with solvent removal of varnish from painted surfaces is the removal of unpolymerized components of the decorative surface, an irreversible process known as leaching. Leaching of oil-painted surfaces as a result of varnish removal is discussed in the section on solvents under section 16.6.3).

Swelling in the decorative surface layer as a result of exposure to solvent during varnish removal will result in damage. The decorative surface, after exposure to solvent, may attempt to swell in all directions but can only freely swell upwards, resulting in plastic compression (*Figure 11.18*). Whilst leaching of soluble low molecular weight components from within the decorative surface may cause shrinkage of around 15% for oil paint, plastic compression may result in up to 80% shrinkage of the paint film on drying. In addition, micro-voids may be created within the paint layer (Michalski, 1990).

Both polar and non-polar solvents can cause irreversible changes in solubility and other properties of protein-based layers. In particu-

(a)

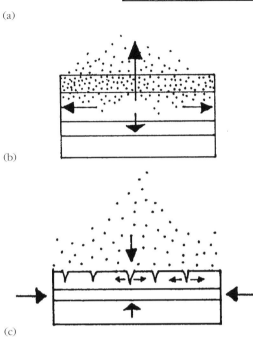

(b)

(c)

**Figure 11.18** Plastic compression
(*a*) Diagrammatic representation of a decorated surface made up of varnish, decorated and ground layers on a wood substrate
(*b*) Solvent is introduced to remove the varnish layer. As varnish is removed, solvent enters the susceptible lower layer, which attempts to swell in all directions, but can only freely swell upwards. In other directions, the susceptible layer/s are compressed (arrows indicate direction of force)
(*c*) Solvent evaporates and swollen layers contract. Where compressive forces have exceeded the elastic properties of the binding material, cracks will develop. Such plastic compression is irreversible

lar, low molecular weight alcohols will tend to remove bound water from the protein structure, altering chemical and physical properties. Some organic solvents may react chemically with specific peptide chains, for example trichloroethylene and cysteine (Karpowicz, 1981).

### Mixing solvents

Miscibility is the capacity of one liquid to mix with another to form a stable solution. When a polar molecular group dominates, the solvent will mix with other polar solvents. When a hydrocarbon, non-polar part of the molecule dominates, the solvent will mix with other non-polar solvents. Solvents may be miscible, partly miscible or immiscible. Miscible solvents will form a stable solution in any proportion. Partly miscible solvents may form a stable solution up to a maximum proportion. Benzyl alcohol, for example is miscible with water only up to around 4%. Immiscible solvents will separate out into distinct layers. They may be shaken to form an emulsion, but will require the addition of a surfactant if a stable emulsion is required.

Solvent blends may exhibit azeotropic behaviour. An azeotrope is a mixture of two or more liquids that has a constant boiling point at a specific concentration. The boiling point of the solution is different from the boiling point of the individual constituents. When two liquids that are capable of forming an azeotrope are mixed, the liquid that is more volatile will evaporate more quickly, until the concentration reaches the azeotropic concentration. At this point the proportion of the solvents in the mixture will remain constant, as both solvents evaporate at the same rate. For example, a mixture of 95% ethanol and 5% water boils at a lower temperature than either pure ethanol or pure water. The proportion of ethanol to water remains constant whilst the mixture is evaporating. Azeotropic behaviour is particularly likely to occur with aqueous solutions. Tables of azeotropic mixtures can be found in Horsley (1952).

### 11.3.4  Proprietary paint strippers

Commercial paint strippers are familiar to anyone who has tried paint or finish removal projects. New products are regularly being developed and may be useful in particular layer removal treatments. In general, these products are either based on solvents, di-basic esters or alkaline solutions. They are designed to remove a wide range of finishes in a non-specific manner, intentionally covering a wide range of Teas' solubility parameters. Thickening agents, waxes, surfactants or chelating agents are often included to increase the effectiveness of the product. It is safer for both the object and the conservator to use materials

specific to a given coating and that cause minimal change or damage to the substrate. Retaining earlier colourants and coatings in the wood as well as remnants of old finish can be of aesthetic, practical and monetary value.

Wollbrinck (1993) reviewed forty-seven proprietary paint strippers and discussed the principles behind their chemical activity. Solvent-based strippers included methylene chloride, acetone, alcohols, toluene or xylene as the primary active ingredients. These materials present significant health risks and measures should be taken to reduce the risk to the conservator. They can be very effective for dissolving coatings quickly but have little selectivity where the stratigraphy of a surface is characterized by similar binding media. This lack of selectivity can be problematic if a treatment requires the removal of a single coating whilst leaving others unaffected.

Dibasic (i.e. possessing two replaceable hydrogen atoms, in this case on the carboxylic acid groups) ester systems function by swelling materials which, like themselves, are characterized by ester linkage structures. Modern synthetic coating materials that incorporate such structures include urethanes and those based on polyesters such as alkyds. They are designed to work after prolonged contact with the coating that is to be removed. Product literature recommends a forty-five minute minimum contact time for cellulose nitrate and shellac, one to three hours for some paints, varnishes and polyurethanes, and overnight for multi-layered coatings. Other sources suggest that the contact times needed to swell or dissolve shellac and cellulose nitrates are significantly longer (Flexner, 1994). The reduced rate of activity in comparison to solvent-based strippers may offer an advantage for the conservator.

N-methyl-2-pyrrolidone will swell or dissolve polar materials such as PVALs, PVACs, carbohydrates or other materials that are easily oxidized such as aged natural resins or aged alkyds. It has been reported as an effective solvent for polysaccharides (Horie, 1992). It has been observed to swell collagen glue based materials such as gesso.

Alkaline removal systems usually contain a strong basic reagent such as sodium hydroxide and their action is chemical rather than solvent based. Strongly basic materials are very effective in breaking down coatings quickly but may also attack the substrate wood. It is rarely necessary to use such strong reagents. Although alkaline pH may be useful in removing some coatings, the potential for severe damage of sensitive substrate materials generally makes the use of such materials undesirable. In addition, unless residues of alkaline strippers are meticulously removed, there is a danger that subsequent coating materials will be damaged. It may be necessary to rinse the surface with a dilute acetic acid solution to neutralize any residues.

## 11.4 Chemical cleaning

Chemical cleaning of decorative surfaces involves the use of reagents, which are chemicals that break primary molecular bonds, converting dirt, varnish or other unwanted material to a different form in order to remove it from the surface. Unlike solvent cleaning, original material cannot be recovered in the same form that was present on the object. After cleaning is complete, any non-volatile reagents must be rinsed from a surface. Common reagents used in furniture conservation include acids and bases, discussed here, and chelating agents and enzymes, discussed in the context of aqueous cleaning. Oxidizing and reducing agents are discussed in the context of bleaching in section 13.5.3.

### 11.4.1 Introduction to acids and bases

Acid–base interactions are a complex area of organic chemistry. Acids and bases are important in cleaning decorative surfaces because acidity and alkalinity (or basicity) may be used to solve problems for which common organic solvents are ineffective. Brønsted and Lowry defined an acid as a proton donor and a base as a proton acceptor. A proton is the same as a positively charged hydrogen ion ($H^+$). Acid–base reactions are equilibrium reactions. In equilibrium reactions the concentration of reactants and products remains the same if external conditions remain unchanged. The reactions do not stop, however, but the forward reaction is equal to the reverse reaction and so the concentrations remain unchanged.

An acid is a substance that releases hydrogen ions in solution, dissociating to form a negatively charged anion and a positively charged hydrogen ion. Acids will turn litmus paper red. In practice hydrogen ions do not exist in solution and are more likely to attach to a water molecule, forming a hydronium ($H_3O^+$) ion. The equation for the ionization of hydrochloric acid is:

$$HCl(aq) + H_2O(l) \rightleftharpoons H_3O^+(aq) + Cl^-(aq)$$

Thus hydrochloric acid is an acid because it loses a $H^+$ ion to form $Cl^-$. In this reaction water is a base because it accepts the $H^+$ ion to form $H_3O^+$.

Generally speaking, inorganic acids are strong and organic acids are weak. The concept of strength (degree of ionization) is different to that of concentration. An acid is said to be strong if a high percentage dissociates to form ions. Thus if solutions of nitric acid (a strong acid) and acetic acid (a weak acid) of the same molar concentration were compared, all of the nitric acid would have become ionized whilst only a very small proportion (about 1/1000) of the acetic acid would have dissociated. It should be remembered that both strong and weak acids can produce highly acidic solutions with a low pH. Formic acid, for example, is a weak organic acid but can be supplied at an 88% concentration with a pH between 0 and 0.5.

A base is a substance that liberates $OH^-$ (hydroxide) ions in solution (that may be non-aqueous), and reacts with an acid to form a salt. Bases will turn litmus paper blue. A base that already contains hydroxide ions, such as sodium hydroxide ($NaOH \rightleftharpoons Na^+ + OH^-$), is considered a strong base. A base that reacts to form hydroxide ions, such as ammonia, is considered a weak base ($NH_3 + H_2O \rightleftharpoons NH_4^+ + OH^-$: note that in this reaction water is acting as an acid). An alkali is a base that produces hydroxide ions in aqueous solutions. Concentrated weak bases and dilute strong bases can both produce solutions with an extremely high pH. pH measures the hydronium ion concentration in an aqueous solution (i.e. measures solution acidity or alkalinity), not the strength of an acid or base.

Acids and bases can play a role in both aqueous and non-aqueous systems. They are reactive because they are very polar and this is the source of both their usefulness and problems they may cause. When an acid and a base react they form a salt and water. For example, hydrochloric acid (HCl) and sodium hydroxide (NaOH) react to form sodium chloride (NaCl) and water ($H_2O$). The reaction of hydronium and hydroxide ions is the basis of this reaction, as it is for all aqueous acid–base reactions. The salt formed may be soluble or insoluble – if it is insoluble it will precipitate out of solution.

Lewis widened the definition of an acid and base by defining an acid as an electron pair acceptor and a base as an electron pair donor. This definition includes acids and bases that would not be recognized using the Brønsted Lowry definition mentioned previously, as it does not require a proton or an aqueous solution.

All acids and bases are damaging to skin and accidental splashes may cause serious damage to eyes. They should be used with extraction, and gloves and goggles should always be worn. Acids should be diluted by slowly adding acid to water, never the reverse. Accidental contact of bases with skin should be washed immediately for about ten minutes under a running tap.

### 11.4.2 Ka and pKa

The molecule or ion formed when an acid dissociates is called its conjugate base and, similarly, the molecule formed when a base dissociates is called its conjugate acid. Consider the equation for the ionization of hydrochloric acid:

$$HCl + H_2O \leftrightarrow H_3O^+ + Cl^-$$
acid    base    conjugate    conjugate
                acid      base

The dissociation into ions and back again is an equilibrium reaction, thus adjusting the pH of the solution changes the ratio of acid to conjugate base.

In order to be able to quantify the potential for dissociation, acids are assigned an acid equilibrium constant (Ka). From this, the acid dissociation constant, or pKa, is derived. pKa (sometimes referred to as pK) is the negative logarithm of the equilibrium constant. This means that, as with pH, a change of one number on the pKa scale indicates a tenfold difference in the potential for dissociation. The stronger the acid, the larger the value of Ka, the smaller the value of the pKa. As with pH, pKa is only valid in aqueous solutions.

Bases may be assigned a Kb, or base equilibrium constant. The pKb, or base dissociation constant, is the negative logarithm of the equilibrium constant. The pKa of the acidic form of a molecule and the pKb of its conjugate base add up to 14, so in practice it is only necessary to tabulate one or the other. The stronger the base, the larger the value of Kb, the smaller the value of pKb. A strong base with a small pKb will have a weak conjugate acid with a large pKa:

strong acid (small pKa) → weak conjugate base (large pKb)

weak acid (large pKa) → strong conjugate base (small pKb)

The pKa of a solution will equal the pH when dissociated and non-dissociated ionic forms are present in equal concentrations. pKa is useful because it gives a measure of the relative acidity or basicity of a non-aqueous solvent (*Table 11.5*).

**Table 11.5** pKa of some acids and bases

| Acid/base | pKa | Conjugate species |
|---|---|---|
| Water | 14 | Hydroxyl ion |
| Abietic acid | 7.6 | Abietate ion |
| Deoxycholic acid | 6.58 | Deoxycholate ion |
| Acetic acid | 4.75 | Acetate ion |
| Citric acid | 3.13 | Citrate ion |
|  | 4.76 |  |
|  | 6.4 |  |
| Oxalic acid | 4.27 | Oxalate ion |
| Formic acid | 3.75 | Formate ion |
| Sulphuric acid | 1.99 | Hydrogen sulphate ion |
| Nitric acid | −1.44 | Nitrate ion |
| Hydrochloric acid | −7 | Chloride ion |
| Ammonia | 9.2 | Ammonium ion |
| Triethanolamine | 7.8 | Triethanolammonium ion |
| Sodium (hydroxide) | −0.8 | Sodium ion |

Citric acid has three pKa's because, with three COOH groups, it has three possible ionization states.
*Sources:* Dean (1992); Perrin (1982); Solomons (1992)

### 11.4.3 Acids

Organic acids have the general formula R-COOH, and the COOH group is called a carboxyl group. Carboxylic acids usually have a pKa in the range of 3–5. Simple organic acids include formic acid, acetic acid and oxalic acid.

$$R - \overset{\overset{\displaystyle O}{\|}}{C} - OH$$

Organic acid functional group

$$H - \overset{\overset{\displaystyle O}{\|}}{C} - OH$$

Formic acid

$$CH_3 - \overset{\overset{\displaystyle O}{\|}}{C} - OH$$

Acetic acid

$$\overset{\overset{\displaystyle O}{\|}}{\underset{\underset{\displaystyle O}{\|}}{\overset{\displaystyle C - OH}{\underset{\displaystyle C - OH}{|}}}}$$

Oxalic acid

Inorganic acids include hydrochloric acid (HCl), sulphuric acid ($H_2SO_4$) and nitric acid ($HNO_3$). Water can act as a weak acid or base.

Alcohols are not ionized to an appreciable degree under normal circumstances but under certain conditions ionization can occur, forming an acid or a base:

$$ROH \rightleftharpoons RO^- + H^+ \text{ and } ROH + H^+ \rightleftharpoons RO^+H_2$$

Acids will react with metals and many metal corrosion products. Pigments that are metal salts (e.g. cadmium sulphide or lead carbonate) may be damaged by acidic solutions. Even though wood itself is weakly acidic, it may be discoloured by exposure to acids. In the context of furniture conservation, acids are used as a component in cleaning solutions, for example pH buffers, chelating agents and resin and bile soaps.

### 11.4.4 Bases

If an organic compound contains an unshared electron pair it is a potential base. Compounds such as amines and amides, which have an unshared electron pair on a nitrogen atom, act as bases. Alkaline solutions may cause alkaline hydrolysis of oils and fats. Waxes and resins, which contain ester bonds, may also be saponified (ester hydrolysis that converts fats and oils to water-soluble soaps).

Ammonia ($NH_3$) is a gas at room temperature and soluble in both water and alcohol. When dissolved in water it forms ammonium hydroxide ($NH_4OH$). Ammonia will reduce the surface tension of water and thereby increase its ability to wet onto surfaces. It is normally supplied at 28% w/v and diluted for most uses. It is a relatively weak base (pKa *c*.9.2). As a base, it can neutralize weak acids to form salts that are usually water-soluble.

In paintings conservation a small amount of ammonia may sometimes be added to deionized water to remove surface dirt or greasy accretions from varnished paintings (pH of 8.5–9) because its volatility ensures that it will not leave a residue and its alkalinity brings thin films of oil and grease into solution. Problems may occur if an ammonium hydroxide solution with an excessively high pH is used to clean alkaline sensitive surfaces or materials (e.g. Prussian blue pigment). As the concentration is increased, ammonia usually begins to solubilize varnish layers (see Alkaline reagents in section 16.6.3). It may be used for this purpose on occasions where it offers more control than solvents and can be used in combination or sequentially with solvents for the removal of varnish layers.

Sodium bicarbonate ($NaHCO_3$), commonly known as baking soda, is an alkaline salt. A 0.1% solution has a pH of around 11.

Strong bases, such as sodium hydroxide, have found occasional use in furniture conservation for removing pH-sensitive adhesives or coatings, or as a component in two-part bleaching systems (see Bleaches in section 13.5.3). They are potentially very damaging and must be thoroughly rinsed away after any treatment.

## 11.5 Aqueous cleaning

Aqueous cleaning has a long history in the cleaning of varnished and decorated surfaces. Water has many advantages as a cleaning agent. It is highly polar, freely available, non-flammable and non-toxic. Like other solvents, the chemical and physical properties of water are defined by its molecular structure. Water is characterized by hydrogen bonding, a type of strongly polar secondary bonding that occurs due to the electro-negative properties of oxygen and the spatial arrangement, or stereochemistry, of the molecule. Water molecules are strongly attracted to each other, resulting in slow evaporation and poor wetting of non-polar surfaces. Wetting refers to the ability of a liquid to displace the air on a surface, to spread out on it and achieve intimate molecular contact with it. The ability of a liquid to wet is a result of the comparative surface tension or energy of liquid and solid. The cleaning properties of water can be enhanced by the addition of a surfactant, which will overcome wetting problems and can enable water to remove non-polar greasy or waxy dirt.

Water has a strong affinity for materials that are partially or wholly hydrogen-bonded, such as wood and proteins, and some affinity for materials that are polar, such as natural resins. It has little affinity for materials that are primarily bonded with van der Waals forces, such as waxes and oils. Most transparent coating materials used on furniture are not primarily hydrogen-bonded. Water, carefully applied and thoroughly removed, is therefore a good choice for cleaning them. Water will, however, soften and swell a wide range of organic materials that are often components of the substrate. Any disruption of the substrate will, in turn, disrupt and potentially damage a decorated surface. Further, the small water molecules may diffuse into and through a coating without dissolving it. This may result in blooming of coatings or disruption of the cohesive bonds within layers, and the adhesive bonds between layers or with the substrate. The diffusion rate of water will be slowest through non-polar materials but, in the context of varnished and decorated surfaces, cannot be completely prevented. The diffusion rate will be affected by the presence of additives such as pigments in the coating. Water should not be considered completely benign for cleaning decorated surfaces consisting of oil paint, natural resins or wax, but is utilized because of its comparatively low affinity for these materials.

Water is often very effective for removing surface dirt. There are several parameters that may be manipulated when working with aqueous solutions. These include pH, conductivity, the addition of surfactants or detergents, the addition of chelators, the addition of enzymes and raising the viscosity of the cleaning solution. Saliva is one of the most commonly used and most effective traditional water-based cleaning materials. The efficacy of saliva for cleaning decorative surfaces has been attributed primarily to the presence of $\alpha$-amylase, an enzyme that breaks down carbohydrates (Romão *et al.*, 1990). Saliva is a thickened aqueous cleaning solution that contains a range of ingredients including pH buffers, a surfactant, a chelating agent, enzymes, a thickening agent, an antibacterial preservative, and has an ionic strength of about 1000 micro-Siemens/cm ($\mu$S/cm) (Wolbers, 2000). These ingredients give an indication of the ways in which a conservator can manipulate aqueous cleaning solutions to extend solubility, to bring a wider range of materials into solution, thereby removing them from a varnished or decorated surface.

Pure water is composed entirely of hydrogen and oxygen. Water is seldom pure, however, and may be acidic, alkaline, or contain dissolved minerals. Tap water contains a range of trace materials, depending on the catchment area, such as dissolved salts, acids, alkalis, fertilizers, domestic sewage, bacteria and fungal spores, industrial and agricultural waste as well as compounds from the water pipes themselves. Distilled or purified water has been treated to remove all contaminants and therefore contains only water molecules. Deionized water has been treated to remove ions (atoms or molecules with an overall negative or positive charge), such as calcium ($Ca^{++}$), magnesium ($Mg^{++}$) and chlorides ($Cl^-$). Both deionized and distilled water have the potential to dissolve carbon dioxide from the ambient atmosphere, which may make them slightly acidic (pH *c.*5.5). This can be minimized by storing them in closed containers, but it may be desirable to check pH before commencing cleaning.

Although varnished and painted surfaces can be cleaned with water based systems they may be damaged by prolonged contact. It is important to work in a controllable area and keep the contact time of both cleaning and rinse solutions to a minimum. Water is a relatively slow evaporator and it may be necessary to remove any excess by blotting or gently swabbing the surface dry.

## 11.5.1 pH and aqueous cleaning

pH is a measure, in moles per litre, of the hydronium ion ($H_3O^+$) concentration in an aqueous solution and is a shorthand way of describing acidity or alkalinity. pH has no meaning for non-aqueous solutions such as organic solvents. The higher the concentration of hydronium ions ($H_3O^+$) in relation to hydroxide ions ($OH^-$), the more acidic the solution. pH is measured on a negative logarithmic scale that runs from 0 to 14. A pH of 7 indicates a neutral solution (an equal ratio of hydronium and hydroxide ions), pH below 7 indicates increasing acidity (a higher concentration of hydronium ions) and pH above 7 indicates increasing alkalinity (a higher concentration of hydroxide ions). Because the scale is logarithmic, a change of one number on the scale indicates a tenfold difference in concentration. A solution of pH 10 contains one-tenth of the number of hydronium ions and ten times as many hydroxide ions as the same volume of solution of pH 9. This means that a solution with a pH of 10 is ten times more alkaline than one with a pH of 9, and one hundred times more alkaline than a solution with a pH of 8.

The pH of an aqueous cleaning solution is critical to its performance. Disregarding pH may cause irreversible damage to a coating or a decorated substrate. A pH between 5.5 and 8.5 has been recommended for oil based films such as oil paint or oil gilding (Wolbers *et al.*, 1990). Below 5.5 there is a risk of acidic attack of pigments such as lead and copper carbonates. Some pigments, such as gamboge, Prussian blue, cochineal, alizarin red, logwood (*Haemotoxylon campechianum*), brazilwood (*Caesalpinia crista*) and indigo are sensitive to, and may be damaged by, alkaline conditions (Daniels, 1982). Above a pH of 8.5 there is an increasing risk of saponifying the oil binder, resulting in a partial breakdown of the polymer matrix and the production of wholly or partially soluble soaps. These may either be removed by the cleaning solution or soften the

oil film if retained within it. Proteins are very sensitive to changes in pH and may be damaged by both acidic and alkaline conditions. Natural resin varnishes are sensitive to, and may be damaged by, elevated pH. Whilst the effects of acidic and alkaline conditions may be unwelcome in a cleaning treatment, they may occasionally be exploited for the removal of unwanted adhesives or coatings, for example the use of elevated pH to remove unformulized casein (Lang, 1999).

Raising pH slightly (*c.*7.5–8.5) will help bring weakly acidic dirt or other materials into solution, prevent precipitates such as insoluble metal salts from forming, and assist surfactants in picking up greasy materials. pH may have an effect on additives in aqueous cleaning solutions. Elevated pH will result in increased deposition of detergent residues, for example, and the activity of enzymes is pH-specific (Wolbers *et al.*, 1990).

The pH of a cleaning solution can be lowered by the addition of an acid or raised by the addition of a base. A basic rule of chemistry states that an acid plus a base will give salt plus water. It is essential for cleaning that any salt thus formed should be soluble, otherwise it will remain as an unwanted residual precipitate on the cleaned surface.

*A Note on calibrating pH meters* pH meters must be calibrated at regular intervals, sometimes daily, to ensure accurate measurements. The first step is usually to condition the pH meter by soaking the electrode tip of the meter in water for 10–30 minutes. Once the meter is conditioned, it can be calibrated. pH meters usually require calibration at two points on the pH scale. If the solution to be tested is known to be acidic, the pH meter should be calibrated at two points in the acidic range (vice versa for known alkaline solutions). If the pH of the solution is unknown, or if the pH meter has only one calibrating screw, the pH meter should be calibrated at 7 (neutral) and a measurement taken of the pH of the solution. If this reading is acidic, the meter should be recalibrated within the acidic pH range (vice versa for alkaline readings). After this second calibration, the meter is ready to accurately measure the pH of the unknown solution. The meter should be rinsed in distilled or deionized water between calibrations and after use.

Buffer tablets and solutions are available from chemical suppliers (e.g. BDH, Sigma). The tablets can be dissolved in a predetermined volume of water (e.g. 100 ml) to produce a solution of a given pH. The conservator will need three buffer tablets in stock to allow for calibrating the pH meter at two points for both acidic and alkaline solutions (e.g. buffer tablets for pH 4, 7 and 10).

### 11.5.2 pH buffers

A simple definition of a buffer is any material that can be dissolved in water that, in the presence of additional acids or bases, resists changes in the pH of the solution. A buffer will hold pH stable against dilution effects and the changes in pH that small additions of acid or base would otherwise cause. A buffered solution has a constant pH that will not change appreciably if the solution is contaminated with traces of acid or alkali.

Weak acids or weak bases can act as buffers because they can sparingly take on and give up hydrogen ions. At their pKa, half the molecules in solution are ionized, and half are not. At that half ionization point (when the pKa of the weak acid or base equals the pH of the aqueous solution) there is a very strong thermodynamic equilibrium, with the result that the addition of a small amount of acid or base does not change the overall pH of the solution. Strong acids or strong bases may be used to adjust the pH of a buffered solution, but are not normally useful as buffers themselves.

Buffers can be used to maintain a specific pH in an aqueous cleaning system. A wide range of organic materials that may be present as soiling materials are weakly acidic. A buffer ensures that as such material is brought into solution, the overall pH of cleaning solution on the object does not fall. A slight alkaline pH will often aid in bringing such materials into solution and prevent the redeposition that would occur if pH were to fall during the cleaning procedure.

The estimated pH of the surface will determine the concentration of buffer required for an aqueous cleaning solution. For example, if the pH of a surface is measured or estimated at 6.5 (e.g. an oil painted or varnished surface), and the target pH for the cleaning solution is within about two pH units, a buffer concentration between 50 and 75 mmol is sufficient.

#### *Choosing a buffer*

Buffers are used wherever there is a need to regulate the pH of an aqueous solution. Lists of common buffers may be found in catalogues of suppliers of biochemical materials (e.g. Sigma or Fluka). Such tables usually list the acid and conjugate base (or base and conjugate acid) along with their effective buffering range. Buffers will only work when both acidic and basic forms of the active agent, e.g. acetic acid and sodium acetate, are in solution at the same time. As a result the effective range of a buffer is generally one pH unit above or below its acid dissociation constant, or pKa.

**Table 11.6**  The pH range and pKa of some common buffers

| Buffer | pH buffering range | pH adjusted with | pKa (25 °C) |
|---|---|---|---|
| Citric acid | 2.0–6.5 | Sodium hydroxide | 3.13<br>4.76<br>6.4 |
| Citric acid | 2.6–7.0 | Disodium hydrogen phosphate | As above |
| Citric acid | 3.0–6.2 | Sodium citrate | As above |
| Acetic acid | 3.6–5.6 | Sodium acetate | 4.6 |
| Potassium dihydrogen phosphate | 5.0–8.0 | Disodium hydrogen phosphate | |
| Potassium dihydrogen phosphate | 5.8–8.0 | Sodium hydroxide | |
| Sodium dihydrogen phosphate | 5.8–8.0 | Disodium hydrogen phosphate | |
| Triethanolamine | 6.8–8.8 | Hydrochloric acid | 7.8 |
| TRIS (2 Amino 2 hydroxy methyl 1, 3 propanediol) | 7.1–9.1 | Hydrochloric acid | 8.1 |
| Diethanolamine | 7.8–9.8 | Hydrochloric acid | 8.8 |
| Ammonium hydroxide | 8.2–10.2 | Ammonium chloride | 9.24 |
| Sodium carbonate | 9.2–10.6 | Sodium hydrogen carbonate | |

The two primary factors in choosing a buffer are the desirable pH for the cleaning solution and the rinse procedure needed to remove the buffer. A range of materials that will act as buffers are listed in *Table 11.6*. The buffer chosen should have a pKa that is the same, or close to, the desired pH of the cleaning solution. The buffer should also be compatible with the substrate, for example buffers containing chlorides (including those in which the pH is adjusted with hydrochloric acid) should be avoided when cleaning metals. Some buffers may be particularly appropriate for specific applications, for example TRIS may be appropriate if buffering an enzymatic cleaning solution.

By definition, buffers are water-soluble materials and residues can therefore be removed using a neutral aqueous rinse. Inorganic buffer compounds can only be rinsed in water, whilst some organic buffers are also soluble in solvents, offering an alternative method of rinsing. Buffers are ionic materials and the conductivity of the surface can be measured and compared to the base line conductivity of the surface before treatment if there are concerns that residues may be present.

pH buffers increase overall ionic strength of a cleaning solution by increasing the concentration of ions in solution. The ionic strength of a buffered solution can be deliberately raised by increasing the overall amount of a buffer in solution, at or close to, its pKa (Wolbers, *et al.*, 1990).

## 11.5.3 Ionic concentration/conductivity

A surface with a weakly acidic character (e.g. the presence of $COO^-$ groups) will attract positively charged ions (ionic 'dirt'). Divalent metal ions such as $Ca^{2+}$, $Mg^{2+}$, $Fe^{2+}$ etc., can form an ionic bond to the acid group and act as a bridge to attract more acidic material. Salts, which are ionic materials, dissociate in water to form ionic solutions. The presence of salts in a cleaning solution can contribute to the general effect of a cleaning solution by creating ion exchange reactions to aid in the removal of ionically bonded material. Thus it may be advantageous to raise the ionic concentration of a cleaning solution.

On some materials, excessive levels of conductivity may damage the substrate. It has been observed that raising conductivity above 5000 µS will begin to damage an oil-painted surface (Wolbers, 1992). Other types of substrates may have similar limiting values, but as yet these have not been quantified. With the exception of archaeological materials that may be contaminated by salts and therefore have substantially higher base level conductivity, a useful rule of thumb may be to limit conductivity of a cleaning solution to about ten times the conductivity of the surface before cleaning.

Ion concentration can be measured in a range of ways. One convenient method is to measure the conductivity of the solution. Conductivity is an overall measure of the total number of ionic species in solution. The standard international unit is the siemen (1 millisiemen (mS) = 1/1000 siemens; 1 microsiemen (µS) = 1/1 000 000 siemens). Conductivity can be measured with a small electrical cell where the electrodes are set a fixed distance apart. A standard one millimolar solution of sodium chloride (0.001 mmol) has a conductivity of 146 µS. Deionized water usually has a conductivity of less than 5 µS, whilst tap water may have a conductivity of around 300 µS, depending on the materials dissolved in it. A 1% solution of triammonium citrate has a conductivity of approximately 8000 µS.

The initial conductivity of a surface may be measured by taking a large swab wetted with deionized water and rolling it gently over the surface for a few seconds. The swab can then be pressed firmly into contact with the two electrodes on the meter and a reading taken. It has been observed, for example, that an oil-painted surface may have an intrinsic conductivity reading of 0–300 µS. As a general rule, the conductivity of a cleaning solution applied to such a surface should not exceed 3000 µS.

Many materials that may be incorporated into an aqueous cleaning solution, such as buffers, chelators, salts, acids and bases, may contribute to the overall conductivity. Once all the ionic materials have been added to a cleaning solution (e.g. the solution has been buffered, the pH set, chelators added etc.) the overall conductivity of the solution can be measured and adjusted. It may be reduced by dilution or increased by the addition of salts that are compatible with the cleaning solution and cleaning objectives as a whole. One advantage of increasing the overall ionic strength may be to decrease the solubility of certain materials, to form insoluble precipitates and 'salt' them out. Proteins, for example, are at their least soluble when close to their isoelectric point or when there is a high concentration of salts in solution.

It is an interesting feature of many surfaces that they are characterized by the presence of a small number of salts or other ionic species (e.g. weak acid groups). In cases where the surface is characterized by an anionic charge, it may be advantageous to rinse with an aqueous solution with a small but measurable amount of salt in solution (e.g. sodium, potassium or ammoniate ions) in order to provide a surface less prone to attract dirt by electrostatic forces. For example, if a surface had an initial conductivity of 300 μS it may be appropriate for the final rinse to have a similar conductivity.

### 11.5.4 Soaps, detergents and surfactants

For centuries the ability of soaps to assist in removing surface dirt from surfaces has been utilized for cleaning furniture and decorative surfaces (Balston, 1956; Caley, 1990). Even relatively recent publications encourage the use of ordinary soap and water solutions to clean or revive furniture finishes (Hayward, 1960/1988). However, traditional soaps have certain drawbacks that make them less useful in conservation than their modern synthetic detergent counterparts. The alkaline component of soaps may result in partial hydrolysis of pH-sensitive materials such as oil-based paint and proteins. Soaps, which are anionic, will form insoluble precipitates (scum) in hard water. If these are formed during cleaning, they will precipitate out of solution and leave a white water-insoluble residue on the surface.

Soaps are derived from naturally occurring fats, e.g. tallow, which have been boiled with an alkali, traditionally derived from wood ash, to create the salt of an organic fatty acid, i.e. a soap. Detergents are similar but are derived synthetically. Both are characterized by a molecular structure that contains a polar 'head' and a non-polar 'tail'. The polar end is hydrophilic and attracted to water and other polar solvents, whilst the non-polar chain is lipophilic and attracted to oils, grease and waxes. This generic structure is normally represented with a wavy or zigzag line to represent the non-polar tail and a circle to represent the polar head.

All soaps and detergents are surfactants. Surfactant is a contraction of the phrase 'surface active agent' and describes a material that lowers the surface tension of a liquid, wetting it onto either a surface or dirt more effectively. Surfactants do this because they preferentially occupy the interface between materials of dissimilar polarity, providing a 'bridge' between materials that would otherwise repel each other.

Both aqueous and solvent cleaning formulations may use surfactants and detergents to bring a wider range of materials into solution than would otherwise be possible. Water/detergent solutions provide a highly polar solvent system that can pick up and suspend dirt, facilitating its removal. Water/detergent solutions can help minimize contact time and avoid the problem of swelling if the solvent is sensitive to polar organic solvents. Natural resins are insoluble in pH neutral or slightly acidic aqueous solutions and are less likely to be harmed by such water-based cleaning systems than by many organic solvents.

The addition of detergent to a solvent may facilitate cleaning by combining solvent action with detergency. The most easily produced systems are those that utilize non-ionic detergents, although the use of co-solvents may be necessary for aliphatic hydrocarbon/detergent solutions. Co-solvents, such as alcohols, glycols, glycol ethers and esters, serve as coupling agents when they are at least slightly miscible in both components of a detergent/solvent solution (Davidsohn and Milwidsky, 1978).

Removal of detergent residues from a surface after cleaning is essential because it is difficult to predict how they might react with the object in the future. It has been observed in the laundry industry that detergent residues increase the rate of resoiling (Moncreiff and Weaver, 1992). The procedure to be adopted for removing detergent or surfactant residues should be clearly understood before these materials are used in a conservation treatment.

### Detergents

Commercially viable synthetic detergents were developed in the 1940s, notably sodium lauryl sulphate $(CH_3(CH_2)_{11}OSO_3^-Na^+)$, a common ingredient in shampoo formulations. Synthetic detergents are in common use in a wide range of industries, from cosmetics to foundry work, and detergents are often custom-designed to accomplish specific tasks in very specific applications. As a result, there are thousands of different formulations of detergents on the market from which to choose. Detergents can be broadly classified according to the ionization of the hydrophilic end of the molecule (anionic, cationic, non-ionic etc.), by their hydrophile–lipophile balance number (HLB), and their critical micelle concentration (CMC).

Cationic detergents have a positively charged hydrophilic head group and include amine salts, quaternary ammonium compounds and amine oxides. They are commonly added to commercial formulations for their antiseptic properties. They are problematic for the cleaning of varnished and decorated surfaces because their strong attraction to aged coatings, which are commonly acidic and therefore negatively charged, can make removal of residues after cleaning very difficult.

Anionic detergents have a negatively charged hydrophilic portion and include alkali carboxylates or soaps, sulphates, sulphonates and phosphates. They work well in neutral or alkaline solutions, but their cleaning properties can be adversely affected by moderate changes in pH and they have a limited electrolyte tolerance. Anionic detergents may precipitate if the solution environment becomes too acidic (Rieger, 1985). Their negatively charged 'head' group means they are more effective than non-ionic detergents for lifting dirt, grime and oil from a surface and keeping it in suspension. The cleaning action of anionic detergents may be inhibited by the presence of $Ca^{2+}$ and $Mg^{2+}$ ions (often present in tap water), which will form insoluble salts with anionic detergent molecules and precipitate out of solution. Commercial detergents often contain chelating agents to prevent this. It may be difficult to completely remove residues of anionic detergents from a surface after cleaning as their polar characteristic makes them more likely to remain fixed to a substrate that is basic (e.g. some proteins) or that is slightly electro-positive.

Non-ionic detergents do not ionize in water and therefore do not have a charged 'head' group. The polar component is generally larger than anionic or cationic detergents and may be as large or even larger than the non-polar tail. Even though they do not ionize, they are water-soluble because of the presence of polar functional groups that are capable of significant hydrogen bonding (Myers, 1992). The absence of a net electrical charge can be an advantage because they have a significantly lower sensitivity to the presence of electrolytes in the cleaning system, are less affected by solution pH, and are unlikely to precipitate. As a class, they are generally weaker detergents than anionics, which can be an advantage when less aggressive cleaning treatments are required. They are equally good at penetrating both polar and non-polar dirt because of the overall structural balance. Branched non-polar tails will slow down or prevent penetration into a surface. Non-ionics have been widely used in conservation because their properties tend to meet conservation cleaning objectives (Moncrieff and Weaver, 1992).

Amphoteric surfactants can be either cationic or anionic depending on the pH of the solution and include zwitteronic surfactants, which possess permanent positive and negative charged groups. They are not in common use in conservation.

### Emulsions and hydrophilic lipophilic balance (HLB) numbers

An emulsion is a liquid/liquid mixture in which globules of one liquid are suspended in another. They are generally found in two forms, either oil-in-water or water-in-oil. Both appear white or opaque and will separate if left to stand. Emulsions can be stabilized by the addition of a surfactant or detergent.

Emulsions can be used to build a cleaning solution that combines polar and non-polar elements. If a surface is sensitive to water, for example, but the dirt would be best removed by an aqueous solution, it is possible to use an emulsion that suspends globules of water (and additives such as pH buffers, chelators etc.) in a non-polar hydrocarbon solvent. Water suspended in a hydrocarbon solvent (an example of a water-in-oil type emulsion) can be used to clean water-sensitive materials such as water gilded surfaces.

The effectiveness of surfactants as emulsifiers can be described by their hydrophilic/lipophilic balance number, or HLB. As previously stated, detergents and surfactants are characterized by a molecular structure that contains both a polar end and a non-polar carbon chain. The balance between the polar (hydrophilic) and non-polar (lipophilic) character of a surfactant molecule is described by its hydrophilic–lipophilic balance number or HLB. The HLB number, usually between 1 and 40, is experimentally determined and measures the ability of a surfactant or detergent to emulsify mineral oil in water. HLB numbers are most successful at predicting the behaviour of non-ionic surfactants but have proven problematic for ionic surfactants.

HLB numbers provide information about the properties of the detergent molecule and act as an empirical guide to a surfactant's wetting and rinsing properties. The higher the HLB, the more balanced its polar and non-polar properties. Emulsions are most efficiently stabilized when the surfactant is more soluble in the continuous phase. As HLB is determined in an oil-in-water system, the higher the HLB, the more water-soluble (and therefore water-rinsable) the detergent.

Detergents with an HLB number less than 10 are considered weak. They usually have a long non-polar (lipophilic) 'tail', and as a result are often soluble in hydrocarbon solvents, for example, but insoluble in water. Thus residues of such detergents will not be removed by an aqueous rinse but will require a hydrocarbon rinse. In contrast, detergents with a high HLB (> 20) are strong surfactants. They are readily soluble in water because the polar (hydrophilic) and non-polar (lipophilic) parts of the molecule are more balanced. Such a detergent, e.g. sodium lauryl sulphate (HLB 40), would be readily water-soluble and very effective for emulsifying oil in water. Detergents with a high HLB (> 20) are very effective for solubilizing oily materials but are not considered appropriate for cleaning decorative surfaces because they may swell or soften surfaces with an oil component and are more likely to result in over-cleaning.

As a general rule conservation cleaning treatments utilize a detergent with a mid-range HLB (*c*.13–20). These detergents have unbalanced polar and non-polar properties but are capable of detergency, that is they can suspend oily dirt in solution. Non-ionics have an upper HLB limit of about 20 and are often used in conservation cleaning treatments because they can effectively disperse most oily dirt and can usually be cleared adequately with water. They are less likely to bond to or swell the substrate than the higher HLB anionics. Even within this narrow mid-range HLB, however, the lower the HLB number, the more unbalanced (and usually non-polar) the surfactant. A detergent such as Triton XL 80N (HLB 13.5) is still predominantly non-polar. It will effectively emulsify water in oil, is sparingly soluble in water but more readily soluble in hydrocarbon solvents. Residue removal requires that the surfactant be more attracted to the rinse solution than to the surface. Thus the lower the HLB, the more likely that a hydrocarbon solvent rinse will be required to remove detergent residues.

### Critical micelle concentration (CMC)

The characteristic that distinguishes soaps and detergents from other surfactants is the ability to form micelles, which aid in detaching and removing dirt from a surface. When a small amount of detergent is added to water it preferentially occupies the interface between the water and other materials, in this case, the interface between the water and its container, and the water and the air. As more and more detergent is added, there comes a point when the detergent molecules will spontaneously re-orient themselves so that the hydrophilic head is pointed outwards into the water and the hydrophobic tail is pointed inwards towards moieties of dirt, grime and other oily materials (*Figure 11.19a*). The orientation of the detergent molecules would be reversed if the solution were predominantly oil-based, e.g. a water-in-oil emulsion (*Figure 11.19b*). This molecular configuration is called a micelle and the concentration at which micelles form is called the critical micelle concentration (CMC). Micelles are aggregates of detergent molecules that are directionally oriented according to the polarity of the cleaning solution. The detergent micelle allows a material to be suspended in a liquid in which it would otherwise be insoluble. Detergents are effective cleaning agents because they penetrate areas of soiling, deflocculate dirt into small particles that are then

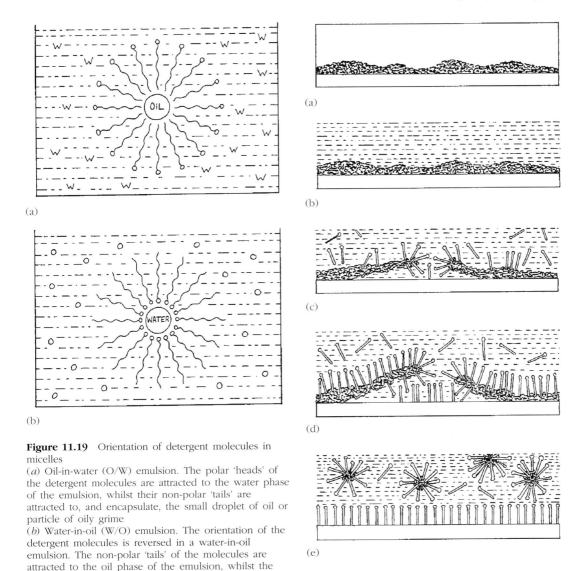

(a)

(b)

**Figure 11.19** Orientation of detergent molecules in micelles
(*a*) Oil-in-water (O/W) emulsion. The polar 'heads' of the detergent molecules are attracted to the water phase of the emulsion, whilst their non-polar 'tails' are attracted to, and encapsulate, the small droplet of oil or particle of oily grime
(*b*) Water-in-oil (W/O) emulsion. The orientation of the detergent molecules is reversed in a water-in-oil emulsion. The non-polar 'tails' of the molecules are attracted to the oil phase of the emulsion, whilst the polar 'heads' are attracted to droplets of water

(a)

(b)

(c)

(d)

(e)

**Figure 11.20** The action of detergents in removing oily dirt from a surface
(*a*) Dirt on a surface
(*b*) An aqueous cleaning solution is applied to surface
(*c*) Detergent molecules are attracted to the interface between the cleaning solution and the dirt, and begin to penetrate the dirt itself, detaching it from the substrate
(*d*) Micelles begin to form, detaching more dirt from the substrate. As the substrate is exposed, detergent molecules are also attracted to the interface between the solution and the substrate
(*e*) Dirt is encapsulated in micelles and suspended in solution. The detergent molecules at the interface of the cleaning solution and the substrate will remain as unwanted residues on the surface unless an appropriate rinse procedure is used

encapsulated by micelles, held in solution and can be rinsed away.

Once beyond their critical micelle concentration, detergents in water suspend or disperse dirt in this micellular structure. In *Figure 11.19a* the hydrophilic ion (or polar 'head') is oriented outward towards the water molecules, while the lipophilic hydrocarbon chain (or non-polar 'tail') is oriented inwards, encapsulating dirt and grime particles and forming a micelle. The strong lipophilic interaction with oily materials can dislodge dirt from a substrate surface and suspend it in solution, facilitating its removal (*Figure 11.20*). The ability of detergents to both remove dirt from a surface and prevent redeposition during cleaning is an important advantage of detergent cleaning systems. Adding a detergent to water will extend the range of dirt that can be brought into solution to include both polar and non-polar material. Water and other solvents on their own are less able to prevent dirt from being redeposited on a surface during the cleaning process.

Detergent cleaning solutions involve a dynamic process of equilibrium where the amount of dirt or varnish held within micelles will, in time, reach equilibrium with that being redeposited (Hofenk de Graaf, 1968). It is important to remove a cleaning solution before such equilibrium can be established because redeposited dirt or varnish is usually very difficult to remove. Redeposition of dirt or varnish is more likely if a single detergent solution remains in contact with a surface for an extended period but may be minimized or prevented if a solution loaded with micellized dirt is removed and replaced.

The CMC is different for each detergent and varies according to temperature, the ionic strength of the solution and the inclusion of water-miscible solvents. In theory, detergents used at their CMC will be capable of detergency. In practice, however, a slight excess of detergent must be maintained to allow for a fall in concentration as micelles form and material is sequestered within detergent micelles. Whilst anionic detergents must be kept above their CMC to prevent dirt redeposition, non-ionic detergents should retain both polar and non-polar dirt in a stable dispersion whether they are above their CMC or not (Tímár-Balázsy and Eastop, 1998). Material that is redeposited onto the surface as a result of a drop in CMC during cleaning may be more difficult to resolubilize and remove than it was originally (Moncrieff and Weaver, 1992). Concentrations of two to five times the CMC have been recommended in conservation literature while solutions as high as ten times the CMC have been described as being necessary in some cases to maintain detergency (Wolbers, 1992). Detergent concentration below the CMC will result in reduced surface tension but will not result in true detergency

(i.e. the formation of micelles). Detergent concentration far in excess of the CMC will not assist the cleaning action of the detergent but will increase the amount of residual detergent left on the surface after cleaning (Wolbers, 1990). It is essential to obtain the CMC of a detergent from the manufacturer since using the wrong concentration may impair the cleaning properties of the detergent, or worse, damage the surface being treated.

For simple detergent structures characterized by a polar head and a non-polar tail, shortening the non-polar tail increases the CMC. The longer the carbon chain, the more the non-polar aspect of the detergent molecule dominates and the less resistance it has to the formation of micelles, that is, the lower the CMC (*Table 11.7*). Wolbers (1992, 2000) has noted that, for these simple structures, detergents with a low CMC (less than 2 mmol) generally have a low HLB, are predominantly non-polar and require a hydrocarbon solvent rinse. Detergents with a high CMC (greater than 20 mmol) also have a low HLB, are predominantly polar in nature and are rinsable in water. Detergents with a mid-range CMC (2–20 mmol), such as lauryl sulphate or deoxycholate, are more balanced in their polar and non-polar aspects and generally have high HLBs (i.e. greater than 20). Triton X-100 has a CMC of 0.24 mmol and an HLB of 13.5. It is just strong enough to act as a detergent, but is dominated by the non-polar portion of the molecule. It will thus have a strong attraction to unoxidized oil paint, will be difficult to remove using an aqueous rinse but will be removed by non-polar solvents. Research on Triton X-100 residue removal has suggested that a clearance procedure that uses an aqueous rinse followed by an aromatic hydro-

**Table 11.7** The CMCs of some simple sodium alkyl sulphonate detergents

| Fatty acid | Detergent structure | Temp (°C) | CMC (mmol) |
|---|---|---|---|
| Caprylic | $C_8H_{17}SO_3^-Na^+$ | 40 | 160 |
| Caproic | $C_{10}H_{21}SO_3^-Na^+$ | 40 | 41 |
| Lauric | $C_{12}H_{25}SO_3^-Na^+$ | 40 | 9.7 |
| Myristic | $C_{14}H_{29}SO_3^-Na^+$ | 40 | 2.5 |
| Palmitic | $C_{16}H_{33}SO_3^-Na^+$ | 40 | 0.7 |

*Source:* Myers, 1992

carbon rinse is required (Burnstock and White, 1990; Koller, 1990). Detergents such as Triton X-100 with a low CMC and fairly low HLB are therefore inappropriate for use on unaged and largely unoxidized oil paint films.

*Calculating the amount of detergent needed*
The manufacturer may give CMC in molar (M) or millimolar (mmol) (1 M = 1000 mmol) quantities, or as a weight percent (wt%). One mole equals the molecular weight in grams and a one molar solution contains this amount of detergent made up to one litre of solution. Thus if the molecular weight is 600 g, a one molar solution will contain 600 g/litre. The general formula used to determine required detergent concentration in grams per litre is:

CMC as molar concentration (mole/litre) × molecular weight = g/litre needed to achieve CMC

For example, the CMC for the non-ionic detergent Triton XL 80N is 0.41mmol. With a molecular weight of 442 the equation is:

0.00041 (CMC in moles) × 442 (MW) = 0.181 grams per litre of solution

Three to five times this amount (0.362–0.905 g/litre; rounded up 0.4–0.9 g/litre) of Triton XL 80N, would be required to maintain detergency in an aqueous cleaning solution. A method for measuring small quantities of liquids is described under section 12.1.1.

Another common way manufacturers express CMC is as a weight percent (wt%). This is a simple unit conversion from grams/litre to grams/millilitre expressed as a percentage. As calculated above, the required detergent concentration for Triton XL 80N is 0.181 g/litre. This can be converted to wt% in the following manner:

0.181 g/litre × (1 litre/1000 millilitre) = 0.000181 g/ml

To express this term as a percentage, multiply by 100:

0.000181 g/ml × 100 = 0.0181%

This is the wt%.

Weight percent CMC can be converted to grams per litre in the following way:

(1) Divide the weight percent by 100 to convert to grams per millilitre:

$$\frac{\text{wt\%}}{100} = \text{grams/millilitre}$$

(2) Divide grams/millilitre by 1/1000 to convert to grams per litre

$$\frac{\text{grams}}{\text{millilitre}} \text{ divided by } \frac{1 \text{ (litre)}}{1000 \text{ millilitres}} =$$
grams/litre

For example, to convert 0.0181 wt% CMC to grams per litre CMC:

Step 1:

$$\frac{0.0181}{100} = 0.000181 \text{ g/ml}$$

Step 2:

$$\frac{0.000181}{1/1000} = 0.181 \text{ g/litre of detergent}$$
solution required to achieve CMC

In order to maintain detergency in use, two to five times this amount (0.362–0.905 g/litre; rounded up 0.4–0.9 g/litre) would be required.

### Choosing a detergent

It may be tempting to use proprietary products such as household detergents for aqueous cleaning. Many of the products marketed for the general consumer have components that may be detrimental to decorative surfaces. Proprietary products often utilize anionic detergents that require them to be buffered at an alkaline pH, and contain additives such as strong chelating agents, bleaches, brighteners, perfumes, dyestuffs etc., that may interfere with treatment objectives or damage the surface being cleaned (Hofenk de Graaf, 1982).

The question of an ideal detergent to meet the needs of a particular treatment should be formulated in terms of the type of dirt to be removed and the nature of the substrate or coating being cleaned. The conservator must know the implications of detergent classification in terms of ionic charge, HLB, and CMC in order to make an informed choice of detergent that will achieve removal of dirt, maximum clearance of residues and minimum damage to the surface. For varnished and decorative surfaces, detergents that are non-ionic and have a mid-range HLB (*c*.13–20) are generally used. A detergent with a mid-range CMC (2–20 mmol) should ideally be used, but in cases where a detergent with a low CMC is used, the rinse procedure may require both an aqueous and aromatic hydrocarbon rinse. *Table 11.8* gives information on several detergents that are, or have been, used in conservation.

Alkyl phenols, such as Igepal CA-630 and 720, Synperonic N and Triton X-100, were phased out of general use in conservation in the late 1990s. Synperonic N, for example, was banned for domestic and industrial use in Europe and the UK because some of the breakdown products are toxic to marine life. In addition, nonyl- and octyl-phenol derivatives, such as Synperonic N and Triton X-100, may be xenoestrogens, that is, they may mimic the effect of oestrogen and have a detrimental effect on humans and other animals.

Alkyl phenols have largely been replaced by linear ethoxylated fatty alcohols such as Synperonic 91/8, Triton XL-80N and Tergitol 15-S-9. Linear ethoxylated fatty alcohols may be less effective in solubilizing unsaturated and aromatic components of grime because they do not have an aromatic ring within their structure. The addition of a small amount of an aromatic solvent to the detergent mixture may be sufficient to bring aromatic components of grime into solution.

Although detergent chemistry is complex, when selecting a replacement for obsolete detergents it is essential to match HLB and to consider the effect of CMC. ICI have recommended Synperonic 91/6 or 91/8 as substitutes for Synperonic N for cleaning 'hard' surfaces. Union Carbide has recommended Tergitol 15-S-9 as a substitute for Triton X-100. Triton XL 80N has also been suggested as a substitute. Stavroudis (1995) has noted that Triton XL-80N dissolves more easily in water than Triton X-100.

***Residues and rinse procedures***

Several factors that can affect the amount of detergent that may be deposited on a surface during cleaning have been identified (Wolbers, 1990). In the case of oil-painted surfaces, for example, elevated pH and detergent concentration significantly in excess of the CMC will result in increased detergent residues. The use of a viscous gel could be expected to significantly reduce detergent residues. Increasing the ionic strength of an aqueous rinse solution beyond 500 µS can remove an additional proportion of residual anionic detergent, such as those used in resin and bile soaps (discussed in section 16.6.3) (Wolbers, 1992). The counter-ion used in anionic soaps can affect residues in the following order: triethanolammonium > ammonium > sodium > potassium. Finally, the use of low CMC detergents on unoxidized oil paint films will result in increased residues.

Detergents and surfactants will require a rinse procedure that is tailored to their particular structure and characteristics, and that is compatible with the substrate. Unlike ordinary rinsing, removal of detergent and surfactant residues is not achieved by progressive dilution. Although detergent micelles will be removed with the bulk cleaning solution, residues on the surface may be more difficult to clear. Surfactants and detergents preferentially occupy the interface between materials of dissimilar polarity. This means that if the surfactant is strongly attracted to the surface, when the bulk cleaning solution is removed, residues will stick to the surface and occupy the interface between the surface and the air. Successful rinsing requires that the surfactant is more strongly attracted to the rinse solution than the surface – if this requirement is not met, no amount of rinsing will remove residues.

### 11.5.5   Chelating agents

The word chelate is derived from the Greek for 'claw' and this metaphor can help to visualize the chelating process. By sequestering metal ions, chelating agents form a soluble complex from a compound otherwise insoluble in water, hold it in solution and allow it to be rinsed away. The use of chelating agents in conservation has been discussed by Carlyle *et al.* (1990), Burgess (1991), Chartier (1991) and Phenix and Burnstock (1992) among others.

Chelating agents used in furniture conservation can be divided into two groups – hydroxy-carboxylic acids such as tartaric acid and citric

**Table 11.8** Properties of some detergents used in conservation

| Trade name | Structure | Type | Molecular weight (g/mole: formula, average or estimated) | HLB | CMC (mM) | CMC (wt%) | Manufacturer |
|---|---|---|---|---|---|---|---|
| Brij 35 | 23 ethoxylate lauryl alcohol | Non-ionic | 1198 | 16.9 | 0.06 | 0.007 | Uniqema (ICI) |
| Brij 72 | 2 ethoxylate stearyl alcohol | Non-ionic | 358 | 4.9 | < 0.2 | < 0.007 | Uniqema (ICI) |
| Brij 78 | 20 ethoxylate stearyl alcohol | Non-ionic | 1096 | 15.3 | < 0.2 | < 0.022 | Uniqema (ICI) |
| Ethomeen C12 | bis(2-hydroxyethyl) cocoalkylamine | Cationic | 275–295 | 12.2 | n/a | n/a | Akzo-Nobel |
| Ethomeen C25 | polyoxyethylene (15) cocoalkylamine | Cationic | 826–909 | 16.8 | n/a | n/a | Akzo-Nobel |
| Igepal CA-630 | octylphenoxy(polyethyleneoxy)(9) ethanol | Non-ionic | 624 | 13.4 | < 0.2 | < 0.013 | Rhodia (Rhône Poulenc) |
| Igepal CA-720 | octylphenoxy(polyethyleneoxy)(12) ethanol | Non-ionic | 756 | 14.6 | < 0.2 | < 0.015 | Rhodia (Rhône Poulenc) |
| Orvus | sodium lauryl sulphate | Anionic | 288.4 | 40 | 8 | 0.231 | Procter and Gamble |
| Photo-flo | 9,10 ethoxylate octyl phenol | Non-ionic | 646 | 14.1 | < 0.2 | < 0.013 | Kodak |
| Surfynol 61 | 3,5 dimethyl 1-hexyn-3-ol | Non-ionic | 126 | 6–7 | n/a | n/a | Air Products |
| Synperonic N | polyoxyethylene 8 nonylphenol alcohol | Non-ionic | 590 | 12.3 | 0.085 | 0.005 | Uniqema (ICI) |
| Synperonic 91/6 | polyethyleneglycol(6) C9–11 alcohol | Non-ionic | 418 | 12.5 | 0.38 | 0.016 | Uniqema (ICI) |
| Synperonic 91/8 | polyethyleneglycol(8) C9–11 alcohol | Non-ionic | 505 | 13.9 | 0.602 | 0.03 | Uniqema (ICI) |
| Tergitol 15-S-9 | polyethyleneglycol(9) C12–14 alcohol | Non-ionic | 584 | 13.3 | 0.0958 | 0.0056 | Union Carbide |
| Triton X-100 | 9–10 ethoxylate nonyl phenol | Non-ionic | 624 | 13.5 | 0.22–0.24 | 0.015 | Union Carbide |
| Triton XL-80N | ethoxylated propoxylated C8-10 alcohol | Non-ionic | 442 | 12–13 | 0.41 | 0.0181 | Union Carbide |
| | triethanolamine deoxycholate | Anionic | 523 | 20 | 4 | 0.209 | Ingredients from chemical suppliers |
| | triethanolamine abietate | Anionic | 433.7 | ~ 8.2 | 12 | 0.52 | Ingredients from chemical suppliers |

The detergents listed here have been used in a variety of conservation disciplines. Orvus (sodium lauryl sulphate) is included for comparative purposes and is not recommended for cleaning varnished or decorated surfaces. Ethomeen C12 and C25 are used for the formulation of solvent gels and their use is not recommended for general cleaning applications. Triethanolamine deoxycholate and triethanolamine abietate are used in resin and bile soaps (see section 16.6).

Alkyl phenols, such as Igepal CA-630 and 720, Synperonic N and Triton X-100 were phased out of general conservation use in the late 1990s due to environmental and/or health and safety concerns. Alkyl phenols have largely been replaced by linear ethoxylated fatty alcohols, for example Synperonic 91/8, Triton XL-80N and Tergitol 15-S-9. Surfynol 61 is a volatile surfactant (nBuAc 0.44; 1040 seconds to 90% evaporation). It is miscible with hydrocarbon solvents, alcohols and ketones, but only slightly miscible with water (0.9% by wt). It is used in commercial glass cleaning formulations and has been used in some conservation treatments.

Vulpex (potassium methylcyclohexyloleate), an anionic detergent, was originally used for the conservation of wall paintings, where its pH of 10.5–11.5 (a result of the addition of potassium hydroxide by the manufacturer) was appropriate. Its high pH makes it unsuitable for cleaning varnished and decorated surfaces.

If a detergent is to be used in a conservation treatment, its properties and possible interactions with the object should be carefully considered. For information on these or other detergents and surfactants see section 11.5.4, *McCutcheon's* (1994), Ash (1993) and/or contact the manufacturer.

(a)

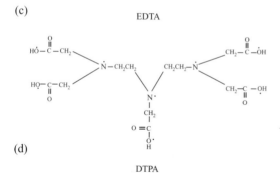

Citric Acid

(b)

NTA

EDTA

(c)

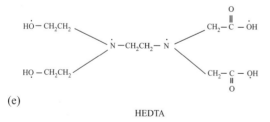

DTPA

(d)

HEDTA

(e)

**Figure 11.21** Molecular structure of five common chelating agents. The electron donating groups are indicated (.): (*a*) citric acid; (*b*) NTA (nitrilotriacetic acid); (*c*) EDTA (ethylenediaminetetraacetic acid); (*d*) DTPA (diethylenetriaminepentaacetic acid); (*e*) HEDTA (N-hydroxyethylenediaminetriacetic acid)

acid (from which di- and tri-ammonium citrate (DAC, TAC) are derived), and aminocarboxylic acids such as nitrilotriacetic acid (NTA), diethylenetriaminepentaacetic acid (DTPA), ethylenediaminetetraacetic acid (EDTA) and N-(2-hydroxyethyl)ethylenediaminetriacetic acid (HEDTA). A third group derived from polyphosphates (e.g. sodium tripolyphosphate or STPP) is no longer used due to concerns about environmental damage. The molecular structure of five chelating agents is illustrated in *Figure 11.21*.

A molecule must have two or more electron donating groups (called ligands) in order to be called a chelating agent. The number of functional groups that participate in chelation is referred to as the co-ordination number. These functional groups can be ionizable groups (e.g. acid or base groups) or neutral groups (such as alcohols and ketones) that have unbonded electrons which can exert weakly attractive forces on metal ions. In order for a molecule to function as a chelator, its structure must allow the formation of a co-ordinated (bonded) structure around a metal ion in solution. Other molecules that have these functional groups but cannot form a ring structure may attract inorganic ions but cannot sequester them in solution. As a general rule divalent metal ions are co-ordinated very strongly to chelating agents. Monovalent ions, such as sodium or potassium, do not form strong co-ordinated bonds with chelating agents and do not interfere with the chelator co-ordinating with other metal ions. This is the reason that sodium salts of chelating agents are often commercially available (e.g. sodium EDTA).

### Formation constants

Both the formation of metal salts (e.g. corrosion products on metals) and chelation are equilibrium reactions. As such, it is possible to assign an equilibrium constant ($k$) to these reactions. In the case of the formation or dissolution of a salt, the $k$ value represents a proportionality constant. That is, the $k$ value represents the proportion of the concentrations of the dissolved species compared to the starting salt concentration at a standard temperature and pressure and at a one molar starting concentration of metal salt.

For example, if the starting reaction is $CaCO_3 \rightleftharpoons Ca^{2+} + CO_3^{2-}$, then the equilibrium constant ($k$) (at standard temperature and pressure) is defined by the following formula (the [ ] brackets indicate concentration):

$$k = \frac{[Ca^{2+}][CO_3^{2-}]}{[CaCO_3]}$$

If the reaction is taken to move in the dissolution direction only (i.e. $CaCO_3 \rightarrow Ca^{2+} + CO_3^{2-}$) then the $k$ from the initial reaction becomes $k_{sp}$, the solubility product (the concentration of calcium and carbonate ions is divided by 1 because the starting point is a one molar solution):

$$k_{sp} = \frac{[Ca^{2+}][CO_3^{2-}]}{1}$$

The $k_{sp}$ number is often very small. For calcium carbonate, for example, the $k_{sp}$ is $2.8 \times 10^{-9}$. For convenience, the negative log of the $k_{sp}$ is often used ($pK_{sp}$). For calcium carbonate, the $pK_{sp}$ is 8.54. The practical importance of this number is that the bigger the $pK_{sp}$, the more insoluble any given salt is in water. In other words, the bigger the $pK_{sp}$, the more stable a salt is in water and the more difficult it will be to remove. Sources such as Dean (1992) provide tables that list solubility products for a large number of salts. The solubility products of some salts that may be encountered in furniture conservation are listed in *Table 11.9*.

**Table 11.9** The solubility products of some salts that may be encountered in furniture conservation

| Substance | Formula | $pK_{sp}$ |
|---|---|---|
| Barium sulphate | $BaSO_4$ | 9.96 |
| Cadmium sulphide | $CdS$ | 26.1 |
| Calcium carbonate | $CaCO_3$ | 8.54 |
| Calcium sulphate | $CaSO_4$ | 5.04 |
| Copper chloride | $CuCl$ | 5.92 |
| Copper carbonate | $CuCO_3$ | 9.86 |
| Copper hydroxide | $Cu(OH)_2$ | 19.66 |
| Copper sulphide | $CuS$ | 35.2 |
| Iron hydroxide | $Fe(OH)_2$ | 15.1 |
| Iron trihydroxide | $Fe(OH)_3$ | 37.4 |
| Lead carbonate | $PbCO_3$ | 13.13 |
| Lead hydroxide | $Pb(OH)_2$ | 14.93 |
| Lead sulphide | $PbS$ | 27.9 |
| Magnesium carbonate | $MgCO_3$ | 7.46 |
| Magnesium hydroxide | $Mg(OH)_2$ | 10.74 |
| Silver sulphide | $Ag_2S$ | 49.2 |
| Titanium trihydroxide | $Ti(OH)_3$ | 40 |
| Zinc carbonate | $ZnCO_3$ | 10.84 |
| Zinc hydroxide | $Zn(OH)_2$ | 16.92 |

*Source:* Dean (1992)

The principle of the formation constant can also be extended to the formation of a bond between chelating agents and metals ions. The same sources that give tables of solubility products also tabulate the formation constants (log $K_f$) for metal ions with chelating agents (which may also be called organic ligands). The log $K_f$ may also be referred to as log $^KM'L'(ML)'$. These numbers are useful in the same way that solubility products are, in that the larger the log $K_f$, the more stable the complex formed between chelator and metal ion. The formation constants of some chelators and metal ions are listed in *Table 11.10*.

To predict whether a salt will be dissolved by a chelator, the log $K_f$ must be bigger than the $pK_{sp}$. If the log $K_f$ is one integer (number) larger than the $pK_{sp}$ it is likely that the salt on a substrate will dissociate and the metal chelate complex will tend to form in solution. For example, EDTA will bind $Ca^{+2}$ with a log $K_f$ of 11.0. If a solution of EDTA is brought to a surface that had calcium carbonate on it, the EDTA will bind calcium ions from the calcium carbonate (which has a $pK_{sp}$ of 8.54). However, $Fe(OH)_3$ iron trihydroxide has a $pK_{sp}$ of 37.4, whilst Fe(III) and EDTA has a log $K_f$ of 24.3. EDTA will not chelate Fe(III) from the iron trihydroxide salt.

In the same way, the solubility product and formation constants can be used to predict whether a chelating agent will have an unwanted effect on the substrate. The solubility constants of materials in the substrate (e.g. $CaSO_4$ in a gesso ground, or pigments such as lead white $Pb(OH)_2.PbCO_3$) can be compared with formation constants of these materials with a given chelating agent.

### Effects of pH and conditional stability constants

The formation constant indicates the preference for formation of the reaction product (or complex) from the ionic species. This calculation does not take into account the affect of pH on the ionic species present. Chelation is an equilibrium reaction and is influenced by the presence of hydrogen and hydroxyl ions. In aqueous cleaning solutions where acidic or basic ligands are involved, chelation is pH-dependent. There is usually an upper pH limit for the effectiveness of a chelator and metal ions. Because chelators are pH-sensitive, a

**Table 11.10** Formation constants of some common chelators and metal ions

| Citric acid Metal ion | Log K$f$ | NTA Metal ion | Log K$f$ | HEDTA Metal ion | Log K$f$ | DTPA Metal ion | Log K$f$ | EDTA Metal ion | Log K$f$ |
|---|---|---|---|---|---|---|---|---|---|
| Aluminium | 7.0 | Aluminium | > 10.0 | Barium(II) | 6.2 | Barium(II) | 8.8 | Aluminium | 16.1 |
| Cadmium | 4.0 | Cadmium | 9.8 | Cadmium(II) | 13.0 | Cadmium(II) | 19.0 | Cadmium | 16.4 |
| Calcium | 4.7 | Calcium | 7.6 | Calcium(II) | 8.4 | Calcium(II) | 10.9 | Calcium | 11.0 |
| Cobalt(II) | 4.8 | Cobalt(II) | 10.4 | Cobalt(II) | 14.4 | Cobalt(II) | 19.0 | Cobalt(II) | 16.3 |
| Copper(II) | 4.4 | Copper(II) | 13.1 | Copper(II) | 17.4 | Copper(II) | 21.1 | Cobalt(III) | 36.0 |
| Iron(II) | 3.0 | Iron(II) | 8.8 | Iron(II) | 12.2 | Iron(II) | 16.0 | Copper(II) | 18.7 |
| Iron(III) | 12.5 | Iron(III) | 15.9 | Iron(III) | 19.8 | Iron(III) | 27.5 | Iron(II) | 14.3 |
| Lead(II) | 6.5 | Lead(II) | 11.8 | Lead(II) | 15.5 | Lead(II) | 18.8 | Iron(III) | 24.2 |
| Magnesium | 3.3 | Magnesium | 5.4 | Magnesium(II) | 5.8 | Magnesium(II) | 9.3 | Lead(II) | 18.3 |
| Manganese(II) | 3.7 | Manganese(II) | 8.6 | Manganese(II) | 10.7 | Manganese(II) | 15.5 | Magnesium | 8.6 |
| Nickel(II) | 5.1 | Mercury(II) | 12.7 | Mercury(II) | 20.1 | Mercury(II) | 27.0 | Manganese(II) | 13.8 |
| Zinc | 4.7 | Nickel(II) | 11.3 | Nickel(II) | 17.0 | Nickel(II) | 20.2 | Mercury(II) | 21.8 |
| | | Zinc | 10.5 | Zinc(II) | 14.5 | Zinc(II) | 18.4 | Nickel(II) | 18.6 |
| | | | | | | | | Silver | 7.3 |

Source: Dean(1992)

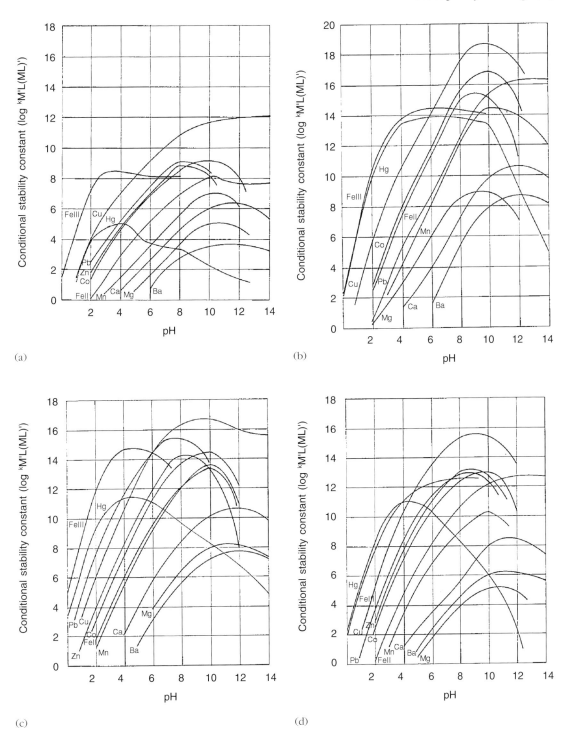

**Figure 11.22** The effect of pH on chelate–metal ion complex formation (derived from tabulated data *in Keys to Chelation: Versene Chelating Agents*, Dow Chemical Company, 1985): (*a*) NTA; (*b*) DTPA; (*c*) EDTA; (*d*) HEDTA
Key to chemical symbols: Ba, barium; Ca, calcium; Co, cobalt; Cu, copper; Fe III, ferric iron; Fe II, ferrous iron; Hg, mercury; Mg, magnesium; Mn, manganese; Pb, lead; Zn, zinc

buffer is usually required to maintain a stable pH.

A conditional stability constant is a formation constant that has been corrected for metal ions which are complexed with hydroxyl ions (OH⁻), the chelating agent corrected for interaction with hydrogen ions (H⁺), and the chelate-metal ion complex corrected for those which include OH⁻ and H⁺. It can be calculated for a range of pH values at a given temperature and concentration. For some chelating agents, such as NTA and DTPA, the effect of pH on the overall formation constant is not very great. For some chelating agents, such as EDTA, the affect of pH is marked. With $Zn^{2+}$, for example, the formation constant increases up to a pH of 9.0 because competition by H⁺ for EDTA is decreasing. At a pH of 10.0, however, the strong attraction of $Zn^{2+}$ for OH⁻ becomes a factor, and there is an increasing tendency for $Zn^{2+}$ to be in solution as an OH⁻ complex (the metal ion hydroxide precipitates from solution). This decreases that amount of $Zn^{2+}$ available for complexing to EDTA, reduces the amount of $[ZnEDTA]^{2+}$ formed, which in turn decreases the conditional stability constant overall. Conditional stability constants, calculated for a single chelating agent, for a range of pH, for different metal ions and plotted against pH provide curves that illustrate the effect of pH on chelate-metal ion complex formation (*Figure 11.22*).

The conditional stability constant and the overall formation constant are not interchangeable. The overall formation constant demonstrates the relative affinity of a particular chelating agent for a particular ion without taking into account the effect of pH. Conditional stability constants are more accurate for determining which metal ions will be complexed by a particular complexing agent at a particular pH. As can be seen in *Figure 11.22*, a chelating agent's affinity for a variety of ions can significantly change with pH. It is critical to know and monitor the pH of the working chelating solution if one is concerned about the ion preference of the chelator.

The solubility of chelators varies with pH. DTPA and EDTA, for example, have low solubility in acidic conditions and pH must be raised (e.g. with a 1M solution of sodium

**Table 11.11**  pKas of some chelating agents

| Chelating agent | pKa |
|---|---|
| Citric acid | 3.13 |
| | 4.76 |
| | 6.4 |
| NTA | 1.9 |
| | 2.5 |
| | 9.8 |
| DTPA | 1.8 |
| | 2.6 |
| | 4.4 |
| | 8.8 |
| | 10.4 |
| EDTA | 2 |
| | 2.7 |
| | 6.2 |
| | 10.3 |
| HEDTA | 2.4 |
| | 5.4 |
| | 9.9 |

Acids such as citric acid, NTA, DTPA, EDTA and HEDTA require at least two of the COO⁻ ions to be dissociated before they can act as chelators. Although this can occur at a low pH, very acidic conditions are unsuitable for most substrates.
*Sources:* Dean (1992); Dawson *et al.* (1986)

hydroxide or other suitable base) to bring them into solution. For example, EDTA is sparingly soluble at a pH of 2, but at a pH of 6.2, is soluble in water and capable of complexing metals ions very strongly. Acids such as citric acid, NTA, DTPA, EDTA and HEDTA require at least two of the COO⁻ ions to be dissociated before they can act as chelators (*Table 11.11*). In the case of citric acid, for example, the pH must be above 4.76. If there is 'cleaning' action below this pH it is the action of the acid reacting with the substrate itself and not a result of chelation.

The chelators discussed above are supplied as free acid or salts in powder form. The free acid is sparingly soluble in water and suitable bases, such as sodium hydroxide, ammonium hydroxide or tri- or di-ethanolamine, may be added to the solution to bring the acid into solution. Where the chelator is purchased in the salt form, for example triammonium citrate or disodium EDTA, this process has already been carried out. The conservator has more scope to formulate a chelating solution to a pH suitable for a given substrate if the free acid form of the chelator is used as the basis for the cleaning solution. The same material can be used to both bring the acid into solution and act as a buffer, e.g. a weak base such as triethanolamine. Residues of chelators could be expected to attract and hold dirt to a surface. The counter-ion used to bring the acid into solution will determine the rinse procedure needed to clear residual chelator from the surface. Inorganic ions such as sodium are very soluble in water but insoluble in solvents. A weak organic base may be soluble in both water and solvents, e.g. an acidic chelate-triethanolammonium salt would be soluble in water, alcohol and ketones.

Cleaning solutions containing chelating agents reported in conservation literature vary in concentration between 0.5 and 5% w/v. Ideally the target amount of chelator in solution should be matched to the amount of metal salt present on the surface (i.e. one millimole of chelator: one millimole of metal salt). Unfortunately it is impossible to measure the exact molar quantity of unwanted material is present on a surface. Commercial suppliers of chelating agents may recommend a 10 millimole concentration for general cleaning purposes. Wolbers (1992, 2000) has recommended a maximum 50 mmol concentration for painted and varnished surfaces. Conservators cleaning decorative surfaces or metal should use the minimum concentration necessary and ensure the surface is rinsed and dried after cleaning. The effect of the pH of the chelating solution on the decorative surface should also be taken into account. The upper safe pH limit for an oil painted surface is 8.5, for example. A chelating solution above this pH would have the potential to damage an oil bound medium by alkaline hydrolysis. Below a pH of 5.5 there is a risk of acidic attack of pigments such as lead and copper carbonates.

Chelators will complex with the metal ions on a surface in a preferential sequence. The preferential sequence can be predicted using the formation constants ($\log K_f$). These sequences form a displacement series and represent the order in which a chelating agent will complex metal ions. The larger the $\log K_f$, the higher the metal ion is in the displacement series.

It is important to be aware of the formation constants at a specified pH, the displacement series and the composition of the decorative surface being cleaned. Many pigments are metal salts that may be sequestered if chelating agents are inappropriately used. Decorative surfaces that include pigments for which a particular chelator has a strong affinity may be vulnerable to damage by it. Citric acid, for example, could potentially chelate $Fe^{3+}$ or $Cu^{2+}$ from pigments such as ochres, earth pigments, malachite and azurite. In addition, citric acid has a proven ability to break up aggregates of particles of clay type minerals (Phenix and Burnstock, 1992). Damage would be unlikely if the paint was medium rich and the pigment well isolated from the cleaning solution, but damage would be inevitable if the pigment were underbound.

The addition of acids, bases or salts will increase the ionic strength of an aqueous solution. It should be noted that excessive ionic strength can disrupt or damage varnished or decorative surfaces (see section 11.6.3). The higher the ionic strength or concentration in solution, the more likely diffusion will take place into an even slightly swollen paint or varnish surface. A 5% TAC solution, for example, may exhibit a conductivity as high as 8–10 mS. Conductivity in excess of 4–5 mS has been observed to blanch oil paint films (Wolbers, 2000). Thus a 5% TAC solution on a painted surface is almost certain to cause irreparable damage. Dilution with deionized water can lower the overall conductivity of an aqueous cleaning solution. Repeated applications of a more dilute solution with a lower conductivity will be as effective in the long run (and safer for the surface) as a single application of a more concentrated solution.

Chelating agents work most efficiently when metal ions are in solution. Chelating solutions used for cleaning may be ineffective if the metal ions in the dirt or corrosion products have low solubility. In such cases they may need to be coupled to another process that converts insoluble compounds into a soluble form. Sodium dithionite (sodium hydrosulphite), a reducing agent, has been used in paper conservation to reduce the insoluble ferric iron to the more water soluble ferrous form (Burgess, 1991). The advantage of using such reducing agents is in converting a more oxidized metal ion that may form very insoluble salts (e.g. hydroxides) in the presence of water, to a lower oxidation state that may be more soluble. This strategy may have limited application on painted or varnished surfaces,

**Figure 11.23** The removal of grime from a nineteenth century Norwegian painted bowl. The bowl was cleaned using hydrocarbon solvent (low aromatic white spirit) followed by the chelating agent triammonium citrate

**Table 11.12**  Formation constants of acetyl acetone and triethanolamine with some metal ions

| Acetyl acetone Metal ion | Log $K_f$ | Triethanolamine Metal ion | Log $K_f$ |
|---|---|---|---|
| Aluminium | 15.5 | Copper(II) | 4.3 |
| Cobalt(II) | 9.54 | Nickel | 2.7 |
| Copper(II) | 16.34 | Silver | 3.64 |
| Iron(II) | 8.67 | Zinc | 2 |
| Iron(III) | 26.7 | | |
| Magnesium | 6.27 | | |
| Manganese | 7.35 | | |
| Nickel(II) | 13.09 | | |
| Zinc | 8.81 | | |

*Source:* Dean (1992)

for example where specific ions (e.g. $Fe^{+3}$, $Cu^{+3}$) are present and available for reduction. Sodium dithionite would be inappropriate, and generally ineffective, for use on varnished and decorative surfaces.

Chelating agents may assist the action of detergents if oily material is present as fatty acid salts of calcium, iron or copper, that would otherwise be insoluble in water. Chelating agents can be used to solubilize inorganic ions forming part of a surface dirt layer (*Figure 11.23*). They may also help remove dirt layers bonded to a surface by the presence of metal ions. It has been noted that citric acid (as the triammonium salt) is effective in removing both organic and inorganic components of dirt (Phenix and Burnstock, 1992).

As well as the chelating agents mentioned above, other substances may also function as chelators. Carboxymethyl cellulose, for example, used in some aqueous gels, may chelate the transition metal ions, $Ca^{2+}$ and $Mg^{2+}$. Some solvents may also function as weak chelators, for example acetyl acetone and triethanolamine (*Table 11.12*).

### 11.5.6   Enzymes

Enzymes are used in cleaning to break down the large molecules of an unwanted material into smaller water-soluble fragments. Enzymes are biologically derived catalysts. They are produced by all living things and have evolved to act as catalysts for specific reactions.

Enzymes catalyse the breakdown of food into constituents that can be converted by an organism into the materials needed to live. Enzymatic reactions may involve oxidation–reduction, hydrolysis, substitution or addition reactions. Because enzymes are catalysts, they are not changed or used up in reactions and therefore only a small amount is required in cleaning preparations. The appeal of enzymes in conservation is that, theoretically, they will serve as catalysts for reactions in a single class of materials whilst leaving others unaffected. Gelling an enzymatic solution may assist in controlled application to a surface.

Enzymes are primarily proteinaceous but may also contain carbohydrates, lipids, and metal ions. Their complex structures become active in water of an appropriate pH and temperature, where the hydrophilic side groups fold outwards and the hydrophobic groups fold inwards. Several theories have been proposed that describe how and why enzymes operate. A simple theory is the 'lock and key' theory. The active site of the enzyme (the lock) has a very particular shape and can only accept a molecule (the key) that matches exactly. Once attached, the chemical bonds of the molecule can be constrained, lengthened, twisted or broken and reformed. The reactivity of the active site will be inhibited outside of a given pH range or distorted by excessive temperature. In either case no reaction will take place.

Enzymes have been utilized in paper conservation for more than twenty years, and more recently have been applied to textiles and paintings conservation (Landi, 1992;

**Figure 11.24** Old residues of a collagen consolidant on this painted surface were removed using a protease gel

Wolbers *et al.*, 1990). Esters in fats and oils (lipids) are broken down into fatty acids by lipase; proteins such as gelatins, collagen and casein are broken down into amino acids by protease; carbohydrates are broken down into sugars by carbohydrases such as amylase. Wolbers has described the use of protease to remove residues of collagen adhesives from painted surfaces, and lipase to remove oil layers applied to paintings in order to increase the specificity of such treatments (Wolbers *et al.*, 1990) (*Figure 11.24, Plate 4*). Whilst protease and amylase have been used for the removal of adhesive residues in paper conservation, the ability of lipase to remove oil applied to painted surfaces has proven somewhat more controversial (Wunderlich and Weser, 1995; Knox, 1995).

Oil has been applied in the past to furniture to saturate colour and from the erroneous belief that wooden surfaces need to be 'fed'. Linseed oil has also been included in many traditional recipes for furniture revivers. The ester linkage between the glycerol backbone and the fatty acids chains that make up the triglyceride molecules in linseed oil is not affected by the polymerization process. Lipases should in theory be capable of breaking down crosslinked oil coatings by hydrolysis but may in fact be hindered by limited access to the ester linkages in a substantially crosslinked oil film. The presence of soiling materials on an oil film, or pigments or a resin component within an oil film will further inhibit enzymatic action.

Resin varnishes will be unaffected by an enzyme cleaning treatment but may be damaged if an excessively alkaline pH solution is used to deliver the enzyme. Lipases will only work at the interface between the cleaning solution and the substrate, which is comparatively small in the case of decorative surfaces. In many cases, partial hydrolysis of a protein or lipid is sufficient to facilitate the removal of an unwanted oily or proteinaceous material.

Enzymes vary in the specificity of their action. Whilst protease will only catalyse reactions that break down proteins, their activity is often not as sharply defined as might be expected. Some proteases, for example, may hydrolyse a wide range of amino acid bonds whilst others may be extremely narrow in their action (e.g. collagenase, which acts only on the peptide bonds in collagen). Lipases are unusually non-specific in their action, catalysing reactions on ester bonds, and can therefore be expected to act on a range of fats and oily material.

Aside from generic considerations such as cost and availability, key factors that influence the choice of enzyme include the degree of specificity to materials present on the object, optimum pH and temperature, and the presence of activators or inhibitors. Slightly alkaline pH (7–8.5) and room temperature are optimal conditions for enzyme performance in decorative surface conservation treatments. Trace minerals such as iron, copper, zinc or calcium are often needed for enzymatic activity (e.g. calcium ions are necessary for lipase activity). Activators are materials that increase the rate of enzyme activity. Inhibitors reduce or prevent enzymes from catalysing reactions by occupying an active site or distorting the enzyme. Both activators and inhibitors are usually well-defined for specific enzymes. Whilst surfactants may be added to an enzymatic solution to increase wetting, particularly for lipases, some surfactants may act as enzyme inhibitors and even a low concentration of some detergents, e.g. Triton X-100, can inhibit the activity of lipases.

The use of enzymes for cleaning requires the enzyme be matched as closely as possible to the material being removed and that the enzyme not act on original material. Thus the general character of a layer or adhesive, the enzyme that will have the most specific activity on this material, and the composition of the underlying layers or substrate should be understood. The conservator should know the specific material or chemical linkage for which the enzyme will catalyse reactions, whether the enzyme is compatible with a desired detergent or chelating agent, the enzyme's optimum temperature and pH range and whether these are safe for the substrate.

The quality and specifications for enzyme products can be obtained from the supplier (e.g. Sigma). Purity of enzyme preparations is an important consideration – technical preparations contain only a small percentage (1–10%) of active enzyme protein. Preparations often include stabilizers that lengthen the shelf life of the product and that may also promote activity due to the presence of various ions such as calcium. Carbohydrates and salts are often added to dilute enzyme concentration to a standard activity (Godfrey and Reichelt, 1983).

Enzyme preparations are sold on the basis of weight and 'unit activity', which is defined as the amount of enzyme required to produce 1 microgram (µg) of product per minute of activity under optimal conditions. A high activity to weight ratio is usually desirable for conservation purposes since 10 mg/ml is usually the upper limit of enzymatic protein that can be dissolved in an aqueous solution (Wolbers *et al.*, 1990). One thousand units of activity per millilitre of solution has been suggested as a target amount for an enzyme solution to have an observable effect within a practical amount of time (Wolbers, 2000).

Enzyme solutions are usually buffered to an optimal pH that is both safe for the substrate and ensures that the enzyme is not denatured. The buffer should match the intended parameters for a given enzyme solution, i.e. the pKa of the buffer should equal the target pH for enzyme activity. As a general rule, chelating agents should not be added to enzymatic cleaning solutions as a small amount of metal ions are often required for enzymatic activity. The formulation of lipase and protease gels is described by Wolbers (2000). General purpose recipes for lipase and protease gels are given below. Amylase recipes can be found in paper conservation literature.

*General purpose lipase gel*

| | |
|---|---|
| 100 ml | deionized water |
| 1 g | deoxycholic acid (free acid) |
| as needed | triethanolamine to adjust pH to 8.0–8.5 |
| 2 g | methyl cellulose (4000 cps) |
| 0.5 g | lipase (Type VII, Sigma) |

Deoxycholic acid is used as part of a buffer but has a dual role as it will also act as a surfactant, wetting the aqueous enzyme preparation onto an oily substrate. One gram of deoxycholic acid per 100 ml of water will give a surfactant concentration of five times the CMC (see under section 11.5.4). TEA is added to raise the pH to 8.0 or 8.5, bringing the deoxycholic acid into solution. The type VII lipase is useful because it has about 800 units of activity per mg at its optimum temperature and pH (i.e. 60 °C and pH 8.5) and contains the calcium required for activity. At the half-gram concentration it should fully dissolve in the solution, and will have a concentration of 5 mg/ml of solution. Using the enzyme at room temperature will result in a loss of around half the stated activity. A concentration of 0.5 grams in 100 ml is equivalent to 5 milligrams per millilitre of solution. The stated activity is 800 units per mg, but the best that can be hoped for at room temperature is half that, 400 units per mg. With 5 milligrams per litre, the effective unit activity of this solution is still 2000 units per ml. It is essential that when the enzyme powder is added that it is gently folded into solution. Brisk stirring will introduce air bubbles that will denature the enzyme. The solution should be pale yellow or straw-coloured when mixed.

The gel may be applied to an area about 25 mm (one inch) square on a surface. The gel may be moved on the surface with a soft brush to increase contact. After about a minute the gel is removed from the surface with a dry swab. The area may be re-treated if necessary. It is important to note that the recipe above uses deoxycholic acid, which will precipitate onto the surface if the pH drops below 7.5, so an aqueous rinse buffered to a pH of 8.0 would be necessary as part of a clearance procedure. The buffer solution might then be cleared with a water or solvent rinse, depending on the counter-ion used in the buffer.

*General purpose protease gel*

| | |
|---|---|
| 100 ml | deionized water |
| 0.73 g | TRIZMA Pre-Set buffer (Sigma T-4253, pH 7.6) |
| 0.1 g | Brij 35 (polyoxyethylene 23 lauryl ether) |
| 2 g | methyl cellulose (4000 cps) |
| 10 mg | trypsin (Sigma Type I, T-8003, 1 mg =10 000 BAEE units) |

At the end of a treatment, enzymes should be denatured to prevent any further reactions. Enzymes are water-soluble and an aqueous rinse is therefore appropriate. Raising or lowering pH, temperature, the use of denaturing solvents, exposure to air or the application of inhibitors may be used as a means of preventing further enzyme activity. Given that lipase must be refrigerated and contact with oxygen minimized to ensure the enzyme is not denatured before it is used, simply air drying Lipase Type VII at room temperature will denature any enzyme residue (Wolbers, 2000).

In their dry form, enzymes should be stored carefully according to the manufacturer's guidelines. Dry enzyme preparations have a shelf life of about one year when refrigerated. As biologically derived catalysts, enzymes will catalyse reactions on and in the human body. Conservators may be exposed to airborne micro-fine powder or splashes when measuring and mixing enzymatic cleaning solutions if simple safety precautions are ignored. Precautions that should be taken when working with enzymes include avoiding inhaling enzyme powder, avoiding contact between powder and eyes, skin and mucous membranes; wearing suitable protective clothing, e.g. masks, goggles, and gloves; working in a well-ventilated, but not draughty, environment; and avoiding contact between liquid enzyme preparations and skin and mucous membranes. Most people will not experience any obvious adverse effects, but some individuals may experience an allergic response. Conservators who suffer from asthma or other respiratory complaints, eczema, dermatitis and hayfever may wish to avoid using enzymes. Spills should be wiped up with a damp cloth, as all enzymes are water-soluble and the priority should be to avoid inhaling enzyme dust.

### 11.5.7 Blanching and blooming

The literal meaning of blanching is to make white by withdrawing colour, and is used to describe an opaque whitish appearance that occurs because of a defect in the paint film (Groen, 1988). Blooming is also an opaque whitish effect but occurs in varnishes, often as a result of exposure to moisture or water. The term blooming has also been used to describe optical changes caused by efflorescence. These terms are often imprecise and often used interchangeably. They do not identify the cause of the problem but indicate that the optical properties of a surface have been altered.

Efflorescence describes a whitish layer encountered on the surface of a material, the components of which originated in the material itself. It may occur independently or as a result of a cleaning treatment. It may occur on wax layers. Efflorescence on oil bound painted surfaces has been ascribed to the migration of free fatty acids, such as palmitic and stearic acids, from the binding medium to the surface of the paint layer (Ordonez and Twilley, 1998).

Blanching may occur as a result of cleaning with organic solvents, reagents, aqueous solutions or consolidation treatments. It may be a result of mechanical disruption of the surface, such as abrasion during cleaning. Granular redeposition of varnish can occur if a fast-drying solvent is used for varnish removal. In such cases the fault can be remedied by either retreating with solvent or revarnishing.

Molecular clusters of water or solvent may be included in a varnish or paint film after cleaning or consolidation. This is common, for example, after treating blisters with a water-based adhesive (particularly in combination with heat), if aqueous solutions have been in contact with water-sensitive areas of the substrate, or as a result of excessive contact time. It may be possible to optically resaturate the affected area by applying fresh varnish. In some cases it may be possible to remedy blanching using a heated spatula isolated from the surface with Melinex/Mylar.

Natural resins are weakly acidic materials that become more acidic as they age and oxidize. Some very degraded natural resin surfaces may be partially soluble in water with a pH of only 8–8.5, a fact that has been exploited in varnish removal treatments (see section 16.6.3). The risk that an aqueous solution will cause bloom in a natural resin varnish increases with the degree of ageing of the varnish and as the pH of the cleaning solution rises. A pH of 6.5 or less may be required to ensure that aqueous cleaning solutions do not cause bloom in very aged natural resin varnishes.

Cleaning may result in components in an underlying layer being deposited on the surface or in the craquelure, resulting in a whitish appearance. Ruhemann (1968) reported one case in which an effect that appeared to be blanching was in fact a deposit of calcium sulphate, a component of the gesso layer. It had apparently been brought to the surface by evaporation of the solvent used in cleaning.

Micro-void blanching may be caused by aqueous cleaning and is characterized by a network of minute pores that form within the paint structure in the presence of susceptible pigments and paint media. Blanching due to inaccessible micro-voids created by pigment/ medium debonding will not resaturate with revarnishing (Michalski, 1990). Adhesive failure resulting in debonding of pigment and medium can occur if there is an affinity between pigments and water or solvent. For example, although water takes days to diffuse through a pure oil medium, it can channel along flocculated pigment surfaces in minutes resulting in blanching, loss of colour saturation, the creation of micro-voids or pigment loss (Michalski, 1990). Water and alcohols have an affinity for inorganic pigments, whilst ketones and less polar solvents are more attracted to organic pigments. Michalski (1990) outlined acid–base affinities between solvents and pigments. There is a potential for interactions between alcohols, water and inorganic pigments that can act as either weak bases or acids. Ketones, ethers and aromatic hydrocarbons are weakly basic and will therefore attach to acidic pigments such as pthalo blues, organic reds and carbon blacks. Browne (1955) identified the affinity of water for zinc white pigments and found that after soaking paint films in distilled water for three days those containing calcium sulphate (such as Venetian red) lost large fractions of the pigment and interconnected voids were found within the paint film. Whilst a conservation treatment should avoid such extreme exposures, Browne's data identified pigments that are very vulnerable to aqueous cleaning as zinc sulphate, zinc oxide, leaded zinc oxides, some iron oxides, Venetian red and most calcium carbonates. Others, such as zinc sulphide, lithopone and any other white pigment with a small amount of zinc oxide, are also vulnerable to a lesser degree. Hedley *et al.* (1990) found that paint films that contain natural earth pigments, e.g. raw sienna, are highly susceptible to water absorption and there is an increased potential for medium erosion by aqueous cleaning solutions.

## 11.6  Thickened solvent delivery systems – pastes, poultices and gels

One of the potential drawbacks of cleaning with free flowing liquids is the difficulty in controlling and containing the material as it is being applied to a surface. Gels, poultices and pastes can be used to contain solvents, reagents and water to provide greater application control. Significantly increasing viscosity reduces the evaporation rate of solvent from the surface being treated and from the surface of the gel by altering the surface/ volume ratio. Increasing viscosity may affect the diffusion gradient and intensify solvent action. The treatment area can be localized and capillary absorption (wicking) of the solvent may be reduced or prevented. The use of thickened solvents occasionally results in a patchy, uneven surface.

Unless the thickened solution is transparent it will not be possible to visually track its progressive action on a surface. Clearance of residues from a surface may present problems since gels, poultices and pastes are, by definition, non-volatile. An effective clearance procedure is therefore essential. Residue problems are more likely on porous surfaces. As a general rule, as the porosity of the surface decreases and the size of the molecule used to thicken the solvent increases, it becomes less likely that clearance will be problematic. Carbopol 980, for example, with a molecular weight of around four million, is comparatively easy to remove and residues are unlikely to be a significant problem.

Wax pastes have traditionally been used in painting restoration for reagents such as ammonia (Burnstock and Learner, 1992; Ruhemann, 1968). They can also be used for increasing the viscosity of hydrocarbon solvents.

Poultices can be used in furniture conservation for the application of solvent and localized removal of stains. Localized application carries a risk of tidelining. In stone conservation, poultices have been used for the removal of salts from within the bulk of an object. When used for cleaning, poultices are usually applied for a limited time, the effects checked and the poultice reapplied if necessary. Stain removal may require application for a longer period, but such extended exposure in a small isolated area may cause deformation, or expansion followed by shrinkage and staining. Any solvent left in pores or cracks may also cause damage.

Poultices may be used to extend the contact time between the surface of the object and the cleaning solution. They are often used to facilitate the softening and removal of dirt when cleaning the surface of porous materials such as ceramics or stone. The aim is to keep the dirt in contact with the poultice rather than allowing it to move deeper into a porous substrate. Poultices may be applied and removed wet, or applied wet and removed when dry. In either case, when the poultice is removed, it is necessary to rinse the surface to remove any softened dirt and remaining poultice material. A poultice that is to be applied and removed wet may be applied directly to the surface in a thick layer and covered with Melinex/Mylar to reduce the evaporation rate. A poultice that is to be applied wet and removed dry would be applied directly to the surface in a thick layer and left uncovered. The aim of a poultice that is removed dry is to move solubilized dirt into the poultice by capillary action as the solvent evaporates. Repeated applications may be necessary.

A poultice that acts as a solvent reservoir can be made using materials such as acid free blotting paper or pulp, clays such as sepiolite and attapulgite, cellulose ether or Carbopol. When using poultices, it is essential to ensure even contact with the surface as the presence of air bubbles may result in patchy cleaning. This may be problematic because such patchy dirt deposits may be difficult to remove without overcleaning the surrounding area.

Aqueous gels can be made using Carbopol, a synthetic colloidal clay (e.g. Laponite RD) or a cellulose ether. These materials will control flow whilst creating few clearance complications. Control of pH is essential for aqueous gels. Water-miscible solvents such as ethanol or acetone can be added to a pre-mixed colloidal clay/water or cellulose ether/water system to create a gelled water/solvent system. Tests will determine the percentage of solvent necessary for dirt or a coating to be softened, swelled or dissolved. Pure solvent gels usually require the use of either a cellulose ether or Carbopol.

### 11.6.1   Controlled vapour delivery

Controlled solvent vapour delivery to, or humidification of, sensitive surfaces can be required in a range of conservation treatments from the removal of paper labels (Navarro, 1997), selective layer removal (Wachowiak and Williams, 1994) or as a necessary first step in a consolidation treatment. These treatments utilize a solvent reservoir suspended over, or in some manner separated from, the surface being treated. Localized humidification may be achieved by suspending barely damp cloth above a water-sensitive surface, or by the use of a moisture reservoir such as acid-free blotting paper in combination with a moisture permeable material such as Gore-Tex or Sympatex (see section 15.2.2). Gels can provide a solvent reservoir for polar and/or non-polar solvents. An intermediate isolating layer will always be necessary and, in some cases, a method of suspending the gel above the surface may need to be found. Various materials have been used for the intermediate layer, from Japanese tissue on its own (Petukhova, 1992), or in combination with a polypropylene screen (Wachowiak and Williams, 1994), to Hollytex (Bluher *et al.*, 1995). If a gel is used as a solvent reservoir it should be very viscous (e.g. 10–40 000 cps/sec).

### 11.6.2   Gelling materials

#### *Clays*

Laponite RD is a synthetic colloidal clay that forms a transparent thixotropic gel when mixed with water. It is free from crystalline silica impurities and is environmentally inert. A 2–5% concentration of the fine white powder in water will produce a clear gel. The gel is made by slowly adding Laponite to water whilst stirring and then leaving the mix for several hours to stand and thicken. The pH of the gel should be checked and adjusted as necessary as a 2% suspension has a pH around 9.8. If a water/solvent gel is required, Laponite should be added to the water and left to sit for approximately 20 minutes. At this point, miscible solvents such as alcohol or acetone may be added, up to around one-third of the total volume of liquid, to produce a water/solvent gel.

When treatment is complete, the bulk of the gel can be removed with swabs and/or a soft bristle brush, followed by a water rinse. Complete removal of residues from porous surfaces may be very difficult. The addition of cellulose fibre (e.g. Arbocel) to a Laponite gel (1:1) will aid in residue removal (Navarro, 2000). The gel is usually applied and removed wet, as dried residues can be particularly problematic. A moisture permeable barrier layer can be used between the gel and a porous or vulnerable surface to prevent the risk of residues remaining on the surface after treatment. The use of a barrier layer will reduce absorption of material from the surface into the gel.

Sepiolite is a naturally occurring clay. It has a fine particle size, is grey–white in colour and contains hydrated magnesium silicate. It will absorb water or solvent to form a thick paste. As with Laponite, complete removal of residues from porous surfaces may be very difficult. As it is a natural material, it may contain some impurities. Attapulgite clays are also naturally occurring and are composed primarily of hydrated magnesium aluminium silicate. They have a three-dimensional chain structure that enables them to absorb large quantities of water. Sepiolite and attapulgite gels are not transparent and are generally used on ceramic or stone surfaces.

### Cellulose ethers

Cellulose ethers are a large family of polymeric materials derived from the etherification of wood pulp (cellulose) resulting in the substitution of hydroxyl groups with alkyl or hydroxyalkyl groups. There are a wide range of products that are fundamentally similar, differing in the number and type of groups added to the glucose monomer. Methyl cellulose (MC) and hydroxypropyl cellulose (HPC) may be used to gel aqueous cleaning solutions. Gel viscosity is dependent on the polymer chain length of the selected cellulose ether. The viscosity of methyl cellulose products supplied by Sigma, for example, ranges from 15 to 4000 cps/sec for a 2% aqueous solution at 20 °C. Several terms are needed to describe the chemical and physical properties of cellulose ethers. The degree of substitution refers to the number of alkyl groups added to each glucose unit of the polymer chain. A low degree of substitution will indicate a material that is water-soluble; a high degree of substitution indicates an alcohol-soluble material. Molar substitution refers to the number of alkene oxide units added per glucose unit.

It is essential to remove all gelled material from the surface after cleaning. The clearance procedure required is dependent on the solubility of the particular cellulose ether used. Gel residues may form a film that will effect the optical properties of the surface and will support mould growth. This propensity for fungal growth means that only fresh solutions should be used and sterile dark conditions are required for storage.

Methyl cellulose is non-ionic, water-soluble (below 90 °C) and produces a thick gel at relatively low concentrations. Methyl cellulose is used in some commercial cleaning products because it holds dirt in suspension and helps prevent redeposition on the surface. Methyl cellulose gels tend to be less viscous than those made with a colloidal clay. A gel can be made by slowly adding the powder whilst continuously stirring the solution. Agitation should be continued for a further 30 minutes. Clumps may form initially but will be broken down by continued stirring. Methyl cellulose does not hydrate immediately but with continuous stirring a uniform solution will form that will gradually become more viscous until hydration is complete. Methyl cellulose is pH tolerant and is stable between pH 3 to 11, although gels will take significantly longer to form in acidic solutions. Concentration may vary between 0.5 and 5% or more depending on the application. It has been suggested that increasing gel viscosity significantly reduces the deposition of surfactant and detergent residues, so if these materials are included in a gelled cleaning solution viscosity should be as high as practicable (Wolbers, 1990). Water-miscible solvents such as ethanol and acetone can be added to a pre-prepared water gel based on a low substitution methyl cellulose. Pure ethanol and acetone gels will require a methyl cellulose with a high substitution number.

Hydroxypropyl cellulose (HPC) has hydroxy propyl groups substituted onto the free hydroxy groups of the cellulose molecule. It is non-ionic, pH-neutral and water-soluble below 60 °C. A range of HPC products are produced by Hercules and marketed under the name Klucel®. Low molecular weight Klucels are more readily soluble in water but produce less viscous solutions (*Table 11.13, Figure 11.25*). The Klucels vary in the viscosity of the gel they produce and their solubility in organic solvents. According to the manufacturer, Klucels tend to hydrate rapidly, leading to the agglomeration of particles into lumps, which significantly increases gel preparation time. They recommend making a slurry of Klucel in either water hotter than 60 °C or in a non-solvent and then adding cold water whilst agitating the mixture. Empirical experience suggests that some Klucels may not thicken in solvents such as alcohol without the inclusion of a small proportion (*c*.4%) of water. Solubility in organic solvents varies from type to type. Acetone will produce a clear gel with Klucel E but will produce a hazy and somewhat granular gel with Klucel G (*Table 11.14*). The solubility of Klucel can be manipulated by the use of small quantities of soluble co-solvents such as water or ethanol in relatively small proportions (5–15%) (*Table 11.15*). Even non-solvents can be used to form solutions if the Klucel is first dissolved in a compatible solvent that is miscible with the non-solvent (e.g. ethanol and toluene).

Klucels are surfactants and will therefore reduce the surface tension of water and play a role in stabilizing emulsions. Hydroxypropyl substitution makes Klucels more lipophilic than other water-soluble cellulose derivatives and they are compatible with a wide range of anionic, non-ionic and cationic surfactants.

**Table 11.13**  Molecular weight of Klucel®

| Klucel type | Molecular weight |
|---|---|
| Klucel H | 1 150 000 |
| Klucel M | 850 000 |
| Klucel G | 370 000 |
| Klucel J | 140 000 |
| Klucel L | 95 000 |
| Klucel E | 80 000 |

Typical properties, these values do not represent a specification.
*Source:* Information courtesy of Hercules

**Table 11.14**  Comparative viscosity of Klucel® in water and some solvents

| Solvent | Viscosity (mP/sec) | | | |
|---|---|---|---|---|
| | Klucel H at 1% conc | Klucel G at 2% conc | Klucel L at 5% conc | Klucel E at 10% conc |
| Water | 2100 | 270 | 80 | 275 |
| Methanol | 800 | 85 | 25 | 75 |
| Ethanol | 1600 | 210 | 65 | 255 |
| Isopropyl alcohol (99%) | B | B | 145 | 570 |
| Isopropyl alcohol (95%) | — | — | 130 | 420 |
| Acetone | B | B | 50 | 175 |
| Methylene chloride | 4500B | — | 1240B | 14 600B |
| Methylene chloride: methanol (9:1) | 5500 | — | 400 | — |
| Propylene glycol | 6000 | 6640 | 5020 | > 10 000 |

B, borderline solvent, solutions are granular and may be hazy.
Typical properties, these values do not represent a specification.
*Source:* Information courtesy of Hercules

**Table 11.15**  Solubility of Klucel® G 2% w/v

| Soluble | Borderline | Insoluble |
|---|---|---|
| Acetic acid | Acetone | Aliphatic hydrocarbons |
| Acetone:water 9:1 | Butyl acetate | |
| Ethanol | Butyl cellosolve | Mineral oils |
| Formic acid | Isopropanol 99% | Toluene |
| Isopropanol 95% | Methylethylketone | Xylene |
| Methanol | Methylene chloride | |
| Methyl cellosolve | Naptha:ethanol 1:1 | |
| Methylene chloride: methanol 9:1 | Xylene:isopropanol 1:3 | |
| Toluene:ethanol 3:2 | | |
| Water | | |

Typical properties, these values do not represent a specification.
*Source:* Information courtesy of Hercules

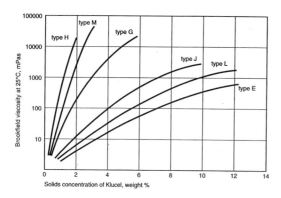

**Figure 11.25** Effect of concentration and type of Klucel® on the viscosity of water solutions. Typical properties, these values do not represent a specification. Source: information courtesy of Hercules

### Polyacrylic acid (Carbopol)

Carbopol, a trademark product of the BF Goodrich company, is a polyacrylic acid polymer used to thicken solvent gels (Wolbers *et al.*, 1990). Various Carbopol polymers are available that vary in molecular weight and degree of intermolecular crosslinks. Carbopol 980, for example, has a molecular weight of four million and forms a transparent and very viscous gel at 40 000–60 000 cps/sec. Concentration of Carbopol can be varied from 0.5% to 6% or more according to the viscosity required to address individual cleaning problems and whether additional solvent/s will be added after formulation of a stock gel.

The gelling or thickening effect occurs when the polyacrylic acid polymer uncoils to form a stable network after the addition of an alkali and a small amount of water (*Figure 11.26*). In the presence of water, the addition of such a 'neutralizing agent' leads to the formation of COO⁻ ions along the polyacrylic acid that bond to the added base via ionic or salt type linkages. The Carbopol uncoils due to electrostatic repulsion and forms a viscous gel. Reactive sites on the carboxylic acid form secondary bonds with some solvents.

A variety of bases can be used to neutralize Carbopol, including triethanolamine, ammonia and sodium hydroxide. Organic amines such as ammonia and triethanolamine may migrate out of the solvent gel, but can be cleared using an aqueous rinse procedure.

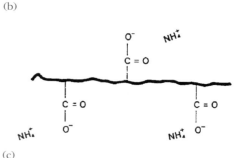

(a)

(b)

(c)

**Figure 11.26** Polyacrylic acid (Carbopol)
(*a*) Polyacrylic acid, monomer unit
(*b*) An unneutralized, partially solvated Carbopol resin molecule
(*c*) A neutralized, fully solvated resin molecule forms the basis for a viscous solvent gel

Bluher *et al.* (1995) reported migration through an intermediate layer. Such migration cannot occur if the gel is suspended above the surface rather than simply placed on an intermediate permeable layer. Inorganic bases such as sodium hydroxide make migration unlikely, but pH control during formulation is more difficult. Ethomeen C12 and C25 (Akzo Nobel), tertiary amine ethoxylates, have been used in a dual role of neutralizing Carbopol and as surfactants within the solvent gel. C-12 is used for non-polar solvent blends and C-25 for polar solvents.

As with gels formulated from cellulose ethers, the exact proportions are dictated by a given treatment. A 2–6% w/v solution of Carbopol will produce a stiff gel to which other solvents may be added if required. Water is present in all Carbopol gels, so pH should be measured and adjusted to a level appropriate to a given treatment.

There are several methods that may be used to formulate Carbopol gels. Solvent components can pre-measured and combined. The Carbopol and neutralizing agent are mixed until a smooth paste is formed. The solvent is then slowly added to the paste while continuously stirring the mixture. Drops of water are added as required. In a second method, the Carbopol is mixed with a small amount of solvent and is stirred until free of lumps. The rest of the solvent is then added followed by the Ethomeen and finally water, drop by drop. In a third method, Carbopol, neutralizing agent and solvent are mixed together, water added, the container sealed and the mixture shaken vigorously. The key to making gels with Carbopol is to add the water last.

The amount of Ethomeen and the proportions of water and solvent vary according to the treatment. An ethanol gel, for example, may include 2–20 ml Ethomeen C25 per gram of Carbopol depending on cleaning requirements and gel viscosity.

*Generic polar solvent gel*
2 g      Carbopol 980
20 ml    Ethomeen C25
100 ml   polar solvent (acetone, IMS etc.)
15 ml    water

*Generic non-polar solvent gel*
2 g      Carbopol 980
20 ml    Ethomeen C12
100 ml   non-polar solvent (white spirit, xylene etc.)
1–2 ml   water

It is possible to make a polar solvent gel and add non-polar solvent to it, and vice versa, up to the tolerance of the gel. Too much non-polar solvent added to a polar gel (and vice versa) will cause the gel to collapse.

*Clearance*   The amount of residue that may be left after use of a Carbopol-based gel was quantified by Stulik *et al.* (2000). Using a worst case scenario, the Ethomeen component of the residue comprised 0.26% of the weight of the paint layer. Burnstock and White (2000) artificially aged a mixture of Ethomeen C-12 and dammar resin. Once the solvent had evaporated, their test varnish film contained approximately 8% Ethomeen C-12, more than thirty times the concentration identified by Stulik *et al.* (2000). After artificially ageing this film for the equivalent of fifty years, Burnstock and White found that a significant degree of additional ageing of the resin.

Conservators considering the use of solvent gels must make a decision based on the relative risk of gelled and ungelled solvents. Neither approach is free from the risk of causing some degree of damage to a sensitive substrate, including japanning, oil paint or light-damaged oriental lacquer. In the case of solvent gels, the risk of future damage can be minimized by a suitable clearance procedure.

Water should not be considered as a rinsing agent unless the gel itself is water-based. Excess gel should be removed with a dry swab followed by rolling over the surface with a swab moistened with an appropriate solvent blend. It is not necessary to use the same blend as was used in the gel as long as the rinse blend is polar enough to dissolve the original gel. If in doubt, take a small amount of the gel and stir it in a small amount of the solvent blend that will be used for rinsing. If the gel dissolves, the blend is appropriate. If the gel does not dissolve or forms a whitish crust, a different solvent blend will be necessary.

## Bibliography

Ash, M. (1993) *Handbook of Industrial Surfactants*, Gower

Ashok, R. and Smith, P. (eds) (2000) *Tradition and Innovation: Advances in Conservation*, IIC

Ashurst, N. (1994) *Cleaning Historic Buildings*, Alden Press

Balston, T. (ed.) (1956) *The Housekeeping Book of Susanna Whatman, 1776–1800*, Geofrey Bles Ltd

Banik, G. and Krist, G. (eds) (1986) *Lösungsmittel in der Restaurierung*, Verlag der Apfel

Barton, A.F.M. (1983) *CRC Handbook of Solubility Parameters and Other Cohesion Parameters*, CRC Press

Beck, J. and Daley, M. (1993) *Art Restoration: The Culture, The Business, The Scandal*, John Murray

Belluci, R., Cremonesi, P. and Pignagnoli, G. (1999) A preliminary note on the use of enzymes in conservation: the removal of aged acrylic resin coatings with lipase, *Studies in Conservation*, 44, 278–81

BFGoodrich Co. (1991) *Carbopol Resins Handbook*

Bluher, A., Haller, U., Banik, G. and Thobois, E. (1995)

The application of Carbopol poultices on paper objects, *Restaurator*, 16, 234–47

Brommelle, N.S. and Smith, P. (1976) *The Conservation and Restoration of Pictorial Art*, Butterworths

Browne, F.L. (1955) Swelling of paint films in water, V: effects of different pigments, *Forest Products Journal*, 5, 192–200

Buck, S. (1993) Three case studies in the treatment of painted furniture, in AIC Wooden Artifacts Group, Conference Papers, Denver

Burgess, H. (1991) The use of chelating agents in conservation treatments, *Journal of Paper Conservation*, 15, 36–44

Burnstock, A. and Learner, T. (1992) Changes in the surface characteristics of artificially aged mastic varnishes after cleaning using alkaline reagents, *Studies in Conservation*, 37, 165–84

Burnstock, A. and White, R. (1990) The effects of selected solvents and soaps on a simulated canvas painting, in *Cleaning, Retouching and Coatings*, Conference Preprints, IIC, pp. 111–18

Burnstock, A. and White, R. (2000) A preliminary assessment of the aging/degredation of Ethomeen C-12 residues from solvent gel formulations and their potential for inducing change in resinous paint media, in Ashok and Smith. pp. 34–8

Caley, T. (1990) Aspects of varnishes and the cleaning of oil paintings before 1700, in *Cleaning, Retouching and Coatings*, Conference Preprints, IIC, pp. 70–2

Carlyle, L., Townsend, J. and Hackney, S. (1990) Triammonium citrate: an investigation into its application for surface cleaning, in *Dirt and Pictures Separated*, UKIC, London

Chartier, D.R. (1991) Cation-selective reagents for conservation treatments, *Material Issues in Art and Archaeology*, 185, 73–9

Cooper, M. (ed.) (1998) *Laser Cleaning in Conservation*, Butterworth-Heinemann

Crank, J. and Park, G.S. (1968) *Diffusion in Polymers*, Academic Press

Daniels, V. (1982) Colour changes of water colour pigments during deacidification, in N.S. Brommelle and G. Thomson (eds), *Science and Technology in the Service of Conservation*, IIC

Davidsohn, A. and Milwidsky, B.M. (1978) *Synthetic Detergents*, George Godwin

Dawson, R.M.C., Elliott, D.C., Elliott W.H. and Jones, K.M. (1986) *Data for Biomedical Research*, Clarendon Press

Dean, J.A. (1992) *Lange's Handbook of Chemistry*, 14th edn, McGraw-Hill

de la Rie, R., Lomax, S.Q., Palmer, M., Glinsman, L.D. and Maines, C.A. (2000) An investigation of the photochemical stability of urea-aldehyde resin retouching paints: removability tests and colour spectroscopy, in R. Ashok and P. Smith (eds), *Tradition and Innovation: Advances in Conservation*, IIC, pp. 51–9

Dorge, V. and Howlett, F.C. (eds) (1998) *Painted Wood: History and Conservation*, Conference Postprints, Getty Conservation Institute

Feller, R.L. (1976a) Problems in the investigation of picture varnishes, in N.S. Brommelle and P. Smith (eds), *The Conservation and Restoration of Pictorial Art*, Butterworths

Feller, R.L. (1976b) The relative solvent power needed to remove various aged solvent-type coatings, in N.S.

Brommelle and P. Smith (eds), *The Conservation and Restoration of Pictorial Art*, Butterworths, pp. 158–61

Feller, R.L., Stolow, N. and Jones, E.H. (1985) *On Picture Varnishes and their Solvents*, Washington, DC: National Gallery of Art

Flexner, B. (1994) *Understanding Wood*, Rodale Press

Godfrey, T. and Reichelt, J. (1983) *Industrial Enzymology*, Macmillan

Groen, K. (1988) Scanning electron microscopy as an aid in the study of blanching, *The Hamilton Kerr Institute Bulletin*, 1

Hackney, S. (1990) The removal of dirt from Turner's unvarnished oil sketches, in S. Hackney, J. Townsend and N. Eastaugh (eds), *Dirt and Pictures Separated*, Conference Postprints, UKIC

Hackney, S., Townsend, J. and Eastaugh, N. (eds) (1990) *Dirt and Pictures Separated*, Conference Postprints, UKIC

Hale, S.J. (1853) *The New Household Receipt-Book*, Long & Bro, New York

Hansen, C. (1967) The three dimensional solubility parameter – a key to paint component affinities, *Journal of Paint Technology*, 39(511), 505–510

Hansen, C.M. (2000) *Hansen Solubility Parameters: A User's Handbook*, CRC Press

Hayward, C.H. (1960, 1988) *Staining and Polishing*, Drake (US)/Unwin Hyman (UK)

Hedley, G., Odlyha, M., Burnstock, A., Tillinghast, J. and Husband, C. (1990) A study of the mechanical and surface properties of oil paint films treated with organic solvents and water, in *Cleaning, Retouching and Coatings*, Conference Preprints, IIC, pp. 98–105

Hildebrand, J. and Scott, R. (1948) *The Solubility of Non-electrolytes*, 3rd edn, Reinhold

Hofenk de Graaf, J.H. (1968) The constitution of detergent in connection with the cleaning of ancient textiles, Studio and Workshop Notes, *Studies in Conservation*, 13, 122–41

Hofenk de Graaf, J.H. (1982) Some recent developments in the cleaning of ancient textiles, in N.S. Brommelle and G. Thomson (eds), *Science and Technology in the Service of Conservation*, pp. 93–5

Horie, V. (1992) *Materials for Conservation*, Butterworth-Heinemann

Horsley, L.H. (1952) *Azeotropic Data*, Advances in Chemistry Series, No. 6, American Chemical Society

Jeffrey, N.A. (1999) Today's art lesson: grime pays, *The Wall Street Journal*, 10 December, W16

Karpowicz, A. (1981) Ageing and deterioration of proteinaceous media, *Studies in Conservation*, 26, 153–60

Keck, S. (1984) Some picture cleaning controversies: past and present, *JAIC*, 23, 73–87

Knox, S. (1995) An assessment of catalytic activity in Wolbers' lipase gel using an enzyme assay, *Conservation News*, UKIC, p. 58

Koller, J. (1990) Cleaning of a nineteenth century painting with deoxycholate soap: mechanism and residue studies, *Cleaning, Retouching and Coatings*, Conference Preprints, IIC, pp. 106–10

Landi, S. (1992) *The Textile Conservator's Manual*, 2nd edn, Butterworths

Lang, S. (1999) Casein plastic: history, chemistry and manufacture, in D. Rogers and G. Marley (eds), *Modern Materials – Modern Problems*, Conference Postprints, UKIC

Leonard, M., Whitten, J., Gamblin, R. and de la Rie, R. (2000) Development of a new material for retouching, in R. Ashok and P. Smith (eds), *Tradition and Innovation: Advances in Conservation*, IIC, pp. 111–13

*McCutcheon's Volume 1 Emulsifiers and Detergents* (1994) North American and International editions, 1994 MC Publishing Co.

Michalski, S. (1990) A physical model of the cleaning of oil paint, in J.S. Mills and P. Smith (eds), *Cleaning, Retouching and Coatings*, Conference Preprints, IIC, pp. 85–91

Mills, J.S. and Smith, P. (eds) (1990) *Cleaning, Retouching and Coatings*, Conference Preprints, IIC

Mills, J. and White, R. (1977) Natural resins of art and archaeology: their sources, chemistry and identification, *Studies in Conservation*, 22(1), 12–31

Mills, J. and White, R. (1994) *The Organic Chemistry of Museum Objects*, Butterworths

Moncrieff, A. and Weaver, G. (1992) *Science for Conservators*, Crafts Council Conservation Teaching Series, Routledge

Myers, D. (1992) *Surfactant Science and Technology*, VCH

Navarro, J. (1997) Removing paper labels from ceramics and glass, *The Conservator*, 21, 21–7

Navarro, J. (2000) Workshop notes: easing the removal of a Laponite RD poultice from ceramics, in *ICOM-CC Glass, Ceramics and Related Materials Working Group Newsletter*, Summer

Neugebauer, J.M. (1990) Detergents: an overview, *Methods in Enzymology*, 182, 239–53

Ordonez, E. and Twilley, J. (1988) Clarifying the haze: efflorescence on works of art, *WAAC Newsletter*, 20, No. 1

Perrin, D.D. (1982) *Ionisation Constants of Inorganic Acids and Bases in Aqueous Solution*, IUPAC Chemical Data Series, No. 29, Pergamon Press

Petukhova, T. (1992) Removal of varnish from paper artifacts, in *The 1992 Book and Paper Group Annual*, AIC, pp. 136–40

Phenix, A. (1998) Solubility parameters and the cleaning of paintings: an update and review, *Kunsttechnologie und Konservierung*, 12(2), 387–409

Phenix, A. and Burnstock, A. (1992) The removal of surface dirt on paintings with chelating agents, in *The Conservator*, UKIC, 16, 28–38

Rieger, M.M. (ed.) (1985) *Surfactants in Cosmetics*, Marcel Dekker

Romão, P. and Alarcão, Viana, C. (1990) Human saliva as a cleaning agent for dirty surfaces, *Studies in Conservation*, 35, 153–5

Rothenberg, G.B. (1978) *Paint Additives: Recent Developments*, Noyes Data Corporation

Ruhemann, H. (1968) *The Cleaning of Paintings*, Faber and Faber

Samet, W. (1998) The philosophy of aesthetic reintegra-tion: paintings and painted furniture, in Dorge and Howlett (1998), op. cit., pp. 412–23

Shelly, M. (1987) *The Care and Handling of Art Objects*, Metropolitan Museum of Art, New York

Solomons, T.W.G. (1992) *Organic Chemistry*, John Wiley and Sons

Stavroudis, C. (1995) Replacement for Triton X-100, *WAAC Newsletter*, 17 (1), 10

Stavroudis, C. (undated) Carbopol resins, *CM Times* (Conservation Materials Ltd), No. 5

Sterlini, P. (1995) Surface cleaning products and their effect on paper, *Paper Conservation News*, No. 76, 3–7

Stulik, D., Dorge, V., Khanjian, H., Khandekar, N., de Tagle, A., Miller, D., Wolbers, R. and Carlson, J. (2000) Surface cleaning: quantitative study of gel residue on cleaned paint surfaces, in R. Ashok and P. Smith (eds), *Tradition and Innovation: Advances in Conservation*, IIC, pp. 188–94

Teas, J.P. (1968) The graphic analysis of resin solubilities, *Journal of Paint Technology*, 40 (516), 19–25

Tímár-Balázsy, Á. and Eastop, D. (1998) *Chemical Principles of Textile Conservation*, Butterworth-Heinemann

Torraca, G. (1975) *Solubility and Solvents for Conservation Problems*, International Center for the Study of Preservation and Restoration of Cultural Property, Rome

Tsang, J. and Erhardt, D. (1992) Current research on the effects of solvent and gelled and aqueous cleaning systems on oil paint films, *JAIC* 31(1), 87–94

Ueberreiter, K. (1968) The solution process, in J. Crank and G.S. Park (eds), *Diffusion in Polymers*, Academic Press

Wachowiak, M. and Williams, D. (1994) Conservation of an 18th century English japanned surface, in *Lacquerwork and Japanning*, Conference Postprints, UKIC

Webb, M. (1989) The removal of an insoluble varnish from an 18th century clock case, AIC Wooden Artifacts Group, Conference Papers, Cincinnati

Wicks, Z.W., Jones, F.N. and Pappas, S.P. (1992) *Organic Coatings: Science and Technology*, Wiley-Interscience

Wolbers, R. (1990) A radio-isotopic assay for the direct measurement of residual cleaning materials on a paint film, in *Cleaning Retouching and Coatings*, Conference Preprints, IIC

Wolbers, R. (1992) Recent developments in the use of gel formulations for the cleaning of paintings, *Restoration 1992*, Conference Preprints, UKIC

Wolbers, R. (2000) *Cleaning Painted Surfaces Aqueous Methods*, Archetype Books

Wolbers, R., Sterman, N. and Stavroudis, C. (1990) Notes for workshop on new methods in the cleaning of paint-ings, Getty Conservation Institute, 1988, 1989, 1990

Wollbrinck, T. (1993) The composition of proprietary paint strippers, *JAIC*, 32, 43–57

Wunderlich, C. and Weser, U. (1995) Gemaldereinigung mit Lipasen?, *Restauro*, 101, 1

# 12

# Principles of consolidation, aesthetic reintegration and coatings

## 12.1 Basic principles

This chapter considers consolidation, aesthetic reintegration (filling and retouching) and the application of coatings. Each section begins with a discussion of principles and then considers materials in common use and the properties that influence selection for a given application. The structure, material properties and deterioration of the materials discussed below are considered in Chapters 4 and 8.

Adhesives, consolidants and coatings often utilize the same classes of polymeric materials. Paraloid B72, for example, may be used as an adhesive, a consolidant or a coating, but the method of application and solution concentration is adapted to the treatment objectives. Thus as an adhesive, it may be used up to 50% w/v concentration, with the solvent chosen to promote or inhibit penetration of the substrate. As a consolidant, it may be used in concentrations as low as 0.5% in a slow-evaporating solvent to prevent reverse migration (see section 12.2.2). As a coating, it may be applied in 10–15% concentration in a solvent that promotes or reduces gloss.

It is important to understand the basic principles of adhesion in order to be able to analyse the cause of a given problem and formulate an appropriate conservation treatment. It may be useful to refer to Chapter 4. The adhesive bond formed by an adhesive, consolidant or coating will depend on the ability of the applied material to achieve intimate interfacial contact by efficiently wetting the surface. The ability to wet is dependent on the compatibility of the intermolecular forces of the applied material and surface, and the viscosity of the applied solution.

Materials whose bulk and surface are strongly bound together, such as metals, oxides, ceramics and glass have a high surface energy between 500 and 5000 mJ/m². Liquids (excluding liquid metals), most solid organic polymers and most organic compounds have a comparatively low surface energy of less than 100 mJ/m². Within this relatively narrow range of less than 100 mJ/m², higher energy surfaces may be considered polar and lower energy surfaces less polar. Lower energy liquids will be attracted to, and spread easily on, higher energy surfaces. If a liquid adhesive has a higher surface energy than the substrate to which is applied will not wet or adhere to it (*Figure 12.1*). Water has a surface energy of 72 mJ/m², wax of around 20 mJ/m² and as a result a water-based adhesive will not wet or adhere well to a surface contaminated by wax.

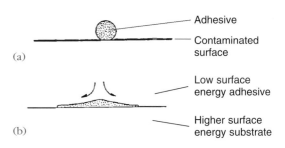

**Figure 12.1** Surface energy and wetting
(*a*) If the surface is contaminated with low surface energy material, such as wax or greasy dirt, the adhesive will not flow out. Even if the adhesive is spread mechanically, any adhesive bond that forms will be very weak
(*b*) When the surface energy (sometimes called surface tension) of the adhesive is lower than that of the substrate, the adhesive will flow out onto the surface, wetting it thoroughly

Viscosity may be manipulated to meet the demands of a given treatment. Adhesive applied as a free-flowing liquid will tend to have a higher bond strength because it will have better penetration of the substrate. In contrast, adhesive applied as a viscous liquid, or in the form of a reactivated solid (e.g. Beva film or a gelled collagen adhesive) will significantly limit wetting and penetration of the substrate, with a concomitant reduction in bond strength. Viscosity may be increased by using higher molecular weight members of a homologous solvent series, by cooling a solution, by increasing concentration or by the use of a thickening agent. Conversely lower members of a homologous series will be less viscous and faster evaporating. The viscosity of all liquids decreases as temperature rises.

## 12.1.1  Making solutions

### Concentration

The calculation of solution concentration has the potential to cause some confusion and has been discussed by Collings (1990), Lomax (1995) and Whitten (1995b, 1998). A true percentage solution is derived by using weight/ weight (w/w) ratio, e.g. 25 g resin in 75 g of solvent. The total weight is 100 g, of which the resin is 25%. The percentage weight/volume (w/v) measurement is often used in conservation and is achieved by weighing dry resin, placing it into a container that measures volume and adding solvent. For example, 25 g resin may be placed in the container and solvent added so that the total volume is 100 ml. This would represent a true 25% w/v solution. In contrast, adding 75 ml of solvent to 25 g of resin would not make a 25% w/v solution because solvents vary in their specific gravity, i.e. the same volume of a different solvent will have a different weight.

Density is the amount of a material per unit volume (e.g. 1 g/ml or 500 mg/m³). Specific gravity is the ratio of the mass of a substance to the mass of an equal volume of water at 4 °C. Because specific gravity is expressed as a ratio, it does not have units of measurement. Thus the density of water is 1 g/cm³ whilst its specific gravity is 1. One gram of acetone occupies less volume than water and has a specific gravity of 0.788, whilst one gram of N-methyl-2-pyrrolidinone occupies more volume than water and has a specific gravity of 1.031. Thus the same weight of resin mixed with the same volume of each of these solvents would produce a different percentage solution, depending on the final volume of the mixture. These mixtures would be most clearly described by specifying the weight of resin and volume of solvent (e.g. 20 g resin:100 ml solvent).

### Molar solutions

A molar solution contains the molecular weight of a substance in grams per litre of solution. Sodium hydroxide, for example, has a molecular weight of 40. Thus a one molar solution of sodium hydroxide would contain 40 grams of sodium hydroxide per litre of solution. Some chemical suppliers' catalogues, e.g. Sigma, list the molecular formula of substances they supply (e.g. NaOH) followed by the molecular weight, (e.g. 40) sometimes called the formula weight (FW).

### Dilution

When experimenting with the application of consolidants or coatings, it is often necessary to try a range of solution concentrations. The following method, derived from Pearson's square, can be used to simplify dilution calculations.

**A**  concentration of original solution
**B**  new desired concentration
**C**  diluent liquid
**D**  new solution concentration
**x**  part of original solution needed for new concentration
**y**  part of diluent needed for new concentration

$x = B–C$
$y = A–B$
$x + y = D$

*Examples*
(1) How much liquid (e.g. water or solvent) has to be added to a 14% solution to make a 6% solution?

A (concentration of original solution) = 14
B (new desired concentration) = 6
C (diluent liquid) = 0 (because there is no concentration of solute, the liquid is pure diluent)
x (part of original solution needed for new concentration) = 6 – 0 = 6
y (part of diluent needed for new concentration) = 14 – 6 = 8

*Answer:* mix 6 parts of the original 14% solution with 8 parts of the diluent liquid to make a new solution with a 6% concentration (D).

(2) How much of a 35% solution has to be added to an 8% solution to obtain a 15% solution?

A (concentration of original solution) = 35

B (new desired concentration) = 15

C (diluent liquid) = 8

x (part of original solution needed for new concentration) = 15 − 8 = 7

y (part of diluent needed for new concentration) = 35 − 15 = 20

*Answer:* mix seven parts of the 35% solution with twenty parts of the 8% diluent solution to make a new solution with a 15% concentration (D).

### Measuring small quantities without a balance

Some liquids are used in very small quantities, which may cause problems if an accurate balance is not available. The detergent Triton XL-80N, and the hindered amine light stabilizer Tinuvin 292, are examples of materials that are added to solutions in very small proportions. Density and specific gravity are defined above. Knowing the density or specific gravity of a material can allow the conservator to make a more accurate measurement using comparatively inaccurate tools. For example, Triton XL-80N and Tinuvin 292 are so close to water in specific gravity that 1 ml of each is approximately equivalent to one ml (pipette) or one cc (syringe) (*Table 12.1*). A graduated pipette or syringe may be used to establish the number of drops per millilitre or cubic centimetre. A pipette, for example, may dispense 30 drops of the liquid per millilitre, thus 3 drops is approximately equal to 0.1 ml or 0.1 gram of liquid.

**Table 12.1** Specific gravity of some materials added to solutions in small quantities

| Substance | Specific gravity |
| --- | --- |
| Water | 1 |
| Triton X-100 | 1.07 |
| Triton XL-80N | 0.98 |
| Tinuvin 292 | 0.9925 |

## 12.2   Consolidation

### 12.2.1   Introduction to consolidation treatment

In the context of conservation, consolidation has been defined as remedial treatment of materials that have lost cohesion as a result of deterioration. The objective is to stabilize an object and make it fit for its intended use (Wermuth, 1990). Consolidation treatment is most often necessary as a result of the breakdown of the material as it ages, the environmental conditions in which an object has been displayed or stored, or a combination of the two. The consolidation treatment will depend on the specific objectives for a given object. These may range from re-establishing full functionality (e.g. wooden structural components), stabilizing a material or layer throughout its thickness (e.g. worm damaged wood or a powdery gesso ground), or consolidating a surface to prevent loss of material (e.g. surface fragments of worm damaged wood, flakes of detached painted or decorated surface) (Schniewind, 1998).

Consolidation is often time consuming and consideration should be given to improving storage or display conditions so that the necessity for future treatment is minimized. Consolidation is the subject of regular discussion in conservation literature and it is essential to keep abreast of current developments. Broadly speaking, such discussion can be divided into the two strands of material evaluation and case histories that consider innovations in technique. The general principles of adhesive bonding have been set out by Cagle (1973). The volume by Brommelle *et al.* (1984) includes articles on both principles of adhesion and consolidation treatments applied in a range of conservation disciplines. The ethical ideal of retreatability has largely superseded reversibility as an ideal requirement for conservation treatments (Appelbaum, 1987; Oddy and Carroll, 1999).

Structural components of furniture must be able to bear the weight of the object, and in some cases may require strengthening in order to withstand use. The aim of consolidation of surface decoration is to halt the loss of original material and to impart sufficient strength to the surface to enable transport, storage or display or to permit essential conservation processes.

### 12.2.2 Penetration of consolidant and reverse migration

Penetration of a consolidant solution is influenced by a large number of variables. These variables include viscosity, the method of application, the particle size and configuration of the resin (e.g. large molecules with branched side chains will penetrate less effectively than small straight chain molecules), the chemical affinity for, and porosity of, the surface, and the presence or absence of inhibiting materials (e.g. a small quantity of wax will prevent penetration of water-borne consolidant). Penetration will also be influenced by the structure of the surface and the drying conditions following consolidative treatment. If there is some doubt about the penetration and distribution of consolidant in a porous surface, it may be possible to test on a facsimile model using sampling and staining techniques (e.g. Ream, 1995), although the limitations of facsimile models should also be appreciated.

Penetration of a consolidant will be greatest with a liquid of low surface tension and low viscosity. Thus conservators often use multiple applications of very dilute consolidant solutions that increase penetration because of their initial low viscosity. Use of differential pressure will also increase consolidant penetration. However, because vacuum impregnation requires a porous structure, it is often not applicable to large wooden components or decorative surfaces applied to wood.

Penetration of consolidant is affected by the evaporation rate of the solvent. The use of a fast evaporating solvent may inhibit penetration of the consolidant as a result of the rapid rise in viscosity as solvent evaporates (Hansen *et al.*, 1996). The use of a fast-evaporating solvent may also cause a higher proportion of consolidant to be deposited on, or near the surface. This phenomenon is called reverse migration, and can affect both wood and decorative surfaces. In decorative surfaces, reverse migration may result in the formation of a consolidated crust lying over unconsolidated material, leaving the surface susceptible to further damage and loss. In addition, excess consolidant on the surface usually results in an undesirable increase in gloss. The use of a low concentration solution combined with a slow-evaporating solvent or a vapour-saturated atmosphere will improve penetration and thereby reduce surface deposits, reverse migration and gloss.

Consolidant migration and distribution may also be affected by the relative solubility of a consolidant in a solvent. The use of a relatively poor solvent can reduce the surface deposition of consolidant in comparison to good solvent solutions. When a relatively poor solvent is used, the polymer will precipitate earlier, within a porous structure, rather than on the surface (Hansen, 1994).

### 12.2.3 Consolidation of wood

In the case of fresh insect infestation of otherwise sound timber, treatment for eradication of woodworm (*Anobium punctatum*) may be all that is required. In some pieces, however, damage may have progressed until parts or the whole of an object may have been reduced to a honeycomb with just a thin skin of intact material on the outside (*Figure 12.2*). The full

(a)

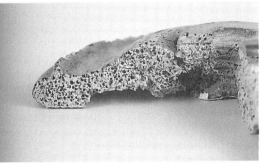

(b)

**Figure 12.2** Woodworm damage
(*a*) Turned wooden component with multiple *Anobium* flight holes and some loss of wood from the surface
(*b*) The extent of damage caused by *Anobium* larvae

extent of damage may not be revealed until everyday stresses or use result in structural failure. This may involve complete breakage of a rail or other component, or the disintegration of edges as a result of handling. The surrounding wood may be too weak to support the cutting edge of tools and/or the pressure of cramps or other apparatus needed to effect repair. Insect infestation of a wooden substrate may disrupt decorative layers as a result of areas of loss, a large number of exit holes or the collapse of larval tunnels. In such cases a consolidant should be compatible with the wood, surface decoration (e.g. not cause darkening) and subsequent treatments such as filling and retouching.

If *Anobium* infestation has caused severe structural damage it may be necessary to impart additional strength to structural components. This can be done by consolidation, reinforcing the structure by introducing dowels or loose tenons, or in severe cases, replacing the entire component or, if the surface is valued, its core. The extent of reinforcement or replacement may be determined by balancing the loss of original material against the risk of further damage to the object or injury to people. An independent support for the structure of the object, such as supports extended from a wall, may provide greater longevity for the object than impregnation with resins.

The purpose of consolidation is to impart strength to the structure of the object so that it can bear its own weight, permit essential conservation processes and ensure it is fit for its purpose, whether that is display or use. Although some properties for consolidants will overlap with those discussed above, such as the need for chemical and mechanical stability, a consolidant for worm-damaged structural components must have good adhesive properties, impart strength, should penetrate the wood fibres well, combine a degree of flexibility with hardness, should not creep, and ideally combine high concentration with low viscosity. Ideally conversion from liquid to solid state should occur at room temperature, at a controlled rate and without shrinkage. Other considerations include the retention and toxicity of solvent, lack of reactivity with non-wood components such as metals, extant adhesive, leather or glass, and compatibility with other adhesives that may be used as part of the conservation

treatment. Some solvents used to deliver consolidant solutions are incompatible with many varnished and decorated surfaces.

The consolidation of wood by impregnation with thermoplastic resins cannot be considered completely reversible. Attempts to remove consolidant, where this is possible, may result in further degradation of the wood. Schniewind (1987, 1988) demonstrated the retention of up to 6% of residual thermoplastic resin used to consolidate small pieces of wood after they had been soaked in solvent to remove the consolidant. The practicality of immersing large components in a suitable solvent may render this finding moot, particularly when varnished or decorated surfaces are present. However, even such partial reversibility is more desirable than a single treatment with a thermoset resin, where the lifetime of the treated wood is extended only by the working life of the resin.

Improvement in strength after consolidation is strongly influenced by the degree of degradation of the wood. More degraded wood allows better penetration of consolidant, increased resin loading, and thus a greater improvement in strength after treatment (Schniewind and Kronkright, 1984). The tensile and compressive strength of the consolidant itself must exceed that of the wood to have a noticeable effect.

The method of application will affect the amount of consolidant absorbed into the wood. Application techniques include brushing or spraying the surface, injecting wormholes, vapour phase (Schniewind and Kronkright, 1984), vacuum impregnation (Schaffer and Brisebois, 1974) and total immersion, though the last two are only feasible for smaller objects or components uncomplicated by the presence of coatings. Barclay (1981) reported that, in comparison to brushing, the use of a portable vacuum chamber increased the amount of consolidant introduced into the wood by a factor of ten. Carlson and Schniewind (1990) considered the effects of solvent retention on the glass transition temperature of thermoplastic resin used for consolidating wood, whilst Schniewind and Eastman (1994) examined consolidant distribution in deteriorated wood.

### Materials used to consolidate wood

A wide variety of materials have been used to consolidate wood. These materials have been reviewed by Schniewind (1998).

*Natural materials* Wax has been used with varying success in the past but imparts little strength and is incompatible with most other adhesives. Animal glue has been used as a consolidant, sometimes mixed with sawdust, but its principal disadvantages are that its comparatively high molecular weight leads to high viscosity in low solution concentration and thus poor penetration. Collagen glues are hygroscopic and become brittle in conditions of low RH. In addition, water-based delivery leads to potential problems from swelling of the wood and shrinkage of the adhesive as it dries, and it provides a nutritious supplement should the object be attacked by wood-boring beetles in the future. Natural resins produce only a moderate increase in strength, must be delivered in polar solvents that may swell the wood, and may be incompatible with varnish or decorated surfaces.

*Synthetic materials* Thermoset resins are capable of imparting strength to damaged or degraded wood. Thermosetting resins have largely been rejected for consolidation, however, because of their inherent non-reversibility and, with the exception of low viscosity epoxies, poor penetration. In addition, although thermoset resins initially produce strong and hard films, significant loss of strength of some resins has been found within forty years (Rodwell, 1984). Low viscosity epoxies have been used to consolidate wood, but, as with other thermosets, their disadvantages are often considered to outweigh their advantages. These disadvantages include that a single application determines degree of penetration, there is potential for human error to result in unsatisfactory and unstable polymers, heat is generated in curing of epoxies, and the surface of the wood may be unacceptably darkened (Grattan, 1980).

Thermoplastic resins, such as poly(vinyl acetate) (PVAC), poly(vinyl butyral) (PVB) and Paraloid B72 have been used for the consolidation of wood. Although the strengthening effect is less than that which can be achieved with thermosets, these resins are, in principle at least, reversible. They can be applied using a variety of techniques, and both PVAC and Paraloid B72 are class A conservation materials that exhibit long term chemical stability. The choice of resin and solution concentration is dependent on the priorities of the consolidation treatment.

Many PVACs are softer than the wood or have a glass transition temperature lower than the ambient environmental temperature. This means they have a rubbery consistency rather than a rigid structure and have a tendency to cold flow (creep). Lower molecular weight PVAC resins (such as AYAC, AYAA and AYAF, MW 12 800, 83 000 and 113 000 respectively) may not impart additional strength or stiffness to degraded wood. Higher molecular weight PVAC (AYAT, MW 167 000) imparted less strength than either Paraloid B72 or PVB (Schniewind and Kronkright, 1984).

Paraloid B72 and PVB are often used by conservators to consolidate degraded wood. Paraloid B72 produces less viscous solutions and has a greater degree of reversibility than Butvar B98, a PVB that has often been used to consolidate wood (Schniewind, 1998). Butvar B98 imparted slightly more strength for the same resin loading in comparison to Paraloid B72 (Schniewind and Kronkright, 1984). Carlson and Schniewind (1990) suggested that this finding may have been influenced by inadequate drying times for B72 in acetone. Schniewind (1998) noted that the adhesion to wood of Paraloid B72 delivered in toluene was a fraction of that found when this consolidant was delivered in ethanol or acetone.

Poly(vinyl butyral) offers a combination of tensile strength, hardness and elongation at break, which allows for some movement of wood in response to changes in RH. The primary disadvantage of PVBs is their high viscosity in low concentration solutions. Butvar B98 (Monsanto) has slightly lower molecular weight than other PVBs and is therefore slightly less viscous, though more viscous than comparable solutions of Paraloid B72. Barclay (1981) reported the use of a 5% solution for brushing, and a 20% solution for vacuum impregnation. Poly(vinyl butyral) may chalk on drying if applied in pure ethanol, but this effect can be avoided by using IMS/toluene solvent mixtures or adding 5% n-butanol (Grattan, 1980). Poly(vinyl butyral) is known to crosslink in acid conditions, leading to insolubility, thus PVBs may not be appropriate for use with very acidic woods (see section 10.1.3). Butvar B98 has been shown to have adhesive properties comparable to Paraloid B72 in acetone and superior to B72 in toluene (Sakuno and Schniewind, 1990).

The effect of synthetic materials on the hygroscopicity of consolidated wood is dependent on resin loading (Schniewind, 1998). The extent of such changes is proportional to polymer loading, though Schniewind (1990) noted no effect at 24% resin loading.

*Solvent selection for thermoplastic resins* The choice of solvent used with a thermoplastic resin can influence a range of physical properties. Though largely a function of resin concentration, penetration of consolidant may be influenced by solvent polarity or the solvent effect on solution viscosity. Although non-polar solvents penetrate wood more than polar solvents, Paraloid B72 and AYAT resin delivered in polar solvents imparted greater strength to treated wood (Wang and Schniewind, 1985). Although solvents with a higher boiling point are retained for longer, their slower evaporation rate may allow deeper penetration of the resin and prevent reverse migration of consolidant to the surface. Reverse migration will result in a concentration of solvent at, or close to, the surface of the wood, which will in turn result in an increase in bending strength. Brewer (1994) suggested the use of consolidant reservoir under Melinex/Mylar in order to facilitate penetration of consolidant and address concerns of reverse migration. The presence of a decorative surface or varnish may complicate solvent selection.

## 12.2.4   Consolidation of painted and decorated surfaces

All decorated (e.g. painted, japanned, gilded or urushi) surfaces have a laminate structure that is comprised of materials with different physical and chemical properties. The laminate structure may be very complex and inevitably has inherent flaws and incompatibilities. These may lead to adhesive failure between, or cohesive failure within, any of the layers. In many cases some sort of consolidation treatment may be necessary if the decorative surface is to survive in a coherent and 'readable' state. It is often helpful to examine a surface that requires consolidation with a binocular microscope before, during and after treatment to assist in understanding the object and the locus of failure, monitor treatment and evaluate its success.

Damage to decorative surfaces is overwhelmingly caused by three main agents of deterioration. First, the materials used in the original manufacture of the object and the techniques used to create it can cause premature deterioration of a decorative surface. This category includes the deliberate or accidental use of adulterated materials, the construction methods used for the substrate such as cleated boards, or short cuts taken by the manufacturer to reduce the time or cost of production. Secondly, unsuitable environmental conditions, particularly high light levels and excessively low, high or widely fluctuating relative humidity (RH), will radically shorten the life of most decorated surfaces. RH levels play an important role in the adhesive failure between gesso-type layers and wood substrates. Long exposure to high humidity will result in a friable, crumbling gesso layer, whilst long exposure to low humidity may lead to gesso cleaving away from the substrate. The third category includes wear and tear, poor handling and unsuitable past restorations. Unsuitable consolidation treatments can be included in this last category, either as a result of the use of inappropriate materials or by stress between consolidated and unconsolidated areas. Unsuitable consolidation treatments may have been the result of inexpert treatment, or the use of materials that have since been proven unsuitable.

There is no one definitive answer to the question of consolidation. Each surface or object must be considered carefully, its problems identified and addressed. In some cases the priority may be a minimal change of appearance (e.g. avoiding excessive saturation of matte paint) whilst in others a strong (or weak) adhesive bond may be the primary consideration. In every case, however, compatibility with existing materials, previous and subsequent treatment stages (e.g. infilling, retouching or the application of a coating) is essential. The potential for future treatments (retreatability) should be clear, and the mechanism and future consequences of deterioration understood as far as possible.

In some cases, for example where the surface is extremely friable, it may be necessary to consolidate before cleaning. In the past such treatment has often involved applying a consolidant and, once dry, removing excess consolidant and some surface dirt. This inevitably consolidates dirt onto the object, but for underbound or very fragile surfaces there may be no alternative. Volatile 'binding' media such as cyclodo-decane may be an alternative in such cases (see under Facing below).

### Traditional vs. modern materials

Historically, when objects required repair they were sent to craftspeople skilled in the techniques originally used for their manufacture. Thus many artists also restored paintings, whilst cabinetmakers or the house carpenter would undertake repairs to furniture and other wooden fittings. Within the vernacular tradition, a wide range of trades were involved in both the manufacture and repair of furniture. Artisans usually employed the same range of materials in the repair process that they used to produce such objects. In skilled hands, many of these materials were compatible with the original but lack of knowledge could cause future problems. In the case of gilded furniture, for example, a strong layer of gesso applied over a weak layer could cause excessive contraction of the upper layer, cleaving the whole of the decorative surface from the substrate.

The advantages of traditional materials lie in their compatibility with the original, a well-understood, predictable deterioration process and, usually, retreatability. Traditional materials are derived from naturally occurring sources and may contain a variety of contaminants. They are often prone to discoloration within a relatively short period and may therefore require more frequent interventive treatment. They may be physically and chemically inseparable from original material and, except in their degree of oxidation, may also be indistinguishable from it, compromising historical and technical understanding of objects or techniques.

The development of synthetic materials has led to a wider range of materials that can be used for consolidation (and coatings). In many cases they can be distinguished easily from the original and have a wider range of chemical and physical properties than natural materials. In some cases it may be more difficult to replicate the exact appearance of the original material on the object. Although they may have better adhesive properties, in some cases the use of synthetic consolidants may make retreatment more difficult. The conservator should be aware of potential problems associated with breakdown products and future removal. Many synthetic consolidants applied in the past have proven problematic, having become cross-linked, discoloured and insoluble (e.g. soluble nylon). The list of consolidants that have been used in the past but are now considered inappropriate is long and it is essential that conservators keep abreast of current literature.

Some conservators have adopted a mixed approach by using traditional materials for repairs or fills but isolating them from the original surface using modern materials, or vice versa. It is essential that conservators are familiar with both traditional and modern materials and techniques and are able to make informed choices when choosing a suitable consolidant.

### Materials used for the consolidation of decorative surfaces

Selection of a consolidant is a problem-solving process. It requires understanding what the decorative surface is made from, what its chemical and physical properties are, what condition is it in, why adhesive/cohesive failure has occurred and possible future use or analysis. Consolidants used for conservation should ideally have long-term stability, good working properties, be compatible with both decorative surface layers and the substrate, and maintain an effective bond between them under variable environmental conditions (Horton-Jones *et al.*, 1991). The properties of available consolidants, such as flexibility, hygroscopicity, shrinkage, chemical reactivity and visual stability must also be understood so that an informed choice can be made to find the best solution to a given problem. If the only suitable carrier for the consolidant may affect the surface, decorative layers can be protected with an isolating layer before the application of consolidant.

*Waxes* Waxes have been used as consolidants in the past but their general use is not recommended. There may be some cases, for example where wax has been used previously and no other consolidant will adhere, where their use is appropriate. Wax/resin mixtures have been used as a consolidant in easel paintings conservation. The proportion of wax to resin varies between 10% and 50% resin. Like waxes, wax/resin mixtures are generally soluble in aliphatic and aromatic hydrocarbon solvents and are applied as a hot melt. Although in theory wax should be removable with a suitable hydrocarbon solvent, in practice it is extremely difficult to remove all residues. Those that remain are likely to interfere with the adhesion of non-wax consolidants, limiting future treatment to either more wax or a waxy material such as Beva 371. It has been observed that waxes can migrate into adjacent porous materials (e.g. ground layers), disrupting them and causing further problems.

Beva 371 contains 40% solids (ethylene vinyl acetate copolymer, cyclohexanone resin, pthalate plasticizer) in toluene and heptane. It has a softening point of 50–55 °C and can be diluted in aliphatic or aromatic hydrocarbon solvents. When the solvent has evaporated, a heated spatula can be used to heat-seal the Beva to the surface. Beva will act as a gap filler, and any excess on the surface after treatment can be removed with mineral spirits. Beva 371 is also available in film form. It is supplied with two barrier layers that must be removed before the film is heat-set between the layers that are being consolidated. When laying flakes, one barrier layer can be removed and the Beva heat set onto the substrate. The second barrier can be removed, the flake positioned, and a heated spatula used to set the flake in place. Beva film can be made by the conservator at a desired strength by casting a film onto silicone release paper. Beva 371 can also be used to impregnate a support material, such as Japanese paper, and allowed to dry. The Beva impregnated support material can then be heat set into place or a little solvent can be brushed onto the surface to activate the adhesive, or both. Liquid application of Beva will have a higher bond strength than heat set film because the liquid will have better penetration of the substrate.

*Collagen adhesives*  Collagen adhesives, such as fish glue, gelatin, isinglass and rabbit skin glue, have many useful properties as consolidants, ensuring their continued use from antiquity to today. The coiled helical structure of the protein chains imparts a degree of flexibility. Collagen adhesives shrink as they dry, are hygroscopic, are brittle at low RH and are prone to mould growth in conditions of high relative humidity. They are degraded by exposure to UV and tend to yellow and darken as they age. Their hygroscopic nature results in expansion and contraction as RH fluctuates, and excessively strong solutions have the

(a)

(b)

**Figure 12.3**  Damage caused by residues of collagen adhesive
(*a*) A painted surface with residual collagen adhesive from a previous consolidation treatment. Residues have adhered strongly to the paint. Shrinkage of the residues has caused cracks to form
(*b*) In places, shrinkage was severe enough to cause flaking and loss of original paint layers

potential to pull a fragile decorative surface apart (*Figure 12.3*). Retreatment with a range of other consolidants is possible and retreatment with a collagen glue can reactivate bonding sites on the original adhesive. They are easy to use and their mechanism of deterioration is well understood. Their effective use as consolidants usually requires that they penetrate a surface before they cool and gel. For a comparison of the properties of isinglass, gelatin and rabbit skin glue see Haupt *et al.* (1990).

Collagen consolidants are usually applied dilute (up to *c*.5% w/v concentration) in a warmed aqueous solution. The main property that influences the choice of gelatin for a given application is Bloom strength, sometimes called gram weight strength (see section 4.7.4), which correlates with molecular weight. The higher the Bloom strength the faster the glue will gel, the better its adhesive properties and the more flexible the dried adhesive. Thus if consolidating a powdery ground, a lower molecular weight gelatin will penetrate more effectively and, because low Bloom strength glues gel more slowly, there is more time for the gelatin to penetrate before it becomes an immobile gel. If adhering flakes, however, slow gelling may be undesirable and a higher Bloom strength may be more appropriate.

Gelatin used in conservation should be highly purified and can be obtained from suppliers such as Sigma or Fisher in a variety of Bloom or gram weight strengths. The longevity of gelatin, and thus consolidation treatments that utilize it, is dependent on good environmental conditions. Gelatin may last for several hundred years in an environment with minimal exposure to light and a moderate, stable RH and temperature. Excessively high, low or fluctuating RH and temperature, and exposure to high light levels and UV will result in rapid degradation (Hansen *et al.*, 1996).

Isinglass is a traditional consolidant for painted surfaces and is utilized in both easel paintings and polychrome sculpture conservation. As with other glues derived from fish, isinglass has a different amino acid composition than mammalian collagen, and as a result does not gel at room temperature. Isinglass and other fish glues do not, therefore, have a Bloom strength. The chain length of the collagen, however, can be comparable to the best-quality mammalian animal glues, and isinglass can therefore be very strong. The viscosity of isinglass and other fish glues is not as closely related to chain length as is the case for mammalian derived glues. The best isinglass was traditionally derived from the swim bladder of the Russian sturgeon fish (*Acipenser stallatus* and *A. güldenstädtii*). Sturgeon glue has more tack and less is needed to achieve a given viscosity in comparison to many commonly available types of isinglass.

Refined isinglass can be purchased through suppliers of artists' materials (e.g. in Europe, Kremer Pigmente www.kremer-pigmente.de). Isinglass may be prepared in the following way.

Four grams of isinglass are soaked overnight in deionized water. The water is then drained and discarded. Eighty millilitres of fresh deionized water is added to the isinglass, which is then warmed (temperature not exceeding 55 °C), in a double boiler for about an hour. It is then strained through a double layer of fine silk or nylon. If the isinglass has been prepared from the dried bladder itself, the conservator may wish to skim the detritus from the surface before straining the mixture. When warmed, the strained isinglass solution (*c.*5% w/v) is ready to be used as a consolidant. Isinglass prepared in this way can be brushed out onto Melinex for later use. Once dry, the isinglass can be broken up and stored. This thin prepared isinglass will dissolve rapidly in warm water and can be used to make up 'instant' isinglass as required. Honey is added to the isinglass as a plasticizer in some traditional recipes but will produce a mix with a yellow-brown colour (Petukhova and Bonadies, 1993). Long periods of heating will denature collagen, so it is better to pour off a small amount to use rather than repeatedly heating a large quantity. A few drops of alcohol may be added to collagen mixtures to reduce surface tension or a surface may be pre-wet with ethanol to increase penetration.

Rabbit skin glue, when used as a consolidant for gilding, should always be weaker than that used for preparation of gesso. A proportion of one part rabbit skin glue to fifteen parts water usually provides a reasonable margin of safety. Traditionally rabbit skin glue is prepared the day before use, allowed to gel overnight and the strength of the gel then assessed (see section 14.2.4). The grains are dissolved in warm water, heated (*c.*55 °C) in a double boiler until dissolved, then strained to remove any gritty particles.

Collagen glues are an option where a water-based consolidant is safe for the object. They can be applied drop-wise from a brush to an affected area. Surface tension may be reduced by pre-wetting with, or adding a drop of, ethanol. Moderate heat (such that a heated spatula can be held without discomfort in the hand) can help to keep collagen glue warm as it infuses into the decorative surface. The spatula should be isolated from the surface by protective tissue, blotting paper or Melinex/Mylar. Gelatin and isinglass are compatible with many other traditional materials but introduce moisture into the coating. This may be an advantage in reducing the brittleness of the decorative surface and, combined with moderate heat, may allow otherwise fragile flakes to be laid. Conversely, it may be a disadvantage where materials within or on the decorative layer are water-sensitive. If the spatula is too hot it may cause a surface coating to bloom. More information on blooming can be found in section 11.5.7.

*Acrylics and PVAC* Paraloid B72 and PVAC are defined as Class A conservation materials according to the criteria proposed by Feller (1978). Such materials may be expected to last in excess of 100 years with less than a 20% change in properties such as photo-chemical stability and solubility parameters. There is an inverse relationship between flexibility and film strength. PVAC adhesives are generally stronger and less flexible than acrylics (Down *et al.*, 1996).

Acrylics such as Paraloid (Rohm and Haas), Rhoplex (Rohm and Haas), Lascaux (Lascaux) and Elvacite, previously Lucite (Du Pont) have been used as consolidants, retouching media and varnishes for decorative surfaces. Many have demonstrated good long-term chemical and visual stability, and are soluble in a range of organic solvents such as ketones and aromatic hydrocarbons. Solid resins such as B72 may be dissolved in a solvent and applied in concentrations generally ranging from 1 to 15% but on occasion up to 20 or even 50% (e.g. Thornton, 1993). The choice of solvent can significantly affect the mechanical, physical and ageing properties and resolubility of the dry polymer film (see section 12.4.3).

Pure resin forms of PVAC (Union Carbide: AYAA, AYAC etc.) have been used as both consolidants and retouch media for decorative surfaces. They have the advantage of reversibility in ketones, alcohols and aromatic hydrocarbons. PVAC adhesives are generally more acidic than acrylics and are known to release appreciable amounts of acetic acid for about a month after application (Down *et al.*, 1996). AYAT films cast from a toluene solution retained more than 4% solvent whilst those cast from acetone, ethanol or water retained less than 0.3% (Hansen *et al.*, 1991). PVAC-type wood adhesives (white glue, Resin W, Elmers

etc.) are unsuitable for consolidation as they are usually very difficult to remove and may crosslink as they age.

*Emulsions and dispersions* There are a large number of adhesives based on thermoplastic resins and supplied in the form of emulsions (liquid polymer droplets in liquid) and dispersions (solid polymer particles in liquid). They may be homo- or co-polymeric materials and are generally divided into acrylics and PVAC derivatives. They are often used as an alternative to solvent-based adhesives and consolidants. PVAC and acrylics in the form of proprietary emulsions and dispersions should not be presumed to be Class A conservation materials. The formulation of individual products affects long-term stability and wide variations in ageing properties have been observed.

Conservation forms a minuscule part of the commercial adhesives market and as a result adhesives that are suitable for conservation may go out of production. Rather than discussing individual examples it is therefore more useful to discuss the properties of these adhesives that may be used to select one that is currently manufactured. Information about ageing characteristics are not usually supplied by the manufacturer, so conservation literature on the subject should be consulted, e.g. De Witte *et al.* (1984), Down *et al.* (1996), Duffy (1989), Horton-Jones *et al.* (1991) and Howells *et al.* (1984).

The viscosity of emulsions and dispersions varies widely (*c.*150 to 25 000 cps) and conservators often dilute viscous adhesive preparations before application. Both emulsions and dispersions contain stabilizing ingredients (e.g. natural gums, dextrine, poly(vinyl alcohol), cellulose) and some also contain surfactants and plasticizers. Although plasticizers increase the flexibility of the adhesive film, some have a tendency to migrate into adjacent materials. Where possible, plasticizers should be avoided in conservation adhesives and consolidants.

Dispersions and emulsions are available across a wide pH range (3–10). The lower the pH, the higher the emission of acetic acid. The pH of a consolidant should be appropriate for the decorative surface that is to be treated. Excessively alkaline pH may damage some binding media and discolour wood substrates with a high tannin content such as oak. Excessively acidic pH may affect carbonate pigments such as malachite and azurite. Decorative surfaces containing these pigments should be treated with pH neutral or slightly alkaline consolidants. Ideally a consolidant should have a neutral pH that remains so on ageing, however a range between 5.5 and 8.0 has been suggested as acceptable for most artefacts (Down *et al.*, 1996).

Solids content, which describes the proportion of polymer in a dispersion, can vary from around 30% to 60%. A higher proportion of solids will increase gap filling properties, decrease shrinkage, increase viscosity and result in harder films. Particle diameter in dispersions is measured in microns and may vary from 0.2 to 1 μm. Smaller particle size will increase penetration of the consolidant.

The properties required of an emulsion or dispersion will vary with the object being treated. In general simple formulations of colourless conservation grade adhesive (i.e. one whose colour and solubility region do not shift markedly as it ages), a neutral pH, and a balance between high solids content and low viscosity may be suitable for a range of consolidative treatments.

*Poly(vinyl alcohol)* Poly(vinyl alcohols) (PVALs) such as Gelvatol (Monsanto), Mowiol (Hoechst) and Rhodoviol (Rhône Poulenc), have been used in conservation as consolidants and fill materials. Their poor adhesive properties and a tendency to crosslink and become insoluble as a result of exposure to UV means they are unsuitable for many applications. PVAL was given a Class C rating by Feller (1978), that is such materials are expected to last less than 20 years with less than a 20% change in properties such as photochemical stability and solubility parameters. This classification was broadly confirmed by Feller and Wilt (1990) in accelerated thermal ageing tests, however Bicchieri *et al.* (1993) suggested that PVAL is not a particularly unstable resin. The use of PVAL in fills is discussed below.

*Aquazol* Aquazol (poly(2-ethyl-2 oxazoline) has been discussed by Wolbers *et al.* (1998) and Shelton (1996). The primary advantage of this consolidant is its wide solubility range.

*Cellulose ethers* Cellulose ethers, such as methyl cellulose and hydroxypropyl methyl cellulose (e.g. Klucel®), have been used as con-

solidants for decorative surfaces. Their properties are discussed in section 11.6.2 in the context of their use as gelling materials. As consolidants they are usually used in concentrations between 0.5 and 5% but have been associated with consolidative failure due to poor adhesive properties (Stone, 1998). Methyl cellulose used for consolidation usually requires low viscosity (e.g. *c.*330–630 cps for a 2% solution) and low substitution. Cellulose ethers have been used to consolidate matte paint, where minimal darkening may be a result of poor wetting or low solution concentration. Cellulose ethers with a high degree of substitution have often been selected as consolidants because they have increased plasticity and solubility in polar organic solvents. Feller and Wilt (1990) found that the long-term stability of cellulose ethers decreased as the degree of substitution increased.

### Application techniques

The choice of application technique will depend on the size of the object or the area of surface that has deteriorated and the nature of that deterioration. In some cases a consolidant solution may be brushed on to a surface and allowed to dry. Excess that has not soaked in to damaged areas may be removed with a swab dampened with a suitable solvent. It may be important when carrying out localized treatment such as laying flakes or cupped areas to avoid leaving excess adhesive on the surface, particularly if the surface is sensitive to the solvent carrier used for the consolidant. In such cases the conservator may apply pressure, release it, remove excess adhesive, and repeat this procedure until no excess remains on the surface. Consolidant may be delivered through facing tissue (see section on Facing below). If the surface is friable or localized application is required, consolidant may be applied drop by drop from a brush of suitable size. Pipettes and micropipettes can be used for controlled and localized application of a measured amount of consolidant. Syringes may be used to inject consolidant into woodworm exit holes or very friable substrates. An airbrush may be used to spray a large area, though the air pressure should be kept as low as possible. If the surface is too fragile for brush or spray application it may be possible to utilize an ultrasonic mister (Michalski and Dignard, 1997; Michalski *et al.,* 1998). Immersion and vacuum impregnation have been used in ceramics, paper and paintings conservation but are generally impractical for large pieces of furniture.

In all the methods described above the liquid consolidant is introduced onto or into a surface and converts in situ to a solid. It may be possible to combine this approach with the use of heat, for example if a liquid adhesive is introduced, allowed to solidify and then treated with a heated spatula. It is also possible to cast a thin sheet of consolidant on Melinex/Mylar or silicon release paper. A piece of cast consolidant can be cut to the required shape and placed under a flake. The consolidant can then be activated with a small amount of solvent, a heated spatula or both. The spatula should be hot enough to soften or melt the consolidant without damaging the decorative surface, and should be isolated from the surface by Melinex/Mylar. Heat sealing is suitable for Beva 371, or PVAC and acrylic adhesives with a Tg lower than the temperature sensitivity of the surface being consolidated. Heat sealing sometimes has the advantage of softening flakes and allowing them to be relaid flat.

### Flakes, cups, tents and blisters

In the context of painted and decorative surfaces, the term crack describes the fracture of layer/s perpendicular to the plane of the surface. Cracks may be caused by shrinkage of the decorative layers as the binding medium dries. Such cracks are not necessarily accompanied by loss of adhesion or distortion from plane. In some cases, cracks in a decorative surface may lead to the formation of cups and flakes as a result of internal stress, environmental conditions, or a combination of both these factors. Craquelure describes a fine network of shallow cracks.

Strong cohesive properties within a particular layer combined with weak adhesive properties between layers will result in the formation of flakes, cups, tents or blisters. These are vulnerable to damage during handling, transport or display and may result in loss if left untreated.

The term cleavage describes loss of adhesion, and may occur between paint or other applied layers, between upper layers and ground, or between ground and substrate. Loss of adhesion can cause several types of charac-

teristic damage. Cups are usually small islands, the edges of which have cleaved from the lower layers or substrate and usually curl upwards (out of plane distortion). Tents are raised areas, cleaved from the lower layers or substrate. The characteristic tent shape, in which adjacent edges of the decorative surface along a crack are forced upwards, is usually a result of substrate shrinkage. Blisters combine loss of adhesion with a bubble-shaped distortion out of plane and are often a result of exposure to heat. Blisters can be extremely difficult to treat as there may be no way to introduce consolidant without causing additional damage. Flakes are a result of a total loss of adhesion, resulting in loss of surface decoration.

If flaking, cupping or tenting is fresh it may be possible to introduce consolidant underneath and press it gently back into place. More commonly, detached areas are brittle and require additional treatment to allow them to be laid without breaking them. Three options for reducing the internal stress in a brittle detached area are heat (alone or in combination with), localized humidity or solvent. If the surface cannot be rendered flexible by these treatments it may be necessary to prevent loss by supporting and adhering the detached area from below using adhesive and an inert filler, e.g. microballoons.

Moderate and localized heat, the temperature dictated by the surface being treated, may be applied with a heated spatula. Heat may be applied to increase the penetration or working time of a collagen or other heat sensitive/thermoplastic adhesive or to soften a decorative surface layer so that a detached area may be flattened. Heat may also be applied after a thermoplastic consolidant has set, for example the following day. Humidity may be applied in a variety of ways. A water-based consolidant introduced under the flake, cup or tent may be sufficient after a minute or two to soften it and allow it to be laid flat. An ultrasonic pencil may be used to introduce water vapour in a controlled and localized manner. Moisture-sensitive surfaces may be treated by indirect humidification, e.g. a Gore-Tex sandwich (see section 15.2.2). The effect on the detached area should be assessed regularly to check the effect on the flake or cup and to ensure the surrounding area is unaffected. Heat and localized humidity are particularly effective in reducing the brittleness of flakes and cups but care should be taken to avoid causing bloom in varnish or otherwise damaging moisture-sensitive surfaces. Finally, an appropriate solvent may be introduced, either as the consolidant carrier, added to an aqueous consolidant or using a solvent-saturated atmosphere, to achieve controlled solvent vapour exposure. The swelling effect of such a solvent should be minimized because a large amount of swelling may cause further damage as a result of plastic compression. If a large area has become detached and is too brittle to be laid in one go, it may be possible to work across it in stages, though it is essential to avoid the formation of ridges of consolidant underneath.

It is not unusual for the wooden substrate under a decorative surface to shrink as a result of sustained low RH. The shrinkage may be significant enough that the cracked edges of decorative surface overlap when relaid. There are four options for treatment in such a case. The first is to introduce and maintain environmental conditions that will reverse or minimize such shrinkage, but in reality this is rarely possible. Alternatively the conservator can retain all original material by laying the edges down so that they overlap, remove original material by trimming the edges to allow the area to be laid flat and flush, or support the surface decoration in its raised state (Webb, 1994). Removal of original material is a decision that should not be taken lightly. Furniture in general, and decorative surfaces in particular, rarely survive the vicissitudes of time unscathed and faults should perhaps be accepted rather than hidden.

### Facing

Facing a decorative surface has traditionally involved securing loose or vulnerable material to a surface by adhering paper over the area. Facing is always intended to be a temporary treatment. It is commonly used to prevent loss of material if an object cannot be treated immediately, to allow an object to be transported without further loss, or to facilitate other conservation treatments.

Facing paper should ideally be non-wet strength, acid-free and with a random fibre. Japanese tissue, rice paper, mulberry paper or Eltoline tissues are suitable facing papers, though in an emergency other materials such as toilet tissue or cigarette papers may be used.

The amount the facing paper shrinks as it dries will depend on the type of adhesive and the size of the facing paper used. Non-water-based adhesives will cause least or no shrinkage. When water-based adhesives are used, the larger the area of the paper the more it will shrink, so the maximum size that should be used is around 10 cm. Any edges should be feathered to avoid the formation of adhesive ridges on the surface. This can be done quickly and accurately by brushing a line of water onto the paper, leaving it a moment and then pulling it apart, or by folding the paper, licking the edge and then tearing it. If more than one piece of paper is used, the edges should be overlapped. If the object is being prepared for transport or structural work, several layers, each slightly misaligned with the one before, may be applied. Small strips may be used to bridge splits or tears in materials such as leather.

Although water-based adhesives are the most compatible with paper, allowing it to conform to the vulnerable surface, moisture may damage a varnished or decorated surface and non-aqueous facing adhesives may be required. Aqueous adhesives should not be used for localized facing on canvas, for example, because they may result in the formation of a permanent ridge as a result of uneven exposure to moisture. Blooming as a result of aqueous consolidants may be avoided by applying an isolating varnish, which should be selected so as not to narrow later treatment options. The adhesive mixture should be dilute to weaken it and avoid shrinkage. Long-term stability is not usually a criterion for the selection of a facing adhesive, but may be a consideration if a large number of objects are treated in an emergency.

If the surface to be faced is porous, the facing adhesive should be compatible with original materials and intended future treatment (consolidation, infilling and retouching media). If the nature of the surface that is to be faced is unknown, it may be necessary to undertake solvent tests to establish solubility parameters in order to select an adhesive that will not damage the surface. The adhesive selected will be dependent on nature of surface to be faced. Methyl cellulose, Beva 371, isinglass/gelatin, PVAL, PVAC and acrylic emulsions and dispersions, Paraloid B72 and B67 have all been successfully used as facing adhesives. Wax/resin mixtures may be problematic but can be useful if a surface has been treated with a wax/resin in the past. Both Beva 371 and wax/resin can be used to impregnate facing paper and then applied to a surface with a hot spatula to quickly secure large areas of vulnerable surface.

Consolidant may be applied to a fragile surface through facing paper (*Figure 12.4*). It may be necessary to apply a thin isolating layer as a pre-treatment, or to pre-wet to assist the penetration of consolidant. The facing paper is laid onto the surface and the consolidant applied on top. When the consolidant is almost dry it may be ironed with a heated spatula or massaged gently with a fingertip. Drying time may be partly dependent on the nature of the ground, for example consolidant applied to a thick gesso layer may take longer to dry than that applied to a thin layer. The facing paper may be left in place until the consolidant has dried, and if necessary the treatment can be repeated. When the area is dry and stable the facing paper can be removed using a swab dampened with a suitable solvent.

Volatile binding media offer an alternative to traditional methods of facing. The use of volatile binding media, such as cyclododecane, to temporarily consolidate, face or isolate a surface has been described by Stein *et al.* (2000) and Jägers and Jägers (1999). These materials are waxy solids at room temperature but are characterized by an appreciable vapour pressure with the result that they sublime (i.e. pass from a solid to a gaseous phase without passing through a liquid phase) within a comparatively short time, leaving no residue on the object. They have been used as temporary consolidants to allow transport of damaged surfaces for treatment. They can be applied selectively and their hydrophobic character allows treatment of adjacent areas with chemical or aqueous treatments. They have been applied to water-sensitive surfaces and the upper layer of consolidant then removed to allow aqueous treatment (e.g. cleaning) that would otherwise be impossible.

## 12.3   Aesthetic reintegration

The term aesthetic reintegration is used to describe the addition of new material in order to bring a surface to an acceptable visual condition. Aesthetic reintegration may include infilling, retouching and the application of a coating. It is important to consider the entire process of reintegration before commencing a treatment to ensure that the intended systems and materials of treatment are compatible with one another. It may be useful to think through the process in reverse, with a clear final objective in mind, considering the alternatives and choices for each stage and the possible effects of each successive layer on the next.

### 12.3.1   Fills

#### *Introduction to filling*
This section deals with filling losses to decorated surfaces, though some materials may be suitable for filling non-structural damage to wood. Structural fills for wood are discussed in Chapter 10. General information on filled polymer systems can be found in Nielson (1966) and Manson and Sperling (1976). Aspects of filling decorative surfaces have been discussed by Green and Seddon (1981), Hatchfield (1986), Hebrard and Small (1991), Mecklenburg (1991), Thornton, (1991a, 1991b), Von Endt and Baker (1991) and Webb (1994). Thornton (1998) has reviewed early gap-filling materials used in the West.

Ethical arguments related to filling are similar to those raised in relation to retouching. The decision whether to infill a loss or not may depend on the conservator and their conservation discipline. Broadly speaking, there are three approaches to the treatment of losses from a decorated surface. These are to leave the surface consolidated, well sealed but unfilled; leave the surface unfilled but retouched; or fill and retouch the decorative layers. This first approach is not one that may be acceptable in easel paintings conservation but may be appropriate where an object is treated to stabilize it, historical information is paramount and damage is considered aesthetically acceptable. Leaving the surface unfilled but retouched may allow a design to be read without disruption at a normal viewing distance whilst allowing identification of retouching on close inspection, often called the 'six foot-six inch' rule.

Traditionally, many restorers filled before varnishing because this gave a crisper edge to the fill and made levelling easier. Localized varnishing was often required to prevent abrasion damage when levelling the fill and to prevent fill materials contaminating the adjacent surface. Many conservators now prefer to varnish the whole surface before filling and retouching. Though this can make filling more difficult because it creates a less sharply defined edge

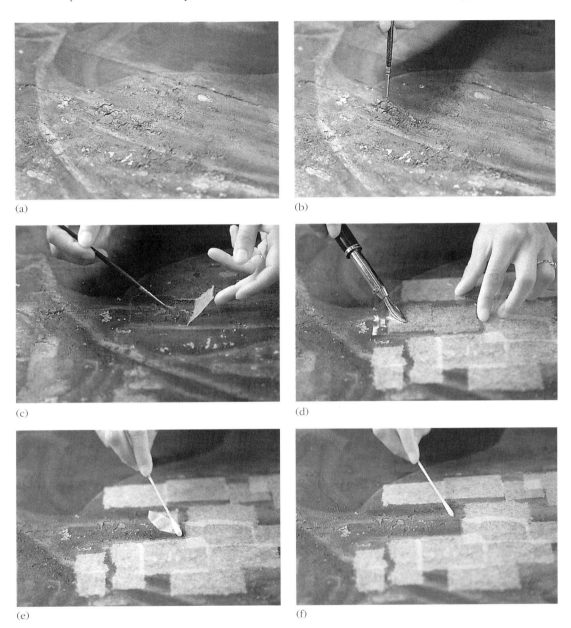

(a)

(b)

(c)

(d)

(e)

(f)

**Figure 12.4** This sequence illustrates the process of applying consolidant through facing paper onto a painted polychrome panel, German, *c*.1520. (*a*) Detail of panel before consolidation with 5% w/v isinglass. (*b*) Pre-wetting using water with a drop or two of alcohol added to reduce surface tension. There is a risk of disrupting varnish if excessive alcohol is added to the pre-wetting solution. Pre-wetting increases the penetration of the consolidant. (*c*) Facing paper is laid onto the surface and consolidant applied through it. (*d*) Some time is allowed for the consolidant to penetrate, softening the paint layers. Flakes are flattened using a heated spatula, which is isolated from the surface with Melinex/Mylar. (*e*) The consolidant is left to dry completely before removing facing paper with a dampened swab. (*f*) Residual consolidant is removed from the surface using a dampened swab

to the loss, it ensures that all restorative work is isolated from the original. Pre-varnishing also prevents 'ghosting', which often occurs if the area surrounding the fill is unvarnished and dust created when a fill is levelled becomes lodged in cracks and other interstices.

Filler should ideally never cover original decorative surface. Fills should be reversible without damage to, and ideally have a lower modulus of compression than, the original material. The inclusion of X-ray dense barium sulphate has been suggested as a means of tagging gesso fills, although the possibility that this may obscure constructional information below should be considered (Thornton, 1991a, 1991b). Unlike other compounds of barium, which are highly toxic, barium sulphate is chemically inert and may safely be used as a bulking agent (Thornton, 1998). Other approaches include the addition of a small proportion of pigment so that a restoration fill can be distinguished from adjacent original material. Documentation should include an accurate record of the extent of repair.

Many conservators isolate a fill from original material using either a collagen adhesive or a synthetic. Collagens may not be easily distinguished from original material whilst synthetics may interfere with the absorptive properties of the ground. The area to be filled should be cleaned and sized to reduce porosity and ensure a good adhesive bond for the fill. A gesso type fill may be built up in stages to prevent excessive shrinkage. Dried fills can be levelled using a scalpel, with a damp swab, abrasive paper (taking care not to touch the original surface) or with a suitable solvent. Fills may be textured with tools such as scalpels or swab sticks or by pressing a mould prepared from the original surface into the fill whilst it is still slightly damp. Leaving fills untextured can be a way of ensuring that repairs are identifiable but not obtrusive. The quality of the fill defines the quality of the finished repair. No amount of expert retouching will conceal a poorly executed fill. Information on casting fills for large areas of loss can be found in section 10.5.

As with consolidation, adhesives in fills are usually used in dilute concentrations. Collagens have been utilized in concentrations between 2 and 5%. They are easy to manipulate when wet and are easy to level after drying. Animal glue

bound fillers are prone to shrinkage as they dry and are unstable if exposed to fluctuations in RH. Other adhesives such as methyl cellulose and Paraloid B72 may also be used as the binder in fills. PVALs and PVACs have been used between 5% and 15% concentration. Synthetics may provide a better adhesive bond to the substrate. A few drops of PVAC added to a collagen gesso, for example, will often improve adhesion, inhibit gelling to allow the fill to be worked longer, and may impart easier reversibility. If adding resin in this way, it is important to be aware of the overall proportion of resin in the fill after volatile solvents have evaporated. One way to conceptualize this is to consider the traditional practice of adding 10% v/v linseed oil to a natural resin varnish composed of, for example, 30% w/v resin dissolved in solvent. Although the oil composes only 10% of the varnish solution, when solvent has evaporated off the proportion of oil will in fact be 25%. The same principle applies to the addition of synthetic resins to a fill mixture, which can result in an unintentionally hard fill.

Small areas of woodworm damage can either be accepted or filled and retouched. In the case of a large number of exit holes, it may be desirable to clean the exit holes to a depth of one or two millimetres and fill them with a neutral-coloured filler. Though often used for wood, as a general rule the use of wax-based materials should be avoided on decorated surfaces. Care may be needed to ensure that the overall effect is in balance with the colour and appearance of the surface.

### *Fill materials*

A combination of adhesive and an inert filler with the possible addition of a colorant can be used to repair losses. The adhesive component can potentially be any of the materials discussed as consolidants above. Factors that will affect the properties of fills include the degree of secondary molecular bonding between adhesive and filler, the percentage concentration of the adhesive solution and the proportion of filler that is added to it. Considerations for filling materials include how well the fill adheres to the surface, the amount of shrinkage that occurs as it dries, the elasticity of the fill, the length of time it takes to dry, how easy it is to level the dried fill and reversibility/retreatability. The flexibility of the fill should be a property of the adhesive polymer rather than the result of the presence of retained solvent or plasticizers. The effect of the fill on adjacent material should also be considered; for example, water-based fills with a high water content may swell unsealed adjacent original gesso, whilst some solvents may swell adjacent pigmented layers.

*Bulking agents* Calcium carbonate (chalk, whiting) is the traditional material used to bulk out a fill. It does not chemically interact with many adhesives and results in a comparatively weak fill, which may be an advantage in conservation. The amount of chalk to be added is gauged in terms of the viscosity of the mixture – a dough-like material for deep fills or a cream-like material that can be applied in stages. Glass (3M) and phenolic (Union Carbide) microballoons have been used as fillers for conservation. Cellulose or paper pulp may be used for low density fills.

*Wax* Wax has been used as a filling material in the past but is no longer generally used as a filler in decorated surfaces, though it may find application for shallow losses. Residues of wax may be difficult to remove completely and are likely to interfere with the adhesion of non-wax fills in the future. If wax is used as a filler, it should be isolated from the original surface, particularly where the fill would otherwise be in contact with a porous ground or decorative layer. Although wax fills are easily levelled, many coatings will not adhere to them due to their low surface energy and this may make sealing and retouching difficult. Further, many conservation inpainting media have a hydrocarbon solvent component, which may disturb the surface of a wax fill. Shellac, often used for sealing and retouching wax fills in wood, is not generally used in the conservation of decorative surfaces due to the polarity of the solvents needed to reverse it and a reported tendency to crosslink over time (Horie, 1992).

*Gesso* Gesso is widely used in the West as a ground for many decorated surfaces and, as the interface between the substrate and the surface layers, is often the locus for adhesive failure. The term gesso originally referred to a gypsum-based ground such as those commonly used in southern Europe, and in some conservation disciplines this specific definition remains. In the context of furniture conservation, the term gesso commonly includes ground layers based on collagen glue and calcium carbonate (chalk). Mecklenburg (1991) has demonstrated that the proportion of chalk in the gesso will affect both its strength and stiffness. Mecklenburg's experiments demonstrated that the tensile strength of gesso is inversely proportional to the chalk-to-glue ratio. A higher proportion of chalk will reduce shrinkage and produce a fill that is softer and more easily reversed. Fills with a high proportion of chalk can be very porous and may require sealing (e.g. with varnish) before they are retouched, in order to prevent the binding medium being absorbed into the filler and leaving an underbound retouch.

*PVAL* PVALs will not be exposed to UV when used as fill materials and therefore crosslinking should not be an issue. PVAL and whiting can be used instead of the traditional rabbit skin glue gesso. Such fills are water soluble and readily reversible using only slightly dampened swabs. The surface of the fill can be dampened to allow easier removal of excess or light moulding of the surface. For use as a fill, PVAL is dissolved in water to make a solution between 6% and 8%. Calcium carbonate is added to the solution until the mixture reaches the desired consistency, a dough for deep fills or much less viscous for shallow fills. The resulting mixture is thixotropic, which makes it difficult to apply in the same way as a traditional gesso is applied. It is best to spread it with a rubber spatula in order to obtain a smooth finish. It can be wetted again later for further smoothing, but can be dry sanded for the final finish. As with any fill material, care should be taken not to expose the adjacent surface to the fill material. PVAL has good working properties, porosity comparable to gesso and is reversible in organic solvents such as alcohol. The use of PVAL as a filling material is discussed by Hebrard and Small (1991) and Webb (1998).

*Commercial preparations* Commercial preparations such as Polyfix (calcium carbonate and other fillers in a vinyl acetate emulsion), Polyfilla (Canada) (cellulose ether and plaster) and fine surface Polyfilla (UK) (vinyl acetate copolymer with inorganic mineral filler) are used by some conservators. Commercial preparations called Polyfilla are marketed in both North America and the UK but the formulations are very different. Product information or technical specification sheets supplied by the manufacturer should be consulted for information on ingredients since formulations can change. Caley (2000) noted a change in the formulation of Fine Surface Polyfilla (UK) and suggested the use of Vinamul 6975 mixed with an inert filler such as whiting or china clay with the addition of a thixotropic material such as sepiolite or bentonite as a stabilizer, as an alternative. Some commercial preparations contain solvents that may affect modern paints, leaving an irreversible halo around the fill. Residues that remain on the surface after levelling should be removed otherwise they may be visible after varnishing. A range of commercial vinyl and acrylic fill materials were evaluated by Craft and Solz (1998).

### 12.3.2 Retouching

#### *Introduction to retouching*

The retouching of decorative surfaces is perhaps the most controversial activity, after cleaning, that conservators undertake. It is, after all, a restoration and, depending on the degree of loss, can be a subjective reinterpretation of the original picture or design. Retouching seeks to reduce the visual impact of damage in order to improve the legibility of an object, enabling it to be more readily understood. In the case of furniture, evidence of wear is often seen as legitimate and it is not necessary to slavishly make good all losses. The significance of loss may be open to interpretation. If the 'unity' of an object is intact despite losses to the surface or decoration, retouching may be considered unnecessary. There may be a conflict between unreconstructed decoration and what the museum-going public or a private owner expects to see. Any treatment should therefore seek to find a balance between aesthetics and the object's role as historical or cultural document. Philosophies of retouching vary between countries, cultures, conservation disciplines and conservators. Bomford (1994) has reviewed historical attitudes to the retouching of paintings, whilst Samet (1998a) has contrasted approaches to the retouching of paintings and painted furniture.

In a reaction against 'deceptive reconstruction' several non-mimetic methods have been developed in an effort to find a compromise between the disturbance of an unreconstructed loss and the subjective reinterpretation of retouching. The first proponents of visible retouching were Cesare Brandi and Paolo and Laura Mora at the Instituto Centrale in Rome, who developed the tratteggio technique. This was devised as a way of retrieving the aesthetic unity of a damaged work of art whilst respecting changes that have occurred due to the passage of time (Ramsay, 2000). Tratteggio is based on the principle of decomposition of the tones in pure colour and recomposition in the eye due to luminous images on the retina. It utilizes a network of parallel, vertical lines of pure colours on a white ground. A variation, called modulated tratteggio, varies the density and the length of the lines to render a more realistic approximation of the image (Bergeon, 1990). Tratteggio is often considered to have been successful on Italian Primitive paintings, but the success of this technique in other contexts remains a matter for debate. An alternative approach, called pointillism, was executed in dots of varying sizes. This technique was generally utilized as a visible retouching technique but could be invisible when the points were extremely fine. Other techniques that rely on chromatic abstraction, such as selezione cromatica and astrazione cromatica, have also been applied to the retouching of paintings (Ackroyd and Keith, 2000; Ciatti, 1990). Thus retouching may range from the use of a neutral background to recreating the loss. Ethical considerations include the nature of the object, the impact and cause of the loss and how the object will be displayed or used after treatment. It should be noted that not all critics believe such techniques were successful and, as is the case with cleaning, retouching is a subject that will continue to provoke controversy and discussion.

Whilst the need for consolidation or the application of a coating to a previously varnished surface can be argued on the basis of preservation, the decision to retouch losses is based primarily on aesthetic and interpretative criteria. There is a wide range of choices between no retouching and complete and invisible retouching. Retouching without filling, for example, may work particularly well on three-dimensional forms such as curved components or carving. Decisions about the type and extent of retouching should be made on a case by case basis with a clear aim in mind. Reconstruction may be partial or complete and incorporate or exclude fills, colour and imitating texture or craquelure. The decision to undertake non-mimetic retouching may allow the object to be presented in a variety of ways. It may allow, for example, a conjectural reinterpretation whilst retaining the viewer's ability to distinguish original from non-original work.

Some conservators have favoured replicating the original structure and pigments in their reconstruction of losses. This approach may be adopted in the hope that the retouching will match the original more closely, and that as the retouching ages any divergence from the appearance of the original will be minimized. Even though original pigments and layer structure may be faithfully reproduced, however, it is impossible to replicate the original method of application or ageing. Other conservators have favoured approaching retouching as a colour matching problem, believing that the use of original pigments is not essential to match the repair to the original. In both cases, retouching is a step by step process, built up in thin layers. Each layer of pigment or glaze applied during colour matching will have some effect on the final result. Replicating the original structure can impart a degree of optical complexity to a retouch, as light penetrating the layers can replicate the look of an aged paint more accurately than a simple structure, which may appear flat in comparison.

General ethical principles relating to retouching include documenting original condition and the extent of retouching. Retouching should be restricted to areas of loss. In the past, restorers have often extended retouching past the area of damage in order to blend it in with the original. Ideally, retouching undertaken as part of a conservation treatment should not obscure original material or decoration on an object. Artist's quality sable brushes can be used to ensure accuracy. It is widely accepted that retouching materials should be distinguishable and safely removable from the original (Perry, 2000).

### Light, colour and metamerism
Light can be defined as the range of electromagnetic radiation to which our eyes are sensitive. Colour perception is not an absolute but relies on an interaction between a light source, an object and the eye of an observer. This interaction must be reproduced if colour perception is to remain constant.

Colour matching requires a strong diffuse light source. When light strikes a coloured object, individual wavelengths may be transmitted, reflected or absorbed. Different light sources contain differing proportions of coloured light (*Figure 12.5*). The proportion of each wavelength available to be transmitted, reflected or absorbed will vary with the light source and, in combination with the spectral reflectance of the surface, will change the colour perceived by an observer (*Figure 12.6*). Ideally the colour temperature and colour rendering quality of light used to retouch should match that used to display the object. Since an exact match for each object is rarely achievable, a good light source for colour matching is generally considered to be natural light from a large north-facing window (south-facing in the southern hemisphere) due to the significant proportion of blue light. Artificial light sources that approximate natural light include colour matching lamps, colour-corrected halogen lights or a mixture of normal incandescent bulbs and fluorescent light sources. Although a good light source is essential for retouching, matching colour is only part of the process. It is possible, for example, to resolve a degree of loss with the 'wrong' colour. Thomson (1988) discusses the effect of colour temperature and colour rendering in the museum environment. For a thorough discussion of colour see McLaren (1983); for information on light see Brill (1980).

Metamerism is a term used in colour science to describe the effect when two colours that match each other under one light source differ when viewed under a second light source of a different colour temperature (see *Figure 12.6*). Metamerism will not occur if pigment identical to the original is used. In many cases, however, this is not possible and a modern substitute must be used. For example, although Prussian blue may be colour-matched using cobalt blue, French ultramarine or cerulean blue, the result will prove metameric because these three modern pigments have a high reflectance of red in comparison with Prussian blue (Staniforth, 1985). It may be helpful to try to match the

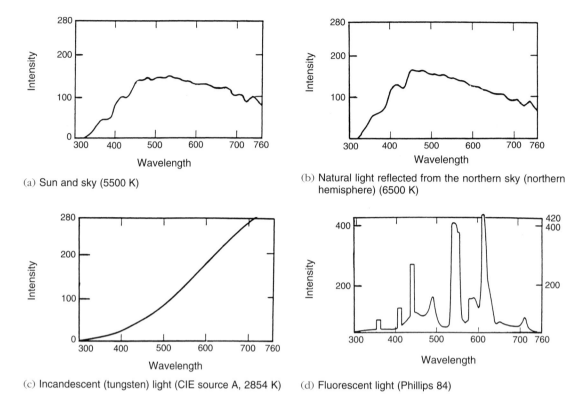

(a) Sun and sky (5500 K)

(b) Natural light reflected from the northern sky (northern hemisphere) (6500 K)

(c) Incandescent (tungsten) light (CIE source A, 2854 K)

(d) Fluorescent light (Phillips 84)

**Figure 12.5** Although they may appear 'white', different lights sources contain different energy distributions of the wavelengths that make up white light. These variations impart a slightly different hue to sunlight, north facing natural light (northern hemisphere), incandescent, tungsten and fluorescent light (Thomson, 1988)
(*a*) Sunlight. In comparison to artificial light, the distribution of relative light energy of different wavelengths in sunlight is roughly equal. When sunlight enters the earth's atmosphere, some of the blue light is scattered. This decreases the blue component of sunlight's spectral distribution and imparts a slight yellow hue
(*b*) Natural light reflected from the northern sky (northern hemisphere) contains a higher proportion of blue light energy that direct sunlight. This gives a bluer light source that has better overall colour balance than sunlight, incandescent or fluorescent light and is therefore better for colour matching. A variety of 'colour matching' electric bulbs are available as an alternative, such as those that conform to the 6500 K standard
(*c*) Incandescent (tungsten) light emitted from an electric light bulb has a very high proportion of yellow–red light and a comparatively low proportion of blue light. As a result it has a marked yellow tinge in comparison to other light sources and is unsuitable for colour matching
(*d*) Fluorescent light contains a high proportion of blue-green light in combination with very little red light. As a result it has a marked blue tinge and is unsuitable for colour matching

spectral curves of retouching pigment/s to the original to minimize metamerism. Spectral curves show the range and amount of each wavelength present in the light reflected from a coloured surface. The spectral curves of many common artists pigments can be found in Barnes (1939), Johnston and Feller (1963) and Mayer (1991).

Although colour may be measured using instrumentation, conservators usually colour-match by eye. The ability to accurately distin-guish colour varies from person to person and with age. The ability to match colour depends on practice, skill and experience but may be aided by knowledge of the theory of colour. Information on the theory of colour and colour matching can be found in Brill (1980) and Wilcox (1989). Information on the instrumental measurement of colour can be found in McLaren (1983).

The language used by artists to describe colour is often vague. The terms hue, value and

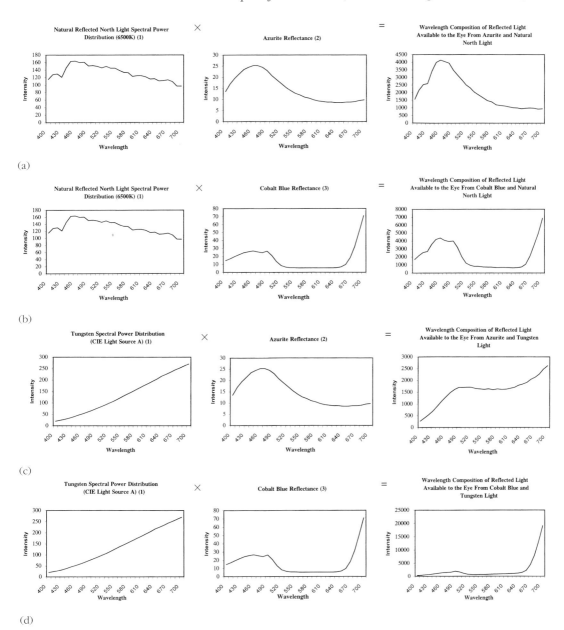

**Figure 12.6** The colour perceived by the eye is dependent on the combination of the energy distribution of the light source and the spectral reflectance of the surface. The human eye is relatively more sensitive to blue light than to green and red (McLaren, 1983), thus metamerism is most noticeable and most easily demonstrable with variations in blue pigments (Staniforth, 1985). Some blue pigments, such as azurite, Prussian blue and manganese blue, have reflectance spectra that peak in the blue part of the spectrum and fall away in the red end of the spectrum. Others, such as cobalt blue and ultramarine blue, have a significant proportion of reflectance in the red end of the spectrum. These representational graphs compare the effect of different light sources on two pigments, as perceived by the human eye. If cobalt blue were used to colour match azurite, the two would be well matched under a north natural light (6500 K, standard equivalent), but under tungsten light (CiE Source A), the cobalt blue would take on a purple cast. The change in hue perceived by the observer is a result of the increase in reflectance from the surface at the red end of the spectrum and the decrease in reflectance from the blue end of the spectrum. Thus a surface that was well matched under one type of light source can appear poorly matched when viewed under a different type of light source. This is known as metamerism. (*Sources:* (1) Thomson, 1988; (2) Staniforth, 1985; (3) Mayer, 1991)

chroma describe the three independent variables of colour and were developed to assist in the description and identification of colour for scientific and industrial purposes (Thomson, 1988). Hue refers to colour – red, blue etc. Value describes the apparent ability of a colour to reflect a greater or lesser proportion of the incident light, making it appear darker or lighter. This property is also sometimes called luminosity. Chroma, which describes the saturation of a colour, is defined as the strength of the hue compared to a neutral grey. Chroma may also be called intensity, purity or vividness (McLaren, 1983; Thomson, 1988).

Other terms are used by artists to describe the effects of mixing and working with pigments and paints. Tinting strength refers to the amount of pigment that must be added to achieve a desired shade of colour. The degree of opacity or transparency of a given pigment is dependent on the binding medium. The closer the refractive index of a pigment to the refractive index of the binder, the more transparent it will appear. Colour index names are an international system of identifying the pigment in a commercially prepared paint and are usually printed on the label, e.g. pigment yellow 29 may be abbreviated to PY29. Mayer (1991) includes a comprehensive list of pigments with their colour index name.

### Materials for retouching

*Pigments* Pigments vary in their tinting strength, opacity and working properties in various binding media and it is therefore important to experiment and become familiar with the theory and practice of colour mixing. Pigments also vary in their light-fastness (Thomson, 1988: Table 1). As a general rule, pigments used in conservation should be photochemically stable, to prevent future retreatment as a result of discoloured retouching.

A retouching palette for decorated surfaces may contain a selection of the following pigments:

titanium white, Chinese (zinc) white, Naples yellow, yellow ochre, raw sienna, cadmium yellow light, Indian yellow, cadmium yellow medium, cadmium orange hue, burnt sienna, cadmium red light, vermilion, Venetian red, alizarin crimson, light red, Indian red, permanent brown madder alizarin, raw umber,

burnt umber, brown madder, oxide of chromium, viridian, Prussian green, terre verte, cobalt blue, ultramarine, Prussian blue, Payne's grey, Davy's grey, ivory/bone black.

It is not necessary to have all these pigments, because a good knowledge of colour-mixing theory should allow most colours to be matched from a comparatively small palette.

*Diluents* The selection of diluents for the retouching paint requires some consideration. The diluent should not, for example, cause original adjacent binding medium to swell. In the past diluents were primarily selected for compatibility with the binding media and for a workable evaporation rate. Greater understanding of the impact of solvents on health has resulted in a move to less harmful alternatives. Thus B72, previously dissolved in xylene to make a retouching vehicle, is now often used with a less harmful aromatic hydrocarbon solvent or 1-methoxypropan-2-ol (also known as methyl proxitol, glycol ether PM, Arcosolv® PM and propylene glycol monomethyl) (Phenix, 1992). The proportion of solvent required will vary according to the way the paint is applied. Translucent glazes, for example, usually require a higher proportion of solvent to slow the onset of the gel phase and ensure the paint does not become rubbery before the glaze layer has been completely finished.

*Binding media* Pigments and glazes used for retouching may be used in a variety of binding media. The properties required of a retouch medium are similar to those required for adhesives and coatings, thus it is not surprising that some materials, such as Paraloid B72 and PVAC, are used in more than one role. Pigments have been mixed with dammar, PVACs, Paraloids, MS2A and other ketone resins. The traditional medium of oil paint is rarely used in conservation because it darkens over time and is often difficult to remove without damaging original decoration. Although not suitable for retouching decorated surfaces, shellac has been the traditional medium used for retouching varnished wood surfaces in furniture restoration. The use of shellac in this context is discussed in section 13.5.6.

The most important properties of binding media for conservation retouching are photochemical stability, flexibility and solubility parameters or application technique that ensures that future removal will not damage original material. Retouching media with proven long term photo-chemical stability include Paraloid B72, Laropal A81 and PVAC (de la Rie *et al.*, 2000). Retouching media need to be compatible with both the surface to which they are applied and any subsequent coating that may be applied. For example, retouching a resin-based japanned surface requires a retouching medium that will not affect the original surface (e.g. one soluble in hydrocarbon solvents), and that in turn will not be affected if a varnish is to be applied. Other important properties of retouching media include refractive index and molecular weight.

The refractive index of many synthetic materials is slightly lower than that of many traditional binding media (*Table 12.2*). This lowered refractive index can reduce the chroma of the paint because it is perceived as greyness (see section 12.4.2). This effect can be reduced or overcome by ensuring good wetting of pigment particles, by careful selection of pigments used for retouching, or by glazing with a higher refractive index material.

The handling properties of a binding medium are a result of both the molecular weight of the medium and the compatibility and evaporation rate of the diluent. The higher the molecular weight and the faster the diluent evaporates, the more rapid the onset of the formation of a gel phase and the more likely the paint will begin to feel 'rubbery'. Low molecular weight resins stay mobile longer because of the later onset of the gel phase, and often have better wetting of both the pigment particles in the paint and the surface being retouched. The compatibility of solvent and resin will affect the appearance and 'feel' of the paint, particularly for high molecular weight polymers such as Paraloid B72. A good solvent will allow the polymer to 'uncoil' to a greater degree, increasing viscosity (Hansen, 1994). The more uncoiled the polymer, the better it can wet individual pigment particles and the more saturated the paint will appear.

Retouching requires that the application of successive thin layers does not disturb those lying underneath. Some binding media need only adequate drying time between coats, whilst others may require the use of isolating layers

**Table 12.2** Comparative glass transition temperature (Tg) and refractive indices (RI) of some natural and synthetic resins

| Resin | Tg °C | RI |
|-------|-------|-----|
| Dammar | 39.3 | 1.539 |
| Mastic | 34.7 | 1.536 |
| Sandarac[a] | | 1.545 |
| Shellac[b] | | 1.52 |
| Laropal K80 | 50.8 | 1.529 |
| MS2A | 54.1 | 1.518 |
| Paraloid B67[c] | 50 | 1.486 |
| Paraloid B72[c] | 40 | 1.487 |
| Paraloid F10 | 20[d] | 1.476[e] |
| Arkon P90 | 35.6 | 1.522 |
| Regalrez 1094 | 33[f]/43.8 | 1.519 |

*Source:* de la Rie and McGlinchey (1990b) except:
[a]Gettens and Stout (1966)
[b]Angelo Bros (1965)
[c]Manufacturer's literature and Samet (1998)
[d]Manufacturer's literature
[e]Tennant and Townsend (1984)
[f]Manufacturer's literature – differences may be due to experimental conditions

with a different solubility parameter. Although the substrate and any adjacent area are usually isolated from retouching materials, reversibility is a property of an integrated system rather than a material. Thus the use of a binding medium that is only re-soluble in acetone or alcohol may be unsuitable for resin-based japanned surfaces. In other cases it may be possible to select a retouching medium that is soluble in acetone or alcohol, which will allow the application and future removal of a hydrocarbon soluble varnish without disturbing the retouch.

In an ideal world the appearance of the paint used for retouching would remain the same on the palette, on the retouching, and before and after varnishing. It may be difficult for an inexperienced retoucher to compensate for colour or saturation changes that may occur at each of these stages. One way of minimizing such change in appearance is to aim to use a paint that is sufficiently medium rich to match the gloss of the surface being retouched. Some conservators wet out with white spirit to replicate the appearance after varnishing, but it may be difficult to remember detail accurately after the solvent has evaporated. Other conservators prefer to saturate and isolate progressive retouching layers with a thin coat of varnish. If this approach is to be successful, the isolating/

saturating layers must be as thin as possible, and the best results are often achieved using spray application. It is essential to avoid building up excessive thickness in these layers.

Different binding media lend themselves to particular methods of application. Some synthetics may require fine hatching whilst others may be used to lay down a smooth base of solid colour. As a result, different binding media may be employed by conservators for different purposes within the same retouch, such as base coats and glazes.

*Paraloid B72*   Given the photochemical and thermal stability of Paraloid B72, it is hardly surprising that conservators have used it as a retouching medium. Although in the past it was often used with xylene or toluene, a less harmful aromatic hydrocarbon solvent or 1-methoxypropan-2-ol can be substituted (Phenix, 1992a,b). B72 can have a 'rubbery' feel if the solvent level drops too far before application is complete. As solvent content drops the resin begins to form a gel phase and thus it may be necessary to add diluent to maintain good handling properties. Inexperienced retouchers may be tempted to reduce the concentration of medium to help prevent this problem, but this will produce a matte retouch with a high pigment volume concentration. As a general rule, underbound or matte paint makes refined judgement about the degree of retouching necessary more difficult, because underbound paint compromises the colour and saturation of the retouching. Although it may be possible to locally introduce a thin varnish or resin solution to 'feed' a retouch (and in some cases this will be necessary), this often makes the task of producing a final surface with even gloss more difficult.

*PVAC*   Conservation grade PVAC is widely used as a retouch medium because it is photochemically stable, soluble in xylene and mixtures of IMS and water, and the base resin can be selected for the desired characteristics (e.g. Tg, molecular weight). It is very versatile and easy to use. PVAC can be used in a viscous solution for texturing or in very thin solutions for wash-like glazes. Some conservators find it easier to control gloss with PVAC in comparison to Paraloid B72. PVAC resins with a Tg around room temperature have a tendency to cold flow (creep).

As a general rule, pure PVAC resin is used as a retouching medium. Commercial emulsions and dispersions may not be appropriate because they contain a wide range of additives, including plasticizers and stabilizers, and vary widely in their photochemical stability. Union Carbide PVAC resins (AYAA etc.) are widely used in North America. Other pure PVAC resins are listed in Down *et al.* (1996). Although there are variations in the PVAC resins used, a standard recipe may utilize 1:1 or 2:1 AYAA:AYAC (see, e.g., Berger, 1990). 1-methoxypropan-2-ol or an aromatic hydrocarbon can be used as the diluent.

*Low molecular weight synthetics*   MS2A and ketone resins may be used as binding media for retouching. MS2A may be stabilized against photochemical degradation using Tinuvin 292 (see section 12.4.5). Although MS2A and ketone resins have a longer induction period (the period before photochemically induced changes occur) than natural resins, polar solvent mixtures similar to those necessary for the removal of aged natural resins are required for the removal of unstabilized aged formulations of MS2A and ketone resins. It may be necessary to isolate unstabilized MS2A and ketone retouches from the original surface. MS2A and ketone resins are soluble in aliphatic and aromatic hydrocarbons. They flow out well and their behaviour is closer to that of a natural resin than a paint. They may be used for scumbles and are very effective for glazes. They can be applied over a base coat of Paraloid B72 to increase optical complexity.

Though Regalrez 1094 and Arkon P-90 stabilized with Tinuvin 292 offer the advantages of solubility in aliphatic hydrocarbons and long-term photochemical stability, their ready solubility makes the application of multiple layers extremely difficult without the use of a less soluble intermediate varnish such as Paraloid B72.

Laropal A81 (BASF) is a LMW resin that is a condensation product of formaldehyde and urea. It has good photochemical stability and has been developed as a commercially available medium for inpainting (de la Rie *et al.*, 2000; Leonard *et al.*, 2000).

*Water colours*   Water colours or gouache tend to be used when a surface is incompatible with solvent-based retouching systems. Water colours are ideal for under-saturated base coats, and can be glazed with a resinous medium to adjust colour or gloss. They may be used to retouch a (non-water soluble) unvarnished matte surface.

Water colours are available in pan and tube form. Pan water colours have a comparatively high glycerine content, which makes them more sensitive to changes in RH and may impair their adhesion to a varnished surface (Caley, 1997). Water colours are notorious for changing hue when varnished and require either wetting out with white spirit or the use of a thin saturating varnish layer. It is possible for conservators to make their own slightly glossier water colours using fresh gum arabic, which can give better saturation. Producing a water colour with the right body, viscosity and gloss when dry may require some experimentation. The organic binding medium used in water colours is hygroscopic and there is the potential for fungal growth in conditions of high RH. Aged water colour retouchings often have a white or cloudy appearance when the varnish lying over them is very thin and has not prevented contact with moisture or pollutants.

*Tempera*   Egg tempera, utilizing egg yolk as the binding medium, has been used as a retouching medium (Kempski, 2000; Lank, 1990). Whilst freshly applied tempera can remain soft for some time, aged tempera forms a very durable paint layer. Potential problems with reversibility mean that it must be isolated from the original surface. Tempera is particularly useful for smooth opaque and bodied base coats, over which resinous glazing can be applied. Whilst this effect can also be achieved with synthetics, it is more easily executed in tempera.

### Making paint tablets

Although hand mixing of paint does not achieve the same consistency of wetting as industrial milling, conservators often formulate their own paint using a range of pigments, binding media and diluents. The role of these constituents in paint is considered in section 4.4.3. Whichever binder is selected, it is essential to ensure that pigment particles are as thoroughly wetted in medium as possible. Traditionally, a muller and slab were used to grind pigment into a binding medium thinned with diluent (e.g. linseed oil thinned in turpentine). The paste thus produced was mixed with the paint vehicle (medium and diluent) and was then ready for use. This ensured both that pigment was evenly ground and that each particle was thoroughly wetted by the medium. Whilst muller and slab are rarely employed for the preparation of small amounts of paint, the essential principle of ensuring that pigment powder and medium are thoroughly mixed remains. Using an artist's spatula and a firm surface such as a tile, many conservators work the dry pigment, binding medium and diluent thoroughly together to ensure the best possible dispersion and wetting of pigment by binding medium. It is important to ensure that binding medium and diluent are also well mixed to ensure that pigment has not been wetted only by solvent. Paint films characterized by well-dispersed pigment will appear more saturated and are usually more physically stable than those in which pigment is poorly dispersed.

Whilst some conservators opt to mix pigment and binding medium on the palette, others prefer to use paint in tablet form. There are advantages and disadvantages for each method. Mixing paint on the palette can be faster for more extensive areas of loss, as it is easier to make a larger amount of evenly coloured paint. Preparation on the palette may produce a better dispersion of pigment in medium because the paint is 'worked' more thoroughly. Mixing paint on a palette is messier than using tablets and requires a bigger palette to accommodate larger paint 'puddles'. Tablets are less wasteful of paint and are less messy in use. They are harder on brushes and it is comparatively easy to cross-contaminate colours, particularly whites.

Paint tablets can be made by the conservator using most of the binding media described above in the section on materials for retouching. Dry resin is weighed, placed in a muslin bag and suspended in solvent to prevent the formation of a slow dissolving semi-solid mass at the bottom of the container. Dissolution will be fastest with the use of a magnetic mixer. In the absence of a mixer, the solution should be stirred periodically until the resin has dissolved. The proportion of resin to solvent is dependent on the molecular weight of the resin and the intended final use. Low molecular weight resins are often used at a 20–50% w/v concentration whilst high molecular weight resins might be used at a 10–30% w/v concentration, or for texturing fills a 50% w/v concentration may be useful. When the resin has dissolved, the solution can be used to make tablets of colour.

To make paint tablets, take some of the resin-in-solvent mixture and add pigment. Use an artist's palette knife on a flat surface (or a muller and slab) to work the pigment evenly into the resin, breaking up lumps to make a smooth paste. Add this mix to the main resin-in-solvent mixture, repeating the process until enough pigment is dispersed to create an opaque paint. Pigment particles vary in shape, size and polarity and thus the amount of medium they absorb. These differences will affect the pigment to binder ratio, as well as the gloss and final texture of each paint (Leonard *et al.*, 2000). It may be desirable for tablets to be slightly underbound rather than resin rich because it is easier to add gloss than take it away. Retouching is a dynamic process and the conservator usually has to judge the ratio of pigment, diluent and medium as they work, on the basis of the saturation and gloss that is required in each instance.

Resins in solution tend to deteriorate much faster than those in solid form. Once the paint has been made, it can be poured off into a container, the solvent allowed to evaporate so that the paint forms a solid block, and the container then sealed. At the beginning of the retouching session, a small amount of solvent is added to the tablets to produce a workable paint. Alternatively, paint can spread on a sheet of Melinex/Mylar. Once dry, it can be broken into flakes and stored in a container ready for use.

### Commercial preparations

Some conservators prefer to use pre-mixed proprietary materials that offer the advantage of finely ground pigments well dispersed in a binding medium. Le Franc & Bourgeois 'Charbonnel Restoring Colours' are based on a mixture of ketone and acrylic resins (poly isobutyl- or poly n-butyl acrylate) in a hydrocarbon solvent. The potential crosslinking of butyl acrylate means that these retouch materials should be applied over a reversible isolating layer. Maimeri 'Restauro Colours' have a marked tendency to discolour as a result of the mastic binder but give excellent saturation, particularly of dark colours. Bocour 'Magna' paints, based

on a poly(n-butyl methacrylate) medium, are no longer available. Golden 'Polyvinyl Acetate Conservation Paints' contain pigment ground in a PVAC binder. Gamblin Conservation Colours are based on Laropal A81, a photochemically stable urea formaldehyde resin. Artists 'Acrylic' colours are readily available and easy to use but there is a colour shift as they dry and they tend to become darker as a result. De la Rie *et al.* (2000) found that retouch paint based on Paraloid B72, PVAC or Laropal A81 resins offered the best photochemical stability.

## 12.4 Coatings

### 12.4.1 Introduction to coatings

Coatings applied to furniture and other decorative art objects perform a dual aesthetic and protective role. Transparent coatings saturate the colour of the wood or decorative surface, offer some protection against accretions of dirt and grime, and can slow the permeation of atmospheric moisture and pollutants. A coating applied in the course of a conservation treatment must balance these functions with the additional constraints imposed by conservation ethics. Aesthetic considerations usually require a transparent coating that saturates the surface. The protective function requires a coating that will allow dust and other accretions to be removed without damaging the surface below. Permeability to moisture and pollutants varies widely according to coating type and thickness (Schniewind and Arganbright, 1984; Brewer, 1991). Conservation ethics require a coating that resists photochemical degradation (e.g. oxidation, yellowing, crosslinking) and allows removability without damaging the substrate. It may be necessary to consider the shrinkage stresses that the coating will cause (Whitmore *et al.*, 1999). In some cases application of a coating may not be appropriate. For example, a painted surface characterized by high pigment volume will appear matte, and application of a varnish may completely and irrevocably alter its appearance.

In the context of furniture, hardness may be an additional coating consideration. Although there has historically been some overlap between the coatings applied to furniture and painted surfaces, a distinction is necessary between surfaces that are essentially decorative and those that must withstand use. Surfaces that must resist wear and tear require harder, tougher coatings. As a general rule coatings with a glass transition temperature (Tg) above the ambient temperature do not imbibe dirt (see *Plate 3*) and are harder but more brittle than coatings with a lower Tg. This hardness is the basis for the use of furniture varnishes based on sandarac and shellac (see section 13.7.2). However, 'hard' coatings tend to dry with substantial shrinkage stresses, and thus the furniture conservator may need to balance the effect of such stresses on an underlying decorative surface (see *Figure 8.6*) against the need for a harder wearing coating (Whitmore *et al.*, 1999). Mastic and dammar are not usually durable enough for use on furniture that has a functional as well as decorative role, although they may have been added as a secondary component to furniture varnish formulations.

Photochemical degradation is the main agent of deterioration of varnishes and causes changes in optical, physical and chemical properties. Optical changes include yellowing, increase in opacity and loss of gloss. Varnishes that tend to yellow more quickly contribute to a cleaning cycle of frequent varnish removal and reapplication and thus increase the risk of damage to the decorative surface from leaching and abrasion. Physical changes include an increase in brittleness and the development of craquelure, crazing or crocodiling (see section 13.8). Chemical changes include crosslinking or a shift toward more polar solubility parameters (oxidation), particularly through the formation of carboxylic acid groups (de la Rie, 1988b). The use of polar solvent blends to remove discoloured varnish often has the potential to damage the decorative surface underneath (see Solvents under section 16.6.3).

The application of varnish can leach paint films in a similar manner to that which occurs during the removal of varnish with solvents. The leaching effect of a varnish solution on an oil paint film is dependent on the polarity of both solvent and resin components of the varnish. The leaching of oil paint films by varnish solutions is discussed in more detail in section 16.6.7.

The chemistry of natural resins is discussed by Mills and White (1977), their degradation by de la Rie (1988b). Samet (1998b) considers varnish and coatings for paintings in considerable

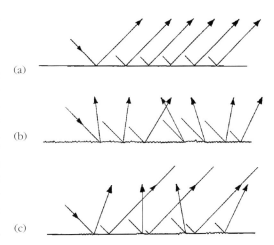

**Figure 12.7** Gloss and matteness
(*a*) Glossy surface (e.g. a newly French polished surface). Specular reflection of light occurs when the angle of the reflected light is the same as the angle of incident light. The greater the degree of specular reflection, the glossier a surface appears
(*b*) Matte surface (e.g. underbound paint with exposed pigment particles). Diffuse reflection of light occurs when light is randomly scattered from an irregular surface. The greater the degree of diffuse reflection, the more matte the surface will appear
(*c*) Semi-matte surface (e.g. an aged varnish). Semi-matte surfaces combine both specular and diffuse reflection of light

depth. The principles of adhesion outlined in Chapter 4 also apply to the application of coatings. The chemical properties of many of the materials discussed below are considered in Chapter 4 and their deterioration is discussed in Chapter 8.

### 12.4.2 Saturation and gloss

Saturation and gloss are inter-related optical properties of a surface. Saturation describes the degree of intensity or vividness of a colour (Mayer, 1991). A glossy surface has a high degree of specular (mirror-like) reflection of incident light, whilst a matte surface has a high degree of diffuse reflection of light (*Figure 12.7*).

The molecular weight, refractive index and gloss of a varnish will affect the saturation of a painted or decorated surface below. Saturation also depends on the ability of a varnish to wet a surface thoroughly, i.e. to displace the air on

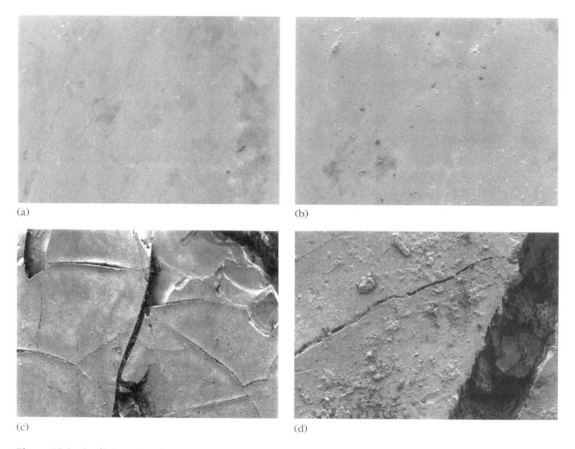

**Figure 12.8**   (*a, b*) Scanning electron microscopy (SEM) photomicrographs of a glossy surface (synthetic coating on a hardwood substrate). Although some roughening of the surface is apparent in (*b*), specular reflection predominates and the surface appears glossy
(*c*) SEM photomicrograph of a semi-matte surface (aged natural resin coating on hardwood) that combines both specular and diffuse reflection of light
(*d*) SEM photomicrograph of a matte surface (aged natural resin coating on hardwood) from which diffuse reflection predominates

the surface, spread out and achieve intimate molecular contact with it. Although wetting is influenced by viscosity and the chemical compatibility of solvent/resin and resin/surface, de la Rie (1987) suggested that refractive index and molecular weight are key factors in determining the optical properties of varnishes.

Some surfaces may require a high degree of saturation in combination with low gloss, for example where there are large dark passages in the design, or where the surface has been abraded in the past. The combination of good saturation and low gloss can be achieved using a multi-layered coating system. An initial layer of a natural or synthetic low molecular weight

resin will provide good saturation, whilst subsequent layer/s of a high molecular weight resin can be used to adjust gloss. If a natural resin is used for the lower saturating layer, it is prudent to incorporate a radical scavenger into the natural resin layer and a UV blocker in synthetic upper layers (see section 12.4.5).

### Refractive index
Refraction describes the change in velocity (and hence direction) of light as it passes from one medium to another. Refractive index ($\eta$) refers to the ratio of the velocity of light in a vacuum to the velocity of light in a given medium. The refractive index for a vacuum is 1, and the

refractive index for air is 1.003 (Brill, 1980). Therefore, in practical terms, refractive index describes the degree to which a material bends light in comparison to air. Linseed oil films have a refractive index of around 1.57, which means that visible light will travel 1.57 times slower through them than air.

Where there is an interface between any two materials (e.g. binding medium and pigment particle or varnish and binding medium), the opacity perceived by a viewer depends on the amount of light that is refracted (bent) at the interface. The greater the difference between the refractive indices of two materials, the more light is reflected (as opposed to transmitted) at the interface and the more opaque the system will appear.

The interface between the varnish and the binding medium will affect the saturation of colour of painted surfaces. The closer the indices of varnish and binder, the less light is reflected at the interface, the more light is transmitted into the paint layer, the more light is absorbed by the pigment particles, and the more saturated the observed colours. Linseed oil has a refractive index of about 1.57 and is well saturated by natural resins such as dammar, mastic and sandarac but comparatively poorly saturated by synthetic resins such as Paraloid B72 (see *Table 12.2*).

### Gloss

Colour saturation is dependent on surface topography as well as the relative indices of binding medium and varnish. The gloss of a surface is inversely proportional to its roughness. A surface that is smooth and reflects light uniformly to the eye of the observer will be perceived as glossy whilst an uneven surface that scatters light will be perceived as matte. Gloss affects colour saturation because the rougher the surface, the more light is scattered. Mixing scattered white light with the coloured light reflected from the substrate desaturates the appearance of the substrate. The darker the colour of the substrate, the greater the desaturating effect of the additional scattered white light.

In the case of matte paint, pigment particles are not thoroughly bound (wetted) by a binding medium. Applying a varnish will result in a varnish/pigment interface replacing an air/pigment interface, with a dramatic increase in saturation.

Wear, abrasion and the accumulation of dirt and grime will reduce the gloss of a coating (*Figure 12.8d*). The final appearance of furniture may require a balance between the original intended aesthetic and the effects of the passage of time. In some cases a high gloss finish is appropriate, whilst in others a matte varnish, or a surface with variations in matteness and gloss, may be a more sympathetic aesthetic.

### Molecular weight

The molecular weight of the resin used in a coating and the evaporation rate of the solvent in which it is dissolved will affect saturation and gloss. The higher the molecular weight of the resin and the faster the diluent evaporates, the more rapid the onset of an immobile gel phase and the less opportunity the varnish has to level. The ability of a varnish to flow out and level contributes to gloss. If a varnish that cures by solvent evaporation forms an immobile gel at a point when considerable solvent remains, it will tend to form a surface that follows the irregularities of the paint underneath the varnish. This increase in roughness produces a decrease in saturation.

Viscosity is a measure of resistance to flow. Low molecular weight resins (e.g. dammar, MS2A, Regalrez 1094) tend to produce low viscosity solutions, whilst high molecular weight resins such as Paraloid B72 produce comparatively high viscosity solutions. This is reflected in the concentrations of varnish solutions in which these resins are used. Brush varnish solutions of low molecular weight resins may be as high as 30% w/v or more, whilst brush solutions of high molecular weight synthetics are often around 10–15% w/v. More viscous varnish solutions will stop flowing over a surface sooner and will have less time to level. The rougher surface that results will result in a slight reduction in gloss and will appear less saturated.

The evaporation rate of the solvent will also affect the physical properties of the film. The use of slow evaporating solvents will allow the maximum amount of levelling to occur and therefore produce glossier surfaces (de la Rie, 1987). It should be noted that a slow-drying coating is likely to pick up more dust particles than a quick-drying finish. Solvent evaporation that is rapid enough to inhibit wetting will reduce the strength of the adhesive bond and colour saturation of the surface.

### 12.4.3    Varnish formulation

The use of different solvents has been shown to affect physical properties of films cast from polymers, such as density and permeability (Lawrence, 1990; Malkin, 1983). Solutions of polymers in different solvents have different viscosities, indicating the degree to which a given solvent allows the polymer molecule to extend. For example, at 25 °C, a 40% w/v solution of Paraloid B72 in acetone has a viscosity of 200 cps, toluene 600 cps and xylene 980 cps (Lascaux technical data sheet R138/1996). The more viscous the solution produced for a given solvent–resin proportion, the greater the degree of uncoiling of the polymer molecule in that solvent. Good solvents produce films that have interpenetrating polymer chains and a dense structure, whilst poor solvents produce films with aggregated chains and a porous structure (Hansen, 1994).

Different solvents can also affect the mechanical properties of polymer films. Paraloid B72 films cast from acetone (a comparatively poor solvent for this polymer), for example, have an extendibility of less than 10% strain to break. In comparison, films cast from toluene, a comparatively good solvent for this polymer, have an extendibility of over 100% strain to break (Hansen *et al.*, 1996). The chemical compatibility of solvent and substrate also has a role in the final performance of the film. For example, Schniewind (1998) noted that the adhesion to wood of Paraloid B72 and PVAC AYAT delivered in toluene were a fraction of that found when these materials were delivered in ethanol or acetone. Factors that affect the physical properties of films of thermoplastic polymers that are cast from solution include solution concentration, retained solvent and film thickness (Hansen *et al.*, 1991).

Turpentine was the traditional solvent for dammar and mastic but contributes to the photochemical instability of varnish films (Feller *et al.*, 1985). A hydrocarbon solvent with an equivalent K-B value (see discussion of hydrocarbon solvents under section 11.3.1) and evaporation rate should be substituted for conservation applications. The properties of a range of hydrocarbon solvents referred to in conservation literature can be found in *Table 11.1*. Many traditional varnish formulations contained linseed oil but this ingredient should

**Figure 12.9** Photomicrograph of the roughened surface of a coating that incorporates a matting agent (raking light)

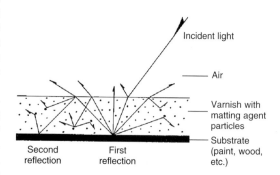

**Figure 12.10** Second order internal reflections occur when light is scattered within a varnish layer. Matteness is increased as light is scattered by particulate matting agent

be avoided due to its propensity to darken and crosslink.

Many varnishes may be made up by the conservator. Resin can be placed in a muslin bag, suspended in solvent and agitated occasionally until most or all of the resin has dissolved. This process may be speeded up by use of a magnetic mixer. Undissolved resin should be discarded before the varnish is strained, e.g. through a double layer of stockings or finely woven silk, to remove detritus. Two to three thin even layers of varnish may be required to achieve even saturation and gloss.

Reactions that contribute to the degradation of natural and synthetic varnishes occur faster in the liquid varnish formulations that in solid resins (de la Rie and McGlinchey, 1989). This effect may be visible, for example, in unused preparations that have yellowed in storage. Coating mixtures used by the conservator should therefore be mixed immediately prior to use whenever possible and many conservators dispose of such solutions after one month. The increased potential for degradation of liquid formulations has implications for pre-mixed proprietary products.

### 12.4.4 Matting down varnishes

Gloss may be reduced by the addition of matting agents. Matting agents reduce gloss by increasing the proportion of diffusely reflected light from the surface (see *Figure 12.7*). The two main mechanisms are roughening the surface (*Figure. 12.9*) and/or increasing second order internal reflection of light within the varnish layer (*Figure 12.10*).

Amorphous fumed silica (silica dioxide) is used as a matting agent by many conservators. Some fumed silicas are used in industry as thickening agents (thixotropes) but agglomerates must be well dispersed if they are to function in this way (see section 13.9). Hydrophobic and hydrophilic grades of fumed silica are produced to match the polarity of the polymer in which they will be mixed. As a general rule (but with a few notable exceptions), well dispersed fumed silica does not have a matting effect. However, the inclusion of any type of poorly dispersed particles in a varnish film will increase second-order internal reflections, scattering light as it passes through the varnish, thus producing a matte surface. Excessive poorly dispersed fumed silica can cause a pebbled appearance.

Precipitated silica is used in matting agents such as Acematt® (Degussa-Hüls). The proportion of silica required varies depending on the degree of matteness required and the type of silica used. Acematt® TS 100, for example, can significantly reduce gloss at around 4–8% concentration in some coatings, whilst Acematt® OK 412 may require 8–12% to achieve the same effect (*Figure 12.11*). The silica is added just before the varnish is to be applied, and dispersed using a high speed stirrer (2000–2500 rpm) for about 15 minutes to break down particle agglomerates. Alternatively, silica powder can be added to a small amount of varnish and worked with a palette knife. This will break up large agglomerates and ensure the particles are wetted by the varnish. When the particles are fully dispersed, the mixture can be added to the bulk varnish solution. As the

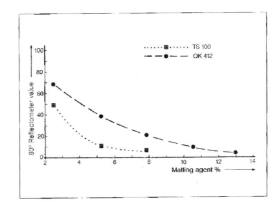

**Figure 12.11** Graphical representation of the relationship between the degree of gloss and the concentration of two types of matting agents (Degussa-Hüls) in a modern acid cured coating. Gloss decreases as more matting agent is added to the varnish

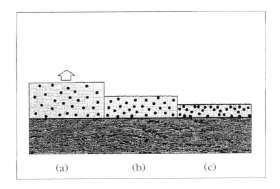

**Figure 12.12** Diagrammatic representation of the effect of film thickness on gloss, assuming the same concentration of matting agent. On application, matting agent particles are uniformly distributed in the varnish film (*a*). The thickness of the coating decreases as solvent evaporates (indicated by the arrow). A thicker varnish layer (*b*) results in a glossier surface because less matting agent is concentrated at the surface. The higher concentration of matting agent particles at the surface of a thin varnish layer (*c*) produces greater scattering of light and reduced gloss

solvent evaporates from the varnish film, the silica particles move to the surface, roughening it and scattering light. The thinner the coating, the more matting agent is concentrated at the surface, the more light is scattered and the more matte the surface will appear (*Figure 12.12*). Since it is usually easier to apply very thin layers using spray equipment rather than by brush application, it is not surprising that spray application can produce a significantly more matte surface than brush application of a varnish with the same concentration of matting agent.

Traditionally, a small proportion of light-coloured beeswax was added to natural resin varnishes to reduce gloss. The amount was determined empirically. Microcrystalline wax may be used in the same way. Microcrystalline wax, which is insoluble in room temperature hydrocarbon solvents, is dispersed in the varnish by gently heating the solution. Varnish removal may not ensure complete removal of wax residues (Horie, 1992). Proprietary formulations may utilize metallic soaps as matting agents (Wolbers, 1996).

Gloss may also be manipulated by the method of application. Brushing a dry badger-hair brush across the surface before the varnish has completely dried will roughen the surface and reduce gloss. The distance between a spray gun and the surface can be used to manipulate gloss. A greater distance may produce a matte surface. However if the distance is excessive, it can also produce a 'pebbled' appearance because the atomized particles have begun to dry before they hit the surface. Application technique can be used in conjunction with the selection of solvents with fast, medium or slow evaporation rates. The faster the evaporation rate of the solvent, the less time the varnish has to level and the more matte it will appear.

### 12.4.5   Stabilizers

Several materials, such as phenolic antioxidants, UV absorbers and hindered amine light stabilizers (HALS), have been tested to assess the degree to which they inhibit the photochemical degradation of both synthetic and natural resin varnishes. Bordeau (1996) gives a useful overview of these materials. The addition of UV absorbers or HALS has been used by some in the restoration trade to prevent detection of retouching using UV lamps.

Phenolic antioxidants, such as Irganox 565 (Ciba–Geigy), were proposed as an additive for varnishes to protect them from thermally induced auto-oxidation at room or elevated temperatures (Lafontaine, 1979a). Phenolic antioxidants do not offer protection against photo-oxidation, which is the primary mechanism in the deterioration of varnishes. These materials have poor light stability and contribute to yellowing and insolubility of varnish in the presence of light (Lafontaine, 1979b).

Ultraviolet absorbers, such as Tinuvin 327 and 328 (Ciba–Geigy) or Univil 400, 490, 497 (BASF), may be added to an upper sacrificial layer of a stable acrylic varnish such as Paraloid B72 in order to protect the layers below it. They can interact with reactive sites, polymer impurities or oxidative species within the varnish layer. They may find application in environments with high UV light levels, for example within a sacrificial layer of Paraloid B72 varnish applied over a natural resin varnish. In such cases the solvent used to apply the underlying varnish should be compatible with Paraloid B72 (e.g. xylene), because residual solvent in the underlying varnish will migrate through the upper layer. Aliphatic solvents such as mineral or white spirits can cause fogging of the Paraloid B72 at the interface with the underlying layer (Bordeau, quoted in Samet, 1997). Bordeau (1989, 1990) has suggested that Tinuvin 327 exhibited UV absorption cut off at 400 nm, the best longevity, and the least UV-induced yellowing of top-coated dammar test samples. Up to 3% Tinuvin 327 may be added to a Paraloid B72 varnish, the percentage measured as a proportion of the dry weight of the B72 resin. The B72 varnish is applied in thin coats and its effectiveness as a UV absorber can be assessed by examining the coated surface under UV light – when sufficient thin coats have been applied, the surface will appear non-fluorescent (black). It should be noted that, whilst they can extend the lifetime and UV protective properties of a varnish, the efficacy of UV absorbers is not indefinite.

Hindered amine light stabilizers (HALS), such as Tinuvin 292 (Ciba–Geigy), are effective radical scavengers in the presence of light. Their chemistry and the mechanism by which they stabilize varnish has been described by de la Rie (1988a) and Bordeau (1996). The addition of HALS may result in a change in Tg (de la Rie and McGlinchey, 1989, 1990a; de la Rie, 1993). The addition of Tinuvin 292 imparts long-term photochemical stability to hydrogenated hydrocarbon resins such as Arkon P-90 and Regalrez 1094. Tinuvin 292, in combination with the exclusion of UV radiation below approximately 400 nm, has proven effective in slowing the shift in polarity of films of artificially aged mastic, dammar and MS2A. Window glass excludes almost all light energy below 330 nm, thus UV filters that screen all wavelengths below 400 nm are needed if Tinuvin 292 is to be effective in stabilizing such varnishes.

If Tinuvin 292 is used, it should be added to the varnish solution shortly before application. The amount of Tinuvin to be added is measured as a percentage of the weight of the dry resin. Accurate measurement of Tinuvin 292 is essential —1% added to Arkon P90, for example, causes the polymer to become more polar after ageing than if no stabilizer had been used, whilst excess Tinuvin 292 may form a distinct and separate phase in the varnish solution. The measurement of small quantities of liquid is discussed in section 12.1.2. The MSDS should be consulted before use. Tinuvin 292 has skin-sensitizing potential and conservators should use a respirator when spraying Tinuvin 292 stabilized varnish. Tinuvin 292 is toxic to aquatic organisms and should be disposed of in compliance with local legislation.

### 12.4.6 Selecting a coating

A varnish should produce a final appearance that is appropriate to the object. Increasing importance has been attributed to optical properties such as saturation and gloss. Although natural resin varnishes are the least chemically stable, their optical properties have been a benchmark against which synthetic varnishes have been compared. As a general rule, natural resin varnishes produce glossy films that saturate painted surfaces well. As de la Rie (1987) has pointed out, synthetic resins were not developed for use as varnishes and it would be coincidental if they produced the optical properties that are desired for this purpose. High molecular weight synthetic resins do not reproduce the gloss and colour saturation associated with traditional natural resin varnishes. PVAC, for example, has been used in the past as a picture varnish but proved unsatisfactory in spite of its chemical stability. PVAC varnishes have poor saturation properties and a comparatively low Tg, which makes them soft and prone to absorb atmospheric dirt, whilst PVAL varnishes have poor adhesion to organic substrates.

Physical properties such as glass transition temperature (Tg) affect the suitability of a material for use as a varnish. A varnish with a low Tg will be soft and retain airborne dirt whilst a varnish with a high Tg will tend to be brittle, scratch more easily and be prone to crack as a result of substrate movement. Hansen *et al.* (1991) found that although Tg is considered a basic property of a polymer, the Tg of polymer films may be affected by the process of deposition from solution. Low molecular weight polymers tend to produce varnish films that are more brittle and less flexible than high molecular weight polymers.

A coating applied as part of a conservation treatment should ideally be photochemically stable. Natural resins become yellow, develop craquelure and undergo a shift in solubility toward more polar solvent blends as they age. Some, such as shellac, are reported to crosslink (Horie, 1992). As a result many conservators have turned to synthetic alternatives such as ketone resins, Paraloid B72 and hydrogenated hydrocarbon varnishes (e.g. Regalrez 1094). Whilst some, such as Paraloid B72, are photochemically stable, others have proven as problematic as the natural resin varnishes they replaced. The history of synthetic resin varnishes is given detailed consideration by Epley (1996).

### 12.4.7 Coating materials

#### *Natural resins*

Dammar is a natural resin that appears to have come into wide use as a picture varnish in the mid nineteenth century (Feller, 1966). Dammar is held in high esteem by many painting conservators because it saturates colours well and allows control of gloss. Compared to mastic it is more photochemically stable, slightly less saturating and has less of a tendency to bloom. Although many traditional recipes suggest up to 50% v/v solutions, many conservators prefer solutions of around 10–20% w/v for brush solutions and 5–15% w/v for spray application (Merz-le, 1996). Aromatic hydrocarbon solvents, or aromatic/aliphatic mixtures (approx. 1:9) may be used instead of the traditional turpentine. It has been suggested that the cloudiness of the varnish solution that may result from some solvents does not affect the final appearance of the varnish. If necessary, cloudiness may be removed by filtering the varnish solution or by the addition of a small amount of toluene, an alcohol or ketone (Merz-le,

1996). De la Rie and McGlinchey (1990a) stated that the exclusion of UV light below 400 nm in combination with the addition of 3% Tinuvin 292 (measured as a percentage of the weight of the dry resin) would transform what would otherwise be a photochemically unstable varnish into a class A conservation material according to the criteria proposed by Feller (1978). The addition of Tinuvin 292 will lower the Tg of dammar from 39.3 °C to 29.2 °C and reduce the brittleness of the varnish film (de la Rie and McGlinchey, 1990a).

Mastic has had centuries of use as a picture varnish. It is glossy and saturates painted surfaces well. As with other natural resins, mastic has a tendency to yellow with time. It is slightly more photochemically unstable than dammar and thus requires the use of comparatively more polar solvents to remove an aged varnish. Solvents that may be substituted for the more traditional turpentine include aromatic hydrocarbon solvents, or aromatic/aliphatic mixtures (approx. 1:9). Mastic is also soluble in alcohols and ketones, though these are unsuitable solvents for coatings applied to oil or protein-based paints because of their polarity. Although many traditional recipes report 25–30% w/v solutions, most conservators prefer a range of about 5–10% w/v, using second or third coats if required. A small percentage (*c.*3%) of resin is usually insoluble, which will reduce the overall percentage concentration of the final solution (Mention, 1995). If the varnish solution appears cloudy it may be left to stand until partially dissolved material settles to the bottom. The clear varnish solution can then be poured off and the insoluble residue discarded. The exclusion of UV light below 400 nm combined with the addition of 4% Tinuvin 292 should provide stabilization of mastic varnish against photochemical degradation (de la Rie and McGlinchey, 1990a). The addition of Tinuvin 292 will also slightly lower the Tg of mastic and reduce the brittleness of the varnish film. A small amount of varnish may be brushed onto a surface then brushed out until it is completely absorbed, or until it becomes tacky (which will occur with second or third coats). If a week or more is left between applying coats, successive coats will not dissolve the previous one (Leonard, 1990).

Sandarac resin was used in both picture varnishes and for transparent coatings on furniture and decorative surfaces, such as marbling or graining, that required a colourless, hard coating (Caley, 1990; Walch and Koller, 1997). It could be dissolved in alcohol to create a spirit varnish or heated with turpentine and linseed oil to create an oil–resin varnish. Brittleness could be reduced by the addition of materials such as gum elemi and Venice turpentine (Gettens and Stout, 1966; Walch and Koller, 1997). Sandarac-based spirit varnishes require the use of polar solvents for removal and thus sandarac is not appropriate as a coating applied directly onto decorative surfaces. It may find application for furniture that requires a hard-wearing coating if the surface has been isolated with a photochemically stable hydrocarbon soluble varnish that is not soluble in alcohols such as Regalrez 1094.

Shellac, the staple varnish of the furniture restorer for at least the past hundred years, is unsuitable as a coating for varnished, painted and decorated surfaces because of its tendency to yellow, its polar solubility parameters and the possibility that it may crosslink with time. If the hardness of shellac is desired, it may be possible to use if the vulnerable surface is isolated with a coating that is insoluble in alcohols such as Regalrez 1094.

### *Acrylics*

Paraloid B72 is an ethyl methacrylate/methyl acrylate copolymer (70:30). Proprietary formulations include Univar varnish (production ceased early 1990s) and Lascaux Fixativ, a fixative spray. Paraloid B72 has been used as a coating material because it is very chemically stable. Its high molecular weight and low refractive index (in comparison to natural resins) result in moderate saturation of some oil painted surfaces, particularly those that are damaged or have large dark areas (e.g. earth or carbon black pigments). The resin is soluble in aromatic hydrocarbons as well as polar solvents such as alcohols and ketones. The choice of solvent will significantly affect the mechanical and optical properties of the film (see section 12.4.3).

Paraloid B72 is roughly equivalent to dammar in hardness (Feller *et al.*, 1985). It can be applied by brush (up to 20% solution, usually *c.*10%) or sprayed (3–15%, usually *c.*10%), usually in xylene (sometimes with the addition of a small proportion (2%) of acetone), although slower evaporating solvents, such as diethylbenzene, diacetone alcohol or Cyclo Sol 100 (Shell) may be used to adjust working properties. If the varnish is applied to a painted surface, consideration should be given to the effect of the solvent on the paint film. Even a small amount of benzyl alcohol or diacetone alcohol, for example, can have a significant swelling effect on oil paint and this may cause the varnish to penetrate into an oil paint layer below and complicate future removal. Paraloid B72 exhibits poor wetting on unevenly cleaned surfaces where residues of old varnish remain. It is less 'forgiving' than natural resin varnishes such as dammar and mastic and must be worked very quickly. Once the varnish begins to dry a softer brush must be substituted for the stiff natural bristle brush if the surface is to be worked further (Buckley and Houp, 1996). Spraying may produce a surface that is electrostatic and will attract dirt. This effect may be exacerbated by a matte finish (Hackney, 1990). Paraloid B72 has been used in conjunction with other varnishes, for example more saturating varnishes (e.g. dammar, MS2A) have been applied over B72 to improve the optical properties of the surface. It should be noted that, in a multi-layer system, the final varnish layer has the most marked effect on gloss.

Paraloid B67, poly(isobutyl methacrylate), is soluble in hydrocarbon solvents with a K-B value above *c*.35, such as VM&P naptha, white spirit and polar solvents such as alcohols and ketones. A small proportion of aromatic hydrocarbon solvent (10–15%) may be added if difficulties are encountered dissolving the resin in aliphatic solvents. Paraloid B67 saturates somewhat better than B72 but exposure to UV causes crosslinking and the aged resin requires the use of comparatively polar solvent combinations for removal (Feller *et al.*, 1985; Thomson, 1957). In some experiments, aged poly(isobutyl methacrylate) films have become completely insoluble. Horie (1992) has suggested that the addition of an unspecified additive to B67 renders it more stable than might otherwise be expected, but concerns about photochemical stability have resulted in most painting conservators discontinuing use of this resin (Vagts, 1996). B67 can be brushed or sprayed in solutions of 5–20% (usually *c*.10%) w/v in a solvent mix of aliphatic and aromatic hydrocarbon solvents. It produces a glossy finish, though this may diminish with time, which may be prone to attract dust, particularly as a result of spray application. B67's comparatively high Tg makes the varnish film very brittle, prone to fracture and scratch. Other products based on poly(isobutyl methacrylate) include Elvacite 2045 (previously known as Lucite 45).

Paraloid F10, Elvacite 2044 and Plexisol 550, all poly(n-butyl methacrylate)s, are soluble in hydrocarbon solvents with a K-B value of 35–55 or more, as well as polar solvents such as alcohols and ketones. These resins, with a Tg around 20 °C, will retain dirt and dust and are therefore unsuitable for use as coatings, particularly for horizontal surfaces on furniture, though they may be added to other formulations to reduce overall Tg and brittleness. After a comparatively short period of artificial ageing, de la Rie (1993) found that a significant amount of material insoluble in either toluene or acetone had formed in test films of Elvacite 2044 (poly n-butyl methacrylate) and 2045 (poly isobutyl methacrylate). The addition of Tinuvin 292 had little effect on the formation of crosslinked material in these two resins.

### Synthetic low molecular weight varnishes

*Ketone resins* Ketone resins, also known as polycyclohexanones, are a class of synthetic low molecular weight varnishes developed in the second quarter of the twentieth century. They have been used as retouching media and as varnishes. Proprietary products available since 1970 include MS2A (Linden Nazareth), Ketone Resin N and Laropal K80 (BASF). De la Rie and Shedrinsky (1989) found Ketone Resin N and Laropal K80 to be chemically indistinguishable. As a class, ketone resin films are comparatively weak, hard and brittle (Horie, 1992). They are prone to yellow in the absence of light, have a tendency to bloom, and although they are initially more stable than the natural resins, in the long term oxidation results in the need for polar solvent mixtures for their removal. Additives tested to date have had no effect on the photo-oxidation of Laropal K80 (Lafontaine, 1978; de la Rie and McGlinchey, 1990a), though it has been suggested that the addition of bleached beeswax reduces the effect of photo-oxidation and improves resolubility (Raft, 1985). Ketone Resin N/Laropal K80 are the primary ingredients in many proprietary varnishes, including Artists' Gloss Varnish (formerly Winton), Talens Picture Varnish (formerly Rembrandt), Artists' Original Matt Varnish and Artists' Retouching Varnish (Winsor and Newton).

MS2A is a reduced ketone resin that is currently available through a small-scale batch production process. It is brittle, less prone to yellow than Ketone Resin N and Laropal K80, and produces a glossy finish, though this may diminish with time. Brittleness can be reduced by the addition of a small proportion of wax. De la Rie and McGlinchey (1990a) found that the photochemical degradation of MS2A can be stabilized by the addition of 2% (of the dry weight of the MS2A resin) Tinuvin 292. Unstabilized MS2A has a longer induction time than natural resins but, once it has begun to oxidize, removal requires similarly polar solvent blends (de la Rie, 1993). Unaged MS2A is soluble in a wide range of solvents such as aliphatic and aromatic hydrocarbon solvents, isopropanol and 1-methoxy-2-propanol. Stabilized MS2A offers greater photochemical stability than natural resins, and has good saturation and gloss. The resin is, however, comparatively expensive (£375 per kilo).

Lank (1976) outlined several formulations for MS2A, including a standard formulation, brushing varnish, matte varnish for spray application and a final varnish. Some formulations have since been adjusted, for example Lank no longer uses the n-butyl acetate referred to in his 1976 paper (Fisher, 1996).

| | |
|---|---|
| Standard solution | 30% w/v in an aliphatic hydrocarbon solvent (low aromatic white spirit, odourless mineral spirits) |
| Brushing solution | 8 parts standard solution: 2 parts low aromatic white spirit v/v |
| Matte varnish | 270 ml standard solution, 60 g microcrystalline wax (Cosmolloid 80H), 1300 ml white spirit; (proportionately 4.5 parts standard solution: 22 parts additional solvent: 1 part microcrystalline wax) |
| Final varnish | 6 parts standard solution: 1 part matte varnish solution v/v produces a varnish with reduced gloss |

Standard, matte and final varnish formulations of MS2A are suitable for spray application at 2–5 kg/cm². The presence of a significant proportion of aromatics in the solvent may prevent film formation using spray application. Surfaces that are to be sprayed should be given a brush coating first, otherwise the coating may not adhere to the surface. The initial brush coat can be worked until the varnish becomes tacky, whilst subsequent coats require spray application. Reticulation of the varnish has been reported by some conservators but may be avoided by allowing up to a week between spray coats, using thin solutions or using a badger brush with a brushing or tamping action to level the varnish (Fisher, 1996). Varnish solutions can have a wide range of resin concentration (5–20% brush solutions, 5–30% spray solutions).

A wide range of proprietary varnishes are based on mixtures of acrylics and/or ketone resins. Soluvar, for example, is a proprietary blend of poly(isobutyl methacrylate) (Paraloid B67) and poly(n-butyl methacrylate) (Paraloid F10). Silica powder is dispersed in Soluvar Matte varnish. Golden MSA Varnish is a blend of butyl methacrylate polymers, whilst Winsor and Newton's Conserv Art Varnish is a mixture of acrylic and ketone resins. These materials are given detailed consideration in Samet (1998b).

*Hydrogenated hydrocarbon resins* Research published in early 1990s proposed low molecular weight hydrogenated hydrocarbon resins as an alternative to natural resins and low refractive index/high molecular weight synthetics such as Paraloid B72 (de la Rie and McGlinchey, 1990b; de la Rie, 1993). The hydrogenated hydrocarbon resins tested had molecular weights and refractive indices comparable with natural resins. Some resins, such as Arkon P90 (Arakawa) and Regalrez 1094 (Hercules), in combination with the hindered amine light stabilizer Tinuvin 292 (2% of the dry weight of the resin), resist photochemical oxidation for significantly longer than dammar or MS2A in conditions where UV light is filtered only by normal window glass. This photochemical stability is a result of the hydrogenation of unsaturated bonds during manufacture and an absence of reactive functional groups. Some hydrogenated hydrocarbon resins are soluble in aliphatic and aromatic hydrocarbons but insoluble in acetone and lower alcohols. They may be used to coat a surface or applied in small areas to adjust gloss or saturation. Stabilized formulations have the advantages of long-term removability in non-polar low aromatic solvent mixtures. However, ageing of test films of both Arkon P90 and Regalrez 1094, without the addition of Tinuvin 292, resulted in severe embrittlement.

The addition of polymeric additives from the Kraton G rubber series (Shell) to hydrogenated hydrocarbon resins has been tested to assess whether this would allow these synthetic resins to mimic the handling properties of natural resins, which incorporate a naturally occurring polymeric fraction (de la Rie, 1993). The addition of 10% polymer additive resulted in reduction of gloss, increased mar resistance and may reduce brittleness. Oxidation of these materials was effectively inhibited when Tinuvin 292 was added. Tinuvin 292 is added at 2% of the combined weight of resin and Kraton G. Whitten and Proctor (1996) have reported that the addition of 1–3% of a Kraton G1650 or 1657 to Regalrez 1094 increases drying time, gives a feeling of resistance when the varnish is applied and may prevent the varnish 'sinking in', but above this percentage the varnish begins to resemble the appearance of a synthetic polymer rather than a natural resin.

Some experimentation may be necessary to achieve satisfactory results with these materials. Leonard (1990) reported a slight excessive gloss using brush application of 35% Arkon P90 in odourless mineral spirits (Shellsol OMS). Other, faster-evaporating solvents, such as Shellsol 340 HT (Shellsol D38) or Shellsol D40 (UK), may reduce the extended drying time associated with odourless mineral spirits (previously known as Shellsol 71). A 25% brush solution, followed by application of several thin spray coats (also 25%), all of which had had excess resin removed by brushing lightly over the wet surface with a dry badger brush, produced a surface that was indistinguishable from that produced by mastic.

Escorez resins (Exxon) were used for varnishing in the 1990s. Escorez 5380 has been used in preference to Escorez 5300 because of its lower Tg. Proprietary varnishes products have utilized this resin and it was the basis of UVS (ultraviolet stabilized) Finishing Varnish (Conservator's Products Company) from 1991

to 1996. Regalrez proved to have better optical and handling properties and this varnish is now based on Regalrez 1094 (Swicklik *et al.*, 1997).

Regalrez 1094 (Hercules), based on 100% hydrogenated oligomers of styrene and α-methyl styrene, was the most stable of the commercially available synthetic resins evaluated by de la Rie and McGlinchey (1990b) and de la Rie (1993). Gamvar (Gamblin Artist's Colors Co, USA) is a proprietary varnish based on this resin. Brush application may utilize 10–40 g resin per 100 ml of solvent, though a mid range (20–25 g resin) is more usual for the initial coat, whether brushed or sprayed. Good results have been achieved using airbrush or HVLP spray equipment. Shellsol 340 HT (Shellsol D38) or Shellsol D40 are suitable solvents for brush application (Whitten, 1995b; Whitten and Proctor, 1996). Subsequent layers must be sprayed to avoid disturbing the lower layer/s and this may be assisted by the use of a faster evaporating solvent. Problems of subsequent sprayed coating dissolving previous ones can be overcome with the use of a faster-evaporating solvent, or an isolating layer of Paraloid B72 or stabilized dammar. Whitten (1995a) has suggested that Regalrez mimics the appearance of natural resins better when applied to a weathered or aged surface, rather than a fresh or oil rich surface. When applied to a rough or weathered surface, a higher concentration of 30–40 g resin per 100 ml solvent may result in a more even coating. Matteness can be manipulated to some degree by application technique, the addition of wax or matting agents, low resin concentration (*c*.10% or less) or the use of fast evaporating solvents. However, the inherent gloss of Regalrez 1094 means it is a poor choice if a completely matte effect is desired. The following recipe may be useful in formulating Regalrez 1094 varnishes (National Gallery of Washington, 1998). The amount of solvent added is dependent on the desired working properties of the varnish.

| | |
|---|---|
| Regalrez 1094 | 20.0 g |
| Kraton G1657 (3% weight of Regalrez) | 0.6 g |
| Total Regalrez + Kraton G | 20.6 g |
| Tinuvin 292 (2% weight Regalrez and Kraton) 0.4 g (rounded down from 0.412 g) | |

Piena (2001) reported that Regalrez 1094 applied to a bed in a domestic interior had proven unsatisfactory because the varnish became tacky when handled and had begun to adsorb dust. Piena recommended the use of Regalrez 1126 (Tg 65 °C, MW 1250) as an alternative, stating that, like Regalrez 1094, it has a non-reactive chemical structure and Regalrez 1126 does not become tacky when handled. Regalrez 1126 is soluble in non polar solvents (e.g. low aromatic white spirit) and may be used in concentrations varying from 5–40% w/v.

Stabilized hydrogenated hydrocarbon resins such as Regalrez have the advantages of high gloss, good saturation properties, photochemical stability and can be applied and removed in solvent blends that are less harmful both to the conservator and many painted and decorated surfaces (e.g. water gilding). They have the disadvantages that they can be difficult to retouch onto, and may require alternating or separating layers of a resin with different solubility parameters. This may be difficult in practice and success relies on the skill and experience of the conservator. When excess is applied to a surface, for example when brush coating, the varnish solution can over-penetrate, though this problem can be prevented by thin-sprayed coats.

*Aldehyde resins*   The use of low molecular weight aldehyde resins for varnishing has been investigated (de la Rie and McGlinchey, 1990b; de la Rie *et al.*, forthcoming). Laropal A81 (BASF) is a commercially available aldehyde resin. It is photochemically stable and saturates well, but gloss can be difficult to control.

## 12.4.8   Application methods for coatings

Varnish may be applied with a brush or spray equipment. Choose the application method that gives the desired result and is compatible with the nature and shape of the surface. Varnish application has been reviewed by Bernstein (1992). Initial coats of synthetic resins such as Paraloid B72, MS2A and hydrogenated hydrocarbon resins can be applied with a brush, but spray application is usually necessary for subsequent coats. In either case the aim is to apply varnish in a thin, even layer. Areas that may absorb more varnish may be selectively pre-varnished before the application of a coating to the whole surface. Several thin layers produce a coating with better optical properties than a

single thick coat. If several layers are to be applied it should be noted the use of slow evaporating solvents will extend drying time and may cause the lower layer to be disturbed if it is not completely dry before subsequent coats are applied. Conditions of high humidity should be avoided when varnishing as they can contribute to bloom in the varnish.

### Brush application

Brushes used for the application of varnish to paintings are given detailed consideration by Jaworski (1996) whilst those used for varnishing furniture, usually squirrel mops, are illustrated by Hayward (1988). A chiselled edge hog's hair brush is used by many painting conservators to apply varnish. The method is dependent on the working time of the varnish, which in turn is influenced by the evaporation rate of the solvent in which the resin is dissolved. A small amount of mastic, dammar or MS2A, for example, may be applied in the middle of the surface and brushed out towards the edges until the brush begins to drag slightly. Other techniques include diagonal stripes from which the varnish is feathered out, and overlapping vertical and horizontal strokes. The brush and method differ from that used by traditional finishers in the furniture trade who used a polisher's squirrel hair mop and applied spirit varnishes using rapid slightly overlapping strokes along the direction of the wood grain.

### Spray application

Spray application has the advantage that it can allow micro-thin coatings. It is essential when using spray equipment to take precautions against inhaling solvent fumes, resin or pigment particles. Health and safety precautions provided by the manufacturer of such equipment (and the materials being sprayed) should be followed but other common sense precautions, including not smoking when spraying and avoiding trying to clear blocked nozzles whilst the compressor is still running and the gun attached to it, will help avoid injuries.

A thin even coat of varnish may be sprayed on to a surface, sometimes followed by briskly brushing over the surface with a fine badger brush to remove any excess. Continuing to brush the surface once it has become tacky will roughen it and reduce gloss. As a general rule solutions applied by spray gun are more dilute

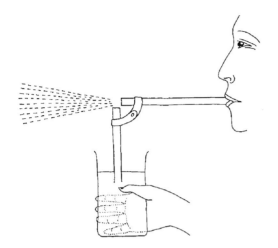

**Figure 12.13** Diagrammatic representation of a mouth diffuser or blow atomizer

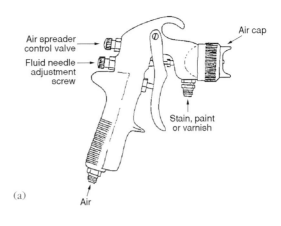

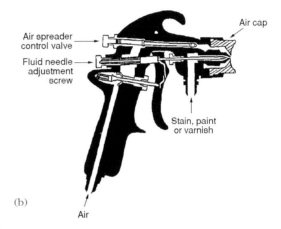

**Figure 12.14** Diagram (*a*) and simplified cutaway (*b*) of a typical suction cup spray gun showing the air spreader control valve, the fluid needle adjusting screw, and the air cap. The air spreader control valve is used to adjust the shape of the cone of mixed air and coating produced by the gun. The less air travelling through the gun, the more circular the discharged mix. Generally a circular fan shape is required. The size of the fan can be adjusted by either a knob on the body of the gun or a ring on the air cap. The fluid needle adjusting screw regulates the flow of coating. The further the adjusting screw is screwed in, the less coating is sprayed from the nozzle. Air horns on the air cap are positioned in the direction of the hand motion used when spraying

than those applied with a brush. Fast evaporating solvents (e.g. acetone) are not usually used for spraying varnishes. The spray gun atomizes the varnish into fine droplets and vastly increases the surface area to volume ratio. If an excessively fast evaporating solvent is used, the droplets will dry before they reach the surface and will produce a frosted appearance. In some cases this effect can be used deliberately. Mention (1995) describes the use of mastic in ethanol to create a frosted surface, followed by reforming these layers by the application of a thin mastic solution in the usual solvent to which a small amount of benzyl alcohol had been added. This allowed an even varnish layer to be applied to a pitted, dry and uneven paint surface. Some painting conservators recommend against spray application of varnish on panel paintings (Gordon, quoted in Samet, 1997).

*Mouth diffuser/blow atomizer*  The mouth diffuser or blow atomizer may be used to apply varnish to small areas of a surface although it has a tendency to produce a somewhat irregular coating (*Figure 12.13*). Air is blown through the tube and creates an area of negative pressure, drawing varnish from the cup from where it is distributed as a fine mist onto the surface. Blowing must produce a forceful and steady air pressure in order to evenly atomize the varnish droplets. If pressure is inadequate, large and irregular droplets of varnish will mar the sur-

face. The varnish should be thin enough to allow very fine droplets to form – a pebbled surface will result if the varnish is too thick. Varnishing horizontal surfaces is easier than vertical surfaces and avoids the formation of sags and drips. Adequate ventilation is necessary and a gentle airflow that moves from behind the person applying the varnish, across

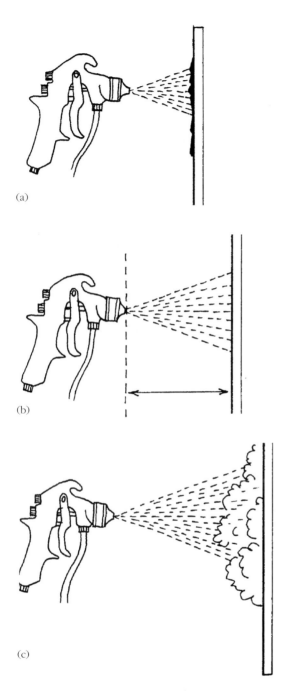

(a)

(b)

(c)

**Figure 12.15** Diagrammatic representation of the effect of spray gun distance from the surface. The correct distance, usually 20–30 cm, is indicated by an arrow in (*b*). If the gun is held too close to the surface, excess coating will be deposited and may result in an orange peel effect (*a*). If the distance is too far, the coating begins to dry before coming into contact with the surface and may result in a pebbled effect (*c*)

and away from the varnished surface is best. Varying the distance and angle between the atomizer and the surface will alter the thickness and saturation of the varnish coat (Zuccari, 1997).

*Spray guns*   Spray guns used in furniture conservation generally utilize compressed air combined with a gravity feed or suction cup on the gun. The liquid surface coating is atomized by the flow of a low volume of air compressed to around 30 psi and carried to the surface by the air stream. This system is known as high-pressure–low-volume (HPLV). It requires strong ventilation to remove excess solvent and coating and there is usually significant overspray. It is essential that the gun is adjusted correctly, good spray technique used, the nozzles, needles and air cap sizes correspond and that the output of the compressor matches the throughput of the gun and nozzle. There are two primary adjustments that can be made to regulate the flow and distribution of finish from the gun. These are the air spreader control valve and the fluid needle adjusting screw (*Figure 12.14*). Other adjustments that can be made include the viscosity of the medium, by increasing or reducing solvent (or pigment) content, air pressure, air flow, the distance between the nozzle and the surface, the evaporation rate of the solution, and the speed of movement across the surface.

The spray gun is usually held approximately 20–30 cm (8–12 inches) from the surface, though the exact distance is dependent on the equipment being used (*Figure 12.15*). Movement of the gun across the face of the surface should maintain this distance evenly (*Figure 12.16*). The spray gun is usually moved across the surface in horizontal bands, with each successive band slightly overlapping the one before to compensate for the lighter covering at the edge of the fan. The beginning and end of each stroke are prone to receive excess coating, so it may be useful to spray beyond the beginning and end of the surface to ensure even coverage at the edges. A black tile may be used as a test surface for transparent coatings to assess whether the correct adjustments have been made, that spray technique is correct and that the level of gloss is satisfactory. Full sized spray guns are useful for dealing with large areas in a very uniform manner, whilst so-called

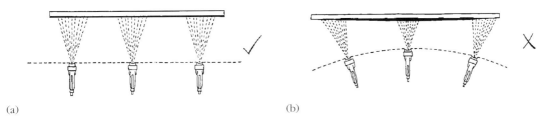

(a)                                      (b)

**Figure 12.16** Spray action: (*a*) maintaining the same distance between the gun and surface through the whole pass will give a coating of even thickness, while (*b*) a curved arc will result in more material being deposited in the centre of the arc and less at the edges, resulting in an uneven coating

'touch-up' guns may be appropriate for fine work or treating areas selectively.

The need to control airborne pollutants has resulted in the development of high-volume–low-pressure (HVLP) spray systems, such as the Chiron SG90, which operate at 2–10 psi. An air 'dome' is formed around the cone of sprayed material as it exits the gun, which reduces solvent vapour in the work atmosphere, overspray and bounceback. These systems deposit a much higher percentage of the coating material onto the object. Manufacturers claim up to 80% transfer efficiency (TE: the total amount deposited on the surface as a percentage of the total amount of material sprayed) in comparison with 30–35% from conventional HPLV spray systems. In some states in the USA conversion to HVLP systems may be mandated by law. HVLP systems may prove to be more sensitive for the selective treatment of objects or new parts because there is less overspray to contend with. They tend to be slightly more expensive to purchase, but may be used with the same air compressor as a traditional spray gun so long as it is sufficiently powerful. An operator used to traditional spray equipment may need to practise and adjust spray technique, e.g. reducing the distance between gun and surface or changing the speed the gun is moved across the surface, as well as experimenting with coating viscosity to produce good results. Ocon and Miller (1996) give useful tips on HVLP conversion guns.

Regardless of which system is used, the gun must be cleaned thoroughly after use. The cup that contained the material that was sprayed should be emptied and any coating that remains in the gun sprayed through. Solvent is then sprayed through until the working parts of the gun have been thoroughly flushed and are

clean. If the gun is used regularly it may assist in preventing clogging if the gun is dismantled and components such as the fluid adjustment needle and nozzles are soaked in solvent overnight. The same solvent may be reused for this purpose many times, but a gun used the following day should be preceded by pre-spraying this solvent out of the gun until a clean film of fresh solvent or coating is produced.

*Air brushes* Air brushes work on the same principle as high-pressure–low-volume spray guns described above, although the air is compressed to about 20 psi. As with other HPLV spray equipment, air brushes have the disadvantages of overspray and the production of solvent vapour in the work atmosphere. Originally designed for the art and craft market, they are well suited to localized or detailed spray work, give quick coverage of large surfaces, produce a smooth coating, facilitate the application of thin layers and may be manipulated to near pin-point accuracy for the application of coating materials. Spraying transparent coatings is usually considered to be heavy duty use of such equipment.

The choice of air brush for spraying transparent coatings is a matter of personal preference, but when purchasing equipment the primary working parts of the head (cap, tip and needle) should be examined to ensure that these parts have been manufactured to a high standard. The size and shape of the areas that the air brush will be used to retouch should be considered. The ability to produce very fine detail may be less important than the ability to deliver varnish solutions. Although working parts in the head of the airbrush may need periodic replacement, the body of a well maintained airbrush will last a lifetime if the airbrush is cleaned thoroughly after every use and oiled periodically. The spray pattern of an airbrush should be circular and symmetrical. Different needles and heads may be used to adjust the shape and size of the spray. As with spray guns, the needle is adjusted within the cone to reduce or increase the flow of varnish. Although most problems are caused by the operator, either by faulty technique or poor maintenance of equipment, faults in spray pattern will occur when the washer in the head wears out or if the needle is bent or damaged. As with spray guns, a black tile may be used as a test surface for transparent coatings to assess whether the correct adjustments have been made, that spray technique is correct and that the level of gloss is satisfactory.

Williams (1983) gave clear and detailed instructions on how airbrushes work, preparation and assembly, problems that are commonly encountered, cleaning and application techniques. Textbooks on air brushing are regularly produced for the graphic arts market (e.g. Owen and Sutcliffe, 1988).

Spray equipment used with compressed air should have three additional devices – a dehumidifier, a pressure regulator and a pressure gauge. The dehumidifier removes droplets of water formed by condensation when the air is compressed. A pressure regulator will maintain pressure from day to day and is used to change the air pressure depending on the equipment that is being used. Many compressors have a built-in pressure gauge for checking the air pressure.

# Bibliography

Ackroyd, P. and Keith, L. (2000) The restoration and reconstruction of Lorenzo Monaco's Coronation of the Virgin, in *Filling and Retouching*, Conference Preprints, Association of British Picture Restorers, pp. 14–18

Angelo Bros (1965) *Shellac*, Angelo Bros

Appelbaum, B. (1987) Criteria for treatment: reversibility, *JAIC*, 26(2), 65–73

Barclay, R. (1981) Wood consolidation on an eighteenth century English fire engine, *Studies in Conservation*, 26, 133–9

Barnes, N.F. (1939) A spectrophotometric study of artists' pigments, in *Technical Studies in the Field of the Fine Arts*, VII, 120–38

Bergeon, S. (1990) Science et patience ou la restoration des peintures, Editions de la Réunion des Musées Nationaux, Paris

Berger, G. (1990) Inpainting using PVA medium, in *Cleaning, Retouching and Coatings*, Conference Preprints, IIC, pp. 150–55

Bernstein, J. (1992) A review of varnish application fundamentals, in AIC Paintings Specialty Group, Conference Postprints, pp. 111–19

Bicchieri, M., Bortolani, M. and Veca, E. (1993) Characterisation of low-molecular-weight polyvinyl alcohol for restoration purposes, *Restaurator*, 14 (1), 11–29

Bigelow, D., Cornu, E., Landrey, G. and van Horne, C. (eds) (1991) *Gilded Wood, Conservation and History*, Sound View Press

Bomford, D. (1994) Changing tastes in the restoration of paintings, in *Restoration: Is It Acceptable?* British Museum Occasional Paper No. 99, pp. 33–40

Bourdeau, J. (1989) An examination of the barrier properties of selected ultraviolet absorbers within acrylic surface coatings, in *Papers presented at the fourteenth Conservation Training Programs Annual Conference*, Buffalo State College, NY, pp. 41–61

Bourdeau, J. (1990) A further examination of the barrier properties of Tinuvin 327 ultraviolet absorber in the protection of dammar films, in *Cleaning, Retouching and Coatings*, Conference Preprints, IIC, pp. 165–67

Bourdeau, J. (1996) Additives: phenolics, antioxidants, stabilisers and UV absorbers, in W. Samet (compiler) (1998), *Painting Conservation Catalogue: Varnish and Surface Coatings*, AIC Paintings Specialty Group, pp. 213–20

Brewer, A. (1994) A consolidation/filler system for insect damaged wood, in *Hamilton Kerr Institute Bulletin*, 2, 69–73

Brewer, J.A. (1991) Effect of selected coatings on moisture sorption of selected wood test panels, *Studies in Conservation*, 36, 9–23

Brill, T.B. (1980) *Light: Its Interaction with Art and Antiquities*, Plenum Press, pp. 63–77

Brommelle, N.S. and Smith, P. (eds) (1976) *The Conservation and Restoration of Pictorial Art*, Butterworths

Brommelle, N.S., Pye, E.M., Smith, P. and Thomson, G. (eds) (1984) *Adhesives and Consolidants*, Conference Preprints, IIC

Buckley, B.A. and Houp, H. (1996) Paraloid B72, in W. Samet (compiler) (1998), *Painting Conservation Catalogue: Varnish and Surface Coatings*, AIC Paintings Specialty Group, pp. 137–52

Cagle, C.V. (1973) *Handbook of Adhesive Bonding*, McGraw-Hill

Caley, T. (1990) Aspects of varnishes and the cleaning of oil paintings before 1700, in *Cleaning, Retouching and Coatings*, Conference Preprints, IIC, pp. 70–2

Caley, T. (1997) Drained water colour as a retouching medium, *The Picture Restorer*, Spring, pp. 5–8

Caley, T. (2000) A change in the formulation of Polyfilla Fine Surface, *Conservation News*, 71, 40

Carlson, S.M. and Schniewind, A.P. (1990) Residual solvents in wood consolidant composites, *Studies in Conservation*, 35, 26–32

Ciatti, M. (1990) Cleaning and retouching: an analytical review, *Cleaning, Retouching and Coatings*, Conference Preprints, IIC, pp. 59–62

Collings, T. (1990) A solution to solutions? Some elementary guidelines, *WAAC Newsletter*, 12 (3), 11–12

Craft, M.L. and Solz, J.A. (1998) Commercial vinyl and acrylic fill materials, *JAIC*, 37, 23–34

Dardes, K. and Rothe, A. (eds) (1998) *The Structural Conservation of Panel Paintings*, Getty Conservation Institute

de la Rie, R. (1987) The influence of varnishes on the

appearance of paintings, *Studies in Conservation*, 32, 1–13

de la Rie, R. (1988a) Polymer stabilisers: a survey with reference to possible applications in the conservation field, *Studies in Conservation*, 33 (1), 9–22

de la Rie, R. (1988b) Photochemical and thermal degradation of films of dammar resin, *Studies in Conservation*, 33 (2), 53–70

de la Rie, R. (1993) Polymer additives for synthetic low molecular weight varnishes, in *ICOM Committee for Conservation*, 10th Triennial Meeting, Washington DC, II, pp. 566–75

de la Rie, R. and McGlinchey, C. (1989) Stabilized dammar picture varnish, *Studies in Conservation*, 34, 137–46

de la Rie, R. and McGlinchey, C. (1990a) The effect of a hindered amine light stabiliser on the aging of dammar and mastic varnish in an environment free of ultraviolet light, in *Cleaning, Retouching and Coatings*, Conference Preprints, IIC, pp. 160–4

de la Rie, R. and McGlinchey, C. (1990b) New synthetic resins for picture varnishes, in *Cleaning, Retouching and Coatings*, Conference Preprints, IIC, pp. 168–73

de la Rie, R. and Shedrinsky, A.M. (1989) The chemistry of ketone resins and the synthesis of a derivative with increased stability and flexibility, *Studies in Conservation*, 34 (1), 9–19

de la Rie, R., Lomax, S.Q., Palmer, M., Glinsman, L.D. and Maines, C.A. (2000) An investigation of the photochemical stability of urea-aldehyde resin retouching paints: removability tests and colour spectroscopy, in *Tradition and Innovation*, Conference Preprints, IIC, pp. 51–9

De Witte, E., Florquin, S. and Goessens-Landrie, M. (1984) Influence of the modification of dispersions on film properties, *Adhesives and Consolidants*, Conference Preprints, IIC, pp. 32–35

Dorge, V. and Howlett, F.C. (eds) (1998) *Painted Wood: History and Conservation*, Getty Conservation Institute

Down, J.L., MacDonald, M.A., Tetrealt, J. and Williams, R.S. (1996) Adhesive testing at the Canadian Conservation Institute – an evaluation of selected poly(vinyl acetate) and acrylic adhesives, *Studies in Conservation*, 41, 19–44

Duffy, M.C. (1989) A study of acrylic dispersions used in the treatment of paintings, *JAIC*, 28, 67–77

Epley, B. (1996) The history of synthetic resin varnishes, in W. Samet (compiler) (1998), *Painting Conservation Catalogue: Varnish and Surface Coatings*, AIC Paintings Specialty Group, pp. 35–50

Feller, R.L. (1966) First description of dammar picture varnish translated, *Bulletin of the IIC American Group*, 12 (2), 72–81

Feller, R.L. (1978) Standards in the evaluation of thermoplastic resins, in ICOM Committee for Conservation, Preprints 5th Triennial Meeting, 78/6/4

Feller, R.F. and Wilt, M. (1990) *Evaluation of Cellulose Ethers for Conservation*, Getty Conservation Institute

Feller, R.L., Stolow, N. and Jones, E.H. (1985) *On Picture Varnishes and their Solvents*, Washington, DC, National Gallery of Art (first published 1959)

Fisher, S.L. (1996) MS2A in W. Samet (compiler) (1998), *Painting Conservation Catalogue: Varnish and Surface Coatings*, AIC Paintings Specialty Group, pp. 81–92

Gettens, R.J. and Stout, R. (1966) *Painting Materials: An Encyclopaedia*, Dover

Grattan, D.W. (1980) Consolidants for degraded and damaged wood in Proceedings of the Furniture and Wooden

Objects Symposium, CCI, National Museums of Canada, pp. 27–42

Green, J. and Seddon, J. (1981) A study of materials for filling losses in easel paintings and their receptiveness to casting of textures, in ICOM Committee for Conservation, Preprints 6th Triennial Meeting, Ottawa

Hackney, S. (1990) The removal of dirt from Turner's unvarnished oil sketches, in *Dirt and Pictures Separated*, Conference Postprints, UKIC, pp. 35–39

Hackney, S., Townsend, J. and Eastaugh, N. (eds) (1990) *Dirt and Pictures Separated*, Conference Postprints, UKIC

Hansen, E.F. (1994) The effects of solvent quality on some properties of thermoplastic amorphous polymers used in conservation, in *Material Issues in Art and Archaeology IV*, Materials Research Society, pp. 807–12

Hansen, E.F., Derrick, M.R., Schilling, M.R. and Garcia, R. (1991) The effects of solution application on some mechanical and physical properties of thermoplastic amorphous polymers used in conservation: poly(vinyl acetate)s, *JAIC*, 30, 203–13

Hansen, E.F., Lowinger, R. and Sadoff, E.T. (1993) Consolidation of porous paint in a vapour saturated atmosphere: a technique for minimizing changes in the appearance of powdering matte paint, *JAIC*, 32(1), 1–14

Hansen, E.F., Walston, S. and Bishop, M.H. (1996) Matte paint: its history and technology, analysis, properties and conservation treatment, *WAAC Newsletter*, 18 (2), 15–24

Hatchfield, P. (1986) Notes on a fill material for water sensitive objects, *JAIC*, 25, 93–5

Haupt, M., Dyer, D. and Hanlan, J. (1990) An investigation into three animal glues, *The Conservator*, 14, 10–16

Hayward, C. (1988) *Staining and Polishing*, Evans Bros, London/Unwin Hyman

Hebrard, M. and Small, S. (1991) Experiments in the use of polyvinyl alcohol as a substitute for animal glues in the conservation of gilded wood, in D. Bigelow, E. Cornu, G. Landrey and C. van Horne (eds), *Gilded Wood, Conservation and History*, Sound View Press, pp. 277–90

Horie, V. (1992) *Materials for Conservation*, Butterworth-Heinemann

Horton-Jones, D., Walston S. and Zounis, S. (1991) Evaluation of the stability, appearance and performance of resins for the adhesion of flaking paint on ethnographic objects, *Studies in Conservation*, 36, 203–21

Howells, R., Burnstock, A., Hedley, G. and Hackney, S. (1984) Polymer dispersions artificially aged, *Adhesives and Consolidants*, Conference Preprints, IIC, pp. 36–43

Jägers, E. and Jägers, E. (1999) Volatile binding media – useful tools for conservation, in *Reversibility – Does It Exist?* British Museum Occasional Paper No. 135

Jaworski, M. (1996) Equipment: varnishing brushes, in W. Samet (compiler) (1998), *Painting Conservation Catalogue: Varnish and Surface Coatings*, AIC Paintings Specialty Group, pp. 225–36

Johnston, R.M. and Feller, R.L. (1963) The use of differential spectral curve analysis in the study of museum objects, *Dyestuffs*, 44, 277–86

Kempski, M. (2000) Tempera retouching, case notes, in *Filling and Retouching*, Conference Preprints, Association of British Picture Restorers, pp. 45–9

Lafontaine, R.H. (1978) The effects of inhibitors on the removability of aged ketone resin N (BASF) film, *JIIC–CG*, 3 (2), 7–12

Lafontaine, R.H. (1979a) Decreasing the yellowing rate of

dammar varnish using antioxidants, *Studies in Conservation*, 24 (1), 14–22

Lafontaine, R.H. (1979b) Effect of Irganox 565 on the removability of dammar films, *Studies in Conservation*, 24 (4), 197–81

Lank, H. (1976) Picture varnishes formulated with resin MS2A, in *The Conservation and Restoration of Pictorial Art*, Butterworths, pp. 148–49

Lank, H. (1990) Egg tempera as a retouching medium, in *Cleaning, Retouching and Coatings*, Conference Preprints, IIC, pp. 156–7

Lawrence, C. (1990) The effects of solvent variations on long term properties of resin coatings, in *Papers presented at the Sixteenth Annual Art Conservation Training Programs Conference*, University of Delaware/Winterthur Museum Art Conservation Department, pp. 65–82

Leonard, M. (1990) Some observations on the use and appearance of two new synthetic resins for picture varnishes, in *Cleaning, Retouching and Coatings*, Conference Preprints, IIC, pp. 174–6

Leonard, M., Whitten, J., Gamblin, R. and de la Rie, R. (2000) Development of a new material for retouching, in *Tradition and Innovation*, Conference Preprints, IIC, pp. 111–13

Lomax, S.Q. (1995) How to calculate concentration of solutions, *AIC News*, January

MacKay, A. (1997) Treatment of a painted plaster sculpture: *The Bard* by Emmanuel Hahn, *J. IIC–C*, 22, 31–8

Malkin, A. (1983) Strength and long-term fracture of polymers formed from different solvents, *Polymer Process Engineering*, 1 (1), 93–108

Manson, J.A. and Sperling, L.H. (1976) *Polymer Blends and Composites*, Plenum Press

Masschelein-Kleiner, L. (1985) Ancient Binding Media, Varnishes and Adhesives, ICCROM

Mayer, R. (1991) *The Artist's Handbook of Materials and Techniques*, 5th edn, Faber and Faber

McLaren, K. (1983) *The Colour Science of Pigments and Dyes*, Adam Hilger

Mecklenburg, M.F. (1991) Some mechanical and physical properties of gilding gesso, in D. Bigelow, E. Cornu, G. Landrey and C. van Horne (eds), *Gilded Wood, Conservation and History*, Sound View Press, pp. 163–70

Mention, E. (1995) Mastic, in W. Samet (compiler) (1998), *Painting Conservation Catalogue: Varnish and Surface Coatings*, AIC Paintings Specialty Group, pp. 55–62

Merz-le, (1996) Dammar, in W. Samet (compiler) (1998), *Painting Conservation Catalogue: Varnish and Surface Coatings*, AIC Paintings Specialty Group, pp. 63–74

Michalski, S. and Dignard, C. (1997) Ultrasonic misting. Part 1, experiments on appearance change and improvement in bonding, *JAIC*, 36, 109–26

Michalski, S., Dignard, C., van Handel, L. and Arnold, D. (1998) The ultrasonic mister: applications in the consolidation of powdery paint on wooden artifacts, in V. Dorge and F.C. Howlett (eds), *Painted Wood: History and Conservation*, Getty Conservation Institute, pp. 498–513

Mills, J.S. and Smith, P. (eds) (1990) *Cleaning, Retouching and Coatings*, Conference Preprints, IIC

Mills, J. and White, R. (1977) Natural resins of art and archaeology: their sources, chemistry and identification, *Studies in Conservation*, 22

National Gallery of Washington (1998) *Synthetic Low Molecular Weight Resins Information Sheet*, National Gallery of Art, Washington

Nielson, L.E. (1966) Simple theory of stress–strain properties of filled polymers, *Journal of Applied Polymer Science*, 10 (1), 99

Ocon, N. and Miller, D. (1996) Spray varnishing equipment, in W. Samet (compiler) (1998), *Painting Conservation Catalogue: Varnish and Surface Coatings*, AIC Paintings Specialty Group, pp. 237–48

Oddy, A. and Carroll, S. (eds) (1999) *Reversibility – Does it Exist?* British Museum Occasional Paper No. 135

Owen, P. and Sutcliffe, J. (1988) *The Manual of Airbrushing*, Thames and Hudson

Perry, R.A. (2000) Retouching damaged modern art, in *Filling and Retouching*, Conference Preprints, Association of British Picture Restorers, pp. 19–22

Petukhova, T. and Bonadies, S. (1993) Sturgeon glue for painting consolidation in Russia, *JAIC*, 32, 23–31

Phenix, A. (1992a) Solvents for Paraloid B–72, *Conservation News*, 48, 21–3

Phenix, A. (1992b) Solvents for Paraloid B–72, *Conservation News*, 49, 23–5

Phenix, A. (1993) Solvents for Paraloid B–72, *Conservation News*, 50, 39–40

Piena, H. (2001) Regalrez in furniture conservation, *JAIC*, 40, 59–69

Raft, K. (1985) A preliminary report on the possibility of using bleached beeswax to improve the resolubility of picture varnishes based on polycyclohexanones, *Studies in Conservation*, 30, 143–4

Ramsay, L. (2000) An evaluation of Italian retouching techniques, *Filling and Retouching*, Conference Preprints, Association of British Picture Restorers, pp. 10–13

Ream, J.D. (1995) Observations on the penetration of two consolidants applied to insecure gouache on paper, in *The Book and Paper Group Annual*, 14, 27–40

Rodwell, D.F.G. (1984) Ageing of wood adhesives – loss of strength with time, *Building Research Establishment Information Paper*, No. 8/84, Building Research Establishment, Glasgow, UK

Sakuno, T. and Schniewind, A.P. (1990) Adhesive qualities of consolidants for deteriorated wood, *JAIC*, 29, 33–44

Samet, W. (1997) General application techniques, in W. Samet (compiler) (1998), *Painting Conservation Catalogue: Varnish and Surface Coatings*, AIC Paintings Specialty Group, pp. 251–72

Samet, W. (1998a) The philosophy of aesthetic reintegration: paintings and painted furniture, in V. Dorge and F.C. Howlett (eds), *Painted Wood: History and Conservation*, Getty Conservation Institute, pp. 412–23

Samet, W. (compiler) (1998b) *Painting Conservation Catalogue: Varnish and Surface Coatings*, AIC Paintings Specialty Group

Schaffer, E. and Brisebois, F. (1974) Inexpensive homemade vacuum chamber for impregnation, *Studies in Conservation*, 19 (2), 91–6

Schniewind, A.P. (1987) What goes up must come down ... but is it reversible, in AIC Wooden Artifacts Group, Conference Papers, Vancouver, BC, pp. 107–117

Schniewind, A.P. (1988) On the reversibility of consolidation treatments of deteriorated wood with soluble resins, in AIC Wooden Artifacts Group, Conference Papers, New Orleans

Schniewind, A.P. (1990) Consolidation of dry archaeological wood by impregnation with thermoplastic resins, *Archaeological Wood Properties, Chemistry, and Preservation*, Advances in Chemistry Series No. 225,

American Chemical Society, Washington, DC, pp. 362–71

Schniewind, A.P. (1998) Consolidation of wooden panels in V. Dorge and F.C. Howlett (eds), *Painted Wood: History and Conservation*, Getty Conservation Institute, pp. 87–107

Schniewind, A.P. and Arganbright, D.G. (1984) Coatings and their effect on dimensional stability of wood, *WAAC Newsletter*, 6 (2), 2–5

Schniewind, A.P. and Eastman, P.Y. (1994) Consolidant distribution in deteriorated wood treated with soluble resins, *JAIC*, 33, 246–55

Schniewind, A.P. and Kronkright, D.P. (1984) Strength evaluation of deteriorated wood treated with consolidants, *Adhesives and Consolidants*, IIC, 146–50

Shelton, C. (1996) The use of Aquazol-based gilding preparations, in AIC Wooden Artifacts Group, Conference Papers, Virginia

Staniforth, S. (1985) Retouching and colour matching: the restorer and metamerism, *Studies in Conservation*, 30, 101–11

Stein, R., Kimmel, J., Marincola, M. and Klemm, F. (2000) Observations on cyclododecane as a temporary consolidant for stone, *JAIC*, 39, 355–69

Stone, T.G. (1998) Artifacts revisited: the evaluation of old treatments, *Canadian Association for Conservation of Cultural Property*, 24th Annual Conference, Abstracts

Swicklik, M., Berger, M. and Berger, G. (1997) UVS (ultraviolet stabilised) finishing and matte varnishes, in W. Samet (compiler) (1998), *Painting Conservation Catalogue: Varnish and Surface Coatings*, AIC Paintings Specialty Group, pp. 129–32

Thomson, G. (1957) Some picture varnishes, *Studies in Conservation*, 3, 64–78

Thomson, G. (1988) *The Museum Environment*, Butterworths

Thornton, J. (1991a) Minding the gap: filling losses in gilded and decorated surfaces, *Gilding and Surface Decoration*, Conference Postprints, UKIC, pp. 12–17

Thornton, J. (1991b) The use of non-traditional gilding methods and materials in conservation, in D. Bigelow, E. Cornu, G. Landrey and C. van Horne (eds), *Gilded Wood, Conservation and History*, Sound View Press, pp. 217–28

Thornton, J. (1993) The history, technology and conservation of architectural papier mâché, *JAIC*, 32, 165–76

Thornton, J. (1998) A brief history and review of the early practice and materials of gap-filling in the West, *JAIC*, 37, 3–22

Vagts, L. (1996) Paraloid B–67, in W. Samet (compiler) (1998), *Painting Conservation Catalogue: Varnish and Surface Coatings*, AIC Paintings Specialty Group, pp. 153–60

van der Reyden, D. and Williams, D. (1986) The technology and conservation treatment of a nineteenth century English 'Papier-Mâché' chair, AIC Wooden Artifacts Group, Conference Papers, Chicago

Von Endt, D.W. and Baker, M.T. (1991) The chemistry of filled animal glue systems, in D. Bigelow, E. Cornu, G. Landrey and C. van Horne (eds), *Gilded Wood, Conservation and History*, Sound View Press, pp. 155–62

Walch, K. and Koller, J. (1997) *Baroque and Rococo Lacquers*, Arbeitshefte Des Bayerischen Landesamtes Für Denkmalpflege

Wang, Y. and Schniewind, A.P. (1985) Consolidation of deteriorated wood with soluble resins, *JAIC*, 24(2), 77–91

Webb, M. (1994) An examination of fill materials for use with lacquer objects, *Lacquerwork and Japanning*, Conference Postprints, UKIC, pp. 30–35

Webb, M. (1998) Four Japanned cabinets: a variety of techniques, in V. Dorge and F.C. Howlett (eds), *Painted Wood: History and Conservation*, Getty Conservation Institute, pp. 328–36

Wermuth, J.A. (1990) Simple and integrated consolidation systems for degraded wood, *Archaeological Wood: Properties, Chemistry, and Preservation*, Advances in Chemistry Series, No. 225, American Chemical Society, pp. 301–59

Whitmore, P.M., Moran, D. and Bailie, C. (1999) Shrinkage stresses in art and conservation coatings based on synthetic polymers, *JAIC*, 38, pp. 429–41

Whitten, J. (1995a) Regalrez 1094: properties and uses, *WAAC Newsletter*, 17 (1), 11–12

Whitten, J. (1995b) Low molecular weight resins for picture varnishes, in AIC Paintings Specialty Group Postprints, AIC

Whitten, J. (1998) Notes for Varnish Symposium, Liverpool, UK

Whitten, J. and Proctor, R. (1996) Regalrez 1094, in W. Samet (compiler) (1998), *Painting Conservation Catalogue: Varnish and Surface Coatings*, AIC Paintings Specialty Group, pp. 109–16

Wilcox, M. (1989) *Blue and Yellow Don't Make Green: A New Approach to Colour Mixing for Artists*, William Collins

Williams, N. (1983) *Porcelain Repair and Restoration*, British Museum Publications

Wolbers, R. (1996) Matting agents, in W. Samet (compiler) (1998), *Painting Conservation Catalogue: Varnish and Surface Coatings*, AIC Paintings Specialty Group, p. 221

Wolbers, R., McGinn, M. and Duerbeck, D. (1998) Poly(2-ethyl-2-oxazoline): a new conservation consolidant, in V. Dorge and F.C. Howlett (eds), *Painted Wood: History and Conservation*, Getty Conservation Institute, pp. 514–28

Zuccari, F. (1997) Use of the mouth atomiser to varnish paintings, in W. Samet (compiler) (1998), *Painting Conservation Catalogue: Varnish and Surface Coatings*, AIC Paintings Specialty Group, pp. 249–50

# 13

# Conserving transparent coatings on wood

## 13.1  Introduction to transparent finishes

Transparent finishes were applied to furniture to saturate the colour of the wood and offer some protection for the wood against dirt and grime. The materials used to make transparent coatings for wood vary from region to region and country to country. The finishes applied to vernacular furniture may differ from that found in bourgeois or court furniture. Examples of wooden objects with an intact original transparent varnish are unusual. Transparent surfaces on wood have been viewed in the past primarily in terms of the function of the object. Aged varnished wood surfaces were often planed, scraped or sanded in preparation for refinishing. In some cases the poor survival of transparent varnishes on wood can be ascribed to materials included in their formulation. Colophony, for example, was often used as an additive to transparent varnishes for wood. Although colophony initially reduced the brittleness of the coating, acidic components have a tendency to crystallize and contribute to the degradation of the varnish. Few of the surviving examples of varnished wood have been analysed. Results of research that has been undertaken, e.g. Walch and Koller (1997), have thrown doubt on much received wisdom.

Whilst the artist or craftsperson may have intended a coating to be expendable, transparent coatings on historic and decorated surfaces are rarely perceived this way by the collector, curator or conservator. This inevitably complicates the selection of a conservation treatment. All natural resins oxidize and yellow with time. In contrast to easel paintings conservation, where aged and yellowed varnish is considered unsightly and usually removed, much of the patination that is so valued on historic furniture is often contained within an aged transparent finish. The deterioration of coatings on wood is inevitable but they are an important aspect of the object and may be conserved even when badly damaged. Too often the only options considered are those of leaving a coating untreated or largely removing it. These extremes are only two of many possibilities that may be available when conservation options are reviewed. Removal of an intact but discoloured original finish will significantly reduce both the historical and monetary value of an article of furniture. In general, therefore, furniture conservators and many restorers make strenuous efforts to preserve original aged transparent coatings.

Conservation of transparent surfaces may draw on traditional materials and techniques for finishing furniture. To some extent traditional finishing remains within a craft tradition with the result that authors and practitioners vary in their varnish formulations and nuances of technique. The conservator should apply both an open mind and a critical approach to traditional finishing techniques – there is much to be learned but much also that is not appropriate to ethical conservation practice.

In the past, the application of protective and decorative coatings to furniture was the province of both cabinetmakers and specialist finishers. Cabinetmakers often opted for finishes that were easy to apply and imparted a degree of protection. Historically this may have meant the use of wax, oil, oil–resin or resin varnishes whilst modern cabinetmakers often rely on self-levelling spray finishes such as nitrocellulose and catalysed lacquers. Complex decorative finishes required a wide knowledge of materials and a greater degree of skill. Wood finishing recipes dating from the twelfth century may be found in translations of the work of Theophilis (Dodwell, 1961; Hawthorne and Smith, 1963). The finishing of wood panelling and furniture is mentioned in many historic treatises, including Sheraton (1803), and became the subject of specialist publications with the oft-reprinted and plagiarized *Cabinetmaker's Guide* of 1827 (Mussey, 1987). Twentieth century publications on wood finishing such as Baron (1987), Frank (1981), Hayward (1988) and Oughton (1982) are regularly supplemented by books published for the amateur enthusiast. Information on historical aspects of transparent finishes can be found in Brachert (1978–9), Mussey (1980, 1982a,b), Penn (1966), Walch (1993) and Walch and Koller (1997). Barnes (1938) discusses the chemistry of shellac, whilst Mills and White (1977) discuss the chemistry of a variety of natural resins. A discussion of stains applied to wood furniture can be found in Baumeister *et al.* (1997), Roelop (1994) and Thornton (1998b). Dyes are the subject of specialist periodicals such as *Dyes in History and Archaeology* but articles may also be published in art history journals, e.g. Berrie and Lomax (1996/97), or in conservation literature, e.g. Keijzer (1988).

Many of the materials discussed below are potentially dangerous. *It is the responsibility of the conservator to be fully aware of the hazard presented and to take adequate precautionary measures.* A high standard of workshop and personal hygiene and appropriate health and safety precautions should be maintained when working with finishing materials.

### 13.1.1  Photochemical oxidation and patina

Patination in furniture may be defined as a desirable change in appearance brought about by time and use. It usually has several aspects, such as photochemical degradation of the wood surface and/or surface finish as well as wear and other evidence of use. The subject of patination is somewhat subjective. It is a concept much beloved in the antique trade

and there is undoubtedly an element of selective historicity, a belief that some changes are valid and some are not, associated with it. The more recent the change, the less likely it is to be perceived as patination rather than undesirable damage.

Any piece of furniture that has been in use for a significant period will exhibit wear on exposed surfaces such as arm rests or front stretcher rails, as well as that which results from the working of the piece, such as drawer runners. Surface wear may also develop as a result of regular wax polishing. Stains may be caused by wet vases or drinking glasses whilst ink-spots may be found on a writing surface. Burn marks, scratches and dents may all contribute to a natural worn appearance.

In general, patination is considered an integral part of the object and often adds monetary value as well as historical context. Natural wear is often very subtle in its effect on the overall appearance and can be difficult to simulate, a fact borne out by the large amounts of aptly named 'distressed' reproduction furniture.

### 13.1.2  Revivers

The use of revivers remains widespread in furniture restoration practice and texts and therefore deserves a brief comment here. 'Reviver' is a general term for a mixture of materials used to clean, resaturate surface colour and produce a soft sheen to the surface of everyday articles of furniture. Commercial revivers are available and contain a variety of ingredients – one popular British example contains xylene and methanol. A recipe mentioned by Mrs Beeton in the mid-nineteenth century, which remains in use in the restoration trade, recommended equal parts methylated spirits, turpentine, vinegar and linseed oil. The methylated spirits was intended to remove degraded varnish, the turpentine to remove greasy dirt, the vinegar to remove water-sensitive dirt whilst the linseed oil provided colour saturation and a low sheen to the 'revived' piece. Other recipes have added soap, metal polish or ammonia to the mixture. It is a basic tenet of conservation cleaning that the treatment should be as specific as possible. Traditional revivers are potentially very damaging and cannot be

**Figure 13.1** Detail of marquetry on a longcase clock (*c.*1700). Patchy darkening is a result of past treatment with linseed oil

recommended for conservation treatments because they may cause significant damage to, or loss of, an original coating. In addition, those that contain linseed oil can, in the long term, cause unsightly and sometimes irreversible disfiguration of a surface. The oil penetrates gaps in the varnish, for example along the outline of marquetry designs, or surface checks in the wood. As the oil dries, it darkens and crosslinks, creating patchy darker areas that can mar intricate designs (*Figure 13.1*).

## 13.2   Cleaning

The cleaning of varnished wooden surfaces has a long history. Seventeenth century sources refer to the removal of degraded varnishes and accretions of soot and grime from panelling using caustic solutions (Walch, 1997). Furniture conservators are usually more selective in their approach to cleaning. Care should be taken not to over-clean furniture, which can result in a significant reduction in the market value of an object. The owner or curator should always be consulted before a cleaning treatment is undertaken. The principles of cleaning tests are set out in section 11.1.5. Care should be taken to ensure that test areas are representative of the whole object. The cleaning test area/s should be examined under low magnification before and after the application of cleaning materials to assess the impact of treatment. In the absence of a micro-

scope, a jeweller's loupe can be used to examine the surface for changes, such as a reduction in gloss. Removal of surface dirt and wax may reveal a surface that has aged and become matte. In some cases alkaline pH or the inclusion of polar solvents in cleaning formulations may swell or partially dissolve many coatings, increasing roughness and thereby decreasing gloss.

Old transparent coatings are generally polar, oxidized and therefore slightly acidic materials with dirt and grime affixed to the surface. Different coating materials require a different cleaning approach. Although they are discussed as singular components below it is important to remember that many transparent coatings contain a combination of materials and treatment should be formulated accordingly. It may be necessary for the conservator to apply a protective coating to areas where the original coating has worn away in order to prevent penetration of cleaning solutions into the wood substrate or between the original coating and the substrate.

Wax finishes are thin and fragile by nature and can be distinguished by a low lustre appearance and solubility in hydrocarbon solvents. Soft wax polish, e.g. that based on pure beeswax, will accumulate dust and grime. Wax finishes may be surfaced-cleaned with a swab or cloth slightly dampened with water but exposure to other solvents will remove them. Applying a thin new wax finish is usually sufficient to rejuvenate an old wax finish.

Oil finishes, like wax, have a low lustre appearance and are non-fluorescent when viewed under UV. Once cured, drying oils are insoluble in hydrocarbon solvents and are swollen (but not dissolved) by alcohols and ketones. Oil finishes are usually thin and well integrated into the wood substrate although later coats, often a result of treatment with revivers, may produce a thick and sticky layer. Oils were used by pre-industrial as well as modern finishers – Sheraton (1803) describes the use of oil and brick dust as 'the general mode of polishing furniture'. Although Erhardt (1998) has asserted that the drying process for linseed oil is complete within three years, empirical evidence suggests that oil-based finishes continue to crosslink for many years. Photochemical oxidation will result in the oil becoming progressively harder and darker (see Mills and White (1994) for a description of the oxidation of drying oils). Dirt may become incorporated into the film structure as it crosslinks. Coatings with a significant oil content are sensitive to, and may be damaged by, aqueous solutions with a pH higher than 8.5, bases, polar organic and chlorinated solvents. Water may be used to clean an oil finish if it is applied sparingly on a damp swab or cloth and the surfaced is wiped immediately with a dry cloth. Although original intent should be a consideration in selecting a treatment, maintaining an oil finish with wax may be preferable to an irreversible re-oiling treatment.

Resinous coatings, e.g. sandarac or shellac, may appear matte, semi-matte or highly glossy depending on age and the use of matting agents or others dulling treatments. They are auto-fluorescent under UV, though the colour of the fluorescence varies according to the resin type/s and the age of the coating. Aged resinous coatings are usually insoluble in hydrocarbon solvents but may be dissolved by alcohols and ketones. In addition, resinous coatings are generally sensitive to elevated pH and polar organic solvents. The removal of dirt from natural resin varnishes that are in good condition is usually straightforward (*Figure 13.2*). Wax or greasy accretions may be removed with a swab dampened with an aliphatic or aromatic hydrocarbon solvent. It should be noted that these solvents will remove some synthetic resins. Cleaning may utilize a swab or cloth dampened with water followed immediately by wiping over with a soft dry cloth. Aqueous cleaning of resinous transparent coatings requires some care as the water molecules may diffuse into the coating and cause blooming. The risk of bloom increases with the degree of ageing of the varnish, exposure time and as the pH of the cleaning solution rises. Some very degraded natural resin surfaces may be partially soluble in water with a pH of only 8–8.5, a fact that has been exploited in varnish removal treatments (Wolbers *et al.*, 1990). The principles of aqueous cleaning are discussed in section 11.5. Blooming of resinous coatings is also often associated with long exposure to moisture or a combination of heat and moisture, for example if excess warmed

(a)                                         (b)

**Figure 13.2** Scanning electron microscopy (SEM) photomicrographs of an aged natural resin varnish (*a*) Before cleaning: accretions darken and obscure the mahogany substrate. (*b*) After cleaning: accretions have been removed and the original varnish remains intact

animal glue used to repair the wood substrate is left in contact with the varnished surface when the repair is cramped up.

Oleo-resinous varnishes were often employed where a hard-wearing surface was required and are particularly associated with the nineteenth century. Drying oils such as linseed or tung oil were used in combination with natural resins such as sandarac, mastic or gum elemi, with fossil resins such as copal or amber, or in combinations of these materials with the addition of colophony.

Limed finishes were created by scrubbing the surface of an open-grained timber such as oak or ash to accentuate and open the large pores associated with early seasonal growth. Traditionally, quick lime (calcium oxide) was dissolved in an equivalent quantity of water to produce highly alkaline slaked lime (calcium hydroxide). A thick mixture was rubbed into the surface of the wood and lodged in the large opened pores of the early wood. Excess was removed from the surface and the lime that remained in the pores created a striking decorative effect. The alkaline liming treatment may have had the additional purpose of disinfecting bare wooden surfaces. Over time the calcium hydroxide absorbs carbon dioxide from the atmosphere and reverts to calcium carbonate, commonly known as chalk. Other more complex chemical reactions may also occur between the alkaline lime and the acidic wood. Where a traditional lime has been used, it is unlikely that a transparent coating was applied. Later, it was more common to achieve a limed effect using grain filling materials that were sealed with a varnish.

Old uncoated liming may have been largely lost and what remains will be discoloured and water-sensitive. Consolidation with a colourless material such as isinglass, PVAC or Paraloid B72 may be necessary, although excessive gloss should be avoided (see section 16.6.8). It may be desirable to utilize a matte coating to protect remnants from dirt and grime. The surface coating should have different solubility parameters to the original material and any consolidant that has been applied.

## 13.3   Selective layer removal

The past practice of 'maintaining' furniture with regular revarnishing or oiling may result in timber or surface decoration becoming completely obscured under thick layers of darkened varnish. It is also possible that an object will have a coating that is historically and aesthetically inappropriate. Walch (1997) has discussed the nineteenth-century practice of applying a stand oil-based coating to varnished wood. In indirect light such coatings have a marked tendency to darken, whilst exposure to strong light may bleach them. They also have a tendency to 'alligator', a problem that is also associated with some oil–resin varnishes (see section 13.8). In addition, furniture with a transparent finish may have been maintained using a range of disparate materials, including waxes, revivers and oils. In some cases it may be possible to selectively remove upper varnish layers using methods outlined in Chapter 11. The selective removal of polyurethane varnish is described by Landrey *et al.* (1988).

A prerequisite to selective layer removal is the identification and characterization of the stratigraphy of the surface. Many conservators are limited to observing the auto-fluorescence

of a surface under a hand-held UV source (in combination with UV protective goggles) and establishing solubility parameters using solvent testing. Retouching and old repairs are often detectable under UV. Non-fluorescent materials, including dirt and grime, appear black under UV. The auto-fluorescence of modern coatings will be muted or blocked if UV absorbers have been included. Although some waxes are auto-fluorescent, e.g. paraffin (blue fluorescence) and carnauba (yellow-brown fluorescence), thin wax coatings on furniture are generally non-fluorescent under hand-held UV (Radley and Grant, 1954). Synthetic resins vary from no auto-fluorescence to blue-white or lavender. The auto-fluorescence of natural resins viewed under UV light may vary from greenish-white (usually associated with resins such as dammar and mastic) to a creamy-orange colour (sometimes associated with sandarac). Some aged synthetic resins may exhibit a greenish white auto-fluorescence. Shellac films that are comparatively young or have not been exposed to high levels of sunlight appear a distinctive bright orange when viewed under UV. The fluorescence of oriental lacquer varies from none, to muted orange to bright orange (see, for example, *Plate 2e*). Cellulose and many proteinaceous materials such as hide glue and keratin have a bright white auto-fluorescence.

Auto-fluorescence is an imprecise tool for identification. Coatings change as they age, particularly as a result of absorbing light energy. Photochemical degradation may result in a shift in the colour of the fluorescence observed. Whilst unaged shellac fluoresces orange, the fluorescence of shellac that has had long exposure to sunlight tends towards yellow-green (*Plate 5a*).

Solvent testing should proceed layer by layer when multiple layers of surface finish are present, as solubility may vary depending on the range of materials present in any one coating. Once the general character of the surface coating has been established, either by solvent testing, microscopy or instrumental analysis, a cleaning treatment can be devised. Attempting to remove all layers with a single solvent blend is, in most cases, the surface coating equivalent of attempting to dismantle furniture using a sledge hammer, i.e. unnecessarily destructive and inevitably damaging.

Identifying a historical progression of transparent coatings may shed light on the history of the object. Microscopy, utilizing both visible and UV light, is very helpful in assessing the stratigraphy (and therefore history) of transparent coatings. General characterizations may be made using UV microscopy, for example white fluorescence may indicate a plant resin, whilst orange fluorescence may indicate the presence of shellac. Identifying specific natural resins is virtually impossible without sophisticated analytical equipment such as gas chromatography coupled with mass spectroscopy (GC–MS). Analytical results may be complicated by the range of materials used in the original formulation and the contamination of earlier layers by later restoration coatings.

The chemical similarity of natural resin varnishes may make selective coating removal problematic or impossible. It may be possible to exploit differing polarity of coatings markedly different in age – a recent coating may be less (or more) polar than an aged coating lying below it. Drying oils become insoluble over time due to crosslinking and enzymes may offer an effective tool for their removal (Landrey, 1993).

## 13.4  Surface blemishes

### 13.4.1  Dents and scratches

Surface blemishes such as dents, bruises and burns may be accepted, patched or filled. Dents in unfinished wood may be steamed out using a damp cloth and warm iron. Such treatment on varnished wood will almost certainly result in damage to the surface finish.

Scratches that are part of the normal wear and tear associated with the use of furniture may not require treatment at all. Scratches on objects in museum collections may result from handling, transport or vandalism. Leaving vandalism untreated can attract more of the same and many museums have a policy of acting quickly to remove or disguise the effects of vandalism to reduce its reoccurrence.

The treatment for scratches will depend on the depth of the scratch. If the scratch is in the varnish and has not penetrated to the wood below, all that may be necessary is to degrease the surface with a non-polar solvent and apply varnish locally. Scratches that have penetrated through the varnish and into the wood are likely to be more obtrusive and may require intervention. Problems may occur if the surface of the wood is oxidized, in which case sealing the scratch with a varnish may darken it and make the scratch more obtrusive. In such cases a pigmented wax fill may be used, followed if necessary by further retouching and localized varnishing.

### 13.4.2  Watermarks

Exposing natural resin varnishes to water for an extended period will result in localized blanching or darkening followed by adhesive disbondment and loss of finish. Whatever the original cause of such a water mark, the treatment will depend on the length of time that has elapsed since exposure.

Fresh white water marks are characterized by the presence of moisture within the varnish. There are several methods to remove the moisture without removing the varnish. The application of a small amount of wax paste followed by vigorous buffing may be sufficient. A traditional method, called 'flashing off', can be used to remove fresh water marks from spirit-based varnishes such as shellac. This method involves using a cotton swab to apply a small amount of methylated spirits to the affected area, and then igniting the solvent on the surface. If too much solvent is applied, the heat generated will be sufficient to burn the varnish. Larger areas can be treated by setting the blanched surface so that it is vertical, applying the spirit in a vertical strip and lighting from the bottom (Hayward, 1988). An area should only be treated once in this way and should then be left to allow the varnish, which will be slightly softened by the heat, to harden off before any further treatment is undertaken. This is an effective remedy for fresh water marks but is a potentially dangerous practice. The use of a heated spatula, isolated from the surface by Melinex/Mylar, may be equally efficacious, if a little less spectacular.

Moisture is not present in all white water marks. The older the water mark, the less likely moisture will be present. Treatments of such marks rely on resaturating or abrading the area of damaged varnish. Camphorated oil has traditionally been used to resaturate old watermarks in varnish, often in conjunction with a mild abrasive. Abrasive creams, including metal polishes, have also been used to reduce old white water marks but such materials are not recommended for conservation treatments. Solvent applied to the blanched area and left to evaporate may remove such blemishes from spirit-based coatings but will probably also result in a slightly dulled appearance. Old water marks are often associated with loss of colour and finish and may require localized colour matching and varnish infilling.

Dark marks usually require an intrusive treatment or acceptance of the blemish. Colour matching from dark to light is usually problematic and requires either the use of pigments to hide the blemish or localized varnish removal, bleaching, colouring and revarnishing. A traditional treatment for such marks is the localized application of an acidic solution, such as oxalic or citric acid. However, it is common to see the surfaces of highly prized pieces of furniture with dark marks that have been left untreated. Historic furniture has usually served both an aesthetic and functional role. In many cases such marks are considered evidence of age and use, and are often viewed as a valid part of the history of the object.

### 13.4.3    In-filling varnish losses

The main reasons for infilling losses from resinous transparent coatings are aesthetics, protection against the accretion of grime and dirt, and to prevent further losses from vulnerable edges. It may be appropriate in some cases to leave areas that have worn away untouched. The decision whether to infill should be taken in the context of the object as a whole.

If an infill is desired, the first step is to degrease the area to be treated in order to remove wax, oily deposits or grime that may inhibit the adhesion of the new varnish. An aliphatic or aromatic hydrocarbon solvent can be used for this purpose, followed by water with the addition of a small proportion of industrial methylated spirits (IMS).

Either natural or synthetic resin varnish can be used for infilling (see section 13.7). In some cases it may be necessary to apply a stain or

pigment wash to adjust the colour of the infill. The surface of the substrate wood must be sealed before the application of any dye or pigment. Stains can be applied between thin layers of, or mixed in with, the in-fill varnish itself (see under section 13.5.6). Stains used to adjust an infill varnish should be selected for compatibility with the infill varnish, ease of application, light fastness and chemical stability. It is possible to utilize dyes with different solubility to the infilling varnish resin. Water stain, for example, may be applied after the surface of the wood has been sealed, and may be tamped, stippled or brushed dry. The stain can be sealed between thin layers of varnish. This technique allows the tone of a varnish infill to be adjusted gradually to match the surrounding surface. When spraying, airbrushing or using a French polishing rubber, there may be some overlap onto the undamaged adjacent surface and an isolating layer may be necessary.

## 13.5    Colour matching repairs to varnished wood

### 13.5.1    Introduction to colour matching processes

The principles of colour matching are discussed in section 12.3.2. This section discusses the materials and techniques that are specific to matching repairs to a varnished wood surface. As is the case with finishing a newly made piece of furniture, colour matching a repair may be a multi-stage process. Although it may be possible in some cases to complete these processes in a day or less, it is usually necessary to allow drying time between them. Although the cumulative time required may be relatively short, it is usually spread out over several days or even weeks.

The degree of colour matching that will be required must be decided on a case-by-case basis. In some cases the aesthetic integrity of an object may require that a repair to a visually prominent section blends in with the surrounding surface and does not disrupt the overall presentation of the object. In other cases it may be desirable to leave a repair or replacement component unmatched, for example an interior component that is not normally seen, so that it can be more easily identified during examination.

Metamerism is a term used in colour technology to describe the effect when two colours that match each other under one light source differ when viewed under a second light source. The problem of metamerism and pigments is discussed in section 12.3.2. Metamerism may occur when colour matching wood, not only as a result of changes in the light source but the direction in which light is reflected from the surface. A piece of wood viewed from one direction may appear to be a light colour but when viewed obliquely or from the opposite direction the same area will appear to be dark. This is particularly evident when viewing timbers such as figured mahogany or satinwood, which derive their striped decorative effect from an alternating grain direction. The light and dark areas of such woods reverse according to the viewer's position and the direction of the light source. The direction light will strike the object and the position of the observer when the object is returned to display must be replicated when retouching wood with pigments and dyes.

Colour matching transparent surfaces on wood may require the subtraction of colour from replacement wood (bleaching). It may be necessary to add colorants in order to match the repair to the original surface. Addition colorants may be opaque pigments or translucent stains. When light strikes an object it will be transmitted, reflected or absorbed thus each layer of pigment or stain that is applied during colour matching will have some effect on the final result. Pigments and stains may be used in a variety of binding media, and may be applied separately or combined as desired. The permanence or colourfastness of materials varies widely and literature from the manufacturer or supplier should be consulted.

A variety of materials and techniques are discussed in general texts on the restoration of antique furniture (Bennett, 1990; Rodd, 1976). Whilst the traditional furniture restorer has relied on materials that vary in their photo-chemical stability, most notably shellac and spirit-soluble stains, a range of more stable materials are available for conservation colour matching. In situations where furniture was exposed to a significant amount of UV light and was in use, periodic refinishing was inevitable. As the colour of the surrounding wood changes with exposure to light, retouched repairs become progressively more obtrusive. Whilst traditional finishers have often tried to avoid the use of fugitive stains in their work, in this context lightfastness was less important than the ability of the surface finish to withstand regular use. With the exclusion of UV light from some domestic and most museum environments, the need for photo-chemically stable retouching materials and binding media has become increasingly important.

The process of matching a repair involves surface preparation, staining, grain filling, colour matching, coating and occasionally distressing. Not all repairs require all these steps but this provides a convenient way of ordering the following discussion.

### 13.5.2 Surface preparation

The purpose of surface preparation is to ensure that the surface of the wood repair is free from blemishes and defects, and to remove oil, wax, dirt and other contaminants that might interfere with the application or subsequent performance of the finish that is to be applied. Materials used to abrade wood are discussed in section 10.1.12. The decision whether to match original tool or abrasion marks may depend on ethical considerations,

**Figure 13.3** Detail of a Victorian tea caddy, rosewood veneer on pine. This is an example of poor workmanship. A patch has been fitted to replace the lost original veneer. In levelling the patch, original finish has been removed from the adjacent surface. As a result, the patch and adjacent area must be separately colour matched

the size of the repair or its aesthetic impact on the object as a whole. Photochemical oxidation may have occurred in both the surface finish and the upper layers of the varnished wood. The process of surface preparation should *never* result in the removal of finish or wood from the original surface that abuts the repair. Such removal is evidence of poor technique and will inevitably complicate any colour matching by creating a fresh and distinct area of damage around the repair (*Figure 13.3*).

Good surface preparation is essential to the successful matching of repairs because no amount of fine colour matching will disguise a poorly prepared substrate. Care should be taken to ensure that repairs are neither proud of nor below the level of the surrounding surface. Gaps around the repair will collect stain and coating materials applied during colour matching and result in a dark outline. It may be necessary to fill gaps with a stopping material before colour matching commences.

### 13.5.3   Materials for colour matching wood repairs

#### Precautionary measures
The colour of a new part can be changed by the subtraction (bleaching) and/or addition (staining) of colour. Bleaches and chemical stains cause a colour change by reacting with components in the wood. Many have been used in the past by furniture restorers but they tend to be hazardous materials (e.g. some may cause blindness if splashed in the eyes) and health and safety precautions must be taken if they are to be used. *It is the responsibility of the conservator to be fully aware of the hazard presented and to take adequate precautionary measures.*

These materials are usually dissolved in water and applied to bare wood and as a result tend to raise the grain. It is advisable to pre-treat an area with water, allow it to dry and denib the raised grain before such treatments are undertaken. All chemical bleaches and stains require care in handling to prevent damage to the object or injury to the user. Eye and skin protection is essential. Staining and bleaching effects will be dependent in part on the type and colour of the wood being treated. Once bleaching or chemical staining has produced the desired colour change, excess is rinsed from the surface of the wood (e.g. with water applied with a swab or rag) and the surface left to dry. It may be necessary to leave the surface untouched for several days to ensure that volatile components have evaporated completely.

#### Bleaches
The term bleaching is used to describe a process that subtracts colour from wood. Restorers have used chemical bleaches over the years in ways that are not acceptable to many conservators today. Bleach can present problems for the longevity of colour matching or surface finishes if it is not completely neutralized or rinsed from the surface. In some cases, however, removing or reducing the existing colour of repair wood may be necessary in order to match it to an aged and faded surface.

Bleaching using direct sunlight is used by some textile conservators and may have some applications in furniture conservation. Direct sunlight may modify the colour of some photosensitive woods comparatively quickly, for example purpleheart (amaranth). It may be useful for a new component that can be light bleached separately from the object to which it will be attached, such as finials or a drawer front. The use of light for bleaching requires advance planning as it may take many weeks, although a strong UV lamp may bleach out colour from a freshly exposed wood surface in a matter of days.

Repairs to a surface must be shaped and levelled and are therefore usually bleached in situ. All chemical bleaches are applied in aqueous solutions and there is a danger that capillary action may draw the bleach solution under the surface coating of adjacent wood, damaging the coating and bleaching original material. If an entire component is to be replaced it should be bleached before it is attached to the object. If a large area is to be bleached it may be necessary to protect other surfaces on the object from inadvertent splashes by applying a water-resistant coating or Parafilm® (*Figure 13.4*).

Bleaches will attack many bristle brushes and are therefore usually applied to large

**Figure 13.4** Parafilm® is a thin waxy film. It can be pressed into contact with the surface adjacent to a patch to protect it from bleach. It is resistant to water and polar solvents such as alcohols and ketones but will be dissolved by many hydrocarbons

$-CH=CH-CH=CH-CH=O$ $\quad+\quad$ $HO_2^-$

conjugated chromophoric system $\quad$ plus $\quad$ hydro-peroxide ions

(alternating double and single bonds)

$$-CH=CH-CH-CH-CH=O$$
$$\diagdown\;\diagup$$
$$O$$

conjugated double bond broken and oxygen gained

In oxidation reactions during bleaching, the conjugated chromophore in the cellulose is disrupted, a double bond is broken in a reaction with the oxidant, resulting in loss of colour

(a)

$\sim CH=CH-CH=CH-CH=CH-CH=O$ $\quad+ H + H$

conjugated chromophoric system $\quad$ plus two hydrogen atoms

$$\sim CH=CH-CH_2-CH_2-CH=CH-CH=O$$

conjugated double bond broken, hydrogen molecules gained

(b)

**Figure 13.5** (*a*) Oxidation reaction; (*b*) reduction reaction

areas with disposable grass type brushes. Bleach may be applied to small areas with a swab. Thorough rinsing with water was the traditional method for removing bleach solutions but some practitioners recommend slightly acidic rinses for non-volatile alkaline bleaching solutions (sodium hypochlorite or those that utilize sodium hydroxide as a pre-treatment) and alkaline rinses for non-volatile acidic bleaching solutions (oxalic acid). Research by German (1989) indicated that residues of oxalic acid crystals remained in the pores of wood that had been rinsed with ammonium hydroxide.

Bleaches work by oxidation and reduction reactions. A simple definition of oxidation is a reaction in which oxygen is gained or hydrogen is lost (*Figure 13.5a*). Oxidation bleaches include hypochlorite and hydrogen peroxide. The oxidative bleaching of wood in sunlight is a result of the combination of atmospheric oxygen and energy from sunlight. Reduction reactions are those in which an oxygen atom is lost or two hydrogen atoms are gained. In a typical example of a reduction reaction during the bleaching of cellulose (i.e. wood), the conjugated chromophore in the cellulose molecule is disrupted and becomes a non-chromophoric system (*Figure 13.5b*). Reduction and oxidation always occur together. The reagent is oxidized when the object is reduced, or vice versa. The reaction is therefore often described as a redox reaction.

Household bleach is usually a 5% aqueous solution of sodium hypochlorite and has a characteristic chlorine smell. It is occasionally used as a weak bleach on wood and is followed by an aqueous rinse.

Proprietary two-pack bleaches consist of an alkali, usually sodium hydroxide (part A), and hydrogen peroxide (part B). An alkaline solution is used because hydrogen peroxide ($H_2O_2$) forms the reactive hydro-peroxide ions ($HO_2^-$) necessary for oxidative bleaching ($H_2O_2$ + $OH^-$ $\rightleftharpoons$ $HO_2^-$ + $H_2O$) (*Figure 13.5a*). Part A is applied to the surface and allowed to penetrate fully, which results in a darkening of the wood. The surface should not be allowed to dry and fresh solution should be applied if necessary to prevent this. Part A is left for two to fifteen minutes before part B is brushed liberally onto the surface. For maximum effect, part B may be left to dry and then the surface rinsed. Two or three repeat treatments usually remove most of the colour from most woods. Any residue that remains after rinsing will attack colouring and finishing materials from below and cause accelerated degradation of the wood. The surface is therefore rinsed with a dilute acetic acid solution (~10%) to neutralize any residual non-volatile alkali. This should then be followed by an aqueous rinse to remove as much acetic acid and hydrogen peroxide as possible. Both these materials are quite tenacious, however, and a small residue will remain. The hydrogen peroxide used in part B is chemically unstable and commercial solutions are often slightly acidic to slow down decomposition. Supplies should be purchased in small quantities as required.

Bennett (1990) recommends a bleaching procedure that produces a less radical change than would be produced by the use of a two part bleach according to the manufacturer's instructions. Part A is applied as usual but part B is left on the surface for only a third to half the application time of part A. At the end of this time, any excess liquid on the surface is wiped away along the grain with a clean rag and a concentrated solution of oxalic acid is applied. The oxalic acid reacts very quickly and is then removed with a damp rag before a 33% solution of acetic acid is applied. The surface is then rinsed two or three times with water and allowed to air dry thoroughly.

Hydrogen peroxide is sometimes sold under the trade name 'Superbleach', which consists of an aqueous solution of hydrogen peroxide. Eight parts of this hydrogen peroxide (35%) is mixed with 1 part ammonia (35%/880) in an open container. Hydrogen peroxide produces up to thirty times its own volume of oxygen as it reacts with the ammonia and the pressure of this gas in a closed container may cause it to explode. The solution is applied immediately to the wood and left there for up to fifteen minutes. Treatment may be repeated if necessary before the surface is rinsed with water. Bleached wood should be left for at least seventy-two hours before the application of other surface coatings or colorants. Since both components are volatile, other methods of neutralization are unnecessary.

Hydrogen peroxide alone may be used, but the absence of an alkali means the hydrogen peroxide is not protonated and the bleaching reaction will therefore be limited. It can be obtained in a variety of concentrations (3%, 35%, 50%, 70% and 90%) in water, but the 35% solution is usually used for bleaching timber. It may be applied to the surface of the timber and left until the desired colour change has taken place. It is neutralized by an aqueous rinse.

It should be noted that hydrogen peroxide will decompose explosively in the presence of acids, platinum, silver, copper, chromium, iron, zinc, lead or manganese, especially in conditions of alkaline pH, and that highly concentrated solutions of hydrogen peroxide (65%) may ignite combustible materials. Hydrogen peroxide is unstable and will decompose if exposed to heat or light.

### Addition of colour to wood repairs: pigments, lakes and stains

*Pigments*   Pigments are insoluble in organic solvents and water and vary in their lightfastness. Pigment properties are listed in *Table 5.3*. They may be classified into three types – inorganic, synthetic inorganic and organic pigments. Inorganic or mineral pigments include the native earths, such as ochre, umber and sienna, and calcined native earths including burnt umber, burnt sienna etc. Synthetic inorganic pigments include cadmium yellow, zinc oxide, titanium oxide etc. Organic pigments may be derived from vegetable sources, such as gamboge, indigo and madder, animal sources such as Indian yellow and cochineal or may be manufactured synthetics. Some pigments present a health hazard and the supplier's or manufacturer's material safety data sheet should be consulted. Some traditional colorants for wood are described in *Table 5.4*. In a few cases chemical reactions with atmospheric pollution may cause pigments to change colour, for example lead white may blacken if exposed to atmospheric hydrogen sulphide.

*Lakes*   Lakes were made by precipitating an organic colouring material or a dye onto an insoluble and inert base. Traditionally the base was aluminium hydrate or calcium sulphate but later a range of materials, including barytes, tin oxide and zinc oxide were used.

*Stains*   Stains (and dyes) are colouring materials that may be dissolved in a solvent (e.g. water or alcohol) and impart a transparent colour that does not obscure the substrate material. Furniture restorers have traditionally classified stains according to their solubility and, given the complexity of modern dye chemistry, this convention will be used below. The solubility of a stain was considered as part of an overall finishing strategy. If, for example, an oil varnish was to be applied, then the use of an oil stain would have been inappropriate as the stain would have been partially redissolved and redistributed during varnishing. Stain can be applied in wax, but such stains often share the weak colourfastness properties of oil and white spirit-soluble stains. Modern paint manufacturers often use 'microfine' pigments in wood staining preparations. These pigments will obscure the figure and grain of the wood if applied too thickly.

Stains applied to wood are usually divided into two categories. First, chemical stains, which change the colour of the wood by chemical reaction, and secondly those stains that are delivered in a solvent, including water stains, spirit stains, oil and NGR (non-grain raising) stains. The manufacture of aniline dyes has proven problematic from a health and safety perspective and these materials have largely been replaced by materials that are less toxic to produce.

The grain structure of a wood surface will influence the uptake of stain. Grain of varying density, direction or anatomical function (e.g. rays), for example, will absorb stain differentially. End-grain absorbs more stain, and this may be problematic on turned components. If this effect is unwanted it will be necessary to seal the surface before the stain is applied. A generous coat of shellac, sanding sealer or other coating may be applied, allowed to dry and then lightly abraded. The sealer will prevent the stain biting into the end-grain whilst the abrasion will ensure that bare wood is exposed to take the stain. The stain may then be applied to the wood, allowed to dry and a surface coating applied.

*Chemical stains* Potassium bi- or di- chromate ($K_2Cr_2O_7$) is supplied as an orange water-soluble powder. It is toxic in liquid and powder forms, whilst the powder is a suspected carcinogen (McCann, 1979). Traditionally a concentrated solution was prepared and thinned as required, but 14 grams (half an ounce) of crystals dissolved in a litre of water (approx. 2 pints) should be sufficient as the stain will operate over a wide concentration range. The stain should be applied evenly to the wood, any excess removed with a clean dry rag and the surface allowed to dry

naturally. Using a saturated solution will result in crystal formation on the wood as the stain dries. This stain reacts with tannic acid in the wood and was traditionally used to enrich the colour of mahogany, as it darkens the wood and imparts a reddish-orange hue. Oak was darkened but the stain tended to produce a greenish quality and softwoods tended not to take the stain (Hayward, 1988). Tannic acid can be painted onto a surface as a pre-treatment, although if this step is necessary the stain may prove to be fugitive. The surface is neutralized after treatment by thorough rinsing with warm water, applied with a clean rag.

Potassium permanganate ($KMnO_4$), also known as permanganate of potash, is supplied as purple crystals. It is prepared and neutralized in the same way as potassium bichromate. Though the liquid is toxic, the stained wood is innocuous. It imparts a rich warm tone to oak and may be the only colorant needed to match an old surface, particularly when applied sparingly in multiple applications. Although considered fugitive, the colour remains true except when exposed to extreme light conditions. An empirical experiment that exposed maple stained with potassium permanganate to one year of direct sunlight in a south-facing window showed minimal colour loss.

Ferrous sulphate ($FeSO_4.7H_2O$), also known as sulphate of iron or green copperas, has been used as a mordant with other dyes. Used in conjunction with logwood, for example, it will create a dark black. It was traditionally used to kill the redness in pale mahogany used as a substitute for walnut (Hayward, 1988). Sycamore stained grey with ferrous sulphate was known as harewood. It imparts a blue-grey tone to many woods including oak, chestnut, ash, beech and birch. Ferrous sulphate was not applied as a concentrated solution and experimentation may be necessary to provide a suitable concentration. A useful starting point may be one teaspoon of crystals dissolved in a pint (450 ml) of water. The effect is not noticeable when the stain is applied but becomes apparent when it has dried. If an excessively strong solution is used an 'air force blue' colour may result. It is neutralized after drying by rinsing thoroughly with water. Ferric nitrate may also be applied to mahoganies to reduce redness.

*Acidic and alkaline stains*   Acids and alkalis have been used as part of the traditional finishing and restoration processes for centuries. Wood is susceptible to damage by acid hydrolysis and will be swollen by exposure to alkalis (Mills and White, 1994). Health and safety data sheets provided by the supplier should be consulted to ensure appropriate precautions are taken when handling these corrosive materials. If diluting acids for workshop use, gloves and goggles should always be worn. Acid should *always* be added to water – the reverse order can be dangerous.

Dilute sulphuric acid ($H_2SO_4$, 5–15%) was traditionally used to treat a French polished surface if excessive oil had been used. It can also be used to neutralize iron stains on oak and will impart a yellowish tone to many woods.

Dilute nitric acid ($HNO_3$) was traditionally used to treat ink stains (Hayward, 1988). A 25–35% solution can be brushed directly on to bare wood, where it will oxidize the surface. It can be used to reproduce the appearance of mellow ageing on timbers such as satinwood, rosewood, tulipwood and occasionally walnut. Bennett (1990) recommends dampening the surface of the wood with nitric acid and then using a (pre-heated) hot air gun. The gun is held a couple of inches away from one end of the surface. After a few seconds a colour change occurs, and this change can be 'chased' across the surface in a slow and continuous movement. Care should be taken not to expose adjacent materials to nitric acid fumes as some, for example most metals, can be severely damaged. Nitric acid can be difficult to neutralize and any residues will attack finishing materials applied over them. Some restorers rinse and leave the surface for up to a week before commencing any further colouring work, whilst others use repeated applications of a weak alkali such as sodium bicarbonate. Treatment with nitric acid may be followed by treatment with oxalic acid or 'Superbleach' (see above) to further chemically modify the colour of bare wood.

Nitric acid vapour is particularly effective in oxidizing organic molecules (Lee, 1967). The fumes produced when a small piece of copper or a copper alloy such as brass is placed into a container of nitric acid have a marked oxidizing effect on many woods and may be particularly effective for matching aged satinwood. Such fuming may be used to oxidize replacement veneer or parts before they are attached to the object, but must be carried out in a sealed fume cupboard, because the fumes are poisonous.

Dilute acetic acid ($CH_3COOH$, *c*.6%) was traditionally used to treat ink stains (Hayward, 1988). Acetic acid can be combined with ferrous material such as old nails or wire wool to produce a stain traditionally used to colour wood with a significant tannic acid content (e.g. oak). The wire wool or nails are steeped in a 30% solution of acid, agitated occasionally, until a dark red brown solution is formed. This is strained to remove large particles and applied as a stain to bare wood. The iron in the stain complexes with tannin in the wood and gives a cold black coloration to the wood.

Oxalic acid (ethanedioic acid, HOOC—COOH) is a weak dibasic organic acid that has been used as a mild bleach and for removing ink and iron stains in traditional furniture restoration. The concentrations recommended in finishing texts vary from saturated to 50/50 w/v solutions. It is brushed liberally onto the surface and allowed to dry before being rinsed from the surface. The dry crystals should not be brushed or wiped from the surface as they are an extreme irritant and are more liable to be dispersed. Research has indicated that residues of oxalic acid can remain within the pores of wood, even after rinsing with ammonium hydroxide. Such residues form crystalline deposits of oxalic acid that have the potential to damage both finishes applied over them and the wood surface in which they are lodged (German, 1989). Oxalic acid is a poisonous substance and ingestion can be fatal but the 5 g dose required is unlikely to be consumed accidentally given its exceedingly unpleasant taste.

Alkalis used to stain wood include sodium hydroxide, ammonia and sodium carbonate. The use of alkalis can cause some woods to turn almost black whilst others, such as mahogany, are reddened. Very dilute solutions of sodium hydroxide (caustic soda, NaOH) will impart an aged brown colour to cherry. Sodium hydroxide was used in dilute solution to darken or degrease wood. It is very corrosive to skin and if splashed in the eyes can cause corneal burns and blindness. It should be used cautiously and with suitable health and safety precautions. A wide range of colour effects may be achieved, from yellow to a dark reddish brown depending on the species of timber, so some experimentation may be needed to achieve the desired result.

Ammonia ($NH_3$) is a gas at room temperature and is soluble in both water and alcohol. When dissolved in water it forms ammonium hydroxide ($NH_4OH$) and it is in this form that it is usually used. Ammonium hydroxide was traditionally used to darken woods that contain tannic acid. Tannic acid may be used in conjunction with ammonium hydroxide or with iron salts to form a brown stain that can be applied to wood. Tannic acid can be painted onto a surface as a pre-treatment, although if this step is necessary the stain may prove to be fugitive. Ammonia is extremely unpleasant to use, so although brushing a large surface is possible, it was generally more practicable to enclose an object and expose it to ammonia fumes. Fuming had the additional advantage that it did not raise the grain of the wood. A test piece may be used to check the progress of colour change. Exposure to ammonia fumes will corrode or discolour many metals and other susceptible materials.

Sodium carbonate (household washing soda, $Na_2CO_3$) may be used to produce an aged effect on some woods. It is one of the few materials that will effectively colour the rays of oak.

*Solvent borne stains* Water stains used in the past by furniture restorers, such as Vandyke or walnut crystals, were derived from natural materials. Most exhibited poor lightfastness and poor resistance to acids and alkalis. In addition they are not compatible with many modern lacquers and these properties lead most traditional materials to be defined as 'poor quality' stains. The term Vandyke brown may refer to a pigment that is a bituminous ferruginous earth, Cassel brown treated with aqueous sodium carbonate or ground and fermented walnut shells. Modern water stains may be based on organo-metallic dyes, complexes of chromium, cobalt or copper with organic molecules, which vary considerably in their lightfastness. Some manufacturer's water stains are not dyes but are based on microfine pigments. Other chemical types are

also used and it may be necessary to contact the manufacturer or supplier for technical specifications and information about chemical stability, lightfastness and compatibility with coating materials.

Water stains may bead slightly on application to bare wood. Some manufacturers recommend the addition of a small amount of ammonia to reduce surface tension and increase penetration (20 ml ammonia to a litre of water stain). The addition of a surfactant such as Photo-Flo may be useful in promoting even wetting of the surface. Water stains are easy to apply and accept all types of traditional coatings. They may be applied to bare wood but can also be applied between sealing coats during retouching using the method outlined below.

Traditional water stains are prepared by mixing about 30 g of powder in a litre of water. Modern water stains should be mixed according to the manufacturer's instructions. Brush, rag or spray application may be used, and any excess wiped away along the grain with a rag. A surface coating may be applied after about 12 hours if the atmosphere in the workshop is warm and dry. The application of a water stain to bare wood swells the wood fibres and raises the grain. This effect can be minimized by pre-wetting the area to be stained, allowing it to dry, and then abrading the uneven surface with 180 grit paper along the grain. Once the stain has dried, a sealing coat can be applied and allowed to dry. The surface can then be lightly abraded to remove any further raised grain caused by the application of the water stain. Subsequent coats of surface coating will need only the usual denibbing with 240 or 400 grit paper between coats.

As their name implies, *spirit stains* are soluble in alcohol and as a result are very quick-drying. They can be sprayed onto a large surface but are not generally brushed onto bare wood because overlapping strokes produce a streaky effect. They were generally used for tinting alcohol-soluble varnishes or for adjusting colour during French polishing. Spirit stains described in twentieth century finishing manuals usually consisted of an aniline dye dissolved in ethyl alcohol or a similar solvent. They were notorious for their tendency to fade, particularly the reds, and were considered 'fugitive'. Modern stains that are soluble in alcohols, ketones and esters include the organo-metallic Orosol dyes (Ciba–Geigy). The best of these dyes exhibit exceptional lightfastness, with 500 hours exposure to carbon arc lighting before a discernible change in colour, but some have poor lightfastness, with change occurring after a mere 10 hours exposure. Brown 2RL, for example, is rated at 250 hours, equivalent to blue wool light fastness 5–6 (Horie, 1992). Orosol and similar dyes are a single pure colour rather than a blend. This means that as they age they may fade in intensity but will not drift in hue. A proprietary product range containing these dyes is available from J.W. Bollom (USA).

Spirit soluble stains may be very useful in colour matching. Some conservators simply add a very small amount of powder directly to the binder on a retouching palette, dissolving and mixing it thereon. Spirit stains may also be pre-mixed in a strongly coloured 5–10% w/v solution in pure solvent. This may be added to the retouch binder to provide control over the colour and intensity of a transparent coloured wash. Pre-mixed stain may also be added drop by drop to a French polishing rubber when it is charged. The stain is then carried through slowly and will subtly adjust the colour of the finish. Applying the stain directly to the face of the pad will produce a streaky result.

*Oil and naptha stains* were traditionally derived from bituminous sources. Oil and naptha stains penetrate wood evenly and well and produce rich colours, especially in the brown shades, but can be slow to dry. The basic material was tinted with oil soluble dyes to produce different coloured stains, but these all tended to fade back to the reddish brown colour of the bitumen. With the exception of some yellows and browns, many modern oil stains share this poor lightfastness. Organo-metallic complexes are utilized by some manufacturers for white spirit soluble stains and these may exhibit improved lightfastness.

*Non-grain raising* (NGR) stains are often produced using a water-soluble acid dye in a glycol ether solvent, which does not raise the grain of the wood and promotes rapid drying. These materials were developed for industrial use so it is not surprising that the best results are achieved by spray application.

Considerable skill is needed to achieve a translucent even colour using hand application methods such as a rag or brush. NGR stains that contain glycol ethers require the use of health and safety precautions. Mixed solvent stains may also be known as NGR stains. They are formulated from lightfast dyestuffs in alcohol and naptha. They are fast-drying but their wide solubility parameters mean they may be disturbed by, or bleed into, subsequent coats of sealer or varnish.

### 13.5.4  Grain fillers

Grain fillers are used to produce a full grain finish on open grain timbers and to speed the finishing process (*Figure 13.6*). Grain filling is generally undertaken after any initial staining process that may have been used, as the binder in the filler could otherwise prevent even take up of the stain. The binder for the filler usually has different solubility to both any stain applied before filling and the coating to be applied afterwards. Hayward (1988), Bennett (1990) and Flexner (1994) discuss filling materials and techniques.

Sheraton refers to the use of brick dust and oil for the finishing of 'plain cabinet work'. Other materials have been used as fillers, with varying success. Pigmented wax may be used as a filler for small repairs, although it may interfere with the adhesion of subsequent coatings. Fillers generally consist of three main ingredients – powder, binder and solvent carrier. Other ingredients were added as necessary, such as driers to home made linseed oil pastes. The fine abrasive effect of some powders also smoothed the surface wood fibres. Powders have included pumice, pigments, plaster of Paris and chalk. The binder was often oil or oil-based, including boiled linseed oil, but could also be gold size, hide or rabbit skin glue. The solvent carrier was dependent on the binder – turpentine for oil-based fillers, water for glue size. The grain of furniture made or veneered in light coloured woods was often filled by brush coating and abrading varnish or in the bodying up stage of applying a French polish. With the passing of time, some of these materials have proved more successful than others. Plaster of Paris, for example, is often responsible for the unsightly white deposit found in the grain of

(a)

(b)

(c)

**Figure 13.6** The use of grain filler. (*a*) Scanning electron microscopy (SEM) photomicrographs of unfilled and uncoated mahogany (*Swietenia macrophylla*): rough areas are a result of poor preparation. (*b*) SEM photomicrographs of unfilled and uncoated mahogany (*Swietenia macrophylla*): this well-prepared surface will take stain and varnish more evenly than that illustrated in (*a*). (*c*) SEM photomicrograph of grain-filled mahogany. The filler is a proprietary linseed oil-based material

nineteenth and early twentieth century mahogany furniture.

The method of application varies with the filling material chosen. Paste fillers, proprietary or home made, are applied using a coarse cloth and working the filler first along the grain, then across the grain. When the grain has been filled, the bulk of the excess is removed across the grain, because working along the grain will simply dislodge the filler from the wood pores. The filler should be left until almost dry and then the surface wiped along the grain with a lint-free rag, barely moistened with solvent if necessary, to remove the excess. Grain filler left on the surface will obscure the figure of the wood. When the filler is completely dry, the surface can be lightly denibbed with 240 or 320 grit paper and the surface is then ready for the next finishing process.

Proprietary oil-based fillers offer as much as 30 minutes' working time and may take one or two days to fully set. They tend to saturate the substrate but may be slow to cure and may darken over time. Water-based fillers tend to dry much more quickly and this can offer an advantage for the integration of small repairs. While acrylic fillers are likely to be more stable and set quickly, their saturating properties may be a little less satisfactory. Either type can be effective and manufacturer's instructions should be followed. Proprietary fillers may be purchased pre-coloured but may also be toned with pigments. As with other colour matching processes, it is helpful to use a test piece to decide whether they are appropriate for colour matching a given repair.

Dilute glue size has been used as a grain filler in preparation for a varnish, and could be pigmented to adjust the tone of the wood. In some cases a small amount of a drying oil was added to the size. Parchment size or isinglass were recommended for the purpose. Fiedler and Walch (1997) have observed different fluorescence of such layers in comparison to the hide/animal glue used as a wood glue. When dry, the surface was worked with a cabinetscraper or abrasive paper. The surface could be treated this way two or three times. When the grain had been filled and excess removed, the surface was varnished.

Traditional oil-based recipes for grain fillers include a mixture of linseed oil and dry pigment powder that was thinned slightly with turpentine to the consistency of a stiff paste before adding a small amount of liquid driers. A mixture of linseed oil, gold size and turpentine (8:4:1) has also been used and both were applied using the method outlined for paste fillers above.

Grain filling can be achieved as part of the French polishing process. The circular motion of bodying up forces polish into the open pores, filling the grain and resulting in a smooth surface. Some polishers apply a brush coat or two of shellac, begin bodying up and then add a small amount of pumice to the polishing rubber. The pumice abrades the surface, acts as a filler, and is bound into the grain by the varnish itself. Pigments may also be added if necessary.

Modern polishers may utilize sanding sealer as a grain filler. The ingredients of sanding sealers vary from manufacturer to manufacturer and may contain nitrocellulose, modified synthetic resins and a fine particulate material (e.g. zinc stearate). A brush coat or two is applied, allowed to dry and the surface abraded. The process is repeated until the grain is full. The disadvantage of this system on very open grain is that solvent may be retained for several weeks or more, and shrinkage that results from solvent evaporation may necessitate further grain filling.

Although modern synthetic materials (e.g. acrylics, polyester) may be used as the binder in grain fillers their main advantage for conservation lies in their reversibility. Since grain fillers are by definition only applied to bare wood used in repairs this criterion is less important than properties such as colourfastness and compatibility with following layers.

### 13.5.5  Stoppings and filling materials

Stoppings and fillers are used to disguise non-structural damage in the presentation surface of furniture. Whilst many of the fill materials discussed in Chapter 12 may be used for non-structural damage to wood, the materials discussed here are specifically associated with varnished wood. Traditional wood fill materials include shellac (sticks or buttons), beaumontage and pigmented wax. These materials were used because they are quick to apply, easy to level and will accept a range of

traditional finishes on top. Dents or holes that are to be filled may need to be cleaned or degreased before the application of a stopping. They may be wiped over with white spirit or a white spirit/IMS mix, depending on the original surface finish.

Thornton (1998a) has considered the wide range of materials used in the past as gap fillers. Fillers perform differently under different circumstances and the type of damage should be evaluated before a filler is chosen (Barclay and Mathias, 1989). The environmental conditions in which an object is stored or displayed will affect the success of a fill. If the object is subject to fluctuations in RH, the fill must have good adhesive properties and a degree of flexibility. The larger the gap or damage that is filled, the greater the degree of flexibility that is required. Grattan and Barclay (1988) tested thirty-three different materials with regard to their suitability as gap fillers in a variety of applications. Materials suitable for wooden objects in an environment in which RH fluctuates must have a low modulus of compression, and include waxes, balsa wood (e.g. for splits), and silicone rubber/microballoon mixtures. These fillers may also be used on objects in an environment with stable RH, as can more rigid materials such as epoxy resin/microballoon mixtures.

Damage caused by an excessive number of woodworm exit holes or exposed tunnelling may be filled with a variety of materials when this is desirable. The decision whether to fill exit holes or exposed tunnelling may depend on their number and to what extent they disturb the aesthetic balance of the object.

Shellac has been used as a filler, in part because of its excellent adhesive properties. It is brittle and only suitable for small areas of damage. Shellac sticks are available in a variety of colours (*Figure 13.7*). The translucent sticks usually contain only shellac whilst opaque sticks are a mixture of shellac and pigments. Two methods can be used to apply shellac. The end of the shellac stick can be held against a soldering iron or heated spatula. The melting shellac is dripped into the hole or dent. If a soldering iron is used, a current regulating plug will help to reduce the temperature of the iron. Alternatively, a flexible palette knife can be heated and used to pare small shavings from the stick. A warm,

**Figure 13.7** Proprietary shellac sticks

(a)

(b)

**Figure 13.8** Wax fills: (*a*) a range of proprietary and home made wax filler sticks; (*b*) Perspex and wood tools for levelling wax fills

softened shaving can then be pressed into position. Excess shellac is removed with a sharp chisel or a scalpel after it has hardened. Buttons of shellac can be used in the same way and may be particularly useful for mid- to dark brown timbers such as unbleached European walnut.

Beaumontage was prepared by the craftsperson by mixing equal parts of beeswax, crushed rosin (colophony), a little shellac and pigment as required (Hayward, 1988). The ingredients were heated together and when cooled were similar in consistency to sealing wax. It was applied and levelled in the same way as stick shellac. Bennett (1990) recommends a similar stopping made with shellac, a small amount of beeswax and powdered pigment. The shellac or rosin content will make both these fill materials brittle.

Pigmented wax can be purchased from a supplier of traditional wood finishing materials or made up as required. As with most traditional finishing materials, recipes vary. Filler sticks can be made from either 100% beeswax or a little carnauba (10–15%) can be added to raise the melting point slightly, though this will also increase brittleness. They can be made in any colour by adding powdered pigments (*Figure 13.8a*). The ingredients are heated gently, mixed and allowed to cool. No solvent is included as this would only lead to shrinkage of the wax fill after it had been applied. A shaving of the filler stick can be heated on a palette knife and pressed into place. Small pieces of pigmented beeswax can be softened in the hand and worked into small defects on the surface of the wood. The wax can be levelled using a piece of Perspex or a wood block with a bevelled edge (*Figure 13.8b*). Shellac will adhere to small areas of wax but adhesion may prove problematic for other surface coatings.

Animal/hide glue, mixed with sawdust or other bulking agents, has been used as a grain filling material in the past. Animal/hide glue remains reversible in water, but animal glue-bound fillers are prone to shrinkage as they dry and are unstable if exposed to fluctuations in RH. Proprietary PVAC wood glues, such as Resin W (UK), are not suitable for use as fill binders unless an isolating layer is used.

Conservation grade materials such as Paraloids, PVAC and PVAL combined with inert filler, such as microballoons, and coloured with pigments, may also be used as stoppings and fillers. They can be levelled with a scalpel or chisel and can be inpainted with water colours or dry pigments in a PVAC binder. These materials, discussed in section

12.3.1, may be more easily and rapidly reversible than fills made from wax, shellac, or a gesso type fill.

Proprietary two-part fillers have been used to fill wood. If used, they must be flexible enough once cured to move with the wood through cycling relative humidity, and soft enough that they do not cause compression set in the original wood. The addition of a compressible bulking agent, such as microballoons, may prevent this problem. Such materials will require an isolating layer to allow future removal.

### 13.5.6  Colour matching methods

Broadly speaking, there are two approaches that can be taken when colour matching a wooden repair (*Figure 13.9*). The first is the traditional method, drawing on techniques used to finish freshly made furniture, in which stain or other colouring material is applied directly to the bare wood. If this method is used, it is *essential* to test all the steps of the intended procedure on scrap wood. The second approach relies on sealing the wood and applying colouring materials on top of this initial isolating layer. Because the sealing coat allows rapid and complete removal of unsatisfactory layers, this method does not require the use of a test piece. It is a quicker method for the experienced conservator and has the advantage of reversibility for the inexperienced colour matcher. The method chosen is a matter of personal preference, though for repairs that may be scuffed, abraded or dented, such as a chair leg in domestic use, the first method is more suitable. If the surface has been bleached or treated with chemicals, the surface must be thoroughly rinsed or neutralized before any other colouring processes are used.

The materials chosen to stain, grain fill, seal, colour match and varnish must be compatible with each successive stage of the colouring process. An oil-based filler, for example, may disrupt an oil-based stain that lies below it, and both may bleed into a hydrocarbon based surface coating applied over them.

Colour matching proceeds in stages with thin coats of colourant. Pigment or stain may be added to a binding medium to lay down a glaze or transparent wash. Stain must be

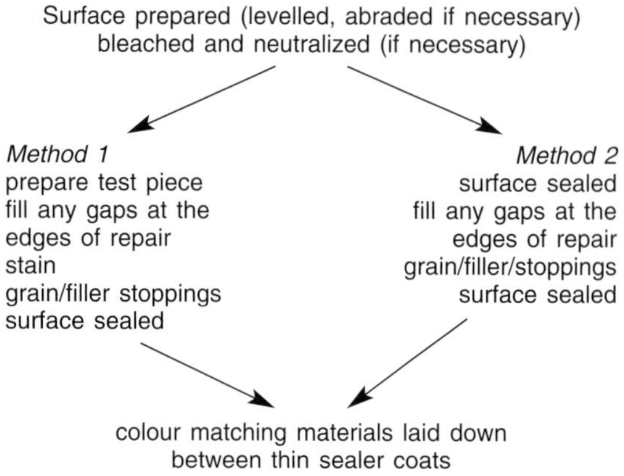

**Figure 13.9** Steps in colour matching repairs to varnished wood

soluble in the diluent, whilst pigment must be well dispersed. Thin sealer coats are often used throughout the colour matching process and serve both to fix each layer of colouring material and offer a protective barrier when light abrasion is necessary. It is essential to avoid an excessive build-up in thickness, thus it is often necessary to lightly abrade a retouched or coated surface once it has hardened off. Fine abrasive paper (320–600 grit), medium grade Micromesh (a cushioned abrasive cloth), or fine (0000) lubricant free wire wool may be used to level brush marks or abrade sealer coats. White-backed Micromesh is usually used in conservation as it does not leave a residue.

### Binding media for colour matching varnished wood

Important properties of binding media for conservation retouching include photochemical stability, good adhesion, flexibility and solubility parameters that will ensure that future removal will not damage original material. Retouching media need to be compatible with both the surface to which they are applied and any coating that may be used. Conservation grade materials used as binding media for colour matching and coatings are discussed in Chapter 12. Many of these materials cannot provide a durable surface for wood surfaces that are intended for regular use. It may be necessary for the furniture conservator to select materials for a specific purpose.

Thus conservation grade materials may be used for retouching or for isolating layers, whilst traditional materials may be used to provide harder wearing, or more aesthetically acceptable surfaces. Whilst the need for accurate documentation is widely accepted in the conservation profession, it is particularly important if different materials are used for isolating, retouching and coating layers. Careful selection of materials can allow future conservators to remove a discoloured upper coating without disturbing retouching below.

Although easel painting conservators avoid the use of shellac as a retouch medium because of its tendency to yellow, shellac has been the retouching binding media of choice for many generations of furniture restorers. Thin coats of shellac dry rapidly and each successive layer partially dissolves and fuses with the preceding layer, a property that is exploited in French polishing. In spite of this, a touch-dry layer of shellac is not immediately dissolved when a subsequent coat is applied. As a result, successive coats do not cause reticulation in lower layers. Shellac-bound colourant, sealer coats and varnish may be applied with a brush, French polishing rubber or sprayed – the latter two methods tend to produce a thinner and flatter surface. It is possible to work in very thin layers, for both coloured glazes or sealer coats, using a French polishing rubber. Although shellac discolours more rapidly than dammar or mastic, it forms a hard wearing durable film.

The apparent lack of concern from furniture restorers about the substantial and relatively quick yellowing of shellac may be a result of its durability in use combined with the fact that the wood itself is subject to colour change as a result of photochemical oxidation. Thus by the time the shellac retouch had yellowed, the background to which it was originally matched had itself altered. Since the aim of modern conservation is to limit such photochemical change of the wood by excluding or limiting exposure to UV, retouching often requires a longer stable lifespan than was previously the case. The use of shellac as a retouching medium may cause problems for the survival of adjacent original or early transparent coatings. Shellac is chemically complex and may partially crosslink, making the whole more resistant to organic solvents after around 150 years (Horie, 1992).

### Applying pigments

Powdered pigments may be applied in an opaque layer to obscure the wood or other filler below or may be thinly dispersed in a binder and applied as wash. Pigments with extremely small particle size, such as microlith pigments (Ciba–Geigy), have made it easier to achieve a translucent wash. A comparatively small palette is required for matching most wood. Such a palette might include flake or Chinese white, yellow ochre, raw sienna, chrome yellow (or its equivalent), burnt sienna, Venetian red, raw umber, light umber, burnt umber and lamp black. Many furniture conservators also use proprietary artist's water colours. Whilst some furniture conservators use the conservation grade materials described in section 12.3.2, others may choose to isolate the adjacent surface and use a shellac binder.

Furniture restorers often used powder pigments in a shellac binder. The process involved using a scrap of used abrasive paper folded into a cone into which a small amount of shellac was poured, diluted with a small amount of methylated spirits. Dry pigment powder was mixed into the resin at the tide edge of the shellac. Whilst there is no doubt this method is convenient, the pigments are not well ground and may not be well integrated into the varnish (i.e. particles may not be thoroughly wetted). The pigment:binder ratio will inevitably vary, sometimes from stroke to stroke. Though more consistent results may be achieved by mixing pigment and resin on an artist's palette, the rapid evaporation of the alcohol binder made this unsuitable for shellac based paint.

If pigment has been as a base coat, colour and tone may be adjusted using transparent glaze layers. Pigmented or transparent glazes may be used to simulate bands of colour. The last step may be simulating the pores or grain of the wood. This may be difficult using pigments. A thick Vandyke brown, made up to the consistency of a paste, is particularly effective for this purpose and can be applied in extremely fine lines. The technique described below for sealing water stain between sealer coats should be used to ensure the fine detail is not removed or disturbed.

### Applying stains

Stains, by definition, are translucent materials. They may be used to adjust the colour and tone of a wood repair. The use of stains requires that the colour of the wood or fill below is lighter than the surrounding wood. If this is not the case and an invisible retouch is required, it will be necessary to bleach the wood or use pigments to create a suitable base colour. Stain can be applied directly to bare wood, between sealing coats, or may be added to the binder for a transparent wash.

*Staining unsealed wood* If stain is to be applied directly to bare wood, the surface must be clean and free from greasy or waxy contaminants. Water-based stains are often used because oil stains are generally not light-fast. Spirit-soluble stains, traditional or modern, are difficult to apply evenly to bare wood and may be disrupted by a solvent-based sealer coat. The use of a water stain requires that the surface be pre-treated to reduce the effect of raised grain. This is done by damping the surface and allowing it to dry before abrading the raised grain. A test piece, taken from the same stock used to make the repair, should be used to prepare a trial run of the entire finishing process. This step is essential because stain applied onto a bare wood surface may prove impossible to completely remove without abrading it below the level of the adjacent surface. The visual properties of both bare and stained wood will change when a surface coating is applied. It may be helpful to saturate the surface of the test piece after staining in order to evaluate the appearance of the stained wood once it has been sealed or varnished. Both bare wood and the test piece can be saturated with a solvent such as white or mineral spirits. The saturated colour of the stained wood should be slightly lighter than the surrounding wood. The colour and tone can be adjusted later in the colour match-ing process if necessary. A brush coat of varnish may be used to seal the stain on the repair wood. When dry, the surface may be further toned with transparent glaze layers.

*Staining sealed wood* It is possible to apply water stain between coats of sealer. The water stain is applied onto a dry, sealed surface. A soft dry brush is used to brush the stain out and prevent it beading, working quickly along the grain until the stain is dry. A suitable brush for large surfaces is a bristle 'jamb duster',

more commonly used by decorators to remove the dust from door jambs and the like after denibbing between coats. Smaller repairs will require a similar, but smaller, brush. When the stain is dry, a thin sealer coat is carefully applied. Shellac may be applied using a French polishing rubber, whilst other coatings may be applied using a brush or an airbrush. It is important that if a French polishing rubber or brush is used, that only a single stroke is applied to any one area. Overlapping strokes on the unsealed stained surface will remove the stain, leaving a streaked effect. If working a large area, it is better to apply the sealer in stages than to risk patchy removal as a result of inadvertent overlapping of strokes. Once the whole surface has been sealed and this coating has dried, additional polish may be applied if desired. Successive layers are applied in the same way and if the effect of one layer is not what was intended, light abrasion will remove the upper layer without disturbing those below.

### Sealing coats

Sealing coats, stains and pigment colour may be applied to small areas using artist's quality sable brushes. These are expensive but will last if properly maintained. The quality of artist's sable brushes varies. If possible, before purchasing dip the bristles into water and shake the excess off. The tip of the brush should come to a fine point – if it does not, the brush is not suitable for fine retouching work. Brushes should be rinsed immediately after use, brought to a fine point and stored in a rack. If a brush is inadvertently left overnight and the bristles bent, the damage can sometimes be undone by rinsing the brush in an appropriate solvent and then soaking it overnight in warm water. A little mild hand soap may be added to the water and the brush supported or positioned so that the bristles are not pressed against the base of the container.

A French polishing rubber may be used for the application of thin sealing coats during the colour matching process and for the applica-tion of thin washes of pigment bound in resin to larger areas. Instructions on making a French polishing rubber are given in the section on French polishing under section 13.7.2. A French polishing rubber is particu-larly useful for sealing wood without saturating the colour. This may be useful where the unsaturated colour of the bare wood provides a better starting point for colour matching than when it is wet out, or if the upper layer of oxidized wood has been inadvertently removed and would be unacceptably dark if the colour was saturated by the application of a surface coating. The rubber is charged with a small amount of shellac polish diluted with methylated spirits. Excess is squeezed out so that the rubber feels almost 'dry', and a single coat of polish applied. This coat must be allowed several minutes to dry and the process repeated until the surface is evenly coated. When dry, the surface may be colour matched or polished as required.

Spray application may utilize a mouth diffuser or blow atomizer, an airbrush or a spray gun. Spraying a stain allows the application of very thin layers to specific areas without physically disturbing lower layers. Spray application is discussed under section 12.4.8 in the context of the application of coatings.

Once a colour match has been achieved, several thin coats of varnish are usually applied to the surface. High gloss may be diminished by lightly abrading the surface with lubricant-free wire wool, pumice or rottenstone and a wax coating applied if appropriate.

## 13.6  Treatment of degraded varnish

There are several options for treating a degraded varnish without removing it. These include the application of a reversible coating, the use of solvents and the traditional technique of 'amalgamation'.

In many cases the application of a fresh coating is sufficient to resaturate a yellowed or degraded varnish. Historically, such treatments used materials that were often very similar to the original and, as time passed, caused further problems. The use of photochemically stable coatings with a different solubility parameter to the original allows the conservator to use this technique and avoid such problems. Reversible coatings that may be used by the conservator in this way include Paraloid B72 (5–10% w/v in an aromatic hydrocarbon solvent) or stabilized coatings such as dammar, MS2A and hydrogenated hydrocarbons (e.g. Regalrez) (10–20% w/v in

an aliphatic hydrocarbon solvent). Note that varnishes that are soluble in white spirit are not compatible with a subsequent wax finish. It may be desirable to reduce the gloss of a newly applied coating using the techniques described in section 12.4.4.

A traditional technique used to resaturate degraded varnish is to apply a thick wax coating, melting it with a hot air gun. If a waxed appearance is desirable, Piena (2001) suggested the use of a wax–resin mixture that utilized Regalrez 1126 in place of the dammar that has traditionally been used. The Regalrez 1126:beeswax:white spirit (10:30:60 g) can be brushed on and evened out with a cotton pad dampened with white spirit. When the solvent has evaporated, the wax-resin coating can be buffed as for a normal wax finish. This technique is a good alternative to the traditional method of applying wax, as it avoids potential heat damage of the original varnish.

Solvent wiped or sprayed over the surface of a transparent coating has been used to resaturate or reform and readhere a resinous coating to the substrate wood (*Figure 13.10*). The solvent must fall within the solubility range of the resin and have a medium to fast evaporation rate. Ethanol or propan-2-ol, for example, would be suitable solvents for a spirit varnish based on sandarac or shellac. The key to successfully treating surfaces in this way is minimal exposure to the solvent, i.e. a single pass with a spray gun or swab. The diffusion of solvent into the coating causes the varnish film to begin to swell and some

**Figure 13.10** Degraded varnish on a seventeenth century japanned surface. The varnish on the left has been resaturated by the careful application of isopropanol

secondary intermolecular bonds are broken. As the solvent evaporates, these secondary bonds reform within the varnish and between the varnish and substrate. It may take up to six months before the re-establishment of secondary bonds is complete (Feller, Stolow and Jones, 1985). It should be noted that many transparent coatings on furniture were polished after their application in order to produce a high gloss finish and that treatment with solvent may not reproduce the original appearance. Further, swelling a natural resin coating by the infusion of solvent may affect its performance as a coating. Although such a treatment may resaturate the finish it will not reverse degradation associated with oxidation.

A traditional method of rejuvenating a resinous coating that is in poor condition is to apply solvent using a French polishing rubber or pad. This technique aims to redistribute partially solvated varnish on the surface and is sometimes referred to as 'amalgamation'. Although such a treatment is not reversible, it may be preferable to wholesale removal of a very degraded original varnish.

## 13.7   Application of coatings to varnished wood

A furniture conservator may apply a new coating to varnished wood in order to preserve the original coating (e.g. if it is friable or vulnerable to damage) or for aesthetic reasons (e.g. to resaturate a degraded surface). In some cases the conservator may be asked to apply a coating in order to better imitate the original appearance of the object. In all cases the treatment chosen should be compatible with the preservation of original varnish or colouring materials. The solubility region of the new coating should be sufficiently different from the original to allow future safe removal. The restoration practice of stripping and repolishing will reduce the historical value of an object and can reduce the monetary value of furniture by up to 80%.

When choosing a material for coating a varnished wood surface, the furniture conservator should consider issues of stability, aesthetics and the time, skill and resources available for the treatment. Historical and physical integrity should be considered and

this may mean assessing the original layer thickness, degree of gloss, original application technique and the use of colourants in the original coating.

Natural resins were historically used as the basis for many transparent varnishes on wood. All natural resins are prone to photochemical degradation, and shellac in particular is known for discolouring comparatively rapidly. Shellac has often been used in the past because of its excellent adhesive properties, colour and refractive index. It is available in a range of colours, such as button or garnet, which may approximate the colour of an original finish more closely than a transparent varnish. The hard-wearing resins associated with furniture varnishes, sandarac, and shellac, require polar solvents for removal. Whilst this is not problematic if they are applied to unfinished wood, it has serious implications if remnants of an original surface finish survive. It is questionable whether the use of natural resins to replicate an original finish can be successful, given that, with a few notable exceptions, the exact formulation of an original varnish is unknown. The main advantages of sandarac and shellac varnishes are that they are hard-wearing and produce an appearance that satisfies the currently accepted aesthetic for varnished wood.

It is essential to avoid a dogmatic approach to the use of traditional or conservation grade materials. In many cases a compromise solution may be possible, for example by using a barrier layer of stabilized varnish soluble in non-polar solvents, followed by a natural resin varnish if this is deemed suitable or essential. This approach may allow an ethical conservation treatment that combines future reversibility/retreatability with practical considerations of durability. It may be necessary to degrease or dewax a surface with white spirit or an aromatic hydrocarbon before a new coating is applied.

### 13.7.1   Non-traditional materials

Synthetic resins that may be suitable for coating a varnished surface include Paraloid B72 or stabilized low molecular weight resins such as dammar, MS2A, Regalrez 1094 or Laropal A81. These materials are discussed in section 12.4.7. The primary advantage of such materials is their photochemical stability. They do not yellow and discolour, they remain removable in non-polar solvents and can be distinguished from original materials. All are suitable for brush or spray application. It has been argued, however, that such materials, particularly the high molecular weight synthetics, do not replicate the original appearance.

Modern varnish manufacturers may produce furniture finishes that are a blend of traditional and modern materials. One example of a hard-wearing varnish that can be applied using French polishing technique is called table top polish (John Myland Ltd, UK), which contains shellac, nitrocellulose and 'some synthetic resins'. This coating does not crosslink and may be reversed in ketones and esters. Adhesion of other coatings applied on top of table top polish is often poor. Such coatings may be applied on top of a traditional French polished finish if a full grain surface is required, as it is can be difficult to abrade once the surface has dried.

### 13.7.2 Traditional materials

#### *Wax*

Wax has been used since antiquity as a protective coating and imparts a soft sheen. It may be applied directly to the wood or over an extant surface coating. A wax coating is not appropriate if a varnished surface is heavily crazed or fragile. Wax layers tend to be thin, photochemically stable, slightly acidic, easily removed from varnished surfaces, have low permeability to moisture and may help prevent scratching of lower resinous coatings during dusting. The properties of wax are discussed in Chapter 4 and in conservation literature including Horie (1992) and Mills and White (1994). Abercauph (1998) has tabulated the physical properties of some commercially available animal, vegetable, mined and microcrystalline waxes.

Sheraton (1803) refers to the use of beeswax in combination with other materials including pigment and copal varnish. Other historical sources refer to the use of beeswax mixed with colophony resin. Walch (1997) has suggested, however, that the use of wax to impart a 'satin sheen' to restored furniture can be traced to a late nineteenth century aesthetic. Such treatment, applied uniformly to furniture from different periods and with total disregard for historical accuracy, has continued throughout the twentieth century and may still be seen in many antique shops and auction rooms.

Beeswax is usually the primary constituent of wax furniture polishes. Although beeswax has a melting point around 65 °C it softens at 37 °C and as a result handling tends to leave the surface marred with smears and fingerprints. Harder waxes may be added to improve the working properties of a wax polish, most notably carnauba wax which has a melting point of around 84 °C but is very brittle. Furniture polishers often prepared their own wax polishes using beeswax, carnauba wax and turpentine with the addition of finely ground pigment or oil stain. Modern tubed artist's pigments are used by some to colour the contemporary mix as these are finely ground and already thoroughly wetted by their oil media. The proportion of beeswax to carnauba varies but the higher the proportion of carnauba added, the more effort is required to buff the polish to a soft and even sheen, and the more brittle the final wax coating. The proportion of carnauba wax may be varied between 10% and 15% to produce a slightly harder-wearing polish that is still easy to buff. The proportion of solvent may vary between roughly 50% to 60% depending on the desired consistency of the final paste. The wax paste may be prepared by melting shavings or blocks of wax in a double boiler, removing from the heat when melted and then adding colouring material (if required) and solvent. A soft thin paste may be made by adding one part carnauba wax, three parts beeswax and six parts solvent, whilst a proportion of 1:2:3 of these ingredients will produce a harder, thicker wax paste for a more durable wax finish. Turpentine was the traditional solvent, though because this solvent contains turpenes, which may leave insoluble polymerized residues, many conservators prefer to use white spirits or mineral spirits.

Proprietary formulations may include soft cheap waxes such as paraffin as extenders and solvents vary from turpentine to white spirit, xylene or toluene. It is not always necessary to clean a wax surface before applying a fresh coating, since the application of a wax paste partially dissolves the extant dirty material.

Products that include xylene and toluene will have wider solubility parameters and therefore are able to clean dirt and grime from a surface during the waxing process. They are, however, more harmful and their use presents an increased health and safety risk.

There are two distinct application methods for wax pastes. The first is used for wax pastes that contain a high proportion of beeswax or similar low melting point constituents. A lump of wax paste may be placed in the centre of a fine cotton or other natural fibre cloth, the corners folded in and a twist formed above the lump. The twist is tightened so that wax begins to squeeze through the cloth, which is then rubbed over the surface, applying a very thin and even wax coating. The wax should be left for a short while to allow most of the solvent to evaporate before a fresh clean soft cloth is rubbed vigorously over the surface, removing excess wax and producing a soft even sheen. If the wax is buffed whilst there is still a large amount of solvent present it will simply be removed from the surface.

The second technique is used for wax pastes that contain a high proportion of carnauba wax or microcrystalline waxes with a high melting point. In this case, the wax paste is applied as above, but buffed immediately. If the solvent is allowed to evaporate, application marks and excess wax may be difficult to remove and it may be difficult to buff the surface to an even sheen.

Dipping the cloth directly into the wax and applying it to the surface usually results in a much thicker and uneven layer that requires more buffing to remove the excess. A light coating of wax may be applied by diluting the wax in solvent and spraying it on using an airbrush or spray gun. This allows the application of a uniform, non-streaky wax film that requires minimal buffing.

Wax pastes may be applied to moulding or carvings using a brush. A paint brush may be used for this purpose once the bristles have been cut to 18–25 mm (¾ to 1 inch) to stiffen them. The polish is usually applied with the brush and excess removed with a soft cloth. A light rub down may be followed by more vigorous buffing when all the solvent has evaporated. A shoe brush may be necessary for carved or other intricate work. Some manufacturers produce brushes with a slight curve to help prevent inadvertent damage to an object when a wax paste is being buffed in this way.

An alternative application method uses techniques derived from French polishing, described below, to create a full grain wax finish on bare wood or that which has only a thin coat of sealer. Apply a heavy coat of wax paste to the surface with a brush and allow the solvent to evaporate. The wax paste may be fortified with up to 25–30% carnauba wax. Using a French polishing rubber slightly dampened with turpentine, body up the surface, working in small circles and figures-of-eight to force wax into the grain. More wax may be applied to fill the grain if necessary, and the bodying up process repeated. A small amount of pumice powder may also be used at this stage. When the surface is smooth, switch to a rubber dampened with methylated spirits to give a smear-free shine. The effect can be almost as glossy as a shellac finish. Bennett (1990) describes a similar technique.

It may be more difficult to produce a soft even sheen with microcrystalline wax. Microcrystalline waxes are prepared to produce a variety of working properties. They can be harder and tougher than natural waxes, and are less acidic. Unpigmented wax lodged in recesses or mouldings is unsightly. Microcrystalline wax may prove more difficult to redissolve than beeswax. Furniture in domestic use does not generally require waxing more than once a year and that in museum collections requires waxing even less frequently.

### Oils

Though unpigmented linseed oil films are not particularly durable, oil polishes based on linseed oil have been used on furniture for centuries and were still recommended until quite recently (Plenderleith and Werner, 1971; Sheraton, 1803). Drying oils such as linseed, poppy seed and walnut oils, could be applied directly to the surface in thin layers over a period of several weeks or months. They could be combined with a grain-filling pigment, for example brick dust on mahogany.

Linseed oil wets efficiently onto most surfaces and enhances appearance through increased saturation. Antique dealers often apply a thin linseed oil coating to furniture in

(a)

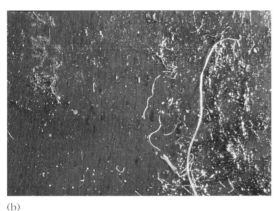

(b)

**Figure 13.11** Use of oils
(*a*) Detail of carving on a Philadelphia Chippendale style side chair. Dust and lint accumulated in the recesses of the carving were adhered to an oiled finish (*b*) Accretions of old linseed oil on a varnished mahogany surface. Patches of darkened oil disfigure the surface

their showrooms for this purpose. Proprietary preparations such as Danish oil and tung oil are often used by the amateur furniture finisher because they are easy to apply. Oils are not usually employed in furniture conservation because they can remain sticky for an extended period of time and trap dirt that becomes incorporated into the surface coating as the oil slowly dries (*Figure 13.11a*). In addition, drying oils darken as they age, crosslinking to produce large insoluble molecules that are difficult to remove without the use of aggressive cleaning methods (*Figure 13.11b*). Oil should never be applied to saturate the colour of a degraded varnished

surface. It should be noted that rags used to apply linseed oil may spontaneously combust, thus used or discarded rags must be stored in a flameproof container.

Non-drying essential oils such as lemon or almond oil are used in numerous proprietary polishes and have been used in the past to saturate polished and decorative surfaces. While they do not polymerize as a drying oil would, they remain sticky and serve to bind dust to the surface. These materials may be removed with white spirit.

### Natural resins

Natural resin varnishes were applied to wood surfaces to saturate the colour and protect the surface from dirt. Some eighteenth century sources refer specifically to the desire that varnishes should impart durability and gloss to a wood surface. Despite a comparatively limited range of natural materials and solvents, historical treatises attest to the many possible permutations for their preparation and combination in varnish formulations. Information on the ingredients and preparation of varnishes can be found in many historical treatises. Walch (1997) has suggested three main classes of varnish were applied to wood in the eighteenth century: oil–resin varnishes, usually based on amber or copal, spirit varnishes and, less commonly, essential oil varnishes.

Oil–resin varnish generally contained a high proportion of a drying oil such as linseed oil. Fossil-type resins, such as amber and copal, could be heated with linseed oil at around 300 °C to produce hard-wearing oil–resin varnishes. Such oleo-resin varnishes could be thinned with turpentine and applied in a few thick layers. Although such varnishes could be diluted with alcohol when fresh, aged films are only sparingly soluble in this solvent. Natural resins, such as sandarac, larch resins and mastic, could be heated with linseed oil to produce an oil–resin type varnish. Natural resins could also be heated and combined with essential oils such as oil of spike, lavender, or rosemary, and diluted to a workable consistency with turpentine. Walch (1997) refers to such formulations as essential oil soluble varnishes.

Whilst a range of natural resins have historically been applied to paintings, only sandarac and later shellac were hard-wearing enough to form the basis for transparent coatings on furniture. Spirit varnishes were applied using a brush, and the surface flattened using fine abrasives after it had dried. This process can be time-consuming, particularly if multiple coats are applied. Shellac is well suited to application from a polishing rubber and this technique, used on furniture since the late eighteenth or early nineteenth century, is described below. The application of varnish from a rubber or fad is substantially faster than applying a similar thickness of coating by brush. Spraying a surface coating allows the application of very thin layers to specific areas without physically disturbing lower layers. Spray application of surface coatings is discussed under section 12.4.8.

Shellac, applied using the technique of French polishing, was a popular furniture finish in the nineteenth century. Alongside this trend was the use of shellac by furniture restorers. Since at least the late nineteenth century, it has been common practice for restorers to apply a shellac varnish, abraded and/or matted down with wax. The result has been that objects from widely differing contexts and regions assume a fairly uniform appearance.

Shellac comes in a variety of colours and types. The colour of the shellac is usually matched to the colour of the wooden object, for example pale timbers such as satinwood require the use of white, 'super blonde' or transparent polish. These are bleached during manufacturing and as a result are slightly denatured. They may be slightly more difficult to apply evenly than the button or garnet varieties. Button polish derived its name from the button shape in which the material was originally supplied. Today it is supplied as a pre-mixed polish, flakes or buttons from specialist suppliers. The ageing properties of the final film may be affected by the length of time the polish has been in solution and it is best to mix a suitable quantity when it is required. The shellac flakes or broken buttons are placed in a glass or plastic container, IMS added and the whole placed on a magnetic mixer until dissolved. Alternatively the shellac may be placed in a muslin bag and then suspended in IMS and agitated occasionally until dissolved. The solution should be strained through a double layer of stockings or finely woven silk to remove detritus.

Hayward (1988) recommends six ounces of shellac to one pint of methylated spirits (170 g to 550 ml). Deller (2000) has reported the addition of Paraloid B72 to shellac-based French polishes. This improves the grain-filling properties when French polishing and will reduce the brittleness of the cured varnish. The inherent photochemical instability of shellac remains unaffected.

Shellac may be applied with a polishing mop, a French polishing rubber or spray equipment (Williams, 1988). Whilst brush application of a single coat of shellac onto bare wood produces an even surface, further coats produce progressively more ropiness that can only be removed by allowing the surface to harden and cutting it back with abrasive paper (*c*.240 grit). This is true of other spirit varnishes and was the method used to create multi-layered japanning in the seventeenth and eighteenth centuries. Shellac has particularly good adhesive properties and may adhere where other, particularly modern, coatings suffer from cissing. Cissing is the partial pulling back of the wet film into beads, craters, islands or pinholes (Hamburg and Morgans, 1979). It is caused by poor wetting and is usually the result of contamination of the surface, e.g. with wax or silicone.

Successful varnish application requires good quality brushes. Brush coats of natural resin varnish to a large surface may be applied using a flat squirrel hair brush or a squirrel hair mop. Polisher's mops may be stored after rinsing in a dilute mix of shellac, with the bristles brought to a point. This prevents both loss of hair and damage that might otherwise occur when the brushes are transported for site work. When required for use, they should be soaked for a few minutes in methylated spirits.

Mastic, dammar, sandarac and synthetic coatings including Paraloid 72 and synthetic low molecular weight varnishes are discussed in section 12.4.7. Surface coatings such as cellulose nitrate, polyurethane, alkyd resins, acid catalysed and pre-catalysed lacquers are inappropriate for antique furniture but may have some application for treating twentieth century objects where they represent an original surface-finishing material. The selective removal of such finishes inappropriately applied to furniture may be problematic.

### French polishing

French polishing describes the skilled application of successive thin coats of shellac to a surface using wadding wrapped in lint-free cotton, known as a polishing rubber or fad. The resulting surface is very glossy, reflective and level. French polishing is thought to have been introduced to English furniture in the early nineteenth century. A finishing manual, published in the United States in 1827, notes that 'Friction varnishing, or French polishing ... is of comparatively modern date' (Mussey, 1987). Prior to the development of French polishing, spirit soluble resin varnishes were applied using a brush. The inevitable unevenness that resulted was smoothed out with a variety of abrasive materials. Time and practice are required to develop the techniques and skill necessary for French polishing. French polishing is particularly suited to polishing large flat areas. Mouldings and the corners of framed panels were particularly difficult areas to French polish evenly. Once mastered, however, the application of very thin surface coats from a polishing rubber can be used in repairing or recreating a resinous surface finish. The techniques used to create a French polished surface may also be used for the application of thin coats of shellac when retouching a repair.

In the past, furniture restorers have applied full gloss French polish finishes somewhat indiscriminately. Care should be taken that resinous finishes applied to furniture are consistent with what is currently understood about historical materials and finishing practice. Hayward (1988), Flexner (1994) and Frank (1986) describe the materials and techniques used in French polishing and may provide a useful adjunct to the information set out below.

French polishing involves six basic steps: making the rubber, colouring the surface if necessary, filling the grain, building up the finish (also known as bodying up), levelling the surface (also known as pulling over) and finally surface treatments such as dulling down. Spiriting out is a step that is only required if oil has been added during polishing. The need for a dust-free workspace for French polishing cannot be overemphasized. As successive coats of shellac are applied the surface may remain soft and sticky for an extended period. Any fibres, dirt or dust that

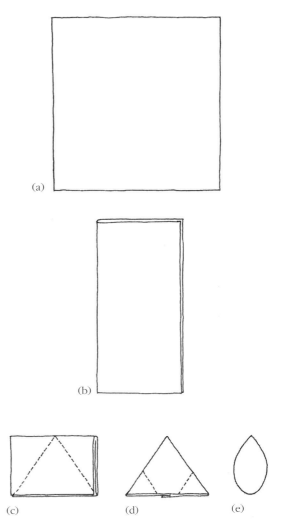

**Figure 13.12** Folding wadding for a French polishing rubber or fad. The square of cloth (*a*) is folded in half (*b*), then into thirds (*c*). Two corners are folded down to make a triangle (*d*). Finally, two corners are folded towards the centre to make the wadding pear-shaped (*e*)

fall onto the surface will cause blemishes that disrupt an otherwise even and glossy surface.

A French polishing rubber or pad consists of fine lint-free cotton wrapped around the wadding that serves as a reservoir for the shellac solution. The wadding is an absorbent and springy material, such as cotton wadding, old linen or wool. A 28 cm (10 inch) square is folded as shown in *Figure 13.12*. The wadding should be slightly pear-shaped, pointed and thinner at one end, round and full at the other. The pointed end may be used for applying polish into corners. Some texts recommend soaking the wadding in polish, allowing it to dry and then moistening it with a little methylated spirits before shaping it. This both prevents the loss of stray fibres that may end up on or in the polished surface and 'pre-charges' the rubber so that it is ready for immediate use. Alternatively the rubber may be prepared and the wadding may simply be charged and squeezed out several times until the varnish solution is evenly dispersed throughout but excess has been removed.

The wadding is wrapped in a 25 cm (9 inch) square of lint-free cotton, such as an old, good quality handkerchief. The twist of cloth is held in the palm of the hand while the index and middle finger are placed just behind the point (*Figure 13.13*). The base of the rubber should be flat and can be made so by pressing it onto a clean dust-free surface, or into the palm of the hand, as was the traditional method. The size of the wadding and rubber may be adjusted to suit the work in hand, for example a small rubber may be useful for the corners of framed panels. There is a degree of 'feel' to the application of French polish and traditionally no gloves were used. After a polishing session it may be difficult to remove all traces of shellac from the hands. Shellac is soluble in water if the pH is raised slightly. Rinsing the hands with a solution of household washing soda, a mild alkali, after a polishing session will usually remove it. A skin cream may be applied to protect against dermatitis. If gloves are used to protect the hands from solvent and stain, they should be thin and tight. Polishing rubbers should be rinsed through with methylated spirits and stored in an airtight container when not in use.

The surface to be French polished is prepared by rubbing over with abrasive paper to remove any scraper marks, glue or other contaminants. Water or oil stain may be applied to the surface and allowed to dry completely. A traditional French polish is a full grain finish, so grain filling was required if the wood was a mid- or dark colour with open or semi-diffuse pores, such as walnut or mahogany. The pores of light-coloured or close-grained woods were filled with polish during an extended bodying up stage.

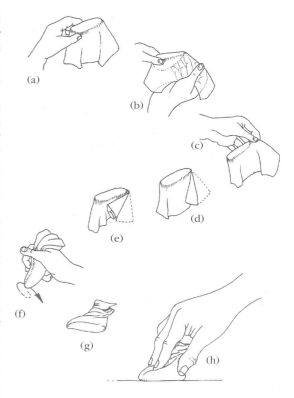

**Figure 13.13** Wrapping wadding for a French polishing rubber. The cloth is twisted from a point at the narrow end of the rubber (*c*), and then along the top of the rubber (*d,e,f*). The twist of cloth is held in the palm of the hand. Two fingers hold the point flat, whilst the body of the rubber is held lightly between the thumb and remaining two fingers (*h*). The base of the rubber should be pear-shaped, uncreased and flat

The application of polish began with a brush coat of shellac. While references for a wide range of concentrations can be found, a two pound 'cut' (i.e. two pounds of shellac to the gallon of spirit, or 100 g to 500 ml) works well through the initial and bodying up stages, after which the alcohol content is gradually increased until it reaches 100% for pulling over or spiriting out. Some polishers prefer to use isopropanol (propan-2-ol) or butanol (butan-1-ol) for spiriting out as they have less 'bite' than IMS or ethanol.

The French polishing rubber is opened and the rear of the wadding charged with polish. Excess is squeezed back into the bottle and the polish applied to the surface using long strokes. The rubber is charged repeatedly during a polishing session. If the rubber is too wet excess polish will squeeze from the edges and create ridges known as ropes or whips. If the rubber is too dry it will drag across the surface, pulling polish away, known as burning. The traditional method of assessing the wetness of a freshly charged rubber was to apply a stroke to the back of the hand – the shellac film thus produced should be very thin and even. The stroke begins in a corner and successive strokes are applied rapidly across the entire surface, working along the grain. The rubber is in constant motion when in contact with the surface. If the rubber should stop it will cause a blemish that must be abraded out after the surface has been allowed to dry. The centre of a panel is usually the easiest part to polish. Part of the skill of French polishing is applying even pressure as the rubber first comes into contact with the surface and making sure it is lifted off at the last moment without dropping or missing any of the edge. Some polishers keep the pad in contact with the surface until the series of strokes has been completed whilst others lift off at the end of each pass (*Figure 13.14a, d*). Polishers may vary the corner in which they start to ensure even application of polish during the bodying up stage and to avoid the inadvertent removal of polish from the corners as the alcohol content is increased. Regular examination of the surface in raking light will reveal faults in technique such as whips or ropiness.

Occasionally shellac will not 'take' on a surface that has been contaminated by oil or grease. If time allows interruption of polishing, the surface is allowed to dry and harden for at least twenty-four hours. The surface is then wiped over with a mild detergent solution and dried thoroughly before recommencing polishing. White spirit or an aromatic hydrocarbon may also be used and a drop of detergent added if necessary. When time does not allow for this, a drop or two of white mineral oil may be applied to the face of the polishing rubber and worked over the area. Although linseed oil was often used in traditional polishing, any excess that remains within the polish may cause crazing. Using oil will necessitate spiriting out at the end of the polishing session. Excess oil that is not removed when spiriting out may work its way

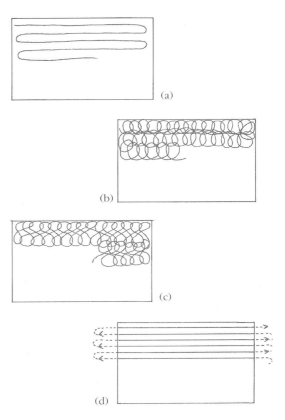

**Figure 13.14** Bodying up a French polish finish: (*a*) long straight motion; (*b*) small circular motions; (*c*) figures of eight (large or small); (*d*) pulling over

through the polish and appear after several days as small beads on the surface. This is known as sweating and may continue for a period of days, weeks or months, depending on the amount and type of oil that was used. The beads of oil that form on the surface must be removed and this is usually done using a combination of abrasion (e.g. fine wire wool or pumice powder) and a cleaning solution such a mild detergent solution. If the problem is minimal, it may be sufficient to use fine wire wool or pumice alone. The surface will require further polishing if a full gloss finish is required; if a dulled surface is acceptable a wax polish may be all that is necessary.

Bodying up involves working the polish into open grain using successive coats of shellac. This can be achieved using a rapid tight circular motion (guaranteed to produce whips from an overcharged rubber) followed by figures of eight (*Figure 13.14b, c*). Some polishers used pumice powder at this stage to speed filling the grain, sprinkling a little on the surface or onto the face of the rubber whilst continuing the polishing process. Pumice used in this way will abrade the outer skin of the polishing rubber and this should be replaced when pumicing is complete. The process of bodying up is labour-intensive and requires speed, energy and concentration. Whips will result if more pressure is applied to one side of the circular or figure of eight motion than the other – part of the skill of French polishing is in applying even pressure in these movements. In addition, the overall pressure applied is greater at the beginning of the bodying up process than at the end.

The technique of 'pulling over' is used at the end of a polishing session in order to give a smooth and level surface. An increasing proportion of alcohol is added to the rubber during pulling over. The rubber should be squeezed almost dry and the alcohol applied to the surface should evaporate in a matter of seconds. While some pressure is used in the filling stage, a light touch is required when pulling over because the finish is soft at this point and easily damaged. The rubber is worked in horizontal strokes along the grain until a level surface with a high gloss is achieved (*Figure 13.15d*). Some polishers add a sprinkle of a mild abrasive such as tripoli powder to the face of the pad as the last step in the polishing process (Frank, 1981).

Filling the grain in this way may require several polishing sessions. The polish should be allowed to dry and harden between sessions and the surface should be levelled using abrasive paper (320 grit) before commencing the next polishing session. Some texts refer to the addition of dilute gum benzoin in the final stages of bodying up. This provided a glossy surface and was a cheap alternative to spiriting out.

Oil was used by some French polishers to lubricate the surface. This allowed more polish to be applied in a single session and increased the productivity of polishing workshops. The oil used was either linseed oil or a non-drying mineral oil such as white oil. Some recommended a few droplets on the surface whilst others limited themselves to several drops on the face of the rubber itself. A great deal of effort in many texts is devoted to the removal of this oil at a later stage in the polishing process and the problems it could cause if it was trapped in the finish. It is entirely possible to French polish a surface without the use of any oil at all and this may be a safer option for novices given the breadth of problems the use of oil may cause.

Once the grain has been filled by bodying up, the surface is allowed to harden off and then denibbed. 'Spiriting out' in traditional texts refers to a process of building up a workable layer of polish using the circular and figure of eight motions described for bodying up. This is followed by the use of a mixture of 50:50 polish and methylated spirits, which is used to pull over the surface in order to level it and remove excess oil applied during the first stage (Hayward, 1988). This process may be repeated as many times as the polisher wishes, increasing the thickness of the varnish layer in each polishing session.

There comes a point in a polishing session when no more polish can be applied, the surface is as smooth as possible and the work must be set aside in a warm dust-free environment for the polish to harden off. Solvent evaporation may result in the polish sinking slightly so that pores filled in a previous session may again become visible. The surface film may lose up to 80% of its initial volume as the solvent evaporates. Minor faults or streaks may disappear as the polish shrinks and 'tightens up'. Specks of dust that are trapped in the surface as it dries are called 'nibs' and light abrasion between polishing sessions is known as 'denibbing'. A fine abrasive paper, 320 grit or above, may be used for this purpose once the surface coating has hardened off. If the surface is particularly uneven it may be lubricated with turpentine or white spirit and the denibbing used to flatten any faults such as whips or ropiness. A French polished surface is built up during successive polishing sessions over a period of a week or more. Once a surface has been French polished it may take up to six months to harden off completely. During this time the surface is susceptible to marking if any object or material is left in contact with it, particularly in warm conditions. If this occurs there is no alternative to abrading the damage out, applying fresh polish before pulling over to ensure a flat finish.

Once the surface has been levelled and has hardened off it may be dulled down using fine pumice or similar abrasive powder. Some polishers sprinkle a little powder onto the surface and use a good quality bristle shoe brush, working along the grain, to dull the surface. Others recommend placing the pumice into a flat container, dampening a cotton pad with linseed oil, and using the pad to pick up a little powder, which is then worked in even strokes along the grain (Oughton, 1982). Still others recommend working over the surface with fine (0000) wire wool sometimes adding a little wax paste to lubricate the surface (Hayward, 1988). It should be noted that French polishing was popular because it produced a glossy surface. Dulling the surface down is not an essential part of the process and may be inappropriate in some cases.

### Glazing

Glazing was used as a cheap alternative to French polishing and was used to impart finish with a high shine without an extended bodying up procedure. It was often used on carved, pierced or fretted surfaces and could be used in the corners of polished panels where it was difficult to create a smooth shiny surface by french polishing. Glaze was made by dissolving gum benzoin in methylated spirits (50/50 v/v). The benzoin was crushed, placed in a jar with the methylated spirits and shaken intermittently over a period of a few days. When the benzoin had dissolved the mix was strained to remove detritus. Hayward (1988) recommends diluting the benzoin until it is similar in colour to champagne. Glaze could be applied using a polishing rubber although strokes should not overlap and a period of about five minutes was needed between successive coats. Glaze could also be applied using a brush or dabbed on with a sponge (Oughton, 1982).

## 13.8  Craquelure, crazing and crocodiling

A byproduct of the ageing process of a transparent coating is a fine network of cracks known as craquelure. Craquelure may contribute to the patina of an aged surface and enhance the object's aesthetic or monetary value. Crazing describes the excessive cracking of a varnished surface, such that the surface below appears disfigured or obscured. Landrey (1984) has described the treatment of a crazed surface finish with abrasives. Crocodiling describes excessive shrinkage of a varnish layer that results in the varnish contracting into small islands, exposing the surface beneath. This effect may also be called alligatoring or traction crackle. Any material that results in a difference in drying rate between the surface of a varnish and the body or interior of this layer will produce some degree of cracking. The more exaggerated the difference, the more extreme the result. Thus thick oil or oil–resin varnish layers that incorporated excess driers are

(a)

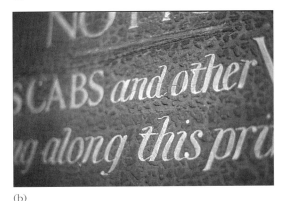

(b)

**Figure 13.15**  Crocodiling
(*a*) Crocodiling on a decorative component from a bed tester. The original red japanning was overpainted black in the nineteenth century. A second red overpaint has been applied over the crocodiled black layer. Accretions of dirt accentuated the crocodiled appearance. (*b*) An example of severe crocodiling on a road sign

particularly prone to this problem. Crocodiling of varnish layers may also be the result of the inclusion of non-drying bituminous materials such as asphaltum. The surface of varnishes that incorporate this material dry, whilst the interior does not. The non-drying interior is pulled into islands as the surface dries and contracts (*Figure 13.15*). It is impossible to reverse this effect. Treatment options will be determined in part by the nature of the object. In some cases, for example where such a finish contains information about an original decorative scheme, such a defect may be acceptable. In other cases, for example where the crocodiled varnish is an unwanted later restoration and can be separated from the original, partial or complete removal may be an option.

It may be difficult to match gloss or areas surrounded by cracked or crazed original surface coating. A crazed surface finish can sometimes be simulated using a two-part system that consists of a slow-drying undercoat and a fast-drying upper coat. A wide variety of materials may be utilized but the size and distribution of the cracks will vary and experimentation will be necessary to produce the desired result. Commercial products, such as 'Vernis à Vieillir et Craqueleur' by Lefranc and Bourgeois, are also available. Techniques that attempt to match craquelure vary in their success. Fairbairn (1988) described casting a silicone rubber mould with the pattern of craquelure and using it to cast a varnish infill that was then adhered with a thin coat of animal glue.

## 13.9   Polishing or dulling a varnished surface

Gloss can be increased if the surface is rubbed over with progressively finer grades of abrasive. This was the method used to polish spirit varnishes that had been applied with a brush to a high gloss. This method requires the use of a hard resin, such as shellac or sandarac. A lubricant, such as white spirit, may be used if required.

Examination of historic objects with aged coatings will demonstrate the variation in gloss present on an object. Recessed areas, for example, may be matte whilst high points may have a high sheen. Sensitivity to such varia-

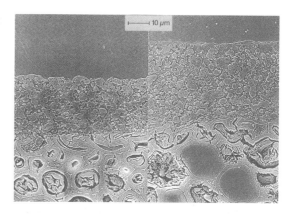

**Figure 13.16** Photomicrograph of cross-sections of a matte paint film applied to a porous wood substrate: (*left*) excessive absorption of binder into the substrate has left non-wetted particles exposed on the surface; (*right*) the inclusion of a thixotropic agent to ensure adequate wetting of particles of matted paint

tions will help in matching a new surface to the old. Gloss may be adjusted by using a mild abrasive to roughen the surface or by the addition of a matting agent such as fumed silica to the varnish. Some fumed silicas act as both matting agents and thixotropes. Thixotropes thicken the lacquer and prevent excessive penetration into absorbent substrates (*Figure 13.16*). If excessive absorption of a transparent matted varnish occurs, the matting agent may be visible as a white deposit in the pores of the wood (*Figure 13.17*). The use of non-thixotropic fumed silicas requires either

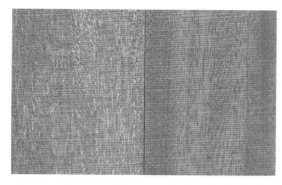

**Figure 13.17** A clear lacquer with a non-thixotropic fumed silica applied to bare wood. Excessive absorption of the binder into the porous substrate has left a white deposit in the open grain of the wood (*left*). Such deposits can be prevented by the addition of a thixotropic agent or by the pre-sealing the surface before applying the matted coating to the wood (*right*)

the addition of a separate thixotrope, or, more commonly in conservation, the surface of bare wood can be pre-sealed. It may be possible to manipulate gloss as a surface coating cures by removing a small amount of the upper layer of a coating or disturbing the surface when it has not completely cured by lightly padding it with a finger to create a textured surface. Misting on a top layer of resin from a spray gun may reduce surface gloss, as will increasing the distance from the object when spraying on a coating. A combination of these gloss modification techniques can be used in to create an appearance consistent with the age and appearance of the object.

Many historical sources refer to the use of powdered abrasives to polish or dull a varnished surface. Powdered abrasives vary in hardness, size and colour. Harder abrasive particles will remove more of the surface with each comparable motion, but particle size will determine whether the scratches produced will be visible. Thus aluminium oxide (Mohs hardness 9) will remove more material than jeweller's rouge (iron oxide, Mohs hardness 5.5–6) but if the particle sizes are the same, the surface appearance will be similar. The abrasive effect of particles on a surface is ameliorated by the presence of a lubricant, such as solvent or a small amount of wax. Precautions must be taken to avoid inhaling abrasive powders or abraded dust.

Pumice, rottenstone, tripoli and crocus powders, precipitated chalk and diatomaceous earth are traditional abrasive powders (see *Table 10.3*). Pumice comes in several grades but even the finest is often too coarse for transparent surfaces. Rottenstone has been used by finishers for centuries as a way to bring a gloss to a surface (Byington manuscript, *c*.1780). Modern materials include aluminium oxide, which can be purchased according to particle size, from 0.05 to 5 μm.

Transparent Plexiglass or Perspex may be used to carry out an empirical evaluation of the degree of scratching produced by different materials. Differences may be more easily visible under UV or raking light than under diffuse natural light. Matte black paper underneath the plastic may also be helpful.

It may be difficult to fully remove powdered abrasive from a surface that has fissures in the coating though a small amount of pigment or dye may be added to make such residues less obtrusive. This problem is less evident with abrasive papers since the abrasive is bound to the backing.

## 13.10 Distressing

Distressing describes the simulation of wear, minor damage, stains and accumulated dirt on a new surface, so that it resembles an aged surface. Many texts on furniture restoration describe methods of distressing repairs in order to simulate age and wear. These can include beating the new wood with bicycle chains, rocks, keys, barbed wire etc., though the effects are often a very poor imitation of the original. Examples of poor distressing include simulating wear evenly on all four arrises of a chair stretcher rather than concentrated on the upper front edge, or the repetitive denting of a surface with the same mark (e.g. a hammer). If distressing is to be undertaken, an old surface should be examined carefully and the type of wear or damage a surface or component would be likely to receive considered. Sharp or sanded edges to dents are rarely appropriate. Surface damage usually occurs long after polishing with the result that dirt is trapped above the surface finish, rather than below it.

Age and accumulated grime may be simulated using a thick solution of Vandyke stain (see, for example, Bennett, 1990). Inert powders such as rottenstone or dry earth pigments may be dusted into recessed areas. Some earth pigments present a health hazard (e.g. raw umber) and the supplier's or manufacturer's material safety data sheet should be consulted (McCann, 1979). A resin binder, preferably with different solubility parameters from the surface coating, may be used to selectively apply particulate material. The success of a matching a repair often depends on the finesse of adding and subtracting from the upper surface until the right visual qualities are achieved.

## Bibliography

Abercauph, C. (1998) Wax as a surface coating, in W. Samet (compiler), *Painting Conservation Catalogue:*

*Varnish and Surface Coatings*, AIC Paintings Specialty Group

Barclay, R. and Mathias, C. (1989) An epoxy microballoon mixture for gap filling in wooden objects, *JAIC*, 28, 31–42

Barnes, C. (1938) Chemical nature of shellac, *Industrial and Engineering Chemistry*, 30 (4), 449–51

Baron, B. (1987) *The Techniques of Traditional Woodfinishing*, Batsford

Baumeister, M., Boonstra, J., Blanchette, R.A., Fischer, C-H. and Schorsch, D. (1997) Stained burl veneer on historic furniture, in K. Walch and J. Koller (eds), *Baroque and Rococo Lacquers*, Arbeitshefte des Bayerischen Landesamtes für Denkmalpflege

Bennett, M. (1990) *Discovering and Restoring Antique Furniture*, Cassell

Bentley, J. and Turner, G.P.A. (1998) *Introduction to Paint Chemistry*, Chapman and Hall

Berrie, B.H. and Lomax, S.Q. (1996/1997) Azo pigments: their history, synthesis, properties and uses in artist's materials, in *Studies in the History of Art*, No. 57, Monograph Series, Conservation Research, National Gallery of Art, Washington

Brachert, T. (1978–9) Furniture varnishes, surfaces of furniture, *Maltechnik Restauro*, I-V

Deller, C. (2000) Some ideas for a better coating, *Conservation News*, 72, 28–9

Dodwell, C.R. (1961) *Theophilus: The Various Arts*, Thomas Nelson and Sons

Erhardt, D. (1998) Paints based on drying-oil media, in V. Dorge and F.C. Howlett (eds), *Painted Wood: History and Conservation*, Getty Conservation Institute, pp. 17–32

Fairbairn, G. (1988) Creating the right impression, in AIC Wooden Artifacts Group, Conference Papers, Vancouver

Feller, R.L., Stolow, N. and Jones, E. (1985) *On Picture Varnishes and Their Solvents*, National Gallery of Art, Washington, DC

Fiedler, I. and Walch, K. (1997) The varying fluorescence of veneer glues, in K. Walch and J. Koller (eds), *Baroque and Rococo Lacquers*, Arbeitshefte des Bayerischen Landesamtes für Denkmalpflege, pp. 297–304

Flexner, B. (1994) *Understanding Wood Finishing*, Rodale Press

Frank, G. (1981) *Adventures in Wood Finishing*, Taunton Press

Frank, G. (1986) French polishing, *Fine Woodworking*, 58, May

German, L. (1989) The physical effects of oxalic acid on wood, in AIC Wooden Artifacts Group, Conference Papers, Cincinnati

Gettens, R.J. and Stout G.L. (1966) *Painting Materials: an Encyclopaedia*, Dover

Grattan, D.W. and Barclay, R. (1988) A study of gap-fillers for wooden objects, *Studies in Conservation*, 33(2), 71–86

Hamburg, H.R. and Morgans, W.M. (1979) *Hess's Paint Film Defects*, Chapman and Hall

Hawthorne, J.G. and Smith, C.S. (1963) *On Divers Arts: The Treatise of Theophilus*, University of Chicago Press

Hayward, C. (1988) *Staining and Polishing*, Evans Bros, London/Unwin Hyman

Horie, V. (1992) *Materials for Conservation*, Butterworth-Heinemann

Jägers, E. and Jägers, E. (1999) Volatile binding media – useful tools for conservation, in *Reversibility – Does It Exist?* British Museum Occasional Paper No. 135

Keijzer, M. (1988) The blue, violet and green modern synthetic organic pigments of the twentieth century used as artist's pigments, in *Modern Organic Materials Meeting*, Conference Preprints, SSCR

Koller, J., Baumer, U., Schmid, A. and Grosser, D. (1997) Sandarac, in K. Walch and J. Koller (eds), *Baroque and Rococo Lacquers*, Arbeitshefte des Bayerischen Landesamtes für Denkmalpflege, pp. 379–94

Koller, J., Schmid, A. and Baumer, U. (1997) Baroque and rococo transparent varnishes on wood surfaces, in K. Walch and J. Koller (eds), *Baroque and Rococo Lacquers*, Arbeitshefte des Bayerischen Landesamtes für Denkmalpflege, pp. 161–96

Landrey, G.J. (1984) The Finish Crack'd: conservator's fix for a fractured film, *Fine Woodworking* 49, November, 74–6

Landrey, G.J. (1993) The conservator as curator, in L. Beckerdite (ed.), *American Furniture*, Chipstone Foundation

Landrey, G., Reinhold, N. and Wolbers, R. (1988) Surface treatment of a Philadelphia pillar and claw snap-top table, in AIC Wooden Artifacts Group, Conference Papers, Louisiana

Lee, W.H. (1967) Nitric acid, in J.J. Lagowski (ed.), *The Chemistry of Non-Aqueous Solvents*, Academic Press

McCann, M. (1979) *Artist Beware*, Watson-Guptill Publications

Mills, J. and White, R. (1977) Natural resins of art and archaeology: their sources, chemistry and identification, *Studies in Conservation*, 22(1), 12–31

Mills, J. and White, R. (1994) *The Organic Chemistry of Museum Objects*, Butterworths

Mussey, R. (1980) Transparent furniture finishes in New England – 1700–1820, in *Proceedings of the Furniture and Wooden Objects Symposium*, CCI

Mussey, R. (1982a) Old finishes – what put the shine on furniture's Golden Age, *Fine Woodworking*, 33, March/April, 71–74

Mussey, R. (1982b) Early varnishes: the 18th century's search for the perfect film finish, *Fine Woodworking*, 35, July/August, 54–8

Mussey, R. (ed.) (1987) *The First American Furniture Finisher's Manual*, Reprint of the 1827 edition of *The Cabinet-Maker's Guide*, Dover

New, S. (1981) The use of stain by furniture makers 1660–1850, *The Journal of the Furniture History Society* 17, 51–60

Oughton, F. (1982) *The Complete Manual of Wood Finishing*, Stobart & Son

Penn, T.Z. (1966) Decorative and protective finishes, 1750–1850: materials, process and craft. Masters thesis, University of Delaware

Piena, H. (2001) Regalrez in furniture conservation, *JAIC*, 40, 59–69

Plenderleith, H.J. and Werner, A.E.A. (1971) *The Conservation of Antiquities and Works of Art*, Oxford University Press

Radley, J.A. and Grant, J. (1954) *Fluorescence Analysis in Ultraviolet Light*, Chapman and Hall

Rodd, J. (1976) *Repairing and Restoring Antique Furniture*, David & Charles

Roelop, W. (1994) Coloured mordants on a set of Dutch marquetry furniture from the late 18th century, in *Contributions of the Central Research Laboratory to the Field of Conservation and Restoration*, Rijksmuseum, Amsterdam

Samet, W. (compiler) (1998) *Painting Conservation Catalogue: Varnish and Surface Coatings*, AIC Paintings Specialty Group

Sheraton, Thomas (1803) *The Cabinet Dictionary*, Praeger facsimile edition, 1970

*Spons Workshop Receipts, for the use of Manufacturers, Mechanics, and Scientific Amateurs* (1884), E&FN Spon

Thornton, J. (1998a) A brief history and review of the early practice and materials of gap-filling in the West, *JAIC*, 37, 3–22

Thornton, J. (1998b) The use of dyes and coloured varnishes in wood polychromy, *Painted Wood: History and Conservation*, Symposium Proceedings Getty Conservation Institute, pp. 226–41

Walch, K. (1993) Traditional coating techniques in Germany: general overview and conservation case studies, in *Conservation of Urushi Objects*, Tokyo National Research Institute of Cultural Properties

Walch, K. (1997) Baroque and Rococo transparent gloss lacquers, in K. Walch and J. Koller (eds), *Baroque and Rococo Lacquers*, Arbeitshefte des Bayerischen Landesamtes für Denkmalpflege

Walch, K. and Koller, J. (1997) *Baroque and Rococo Lacquers*, Arbeitshefte des Bayerischen Landesamtes für Denkmalpflege

Watin (1755), *L'Art du peintre*, reprinted Chez Leonce Larget, 1975

Williams, D.C. (1988) Shellac finishing: a traditional finish still yields outstanding results, *Fine Woodworking*, July, 56–59

Wolbers, R. (1992) Recent developments in the use of gel formulations for the cleaning of paintings, *Restoration 1992*, Conference Preprints, IIC, pp. 74–75

# 14

# Introduction to traditional gilding

## 14.1 Background

Gilding describes the practice of applying extremely thin gold leaf to a surface to imitate solid gold or to otherwise imitate the appearance of solid gold. Gilded surfaces were originally viewed under daylight or candle light, the only forms of illumination. They were often embellished with texture that gave variations in reflectivity and added to the overall decorative effect. The European tradition, later exported to the New World, traditionally applied gold leaf using the distinct processes of water gilding and oil gilding. These processes are distinguished by different methods of preparation and application that result in varying surface appearances. This chapter will outline the traditional materials and techniques used to create gilded surfaces on wood as well as giving a brief introduction to the conservation of such surfaces.

Gilding is a skill with a strong craft tradition, historically passed from master to apprentice, and was traditionally subject to a great deal of secrecy. There is, as a consequence of this tradition, a wide variation in the preparation of materials and application techniques within this craft. Although the principles of gilding are fairly standardized, gilding practice is not. The information presented in this chapter should be considered a guide to the continuum of practice that constitutes traditional gilding.

Techniques to imitate the appearance of solid gold have been used in all cultures that have placed a high value on gold. Using many similar techniques to those used today, the ancient Egyptians, for example, utilized rounded stones and bronze hammers to beat the gold into leaf form, which was laid onto surfaces of gesso and clay (Hatchfield and Newman, 1991). Despite this technical continuity there has been a wide range of stylistic and regional differences in the way gilding has been used as a decorative surface. The context, date, style, country or even region will have a direct bearing on the gilding of an object. As a result a thorough knowledge of historical styles, materials and techniques is essential when trying to reproduce gilding of a particular style or period. The appearance of the gold and groundwork of a sixteenth century Italian icon or altarpiece, for example, is very different to that of a Louis XV console table. The appearance of gilding can vary greatly depending on different treatment of the groundwork, colours of clay and gold, the method of leaf application and treatment of gold after it has been laid.

### 14.1.1 Water and oil gilding

The two basic techniques of gilding onto a wooden substrate are water gilding, which traditionally utilized a collagen glue, and oil gilding, where the gold leaf is adhered to the ground by a mordant, usually an oil-based size. The principle of using thin gold leaf applied to a surface to simulate solid gold is similar in both cases but the materials and techniques used to apply water and oil gilding differ. Water gilding must be laid onto a porous ground, normally gesso, and is a more time-consuming process than oil gilding. It is water soluble and is therefore unsuitable for exterior use. It is primarily, though not exclusively, used on fine furniture and objects. Water gilding can be burnished to a highly reflective shine, whilst oil gilding cannot. Oil gilding can be used on porous and non-porous substrates such as wood, metal, plastics or stone. Oil gilding is used for exterior work because of the water-resistant nature of the oil mordant. It is used for gilding areas when the labour costs associated with water gilding would be prohibitive (for example interior architectural work) or when the style or decorative scheme of a piece demands the lustre of oil gilding, which differs from that of water gilding. Oil gilding is also used where the degree of very fine detail would make water gilding impractical.

The appearance of water gilding will be affected by the use of different coloured clays in the bole layer and the use of different colours and alloys of gold leaf. The gold leaf is so thin that it is translucent and if a single leaf is held up to a light source such as a candle a slight green–blue tinge may be observed. This translucence means that the colour of the bole underneath will affect the perception of colour of the gold leaf. In addition, gold is often abraded (by age or intent). Gilding is seldom absolutely complete, so bole often shows to a limited or large extent. Thus both bole and leaf must be matched to the original if a restoration repair is made.

Prior to gilding, the ground was worked to give varying decorative effects to the finished gilded surface. These effects vary according to regional differences in the nature and application of the gesso, styles of gesso recutting and the tools used, the use of effects such as pastiglia, pressbrokaat, the use of composition and other moulded and applied ornament as well as applications to the surface of the gesso such as sand, poppy seeds, shell and various types of woven netting. The application of these techniques creates a decorative effect by enhancing the play of light over the surface. The variations in reflectivity thus produced give the visual illusion of a greater depth of form in the decorated surface.

Once water gilding has been laid the appearance can be further modified by techniques such as punchwork, scraffito, variations in lustre (matte/burnish) or by the application of coloured glazes. The application of glazes to create decorative effects is called lustrework. The subsequent application of toning layers was also used to enrich the depth and contrasting lustre of the gilded surface. Thus each stage of the gilding process, from the preparation of the ground to the treatment of the gold, plays a vital part in the appearance of a gilded object. The appearance is further modified over time by ageing processes, including wear resulting from use and historical restoration or regilding treatments.

Although conservators may be confronted by the need to repair gilding on furniture, there are comparatively few reliable guides to the gilding process. Cennini's fifteenth century Florentine text (trans. Thompson, 1954), Watin (1755) and Thompson (1956, 1962) provide a fascinating insight into historical materials and techniques. Other texts and articles on methods and materials include Scott-Mitchell (1905), MacTaggart and MacTaggart (1984) and Wetherall (1991a). Green (1991) described the traditional method of gilding spherical balls. Cession (1990) and Koller (1991) discuss the eighteenth century practice of embellishing baroque gilded decoration with coloured varnishes. Powell (1998) examines historical sources and compares English and French gilding techniques.

### 14.1.2　Tools for gilding

As with gilding practice, the tools used by gilders vary according to personal preference and training (*Figure 14.1*).

The gilder's cushion is a hand-held leather pad onto which loose leaves of gold are

**Figure 14.1**　A range of tools and materials that may be used in traditional gilding

**Figure 14.2**  A gilder's cushion

**Figure 14.3**  A gilder's knife, and a gilder's tip being used to pick up cut gold leaf

placed and cut (*Figure 14.2*). It is a rectangular board, usually about six inches by ten inches (150×250 mm), covered very evenly with two or three layers of felt or velvet over which is stretched a piece of very fine calfskin, chamois leather or suede, rough-side up. A piece of parchment is tacked on at one end and encloses the back and half the length of the sides, acting as a windshield. A leather thumb loop, and a loop for storing the knife are attached to the underside of the cushion. Some gilders prefer a larger cushion without a windshield and gild directly from the book of gold. Cushions can be purchased from gilders' suppliers although many gilders make their own.

The cushion is divided into two working areas. The back of the cushion, usually surrounded by the parchment shield, is used for depositing and storing the loose leaves of gold. The front of the cushion is used to blow the leaf flat and cut, once a single leaf has been teased from the pile at the back. The surface of the leather at the front of the cushion must be kept in good condition so that the gold will lie flat and cut cleanly. Loose particles can be removed with a vacuum cleaner or stiff brush. Jewellers rouge may also be worked into the leather and acts as a polishing agent that helps to keep the knife clean and sharp when in use. It also prevents the gold leaf sticking to the cushion, as will the application of a little talc (French chalk) to the leather.

The gilder's knife, used for manipulating and cutting the gold, is similar in appearance to an old fashioned table knife. It should be well balanced and have a flat blade at least six inches (150 mm) long with an angled end (*Figure 14.3*). It is often very lightweight, as it may be held for long periods between the ring finger and little finger of the hand holding the cushion. The blade is usually flexible in order to get underneath the leaves of gold to lift them. The cutting edge must be free from imperfections, burrs, nicks or other damage, which will tear the gold. The blade of the knife must be sharp enough to cut the gold without damaging the cushion. Unlubricated fine grade wet-and-dry abrasive paper may be used to sharpen the knife if necessary during gilding. Every now and then the knife will need to be sharpened with a fine water stone. An 800 grit water stone can be used to grind a bevel of about 45° on both sides of the knife. This will make the knife too sharp to use without damaging the cushion and as a result it may be necessary to blunt the edge slightly. This can be done by rubbing the edge with 600 grit wet and dry silicon carbide paper, or by pulling it across a piece of softwood or cork. If the knife becomes contaminated with grease, water or static, which will cause the gold leaf to stick to it, the blade may be wiped or buffed with talc (French chalk).

Gilders' tips are used for picking up loose leaf gold from the cushion and laying it onto the work (*Figure 14.3*, and see also *Figure 14.15*). Tips consist of a thin layer of hair sandwiched between two pieces of cardboard. The width is usually standard but there are different thicknesses and lengths of hair. The hair is usually of squirrel or badger. Squirrel is used for laying gold and silver leaf whilst badger is only suitable for leaf and foil made from lesser metals, which are usually heavier and thicker than gold leaf. Old tips can be cut up to make smaller ones that are useful for gilding into deep or awkward areas of carving. Tips for laying whole leaves of gold can be made by gluing one tip behind another to create a longer hair surface. A cork can then be adhered to the upper surface. To prevent the hairs from shedding from new tips, a very fine line of shellac polish can be applied to the edge of both sides where the hair meets the cardboard. Tips may be cleaned by placing them on a clean flat surface and combing through the hair with chalk on a stiff brush or a ball of cotton wool soaked in methylated spirits (denatured ethanol).

Gesso hooks are used to recut and engrave the gesso before the application of bole and water gilding (see section 14.2.11). They are made of hardened steel that is bent, profiled and sharpened at one end with a handle attached to the other. Gesso hooks were extensively used in France, where recutting became highly developed during the eighteenth century. The best quality and widest range of gesso hooks are still found in France. Gesso hooks are sharpened in a similar manner to carving tools, but as the cutting bevel is used to scrape rather than cut it is ground at a less acute angle, usually between 10 and 15 degrees. Gesso hooks are used by drawing the tool into the gesso, towards the recutter (see *Figure 14.7*). English and American carvers and gilders commonly used ordinary carving tools for recutting, often reserving a simple set for working 'in the white'.

Metal punches may be used for stamping decoration into the finished water gilded surface. Punches may be purchased in a variety of designs but it is usually necessary to custom-make one's own if an original punched surface is being matched. Ring punches and double ring punches may be made on an engineer's lathe but designs such as stars and pin groups are usually shaped using a grinder, needle files, a graver or burin. The cutting edge of punches are polished, as they lack cutting edges. This gives a burnish in the indented punched pattern without cutting the gold.

Burnishers are used for polishing water gilding to a high lustre, sometimes known as burnish gilding, and come in many different shapes. A selection of profiles may be required by a gilder but one of the more useful shapes is the hockey-stick or dog's-tooth type (see *Figure 14.18*). Highly polished agate (silicon dioxide) stones attached to a wooden handle are most commonly used to make modern burnishers as they are hard wearing and can be repolished several times. Other stones that may be utilized in this way include flint, black flint (both types of silicon dioxide) and hematite. Hematite is an iron oxide and is softer than agate. Cennini recommended 'sapphires, emeralds, balas rubies, topazes, rubies and garnets or the tooth of any flesh-eating animal'. Burnishing stones should be treated with care and stored in a soft cloth cover, such as a tool roll or the cut off fingers of cotton gloves. Any scratches in the stone will damage the gold when attempting to burnish it. Professional repolishing will produce the best burnishing surface.

Round stringed hog-hair brushes are often used for applying the protein size coat, yellow ochre or clay and in most cases the gesso. Two types are available – long-haired brushes, most often used and supplied in England and Italy, and the short-haired type used in France. Gilding mops are round with domed heads, made from squirrel hair. Many different sizes of both types of brushes are available. Their primary use is applying the gilding water as they hold the liquid well and distribute it evenly onto the clay bole. In oil gilding, large mops may be used to brush lightly over the surface in order to press the gold gently onto the oil size. Squirrel dabbers or sable tampers are used to press down on the gold once it has been laid in order to remove any air bubbles. Traditionally the soft, supple hairs are cut to a flat tip and are attached to a quill, which can be placed over the end of a gilding mop. Chisel-ended sable writer's brushes may also be used for this purpose. Dabbers and tampers can be purchased individually or as a set and range in size from 'lark' to 'swan', names that derive from the birds that historically supplied the quills. These brushes must be kept clean and dry. They may be washed with very mild soap and water and brushed out so that they dry straight. Sable brushes are considered the best brushes to use for apply-ing clay, although ox hair or even nylon are cheaper and can work well. Round brushes are ideal as they hold and distribute the clay evenly. Flat or round sable brushes may also be used for applying a coating to the gold. Sable-ox hair mixtures for larger sizes offer some economy over pure sable whilst retain-ing good working properties. Separate brushes should be used for water gilding and oil gilding, as oil residues will prevent adhesion of water gilt leaf.

### 14.1.3   Gold and metal leaf

Modern gold leaf is slightly thinner than that used by the Egyptians or in medieval Europe. Gold leaf is prepared by casting bars that are then rolled and annealed. The leaf was hand beaten to its final thickness. Gold leaf has been machine beaten to its final thickness since the late nineteenth century, though traditional hand beaten gold leaf is still manufactured on a small scale. Commercial twenty-four carat gold leaf may vary between 0.3 and 0.8 μm. Pure gold leaf is available in 'single' and 'double' weight. There is no industry standard for the thickness of gold leaf and as a result the thickness of one manufacturer's leaf may be nearly double that of another, but both may still be named 'regular'. Gold leaf is available as loose leaf and transfer leaf. Loose leaf may be used in water or oil gilding and is applied with a gilder's tip, whereas transfer leaf, also available in rolls, is pressed onto a mordanted or oil sized surface and cannot be burnished to a high lustre. Other metals such as copper or silver may be alloyed with the gold to produce leaves of differing colour and hardness (*Plate 7* and see *Table 5.2*). The presence of alloy metals may cause gold leaf to oxidize and change colour over time, partic-ularly in lower carat weight leafs where the non-gold content is higher. Other types of metal leaf include silver, white gold, copper, aluminium, palladium and platinum. Silver, platinum and palladium leaf are slightly thicker than gold leaf. Schlag leaf, also known as Dutch metal, is a thick leaf alloyed from copper and zinc with a marked tendency to tarnish if it is left uncoated. Aluminium, copper and schlag, used only in oil gilding, require slightly different handling techniques, which

are outlined by MacTaggart and MacTaggart (1984). Lewis (1763–5) describes the process used to manufacture gold leaf in the eighteenth century whilst MacTaggart and MacTaggart (1984) outline the modern process.

Any excess pieces of gold that are too small to be used on the piece, or are brushed from the surface after gilding is complete, are called skewings. They may be collected separately according to the colour of the leaf and used to make gold powder, which is expensive and may be difficult to obtain from commercial suppliers. When a sufficient quantity of skewings have been collected they are mixed with a small amount of honey and ground into a powder using a mortar and pestle or a slab and muller (Cennini, trans. Thompson, 1954). Although the process should take only 10 or 15 minutes, the longer the skewings are ground, the finer the resulting gold powder will be. Very fine powder will appear slightly dull whereas very large particles will tend to clump together in use. The gold powder may be separated from the honey by placing the honey and gold mixture into a container and covering it with hot water. When the gold has settled to the bottom the water may be poured off. This process may be repeated five times, the last two rinses with deionized water. If making powdered gold, most of the last rinse water may be poured away and the remain-der left to evaporate. The powder may be made into a gold paint, also known as shell gold, by the addition of a drop of concen-trated gum arabic when most of the water has evaporated (MacTaggart and MacTaggart, 1984). Shell gold and powdered gold are painted on with a brush or rubbed onto the surface with a finger. Shell gold, in gum arabic, requires only the humidity of a breath to reactivate the medium, whilst powdered gold requires the application of a layer of size or mordant. Shell and powdered gold are mostly used for letter-writing, drawing small designs, repairs to small abrasions or may be used in deeply carved recesses that would be inaccessible to gold leaf.

### 14.1.4   Surface preparation

A surface that is to be gilded should be clean, stable and free from defects. In the case of water gilding on wood, it is critical that the wood be dry, free of grime, oil and finger marks, or traces of varnish, strippers or other chemicals. All these contaminants will interfere with the adhesion of gesso to the wood. Wood that has been prepared for gilding should be kept covered so that airborne grime does not settle on it.

Degreasing cleans the surface of the wood in preparation for gilding new work. It may raise the grain so that the subsequent coat of rabbit skin size is able to penetrate the surface of the wood slightly, providing a mechanical key to strengthen the adhesive bond. If the wood is clean and has not been handled then degreasing may be unnecessary. The choice of degreaser will depend on the type of wood and the level of dirt and grease. A 3–10% solution of .880 ammonium hydroxide in cold water may be used for cleaning wood that has been handled a great deal or is particularly dirty. It should be applied with a hogs hair brush of a suitable size for the job. The effectiveness of the mixture will be seen almost immediately as the dirt and grease rise quickly to the surface. A sponge may be used to mop up any excess that may have collected in the recesses of carving. The work must be thoroughly rinsed and allowed to dry afterwards to allow the evaporation of any residual ammonia. This method is only used with new work and is not appropriate for historical artefacts.

Cellulose thinners or methylated spirits (denatured ethanol) may also be used to degrease surfaces but will not raise the grain of the wood. They may be applied with a hog's-hair brush but extra care should be taken to ensure that dirt and deposits are removed from the recesses of carving. It is not usually necessary to rinse the work, but if it has been handled a great deal or if it is particularly dirty the surface should be rinsed with fresh solvent. The use of solvents or ammonium hydroxide for degreasing will require efficient extraction and good workshop ventilation.

Surface defects, such as splits in the wood, minor losses to carved details or excessive roughness, can be patched with a gesso putty. Larger losses may require a wood patch. Knots on resinous woods must be sealed and this is usually done with a shellac varnish, such as button polish. Joints, splits or shakes in wood that is to be water gilded are sometimes covered with a fine fabric such as cotton or silk. On some larger pieces the surface is overlaid with linen before the application of gesso. In both cases the surface must be sized before fabric is applied and the material is then applied using the same glue size mix.

### 14.1.5 Gesso putty

Gesso putty may be used as a filling material for small faults in the wood or gesso. It may be made by adding the stock glue size to the whiting, or whiting to the glue. A quantity of warmed stock glue size is poured into a well in the whiting. The wetted whiting from the sides of the well is mixed into the size until it forms a ball. The hands of the gilder are dusted with whiting and the ball picked up and pressed into the whiting, to gather more whiting onto the ball. The ball is then rolled in the hands to give a uniform mix, with a consistency similar to Plasticene. Alternatively, whiting may be added to a small amount of stock glue size until a putty-like consistency is achieved. Small quantities may be mixed in the palm of the hand and kept warm for use by wrapping the putty in film wrap and keeping it next to one's skin. Putty fills may be shaped as they are applied using a fine potter's spatula with an elongated head and rounded edges.

## 14.2 Water gilding

### 14.2.1 Conditions for gilding

Stable temperature and relative humidity are important because movement in the wood during the process of gessoing may cause cracking or flaking of the gesso. Workshop temperature should ideally be around 22 °C so that the glue does not gel before penetrating into the pores of the wood. Dust should be kept to an absolute minimum so that it does not settle on the surface of work in progress or contaminate the gesso.

### 14.2.2 Size

In its broadest sense, the term 'size' refers to any material used to seal or pre-treat a porous surface. In the context of water gilding, the term size refers to rabbit skin or parchment glue mixed with water. It is used to seal the substrate and provides the base for the gesso. Rabbit skin size is now most commonly used throughout the gilding process, but traditionally parchment cuttings were used. Parchment size is finer and less viscous than rabbit skin size and is still used by some modern gilders, even though it is inconvenient and more time-consuming to prepare in the quantities necessary for the size coats and gesso layers. Rabbit skin granules and sheets are readily available, easy to prepare in quantity, and are more consistent in strength. They are therefore ideal to use for preparing the size coat and binder in the gesso.

### 14.2.3    Preparation of glue size

Glue size and gesso should always be prepared in a double boiler or 'bain marie'. The temperature of the mixture should be no higher than 55 °C in the preparation and subsequent reheating of the rabbit skin size. Higher temperatures will denature the protein, impairing the elasticity and adhesive properties of the glue.

The strength of the prepared size is determined by the ratio of dry glue to water. Some gilders prefer a very strong solution of four parts of water to one part of dry glue whilst others use a medium strength solution of ten parts water to one part dry glue. There are dangers in making the glue too strong or too weak: if it is very strong it will be difficult to smooth once dry and will burnish poorly, whilst if it is too weak the gesso will have little strength and may crumble.

A medium strength solution of 1:10 v/v rabbit skin granules to water is recommended here. After pre-soaking in water, preferably overnight or for at least four hours, the rabbit skin granules should be gently warmed (40–50 °C) in a double boiler and occasionally stirred until the glue has dissolved. If a skin forms it indicates that either the glue is too hot or the room is too cold. Once evenly melted, the size should be set aside, allowed to cool and the gel assessed for strength.

Parchment size may be prepared by cutting the parchment into small pieces about an inch square and soaking them in cold water for at least an hour. The water is discarded and the clippings rinsed in clean running water. The cuttings are placed in a double boiler and the outer water simmered for two to four hours.

One pound (454 g, dry weight) of cuttings may be simmered in four pints (approx. two litres) of water and will result in a fairly strong size roughly equivalent to a 1:6 or 1:7 (v/v water:glue granules) mix prepared with rabbit skin glue. Some gilders prefer a slightly weaker size prepared with ¼ pound parchment clippings (113 g) in two pints (1.137 litres) of water (Green, 1979; Sheraton, 1803). In either case the clippings are discarded before the parchment size is strained through two thicknesses of fine tights or silk, allowed to set and assessed for gel strength. The liquid should be clear and when it has set should appear transparent with a yellowish tinge. Although believed to be necessary for the best quality gesso, parchment may be difficult to acquire in large quantities. Parchment size may be reserved for mixing with the bole or for matting and protecting the gold.

### 14.2.4    Assessing gel strength

Rabbit skin glue and parchment size may vary in the gel strength produced from batch to batch. Since the gel strength is critical to the success of the gessoing, it is essential that each mix of size is allowed to cool and set to allow gel strength to be assessed. The size should be left overnight for this purpose. Gel strength is a matter of feel. Run a fingertip over the surface of the size – it should have the feel of a medium to stiff table jelly. If the gel is broken easily and cleanly it is the right strength. If a fingertip can be pushed into the size without the glue breaking apart, it is too strong and must be warmed and diluted before testing gel strength again. If the gesso cannot be cleanly parted it is too weak and a fresh batch should be made.

### 14.2.5    Sizing the wood

Once the surface has been cleaned and dried a thin layer of glue size is applied to the surface. It is important for this coat of size to penetrate the wooden support as much as possible in order to provide adhesion and stability to the subsequent gesso layers.

The wood may be coated with pure size, or size with a little whiting added, this last known as clair colle or clearcole. If the wood is very absorbent and open grained it may be necessary to use a size coat as strong as six parts water to one part glue and to apply a second coat. The strength of the size coat may vary from a glue strength of 4:1 to 10:1 v/v water to dry glue – the fundamental principle of gilding is that size and gesso should progress from strong to weak as the layers are built up – subsequent gesso layers should *never* be based on a stronger mix than was used for the size coat. Care should be taken to avoid applying too much size or allowing it to puddle. The wood should not have a shiny appearance after the size has dried.

Sufficient size to cover the job should be warmed in a double boiler. Some gilders apply the hot glue to the surface using a stiff gesso brush to work the size into the grain, using a tamping motion to reach recesses and under-cut carving. Some gilders stiffen a hog's-hair brush by wrapping the hairs to within a couple of inches of the end with butcher's twine and coating the wrapping with epoxy. Some gilders prefer to use a second size coat of clair colle (thin white), made by adding a small quantity of whiting (calcium carbonate) or calcium sulphate to the size. This allows the gilder to see where the size has been applied and may provide a mechanical key for the subsequent gesso layer (Watin, 1755). The whiting should be added when the glue has been warmed to around 37–40 °C (blood temperature). The amount of whiting is not critical but should be enough to give the size a milky appearance – a rounded tablespoon of whiting added to 300 ml (10 fl oz) will be sufficient. The whiting should be sieved and then sprinkled onto the surface of the size, allowed to settle and then stirred very gently with a hog's hair gesso brush gently backwards and forwards on the bottom of the container until the whiting is mixed into the size. A wetting agent, such as few drops of methylated spirits (denatured ethanol) or Photoflo, may be added to reduce the surface tension of the size coat. Whether size or clair colle is used, the surface should be allowed to dry thoroughly before subsequent coats of gesso are applied.

### 14.2.6 Gesso

The function of the gesso layer is to provide a surface that can be smoothed to a fine finish onto which gold can be laid. The gesso layers obscure both the grain and any imperfections in the wooden substrate and provide a cushioning layer that allows the gold to be burnished. Gesso is an adaptable material that can be textured, recut, incised or engraved and can also be used to make raised designs. The polymeric coiled structure of collagen glue produces a material that is slightly elastic, even when dried to equilibrium with the ambient environment. This allows the gesso to tolerate a certain amount of substrate movement without flaking. Gesso provides a fine, white, uniform surface and has traditionally been used as a ground for painting, water gilding and, on occasion, oil gilding. Additional information on gesso can be found in Chapter 4.

The term gesso originally referred to a gypsum-based ground such as those commonly used in southern Europe, and in some conservation disciplines this specific definition remains. In the context of gilded furniture, the term gesso now commonly includes gesso based on calcium carbonate. Thus 'gesso' describes a mixture of either rabbit skin or parchment size combined with an inert filler. In Northern European regions, particularly England and France, a very fine variety of calcium carbonate (chalk whiting – $CaCO_3$), known as gilder's whiting, is used to make gesso. This whiting produces a gesso that is fine and hard, suitable for recutting and crisp outlines. In Italy and other regions of Southern Europe, calcined gypsum (plaster of Paris) is used as a filler to make gesso.

The use of different fillers produces gessoes with distinct characteristics. Each type will produce a different appearance on the final surface. It is not possible, for example, to recut Italian gesso sottile as finely as is necessary to reproduce the sharp and intricate designs on many pieces of French furniture. Similarly, the soft look and fluid feel of Italian and Spanish gilded works, which is partly achieved by the malleable nature of gesso sottile, cannot be reproduced using calcium carbonate as a filler. Kaolin (China clay) has also been used occasionally as a filler, for example on highly detailed French carving in the nineteenth century and on oriental objects (see, for example, Larson and Kerr, 1985). The detail in the carving is not lost because only one or two coats are applied and a relatively good burnish can be achieved using this method. Thin coats of gesso, however, have a tendency to flake and gesso made with kaolin cannot be built up as successfully as calcium carbonate into a thick gesso layer.

The strength of glue size used in gesso recipes varies widely, but in general varies between 15:1 and 10:1 v/v water to rabbit skin glue granules. It is essential to prepare enough gesso to complete the whole job because if more than one preparation of gesso is used on the same piece of work the glue strength may vary between the batches. This can lead to delamination if later layers have utilized a stronger size. The gesso should be made using size that has been pre-prepared and tested for gel strength. The size should be warmed in a double boiler and allowed to cool slightly before adding the whiting. The whiting may be ground in a mortar and pestle and/or sieved to remove lumps and large particles. The whiting should be sprinkled slowly onto the surface of the glue. The amount of whiting added will depend upon the thickness of gesso required for the job. Some sources recommend a thinner gesso mix for softwoods (Wetherall, 1992). Some types of carving may require only two or three thin coats of gesso in order to fill the grain and smooth out any tool marks. Work that requires extensive recutting should receive more coats of gesso.

A medium viscosity gesso may be produced by sprinkling the whiting into the glue until a cone covers about half the surface of the size (approximately a 2:1 w/w ratio of whiting to glue) or until the whiting is level just below the surface of the size. Some gilders allow the whiting to settle and absorb the size and then stir gently with a wooden stick, whilst others stir the mixture as the whiting is added. Stirring should always be gentle – excessive or vigorous stirring will cause air bubbles in the gesso. The mixture should be about the consistency of thick cream and may be brushed out on a test piece of wood to check that it produces a smooth even layer. Some gilders add a few drops of linseed oil, a pea size lump of tallow wax, a drop of alcohol or other surfactant to the gesso to improve the working properties of the gesso, prevent a skin forming on the top and reduce the number of pin holes. It is critical to avoid or minimize the formation of bubbles in the

gesso. The likelihood of bubbles increases as temperature rises, or if excessive agitation is used when stirring the whiting into the glue. The gesso may be strained through a double layer of fine nylon tights or silk. Once the gesso is made it may be left to sit. This allows for better absorption of glue in the whiting and gives any air bubbles time to rise to the surface where they can be removed once the gesso has cooled. If the gesso has gelled it should be slowly reheated to around 37–40 °C.

### 14.2.7　Application of gesso

Some gilders prefer to work by slicing enough gelled gesso from the stock batch to apply a coat to the work whilst others simply use one large batch. In either case, warm the pre-prepared gesso in a double boiler and ensure that the temperature of the gesso does not exceed 45 °C. Once warmed, the gesso should be applied to the work. Some gilders take gesso onto the brush from the centre to bottom of the gesso container, swirling the gesso gently each time to avoid the formation of a skin on the surface, whilst others take slowly from the side of the container. In either case excess gesso should be removed from the brush before it is applied to the work. Always try to brush on each gesso layer in one application without breaking off, which will avoid the formation of ridges or an uneven build-up in the gesso.

All the necessary coats should ideally be applied on the same day, using the same batch of gesso, to avoid the possibility of the layers delaminating. If this is not achievable it is possible to go over the dry gesso with a damp brush. This will reactivate the glue in the dry gesso reducing both the possibility of 'shelling' and the occurrence of pinholes in the next layer. Each subsequent layer should be applied once the preceding layer has become dull or matte, which indicates that the glue has gelled but is not yet completely dry. The gesso will tend to thicken during the extended process of applying multiple gesso coats. Some gilders add a little water to reduce the viscosity of the gesso and to slightly reduce the strength of the upper layers, reducing the risk of delamination and allowing for a better burnish to the gold. Adding water in this way, however, makes it more difficult to assess the relative strength of the bole size. Care should be taken to avoid brushing gesso onto the side of the bowl where it may congeal, dry and then form lumps that fall into the liquid gesso below.

The method of application of the gesso varies according to the style and period of the work, the type of gesso and the number of coats required. A flat panel may require a minimum of eight coats, whilst a carved panel may require four even coats over the whole surface followed by a further four coats on raised areas that are to be burnished. A thin gesso, with a lower proportion of whiting (calcium carbonate), may be used for carved work that is very crisply gessoed and will not be recut. This gesso takes longer to apply and will tend to thicken if left on the heat source. Some gilders prevent the gesso from overheating and thickening by removing the inner container with the gesso from the heat completely and exchanging external bowls. The bowl not in use is placed on the heat source, and exchanged when the other cools.

The gesso may be applied quickly and carefully with a soft brush small enough to reach into the depths of the carving (*Figure 14.4*). Once enough coats have been laid on, the surface should show no tool marks or wood grain, there should be no ridges, puddles, or brush marks in the gesso, and carving details should still be sharp. If necessary extra coats may be applied to areas that are to be burnished. Cut gesso may require twenty coats or more of gesso and some gilders add a little pigment to the fourth or fifth coat to act as a depth guide for the recutter (Wetherall, 1992). Gesso made with chalk whiting is used for carved work that requires extensive and detailed recutting. The large number of coats required means that gesso layers may be thicker, with a higher proportion of whiting, to enable them to be built up quickly. The layers may be stippled on using a short-haired, stringed, hog's-hair gesso brush. Applying the gesso in this way will ensure that the depths of the carving do not become clogged and a thick, even layer can be built up over the entire piece of work. The last coat is usually less viscous and is brushed on to even out the orange peel effect caused by the stippling. If a carving is to be recut, it

**Figure 14.4** Application of gesso to a carved surface

is essential that the gesso is applied thickly enough to carve into without penetrating to the wooden support, but the gesso must also be carefully applied so as not to loose the shape of the carving.

Some gilders simply apply successive brush coats of gesso, whilst others use a tapping stroke to ensure good adhesion between successive coats of gesso by increasing the interface with the very fine peaks and by mechanically forcing them together. The emphasis in this approach is to use the tapping stroke to pull the gesso up out of the interstices, which would otherwise become clogged, and deposit it on the high spots of the carving if it is needed there for recutting.

Traditional Italian gesso sottile may be applied using a long-haired, stringed, hog's-hair gesso brush or softer flat ox hair. It is laid on, rather than brushed, in a smooth, fluid and even layer. While liquid the gesso can be worked with the brush to even out the surface, but once the gesso has started to gel it can no longer be worked. The layers of gesso sottile will build up quickly and should appear soft and fluid while still retaining the outlines of the carving.

Gesso may be built up on plain mouldings using long, smooth brush strokes. Some gilders prefer a long-haired, stringed gesso brush for this type of work whilst other use a round ox-hair brush. Some objects will involve both carving (to be stippled) and plain mouldings (to be brushed), in which case the stippling brush may be used for both processes but a brushing motion used for applying the gesso to the plain mouldings.

The final coat is brushed on and may be smoothed out immediately with a clean damp brush or with a finger wrapped in slightly dampened silk worked in a circular motion (ragged). Although airbrushes have been used for the application of gesso (Thornton, 1991b), this technique may not accurately reproduce the brush application of gesso on a complex carved surface.

### 14.2.8   Faults in the gesso

Some faults in the gesso, such as pinholes, may be noticed immediately whilst others are detected either once the surface has been gilded or even a few years after the work has been completed.

Air bubbles in the gesso will result in pinholes in the finished work. These are caused in the preparatory stage by adding the whiting to size that is too hot, by adding too much whiting, or by excessive or vigorous stirring of the whiting and size. If there are no air bubbles in the gesso but pinholes appear in the work they may be caused by overheating of the gesso, the gesso layer being applied too thickly or too hot, or by the preceding layer being too cold or dry. The only way of treating pinholes once they are in the gesso is to tediously work a thin gesso into the pitted surface with a finger, so it is best to prevent the conditions that cause them. Pin holes will reappear if more gesso is simply applied over the top, and may actually increase in size.

An excessively strong size will make the gesso brittle and lead to the possibility of it delaminating from the support after a few years. If the size is too weak or if too much whiting has been used then the gesso will flake and may crumble when the burnisher is applied to the gold.

Delamination between layers of gesso may be due to the individual layers drying too quickly or by too great a variation in the strength of the size between layers. Cracks may be caused by excessively thick layers of gesso or by not allowing sufficient drying time between each successive coat.

### 14.2.9   Smoothing the gesso

Various methods may be used to smooth the gesso. The method used is important because it gives the finished work some of its character. The sharpness and crispness of the gesso on nineteenth century plain mouldings, for instance, cannot be achieved by using pumice and water or simply by washing in. If an attempt were made to sharpen a sixteenth century Italian gesso sottile with straight edges and abrasive paper the result would be completely out of character.

Pumice stones, used with water, are often used in commercial workshops for work that requires a soft, fluid look and for fillets and plain mouldings (*Figure 14.5*). Dutch reeds or horsetail plants, called 'prelle' in France, used with water are useful for getting into awkward areas such as carving and small grooves. Pumice stones may be cut into a suitable shape using a hacksaw and smoothed with abrasive paper. The shaped pieces of pumice should be soaked in water until they are needed for use. Reeds may be used in bundles or individually depending upon the area of work to be covered and are particularly good for softening the sharpness of recut carving.

Once the gesso has been shaped and smoothed to the effect required it should be treated using a slightly dampened fine cotton cloth or silk worked in a circular motion over the surface. This process, called ragging, dissolves the glue in the uppermost gesso layer, allowing the surface to be smoother. Excessive ragging or over-wetting the surface will draw glue from the underlying layers by capillary action and will cause delamination at a later date. A damp cloth may be wrapped around shaped pieces of wood to sharpen up

**Figure 14.5**   Smoothing gesso with pumice stones

flutes or other details in the carving. Ragging will remove marks left by fine abrasive paper or pumice and, if necessary, smooth sharp edges left by recutting. It will result in a smooth but sometimes uneven surface with undulations and discrepancies in the thickness of the gesso on the mouldings, which would, for instance, be a surface typical of seventeenth century Italian gilding.

Shaped blocks and straight edges may be used for fillets, edges, plain hollows and mouldings. Abrasive paper of increasing grades of fineness, used either wet or dry, may be wrapped over the cowl or straight edge and used against the moulding with a long, straight motion. These mouldings should be finished with a very fine dry abrasive paper and then with a quick wipe of a fine cotton cloth or natural sponge dipped in water. The end result should be a perfectly even and smooth surface without abrasive paper marks or undulations in the mouldings.

It may be necessary to rag gesso that has been stippled on. For areas that are to be recut the gesso need only be worked far enough to smooth out the effects of the stippling. Ragging should be left until after the work has been recut.

### 14.2.10 Decorative details

The gessoed or gilded surface was often embellished with fine decorative detail to define elements of the design or provide overall aesthetic balance to the piece. In some cases it may have the additional role of providing a key for later toning. Sands of differing particle size were sometimes sprinkled onto flat decorative elements either when the gesso was wet or after application of fresh rabbit skin size. Oil mordants were also used to adhere sands. Thin gesso could be applied over the sand to soften the effect or the gold leaf could be applied directly over the sand. Both narrow crosshatching and wider hatching, often with additional punched centre dots, have been used for background areas of the design. Fluting, without any flat areas between the cuts, so that it has a 'wave' cross-section, is often found on the inner edges (called site edges) of frames and could be burnished or matte. Hazzling or hassling was incised into many flat or gently curved elements by using

a flat or very gently curved chisel upright on the surface and using a rolling motion of the wrist to 'walk' the tool to create a zigzag pattern. Punchwork was carried out after gold leaf had been applied. It is particularly common around haloes or nimbi on panel paintings and the indentation is burnished slightly as the gesso is compressed. Cut gesso or intaglio, described below, requires a thick gesso layer into which intricate low relief sharply detailed designs are carved. It was used for flat surfaces such as table tops and chests. Raised designs in gesso, called pastiglia, were created by applying the gesso from a brush to create smooth, rounded decorative detail (Wetherall, 1992). Pressbrokaat is the name given to wax or gesso appliqué work that imitated the texture of fine cloth (Richardson, 1991). Scraffito is not a texture but a decorative treatment that utilized egg tempera over a previously water-gilt and burnished surface. This Italian decorative technique removed paint to reveal the gold underneath and may be found on borders and polychrome objects (Wetherall, 1992).

### 14.2.11 Recutting

Gesso applied to carving causes the carving to lose its sharpness and definition and gives it a smooth and rounded appearance. If this type of appearance was the intended aesthetic, the work required only careful smoothing and washing in. If, however, sharply defined decoration was the intention of the work then recutting was necessary.

As its name implies, recutting refers to a second carving operation, after the application of the gesso. Recutting varies widely according to the style and origin of a piece of furniture. Historically it has involved not only sharpening or redefining carving clogged by the gesso, but more importantly, the addition of decorative details and motifs too fine to be carved in the wood. The very rich and inventive ground patterns added to European baroque furniture are good examples of this technique. The aim of recutting on neo-classical furniture, however, is not to embellish the surface but to sharpen the definition of the carving by cleaning undercuts and interstices. In recutting gesso sottile, the aim was to redefine carving outlines and restore the detail lost through gessoing. Italian recutting tends to be much looser than English work, and much of the rounded appearance that results from the use of gesso sottile was deliberately kept.

It is important that a gilder gain as much knowledge as possible about the appropriate recutting of a given style before undertaking the recutting of a repair to a period object. Having an authentic model to copy of a very similar object from the same period, country and level of sophistication is the best way to ensure a faithful interpretation and an appropriate recutting scheme for reproduction pieces. The study of recutting may also be helpful in determining if an object that is not presently gilded was originally meant to be gilded. If, for example, there are very fine details carved into the wood that would be completely filled in by the gesso, it is a good indication that the object was not made to be gilded because those details would only have been added at the recutting stage. Craftspeople in the seventeenth and eighteenth centuries did not repeat lengthy operations unnecessarily.

In general, recutting falls into the two categories of either redefining work that was highly detailed in the wood or completely reworking the gesso layer with elaborate detail that was not put into the initial carving. The first is characteristic of English and Italian work whilst the French excelled at the second.

Some carving was very highly finished in the wood to minimize recutting. The gesso on this kind of work was relatively thin and the recutting limited to sharpening the outlines and flutes that became clogged with gesso. This type of recutting was executed with the same tools and techniques used for carving the wood. Examples of this can be seen on some English Georgian parcel gilt mirrors. It may be reproduced by gently smoothing the high points of the gesso with a fine grade abrasive paper (320 grit). The outlines of the leaves and ornament are redefined using carving tools and fine decorative detail, such as fluting, are then carved in. Surface texturing in the gesso, such as hassling, is the last step.

Some carving was roughly carved in the wood, aiming only to give a base for a thick layer of gesso. Sufficient gesso was applied so that extensive working of the surface was possible without cutting back to the wood. This type of recutting suited the very fine and

intricate surface decoration typical of much eighteenth century French work. As with gesso sottile, the recutting was defined and then the fine fluting and other detail added. A characteristic of French work is the extensive decoration worked into the ground. After the ornamental detail has been finished the ground is smoothed and fine crosshatching, diamonds or hassling may be added.

Recutting is the most challenging of the gilding operations and was traditionally the responsibility of the most skilled and highest paid gilder in a workshop. The finest recutting displays deftness, sureness of hand and spontaneity. Skilled recutting requires not only an understanding of historical techniques and design, but a great deal of practice. It is essential to practice recutting on a gessoed board before undertaking a restoration project. The cutting edge of the hook should be held as near as possible to the end with one hand (for maximum control), placing the other hand on the handle and pulling the tool (*Figure 14.6*). Moistening the gesso will make it easier to carve, but it must not be soaked so much that the gesso becomes damaged. Sharp tools are essential. The hardness of the gesso will affect recutting – if the gesso is too hard the strokes will be wavy and difficult whilst if the gesso is too soft the recutting will lack crispness.

Once the recutting and smoothing are complete the loose particles of gesso must be removed from the surface. Work should be ragged if necessary and the recut areas examined to see if the outlines need to be softened. If so, they may be carefully ragged with shaped pieces of wood wrapped in cloth.

**Figure 14.6**  Recutting a gesso repair

### 14.2.12 Yellow ochre

A coat of size pigmented with yellow ochre was applied to a carved surface that was to be gilded. This wash was intended to disguise any recesses or undercutting that may be inaccessible during gilding so that they would not be noticeable. Traditionally, yellow ochre mixed with size was used for this purpose but modern gilders often omit this step and rely on the yellow bole instead.

A stock preparation of yellow ochre may be made by immersing some yellow ochre in water so that, with time, the grit in the pigment will sink to the bottom of the container. The wet yellow ochre should be taken from the top of this stock solution and mixed with a pre-prepared 6–8% rabbit skin size (15:1–12:1 v/v water:glue granules). Avoid the sediment at the bottom because it is too thick and may contain grit. The amount of pigment used is not critical but should be sufficient to colour the work in one application. The size and yellow ochre mix should be warmed in a double boiler and, if a large area is to be covered, left in the double boiler to ensure it remains hot. The yellow ochre and size should be applied hot (around 55 °C) to ensure that the colour reaches all the depths of the carving and recutting. The yellow size should flow on fluidly and easily and should not need to be worked in with the brush. A long-haired hog's-hair brush large enough to cover the work quickly should be used. Do not expect the finished colour to be uniform; overlaps in colour do not matter so long as no ridges form. The colour should be more concentrated in the depths and hollows of the carving where it is needed most.

### 14.2.13 Bole

Bole is a coloured clay applied onto the gesso before gold leaf is applied. The platelet structure of the clay, in combination with the cushioning effect of the underlying gesso layers, allows the gold leaf laid over it to be burnished to a high sheen. In addition, the bole layer partly seals the gesso layer and prevents free absorption of the size water into the gesso layer below. The use and choice of clay colour applied as a foundation for the gold leaf has a great effect on the colour and lustre of the finished work. Matching and using the correct clay colours is of the utmost importance, because the colour of the bole will affect the final appearance of the gold. It is essential that the gilder is aware of the intended subtleties of semi-burnished, matte and burnished areas before applying the clay.

Bole comes in many colours and is sold either pre-mixed with water or, in a more limited range of colours, in dry lumps or cone form. Modern clays are manufactured from kaolin (pipe clay) combined with a colouring agent (usually ground earth pigments) and water and may contain additives such as dyes, lanolin or glycerine and preservatives (Thorn, 1987). Any grit in the bole will cause lumps and scratch the gold leaf when it is being burnished.

Many gilders prefer to use proprietary bole that has been ground and pre-mixed with water. Others prefer to start with the dry clays or cones. A stock solution may be prepared from dry clay or cones by grinding the clay into very small particles using a mortar and pestle and mixing with water to form a thick, unctuous paste. The paste should be strained once or twice through a fine nylon stocking to remove grit and lumps, and placed in a glass jar. This stock solution may then be used in the same manner as proprietary wet clays. Any clay has a limited shelf life once the glue size has been added.

Colours in common use are yellow, red, white, black and blue. Most traditional clay colours can be achieved by blending these basic colours and if necessary by adding a small amount of an appropriate pigment. Some pigments, such as terre verte, will give a gritty finish and are therefore inappropriate. Traditional bole varied in burnishing properties depending on the colour. Yellow bole burnished poorly and was used for the background, red burnished well and was used on highlights whilst Victorian black could be highly burnished and was used on isolated areas of highlighting. English clay could not be burnished without the addition of graphite and English burnish clay was made by mixing equal parts of clay and mutton suet with a small amount of graphite (Wetherall, 1992).

Bole may be prepared by warming enough pre-prepared rabbit skin size to cover the surface of the work three or four times. The size should be considerably weaker than that used for the gesso. This is one reason for not diluting the gesso during the application of the layers, as the size strength in comparison to the bole size strength is then unknown. To make a bole size, the strength of the stock parchment or rabbit skin size should be reduced by adding an equal volume of water. The wet clays may be blended to produce the desired colour and then gradually the warm glue should be added to the clay whilst stirring the mixture continuously and gently. A small amount of finely ground pigment may be added at this stage to adjust the colour if necessary but should be thoroughly mixed in before adding the remainder of the warm size. The clay should be about the viscosity of milk and of a strength so that when left at normal room temperature should not quite set.

It is a good practice to assess the colour and consistency of the bole by applying it to a gessoed test board, allowing it to dry and then burnishing it. If the clay does not burnish well it may be because too much pigment has been added, that the size is too strong, or that there is insufficient clay in the mixture. Adjust the clay mixture or start again. Once burnished, test the strength of the size in the clay by running cold water over the test piece for a few seconds. If the clay washes off adjust the strength and test again until the clay remains undisturbed on the board.

Traditional recipes mention the use of clay mixed with egg white or isinglass instead of rabbit skin or parchment size. Clay mixed with isinglass gives a mixture that is easy to apply and results in a good, soft burnish. The glue solution is prepared by soaking an appropriate amount of dried material in just enough water to cover the pieces. Excess water is poured off and the swollen glue mass is kneaded into a uniform consistency. The glue is transferred to a double boiler with enough water to cover the mass and heated and stirred until the glue is dissolved. Allow to set and check for gel strength. The stock isinglass will need to be diluted with water until a strength equivalent to that of the parchment size for clay is achieved and then added and used in the same way (see p. 648). Clay mixed with egg white, a southern European gilding technique, also gives a good burnish but has a tendency to be rather hard and brittle when

dry. To prepare for use, beat an egg white until stiff and leave to settle overnight on a tilted plate. The liquid that will have collected in the bottom of the plate is called glair. Mix this with an equivalent amount of cold water and add to the clay.

Bole may be applied after heating the size/clay mixture in a double boiler and straining it through a nylon stocking into a warm container. The bole should be applied with a round soft brush, preferably sable, at a temperature of around 37 °C. To achieve a consistent temperature and an even amount of clay on the brush some gilders take the clay on the brush from the container and rub the brush into the palm of their hand, using the palm as an intermediate palette, before applying to the work (*Figure 14.7*). The clay is then brushed lightly onto the work in long even strokes. Individual coats should be thin and transparent and should brush on easily without runs or build-ups, but the clay should not flow into or collect in the depths of the carving. Subsequent coats may be applied when the preceding coat has dried and until the desired opacity is achieved. Usually three coats is enough but up to five coats may be selectively applied to areas that are to be highly burnished. Matte areas may receive one or two coats of clay and the background and recesses of carving should remain yellow.

Two layers of colour were sometimes applied – a yellow base coat applied evenly over the surface to conceal small faults in the gilding followed by a second coloured coat,

**Figure 14.7** Applying bole to a gessoed repair whilst keeping the bole warm in the hand

applied only to highlight areas (*Figure 14.8*). The second bole was usually a darker colour, such as red, orange, plum, but sometimes blue, grey or even black. The application of the darker bole should be studied very carefully because there are several different approaches to it. French gilders often applied a solid coat of bole only to areas that were to be burnished and only a thin, transparent coat, if any, to areas that were to be left matte. These details should be reproduced accurately in restoration treatments. The dark bole may be applied with a flat sable brush held at a low angle to the work, so that it is applied only to the high spots. Two or three coats are required for areas that are to be burnished. The end result is a pattern of the yellow bole in the depths with the dark bole lying over it.

Once completely dry the clay must be polished to remove any grit or dust to prevent raised particles being dragged across the surface and causing scratches and holes when the gold is burnished. The finished bole can be lightly buffed or polished with a very stiff brush (*Figure 14.9*), 0000 oil-free wire wool or a chamois leather. If the surface is very gritty or rough, a very fine abrasive paper (1000 grit) may be worked lightly over the clay to ensure a smooth surface. A Perspex/ Plexiglass scraper can also be used for this purpose and may give greater control (*Figure 14.10*). As well as smoothing out irregularities, the abrasive paper will also buff the clay to a satin finish. On carved areas, a hessian or cotton cloth may be used to remove any dust particles before using a bristle brush to buff the areas that are to be burnished. Finally, the bole may be degreased with alcohol before gilding. Care must be taken to keep the work clean during all of these steps, but especially after the bole has been applied.

### 14.2.14 Laying the leaf

Gold leaf is applied to the surface after wetting it with 'size water'. This is usually comprised of clean water with a small quantity of methylated spirits (denatured ethanol) and either rabbit skin or parchment size. The quantity of methylated spirits (denatured ethanol) and size added to the water may vary according to the work and the behaviour of the size water on the surface – for example if the size water is

**Figure 14.8** Applying a darker bole to highlights of the carved surface

**Figure 14.9** Denibbing and buffing dry bole with a stiff brush

**Figure 14.10** Smoothing bole with a Perspex/Plexiglass scraper shaped to fit the profile of the moulding

wetting too quickly, reduce the quantity of methylated spirits (denatured ethanol), or if wetting too slowly increase the methylated spirits (denatured ethanol). Recipes vary but a common one uses approximately one-quarter of a teaspoon of glue size mixed with one-quarter of a pint of water and one teaspoon of methylated spirits (denatured ethanol) (Wetherall, 1992). A little more size may be added to the water and alcohol mixture when matte gilding. Five per cent is usually considered the upper limit because more may cause the gilding water to pull and adhere the gold leaf to the surface too quickly, resulting in webs or unwanted overlapping of the gold. Size water will stain previously laid gold.

It is important to carefully plan the order in which parts are gilded and to burnish work as a project progresses in order to avoid water marks. The size water run off necessitates working from the top down, because any water that flows on leaf will leave a mark. Care must also be taken that size water does not sit on the preparation as it will dissolve the gesso. If there is a place where it collects, absorb it frequently with a dry brush or surgical cotton. The insides of the legs of a chair and then the insides of the arms, for example, are gilded first and then the back, the aprons and the outsides of the legs.

With the matte and burnish scheme decided upon and the colour of the gold leaf chosen from the many that are now available, the actual laying of the gold can proceed. Laying the gold requires dexterity and concentration and it takes much practice to perfect the technique. Draughts must be excluded and breathing directed in such as way so as not to disturb the flattened gold leaf on the cushion.

Place the work on a tilt so that when the gilding water is applied it will run away from the piece of gold that is being laid. Gather together all the tools and materials that are required, i.e. the books of loose leaf gold, a gilder's cushion and knife, gilder's tips, lip salve, a selection of mops for laying on the gilding water, cotton wool or squirrel dabbers for tamping down, and a jar of gilding water.

It is almost impossible to describe how to handle gold leaf without a practical demonstration. There are a variety of techniques that may be used. In addition to the method described, some gilders strap the book of gold directly onto the back of their cushion, without the parchment wind screen, and work directly from the book, although this may present some difficulty when handling off cuts. Some gilders dispense with the gilder's cushion altogether and take the gold directly from the book, using a small finger ring knife to cut it. The gold is taken out from the back of the book to the front, and a piece of cardboard is put under the sheets that are being cut to stiffen the book as this is done. The gold may then be moved directly from the book to the sized surface.

The directions that follow will be most useful in conjunction with a demonstration by a practising gilder. Place the gold leaves onto the back on the cushion, where they are protected by the parchment shield, by holding the book of gold by the spine with one hand and flipping the leaves open one by one with the thumb of the other hand (*Figure 14.11*). If the leaves do not fall easily onto the cushion shake the book a little or gently blow onto the leaf. If working on a large project, a book of gold may be emptied into the back of the cushion.

If right-handed, take the cushion up in your left hand and hold it by means of the thumb loop attached beneath. Rub a little lip salve or Vaseline either onto the wrist of the hand holding the cushion or onto the right cheek. Take a leaf of gold with the flat of the knife from the back of the cushion to the front and with a short sharp puff of breath to the centre of the leaf, blow it flat. It is important that the leaf lies flat and evenly stretched onto the cushion otherwise it will not cut neatly. The leaf may be manipulated on the cushion with the knife, which must be kept very clean

**Figure 14.11** Transferring gold leaf from a book to the gilders cushion

**Figure 14.12** Manipulating the gold leaf on the cushion with a gilder's knife

**Figure 14.13** Applying gilding 'water' (thin rabbit skin size) to gesso repair in preparation for laying gold leaf

(*Figure 14.12*). It can be degreased with alcohol and then rubbed with whiting. It should be sharp enough to cut the leaf rather than tearing it, but not so sharp that it will cut the cushion. To cut the leaf into the required size, lay the cutting edge of the knife over the gold and push the knife forward a little and then pull it back in one even stroke, keeping the cutting edge flat on the cushion all the time.

When the leaf has been cut to the required size, place the knife between the ring and little finger of the hand that is holding the cushion. Pass the end of the gilder's tip lightly across the lip salve on the cheek or wrist and pick up the leaf swiftly, by positioning the tip directly over the leaf and placing the end of the tip onto the leaf. Place the tip with the adhering leaf between the first and second fingers of the hand holding the cushion. Take the mop from the gilding water, wet the clay with an even unbroken film and return the mop to the jar of water (*Figure 14.13*). Take the tip with the leaf attached in the right hand and apply the leaf to the water on the work. A sure gesture without hesitation is required. This will have the 'wind' against the face of the leaf so that the tip can push it into the work without getting wet (*Figure 14.14*).

Pick up the next piece of gold leaf, wet the surface up to the edge of the previous piece, and apply in the same way but allow it to overlap the last piece. The amount of overlap varies; in nineteenth century English and French work the gilding is very precise, the overlaps are usually no more than one-

**Figure 14.14** Laying gold leaf (water gilding)

sixteenth of an inch (about 1.5 mm) and the lay lines are very regular. Spanish and Italian gilding may have overlaps of up to one-quarter of an inch (about 6 mm) and the laying of the leaf is far less precise.

Once five or six pieces of gold have been laid in this manner, pick up a piece of dry cotton wool or a dry squirrel brush with a flat end (known as a dabber) and press down the first piece of gold that was laid in order to remove any air trapped underneath the gold (*Figure 14.15*). The time to do this is when the gilding water has been absorbed into the preparation but when the clay is still damp enough for the gold being pressed down to stick to it. If size water seeps through the gold when damping down go back to the work when it is a little drier. If the work is too dry the gold trapped above the air bubble will

**Figure 14.15** Pressing freshly laid leaf with cotton wool to remove any air trapped underneath the gold

simply wipe off leaving an ugly speckled surface. Always ensure that the brush or cotton wool used for damping down is dry, otherwise the gold will either lift off or be spoiled by water marks. Some gilders prefer to use both hands, laying gold with one hand, and tamping the gold with the other as they work. This requires the cushion to be placed on a work surface rather than held in the hand.

When applying the gilding water to carved areas, bear in mind that the gold will pull towards it and stick to the high points. To avoid bridging the gold leaf, make sure that the water is applied only to the areas where you want the gold leaf to fall. On plain mouldings, however, it helps if the gilding water is applied to the area where the next piece of gold is to be laid at the same time as wetting for the first piece, so that when this area is wetted again to take the gold, the glue in the clay will already be reactivated and better adhesion will be achieved. If laying leaf onto an undulating surface, let one end of the gold on the tip attach itself to the work and angle the tip so that the speed at which the gold is taken up by the water is controlled by the tip.

Wetherall (1992) emphasizes the following points. The presence of excess size water will prevent the gold from pulling down evenly. Hold the tip parallel to the surface and avoid any hesitation in approach because the gold may 'jump' as it nears the moisture. Having laid the leaf, avoid pulling the tip towards you as it is lifted away or it may cause the gold to tear. Only use a tamping brush once the

gold has left the tip, and hold the brush at 90° to the surface. When gilding sharp angles or mouldings lay the leaf so that the edge aligns exactly with the bottom of the carved angle – this will mean you will need two pieces of gold, one for each side of the cut.

### 14.2.15 Faulting

Once the gold has dried, wipe over the surface with dry cotton wool to remove any loose pieces of gold leaf. Any faults or breaks in the gilded surface must be patched with smaller pieces of gold. It is especially important to do this on areas that are burnished, as the coloured clay clearly shows the imperfections in the gilding. Faulting can be done while gilding or after burnishing. Use a small brush to apply the gilding water and ensure that the patch of gold is large enough so that the water does not seep from under it and cause water marks on the previous gilding. Burnish the faulting when it is dry. Another way of faulting on burnished work is to breathe onto the clay to be patched, place a small piece of gold onto the site and burnish the piece immediately. It is not usually necessary to fault into the depths of the carving as the yellow size underneath will usually hide faults in the gold.

### 14.2.16 Matte water gilding

If the surface to be gilded requires a matte finish, a coat of thin parchment or rabbit skin size should be applied to the surface before gilding and allowed to dry. The strength of this size should be no more than 16:1 v/v water:glue granules. If the size is too strong the gold being laid will dry with spiders webs and overlaps, which will ruin the appearance of a matte surface. If the size coat is too weak or too wet the gilding water will break through it and the gilding will have to be set aside, allowed to dry and the size layer replaced before gilding of the area can recommence.

A matte effect may also be achieved by applying a size after gilding has been completed. Brush strokes used to apply the size should be directed in the opposite direction in which the gold was laid so that the brush does not lift the edges of the gold.

## 14.2.17   Double gilding

Water gilding on flat surfaces is more effective
if double laid. Nineteenth century English work
was often double gilded in order to give a
more solid and rich appearance. If double
gilding, do not bother to fault the first layer of
gold as the second application should cover
most imperfections. The second layer of gold
is usually applied without disturbing or
burnishing the first. In some cases, however,
the first layer of gilding may be burnished
before the application of the second layer of
leaf, which is left unburnished. This technique
may be used to give greater depth to a gilded
surface. Handle the work as little as possible
to keep the surface free from grease otherwise
the gilding water, which must contain a small
amount of size when double gilding, will bead.
Lay a thin parchment size on the first layer of
gold if the finished effect is to be left matte.

## 14.2.18   Burnishing

A variety of burnisher shapes is available and
should be matched to the surface in hand.
Convex and flat surfaces, for example, should
be burnished with a slightly convex burnisher.
The burnisher should be smooth and have a
good polish. A well burnished surface should
appear as though it was made from highly
polished metal. The brilliance of the burnish
depends on the condition of the gesso underneath and decorative elements should be
burnished as a whole, where possible, to
ensure a coherent appearance (MacTaggart
and MacTaggarat, 1984).

Select the areas to burnish and which to
leave matte, according to style and period of
the work (*Figure 14.16*). There is an optimum
time to burnish after the gold has been laid
but the time lapse is variable and depends to
a great extent on climatic conditions. A humid
atmosphere is good for burnishing as the
'window' to catch the burnish remains open
for much longer. In most instances, if the work
was laid in the morning it should be ready to
burnish in the afternoon. Ambient conditions
will affect how soon burnishing is possible. In
some cases the surface may be ready in thirty
minutes, whilst in others a burnish may only
be possible after twenty-four hours. Select an
agate burnisher and test a small area to see if

**Figure 14.16**   Burnishing water gilding using a dog's-
tooth agate burnisher

the gold is dry enough. If the burnisher pulls
against the gold or rubs through it, it is still
too wet. If the gold does not burnish well and
the burnisher scratches against surface then it
is too dry. The burnisher should easily glide
over the surface leaving polished gold in its
wake. Some gilders test for the right burnishing time by gently tapping the gold with the
burnisher. If the burnisher makes a high click,
it may be too dry to burnish well, and if it
makes a lower thudding sound it may be too
damp. Judging when a surface is ready to
burnish requires practice.

Hold the burnisher firmly in one hand and
work the agate backwards and forwards against
the gold. Restrain the burnisher with the tips of
the fingers of the other hand when burnishing
delicate details and when burnishing close to
matte areas (*Figure 14.17*). Compress the gold
with light pressure to begin with and then
increase the pressure as required, as the
burnish begins to form. Small pieces of gold
that stick to the burnisher should be removed
with a clean dry cloth as they may otherwise
scratch the surface. Remember that excessive
burnishing may cause exfoliation of the upper
surface. Remember also to maintain a balance
between burnished and unburnished areas –
too much burnishing may disrupt the overall
decorative form of the surface.

If the gold is not ready to burnish at the
end of the day it may be possible to extend
the burnishing time until the following
morning by placing one or two shallow bowls
of water next to the piece and covering it with
a plastic sheet. Burnishing should be under-

**Figure 14.17** Burnishing water gilded highlights on architectural moulding using a dog's-tooth agate burnisher

taken as soon as possible after gilding. If gilding is undertaken on more than one day always ensure that the previous day's gilding is burnished before proceeding with new gilding. It is possible to rehumidify a repaired area, using a Gore-Tex sandwich (see section 15.2.2), to allow the gold to be burnished.

### 14.2.19 Punched decoration

Many examples of gilded work incorporate punched designs. These are usually on the background of English work or on the frieze or background of Italian work. Punchwork may be used to relieve large, flat areas of gilding or to disguise an uneven or irregular background. Punching is done after the gold has been laid. The gold is pushed into the punched recess and burnished with the same action. The work should be thoroughly dry otherwise the preparation will be soft and the punching will damage the gesso. A metal punch, made from a suitable nail or dental tool, may be ground or filed to the required design and punched into the work either using a small hammer or pressure from the palm of the hand. Punching will have the immediate effect of breaking up plain flat areas and backgrounds and result in changing the play of light over the surface.

### 14.2.20 Coatings

Any varnish or coating applied over gold leaf will alter the brilliant metallic quality of the surface. Tinted and clear varnishes have been used for specific decorative purposes (e.g. lustrework) in the past but were not routinely applied to gilded objects. The seventeenth and eighteenth centuries saw a popular trend in Europe of glazing silver leaf in imitation of gold and the application of decorative surfaces such as turtleshell over metal leaf. Other effects included the use of green copper resinate glazes and highlights picked out in opaque overpaint (Portell, 1991; Wetherall, 1992).

English gilders in the Victorian period utilized shellac-based coatings, matting coats and surface colour (Wetherall, 1992). This coating was called ormolu, but it should not be confused with the mercury gilt metal mounts found on furniture that are also known as ormolu. The gilder's ormolu coating was applied to water gilding and pigment colour or traditional materials such as red Saunders' wood (*Pterocarpus santalinus*), turmeric, saffron and dragon's blood could be added if desired. All these natural colourants fade rapidly and modern lightfast dyes, such as some Orosol dyes (Ciba–Geigy) are better for modern practice. Gilder's ormolu was made by dissolving 20 g (½–¾ ounce) of shellac in 300 ml (10 fl oz) of alcohol and then straining to remove lumps and impurities (MacTaggart and MacTaggart, 1984). If a milky appearance was required, talc (French chalk) or rotten-stone could be added. It was applied to local-ized areas with a soft brush and care was taken to avoid over-brushing and runs. Some sources recommend combining gilder's ormolu with parchment size (1:10) for use as a matting agent on oil or water gilding (Green, 1979; Scott-Mitchell, 1905). A traditional coating, still used in many workshops, is a thin layer of rabbit skin, gelatin or parchment glue.

### 14.3 Oil gilding

Oil gilding has been practised since ancient times and is used primarily for gilding matte areas, to provide contrast next to water gilding, for architectural gilding and exterior gilding. In the eighteenth and nineteenth centuries, especially on English and French work, the different appearance of oil gilding, burnished water gilding and matte water gilding was exploited to create an attractive play of light across the gilded surface. In such work the ground would be prepared uniformly to the same high standard necessary for water gilding. Although the process of oil gilding is simpler than water gilding, it was not perceived as producing an inferior decorative surface and was applied to furniture of the highest quality.

At its most basic, oil gilding can be applied to any non-porous surface (or a sealed porous surface) simply by applying oil size and gold. This is the method used commonly on exterior work and particularly on metals, but oil gilding on furniture is usually applied onto a more thoroughly prepared ground. The layers of gesso applied under water gilding to provide a cushion for burnishing are unnecessary for oil gilding, although a thin gesso layer will act as a grain filler and provide an even surface. As with water gilding, the final appearance of oil gilding is dependent on the quality of preparation of the underlying layer/s. The greatest visual difference between oil gilding and water gilding is the degree of lustre. Although oil gilding can be lightly buffed after application, it cannot be burnished in the same way as water gilding and so has a comparatively matte appearance. The oil size and sealant give oil gilding a sheen that distinguishes it from matte water gilding. Even though it cannot be burnished, well executed oil gilding can appear as rich and lustrous as water gilding.

One advantage that oil gilding has over water gilding is that the water-based preparation essential for burnished water gilding is not a prerequisite. Oil gilding onto bare wood, usually oak, was a popular decorative surface in the England in the nineteenth century (e.g. the chancel screen designed by Gilbert Scott in Worcester Cathedral, UK). The usual preparation for exterior oil gilding is a waterproof oil-based paint or primer onto which the oil size and gold are laid.

If water gilding and oil gilding are to take place on the same piece of work, follow the preparation for water gilding up until the yellow ochre stage. Complete the remainder of the preparatory stages for water gilding on areas that are to be water gilded and finish all the water gilding before commencing oil gilding.

### 14.3.1 Mordants for oil gilding

Oil gilding derives its name from the use of the oil-based adhesive, or mordant, used to adhere the gold leaf to the surface. The main constituent of this mordant, known as gold size, is usually linseed oil that has been treated with a siccative, traditionally lead acetate ('sugar of lead'). Other materials, such as copal varnish and turpentine, could be added to manipulate the working characteristics (MacTaggart and MacTaggart, 1984). Gold size is sold according to designated drying times, such as two to four hours, twelve hours and twenty-four hours, which gives a general comparison between sizes rather than indicating absolute drying properties. The longer the drying time, the more lustrous the final effect. In addition to different drying times, the various sizes have a different 'window' during which time the size has reached the appropriate level of tack for the gold leaf to be applied to it. The shorter the drying time the narrower the window of time during which gold may be applied.

Japan gold size, also known as 'Quick Japan', dries in about one-half to two hours. It produces a brittle adhesive layer and may suffer from uneven drying but may be useful for small areas or when working outdoors, when the fast drying time may help avoid dust or inclement weather. Three hour gold size is thinner than Japan size and may take two to five hours to dry. Twelve hour gold size is the most commonly used as it is less viscous and therefore dries evenly. It has a window of four to five hours but may take eighteen to twenty-four hours before it is ready to gild. Twenty-four hour size is usually used on large scale architectural gilding. Modern alternatives based on acrylics are also available but are often less reliable in use.

### 14.3.2 Surface preparation

A yellow ground is often used to enhance the colour of the gold and to disguise any small faults in the gilding. A porous surface that is to be oil gilded must be sealed before applying the oil size to prevent loss of adhesion or patchy drying. If oil gilding directly onto wood, the surface should be degreased, cleaned and, if required, the grain should be raised and abraded before applying a thin sealant. If the oil gilding requires a lustre, a sealant such as shellac may be applied, allowed to dry, lightly denibbed and then buffed with a cotton cloth. If the gilding is intended to have a matte finish, select a matte varnish or add a little matting agent to the sealant.

A thin gold size may be used to seal the surface. The size is thinned with turpentine and may be tinted with yellow ochre, applied to the surface and allowed to dry thoroughly. Two to three coats may be brushed on evenly, each allowed to dry and lightly denibbed to seal the surface. Some gilders simply apply two or three coats of a thinned yellow oil-based paint to seal the surface, rubbing each layer down with a fine abrasive paper (Wetherall, 1992).

Whatever sealant is used, it should be applied in thin coats to allow it to soak into the surface and seal it thoroughly. If the sealer is too thick brush marks may occur, the coating will sit on the surface and may appear lumpy, ill-defined or streaky. The porosity of the surface must be judged on a case by case basis and the viscosity and number of sealer coats adjusted accordingly. If gilding onto an oil-painted surface, for example, no varnish need be applied as the surface is already sealed and ready for the oil size. If gilding directly onto oak, where the open grain is a feature in the gilding (for example pre-Raphaelite picture frames), then thin coats of sealant should be applied so that the grain does not become clogged, and more than one application will be necessary as the wood will soak up the varnish.

### 14.3.3 Applying the oil size

Tinting the clear size yellow can allow easy identification of where the size has been laid and prevent holidays in the size coat. Tinted size may be made by adding artist's quality oil paint to clear size but this will lengthen the drying time.

Select a time of day to apply the oil size that will correspond to the drying time of the size. The longer the drying time the better the lustre of the gold will be, but also bear in mind that the longer the size is left the more susceptible it will be to dust and abrasions. A fairly stiff short-haired brush is usually used to apply a thin layer of oil size to the surface. The size should be applied in a systematic manner from the bottom to the top of the surface, thinly and evenly and avoiding brush marks, drips, sags or runs. An excessively thick layer will cause

the gold laid over it to wrinkle. Size that has settled or pooled into the depths and hollows of the support should be removed. Some gilders work over the surface with a dry brush to even out the oil size layer.

### 14.3.4 Applying gold leaf

The gold leaf cannot be applied until the size has reached an appropriate level of tackiness. Several factors may affect the drying time of gold size, including the thickness of the application, temperature of the room, viscosity of the size, airflow over the surface and the addition of drying or colouring agents. There are several ways of checking the tack of the size. The traditional method was to touch the surface with the hairs on the back of the fingers – when they were just barely dragged by the size the surface was deemed ready for gilding. A second method involves running the little finger over an unobtrusive part of the surface – if the surface 'squeaks' it is ready. Either of these methods may be used to assess whether the surface is touch dry and ready for gilding. If the gold is laid onto size that is too tacky or soft, the lustre of the finished work will be impaired and the gilded surface will remain vulnerable to scratches and fingerprints for many days or even weeks. If the tack time has been missed and the oil size is too dry for the gold to adhere, then the size must either be wiped off with white spirit and new size applied, or allowed to dry thoroughly and a second layer applied. The varnish coat used to seal the surface may also have to be removed and replaced if it has been disturbed by the solvent.

As with water gilding, loose gold leaf is applied from the cushion using the knife to cut the gold and the tip to transport the leaf from the cushion to the oil-sized surface (*Figure 14.18*). The leaf should be laid quickly and in the same order that the size was applied, from the bottom towards the top, to avoid loose, falling leaf adhering to the tacky work below. Once the gold has been applied to an entire piece or area, dab the loose leaves down with a large, soft round brush such as a large squirrel gilding mop (*Figure 14.19*). This mop should only be used for this purpose and not for water gilding. This will adhere the loose leaves and fragments of gold into all the

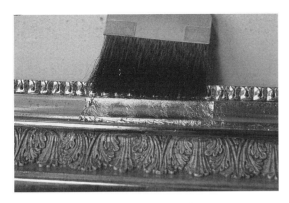

**Figure 14.18** Laying gold leaf on oil size

**Figure 14.19** Laying down wrinkles in gold leaf on oil size with a sable brush

areas, however deep, that have been oil sized. At this stage, the gilded surface is very vulnerable to finger prints and abrasion as the oil size beneath the gold is still soft, so leave the work undisturbed for at least 48 hours to give the size time to dry and harden. Once it is dry, brush it over with a large dry gilder's mop and, if desired, buff the gold with cotton wool, taking care not to scratch the surface.

Transfer gold, loose leaves of gold that have been adhered to tissue paper by pressure or wax, is used in conditions where the loose leaves of gold cannot be controlled, e.g. exterior conditions. An experienced gilder will find transfer leaf more time-consuming to apply and therefore a more costly method of applying the leaf. As a result it is usually limited to exterior oil gilding or other areas where draughts are a problem. Transfer leaf is particularly useful for signwriting. It is less lustrous than loose leaf as it conforms to the texture of the supporting tissue.

### 14.3.5 Coatings

Oil gilding, once dry, is very durable and a protective coating should not be necessary unless heavy wear is anticipated. A thin coat of a natural resin varnish such as dammar, mastic or shellac may be found on some objects. The colour of these materials may have been enhanced by resinous coatings such as dragon's blood, gamboge and button or garnet shellacs. Interior oil gilding may be given a matte appearance by the application of a thin rabbit skin, parchment size, or glair coating. Weak parchment or rabbit skin size

mixed with pigments may be used in the same way as for matting water gilding. Glair may be prepared by beating egg white to a stiff froth and diluting the liquid that runs off with a little cold water (see p. 656). Pigments may be added to alter the colour and the glaze may be applied with a soft brush. Egg white used in this way is delicate and brittle.

### 14.4 Composition

Composition was used as a cheaper alternative to ornamentation that would otherwise have been carved in wood. Composition was made traditionally from a mixture of colophony, linseed oil, hide glue and whiting, although other materials such as lead fillers, paper, starch pastes, pitch and eggs have also been incorporated on occasion. The moist thermoplastic material was pressed into reverse carved reusable boxwood or fruitwood moulds. Recent interest in composition has generated several articles touching on both the history and manufacture of this material, including Thornton (1985, 1991a, 1991b), Rees (1985) and Wetherall (1991b). Composition is further discussed in section 10.5.7.

### Bibliography

Anon. (1874) *The Illustrated Carver and Gilders Guide and Picture Frame Makers Companion* London
Budden, S. (ed.) (1991) *Gilding and Surface Decoration*, Conference Preprints, UKIC
Cennini (trans. Thompson, 1954), *The Craftsman's Handbook*, Dover

Cession, C. (1990) The surface layers of Baroque gildings: examination, conservation, restoration, in J.S. Mills and P. Smith (eds), *Cleaning, Retouching and Coatings*, Conference Preprints, IIC, pp. 33–35

Green, M. (1979) Conservation and restoration of gilded antiques, *The Conservator*, 3, 39–42

Green, M. (1991) Thirty years of gilding conservation at the Victoria and Albert Museum, in D. Bigelow, E. Cornu, G. Landrey and C. van Horne (eds), *Gilded Wood, Conservation and History*, Sound View Press, pp. 239–48

Hatchfield, P. and Newman, R. (1991) Ancient Egyptian gilding methods, in D. Bigelow, E. Cornu, G. Landrey and C. van Horne (eds), *Gilded Wood, Conservation and History*, Sound View Press, pp. 27–47

Koller, M. (1991) Leaf gilded surfaces: burnishing and varnishing in Central Europe, in D. Bigelow, E. Cornu, G. Landrey and C. van Horne (eds), *Gilded Wood, Conservation and History*, Sound View Press, pp. 291–99

Larson, J. and Kerr, R. (1985) *Guanyin: A Masterpiece Revealed*, Victoria and Albert Museum, London

Lewis, W. (1763–5) *Commercium Philisophico-Technicum*

MacTaggart, P. and MacTaggart, A. (1984) *Practical Gilding*, Mac and Me

Portell, J.D. (1991) Altered silver gilding, in D. Bigelow, E. Cornu, G. Landrey and C. van Horne (eds), *Gilded Wood, Conservation and History*, Sound View Press, pp. 205–16

Powell, C. (1998) Some French and English gilding techniques: the making and gilding of an 18th century English style mirror frame, *SSCR Journal*, 9 (4), 5–14

Rees, J. (1985) Compo moulds, in *Tools and Trades History Society*, 3

Richardson, R. (1991) The materials and techniques of pressbrokaat, in S. Budden (ed.), *Gilding and Surface Decoration*, Conference Preprints, UKIC

Scott-Mitchell, F. (1905) *Practical Gilding, Bronzing and Lacquering*, Trade Papers Publishing Co.

Sheraton, Thomas (1803) *The Cabinet Dictionary*, Praeger facsimile edition, 1970

Sutherland, W. (1889) *The Art and Craft of Signwriting, Gilding, and Painting on Glass*, Decorative Arts Journal Co.

Thompson, D.V. (1956) *The Materials and Techniques of Medieval Painting*, Dover

Thompson, D.V. (1962) *The Practice of Tempera Painting: Materials and Methods*, Dover

Thorn, N. (1987) Restoring a pair of gilded girandoles, in AIC Wooden Artifacts Group, Conference Papers, Vancouver

Thornton, J. (1985) Compo: the history and technology of 'plastic' compositions, in AIC Wooden Artifacts Group, Conference Papers, Washington, DC, pp. 113–26

Thornton, J. (1991a) Minding the gap: filling losses in gilded and decorated surfaces, in S. Budden (ed.), *Gilding and Surface Decoration*, Conference Preprints, UKIC, pp. 12–17

Thornton, J. (1991b) The use of non-traditional gilding methods and materials in conservation, in D. Bigelow, E. Cornu, G. Landrey and C. van Horne (eds), *Gilded Wood, Conservation and History*, Sound View Press, pp. 217–28

Watin (1755) *L'Art du Peintre*, reprinted Chez Leonce Larget, 1975

Wetherall, J. (1991a) Going for gold, *Practical Wood-working*, April

Wetherall, J. (1991b) History and techniques of composition, in S. Budden (ed.), *Gilding and Surface Decoration*, Conference Preprints, UKIC

Wetherall, J. (1992) Gilding – notes for short courses, published by the author

# 15

# Conserving other materials I

This chapter introduces the principles and techniques for the conservation of diverse materials often associated with wooden furniture. Each of these materials is a specialist subject in its own right. It is essential that conservators undertake further research, consult references and seek specialist advice rather than undertaking treatments on an unfamiliar material. The conservator should be as well informed as possible about these materials and be alert for potential problems in order to avoid causing irreversible damage.

## 15.1 Ivory, bone and antler, turtleshell and horn, mother-of-pearl

### 15.1.1 Ivory, bone and antler

Ivory and bone are hygroscopic and anisotropic. As a result they are prone to warping and dimensional distortion in fluctuating RH. Cracking is particularly associated with low RH. Dimensional change in conditions of fluctuating RH have been measured at around 4.2% along the radial axis, 1.5% along the tangential axis and 0.5% longitudinally (LaFontaine and Wood, 1982). Ivory and bone are slightly porous and may absorb greasy deposits, e.g. from handling or solubilized dirt during cleaning. Ivory will yellow in the absence of light. Antler is a modified form of bone that is hygroscopic and will be damaged by low RH, which may lead to cracking or splitting. Split pieces may curl open. As a general rule, the factors which affect the behaviour of ivory have a similar effect on bone. Bone tends to be harder and more brittle than ivory. Organic components of ivory, bone and antler will be attacked in excessively alkaline condi-

tions whilst excessively acidic conditions will damage the mineral components. A pH ranging between 5.5 and 8.5 should, as a general rule, be maintained if aqueous treatments are used. Ivory, bone and antler are very variable materials and there will be exceptions to the generalized information provided above. Ivory and bone can be worked with woodworking tools and can be machine or hand sawn, scraped and abraded as required. Snow and Weisser (1984) and Driggers *et al.* (1991) provide useful information on the conservation of ivory. The material properties and identification of ivory and its substitutes are discussed in Chapter 5, Thornton (1981) and Espinoza and Mann (1992) among others.

### *Cleaning*

Before cleaning ivory and bone, the surface should be examined for the presence of original varnish, dye, polychromy or gilding. Ivory may have been finely engraved and material found in engraved areas to highlight the design is usually less vulnerable to damage than that on the surface. Removal of surface dirt and accretions is usually undertaken before re-adhering loose pieces into place to avoid adhering the dirt along with the ivory. Abrasive materials should be avoided.

Cleaning tests are recommended to establish the efficacy of the least potentially harmful cleaning method. Plastic materials such as celluloid and casein were used as ivory substitutes in the late nineteenth and early twentieth centuries and may be sensitive to both aqueous and solvent cleaning. Cellulosic vegetable ivory from the nuts of several palm species may also be encountered. The auto-fluorescence of these materials under UV is discussed by Driggers *et al.* (1991).

Ivory may be cleaned using the dry cleaning methods described in section 11.2.4. A traditional method using dilute hydrochloric acid to clean ivory is known to strip the mineral component from the ivory, eroding the surface, opening cracks and causing increased hygroscopicity. Matienzo and Snow (1986) demonstrated that immersion in toluene can cause an increase in the concentration of organic material on the surface but observed that ethanol and acetone caused no noticeable change. Aromatic hydrocarbon solvents should be avoided, though as yet the effects of aliphatic hydrocarbons have not been quantified. Given the hygroscopic nature of ivory and bone, non-aqueous methods for the removal of surface dirt, such as a swab slightly dampened with white spirit, ethanol or acetone may be preferable. In some cases, however, the most efficacious method for removing dirt is a swab slightly dampened with saliva or deionized water. Care should be taken to avoid dimensional distortion by minimizing contact with water. Some sources recommend a contact time of fifteen or twenty seconds followed by immediately drying the surface (CCI Notes 6/1). Solvent mixtures which combine white spirit, acetone and water may also be effective. Whilst a soft brush may remove dust and dirt from the surface, embedded dust, wax and accretions of dirt may be more difficult to remove, particularly when the surface of the ivory is damaged or cracked. Poulticing (see section 11.6) may be effective in such cases.

Cracks in ivory veneer may be partial or run through the whole thickness of veneer. In cases where ivory veneer is already loose, lifting the veneer completely may give better access for cleaning. Patience may be required to avoid causing further damage. Water is often used to soften residual adhesive, though isopropyl alcohol may be used if there is no risk of damaging adjacent materials or surface. Partial cracks may be cleaned using a medium-soft brush and solvent. Poultices may be used to remove deep accretions of wax.

### Staining

Whilst yellowed ivory that has been kept in the dark may be whitened by simple exposure to light, removal of other stains, such as rust or copper stains, ink or previous use of adhesives such as animal glue or shellac may be more problematic. Darkened residues of animal glue may have penetrated into the body of ivory and the problem is usually exacerbated with porous bone. Oils, both drying (e.g. linseed) and non-drying (e.g. almond) may have been applied in the past to saturate the surface and produce a low sheen. Oiling ivory is no longer considered an acceptable conservation practice. Whilst almond oil can usually be removed with white spirit, linseed oil that has darkened and crosslinked may be more problematic.

The first step in the treatment of such stains is to decide whether stain removal is desirable. Many stains are considered of value because they contribute to patina, an appearance of age or evidence of history of use. Stain removal is often very difficult. Excesses of the past have led to a general presumption against bleaching because of the difficulty of keeping such treatments localized, their irreversibility and the inherently chemically destructive nature of the process. Occasionally localized bleaching may be undertaken, though care must be taken to avoid the formation of a bleached halo around a stained area. Inlay to be bleached is usually removed from the substrate to increase the effectiveness of the treatment (stain are often taken up from the verso side) and to avoid damaging adjacent material. Bleach should be carefully applied to the affected area only. Hydrogen peroxide may be used though it is not combined, in this instance, with a base such as ammonia or sodium hydroxide (see Bleaches under section 13.5.3). Progress should be checked regularly and the action of the bleach may be noticed within fifteen to thirty minutes or longer. Sodium hypochlorite bleaches should not be used as they have been associated with yellowing of ivory weeks or months after the treatment and because they degrade to sodium chloride, giving rise to the potential for salt damage.

Some success has been reported in removing metal stains with chelating agents (Rao and Subbaiah, 1983). There is a possibility that chelating agents may attack mineral components of the ivory. Conditional stability constants should be considered in relation to pH and the sensitivity of the ivory or bone to excessively acidic or alkaline conditions (see section 11.5.5).

## Consolidation

Powdering or flaking is often associated with archaeological ivory, either as a result of age or the presence of salts as a result of burial. Spalling may be caused by the use of adhesives that exhibit excessive shrinkage. Snow and Weisser (1984) have described a consolidation treatment that may be relevant in such cases. Ivory incorporated into non-archaeological furniture is more likely to have cracked, buckled or curled as a result of high, low or fluctuating RH. In such cases two options may be considered – humidifying and flattening the ivory, or supporting it in situ using an adhesive and bulking agent.

## Humidification

The traditional treatment for curled and buckled ivory was removal followed by soaking in hot (but not boiling) water. This is not recommended as it is likely to exacerbate distortion or damage. The use of a humidification chamber is recommended to allow greater control of the process. Whilst humidity may be introduced comparatively rapidly, it is essential to return the ivory to ambient RH in slow stages to avoid splitting. RH may be raised up to 80% in a comparatively short time (days) depending on the thickness of the piece – thicker pieces may require weeks. Ivory often flattens as it is humidified but if it does not, it may be flattened with weights. Wide thin veneer (up to 1 mm) can be weighted fairly quickly, whilst narrow thicker pieces need to be weighted more slowly because of the increased risk that they will snap. Once flat, the weight/s should be kept in place while RH is lowered. RH should be reduced regularly and gradually, with rest periods in between to ensure the ivory has achieved equilibrium. Thicker pieces may require six to eight weeks, whilst the RH for thinner pieces can be returned to ambient in two to four weeks.

Partially detached ivory that has not warped may be readhered using animal glue. This adhesive may be less desirable if the ivory is cracked, when capillary action may draw the adhesive along the cracks and darken them in time. If the adhesive bond has broken but the old glue still forms a coherent layer, it may be possible to introduce solvent-based adhesive. This option may be chosen when it is desirable to leave original adhesive for future analysis or where the adhesive layer is very thick and its removal would require back filling before ivory could be relaid.

## Adhesives

The thinner the ivory the more prone it will be to warp when exposed to aqueous adhesives. Whilst the use of animal glues is not recommended for three-dimensional ivories, it may be appropriate for reattaching ivory to furniture. If a collagen glue is used it should be freshly made and prepared in a non-ferrous glue pot. A good quality medium to high bloom strength glue, such as hide glue, rabbit skin glue or a high tack fish glue may be used, particularly where there is very little mating surface in a break and strength is a paramount concern. Proteinaceous adhesives provide a stronger bond on clean ivory than other adhesives. Paraloid B72 is a good adhesive for ivory. The flexibility of the polymer is affected by the solvent in which it was dissolved (see section 12.4.3). Some conservators prefer PVAC or acrylic dispersions because they are swellable in acetone. PVAC adhesives are generally stronger and less flexible than acrylics (Down *et al.*, 1996). These synthetics may be more liable to exhibit cold flow (creep) under stress than a collagen glue and may retain water for longer, inducing re-curling. Residues of old adhesives must be removed from substrate and ivory to ensure a good adhesive bond. Reversing PVAC or acrylic adhesives often requires solvents that may damage adjacent materials or coatings. Cellulose nitrate adhesives have been used because they have good adhesive properties. They have been associated with yellowing, especially with exposure to light, though this may be less of a problem if applied underneath thick, non-translucent ivory. Epoxies are not usually appropriate because they tend to yellow, and if the joint is good it can be extremely difficult to reverse without damaging the ivory. Whichever adhesive is chosen, the reattached ivory should be weighted or cramped for twenty-four to forty-eight hours, depending on the complexity and size of the piece.

Ivory may be secured in a non-planar position using an adhesive and bulking agent. A paste or putty may be made using Paraloid

B72 or an emulsion/dispersion combined with a filler such as microballoons. Paraloid B72 deposited from a solvent such as xylene or toluene is more flexible than that deposited from acetone. Acetone may be used as the solvent for a putty based on emulsions or dispersions to reduce the water content of the putty. Pigment, toned to the background colour of adjacent material, may be added to stiffer mixes to speed later retouching. Less viscous pastes are more likely to penetrate the ivory, carrying pigmenting material with them and causing discoloration.

Cracks in ivory may be filled using a viscous, non-aqueous bulked mixture, to minimize solvent migration into ivory. In some cases it may be possible to use moulding and casting techniques to fabricate repairs (see section 10.5). In many cases, however, cracks are often stained, and the final appearance of an ivory-coloured fill surrounded by a stained halo may be less desirable than untreated damage.

### Replacements

A variety of materials have been used to replace lost ivory elements. International trade in ivory was banned in 1990 under the Convention on International Trade in Endangered Species of Wild Fauna and Flora (known as CITES). In 1997 the elephants in Zimbabwe, Namibia and Botswana were downlisted to Appendix II, and in theory ivory from these species can be traded with permits. In fact, the stringent conditions imposed has meant that legal trade in ivory remains problematic. Given the cost and difficulty of acquiring ivory, restorers and conservators more often rely on recycling ivory, e.g. Victorian piano keys for escutcheons, or they make their own substitutes from thermosetting resins.

Mammoth tusks are a legal alternative to ivory. Bones with a comparative density to ivory, such as the long bones of cattle, camel (high density) or horses may also be used to replace losses. The joints are cut from the ends and the bone boiled to remove fat, flesh and marrow, until no more scum is formed. This may take several hours, depending on the size of the bone. The water is replaced and the bone boiled again, rinsed and left to soak for a day or two in clean water, then dried. It may

then be sawn and worked to produce veneer or inlay. Large sections of cattle femur bones may be available from pet shops. These are dense and clean and may not require such extensive preparation.

Synthetic ivories are often based on bulked polyester resin and are available in both sheets and rods. It may be possible to replace carved or turned elements using materials and techniques described in section 10.5. A convincing ivory substitute may be made using a light stable epoxy such as HXTAL NYL-1 bulked with calcium carbonate and pigmented as needed with dry pigments. This mixture can be rolled down to an accurate gauge when partially set to produce a sheet. Vegetable ivory may be used, though the main draw back of such material is its small size. Painted wood has often been used though the success of the replacement is often dependent on colour matching skill.

### Staining ivory

Ivory veneer may have been stained and some experimentation may be required to match replacement veneer to extant stained material. A range of nineteenth century recipes may be found in sources such as Siddons (1830) or Mussey (1987), *Spons Workshop Receipts* (1873 and later editions) and Bitmead (1873), among others. Ramond (1989) recommends pre-treating ivory by soaking it in a mordant solution of vinegar and alum for six to eight hours to ensure an even and durable stain, though this is a very harsh method. Saffron may be used to produce a golden-yellow colour, verdigris for green, campeche (logwood, *Haemotoxylon campechianum*) for a purple-pink and pernamouc wood (brazilwood, *Caesalpinia crista*) for a reddish brown. Many traditional stains, such as those produced by saffron, logwood and brazilwood, are fugitive. Modern alternatives include textile dyes – those that stain silk well tend to be effective on ivory.

### Polychrome ivory

It is common for ivory from the Indian subcontinent or the Far East to retain traces of polychromy. Isinglass, though hygroscopic, is often an effective consolidant for cupped flakes of paint. Its water content tends to soften paint and its surface tension may pull flakes down. Some conservators prefer to use synthetic materials, such as Paraloid B72, or acrylic emulsions or dispersions, in low concentrations (2–5%). Current literature on the treatment of matte paint should be consulted in cases where there is a high pigment volume concentration and a comparatively weak bond between the paint and ivory. Inks, sometimes found on ivory from the Indian subcontinent and the Far East, may be soluble in water or white spirit and require a cautious approach.

### Coatings

Ivory has the ability to take a high polish. In cases where ivory is undecorated, a thin microcrystalline wax layer is generally sufficient as a coating. LaFontaine and Wood (1982) found Cosmolloid 80H was a more effective barrier to fluctuations in RH than Renaissance wax. In some cases varnish may be necessary to match original material.

### Antler

Antler has often been incorporated into furniture with minimal change from its natural appearance. In most cases surface finishes were not used. If dusting with a brush is insufficient, dry cleaning methods (section 11.2.4) or water with a drop of detergent may remove accretions of dirt, though care should be taken not to flood the surface. The uneven surface often found on antler may require the use of a medium-hard stiff brush. White spirit may be used to remove greasy material.

### Repair and replacement

Cracks running along the length of the antler are not uncommon, particularly on the tynes. These may be filled using a bulked adhesive though it is essential that the fill material is flexible. Splits in antler may widen and curl away from the axis. This may be remedied by steaming and binding. Direct application of steam, which may be done in situ, softens the antler and allows the split component to be bound closed. When the antler has cooled and dried, usually within 24 hours, the split is then adhered.

Losses are usually replaced with antler, which may be acquired from venison producers. Alternatives include wood or casting replacement pieces. The hollow core requires the use of a fitted dowel to attach the replace-

ment. The dowel and adhesive should be reversible and compatible with original and replacement material. The dowel may be made to fit the hollow in the antler, or the hollow may be filled and the dowel pushed into place or the fill drilled after it has dried.

A tinted wax may be applied if a coating is necessary, though in most cases antler is left unfinished.

### 15.1.2   Turtleshell and horn

Tortoiseshell is actually from marine turtles, particularly the Hawksbill turtle, and in the following section is therefore referred to by the more accurate term turtleshell. Turtleshell and horn are hygroscopic materials. The combined effects of photochemical degradation and accretions of dirt leads to loss of gloss as they age. As with many other surfaces and materials associated with furniture, turtleshell and horn may have been treated with oil in the past. Degradation of such oils often contributes to a poor appearance. Horn may be prone to delaminate in conditions of low RH, though this problem may also be associated with over-processing at the time of manufacture.

### Cleaning

Surface dirt is usually effectively removed using a slightly dampened swab, whilst white spirit may be used to remove waxy accretions.

### Consolidation

Loose turtleshell or horn that is not completely detached may be consolidated using fresh slightly thinned animal glue, rabbit skin glue or fish glue. If pieces are sufficiently loose, a warmed artist's palette knife may assist, otherwise it will be necessary to use a syringe or to gently massage the loose veneer to draw the adhesive underneath. Bubbles in turtleshell are particularly common in the thin shell used on nineteenth century pieces. Fresh glue may be worked under the bubble and then cramped down. If the original glue is not severely degraded, in some cases a combination of water and methylated spirits (3:1) may be sufficient to reactivate it. In cases where the paper used under the turtleshell has delaminated, it may be consolidated with isinglass or another suitable adhesive. Turtleshell may become embrittled with age and it may be necessary to soften old glue with water or a Laponite gel (see under section 11.6.2) to prevent fracturing the edges of adjacent turtleshell when the glue is removed.

In some cases turtleshell or horn may have been applied over a gesso-type base. This may require consolidation with isinglass, a thinned glue size or Paraloid B72 (*c*.5% in a slower evaporating solvent such as xylene) before horn or shell is readhered.

Turtleshell and horn may have partially delaminated. Some conservators have consolidated delaminating turtleshell with thinned animal/hide glue or other saturating adhesive and pinched cramping pressure. Horn that has delaminated may be treated in the following manner. Flat pieces (i.e. not curved or moulded) may be detached from the object and immersed in water just below boiling point, softened and then transferred to a press, using a blotting paper interface to absorb excess moisture. Horn up to 2 mm thick may require immersion for ten to fifteen minutes. Soft horn, such as cow horn, requires pinch pressure only in the press as excess pressure may cause the horn to spread and increase its surface area. Stiffer horn, such as black or brown buffalo horn, may require more pressure. In good conditions, i.e. warm and around 50% RH, the horn will be dry after about forty-eight hours. When dry, it may be removed from the press and a low viscosity adhesive touched to the edge of lamella. The adhesive is drawn by capillary pressure between the delaminated sections. The horn is then placed between Melinex/Mylar, placed in the press and pinch pressure applied and then released. Excess adhesive is removed from the horn and the Melinex/Mylar and the horn replaced in the press until the adhesive has dried.

### Replacing losses

Hawksbill turtle was the major source of the turtleshell found on historic furniture. Although both the hawksbill and green turtle are protected species, farmed green turtle can provide a legitimate source of shell when this is required for replacing losses, without endangering the survival of turtles in the wild. The Cayman Island embassy may be contacted for details of such turtle farms and shell. Hawksbill shell is very thermoplastic and could be heat welded or moulded around compound shapes. The shell of the green turtle is less thermoplastic and less transparent. Freshly killed turtleshell was prepared for use by immersion in hot water. The shell may be cramped flat or shaped after sufficient immersion and will maintain a given shape after it has cooled. It may be thicknessed and surface faults removed by planing, scraping and sanding.

The horn of cattle is most frequently used for replacing lost horn. The tip and base are cut away and the central tubular section cut down the side to allow horn to be opened up. It is flattened using heat and pressure. Horn has a laminate structure and it is possible, though difficult, to cleave away successive individual layers to reduce the thickness. If this is not possible the horn must be filed or abraded to thickness. Horn is not usually pale or clear and the traditional method of preparing it involved covering the surface with a layer of tallow or animal fat and heating it to around 200 °C followed by heavy pressure in a press. The surface was then buffed and polished (Hawkins, 1986). Such treatment is usually unnecessary and excessive heat can lead to delamination. It is usually sufficient to simply remove the core from the horn, cut it into veneer and use it. Horn may be bleached with hydrogen peroxide.

Both horn and turtleshell may be polished with traditional materials such as pumice and linseed oil, or modern materials such as progressively finer grades of Micromesh cushioned abrasive cloths. A final treatment with a nail buffer will impart a high sheen. Turtleshell and horn may require the use of a support layer of veneer or thin wood when it is thicknessed and may be adhered to this support with a non-aqueous contact adhesive such as Cow Gum or Thixofix. The surface must be degreased before the shell is laid.

Shell and horn have often been tinted by adhering them with an adhesive mixed with pigment or using coloured paper. Shell and horn replacements may be coloured using colour fast proprietary paints or pigments mixed with animal glue. It may be necessary to polish both sides of the shell or horn to allow good transmission of colour. Non-laminated white paper may be used to increase reflectivity. The upper layers of the shell or horn itself may be dyed with a light fast water soluble dye by simmering the shell gently for a few minutes, though extended simmering will cause shell and horn to delaminate. The overall tone of the dyed shell may then be adjusted by using pigmented glue or paper underneath. In some cases, for example when matching an adjacent surface, it may be necessary to apply a varnish or tinted glaze.

Many alternatives to turtleshell and horn have been utilized and include a variety of pigmented fill materials from sealing wax, shellac, epoxy resin, polyester resin, guitar picks and acetate sheets (Lochhead, 1989). It may be possible to cast replacements, though polyesters may require the addition of an inert powder to impart opacity. Imitation turtle shell can be made from epoxy resin tinted with Orasol dyes (Ciba–Geigy). As with the ivory substitute described above, the dyed epoxy can be accurately rolled to thickness between guides or in a rolling mill before it has completely set (*Figure 15.1a,b*). If a thermoset is cast directly into the surface a reversible isolating layer should be used.

### Coatings

Wax may be used as a coating to resaturate an aged surface, matte surface. A mixture of beeswax and carnauba wax paste may impart a high sheen.

### 15.1.3   Mother-of-pearl

Although mother-of-pearl is an organic material, it has a high inorganic content. It is non-porous, brittle and may be prone to delamination. Calcium in the shell will be attacked in acidic conditions. Shells and shell material can be attacked by organic acids in the air and show fuzzy crystals of calcium formate, sometimes known as Bynes disease (Tennent and Baird, 1985). Long exposure to acidic conditions may completely destroy the shell. The susceptibility to acids was exploited in the past to etch shell. Wax was applied to the shell, a design traced through the wax, and the shell then dipped into an acidic solution, etching the surface of the shell where it was exposed.

### Cleaning

A dampened swab is usually sufficient to clean mother-of-pearl, though acidic solutions

(a)

(b)

**Figure 15.1**  Epoxy turtleshell substitute: (*a*) rolling to the required thickness using a rolling mill; (*b*) substitute ready to be cut to shape

should be avoided. Organic solvents may be used if they are compatible with the adjacent surfaces. Hydrocarbon solvents are effective in removing greasy accretions. Atmospheric pollution may lead to degradation and the formation of a powdery surface. This may be left untouched, but if removal is required it will require a stiff brush and will reveal a dull white surface. This may be left intact, or the original surface approximated by the use of fine abrasives or the application or a coating such as varnish, with the possible addition of mica or lustre pigments.

Painted or gilded decoration was often applied to mother-of-pearl, for example on many nineteenth-century papier mâché objects. Swabs should be lightly rolled over the surface as paint may be poorly adhered and easily lost through careless cleaning. Poorly adhered paint may require consolidation before cleaning and the removal of discoloured varnish may be problematic.

### Consolidation

It can be difficult to achieve a good adhesive bond with mother-of-pearl. Loss frequently occurs as a result of substrate unevenness or movement. Careful examination may reveal a shimmer of nacreous residue, particularly after loss from an urushi surface.

The adhesive used to adhere shell should be flexible. A high bloom strength collagen or high tack fish glue may be used. Acrylic emulsions/dispersions are less acidic than PVAC and give a weaker adhesive bond but a more flexible film. The adhesive chosen should be compatible with adjacent material. So, for example, whilst the acetone necessary to swell many acrylics is compatible with mother-of-pearl, it will damage resinous japanning and may be problematic for oil based japanning. In cases where the shell is thin and has been laid onto a dark ground, it may be necessary to add a small amount of white pigment to the adhesive. If loss has occurred because the substrate is uneven, it may be necessary to back fill to provide a flat surface to readhere original or replacement shell. A microballoon bulked adhesive may be used and should be compatible with the adhesive used to readhere the shell. Cracked shell may be lifted, cleaned and relaid.

### Replacing losses

It can be difficult to match the reflectivity and colour of original shell, and a successful match requires a wide selection of replacement material or a good supplier. Mother-of-pearl may be cut and shaped using small and thin high-speed diamond impregnated saw blades and burrs in a flexible shaft machine or Dremel machine. A traditional method of cutting mother-of-pearl replacements is to use a piercing or fret saw on a vice held fretsaw frame (see *Figure 10.22*). The brittle shell will require a support such as thin plywood, which may be adhered with thinned animal glue. An isolating layer of paper will speed separation when the shaped piece is soaked in water.

Very thin shell, such as Japanese awabe or abalone, may be difficult to cut using a saw. Pieces may be acid cut by coating the area required with wax and dipping the shell in vinegar, weak hydrochloric or acetic acid to dissolve excess. Although such thin shell will split if sawn, it may be possible to cut straight lined replacements with a scalpel. Areas of black shell may be matched by treating the replacement with silver nitrate and leaving it in the sun.

Mica pigments have been used as an alternative to shell. A filler such as plaster or gesso may be used to create a smooth surface. Mica pigments give the best results when brushed onto a tacky adhesive so that the thin platelet particles align parallel to the eye. Such inpainting, skilfully executed, is extremely effective and avoids potential future problems in distinguishing original material from replacements. Materials and techniques used for filling glass may be applicable in some cases (Davison, 1998).

### Coatings

Coatings on mother-of-pearl are usually applied as part of treatment of an entire surface. Coatings that require polar solvents for removal should not be applied over polychromed shell. In such cases a photochemically stabilized varnish, discussed in section 12.4.1, may be appropriate.

## 15.2    Paper labels and linings on furniture

Paper, which is usually alkaline, is most stable in an environment close to neutral pH or in alkaline conditions. As paper ages and oxidizes it becomes acidic, causing discoloration and brittleness. The cellulose chains break into shorter and shorter pieces (chain scission), destabilizing the paper from within. This process may be exacerbated for paper associated with furniture, particularly that in a micro-climate such as a drawer interior. Wood is acidic, and many species off-gas volatile organic acids, particularly acetic acid (see *Table 10.1*). The glue used to attach a label or lining will in most cases have been animal glue, also an acidic substance. These factors can present a significant challenge to the survival of paper labels and linings.

### 15.2.1 Labels

Labels are an essential part of an object and should be altered as little as possible, lest value or context be disrupted. An intact label on an object provides important information regarding provenance and can indicate place of origin, date and maker. For the most part, treatment of a paper label should involve a professional paper conservator. There are, however, some procedures that can be carried out by a non-specialist.

The types of problems a paper conservator may address include, but are not limited to, securing a lifting label, humidifying a distorted or wrinkled label, consolidation, repairing tears, removing a label for treatment and readhering it to the object. The non-specialist can address minor problems with a label, for example if the label is beginning to lift from the substrate, or if it needs to be protected or secured into place by a cover of Melinex/Mylar or Plexiglas.

#### *Options for dealing with a label on furniture*

The intended use of the object, such as museum display or domestic use, may determine treatment options. In most cases, paper should be treated by an experienced paper conservator.

If a decision is made not to treat the label, both the object and its label should be photographed to document current condition. This allows for the retention of information from the label, and records its context on the wooden object. A better solution for treatment may be developed in the future. Waiting and leaving the label alone may prevent unnecessary damage.

If a label needs to be protected from abrasion or might be damaged in handling, it can be covered by materials such as Plexiglas or Melinex/Mylar. In either case an 'open' system is necessary to allow airflow. This will avoid the creation of an acidic micro-climate that would cause the paper to deteriorate more quickly than if left uncovered. A Plexiglas cover, secured to wood or Plexiglas spacers 1.5–3 mm (¹⁄₁₆–⅛ inch) thick, can be constructed to protect the label. The spacers may be anchored into place around the label using animal/hide or fish glue, which is easily reversible. Once the glue has set, the Plexiglas cover can be screwed to the spacers. Labels that are fragmented or brittle can be held in place by covering an area slightly larger than the label with a piece of Melinex/Mylar, secured along three sides to allow some air circulation. The Melinex/Mylar can be secured in place using stainless steel pins, nipped off to the right length, or an acrylic adhesive. The acrylic adhesive can be isolated from the wood with a layer of animal glue if necessary. The use of PVAC should be avoided for this task due to off-gassing of acetic acid (Down *et al.*, 1996).

A paper conservator is best qualified to make a decision about whether deacidification is necessary. Labels can be on poor quality paper. When a proprietary deacidification product is used to impart an alkaline reserve into a paper containing lignin, the paper can significantly discolour with age and become prematurely embrittled. Deacidification using a proprietary solvent-based product is not recommended. When a proprietary deacidification product is used, the pH of the paper rises dramatically, and tide-lines may result if the paper is subsequently exposed to moisture. After the application of a deacidification product, a white precipitate can sometimes form on the surface of the paper label.

A paper conservator should be involved if the paper is embrittled, fragmented, burnt, distorted, torn, needs consolidation or in cases where the label needs to be removed for treatment before being re-adhered to the object. If a label is brittle and weak, the paper conservator might consider lining or reinforcement. If the label is detached from the object this is easily done, though reinforcement is also possible if the label is still attached. Care should be taken to leave a label on an object if at all possible. A paper conservator may be inclined to remove the label and place an alkaline barrier layer between the label and the object. This treatment should not be undertaken unless the conservation of the wooden object overall calls for the label's removal. Removing the label may call the authenticity of the label and the object into question and affect provenance. A label might be removed if it were bridging a break or if it were in danger of damage during treatment. If the label has been removed and then stabilized, it can be reattached either directly to the object, or placed between Melinex/Mylar and attached to the object. If the label will not be reattached, it can be kept with documentation records. Photo-documentation is essential in such cases to record pre-treatment condition and information contained in a label in its original site.

Certain practices have been used in the past to treat lifting labels, such as brushing on varnish, oil, wax or a white glue/water mixture. All of these methods are undesirable. Another unsatisfactory method used a 50:50 mixture of white glue (PVAC emulsion) and water brushed onto the surface of paper in an attempt to consolidate it. This can cause embrittlement due to differing rates of expansion and contraction between the consolidant and the paper label. A more appropriate way to adhere a lifting or fragmented label is to use an adhesive such as methyl cellulose. It should be noted, however, that methyl cellulose will not adhere well to a finished or 'slick' surface.

## 15.2.2   Paper liners

Paper liners are sometimes found in furniture and related wooden objects. Due to the difference in pH between paper and wood, a paper liner in a wooden drawer is likely to be somewhat discoloured and/or embrittled. Depending on the degree of degradation, the paper may be visually unaffected or fragile and flaking. If the paper liner is falling to pieces or very fragile, a paper conservator is needed to stabilize the liner. If the paper liner is stable but distorted or cockled, local humidification may be used to reduce planar distortion. Listed below are two methods to humidify paper followed by various choices for readhering lifting paper.

Water vapour or steam can be used to humidify paper. An ultrasonic mister produces a fine mist of water vapour, which can be delivered through various attachments. A small opening will concentrate and direct a fine mist of vapour in a relatively small area. The use of an ultrasonic mister can be time-consuming, especially when humidifying large areas. The use of water in mist or steam form is not very specific and can be difficult to control, resulting in the introduction of excess moisture to the object.

Gore-Tex can be used to humidify a paper lining. Gore-Tex is a sheet of Teflon, available in two weights, that allows the passage of water vapour but prevents the passage of liquid water (Purinton and Filter, 1992). To humidify an area, a Gore-Tex sheet is placed with the smooth side against the area to be humidified. A damp blotter, slightly smaller than the Gore-Tex, is placed on top and the whole 'sandwich' covered by a larger piece of Melinex/Mylar. Water vapour diffuses through the Gore-Tex, allowing even moisture-sensitive paper to be relaxed thoroughly and quickly. When using thin Gore-Tex, one can expect to see the desired result within one to five minutes, whilst thick, felted Gore-Tex takes longer. Although Gore-Tex permits controllable humidification, it is possible to over-wet using this material and such treatments must be continuously monitored.

Paper liners can lift away from their wooden substrate. Differential movement between the paper and the wood substrate causes stress on the original liner adhesive and may cause it to fail. Various materials that can be used to secure lifting paper are discussed below. Gelatin is a good choice for stabilization, whilst synthetic adhesives and wheat starch paste are less appropriate for this particular task.

Gelatin is often the most appropriate adhesive for re-adhering a paper liner. An alkaline processed, high bloom strength gelatin, used in a 2–5% concentration, will bond strongly with wood (see discussion of materials used for the consolidation of decorative surfaces in section 12.2.4). After application to the wooden substrate, the adhesive should be allowed to gel, and the paper liner tacked into place using a heated spatula (c.50–55 °C). Gelatin applied in this way has a weaker bond to the paper because it does not penetrate into the paper, making it easier to reverse if necessary. Gelatin may not adhere to a surface that has been treated with synthetics in the past.

The application of wheat starch paste to large areas is not advisable, even when a 'dry' solution is used. The paper lining is unlikely to have been, and probably cannot be, washed. As a result, moisture from the wheat starch paste will bring some degradation products present in the paper into solution. A brown tide line will form as the solubilized degradation products migrate and stain the paper as it dries (*Figure 15.2*). In smaller areas, 'dry' wheat starch paste can be applied to a surface, and allowed to dry slightly before pressure is applied. A heated spatula can be used to speed drying. This is a very time-consuming process and may not be practicable for securing large areas of a lifting paper liner. The resultant bond between the wheat starch paste, liner and wood substrate might not be as strong as gelatin. The drying time will be considerably longer than if gelatin or

**Figure 15.2** An example of tide lining on a colour lithograph entitled 'The St Sebastian Society of Archers at Bruges'. Water-soluble degradation products in the paper move with water through the sheet. When the water dries they are redeposited and form a brown tide line. Once dry, tide lines can be permanently disfiguring

BEVA® film had been used. Huxtable and Webber (1986) give comprehensive directions for preparing wheat starch paste. 'Dry' wheat starch paste is prepared by placing a small amount of paste onto blotting paper before use to draw off excess moisture.

BEVA® film can be used to secure a lifting lining. The film is placed between the paper and wood substrate and a heated spatula is used to tack the lining into place. BEVA® film may not bond well or evenly to a wood substrate because tacking takes place through the drawer lining.

Synthetic adhesives may be appropriate if gelatin is unsuccessful. A degree of flexibility is necessary to accommodate the differential expansion and contraction of the paper and wood substrate. The adhesive chosen must be flexible, with a glass transition temperature (Tg) around room temperature. The flexibility of thermoplastic polymers is affected by the solvent in which they are dissolved (see section 12.4.3). Future removal of such adhesives may be difficult in a small drawer interior. In addition, solvent applied to remove the adhesive may cause migration of the adhesive into the paper and, by saturating the liner in places, may cause tide lines or future oxidative discoloration.

PVAC adhesives are not usually a good choice for paper because their reversibility is limited and the adhesive is stronger than the paper. The reversibility of PVAC is limited even in low concentrations. PVAC will swell in polar solvents, such as acetone, but still requires mechanical action for removal. The paper substrate would typically fail before the adhesive. In addition, it should be noted that PVAC off-gasses acetic acid for up to a year and the pH of many emulsions and dispersions falls as they age (Down *et al.*, 1996). As a result many PVAC adhesives are not appropriate for use with paper, particularly where there is a risk that an acidic micro-climate will form, e.g. a drawer interior.

## 15.3 Metals

### 15.3.1 Introduction

The basic principles of metal conservation are to preserve aesthetic value and historical and technical evidence. Information on the conservation of metals may be found in conservation literature that deals with the treatment of archaeological and historical metal objects, although articles on the conservation of industrial collections and modern metal artefacts may also be useful. Related disciplines such as the conservation of scientific instruments and horology may also provide helpful references. Publications that may prove useful include MacLeod *et al.* (1995), Mourey and Robbiola (1998), Scott *et al.* (1994) and Slater and Tennent (1979). Spot tests for the identification of metals are described Ganiaris (1985) and Townsend (1985, 1988).

Ethical issues have generated significant debate in the discipline of metal conservation. An issue specific to metal conservation is the effect of repairs that utilize heat treatments. Hot metal joins such as soldering, welding or brazing alter metallographic structure, will change metal colour and patination and may interfere with future analysis. Repairs utilizing heat may affect function, for example springs that are heated may no longer function as springs. If welding is necessary, TIG or MIG welding are the best alternatives because fluxes are not necessary and the heat is intense, brief and localized, minimizing conduction and metallographic alteration.

The treatment of metal fittings on furniture, or metal furniture itself, must be considered within the broader context of furniture conservation. Bending metal back to its original shape changes the metallographic structure. In the context of furniture, the retention of original, functional fittings is usually ascribed a higher priority than unchanged metallographic structure.

### Patina

Some corrosion layers are considered attractive or may attest to the passage of time and are therefore considered to be of value whilst others, such as the tarnishing of silver, may not. The term 'patina' is often used as a value judgement for any corrosion product that is considered to enhance the appearance and value of an object. Metal conservators generally use the term to denote an artist- or manufacturer-applied corrosion product that was part of the original intent.

Perceptions of appropriate appearance are influenced by culture and fashion. The owner or curator's opinion should be sought before undertaking treatments that may radically alter the appearance of metal. Consideration should be given to the overall aesthetic balance of the object. Furniture decorated with marquetry and metal may appear unbalanced, for example, if the metal is highly polished whilst the colour contrast of the wood has faded to a mellow interplay of shades of brown.

Metals and their surface finishes, including ferrous metals, are softer and more porous than is often imagined. Decorative layers, such as gold or silver, are not only soft but may have been applied in very thin layers and are very easily damaged. In some cases, including gilding, ormolu and other surfaces, finishes were deliberately left with a 'frosted' or matte finish, patinated or painted. It should not be automatically assumed that the original finish was brightly polished, and buffing or polishing surfaces is often inappropriate. The blanket treatment of metal fittings on furniture with abrasives is not acceptable because metal treated in this way will not reflect the age or use of the object.

Wood in contact with hardware, for example iron hinges, screws or nails, is often discoloured. High moisture content as a result of elevated RH may cause leaching of iron ions and produce a blue/black (iron tannate) discoloration in oak and other woods with high tannic acid content (Panshin and de Zeeuw, 1980). Such discoloration is often considered to be evidence of age.

### Removal of metal fittings

The removal of original hardware and fittings should be avoided wherever possible. Items of hardware, such as screws or handles, that are removed to allow conservation should be labelled and stored so that they can be returned to their original position. Soft white foam may be used for this purpose, or a tag of masking tape that notes the original position may be attached to the thread. Techniques for the removal of screws are discussed in section 10.2.1.

### 15.3.2   Cleaning

As a general rule, accretions of dirt or grease are removed before dealing with active corrosion so they do not interfere with tarnish removal. Dusting or wiping over the surface will remove loose material. The presence or absence of original paint, lacquer or more recent coatings should be established before undertaking solvent cleaning. If such coatings are not present, the surface may be degreased using white spirit or industrial methylated spirits (IMS). As a general rule, immersion in water should be avoided unless followed by a thorough rinsing and drying procedure (see section 15.3.4).

Coatings are often applied to metal in an attempt to prevent or slow corrosion. Two common types of coating that have been applied to the metal components of furniture include paint and varnish, called lacquer when applied to metal. In many cases metal components have been varnished with the same materials used to finish adjacent woodwork. In some cases, however, coatings were applied which incorporated dyes or other materials that were specifically intended to enhance the appearance of metal components on furniture metal (Thomson, 1991). Before a conservation treatment is undertaken, the presence of such lacquer, which it may be desirable to conserve, should be identified. Indications of the presence of such coatings include the absence of tarnish or corrosion on a metal that would normally be expected to tarnish. The presence of areas of metal that are well preserved but adjacent to areas with a degraded or corroded surface, such as tarnish on the high areas and bright metal in the low areas, may indicate a lacquer that has begun to degrade. The presence of original patination may be indicated by the presence of a high polish or an even colour that differs from the natural appearance of the polished metal, which may itself be visible if the surface has been scratched.

### 15.3.3 Removal of corrosion products

Removal of corrosion products always involves the removal of what was once material original to the object. Some loss is inevitable, whether mechanical or chemical methods are used. The removal of corrosion from metals requires the conservator and/or curator or owner to make an informed decision that balances the degree of corrosion product removal against the potential for, or degree of

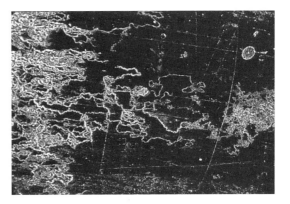

**Figure 15.3** Filiform corrosion on a seventeenth century strongbox. Filiform corrosion occurs under coatings and has a threadlike appearance. It is caused by poor surface preparation of the metal before a coating is applied in combination with elevated RH (*c*.80%) once the coating has dried. The corrosion mechanism is similar to pitting corrosion

acceptable, damage. Repeated use of abrasive or chemical polishes, for example, may eventually lead to the loss of decorative detail, plating, chasing, filigree work or hallmarks.

The successful removal of corrosion from metal requires skill and experience. There are subtle differences in metal alloys and corrosion products. A chemical or process applied by an experienced conservator may be successful whilst inexperience may cause irreparable damage. Given the damage that may be caused by repeated corrosion removal treatments, consideration must be given to storage or display conditions so that further corrosion and future treatment is minimized (*Figure 15.3*). RH should be minimized as far as is practicable within the context of the object as a whole, and gloves should be worn when handling metal to protect it from salts and oils present on skin which, if left on the surface of metal, will permanently etch it. Coatings may not be sufficient to protect the metal from volatile organic acids or residues left by ungloved handling.

There are three methods of treating accretions of corrosion products on metal objects – mechanical removal, electrolytic and electrochemical reduction, and the use of chemical reagents to remove corrosion products or stabilize the metal against further attack. The first and last are most commonly used in furniture conservation. All may be used over the whole surface or applied selectively. Deionized water rinses may be used to remove soluble corrosion products and residues from chemical cleaning agents (Fiorentino, 1994).

### Mechanical removal of corrosion products

The mechanical removal of corrosion products is generally more selective and controllable than chemical methods, but chemical and mechanical methods are often used in combination. It is often useful to remove the bulk of heavy corrosion by mechanical means before chemical removal of corrosion products or stabilization is carried out. Mechanical methods must be selected on the basis of the condition and the delicacy and level of detail on the object.

Mechanical removal is usually undertaken with the aid of a low magnification microscope. It is helpful to examine metal surfaces under magnification before treatment, as original surface treatments may be detected in the corrosion layer, for example gold overlay on iron may not be visible to the naked eye. This type of treatment of corrosion products may utilize a scalpel or other sharp tool to pick thick brittle corrosion layers from a surface. The point of the tool is used to pick off small flakes of corrosion. Although a scalpel can be used if corrosion layers are very thick, care must be taken to avoid scratching underlying or adjacent metal. Bone and ivory tools are often useful because they are hard enough to remove many corrosion products, but soft enough not to damage the metal surface. A variety of abrasive materials may be used, such as Garryflex (an abrasive block) or proprietary polishing compounds that utilize abrasive powders in paste form. Glass fibre bristle brushes are equivalent in hardness to hardened and tempered steel. They are inappropriate for the removal of corrosion products from brass and other copper alloys, gold and silver, but may find occasional use for very resistant corrosion products. Gloves should be worn when using these pens as the glass fibres break off in minute pieces that cause painful irritation if lodged in the skin.

Abrasives polish metal by scratching the surface to remove a small amount of metal. Abrasive powders vary in hardness and particle size. Harder particles will remove more

metal, but particle size will determine whether the scratches produced will be visible. Thus fine alumina (Mohs hardness 9) will remove more metal than jeweller's rouge (iron oxide, Mohs hardness 5.5–6) but if the particle sizes are the same, the final surface appearance will be similar. The abrasive effect of particles on metal will be ameliorated by a lubricant such as solvent or wax. Transparent Plexiglass or Perspex may be used to carry out an empirical evaluation of the degree of scratching produced by different materials. Properties of modern and traditional abrasives can be found in *Table 10.3*. Buffing wheels should not be used to polish metal fittings from furniture because they rapidly erode the surface.

Proprietary polishing compounds often combine mechanical and chemical removal of corrosion products, for example proprietary silver and brass polishes may contain chemically active agents such as ammonia or amines and may have a pH of up to 10. In addition to fatty acids, surfactants and other additives, they often contain very hard abrasive material such as quartz ($SiO_2$) and alumina powder ($Al_2O_3$, corundum). Conservators usually prefer to split the mechanical and chemical processes to give greater control of the corrosion removal process.

Mechanical removal of corrosion products has several limitations. Unless the surface is abraded to the depth of corrosion pits, corrosion products cannot be completely removed. In many cases the pits are too deep for this to be practicable and, if it is essential to remove all corrosion products, chemical methods may be required. In cases where the underlying metal is very soft and is obscured by corrosion products, e.g. lead acetate (lead ethanoate), mechanical removal of corrosion products can cause significant damage. It is possible to do a great deal of damage using abrasives, which are usually harder than the underlying metal. It may be difficult to remove all abrasive particles or polish residues, though a small amount of pigment or dye may be added to disguise such deposits. Wood adjacent to metal fittings has often been discoloured by deposits of metal cleaning pastes and the residues of metal within them. Such damage may be prevented by removing hardware when corrosion removal is required, or inserting Melinex/Mylar or Parafilm

**Figure 15.4**
Reverse side of a music stand, English, *c*.1810, before treatment. Parafilm has been used to protect the varnished and decorated paper surface adjacent to the metal

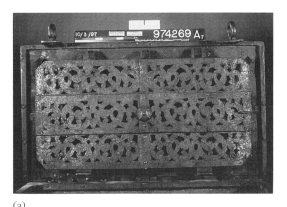

(a)

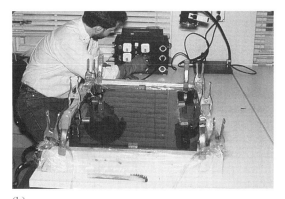

(b)

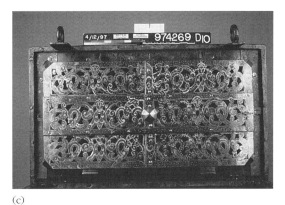

(c)

between the metal fitting and adjacent wood (*Figure 15.4*).

## *Electrochemical and electrolytic reduction*

Electrochemical reduction of corrosion products, described by Plenderleith and Werner (1971), was often used in the past. It relies on the corrosion of an anodic metal to supply electrons to the cathodic metal, which reduces the corrosion products (see section 8.4). Copper objects, for example, were immersed in zinc, in the form of pellets, powder or granules, and sodium hydroxide or sulphuric acid added and heated. A similar technique utilized strips of aluminium foil for the treatment of silver. Such treatments may be problematic because observation of the progression of the reduction treatment may be difficult and corrosion products were sometimes redeposited on the surface. Such products were often not originally present on the surface and were difficult to remove.

Electrolytic reduction, which utilizes an electric current and an electrolyte to reduce corrosion products, has become more sophisticated and is particularly suitable for the treatment of lead. Electrons are given up by the metal in the process of forming corrosion products. Electrolytic reduction 'reverses' this process by supplying electrons from a direct current source. In electrolytic reduction, the object is wired as a cathode in an electrolytic solution and corrosion products are converted back to free metal or to a lower oxidation state

**Figure 15.5** Electrolytic reduction
(*a*) The inner lock cover of a seventeenth-century strongbox before treatment. Corrosion and previous applications of oil and wax coatings have darkened formerly bright surfaces. (*b*) Tank and treatment set up for electrolytic cleaning of the lock cover. Corrosion on the lock cover was reduced and removed using direct current in an electrolytic solution of sodium carbonate (*c*) Lock cover after treatment. Coatings were removed with sodium hydroxide, corrosion removed by electrolytic reduction and mechanical polishing

compound (*Figure 15.5*). After reduction, loose corrosion products are brushed away under running water, and the object is rinsed repeatedly in deionized water. Electrolytic reduction can also be carried out locally using small hand-held anode swabs. This is a useful technique where composite objects cannot be immersed in electrolyte, but it is very slow. On wood–metal composites, consideration must be given to the feasibility of post-treatment rinsing. The advice of an experienced specialist should be sought before undertaking reduction treatments.

Both electrochemical and electrolytic reduction often produce a dull, matte surface that requires polishing. In addition, although the original metal is recovered, it is unlikely that the exact original surface would be reproduced or recovered.

### Chemical removal of corrosion products

Chemical reagents are often used to soften corrosion products in order to facilitate mechanical removal. Chemical removal of corrosion products has been extensively used in the past, particularly for softer metals such as gold, silver and copper, and in cases where a large number of objects, such as coins, have required treatment to stabilize them or to allow examination and study. Many objects that were chemically cleaned in the past are no longer considered displayable as they have lost their original surface and any patina associated with it, whilst the surface of the metal that has been revealed may be etched, pitted, porous or grainy. In some cases it may be possible to incorporate a corrosion inhibitor. Chemicals used to clean metal may attack and irreparably damage adjacent materials such as wood, enamel, glass, stone, paper and textiles.

Chemical reagents used to remove corrosion products from metal include acids, alkalis and chelating agents. All these reagents require an aqueous system. If aqueous systems are used, very high or very low pH should be avoided. Very low pH solutions in particular will increase the rate of dissolution of the base metal and therefore etch the surface. As a general rule the conservator should aim to work with an alkaline solution. It may be necessary to use a buffer to ensure an aqueous solution remains at a stable and given pH (see section 11.5.2).

Materials that can be used for thickening corrosion removal solutions are described in section 11.6. Carbopol gels contain a small percentage of water and will collapse if pH falls too low. Cellulose ethers are stable over a wider pH range. Examples of the use of gels in the conservation of metals may be found in Lupu and Balta (1998) and Sawada (1993).

The use of chemical reagents to remove corrosion products is often problematic. Chemicals may preferentially attack components within a metal alloy, leaching material or depositing insoluble complexes on the surface. Reaction products may remain after treatment. Such residues may remain even after rinsing of the surface and may interfere with future analysis. Whilst the use of chemicals may facilitate the removal of corrosion products, it is essential that objects or surfaces treated in this way are thoroughly rinsed and dried. All residues must be removed after treatment or further, more aggressive, corrosion may result. Chelating agents are discussed in sections 11.5.5 and 15.3.9.

Mechanical and chemical removal of corrosion products will reveal a fresh reactive surface. In some cases, noticeable re-corrosion may occur within a matter of hours, days or, in the case of electrolytically reduced iron, minutes. If this is undesirable, a coating should be applied shortly after the removal of corrosion products, when the rinsing or drying procedure has been completed.

Many chemicals used to remove corrosion products from metals are potentially dangerous. *It is the responsibility of the conservator to be fully aware of the hazards presented and to take adequate precautionary measures.* A high standard of workshop and personal hygiene should be maintained and appropriate health and safety precautions taken when working with chemicals.

### 15.3.4   Rinsing and drying

A rigorous rinsing and drying procedure is essential to prevent residues of moisture or reagents initiating further corrosion. Several rinsing procedures may be used. Where an object has been immersed in an aqueous solution it may be rinsed by further repeated immersion in distilled water. Conductivity and pH meters may be used to detect the presence of electrolytes (e.g. after removing corrosion products with silver dip) and rinsing repeated until conductivity has fallen off or levelled out. Immersion in an IMS or acetone bath is a common procedure and relies on the faster-evaporating, water-miscible solvent rinsing excess water from the metal. As a final stage, many conservators gently warm the object (*c.*60 °C) to ensure the evaporation of any residual moisture. Water spotting can be avoided by solvent drying, or drying the metal with a well-washed cotton cloth. Jewellers sometimes dry smaller pieces in dust-free boxwood sawdust, which can be bought from jewellers supply catalogues.

### 15.3.5   Repairs

Repairs to metal components on furniture will be dependent on position, use, loading, or whether the metal has been heated during or after manufacture. Ferrous hinge plates, for example, are unlikely to have been hardened and silver soldering may be appropriate as an alternative to replacement. It is usually possible to straighten ferrous hinge plates without the risk of the metal breaking. Mechanical repairs, such as riveting and stitching (a technique used for cast iron), are not as strong as hot metal joins and are often visually obtrusive but may be preferable to wholesale replacement of components. Complex straightening and reforming should be attempted only by conservators with extensive practical experience of metal working. Metal must be examined frequently under high magnification during straightening so that incipient cracks can be spotted. It is seldom possible to straighten highly stressed metal objects. Severely corroded objects cannot normally be straightened due to intergranular corrosion leading to the presence of 'stress raisers', which cause the metal to crack at these points. Repairs to hardware such as locks, hinges, castors and escutcheons have been described in general literature on furniture restoration, including Rodd (1976) and Bennett (1990).

Adhesives may be appropriate for non-structural repair. Adhesive bonding requires that the surface be clean and free from loose corrosion products. If a metal oxide layer is tightly bound to the metal layer beneath, a durable adhesive bond can be formed (Cagle, 1973). Adhesives must be stable and non-reactive to uncorroded metal. The glass transition temperature should be high enough to avoid cold flow (creep). Paraloid B48N is specifically designed for use with metals and can be used in conjunction with fine fibre glass mesh and microballoon fillers to strengthen vulnerable components. Paraloid B72 is satisfactory when used at a 50% concentration in acetone. PVAC (pure resin) has been used in metal conservation. PVACs are not desirable for use on lead, leaded bronze, silver or copper alloys because of the potential for corrosion due to acetic acid off-gassing from the PVAC. Cellulose nitrate adhesives, e.g. HMG and Duco, have been used for many years, particularly in the UK. Some doubts have been expressed regarding the stability of cellulose nitrates, but this concern is disputed by many. Epoxy resins are useful where more strength is required. Epoxies with amine hardeners can react with metals, particularly copper alloys, and cause corrosion. They should be isolated from metal with Paraloid B72. An isolation layer is also important to prevent penetration of epoxy into porous areas. In cases where consolidation of corrosion products is necessary, adhesives should not penetrate the porous corrosion products and thus change their optical saturation.

### 15.3.6   Replacement elements

Replacement of lost fittings is often problematic, a fact that in the past has often led to the wholesale replacement of, for example,

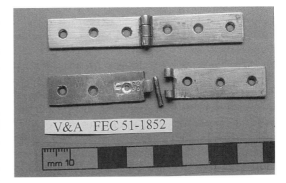

**Figure 15.6**  Mercury silvered copper hinges from a nineteenth century Japanese lacquered writing box. A broken old repair was replaced and the new repair stamped V&A 2000. The repaired section of the hinge was then silver plated

handles on carcase furniture. Furniture that survives with its original hardware intact usually has increased historical and monetary value. Metal components replaced during a conservation treatment should be given a durable unobtrusive mark, such as stamping or engraving, to indicate their non-original nature. Such marking should include dating where possible (*Figure 15.6*).

Some small firms offer a casting service and use an original fitting as a pattern from which a replacement is cast. Since metals shrink slightly on cooling, the replacement will be slightly smaller than the original. In other cases it may be possible to purchase a replacement from specialist suppliers but as a general rule these require some finishing by the conservator before they are fixed to the object. This may involve, for example, the addition of a bevel to the backplate of a drawer handle or polishing the surface, having first closely inspected such details on the original fittings.

Electrotypes can be made from existing elements by electrically depositing metal into a mould made from an existing element. This technique produces a metal copy without any shrinkage, which can be bent, soldered etc., and is faithful to the original in all details. Copper electrotyping is easy and safe in a small lab setting.

There are a wide variety of colours and effects that may be used in the patination of metal replacements. The one proviso in regard to patination is that conservators should be wary of conjectural restoration where no original exists. Conservators are encouraged to consult specialist texts (Hughes and Rowe, 1982), restoration manuals (Bennett, 1990; Rodd, 1976) historical treatises (e.g. Smith, 1810; *Spons Workshop Receipts*, 1873 etc.) and sources in related disciplines such as engineering and horological manuals. It should be borne in mind that chemically patinated metal may need to be thoroughly rinsed and dried to remove residues that might otherwise catalyse corrosion. Toning using dyes and transparent coatings is also often effective.

In some cases it may be sufficient, if time allows, to thoroughly clean the surface and then leave the metal to slowly oxidize. Proprietary patinating mixtures such as 'gun blue' have been used for arms and armour. Brass has been toned using a wide variety of

materials including proprietary products such as the Armatone range, copper nitrate and spirit stains in shellac. A simple method of removing the high shine from new brass is to simmer the part in deionized water. The oxidation layer thus formed will be even and stable.

In some cases replacements may be cast using the materials described in section 10.5. Polyester resin or epoxy resin may be coloured using metal powders. The metallic effect is particularly convincing if these are dusted into a rubber mould prior to pouring the resin. In addition to these materials, it may be possible to cast a replacement using low melt ('white') metals such as tin/lead alloys or pewter.

Epoxies and polyesters are often chosen for filling large losses in metal objects. They may be cast separately and adhered into place, or cast in place using techniques borrowed from glass conservation. Epoxies should be isolated from direct contact with the metal (see section 15.3.5). Glass fibre cloth or randomly oriented glass fibre 'mat' may be used to reinforce fills, or used to support fills as they are modelled in place. Epoxies bulked with microballoons are very useful because the density and weight may be more sympathetic to damaged, corroded and weak metal, and they are more easily carved, filed and manipulated after curing. Denser epoxy putties such as Pliacre (grey) and Milliput (white) may be useful in some instances, and can be made less dense by the addition of microballoons by the conservator.

### 15.3.7   Application of coatings after conservation

There has been some debate in the field of metal conservation about the appropriateness of lacquering. Some metals or types of object have traditionally been lacquered whilst others were not. Some metals surfaces are not suitable for coating, e.g. blued steel and other patinated finishes. Consideration should also be given to ease of future removal.

Small amounts of water, ions, pollution and oxygen that penetrate a coating applied to metal may cause corrosion to occur at a similar rate to bare metal. The protection offered by a coating is dependent on several factors, including physical and chemical properties and resistance to the permeation of gases, vapours, liquids and ions. The application of a coating may slow or prevent corrosion caused by external factors such as pollutants and moisture. However, if unstabilized corrosion remains in pits or in the body of the metal, corrosion will continue regardless of the coating applied.

The addition of corrosion inhibitors may enhance the ability of organic coatings to resist corrosion. Some proprietary products contain corrosion inhibitors, e.g. silver cloths, or acrylic-based Incralac lacquer, which contains benzotriazole (BTA), although the BTA may volatilize from a protective film within a couple of years. BTA has been recommended for stabilizing cuprous chloride on archaeological artefacts (Madsen, 1967; Sease, 1978). The protective layer provided by the corrosion inhibitor is chemically bonded to the metal. The use of corrosion inhibitors on composite or alloyed metals may be problematic because whilst the corrosion inhibitor may be effective for one metal it may attack the other. Some corrosion inhibitors that are used for industrial applications rely on a corrosion free surface and may therefore require harsher surface preparation than would be acceptable in conservation. Some corrosion inhibitors, such as phosphoric acid on ferrous metals, form part of a multi-stage coating system, applied to prevent physical disruption of the inhibitor layer. Information on the principles and use of corrosion inhibitors in conservation may be found in Keene (1985). Before using corrosion inhibitors, conservators should be aware of the likely occurrence of the corrosion products inhibited by a specific product.

The application of coatings to metal in industry is usually preceded by cleaning the surface using abrasion or solvents. In the context of conservation, where it may not be appropriate to abrade a surface, it is considered sufficient to remove loose flakes of corrosion and degrease the surface with white spirit followed by ethanol. Acetone can be problematic because its fast evaporation rate can cool the metal sufficiently to cause condensation of water vapour, visible as a white misty bloom on the surface.

### Method of application

The method chosen to apply a coating will be dependent on several factors, including scale, ease of removability of hardware, temperature and RH, the surface finish of the metal etc. The surface of the metal must be thoroughly degreased before lacquer is applied. Three methods that may be applicable to the conservator are brush coating, spray coating and dipping. The success of all these methods is largely dependent on operator skill. Brush application is very versatile, whilst spraying or dipping can produce coatings with good continuity and even thickness. Lacquering metal is a difficult skill to master, and requires practice.

Brush coating may be problematic because brush marks produce a coating of variable thickness. Thin areas tend to break down before thick areas and preferential corrosion occurs in a brush-stroke pattern that may be difficult to remove. Other factors, such as the solvent carrier, may also have an effect. A slow-evaporating solvent may allow time for the surface to flow and level but may not be appropriate for vertical surfaces. The type of brush used will also affect the lacquer layer and specialist suppliers sell brushes manufactured for lacquering metal. Traditionally these were flat, wide, thin squirrel hair brushes that minimized brush marks, though the expense of squirrel brushes has led to the use of cheaper mixed hair brushes.

Spray application of coatings is discussed in section 12.4.8. A turn-table is necessary for spray coating larger objects. Dipping can provide a coherent and even coating, though it may not always be practicable (Rymuza, 1989). Dipped objects may be hung on wires, and drips collected with blotting paper as the lacquer dries. Some experimentation may be required to ensure that the coating is even, rather than thin at the top (which will produce a rainbow interference pattern) and thick at the bottom.

### Preferential corrosion

The problem of preferential corrosion is likely to arise where there is uneven exposure of the metal to the ambient atmosphere. This may occur as a result of holidays (voids) in the coating or where lacquer begins to degrade (*Figure 15.7*). In such cases the coated metal behaves as a more noble metal whilst the uncoated metal is more reactive. An air corrosion cell, which may lead to the formation of disfiguring pits, can occur on the uncoated

**Figure 15.7** An eighteenth century Sheffield silvered plated candlestick. Preferential corrosion has occurred as a result of poor application technique when the object was lacquered

atmospheric moisture and appearance. Often the primary criterion in metal coating research is corrosion resistance. Whilst this is undoubtedly important for metal components in furniture, an appearance consistent with the object as a whole may be given greater emphasis in many cases.

It should be noted that historic lacquers on metal fittings have probably yellowed over time, or may have originally been intentionally coloured to simulate gold on brass or polished iron and tin. Historical recipes for brass lacquers usually contain colorants. The replacement of such coatings with a modern clear coating is inappropriate.

Given the potential damage to objects and expense of repeated conservation treatment, many museums aim to reduce exposure to corrosive agents by filtering gallery air or placing moisture or pollutant absorbers, e.g. silica gel or activated carbon, within display cases. There has also been increasing awareness of need to consider the materials incorporated into display cases, e.g. paints, lacquers, textiles, showcase frames etc., which may off-gas corrosive chemicals (see, e.g., Thickett *et al.*, 1998).

Microcrystalline and polyethylene waxes have been used for coating metals, whilst the chemical reactivity of beeswax and carnauba wax make them unsuitable for this purpose. Most natural oils and waxes will form organo-metallic complexes, for example copper oleates and stearates, which can complicate the removal of these coatings. Microcrystalline waxes are preferable to natural waxes because they are chemically inert and free from fatty acids. Crystalline regions make these waxes less permeable to moisture and atmospheric pollutants than natural waxes. Proprietary formulations have a range of softening and melting points, allowing a product to be selected according to the requirements of the object, its display and handling. Waxes are premixed into a thin paste and applied using a soft cloth or brush. The surface is left to allow solvent to evaporate and then excess wax is buffed from the surface with a soft lint-free cloth. Two or three coats may be applied in this way to minimize the possibility of voids in the film.

In comparison to lacquers, wax coatings on polished surfaces are more easily disrupted

metal. In such cases the uncoated area will corrode more rapidly than if the surface had not been coated. It is therefore essential that a coating applied to a metal surface should be without holidays and evenly applied. If this is not possible it may be better to leave the metal uncoated.

### Coating materials for metals

Coatings applied to metal on historical artefacts encompass the range of materials available at the time of manufacture (e.g. waxes and solvent-borne coatings). The twentieth century saw the use of cellulose nitrate coatings and, more recently, acrylics such as the Paraloids. The criteria used for selecting a coating for metal include longevity, removability, impermeability to pollutants or

when the object is handled. Research on wax coatings for metal has largely been focused on outdoor objects that are exposed to weathering, such as industrial collections and bronze sculptures (Price *et al.*, 1997; Siepelt *et al.*, 1998). Selwyn (1990) has observed that although wax coatings are commonly held to be easily removed with hydrocarbon solvents, this may not be true for surfaces that are porous, pitted, ornate or detailed. It can be difficult to remove all traces of wax from crevices etc., and residues may interfere with the adhesion of subsequent coatings. Moffett (1996) noted that polyethylene wax could only effectively be removed using hot xylene.

Shellac has been applied to many metal fittings and mounts associated with furniture since at least the mid-eighteenth century (Dossie, 1758). It has the advantage of being easy to apply, has very good adhesive properties and is usually easily reversible in alcohols such as IMS, ethanol or diacetone alcohol. Conservators coating boullework have sometimes used a cellulose nitrate coating followed by shellac.

Cellulose nitrate (CN) is favoured by many metal conservators because of its aesthetic properties. The film is considered very unobtrusive in contrast with the plastic appearance associated with acrylics. For many conservators, this has outweighed the fact that CN is less than ideal in a conservation context because it produces nitric acid as it degrades (Heller, 1983). Advantages of CN include good levelling and rapid solvent release, which produces a dry coating within minutes and reduces contamination from dust. It is comparatively easy to apply a single coat, which usually produces a coherent film. Thin coats may produce a rainbow interference pattern. Brush application of subsequent coats is often problematic as lower layer/s are easily redissolved and subsequent coats usually require the use of spray equipment. When CN is applied to a large area it is essential to work very quickly, though this makes it more difficult to apply a coating that is even and without holidays. The use of a proprietary CN 'pull-over' solution may allow a brushed or sprayed surface to be levelled using a chamois leather and French polishing technique. Coatings may have a projected lifetime of up to ten or fifteen years, though cast films kept out of bright light have been reported to have lasted for over sixty years (Selwitz, 1988). Aged cellulose nitrate may be somewhat resistant to dissolution in acetone and removal may be assisted by extending the contact time via a solvent gel (*Figure 15.8*).

Acrylic resins, such as the Paraloids, vary in their hardness and resistance to atmospheric pollutants. Thin films are often relatively brittle

(a)

(b)

(c)

**Figure 15.8** Removing degraded coating
(*a*) Detail of the base of a music stand pole, English *c*.1810. The coating on the pole was severely degraded and appeared almost black in places. Swabbing with acetone was insufficient to remove the coating
(*b*) Acetone gel was applied to the upper feather and right hand section of the pole in order to increase the contact time of the solvent
(*c*) Base of a music stand pole after removal of gel and degraded coating. Corrosion pitting was treated with a combination of mechanical and chemical methods

and may fracture if the substrate metal is flexed. Their appearance is often considered somewhat plastic, though this may be modified by the addition of matting agents or by using a slower evaporating solvent. Incralac, a proprietary mixture of Paraloid B-44 and benzotriazole, is widely used for copper and copper alloys. Acrylic resins may be used to provide an easily removable isolating layer over which other coatings, with different solubility parameters, may be applied. Solutions of 10–12% w/v of Paraloid B72 in acetone have been used to spray coat brass. Successful brush application may be more problematic and some conservators have used B72 in xylene or a slower evaporating solvent mixture such as 3:1 diacetone alcohol: ethanol.

Many proprietary metal coatings are available. These may be based on Paraloid (e.g. Incralac) or cellulose derivatives such as propionate and butyrate (e.g. Ercalene, Agateen). Frigilene, a CN-based lacquer, has been recommended for coating silver. Such lacquers are often marketed as product lines and are available in a variety of formulations that may contain stabilizers, plasticizers, colorants and other additives. De Witte (1973/74) compared coatings applied to silver objects and found that the permeability to hydrogen sulphide ($H_2S$) was higher through polymethacrylates (PMAs) than cellulose nitrate (CN). The adhesive properties of CN were better than PMAs (except B72) and the CN exhibited better elastic properties. The PMAs resisted abrasion very well and were easily removable after accelerated ageing, whilst the CN performed poorly in comparison. Selwitz (1988) has pointed out that De Witte's accelerated ageing conditions were selectively destructive for cellulose nitrate, which suggest CN may exhibit better ageing properties than DeWitte's results indicate.

## 15.3.8 Ferrous metals

Iron is one of the most reactive of the common and useful metals, with rust being the inevitable consequence of neglect and disuse. The corrosion products of ferrous metals are larger in volume than the original metal and it is common to find corrosion products on the surface that may have been generated from a small corrosion pit. Although the corrosion product may be present over the surface of the metal component, careful removal of rust or other corrosion products may reveal a surface that is relatively undamaged. Information on the conservation of ferrous metals may be found in Clarke and Blackshaw (1982) and Stambolov (1979). The stability imparted by various treatment methods has been reviewed by Selwyn and Logan (1993).

The chief electrolyte in iron corrosion is chloride ($Cl^-$). Historic iron that is free from chlorides can be stable even when heavily rusted and subject to high humidity. Iron that is contaminated with chlorides will not be stable even when humidity is very low. Objects with intact coatings or a stable patina will be more resistant to corrosion than uncoated surfaces. The material commonly called 'rust' usually consists of a mixture of ferric oxy-hydroxide corrosion products, particularly goethite (yellow/ochre), akaganeite (dark red-brown/burnt sienna) and lepidocrocite (bright orange red).

### Patination of iron

In order to treat ferrous artefacts responsibly it is important to understand what the original surface treatments and coatings may have been, and their appearance. Heat or fire bluing is the blue temper colour sometimes used as a decorative and somewhat protective layer. Fire bluing is often found on scientific instruments and barometers, particularly on indicator needles. Chemical bluing/browning describes a range of chemical treatments used to yield a coloured, protective patina. These are often generically called bluing even though they produce a range of browns. Fire or mill scale is the silvery-grey layer of magnetite that forms as iron is being forged. When the layer builds up to a certain thickness, it spalls off the object in fine flakes. Smiths would often finish objects by wire brushing off all of the loose material, and re-heating the object evenly to form a thin adherent layer of magnetite. This treatment was, in some cases, followed by rubbing oil onto the hot surface and allowing it to char and bake on. This resulted in a brownish-black semi-glossy surface. Stove blackings and grate polishes were proprietary polishes consisting of waxes and pigments, usually lamp black and graphite. They were commonly used on cast iron domestic objects such as stoves, grates, fenders, hobs etc., and gave a shiny black polished surface. These products were common in the nineteenth and early twentieth centuries and are still available in the UK (e.g. Z-Brite).

After the introduction of electroplating in the 1840s, a variety of metals were plated onto iron. Chromium and nickel plates were especially popular for iron. Since relatively few metals will plate onto iron, it is common to find a copper layer, which is easy to deposit on iron, underneath the surface metal plate. Modern tin electroplating replaced the older method of hot dipping in molten tin. Mercury gilding (fire gilding or amalgam gilding) can be done on iron that has first been coated with copper, which was usually done by boiling in copper sulphate or 'blue vitriol'. Electrochemical gilding using cold gold solutions (gold dissolved in aqua regia, a mixture of nitric and hydrochloric acids) were also used, but gave only a very thin gold 'wash' that was easily abraded.

Japanned coatings for iron were black pigmented, baked-on (stoved) oil-resin varnishes. Japan coatings were popular on sheet iron and tinned iron as a base for polychrome and gilded decoration, and on utilitarian iron objects such as tools, boxes, hardware etc.

Tin has been a common decoration or overall coating on iron from ancient times to the present. It is shiny and more resistant to corrosion than iron, but unlike zinc, it does not confer cathodic protection to the iron, but protects it only as long as the tin layer is continuous. Tinned iron is commonly referred to as 'tin', and has been used extensively to make decorative and functional artefacts since the eighteenth century.

Galvanizing is the term for a protective coating of zinc on iron. The zinc will be preferentially corroded as long as there is any metallic zinc in electrical contact with the iron, and so does not rely on a continuous barrier layer.

Various metallic compounds have been used extensively as paint pigments or as primers where another colour is coated on top of them. Red lead ($Pb_3O_4$) has been used as a protective paint for iron.

## *Mechanical removal of corrosion products*

Mechanical corrosion removal methods are commonly used to remove corrosion products from ferrous metals. It is helpful to establish whether the corrosion problem is one of small areas of corrosion that have generated a large amount of products or whether surface as a whole has suffered. The least interventive methods should be tried first. The use of a sharp tool to pick away flakes is appropriate for small discrete areas of corrosion. Where possible this should be undertaken using

(a)

(b)

**Figure 15.9** Removal of corrosion products
(*a*) Detail of a quoit from a ceremonial Akali (quoit) turban, mid-nineteenth century, Punjab, India, before treatment. Gold wire overlaid on blued steel. Ferrous corrosion products were present below, beside and over the gold decoration. (*b*) Detail of quoit after treatment. The gold was pre-consolidated with Paraloid B72 to prevent further loss. Working under magnification, ferrous corrosion products were removed from on and around the gold using a scalpel. The turban was coated with three thin applications of microcrystalline wax after treatment

magnification, taking care to remove rust without scratching the surface (*Figure 15.9*). This technique is very time-consuming. Larger scale problems, for example tubular steel furniture on which the whole finish has been affected, may require the use of mild abrasives such as talc, fuller's earth or jeweller's rouge. The removal of abrasive particles after treatment is often problematic and residues are potentially visually obtrusive. Proprietary products such as Autosol are not recommended as they often contain particles that are large, excessively coarse and may leave deep scratches.

Fine (0000) wire wool has been recommended for the removal of corrosion products from ferrous metals (CCI Notes 9/6, 1995). Fine wire wool is a comparatively harsh abrasive but can be effective for removing rust, particularly if the corrosion is softened up by soaking in aliphatic hydrocarbon solvent (e.g. Stoddard solvent, petroleum benzine) or penetrating oil (e.g. WD-40). Wire wool may find application for large scale corrosion, for example the removal of rust from the underside of an object, but will obliterate any fine detail, tends to leave a surface covered with fine scratches and will round over sharp edges. It is used in combination with a light mineral oil, residues of which may be removed with solvent. Some steel wool is coated with silicone-based lubricants that can cause subsequent problems with coatings, so conservators generally use lubricant-free grades. Stainless steel wool could also leave chromium and other trace metals on surfaces, which could confuse instrumental analysis.

Dry brushing will remove loose flakes and may utilize a watchmaker's bristle brush or a medium hard toothbrush. In some cases a swab and solvent such as petroleum spirits or alcohol may be successful, though the presence of coatings that may be damaged by the solvent should be ruled out first. If solvent splashes will not damage the surrounding area, a brush may also be used.

Air-abrasive methods may find occasional application for ferrous components of furniture. Various grits are available for different jobs requiring more or less removal and delicacy. Organic grits of corn-cobs and walnut shells are most gentle, but do not remove tightly adhering corrosion. Glass bead

'peening' may be useful for parts such as screw threads where appearance is not an issue and complete corrosion removal and smooth functioning is important.

### Rust converters

Rust converters may be used to treat lightly corroded historic iron. These chemicals convert unstable corrosion products into more stable iron compounds. The most common are phosphoric acid and tannic acid. The compounds formed are bonded to the surface of the metal by an irreversible chemical reaction. Ethical debate on the use of rust converters has centred on the change in appearance and the appropriateness of such a non-original layer chemically bonded to the surface. The decision whether to use a rust converter must balance these factors against the probability of removing all corrosion products and the environment to which an object will be returned. Commercial rust removers usually consist of citric and ortho-phosphoric acids with passivating agents such as amines (hexamine) to prevent them from aggressively etching uncorroded metal. Although rust converters can be applied selectively, the effect can be visually disruptive. The use of tannic acid on surfaces that have been painted black is an exception to this – loose flakes of corrosion can be picked off and the tannic acid then applied. Binnie *et al.* (1995) tested a range of rust converters for ferrous objects displayed outdoors.

Phosphoric acid can remove corrosion products and additionally forms a stable phosphate layer that resists corrosion. The conversion products from phosphoric acid are more stable than those produced by tannic acid. Phosphoric acid is often a component in metal primers. The light grey appearance of treated metal is often considered unsightly. It is often used as the first stage in a treatment, followed by the application of lacquer or paint. Acidic rust removers based on hydrochloric acid or phosphoric acid, thickened with cellulose ethers, are called naval jellies.

Tannic acid forms a stable black iron-tannate layer (Logan, 1989). Tannic acid effectively converts and passivates light corrosion, and the black colour is often in harmony with blacksmithed objects. Tannic acid does not penetrate or react with an uncorroded surface,

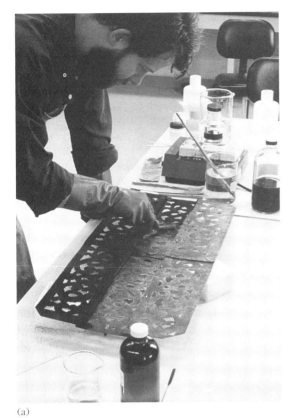

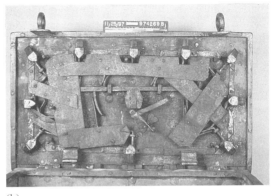

(a)

(b)

(c)

**Figure 15.10** Rust conversion
(*a*) The reverse side of the lock cover illustrated in *Figure 15.5* being treated with tannic acid to passivate
corrosion. (*b*) Lock mechanism, iron and steel, of a seventeenth-century strongbox before treatment with tannic acid.
(*c*) Strongbox lock mechanism after removal of old coatings and passivation of corrosion with tannic acid.
Mechanism has had all working parts greased with a horological grade of grease

so if the treatment is to appear even, light oxide should be present over the entire object. Mixtures of tannic and phosphoric acids have been found to be most effective. One recipe is:

> 1 part (by weight) 10–40% phosphoric acid
> 1 part (by weight) tannic acid powder

These ingredients are diluted in a 50/50 solution of ethanol and water to a concentration of 10–20% w/v. Objects can be soaked in this solution or it can be swabbed on (*Figure 15.10*). This is followed by rinsing and drying. The use of an additional protective coating is unnecessary for surfaces that have been treated with tannic acid.

### Chemical removal of corrosion products

Citric acid, a weak chelator, forms a water-soluble colourless complex with iron (see *Table 11.10* for formation constants). Examples of commercial rust removers based on citric acid are Modelene (UK) and Brownell's Rust Remover (USA). The rate of removal can be controlled by the strength of the solution, as directed by the manufacturer's instructions. The metal will appear clean and bright. Rust patinas, fire bluing and temper colours will be completely removed.

EDTA is a generally effective chelating agent for a variety of metal ions. *Figure 11.22c*, which plots the conditional stability constants of EDTA and several metal ions, shows that between a pH of *c.*4 and 7 EDTA can form stable complexes with ferric iron (Fe(III)). It should be remembered that the more acidic the solution, the more likely the base metal will be attacked and etched. Between a pH of 8 and 10 EDTA can form stable complexes with ferrous iron Fe(II). Above a pH of about 10, hydroxyl ions successfully compete to bind $Fe^{2+}$ ions, thus EDTA complexing of such ions drops off markedly as pH rises beyond this point. DTPA complexes most strongly with Fe(III) between a pH of 5 and 7, whilst the DTPA-Fe(II) complex formed at a pH of 10 or above is significantly more stable than that formed by EDTA-Fe(II) (*Figure 11.22b*).

Enzymes have also been used to remove light rusting from iron objects. One commercial product is Rust Biox. Removal is quite slow and removal is less even than with the acid cleaners, but enzymatic cleaners are useful where sensitive coatings or associated material is present (e.g. tin-types).

Some organic amines are excellent corrosion inhibitors, and may have the ability to reduce some iron corrosion products. Ethylenediamine and triethanolamine (TEA) have both been used, but TEA is less toxic and appears to work well. Archaeological iron has apparently been stabilized by TEA soaks. Amines can be thickened to a gel and applied as a poultice, or can be added to wax coatings to passivate iron surfaces (Argo and Turgoose, 1985).

Thioglycolic acid has been found to etch uncorroded iron, has an unpleasant odour and is no longer used. Electrolytic reduction has been used to strip corrosion products from ferrous metals but its success is dependent on operator skill. Thermal reduction has been used successfully to remove chlorides and reduce corrosion products on large iron objects recovered from marine environments, whilst plasma reduction has been used to reduce corrosion products on small archaeological objects.

### Coatings
Any coating on heat or chemically blued iron will change its visual properties. Such surfaces should be kept clean and uncoated. Iron components of furniture were not usually waxed or lacquered unless as a side effect of finishing the adjacent wood. Polished and clean iron may be coated with a lacquer or waxed. If corrosion is likely to be a problem in the future it may be appropriate to apply a corrosion inhibitor as part of a coating process. Paraloid B72 or cellulose nitrate lacquers may be used if required. Brewer (1991) found wax coatings were less permeable to moisture than Paraloid B72, however waxes may be difficult to remove from pitted iron surfaces. A combination of a coating of B72 followed by a wax coating may reduce permeability to moisture and ensure the future removability of a wax coating.

A hot wax application provides good penetration and is less likely to be damaged than a lacquer layer. The component is heated with a heat gun until a mixture of microcrystalline wax, made to a paste consistency with petroleum benzine or white spirit, melts into and saturates the surface. Care should be taken not to overheat the metal and thereby compromise metallographic evidence. Excess wax is removed by buffing with a soft cloth and the component left to cool. A higher shine can be obtained by buffing the wax after it has cooled.

### 15.3.9    Brass and bronze

In modern usage, brass refers to an alloy of copper and zinc, whilst bronze refers to an alloy of copper and tin. Such nomenclature does not necessarily reflect historic practice. The Latin, and hence medieval, term for brass was auricalcum (gold copper). Many historic copper alloy objects contain both zinc and tin, and so the term 'copper alloy' is prudent if the exact composition is not known. Brass components in furniture may have been polished or matte, patinated or lacquered. Copper alloys that were stamped, rolled or hammered during manufacture may become embrittled over time. They are vulnerable to damage – for example if levered up, they may snap. Casting bronzes may contain 10–18% tin, though a common alloy composition for 'bronze' statuary is 85% copper and 5% each of zinc, tin and lead.

### Stabilization
Stabilization treatments are designed to retain all of the corrosion products and render them stable. Stabilization treatments may alter the appearance of the metal. The decision to undertake a stabilization treatment should take

into consideration the importance and vulnerability of extant patina and whether a change in appearance will be acceptable.

Benzotriazole (BTA, $C_6H_5N_3$) is a common treatment for archaeological copper alloy objects and for bronze disease. BTA is a copper complexing agent designed to form a polymeric film of copper and BTA, tying up free copper at the surface of the metal so that it is unavailable for further corrosion reactions. The polymer layer may also slow down the diffusion of $O_2$ and other aggressive species. It is incorporated into some lacquers, e.g. Incralac, applied to historic objects.

Zinc dust has been proposed as a method of stabilizing bronze disease without overall treatment. Zinc will form stable and adherent layers of basic zinc hydroxide chlorides that can seal off areas of local corrosion. Active corrosion on bronze objects were treated with zinc dust, exposed to artificially high relative humidity, then to five years of uncontrolled tropical environment in India without renewed activity (Sharma *et al.*, 1995).

### Mechanical removal of corrosion products

Conservators often combine chemical and mechanical methods for the removal of corrosion products from copper and brass. Stabilization, for example, is usually improved by mechanical corrosion removal methods because corrosion crusts have been reduced, and penetration of BTA is better. The selective mechanical removal of corrosion products of brass and copper can be difficult because the corrosion products are hard, whilst the surrounding metal is comparatively soft. Abrasive removal of corrosion products often leads to excessive polishing of the surface adjacent to the corrosion products.

Original brass may have had a brushed or satin finish. Corrosion can disrupt this finish so that, after removal of corrosion products, the surface appears a characteristic yellow but roughened. In the past such surfaces were often restored by abrasive polishing, but this practice has become less acceptable and is not compatible with the conservation principle of minimal intervention. The historical and monetary value of many bronzes in enhanced by the effects of age and corrosion. Many bronzes, for example those from cultures with a strong reverence for the past, e.g. China or Rome, should not be polished.

Problems associated with mechanical removal of corrosion products mean chemical methods are often used as a first stage treatment. Where metal is not detachable or is adjacent to vulnerable material, e.g. metal inlay, it may be necessary to avoid chemical methods. Fine particle abrasive powders that may be useful include charcoal, jeweller's rouge (particularly useful after chemical removal of corrosion products), rottenstone and finely ground pumice powder. Proprietary polishes that contain coarse particles or ammonia should be avoided (e.g. Autosol). Start with softer abrasives and move to harder types if these are unsuccessful (see *Table 10.3*). Abrasives may be applied using a hydrocarbon solvent as a lubricant. On flat surfaces, some conservators have used abrasives applied to the face of a French polishing rubber, in combination with solvent, to allow moderate to heavy pressure to be applied evenly. It may be impossible to remove residual abrasive particles, for example from boulle surfaces, though some conservators add a small amount of pigment to disguise such deposits.

### Chemical removal of corrosion products

Chemical methods are often effective in removing corrosion products or softening them sufficiently to allow mechanical removal. Vacuum impregnation with benzotriazole has made it feasible to retain corrosion product crusts even if aggressive chlorides are present, but many treatments in the past relied on stripping the metal surface so that chlorides and chloride-containing products could be removed. When corrosion products are relatively light and their removal is likely to improve the appearance and stability of the object, chemical removal of corrosion products can be an option. The are several potential problems associated with chemical removal of corrosion products from copper alloys including etching of the surface of adjacent or underlying metal, stress corrosion cracking, dezincification and the deposition of insoluble metal complexes.

### Stress corrosion cracking

Stress corrosion cracking (SCC) is a progressive fracture mechanism that occurs in metals

(Scully, 1971). It is caused by the interaction of a corrodent, particularly ammonia, chlorides and nitrogen compounds, in combination with tensile stress. Such stress may be applied, or residual from forming or manufacture. SCC is a complex phenomenon that may be confused with embrittlement and the exact mechanism is still a subject for metallurgical debate. SCC results in sudden and unpredictable catastrophic failure of metal and occurs some time (hours, months or years) after the metal has been exposed to the corrodent. Initiation of SCC requires the presence of water or moisture and a suitable hydrogen donating material, such as acids or ammoniate ions (the conjugate acid of ammonia). Chemical treatment of copper alloys with these chemicals should be avoided. Each treatment of a susceptible metal with such materials can contribute to the SCC process, which in the long term can lead to the complete destruction of the object. SCC has been initiated by deionized water in laboratory conditions.

Although all alloyed metals are susceptible to SCC in particular corrosive environments (e.g. high or low pH-induced SCC in pipeline steel), concern in the context of conservation usually focuses on the susceptibility of brass. Brasses nominally composed of 70/30 copper/zinc that have been work hardened by rolling, stamping, pressing or hammering during manufacture are most susceptible, but any brass with a zinc content above about 15% is vulnerable. Metal that has been annealed is not affected. Chemical removal of corrosion products should not be carried out on stressed sheet metal objects (such as spun or die-struck brass) due to the danger of preferential intergranular attack leading to stress cracking. Although it has been suggested that stress in cold-worked brass can be relieved ('normalized'), without unduly softening the metal, by raising the temperature of the metal to around 250 °C for about thirty minutes, this is not a recommended conservation process.

### Dezincification and the deposition of insoluble metal complexes

The use of acidic, alkaline and chelating solutions can result in a pinkish, coppery appearance to brass surfaces. This is aesthetically undesirable and is usually followed by polishing, which removes the offending layer.

Two mechanisms, dezincification and redeposition, have been proposed to explain this phenomenon. De-alloying is the selective removal of the more electrochemically active component (anode) of an alloyed metal to leave a porous weak deposit of the more noble component. In brass, de-alloying usually takes the form of dezincification and may be visible as a pinkish copper blush on the surface. The metal becomes more coppery in appearance because zinc has been stripped out of the alloy. This process may also be referred to as leaching.

It has also been suggested that the pinkish appearance may be the result of the deposition of insoluble metal complexes onto the surface. The complexes may form between the chemical used to clean the surface and corrosion products or may be a result of incomplete breakdown of corrosion products. The exact mechanism that results in the deposit or formation of such a layer is often unclear, but whatever the cause, the result is undesirable. The pinkish coloration can be difficult to remove chemically and polishing compounds are usually used to abrade away the offending layer of metal.

### Reagents for the chemical removal of corrosion products

A wide range of reagents have been used to remove corrosion products from brass. Some, such as Graham's salt (sodium hexametaphosphate), sodium tripolyphosphate (STPP), alkaline glycerol (propane-1,2,3-triol), Rochelle salts (sodium potassium tartrate) in sodium hydroxide (known as alkaline Rochelle salts) and citric acid, have been used to remove cuprous chlorides from archaeological metal. They are not necessarily appropriate for the treatment of historical metal because all are comparatively harsh reagents and may cause severe etching (Merk, 1978). STPP is no longer widely used because of environmental concerns associated with phosphates. Hjelm-Hansen (1984) proposed the use of substituted sodium dithiolates for the removal of sulphide corrosion (black spot disease) from copper alloys. Chloride or ammoniate containing materials should not be used on copper containing alloys. As a general rule, the use of acids or acidic solutions for the removal of corrosion products from metals should be avoided.

Alkaline glycerol solution will remove cupric ($Cu^{3+}$) salts and will also act slowly on cuprous ($Cu^{2+}$) salts. The solution is made from 120 g sodium hydroxide, 40 ml glycerol (glycerine) and 1 litre of deionized water. The NaOH dissolves the corrosion products, at the same time that the copper is complexed by the glycerol. The addition of 1% BTA can reduce pitting of uncorroded copper. Since this method will not remove cuprite effectively, the surface will appear reddish after treatment. Treatment with alkaline glycerol can be followed by another treatment (such as citric acid) to remove the cuprous products. Because of the combined alkalinity and complexing agent, this method may be useful for removing copper soaps of fatty and resin acids from objects. Such films result from organic coating materials and can be very hard to remove.

Alkaline Rochelle salts function as a chelating agent but do not remove cuprous products effectively. It is more expensive than alkaline glycerol, but may etch uncorroded metal less, especially if 1% BTA is added. The reagent mixture is composed of 5% sodium hydroxide, 15% sodium potassium tartrate and 80% deionized water.

Citric acid at an alkaline pH is more effective for removing cuprous and cupric corrosion products than alkaline glycerol or alkaline Rochelle salts because it is a stronger chelating agent (log $k_f$ for copper citrate is 14.2 in comparison to tartaric acid at 4.78). At a pH below about 5, however, the removal of corrosion products is a result of the acidity of the solution, rather than chelation.

Formic acid has been used to dissolve (but does not chelate) copper corrosion products, but its use has been largely abandoned for stripping bronzes. Dilute solutions of formic acid have been used as a pre-treatment before mechanical removal of corrosion products. Formic acid has the advantage of being a weak organic acid whose volatility precludes the need for extensive rinsing after treatment. Formic acid has the disadvantage that, as an acid, it will act to dissolve the base metals themselves, particularly the zinc component of brasses. It may cause a pinkish deposit on the surface of the brass. The use of formic acid should generally be avoided. If this material is used, the least damaging approach is to use the least acidic pH at which it is still effective.

Ammonium hydroxide was the reagent traditionally used by furniture restorers for removing corrosion from brass. Ammonium hydroxide is a very effective complexing agent for copper ions. It dissolves cupric and cuprous corrosion products to form cuprammonium ions, which have an intense blue colour in solution. The traditional method used to remove corrosion products from brass was to swab the surface with, or to immerse a component in, an aqueous ammonia solution. Brass components left too long in an ammonia solution can completely disintegrate. Ammonium hydroxide is effective not only in attacking cuprous corrosion products but will attack the metal itself. Thus after such treatments the surface of the brass was often pitted as a result of the removal of corrosion, whilst uncorroded metal was often etched. The surface was free from corrosion products but matte due to loss of specular reflection, so treatment was often followed by polishing, i.e. the removal of a layer of metal in order to smooth the surface and restore a bright and shiny finish.

As a general rule the use of ammonia-based solutions should be avoided because of the risk of etching the surface and the danger of stress corrosion cracking. Ammonium hydroxide can diffuse very deeply into the grain structure of the metal. Ammonium hydroxide in contact with a metal will be reduced to produce ammonia gas and hydrogen gas and SCC will result. Ammonia will darken many woods, attack transparent and decorative surfaces and cuprammonium ions will attack cellulose. Cast brass or bronze is porous and the longer the contact with aqueous ammonia, the greater the danger of deep penetration of both water and ammonia into the body of the metal. In some cases ammonium hydroxide may leave the surface with an undesirable pink coloration. In addition, the newly cleaned surfaces are liable to rapid oxidation and thus soon lose their brightness. The use of ammonium hydroxide on copper alloys should be avoided, and mounts should not be immersed in ammonium hydroxide solutions. The risks associated with ammonium hydroxide far outweigh potential benefits for cleaning.

Chelating agents may be used for the removal of corrosion products from the surface of metal artefacts. The two chelating agents most commonly used to remove corrosion products from brass are EDTA and DTPA. Uncorroded metal is not attacked by the chelating agent because it does not exist in the ionic form. However, if these materials are used at an acidic pH, the acidic conditions can etch the metal. These materials are discussed in section 11.5.5.

DTPA and EDTA have been used for the removal of corrosion products because they form complexes with many metal ions. DTPA has been used to remove corrosion products from brass because it is believed to have a slower and more controllable rate of reaction. The action of chelators on metal ions is pH dependent, thus the pH of chelating solutions should be buffered to the desired (preferably alkaline) pH. Adding sodium hydroxide to EDTA (free acid) will raise the pH of the solution and, if pH is raised high enough, will affect both the displacement series and EDTA's effectiveness at picking up a given metal ion (see *Figure 11.22c*). Complexes with divalent metals (e.g. $Cu^{2+}$, $Fe^{2+}$) may be displaced from the chelator and redeposited on the surface in acidic conditions. Some trivalent metal complexes are stable even in acidic solutions.

In some cases different metals or alloys are present on the same object, e.g. ferrous metals and brass may be present in the same component. *Table 11.10* and *Figure 11.21* can be used to compare the chelating agents and to predict the selectivity of the chelating solution. At a pH of 5, for example, EDTA would selectively chelate Fe(III) ions over Cu(II) ions, whilst at a pH of 10, EDTA would selectively chelate Cu(II) over Fe(III). This selectivity is also dependent on the molar ratios of the chelating agents. At a pH of 10, for example, EDTA would chelate Cu(II) ions, but when these were no longer available would chelate other ions (Zn, Mn, Fe(III), Ca, Mg) etc. This is the reason for using repeated applications of a less concentrated solution, rather than using a single strong solution for an extended period.

The technique used to apply the chelating agent can affect the result. Problems may occur with the formation of copper complexes, so it is important to clear such complexes from the surface as they are formed. It is therefore important to use fresh solution on each swab and to discard used

swabs rather than re-immersing them in the cleaning solution. Whether metal is swabbed or dipped, it is important to watch for unwanted reactions. Any change in the colour of the cleaning solution indicates that the solution should be changed immediately.

It is possible that an overly strong solution of any given chelating agent may simply provide a high concentration of an electrolytic solution that will encourage dissolution reactions on the surface of the metal itself. Although at present this phenomenon has not been studied, limiting the concentration of chelating solutions used to clean metals to 5% or the overall conductivity of a cleaning solution to 15 000–20 000 microsiemens may represent a safer corrosion removal strategy.

### 15.3.10   Ormolu

Ormolu is a term used to describe gilt brass and is particularly applied to gilded mounts on furniture, such as those found on eighteenth and nineteenth century French furniture. Eighteenth century mercury gilding techniques have been considered by Goodison (1974) and Chapman (1994). Thornton (2000) has discussed the wide range of materials that have been used to imitate gold as well as unintended gold-coloured corrosion products and thin-layer interference patterns that may produce gold-like surfaces. Comparatively little has been published on the conservation of ormolu, however useful information may be found in Drayman-Weisser (2000), Fiorentino (1994), Sawada (1993) and Scott (1983).

Under normal conditions gold does not corrode and alloys with a gold content of more than 50 atomic per cent gold are usually corrosion resistant (*Figure 15.11*). In binary gold-copper alloys, for example, this corresponds to 75.6 wt% gold and 24.4% copper (Scott, 1983). In the context of furniture, the metal mounts onto which the gold is applied are usually brass with a high copper content. Matthew Boulton, for example, who produced ormolu in England in the late eighteenth century, recommended an alloy of about 95% copper and 5% zinc (Chapman, 1994). Mercury gilding produces a porous gold layer. The galvanic effect of cathodic gold in contact with anodic brass or bronze can accelerate corrosion. In the presence of moisture, copper

**Figure 15.11** A gold snuff box, *c.*1814. Disfiguring tarnish caused by the corrosion of metals alloyed with the gold

(a)

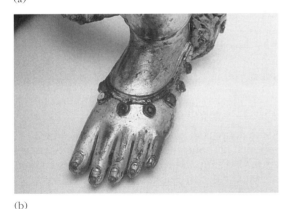

(b)

**Figure 15.12** Eighteenth century statue of Tara, Nepal (*a*) Detail of foot before removal of corrosion products. The metal is a gilded copper alloy. Corrosion products from the copper obscure the gilt surface
(*b*) Detail of foot of statue, after cleaning. The gilded surface was revealed by the removal of copper corrosion products. This is the type of alloy that might have been cleaned with ammonia in the past but is now more safely cleaned using chelating agents, followed by rinses of deionized water and acetone

corrosion products can emerge from the pores and spread over the surface of the gold (*Figure 15.12a*). This may also occur where the gold layer is not continuous, for example if it has been worn away.

Electroplating will result in an even layer of gold over the whole mount, whilst mercury gilding was applied only to the presentation surface. Gilding has often been imitated and reproductions, particularly neo-classical objects and designs, were cast in zinc alloys (e.g. spelter) or Britannia metal. Such pieces cannot be cleaned using the materials set out below.

### Cleaning

All gilding layers tend to be fairly thin and are vulnerable to wear. Dirt may be removed with hydrocarbon solvents. This treatment is often sufficient if the surface is not corroded. Ormolu was often left partly matte as a decorative contrast to adjacent burnished areas. Care must be taken to avoid burnishing the surface – it may be possible, for example, to burnish the gold using cotton wool and heavy pressure. Non-original varnish or splashes as a result of finish applied to adjacent wood can usually be removed using organic solvents.

In some cases mounts were not gilded at all. In the early eighteenth century brass mounts were often polished or acid dipped and then lacquered, a technique known as mise en couleur de l'or (Tear, 1996). In many cases a colouring agent, such as crushed liquorice, turmeric or saffron, was added to the lacquer.

### Removal of corrosion products

When considering chemical treatment for removing corrosion products it should be borne in mind that the overall appearance of the object should be consistent, for example the balance between cleaned mounts and inlaid brass, or mounts and faded wood.

Removing corrosion products without damaging the gold layer may be problematic. Mechanical removal of corrosion products will result in damage to the gold and mechanical removal of corrosion products is usually limited to brushing over the surface with a very soft brush. In some cases it may be possible to pick corrosion products from the surface with the point of a scalpel.

The vulnerability of gilding to wear and physical damage means that it is usually cleaned chemically rather than mechanically. The corrosion products found on ormolu, and the chemicals used to remove them, are usually the same as those associated with brass. The chemical removal of corrosion products of ormolu is complicated by the presence of the vulnerable layer of gold. Corrosion products may be present underneath, as well as on the surface of the gold. In some cases, removal of corrosion products may undercut the gold layer itself, leading to loss. As with copper alloys in general, reagents used to clean ormolu should not contain chloride or ammoniate ions, and cleaning solutions with an acidic pH should be avoided.

Whilst an unwanted pink coloration on brass can be polished away, such an effect on gilt metal, which may be caused by all the reagents mentioned below, may be unsightly and permanent. Once this layer has formed the conservator is faced with the choice of damaging the gold by using abrasives (which is never desirable and in any case not possible on many surfaces, e.g. those that have been textured) or accepting the non-original obtrusive pinkish tinge.

It may be possible to gel corrosion removal solutions and apply them to the surface, though localized treatment may result in formation of distinct cleaned area that may be obtrusive. Another complication of chemical corrosion removal is the potential for stress corrosion cracking (SCC). Wise (1964) noted that burnishing operations can create enough internal stress to induce SCC in cast gold-copper alloys.

Chelating agents are often very effective for the removal of corrosion products from ormolu (*Figure 15.12*). As a general rule they should be used at an alkaline pH, with multiple dilute treatments rather than a single concentrated treatment. A thorough rinsing procedure is necessary to ensure the removal of all residues. This may take the form of a deionized water rinse to remove any residues of the chelating agent, followed by an acetone rinse to remove residual water. During aqueous rinsing, a conductivity meter can be used to check for the presence of residues by comparing conductivity before and after cleaning (the conductivity of historic metal should

be near or at zero). Fiorentino (1994) reported successful treatment of gilt bronze with trisodium EDTA, ammonium tartrate and a cationic resin in acid form.

Formic acid has been used in the past for removing copper corrosion products from ormolu. Formic acid is volatile so rinsing is not necessary, but fumes present a significant hazard to the conservator (OEL 5ppm, 1993, UK). Formic acid does not attack silver or gold but will attack the base metal and may cause an undesirable pink discoloration of the gilding. Sawada (1993) reported increased controllability by gelling formic acid. He reported rapid removal of basic copper carbonate, whilst removal of copper oxide was much slower. As a general rule, formic acid is not recommended for the removal of corrosion products from ormolu.

Ammonium hydroxide was commonly used in the past for the removal of corrosion products from ormolu. Restorers either made up a dilute solution (5–10% solution of .880 ammonia in water) or used proprietary ammonia solutions that incorporated ingredients such as oleic acid, solvents (e.g. acetone) and detergents. As with copper alloys, the use of ammonia based solutions for the removal of corrosion products from ormolu is not recommended.

Although in many cases ormolu mounts were not originally lacquered, there may be a case for the application of a coating if the mount is vulnerable to wear or further corrosion.

### 15.3.11   Silver

Silver may be encountered in the form of mounts or equipment associated with writing and dressing tables. Silver is most often alloyed with a variable amount of copper (e.g. sterling silver 92.5% Ag/7.5% Cu). The greater the copper content, the harder the alloy and the more it is prone to corrosion. Corrosive species selectively attack the Cu-rich phase that surrounds silver-rich dendrites in Cu/Ag alloys. As a result, copper corrosion products will predominate on many silver alloy objects. A significant body of literature exists on the conservation of historical silverware, including storage and display, corrosion prevention and treatments, e.g. Wharton *et al.* (1990), Selwyn

(1990) and CCI notes 9/7 (1993). The components of some proprietary silver corrosion removal products have been analysed by Selwyn and Costain (1991).

Silver may have been deliberately patinated. Other deliberate decorative effects include niello, an enamel-like mixture of metallic sulphides that was intentionally fired into recesses on silver and gold objects. Such patination adds historical and monetary value to the object as a whole and should not be removed. The presence of niello can be obscured by silver tarnish. Proprietary products such as silver dip will severely damage or destroy niello.

Although silver corrosion products are stable they do not protect the underlying metal, which will continue to corrode as long as there are reactants. The reactive species are hydrogen sulphide ($H_2S$), carbonyl sulphide (COS), which is the reactive component of organic sulphides, and sulphur dioxide ($SO_2$).

### Removal of corrosion products

Silver is soft and easily damaged by mechanical corrosion removal methods. Silver plating is very vulnerable and any method of tarnish removal is potentially damaging. Surfaces are normally blackened by silver sulphide, and copper oxides and sulphides. In some cases, light coatings of these corrosion products may be mistaken for gilding due to thin-layer optical interference phenomena. True gilding will not be removed by acidic thiourea, however, and this can be used as a spot test. Tarnish may be removed from silver using electrochemical reduction, polishes or chemical dips.

Electrochemical reduction, described in CCI Notes 9/7, reduces the corrosion products back to silver, which is redeposited on the surface. The dull, matte finish that results often requires polishing to produce an acceptable appearance. Care is needed to ensure that the final finish remains in balance with the object as a whole.

Polishing tarnished silver with a mild abrasive is the traditional method of removing corrosion products. Precipitated chalk, mixed with ethanol to the consistency of a paste, may be used for this purpose. The advantages of polishing are that sulphide is left in low spots heightening the visual detail of chasing and engraving. By the same token, abrasives wear away high spots, change the surface topography, obliterate detail and reveal sub-surface copper oxides (fire scale) over time.

Silver polishes may be used to clean in situ though care must be taken to avoid leaving residues on adjacent material (*Figure 15.13*). Minimal pressure, mild abrasives and fine particle size will minimize the immediate and cumulative effect of abrasive polishes. Wharton *et al.* (1990) found that it is less damaging to clean silver with a mild abrasive for a longer time than a harder, more aggressive material for a shorter time. Selwyn and Costain (1991) ranked common proprietary silver corrosion removal products according to the amount of silver removed, the degree of scratching caused and rate of retarnishing. They found that multipurpose polishes were not suitable for removing tarnish from silver as they contain harsher alumina abrasives, rather than the softer silica found in silver polishes.

**Figure 15.13** Ebony clock case, London, *c.*1680–1700, with pierced and engraved silver mounts. In order to avoid metal cleaning residues, mounts may be removed or vulnerable areas protected, e.g. with Melinex/Mylar

Many silver polishes contain a tarnish inhibitor. North (1980) reported that removing the tarnish layer that had formed after the application of a tarnish inhibitor required more effort and resulted in greater removal of silver. Tarnish inhibitors will fail eventually and the tarnish that then forms may be uneven. Lins (1989) found that a film of tarnish inhibitor resulted in a silver surface that could not be wetted easily, polished evenly or adequately lacquered.

Silver dips are usually composed of a mineral or organic acid (e.g. sulphuric or formic acid) and a complexing agent such as thiourea (Brenner, 1953). It should be noted that silver sulphide has a $pK_{sp}$ of 49.2, which far exceeds the $K_f$ of most chelators with the metal ion (see section 11.5.5). Thiourea, for example, binds silver with a $K_f$ of only 13.1, thus the removal of silver sulphide is a result of acidic conditions rather than chelation. Although dips will dissolve tarnish, they tend to leave a rougher, more granular surface with a larger surface area than polishes (Selwyn and Costain, 1991). They may be applied to mounts in situ, using a swab, or mounts may be removed from the object and immersed. Contact with silver dip should be minimized to limit acidic attack of the surface of the metal. Silver dips have the advantage of being quick and sometimes avoid the need for mechanical removal of corrosion products. However, dips tend to be an all or nothing process and the ultra clean appearance produced may not be desirable. In some cases it may be necessary to use polish after an object has been dipped. Silver treated with dip retarnishes more quickly than that cleaned with polishes.

### Reshaping
Silver/copper alloys are metastable. Copper, as well as unintentional metallic impurities, will often migrate to the grain boundaries over time, leading to a loss of malleability called precipitation hardening. Because of this effect, it is considered unwise to attempt mechanical straightening of objects over 100 years old, and in practice, less time may be needed to make an object unsuitable for cold reforming. The techniques of polymer casting and electrotyping are both suitable for supplying missing parts on silver objects.

### Prevention of tarnish
Given that the primary mechanism for the formation of tarnish on silver is exposure to atmospheric pollutants, the exclusion or absorption of such pollutants should be given a high priority for furniture that incorporates silver components.

### Coatings
Lacquering is probably the best means of protecting silver from tarnishing while on open display in period rooms, houses etc. Various organic coatings have been used but many conservators prefer the appearance of cellulose nitrate lacquers (e.g. Frigilene, Agateen) on highly polished historic silver. They level very well and a skilfully lacquered object cannot be distinguished from an uncoated piece.

### 15.3.12    Lead

Lead may be encountered in furniture, for example in lead linings to urns or wine coolers, or in the form of lead-based repairs. Lead is relatively inert. Inorganic acids may form salts on the surface that stop or slow further corrosion. Organic acids, particularly acetic acid, are the chief agents of deterioration in collections. Organic acid attack will produce fuzzy white deposits of lead formate (methanoate), lead acetate (ethanoate) and ultimately, lead carbonate. Whilst lead carbonate is considered stable under most circumstances, lead acetate and formate are not, because they may convert to lead carbonate. Care should be taken when removing these corrosion products, and in the disposal of both removed material and cleaning materials such as swabs, as they are a health hazard. Thickett et al. (1998) considered the risk posed to metal artefacts by carbonyl pollutants.

Lead was often added to bronze casting alloys to improve the flow characteristics. Lead does not form an alloy with bronze, but segregates out as the metal cools. These lead pockets or inclusions can be preferentially attacked by organic acids under some display and storage conditions.

Lead exposure in the workplace is subject to health and safety legislation. Protection measures against exposure are geared towards reducing escape of lead dust, fumes or vapour into the workplace. The type of exposure where there is liable to be significant exposure to lead unless adequate controls provided include high temperature work (>500 °C), abrasion of lead giving rise to dust in the air (i.e. grinding, cutting with power tools), the spraying of lead paint, and work with lead compounds that gives rise to lead dust in the air. Conservators must comply with current local legislation. Basic safety precautions include a high standard of workshop hygiene. In the context of furniture conservation, small particles of lead pose the greatest hazard. If a vacuum cleaner is used, a filtered model is essential as small particles of lead will pass through a conventional vacuum cleaner, becoming airborne and increasing the risk that lead will be ingested.

### Removal of corrosion products

Lead is soft and can be marked easily, for example with a thumbnail. The surface should be left untouched unless corrosion is active. It may be possible to mechanically remove corrosion products, but, as corrosion products are harder than the original metal, care is necessary. Polishing the surface with a mild abrasive may be sufficient to remove minor accretions of corrosion products. In some cases lead may have corroded through the thickness of the metal, and removal of corrosion products may expose a hole in the metal. The removal of corrosion products from lead has been considered by Degrigny and Le Gall (1999), Green (1989) and Lane (1975, 1979).

Electrolytic reduction has been used both to remove lead corrosion products (using high current densities for short duration) and to consolidatively reduce lead corrosion products in situ, forming porous lead metal in place of corrosion. Consolidative reduction is usually carried out in a sulphuric acid electrolyte using partially rectified current at low current density for long periods of time. Localized treatment may be possible using gelled electrolytes.

Lead corrosion products can be removed with chelating agents such as DTPA, EDTA and HEDTA. Lead chelation by these agents is most effective at a pH of 8–9 (*Figure 11.22*). This must be followed by thorough rinsing. Lead will slowly dissolve in deionized water because of dissolved carbonic acid, so a rinse solution buffered to a neutral or alkaline pH

must be used, and the object or surface thoroughly dried.

### Coatings

Further corrosion may be reduced by applying a coating, as long as unstable corrosion products are not present within the body of the metal. Organic coatings based on natural and cellulose nitrate resins should not be used on lead, because their degradation products may encourage further corrosion. Paraloid B72 may be used, incorporating matting agents if necessary. Microcrystalline wax can also be used. Neither of these coatings is impermeable to airborne organic acids but may reduce the diffusion rate.

## 15.4 Ceramics and enamels

Ceramics may be incorporated in furniture as tiles, ceramic plaques, handles, castors, inset panels and other decorative elements. The physical properties of ceramics are determined largely by their firing temperature and the materials from which they are made. Low fired wares, such as earthenwares and terracottas, are porous and often thickly potted. They are more prone to staining and deterioration than higher fired wares. The principles discussed for the cleaning of stone apply to low fired wares (see section 16.1). High fired ceramics, such as stoneware and porcelain, are as a general rule markedly less porous and more robust. Glaze, which can be regarded as a thin layer of glass fired onto the ceramic body, is impervious, adds strength to the object and may act as a decorative surface.

Glazes may act as a substrate for enamel decoration and metallic lustrous finishes, including gilding. Glazes are fired to a lower temperature than the body and are vulnerable to damage during use and conservation treatments. The conservation treatment employed depends on the type of ceramic and its method of fabrication. It is essential to identify this and carefully examine the object before treatment in order to identify surface decoration and old restorations and assess potential areas of weakness such as unstable cracks. All surface decoration, especially low fired on-glaze colours and unfired decoration, is vulnerable to damage during treatment and should be treated with care. Information on the technology of ceramics may be found in Hamer (1986). The conservation of ceramics is given detailed consideration by Buys and Oakley (1996).

### 15.4.1   Cleaning

Cleaning of ceramics can involve the removal of previous restoration materials, surface dust and dirt, ingrained dirt, stains and soluble salts within the body of an object. Surface dirt may need to be removed so that it does not penetrate a porous body or cause disfiguration. It can be removed mechanically using a soft brush, such as an artist's sable paint brush, or a cotton wool swab. A swab can be dampened with the appropriate solvent such as water, acetone, IMS or white spirit. The swab should be rolled across the surface to lift the dirt rather than using a wiping action. There is a risk of dirt being absorbed into the ceramic body if the swab is too wet.

Low fired porous wares should not be immersed in water or organic solvents as this may result in damage to the object, such as the formation or exacerbation of cracks, migration of soluble salts to the surface and staining. High fired wares in good condition are markedly less vulnerable to damage during cleaning. They may be surface cleaned with water or organic solvents or carefully immersed in lukewarm water to which a few drops of non-ionic detergent has been added. This should be followed by a thorough rinse procedure. The object can be blotted dry with paper towels and left to dry thoroughly.

It is recommended that only surface cleaning should be undertaken by the non-specialist and that further cleaning treatments, including stain removal, are referred to a ceramics conservator. Natural resin varnishes, synthetic resins, organic materials, metal fixings and mounts may all stain ceramics. Stains or dirt which have penetrated into the body of a low or high fired ceramic require solvents that will reach the dirt, mobilizing it and enabling it to be drawn out of the body with the dirt. There is a risk that the stain or dirt can be spread throughout the body during an attempt to remove it and that the cleaning material can remain in the body. As in stone conservation, packs and poultices are commonly used by ceramics conservators. Although Laponite RD has been used for this purpose there may be problems in removing residues (Lee *et al.*, 1997; Ling, 1991). Chelating agents have been used by some conservators for the removal of metal stains but there is a risk of stripping metal ions from the ceramic body and glaze. Problems relating to the presence of soluble salts should be referred to a specialist.

### 15.4.2   Bonding

There may be instances when a minor repair such as a ceramic component broken cleanly in two pieces may be attempted by a non-specialist. The object should be carefully examined first and if the conservator is in any doubt as to the condition of the object, advice should be sought. The edges to be bonded must be absolutely clean, as any dirt will be visually obtrusive and prevent the formation of a tight adhesive join. Work surfaces, tools and hands should be cleaned and care taken not to touch the break-edges. The break-edges can be swabbed with a solvent prior to the application of an adhesive. The choice of adhesive is dependent on the type of ceramic body, colour and weight of the object and its viscosity is important in relation to the porosity of the body. In general the bond should be weaker than the ceramic itself.

As a general rule the break edges of low fired ceramics should be sealed with a thin, even coat of a dilute solution of resin, e.g. 5–10% w/v Paraloid B72 in acetone, applied with an artist's paintbrush. The adhesive solution used to bond the edges should be more viscous, for example a 40–50% w/v Paraloid B72 in acetone (Koob, 1986). Pre-sealing the edges combined with the use of a viscous adhesive will minimize penetration of adhesive into the body of the ceramic and staining that may result from this. In contrast high fired wares usually require a low viscosity, water white adhesive such as HXTAL NYL-1 epoxy resin to facilitate a tight join. Only a small amount of resin is required and this is usually applied to one break-edge only. Support whilst the adhesive cures can be provided by small strips of pressure-sensitive tape (*Figure 15.14*). The tape must be compatible with the bonding material and not cause

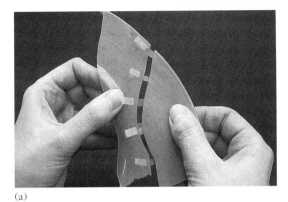

(a)

(b)

**Figure 15.14** Use of pressure-sensitive tape to provide support during bonding. (*a*) Fragments of a plate prepared for bonding. Strips of pressure sensitive tape should be placed at right-angles to the join, on both sides of the body and directly opposite each other. (*b*) Fragments adhered and supported in position by pressure-sensitive tape until the adhesive has cured

any adverse reactions such as colour change. Ensure that the join is correctly aligned before the adhesive cures.

### 15.4.3 Filling losses

It is not always necessary to fill all areas of loss. Factors such as structural implications, aesthetics, the potential for trapping dirt in unfilled chips and ethical implications, such as whether there is sufficient evidence to replace a loss, may play a role in the decision to fill. Small unobtrusive losses are often not filled.

In general, ceramics conservators make use of synthetic resins modified by the addition of pigments and appropriate aggregates to fill damaged ceramic objects. Fill materials should

be weaker than the body of the ceramic but cure to give a hard surface. Standard conservation criteria such as chemical stability and reversibility apply. Small chips along a break line may be filled using the bond material with the addition of a small amount of a compatible aggregate and colorant. Glass microballoons may be used with acrylics such as Paraloid B67 or B72 on low fired wares (Walker and Shashoua, 1996). Fumed silica may be used with an epoxy such as HXTAL NYL-1 on high fired wares. The working properties of the fill materials can be modified by adding them in different proportions.

Low fired wares are usually filled with calcium-based fillers, including proprietary materials such as All Purpose Polyfilla (UK), Fine Surface Polyfilla (UK) or dental and casting plasters. An isolating layer of acrylic resin between the fill and the ceramic body will prevent absorption of the filler into the body and, in the case of plaster, the risk of salt contamination.

Epoxy resins combined with aggregates to form a workable paste are often used to fill high fired wares. Missing areas can either be filled with a material matched in colour and density to the body and glaze of the object, or with opaque materials that will require a colour matched surface coating. An example of an opaque fill is an epoxy resin, French chalk and titanium dioxide. A water-white epoxy such as HXTAL NYL-1, fumed silica and dry artists pigments may be used to form colour matched fillings in porcelain (Jordan, 1999a). After curing, fillings can be adjusted with a scalpel blade, solvents and abrasive papers. These should never come into contact with the ceramic surface, which scratches very easily.

### 15.4.4 Retouching

Retouching is only carried out on restored areas and should not obscure original material. The broadly accepted ethic in ceramics conservation is that retouching should render fills visually unobtrusive but not invisible (Smith, 1994; see, for example, Oddy, 1992). Ceramics conservators use a variety of different retouching mediums. Artist's acrylic paints have commonly been used for retouching earthenwares and are now increasingly used on high fired wares. An alternative method is the use of powder pigments mixed in a resin, for example an acrylic varnish, as a binding medium. The retouching medium is usually applied with a soft bristle (sable) artist's paintbrush. If an airbrush is used to spray a large filled area, the surrounding ceramic should be masked off or the overlapping spray removed after airbrushing.

It may be necessary to replicate the colour or translucency of a glaze or body in layers. These should be as thin and even as possible so that the restored area does not sit proud of the surface. Brush strokes and excess paint can be removed by abrading the restored area with fine abrasive papers or cushioned abrasive cloths such as Micromesh. It is sometimes necessary to polish the retouched area in order to alter the surface reflectance. A cushioned abrasive cloth and/or a liquid polish used on acrylic and plastic surfaces such as Aeroglym Finishing Polish can be used for this purpose. A coating on retouched and filled areas is not usually necessary and can complicate the repair by adding unwanted thickness, causing a shadow or darkening the fill. As a general rule, the application of a coating is unnecessary and is not recommended for ceramics.

Matte finishes, gilding, silvering and lustre finishes may be required. Lustre finishes are difficult to replicate. Mica or opalescent pigments can be used to approximate such glazes used on their own or over a metal leaf base. Gilding is best reproduced using gold leaf, powder or tablet gold rather than bronze paints. It can be applied on oil size or by water gilding. Silver leaf will require a coating to protect against tarnishing.

On occasion it may be necessary to mount tiles onto a backboard. Aluminium honeycomb board, sold under trade names such as Hexlite®, has been used as a strong, rigid and lightweight backing material (see, for example, Jordan, 1999b).

### 15.4.5 Enamels

Enamel may be encountered in the form of plaques or panels on boxes, bureaux or incorporated into chair backs. Enamel is a vitreous (glassy) material, fused to a metal substrate by heat. Small amounts of metal oxides impart colour to the glass. The metal substrate is usually copper or a copper alloy. The structure is inherently problematic because the expansion coefficients of the enamel and metal can significantly differ and this can cause the enamel to flake from the metal substrate. Enamel is brittle, and flaking can also be a result of impact damage caused by poor handling. Corrosion of the metal substrate will be precipitated by the presence of moisture and exacerbated by exposure to organic acid vapour. Enamels may be embellished with gilding, which is often fragile. Enamels should ideally be kept in an environment with minimal fluctuations in temperature and low RH (35–42%), but this is not usually possible when the enamel has been incorporated into furniture. The techniques and materials used to create enamel have been considered by Speel (1998) and Benjamin (1987).

The chemical composition of some enamels has been found to be unstable (Smith *et al.*, 1987). The surface of the enamel should be examined for signs of deterioration before any treatment is undertaken. Deterioration can be visible as a loss in glass transparency (matteness), efflorescence on the surface, a network of fine cracks (crizzling) or spalled enamel. Other problems include surface cracks, flaking, chips and corrosion of the metal substrate, which can be found in the form of green cupric corrosion products, sometimes along cracks but more often where the metal is exposed. Cracks, which may be accentuated by the accumulation of dirt, are always problematic because of the potential for capillary action to pull solvent or solubilized dirt further down into the crack and into contact with the metal substrate. If there are *any* signs of deterioration the enamel should be referred to a specialist for treatment.

If the enamel is in good condition dust can be removed using a soft bristle brush and a miniature vacuum cleaner. Enamels should never be immersed in water. A cotton wool swab, slightly dampened with saliva, deionized water or IMS, can be rolled lightly over the surface. If saliva or deionized water have been used, it is essential that the surface of the enamel is completely dry after treatment and the surface can be wiped over with a swab slightly dampened with acetone to ensure that any water residues are removed. Any other treatment should be undertaken by a specialist.

## 15.5 Flat glass, mirrors, reverse painted and gilded glass

Glass may be found association with many different forms of furniture including glazed doors and door lights, wall mounted framed mirrors and reverse paintings on glass, mirrors within dressing tables and boxes or as small decorative elements such as painted or gilded glass on frames and drawer fronts. These glasses cannot be considered in isolation from the furniture of which they form a part. As with a framed painting, the glass is the functional part of a framed mirror. The mirror frame, like the picture frame, is a support for, and an enhancement of the looking glass. Both glass and frame make up the mirror and it would be unethical to separate them. Where both furniture and glass are to be conserved, it is necessary to consider the level of conservation treatment in order that visual harmony is maintained. All glass can be conserved if the budget allows and the owner really wants to keep the original. Replacing original glass with a reproduction can significantly reduce the value of the whole object.

### 15.5.1 Flat glass

Flat glass can be made by various methods (see section 5.6) that can be determined by visual examination and analysis (Frank, 1982). Glass is a non-porous, brittle and may be considered a comparatively 'unforgiving' material. Mechanical damage is the most common cause of deterioration because of the inherent brittleness of the material. Scratches can be ground from the glass, but will leave a dip that may prove obtrusive, particularly on mirrored glass. Handling glass can be problematic. Not only can it be very heavy and unwieldy, but also there is a possibility that cracks may propagate rapidly and lead to breakage. Such cracks may be small or invisible to the naked eye but may extend when the glass is handled. Changes in temperature, especially sudden cooling known as thermal shock, may cause glass to crack.

Broken glass is difficult to re-assemble and bond, both because of the nature of the glass and the relatively few materials with a refractive index suitable for glass repair (Tennent and Townsend, 1984). Although generally found in vessel glass, 'glass disease' may also be encountered in furniture, particularly where the glass is enclosed, for example in toilet boxes, clocks or barometers. Much of the information on the conservation of glass deals with vessel glass rather than the flat glass that is likely to be encountered in furniture (e.g. Tennent, 1999).

### 15.5.2 Mirrored glass

Glass may be decorated in many different ways. The most common forms are mirrors, reverse painted glass (hinterglasmalerei) and verre eglomisé. These decorative techniques may be found together on the same object or even on the same plate of glass.

Mirrors have been produced since early in the fourteenth century by applying a metallic layer to the reverse side of a flat sheet of glass (Child, 1990; Wills, 1965). Two distinct types are mercury/tin amalgam and silvered mirrors (see section 5.6). Tin/mercury mirrors were produced up to the beginning of the twentieth century, whilst silver-backed mirrors were produced from the middle of the nineteenth century. The two differ in both colour and reflectivity. Tin/mercury mirrors reflect darkly and have a grey tint, whilst silvered mirrors are brighter and have a slight yellow reflection. Whilst the back of silvered mirrors were always given a protective coat of paint, tin/mercury mirrors were rarely painted, except, for example, those used at sea. Mercury mirrors can be recognized by the rough matt grey (verso) and by the distinctive characteristics of the deterioration seen from the front.

The tin/mercury surface is a two-phase system in which crystals of a tin–mercury compound are surrounded by a mercury-rich liquid phase. This two-phase amalgam layer is unstable. The crystals change shape and grow larger whilst the amalgam layer oxidizes and releases liquid mercury that slowly evaporates. The liquid phase moves slowly to the bottom edge of the mirror, where it is not uncommon to find droplets of mercury. Whilst the upper

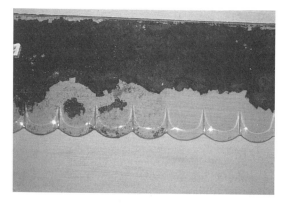

**Figure 15.15** Loss of tin-mercury amalgam from the edge of a seventeenth-century mirror glass

(a)

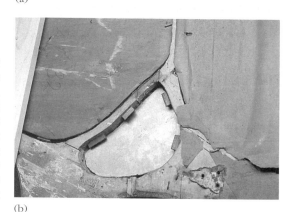

(b)

**Figure 15.16** Deterioration of a mirrored surface (*a*) Accretions of dirt and soot can accelerate degradation of the mercury amalgam (*b*) Fingerprints left by ungloved handling may eventually corrode through the entire depth of the amalgam

section may be hard and brittle, the lower edge may be soft and vulnerable to damage from handling (Hadsund, 1993) (*Figure 15.15*).

The deterioration of tin/mercury mirrored surfaces is irreversible. Although the process may be slowed by a low and constant ambient temperature, this is often unsuitable for the preservation of the frame or other components of the object. The separation of the tin/mercury amalgam into its constituent components followed by oxidation of the tin creates a dark and cloudy appearance. Concentric circles of corroded material may appear dark grey, yellow-brown or white. Corrosion occurs where the amalgam layer is exposed to the external environment and will be accelerated by the presence of dust, spiders' webs and fingerprints (*Figure 15.16*). This is most common along the edges or where there are splits in the backboard.

### 15.5.3　Painted and decorated glass

From antiquity, icons and altarpieces were produced with reverse painted and gilded glass. The Italians used reverse painting on glass in the fourteenth century and the technique spread through Europe in the sixteenth century. Glass was very expensive and items with reverse paintings, such as mirrors and cabinets, were highly valued. Large painted glass panels were produced in southern Germany from 1780, and as folk art until 1920. By the early twentieth century mass production using cheap glass, pigments and binders, resulted in a poor quality item.

Reverse painted glass is generally used as a decorative element above mirrors, or inset into furniture. It was executed in oils and water colours and sometimes incorporated coloured paper or vellum prints adhered to the glass.

Verre eglomisé, a Roman art revived in Italy during the fourteenth century, is the process of decorating the underside of a glass with metal leaf (usually gold or silver) against a red, black or green ground. Translucent lacquers were used to produce a brilliance of colour that was intended as an imitation of stained glass. Cennini described the technique in 1390 (trans. Thompson, 1954). It is often found decorating a border for mirror and picture frames and as panels on furniture.

The materials used in the decoration of glass are fragile and easily damaged by abrasion, moisture, organic solvents and corrosive vapours (e.g. carbonyl pollutants). The glass was intended to be a protective face and the reverse was almost always enclosed by a backboard or mounted onto the furniture and thus protected by it.

Glass exhibits a degree of shrinkage and expansion in response to changes in temperature. Unlike a painting on canvas, the binding media of the paint cannot physically soak into the glass support, thus the two layers are not mechanically bound together. Over time, the painted layer will become brittle and shrink due to loss of solvent. Thus the main problem associated with decorated glass is the detachment of the painted or gilded layer from the glass and its subsequent loss.

Cupping and shrinkage of the paint result in losses of the metal leaf. The painted glass will appear grey where leaf has detached. Corrosion of silver leaf will occur wherever it is exposed to the environment, mainly along the edges or where there are splits in the backboard. Animal glue may have been used to attach backing papers and can also cause deterioration as it ages and becomes brittle. The pressure exerted by the glue can pull the painted layer and metal leaf away from the glass. Oxidation of the paint may also cause colour change. Although the painted layer is protected from the front where it is securely bound to the glass, the reverse may be discoloured. UV light can penetrate the glass and cause bleaching, particularly of dark colours, but even in the same media, various pigments are affected differently. Humidity can also cause a problem as animal glue or gelatin may have been used as a coating on the glass. Mould growth can develop in damp conditions.

### 15.5.4 Repairs to adjacent wood

Potential damage to the glass as a result of the handling or transport of the object must be considered before repairs to adjacent wood or a frame are undertaken. As a general rule, if the glass is well supported, then it is safer for it to travel with the object (see section 10.2.5 for guidelines for handling mirrors). Where the glass and furniture are to be treated separately the object should be first delivered to the glass conservator where it can be taken apart.

**Figure 15.17** Missing sections of a mirror backboard replaced with seasoned obeche wood

Depending on the work to be carried out on the furniture, it may be possible for the glass to remain in situ. However, the risk of breakage or scratching from the use of hand tools or abrasive papers near glass cannot be over-emphasized.

The potential for chemical contamination must also be considered. Off-gassing from adhesives or wood used for the repair of adjacent wood can corrode metal, particularly if a microclimate has been created. PVAC adhesives, for example, off-gas acetic acid (Down *et al.*, 1996), whilst polyester resins off-gas styrene that will blacken silver and tin. Wood preservatives, varnishes and paints that off-gas carbonyl pollutants should be avoided. One of the criteria in the selection of wood for repairs or board materials for backing should be minimal off-gassing of acetic acid (see *Table 10.1*) (*Figure 15.17*). Repair wood or backing board may be isolated from the decorated or mirrored glass by a strip of Melinex/Mylar placed between the glass and the wood. This reduces the rate of, but does not completely prevent the, emission of carbonyl pollutants. It is extremely important to allow for some air movement, whilst also minimizing the ingress of dust and dirt, to prevent the formation of a destructive microclimate (Thickett *et al.*, 1998).

### 15.5.5 Removing glass

As a general rule the glass should be treated in situ wherever possible. However in some cases it may be necessary to remove glass to facilitate its treatment, to protect it from physical or chemical hazards during the conservation treatment of adjacent areas, or if the glass is not adequately supported in its original mount. It is necessary to balance the risk to the glass if it remains in situ against the risk of damage from removing it. Considerations will include the size and weight of the glass, its condition (cracks or breaks, strength/thickness of the glass), ease of removal of fixings that secure the glass in the mount, the condition of a mirrored or painted surface (corrosion, flaking, losses), and storage and transport, if necessary, to a glass conservator. Before dismantling, the orientation of the glass and the backboard must be documented, original fixings should be labelled and their position marked on a diagram. It is important to check that all fixings holding the glasses are removed otherwise they might crack or scratch the glass as it is lifted out. The most commonly found fixings include nails, screws, wooden wedges, metal clasps or frames, putty, paper or fabric tape.

If glass is to be removed, there should be adequate room to manoeuvre it. If the glass is to be laid flat, it should be placed onto a layer of clean, cushioned, non-abrasive and non-slip material such as Plastazote. Although apparently flat, it is rare for the surface of old glass to lie in a single plane and it should be well supported to avoid stress concentrations, which will result in breakage. It is advisable to protect glass in a workshop from accidental damage by enclosing or covering it with a rigid wooden box frame or polypropylene tray. It is essential when handling metalled glass to wear gloves to protect both object and conservator. Acids from fingerprints may cause corrosion on metalled surfaces, whilst mercury, a heavy metal associated with nervous system damage, may be absorbed directly through the skin.

### 15.5.6   Refitting decorated and mirrored glass

The frame and backboard act as a support, isolate vulnerable surfaces from physical damage and, when well made, prevent the ingress of dust and dirt. Whilst the backboard should be well sealed it should not be airtight, to avoid the build up of potentially harmful

**Figure 15.18**   A temporary fitting, padded to protect and secure mirror glass during transit to the conservation studio, where mouldings were reattached

products in a micro-climate. In cases where the original backboard is refitted but has splits, these should be lined on the interior surface with Melinex to prevent the ingress of dust and dirt. Hadsund (1993) illustrated a system for mounting and supporting mercury amalgam mirrors. Suitable new backings for glass include conservation grade fabrics, acid free card and paper. Whilst original wedges and nails that secured the mirror in place should be reused where possible, it may be necessary to incorporate new fittings to secure the glass (*Figure 15.18*).

### 15.5.7   Cleaning undecorated glass

The cleaning of undecorated glass should be preceded by careful visual inspection to identify presence of cracks, breaks or the presence of original decoration, such as gilding applied between panes. Minimum pressure is required when cleaning glass. A soft, clean brush, used in combination with a vacuum cleaner, may be used to remove dust. It is advisable to use tissue to protect the frame from the cumulative effects of abrasion when dusting. Large dusting cloths may snag on delicate elements of the frame or surround and should therefore be avoided. Small pads made from silk or a lint-free cotton may be used.

Aqueous and solvent cleaning solutions may be used, with caution, to clean undecorated glass. Swabs should be damp, not wet, and care should be taken to prevent water or solvent creeping behind or underneath the surface of the glass that is being cleaned. The frame or surround should be protected from cleaning solutions; Melinex/Mylar may be inserted into the rebate between the glass and frame for this purpose. Aqueous or solvent cleaning should be avoided if the glass is cracked because dirt will be drawn into the cracks by capillary action. The traditional method of cleaning glass was to add a little vinegar or ammonium hydroxide to water. Raising pH slightly, with a drop of ammonium hydroxide, will saponify grease and oil and make it water-soluble. A cleaning solution with an excessively high pH may attack the silica in the glass. Consideration should be given to the potential for damaging adjacent materials or finishes if pH is adjusted. A pH of 5.5–8.5 is broadly accepted as safe for many organic surfaces. Adding a drop of a non-ionic detergent (e.g. Triton XL-80N) will also assist in bringing oil and grease into solution but as detergents are non-volatile, a clearance procedure will be necessary (see section 11.5.4). Wiping over the surface with a swab dampened with deionized water should be sufficient to remove detergent residues from glass. Solvent cleaning may utilize IMS, acetone, 50/50 water and IMS, or white spirit. Proprietary window cleaning products should be avoided because the constituents are often unknown. Spray application is inappropriate because of the risk of damage from the inevitable overspray. Proprietary abrasive pastes generally contain particles of alumina or silicon. These abrasives are not suitable as they are too hard and will scratch the glass. A home made paste may be made from whiting and deionized water, to which a drop of dilute ammonium hydroxide may be added if necessary.

### 15.5.8 Cleaning mirrored and decorated glass

Painted and gilded surfaces that are well adhered may be cleaned with a soft brush and vacuum cleaner. Gilded glass has usually been water gilded and aqueous cleaning should therefore be avoided. The use of solvents with a hydrogen-bonding component, such as alcohol, should also be minimized. Davison and Jackson (1985) have considered the

conservation of reverse painted glass and mirrors. Caldararo (1997) discussed the treatment of paintings on ceramics and glass.

Tin/mercury surfaces should not be vacuumed because the mercury will be vaporized and expelled into the ambient environment where it will present a health hazard. A soft brush, used only for mirrored surfaces and stored in a plastic bag, may be used to lightly brush over the surface. Mercury may be collected using a mercury salvage kit (e.g. Chemizorb Hg, available through Merck) and disposed of in accordance with current guidelines or legislation. Mercury sponges are not recommended for use on mercury amalgam surfaces as they are not particularly effective for this application and may cause damage. Silvered surfaces are usually sealed with paint and, if well adhered, may be vacuumed.

### 15.5.9 Repair of glass

Cracked or broken glass should be referred to a specialist for repair and adhesive bonding. Such treatments are difficult and require experience and skill. A glass conservator may be able to cast infills or readhere chips using techniques developed for vessel glass, although such treatments are usually only justified for small areas on very valuable mirrors (Jackson, 1984). Whilst reproduction glass is available from a few specialist companies, it is difficult to match the replacement to the original. Bevelling and cutting complex shapes was previously done by hand. Copying it is often beyond the skill of glaziers and may require the skills of a glass conservator. Repair of painted, gilded or mirrored glass presents additional difficulty, as there is the potential that adhesive used to bond the glass may creep between the glass and the painted or mirrored surface, disfiguring it.

### 15.5.10 Consolidation

Flaking on painted, gilded or mirrored surfaces should be referred to a specialist with experience of painted glass, as the association of these materials can present particular problems. The decorated surface itself is often complex, a wide variety of binding media may have been used and problems are often complicated.

The consolidation of flakes on a mercury amalgam mirror may be problematic as the oxidized tin layer is very brittle. The traditional method of laying a flake by applying consolidant under the flake and then adhering it to the substrate with a heated spatula is not appropriate for mercury amalgam surfaces. The application of pressure to the flake will break or shatter it. In addition to problems with appearance, the crystal structure of the mercury amalgam phase has an upper limit of 58 °C (Hadsund, 1993). In some cases the application of a small amount of consolidant to the thin edge of a flake may provide a bridge that secures the flake in place. Such consolidant should be very viscous (e.g. 50/50 w/v Paraloid B72 in acetone). If this procedure is undertaken the minimum amount of consolidant should be used and it should not end up under the flake.

Techniques for consolidation of the painted layer of reverse painted glass are unlike those used in painting conservation. The glass is an inflexible support of a very different nature to canvas or panel paintings. Traditional methods of varnishing the reverse or injecting voids with resin have usually been unsatisfactory and, due to shrinkage of the consolidant, may have exacerbated the problem. Refixing flakes of detached paint is a specialist task that should be referred to a conservator with experience of reverse painted glass.

### 15.5.11   Restoration and retouching

The use of metal foils to patch areas of loss is inadvisable because of the probability that the mercury will react with the repair material and that galvanic corrosion will occur (see section 8.4). Jackson (1987) used a technique in which mirrored Melinex/Mylar sheet was laid behind the mirror to disguise areas where the amalgam had been lost. A similar technique may be used for areas of loss on reverse painted glass. A coloured background acid free paper, tinted with water colours if necessary, may be laid behind the reverse painting for small areas of loss. Larger details may be painted onto a sheet of Melinex/Mylar and positioned so that the replacement is aligned with the original design. This should be secured to the backing and not the glass.

### 15.5.12   Coatings

Coatings are not appropriate for undecorated, reverse painted or mirrored glass. The application of a coating to a mercury amalgam surface is not recommended. The deterioration of tin/mercury mirrored surfaces is irreversible. Blackened areas result from the separation of the tin/mercury amalgam into constituent components followed by oxidation of the tin. Impregnation or coating with a resin will not slow down or prevent this deterioration and cannot prevent crystal growth or other changes in the amalgam. Further, attempts to remove such a coating in the future are likely to damage the amalgam surface. The most effective way of ensuring longevity to mirrored or decorated glass is to ensure that it is protected from physical and environmental damage.

## Bibliography

### 15.1   Ivory, bone, antler, turtleshell, horn and mother-of-pearl

Bitmead, R. (1873) *The London Cabinet Maker's Guide*, London

Davison, S. (1998) Reversible fills for transparent and translucent materials, *JAIC*, 37(1), 35–47

Down, J.L., MacDonald, M.A., Williams, J.T. and Williams, R.S. (1996) Adhesive testing at the Canadian Conservation Institute – an evaluation of selected poly(vinyl acetate) and acrylic adhesives, *Studies in Conservation*, 41(1), 19–44

Driggers, J.M., Mussey, R.D. and Garvin, S.M. (1991) Treatment of an ivory inlaid Anglo-Indian desk bookcase, in AIC Wooden Artifacts Group Conference papers, Albuquerque

Espinoza, E.O. and Mann, M. (1992) *Identification Guide for Ivory and Ivory Substitutes*, World Wildlife Fund, Washington, DC

Hawkins, D. (1986) *The Technique of Wood Surface Decoration*, Batsford

LaFontaine, R.H. and Wood, P.A. (1982) The stabilization of ivory against relative humidity fluctuations, *Studies in Conservation*, 27(3), 109–17

Lochhead, V. (1989) Tortoise-shell substitute veneer, *Conservation News*, 38, 31–2

Matienzo, L.J. and Snow, C.E. (1986) The chemical effects of hydrochloric acid and organic solvents on the surface of ivory, *Studies in Conservation*, 31(3), 133–9

Mussey, R. (ed.) (1987) *The First American Furniture Finisher's Manual*, reprint of the 1827 edition of *The Cabinet-Maker's Guide*, Dover

Ramond, P. (1989) *Marquetry*, Taunton Press

Rao, S. and Subbaiah, K.V. (1983) Indian ivory, *Journal of Archaeological Chemistry*, 1 (1), 1–10

Siddons, G.A. (1830) *The Cabinet Maker's Guide*, Sherwood, Gilbert and Piper

Snow, C.E. and Weisser, T.D. (1984) The examination and treatment of ivory and related materials, in *Adhesives and Consolidants*, Conference Preprints, IIC, pp. 141–45

*Spons Workshop Receipts for Manufacturers and Scientific Amateurs* (1873/1921), E&F.N. Spon, London

Tennent, N.H. and Baird, T. (1985) The deterioration of mollusca collections: identification of shell efflorescence, *Studies in Conservation*, 30(2), 73–85

Thornton, J. (1981) The structure of ivory and ivory substitutes, in Preprints of the AIC Philadelphia meeting, pp. 173–81

## 15.2   Paper labels and linings on furniture

Down, J.L., MacDonald, M.A., Tetrealt, J. and Williams, R.S. (1996) Adhesive testing at the Canadian Conservation Institute – an evaluation of selected poly(vinyl acetate) and acrylic adhesives, *Studies in Conservation*, 41(1), 19–44

Huxtable, M. and Webber, P. (1987) Some adaptations of Oriental techniques and materials used in the Prints and Drawings Conservation Department of the Victoria and Albert Museum, *The Paper Conservator*, 11, 46–57

Purinton, N. and Filter, S. (1992) Gore-Tex: an introduction to the material and treatments, in AIC Conference Postprints, pp. 141–55

## 5.3   Metals

Argo, J. and Turgoose, S. (1985) Amines for iron: discussion, in S. Keene (ed.), *Corrosion Inhibitors in Conservation*, UKIC

Bennett, M. (1990) *Discovering and Restoring Antique Furniture*, Cassell

Binnie, N.E., Selwyn, L.S., Schlichting, C. and Rennie-Bisaillion, D.A. (1995) Corrosion protection of outdoor iron artifacts using commercial rust converters, *J.IIC-CG*, 20, 26–40

Brenner, H. (1953) Silver dips, *Soap and Sanitation Chemistry*, 29(5), 161, 163, 165, 167, 187

Brewer, J.A. (1991) Effect of selected coatings on moisture sorption of selected wood test panels, *Studies in Conservation*, 36, 9–23

Brown, Burnett, Chase, Goodway, Kruger, Pourbaix (eds) (1977) *Corrosion and Metal Artifacts – A Dialogue Between Conservators and Archaeologists and Corrosion Scientists*, National Bureau of Standards, Washington, DC

Cagle, C.V. (1973) *Handbook of Adhesive Bonding*, McGraw-Hill

CCI Notes (1988) 9/3 *The Cleaning, Polishing and Protective Waxing of Brass and Copper*, Canadian Conservation Institute

CCI Notes (1989) 9/1 *Recognising Active Corrosion*, Canadian Conservation Institute

CCI Notes (1993) 9/7 *Silver – Care and Tarnish Removal*, Canadian Conservation Institute

CCI Notes (1995) 9/6 *Care and Cleaning of Iron*, Canadian Conservation Institute

Chapman, M. (1994) Techniques of mercury gilding in the eighteenth century, in D.A. Scott, J. Podany and B.B. Considine (eds), *Ancient and Historic Metals Conservation and Scientific Research*, Conference Proceedings, Getty Conservation Institute, pp. 229–38

Clarke, R.W. and Blackshaw, S.M. (eds) (1982) *Conservation of Iron*, National Maritime Museum, Greenwich (UK)

Degrigny, C. and Le Gall, R. (1999) Conservation of ancient lead artifacts corroded in organic acid environments: electrolytic stabilization/consolidation, *Studies in Conservation*, 44(3), 157–69

De Witte, E. (1973/74) The protection of silverware with varnishes, *Bulletin Institute Royal du Patrimonie Artistique*, 14, 140–51

Dossie, R. (1758) *The Handmaid to the Arts*, London

Drayman-Weisser, T. (ed) (2000) *Gilded Metals: History, Technology and Conservation*, Archetype

Fiorentino, P. (1994) Restoration of the Monument of Marcus Aurelius: facts and comments, in D.A. Scott, J. Podany and B.B. Considine (eds), *Ancient and Historic Metals Conservation and Scientific Research*, Conference Proceedings, Getty Conservation Institute, pp. 21–31

Ganiaris, H. (1985) A portable spot-test kit, *Conservation News*, 27, 25–6

Goodison, N. (1974) *Ormolu, the Work of Matthew Boulton*, Phaidon

Green, L. (1989) A re-evaluation of lead conservation techniques at the British Museum, *International Restorer Seminar*, Központi Muzemi Igazgatóság, Hungary

Heller, D. (1983) Coating of metal objects at Winterthur, in AIC Conference Preprints, pp. 57–64

Hjelm-Hansen, N. (1984) Cleaning and stabilization of sulphide-corroded bronzes, *Studies in Conservation*, 29(1), 17–20

Hughes, R. and Rowe, M. (1982) *The Colouring, Bronzing and Patination of Metals*, Crafts Council

Jones, R.H. (ed.) (1992) *Stress Corrosion Cracking*, ASM International

Keene, S. (ed.) (1985) *Corrosion Inhibitors in Conservation*, UKIC

Lane, H. (1975) The reduction of lead, in *Conservation in Archaeology and the Applied Arts*, IIC Preprints, pp. 215–19

Lane, H. (1979) Some comparisons of lead conservation methods, including consolidative reduction, in E.A. Slater and N.H. Tennent (eds), *The Conservation and Restoration of Metals*, Conference Proceedings, SSCR, pp. 50–60

Lins, A. (1989) The inhibition of silver tarnishing, in *Current Problems in the Conservation of Metal Antiquities*, 13th International Symposium on the Conservation and Restoration of Cultural Property, Tokyo National Research Institute, pp. 119–31

Logan, J. (1989) Tannic acid treatment, *CCI Notes*, 9/5

Lupu, M.I.A. and Balta, Z.I. (1998) A possible method based on CMC for cleaning metalwork decorative art objects, in *Metal 98* (James and James), pp. 173–6

MacLeod, I.D., Pennec, S.L. and Robbiola, L. (eds) (1995) *Metal 95* (James and James)

Madsen, H.B. (1967) A preliminary note on the use of benzotriazole for stabilising bronze objects, *Studies in Conservation*, 12 (4), 163–6

Meehan, P. and Green, L.R. (1992) Evaluation of DTPA (diethylenetriaminepenta-acetic acid) as an alternative to EDTA (ethylenediaminetetra-acetic acid) to clean copper alloys, British Museum Report 1992/3

Merk, L.E. (1978) A study of reagents used in the stripping of bronzes, *Studies in Conservation*, 23 (1), 15–22

Moffett, D.L. (1996) Wax coatings on ethnographic objects: justifications for allowing a tradition to wane, *JAIC*, 35, 1–7

Mourey, W. and Robbiola, L. (eds) (1998) *Metal 98* (James and James)

North, N.A. (1980) Proprietary silver cleaners, *ICCM Bulletin*, 6, 3–4, 41–5

Oddy, W.A., Bimson, M. and La Niece, S. (1983) The composition of niello decoration on gold, silver and bronze in the antique and medieval periods, *Studies in Conservation*, 28(1), 29–35

Panshin, A.J. and de Zeeuw, C. (1980) *Textbook of Wood Technology*, 4th edn, McGraw–Hill

Pearson, C. (ed.) (1987) *Conservation of Marine Archaeological Objects*, Butterworths

Plenderleith, H.J. and Werner, A.E.A. (1971) *The Conservation of Antiquities and Works of Art*, Oxford University Press

Price, C., Hallam, D., Heath, G., Creagh, D. and Ashton, J. (1997) An electrochemical study of waxes for bronze sculpture, in *Metal 95* (James and James), pp. 233–41

Rodd, J. (1976) *Repairing and Restoring Antique Furniture*, David & Charles

Rymuza, Z. (1989) *Tribology of Miniature Systems*, Elsevier

Sawada, M. (1993) A new technique for removal of corrosion products on gilded copper alloy artifacts, in Shigeo, A. (ed.), *Current Problems in the Conservation of Metal Antiquities*, Bunka-cho Tokyo Kokuritsu Bunkazai Kenkyujo Hozon Kagakubu, Tokyo, pp. 215–24

Scott, D.A. (1983) The deterioration of gold alloys and some aspects of their conservation, *Studies in Conservation*, 28(4), 144–203

Scott, D.A., Podany, J. and Considine, B.B. (1994) *Ancient and Historic Metals Conservation and Scientific Research*, Conference Proceedings, Getty Conservation Institute

Scully, J.C. (ed.) (1971) *The Theory of Stress Corrosion Cracking in Alloys*, Conference Proceedings, NATO Scientific Affairs Division, Brussels

Sease, C. (1978) Benzotriazole: A Review for Conservators, *Studies in Conservation*, 23 (2), 76–85

Selwitz, C.M. (1988) *Cellulose Nitrate in Conservation*, Getty Conservation Institute

Selwyn, L.S. (1990) Historical silver: storage, display and tarnish removal, *J.IIC-CG*, 15, 12–22

Selwyn, L.S. (1995) Corrosion chemistry of gilded silver and copper, in Gilded Metal Surfaces Conference Abstracts (AIC Objects Specialty Group), pp. 6–7

Selwyn, L.S. and Costain, C.G. (1991) Evaluation of silver cleaning products, *J.IIC-CG*, 16, 3–16

Selwyn, L.S. and Logan, J. (1993) Stability of treated iron: a comparison of treatment methods, in ICOM Committee for Conservation, Preprints 10th Triennial Meeting, Washington, DC, pp. 803–7

Sharma, V.C., Lal, U.S. and Nair, M.V. (1995) Zinc dust treatment – an effective method for the control of bronze disease on excavated objects, *Studies in Conservation*, 40(2), 110–19

Siepelt, B., Pilz, M. and Kiesenberg, J. (1998) Transparent coatings – suitable corrosion protection for industrial heritage made of iron?, in *Metal 98* (James and James), pp. 291–6

Slater, E.A. and Tennent, N.H. (eds) (1979) *The Conservation and Restoration of Metals*, Conference Proceedings, SSCR

Smith, G. (1810) *The Laboratory and School of Arts*, London

*Spons Workshop Receipts for manufacturers and scientific amateurs* (1873/1921), E&F.N. Spon, London

Stambolov, T. (1979) Introduction to the conservation of ferrous and non-ferrous metals, in E.A. Slater and N.H. Tennent (eds), *The Conservation and Restoration of Metals*, Conference Proceedings, SSCR, pp. 9–18

Tear, P. (1996) The cleaning and conservation of the balustrade of the main staircase of Hertford House, in P. van Duin, D. van Loosdrecht and D. Wheeler (eds), *Proceedings of the 3rd International Symposium on Wood and Furniture Conservation*, Rijksmuseum/VeRes, Amsterdam

Thickett, D., Bradley, S. and Lee, L. (1998) Assessment of the risks to metal artifacts posed by volatile carbonyl pollutants, in *Metal 98* (James and James), pp. 260–4

Thomson, C. (1991) Last but not least – examination and interpretation of coatings on brass hardware, in AIC Wooden Artifacts Group, Conference Papers, Albuquerque

Thornton, J. (2000) All that glitters is not gold: other surfaces that appear to be gilded, in Drayman-Weisser, T. (ed) *Gilded Metals History, Technology and Conservation*, Archetype, pp. 307–17

Townsend, J. (1985) Spot tests for metals, *Conservation News*, p. 28

Townsend, J. (1988) The identification of metals: chemical spot tests, in R.E. Child and J.H. Townsend (eds), *Modern Metals in Museums*, Institute of Archaeology Publications, pp. 15–22

Uhlig, H.H. and Revie, R.W. (1985) *Corrosion and Corrosion Control: An Introduction to Corrosion Science*, Wiley

West, T. (1969) *Complexometry with EDTA and Related Agents*, 3rd edn, BDH Chemicals Ltd

Wharton, G., Maish, S.L. and Ginell, W.S. (1990) A comparative study of silver cleaning abrasives, *JAIC*, 29, 13–31

Wise, E.M. (ed.) (1964) *Gold: Recovery, Properties and Applications*, Van Nostrand

Yaseen, M. (1981) Permeation properties of organic coatings in the control of metallic corrosion, in H. Leidheiser (ed.), *Corrosion Control by Organic Coatings*, National Association of Corrosion Engineers, Houston

## 15.4   Ceramics and enamels

Benjamin, S. (1987) *English Enamel Boxes from the Eighteenth to the Twentieth Centuries*, Macdonald Orbis

Buys, S. and Oakley, V. (1996) *The Conservation and Restoration of Ceramics*, Butterworth-Heinemann

Hamer, F & J. (1986) *The Potter's Dictionary of Materials and Techniques*, A&C Black

Jordan, F. (1999a) The practical application of tinted epoxy resins for filling, casting and retouching porcelain, in N.H. Tennent (ed.), *The Conservation of Glass and Ceramics: Research, Practice and Training*, James and James (Science Publications), pp. 138–45

Jordan, F. (1999b) The remounting of a Victorian tile panel, *V&A Conservation Journal*, 33, 10–12

Koob, S.P. (1986) The use of Paraloid B72 as an adhesive: its application for archaeological ceramics and other materials, *Studies in Conservation*, 31(1), 7–14

Lee, L-M., Rogers, P., Oakley, V. and Navarro, J. (1997) Investigations into the use of laponite as a poulticing material in ceramics conservation, *V&A Conservation Journal*, 22, 9–11

Ling, D. (1991) Laponite poulticing, *Conservation News*, 46, 10–11

Oddy, A. (ed.). (1992) *The Art of the Conservator*, British Museum Press

Smith, R., Carlson, J.H. and Newman, R.M. (1987) An investigation into the deterioration of painted Limoges enamel plaques *c.*1470–1530, *Studies in Conservation*, 32(3), 102–33

Smith, S. (1994) Filling and painting of ceramics for exhibition in the British Museum – is it acceptable?, in A. Oddy (ed.), *Restoration: Is It Acceptable?*, British Museum Occasional Paper 99, pp. 159–69

Speel, E. (1998) *Dictionary of Enamelling. History and Techniques*, Ashgate Publishing

Walker, W. and Shashoua, Y. (1996) Paraloid resins/microballoon mixtures as gap filling materials for friable ceramics, British Museum Conservation Research Group Report 1996/5

## 15.5 Flat glass, mirrors, reverse painted and gilded glass

Caldararo, N. (1997) Conservation treatments of paintings on ceramics and glass: two case studies, *Studies in Conservation*, 42(3), 157–64

Cennini, C. (trans. Thompson, 1954), *The Craftsman's Handbook*, Dover

Child, G. (1990) *World Mirrors 1650–1900*, Sothebys Publications

Davison, S. and Jackson, P.R. (1985) The restoration of decorative flat glass: four case histories, *The Conservator*, 9, 3–13

Down, J.L., MacDonald, M.A., Tetrealt, J. and Williams, R.S. (1996) Adhesive testing at the Canadian Conservation Institute – an evaluation of selected poly(vinyl acetate) and acrylic adhesives, *Studies in Conservation*, 41(1), 19–44

Frank, S. (1982) *Glass and Archaeology*, Academic Press

Hadsund, P. (1993) The tin–mercury mirror: its manufacturing technique and deterioration processes, *Studies in Conservation*, 38(1), 3–16

Jackson, P.R. (1984) Restoration of glass antiquities, in ICOM Committee for Conservation, Preprints 7th Triennial Meeting, Copenhagen, pp. 84.20.13–84.20.17

Jackson, P.R. (1987) The Hampton Court Palace fire – rescuing pier glasses, in J. Black (compiler), *Recent Advances in the Conservation and Analysis of Artefacts*, UKIC, pp. 59–62

Tennent, N.H. (ed.) (1999) *The Conservation of Glass and Ceramics: Research, Practice and Training*, James and James (Science Publications)

Tennent, N.H. and Townsend, J.H. (1984) The significance of the refractive index of adhesives for glass repair, in A. Brommelle *et al.* (eds), *Adhesives and Consolidants*, Conference Preprints, IIC, pp. 205–12

Thickett, D., Bradley, S. and Lee, L. (1998) Assessment of the risks to metal artifacts posed by volatile carbonyl pollutants, in *Metal 98* (James and James), pp. 260–4

Wills, G. (1965) *English Looking Glasses: A Study of the Glass, Frames and Makers, 1670–1820*, Country Life, London

# 16

# Conserving other materials II

This chapter introduces the principles and techniques for the conservation of diverse materials often associated with wooden furniture. Each of these materials is a specialist subject in its own right. It is essential that conservators undertake further research, consult references and seek specialist advice rather than undertaking treatments on an unfamiliar material. The conservator should be as well informed as possible about these materials and be alert for potential problems in order to avoid causing irreversible damage.

## 16.1 Stone and related materials

Stone is a porous material. Porosity varies according to the type of stone and the type of finish. A highly polished marble surface, for example, is usually less porous than an eroded surface. Surface coatings that may have been applied, such as wax, will also affect the porosity of the surface. Porosity will affect the way dirt collects on the surface and the behaviour of liquids applied to clean it. Capillary action will draw liquids into the body of the stone and there is a risk that dirt in solution may be carried with them. Polishable stones, such as marble, become more porous if the polished surface becomes degraded. A furniture conservator may undertake cleaning of a surface that is in good condition. Problematic surfaces, such as those that are degraded, should be treated by a specialist.

A range of stone and stone-like materials have been incorporated into furniture. The first step in treatment is to identify the material/s that are present. It may be helpful to examine an unpolished surface, such as the underside of a table top. Compare the top and bottom surface but keep in mind that plaster may have been used as an adhesive layer. Specialist advice should be sought if identification is difficult. Materials such as slate, coadestone and alabaster may be encountered, and conservation treatment will vary accordingly. Alabaster, for example, is readily soluble in water so irreversible damage may occur if aqueous cleaning solutions are used.

Much of the literature available about cleaning and repair of stone is geared towards the conservation of historic buildings, e.g. Ashurst and Dimes (1990) and Winckler (1973). There is a difference in approach between major structural buildings conservation and that required for stone found as a component of furniture. Whilst much useful information may be gained from general texts, this difference should be borne in mind when considering adopting the approaches or techniques outlined in them.

Although stone is a durable material it is vulnerable to damage from abrasive cleaning. Proprietary metal polishes such as Autosol, abrasive powders such as pumice, or abrasive materials such as 0000 wire wool are not appropriate for stone surfaces.

### 16.1.1 Marble

Whilst fine white marble has been prized as a stone for statuary, marble used in furniture tends to be highly figured, coloured and veined. Veins may be a point of structural weakness or more easily eroded in use.

#### Cleaning
The types of unwanted surface accretions encountered on marble table tops may be broadly characterized as a general build up of dirt, grease or finger marks, paint marks, food and drink stains, copper or iron stains and

coatings that may have been applied in a previous restoration treatment. The removal of graffiti from stone is described by Ashurst (1994). The decision to clean a table top in situ or remove and treat it separately may depend on the relative risk of damage from cleaning versus potential damage from handling or the sensitivity of the adjacent wood to inadvertent splashes from cleaning solutions.

As with cleaning other surfaces, the materials chosen should progress from the least aggressive and cleaning tests should be undertaken to assess the efficacy of a given choice. Bleaches, acids, cleaning solutions with an acidic pH, and proprietary cleaning materials should not be used to clean marble and other polishable stones. Any acidic material will etch the surface.

Water is often an effective cleaning agent and a non-ionic detergent may be added if required. The use of non-volatile cleaning materials such as detergents will necessitate the use of a rinse procedure to ensure that residues do not remain on the surface after treatment has been completed. A pH between 7 and 9 is suitable for aqueous cleaning solutions to be used on marble or plaster. If there are inclusions of iron pyrites that are oxidizing within the stone, contact with water should be avoided. Pyrites will appear as pinhead sized black/silver or rust coloured inclusions, sometimes beneath the surface and sometimes at the surface. They may have fallen, or been picked, out and the holes filled with wax. Water/solvent or solvent/solvent mixtures may also be used for cleaning stone. An effective general cleaning solution is a fifty/fifty mixture of water and white spirit with non-ionic detergent at two to three times CMC (see section 11.5.4). The resulting emulsion should be shaken during use and the rinse required will be dependent on the detergent used. A mixture of water and acetone may also prove effective for cleaning.

Cleaning solutions may be applied with a cotton swab or a small natural bristle brush, such as a stencil brush. Nylon bristles, such as those on toothbrushes, may scratch the surface and should therefore be avoided. Paint splashes may be removed mechanically or with a proprietary solvent-based paint stripper.

In some cases the dirt may appear to be on the surface but is not affected by these mixtures and it is possible that a poultice may be more effective. The cleaning solutions described above, particularly water, white spirit or water/acetone, may be used in poultices. A variety of materials, such as methyl cellulose, Laponite or Carbopol, may be used to thicken or gel cleaning solutions to provide greater application control. Poultices and gels are described in section 11.6. When cleaning calcitic materials (such as marble and plaster), poultices should be applied and removed wet. As a general rule, tap water is inappropriate for cleaning solutions for stone. Deionized water, left in contact with calcitic materials for prolonged periods can dissolve calcite (Lauffenburger *et al.*, 1992; Livingston, 1992). Water used in packs and poultices for cleaning calcitic materials should be pre-treated so that it is already saturated with respect to calcite. This may be done by soaking limestone or marble chips in deionized water, in an open container (Livingston, 1992). This will prevent the cleaning solution leaching the surface of the calcitic material and causing loss of gloss.

Iron and copper stains may occur if metal objects such as a clocks, metal vases or candlestands are in contact with the stone in combination with water on the surface, e.g. high RH, spills, flooding etc. Copper stains may be reduced by poulticing with 5% ammonium bicarbonate in water. When the copper becomes visible as a pale green coloration in the poultice, it should be replaced. This treatment will reduce, but not remove, copper stains and it is likely that the green colour of copper stain will recur. Iron stains may also be reduced by this ammonium bicarbonate solution. Although many texts recommend using chelating agents such as EDTA or TAC in this cleaning solution there is a danger that a low pH solution will affect the carbonate and chelating solutions may attack the calcium (de Witte and Dupas, 1992; Livingston, 1992; Matero and Tagle, 1995; Thickett, 1995). The use of chelating agents is therefore not recommended on stone components of furniture. Iron stains that occur as a result of iron pyrites in the stone itself should be left untreated. The continued presence of pyrites is a source of further iron oxidation, which may be exacerbated by cleaning materials.

Food and drink stains may be treated using the treatments outlined above. Repeated applications of poultices may be necessary if the stains have penetrated some distance into the stone. Solvent cleaning, outlined in 11.3, may be used for the removal of aged, non-original coatings. There have been suggestions that steam cleaning of stone is an excessively aggressive treatment and current research should be considered before such a treatment is undertaken.

Alabaster may be cleaned with non-polar solvents, although a small amount of alcohol may be used if a more polar mix is required. The efficacy of solvent cleaning solutions may be improved if they are applied in gel form. Poultices for use on alabaster may be made with a non-polar solvent and sepiolite or atta-pulgite.

### Consolidation

Stone that requires consolidation should be referred to a specialist for treatment.

### Repair and reintegration

Once a slab has broken it is likely to be more fragile than a comparable unbroken piece, regardless of the method used to repair it. The treatment of major structural repairs will be dependent on the thickness of the slab and the type of break. The most common methods used by stone conservators to support breaks are stainless steel dowels, cramps or flat rods set into a thixotropic knife grade polyester resin. Such treatments should be undertaken by an experienced stone conservator. Structural fills for stone, i.e. those that contribute to overall structural integrity, have been considered by Griswold and Uricheck (1998). An aluminium honeycomb support, such as Hexlite®, may be used underneath a broken slab to support it. Such supports offer the advantage of minimal intervention coupled with a uniform lightweight support but will change the thickness of the slab component. Although Hexlite® is often used in conjunction with epoxy resins, the use of a range of other adhesives, including PVAC and Beva 371, has been described in conservation literature.

Marble chips may be reattached using a thixotropic knife grade polyester resin. Fills may be necessary if small losses have occurred. Fills may be made using water clear polyester or two part acrylic resins such as Akemi® (*Figure 16.1a*). The choice of polyester resin for fills is dependent on the required working

(a)

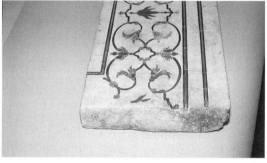
(b)

**Figure 16.1**  Infilling marble
(*a*) An area of loss on a seventeenth century Indian marble Agrawork panel, prepared to receive a fill. Aluminium foil tape has been used to 'wall' the fill, which is built up in stages. Water clear polyester resin has been matched to the colour of the background marble using alabaster powder and pigment. The pigmented polyester resin forms a thick but fluid paste (*b*) Fill completed and matched to the background colour of the marble. Although the Agrawork design has been reproduced where the design elements were known, conjectural restoration has not been undertaken

time. Ground white alabaster or white marble dust may be used in combination with pigments to obtain the required texture and colour (*Figure 16.1b*). Melinex/Mylar may be used between a piece of Perspex/Plexiglass and the surface to ensure a level fill. An uneven fill may be levelled using a sharp blade and polished using fine abrasive papers, but care must be taken to avoid damaging the adjacent stone surface. Very small fills may utilize Polyfilla or pigmented wax. If local retouching is necessary finely ground pigments in a thin solution (less than 5%) of a Paraloid resin or other conservation grade binder may be used. Artist's acrylic paint may be used if it is diluted to the consistency of water colours. Nagy (1998) has considered a range of materials for filling losses to white marble in an outdoor environment.

### Coatings

The application of a coating should be considered on a case-by-case basis. A thin coating of microcrystalline wax may be appropriate for polished and eroded polishable surfaces if the furniture is in use (*Figure 16.2*). This will facilitate future cleaning and act as a barrier to spills and dirt that result from handling. A thin layer of wax paste, diluted with solvent to the consistency of cream, may be applied using a brush or soft cloth and buffed to a low sheen. As a general rule varnish type coatings are difficult to remove from porous stone surfaces and should not be used.

**Figure 16.2** A seventeenth century Italian table top, slate with scagliola inlay. Detail showing loss of surface polish from the scagliola and deterioration of the slate surface. A thin layer of microcrystalline wax can be used to resaturate the colour

### 16.1.2    Scagliola

There are comparatively few sources available on the conservation of scagliola. Zecchini (1992) described the history and construction of scagliola. Agnini *et al.* (1998) described the restoration treatment of scagliola choir stalls in Kempten, Germany. Wittenburg (1999) outlines the results of a two-year research project into Baroque artificial marble and includes bibliographic material as well as recommendations for conservation.

### Cleaning

Like marble, scagliola is a porous surface and skilled solvent or aqueous cleaning involves application of a small amount of liquid, which solubilizes the dirt and is rapidly removed. If solvent penetrates the porous surface, it will carry any solubilized dirt deeper into the body of the plaster, thus swabs allow controlled cleaning.

When scagliola is in good condition and its polished surface is intact, it may be cleaned using the techniques described for marble, with the exception that bristle brushes should not be used. In contrast, broken or worn surfaces will be very porous. In such cases cleaning will be more problematic and cleaning methods used for plaster may be more applicable (see for example, Haller and Schliessl, 1998). Dry cleaning methods, described in section 11.2.4, may be effective on a stable surface either on their own or in combination with a swab slightly dampened with water or solvent. Preservation pencils produce nebulized water vapour, the flow and temperature of which can be adjusted to allow controlled and localized application of moisture whilst using a swab to remove surface dirt.

Scagliola may have been treated in the past by the application of oils or varnish. In some cases these may be removed using solvent poultices but such treatments may be problematic and should be referred to a specialist.

### Consolidation

One of the difficulties associated with the consolidation of a crumbling scagliola surface is that there is a danger of causing darkening, tidelines and discoloration when applying a consolidant. One way of avoiding this is to use repeated applications of a very weak consolidant solution, such 0.5% Paraloid B72 in a solvent with a slow to medium evaporation rate. Penetration of the consolidant may be assisted by pre-wetting the surface with a solvent compatible with the consolidant. Once applied, the consolidant should be allowed to dry and the surface checked for discoloration before further application.

Cracks may be consolidated in a variety of ways. Two or three applications, by syringe if necessary, of 0.5% Paraloid B72 solution or a very dilute conservation grade PVAC may be followed by a thicker conservation grade PVAC adhesive. Gentle cramping pressure may be applied to bring the edges of the crack into contact but potential weakness in the structure of the scagliola should be considered. The edges and surface of the object should be protected if cramps are used.

Chips may be readhered using a conservation grade PVAC. The chipped surfaces should be clean and pre-sealed with a weak solution of consolidant as described above. Repair of major breaks should be referred to a specialist.

### Fills

Areas that are to be filled should be cleaned and coated with an isolating layer. Proprietary products such as interior Polyfilla may be used. A more accurate colour match may be produced by mixing dry pigment powder with the Polyfilla powder. Water is added once a satisfactory colour has been achieved. Pigments used to make scagliola were selected for lightfastness and compatibility with lime, and as a result natural earths and mineral colours were commonly used. Fills may also be made using whiting and pigment and may include aggregate material such as ground alabaster powder and an adhesive such as rabbit skin glue, PVAC, or other materials discussed in section 12.3.1. Colour matching is most effective when the fill itself matches the adjacent scagliola but water colours, pigment in Paraloid etc., may be used to match a marbled effect. Surface polish may be simulated by burnishing with a fine polishing cloth, an agate stone, or by repeat applications of microcrystalline wax, buffing between each layer, or a combination of these methods.

### Coatings

A scagliola surface that is clean and has retained its original polish may be given a thin coat of microcrystalline wax. The wax should be buffed to a low sheen using a soft cloth. As a general rule varnish type coatings are difficult to remove from porous surfaces such as scagliola and should not be used.

### 16.1.3   Piètre dure

The history, materials and techniques used to create piètre dure surfaces have been described by Giusti (1992). There are two main methods of constructing pietre dure decora-

tion. One method is known as intarsia and, using a technique similar to wood intarsia, the pre-cut pieces of coloured stone are laid into a recessed stone ground, usually marble, which forms part of the design. The other method, known as mosaic or commesso, similar to marquetry used for wood, is to assemble the pieces of the design and adhere them to a stone support. In both cases the pieces are adhered in place with cement or a wax–resin (usually beeswax and colophony) mixture.

### Cleaning

The condition of the structure will define the parameters of the cleaning procedure. If the structure is in good condition and the decorative stone is sound and well adhered, then the materials and techniques described for cleaning marble may be used. Before cleaning, the surface should be checked for evidence of replacements or fills as this may affect the choices for cleaning. Losses or loose pieces should be treated before the surface is cleaned to prevent penetration of cleaning solutions into the adhesive and substrate.

Loose decorative elements may be reattached using a variety of materials depending on the nature and condition of the existing adhesive. If the element is loose but not separate, a consolidant such as Paraloid B72 may be injected underneath to avoid the risk of breakage when trying to lift and relay pieces. A traditional method was to run a melted wax–resin mixture between the pieces. Separated pieces may be readhered using these materials or a two part knife grade polyester, which is usually available in black, white or straw colour. A two part acrylic, such as Akemi®, which is available in both liquid and knife grades, may also be used.

### Fills/losses

Losses may be filled with the materials described above and these may be tinted with pigment as required. Some epoxies, such as HXTAL NYL-1, may provide a higher gloss to the surface of the fill than the materials described above but will require the use of an isolating layer.

### Coatings

The principles and materials outlined above for marble may also be applied to piètre dure.

## 16.2 Plastics

### 16.2.1 Introduction to plastics

Plastic is a generic term incorporating all types of synthetic polymeric materials. These range from the early semi-synthetic materials such as cellulose nitrate to the latest fibre-reinforced composite. Plastic may be used in furniture as a decorative inlay or, in modern objects, it may be the primary material. Different types of plastics have diverse requirements in terms of care and conservation, so it is important to have some idea of the class of material you are dealing with. In some cases knowledge of the date of the plastic, its appearance and properties may be sufficient to allow identification whilst in other cases analytical methods may be required. Techniques for the identification of plastics have been described by Blank (1990), Braun (1982), Morgan (1991), Mossman (1988), van Oosten (1999) and Williamson (1999), whilst Coxon (1993) has discussed the limitations of simple identification methods. An historical overview of the development of plastics may be found in Katz (1986) and Mossman and Morris (1994). Brydson (1995) provides an overview of the properties of historical and modern plastics. Blank (1988, 1990), Grattan (1993), Quye and Williamson (1999) and Sale (1988) provide a useful introduction to the conservation of plastics.

Some plastics, such as cellulose nitrate and poly(vinyl chloride) (PVC), produce acidic off-gassing and/or surface droplets as a side effect of their degradation process. Many polymers, especially those used to produce flexible plastics, may have a sticky surface. This may be a result of degradation (e.g. cellulose nitrate) or oxidation (e.g. rubber). Plasticizers, added to regulate flexibility, may migrate to the surface of the material causing it to become sticky and attract dust and dirt, for example poly(vinyl chloride).

Conservation of plastic can be divided into preventive treatments, designed to control agents of degradation in order to retard the deterioration rate, and interventive conservation, designed to stabilize an object to allow storage or display. Preventive treatments have focused on retarding the rate of degradation. Oxidation and the build up of damaging gases have been identified as the primary mechan-

**Figure 16.3** Detail of red and white polyurethane upholstery from 'Armadillo' designed by Designers Associated Milan, Italy, 1969. Oxidation and loss of plasticizer have caused cracking and peeling of the plastic

isms of degradation of polymers in museum collections. Oxygen scavengers such as Ageless® have been used in closed systems, whilst ventilated storage combined with activated charcoal cloth has been used to address the problem of auto-catalytic reactions as a result of off-gassing (Shashoua and Thomsen, 1993; Ward and Shashoua, 1999).

The conservation of plastics presents many ethical dilemmas as conservators try to balance the requirements for long-term stability or display against removal of original material or reversibility. Treatment may be complicated by accurate identification, complexity of formulation (e.g. co-polymers, plasticizers and other additives), as well as the degree and effects of degradation (*Figure 16.3*). As a result all treatments should be tested cautiously before use. Fenn (1993) has considered the problem of applying acquisition numbers to plastic objects.

### 16.2.2 Cleaning

Accretions of dirt and dust on plastics may be complicated by the presence of plasticizers or acidic degradation products. Although mechanical cleaning is often the least damaging alternative for non-sticky plastics, many plastics are vulnerable to scratching and abrasion, and those with a Tg around room temperature may be vulnerable to indentation. Vigorous polishing may result in a localized temperature rise above Tg and cause softening and damage.

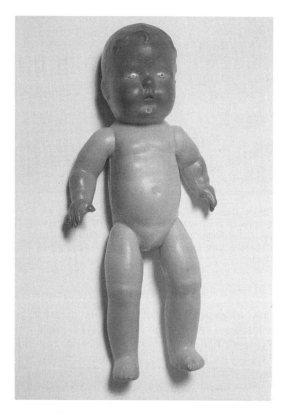

**Figure 16.4**   PVC doll. Discoloration of the face, arms and legs is a result of photochemical degradation and cannot be removed by cleaning

Some plastics, such as casein, may have been surface dyed and such dyes may be mobilized or removed by the use of water or solvents. Many plastic materials may yellow, darken or fade with time but this is a chemical change and no amount of cleaning will return them to their original state (*Figure 16.4*).

As a general rule, plastics have a low surface energy that results in a hydrophobic surface. Urea formaldehyde, for example, has a surface energy of around 61 mJ/m², casein has a surface energy around 43 mJ/m², whilst PVAC and PVAL have a surface energy of around 37 mJ/m² (Blomquist *et al.*, 1983). Liquids can only wet (i.e. spread out) onto materials with a higher surface energy. As a result, water, with a surface energy of 72 mJ/m², will not wet on to many plastics. In spite of this, a swab slightly dampened with water combined with gentle mechanical action is often effective in removing accretions of dirt. The addition of a

small amount of detergent will lower the surface energy of water and allow it to wet plastic surfaces. Whilst detergents may be useful in some cases they can cause stress cracking of some plastics, e.g. poly(ethylene). Detergent residues may cause further degradation, so careful rinsing is required.

Organic solvents may react with many plastics and cause swelling, stress cracking or crazing, and as a result it is often preferable to avoid their use for cleaning and other treatments. Stress is inherent in extruded plastics that have not been annealed and such plastics may be prone to stress cracking if exposed to solvents. This may occur within days after exposure but damage may not become evident for some time. In cases where it is necessary to use a solvent, minimal amounts may be applied by swab to test pieces of a similar material and the surface inspected both immediately afterwards and several days later to see if there is any adverse reaction. The solvent sensitivity of many plastics has been described by Blank (1990) and Sale (1988). This data should be taken as a guide only as there may be more than one formulation of the same plastic, giving rise to different sensitivities.

### 16.2.3   Adhesives and consolidation

Adhesives for plastics are often chosen on the basis of identifying a solvent that will minimize damage, and then choosing an adhesive soluble in this diluent. Ward and Shashoua (1999), for example, selected PVAC in acetone to adhere polyvinyl chloride, due to the low solubility of the material in this solvent. The use of adhesives in general, and consolidation treatments in particular, is often ethically problematic as they are often partially or totally irreversible. The mobility of molecules within plastics often results in contamination of the plastic beyond the adhesive interface. In some cases, such as degraded polyurethane foams, treatment with irreversible consolidants has been preferable to the complete disintegration of the object.

Adhesives used on plastics usually rely on similar solubility parameters to the plastic or chemical interaction with it. Those adhesives or materials with low surface energies are most likely to be effective and success has been reported using a variety of materials including

PVAC, Paraloid B72, ethylene vinyl acetate, methyl cellulose and even isinglass. It can be difficult to find an adhesive that will bond to solid poly(ethylene), which has a surface energy of only 31 mJ/m$^2$.

### 16.2.4 Filling

Many fillers used on other materials can also be used for plastics. The main consideration is that they may not be reversible due to chemical interaction with the plastic. Care must be taken to ensure that the carrier solvent for the filler or resin is compatible with the base polymer of the plastic. Fills can retain solvent for an extended period, acting as a solvent reservoir, and this will exacerbate potential problems. It may be necessary to make allowances for shrinkage as solvent evaporates from the fill or resin polymerizes. Examples of resins that have been used are ethylene vinyl acetate, silicone rubber, epoxy resins, polyester resin and water-based resins.

### 16.2.5 Retouching

Paint media must be able to adhere to the plastic or filler. Acrylic paints in various solvents have been successfully employed for this, though colour matching may be complicated by their tendency to darken slightly as they dry. As with all conservation processes carried out on plastics, the effect of the carrier solvent used in the paint on the base polymer in the plastic must be considered.

### 16.2.6 Coatings

Coatings are not generally recommended for plastics, although in some cases wax has been used to improve the appearance of hard plastics such as bakelite, ebonite and casein.

## 16.3 Upholstery

### 16.3.1 Introduction to upholstery conservation

The primary aim of upholstery conservation is the preservation, examination and documentation of upholstered furniture. Accurate interpretation of the piece within the historical and social context of its setting is another aspect of the work. Upholstery conservation often requires collaboration with conservators experienced in the treatment of textiles, wood, leather, plastic and metal.

Conservation of upholstery is a comparatively recent development in the field of conservation. Until the late 1970s, greater emphasis was placed on aesthetics than on the preservation of upholstery as an important document of historic craft and trade practice. Furniture was often made to look clean, new, tidy and functional by a change of upholstery. Sometimes the top cover was removed, treated if required, and replaced but the supporting structural materials were nearly always removed and generally discarded without being sampled, documented, or stored. The frame was reupholstered with new materials as if it were still functional, the original profiles were lost and the materials were often different and usually of lesser quality than those replaced. Perhaps less than 10% of upholstered furniture in museum collections retains its original upholstery.

The increasing rarity of original upholstery has given it a cachet, linked in part to increased monetary value, which has resulted in a new attitude of respect. An appreciation of the upholders' trade has developed through historic and technological studies and the need to preserve original material has increasingly been recognized. This shift in attitude has resulted in a change in the acquisition policies of some institutions that has a knock-on effect on the commercial market.

General references on the conservation of upholstery include Gill and Eastop (2001) and Williams (1990). James (1990) describes upholstery techniques clearly. French (1990) and Landi (1992) are valuable sources on the conservation of textiles associated with upholstery. White (1993) describes gaining access to loose joints in the frame with minimal disturbance of upholstery layers.

Increased interest and awareness of the development and history of upholstery under structures, materials and technological advancements has influenced approaches to treatments. Conservation treatments have been developed that consider the object in its entirety, that is the frame, outer-covering, trimmings and concealed inner structure. Treatments may range from minimal in situ work to the removal, conservation and reapplication of all materials or, alternatively, to the replacement of inaccurate interventions (upholstery additions or replacements) with more appropriate materials or historically based interventions. Where practicable, the objects are placed in a controlled environment. It is necessary to differentiate between objects with upholstery which merit conservation and those that do not. Whilst a specialist upholstery conservator is in the best position to either treat or advise, some objects may be treated by reputable craftspeople, using materials and techniques specified by a historian or conservator.

All objects should be assessed individually and treatments proposed on a case-by-case basis in the context of current conservation ethics. Broadly speaking, the treatment factors to be considered for upholstery are based on the same principles as for other furniture types. They include the nature of the materials and current condition, the end use of the furnishing, the nature of the furniture collection, the significance and effects of later interventions, budget and time constraints, availability of materials, facilities and expertise. Thorough examination of the object and documentation is essential before treatment begins.

## 16.3.2   Ethics

The ethical dilemmas that face an upholstery conservator often mirror those in the broader profession, for example balancing preservation requirements against demands for study, display or use. Other dilemmas have their roots in historical approaches to the presentation of interiors. The incorporation of historic colours into furnishing textiles, for example, has often drawn on an aesthetic with roots in the nineteenth century revivalist movement. Furnishings have been based on 'authentic' colours derived from aged textiles rather than an original unfaded state. Dress fabrics from previous centuries have on occasion been re-interpreted in a similar way. In some cases this approach has been taken a step further, with the desire to incorporate surviving textiles into new interpretations of historical interiors. Thus, on occasion, upholstery conservators may be asked to marry historic textiles to upholstery with which they have not been associated.

Many upholstery conservators believe such marriages are in conflict with professional ethical guidelines. Such requests often pay little heed to the historical use of fabric weight and construction, fibre type, design, size or trimmings. Practical concerns in using historic textiles include the time and costs entailed in preparing these degraded artefacts for use. Such textiles may require cleaning and conservation to make them stable enough to withstand the handling necessary for re-application to the frame. Historical textiles, even after conservation, are likely to require replacement sooner than replicas.

Advances in furniture and textile studies by historians, curators and conservators have resulted in a re-examination of the presentation of upholstered furniture and the use of historic textiles as replacement top coverings. The use of historic textiles has become less acceptable within the context of a greater respect for preservation and accurate interpretation of upholstery. The use of reproduction period fabrics based on document textiles (those with documentary evidence to support an ascribed date) has become an accepted practice among conservators and curators (Gill and Eastop, 2001; Nylander, 1990). The quality, choice and cost of reproduction has often been a factor in the choice of treatment. However, the quality of reproduction fabrics has improved in response to the demands of museums as discerning customers. The increased acceptance of the practice of using reproductions has resulted in collaborative ordering and purchase by museums and a wider choice being available from stock. This has reduced costs, as may the purchase of undyed yardage for piece dyeing different colours.

Curators often have legitimate concerns in using reproduction textiles. For example, a new textile or leather reproduction used as an upholstery covering often appears too lustrous and bright against the patina of an aged historic finish or mellowed wood. To overcome the high lustre, a different material may be substituted. Mercerized cotton, for example, is closer in appearance than new silk as a replacement for aged silk. Textile and leathers may be purchased in an undyed state to allow them to be dyed to a more appropriate tone. Small yardage can be dyed in-house by a conservator, whilst bulk quantities may be piece-dyed by contract. Although this may raise new issues of interpretation, these may be overcome by accurate labelling and/or display of mounted document textiles or leather in close proximity to the upholstered furniture.

### 16.3.3 Examination and documentation of upholstery

Although upholstery structures present some problems of examination, it is not essential to dismantle an object for documentation. Inaccessible layers may be observed through areas of damage or the use of X-ray photography may allow a limited record to be made (Gill and Eastop, 2001). A small area of upholstery may sometimes be temporarily lifted for examination, for example if authentication before purchase is necessary. Such examination may establish the presence or absence of extra tack holes. An absence of extra tack holes can indicate that extant upholstery materials are original to the frame, if the section of frame under examination is contemporary with the rest of the object. The type of metal fastener or upholstery material may provide further information on the date of the artefact or the intervention. A machine stamped tack, for example, might indicate the addition of new material or a dealers 'marriage' if found securing an eighteenth-century fabric to an eighteenth-century frame. Similarly, woven jute cloth indicates a date of application of *c*.1850 or later.

### 16.3.4 Previous interventions

Upholstery is subject to change as a result of changes in taste and physical decay. Previous interventions may include revisions of upholstery such as additional stuffing to change profile, previous repairs or modernizations. Upholstery may be significant to the collector because of, rather than in spite of, such changes.

Previous interventions may be retained if they are considered to be of historic significance. One example of this is a chair designed by William Burges with rush seating that was later upholstered with a William Morris fabric by the designer himself for his own use. The object is now in a collection displaying material associated with William Morris (Gill and Eastop, 2001).

Previous interventions may be removed if they are causing damage to original materials or visually distort the artist, designer, or makers' original intentions. Such decisions should be made jointly between conservator and curator or owner. They should be based on sound evidence gleaned from the object and from contemporary sources including photographs, written descriptions and original textile fragments. Treatment to reverse previous interventions should ideally stabilize original material, whilst replacement materials and techniques should be based on sound historical evidence. Decisions made in the context of an historic interior may not be easily resolved. The way in which notions of intention, identity, context and aesthetics lead to one course of action rather than another have been considered by Trupin and Moore (1990).

Degraded or unstable frames may require stabilization, which may be achieved by introducing additional external support in situ. A chair seat, for example, may be supported from underneath by means of an independent frame, across which is stretched new webbing or other suitable support material (*Figure 16.5*). In situ treatments may be the only options available. Some materials, for example, may be too weak to withstand the handling necessary for removal and reapplication. In other instances the components of some pieces, particularly those manufactured in the twentieth century, were applied with special tools and machinery, making it difficult or impossible to dismantle individual layers. Materials that could otherwise be removed for treatment may not fit back on the frame correctly after treatment due to extra thickness created by support fabric(s) used in the treatment. In cases where materials can be removed and reapplied, the original method of reapplication may have to be modified to reduce further damage to the frame and upholstery layers.

Previous adhesive conservation or repair treatments are often a cause for concern, for example where yellowing and embrittlement occur. The use of synthetic adhesives on upholstery dates from the first quarter of the twentieth century. One example, found in a publication by the UK Department of Scientific and Industrial Research (1926), describes the use of a 2.5% solution of cellulose acetate in

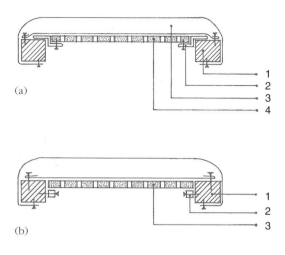

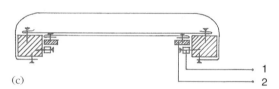

**Figure 16.5** Cross sectional views of different support systems for the underside of a seat or an outer back upholstery section. Parts (*a*) and (*b*) illustrate two systems suitable for a rigid or semi-rigid material such as acid-free card or acrylic sheet. Part (*c*) illustrates a system suitable for a flexible support such as polypropylene mesh
(*a*) Vented rigid support (4), attached to an 'S' shaped metal fixing system (2) that slips between the upholstery (3) and the rail (1)
(*b*) A more invasive method: it relies on wooden batons (2) screwed directly into the rail (1) to hold the vented rigid support (3)
(*c*) System suitable for a flexible support such as polypropylene mesh: the mesh is attached to an independent stretcher (2) that in turn is held to the frame with a baton (1) in the same way as in (*b*). This system could be adapted to the bracket system illustrated in (*a*)

acetone as a consolidant for the surface of a tapestry chair cover. Whilst some old adhesives can be removed by aqueous or solvent solutions, these are often inappropriate for uphol-stered objects. Another problem that may be encountered on some textiles associated with furniture, e.g. beds, is the combination of residues composed of starch and protein. Starch may have been applied to textiles to 'set' the stitches or act as a moisture barrier to pre-vent wetting, staining and distortion before the textile was adhered to wood with animal glue. Enzyme gels (see section 11.5.6) may be an alternative for removing adhesive residues from textiles on furniture, such as desk tops, card tables, boxes. In cases where starch and protein are combined, enzymatic treatment may combine protease and amylase (Bott, 1990). Enzymatic treatments are potentially problematic as many materials, such as silk and leather, may also be attacked by enzymes. The removal of latex adhesives has been consid-ered by Leach (1995).

### 16.3.5 Condition of the frame

An upholstered piece may have undergone several re-upholstery treatments before acquisi-tion. Repeated treatments may damage a frame to the extent that some intervention is required to preserve it. In the examination of uphol-stered furniture it is common to encounter frame repairs, disparagingly known as 'uphol-sterer's repairs' by furniture conservators. These repairs are usually the product of an upholsterer working in isolation with few (if any) woodworking skills. Simple, cheap and quick repairs of this type include bandages glued to rails, sawdust and glue fillings, and cardboard fills. From the upholstery conserva-tor's viewpoint, such repairs are preferable to alternatives such as replacement of whole rails or cutting out split or damaged sections and replacing them with new wood, which destroys all information about the original upholstery and devalues the object as an his-torical artefact.

Crude modifications to the frame may also be encountered. Two of the more commonly occurring ones are chamfering or rasping rails to provide a tacking surface, and the addition of horizontal and vertical tacking rails to pre-nineteenth century wing chairs or settees in order to simplify reupholstery.

### 16.3.6 Materials

Materials generally available to trade uphol-sterers are often inappropriate for use in con-servation because of modern manufacturing methods such as finishes, quality and the use of fire retardants.

Textiles used in upholstery conservation should be ordered in the loom state and finish-free. The advice of a textile conservator should be sought to assess whether finishes applied to the textile are compatible with conservation requirements and to advise on methods to test for finishes and techniques to remove those that are not appropriate (see, for example, Landi's (1992) comments on testing materials, preparation of support fabrics and pre-shrinking).

Where additions for rebuilding or supplements to existing layers are required, stable synthetic filling materials may be substituted for natural or unstable synthetic materials. Corrosion resistant metals such as Monel metal, a nickel–copper alloy or stainless steel are usually chosen for conservation use, and the smallest size and least number appropriate to the job are used. In addition to materials that would be familiar to any upholsterer, upholstery conservators often make supports for museum materials that are based on stabilizing the object rather than the traditional criteria of seating comfort.

### 16.3.7  Non-invasive treatments

#### *Surface cleaning*
Loose dust and dirt may be removed with a low powered vacuum cleaner through a screening material made from a conservation grade non-woven fabric net (e.g. Reemay™, a polyester fibre fabric with a non-woven structure) to prevent loss of material into the vacuum cleaner. This material can be used loose or stretched on a frame between the object and the vacuum cleaner. Alternatively, it can cover the nozzle or be inserted between extension tubes. A filter attached to the cleaner should not severely interrupt the vacuum flow or lead to overheating. A water trap may be used on micro-vacuums. This is important as it is possible to check what is being removed from the object. Fragile fibre surfaces may be vacuumed from a textile, and a filter check allows the conservator top check whether too much fibre is being removed. Soils collected in vacuum traps may be saved for analysis.

In cases where the upholstery filling is in robust condition, vibration with gentle tamping may be used to dislodge loose soiling, such as dust or frass, trapped in the layer structure.

Dust raised in this way should be removed with a vacuum cleaner. It may be possible, for example with cane or fibre-bottom seating, to remove such loose soiling using two vacuum cleaners, the first set to blow on a slightly lower power setting than the second, used to vacuum dirt away.

Some surface soils may require gentle mechanical cleaning using brushes, dry cleaning materials (see section 11.2.4) or, for example in the case of encrustations, the cautious use of a sharp blade. Short stiff brushes may be used with a tamping action to break up encrusted surface deposits, whilst soft long-haired brushes may be used to stroke loose surface deposits away from the surface in combination with a vacuum cleaner. Solvent swab cleaning, subject to spot tests, may be considered for lightly bound greasy surface soils.

The use of proprietary upholstery cleaners is not recommended. These products work by a foaming action that pushes soiling material from the surface of the piece, before foam and soil are vacuumed away. Since residues are not rinsed from the textile, there is a danger they will interact with original material and cause damage. Other problems may include over-wetting of the textile and support, pH changes and stains being drawn from the upholstery filling into the top cover. Steam cleaning is inappropriate for historic material as the evaporating water may pull more soiling to the surface and the heat may cause damage. The combination of heat and water may in fact act to prevent the removal of dirt or cause differential shrinkage or staining. 'Wet and dry' vacuum cleaners are also not appropriate because the suction required to lift out water will damage weak textile or upholstery materials. Fabric protector spray finishes are inappropriate for historic upholstery as they may break down over time and attract dirt (Smith, 1983).

#### *Semi-transparent coverings*
A fragile top cover may be protected by a semi-transparent fabric with an open structure. This may enclose the whole upholstery component and either be fastened to itself at the rear/underside of the component or to an independent panel by means of stitching or a fastener such as Velcro®. Similar treatments were utilized in the nineteenth century, when coarse (fishing net quality) nets of cotton or wool were used. The

principle behind the treatment remains the same, although modern materials, such as net, leno, gauze or knits, offer fine mesh size, better width of material and may be based on silk or nylon net and silk or polyester crepeline.

### Case covers

Upholstery can be protected from dust and light damage with case covers. Fine furniture was often historically protected with 'cases' of fabric or leather. These were distinct from storage dust covers and were often of a decorative quality. They were used as daily furnishings and could be removed for special occasions. A conservator or curator may design reproductions of period case covers. Cases should be lined with a light, smooth, slippery fabric that will prevent abrasion of the top covers when the cases are applied or removed.

### Stabilizing with repairs

Detached, loose and missing areas may be stabilized by means of patches, either over top surfaces or inserted through missing areas to rest between layers. The technique used to attach patches, e.g. stitching or adhesives, should be reversible and suitable to the type of material and its condition. Further discussion on patching may be found in Landi (1992) and Brooks *et al.* (1995).

### Supports

The underside of a seat or outer back panel may be supported with a rigid or semi-rigid material such as acid-free card, acrylic sheet or polypropylene mesh. The support should be vented with holes to allow free passage of air, and may use a fixing system that slips between the upholstery and the rail (see *Figure 16.5*; Balfour *et al.*, 1999; Sheetz, 1989).

## 16.3.8   Invasive treatments

To some degree most invasive treatments will irreversibly change some aspect(s) of the original construction. Some forethought is required to decide if and how the removed layers will be reapplied. Consider what will be used to replace the layers if they are retired to storage.

### Removal and documentation

It is important to document dimensions, order of application and condition as far as possible before disassembly. This information is required both to meet professional standards of ethics and to reassemble the object. Note the number of metal fasteners and their corresponding holes. Any extra holes and metal fasteners may suggest earlier interventions or that the layer has been removed and reapplied. To the practised eye, location and size of holes may suggest specific layers and an original style of upholstery and trim. Sometimes fragments of fibres will be found embedded in the corrosion products of hardware. Oxidized or compressed wood may show the location of a former layer, for example webbing, caning,

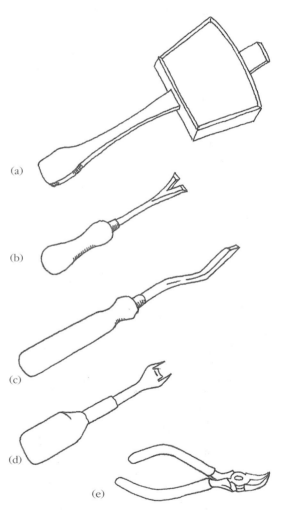

**Figure 16.6**   A selection of tools used for removing metal fastenings: (*a*) mallet; (*b*) tack lifter; (*c*) ripping chisel; (*d*) staple lifter; (*e*) oblique-headed side cutters

springs, iron tacks, or brass nailing patterns. Rubbings taken from rails may be useful for recording this type of information.

### Metal fixings

It is often necessary to remove decorative and other nails to carry out full conservation treatment of the upholstery layers. During removal, aim to minimize damage to the metal fasteners, frame and upholstery materials. A variety of small blunt-ended tools are used for this purpose, including tack lifters, blunt screw drivers, small blunt side pincers and staple lifters (*Figure 16.6*). They are usually inserted under, or used to grip round, the head of a tack or bar of a staple, which are then eased out by levering the tool to gently dislodge the shank. Both textile and frame should be cushioned from damage using small softwood wedges or expanded polyethylene foam pads. If the fasteners are to be replaced in the same holes after treatment, they may be stored by pushing them into a piece of card or a block of soft material, with their location recorded both next to each nail and on a photo or diagram of the object. It is advisable to place a sheet of acid-free blotter between the block and the tack/nail head to absorb any condensation that may occur. In cases where a metal fastener is embedded into a fragile material or if the fastener is corroded, a scalpel cut around the tack or staple may be the only way to release the material and allow removal without the danger of bruising the wood, breaking the fastener or tearing the material.

The cleaning and conservation of metal is discussed in section 15.3. Chemical removal of corrosion products is often unsuitable for in situ treatments on upholstery because of the risk that the solution will wick into and stain the adjacent textile. Corrosion products on iron, brass and other copper alloys may be removed with gentle mechanical action. A coating may be required after such treatment.

With the exception of staples, which cannot be reused, reapplication using the original metal fasteners in their original holes has the advantage of not damaging the frame by creating more holes. This approach often requires an existing hole to be packed, for example with Ethafoam™ or bamboo, to ensure the metal fastener is firmly attached to the frame. This can be very time-consuming, however, and may not always provide enough tension.

In many cases original nails may be severely corroded or damaged and cannot be reused. Often the shanks of nails snap off, either during removal due to the twisted angle of the shank within the wood, or during reapplication. It is possible to solder such breaks but the joint remains weak and the heat required may damage original coatings. Small or unusual-sized nails can be difficult to obtain, especially in small quantities. If new metal fasteners are to be used, a corrosion resistant metal such as Monel metal (largely nickel and copper with traces of aluminium, silicon, iron, manganese), copper, brass, or stainless steel is preferable to iron.

Dome-headed decorative nails with damaged or missing shanks may be converted to buttons and stitched back in place. A small ring, such as a jewellery fitting, may be embedded into resin in the head of the nail, which can then be stitched into place on the object. It may be possible for the conservator to make their own replacement decorative nails. The blank for a domed nail can be punched from a sheet of brass using an ordinary metal punch and then shaped using a dapping (or doming) punch. The slight variations produced by this do-it-yourself technique are an advantage when matching hand-wrought fasteners. The domes can be 'pickled' to dull them or toned with tinted varnish. If the brass sheet was lacquered, the coating should be removed (e.g. with paint stripper) before pickling. The brass domes can be fumed using ammonium hydroxide on cotton wool in a plastic container. About twenty minutes is a guide time but experimentation will be required to match the colour of historic fasteners. White spirit should be used to degrease the surface before the application of a coating.

The domes may be soldered or adhered to shanks or tacks, though this is usually time-consuming. The heads can also be applied to replica top covers fabrics or leathers with hot-melt polyamide adhesive or can be converted to buttons for application to period covers. A line of stitching with a curved needle is often required to create dimples in the fabric to give the appearance of the nail 'biting' into the textile and frame.

### Cleaning

Individual layers or whole upholstery fillings may be cleaned using water or solvents.

Aqueous cleaning will remove water-soluble soils and often improve flexibility. It may raise post-treatment pH because acidic degradation materials have been removed. Cleaning bath additives can enhance control of pH during washing and the removal of dirt. Weak and fragile textiles may require support during cleaning to minimize further damage and fibre loss. Disadvantages of aqueous cleaning include the possible presence of dyes that are fugitive or pH-sensitive, and water-soluble finishes. There is a danger that aqueous cleaning will cause distortion (e.g. tent stitched canvas) or result in the shrinkage of cellulosic materials in the filling or its covers as they are wetted. Differential drying may cause ring staining (e.g. crewel work). Textiles that are not sufficiently robust to be restretched to their original dimensions should not be aqueously cleaned.

Solvent cleaning will remove oily or greasy soiling. Systems that include some detergent-bound water, known as charged systems, may remove some water-based soils as well. Whilst small quantities of solvents may be used within a fume hood, large quantities require the use of a closed system, though the mechanical action of some large systems may prevent their use for conservation treatments. Solvent cleaning has a tendency to over-dry the textile and humidification may be needed afterwards. As a general rule, commercial dry cleaning should be avoided.

### Supports

It may be necessary to introduce a supporting element in cases where the original upholstery or any of its elements is no longer strong enough to support its own weight, or where webbing is being damaged by tension or pressure from springs. A support may consist of a solid element introduced to support the structure from underneath secured with clips, hooks, tacks or staples (*Figure 16.5a,b*). Weakened textiles or cane may be supported with patches or fully lined with a textile so that they are stable enough to support their own weight and reapplication to the unit under the required tension.

Compression springs incorporated into an upholstery structure are compressed and tied down into position with twine. When the twine degrades, the compression is released and the springs can burst through the top or bottom of the upholstery. In such cases individual springs may be recompressed using three lengths of wire, secured at equally spaced points around the circumference of the spring and around the upper and lower section of the spring.

Supporting or lining materials need to be both flexible and strong enough not to be readily deformed by movement in objects. The materials used often compromise between these requirements. Factors that guide the choice of supporting materials include:

- The support material should not contribute to the further degradation of an object by chemical or physical means – for example, it should not give off acidic vapours or have markedly different responses to environmental conditions than the material to be supported
- The support material should be of appropriate colour, thickness, lustre, ease of application, availability and cost
- Textiles should be finish-free or have a finish that is easily removed and should be easily dyed, if required, using simple methods and equipment
- The movement and strength of the support or lining should be compatible with that of the object, i.e. strong enough to function well but not so strong that it might cut through or damage an aged textile – compatibility remains an important issue during ageing
- The material should have long-term stability and good ageing properties
- Additions to the object should be able to be isolated or easily detected on examination so as not to devalue the item for analysis as a historical document
- Choice of a support fabric is important as a fabric that is too thick or heavy may cause bulkiness, spoil the line of the furniture or the frame, or prevent a detachable unit, for example a slip seat, from fitting back into the main frame
- Hygroscopic properties are a consideration in choosing a support fabric. Moisture may be wicked away from the original materials by the support fabric so that the support fabric acts as an environmental buffer. Conversely, moisture absorption may add weight to the support fabric. Moisture may also be attracted from the atmosphere by the support fabric, transferring it to the object.

### Reapplication of lined textiles

Stapling a textile can cause less damage to the textile and frame than the use of tacks. A wide range of corrosion-resistant staples is available, and staple guns will cause less vibration than a tack hammer. Where possible, one staples only through the support lining of a conserved textile and not through the textile itself, although textiles may be stapled directly to the frame where the extra bulk of a lining would be a problem. When extra bulk is not a major concern, cloth covered card or polyester/polypropylene strips stapled to the frame will provide a stitching ground for the lined textile. Use of a stitching ground reduces the number of metal fasteners required and therefore reduces damage to the frame. Stitching the lined textile to such a ground gives more even tension since the line of stitching is continuous, unlike the localized tension of metal fasteners. Pins are used to apply and maintain tension during stitching.

### Storage for study as an alternative to reapplication

If the upholstery is too fragile or distorted to be conserved in situ, then documentation, removal and preparation for study or storage may be the best option. With a detachable upholstery unit such as a slip seat, the whole frame could be retired to storage and a new one made for display. This is also a good option for upholstered furniture in private collections where the owner wishes objects to remain in use. A disadvantage of removing fixed upholstery from the frame is that the unit will lose its form unless reattached to a replica rigid frame for study.

### Independent sub-frames

Independent sub-frames may be used to provide the foundation to which new materials are attached. The aim of such treatment is to simulate the appearance of conventional upholstery whilst minimizing or eliminating the use of metal fasteners, thus preventing further damage to the frame. Independent detachable sub-frames may be slotted into, clamped to, or simply rest on, the surface of the original frame, to allow access to the original frame for study or display. Textile extensions on the sub-frame may be wrapped around the original frame to secure and position the new frame. The uphol-

stery profile may be built up onto the sub-frame using conventional techniques or high density expanded polyethylene foam. High density expanded polyethylene foam can itself be cut to slot onto the original frame, eliminating the need for a separate sub-frame. Expanded polyethylene foam may be shaped to the desired profile, lightly padded and covered in the appropriate fabric. Further damage to the frame from the use of reproduction dome headed decorative nails can be avoided by converting them to buttons, which are then stitched in place or glued directly to the reproduction textile (see discussion of metal fixings on p. 727 and Gill and Eastop, 2001).

### 16.3.9 Rush, reed and cane

Treatment of plant materials such as rush, reed and cane may be aimed at stabilization and prevention of loss of material, replacement of areas of disfiguring loss or humidification to allow distortions to be reshaped. A conservator with experience of these materials should be consulted before humidification, deacidification or repairs are undertaken. Although there are many craft books available, the techniques described in them are often inappropriate for conservation treatments.

Examination will reveal whether a woven component is structurally sound. Documentation may include the size(s) of cane and mesh, the number of holes in the frame and position of pegs, and the pattern of weave. Previous repairs may be revealed under UV light. Surface dirt and dust may be removed using a low powered vacuum cleaner. Florian *et al.* (1990) discuss the conservation of artefacts fashioned from plant materials whilst Doyal (1999) discussed the use of traditional and innovative materials in twentieth century cordage and basketry seating.

### Rehumidification

Plant material loses its ability to recover its shape over a period of use. In use, the durability of these materials is linked to flexibility. Rewetting plant materials was often advocated as a maintenance treatment in the past. Stokes (1852) for example, recommended that

*To clean and restore the elasticity of cane chair bottoms, couches & c. Turn up the chair bottom, and with hot water and a sponge wash the cane-work so that it may be thoroughly soaked. Should it be dirty, use a little soap, let it dry in the air, and it will be as tight and firm as when new, provided the cane be not broken.*

Such treatment of plant material in historic furniture is inappropriate because it may be too weak to withstand the stress caused by tightening as it dries. Reshaping using rehumidification may be possible but differential shrinkage, staining or colour loss may occur. Previous 'maintenance' treatments, such as annual oiling, coating with shellac, other varnishes or paint may have been undertaken to allow the surface to be easily wiped down. On balance, there is no evidence that these treatments did any good and they may have caused harm in some cases. Such coatings may preclude humidification treatments.

Plant materials may be humidified by a variety of techniques including contact humidification, misting with a spray or ultrasonic humidifier, by enclosing the object in a humidity chamber or the use of moisture-permeable membranes such as Gore-Tex (Britton, 1994; Doyal, 1999). 'Contact' humidification involves sandwiching the object between layers of wet and dry materials to elevate humidity without saturation or direct contact with water. The bottom layer of the sandwich may contain wet linen or damp acid-free blotting paper over which are placed at least six layers of dry linen or acid free blotting paper. The object is placed on top and a spacer layer is suspended over the object. A layer of polythene sheet is placed over the top to contain the humidity, which rises through the object. The spacer layer, which may be acid-free tissue or a permeable membrane such as Gore-Tex™ or Sympatex™, stops the polythene from coming into contact with the object and prevents any condensation that may form on the polythene from dripping back down onto the object.

A humidity chamber can be a simple polythene tent or a purpose-built climate chamber. Water or a range of conditioned gels or buffering agents can be used to increase control of humidity changes around the object.

### Deacidification
As with other organic materials, cellulosic materials become more acidic in time. There may be concerns that excessive acidity can lead to accelerated autocatalytic degradation and conservators may wish to measure pH. The standard method for measuring pH requires maceration of a sample in water. In cases where destructive sampling is not acceptable, a drop of distilled water may be applied to a dust-free surface. A non-bleeding pH paper may then be applied, weighted (e.g. with a glass plate) and left for a few minutes. Although this is not a very accurate method it can be a less intrusive alternative to destructive sampling. A pH of 3 or below might be considered a problem, as may a slightly less acidic pH that is associated with embrittlement. If a small test deacidification provided an increase in flexibility, overall deacidification may be appropriate. Deacidification need not necessarily be undertaken for its own sake.

Deacidification of plant materials has been achieved in some cases by washing in water, application of neutralizing buffer solutions by spray or immersion, exposure to alkaline vapours, or by the use of particulate alkaline buffers that are then brushed and vacuumed away. All of these treatments should be approached with extreme caution and may cause darkening of plant material.

### Repair
Techniques used to repair plant materials are often based on techniques of manufacture, for example, patching with new material. Other techniques rely on mechanical (stitched) or adhesive repairs. These can include sandwiching the original between two layers of semi-transparent fabric stitched around the breaks.

### 16.3.10   Imitation leather

Imitation leather, often called leatherette, is often based on vinyl polymers. Thorp (1990) has considered its structure, composition and conservation treatments. Previous repairs to this type of material may have encompassed the repair of cigarette burns, cuts, tears and surface abrasions. Repairs may have been undertaken using proprietary kits based on a thermoplastic resinous filling, textured when still soft using grained papers. This technique may be adopted by conservators using reversible materials.

## 16.4 Leather, parchment and shagreen

### 16.4.1 Leather

Leather is often incorporated into furniture as an upholstery material, writing surfaces (often called skivers) and drawer pulls, laid onto the outside surface of boxes and chests and occasionally leather handles on chests. Leather associated with furniture often has a dyed finish, either as part of the processing and preparation of the leather or applied when the leather was incorporated into the object. Dyes are typically fugitive and will fade if exposed to light/UV. Leather often has tooled or stamped decoration, which may be blind (i.e. just tooled) or gilded. On occasions, leather may have been painted, gilded and varnished, for example some nineteenth century English furniture has painted decoration on top of a varnish applied to the leather. Shrinkage temperature may be used to identify new leather, but is progressively less accurate as the leather degrades.

At present there is no standard text for the conservation of leather, though one is planned in the Butterworths Museology series (Kite and Thomson, eds). The structure, material properties, composition and ageing of leather are discussed in Chapter 3 of this present text, the Leather Conservation Centre (1981) and Calnan and Haines (1991). Articles on the history and technology of leather may be found in the *Journal of the Society of Leather Technologists and Chemists*. General references on the conservation of leather include Sturge (2000), van Soest *et al.* (1984), Calnan (1991) and Hallebeek *et al.* (1992). Conservation periodicals include *Leather Conservation News* (US) and the ICOM Leather Group Newsletter. Koldeweij (1992) provides an overview of the history of gilt or 'Spanish' leather, although specialist advice should be sought before undertaking the treatment of such decorated leather. Bennett (1990) describes the process of laying a new leather writing surface.

#### *Evaluating the surface of the leather*
The first step in the conservation treatment of leather is to evaluate its condition. Conservators should examine leather for evidence of physical damage, biological attack, chemical degradation and the presence and effects of previous dressings.

Physical deterioration may range from leather with its surface and any coatings intact, to light wear such as abrasion, scratches or dents, to that which has been subject to heavy wear and may be torn, the surface of the leather worn or abraded away, exposing the fibre bundles. Biological damage may occur in the form of mould growth that results in spotting on the surface, or holes from woodworm which have attacked substrate material and exited the object through the leather. Mould is particularly associated with leather that has been excessively dressed or oiled in the past. Both forms of biological attack will only occur in conditions of excessively high RH and will cease if RH falls below 68%.

Chemical deterioration of leather can have many causes, including atmospheric pollutants, metal contaminants and previous maintenance treatments. Acidic deterioration, also known as red rot, attacks vegetable tanned leather. Acid induced oxidative breakdown of leather causes the layers of fibre bundles to separate. The term red rot refers to the characteristic appearance of the leather, which is powdery, red and brittle, and is often accompanied by an acrid odour. Red rot is particularly associated with poor environmental conditions. It is caused by atmospheric pollutants which produce highly acidic reaction products ($H_2SO_4$) and is exacerbated by low RH. Black rot, partly caused by iron contamination, may be found on archeological vegetable and native tanned leather but is uncommon in leather associated with furniture. Affected leather is black, powdery and brittle, though there is no associated odour. Surface salts, which are also uncommon on leather in furniture, may be visible as small white crystalline deposits and are caused by improper tanning or inappropriate past treatments, often linked to poor environmental conditions.

Previous maintenance treatments and dressings are a significant cause of the deterioration of leather. Dressings are based on various types of fats and oils and are often applied in the mistaken belief that they will 'feed', preserve or soften leather. In some cases, particularly social history objects such as leather buckets, 50% of the overall weight of an object may be composed of old dressings. Oxidized oily dressings within the leather cause it to darken and become embrittled. In time, components such as free fatty acids that are solid at room temperature may crystallize out on the surface of the leather to form spews (or spues), which are often visible as white spots. The previous use of saddle soap, which has a pH of 9–10, may cause significant deterioration because it destabilizes the acidity level of the surface of the leather (Haines and Calnan, 1988). In the long term this lowers the shrinkage temperature at the surface of the leather and causes severe cracking. In some cases the cracked leather may cup and expose the flesh below.

### Cleaning

As well as the dirt encountered on many objects (e.g. dust, soot, fungal spores etc.), there are particular types of soiling associated with leather. Oils that have been applied in the past to dress the leather, as well as fats and oils from within the leather itself, can migrate to the surface and are known as known as 'fatty spues'. Writing and other horizontal surfaces may have stains associated with their use such as ink, water, wine, food etc. Staining may result from residues of metal polishing compounds, particularly around metal studs. White residues mixed with small amounts of abraded metal are not uncommon, whilst components from metal polishes which are absorbed into the body of the leather may leave a dark halo around the studs. Staining from metal corrosion products is not usually a significant problem. Unvarnished surfaces are prone to a build up of ingrained oily dirt, e.g. from handling and fingermarks. Past maintenance treatments such as wax, oil and leather dressings are often discoloured and serve to bind dirt to the leather.

It is essential to evaluate the type of soiling that is present and consider the effect of a proposed treatment on both unwanted dirt or coatings and on the leather itself. Leather is a porous material and acts as a sponge, drawing liquid and solubilized dirt deeper into the body of the leather. This behaviour is minimized when the surface of the leather is freshly tanned and intact, but is exacerbated in old and abraded leather. Dirt may be lifted from the surface using swabs slightly dampened with solvent. As a general rule the surface should not be flooded with solvent or other cleaning solutions. Polar solvents (e.g. acetone) can affect the chemical additives applied to the leather in the tanning process, known as tannage. Non-polar solvents are markedly less likely to damage the leather.

Loose dirt may be removed with a soft brush and a vacuum cleaner. This is usually safe for leather with an intact or abraded surface. Dry cleaning methods, described in section 11.2.4, may be used if the surface is sufficiently robust. Such treatments should always be pre-tested in an inconspicuous area because in some cases, particularly when the leather has a low pH, the fibre bundles may have deteriorated to such an extent that even light pressure will remove the whole surface. Non-polar hydrocarbon solvents may be used to remove wax or oily deposits from intact or abraded leather. The use of a swab slightly dampened with solvent should reduce the likelihood of solubilized material being absorbed into the body of uncoated, porous leather. Leather with an intact surface may be cleaned with a swab slightly dampened with water. Water is problematic for abraded leather because it can cause stains, tidelines and can catalyse acidic deterioration. Further, capillary action may pull solubilized soils from the surface into the body of the leather. Fungal accretions may be removed by vacuuming or swabs dampened with IMS or ethanol swabs, having pre-tested these in an inconspicuous area. Mould stains cannot be easily removed.

### Chemical stabilization

The porous nature of leather results in the absorption of both acidic and alkaline pollutants which catalyse degradation. pH measurement has been used to gauge the condition of leather because acidic deterioration will occur at a pH of 3 or below. If the leather has absorbed alkaline pollutants a pH measurement may indicate a higher overall pH but is not necessarily an accurate indicator of chemical stability. Whilst pH measurement may be useful, a careful visual inspection of the overall condition of the leather, checking for a dry appearance, acrid smell, or powdery structure is often a better indicator of overall condition.

Treatments intended to stabilize the acidity of vegetable tanned leather and thus halt chemical degradation have often used aluminium salts such as aluminium sulphate, aluminium triformate or aluminium alkoxide. These salts were used to saturate the flesh (underside) of the leather. Because aluminium sulphate and aluminium triformate were added from aqueous solutions, the benefit of the salts on the leather was often outweighed by the damage caused by the water carrier. Aluminium alkoxide, however, is applied in a non-polar solvent carrier and is therefore inherently safer. There have often been unrealistic expectation of what can be achieved using such treatments, which can stabilize pH and the chemical deterioration of the collagen/tannin complex, resulting in a significant increase in shrinkage temperature. The mechanical properties of the leather, however, remain unchanged. Success is somewhat dependent on operator skill and treatments have caused surface darkening of the leather. Accelerated aging experiments have suggested that retanning treatments may exacerbate deterioration in the long term (Larsen *et al.*, 1996).

### Consolidation

Leather that is powdery or flaking may require consolidation. Whilst maximum penetration of consolidant into the leather is desirable to prevent later delamination, it has been suggested that the maximum average penetration of a consolidating material is approximately 50% of the thickness of the leather. Penetration will be assisted by the use of dilute solutions and low molecular weight and small particle size.

The fundamental principle of the consolidation of leather is to avoid solidifying the structure of the leather. This means that many common conservation consolidants are inappropriate. Paraloid B72, for example, saturates and darkens the surface of the leather and has a solidifying effect on the structure. Other resins with a glass transition temperature (Tg) higher than the ambient room, display or storage temperature are similarly inappropriate. Although cellulose ethers such as Klucel® have been used in the past because they do not darken abraded leather, they are no longer widely used because they are comparatively chemically unstable and there are better alternatives for the consolidation of leather.

Ideally, consolidants for leather should have a Tg around room temperature for maximum flexibility, a pH in the range of 5.5–8, though within this range adhesives with a higher pH

(a)

(b)

**Figure 16.7** Application of consolidant from a pipette (a) on a nineteenth century shoe from Northampton Central Museum and using a heated spatula (b) to heat set the consolidant

may be more appropriate. Adhesives should exhibit minimal or no off-gassing of volatile acids or alkalis and minimal or no yellowing on ageing. Flexibility is more important than strength for the consolidation of leather. PVAC adhesives generally have a lower, more acidic pH than acrylics and may off-gas acetic acid for up to a year. PVAC adhesives are generally stronger and less flexible than acrylics (Down *et al.*, 1996). For these reasons acrylics emulsions and dispersions are usually selected for the consolidation of leather. Although as a general rule aqueous adhesives should be avoided, acrylic emulsions and dispersions may be used if diluted (1:2 to 1:3) in a compatible non-polar solvent.

Lascaux 360 HV has been used to consolidate leather. It is a butyl acrylate (>50%)/methyl methacrylate copolymer. Butyl acrylate/methyl methacrylate copolymers with a higher proportion of butyl acetate produce weaker but more flexible films. Lascaux 360 HV has a slightly alkaline pH (*c*.7.8) which, after four years of dark ageing, dropped to *c*.6.7, and thus fell within limits defined as acceptable by Down *et al.* (1996). Lascaux 360 HV did emit a small quantity of acetic acid and freeze/thaw cycling will cause the emulsion to collapse. Even though it has a Tg of –8 °C, 360 HV is very flexible, with 1000% elongation at break.

Pliantex has been widely used for the consolidation of archeological leather because it produces a soft film, is flexible (410% elongation at break) and does not crosslink (*Figure 16.7a,b*). It is an ethyl acrylate/methyl methacrylate copolymer (> 66% ethyl acrylate) solution in organic solvents. Tests by Down *et al.* (1996) indicate it is significantly less flexible than Lascaux 360 HV, and after dark ageing for four years pH had dropped to *c*.5.

### Infills

The materials used for infilling losses partly depend on the size of the loss. Large areas of loss are often replaced with leather whilst smaller areas often use polymeric materials.

*Leather infill techniques* Semi-alum leather, that is leather which has been vegetable-tanned and then retanned with aluminium salts, is often the best option and is suitable for general repair work. Chromium tanned leather may offer the advantage of durability and is generally softer and more flexible than semi-alum leather. It has different flexing characteristics to the original, however, and is generally much more difficult to pare and manipulate. Vegetable tanned leather is not usually considered chemically stable enough for repairs unless it has been retanned. The skin type and grain of the leather used in the infill should be matched as closely as possible to the original, although it is often difficult to match the texture of the original exactly.

Four methods of infilling with leather are illustrated in *Figure 16.8*. In all cases the leather is glued into position. In cases where the leather must be able to flex, a good adhesive bond on leather requires limited penetration of the adhesive into the nap. Deep penetration will reduce the flexibility of the

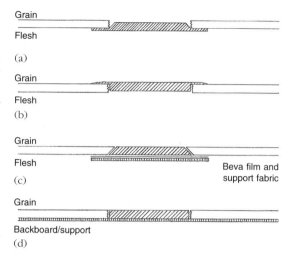

**Figure 16.8** Four methods of infilling with leather: (*a*) a stepped infill; (*b*) an overlapping in situ leather fill; (*c*) a skived infill, which has better visual and structural properties than a stepped infill (*a*): thin skived infills can be strengthened with a backing fabric; (*d*) a plug infill. In cases where the leather is supported by a solid backboard (e.g. chests or panels), the infill can be adhered to the backboard or support

leather. Stepped or overlapping in situ fills may add undue bulk, particularly for leather adhered to wood, e.g. writing surfaces. Skived or plug infills require the use of a thin flexible support fabric.

Unfinished leather, buff in colour, has not been glazed or dyed and is therefore easier to colour match. Leather may be coloured using azo metal complex dyes (available through the Leather Conservation Centre, UK). These dyes are water-soluble, light-fast and formulated for use on leather. The dyes are supplied in four colours (blue, brown, yellow, and red) that are mixed as required.

*Adhesives for leather infills* Protein-based glues are generally inappropriate for leather because of their moisture content and because most are applied hot. Shrinkage temperature may be lower than expected in untanned or aged and degraded leathers and exceeding the shrinkage temperature will cause irreversible damage. Future removal of collagen adhesive may be problematic, particularly in the light of the need to minimize contact between old leather and water.

Acrylic emulsions and dispersions are usually selected for the consolidation of leather (see discussion of consolidation below). Selm

(1991) reported that stronger bonds were formed when adhesive was applied to the support fabric rather than the leather. The adhesive should be applied as a continuous coat. Although Selm recommended a dot pattern for upholstery leathers and other three-dimensional surfaces, in practice such discontinuous application often fails. Many conservators prefer to apply acrylic emulsions (e.g. Lascaux 360 HV: 498 HV 1:3) adhesive to the backing material and allow the diluent to evaporate. The film may be reactivated with solvent and pressed onto the leather and moderate heat may be used to improve the adhesive bond. This technique will ensure a good adhesive bond but minimize adhesive penetration of the leather and may be particularly useful for spot repairs on vulnerable or damaged leathers.

Beva 371 film or solution can be useful for large areas, such as panels, is easy to apply and has good tack. Solutions of Beva can be pigmented to match the leather. Paraloid B72 may be useful for adhering small flakes or for small structural repairs. Solutions should have a high resin content (up to 50%) and may utilize faster evaporating solvents to limit the penetration of the adhesive into the leather.

*Non-leather infills* Often damage to leather surfaces may be too small or irregular to fill with leather. The infill material should be flexible and chemically stable. Pigmented natural waxes such beeswax or carnauba wax have been used in the past for leather to infill losses in leather which cannot flex and is not in use. Natural waxes have several disadvantages, including their acidity and a propensity to hold dust. Mixtures with a high proportion of beeswax have a low softening point. Beva 371 has been used as an alternative to these natural materials (*Figure 16.9*). In all cases it may be difficult to remove all residues and any accretions on the leather usually prevent the adhesion of subsequent non-wax fills. Pre-sealing the leather may lead to solidification of the structure unless a very flexible material is used with minimal penetration. Selm (1991) reported success using a formulation based on Encryl E, an acrylic emulsion based on ethyl and butyl acrylates, a wax emulsion, thickener and microballoons. Beva 371 film, though less easy to apply, also produced satisfactory results.

Nieuwenhuizen (1998) discussed the use of Beva 371 or Paraloid F10 bulked with glass microspheres. Non-leather infills may be colour matched to the surrounding surface using a

(a)

(b)

**Figure 16.9** Non-leather infills
(*a*) Filling a gap in eighteenth-century gilt leather, from Levens Hall, Cumbria, using hot-melt pigmented Beva 371. (*b*) Cleaning excess infill from the seat of a seventeenth-century chair

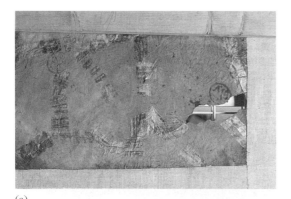

(a)

(b)

**Figure 16.10** Supporting tears in leather
(*a*) First-aid treatment to the reverse side of a torn
seventeenth century gilt leather panel. The torn edges
have been supported with Japanese tissue secured with
an acrylic adhesive. (*b*) The front of the gilt leather
panel pictured in (*a*). The wire of the storage rack can
be seen through a hole in the left-hand side of the
panel

variety of materials including acrylic paints,
gouache or water colours.

### Backing materials
Fabric may be bonded to the underside (flesh
side) of leather to support leather infills or torn
edges. Thin, non-woven fabrics such as Cerex
30 (0.08 mm) or Reemay 2410 (0.25 mm) have
been recommended for general lightweight use
on upholstery leathers (Selm, 1991). They may
also find application for supporting tears, such
as those found on folding screens or skivers
laid across hinged fall fronts. They are flexible,
but do not add undue bulk to a repair and do
not exert directional distortion on already fragile leather. Other alternatives include Tnjugo, a
hand-made Japanese paper, which is weaker

than the leather and will break before causing
damage to fragile leather (*Figure 16.10*).

The following procedure may be used for
applying a backing material to support torn or
friable leather. Lay the support material onto silicone release paper. Coat the support material
with an adhesive (e.g. Lascaux 360 HV) and
leave to dry. Cut the support material to the
required shape or size and remove the silicon
release paper. Lay the support, adhesive side
down to the flesh side (underside) of the
leather. Brush the adhesive impregnated support fabric with a suitable solvent to reactivate
the adhesive and press onto the leather.
Moderate heat may be used to improve the
adhesive bond. Where this technique is used on
a flat surface, e.g. a writing surface, weights may
be applied, though they should be isolated from
the support fabric (e.g. with Melinex/Mylar).

### Coatings
The historical application of varnish-type coatings on writing surfaces has not been systematically researched as yet. Such coatings are not
recommended as part of a conservation treatment because they will penetrate the leather
and reduce its flexibility. Removal of oxidized,
aged and discoloured varnish from a porous
and absorbent leather ground is likely to be
problematic and may damage the leather.

Leather dressings have often been applied in
the past in the mistaken belief that they will
'feed', lubricate or preserve leather. Oil based
dressings penetrate the leather, degrade and
embrittle the leather, discolour and bind dirt to
the surface. The application of such dressings
is often a primary cause of deterioration.
Modern dressings are prepared for the eques-
trian market and are not suitable for fine
leathers or conservation applications. Dressings, creams or hide foods should not be
applied to leather as part of a conservation
treatment. Saddle soap should never be used.

If a leather surface is intact and has not been
abraded, the surface may be given a low sheen
by the application of a thin coat of microcrystalline wax. Leather with an abraded surface
should be left unwaxed.

### 16.4.2   Parchment and vellum

Parchment is a generic term used to describe
untanned animal pelt which has been dehaired

by enzymatic or lime action and which has been stretched in a wet state on a frame and left to dry under tension (Clarkson, 1992). Vellum describes a superior quality of parchment which may be made from calfskin, goatskin or the skin of a young, or fetal, animal (Cains, 1992). Parchment is most commonly found in books and documents and is usually treated by book or paper conservators. On occasion parchment may be found incorporated into furniture, for example that designed by Carlo Bugatti (see Figure 3.4). Parchment incorporated into passmenterie and decorative textile trimmings on furniture is commonplace. Parchment incorporated into furniture may have been treated very differently from that found in manuscripts or prints. It may have been oiled, waxed, painted or varnished as a protective or decorative treatment.

Manufacturing processes will determine pH with alkaline processed skin generally having a higher pH, although certain parchments have had some or all of the lime removed during processing to impart translucency or other properties. Parchment is an extremely hygroscopic material and whilst this has general implications for preventative conservation it will also influence the type of conservation treatments which may be undertaken. If parchment is resoaked or left in a very damp environment it will become a gelatinous mass and may putrefy. If the environment is too dry it may become inflexible, hard and brittle. Clarkson (1992) stated:

> The addition of moisture, whether accidental or through deliberate treatment, without also renewing the tension on drying, allows reorientation of the fibre network. The affected part will swell, thicken, and contract. The fusing together of fibres will also cause transparency and inflexibility. Even a small amount of liquid spilt or left lying on the surface will alter the original surface treatments, with a tendency towards reglazing (with or without retensioning the membrane).

Much of the damage done to parchment can be ascribed to equating it with paper and using inappropriate techniques such as pressing, wetting, gluing or backing.

When incorporated into furniture, parchment may have been subjected to wear and tear as a result of use. Light damage may cause fading of original painted or stained design elements. When it has been used as an upholstery material the tension exerted by the restrained parchment is immense, particularly if the object has been subjected to cycles of fluctuating RH. This may result in damage to poorly constructed frames, tears in the parchment at the fixing points or large tears at the weakest point across the skin.

General references on parchment include de Hamel (1992), Haines (1999), Reed (1972) and Ruck (1991). Among conservators experienced in treating parchment there is wide variation about which treatment methods are effective or acceptable. *Parchment Treatments*, produced by the AIC Book and Paper Group in 1994, provides a useful overview.

### Cleaning

Soiling may turn the parchment from a creamy yellow or light brown colour to a grubby and unattractive grey. The primary consideration for cleaning parchment is to avoid any treatment that will affect the tension of the parchment. Aqueous cleaning solutions should not be used. Although polar organic solvents have been used, for example in book and document conservation, parchment incorporated into furniture is usually restrained and polar solvents may result in changes in tension and should therefore, as a general rule, be avoided.

The cleaning of parchment incorporated into furniture is dependent on whether the surface has been painted and/or varnished. Parchment surfaces which are undecorated and uncomplicated by the presence of varnish or wax may be surface cleaned using dry cleaning materials described in section 11.2.4 (*Figure 16.11*). Residues should be removed using a soft brush and a vacuum cleaner. Non-polar solvents will not affect the tension of the skin but may temporarily cause the parchment to become transparent. Cleaning of varnished and decorated surfaces applied to parchment may utilize the principles, materials and techniques outlined in Chapter 11 with the proviso that aqueous cleaning solutions should be avoided and the use of polar organic solvents minimized. Chapter 13 and section 16.6 provide specific information on the treatment of varnished and painted surfaces respectively.

(a)

(b)

**Figure 16.11**  Cleaning painted parchment
(*a*) Detail of a painted parchment panel before cleaning
(*b*) After cleaning. Dry cleaning materials were used to
remove dirt from the unpainted background

### *Repair and support*

Parchment may be stiff, distorted or brittle and
often requires indirect humidification before lifting edges or tears may be treated. Water in liquid form should never come into contact with
the parchment. Spray application of water, for
example from ultrasonic humidifiers or steam
pencils, should not be used. The combination of
heat and water is potentially disastrous.

Localized humidification may be sufficient to
soften the edges of the parchment to allow
them to be flattened and realigned. Dampened
blotting paper may be used as a reservoir for
moisture. It must be isolated from the surface
of the parchment using a semi-permeable membrane such as Gore-tex. The blotting paper may
be covered with Melinex/Mylar to prevent
evaporation of moisture from the blotting
paper. As the parchment begins to soften,

increasing pressure may be applied. When the
parchment has been flattened, dry blotting
paper may be substituted in order to reduce the
moisture content. Heat should not be used in
any conservation treatment (e.g. consolidation)
until the parchment has been returned to ambient conditions and moisture content has stabilized.

Once the edges of a tear have been
realigned they may be supported from the rear
of the parchment. The support material should
have similar physical characteristics to the
parchment and in particular should approximate the behaviour of parchment to fluctuations in relative humidity. It should also be
mechanically weaker than the parchment.
Materials such as artificial sausage casings,
goldbeaters skin (processed sheep intestine),
parchment or non-woven synthetic textiles
(e.g. Reemay) have been used (Woods, 1995).

Adhesive applied to parchment should form
an adhesive bond to the surface it is applied
to, but should not penetrate through the thickness of the parchment. Any adhesive which
wets through to the upper surface of the parchment will cause it to become translucent. The
adhesive should be flexible.

Beva 371 may be used to adhere a support
to the rear of the parchment. As is the case
with leather, stronger bonds may be formed
when adhesive is applied to the support material rather than the parchment. A thin even
layer of Beva 371 may be applied, either as a
slightly warmed 40% solution as supplied or
diluted with half the quantity of aromatic solvent to both the surface of the support. The
solvent is allowed to evaporate, before reacti-
vating the surface with solvent and pressing it
into position. Moderate heat may be used to
improve the adhesive bond. This technique
will ensure a good adhesive bond but minimize adhesive penetration of the parchment.

Aqueous adhesives are likely to be problematic for a conservator who is inexperienced in
treating parchment and as a general rule
should be avoided. More experienced conservators have used 'dry' solutions of wheat starch
paste or collagen-based adhesives such as
parchment size, rabbit skin glue or fish glue.
PVAC and acrylic emulsions and dispersions
which have a high aqueous content should be
avoided unless diluted with a compatible
hydrocarbon solvent.

The principles outlined above for supporting tears may be applied to loose areas and lifting edges. Losses may be infilled using parchment matched to the colour, texture and surface treatment of the original. The patch should be supported using the technique described above. In some cases it may be appropriate to laminate new parchment for full support, though this should be undertaken by an experienced specialist.

### *Coatings*

Any coating which is applied to previously untreated parchment will change its appearance, texture and patina and there is, therefore, a general presumption against such treatments. Where parchment has been varnished in the past there may be areas where the substrate parchment is exposed. In such cases, the application of a coating runs the risk of differential take-up between varnished and unvarnished areas.

### 16.4.3 Shagreen

In furniture conservation, the term shagreen usually refers to the skins of sharks and rays. The term shagreen is derived from an entirely different material, sometimes known as 'shagreen leather', derived from the back of a horse or donkey and embossed with seeds. The historical derivation of the term can cause some confusion and it is important to identify which material is actually present on an object.

The physical characteristic that produces the decorative effect on ray skins is the presence of cartillagenous nodules in the grain surface of the skin. These nodules are hard and the skins have been used as an abrasive material in the past. The skin itself could be processed and abraded to reveal the small white circular pattern which is characteristic of this material and produced a hard wearing and decorative surface. Gopfrich (1999) describes the history and conservation of shagreen leather, specifically an untanned hide that had been embossed with seeds.

The skin of other aquatic animals such as chat (*Squalus catalus*) and dogfish have also been used and are often also called shagreen. Kite (forthcoming) mentions the use of untanned shagreen to bind European ceremonial sword hilts and its incorporation into the handles of Samurai swords and dirks during the Edo period in Japan (1615–1868). When used in this way the surface of the shagreen was not abraded, as the nodules on the skin provided additional grip.

Shagreen was used in Europe, from the seventeenth century onwards, as a decorative covering material for boxes and was also utilized in instrument cases and jewellery (Willemsen, 1997). The French cabinetmaker Ruhlman often used shagreen to great decorative effect and this material enjoyed a period of popularity in England in the 1920s when it was favoured by the Duke of Windsor (Springer, 1984).

Both tanned and untanned shagreen may be encountered as a decorative surface. Although tanning raises the shrinkage temperature of leather, in many cases the shagreen used on articles of furniture was untanned. Although dry heat is usually tolerated, it may be helpful to establish the shrinkage temperature before undertaking a conservation treatment that utilizes heat, e.g. heat setting of adhesives. The sudden contraction of the skin at the shrinkage temperature usually requires both heat and moisture, but it is possible, for example if aqueous adhesives have been used, or in conditions of high ambient RH, or if the shagreen has been humidified and has not yet returned to equilibrium with the ambient environment, for contraction to occur without additional moisture.

Shrinkage temperature may be established by taking a small sample, which is thoroughly soaked in cold water overnight. The temperature of the water is then raised, ideally at 2 °C per minute, and the temperature at which the sample suddenly and irreversibly shrinks is noted. Microscopic examination using a heated stage may allow the use of a very small sample and has been described by Young (1990) and Larsen *et al.* (1993). If taking a sample to establish shrinkage temperature is impracticable it should be assumed that untanned shagreen has been used.

The shrinkage temperature of fish collagen is significantly lower than that of mammalian collagen (*c*.65 °C). Generally speaking, the shrinkage temperature of cold water species is around 38–45 °C, whilst that of warm water species is around 50–56 °C. Shrinkage temperature has a direct relationship with the hydroxyproline content of the collagen – low hydroxyproline content results in low shrinkage temperature (O'Flaherty *et al.*, 1958). Conservation treatments, such as humidification or the use of heat-set or aqueous adhesives, may be potentially harmful for degraded shagreen derived from cold water fish species.

Shagreen was coloured in a variety of ways. Gopfrich (1999) reported the use of natural dyes or precipitated metallic salts in the grain surface of untanned horse or donkey hide. Willemsen (1997) reported the use of green pigment (terre verte) on shark and ray skin. In addition, transparently thin shark and rayskin could be dyed and then laid onto coloured paper to enhance the effect. Eighteenth century shagreen boxes may have a natural resin varnish and/or wax coating whilst those manufactured in the 1930s often had a cellulose nitrate coating applied.

### Cleaning
Dry cleaning methods, described in section 11.2.4, may be used if the surface is sufficiently robust. Shagreen may also be surface cleaned using a non polar hydrocarbon solvent or by swabs slightly dampened with water. Care must be taken to ensure that any solvent used for cleaning does not dissolve dyestuffs which may have been used to colour the shagreen. Although slightly dampened swabs should be safe, it is important to avoid excessive exposure to water, particularly if the shagreen is untanned or has deteriorated significantly. If a surface coating has deteriorated and must be removed, the least polar solvent blend possible should be used.

### Lifting edges and tears
Treatment possibilities will be defined by the material properties of the skin such as thickness, shrinkage temperature and the skin's inherent flexibility. The principle underlying treatment is humidification without direct contact with water, to allow the skin to be manipulated, flattened and readhered. The treatment for lifting edges and tears described for parchment may also be used for shagreen. A 'dry' wheat starch paste or acrylic emulsions and dispersions may be used to readhere the shagreen after it has been flattened but care should be taken to minimize wetting of the skin, which may result in staining or the formation of tidelines if dyestuffs or tanning materials are solubilized and move through the skin to the surface. As a general rule collagen adhesives should be avoided as they may be difficult to reverse without damaging the skin. Conservators experienced in treating parchment have used slight dampness to facilitate the removal of old collagen adhesive. After consolidation of loose edges, losses may be infilled using leather or the materials discussed in the context of leather.

The application of a coating may be dependent on the level of use or handling, the presence and solubility of dyestuffs and the presence of any original coating. A thin coating of microcrystalline wax may be applied if required. Oil-based leather dressings should never be used.

## 16.5 Textiles

Textiles incorporated into furniture include silks or velvet linings in dressing cases or clocks, on writing surfaces and as part of sewing boxes (*Figure 16.12*). Some boxes or caskets may incorporate quilted or padded linings trimmed with metal thread ribbons or braids, which may have been secured with animal glue. Textiles are not confined to small objects but will also be found incorporated into cradles, screens and beds as hangings, drapes, testers etc. Sedan chairs, carriages and assorted carts and sledges may fall within the remit of furniture conservation. All incorporate textile, leather and metal elements and are complex composite objects that require a multi-disciplinary approach. Although in some cases textile elements may be treated in situ, in other cases it may be necessary to remove the textile and framing elements for separate treatment. Removal should be undertaken in partnership with a textile conservator as the fabric may be very vulnerable to damage.

Textiles are vulnerable to damage from light, heat, wear and chemical degradation. When incorporated into furniture, chemical degradation may be exacerbated by adhesives or acidic vapours that off-gas from many species of wood. Comprehensive information about the conservation of textiles may be found in Landi (1992) and Tímár-Balázsy and Eastop (1998).

Baize was often used as a writing surface. Baize is a thick strong woven wool cloth and

**Figure 16.12** Front rail of a nineteenth century chair designed by Pugin. Red velvet and gilded rosettes embellish the gothic detail of the front rail

**Figure 16.13** An embroidered casket (1671) worked by Martha Edlin using silks, metal threads and feathers on a silk satin ground. Each embroidered panel is adhered to the wood substrate

should not be confused with or replaced by felt, which is a cloth with a weak structure made by matting and pressing fibres together. A comprehensive description of the process of laying new baize has been provided by Bennett (1990).

A particular form found in the seventeenth century was the stumpwork box (*Figure 16.13*). This was a ladies' dressing case, writing box and jewel casket, all rolled into one. A feature of this form was outside panels decorated in raised embroidery (sometimes also beaded) with free-standing three-dimensional elements. Examples of such decorative elements include needlewoven leaves, insect wings, fruits and berries, embroidered skirts and draperies, and also occasionally small lace components. These decorative elements were worked onto a silk-satin ground fabric that was glued onto the wooden substrate. These boxes always incorporated secret compartments and were lined with silk or velvet and sometimes paper. The condition of the decoration is dependent on the degree of damage caused by use, light or surface soiling. As a general rule, the decoration should be treated in situ if possible because of the fragility of the textile and the likelihood of causing extensive damage to the ground fabric if removal is attempted. The treatment of a textile adhered to a wood substrate has been considered by Kite and Webber (1995).

Other forms, such as curiosity cabinets, may incorporate ornate embroidered linings to the doors and drawer fronts. Some are simple and

**Figure 16.14** A late seventeenth or early eighteenth century passementerie furnishing trimming, worked in silk. The loops are parchment bound with silk thread

are of laid silk embroidery. Others are very elaborate and may have portraits embroidered on the central panels, often surrounded by decorative silk covered wire loops, silk wrapped parchment loops or passmenterie (*Figure 16.14*). The treatment of such decorative textile elements that have been worn, damaged or crushed should be undertaken by an experienced textile conservator.

The wooden carcase of stumpwork boxes is often crudely made in a lightweight timber. The value of the object was in the rich and ornate embroidery. Damage in the carcase is often associated with glued joints or stress points such as hinges. In some cases, for example where access to a broken hinge or associated damaged wood is required, it may be necessary to lift a small area of textile. This may be undertaken using a small, very thin spatula (0.2–0.3 mm thick), inserted carefully between textile and wooden substrate. Note that an artist's palette knife is too coarse for this procedure. In some cases, localized cool humidity from a preservation pencil may be helpful in breaking the adhesive bond. After the hinge or carcase wood has been treated, the textile may be relaid using 'dry' wheat starch paste. Huxtable and Webber (1986) give comprehensive directions for preparing wheat starch paste. To make a 'dry' paste, excess water may be removed from a standard formulation of paste by placing a small amount onto blotting paper before use. Although animal glue may have been used originally, it is often not appropriate for regluing fragile textiles in this context.

### 16.5.1 Cleaning

The textile interiors of boxes have often become very dusty, particularly in the corners. Surfaces such as these are ideally cleaned using a vacuum tweezer unit. A conventional handheld vacuum cleaner may be used, in which case the suction should be reduced if possible. The suction of the vacuum cleaner should be just enough to dislodge dust and particulate matter without exerting pull on the textile. In addition, the hand held nozzle should be covered with two layers of nylon to prevent loose threads being sucked up and lost, with the result of further unravelling of the textile. Care should be taken that the nozzle does not come into contact with the textile because it will leave an irreversible scuff mark. A soft brush may be used to assist in dislodging dust and particulate matter but should not be used where the surface of the textile is degraded to the point of turning to dust. Dry cleaning materials (not solvent cleaning), discussed in section 11.2.4, may be appropriate for removing ingrained dust from robust textiles in good condition but are unlikely to affect wax or stains.

Wax accretions are difficult to remove from well adhered fabric. It may be appropriate to mechanically remove the bulk of the wax before using heat and absorbent paper. Although Stoddard solvent is a good solvent for wax, its use may be problematic if the textile is adhered to wood, in which case there may be a danger of solubilizing the adhesive or bringing a stain through from below. It may

be prudent to leave such marks untreated. Other stains or ink marks should be treated by a specialist textile conservator but in many cases should also be left untreated.

### 16.5.2 Loose and lifting linings

Wear and use has often led to repair or replacement of original lining fabrics but in some cases, such as dressing cases, writing boxes and stumpwork boxes, the original lining may be found beneath a later additional repair. Original linings may be extremely damaged and fragile. Their conservation should be undertaken by an experienced textile conservator, who may be able to support original remnants and reconstruct lost material. If relining has occurred, the owner or curator should be consulted about the potential historic importance of the relining and therefore the conservation treatment required.

In cases where the original lining has been removed, remnants are often found adhered to old adhesive, edges or fixings. A single thread may provide important evidence of original material and colour. The colour of later linings were subject to the fashion of the day rather than concerns of historical accuracy. Velvet may have replaced silk, or vice versa, depending on the prevailing taste. If it is necessary to remove old adhesive, the area should be examined under a binocular microscope for remnant fibres. If found, fibres should be documented, photographed and kept.

Where a lining has become loose or is lifting, it may be possible to relay the material. An adhesive should be selected on the basis of the weight, weave and porosity of the material. The original adhesive should be identified in order to choose a compatible adhesive so, for example, a wheat starch may be used where a starch paste was used originally. A critical parameter of the use of this adhesive is that it should be used 'dry' so that it does not soak through the material and cause irreversible staining. Capillary action in the fibres of the lining will tend to pull excess moisture and adhesive through to the upper surface. The more damaged or tendered the material, the more porous it is likely to be. Conservation grade PVAC is not generally appropriate for linings, though it may be used to secure loose braid, trimming and passmenterie. Animal/hide glue may be appropriate for leather linings or skivers but is not appropriate for lightweight textile linings. Animal glue may have been used originally to adhere textile writing surfaces such as a heavy moire silk and it may be appropriate to use animal glue to readhere lifting areas on such a material. If reinstating a textile writing surface, animal glue may be used and should be applied in a thin even layer and allowed to gel, so that there is tack but no excess moisture. A paste brush, used dry, may be used to smooth and lay the fabric.

In some cases the pleated textile of Regency sewing or games tables may be missing, or degraded and damaged. Nineteenth-century tin-weighted silk may have shattered. In such cases it may be appropriate to replace or reconstruct the textile element of the furniture. Evidence of original textile and colour may be found under nails, in nail holes or inside the top compartment, where one exists. Care should be taken to match the quality of the original fabric. Silk taffeta, for example, should be replaced with a silk taffeta dyed or matched to the original. A modern synthetic fabric is inappropriate as a replacement material because it will not reproduce crease and drape in the same manner as the original or be in keeping with the object.

## 16.6 Painted furniture

### 16.6.1 Introduction to conservation of painted furniture

Painted furniture encompasses a wide range of objects, from the highest quality 'court' furniture, to humble vernacular pieces. Furniture functions within the context of daily life and, in addition to art historical information, carries evidence of social history. Whenever possible, painted furniture should be treated by a conservator with experience in decorated surfaces. There is an inherent risk that treatment by a non-specialist will cause further damage and reduce both the historical and monetary value of the object. The painted surface, which carries much of the 'meaning' and value of the piece, is often the most important part of the object. It is also very vulnerable to damage as a result of the vicissitudes of time and use. Treating painted furniture can present many unique challenges, for exam-

ple the conservator may need to balance the 'readability' of a surface with the need to preserve evidence of wear.

Information on the chemistry, structure and materials found in painted surfaces can be gained from a variety of sources, such as Dorge and Howlett (1998) and Dardes and Rothe (1998). Conference papers from the related disciplines of painting and polychrome sculpture conservation, such as Brommelle and Smith (1976), Hackney, Townsend and Eastaugh (1990), Hodges, Mills and Smith (1992) and Mills and Smith (1990), cover a wide range of materials and conservation techniques. Although far fewer in number, there are excellent articles available on the conservation of painted furniture, e.g. Buck (1993, 1994, 1995). Information on architectural paint such as Bristow (1996, 1998) may prove useful, particularly for furniture decorated as part of an overall interior design. Literature from the paint industry, such as Dintenfass (1958), Lambourne (1993), Marrion (1994) or Martens (1974), can provide detailed information on the chemistry and physics of coatings in general and industrial paint in particular. Information on historic binding materials and pigments can be found in Erhardt (1998), Feller (1986), Gettens and Stout (1966), Harley (1982), Mayer (1991), Newman (1998) and Roy (1993).

The conservation of painted surfaces on furniture has much in common with the related disciplines of panel paintings and polychrome wooden sculpture conservation. Painted surfaces on furniture are often characterized by a variety of materials applied in thin films. The types of paint found on furniture may range from artists' type materials to paints formulated for interior decorative schemes. The materials added to a paint to create an appropriate rheology for the intended use will affect the solubility of the final aged film. Artists' paints are often formulated to allow the use of brushmarks or impasto and may incorporate a small amount of a gum or glue emulsified into the paint. In contrast, decorators' paints are often designed to flow out and level to create a smooth surface. The addition of a material such as a monoterpene (an essential oil) or a slow evaporating solvent will facilitate the levelling process.

Conservation treatment of painted furniture requires care and experience because of the potential to alter original intended appearance and the fact that such surfaces often have complex structures. Thin glazes were often used to create a surface aesthetic. If the arrangement of layers is disrupted when the surface is cleaned, the effect on the original intended design can be devastating. It is important to understand the multi-component character of painted furniture. Even simple decorative schemes on furniture may make use of multiple layers of materials with widely differing properties, such as oils, resins, casein, tempera, collagen glues and gums. It is common for a wide variety of materials to be incorporated in a complex layer structure to allow complex designs to be created comparatively quickly. Grained surfaces, for example, may have utilized a casein base coat, figured with oil and toned glazes before being varnished with an oil or oil-resin varnish. Alternatively, the system used to create the graining may have incorporated an oil base coat, figured utilizing a binder of stale beer or a gum, before the final varnish coating/s were applied. The surfaces thus created may appear very similar but may respond very differently to a cleaning treatment.

Research has indicated that, in parts of seventeenth and eighteenth century Europe, the primary constituent of the best and palest transparent spirit varnish was sandarac. Ingredients such as mastic, elemi, camphor and turpentine resin were also added to manipulate working and drying properties and the appearance of the cured finish. Copal and amber were rarely added (Walch, 1997). Sandarac varnishes are characterized by hardness and polishability (in contrast to mastic, dammar, colophony etc.), translucence and colourlessness (in contrast to unbleached shellac and colophony) and resolubility in alcohol (in contrast to aged shellac, copal resins, amber etc.) (Koller *et al.*, 1997). In the nineteenth century oleo-resinous varnishes were often employed where a hard-wearing surface was required. Drying oils such as linseed or tung oil may have been used, whilst rosin and rosin esters were used in place of dammar and mastic when import of these materials was disrupted. Shellac was usually avoided as a varnish layer for painted surfaces because of its inherent colour and its tendency to rapid yellowing, though it may be encountered as a late nineteenth century or restoration varnish. Decolouring of shellac was developed in the latter part of the nineteenth century. *Spons Workshop Receipts* (1873) recommends removing the colour from shellac by boiling it with charcoal, whilst the 1919 edition of *Staining and Polishing* (Woodworker Series, Evans Bros) states that shellac was bleached using chlorine.

### 16.6.2   Cleaning

As a general rule, painted surfaces on furniture were varnished. The presence of a natural resin varnish can be established using UV, as these materials exhibit auto-fluorescence. Plant resins usually exhibit a green white fluorescence, whilst freshly applied shellac has a characteristic orange fluorescence. Extended exposure to natural light will cause a shift in the fluorescence of shellac from orange to yellow–green (see *Plate 5*). An accumulation of grime or wax, or the presence of an overlying oil or oil containing layer may mask such auto-fluorescence.

The condition of the paint layer, which may range from underbound or matte paint to well-bound intact films, will determine treatment options. Removal of surface dirt from a painted surface is usually straightforward unless there is no coating, or where the varnish has been damaged, abraded or lost.

In cases where the paint layers are in good condition and the varnish intact, the use of dry cleaning methods (see section 11.2.4) may be effective, as illustrated in *Figure 11.7*. The use of water-based cleaning solutions or saliva on such surfaces is common. Swabs moistened with saliva or deionized water are usually sufficient to remove accretions of dust and dirt from painted surfaces protected by an intact varnish. Although these materials are widely used and are comparatively innocuous to oil-based paint substrates, spot tests will establish whether the surface is sensitive to them. Ground layers often have a water sensitive proteinaceous binder, which may be vulnerable to cleaning solutions via ageing or other cracks in the paint and varnish layers, so aqueous cleaning should be carried out cautiously. Cleaning may result in components in a ground or other layer being deposited on the surface or in the craquelure, resulting in a whitish appearance. Aqueous solutions with an acidic pH may interact with sensitive materials such as calcium carbonate ($CaCO_3$) grounds.

If the surface is unaffected by spot tests, there are five parameters that may be manipulated when working with aqueous solutions. These are pH, conductivity, the addition of surfactants or detergents, the addition of chelators and raising the viscosity of the cleaning solution. The principles behind the manipulation of these parameters are discussed in detail in sections 11.5 and 11.6. As a general rule the following may be useful guidelines for aqueous cleaning solutions applied to painted surfaces:

- pH 5.5–8.5 for oil paint films. The older the oil paint film, the greater the risk that it will be damaged by elevated pH, so the upper limit of 8.5 should be adjusted downwards according to the age of the paint film.
- pH 5.5–7.0 for casein based paints, although in some cases the use of water to clean casein-based paints may be inappropriate. At a pH around 4.6 (the isoelectric point) casein is at its least soluble in water.
- Natural resins are weakly acidic materials and ageing will also contribute to this acidity. As pH rises above 7, alkaline solutions will increasingly interact with such surfaces, and there is a concomitant risk that blooming will occur in the varnish.
- The presence of distemper (collagen glue-based paint) or gums may preclude the use of water-based cleaning solutions.
- As a general rule, the conductivity of aqueous solutions used to clean painted surfaces should not exceed 5000 µS. Conductivity may be excessive if ionic materials such as buffers or chelators are incorporated into a cleaning solution (see section 11.5.3).
- The HLB of surfactants should, as a general rule, fall between 13 and 20. Low CMC surfactants may be difficult to clear from lipophilic surfaces such as unaged oil paint films. Surfactants with an HLB above 20 have an increasing ability to emulsify water into oil, and thus blanch an original paint layer.
- Weak chelators (such as citric acid), should be used in preference to stronger chelators (such as EDTA) (see section 11.5.5).
- Viscosity may be raised, for example with a cellulose ether or polyacrylic acid (e.g. Carbopol), to give greater application control (see section 11.6). The thicker the gel, the less the possibility of liquid water (or solvent) penetrating a complex surface and disrupting sensitive layers below.

Unvarnished paint is more susceptible to damage during cleaning. In some cases, for example if the surface was originally varnished, such areas may be sealed before cleaning commences. Hackney *et al.* (1990) and Green (1990) set out strategies for cleaning unvarnished painted surfaces including the use of erasers, aqueous cleaning solutions and solvent/detergent emulsions.

Removal of surface dirt from painted furniture may be complicated by the presence of grease, wax or oil. In some cases varnish or oil layers may have been applied over disfiguring soiling material. Aliphatic hydrocarbon solvents may be used to remove wax and grease from natural resin varnish coatings, but will remove many synthetic coatings such as dammar, MS2A and hydrogenated hydrocarbon varnishes, particularly where these varnishes are unaged or have been stabilized with Tinuvin 292 (see section 12.4). Aromatic solvents will remove Paraloid B72, moderately aged unstabilized dammar and MS2A. Small spot tests will establish whether a surface coating is sensitive to a particular hydrocarbon solvent.

Traditional recipes for varnish removal or degreasers often relied on the addition of a small amount of a reagent such as ammonium hydroxide to water. If this approach is used, the pH of the solution should not exceed 8.5 (Wolbers *et al.*, 1990). Proprietary cleaning solutions should be avoided because they are often formulated at alkaline pHs, often incorporate an excess of strong chelating materials and may contain high HLB detergents. As a general rule such conditions are not appropriate for historic finishes or surfaces.

### 16.6.3  Removal of varnish

Discoloured varnish may be considered more of a problem on painted surfaces than on varnished wood. Discoloured varnish may disrupt the intended aesthetic of the decorative scheme. As varnish yellows or darkens it may obscure the colours below and can alter colour relationships and balance within a decorative scheme (*Figure 16.15*). The goal of treatment in such cases may be to remove a layer that has significantly disturbed the original intended

(a)

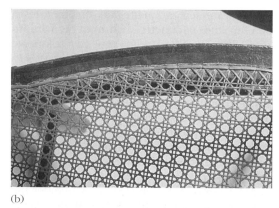

(b)

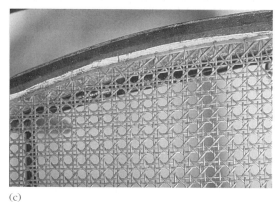

(c)

**Figure 16.15** Effect of discoloured varnish
(*a*) A fancy painted chair, Baltimore, early nineteenth century, during conservation. Darkened and degraded varnish (right front leg) gave an entirely different effect from the original paint scheme, revealed on the left front leg
(*b*) Detail of the seat rail of the chair, before conservation
(*c*) Detail of the seat rail of the chair, after conservation. Removal of discoloured varnish with an enzyme gel revealed an elaborate decorative scheme

aesthetic. The decision to remove a discoloured varnish layer should be made in consultation with the owner or curator, and may be influenced by whether such a coating was part of the original surface. An original coating may be left intact even though it has discoloured whilst a similar non-original coating may be more likely to be removed. The services of a paint analyst or microscopist skilled in the analysis of historic paint films may be helpful. The removal of a coating from a painted surface is a major conservation treatment and should be undertaken only with the guidance of an experienced specialist.

Treatment options for the removal of varnish from painted furniture will depend on the nature of the binding media. A wide range of

binding media have been used on painted furniture, including drying oils, resins, egg white, egg yolk, gums, glue size, oil and beer. Casein paint was usually prepared by mixing milk curd with an alkali. The resulting material could be used as an adhesive or as a binder for paint. In some cases, for example on vernacular furniture, milk paint was made by simply mixing pigment with milk. The proportion of pigment could be as high as 10%. The options for treating an oil-based paint are different to that for a distemper, a mixed media finish such as graining or marbling, or a surface composed predominantly of pigmented natural resins.

The responsible removal of varnish layers from painted furniture requires accurate identification and characterization of the stratigraphy of the decorative surface. Wolbers and Landrey (1987) described the use of reactive fluorescent dyes for the characterization of binding media in decorative surfaces. Sigel (1993) tabulated many reactive fluorescent dyes and the materials they tag. If access to a UV microscope can be gained, this can be an effective tool that allows the conservator to formulate cleaning, consolidation and recoating strategies specifically designed for a given painted surface. The microscopic examination of paint layers has been considered by Plesters (1956) and reviewed by Martin (1998). Such microscopic analysis is usually conducted in conjunction with careful solvent testing. If microscopy or other analytical techniques are not available, examining the surface under hand-held UV, before and after surface cleaning, will identify the presence of an auto-fluorescent natural resin varnish. Removal of discoloured varnish may be complicated by the presence of 'maintenance' coatings such as wax, linseed oil, or multiple layers that may comprise natural resins or oil-resin varnish/es.

A variety of techniques have been used to remove discoloured varnish from painted surfaces. These techniques include mechanical removal, the use of solvents and solvent gels, alkaline reagents and, more recently, aqueous methods (Wolbers, 2000), each of which has advantages and disadvantages.

### Mechanical removal

Mechanical reduction of varnish may be an option when other methods are precluded. A traditional technique for the removal of varnish from easel paintings was to grind a natural resin such as dammar, mastic or colophony, which had originally been used to varnish the painting, and to rub it over the surface with a finger. This method has the advantage of not requiring the use of solvents or water, and may be a controllable technique in skilled hands. It is not usually used in conservation treatments because there is a significant danger of abrading the paint below. In some cases, however, where the varnish is very oxidized and brittle, this may be considered less damaging than other cleaning options.

### Solvents

The most common method of removing a varnish from a painted surface is the use of sol-

vents. Varnishes are prone to oxidize, discolour and become soluble in more polar solvents over time. The strategy for solvent removal of varnish is to find a solvent or solvent mixture that is polar enough to rapidly swell or dissolve the bulk of the varnish film without affecting underlying materials. Thus a typical blend may be based on acetone, isopropanol or IMS, often mixed with a non-polar solvent such as white spirits to adjust the degree of polarity and position of the mix on a TEAS diagram (see discussion of solubility parameters under section 11.3.3). Ruhemann (1968) and Feller *et al.* (1985) describe this cleaning strategy.

The advantages of solvent cleaning are easy formulation if the conservator can find a blend with suitable solubility parameters, rapid dissolution and removal of a coating. The materials are volatile, leave no residues and the treatment is therefore uncomplicated by problems of clearance. The disadvantages of solvent cleaning are that it is often difficult to get the solubility parameters exactly right. Varnishes used on furniture are often complicated by the presence of oil, fossil resins or other polymer containing or forming materials. Simple solvent mixtures may not work well with such complex films. As both the varnish and decorative layers age and oxidize, solubility parameters may increasingly overlap. In some cases, the original materials and coating may have originally had similar solubility parameters, e.g. Victorian reds and browns often contain an admixture of natural resin. One strategy for dealing with this problem is to limit the diffusion of solvent into the surface by using a viscous solvent gel (see section 11.6).

*Leaching and swelling* A serious problem associated with solvent cleaning, particularly of oil painted surfaces, is the removal of unpolymerized components of the decorative surface, an irreversible process known as leaching. The leaching of unaged oil paint films was quantified by Feller *et al.* (1985). The loss of soluble components occurs during cleaning as the solvent diffuses into the paint film. Small soluble molecules will be lost independently of swelling, but leaching will markedly increase when accompanied by swelling (*Figure 16.16*). Thus the relationship between swelling and leaching is not directly proportional. The overlap of solubility parameters of the solvent and

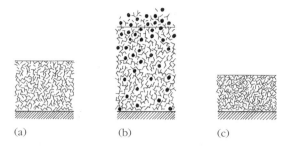

**Figure 16.16** Diagrammatic representation of the effects of solvent-induced swelling and leaching on an oil paint film
(*a*) A dried linseed oil film. It is composed of an insoluble polymerized network of triglycerides but also includes soluble components such as oxidation products (carboxylic and dicarboxylic acids), saturated triglycerides and low molecular weight triglycerides (those formed from stearic, palmitic or oleic acids)
(*b*) Diffusion of solvent into the linseed oil film. The film swells and some low molecular weight components are dissolved and removed
(*c*) A linseed film that has been leached by solvent removal of varnish. It has reduced in thickness and weight, increased in density and is embrittled due to the loss of low molecular weight components that act as plasticizers within the film

the extractable compounds plays an important role, as do diffusion characteristics (Sutherland and Shibayama, 1999). The degree of leaching is dependent on factors such as contact time, type of solvent, film thickness, the pigmentation of the decorative surface and its composition, and the previous cleaning history of the surface.

The molecules that may be removed by leaching function as plasticizers and their removal results in a surface film that has shrunk to occupy less volume, is reduced in weight, increased in density and is embrittled. Loss of soluble material from an unaged oil paint film is very rapid and may begin within seconds of initial contact with solvent. One study reported 50% of soluble material was removed from both pigmented and unpigmented unaged oil paint films within 100 seconds (Feller *et al.*, 1985). Timed studies showed that the lower weight molecular species such as alcohols, ketones and aldehydes are removed first, followed by saturated triglycerides and, lastly, dicarboxylic components. Leaching can remove 20–50% of the organic content of an oil-based film, depending on the age and type of paint film and its previous cleaning history. Where the pigment

in the film has had no effect on, or has retarded the drying of the film (e.g. iron oxides), solubility of organic content may be significantly higher.

Feller *et al.* (1985) recommended balancing the potential swelling of a solvent and its rate of diffusion into the paint layer and suggested that the leaching of oil paint could be minimized by utilizing a slow-diffusing solvent with a low swelling action and a low leaching rate. Michalski (1990) has summarized and tabulated data on the swelling of oil media by organic solvents and their speed of penetration. A fast diffusing solvent such as acetone can be used relatively safely if contact time with the surface is minimized, small quantities are used and adequate time for evaporation allowed (see *Figure 11.9*). Repeated solvent application in one area will build up dangerously high levels of solvent within the paint layers and any mechanical action from swab cleaning can cause significant damage. Phenix (1998) has suggested that certain polar solvents have a greater swelling effect on oil paint films than had previously been suggested.

The swelling process itself will result in damage to a decorative surface layer. The decorative surface coating, after exposure to solvent, will attempt to swell in all directions but can only freely swell outwards, resulting in plastic compression. Whilst leaching may cause shrinkage of around 15%, plastic compression may result in up to 80% shrinkage of the paint film on drying and the creation of micro-voids within the paint layer (Michalski, 1990).

It is not uncommon for conservators to utilize immiscible solvents, such as acetone and white spirits, to reduce the overall polarity of an effective solvent that is working too fast or to remove coatings that contain components with widely differing solubility parameters. It is worth noting that that some solvent blends may result in enhanced swelling of an oil paint film with an increased risk of damage from mechanical cleaning action such as swabbing.

Feller *et al.* (1985) observed significant leaching in comparatively young, unoxidized oil paint films. White and Roy (1998) suggested that leaching is not a significant factor in typical solvent blends used to remove varnish from old master easel paintings that had been subjected to many cleaning/restoration cycles in the past. In both cases, these results may or may not be representative of the kinds of surfaces encountered in decorative paints on furniture. It is therefore safer to assume that leaching will be a problem and to choose a cleaning strategy accordingly, rather than assuming it is not and potentially causing significant damage.

### Alkaline reagents

Natural resin varnishes become increasingly acidic in character as they oxidize and age. Alkaline liquids, such as ammonium hydroxide, will have some effect on those materials and, in some cases, will dissolve them. Unfortunately, many paint binding materials also become more acidic as they age and become increasingly susceptible to damage from alkaline cleaning solutions. The traditional approach with ammonium hydroxide has been to rely on its comparatively fast evaporation to limit penetration and potential damage to an underlying surface. The most dramatic effects are usually observed at significantly elevated pH (i.e. above 8.5), but there is a concomitantly high risk of damaging the substrate, e.g. by the saponification of oil paint films or the dissolution of proteinaceous films. In some cases, where the pH is buffered, e.g. to 8.5 or less for oil bound paint, an alkaline solution such as ammonium hydroxide may cause less swelling than a solvent-based system.

### Aqueous methods

Water has been suggested as a method for removing varnish from oil paintings (Wolbers *et al.*, 1990; Wolbers, 2000). The primary advantage of aqueous varnish removal solutions is that water is a poor solvent for oil-based paints. Where varnish is very degraded (and therefore more polar), the use of an aqueous solution may have less potential to damage the paint layer than the use of a very polar solvent blend. Aqueous cleaning solutions offer the conservator the potential to manipulate, monitor and control the parameters of pH, conductivity, the addition of surfactants or detergents, the addition of chelators, and viscosity. It is important to use measured amounts of these materials and to define safe limits for their use (Wolbers, 1992). The use of non-volatile materials will, however, require a well-formulated clearance protocol. The disadvantages of aqueous cleaning include the fact that the formulation of aqueous cleaning solutions is often more complex than solvent blends and is not easily undertaken without a good grasp of the theory and chemistry involved. The aspect of aqueous cleaning solutions that has caused most concern is the use of non-volatile materials, the effectiveness of clearance procedures, and the ageing characteristics of any residues that may be left on the surface. The research that has been undertaken on the subject of residues varies in quality (Lang, 1998). It is important that conservators keep abreast of current research in this specialized field.

*Resin and bile soaps* Resin and bile soaps are aqueous systems developed for the removal of aged and degraded natural resin varnishes, usually dammar or mastic, from painted surfaces (usually nineteenth-century paintings with an oil–resin binding media) (Wolbers *et al.*, 1990). Varnish removal relies on the differential solubility of varnish and paint. As natural resin varnishes age they become more polar, and require polar solvents in order to dissolve them. These polar solvents are more likely to swell or leach an aged oil paint below, particularly where an oil–resin binder has been used for the paint. In contrast, within the time an oil paint film may be exposed to water during cleaning, it is unlikely to swell oil-based paint (Browne, 1954). Water can be used to provide the necessary polarity for removing degraded varnish, whilst the addition of a detergent or a small amount of an aromatic solvent such as benzyl alcohol can be used to bring non-polar components of degraded natural resin varnishes into solution.

Dammar and mastic do not polymerize as they age, though they do oxidize and become more polar. This lack of polymerization implies a low molecular weight and the potential for detergent micelles to bring moieties into solution. Oxidized varnish may contain relatively polar material that may be sparingly soluble in water, but the bulk of natural resins such as dammar and mastic is made up of non-polar molecular groups. Any detergent would aid in solubilizing such material, but Wolbers based his selection of certain soaps for solubilizing aged resin varnishes on the principle of 'like dissolves like'. He argued that, at any given HLB, a close structural similarity of soap and resin would maximize intermolecular interactions and therefore have a higher 'affinity' for, or be more effective in, bringing non-polar components into solution.

The majority of natural resins are terpenoids. They exude from trees as liquids and subsequently harden by evaporation of volatile components or partial oxidative polymerization of some components. Dammar and mastic are both triterpenoid resins, i.e. they have thirty carbon atoms per molecule (Mills and White, 1977). Dammar is formed from a complex mixture of cyclic compounds, whilst mastic also contains a proportion of polymeric hydrocarbon material. Wolbers chose weak organic (i.e. carboxylic) acids with an aromatic structure, similar to that found in natural resins, as the fatty acids on which to base his soaps. Abietic acid, used in resin soaps, is a component of diterpenoid (20 carbon) resins and has lipophilic and unsaturated groups at one end of the molecule and a hydrophilic carboxylic acid at the other. Deoxycholic acid, used in bile soaps, occurs naturally in the blood and bile of mammals and has a saturated polycyclic structure with hydrophilic hydroxyl and carboxylic acid groups attached (*Figure 16.17*).

A soap is the salt of an organic fatty acid. The addition of a base such as triethanolamine to abietic acid produces triethanolammonium abietate, whilst the addition of a base such as triethanolamine to deoxycholic acid produces triethanolammonium deoxycholate. These soaps are known as resin and bile soaps respectively because these were the original sources of the fatty acids used to make the soap. Deoxycholate is more polar than abietate and is more appropriate for the removal of older, more degraded varnish.

*Abietate resin soap recipe*

   2 g     abietic acid (free acid)
   5–6 m  triethanolamine (TEA)
             HCl (1M) to adjust pH to 8.5, as
             needed
   1 ml   Triton XL-80N
   2 g     hydroxypropyl methyl cellulose
             (HPMC)
   100 ml distilled or deionized water

The abietic acid is dissolved in water with the TEA to form triethanolamine abietate. Hydrochloric acid is used to reduce the pH to

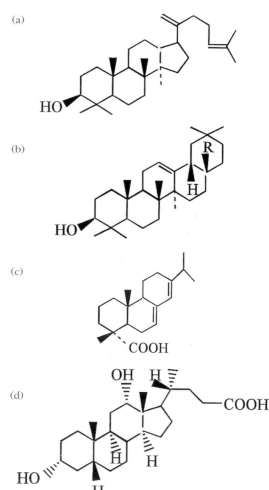

**Figure 16.17**
(*a*) Molecular structure of dammaradienol, a typical component of dammar
(*b*) Molecular structure of oleanolic acid, a typical component of mastic
(*c*) Molecular structure of abietic acid, a component of rosin
(*d*) Molecular structure of deoxycholic acid, a component of mammalian bile

8.5 (1 M refers to a one molar solution, see section 12.1.1). The solution is then filtered through coarse laboratory filter paper, placed on a magnetic stirrer and Triton XL-80N added if desired. HPMC is added to gel the solution. The gelled solution is usually applied with a cotton swab, stirred with a small soft brush for a moment and then removed.

*Deoxycholate soap recipe*

| | |
|---|---|
| 2 g | deoxycholic acid (free acid) |
| 5–6 ml | triethanolamine (TEA) |
| | HCl (1M) to adjust pH to 8.5, as needed |
| 0.1 g | Triton XL-80N |
| 2 g | hydroxypropyl methyl cellulose (HPMC) |
| 100 ml | distilled or deionized water |

The deoxycholic acid is added to the water and the TEA is stirred in to form triethanolamine deoxycholate. Hydrochloric acid is used to reduce the pH to 8.5. The solution is filtered and the HPMC added to gel the solution. An additional detergent such as Triton XL-80N can be added if required.

Resin and bile soaps require a three-stage rinse procedure. An initial rinse with a buffered solution of 0.5% to 1% ammonium acetate of the same pH as the original cleaning solution has been recommended. The buffer can be made from a 0.5% to 1% ammonia solution to which acetic acid has been added to adjust pH (information on buffers can be found in section 11.5.2). This should be followed by a neutral aqueous rinse or spit clean, followed by an aromatic hydrocarbon rinse if Triton X-100 or XL-80N has been included in the formulation (Stavroudis and Blank, 1990).

Aqueous cleaning systems can be expected to swell and possibly leach water-sensitive materials. Because water is a poor solubilizer of oil-based paint, aqueous cleaning systems were originally thought to avoid the swelling and leaching of oil paint substrates that occur as a side effect of solvent cleaning. Whilst it is undoubtedly true that swelling of oil paint films is virtually eliminated by using aqueous systems, leaching remains a problem. Research indicates that the amount of leaching by resin and bile soaps is roughly equivalent to typical solvent cleaning formulations, although most leaching occurred as a result of rinsing procedures rather than from the soaps themselves (Ford and Byrne, 1991). Other research has indicated that abietate gel leached slightly less than solvents such as hexane, toluene or acetone (Tsang and Erhardt, 1992). Factors that can affect the amount of detergent residues that are deposited during treatment or cleared in a rinse procedure are discussed in section 11.5.4.

### Removal of synthetic varnishes

Modern synthetic varnishes may have been applied to historic pieces, or may represent the original finish, for example on twentieth and twenty-first century objects. As with natural resin varnishes, the solubility parameters of most synthetic coatings change as they age. Many materials (both traditional and modern) applied to furniture have a tendency to crosslink. They can be difficult to resolubilize using solvents and may require a different strategy for removal. Incorporating surfactants may aid in dispersing such coatings. Polyurethane, for example, will swell in aromatic solvents, so an aromatic solvent gel may be effective (Landrey *et al.*, 1988). Some synthetic coatings, for example acrylics, don't necessarily oxidize, so the traditional approach of increasing the polarity of a solvent blend is less likely to be successful for removing them. In some cases non-polar solvents may be successful in removing such coatings, particularly in conjunction with a surfactant. As with all cleaning or varnish removal, it is helpful to understand the forces holding the coating together, and then formulate a strategy based on that particular polymeric material.

### 16.6.4 Removal of overpaint

Removal of old overpaint can be problematic, particularly where the retouch has the same binding medium as the original surface and was not isolated from it. In cases where overpaint is comprised of natural materials such as oils or resins, the strategy of swelling or dissolving overpaint follows the principles used for the solvent removal of varnishes. Standard solvents and mixtures (e.g. white spirit, xylene, IMS, acetone) may be successful. Mechanical methods may be successful in some cases, or may be required to reduce the amount of overpaint before other methods are used. Mechanical methods may also be used in combination with solvent-based solutions. In some cases may be possible to cleave an overlying layer from an underlying layer. It may be possible, by understanding the chemical nature of the materials involved, to develop a removal strategy on the basis of the specific materials present (Wolbers *et al.*, 1990).

The incorporation of pigments or metal soaps used as dispersing agents can make overpaint more resistant to dissolution than a coating composed of the same binder. Bronze powder retouchings, for example, often bound with an oil–resin mixture, were often applied to both water and oil gilded surfaces. As the binder ages and oxidizes it becomes more acidic and can catalyse the corrosion and discoloration of the metal flakes in the bronze paint. Metal salts can form within the film and crosslink it, making it even more difficult to swell or disperse in the solvents or solvent blends that might otherwise be expected to have an effect.

Where the retouch is very resistant it may be necessary to combine mechanical removal with the use of an alkali such as ammonium hydroxide, Vulpex (an alkaline detergent) or a chlorinated solvent such as dichloromethane. In the past dimethyl formamide has been a last resort but the toxicity of this solvent usually precludes its use. These materials work because they are strongly alkaline or very polar, but as such carry the very real danger that they will damage the original surface where they come into contact with it. Commercial paint strippers are often formulated with methanol, methanol chloride, toluene or dichloromethane, and may contain water and a surfactant. They are often effective in removing overpaint but will also tend to damage underlying original material. The more aggressive the removal method used, the more risk of damage to the surrounding paint. It may be a more ethical decision to leave the retouch intact rather than risking damage to the surrounding original decoration.

### 16.6.5    Consolidation

Paint surfaces that are flaking or friable often require consolidation before the surface is cleaned. Flaking, peeling and lifting paint can be treated by introducing a consolidant under the paint film to renew the adhesion of the paint film to the substrate and prevent further losses. The choice of consolidant is determined by the condition and sensitivity of the surface. Although wax has been used as a consolidant in the past, it is a poor adhesive and limits future treatment options and is therefore not recommended as a consolidant for painted surfaces. Where it has been used as a consolidant in the past it may be necessary to re-treat using wax or Beva 371. Common materials used for the consolidation of paint on wood include

protein based consolidants such as gelatin, sturgeon glue or isinglass, methyl cellulose, PVAC, acrylic dispersions and acrylic resins such as Paraloid B72. The advantages and disadvantages of common consolidants are discussed in section 12.2.4.

### 16.6.6    Reintegration

Samet (1998) has contrasted approaches to the aesthetic reintegration of paintings and painted furniture. Infilling and retouching media should ideally possess different solubility parameters from the original paint and be separated from it by a reversible isolating layer. They should also be undisturbed by the application of a final coating. Materials and approaches to infilling and retouching are considered in section 12.3. It is important to consider the sensitivity of the surface because a fill can act as a solvent reservoir and swell or damage adjacent original paint. Infilling of losses to painted surfaces may utilize a collagen, PVAL, PVAC or Paraloid adhesive and traditional whiting or microballoons may be used as a bulking agent. Aqueous pastes such as collagen or PVAL-based fills are often similar in density to gesso type grounds and are easy to manipulate, apply, level and clean up around the fill. Commercial spackles, which may be based on an acrylic dispersion, are used by some, but as with other fills, should be isolated from the original to ensure future reversibility or retreatability. A range of commercial vinyl and acrylic fill materials have been evaluated by Craft and Solz (1998).

### 16.6.7    Coatings

Common materials used for the coating of painted surfaces, their advantages and disadvantages, and application methods are discussed in section 12.4. It is essential that the final surface of the object is appropriate to current knowledge of its historical appearance. Coatings that appear to be thick, plastic and/or excessively glossy may be inappropriate for painted furniture. Painted furniture that is to be used or displayed in a domestic context may require a harder wearing coating than that needed for a museum context.

The application of varnish can result in leaching of paint films in a similar manner to that which occurs during the removal of varnish with solvents. Although solvent evaporates from the surface of an applied varnish coating, it also diffuses into the underlying paint film and will dissolve soluble components, carrying them into the varnish layer as the solvent diffuses through it and evaporates. Tsang and Erhardt (1992) demonstrated that the amount of leachable material found in varnish after only several days of drying was comparable to what would be extracted from the paint during solvent cleaning. Thus the selection of solvent used to apply varnish is as important as the choice of solvents used in cleaning. The bulk of solvent will evaporate out of the varnish film relatively quickly, but a small percentage will be retained and released slowly. The rate of release will depend on the chemical affinity between solvent and polymer and the stereochemistry of the solvent molecules – small linear unbranched solvents molecules will be retained least by a polymer film (Newman *et al.*, 1975). Films of Paraloid B72 retain a significant amount of toluene, for example, for many months. In comparison, *p*-xylene evaporates more slowly during the initial drying stage but is not retained by the B72 in the later stages (Dauchot-Dehon and De Witte, 1978).

Sutherland (2000) found that the leaching effect of a varnish solution on an oil paint film depended on the polarity of both the solvent and the resin component/s of the varnish. Of the resins tested, he found the following order of leaching effect: dammar > MS2A > Paraloid B72 > Regalrez 1094. He suggested this order was a result of polar functional groups, e.g. hydroxyl, carbonyl and carboxylic acid groups, contained in the structure of the resin. The use of a varnish composed of non-polar solvent and resin is indicated in cases where a painted surface has exhibited sensitivity to polar solvents.

### 16.6.8 Matte paint

Matte paint is characterized by a high pigment volume concentration (PVC). In other words, matte paint contains a high proportion of pigment and comparatively little binder. The treatment of matte paint has been considered by Feller and Kunz (1981), Hansen, (1990), Hansen and Bishop (1998), Hansen *et al.* (1993), Hansen *et al.* (1994) and Welsh (1980).

Cleaning matte paint is often problematic because the underbound paint surface may be damaged by contact with a swab or other cleaning tool. Consolidation is often required before cleaning can be undertaken. Consolidation is complicated by the fact that the surface of the paint is often characterized by voids between the pigment particles that are not filled by binder. If the consolidant fills these voids, some change in appearance is inevitable. The degree of change will in part depend on the amount of consolidant added and its distribution within the paint layer (Hansen, 1990). As a general rule, the darkening effect of a given consolidant can be minimized by using low concentrations (< 5%) in a slow-evaporating solvent that prevents reverse migration and deposition of consolidant on the surface. Thus Welsh (1980) reported success using a 4% solution of Paraloid B72 in diethylbenzene. Application techniques such as ultrasonic misting of aqueous consolidants with a concentration as low as 0.5% will prevent the treatment physically disturbing the surface and can minimize darkening as a result of consolidation (Michalski and Dignard, 1997; Michalski *et al.*, 1998).

The application of a coating to matte paint surfaces should be considered on a case-by-case basis but is usually inappropriate. In some cases the original decorative effect exploited differences in matte and gloss, for example chairs decorated as part of an overall interior scheme may contrast areas of matte paint with adjacent areas of highly burnished water gilding. It may be possible to apply a micro-thin coating using spray application that does not disrupt such original intent, or an aesthetic that accurately represents age and use. As a general rule, however, coatings will tend to fill the voids between the pigment particles and saturate the appearance of the surface.

## 16.7 Japanned furniture

### 16.7.1 Introduction to japanning

Japanning is a comparatively non-specific term and, in its broadest meaning, can encompass any surface finish produced in the West that approximated the appearance of Oriental lacquer, known in Japan as urushi. The conservation treatment of japanning is quite different to the conservation of Asian lacquer because the materials used to create each have little in common. Conservation treatments recommended for Asian lacquer are often inappropriate for japanning. In no case should urushi be used to restore European japanning. Information on the conservation of Oriental lacquer can be found in section 16.8.

Early sources, such as Evelyn (1670) and Stalker and Parker (1688/1960), refer to the use of alcohol soluble resins, whilst eighteenth century sources such as Dossie (1758) also refer to the use of oil–resin formulations. In the nineteenth century oil–resin formulations were adapted for use with papier mâché and were oven-baked to increase the durability of the finish. Such japanning is, in turn, distinct from the black paint applied to some English furniture, as a sign of mourning, after the death of Queen Victoria's consort, Albert. Finishes applied during the Edwardian revival of japanning may include materials newly developed in the early part of the twentieth century. Thus familiarity with historical sources, materials and techniques, such as Sayer (1762/1966), Tingry (1804) and Watin (1755) is essential for a conservator of japanned surfaces. More recent texts, such as Huth (1971) and John (1953), may also be helpful.

Broadly speaking, japanning can be divided into two types – spirit varnishes and oil varnishes. The first step in a conservation treatment is to identify the type of japanning present and its solubility parameters. Solubility parameters will affect options for cleaning, consolidation and the possible application of a coating.

In general, japanned finishes that were primarily based on spirit-soluble natural resins are not soluble in non-polar solvents such as hydrocarbons but remain soluble in alcohols and ketones, even after hundreds of years. Nineteenth century japanning based on baked oil finishes are usually insoluble in most common solvents and, as a result, there is a greater choice of mediums and solvents that may be applied to the surface. None the less, solubility tests should always be carried out prior to commencing work.

To develop methods of conservation that are compatible with either type of japanning, understanding the original processes is paramount. Through chemical analysis, examination of historical texts and the reproduction of original recipes, conservators realize that often the method of application is as important as the materials used. With an improved understanding of techniques we are able to develop better conservation treatments. See section 4.4.7 on japanning for further information on original techniques.

Case histories on the treatment of japanned surfaces include Bigelow (1990), Budden and Halahan (1994), Derrick *et al.* (1988), Hill (1976), Kühlenthal (2000), Webb (1998a, 1998b, 1989, 2000) and Wolbers *et al.* (1990). Ballardie (1996) has experimented with recreating historical recipes whilst other authors have focused on identifying original materials and techniques (Bernstein, 1992; Kühlenthal, 2000; Walch *et al.*, 1996). Resinous surfaces found on objects from Persia, India and the Near East have been discussed by Agrawal (1971, 1978) and Skálová (1993).

### 16.7.2    Examination of objects

Choosing the correct course of action is vital to the proper treatment of japanned finishes. A thorough examination should be undertaken. Ideally, detailed chemical analysis of the layers of varnish should be done, but for most conservators this may not be possible. Fortunately complex analysis is not always necessary to carry out a conservation treatment.

Cross-sections, which can be made with a minimum of equipment, will reveal much about the composition of the japanning. A microscopic examination of a cross-section under normal light conditions should enable one to distinguish the original layers from any later coatings (*Figure 16.18a,b*). Dirt, appearing as a black layer of particles, may be embedded in between the layers. The later coatings may not have the same degree of transparency as the original layers. UV microscopy, if available, is a particularly useful tool for examining and understanding japanned surfaces (*Figure 16.18c,d*). Examination of the object under hand-held ultraviolet light will often identify areas that have been overvarnished or repainted. Repainted or retouched areas may exhibit a different colour or intensity of fluorescence to the original (see section 13.3). An unaged varnish layer may appear very even in appearance in comparison to an aged varnish.

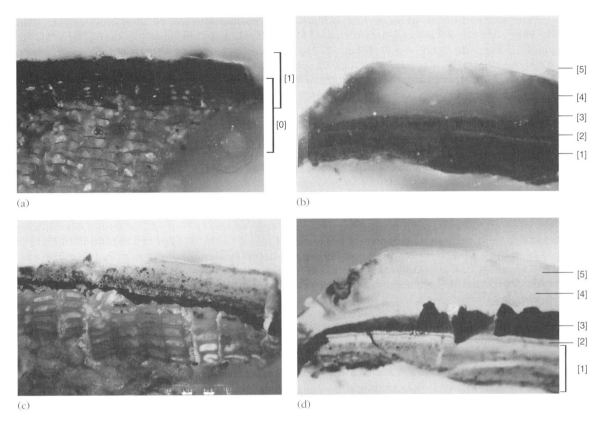

(a)  (b)  (c)  (d)

**Figure 16.18** Cross-sections of japanning
(*a*) Photomicrograph of a cross-section of a seventeenth century japanned surface viewed under visible light. (*a*) and (*b*) combined illustrate the entire stratigraphy of a seventeenth century japanned surface. The layers in (*a*) represent the original japanned surface (1). In this case no gesso layer was used, and the resinous japanning layers have penetrated into the cellular structure of the substrate wood (0). (*b*) Photomicrograph of a cross-section of upper restoration layers on a seventeenth century japanned surface viewed under visible light. The dark layers seen at the bottom right-hand side are the original japanning layers (1). The light line represents the first restoration layer (2). Above this is a thick black layer (3), which has partially dissolved in the white spirit used in conjunction with the coverslip when the section is viewed under the microscope. The thick translucent brown layer above this is a restoration varnish (4). Lastly, a thin modern varnish has been applied (5). (*c*) Photomicrograph of (*a*) viewed under UV. The natural resin component of the original japanning exhibits a bright white auto-fluorescence, whilst the non-fluorescent black pigments appear dark. The original japanning is comprised of four layers. The lowest, applied directly to the substrate wood, is densely pigmented. Pigment content is progressively reduced in the succeeding layers. The yellowish topmost layer in this photomicrograph represents the first restoration layer. (*d*) Photomicrograph of (*b*) viewed under UV. Three layers of the original auto-fluorescent resin-based japanning are visible (1). The orange auto-fluorescence of the first restoration varnish (2) indicates that it may be a shellac coating. The solubility of the second restoration layer (3) in white spirit may indicate significant bituminous content. The thick varnish in layer (4) is auto-fluorescing white, indicating a natural resin varnish. The modern synthetic coating (5) appears pale lavender

## 16.7.3 Cleaning

As stated in Chapter 11, the practitioner should be reminded that there is a vast difference between cleaning, which is the simple removal of dirt from the surface, and the removal of varnish layers. The removal of discoloured varnish on a work of japanning should not be considered part of any routine cleaning process. Japanned objects are created in a layered process, each layer serving to create the appearance of depth and translucency. The accidental (or deliberate) removal of original upper layers can seriously distort the original aesthetic of the surface.

If the japanned layers are in good condition, the first step in a cleaning treatment is to remove loose dirt with a soft brush. If the japanning is poorly adhered, lifting, flaking, or if the surface is broken up, the brushing must be undertaken with care. In some cases it may be possible to dust individual flakes, whilst in others consolidation may be required before, or at the same time as, cleaning.

Should the layer of dirt be more firmly attached than can be removed with a brush, dry cleaning methods, discussed in section 11.2.4, may be appropriate. If neither of these methods is effective, one must move to the next step in cleaning, which is the use of liquids. Liquids must be used with caution and solubility tests should be carried out prior to use. One must not only consider the solubility of the surface but the possible solubility of the underlying layers as well. The liquid must not be allowed to penetrate through the surface to dissolve an underlying layer. Underlying layers may be soluble in alcohol, aliphatic or aromatic hydrocarbon solvents or water. If one of the underlying layers is more soluble than the surface, cleaning should be discontinued. Liquids can be applied on a cotton swab, which is then rolled over the surface to remove dirt. If the surface is sound, some pressure may be applied. Avoid scrubbing the surface as even the finest cotton may abrade a highly polished surface. Many fabulous surfaces have been ruined from over-zealous cleaning. The cleaned areas should be dried with a wad of the same soft cotton. Only the finest, purest cotton should be used for cleaning japanned surfaces.

Since a great many japanned surfaces remain soluble in alcohol, it is not recommended for cleaning. Most japanned surfaces are not soluble in aliphatic hydrocarbons so these would be the first solvents to try. In the eighteenth and nineteenth century a large portion of asphaltum may have been included in the original formulation of oil-based japanning. Because asphaltum remains partially soluble in petroleum based products, it is advisable to carry out solubility test even with solvents considered benign to natural resin finishes. Although hydrocarbon solvents will remove fingerprints and any applied wax coating, much grime may require a polar solvent to remove it.

It is possible to clean some surfaces with water, but certain situations should be avoided. Aqueous solutions should not be used where damage to the surface means that water may penetrate to the ground or substrate. Water-soluble size on the surface, although rare in japanning, would also be removed by this approach to cleaning. Water should not be used on japanned metals since the water may accelerate the corrosion of the underlying metal.

If the surface is sound and insoluble, cleaning with water is not difficult. Moisture can be applied using a swab dampened with deionized water or saliva. Moisture should be applied to the surface only and thus the swab should be damp but not dripping wet. The surface should be dried immediately with soft cotton. Extended exposure to moisture may cause the japanned surface to bloom. The risk of bloom increases with the degree of ageing of the varnish and as the pH of the cleaning solution rises. Some very degraded natural resin surfaces may be partially soluble in water with a pH of only 8–8.5, a fact that has been exploited in varnish removal treatments (Wolbers *et al.*, 1990). The principles of aqueous cleaning, including the use of pH buffers, are discussed in section 11.5.

An alternative to wet or solvent cleaning is mechanical cleaning with abrasives. Fine abrasives can only be used on an undamaged, robust and relatively smooth surface. The methods outlined would not be the conservator's first choice but can be used in some cases when the use of solvent is not possible. A fragile surface may be lost due to the inappropriate use of abrasives. Using this technique will remove not only the dirt but a thin layer of the varnish as well. This method should be confined to circumstances where the varnish on the surface is not original. The disadvantages of using abrasives are that fine powder can become embedded in the craquelure, and a patchy appearance may result if abrasives are used on an uneven surface. This is often found in situations where the surface has previously cupped and then been consolidated. In such cases the raised areas will be abraded while the pits remain filled with discoloured varnish.

There are a number of different methods for the use of abrasives. Fine powders can be applied in mineral spirits or a non-drying oil.

In the past, abrasives such as rottenstone or tripoli powders were used, however there are many much finer abrasives available today. Abrasive particle size, hardness and the use of lubricants is considered in section 13.9. Micromesh polishing cloths are a good alternative to traditional abrasive powders. This product was developed for removing scratches from acrylic panels. A cushioned cloth holds particles of uniform size, which avoids both abrasive particles lodging in the craquelure and scratches caused by the inclusion of stray large particles. Micromesh cloths are available from 1500 to 12 000 grit, allowing the conservator a great deal of control over the amount of material removed and the final finish.

### 16.7.4 Removal of overpaint and later varnishes

Japanned furniture has often suffered from frequent applications of varnish – in one case up to thirty-three layers of overvarnish were found (Wachowiak and Williams, 1994). Removal of non-original varnish from japanned surfaces is often complicated by the similarity in solubility parameters between the original material and subsequent additions. This can be exacerbated if nineteenth-century oleo-resin varnishes have been applied over seventeenth- and early eighteenth-century resinous japanning. In some cases, for example where the upper layer is more aged and oxidized than a lower layer, the lower layer will dissolve more readily in solvents than the upper, unwanted layer.

The question of whether to remove non-original restoration varnishes often involves balancing aesthetic considerations, for example where an original design is obscured or distorted by multiple layers of discoloured varnish, against the potential risk of damaging the original layers. If such layer removal treatments are undertaken, analytical techniques such as microscopy (both visible light and UV) can help characterize or identify components in the layer structure and allow a more selective treatment.

The presence of water-sensitive metal leaf or powders often precludes the use of aqueous solutions. A more common approach is the use of solvents. The process of choosing the appropriate solvent is outlined in section 11.3.3. The advantage of a fast-acting solvent is that the solvent will be in contact with the surface for a shorter period of time, however, the solvent may act too quickly resulting in damage to the underlying surface. A slower solvent will give the conservator more control over the dissolution of the varnish, however, the underlying surface will be exposed longer which may cause damage by swelling (Michalski, 1990; see also section 11.3.3). Using a solvent gel may slow penetration of the solvent into the substrate and thus provide more control over the rate of dissolution of the varnish layers (*Plate 6*). Solvent gels are discussed in section 11.6.

Enzymes can be very useful to remove an oil varnish that has been applied over a natural resin coating. A water-based system using enzymes may be safer than solvents in many cases (Wolbers *et al*, 1990). Enzymes are discussed in section 11.5.6.

At first glance often the mechanical removal of later varnishes seems to be an attractive option. This is especially true if the layers are not well bonded to one another or a layer of dirt separates them. The principles and problems associated with cleaving are discussed in section 11.2.2. This method of 'pinging' off dirt or unwanted upper layers is limited by differences in adhesion and cohesion between different layers on the surface and by the skill of the conservator. Abrasives can be used to remove an unwanted varnish layer, subject to the limitations outlined in the discussion on cleaning above. Abrasives are considered in sections 11.2.3 and 13.9.

### 16.7.5 Consolidation

Materials and techniques for consolidation, outlined in Chapter 12, can be used on japanned surfaces. Many japanned surfaces have been applied over a protein-based ground layer. Often this gesso is a thin layer merely filling the pores of the wood. However, it is this layer that is the cause of much damage. Protein glues are hygroscopic and, in comparison to many synthetic adhesives, brittle. Fluctuations in RH cause corresponding expansion and contraction of the adhesive. The resultant stress often causes adhesive failure between the gesso ground and the substrate.

The other main form of cleavage occurs between the layers of varnish themselves. This may have been caused by a change in the formulation of the varnish or contamination of the surface between layers. Sometimes the clear varnish applied over the painted or gilded decorative layer is the one to separate. The approach to consolidation must take into account which layer of the japanned object is in need of consolidation.

Collagen glues such as rabbit skin glue, gelatin, or fish glues have been traditionally used in the repair of japanned objects when the gesso ground layer has delaminated from the substrate. The glues penetrate to the ground well, and since they shrink as they dry, the bond between the lifting flake and the substrate is quite good. However, water-based adhesives may cause blooming of the varnish layers. The risk of bloom increases as the pH of the adhesive rises, or with prolonged exposure of the surface to heat and moisture. Solutions from 2% to 5% have been used to successfully consolidate japanned ground layers. Different protein based glues can be used for different objects. Paler adhesives such as isinglass or gelatin can be used enough to consolidate light japanned pieces, where there is a danger that darker collagen adhesives may cause a colour change.

Synthetic adhesives such as emulsions or dispersions based on PVAC or acrylics are discussed in section 12.2.4. If such materials are used to consolidate the ground layer, the particular adhesive should be chosen with particular attention to long-term stability and flexibility. Acrylics are generally weaker and more flexible than PVAC (Down *et al.*, 1996) and may therefore be more appropriate in this context. Resolubility is also an important consideration. Ideally the dried consolidant should be resoluble in a solvent that does not affect either ground or varnish layers, such as aromatic hydrocarbons. Those that are resoluble only in water or very polar solvents such as acetone are inappropriate for use on japanned surfaces.

Paraloid B72 and Paraloid B67 have been used successfully over the past few decades in the consolidation of japanned surfaces and are a popular choice because of their excellent ageing characteristics. These are best used for separation between the varnish layers. Paraloid B72 should be used in situations where it is not left on the surface because it can impart an unnatural plastic appearance. Paraloid P67 has an appearance closer to those found on japan-

ning. Since both B72 and B67 can be dissolved in a number of solvents, it is possible to choose a medium that does not affect the surface. Hydrocarbon and aromatic solvents are good choices. When mixing either acrylic, the percentage should be kept fairly low. Several applications of 2% are better than a single application of 10%. The low concentration will aid penetration and prevent an unnecessary build up on the surface. Ideally one should have little or no consolidant remaining on the surface.

### 16.7.6    Infilling

#### *Fills for grounds*

When filling losses to japanned surfaces it is better to consider the ground layers and the varnish layers separately. To ensure reversibility of any of the fills listed below one should isolate the substrate from the fill with a readily soluble material before proceeding. One must remember that the fill should be weaker than the original surface. Should the wooden substrate move, it is better that the fill fall out than cause more damage to the original surface.

Traditional gesso fills of rabbit skin glue and calcium carbonate are appropriate for the ground layers since they are similar to the original. Barium sulphate can be added to the gesso to ensure that the fill can be identified as non-original. Before filling, the area surrounding the loss should be consolidated and the surface protected with a removable varnish. A very weak pigmented gesso can be used for a very fragile surface with numerous losses (Ballardie, 1994). For deeper losses, gesso dough is preferable to several applications of liquid gesso. This prevents the damage to the japanning from excess exposure to moisture.

The combination of PVAL and whiting can be used instead of the traditional rabbit skin glue gesso. Since the PVAL can be applied easily, dries fast and also can be burnished to a very smooth finish, it seems a good candidate for use as a fill in japanning (see section 12.3.1). As with any fill material, care should be taken not to expose the surface of the japanning to this material. Webb (1998a) reported the use of 6% PVAL in water, whiting and dry pigments to infill losses on a late seventeenth-century cabinet in the Royal Ontario Museum collection.

Wax has been used many times to infill loss in japanning. Unfortunately, once it has been used it is very difficult to remove. For this reason wax is not recommended for fills to japanning. However, wax fills have been used quite successfully for raised areas where the wax is prevented from entering the substrate. John Hill describes the use of microcrystalline wax, rottenstone and pigment mixed together to replace missing raised areas on the Pimm Highboy (Hill, 1976). Beeswax, carnauba or microcrystalline wax formulations could be used for fills that only involve the surface layer.

### Fills for papier mâché

Paraloid B72 mixed with black pigment and glass microballoons works quite well to fill small losses around mother-of-pearl on papier mâché. It is applied as a bulked paint to the small areas. It is also useful for small cracks.

The baked paper substrate of papier mâché is best filled with similar materials. Heavy rigid materials such as plaster and wood filler should be avoided. Fills can be made by building up layers of paper adhered with 3% methyl cellulose or wheat starch paste. Huxtable and Webber (1986) give comprehensive directions for preparing wheat starch paste. Long fibre paper, such as Japanese paper, is the best choice for such fills.

Paper fills can also be made in the original fashion. A mould can be taken of the desired shape from similar area of the piece, then paper and wheat starch can be used to build up the layers within the mould. Leaving the paper in the mould, it should be baked at 100 °F until the paper is hard. The resulting fill can be carved to fit precisely then be glued into place (Van der Reyden and Williams, 1986).

### Fills for japanned layers

Paraloid B67 or B72 can be mixed with dye to achieve a good approximation of the aged varnishes for both resin and oleo-resinous japanning. Orasol dyes (Ciba–Geigy) are particularly useful for this purpose. These dyed resins can be applied in layers over fills made of paper, traditional gesso, acrylic gesso, or PVAL and whiting. Either synthetic resin can be used, but the gloss of Paraloid B67 is more similar to the original japanned surface. The potential crosslinking of B67 should not present a sig-

nificant problem if retouch materials are applied over a reversible isolating layer (see section 12.3.2). The addition of microcrystalline wax will give a sheen similar to the japanned surface (Park, 1994).

Acrylic paints are suitable for inpainting japanning on papier mâché or metal. The opaque quality of the paint is not readily apparent on these materials. The gloss can be matched to the surrounding areas by building up thin applications. Acrylic gloss medium used with mica based pigment works well to inpaint losses in deteriorated gilded decoration. Dry pigment can also be mixed with Paraloid B72, B67 or PVA AYAF and used in a traditional inpainting approach.

Oil paints have often been used in the past to imitate the decorative layer. Their use is not recommended because paint based on drying oil crosslinks. This will present a serious problem for future removal from a spirit varnished surface.

### 16.7.7 Varnishes

Overall varnishing of japanned pieces will help to integrate fills and give a uniform appearance. However this should only be carried out if the application and future removal will not affect the original layers of japanning. Satisfactory, but not always invisible, fills can be achieved without revarnishing the entire piece.

High molecular weight synthetic varnishes, such as Paraloid B72, do not have the same appearance as natural resins (see section 12.4). Many pieces coated with high molecular weight synthetic resins in the past have an unnatural 'plastic' appearance, although this problem can be minimized if thin coats are used. The development of stabilized low molecular weight synthetic resins is of particular importance for the conservation of japanned surfaces. These resins, discussed in detail in section 12.4.7, share the optical properties of traditional natural resins but remain soluble in hydrocarbon solvents. Stabilized dammar or MS2A can also be used as a protective coating. Although many of these resins are softer than the original surface, they can be formulated or applied so that they approximate the sheen of an aged japanned finish. It may be possible to use a matting agent, spray technique or a mild abrasive (if the surface is sufficiently robust to withstand it) to reduce the gloss of such a coating.

It may be tempting to imitate the original surface using traditional japanning materials and techniques. However, for most losses the risk of damage to the surrounding area from the solvents and abrasive is too high. In the future it may also become difficult to distinguish the original surface from the later restoration. However, it is still a viable option for replacing missing parts or large isolated areas on a piece of furniture. Using chemical analysis of the existing japanning and a thorough understanding the original formulas, one can reproduce japanning quite close in appearance to the original (Walch, 1997).

## 16.8   Lacquered (urushi) furniture

### 16.8.1   Introduction and definition

The term lacquer is very non-specific and can encompass Oriental lacquer (called urushi in Japan), surfaces created in the West to simulate the appearance of Oriental lacquer (called japanning in Britain and North America), and is also applied to modern synthetic coatings such as nitrocellulose. The decorative surface discussed here is Oriental lacquer created from the sap of *Rhus verniciflua* (China, Korea and Japan), *Rhus succedanea* (Taiwan and Vietnam) or *Melanorrhoea usitata* (Thailand and Burma).

Oriental lacquer is a natural material and as a result there is considerable variation between lacquers from different sources. The quality of lacquer surfaces and objects varies depending on the raw materials used, methods of preparation, manufacturing techniques and the artisan's skill. The response of the material to conservation treatments will reflect these variations. As a general rule, objects made for export were of a significantly lower quality than those created for the domestic market. An exception to this rule was the Japanese export lacquer produced in the seventeenth century, e.g. the Mazarin chest (V&A Museum). Although wood is a common substrate, lacquer has been applied to metal, leather, ceramic, turtleshell, ivory, horn and cloth. Decorative lacquer surfaces are usually pigmented and may include metal foils or powders, ivory, coral or mother-of-pearl.

Material aspects of Oriental lacquer are discussed in Chapter 4. The conservation of lacquer objects has been considered by Webb (2000). Kumanotani (1988, 1995, 1998) discussed the chemistry of Oriental lacquer, whilst Umney (1987a, 1987b) considered chemistry and conservation. Proceedings of conferences, such as Barrington and Fryer (1999), Brommelle and Smith (1988), Kühlenthal (2000b) and those held by the Tokyo National Research Institute of Cultural Properties (1978, 1980, 1995) cover chemistry, history and conservation case histories in Japan and the West using both traditional and non-traditional materials. Case histories of the conservation treatment a variety of Oriental lacquer objects have been presented by Budden and Halahan (1994), Minney (1994) and Chase *et al.* (1988), among others. The corrosion of lead and lead/tin alloy inlay in lacquer objects is discussed by Heath and Martin (1988).

### 16.8.2   Handling lacquer

The best quality lacquer is very durable and, at least initially, highly resistant to water and organic solvents. Water forms a small but essential part of the structure of the lacquer film. Loss of water due to excessively low relative humidity will lead to loss of toughness, an increase in brittleness and changes in barrier properties to water and oxygen. Exposure to short wavelength light and UV radiation causes the surface of the lacquer to become hydrophilic and results in a reduction of surface gloss. One consequence of this is the tendency of residues from ungloved handling to

**Figure 16.19**   Fingerprint etched into the surface of a nineteenth century Japanese lacquer writing box

permanently etch the lacquer, leaving the surface irreversibly marred by fingerprints (*Figure 16.19*). When handling lacquer objects, it is essential either to wear gloves or, after ungloved contact, to wipe down a surface with mineral or white spirits.

### 16.8.3  Distinguishing Oriental lacquer from japanning

Japanning and lacquer on furniture may appear similar at first sight. Both are characterized by a pigmented background that originally often had a lustrous appearance and was frequently decorated with raised and gilded detail. Designs for japanned ornament were often derived from porcelain or fanciful interpretations from other sources. The two surfaces are often found on the same object and lacquer may have been restored, altered or embellished using japanning materials and techniques. Japanning and Oriental lacquer can usually be distinguished on the basis of the nature and quality of their decorative elements. Close inspection of areas of loss or cleavage may allow identification by revealing lower layers. Examination under UV light, microscopy and solvent testing can also be used to distinguish these materials.

The imprecise nature of identification of coatings under UV is discussed in section 13.3. When studying a surface under UV, conservators should bear in mind that they can only see the uppermost layer of the object. This may represent an original surface or merely the latest in a long line of 'restoration' varnishes. Within the context of these limitations, japanning based on natural European resins may fluoresce greenish-yellow or pale creamy-orange. The appearance of Oriental lacquer under UV varies considerably, probably as a result of the type of lacquer used for the final coat. Thus nashiji lacquer, which may have been applied as the final coating over sprinkled nashiji gold powder, may have a startlingly bright orange auto-fluorescence. Black lacquer may exhibit a muted or bright orange auto-fluorescence (see *Plate 2*). Makie decoration may appear black (non-fluorescent) or exhibit an orange auto-fluorescence. Unaged shellac has a distinctive bright orange auto-fluorescence. It is important that the conservator does not mistakenly interpret orange fluorescence on lacquer as indicat-

**Figure 16.20**  Photomicrograph of a thin section of Oriental lacquer viewed under visible light. The layer structure of both ground (1) and lacquer (2) is clearly visible

ing the presence of a shellac varnish. Under UV the presence of non-fluorescing makie decoration against an autofluorescent orange background is indicative of Oriental lacquer. Conservators may wish to confirm the presence of a European varnish with additional analysis.

Cross-sections of seventeenth and eighteenth century japanning executed in resin or oil–resin varnishes will reveal a surface similar in many ways to a painted surface. There may be a gesso type ground, layers of autofluorescent resin in which the pigment content is reduced in stages and finally clear varnish on top. Lacquer sections viewed in cross-section will reveal ground layers below the decorative layers (*Plate 8a*). Viewed under UV, Oriental lacquer may autofluoresce bright or pale orange (*Plate 8b*), or not at all. Natural resin varnish layers added in the west may be found autofluorescing above the lacquer (*Plate 8c*). Samples viewed in thin section will reveal the structure of the lacquer layers (*Figure 16.20*). The process of mounting cross-sections producing a thin section is illustrated in *Figure 16.21*.

Solvent testing has also been proposed as a method of distinguishing japanning and Oriental lacquer (Westmoreland, 1988). When newly manufactured, lacquer is impervious to water or organic solvents and reputedly loses gloss when exposed to nitric acid (80%) or sodium hydroxide (50%) (Nagase, 1986). Oriental lacquer remains insoluble as it ages, though its degradation products are soluble in

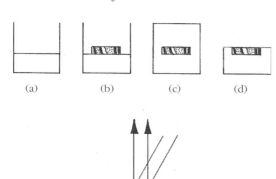

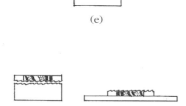

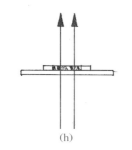

**Figure 16.21** Producing thin sections is done in several stages. The first step is to embed a sample in polyester resin, as for samples that will be examined under reflected light (*a–e*). The polished and mounted sample is sawn from the polyester resin mounting block (*f*) and glued, polished side down, to a glass microscope slide. It is then ground and polished until it is thin enough for light to pass through the sample: (*a*) Half pan of cured polyester resin. (*b*) Sample placed onto half pan. (*c*) Polyester resin poured to enclose the sample. (*d*) Once cured, polyester is ground and polished to reveal a cross-section. (*e*) Reflected light is used to examine cross-section
(*f*) The lower part of the polyester resin block is sawn away. (*g*) The polished surface of the cross-section is glued to a glass microscope slide and polished. (*h*) Transmitted light is used to examine the thin section produced

water and polar organic solvents. In contrast, japanning manufactured from natural resins and oil–resin varnishes begins and remains wholly or partially soluble in polar organic sol-

vents. Solvent tests should be carried out in an area that is both unobtrusive and that accurately represents the surface. If the object has mounts, for example, it may be possible to test the surface after a mount has been removed. Areas that may have undergone selective past restoration should be avoided. Solvents such as ethanol or acetone will dissolve natural resins and swell crosslinked linseed oil (see *Figures 11.10, 11.11*; Gettens and Stout, 1966).

### 16.8.4 Eastern and Western approaches to restoration and conservation

Repair of lacquer objects in the Far East has traditionally involved the use of lacquer-type materials. Artisans and artists skilled in the making of lacquer objects also undertake repairs. The long-term success of such repairs is dependent on the skill, experience and sensitivity of the craftsperson. As in the West, lacquer objects in Japan are esteemed for their decorative and historical value, but also have additional cultural resonance. Lacquer continues to be used to create functional, artistic and religious objects. Japanese artists, in addition to preserving an object, may wish to identify and recreate traditional techniques in order to pass them on to future generations.

Lacquer objects in the West have often been treated with a range of materials, such as natural resins, waxes and oils, with varying degrees of success. Though these materials may have been satisfactory when they were applied, they have poor ageing properties and usually become dull and discoloured. In the more recent past, lacquer objects in the West have been treated with principles of conservation in mind, with non-traditional materials that are photochemically stable and, at least in theory, reversible. Some of the techniques used in the West, e.g. wax fills, are not compatible with traditional materials (Nakajima, 1988).

Cultural exchange has engendered a variety of approaches in both East and West. Some Western conservators use Oriental lacquer-based materials, whilst synthetic resins may be utilized in Japan. Approaches to the conservation of lacquer vary according to the ethics, experience and skills of the individual undertaking the treatment. The use of lacquer-based materials for the consolidation, infilling, retouching and coating of lacquer objects is, however, beyond the scope of this section.

## 16.8.5 Cleaning

### *Potential problems*

As with other varnished or decorative surfaces, different areas on the same lacquer object may exhibit different responses to an identical treatment. The cleaning of Oriental lacquer may be complicated by previous treatments or by a differing history of exposure to light. The exterior of a box, for example, may respond differently to an interior that has been protected from exposure to UV. Black lacquer made by a reaction between raw lacquer and iron hydroxides, and dark brown lacquer are particularly prone to UV damage as they age. Black lacquer that has been coloured with pigment is the least sensitive to such changes.

Exposure to short-wave light and UV changes the physical and chemical properties of Oriental lacquer. There is an inverse relationship between the previous exposure to UV of a lacquer surface and its resistance to water and polar organic solvents. The more UV exposure Oriental lacquer has received, the more polar the surface, the more polar the dirt adhering to it and the more polar the solvents needed to separate the two. Light-damaged lacquer is extremely hydrophilic. With reference to cleaning, the most important changes are the development of cracks in the lacquer layer and an overall increase in sensitivity to water, polar solvents and elevated pH.

Cracks in Oriental lacquer may extend through the entire thickness of the lacquer coating (*Figure 16.22*). Such cracks can act as capillaries for solvents or water used to clean or deliver consolidant, allowing liquid to penetrate through to the ground layers. The effect of the capillarity is that liquid may wick in rapidly but evaporate out very slowly. As a result, solvents may be retained in both ground layers and lacquer for an extended period. Retained water or polar solvents may cause delamination or discoloration of the lacquer. If the surface is very light-damaged, the degree of penetration (and retention) of solvent during cleaning is best limited by using minimal solvent, e.g. a barely dampened swab or soft cotton cloth. Gelled solutions do not sufficiently limit exposure of the lacquer surface and, as a general rule, should be avoided.

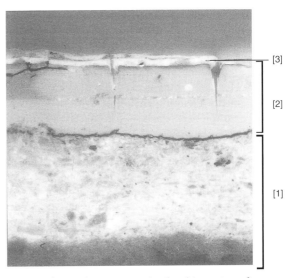

**Figure 16.22** Photomicrograph of a thin section of Oriental lacquer. Long exposure to light has led to photochemical degradation of the lacquer and the resultant cracks extend through the decorative layers (2). In some cases such cracks can extend through to the ground layers (1). Old restoration varnishes are visible on the surface of the lacquer (3)

The effect of pH and conductivity on the water-sensitivity of aged lacquer coatings has not been quantified as yet. The sap of urushi, when initially collected, has a pH between 5.5 and 7. This corresponds to the optimal pH for enzyme activity as the sap matures. The pH of matured liquid raw urushi is around 4.5 (Kenjo, 1988). It seems safe to assume that pH of dried lacquer films starts similarly low, and may drop even further as it ages. Certainly, aged urushi coatings can be completely solubilized by aqueous solutions with a pH of 8.5–9.5. It is prudent to assume that the more light damaged and oxidized the surface, the more sensitive to elevated pH it will be.

### *Removal of surface dirt and accretions*

Aliphatic hydrocarbon solvents are unlikely to damage Oriental lacquer because degradation products are not soluble in these solvents. Swabs slightly dampened with solvent (e.g. white spirit) should be lightly rolled, not rubbed, over the surface. The exposure of the lacquer to solvent can be limited by using a soft cotton cloth. The cloth can be wrapped around a (gloved) fingertip, a drop or two of solvent applied with a pipette, and the cloth wiped very lightly over the surface.

Dry cleaning materials such as a smoke sponge or Draft Clean granules, described in section 11.2.4, may be used to remove dust from lacquer. Care must be taken not to scratch the surface of the lacquer and a lubricating solvent (white or mineral spirits) may be useful. Not all dry cleaning materials are appropriate; for example erasers are too harsh for many lacquer surfaces.

Due to the polar nature of aged lacquer surfaces, water is often very effective for removing surface dirt. There is a danger, however, of solubilizing and removing lacquer degradation products. The safety of cleaning lacquer with water is in part dependent on condition of lacquer surface (e.g. the history of exposure to UV, previous treatments) and partly dependent on the skill and experience of the conservator. Water will remove surface dirt, which will often have a black appearance on a swab. Continued swabbing of a degraded surface with water will begin to solubilize degradation products, which are light brown in colour. As a general rule, if the surface is glossy and lustrous water is less likely to cause damage. Water should be avoided for cleaning surfaces that are dull and degraded. If water is used to remove dirt, a slightly dampened swab may be applied to a small area that is immediately dried with clean fresh cotton wool. Using a swab that is too wet, or leaving the moisture in contact with the surface for too long can result in unsightly water marks and tidelining.

The use of water is much favoured by Japanese conservators. One method involves two soft cotton cloths (e.g. cut from an old white T-shirt). The first piece of cloth is dipped in water and then wrung out to remove excess liquid. The second (dry) cloth is then rolled in the first and the two squeezed together. The second cloth, now slightly dampened, is wrapped around a fingertip and, with a circular motion, used to gently wipe a small area (a square inch or so) of the urushi surface. Although this sounds a simple procedure, the wrong amount of moisture, the wrong cloth, or this technique applied inappropriately to a sensitive surface, can all cause damage (Murose, 1996).

### Cleaning decorative elements
The effect of a cleaning treatment on decorative elements within a lacquer surface may differ from the effects observed on the background element of the design. Makie (sprinkled metal powder) decoration may be poorly adhered and is very vulnerable to the cumulative abrasive effects of cleaning treatments. Cleaning makie decoration involves a judgement about the original intent of the maker, as 'discoloration' may be a result of deliberate patination rather than ageing and corrosion. Tarnish on silver makie, for example, was often an intended patina. Such deliberate patination should not be removed. If the original intent is unknown or unclear, treatment should be limited to the removal of surface dirt.

Kirikane (cut metal) and other types of metal foil decoration are particularly vulnerable to damage during cleaning as they may be loose. Before cleaning commences, metal foil decoration should be carefully examined, under a low magnification bench microscope if necessary, to ensure that it is well adhered. If not, it should be consolidated before being cleaned.

Water is very effective for cleaning mother-of-pearl, which is often fragile and brittle. It is important to avoid over-cleaning or excess pressure that will change the appearance of the shell and the overall aesthetic balance of the object. Shell may have been adhered with a water-soluble adhesive such as animal glue and a slightly dampened swab will limit the potential for water to penetrate under the shell. Delicate surfaces, such as aogai (blue–green) shell inlay, may be cleaned through paper. A thin flexible paper can be laid over the surface, solvent applied and a soft brush pounced on the surface. Dirt will become attached to the paper whilst the surface is protected from excessive mechanical action. Different papers will absorb slightly different materials, so some experimentation may be called for.

### Removing unwanted coatings
Wax has often been applied to Oriental lacquer. Excess wax will result in a cloudy or smeared surface and a halo of wax may build up around raised decorative elements (*Figure 16.23*). Wax may be removed with aliphatic or aromatic hydrocarbon solvents, though some additional mechanical action with cotton wool or a dry cleaning material may also be necessary. Chloroform may be an effective solvent in particularly refractory cases.

(a)

(b)

**Figure 16.23** Japanese inro
(*a*) Before conservation: accretions of wax form a halo around raised decoration
(*b*) After conservation: wax was removed with an aromatic hydrocarbon solvent

**Figure 16.24** Detail of a lacquer panel (*c.*1640) incorporated into a French fall front secretaire (*c.*1790–1810) during conservation. Degraded varnish was removed from the lacquer panel with ethanol

Oriental lacquer objects in the west were often given a coat of a natural resin varnish to restore lustre to the surface or as part of a restoration treatment. In many cases, the subtlety of lacquer decoration is compromised by such coatings, for example loss of contrast between matte and gloss areas or variations in makie decoration (*Figure 16.24*). The difficulty in removing an aged, natural resin varnish from a light-damaged lacquer surface is that the materials which will most readily remove the natural resin varnish are also the most likely to blanch or damage the underlying lacquer. If the removal of varnish is deemed necessary, it should be undertaken with the least polar solvent or solvent blend possible. It has been observed that the more hydrogen bonding plays a role in the cleaning action of a solvent or solvent blend, the more potential there is to disrupt or damage the surface of the lacquer (Rivers, 2003).

It is important that solvents do not penetrate the lacquer, via cracks in the surface, to the ground layers below. Gelled solutions do not sufficiently limit exposure of the lacquer surface and, as a general rule, should be avoided. In a few cases, where the underlying lacquer is in good condition, or where its surface has been so harshly treated in the past that the very water/solvent sensitive upper layers have been removed, it may be possible to remove an unwanted varnish using swabs moistened with solvents. In most cases, however, this treatment is unsuitable and a method that uses minimal solvent may be tested. A few drops of acetone, ethanol, or 80:20 ethanol and water, can be applied to a small piece of soft cotton cloth. The cloth may be wrapped around a fingertip and moved with very light pressure in a circular motion across a small area (a square inch or so) of the surface. As solvent diffuses into the resin coating it will start to swell and may blanch (become white). Continued treatment with *very* light pressure will remove the coating. This technique requires caution and patience. All the solvents mentioned above can damage lacquer if used insensitively and, even if a particular solvent is successful, this is a time-consuming process.

Non-drying oils such as almond oil can be removed with white spirit. Coatings of a drying oil or oil–resin varnish may be problematic. Removal of linseed oil, for example, usually requires polar solvents, elevated pH or enzymes. Polar solvents and elevated pH may cause significant damage to the underlying lacquer surface, depending on its condition. Michalski (1990) has tabulated data on the swelling effect of some solvents and solvent blends on linseed oil films. The use of a lipase treatment is dependent on the sensitivity of the underlying lacquer to aqueous solutions, and whether the enzyme can function at a pH that will not damage the lacquer.

### 16.8.6  Consolidation

Separation of upper layers from lower foundation layers is perhaps the most common consolidation problem that will be encountered on Oriental lacquer objects. This is most often a result of environmental conditions, particularly low or fluctuating RH, or the original manufacturing technique. Protein adhesives such as animal glue or animal blood were used in some foundation layers. Grounds based on clay and animal glue, typical of Japanese Meiji period (1868–1912) lacquerware, are comparatively weak and often fail. In the case of lacquer-based foundation layers, the amount of lacquer binder used at the time of manufacture was often reduced to speed drying. As the object ages, however, insufficient binder can lead to detachment between upper layers and foundation, and between foundation layers and the substrate (Minney, 1999).

Consolidation of lacquer can be undertaken using lacquer-based materials or synthetic resins. Lacquer-based materials, which crosslink, are irreversible. Synthetic resins applied to a porous and fragile substrate or layer offer the advantage of retreatability and a degree of reversibility.

### Softening brittle lacquer before consolidation

Cups, blisters or flakes on an Oriental lacquer surface are often brittle and may require softening before consolidation can be undertaken. Humidification, heat and the use of polar solvents may soften lacquer sufficiently to allow it to be relaid flat onto the substrate.

Humidification at around 70% RH is often effective for softening brittle lacquer. A Gore-Tex sandwich may be useful for localized short-term humidification (see section 15.2.2). Humidification for an extended period, e.g. one to six months, may be necessary, depending on the thickness of the lacquer and the nature and thickness of the substrate. The traditional method for humidifying lacquer furniture is to use a wooden box, though polythene or Perspex may be substituted. If wood is used for a humidification box, the conservator should be aware of the acidity of the wood and its potential for off-gassing volatile organic acids, particularly acetic acid (*Table 10.1*). Such off-gassing increases as temperature and RH increase, and will damage many metals used for decorative inlay. Consideration should be given to the long-term effect of humidification on the substrate. Humidifying lacquer furniture that has been stored or displayed in an environment with low RH may be problematic. If a wooden substrate has split, for example, a sustained cycle of high RH, followed by a return to ambient low RH conditions can exacerbate compression set. It may also cause additional stress on the lacquer or ground that has been consolidated.

Heat can be used to soften and 'relax' distorted lacquer but as the lacquer cools it usually resumes the distorted shape. A heated spatula, isolated from the surface with silicone release paper or Melinex/Mylar, may be used to apply heat (*c.*55–60 °C) to a small localized area. Short exposure to heat may be insufficient to soften the lacquer. Webb (1995) described the use of a thermal sheet in combination with weights, applied over a period of several days, to flatten distorted lacquer. The combined use of heat and moisture has the potential to discolour lacquer. Webb (2000) reported that the combination of moisture and heat as low as 50 °C from a spatula could result in a colour change on the surface of light-damaged lacquer.

Extended exposure to polar solvents of the underside of a flake may soften the lacquer sufficiently to allow it to be eased back into place with small weights or a heated spatula. Unfortunately extended exposure to polar solvents may also cause significant damage to the surface of the lacquer.

### Flattening distorted lacquer

General techniques for cramping are discussed in section 10.1.10. The traditional Japanese method for cramping consolidated lacquer deserves a brief mention. Flexible sticks braced against a frame to apply pressure to lacquer-ware objects are called shimbari (*Figure 16.25*). The amount of pressure applied depends on the thickness of the stick and the degree to which it is bent. Foam or small pieces of rubber can be used to protect the surface and prevent the sticks slipping. The use of small pieces of Perspex allows the conservator to see the surface as progressive cramping pressure is applied.

Flakes, cups or tenting may be flattened incrementally, after humidification, by introducing a *small* amount of ethanol or a blend of 95% ethanol and 5% water to the underside. Shimbari can then be used to apply very gentle pressure, flattening the distorted lacquer by 0.5–1 mm. The pressure and the humidified state of the lacquer should be maintained for some time, depending on the thickness and condition of the lacquer. The process is repeated until the distorted lacquer is flat and can be adhered to the substrate.

If an area of a lacquer surface has become fragmented, the pieces may be assembled using tiny pieces of transparent pressure-sensitive tape. A thermoplastic adhesive may then be applied to the underside and the ground and the whole relaid in a manner appropriate to the chosen adhesive. The amount of adhesive applied should be just sufficient to adhere the lacquer to the object. Excess pressure may force adhesive out onto the surface, where extended contact during drying may damage the lacquer. A thermoplastic adhesive will allow the additional use of a heated spatula, isolated from the surface with Melinex/Mylar, during the consolidation treatment. Any remnants of adhesive from pressure-sensitive tape may be removed with a hydrocarbon solvent.

(a)

(b)

**Figure 16.25** Shimbari
(*a*) Applying shimbari to a nineteenth century Japanese lacquer tea table
(*b*) Detail of shimbari used to apply pressure to a lacquer surface. Consolidation utilized traditional materials (mugi urushi)

### Materials

Webb (1995, 1999, 2000) has reviewed the use of synthetic consolidants for lacquer. This section identifies problems that may be encountered and approaches that may be used when consolidating Oriental lacquer. The advantages and disadvantages of various materials used for consolidation are discussed in section 12.2.4.

Wax and wax/resin mixtures have been used with varying success in the past but impart little strength and are incompatible with most other adhesives. These materials are not recommended for consolidating Oriental lacquer.

Water-based consolidants are often useful for consolidating lacquer because they can penetrate and adhere well. Although some may be used in conjunction with heat, the combination of water and heat has the potential to cause thermochromatic discoloration of lacquer (Webb, 2000). It is necessary to balance consolidant concentration (degree of adhesion) against solution viscosity (degree of penetration). Water-based consolidants, particularly those based on collagen adhesives, must often be very dilute (2–5%) and, at this concentration, may be insufficient to consolidate very degraded porous grounds. PVAC based consolidants can offer a combination of good penetration and adhesion.

Consolidant solutions applied in polar solvents or water may act as solvent reservoirs until they have completely dried, leading to softening or distortion of the lacquer surface. Where the ground is friable and porous this may lead to spalling. It is essential to avoid leaving excess adhesive on the surface when carrying out localized treatment such as laying flakes. The conservator should apply pressure, release it, remove excess adhesive and repeat this procedure until no excess remains on the surface.

### Shell inlay

The brittleness and translucence of shell inlay may complicate consolidation. The ground layer under shell inlay varies in colour and in the adhesive material used. Many consolidants will saturate the colour of the ground, darkening it and changing the colour or reflectance of shell inlay. The effect of consolidants may be tested using glass or a facsimile that mimics the colour of the ground. If it is necessary to add pigment or filler to the consolidant, matte combinations will cause the least colour change, but adhere poorly in the long term. Very dilute animal or fish glue has been successful in some cases.

### 16.8.7 Infilling

If an area of loss that exposes the substrate and ground to the ambient environment is left unsealed or unfilled it can lead to a continuing process of adhesive failure and damage to adjacent areas of lacquer. The use of an inappropriate fill material can have the same result. Webb (1994, 1998, 2000) has reviewed the use of a range of filling materials for lacquer. Considerations that may influence the choice of fill materials include the condition of the surrounding lacquer surface, the sensitivity of

the lacquer to the fill medium, ease of levelling and possible abrasive effect on adjacent lacquer, and reversibility or retreatability.

Wax and wax–resin mixtures have been used as filling materials in the past, when they were often heated and applied directly into the area of loss. It has been suggested that, in addition to the difficulty of removing residues, wax may migrate into the areas immediately adjacent to the fill and lead to further adhesive failure (Nakajima, 1988). Many Eastern and Occidental lacquer conservators are opposed to the use of wax as a fill material. Wax fills may be applied to small areas of damage where an isolating layer has been used, but should not be applied directly into a loss from a lacquer surface.

Paraloid B72 bulked out with microballoons has been used to fill deep cracks and to support tented lacquer where substrate shrinkage meant relaying the lacquer flush with the substrate was not possible (Webb, 1994). PVAL has been used with some success for filling losses in the ground layers. Acrylic emulsions and dispersions may be mixed with an inert filler to create a reversible fill (see Fill materials, section 12.3.1).

Two approaches may be useful when filling losses to lacquer. A filler paste may be made with minimal solvent and applied in a single operation. Alternatively, the fill may be built up in thin layers and allowed to dry before the following layer is applied. In both cases the underlying principle is to minimize exposing the adjacent lacquer to solvent whilst the fill is drying.

Thermosetting resins such as polyesters or epoxies may be cast and used as fill materials. It may be necessary to seal the original surface to prevent its contamination by the release agent or the casting material. Such a sealant should be compatible with the adhesive that will be used to fix the cast replacement into position. A volatile 'binding' media such as cyclododecane may prove useful (Brückle *et al.*, 1999). Materials and techniques used for casting are discussed in section 10.5. Carr and Driggers (1997) reported success with the use of silicone moulds and an epoxy bulked with pigment.

### 16.8.8 Retouching

Once a surface has been filled, it may be desirable to match the repair to the existing surface.

Retouching may involve reproducing not just the colour of the original, but also the translucence and reflective properties of the surrounding area, and in some cases, texture. The retouching materials and techniques discussed in section 12.3.2 may be useful, with the proviso that those in a non-polar binding medium will have the least potentially detrimental effect on adjacent lacquer. One of the characteristics of Oriental lacquer that proved so attractive to Europeans in the past, the translucence of the surface, is one of the characteristics that can cause difficulty when retouching. It may be possible to partially simulate this property with a gradual transition from pigment-rich to medium-rich layers. This process will be assisted if the retouch medium can be abraded smooth between layers. Some paints mediums, such as the Intenso range, may be burnished instead of abraded. This can be helpful because the retouching is easier to level and the burnished paint can simulate Oriental lacquer better than a gloss medium. Webb (1994, 1998, 2000) reported success using dyes and pigments in an acrylic emulsion. Natural resin varnishes such as dammar, and the traditional furniture retouching medium, shellac, can be used, though they have a tendency to yellow, and will develop craquelure as they age. Stabilized hydrogenated hydrocarbon resins, discussed in the section on synthetic low molecular weight varnishes (section 12.4.7), may be a better alternative. They can be applied and removed without exposing the lacquer to polar solvents and are more photochemically stable than their traditional counterparts.

### 16.8.9 Restoring a degraded matte surface

In some cases it is possible to remove a thin upper layer from a degraded and dull lacquer surface in order to restore a degree of gloss to the surface. Such treatments are not generally recommended because they may damage decoration and are irreversible. In addition, some subtleties in the original design may be lost and the restored surface may not accurately represent the age or history of the object. As with Western furniture, signs of age may add to a lacquer object's financial and historical value. Some collectors prize dull surfaces as an indication of age. The decision to restore a matte surface should only be taken in consultation with an owner or curator. Speculative restoration should be avoided. Care should be taken to avoid localized treatment that may result in a patchy appearance.

Two approaches can be used. In the first, the surface of the lacquer is rubbed gently with a soft cotton cloth slightly dampened with water, until the upper layer of lacquer that has been dulled by photo-oxidation is removed (see section 16.8.5 on removal of surface dirt and accretions). The second method makes use of abrasives. If the surface of the Oriental lacquer is treated with abrasives, only those that are soft and have finely divided particles should be used, in combination with a lubricant such as white or mineral spirits (see *Table 10.3*). Progress should be checked frequently by clearing the surface of slurry and examining the effect. Abrasives may be applied on a small pad made from high quality cotton wool and a soft cotton cloth. The method illustrated in *Figures 13.12* and *13.13* for making a French polishing rubber can be adapted for this purpose. Swabs are not recommended because they may cause excessive localized abrasion. Proprietary abrasive mixtures should be avoided because the abrasive particles are often large, excessively hard and may irreversibly damage lacquer surfaces. It is important to ensure that all residues of cleaning materials are removed when the treatment is complete.

### 16.8.10 Coatings

The decision whether to apply a coating to a lacquer object after a conservation treatment must be taken on a case-by-case basis after considering conditions of use, display or storage. Although there may be occasions when the application of a coating is appropriate, as a general rule coatings should not be applied to lacquer unless they meet a specific need and can be removed in the future without damaging the original surface. Restoration coatings are rarely consistent with the original intended appearance and may be misleading to an inexperienced viewer.

If a coating is applied, its intended role should be clear. If a coating is to provide a UV barrier, for example, it must incorporate a UV inhibitor as transparent coatings *per se* do not prevent the transmission of UV to the substrate.

A better long-term option would be to remove UV from the ambient environment.

Wax has been applied to lacquer surfaces both as a protective coating and to increase the lustre of a degraded surface. Wax coatings can be a comparatively effective moisture barrier (Brewer, 1991). Wax coatings can, however, also exacerbate accretions of dirt, create a cloudy appearance and may be problematic to remove (Webb, 1995).

A resin-type coating may be a compromise decision if the appearance of the surface is not acceptable and a suitable surface cannot be recovered. In some cases a coating may unify a surface decorated with both japanning and Oriental lacquer. The application of very thin layers is easier with a spray gun than a brush. Coating materials and photochemical stabilizers are discussed in section 12.4. Stabilized hydrogenated hydrocarbon resins represent a more ethical option than the use of traditional natural resins.

## 16.9   Gilded furniture

### 16.9.1   Introduction to conservation of gilded surfaces

The conservation of gilded surfaces is a comparatively young discipline that requires familiarity and experience with both traditional and modern materials and techniques. It is essential that the conservator keeps abreast with current conservation literature and ongoing developments in the field. The use of synthetic materials and conservation techniques has been accompanied by a great deal of debate and decisions should be made on a case by case basis, with a clear understanding of the aims and principles of treatment, and the needs of the object in mind. Thompson (1956, 1962) and Cennini (trans. Thompson, 1954) discuss historical recipes and gesso formulation. Historical gilding techniques, research and case histories that utilize both traditional and modern materials are discussed in Bigelow *et al.* (1991) and Budden (1991). Considine (1989) considered the ethical implications of the treatment of gilded objects. Case histories of gilding conservation such as Cession (1990), Hanlon (1992) and Thorn (1987) may be found in conference papers and conservation period-

icals. Binnington (1991) has discussed verre eglomisé (gilding on glass) and Richardson (1991) has considered materials and techniques relating to pressbrokaat decoration.

As with other decorative surfaces, the conservation of gilded surfaces does not lend itself to a dogmatic or categorical approach. The conservator must be prepared to recognize and deal with a wide variety of complex surfaces and binding media and to identify treatment objectives on a case by case basis. Treatment objectives should be informed by accurate surface characterization when possible, for example microscopic analysis.

It is helpful to understand the types of gilding, surface coatings and underlying layers that are present on an object. A gilding conservator should have a good knowledge of historical methods and materials, such as how gesso would have been recut, the appropriate bole colour for a given period, when two tones of leaf were commonly used or when a surface coating might be an original glaze. Technical examination and analysis of stylistic and historical information is essential in formulating a balanced conservation treatment. The treatment should take into account knowledge of historical materials and methods, as well as the evidence presented by the object itself.

Every conservation treatment of a decorative surface involves weighing the documentary value of an existing surface against the aesthetics of a chosen interpretation. It is important to establish ethical criteria for making these decisions that will have validity for most cases so that treatments are based on broadly applied principles rather than expedience. Some of these principle are widely held throughout conservation and are discussed in Chapter 9. Other considerations specific to gilding conservation can include the preservation of original preparative layers even when regilding is indicated, recognition of the nature and extent of aesthetic intervention, a commitment to leave a physical document of altered surfaces on any object, and to differentiate between old or original surfaces and current treatment (especially where original gilding is involved).

One of the most rewarding challenges for a gilding conservator is treating original gilding. In such cases the desire for preservation and historical integrity are often the most important ethical considerations. Objects that have survived with their original gilding intact usually have significant historical, and often monetary, value. Many gilding conservators prefer in-painting to in-gilding. If in-gilding is deemed necessary for the interpretation of the object, it should be reversible without damage to original material and clearly delineated from it. This consideration may rule out the use of traditional materials that are identical to the original in composition and solubility.

As is the case with other decorated surfaces, the conservation of gilded surfaces is often complicated by past restoration treatments of an object. Some areas may have been over-cleaned and then coated with bronze powder paint, whilst other areas may have been regilded or left untouched. The appearance of the object may have been unified by the application of a pigmented toning coat. Any decisions about cleaning, consolidation or aesthetic reintegration depend on identifying the gilding type and the stratigraphy of the surface decoration. Although a trained eye can usually distinguish oil and water gilding, there are occasions when it can be difficult to distinguish the two. Generally speaking, oil gilding is matte, often laid onto a yellow, white or cream layer, and may be found on furniture, frames, architectural mouldings, metal objects, lettering and exterior decoration (Halahan, 1991). It can be swollen by aromatic hydrocarbons such as xylene and toluene, is usually soluble in polar solvents such as alcohol or acetone and will be completely removed by strongly polar solvents such as dichloromethane. Water gilding is often burnished, may be laid onto a coloured bole and is limited to interior decoration. It can be found on picture frames, furniture and sculpture. Water gilding is soluble in aqueous cleaning solutions and may be damaged by organic solvents characterized by a degree of hydrogen bonding. Polar solvents that have no hydrogen bonding such as dichloromethane can be used on water gilding as they present a low risk of damage to the surface.

Clues about previous treatments may be offered by the overall appearance of the object – whether the carving appears clogged by gesso added during previous restorations, whether the wood substrate is a species typically found under gilding or whether there are traces of earlier or different surfaces. Analytical techniques such as examination under UV, low power magnification, visible light and fluorescence microscopy or thin layer chromatography can also be utilized to characterize gilded surfaces, assess whether the object was originally gilded and whether more than one layer of gilding is present. Microscopy can assist in understanding the condition and extent of any original layer/s (see, for example, Powell, 1999). The information gained from visual and technical examination of a surface should be used to identify goals and formulate an appropriate treatment. Consolidation and cleaning are generally the first treatment steps following examination.

### 16.9.2 General care

Gilded wood is susceptible to significant and sometimes irreversible damage as a result of excessively high, low or repeated cycling of RH extremes. Robertson (1991) recommended aiming for a temperature around 60–70 °F (15–22 °C) and a relative humidity of 45–55%. Water gilding can be damaged by moisture from hands, flower vases, spraying of flowers, spilt drinks or condensation on the base of drinking glasses. Oil gilding can be damaged by spilt solvents or alcoholic drinks (Halahan, 1991). Gilded frames should not be hung against an exterior wall, above a radiator or air conditioning outlet. As with all light-sensitive objects, gilded furniture should not be placed in direct sunlight. Although the gold leaf itself is photo-chemically stable, exposure to light will accelerate the deterioration of any coatings on the surface of the gold and localized heat can affect the gesso underneath.

### 16.9.3 Cleaning

Preventive conservation is the most important part of keeping an object in good condition. Giltwood objects can be dusted with a sable brush and the dust removed with a low suction vacuum cleaner with gauze over the nozzle to avoid the loss of any loose flakes. The use of feather dusters or loosely woven cloth should be avoided. If a cloth is used it must be absolutely clean, lint-free, soft and smooth and should not be used for any other cleaning tasks.

Before undertaking a cleaning treatment, it is essential to identify areas of water gilding, oil gilding, decorative elements composed of composition, or the presence of water or spirit soluble surface layers. Material that can be safely applied to one type of surface may seriously damage others in areas that are immediately adjacent. A great deal of skill is also required. Materials that can be used safely by an experienced gilding conservator may prove disastrous in less skilled hands. The conservator should be sensitive to the different reactions of burnished and matte gilding to a cleaning solution – in general burnished gilding is more tenacious and will clean more easily than matte gilding. Cleaning should be incremental to avoid over-cleaning and detrimental aesthetic consequences. It is important to start with a very mild solution and to test cautiously, advancing to more 'active' materials only if necessary.

The application of tinted varnish to water gilding was common in seventeenth and eighteenth century England. Removal of discoloured varnish can be inappropriate if it represents an original decorative finish. Solvents can be used for removing discoloured shellac from water gilding but it is essential to pre-test on an inconspicuous area and to adopt a cautious approach.

Water gilding that has been burnished to a high lustre is unlikely to have received any coating, which would have interfered with the intended decorative effect. It is therefore particularly vulnerable to damage from abrasion during cleaning. Aliphatic or aromatic hydrocarbon solvents, applied with soft cotton wool, can be used to remove surface dirt from water gilding. Such solvents will also remove wax-based toning that may have been applied in previous restorations. The more hydrogen bonding plays a role in the solvent or solvent mix used the more likely it is that the water gilded surface can be damaged. Very polar solvents that exhibit no hydrogen bonding, such as dichloromethane, can be used to clean water gilded surfaces. In some cases, water gilding may be surface-cleaned with a detergent in a solvent. Hydrocarbon solvent-based emulsions that incorporate a small amount of detergent and water can be a useful tool. Gelled cleaning mixtures may offer advantages, but any appreciable water content is likely to cause damage to water gilding. Cellulose ethers can be used to formulate water-free systems (see section 11.6.2).

A traditional technique of surface cleaning, which is essentially an early form of gel cleaning, involves applying a very weak parchment or rabbit skin size to the surface, allowing it to cool and gel before rolling or peeling it from the surface. This technique requires that the gold and gesso are stable and well adhered, otherwise consolidation will be necessary before such a treatment can be attempted.

The mordant used for oil gilding is based on linseed oil and the constraints this imposes on cleaning are similar to those found in the cleaning of oil-painted surfaces. The mordant is susceptible to swelling and leaching as a result of exposure to polar solvents such as IMS or acetone. Oil gilding can be surface-cleaned with an aqueous solution, sometimes with the addition of a little detergent. The mordant may be saponified if the pH of aqueous cleaning solutions exceeds 8.5, whilst calcium carbonate in the gesso is susceptible to damage from a pH below 5.5. The use of deionized water with the addition of a small percentage of a non-ionic detergent may be effective in some cases. The use of a few drops of ammonium hydroxide in water for cleaning oil gilded surfaces has been reported in case histories but is not recommended as a general rule. Microscopic examination can reveal that gold has been removed with ammonium hydroxide even when this is not apparent from visual examination.

Ammonium citrate is very useful as a general cleaning agent for oil gilding (*Figure 16.26*). The pH may be adjusted, and buffered if necessary, to keep it in a safe range for the gilding that is being cleaned. As gilding ages the oil size becomes more polar, so the upper limit of the pH range of the ammonium citrate solu-

**Figure 16.26** Cleaning of a gilded frame with a pH buffered solution of ammonium citrate

tion will need to be reduced accordingly. An excessively strong concentration of citrate can damage oil gilding (see section 11.5.3).

### 16.9.4 Removal of overgilding

The opportunity to uncover original gilding that has been overgilded, often with intervening gesso layers, is encountered with some frequency because restorers in the past often found it easier and more profitable to regild an object than to carefully clean and patch the original. Microscopy, both reflected visible light and UV light combined with staining, can be used to characterize the stratigraphy and class of binding media. This can help the conservator select a treatment to remove upper layers whilst minimizing the risk of damaging original material below. The removal of one or more subsequent layers of gesso, bole and leaf will restore legibility to carving although other factors such as the historical importance of the upper layer/s and the overall condition of the underlying layer must also be considered. Conservators of polychrome sculptures with several generations of paint have often considered which layer to present.

Hanlon (1992) reported the use of aqueous poultices to swell water gilding that had been applied over an original oil gilded surface. The poultices gave a degree of control over the penetration of moisture into the gesso layers and facilitated the mechanical removal of the softened gesso. Polar chlorinated hydrocarbons, such as dichloromethane, can be used to remove oil gilding that has been applied over water gilding. Dry stripping of overgilding may utilize any sharp flexible tool such as a scalpel or a leather worker's bent awl (Green, 1991). Tools made of ivory, bone or Perspex (Plexiglas) are hard enough to do the job and can reduce the risk of damaging an original surface. Dry stripping is time-consuming and usually carried out where the burnished water gilding forms the original substrate because this provides a poor adhesive bond to subsequent layers. Dry stripping may not be successful where oil gilding or textured gilding forms the original decorative layer.

### 16.9.5 Removal of bronze paint

Although bronze powder has a long history of use in the creation of decorative surfaces,

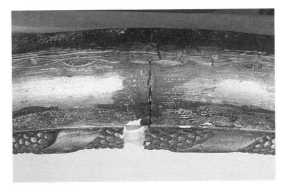

**Figure 16.27** Detail of darkened and discoloured brass particle ('bronze') paint on a nineteenth century gilded picture frame

including japanning and stencilling, it is often encountered in the context of poor quality restorations on gilded objects. Bronze paint, sometimes called gold paint, usually consists of brass powders that may have been bound in a variety of vehicles (oil-based, resin-based, cellulose nitrate etc.). Bronze paint has often been applied to gilded surfaces during previous restoration attempts in order to compensate for losses or to brighten up the appearance of the surface. Removal is problematic when the solubility parameters of the bronze paint binder overlap with the mordant used in the original gilding, for example when oil-based bronze paint has been applied directly onto an oil gilded surface. Bronze powders or paint should not be used on gilded surfaces because they tarnish and discolour over time (*Figure 16.27*).

It is important to characterize the solubility of the bronze paint vehicle and the underlying gilding in order to assess whether the bronze paint can be removed with solvents. Bronze paints bound in a cellulose nitrate medium are soluble in acetone. Buck (1993) reported success in removing bronze paint from both water and oil gilded surfaces using solvent gels and considered the use of an aqueous cleaning solution that incorporated a chelating agent.

### 16.9.6 Consolidation

A gilded surface is vulnerable to damage from wear, abrasion and breakage. Aside from these, major categories of gesso damage include delamination from the substrate, delamination between layers of gesso and internal adhesive failure (Von Reventlow, 1991). Delamination from the substrate can be localized and take the form of bulges or blisters or may be more widespread, in which case it can be detected by tapping the surface. A well-adhered surface will sound dull when tapped lightly whereas loose gesso will produce a more resonant and sharper sound with a slightly higher pitch. Adhesive failure between substrate and gesso that results in delamination may be a result of substrate shrinkage, stress around localized faults such as knots, or weak or uneven size application. Delamination between layers of gesso can be caused by the use of a strong size over a weak size or by overgilding in a previous restoration. Internal adhesive failure, which results in a friable powdery gesso, may be caused by the use of a weak glue size or long exposure to excessive high humidity, sometimes in combination with fungal attack. This last is usually a difficult and time-consuming problem to address and in some cases consolidation may prove impossible. Consolidant may be delivered through facing tissue if a surface is very flaky or unstable and this technique is described on p. 574 and in *Figure 12.4*.

As is the case with other decorative surfaces, a decision must be made about whether to use traditional or modern materials for consolidation. This issue is discussed in section 12.2.4 in the general context of decorative surfaces. Opinions on the subject are divided and the conservator should consider the long-term needs of the object within an ethical framework. Whether a traditional or modern adhesive is used, when carrying out localized treatment such as laying flakes or cupped areas, it is important to avoid leaving excess adhesive on the surface. A heated spatula can be used in conjunction with traditional and many modern adhesives.

Consolidation of gesso layers on shaped areas such as intricate carving may require the use of a collagen consolidant that will gel and may remove the need for the lengthy application of pressure to the surface. Alternatives such as flexible cauls, or the use of cling film/Saran wrap can allow the use of consolidants with a longer drying time. The use of low vacuum pressure can be appropriate for treating large areas of friable gilding. Water-based adhesives will soften the gesso and may allow

flakes to be gently repositioned and flattened. A small amount of alcohol, which acts as a surfactant, can be added to the size to aid penetration of the gesso. Powdery, friable gesso, however, can become an amorphous slurry and if this occurs the need for a non-aqueous consolidant is indicated. If applying a water-based consolidant to a water-gilded surface, it may be necessary to protect the surface by applying a temporary hydrocarbon-soluble protective coating (see section 12.4.7). Such coatings can be tinted with pigment to identify where they have been used and ensure their removal after treatment is complete.

Rabbit skin glue or gelatin, when used as a consolidant for gilding, should always be weaker than that used for preparation of gesso. A solution of one part dry glue granules to twenty parts water (5% v/v) may provide a reasonable margin of safety. Paraloid B72, PVAC and acrylic dispersions or emulsions can also be used as consolidants for gesso. The primary issue with these materials is retreatability, since removal of a consolidant from a porous surface is rarely practicable. Some conservators have expressed concern that the use of such materials may inhibit the future penetration of aqueous consolidants and Thornton (1991b) alludes to this problem when discussing the use of isolating layers. The use of Aquazol, poly(2-ethyl-2-oxazoline) as a consolidant for gilded surfaces has been examined by Friend (1996), Shelton (1996) and Wolbers *et al.* (1998). The use of wax-based materials for the consolidation of porous gesso surfaces is not recommended because they cannot be completely removed and can inhibit or prevent the future use of most other consolidants.

### 16.9.7 Reintegration

The material selected to replace losses to the wooden substrate will depend on the size and position of the damage. Wood may be the material of choice where repairs must be weight-bearing or where the loss has occurred on an edge and wood movement related to fluctuations in relative humidity will not add to the instability of the surface. Hanlon (1992) utilized a carvable epoxy resin (Araldite 1253), isolated from the original wood with animal glue, to fill losses from a wooden substrate (*Figure 16.28*).

(a)

(b)

**Figure 16.28** Filling with a carvable epoxy resin (*a*) Epoxy putty used to adhere and fill the joint between a large decorative element and the gilded frame where the fit was poor. An isolating layer should be used in conjunction with epoxy adhesives (*b*) Detail of the in-gilded repair

In general a fill should be softer than the surrounding original material so that, in the event of substrate shrinkage, the fill is compressed and the original remains undamaged. For gesso fills this may mean the use of a size slightly weaker than the standard mix, or the addition of a slightly higher proportion of whiting, to produce a 'soft' fill. In situations where hygrometric swings are unavoidable, the use of a fill that remains slightly plastic may be indicated, such as microballoons in a synthetic resin with a low Tg and a low softening point. All filling should be preceded by cleaning and degreasing the site of loss before sizing it with the adhesive used as the binder for the fill.

Infilling of losses to the gesso can utilize traditional or modern materials. Traditional mater-

ials are often applied using the same materials and techniques used to manufacture the original surface and, with the exception of a reduction in strength of the size, are carried out using the procedures outlined in Chapter 14. Some conservators adopt a mixed approach by applying a weak size to consolidate the edges of the loss, allowing it to dry and then applying an isolating layer of a dissimilar material such as an acrylic dispersion or a Paraloid. The fill is then carried out using rabbit skin gesso or gesso putty. The use of barium sulphate, an X-ray dense material, has been suggested as a method of tagging repairs to the gesso that would otherwise be difficult to locate in the future (Thornton, 1991a, 1991b). Unlike other compounds of barium, which are highly toxic, barium sulphate is chemically inert and can be safely used as a bulking agent (Thornton, 1998). The use of PVAL as a filling material discussed by Hebrard and Small (1991). PVAL is relatively chemically stable, has good working properties, porosity comparable to gesso and is reversible in organic solvents such as alcohol. Thornton (1991a) suggests that the criteria of reversibility can be met by isolating the fill from the original with a stable material such as a PVAC or Paraloid B72. He also discusses the use of composition, fillers based on a binding medium and calcium carbonate or microballoons, waxes and wood. Synthetic fillers, such as Paraloid B72 bulked with microballoons, may also find application in some cases.

Great care must be taken to match bole colours exactly if intending to match new gilding to old. Proprietary wet clays can be blended to produce the desired colour. Green (1991) recommends using pipe clay mixed with pigment colour and parchment size to which a little graphite may be added to aid burnishing the bole or gold. With this mixture, the colour of the wet bole matches that of the dry burnished bole, thus a small amount of wet bole applied to a thumbnail can be used to test the colour-match at different points on the object.

Broadly speaking, there are three approaches that can be taken to in gilding. The first is purely restorative and utilizes the same materials and techniques as were used on the original. In the past this has resulted in repairs that cannot be separated from the original. Shell gold can be applied to a surface when only a hint of burnished gold is required to simulate the original finish (Green, 1991). It can also be used where original bole is intact, wear is visually distracting but the conservator wishes to avoid excessive in gilding. The second approach is to in-gild using a variety of synthetic mordants such as Paraloid B72, acrylic emulsions, PVAL or proprietary materials such as those produced by Kölner (Thornton, 1991b). The third approach is not to ingild at all but to compensate for loss using pigments, water colour or gouache. Iridescent pigments made from mica have been used by conservators who do not wish to in-gild but want greater reflectance than water colours offer (Moyer and Hanlon, 1996; Thornton, 1991b; Webb, 1994). Such metallic sheen pigments, sometimes called pearlescent pigments, are produced by the vapour deposition of thin layers of titanium and iron oxide on mica flakes and offer great stability (Thornton, 2000).

### 16.9.8   Composition

Composition tends to crack with age and this can lead to breakage and loss. It also exhibits a tendency to shrinkage, warping, cupping and loss of the adhesive bond with the substrate (Wetherall, 1991). These problems can be caused or exacerbated by fluctuations in relative humidity or if excessive solvent applied during cleaning treatments runs through ageing cracks and weakens the adhesive bond between applied ornament and substrate (Green, 1991). The mixture of animal glue, resin and linseed oil means that composition may be damaged by water, polar solvents such as alcohol or acetone, and exposure to chlorinated hydrocarbon solvents such as dichloromethane, a component in many commercial paint strippers. Where loss of parts of the compo moulding have occurred it may be possible to take an impression from another part of the object and cast a replacement. Thornton (1991a) discusses a range of materials and techniques that can be used for this purpose. Composition is discussed in the context of moulding and casting in section 10.5.

### 16.9.9   Coatings

As with other decorative surfaces, the decision whether to apply a coating to a gilded surface after a conservation treatment must be taken on a case-by-case basis, taking into consideration the desired aesthetic appearance, conditions of use, handling, display or storage. Although gilding is rarely varnished, a thin synthetic coating may offer a degree of protection for areas that will be exposed to wear in use, although such a coating is unlikely to reproduce the original appearance of a gilded surface.

Rabbit skin or parchment size has traditionally been used as a coating and some gilders are able to remove this with minimal damage. Rabbit skin or parchment size is sometimes applied to an object when a similar layer was removed during cleaning. Collagen glues are hygroscopic and will shrink markedly in conditions of low RH. This can cause exfoliation of the gold leaf surface. Thorn (1987) has suggested that rabbit skin size will discolour over time and, if applied over water gilding, may prove difficult to remove without damaging the underlying gold.

### 16.9.10   Distressing

The concept of patina is applied to gilded pieces in much the same way as it is to furniture. Patina represents the mark of the passage of time and is considered to add aesthetic, historic and monetary value to an object. Distressing is the process by which wear and minor damage that would occur as a normal result of handling, cleaning and use of the object is simulated on a new surface or repair. A current aesthetic is for the surface to appear old and in good condition but not overly restored, thus distressing is required to blend in areas that have been repaired which might otherwise appear glaring in comparison to the rest of the object. It is essential to study the surface of an old piece carefully to understand the degree of wear, where it has occurred, and the overall effect on the appearance of the object. It is important to remember that current perceptions of how a surface 'should' appear may be far removed from the intended original appearance.

Distressing imitates original wear by rubbing carefully through the gold to expose the underlying layers. Any abrasive material may be used that produces acceptable results. Fine wire wool, fibreglass pens, abrasive powders such as pumice, rottenstone or talc (French chalk) may be used. Gilders whiting is a comparatively mild abrasive that allows the conservator to worked through the gold leaf slowly and in a more controlled way. Cracks can be carefully inpainted or incised using a scalpel prior to distressing and toning (Green, 1979).

## 16.9.11   Toning

Toning describes the application of colour or surface coating to a gilded surface. Toning that utilized a thin size was usually applied as part of an original gilding system to create areas of matte gilding, which brings greater contrast to adjacent areas of burnished gilding.

Conservators may apply toning to integrate a repair to an existing surface (*Figure 16.29*). There is little published on toning and gilders are often reluctant to share trade secrets. However, the conservator has a wide range of materials to choose from – one source stated the case simply when she suggested that the gilder is free to use anything that will give the desired result and which is ethically acceptable (Wetherall, 1992). The guiding principle is to avoid the binding medium used in the gold below so, for example, water colours or gouache may be used on oil gilding and oil colours or japan size on water gilding. Some gilders apply a sealing coat of transparent shellac onto water gilding, allow it to dry and then use water colours. Colour can be applied as a thin wash, stippled or brushed on the surface or, for large areas, applied with an airbrush. Wax and wax based emulsions have been widely used in the past. Other possible materials include commercial water or oil colours used in conjunction with conservation grade materials such as Paraloid B72, stabilized dammar or Regalrez 1094. Green (1979) recommended toning using parchment size and gilder's ormolu for oil gilding and emphasized the need for transparency, which allows the gold to be seen below the toning. Rogers (1991) utilized parchment size tinted with water colours and added a small amount of an acrylic matte medium to prevent the wet surface coating contracting into beads or islands.

# Bibliography

## 16.1   Stone and related materials

Agnini, E., Haagh-Christiansen, A., Schmidt, G. and Stümmer, I. (1998) Production, technique and restoration of marbled stucco objects, *Kermes*, 11(33), 13–20, 22

Ashurst, J. and Dimes, F.G. (1990) *Conservation of Building and Decorative Stone*, Butterworth-Heinemann

Ashurst, N. (1994) *Cleaning Historic Buildings*, Alden Press

de Witte, E. and Dupas, M. (1992) Cleaning poultices based on E.D.T.A., in *Proceedings of the Seventh International Congress on Deterioration and Conservation of Stone*, Laboratorio Nacional de Engenharia Civil, Lisbon, pp. 1023–1031

Giusti, A.M. (1992) *Pietre Dure, Hardstone in Furniture and Decoration*, Phillip Wilson

Griswold, J. and Uricheck, S. (1998) Loss compensation methods for stone, *JAIC*, 37, 89–110

Haller, U. and Schiessl, U. (1998) Reinigung ungefasster Gipsoberflachen – eine neue Methode (Conservation of undecorated gypsum surfaces: a new method), *Kunstechnologie und Konservierung*, 12(2), 274–82

Lauffenburger, J.A., Grissom, C.A. and Charola, A.E. (1992) Changes in gloss of marble surfaces as a result of methylcellulose poulticing, *Studies in Conservation*, 37(3), 155–64

Livingston, R. (1992) Geochemical considerations in the cleaning of carbonate stone, in Webster, R.G.M. (ed.), *Stone Cleaning and the Nature, Soiling and Decay Mechanisms of Stone*, Conference postscripts, Donhead, pp. 166–79

Matero, F.G. and Tagle, A.A. (1995) Cleaning, iron stain removal and surface repair of architectural marble and crystalline limestone: The Metropolitan Club, *JAIC*, 34, 49–68

Nagy, E.E. (1998) Fills for white marble: properties of seven fillers and two thermosetting resins, *JAIC*, 37, 69–87

Thickett, D. (1995) Evaluation of the Effects of Triammonium Citrate on Painted Plaster Busts and Unpolished Marble Surfaces, British Museum Report 1995/24

Winckler, E.M. (1973) *Stone: Properties, Durability in Man's Environment*, Springer-Verlag

Wittenburg, C. (ed.) (1999) *Baroque Artificial Marble Environmental Impacts, Degradation and Protection*, ENVIART Research Report No. 9, European Communities (EEC)

Zecchini, A. (1992) *Arte della scagliola sul Lario*, Milan

**Figure 16.29**  Coating and toning of a conserved frame with spray application of cellulose nitrate lacquer

## 16.2  Plastics

Blank, S. (1988) Practical answers to plastic problems, in *Modern Organic Materials Meeting*, Conference Preprints, SSCR, pp. 115–21

Blank, S. (1990) An introduction to plastics and rubbers in collections, *Studies in Conservation*, 35(2), 53–63

Blomquist, R.F., Christiansen, A.W., Gillespie, R.H. and Myers, G.E. (eds) (1983) *Adhesive Bonding of Wood and Other Structural Materials*, Pennsylvania State University Press

Braun, D. (1982) *Simple Methods for the Identification of Plastic*, Carl Hanser Verlag

Brydson, J.A. (1995) *Plastics Materials*, Butterworth-Heinemann

Coxon, H. (1993) Practical pitfalls in the identification of plastics, in D. Grattan (ed.), *Saving the Twentieth Century: The Conservation of Modern Materials*, Conference Proceedings, CCI/Communications Canada, pp. 395–410

Fenn, J. (1993) Labelling plastic artefacts, in D. Grattan (ed.), *Saving the Twentieth Century: The Conservation of Modern Materials*, Conference Proceedings, CCI/Communications Canada, pp. 341–50

Grattan, D. (ed.) (1993) *Saving the Twentieth Century: The Conservation of Modern Materials* Conference Proceedings, CCI/Communications Canada

Katz, S. (1986) *Early Plastics*, Shire Publications

Morgan, J. (1991) *The Conservation of Plastics*, Conservation Unit/Plastics Historical Society

Mossman, S. (1988) Simple methods of identifying plastics, in *Modern Organic Materials Meeting*, Conference Preprints, SSCR, pp. 41–45

Mossman, S.T.I. and Morris, P.J.T. (1994) *The Development of Plastics*, Royal Society of Chemists

Quye, A. and Williamson, C. (eds) (1999) *Plastics: Collecting and Conserving*, NMS Publishing

Sale, D. (1988) The effect of solvents on four plastics found in museum collections, in *Modern Organic Materials Meeting*, Conference Preprints, SSCR, pp. 105–14

Shashoua, Y. and Thomsen, S. (1993) A field trial for the use of Ageless in the preservation of rubber in museum collections, in D. Grattan (ed.), *Saving the Twentieth Century: The Conservation of Modern Materials*, Conference Proceedings, CCI/Communications Canada, pp. 363–72

van Oosten, T.B. (1999) Identifying plastics: analytical methods, in A. Quye and C. Williamson (eds), *Plastics: Collecting and Conserving*, NMS Publishing, pp. 70–83

Ward, C. and Shashoua, Y. (1999) Interventive conservation treatments for plastics and rubber artefacts in The British Museum, in ICOM Committee for Conservation, Preprints 11th Triennial Meeting, Edinburgh, pp. 888–93

Williamson, C. (1999) Identifying plastics: physical clues and simple analysis, in A. Quye and C. Williamson (eds), *Plastics: Collecting and Conserving*, NMS Publishing, pp. 55–69

## 16.3  Upholstery

Balfour, D., Metcalf, S. and Collard, F. (1999) The first non-intrusive upholstery treatment at the Victoria and Albert Museum, *The Conservator*, 23, 22–9

Bott, G. (1990) Amylase for starch removal from a set of seventeenth century embroidered panels, *The Conservator*, 14, 23–9

Britton, N. (1994) Basket cases: two upholstery treatments composed of plant materials, in AIC Textile Specialty Group, Conference Postprints, pp. 27–38

Brooks, M., Eastop, D., Hillyer, L. and Lister, A. (1995) Supporting fragile textiles: the evolution of choice, in *Linings and Backings: The Support of Paintings, Paper and Textiles*, UKIC Conference Postprints, pp. 5–13

Department of Scientific and Industrial Research (1926) *The Cleaning and Restoration of Museum Exhibits*, HMSO, London

Doyal, S. (1999) Modern materials problems– Oh, sit on it!, in D. Rogers and G. Marley (eds), *Modern Materials Modern Problems*, UKIC Conference Postprints

Florian, M.L., Norton, R. and Kronkright, D. (1990) *The Conservation of Artifacts Made from Plant Material*, Getty Conservation Unit

French, A. (ed.). (1990) *Conservation of Furnishing Textiles*, SSCR Conference Postprints

Gill, K. and Eastop, D. (2001) *Upholstery Conservation: Principles and Practice*, Butterworth-Heinemann

James, D. (1990) *Upholstery – A Complete Course*, The Guild of Master Craftsman Publications, UK

Landi, S. (1992) *The Textile Conservator's Manual*, 2nd edn, Butterworth-Heinemann

Leach, M. (1995) Blickling Mortlake tapestry – adhesive removal treatment, in K. Marko (ed.), *Textiles in Trust*, Archetype Books, London, pp. 176–78

Nylander, C.F. (1990) *Fabrics for Historic Buildings*, Preservation Press

Sheetz, R. (1989) Conservation of Russian artifact from Sitka, Alaska, in AIC Wooden Artifacts Group Conference, Cincinnati

Smith, A. (1983) Scotchguard, Unpublished internal report, The Textile Conservation Centre, UK

Stokes, J. (1852) *The Cabinet-maker and Upholsterer's Companion*, Philadelphia

Thorp, V. (1990) Imitation leather: structure, composition and conservation, *Leather Conservation News*, 6(2), 7–15

Trupin, D. and Moore, M. (1990) The restoration of the Mills Mansion State Historic Site: a holistic approach to conservation and restoration of upholstery and furnishing fabrics, in M. Williams (ed.), *Upholstery Conservation*, American Conservation Consortium Symposium Preprints

White, A. (1993) On the rack, *Woodworker Magazine*

Williams, M. (ed.) (1990) *Upholstery Conservation*, American Conservation Consortium Symposium Preprints

## 16.4  Leather, parchment and shagreen

Bennett, M. (1990) *Discovering and Restoring Antique Furniture*, Cassell

Cains, A. (1992) The Vellum of the Book of Kells, *The Paper Conservator*, 16, 50–61

Calnan, C. (ed.) (1991) *Conservation of Leather in Transport Collections*, UKIC

Calnan, C. and Haines, B. (1991) *Leather: Its Composition and Changes with Time*, Leather Conservation Centre, UK

Clarkson, C. (1992) Rediscovering parchment: the nature of the beast, *The Paper Conservator*, 16, 5–26

de Hamel, C. (1992) *Scribes and Illuminators*, British Museum

Down, J.L., MacDonald, M.A., Williams, J.T. and Williams, R.S. (1996) Adhesive testing at the Canadian Conservation Institute – an evaluation of selected poly (vinyl acetate) and acrylic adhesives, *Studies in Conservation*, 41(1), 19–44

Gopfrich, J. (1999) The granulated donkey? Shagreen: some aspects of conservation, ICOM Committee for Conservation, Preprints 12th Triennial Meeting, Lyons, Vol. II, James and James (Science Publishers), pp. 685–90

Haines, B. (1999) *Parchment*, Leather Conservation Centre

Haines, B. and Calnan, C. (1988) *Conservation of Skin and Leather*, Course Notes Summer Schools Press (Archetype Books, UK)

Hallebeek, P., Kite, M. and Calnan, C. (eds) (1992) *Conservation of Leathercraft and Related Objects Interim Symposium*, ICOM Committee for Conservation

Kite, M. (forthcoming) An introduction to the use of fish skin and other aquatic leathers which may be found in dress collections, in Wright, M. (ed.) *Unusual Materials*, Archetype

Koldeweij, E. (1992) How Spanish is 'Spanish' leather?, in *Conservation of the Iberian and Latin American Cultural Heritage*, Conference Preprints, IIC, pp. 84–88

Larsen, R., Chahine, C., Wouters, J. and Calnan, C. (1996) Vegetable tanned leather: evaluation of the protective effect of aluminium alkoxide treatment, in ICOM Committee for Conservation, Preprints 11th Triennial Meeting, Edinburgh, pp. 742–50

Larsen, R., Vest, M. and Nielsen, K. (1993) Determination of hydrothermal stability (shrinkage temperature) of historical leather by the micro hot table technique, *Journal of the Society of Leather Technologists and Chemists*, 77, 151–6

Leather Conservation Centre (1981) *The Fibre Structure of Leather*, LCC, UK

O'Flaherty, F., Roddy, W.T. and Lollar, R.M. (eds) (1958) *The Chemistry and Technology of Leather*, Vol. II, Reinhold

Nieuwenhuizen, L. (1998) Synthetic fill materials for skin, leather and furs, *JAIC*, 37, 135–45

Reed, R. (1972) *Ancient Skins*, Seminar Press

Ruck, P. (1991) *Pergament*, Jan Thorbecke Verlag

Selm, R. (1991) The conservation of upholstery leather – an evaluation of materials and techniques, in C. Calnan (ed.), *Conservation of Leather in Transport Collections*, UKIC, pp. 15–22

Springer, K. (1984) *History of Shagreen*, Monograph, Karl Spinger Ltd

Sturge, T. (2000) *The Conservation of Leather Artefacts: Case Studies from the Leather Conservation Centre*, The Leather Conservation Centre

van Soest, H.A.B., Stambolov, T. and Hallebeek, P.B. (1984) Conservation of leather, *Studies in Conservation*, 29(1), 21–31

Waterer, J.W. (1946) *Leather in Life, Art and Industry*, Faber

Willemsen, M. (1997) Shagreen in Western Europe: its use and manufacture in the seventeenth and eighteenth centuries, *Apollo*, Vol. 145, No. 419 (January), pp. 35–8

Woods, C. (1995) Conservation treatments for parchment documents, *Journal of the Society of Archivists*, 16 (2), 221–38

Young, C.S. (1990) Microscopical hydrothermal stability measurements of skin and semi tanned leather, in ICOM Committee for Conservation, Preprints 9th Triennial Meeting, Dresden, Vol. II, pp. 626–31

## 16.5   Textiles

Bennett, M. (1990) *Discovering and Restoring Antique Furniture*, Cassell

Huxtable, M. and Webber, P. (1987) Some adaptations of Oriental techniques and materials used in the Prints and Drawings Conservation Department of the Victoria and Albert Museum, *The Paper Conservator*, 11, 46–57

Kite, M. and Webber, P. (1995) The conservation of an English embroidered picture using an Oriental paper method: a joint approach, *The Conservator*, 19, 29–35

Landi, S. (1992) *The Textile Conservator's Manual*, Butterworth-Heinemann, 2nd edition

Tímár-Balázsy, Á. and Eastop, D. (1998) *Chemical Principles of Textile Conservation*, Butterworth-Heinemann

## 16.6   Painted furniture

Bristow, Ian (1996) *Interior House Painting: Colours and Technology*, Yale University Press

Bristow, Ian (1998) The imitation of natural materials in architectural interiors, in V. Dorge and F.C. Howlett (eds), *Painted Wood: History and Conservation*, Getty Conservation Institute, pp. 110–19

Brommelle, N.S. and Smith, P. (eds) (1976) *The Conservation and Restoration of Pictorial Art,* Butterworths

Browne, F.L. (1954) Swelling of paint films in water II: absorption and volumetric swelling of bound and free films before and after weathering, *Journal of the Forest Products Research Station*, 4, 391–400

Buck, S. (1993) Three case studies in the treatment of painted furniture, in AIC Wooden Artifacts Group Conference Papers, Denver, pp. 1–6

Buck, S. (1994) A masonic master's chair revealed, in L. Beckerdite (ed.), *American Furniture*, Chipstone Foundation

Buck, S. (1995) Bedsteads should be painted green, in *Old Time New England*, Autumn (Society for the Protection of New England Antiquities), pp. 17–35

Craft, M.L. and Solz, J.A. (1998) Commercial vinyl and acrylic fill materials, *JAIC*, 37, 23–34

Dardes, K. and Rothe, A. (1998) *The Structural Conservation of Panel Paintings*, Getty Conservation Institute

Dauchot-Dehon, M. and De Witte, E. (1978) Etude de temps de sechage du varnis Paraloid B72 sur les peintures, in ICOM Committee for Conservation, Preprints 5th Triennial Meeting, 78/16/2/1–7

Dintenfass, L. (1958) The nature of adhesion in paint films, *Paint Manufacture*, 28, 103–6

Dorge, V. and Howlett, F.C. (1998) *Painted Wood: History and Conservation*, Getty Conservation Institute

Erhardt, D. (1998) Paints based on drying-oil media, in V. Dorge and F.C. Howlett (eds), *Painted Wood: History and Conservation*, Getty Conservation Institute, pp. 17–32

Feller, R.L. (1986) *Artist's Pigments: A Handbook of Their History and Characteristics*, Vol. 1, National Gallery of Art, Washington, DC

Feller, R.L. and Kunz, N. (1981) The effect of pigment volume concentration on the lightness or darkness of porous paints, in AIC Conference Preprints, Philadelphia, pp. 66–74

Feller, R.L., Stolow, N. and Jones, E.H. (1985) *On Picture Varnishes and their Solvents*, Washington, DC, National Gallery of Art

Ford, B. and Byrne, A. (1991) The lipid stripping potential of resin soap gels used for cleaning oil paintings, *AICCM Bulletin*, 17(1&2), 51–60

Gettens, R.J. and Stout, R. (1966) *Painting Materials: An Encyclopaedia*, Dover

Green, T. (1990) Surface dirt removal from unvarnished paint films, in S. Hackney, J. Townsend and N. Eastaugh (eds), *Dirt and Pictures Separated*, Conference Postprints, UKIC, pp. 51–55

Hackney, S. (1990) The removal of dirt from Turner's unvarnished oil sketches, in S. Hackney, J. Townsend and N. Eastaugh (eds), *Dirt and Pictures Separated*, Conference Postprints, UKIC, pp. 35–39

Hackney, S., Townsend, J. and Eastaugh, N. (eds) (1990) *Dirt and Pictures Separated*, Conference Postprints, UKIC

Hansen, E.F. (1990) A review of problems encountered in the consolidation of paint on ethnographic wood objects and potential remedies, in ICOM Committee for Conservation, Preprints 9th Triennial Meeting, Dresden, pp. 163–68

Hansen, E.F. and Bishop, M.H. (1998) Factors affecting the re-treatment of previously consolidated matte painted wooden objects, in V. Dorge and F.C. Howlett (eds), *Painted Wood: History and Conservation*, Getty Conservation Institute, pp. 484–97

Hansen, E.F., Lowinger, R. and Sadoff, E.T. (1993) Consolidation of porous paint in a vapour saturated atmosphere: a technique for minimizing changes in the appearance of powdering matte paint, *JAIC*, 32(1), 1–14

Hansen, E.F., Walston, S. and Bishop, M.H. (1994) *Matte Paint: Its History and Technology, Analysis, Properties, Deterioration and Treatment*, Supplemental Bibliography, AATA, Getty Conservation Institute

Harley, R.D. (1982) *Artist's Pigments: c.1600–1835*, Butterworths

Hodges, H.W.M., Mills, J.S. and Smith, P. (1992) *Conservation of the Iberian and Latin American Cultural Heritage*, Conference Preprints, IIC

Koller, J., Baumer, U., Schmid, A. and Grosser, D. (1997) Sandarac, in K. Walch and J. Koller (eds), *Baroque and Rococo Lacquers*, Arbeitshefte des Bayerischen Landesamtes für Denkmalpflege, pp. 379–94

Lambourne, R. (1993) *Paint and Surface Coatings*, Ellis Horwood

Landrey, G., Reinhold, N. and Wolbers, R. (1988) Surface treatment of a Philadelphia pillar and claw snap-top table, in AIC Wooden Artifacts Group Conference Papers, Louisiana

Lang, S. (1998) A review of literature published in response to Wolbers' resin soaps, bile soaps and solvent gels, MA Dissertation, Royal College of Art/Victoria and Albert Museum, London

Marrion, A. (1994) *The Chemistry and Physics of Coatings*, Royal Society of Chemistry

Martens, C.R. (1974) *Technology of Paints, Varnishes and Lacquers*, Kreiger

Martin, J.S. (1998) Microscopic examination and analysis of the structure and composition of paint and varnish layers, in V. Dorge and F.C. Howlett (eds), *Painted Wood: History and Conservation*, Getty Conservation Institute, pp. 64–79

Mayer, R. (1991) *The Artist's Handbook of Materials and Techniques*, 5th edn, Faber and Faber

Michalski, S. (1990) A physical model of the cleaning of oil paint, in *Cleaning, Retouching and Coatings*, Conference Preprints, IIC, pp. 85–91

Michalski, S. and Dignard, C. (1997) Ultrasonic misting. Part 1: Experiments on appearance change and improvement in bonding, *JAIC*, 36, 109–26

Michalski, S., Dignard, C., van Handel, L. and Arnold, D. (1998) The ultrasonic mister: applications in the consolidation of powdery paint on wooden artifacts, in V. Dorge and F.C. Howlett (eds), *Painted Wood: History and Conservation*, Getty Conservation Institute, pp. 498–513

Mills, J.S. and Smith, P. (eds) (1990) *Cleaning, Retouching and Coatings*, Conference Preprints, IIC

Mills, J. and White, R. (1977) Natural resins of art and archaeology: their sources, chemistry and identification, *Studies in Conservation*, 22(1), 12–31

Newman, R. (1998) Tempera and other nondrying-oil media, in V. Dorge and F.C. Howlett (eds), *Painted Wood: History and Conservation*, Getty Conservation Institute, pp. 33–63

Newman, D.J., Nunn, C.J. and Oliver, J.K. (1975) Release of individual solvents and binary solvent blends from thermoplastic coatings, *Journal of Paint Technology*, 47 (609), 70–88

Phenix, A. (1998) Solvent-induced swelling of paint films: some preliminary results, *WAAC Newsletter*, 20 (3), 15–20

Plesters, J. (1956) Cross-sections and chemical analysis of paint samples, *Studies in Conservation*, 2(3), 110–57

Roy, A. (1993) *Artist's Pigments: A Handbook of their History and Characteristics*, Vol. 2, National Gallery of Art, Washington, DC

Ruhemann, H. (1968) *The Cleaning of Paintings*, Faber and Faber

Samet, W. (1998) The philosophy of aesthetic reintegration: paintings and painted furniture, in V. Dorge and F.C. Howlett (eds), *Painted Wood: History and Conservation*, Getty Conservation Institute, pp. 412–23

Sigel, A. (1993) Computer enhanced UV fluorescence microscopy of aged artists materials, in Art Conservation Training Programs Conference, Art Conservation Department State University of New York at Buffalo

*Spons Workshop Receipts for Manufacturers and Scientific Amateurs* (1873/1921), E&FN Spon, London

Stavroudis, C. and Blank, S. (1990) Authors Reply, *WAAC Newsletter*, 12(2), 31

Sutherland, K. (2000) The extraction of soluble components from an oil paint film by a varnish solution, *Studies in Conservation*, 45(1), 54–62

Sutherland, K. and Shibayama, N. (1999) The components of oil paint films extracted by organic solvents, in ICOM Committee for Conservation, Preprints 12th Triennial Meeting, Lyons, pp. 341–6

Tsang, J. and Erhardt, D. (1992) Current research on the effects of solvent and gelled and aqueous cleaning systems on oil paint films, *JAIC*, 31(1), 87–94

Walch, K. (1997) Baroque and Rococo transparent gloss lacquers, in K. Walch and J. Koller (eds), *Baroque and*

*Rococo Lacquers*, Arbeitshefte des Bayerischen Landesamtes für Denkmalpflege, pp. 21–51

Walch, K. and Koller, J. (1997) *Baroque and Rococo Lacquers*, Arbeitshefte des Bayerischen Landesamtes für Denkmalpflege

Welsh, E. (1980) A consolidant treatment for powdery matte paint, in AIC Preprints, San Francisco, pp. 141–50

White, R. and Roy, A. (1998) GC–MS and SEM studies on the effects of solvent cleaning on old master paintings from the National Gallery, London, *Studies in Conservation*, 43(3), 159–76

Wolbers, R. (1992) Recent developments in the use of gel formulations for the cleaning of paintings, in *Restoration 1992*, Conference Preprints, IIC, pp. 74–75

Wolbers, R. (2000) *Aqueous Methods for Cleaning Painted Surfaces*, Archetype Books

Wolbers, R. and Landrey, G. (1987) The use of direct reactive fluorescent dyes for the characterization of binding media in cross-sectional examinations, in AIC Wooden Artifacts Group, Conference Papers, Vancouver, pp. 168–204

Wolbers, R., McGinn, M. and Duerbeck, D. (1998) Poly(2-ethyl-2-oxazoline): a new conservation adhesive, in V. Dorge and F.C. Howlett (eds), *Painted Wood: History and Conservation*, Getty Conservation Institute, pp. 514–27

Wolbers, R., Sterman, N. and Stavroudis, C. (1990) Notes for workshop on new methods in the cleaning of paintings, Getty Conservation Institute, 1988, 1989, 1990

## 16.7 Japanned furniture

Agrawal, O.P. (1971) A study of Indian polychrome wooden sculpture, *Studies in Conservation*, 16(2), 56–68

Agrawal, O.P. (1978) Technique of wood work in India, in *Conservation of Wood*, Tokyo National Research Institute of Cultural Properties, pp. 77–86

Ballardie, M. (1994) Conservation of an 18th century chest lacquered and japanned, in S. Budden and F. Halahan (eds), *Lacquerwork and Japanning*, Conference Postprints, UKIC, pp. 11–13

Ballardie, M. (1996) Historical colours used in 17th century and 18th century japanning, in ICOM Committee for Conservation, 11th Triennial Meeting, Edinburgh, pp. 911–14

Bernstein, J. (1992) An investigation of the metallic decoration in eighteenth century American japanning, in AIC Wooden Artifacts Group Conference Papers, Buffalo

Bigelow, D. (1990) A review of the consolidation system used in the conservation of a japanned clock, in AIC Wooden Artifacts Group Conference Papers, Richmond

Budden, S. and Halahan, F. (eds) (1994) *Lacquerwork and Japanning*, Conference Postprints, UKIC

Derrick, M., Druzik, C. and Preusser, F. (1988) FTIR analysis of authentic and simulated black lacquer finishes on eighteenth century furniture, in N.S. Bromelle and P. Smith (eds), *Urushi*, Getty Conservation Institute, pp. 227–34

Dossie, R. (1758) *Handmaid to the Arts*, London

Down, J.L., MacDonald, M.A., Williams, J.T. and Williams, R.S. (1996) Adhesive testing at the Canadian Conservation Institute – an evaluation of selected poly (vinyl acetate) and acrylic adhesives, *Studies in Conservation*, 41(1), 19–44

Evelyn, J. (1670) *Silva*, London

Hill, J.H. (1976) The history and technique of japanning and the restoration of the Pimm Highboy, *American Art Journal*, November, 59–84

Huth, H. (1971) *Lacquer of the West*, University of Chicago Press

Huxtable, M. and Webber, P. (1987) Some adaptations of Oriental techniques and materials used in the Prints and Drawings Conservation Department of the Victoria and Albert Museum, *The Paper Conservator*, 11, 46–57

John, W.D. (1953) *Pontypool and Usk Japanned Wares*, Ceramic Book Co

Kühlenthal, M. (ed.) (2000) *Japanese and European Lacquerware*, Arbeitshefte des Bayerischen Landesamtes für Denkmalpflege, Munich

Michalski, S. (1990) A physical model of the cleaning of oil paint, in *Cleaning, Retouching and Coatings*, Conference Preprints, IIC, pp. 85–91

Park, J. (1994) Conservation principals applied to a restoration project: the Allam clock case, in *Lacquerwork and Japanning*, Conference Postprints, UKIC, pp. 41–44

Sayer, R. (1762/1966) *The Ladies Amusement*, Facsimile Edition, Ceramic Book Co.

Skálová, A. (1993) Different types of lacquer techniques, history and restoration, in *Conservation of Urushi Objects*, Tokyo National Research Institute of Cultural Properties, pp. 49–62

Stalker, J. and Parker, G. (1688) *A Treatise of Japanning and Varnishing*, Tiranti reprint, 1960

Tingry, P.F. (1804) *The Painter and Varnisher's Guide*, London

Van der Reyden, D. and Williams, D.C. (1986) The technology and conservation treatment of a nineteenth century English 'papier mâché' chair, in AIC, Conference Preprints of the 14th Annual Meeting, pp. 125–42

Wachowiak, M. and Williams, D. (1994) Conservation of an 18th century English japanned surface, in *Lacquerwork and Japanning*, Conference Postprints, UKIC, pp. 27–29

Walch, K. (1997) Baroque and Rococo red lacquers I: the red lacquer-work in the Miniatureenkabinett of the Munich Residenz. Replicating the Technique on the Basis of Historic Sources and Scientific Investigation, in K. Walch and J. Koller (1997) *Baroque and Rococo Lacquers*, Arbeitshefte des Bayerischen Landesamtes für Denkmalpflege, Munich, pp. 128–44

Walch, K., Koller, J. and Fischer, C-H. (1996) The red lacquer-work in the Cabinet of Miniatures in the Munich Residenz, in ICOM Committee for Conservation 11th Triennial Meeting, Edinburgh, pp. 920–2

Watin. (1755) *L'Art du Peintre*, reprinted Chez Leonce Larget, 1975

Webb, M. (1998a) Four japanned cabinets: a variety of techniques, in V. Dorge and F.C. Howlett (eds), *Painted Wood: History and Conservation*, Getty Conservation Institute, pp. 328–36

Webb, M. (1998b) Methods and materials for filling losses on lacquer objects, *JAIC*, 37, 117–33

Webb, M. (1989) The removal of an insoluble varnish from an 18th century clock case, in AIC Wooden Artifacts Group Conference Papers, Cincinnati

Webb, M. (2000) *Lacquer: Technology and Conservation*, Butterworth-Heinemann

Wolbers, R., Sterman, N. and Stavroudis, C. (1990) Notes for workshop on new methods in the cleaning of paintings, Getty Conservation Institute, 1988, 1989, 1990

## 16.8    Lacquered (urushi) furniture

Barrington, M. and Fryer, H. (eds) (1999) *Oriental Lacquer and Japanning*, Conference Postprints, British Antique Furniture Restorers Association

Brewer, J.A. (1991) Effect of selected coatings on moisture sorption of selected wood test panels, *Studies in Conservation*, 36(1), 9–23

Brommelle, N.S. and Smith, P. (eds) (1988) *Urushi: Proceedings of the 1985 Urushi Study Group*, Getty Conservation Institute

Budden, S. and Halahan, F. (eds) (1994) *Lacquerwork and Japanning*, Conference Postprints, UKIC

Brückle, I., Thornton, J., Nichols, K. and Strickler, G. (1999) Cyclododecane: technical note on some uses in paper and objects conservation, *JAIC*, 38, 162–75

Carr, M.H. and Driggers, J.M. (1997) Loss compensation of lacquer on two Chinese tables, in AIC Wooden Artifacts Group Conference Papers, San Diego, pp. 36–44

Chase, W.T, Jett, P.R, Koob, S.P. and Norman, J. (1988) The treatment of a Chinese red lacquer stationery box, in J.S. Mills, P. Smith and K. Yamasak (eds), *The Conservation of Far Eastern Art*, Conference Preprints, IIC, pp. 142–5

Gettens, R.J. and Stout, R. (1966) *Painting Materials: An Encyclopaedia*, Dover

Heath, D. and Martin, G. (1988) The corrosion of lead and lead/tin alloys occurring on Japanese lacquer objects, in J.S. Mills, P. Smith and K. Yamasak (eds), *The Conservation of Far Eastern Art*, Conference Preprints, IIC, pp. 137–41

Horie, V. (1992) *Materials for Conservation*, Butterworth-Heinemann

Kenjo, T. (1988) Scientific approach to traditional lacquer art, in N.S. Brommelle and P. Smith (eds), *Urushi: Proceedings of the 1985 Urushi Study Group*, Getty Conservation Institute, pp. 155–62

Kühlenthal, M. (ed.) (2000a) *Japanese and European Lacquerware*, Arbeitshefte des Bayerischen Landesamtes für Denkmalpflege, Munich

Kühlenthal, M. (ed.) (2000b) *Ostasiatische und europäische Lacktechniken*, Arbeitshefte des Bayerischen Landesamtes für Denkmalpflege, Munich

Kumanotani, J. (1988) The chemistry of Oriental lacquer (*Rhus verniciflua*), in N.S. Brommelle and P. Smith (eds), *Urushi: Proceedings of the 1985 Urushi Study Group*, Getty Conservation Institute, pp. 243–51

Kumanotani, J. (1995) Urushi (oriental lacquer) – a natural aesthetic durable and future-promising coating, *Progress in Organic Coatings*, 26, 163–95

Kumanotani, J. (1998) Enzyme catalysed durable and authentic oriental lacquer: a natural microgel-printable coating by polysaccharide–glycoprotein–phenolic lipid complexes, *Progress in Organic Coatings*, 34, 135–46

Michalski, S. (1990) A physical model of the cleaning of oil paint, in *Cleaning, Retouching and Coatings*, Conference Preprints, IIC, pp. 85–91

Mills, J.S., Smith, P. and Yamasaki, K. (eds) (1988) *The Conservation of Far Eastern Art*, Conference Preprints, IIC

Minney, F. (1994) The conservation of a Burmese dry lacquer statue of Buddha, *Studies in Conservation* 39(3), 154–60

Minney, F. (1999) The conservation of lacquerware, in M. Barrington and H. Fryer (eds), *Oriental Lacquer and Japanning*, Conference Postprints, British Antique Furniture Restorers Association, pp. 6–11

Murose, K. (1996) On Ryukyu urushi technique and restoration, in ICOM Committee for Conservation 11th Triennial Meeting, Edinburgh, pp. 915–919

Nagase, Y. (1986) Urushi-no-hon (The Book of Urushi) Kensei-sha

Nakajima, T. (1988) Conservation of Chinese urushi: methods and difficulties, in N.S. Brommelle and P. Smith (eds), *Urushi: Proceedings of the 1985 Urushi Study Group*, Getty Conservation Institute, pp. 87–9

Rivers, S. (2003) Removal of varnish from japanned and lacquered surfaces: principles and practice, in *The Meeting of East and West in the Furniture Trade*, Sixth International Symposium on Wood and Furniture Conservation, Stichting Ebenist, Rijksmuseum, Amsterdam

Tokyo National Research Institute of Cultural Properties (1978) *Conservation of Wood*, Proceedings of the First International Conference on the Conservation and Restoration of Cultural Property, 1977

Tokyo National Research Institute of Cultural Properties (1980) *Conservation of Far Eastern Art Objects*, Proceedings of the International Symposium on the Conservation and Restoration of Cultural Property, 1979

Tokyo National Research Institute of Cultural Properties (1995) *Conservation of Urushi Objects*, Proceedings of the International Symposium on the Conservation and Restoration of Cultural Property, 1993

Umney, N. (1987a) Oriental lacquer, *Conservation News*, 32, 23–5

Umney, N. (1987b) Oriental lacquers, *Conservation News*, 33, 13–15

Webb, M. (2000) *Lacquer: Technology and Conservation*, Butterworth–Heinemann

Webb, M. (1999) Cracks, cups and cures: causes and conservation methods and materials for damaged lacquerware, in M. Barrington and H. Fryer (eds), *Oriental Lacquer and Japanning*, Conference Postprints, British Antique Furniture Restorers Association, pp. 35–41

Webb, M. (1998b) Methods and materials for filling losses on lacquer objects, *JAIC*, 37, 117–33

Webb, M. (1995) Conservation treatment of lacquer in the Royal Ontario Museum, in Tokyo National Research Institute of Cultural Properties, *Conservation of Urushi Objects*, pp. 1–16

Webb, M. (1994) An examination of fill materials for use with lacquer objects, in S. Budden and F. Halahan (eds), *Lacquerwork and Japanning*, Conference Postprints, UKIC, pp. 30–5

Westmoreland, R. (1988) Solvent testing method for identification of Oriental lacquer in European furniture, in N.S. Brommelle and P. Smith (eds), *Urushi: Proceedings of the 1985 Urushi Study Group*, Getty Conservation Institute, pp. 235–42

## 16.9    Gilded furniture

Bigelow, D., Cornu, E., Landrey, G. and van Horne, C. (eds) (1991) *Gilded Wood, Conservation and History*, Sound View Press

Binnington, F. (1991) Verre eglomisé, in S. Budden (ed.), *Gilding and Surface Decoration*, Conference Preprints, UKIC, pp. 5–7

Buck, S. (1993) Three case studies in the treatment of painted furniture, in AIC Wooden Artifacts Group Conference Papers, Denver, pp. 1–6

Budden, S. (ed.) (1991) *Gilding and Surface Decoration,* Conference Preprints, UKIC

Cennini (trans. Thompson, 1954) *The Craftsman's Handbook,* Dover

Cession, C. (1990) The surface layers of Baroque gildings: examination, conservation, restoration, in J.S. Mills and P. Smith (eds), *Cleaning, Retouching and Coatings,* Conference Preprints, IIC, pp. 33–35

Considine, B. (1989) Damaged giltwood: a change in ethics, *Apollo* November, pp. 312–331

Friend, S. (1996) Aquazol: one conservator's empirical evaluations, *WAAC Newsletter,* 18(2)

Green, M. (1979) Conservation and restoration of gilded antiques, *The Conservator,* 3, 39–42

Green, M. (1991) Thirty years of gilding conservation at the Victoria and Albert Museum, in D. Bigelow, E. Cornu, G. Landrey and C. van Horne (eds), *Gilded Wood, Conservation and History,* Sound View Press, pp. 239–48

Halahan, F. (1991) Care of gilded objects, in S. Budden (ed.), *Gilding and Surface Decoration,* Conference Preprints, UKIC, p. 25

Hanlon, G. (1992) Examination and treatment of a German gilded console table, *c.*1740, in AIC Wooden Artifacts Group Conference Papers, Buffalo

Hebrard, M. and Small, S. (1991) Experiments in the use of polyvinyl alcohol as a substitute for animal glues in the conservation of gilded wood, in D. Bigelow, E. Cornu, G. Landrey and C. van Horne (eds), *Gilded Wood, Conservation and History,* Sound View Press, pp. 227–90

Moyer, C. and Hanlon, G. (1996) Conservation of the Darnault Mirror: an acrylic emulsion compensation system, *JAIC,* 35, 185–96

Powell, C. (1991) Case study: national gallery frame, in S. Budden (ed.), *Gilding and Surface Decoration,* Conference Preprints, UKIC, pp. 3–4

Powell, C. (1999) Original gilding and over gilding: the examination of the layers on an important English eighteenth century chair, *The Conservator,* 23, 30–6

Richardson, R. (1991) The materials and techniques of pressbrokaat, in S. Budden (ed.), *Gilding and Surface Decoration,* Conference Preprints, UKIC, pp. 36–39

Robertson, S. (1991) The routine maintenance and care of gilder wood objects, in D. Bigelow, E. Cornu, G. Landrey and C. van Horne (eds), *Gilded Wood, Conservation and History,* Sound View Press, pp. 375–81

Rogers, J. (1991) Gilding at Brighton Pavilion, in S. Budden (ed.), *Gilding and Surface Decoration,* Conference Preprints, UKIC, pp. 8–11

Shelton, C. (1996) The use of Aquazol-based gilding preparations, in AIC Wooden Artefacts Group Conference Papers, Virginia

Thompson, D.V. (1956) *The Materials and Techniques of Medieval Painting,* Dover

Thompson, D.V. (1962) *The Practice of Tempera Painting: Materials and Methods,* Dover

Thorn, N. (1984) Water-gilding – how to match the Golden Age, *Fine Woodworking,* 46, May/June, 82–85

Thorn, N. (1987) Restoring a pair of gilded girandoles, in AIC Wooden Artifacts Group Conference Papers, Vancouver

Thornton, J. (1991a) Minding the gap: filling losses in gilded and decorated surfaces, in S. Budden (ed.), *Gilding and Surface Decoration,* Conference Preprints, UKIC, pp. 12–17

Thornton, J. (1991b) The use of non-traditional gilding methods and materials in conservation, in D. Bigelow, E. Cornu, G. Landrey and C. van Horne (eds), *Gilded Wood, Conservation and History,* Sound View Press, pp. 217–30

Thornton, J. (1998) The early practice and materials of gap-filling in the West, *JAIC,* 37, 3–22

Thornton, J. (2000) All that glitters is not gold: other surfaces that appear to be gilded, in Drayman-Weisser, T. (ed.) *Gilded Metals History, Technology and Conservation,* Archetype, pp. 307–17

Von Reventlow, V. (1991) The treatment of gilded objects with rabbit-skin glue size as consolidating adhesive, in D. Bigelow, E. Cornu, G. Landrey and C. van Horne (eds), *Gilded Wood, Conservation and History,* Sound View Press, pp. 269–76

Webb, M. (1994) An examination of fill materials for use with lacquer objects, in *Lacquerwork and Japanning,* Conference Postprints, UKIC, pp. 30–35

Wetherall, J. (1991) History and techniques of composition, in S. Budden (ed.), *Gilding and Surface Decoration,* Conference Preprints, UKIC, pp. 26–29

Wetherall, J. (1992) *Gilding – notes for short courses,* published by the author

Wolbers, R., McGinn, M. and Duerbeck, D. (1998) Poly(2-ethyl-2-oxazoline): a new conservation adhesive, in V. Dorge and F.C. Howlett (eds), *Painted Wood: History and Conservation,* Getty Conservation Institute, pp. 514–27

# Index

Aalto, Alvar, 36, 38
Abalone shells, 204
Abrasive papers, 449–50, 453
Abrasives, 449–54, 503, 638–9
  corrosion product removal, 680,
    693
  japanned furniture cleaning, 756–7
Accelerator Mass Spectrometry
    (AMS), 394
Accident procedures, 430–1
Accountability, 396
  *See also* Documentation
Accretions, surface disfigurement
    and, 310
  *See also* Cleaning
Acematt, 591
Acetic acid, 265, 294, 351, 527
  as stain, 618
  metal corrosion, 322–3
Acetone, 511
Acids, 527–8, 529
  acid dissociation constant (pKa),
    528
  acid equilibrium constant (Ka), 528
  stains, 618
  *See also Specific acids*
Acrylics, 130, 180–1, 185
  as coatings, 594–5
    metals, 687–8
  as consolidants, 570, 735
Acrylonitrile-butadiene rubber (NBR),
    130
Acrylonitrile-butadiene styrene
    (ABS), 130
Activation energy, 245
Adam, Robert, 20, 22, 24, 25
Adhesion, 156, 560
  bonding of ceramic components,
    702–3
  mechanical adhesion, 157
Adhesives, 120–1, 134–5, 156–61,
    441–2, 560–1
  application of, 444

choice of, 159–60, 442–4
  cured adhesive characteristics,
    160
closed time, 159
contact cements, 161
deterioration, 345
failure, 158, 334, 345, 552
for boulle work, 475, 478
for ivory, 669–70
for japanned furniture, 758
for leather, 734–5
for marquetry, 478
for metal repairs, 683
for paper liners, 677
for parchment, 738–9
for plastics, 720–1
for veneers, 473
gap-filling properties, 442
glue line thickness, 158–9
health and safety issues, 160
hot melt adhesives, 161
identification, 187–9
in woodworking, 160–1
open time, 159
phenol-formaldehyde (PF)
    adhesives, 184–5
removal of, 458
roughening surfaces, 159
starch adhesives, 167
starved joints, 159
urea-formaldehyde (UF) adhesives,
    184
  *See also* Glues
Administration area, 410
Aesthetic reintegration, 574–86
  fills, 574–8
    materials, 576–8
  gilded surfaces, 775–6
  marble, 716–17
  painted furniture, 752
  retouching, 578–86
    making paint tablets, 585–6
    materials, 582–5

Afleck, Thomas, 20
Agar-agar, 167, 485
Air brushes, 601–2
Air conditioning, 257–8
Alabaster, 218
  cleaning, 716
Albers, Josef, 36
Albumins, 173
Alcohols, 510, 513, 524
Aldehydes, 510–11
Algerian fibre, 118
Alginates, 167, 485
Alizarin, 220, 326
Alkalis, 527
  stains, 618–19
Alkanes, 505
Alkenes, 505
Alkyds, 185
Alkyl phenols, 540
Alligator crackle, 336
Alloys, 207
Alum tawing, 101, 102
Aluminium, 37, 210
  stable aluminium oxide layer, 317
Amalgam, 212
Amber, 178
  identification, 219
Ambrosia beetles, 286
Amides, 512
Amines, 511–12
  cyclic amines, 512
Amino acids, 168, 169
Amino black test, 111
Ammonia, 529, 619
Ammonium citrate, 773
Ammonium hydroxide, 695, 698,
    749, 773
Amylase, 549
Analysis, 384, 393–4
Angel bed, 23
Angiosperms, 50, 54
Angle joints, 89–90, 91
Aniline dyes, 231

Animal glues, 169–73, 442–3
  as consolidants:
    of decorative surfaces, 568–70
    of wood, 565
  as filling materials, 576, 623
  Bloom strength, 172
  removal of, 458
  use in moulding, 485–6
*Anobium punctatum, See*
  Woodworm
Ant chair, 38
Antler, 197
  conservation, 667, 671
  deterioration, 315–16
  identification, 199–201
Aquazol, 571
Arad, Ron, 37
Arc springs, 120
Arkon P-90, 584, 596, 597
Aromatic solvents, 508
Art and Crafts Exhibition Society, 27
Art Deco style, 35, 41
Art Furniture, 29
Art Gum, 504
Art Moderne, 36
Art Workers Guild, 27
Arts and Crafts movements, 27
Ash, 63
Ashbee, C.R., 27
Aspen, 65
Association for Preservation
  Technology (APT), Canada,
  369–70
Autofluorescence:
  coatings, 610
  finish identification, 188
  wood identification, 74
Auxochromes, 220
AW2 (BASF), 181
Azeotrope, 526
Azurite, 325–6, 571

Bacteria, 296
  relative humidity and, 256
Baekeland, Leo, 129
Bamboo, 31
Banding, 18
Bandsaws, 32
Bantam work, 19
Barcelona chair, 37
Barium sulphate, 576
Barnsley, Sidney, 36
Baroque, 20, 21
Bases, 527–8, 529
  base dissociation constant (pKb),
    528
  base equilibrium constant (Kb), 528
Basketwork, 31

Bast fibre cloths, 120
Baudouine, Charles, 27
Beaumont, Sir George, 500
Beaumontage, 623
Beds, history of:
  early Egypt, 3
  Medieval period, 7
  16th Century, 9–10
  17th Century, 16
  18th Century, 23
Beech, 64
Beeswax, 166, 167, 629, 735
  gloss reduction, 591
Beilstein test, 111
Belter, John Henry, 27, 32
Bench, 418
Bending stresses, 83–4, 302
Bentham, 32
Benzene, 508
Benzoin, 178
Benzophenones, 249
Benzotriazole (BTA), 693
Benzyl alcohol, 510, 526
Bergère chair, 23
Bertoia, Harry, 37
Bessemer, Henry, 209
Beva, 568, 735, 736, 738
Biedermeier style, 29, 30
Bile soaps, 749–51
Binding media, 582–3, 624–5
Birch, 65, 71
Black rot, 349, 731
Blaize, 741
Blanching, 551–2
Bleaches, 614–16
Blisters, 572, 766
Blocking, 22
Blood glues, 184
Bloom, 338, 551, 552, 573, 609
Bloom strength, 172, 569
Blow atomizer, 598–9
Blow chair, 39
Bois-durci, 128
Bole, 143–4, 655–7, 776
Bonded chip foam, 119
Bone, 197
  conservation, 667–71
    cleaning, 667–8
  deterioration, 315–16
  identification, 199–201
Bone glues, 172
Bookcases:
  history of, 15
  sagging of shelves, 303
Boulle, André-Charles, 16, 19, 202,
  304, 470
Boulle work, 19, 33–4, 470
  conservation, 470–1

  cleaning, 473–4
  coatings, 481
  consolidation, 474–6
  lifting, 480
  loss replacement, 476–80
  deterioration, 304
Boulton, Matthew, 696
Bramah, Joseph, 32
Brandi, Cesare, 578
Brass, 209–10
  conservation, 692–6
    chemical removal of corrosion
      products, 693, 694–6
    dezincification and redeposition,
      694
    mechanical removal of
      corrosion products, 693
    stabilization, 692–3
    stress corrosion cracking, 693–4
  inlay, 482
  *See also* Boulle work; Ormolu
Breccia, 218
Breuer, Marcel, 37, 38, 461
Brimstone, 218
Brittle heart, 285
Brocade weave, 110
Bronze, 209
  conservation, 692–6
    chemical removal of corrosion
      products, 693, 694–6
    dezincification and redeposition,
      694
    mechanical removal of
      corrosion products, 693
    stabilization, 692–3
    stress corrosion cracking, 693–4
Brown rots, 294
Brownwell's rust remover, 691
Buffers, 532–3
Bugatti, Carlo, 304, 737
Bullock, George, 482
Bureaux, 15
Burnishers, 645
Burnishing, 454, 661–2
Burrs, 286
Butt joints, 89, 460
  reinforcement, 460–1
Butterfly keys, 306–7
Buttoning, 99
Butyl rubber (BUTYL), 130
Byne's disease, 316–17
Byzantium period, 5–6

Cabinetmakers, 17
Cabinets, history of:
  china cabinets, 16
  early Egypt, 4
  18th Century, 22

Cabinetscraper, 449
Cabriole leg, 21, 22, 303
Calcium carbonate, 143, 577
Calcium sulphate, 142–3
Calendaring, 110, 111
Cameras, 406–7
Cane, 106–7
    conservation, 729–30
        rehumidification, 729–30
    deterioration, 349–50
    identification, 107
Canework, history of, 16, 31
Canvas work, 110
Capillary action, 514
*Caquetoire* chair, 10
Carbamate insecticides, 269
Carbohydrates, 167, 359
    deterioration, 346
Carbon-14 dating, 394–5
Carbonic acid, 324
Carbopol, 552, 553, 556–7
Carboxylic acids, 529
Carboxymethyl cellulose, 548
Cardboard, 89
Carlton House table, 23
Carnauba wax, 166, 629, 630
Carpet beetles, 352
Carving:
    history of, 8, 11–12
        revival, 33
    pressure carving, 33
    recutting, 653–5
Casein, 128, 173
    glues, 173–4, 184
Casting, *See* Moulding and casting
Castle, Wendell, 36
Castors, 14–15
Cataloguing, 243
Catalysts, 246
Cauls, 445, 472, 474, 475, 478
Cavity foam, 119
Cellosolve, 511
Celluloid, 129
Cellulose, 74
    degradation, 349–50
    structure within cell walls, 75–6
Cellulose acetate butyrate (CAB),
    130
Cellulose ethers, 554–5, 571
Cellulose nitrates, 113, 182–3, 669
    degradation, 358
    metal coating, 687, 692
Cellulosic esters, 130
    fibres, 108
Ceramics, 213, 214
    conservation, 701–4
        bonding, 702–3
        cleaning, 702

filling losses, 703
    retouching, 703–4
    deterioration, 323
    identification, 217
Ceresin, 166–7
Cesca chair, 37
Chairs:
    damage to, 310–11
    dismantling, 454–5
    history of:
        Byzantium period, 5, 6
        16th Century, 9
        17th Century, 13–14
        18th Century, 21, 22, 23
        19th Century, 28
        20th Century, 37, 38, 39
    workshop chairs, 420
    *See also* Seats
Chapius, 25
Characterization, 380–1, 384, 385–6,
    496
Charcoal filters, 265–6
Chareau, Pierre, 35–6
Checks, 289, 308, 461
Cheese glues, 173
Chelating agents, 540–8
    ceramics conservation, 702
    corrosion product removal, 695–6,
        698
    formation constants, 542–3, 544
    pH effects, 543–7
Chemical Handling Information and
        Packaging (CHIP)
        Regulations, 424
Chemical hazards, 422, 424–6, 614
    exposure limits, 425–6, 514–15
Chemical reaction thermodynamics,
        244–6
Chemical spills, 431
Chemical spot tests, wood
        identification, 74
Cherry, 64
Chestnut, 62
Chests, history of:
    Byzantium period, 5–6
    early Greece, 5
    Medieval period, 6, 7
    17th Century, 13, 15
China cabinets, 16
Chipboard, 38
Chippendale, Thomas, 20, 24, 26
Chloride ions, metal corrosion and,
        322
Chlorinated fluorocarbons (CFCs),
        112
Chlorinated hydrocarbons, 509–10
Chroma, 580–1
Chroma Cosmos system, 219

Chrome green, 325
Chromium, 37
    plating, 689
Chromophores, 220
Chrysler Corporation, 40
Citric acid, 691, 695
Clamps, 448, 449
Classical revival, 20, 21
Clay, Henry, 156, 206
Clays, 485, 553–4
Clean Air Act (1956), 260
Cleaning, 494–557
    aqueous cleaning, 529–52
        blanching and blooming, 551–2
        chelating agents, 540–8
        enzymes, 548–51
        ionic concentration/conductivity,
            533–4
        pH and, 531–2
        pH buffers, 532–3
        soaps, detergents and
            surfactants, 534–40
        varnish removal, 749–51
    ceramics, 702
    chemical cleaning, 527–9
    dirt, 499–500
    gilded surfaces, 772–3
    glass, 708–9
        mirrored and decorated glass,
            708–9
        undecorated glass, 708–9
    ivory and bone, 667–8
    japanned objects, 756–7
    joint cleaning after dismantling,
        458
    lacquered (urushi) furniture, 763–6
        decorative elements, 764–5
        potential problems, 763–4
        surface dirt and accretions, 764
        unwanted coating removal,
            765–6
    leather, 732
    marble, 714–16
    mechanical cleaning, 501–4
        abrasives, 503
        cleaving, 501–3
        dry cleaning methods, 503–4
        dusting, 501
    metals, 678–9
    mother-of-pearl, 673–4
    objectives, 495–6
    ormolu, 697
    over-cleaning, 495–6
    painted furniture, 744–5
    parchment, 737–8
    pietre dure, 718
    plastics, 719–20
    pre-cleaning checklist, 496

Cleaning (*cont.*)
  scagliola, 717
  shagreen, 740
  solvent cleaning, 504–27
    mixing solvents, 525–6
    proprietary paint strippers,
      526–7
    solubility, 515–24
    varnish removal, 524–5, 747–9
    *See also* Solvents
  textiles, 742
  thickened solvent delivery
    systems, 552–7
    cellulose ethers, 554–5
    clays, 553–4
    controlled vapour delivery, 553
    polyacrylic acid (Carbopol),
      556–7
    poultices, 553
    wax pastes, 553
  turtleshell, 671
  upholstery, 725, 728
  varnished wooden surfaces,
    608–10
  veneer, marquetry and boulle,
    473–4
Cleaning tests, 497–9, 667
Cleats, 303–4
Cleavage, 572
Cleaving, 501–3
Client reception, 410
Close-up photography, 407
Clothes moths, 352–3
Co-polymers, 124–5
Coatings, 134–42, 586–602, 606–39
  ageing, 141
  application methods, 598–602
    brush application, 598
    spray application, 598–602
  application of to varnished wood,
    628–37
    French polishing, 633–7
    glazing, 637
    natural resins, 631–2
    non-traditional materials, 628–9
    oils, 630–1
    wax, 629–30
  barrier properties, 137–8
  boulle work, 481
  cleaning, 608–10
  colour matching repairs to
    varnished wood, 612–27
    grain fillers, 620–2
    materials, 614–20
    methods, 624–7
    stoppings and filling materials,
      622–4
    surface preparation, 613–14

degraded varnish treatment, 627–8
deterioration of, *See* Deterioration
dissolution of, 517–18
examination, 382
gilding, 148–9, 340–2, 662–3, 665,
  776
glass, 710
gloss, 597, 599
grounds, 142–4, 333–5
  bole, 143–4
  composition, 144
  gesso grounds, 142–3, 333,
    340–1
hardness, 136
identification, 187–9, 610–11
ivory, 671
Japanning, 153–6, 343–4
lacquered (urushi) furniture, 770
leather, 736–7
marble, 717
metals, 211–12, 684–8
  application method, 685
  iron, 689, 692
  lead, 701
  materials, 686–8
  preferential corrosion, 685–6
  silver, 700
mother-of-pearl, 674
optical properties, 138–40
  colour, 139–40
  gloss, 138–9
  refractive index, 139
  transparency, 138
oriental lacquer, 149–53, 342–3
oxidative coatings, 147
painted surfaces, 753
parchment, 739
patination, 607
pietre dure, 719
plasticizers, 137, 141
plastics, 721
protection against handling and
  soiling, 136
reactive coatings, 147
revivers, 607–8
saturation, 587–9
scagliola, 718
selection of, 593
selective layer removal, 610–11
solubility and working properties,
  140–1
solvent release coatings, 147
stabilizers, 592
strength and elasticity, 136–7
supports, 142, 332–3
  grain fillers, 142, 620–2
  stoppings, 142
surface blemishes, 611–12

dents and scratches, 611
in-filling varnish losses, 612
watermarks, 611–12
transparent coatings, 146–8,
  337–40, 586, 606–8
turtleshell, 673
*See also* Lacquers; Paints; Resins;
  Varnishes; Waxes
Codes of ethics and practice, 370–1
Cohesion, 156
Coil springs, 99, 120
Coir, 118
Collagen, 101, 169–73
  as consolidant:
    japanned furniture, 758
    of decorative surfaces, 568–70
    of wood, 565
  as filling material, 576
  degradation, 348
  shrinkage temperature, 101
Collapse, 289
Collections:
  cataloguing, 243
  historical background, 367
  inventory, 243
  legal requirement for preservation,
    241
  management, 243–4
  scope of, 243
  use versus preservation, 242–3
  *See also* Objects
Colloidal systems, 165
Colour, 219–21, 579–82
  basis of, 219–21
  metamerism, 415–16, 579–80, 613
  *See also* Dyes; Paints; Pigments;
    Stains
Colour matching, 579–80, 612–27
  grain fillers, 620–2
  materials, 614–20
    bleaches, 614–16
    pigments, lakes and stains,
      616–20
    precautionary measures, 614
  methods, 624–7
    binding media, 624–5
    pigment application, 625
    sealing coats, 626–7
    stain application, 625–6
  stoppings and filling materials,
    622–4
  surface preparation, 613–14
Colour rendering, 415–16
Colour temperature, 247
  photography and, 402–3
Common furniture beetle, *See*
  Woodworm
Commonwealth period, 13, 18

Comparison, 385
Composites, 129
Compression, 83
Compression set, 310, 311
Compression springs, 120, 728
Compression wood, 285
Computer tomography (CT), 395–6
Conditional stability constant, 546
Conduction, 252
Conductivity, 533–4
Conglomerate, 218
Conservation, 241–2
  antler, 667–71
  as a cultural discipline, 372–4
  bone, 667–71
  business of, 370
  cane, 729–30
  ceramics, 701–4
  cost estimation, 386, 397
  definition of profession, 368–9
  enamels, 704–5
  gilded furniture, 770–7
  historical background, 367–8
  horn, 671–3
  ivory, 667–71
  Japanned furniture, 754–60
  labels, 675–6
  lacquered (urushi) furniture, 760–70
  marble, 714–17
  mother-of-pearl, 673–4
  paper liners, 676–7
  parchment, 737–9
  pietre dure, 718–19
  plastics, 330–1, 719–21
  polymers, 330–1
  professional organizations, 369–70
  reed, 729–30
  rush, 729–30
  scagliola, 717–18
  shagreen, 739–40
  textiles, 354, 740–3
  treatment errors, 306–7
  turtleshell, 671–3
  upholstery, 348
  veneer, marquetry and boulle,
    474–6
  *See also* Ethics; Glass; Leather;
    Metal conservation; Painted
    furniture conservation;
    Upholstery conservation;
    Wooden furniture
    conservation
Consolidants, 135, 161–2
  penetration of, 563
  reverse migration, 563, 566
Consolidation, 562–74
  gilded surfaces, 774–5
  glass, 709–10

horn, 671–2
ivory, 669
japanned furniture, 758
lacquered (urushi) furniture, 766–8
  flattening distorted lacquer,
    767–8
  materials, 768
  pre-softening brittle lacquer,
    766–7
  shell inlay, 768
leather, 733–4, 735
mother-of-pearl, 674
painted and decorative surfaces,
    566–74, 752
  application techniques, 571572
  facings, 573–4
  flakes, cups, tents and blisters,
    572–3
  materials used, 567–71
  traditional versus modern
    materials, 567
plastics, 720–1
scagliola, 717–18
turtleshell, 671–2
veneer, marquetry and boulle,
    474–6
wood, 563–6
  materials used, 564–6
Contact cements, 161
Control of Substances Hazardous to
    Health (CoSHH)
    Regulations, 514
Convection, 252
Conversion, 288–9
Cook, Clarence, 27
Copal, 177
Copper alloys, 209–10, 692
  corrosion, 318, 319, 322, 323
  *See also* Brass; Bronze; Ormolu
Coray, Hans, 37
Cordage, 105
Corrosion, *See* Metals
Cotton, 108, 111
  cloths, 120
  fillings, 118
Cotton flock, 119
Covers, 262, 278–9
  upholstery, 725–6
Cracks:
  antler, 671
  decorative surfaces, 572
  environmental stress cracking, 327
  ivory, 670
  stress corrosion cracking, 693–4,
    698
Cramping, 444–8, 449, 474, 767
Craquelure, 336, 337, 572, 637
  examination, 382

Crazing, 327, 337, 637–8
Creep, 127–8, 141
Crewel work, 110
Critical micelle concentration (CMC),
    536–9
Crocodiling, 637–8
Croners Substances Guide, 424, 425
Cross banding, 18
Crown glass, 216
Crude oil, 508
Cultural issues, 372–4
Cupboards, history of:
  Medieval period, 6–7
  16th Century, 10
  17th Century, 13, 15
Cups, 572–3, 766, 767
Curled hair, 116–17
Cyanoacrylates, 186
Cyclododecane, 487, 574
Cyclohexanone resins, 181–2, 339

Dabbers, 645
Damage, *See* Deterioration
Damask, 110
Dammar, 139, 177–8, 339, 347, 586,
    593, 749–50
Daniels planers, 32
Danish cord, 105
Danish oil, 631
Data management system, 400–1
Dating methods, 394–6
  carbon-14 dating, 394–5
  dendrochronology, 395–6
Day, Robin, 39
Death watch beetle, 299–300
  diagnosis, 300
  life cycle, 299
  preventive measures, 300
Deformation, 84
Dehumidifiers, 258–9
Dendrochronology, 395–6
Density, 389, 561
  calculation, 389
  of wood, 50
Dentin, 195–6, 201
Deoxycholic acid, 550, 750–1
Deskey, Donald, 36
Detergents, 534, 535, 536–40, 541
  choice of, 539–40
  critical micelle concentration
    (CMC), 536–9
  rinse procedure, 540
Deterioration, 241, 244
  adhesives, 345
  bone and antler, 315–16
  categories of damage, 383
    structural damage, 383
    surface effects, 383–4

Deterioration (*cont.*)
  ceramics, 323
  coatings, 331–44, 566
    gilding, 340–2
    ground, 333–5
    japanning, 343–4
    oriental lacquer, 342–3
    paint, 335–7
    support, 332–3
    varnishes, 337–40
  enamels, 704
  glass, 323–4
  horn, 315–16
  ivory and teeth, 315–16
  lacquers, 346–8
  metals, 317–23, 359–60
    chloride effects, 322
    heat and, 322
    light and, 322
    mechanical damage, 323
    moisture effects, 321
    pollutant effects, 322–3
  mollusc shell, 316–17
  oils and fats, 345–6
  paper and paper products, 317
  pigments, dyes and stains, 324–6
  plastics and polymers, 326–31,
      338–40, 354–8
    biological damage, 330
    environmental stress cracking
        and crazing, 327
    heat effects, 329
    light effects, 328–9
    oxidation, 327–8, 719
    pollution effects, 329–30
    polyurethanes, 356–7
    poly(vinyl chloride) (PVC),
        357–8
    prevention and care, 330–1
    relative humidity effects, 329
  proteins, 346
  resins, 346–8
  stone, 324
  tortoiseshell, 315–16
  upholstery, 348–60
    biodeterioration, 352–3
    carbohydrates, 346
    cellulose nitrate, 358
    chemical degradation, 351–2
    hardware, 359–60
    leather, skin and parchment,
        348–9
    plastics and rubber, 354–8
    rush, reed and cane, 349–50
    textiles, 350–4
    trimmings, 358–9
    understructures, 359
  waxes, 346

  wood, 285, 290–302
    fungi, 294–6
    heat, 291–2
    insects, 296–301
    light, 290–1
    mechanical deterioration, 301–2
    moisture, 292–4
    pollution, 294
  wooden structures, 302–12
    accretions and surface
        disfigurement, 310
    broken/damaged parts and
        losses, 307
    carcase furniture, 311–12
    chairs, 310–11
    conservation treatment errors,
        306–7
    construction faults, 305–6
    design faults, 303–4
    inappropriate use of material,
        306
    incompatible materials and, 304
    loose and broken joints, 308
    loose and lifting veneer, 307–8
    poor quality materials, 306
    role of fashion and innovation,
        306
    shrinkage splitting and warping,
        308–10
    tables, 312–13
Dezincification, 694
Diacetone alcohol, 511
Diachromatizing, 34
Dichloromethane, 509–10
Dichlorvos, 269, 271
Dielectric moisture meters, 78–9
Diffusion, 137
Diluents, 582
Dimethyl formamide, 512
Diphenylamine spot test, 111
Dirt, 332, 499–500
  *See also* Cleaning
Disaster preparation, 279–82
  disaster management, 281–2
    after a disaster, 282
  disaster planning, 279–81
    preparation, 280–1
    prevention, 279–80
Dismantling objects, *See* Objects
Dispersions, 570–1
Dispersive X-ray analysis, 394
Distressing, 639, 776–7
Do-it-yourself (DIY) furniture, 37
Documentation, 396–401
  condition, 408
  health and safety management,
      422–3
  information needs, 396–8

  methods, 398–400
  results of examination, 380
  risk analysis, 427
  setting up a documentation
      system, 400–1
  treatment, 409
  upholstery, 723, 726–7
  *See also* Photography
Dovetail joints, 89, 91–2
  dismantling, 457
  history of, 17–18
    machine development, 32
Dovetail keys, 306–7
Dowel joints, 93
  failures, 308
Dowels, 468–9
Downing, A.J., 27
Draft Clean granules, 504
Dragon's blood, 178
Drawers:
  construction, 17–18
  damage to, 310, 311
  protection, 312
Dry cleaning methods, 503–4
Dry rot, 294–5
DTPA, corrosion product removal,
    696
Dunand, Jean, 35–6, 41
Dunlop, 112
Dust:
  control of, 261–3
  covers, 262, 278–9
  health risk, 417
Dusting, 501
Dyes, 109, 230
  deterioration, 325, 353–4
  identification, 232

Eames, Charles, 36, 38, 39, 40, 461
Eames, Ray, 36
Eastlake style, 27
EDTA, 542, 543–6
  corrosion product removal, 696
  rust, 691–2
Edwards hydrogen bonding index,
    524
Efflorescence, 551
Egypt, early history of furniture, 3–4
Eighteenth Century, 20–6
  design and construction, 21–3
  functional types, 20–1
  materials used, 23–4
  surface decoration and finish,
      25–6
  tools and techniques, 24–5
  trade organization, 26
Elastic limit, 85
Elastomers, 118–19, 125

Electromotive force (EMF) series, 321
Electronic flash, 403–4
Electroplating, 211, 689, 697
Electrostatic dust precipitators, 262–3
Elemis, 178
Elgin marbles, 371
Elm, 62
Elvacite, 570
Embroidery, 110
Emergencies, medical, 430–1
    *See also* Disaster preparation
Empire style, 29
Emulsifiers, 165, 536
Emulsions, 140–1, 165, 535–6
    as consolidants, 570–1
    poly(vinyl acetate) emulsions, 179
Enamels, 145
    conservation, 704–5
    deterioration, 704
Energy Dispersive X-ray
        Spectrometry (EDS) system, 74
Entrance, to workshop, 410
Environment, 244
    management of, 277–9
        stores and storage, 277–9
    *See also* Light; Relative humidity;
        Temperature
Environmental stress cracking, 327
Enzymes, 548–51
    denaturing, 551
    rust removal, 692
    storage, 551
Epoxies, 130, 185–6, 443, 488
    ceramics conservation, 703
Equipment, 417–20
Erasers, 504
Escorez resins, 597
Esherick, Wharton, 36
Ester cellulosic, 130
    fibres, 108
Esters, 511, 524
Estimating, 386, 397
Ethanol, 510
Ethers, 511
Ethics, 370–80
    codes of ethics and practice,
        370–1
    conservation as a cultural
        discipline, 372–4
    restoration versus preservation,
        371–2, 436
    tools for balanced ethical
        judgement, 374–5
    V&A ethics checklist, 375–80
    upholstery conservation, 722–3
Ethylene bromide, 353
Ethylenediamine, 692

Etruscan furniture, 5
Evaporation rates, 513, 589
Evelyn, John, 153–4
Examination, 368, 380–96, 408, 496
    categories of damage, 383
        structural damage, 383
        surface effects, 383–4
    japanned furniture, 754–6
    methods of, 384–96
        dating methods, 394–6
        estimating, 386
        gross examination, 386–8
        mechanical tests, 388–90
        microscopic examination, 390–1
        sampling, 391–3
    purpose of, 380–1
    upholstery, 100, 723
    what to look for, 381–4
    workshop requirements, 411
Exposure limits, 425–6, 514–15
    lead, 700–1
Exposure monitoring, 429
Extenders, 145
Extraction, 416–17

Fabrics, 107
    *See also* Textiles
Facing, 573–4
Factories, 34, 40
Fading, 353–4
Failure Mode and Effect Analysis,
    273
Farthingdale chair, 13
Fats, 162–5
    deterioration, 345–6
Feathers, 117–18
Felt, 110
Ferrous sulphate, 617
Fibre glass, 129
Fibre glass wool filters, 262
Fibre optic lighting, 387
Fibreboard, 89
    medium density fibreboard (MDF),
        38, 89
Fibres, 108–9
    deterioration, 351
    identification, 111
    spinning, 109
    *See also* Textiles
Fibrils, 75–6
Filling, 574–6
Filling materials, 31, 99, 116–19,
    576–8, 622–4
    animal materials, 116–18
        curled hair, 116–17
        feathers, 117–18
    casting materials, 489
    deterioration, 359

elastomers, 118–19
    foams, 119
    japanned furniture, 758–9
        grounds, 758–9
        japanned layers, 759
        papier mâché, 759
    lacquered (urushi) furniture, 768–9
    leather, 734–6
        adhesives for, 734–5
        leather infill techniques, 734
        non-leather infills, 735–6
    marble, 716–17
    painted surfaces, 752
    pietre dure, 718
    plastics, 721
    scagliola, 718
    sheet and moulded materials, 119
    shrinkage splits, 464–5
    vegetable materials, 118
Film, 401–2
Filters:
    charcoal filters, 265–6
    particulate pollution control, 261–2
    UV filters, 248–9
Finishing, 408
    moulding and casting, 489–90
    workshop area, 412
Fir, 68
Fire damage, 281
Fire prevention, 279, 280, 431
    precautions, 431
Fish glues, 172–3, 443, 475
Fixed oil varnishes, 147
Flakes, 572–3, 766, 767
Flammability, 515
Flash photography, 403–4
Flashing off, 611
Flax, 108, 111
Flexure Formula, 84
Floral marquetry, 18
Fluorescence:
    immunofluorescence, 391
    photography, 405–6
    use in examination, 388, 390–1
    *See also* Autofluorescence
Fluorescent lamps, 249, 251
Foams, 119, 129
    deterioration, 355
Folk art furniture, 20
Formaldehyde, 322, 354
Formation constants, 542–3, 544
Formic acid, 265, 527, 695, 698
Formica, 129
Foucault process, 217
Fourier Transform Infra Red (FTIR)
        spectroscopy, 134, 189,
        391
Foxing, 256

Frame and panel construction, 94
  shrinkage splitting, 308–9
Frame conservation, 459–60
  mirror frames, 459–60
Framed construction, 94
Framing joints, 90, 92, 93
Frankl, Paul, 36
Frass, 296, 297–8, 300
French polishing, 34, 41, 148, 633–7
  grain filling and, 622
Fume extraction, 416–17
Fumigants, 271–2
Fungi, 266–7, 294–5
  control of, 267
  effects on wood strength, 86
  hyphae, 267
  relative humidity and, 256
  spores, 267
  wood deterioration, 294–6
Furniture beetle, *See* Woodworm
Furniture history, 3–41
  early history:
    Byzantium and Romanesque
      period, 5–6
    Egypt, 3–4
    Greece, 4–5
    Rome, 5
  Medieval period, 6–9
  16th Century, 9–12
  17th Century, 12–20
  18th Century, 20–6
  19th Century, 26–35
  20th Century, 35–41
  *See also* Objects
Furs, 104

Galvanic series, 321
Galvanizing, 689
Gas chromatography (GC), 188–9, 394
  pyrolysis gas chromatography
    (PGC), 189
Geddes, Bel, 36
Gehry, Frank, 40
Gelatin, 169–71, 346, 676–7
  use as consolidant, 569, 774
  use in moulding, 485–6
Gelling agents, 553–7
  cellulose ethers, 554–5
  clays, 553–4
  polyacrylic acid (Carbopol), 556–7
Georgian period, 20–1
Gesso:
  as filling material, 577
  gilding and, 643, 649–53
    application, 650–2
    consolidation, 774
    faults in the gesso, 642
    smoothing the gesso, 652–3

  grounds, 142–3, 333, 340–1, 643
Gesso hooks, 645
Gesso putty, 647
Gibb's free energy, 244
Gilders composition, 490–1
Gilding, 19, 25, 148–9, 490, 642–66
  composition, 665–6
  conservation, 770–7
    bronze paint removal, 773–4
    cleaning, 772–3
    coatings, 776
    composition, 776
    consolidation, 774–5
    distressing, 776–7
    general care, 771–2
    overgilding removal, 773
    reintegration, 775–6
    toning, 777
  deterioration, 340–2, 697, 698
  gesso putty, 647
  oil gilding, 148, 149, 341, 643,
    663–5, 772–3
    coatings, 665
    gold leaf application, 664–5
    mordants, 663, 772–3
    oil size application, 664
    surface preparation, 664
  on metals, 211–12
  spirit gilding, 342
  surface preparation, 647
  tools for, 643–6
  water gilding, 19, 148–9, 642–3,
    647–63, 772
    bole, 655–7
    burnishing, 661–2
    coatings, 662–3
    conditions for, 647–8
    decorative details, 653
    double gilding, 661
    faulting, 660
    gesso, 649–53
    laying the leaf, 658–60
    matte water gilding, 660–1
    punched decoration, 662
    recutting, 653–5
    size, 648–9, 658
    yellow ochre, 655
  *See also* Ormolu
Gimp pins, 114
Glare, 250
Glass, 40, 213–14
  broad glass, 214–16
  conservation, 705–10
    cleaning, 708–9
    flat glass, 705
    mirrored glass, 705–6
    painted and decorated glass,
      706–7

  refitting, 708
  removing glass, 707–8
  repair, 709
  repairs to adjacent wood, 707
  crown glass, 216
  deterioration, 323–4
  identification, 217
  plate glass, 214
Glass fibre, 39
Glass transition temperature, 126–7,
  593
Glazing, 637, 701
Gloss, 587, 589
  matting down, 590–1, 638–9
Gloves, use in handling of objects,
  274, 385
Glues, 120–1
  blood glues, 184
  casein glues, 173–4
  failures, 308
  glue line thickness, 158–9
  removal of, 458
  SuperGlue, 186
  white glues, 179
  yellow glues, 179–80
  *See also* Adhesives; Animal glues
Glycerol, 163
  alkaline glycerol solution, 695
Godwin, E.W., 29
Gold, 207
  powdered gold, 211
  shell gold, 211
Gold leaf, 210–11, 341, 646
  *See also* Gilding
Gold powder, 646–7
Goodison, Benjamin, 20
Goodyear, Charles, 112, 128
Gore-Tex, 676
Gothic period, *See* Medieval
  furniture
Gothic revival, 27
Gragg, Samuel, 25
Grain, of wood, 52–3, 288
  strength properties and, 85, 86
Grain fillers, 142, 620–2
Graining, 34
Granite, 218
Grasses, 118
Great Exhibition (1851), 27
Greece, early history of furniture,
  4–5
Grey, Eileen, 41
Grime, *See* Cleaning; Dirt
Grinding, samples, 391
Groomstick, 504
Gropius, Walter, 36
Grounds, 142–4, 643
  bole, 143–4

deterioration, 333–5
    gesso grounds, 142–3, 333, 340–1, 643
Growth rings, 50, 51, 52, 287–8
    dendrochronology, 395–6
Guild of Handicraft, 27
Guild system, history of, 9, 12, 26, 35
Gum turpentine, 509
Gum-lac, 153, 344
Gumley family, 20
Gums, 167, 174
Gutta percha, 31, 128, 134
Gymnosperms, 50, 54
Gypsum, 143, 486

Hammer veneering, 471
Handling and moving objects, 273–6, 385
    clothing, 274
    damage, 276
    forces applied to object, 274–5
    mirror frames, 459–60
    protection, 276
    risks involved, 242
    touch, 273–4
Hansen, Fritz, 36
Hansen solubility parameters, 518
Hardboard, 38
Hardness, coatings, 136
Hardwoods, 50
    cell structure, 57–60
    identification, 71–3
    *See also* Woods
Hatton, Leonard, 32
Hazards, 423
    category of danger, 424
    chemical hazards, 422, 424–6, 614
        exposure limits, 425–6, 514–15
    *See also* Health and safety
Heal, Ambrose, 36
Health and safety, 420–32
    accidents and emergencies, 430–1
    audit, 430
    documentation, 422–3
        log book, 423
        personal health and safety folder, 423
    exposure limits, 425–6, 514–15
    health surveillance, 429
    information provision, 430
    legal requirements, 421–2
    maintenance, 428–9
    management of, 422
    monitoring exposure, 429
    risk assessment, 423–7
    risk control, 427–8, 515
    training, 430

workplace inspections, 429–30
Heat, 252
    deterioration and:
        metal corrosion, 322
        polymers, 329
        wood, 291–2
    sources of, 252–3
        lighting, 251–2
    thermal expansion, 291
    transmission of, 252
    *See also* Temperature
Hemicelluloses, 74
Hemp, 108, 120
Henry's law, 137
Hepplewhite, George, 20, 26
Herter Brothers, 30, 399
Heywood, Walter, 31
High-volume-low-pressure (HVLP) spray systems, 600–1
Hildebrand solubility parameters, 518
Hindered amine light stabilizers (HALS), 592
Hinge repairs, 465
History, *See* Furniture history
Hog-hair brushes, 645
Hogarth, William, 22
Holland, Henry, 28
Homo-polymers, 124
Hope, Thomas, 28, 482
Horn, 202–3
    conservation, 671–3
        consolidation, 671–2
        loss replacement, 672–3
    deterioration, 315–16
    identification, 203–4
Horsehair, 108, 117
Hot melt adhesives, 161
Hot-air guns, 419–20
House longhorn beetle, 301
Hue, 580–1
Humidifiers, 258
Humidistat, 258
Humidity, 253
    temperature relationship, 253, 308
    *See also* Relative humidity; Wood-water relationships
HXTAL NYL-1, 703, 718
Hyatt brothers, 129
Hydrocarbon solvents, 505–9, 524
    chlorinated hydrocarbons, 509–10
Hydrochloric acid, 265, 527, 528, 529
    control of, 265
    ivory cleaning, 668
Hydrogen peroxide, 616
Hydrogen sulphide, 264–5, 322
Hydrophilic lipophilic balance (HLB) numbers, 535–6

Hydroxypropyl cellulose (HPC), 554, 555
Hygroscopicity, of wood, 77
*Hylotrupes bajulus* (house longhorn beetle), 301
Hysteresis, 77

Illuminance, 248
    *See also* Light
Immunofluorescence, 391
Ince and Mayhew, 20, 26
Industrial methylated spirits (IMS), 510
Industrial Revolution, 27, 34
Infra red photography, 405
Infra red reflectography, 388
Insect pests, 267–73, 384
    control of, 268–9, 270–3
        fumigants, 271–2
        insecticides, 269, 270–1
        low oxygen environments, 272
        temperature treatments, 272
    dealing with infestation effects, 273
    effects on wood strength, 86
    identification, 270
    ivory and horn veneers, 316
    life cycles, 268
    living trees, 286
    monitoring, 269–70, 272
        traps, 269–70, 272
    relative humidity and, 256–7
    textiles, 352
    trimmings, 358
    wicker, 350
    wood deterioration, 296–301
    wooden furniture repair, 458
        consolidation, 563–4
    *See also Specific insects*
Intarsia, 471
International Council of Museums (ICOM), 368, 369
International Institute for Conservation of Historic and Artistic Works (IIC), 369
Inventory, 243
Iodine number, 163
Ionic concentration, 533–4
Iron, 208–9, 688–92
    cast iron, 208
    coatings, 692
    corrosion, 317, 318, 688
        chemical removal, 691–2
        mechanical removal, 689–90
        rust converters, 690–1
    patination, 688–9
    wrought iron, 208–9
Isinglass, 173, 569
    Japanese isinglass, 485

Isopropanol, 456
Ivory, 194–6
　conservation, 667–71
　　adhesives, 669–70
　　cleaning, 667–8
　　coatings, 671
　　consolidation, 669
　　humidification, 669
　　polychrome ivory, 670–1
　　replacements, 670
　　staining, 670
　deterioration, 315–16
　　staining, 668
　identification, 198, 199–201
　storage, 316
Ivory substitutes, 197–9
　identification, 198, 199–201

Jacobsen, Arne, 36, 38
Japanese isinglass, 485
Japanned furniture conservation,
　　754–60
　cleaning, 756–7
　consolidation, 758
　examination, 654–756
　infilling, 758–9
　　fills for grounds, 758–9
　　fills for japanned layers, 759
　　fills for papier mâché, 759
　overpaint removal, 757
　varnish removal, 757
　varnishes, 759–60
Japanning, 19, 25, 33, 153–6, 754
　application, 154
　deterioration, 343–4
　distinction from Oriental lacquer,
　　761–2
Jennens, Theodore, 206
Jensen, Gerritt, 19
Jewel beetles, 286
Joints, 89–95
　assessment, 454
　critical success factors, 90–1
　dismantling, 454–7, 460
　　cleaning after dismantling, 458
　failure of, 302, 308, 345
　　repair, 460–1
　reinforcement, 459
　types of, 89–90, 91–3
　　angle joints, 89–90, 91
　　butt joints, 89, 460
　　dovetail joints, 17–18, 89, 91–2
　　dowel joints, 93
　　framing joints, 90, 92, 93
　　knuckle joints, 461
　　mitre joints, 93
　　mortise and tenon joints, 92
　　widening joints, 89, 90

Jordan process, 33
Jute, 108, 120, 350

Kapok, 118
Karl Fischer reagent, 78
Kauri-butanol test, 508
Kent, William, 20, 21, 25
Keratin, 201
Kerfing, 467
Ketone resins, 181, 339, 595
　retouching, 584
Ketones, 510–11, 524
Kirikane, 764
Klint, Kaare, 36
Klismos chair, 5
Klucels, 555, 733
Knitted structures, 110
Knock-down (KD) construction, 37,
　41
Knoop Hardness Scale, 453
Knots, 286, 287
Knuckle joints, 461
Kraton G, 596

Labels, 381–2
　conservation, 675–6
　health and safety, 430
Lacquered (urushi) furniture
　　conservation, 760–70
　cleaning, 763–6
　　decorative elements, 764–5
　　potential problems, 763–4
　　surface dirt and accretions, 764
　　unwanted coating removal,
　　　765–6
　coatings, 770
　consolidation, 766–8
　　flattening distorted lacquer,
　　　767–8
　　materials, 768
　　pre-softening brittle lacquer,
　　　766–7
　　shell inlay, 768
　Eastern and Western approaches,
　　762–3
　infilling, 768–9
　lacquer handling, 761
　restoring a degraded matte
　　surface, 769–70
　retouching, 769
Lacquers, 25–6, 41, 145, 760
　deterioration, 346–8
　handling of, 761
　on metals, 212, 686
　　silver, 700
　*See also* Lacquered (urushi)
　　furniture conservation;
　　Oriental lacquer

Lakes, 230, 326, 616
Laminates, 129
Lampas weave, 110
Lane, Danny, 37
Lannuier, Charles Honore, 482
Laponite, 553–4, 702
Larch, 67
Laropal A81, 183, 584, 598
Laropal K80, 595
Lascaux, 570, 734
Latex, 112
　deterioration, 355
　fillings, 118–19
Le Corbusier, 37
Leaching, 747–9
Lead:
　conservation, 700–1
　　coatings, 701
　　corrosion product removal, 701
　corrosion products, 320
　exposure limits, 700–1
　pigments, 221–2, 325
Leather, 101–3
　conservation, 731–7
　　backing materials, 736
　　chemical stabilization, 732–3
　　cleaning, 732
　　coatings, 736–7
　　consolidation, 733–4, 735
　　infills, 734–6
　　surface evaluation, 731–2
　deterioration, 348–9, 731–2
　identification, 105
　imitation leather, 730–1
　post-tanning processing, 102
　pre-tanning processing, 102
　tanning, 101–2
　uses of, 102–3
　working methods, 102–3
Leather cloth, 31
Lecithin, 165
Leg shapes, 14, 15
　cabriole leg, 21, 22, 303
Levelling repairs, 440, 448–9
Lewis acids, 528
Liberty, Arthur, 27
Lifting, *See* Handling and moving
　　objects
Light, 246–52, 579
　colour temperature, 247, 402–3
　control of, 248–51
　　artificial lighting, 251
　　daylight, 250–1
　　time of exposure, 251
　deterioration and:
　　coatings, 331, 342
　　metal corrosion, 322
　　polymers, 328–9

textiles, 351
wood, 290–1
for photography, *See* Photography
heat production by lighting,
251–2
inequalities in lighting, 250
light energy, 247
measurement of, 248
reciprocity, 248
workshop lighting, 415–16
*See also* Ultraviolet radiation
Lignin, 74–5
Lime, 65
Limed finishes, 609–10
Limestone, 218
deterioration, 324
Lindane, 271
Linear ethoxylated fatty alcohols,
540
Linen, 108, 120, 350
Linke, Francois, 35
Linseed oil, 163, 164, 345, 608–9,
630–1
gold size, 663
removal of, 549
Lipases, 549
Lipids, 162–3
*See also* Oils
*Lit de repos*, 10
Lloyd Loom, 40
Loading bay, 410
Loads, 83
Local exhaust ventilation (LEV), 416
Lock, Mathias, 20
Lockheed Lounge, 37
London Court of Alderment, 17
Long-term exposure limit (LTEL),
425
Longhorn beetles, 286
house longhorn beetle, 301
Loss replacement, 468–9
antler, 671
ceramics, 703
gilded surfaces, 775–6
horn, 672–3
ivory, 670
marble, 716–17
metals, 683–4
mother-of-pearl, 674
pietre dure, 718
turtleshell, 672–3
varnish losses, 612
veneer, marquetry and boulle,
476–80
Loudon, J.C., 30
Lubbers, J.H., 215
Lustrework, 643
*Lyctus* (powder post beetle), 300–1

Machine room, 411–12
Machines, development of, 31–2, 40
McIntyre, Samuel, 20
Magnifiers, 387
Magnus, E.G., 30
Mahogany, 23–4, 30, 66
Makepeace, John, 36
Makie decoration, 764
Malachite, 571
Maloof, Sam, 36
Manufacturing:
19th Century, 34–5
20th Century, 51
Maple, 64
Marble, 30, 217–18
conservation, 714–17
cleaning, 714–16
coatings, 717
consolidation, 716
repair and reintegration, 716–17
deterioration, 324
Marbling, 34
Marks, 381–2
Marot, Daniel, 22
Marquetry, 16, 18, 33–4
conservation, 470–1
cleaning, 473–4
consolidation, 474–6
lifting, 480–1
loss replacement, 476–80
floral marquetry, 18
seaweed marquetry, 18
stone marquetry, 218
Masonite, 38
Mastic, 139, 178, 339, 347, 586,
593–4, 749–50
Maximum Exposure Limit (MEL),
425, 514
Mechanical tests, 388–90
Media, 134–5
identification, 187–9
paint media, 145
Medieval furniture, 6–9
design and construction, 7–8
functional types, 6–7
materials used, 8
surface decoration and finish, 8–9
tools and techniques, 8
trade organization, 9
Medium density fibreboard (MDF),
38, 89
Melamine formaldehyde (MF), 131
Metal conservation, 677–701
cleaning, 678–9
coatings, 684–8
application method, 685
materials, 686–8
preferential corrosion, 685–6

corrosion product removal,
679–82, 691–701
chemical removal, 682, 691–2,
693, 694–6
electrochemical and electrolytic
reduction, 681–2
mechanical removal, 680–1,
689–90, 693
rust converters, 690–1
loss replacement, 683–4
patina, 678
removal of metal fittings, 678
repairs, 683
rinsing and drying, 682–3
*See also Specific metals*
Metal fasteners, 115, 727–8
deterioration, 359–60
Metal inlay, 482
Metal leaf, 646–7
*See also* Gilding; Gold leaf
Metal punches, 645
Metals, 206–13
alloys, 207
corrosion, 317–23, 359–60, 384
chlorides and, 322
heat and, 322
humidity and, 257
inhibitors, 685
light and, 322
pollutant effects, 322–3
preferential corrosion, 685–6
removal of, *See* Metal
conservation
crystal structure, 207–8
dating, 213
finishes and coatings on, 211–12
heat treatment, 207–8
history of use, 8, 16, 30, 37
identification, 212
structure and fabrication,
212–13
mechanical damage, 323
properties, 207
*See also* Metal conservation;
*Specific metals*
Metalworking area, 413–14
Metalworking tools, 418
Metamerism, 415–16, 579–80, 613
Methanol, 510
1–Methoxypropan-2–ol, 510
Methyl bromide, 271–2, 353
Methyl cellulose (MC), 554–5, 576
Methyl ethyl ketone, 511
Methyl methacrylate, 147
Methylene blue dye, 261–2
Micelles, 536
critical micelle concentration
(CMC), 536–9

Microscopy, 390–1
  fluorescence microscopy, 390–1
  incident light microscopy, 390–1
  stereo microscopy, 390
  transmitted light microscopy, 391
  wood identification, 70–4
    electron microscopy, 74
Mildew, 266
  *See also* Fungi; Mould
Milk protein adhesives, 173–4, 184
Minerals, 217
Mirrors:
  conservation, 705–6
  handling mirror frames, 459–60
  history of, 16, 217
Mitre joints, 93
Modelene, 691
Modulus of elasticity, 85
Mohs hardness, 136
  scale, 450
Moisture, *See* Relative humidity;
    Wood-water relationships
Moisture meters, 78
Molar solutions, 561
Mollusc shell, 204–5
  deterioration, 316–17
Monitoring:
  exposure to hazards, 429
  insect pests, 269–70, 272
Montan wax, 166–7
Mora, Laura, 578
Mora, Paolo, 578
Mordants, 23, 663, 772–3
Morpholine, 512
Morris, William, 27, 372
Mortise and tenon joints, 92
  dismantling, 456–7
  failures, 308
  woodworm damage, 461
Mother-of-pearl, 204
  conservation, 673–4
    cleaning, 673–4
    coatings, 674
    consolidation, 674
    loss replacement, 674
  deterioration, 316–17
Moths, 352–3
Mould, 266
  on polymers, 330
  on textiles, 353
  relative humidity and, 256
  *See also* Fungi
Moulded materials, 119
Moulding and casting, 33, 482–91
  colorants and fillers, 489
  finishing, 489–90
  gilders composition, 490–1
  making a mould, 489

release agents, 488–9
selection of materials, 483–8
Mouth diffuser, 598–9
Moving objects, *See* Handling and
    moving objects
MS2, 181–2
MS2A, 584, 595–6
Munsell system, 219
Museums, 367
  *See also* Collections

N-methyl-2–pyrrolidinone, 512, 526
Nacre, 205
Nails, removal of, 455–6, 727–8
Nakashima, George, 36
Naphtha, 508
  stains, 620
Naphthalene, 353
Needled fillings, 119
Neo-classical revival, 21
Newberry, William, 32
Newsom, Marc, 37
Nickel plate, 211, 689
Niello, 699
Nineteenth Century, 26–35
  functional types, 28–9
  materials used, 30–1
  style and construction type, 29–30
  surface decoration and finish, 33–4
  tools and techniques, 31–2
  trade organization, 34–5
Nitric acid, 264, 527, 529
  as stain, 618
Nitrogen oxides, 264
  control of, 265
Non-grain raising (NGR) stains, 620

Oak, 14, 16, 62
Objects:
  dismantling, 408, 454–7
  documentation, 398–9
  equipment, 419
  life cycle of, 243–4
  *See also* Collections; Handling and
      moving objects
Occupation Exposure Standard
    (OES), 425, 514
Occupational Exposure Limit (OEL),
    425, 514, 515
Oil chamoising, 101, 102
Oil cloth, 31, 113
Oil gilding, *See* Gilding
Oil of spike, 176
Oil of turpentine, 176
Oil stains, 620
Oils, 146, 147, 148, 162–5, 630–1
  application to varnished wood,
      630–1

deterioration, 345–6
drying oils, 163–4
finishes, 608
iodine number, 163
linseed oil, 163, 164, 345, 608–9
non-drying oils, 163
on metals, 212
Oleo resins, 174, 344, 609
Oriental lacquer, 18–19, 26, 149–53,
    760, 769
  application to substrate, 151–2
  decoration, 152
  deterioration, 342–3
  distinction from japanning, 761–2
  identification, 152–3
  making a cured film, 150–1
  preparation, 149–50
  refining raw lacquer, 150
  *See also* Lacquered (urushi)
      furniture conservation
Ormolu, 662
  conservation, 696–8
    cleaning, 697
    corrosion product removal,
        697–8
Oxalic acid, 616, 618
Oxidation:
  coatings, 331, 337
  metals, 317–18
    *See also* Metals
  oils and fats, 345
  polymers, 327–8, 719
Oyster veneers, 16, 18, 480
Ozokerite, 166–7
Ozone, 263–4
  control of, 265, 266
  wood deterioration, 294

Packing, 275, 276
Painted furniture conservation,
    743–54
  cleaning, 744–5
  coatings, 753
  consolidation, 752
  matte paint, 753–4
  overpaint removal, 751–2
  reintegration, 752
  varnish removal, 746–51
    alkaline reagents, 749
    aqueous methods, 749–51
    mechanical removal, 747
    solvents, 747–9
    synthetic varnishes, 751
Painting, history of, 8–9, 25, 33
Paints, 144–6, 335, 743–4
  deterioration, 334, 335–7
    chalking, 335
    discoloration, 336–7

extenders, 145
identification, 187, 188
making paint tablets, 585–6
matte paint, 753–4
media, 145
pigments, 145
primers, 145
removal of, 500, 751–2
  bronze paint, 773–4
  japanned furniture, 757
  proprietary paint strippers,
    526–7
sealers, 145–6
undercoats, 145
water colours, 584–5
*See also* Coatings; Painted
  furniture conservation;
  Retouching
Paper, 40, 205–6
deterioration, 317
identification, 206
Paper liners, 676–7
Paper products, 205–6
deterioration, 317
identification, 206
Papier mâché, 30, 129, 206
deterioration, 317
fills for, 759
japanned, 156, 759
Paradichlorobenzene, 353
Paraloid B67, 595, 758
Paraloid B72, 339, 560, 669–70
as binding medium, 582, 583
as coating, 593, 594–5, 596, 692
as consolidant, 565, 570, 758
as filling material, 576, 768
metal repairs, 683
retouching, 583–4
Parchment, 104, 173
conservation, 737–9
  cleaning, 737–8
  coatings, 739
  repair and support, 738–9
deterioration, 348
*See also* Size
Parenchyma, 59
longitudinal, 57, 59
Parkes, Alexander, 129
Parquetry, 16, 18
Particle board, 38, 89
Passementerie, 114
Patina, 678
Patination, 607
iron, 688–9
silver, 699
Pearl shell inlaying, 30
Pearls, 204
Pensi, Jorge, 37

Pentimenti, 335
Perkin, William, 230
Permeability, 137
Permissible exposure limit (PEL),
  514, 515
Peroxy acyl nitrate (PAN), 264
control of, 266
Petroleum spirits, 509, 514
Pewter, 210, 479
pH, 531
aqueous cleaning and, 531–2
buffers, 532–3
chelating agents and, 543–7
pH meter calibration, 531
Phenol formaldehyde (PF), 131
adhesives, 184–5
Phenols, 164
Phosphatides, 164–5
Phospholipids, 164–5
Phosphoric acid, 690
Photochemistry, 331
*See also* Light
Photography, 401–7
backgrounds, 404–5
camera, 406–7
close-up photography, 407
film, 401–2
fluorescence photography, 405–6
light source, 402–6
  alternative light sources, 405–6
  colour temperature, 402–3
  diffusion, 404
  electronic flash, 403–4
studio requirements, 411
X-ray radiography, 406
Photosynthesis, 49
Picture frames, history of, 16
Pietre dure, 34, 218
conservation, 718–19
Pigments, 145, 146, 221–9, 325,
  581–2, 616
application of, 625
binding media, 582–3
casting material colorants, 489
chemical properties, 221–2
deterioration, 324–6
identification, 232–3
physical properties, 222–9
retouching, 582
toxicity, 222
Pile woven fabrics, 110
Pin hole borers, 286
Pincore foam, 119
Pine, 67, 70
Pirelli, 112
Plain weave, 110
Plane, 63
Planes, 5, 32

Plant taxonomy, 54–5
Plaster, 218, 486
Plasticene, 485, 489
Plasticizers, 137, 141, 570
Plastics, 38–9, 40, 112, 124–34, 179,
  719
chemical structure, 124–6
conservation, 330–1, 719–21
  adhesives and consolidation,
    720–1
  cleaning, 719–20
  coatings, 721
  filling, 721
  retouching, 721
deterioration of, *See* Deterioration
history, 128–34
identification, 113, 134
physical properties, 126–8
  creep, 127–8
thermoplastics, 179–83
*See also* Polymers; *Specific plastics*
Plate glass, 214
Platinum, 207
Plia chair, 37
Pliantex, 734
Plywood, 38, 88–9
Poiret, Paul, 36
Polishing, 26
corrosion product removal, 680
  lead, 701
  silver, 699–700
samples, 392–3
*See also* French polishing
Pollution, 260–6
deterioration and:
  metal corrosion, 322–3
  polymers, 329–30
  textiles, 351–2
  wood, 294
gaseous pollution, 263–6
  control of, 265–6
particulate pollution, 260–3
  control of, 261–3
*See also Specific pollutants*
Poly acetal (POM), 131
Polyacrylic acid (Carbopol), 552,
  553, 556–7
Polyamides (PA), 131
Polybutadiene (BR), 131
Polycarbonate (PC), 131
Polychloroprene (CR), 131
Polychromy, 146, 325
ivory, 670–1
Polyester, 119, 131–2
use in moulding and casting,
  487488
Polyester urethane, 112, 133
Polyether urethane, 112, 133

Polyethylene (PE), 327
Polyethylene glycol (PEG), 467–8
Polyfilla, 577–8, 703, 716, 718
Polyfix, 577
Polymers, 112, 113, 124–34, 179
    as sources of pollutants, 329–30
    chemical structure, 124–6
        tacticity, 126
    conservation, 330–1
    deterioration of, *See* Deterioration
    dissolution of, 517–18
    fillings, 118–19
    history, 128–34
    identification, 113, 134, 330
    physical properties, 126–8
        creep, 127–8, 141
        glass transition temperature,
            126–7, 593
        minimum film formation
            temperature (MFFT), 140–1
        rigidity, 127
    use in moulding and casting,
        486–7
    *See also* Plastics; *Specific polymers*
Polyolefins, 132
Polysaccharides, 167
    deterioration, 346
Polystyrene, 112, 132
Polytetrafluoroethylene (PTFE), 132
Polyurethanes (PUR), 112, 133, 185,
    751
    deterioration, 356–7
Poly(vinyl acetals), 180
Poly(vinyl acetate) (PVAC), 125, 133,
    179–80
    adhesives, 443, 669, 733–4
    as consolidant, 565, 718
    as filling material, 576, 718
    as varnish, 593
    emulsions, 179
    retouching, 584
Poly(vinyl alcohol) (PVAL), 180
    as consolidant, 571
    as filling material, 576, 577
Poly(vinyl butyral) (PVB), 180, 565
Poly(vinyl chloride) (PVC), 105, 113,
    133
    as binding medium, 582
    as consolidant, 570
    deterioration, 357–8
    use in moulding, 486
Poly(vinyl fluoride) (PVF), 133
Poplar, 65
Pore size, hardwoods, 58
Porphyry, 218
Potassium permanganate, 617
Poultices, 553
Powder post beetle, 300–1

Precipitation hardening, 323
Preservation, 368
    legal requirement, 241
    use versus preservation, 242–3
    versus restoration, 371–2
    *See also* Conservation
Pressure carving, 33
Primers, 145
Professional organizations, 369–70
Proportional limit, 85
Protease, 549
Proteinaceous fibres, 108
Proteins, 169–74
    albumins, 173
    casein, 128, 173–4
    collagen, 101, 169–73
    denatured, 169, 346
    deterioration, 346
    keratin, 201
    structure of, 169
Prussian blue, 325, 579
Pumice, 639, 652
Pyrethins, 269
Pyrethoids, 269, 271
Pyrography, 33
Pyrolysis gas chromatography (PGC),
    189

Queen Anne chairs, 21
Quick Japan, 663
Quick lime, 609

Rabbit skin glue, 172, 569, 758, 774
    *See also* Size
Race, Ernest, 37
Radiation, 252
Ragging, 653
Randolph, Benjamin, 20
Rattan, 31, 106–7
Rawhide, 101
Ray skin, 104, 739
    *See also* Shagreen
Rays, 52
    hardwoods, 58, 59–60
    softwoods, 57
Reaction wood, 286
Reciprocity Law, 248, 407
Recommended exposure limit (REL),
    515
Reconstituted wood products, 89
Red rot, 731
Reed, 107
    conservation, 729–30
    deterioration, 349–50
Reflectance, 138
Refractive index, 222–9, 588–9
Regalrez, 183, 584, 596, 597

Regency period, 21, 29, 30
Reintegration, *See* Aesthetic
    reintegration
Relative humidity, 253–60
    control of, 257–60
        in display cases, 259–60
    definition of, 253–4
    dehumidifiers, 258–9
    deterioration and, 256–7
        metal corrosion, 321
        oriental lacquer, 342–3
        polymers, 329
        textiles, 351
        wood, 293–4
    humidifiers, 258
    measurement of, 254–6
    temperature relationship, 253, 308
    wood moisture content
        relationship, 77
    shrinkage and, 82
    *See also* Wood-water relationships
Renaissance, 9
Replacements, *See* Loss replacement
Resin canals, 57
Resin W, 443
Resins, 174–9, 749–51
    aldehyde resins, 598
    as coatings, 593–4, 631–2
        on metals, 687–8
        synthetic resins, 628–9
    as consolidants, 565–6, 570
    cyclohexanone resins, 181–2
    deterioration, 346–8, 551–2
    epoxy resins, 185–6
    hydrogenated hydrocarbon resins,
        596–8
    identification, 187
    molecular weight, 589
    thermoplastic resins, 565–6
    thermosetting resins, 184–5, 566
    use in moulding and casting,
        487–8
    *See also* Specific resins
Resistance meters, 78
Resorcinol-formaldehyde (RF) resins,
    185
Restoration, 368
    treatment errors, 306–7
    versus preservation, 371–2
Retail outlets, 34–5
Retouching, 578–86, 624–5
    ceramics, 703–4
    commercial preparations, 586
    glass, 710
    lacquered (urushi) furniture, 769
    making paint tablets, 585–6
    materials, 582–5
    painted furniture, 751–2

plastics, 721
*See also* Coatings
Reverse migration, 563, 566
Revivers, 607–8
Rexine, 31
Rhoplex, 570
Risk assessment, 277
  health and safety, 423–7
Risk controls, 427–8
  hierarchy of control, 428
  life cycle of control, 428
  maintenance, 428–9
Risk phrases, 424–5
Rochelle salts, 695
Rocks, 217
Rococo style, 20, 21–2, 25
  revival, 27
Rohde, Gilbert, 36
Rohe, Mies van der, 36, 37
Romanesque period, 5–6
Romayne panels, 12
Rome, early history of furniture, 5
Rosewood, 67
Rottenstone, 639
Roux, Alexander, 27
Rubber, 112, 128
  cloths, 113
  deterioration, 355–6
  fillings, 118–19
  use in moulding and casting,
    486–7
Ruhlmann, Jacques Emile, 36, 104
Rush, 106
  conservation, 729–30
  deterioration, 349–50
  identification, 107
Ruskin, John, 372
Russell, Gordon, 36
Rust, 317
  converters, 690–1

Saarinen, Eero, 36, 39
Sacco chair, 39, 112
Safety issues, *See* Health and safety
Saliva, 530
Sampling, 391–3
Sandarac, 176–7, 344, 586, 594, 609,
  631–2
Sanding, 453
Satin weave, 110
Satinwood, 24
Saturation, 587–9
Savery, William, 20
Saw kerfing, 467
Saws, 32
Scagliola, 24, 218
  conservation, 717–18
    cleaning, 717

coatings, 718
consolidation, 717–18
fills, 718
Scanning electron microscopy (SEM),
  wood identification, 74
Schreger lines, 200
Screws, removal of, 455
Sealers, 145–6, 626–7
  pre-cleaning sealing, 497
Seasoning defects, 289–90
Seats:
  history of:
    early Egypt, 4
    early Greece, 4–5
  *See also* Chairs
Seaweed marquetry, 18
Secretaire, 15
Seed-lac, 154–5, 175
Sepiolite, 554
Seventeenth Century, 12–20
  design and construction, 14–16
  functional types, 13–14
  materials used, 16
  surface decoration and finish,
    18–20
  trade practice, tools and
    techniques, 16–18
Seymour, John, 20
Shagreen, 739
  conservation, 739–40
    cleaning, 740
    lifting edges and tears, 740
Shakers, 28
Shakes, 286
Shark skin, 104, 739
  *See also* Shagreen
Shear, 83
Sheepskin, 104
Sheet materials, 119
Shell inlay, 30, 768
Shellac, 136, 147, 174–9, 586, 594,
  609, 631–2
  application to varnished wood,
    631–2
  as filler, 622–3
  deterioration, 344, 348
  history of, 128
  identification, 188, 610
  on metal, 687
  retouching, 625
  solubility, 519–20
  *See also* French polishing
Shells, 204–5
  deterioration, 316–17
Shellsol, 597
Sheraton, Thomas, 20, 24, 25, 26, 33
Short-term exposure limit (STEL),
  425–6

Shrinkage, of wood, 79–80
  compression shrinkage, 310,
    311
  differential shrinkage, 292–3
  estimation of, 81–2
  splitting and, 308–9, 311, 461–5
    repair, 461–5
Silica:
  gel, 259
  matting agent, 590–1
Silicone (SI), 133
Silicone rubbers, 487, 488
Silk, 108
Silver, 210
  conservation, 698–700
    coatings, 700
    corrosion product removal,
      699–700
    patination, 699
    reshaping, 700
    silver polishes, 699–700
    tarnish prevention, 700
  corrosion, 319, 322
Silver leaf, 210, 341–2
  *See also* Gilding
Sixteenth Century, 9–12
  design and construction, 10
  functional types, 9–10
  materials used, 11
  surface decoration and finish,
    11–12
  tools and techniques, 11
  trade organization, 12
Size, 648–9, 657
  application of, 649
  gel strength assessment, 648–9
  gold size, 663
  oil size, 664
Skewings, 646
Skin, 100–1
  deterioration, 348–9
  identification, 105
  shark and ray skin, 104
  skins 'in the hair', 104
  *See also* Leather; Shagreen
Sling seat, 98
Smalt, 325
Smith, George, 28
Soaps, 534, 750
  bile soaps, 749–51
Sodium bicarbonate, 529
Sodium hydroxide, 527, 528, 615
Sodium lauryl sulphate, 535, 536
Soft rots, 294
Softwoods, 50
  anatomy, 55–7
  identification, 70
  *See also* Woods

Solid wood composites, 89
Solubility, 140, 515–24
  chelating agents, 546
  dissolution process, 515–18
  parameters, 518
  prediction of, 518–24
  Teas diagram, 394
  tests of, 393–4
Solutions, 561–2
  concentration, 561
  dilution, 561–2
  measuring small quantities, 562
  molar solutions, 561
Soluvar, 596
Solvent release coatings, 147
Solvents, 140, 146–7, 148, 504–15
  alcohols, 510
  aldehydes, 510–11
  cleaning with, *See* Cleaning
  esters, 511
  ethers, 511
  hydrocarbon solvents, 505–9
    chlorinated hydrocarbons,
      509–10
  ketones, 510–11
  mixing solvents, 525–6
  organic nitrogenous compounds,
    511–12
  physical properties of, 512–15
    capillary action, 514
    evaporation rates, 513
    flammability, 515
    surface tension, 514
    toxicity, 514–15
    vapour pressure, 513
    viscosity, 513–14
  storage, 415
  varnish removal, 524–5
  *See also* Solubility
Spanish leather, 103
Spanish moss, 118
Spinning, 109
Spirit gilding, 342
Spirit stains, 619–20
Spirit varnishes, 147
Splints, 107
Spray guns, 599–601
Springs, 39, 40, 99, 120
  arc springs, 120
  coil springs, 99, 120
  compression springs, 120, 728
  deterioration and, 359
  tension springs, 120
Spruce, 67–8
Stabilization, 592, 692–3
  leather, 732–3
  upholstery, 726
Stain removal, *See* Cleaning

Staining, 34, 625–6
  ivory, 670
  sealed wood, 626
  unsealed wood, 626
Stains, 230–1, 616–20
  acidic and alkaline stains, 618–19
  application of, 625–6
  chemical stains, 617
  identification, 188, 232–3
  non-grain raising (NGR) stains,
    620
  oil and naphtha stains, 620
  solvent borne stains, 619–20
Stam, Mart, 37
Staples, 114–15
Starches, 167, 354
Starck, Phillipe, 37
Staudinger, Hermann, 129
Steel, 209
Steel wool, 454
Stereo microscopy, 390
Stoddard solvent, 508–9
Stone, 217, 714
  deterioration, 324
  identification, 218–19, 714
  *See also* Marble
Stoppings, 142, 622
Storage, 277–9
  at workshop, 410–11, 414–15
    solvents, 415
    tools, 415
    wood store, 412
  enzymes, 551
  ivory, 316
  upholstery, 729
Strain, 84–5
Straw, 118
Straw work, 19
Strength, of wood, 83–7
  affecting factors, 85–6
  relative strength properties, 85
  role in furniture, 86–7
Stress corrosion cracking (SCC),
  693–4, 698
Stresses, 83–5
Stringing, 481–2
Studio, *See* Workshop
Stumpwork box, 741
Styrene acrylonitrile (SAN), 133
Styrene butadiene (SBR), 133
Sue et Mare, 36
Sugars, 167
  deterioration, 346
Sulphur, 218
Sulphur dioxide (SO2), 263, 322
  control of, 265
  wood deterioration, 294
Sulphuric acid, 322, 324, 351, 529

  as stain, 618
Sulphuryl fluoride, 353
Summers, Gerald, 38
Supports, for upholstery, 726, 728–9
  independent sub-frames, 729
Surface energy, 157–8, 560
Surface tension, 157, 514
Surfactants, 534, 535
  hydrophilic lipophilic balance
    (HLB) number, 536
  rinse procedure, 540
Synthetic fibres, 108, 129
Synthetic polymers, *See* Polymers

Tabby weave, 110
Table top polish, 629
Tables:
  damage to, 312–13
  history of:
    early Egypt, 4
    early Greece, 5
    16th Century, 9
    17th Century, 13
    18th Century, 21, 22–3
    19th Century, 28
Tacks, 114, 115, 359
Talbert, Bruce, 29
Tampers, 645
Tannic acid, 690–1
Tanning, 101–2
Tapestry weave, 110
Tar varnish, 156
Tarsia, 471
Taxonomy, of plants, 54–5
Teak, 66–7
Teas chart (solubility parameters),
  394, 518–24, 747
Teeth, 194, 195–6
  deterioration, 315–16
Tempera, 585
Temperature:
  control of, 252–3
  deterioration and:
    metal corrosion, 322
    polymers, 329
    wood, 291–2
  humidity relationship, 253, 308
  insect pest control, 272
  measurement of, 252
  wood strength and, 86
  work space, 416
  *See also* Heat
Tendering, 354
Tension, 83
Tension springs, 120
Tension wood, 285–6
Tents, 572, 767
Terpenoids, 174

Textiles, 107–12, 120
  conservation, 740–3
    cleaning, 742
    loose and lifting linings, 742–3
  deterioration, 350–4, 741
    biodeterioration, 352–3
    chemical degradation, 351–2
    dyes and finishes, 353–4
    structure and, 353
  dyeing, 109
  fibres, 108–9
    spinning, 109
  finishes, 111
  identification, 111
  preventive conservation, 354
  reapplication of, 729
  structures, 109–10
    non-woven, 110
    woven, 109–10
  surface decoration, 110–11
Thermal expansion, 291
Thermodynamics, 244–6
Thioglycolic acid, 692
Thixotropes, 638
Thonet, 32, 35, 40
Threshold Limit Value (TLV), 426, 515
Thrones, history of, 4, 6
Tiffany, Louis Comfort, 30
Timber:
  history of use, 8, 11
  international trade, 24
  *See also* Woods
Tin, 210
  coatings, 211
  plating, 689
Tinuvin 292, 596
Toluene, 508, 515
Toning, 777
Tools, 417–20
  bench, 418
  gilding tools, 643–6
  metalworking tools, 418
  storage, 415
  woodworking tools, 417–18
Tortoiseshell, 16, 201–2, 470–1
  deterioration, 315–16, 475
  identification, 203–4
  properties, 202–3
  *See also* Boulle work; Turtleshell
Tow, 118
Townsend-Goddard family, 20
Tracheids, 55–7, 59
Trade organization:
  Medieval period, 9
  16th Century, 12
  17th Century, 16–17
  18th Century, 26

19th Century, 34–5
20th Century, 41
Traditional Paint Forum, 146
Transmission electron microscopy
    (TEM), wood
    identification, 74
Transmittance, 138
Tratteggio, 578
Travertine, 218
Triethanolamine (TEA), 512, 692, 751
Triglycerides, 162–3, 164
Trimmings, 113–14
  deterioration, 358–9
Tripoli powder, 154, 155
Tulip chair, 36, 39
Tunbridge ware, 19, 34
Tung oil, 631
Tungsten lamps, 251
Turitella, 218
Turning, *See* Wood-turning
Turpentine, 509, 590
Turtleshell, 16, 201–2
  conservation, 671–3
    cleaning, 671
    coatings, 673
    consolidation, 671–2
    loss replacement, 672–3
  identification, 203–4
  properties, 202–3
  *See also* Tortoiseshell
Tusks, 194–5, 196
Tutankhamen's gold throne, 4
Twentieth Century, 35–41
  context, 35–7
  materials used, 37–40
  surface decoration and finish, 40–1
  tools and techniques, 40
  trade organization, 41
Twill weave, 110

Ultramarine, 325
Ultraviolet radiation, 247–8
  absorbers, 592
  control of, 248–9, 415
  use in examination, 387–8
  use in photography, 405
*Ulva marina*, 118
Undercoats, 145
Upholstery, 97–121
  adhesives, 120–1
  buttoning, 99
  classification, 97
  conservation, *See* Upholstery
    conservation
  deterioration of, *See* Deterioration
  examination, 100

fillings, 31, 99, 116–19, 359
  animal materials, 116–18
  elastomers, 118–19
  foams, 119
  sheet and moulded materials, 119
  vegetable materials, 118
hardware, 114–15, 359–60, 727–8
history of, 13, 31, 39–40, 98–100
springs, 39, 40, 99, 120, 728
support systems, 119–20
  fabrics and twines, 120
  springs, 120
  webbing, 119–20
terminology, 97–8
top coverings/simple structures, 100–14, 348–59
  coated fabrics and leather
    cloths, 113
  interworked materials, 105–7, 349–50
  leather, skin and parchment, 101–5, 348–9
  synthetic polymers and plastics, 112–13, 354–8
  textiles, 107–12, 350–4
  trimmings, 113–14, 358–9
understructures, 115–16, 359
workshop requirements, 412–13
Upholstery conservation, 348, 721–9
  documentation, 723, 726–7
  ethics, 722–3
  examination, 723
  frame condition, 724
  invasive treatments, 726–9
    cleaning, 728
    independent sub-frames, 729
    metal fixings, 727–8
    reapplication of lined textiles, 729
    removal and documentation, 726–7
    storage for study, 729
    supports, 728–9
  materials, 725
  non-invasive treatments, 725–6
    case covers, 726
    semi-transparent coverings, 725–6
    stabilizing with repairs, 726
    supports, 726
    surface cleaning, 725
  previous interventions, 723–4
Urea formaldehyde (UF), 134
  adhesives, 184, 443
Urushi, *See* Lacquered (urushi)
    furniture conservation;
    Oriental lacquer

Vapour pressure, 513
Varnishes, 146, 174, 595–8
    cleaning, 608–10
    degraded varnish treatment,
        627–8
    deterioration, 337–40, 586–7, 590
        development of insoluble
            matter, 339–40
    dulling/matting down, 590–2,
        638–9
    fixed oil varnishes, 147
    formulation, 589–90
    historical use of, 147–8
    identification, 187
    in-filling losses, 612
    japanned furniture, 759–60
    pigmented, 145
    removal of, 496, 500, 524–5,
        746–51
        alkaline reagents, 749
        aqueous methods, 749–51
        dissolution process, 517–18
        from lacquered surfaces, 765–6
        japanned furniture, 757
        mechanical removal, 747
        solvents, 747–9
        synthetic varnishes, 751
    selection of, 593
    spirit varnishes, 147
    stabilizers, 592
    tar varnish, 156
    thermoplastic resin varnishes, 147
    thermosetting varnishes, 147
    *See also* Coatings
Varnishing, 19, 25
Vegetable tanning, 101–2
Vellum, 104, 737
    *See also* Parchment
Veneers, 87–8
    application, 445, 471–3
    conservation, 470–81
        cleaning, 473–4
        consolidation, 474–6
        laying veneer, 471–3
        lifting original veneer, 480–1
        loss replacement, 476–80
    deterioration, 304, 306, 312, 316,
        333
        loose and lifting veneer, 307–8
    history of, 14, 16, 18
    oyster veneers, 16, 18, 480
    production, 87–8
    repair, warping and, 467
Verdigris, 325
Vermilion, 325
Vernis Martin, 25–6
Verre eglomisé, 19
Vessel elements, 58

Victoria and Albert Museum *Ethics
    Checklist*, 375–80
Victorian period, 29, 30
Viscosity, 513–14
Vulcanization, 112

Wakefield, Cyrus, 31
Wallmaster Chemical Sponge, 504
Walnut, 23, 30, 63, 73
Warping, 289, 290, 309–10
    repair, 465–8
Wassily chair, 37
Water, 529–30
Water aerosol, 262
Water clays, 485
Water colours, 584–5
Water damage, 281–2
Water gilding, *See* Gilding
Water marks, 338
    treatment, 611–12
Water spray, 265
Water stains, 619
Wax pastes, 553
Waxes, 138, 146, 165–7, 629–30
    animal waxes, 166
    application to varnished wood,
        629–30
    as consolidants, 162
        for decorative surfaces, 567–8
        for wood, 565
    as filling materials, 577, 623, 735,
        759, 768
    commercial products, 167
    deterioration, 346
    finishes, 608
    identification, 187–8
    melting point, 187–8
    metal coatings, 212, 686–7, 692
    mineral waxes, 166–7
    plant waxes, 166
    removal from lacquered surfaces,
        765
    use in moulding and casting,
        483–5
Weathering, 326
Weaves, 110–11
Webbing, 119–20, 350
Weber, Kem, 36
Wegner, Hans, 36
Wet rot, 294–5
Wetting, 157–8, 560
White rot, 294
White spirit, 508, 509
Whittock, Nathaniel, 34
Wholesalers, 34–5
Wicker, 31, 106
    deterioration, 350
    identification, 107

Widening joints, 89, 90
Williamson, Rupert, 36
Windsor chairs, 22
Wing chair, 23
Wire, 37
Wire wool, 454, 690
Wishab sponge, 504
Wood swelling agents, 460
Wood-inhabiting insects, *See* Insect
    pests
Wood-turning, history of, 10, 11, 18
    origins, 4
Wood-water relationships, 50–1,
    76–83, 256
    deterioration and, 292–4
    dimensional changes, 79–80, 256,
        292–3
        estimation of, 80–3
        shrinkage, 79–80, 292–3
    fibre saturation point (FSP), 76, 77
    hygroscopicity, 77
    moisture content (MC), 76
        equilibrium moisture content
            (EMC), 77
        measurement of, 77–9
    *See also* Relative humidity
Wooden furniture conservation,
    436–91
    adhesion, 440–2, 444
        selection of adhesive, 442–4
    assembly, 444
    construction of repair piece, 439
    cramping/clamping, 444–8
    diagnosis of cause of failure, 437
    dismantling, 454–7
        joint cleaning after dismantling,
            458
    fitting the repair to the object,
        439–40
    frames, 459–60
    insect damage repair, 458
    joint reinforcement, 459
    levelling repairs, 440, 448–9
    moulding and casting, 482–91
        colorants and fillers, 489
        finishing, 489–90
        gilders composition, 490–1
        making a mould, 489
        release agents, 488–9
        selection of materials, 483–8
    repair by damage type, 460–570
        breaks and losses, 468–9
        faulty construction, 470
        hinges, 465
        joint failures, 460–1
        shrinkage checks and splits,
            461–5
        warping, 465–8

repair material selection, 437–9
  wood selection, 438–9
surface preparation, 439–40
  for finishing, 449–54
transfer of shapes, profiles and
    measurements, 439
veneer, marquetry and boulle,
    470–82
  cleaning, 473–4
  coatings for boulle, 481
  consolidation, 474–6
  laying veneer, 471–3
  lifting original veneer, 480–1
  loss replacement, 476–80
  stringing and metal inlay, 481–2
Woods, 49–95
  cellular structure, 50, 51–2
    hardwoods, 57–60
    softwoods, 55–7
  chemical nature of, 74–6
    cellulose structure, 75–6
    chemical constituents, 74–5
  classification of, 50
  consolidation, 563–6
    materials used, 564–6
  dating methods, 394–6
    carbon-14 dating, 394–5
    dendrochronology, 395–6
  defects in, 285–90
    conversion, 288–9
    natural defects, 285–8
    seasoning defects, 289–90
  density, 50
  deterioration of, *See* Deterioration
  dimensional changes, 79–80
    estimation of, 80–3
  finishes, 12, 18–19, 25–6, 34
  gross features, 51–4
    colour, 54
    figure, 53–4
    grain, 52–3, 288
    texture, 53
  growth rings, 50, 51, 52, 287–8
  history of use:
    Medieval period, 8
    16th Century, 11
    17th Century, 16
    18th Century, 23–4

19th Century, 30
20th Century, 38
identification of, 60–74
  electron microscopy, 74
  hand lens examination, 61–70
  keys, 60–1
  microscopic examination, 70–3
inlays, 12
mechanical properties, 83–7,
    301–2
  definitions, 83–5
  factors affecting strength, 85–6
  relative strength properties, 85
  role of wood strength in
      furniture, 86–7
metal corrosion and, 322–3
moisture relationships, *See* Wood-
    water relationships
plies, 25, 30, 88
plywood, 38, 88–9
reconstituted wood products, 89
samples, 393
shrinkage, 79–80
  estimation of, 81–2
  splitting and, 308–9, 311, 461–5
stains, 230–1
storage at workshop, 412
taxonomy, 54–5
treatment, 38
veneers, 87–8
  *See also Specific types of wood*;
      Timber; Wooden furniture
      conservation
Woodworking tools, 417–18
Woodworm, 296–9, 564, 622
  diagnosis, 297–9
  factors influencing infestation, 299
  joint damage, 461
  life cycle, 296
  monitoring, 272
  treatment, 270, 299
  *See also* Insect pests
Wool, 108, 111
Workshop, 407–17
  clean area, 413
  client reception and
      administration, 410
  dust area, 413

electrical power supply, 415
entrance/loading bay, 410
examination and photography, 411
extraction, 416–17
heating, 415–16
inspections, 429–30
lighting, 415–16
location, 409
machine room, 411–12
main work area, 411
metalworking area, 413–14
processes and procedures, 408–9
  dismantling, 408
  examination, 408
  finishing and colouring, 408
  re-assembly, 408
  recording and reporting, 408,
      409
  repair, 408
recreational areas, 414
retouching area/clean room, 412
storage, 410–11, 414–15
  solvents, 415
  tools, 415
  wood store, 412
upholstery workshop, 412–13
wet area, 413, 415
wood store, 412
*See also* Health and safety
Woven fabrics, 109–10
Wright, Frank Lloyd, 37
Writing tables, 15

X-ray radiography, 395, 406
*Xestobium rufovillosum* (deathwatch
    beetle), 299–300
Xylene, 508, 509, 515, 524
Xylonite, 129

Yellow ochre, 655
Young's Modulus, 85, 127

Zeolite pellets, 357
Zinc, 210
  coatings, 211, 689
  dust, 693
  pigments, 221–2
Zwiener, Joseph-Emanuel, 35